CW00950268

ERIC SHIPTON

THE SIX MOUNTAIN-TRAVEL BOOKS

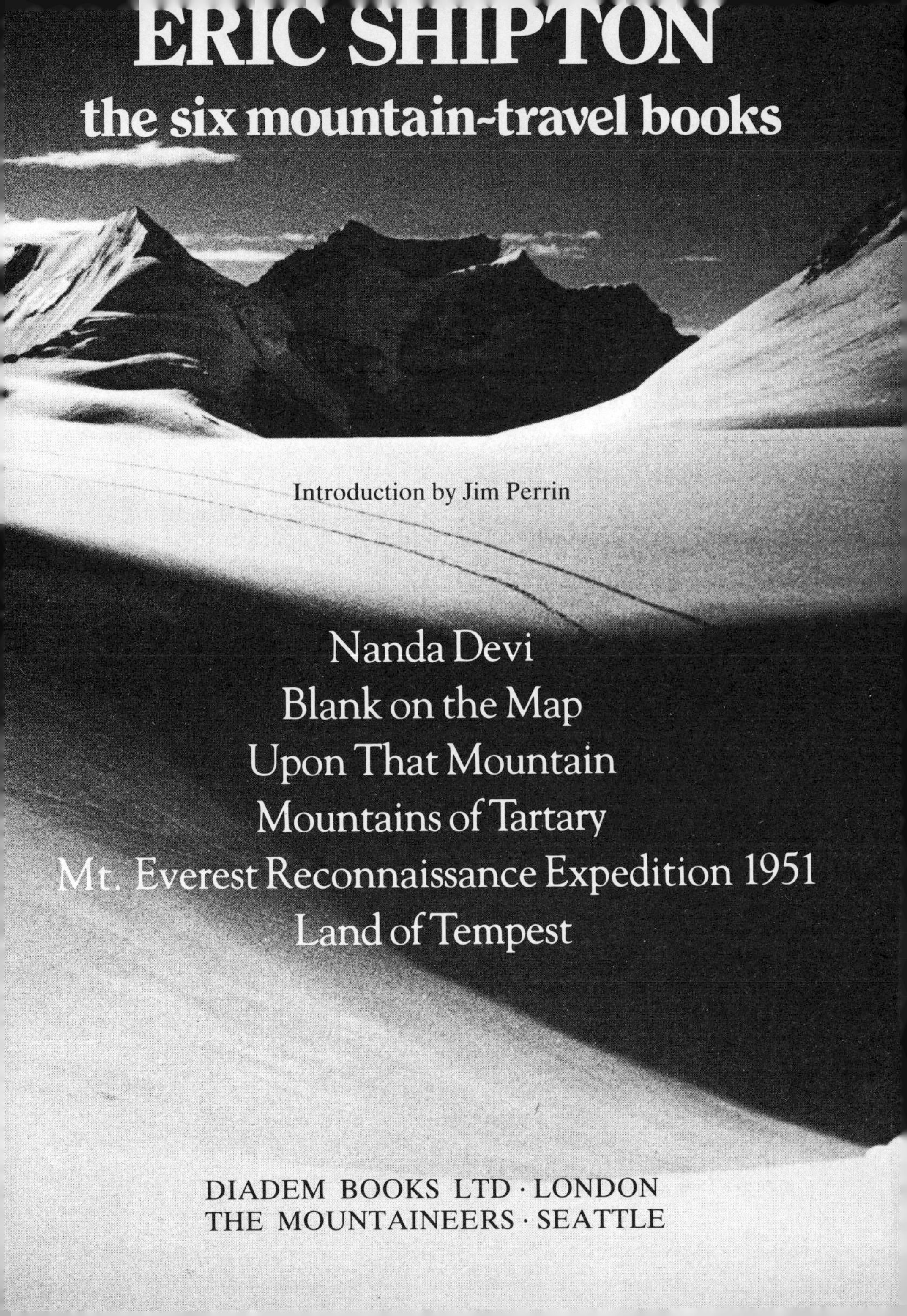

ERIC SHIPTON

the six mountain-travel books

Introduction by Jim Perrin

Nanda Devi
Blank on the Map
Upon That Mountain
Mountains of Tartary
Mt. Everest Reconnaissance Expedition 1951
Land of Tempest

DIADEM BOOKS LTD · LONDON
THE MOUNTAINEERS · SEATTLE

Published simultaneously in Great Britain and the United States
by Diadem Books Ltd., London and The Mountaineers, Seattle

Reprinted 1990

All trade enquiries in the U.K., Europe and Commonwealth (except Canada) to
Hodder and Stoughton, Mill Road, Dunton Green, Sevenoaks, Kent

All trade enquiries in the U.S.A. and Canada to
The Mountaineers, 306 2nd Avenue West, Seattle,
Washington 98119, USA

British Library Cataloguing in Publication Data:
Shipton, Eric
The six mountain-travel books.
1. Shipton, Eric 2. Mountaineers – Great Britain – Biography
I. Title
796.5′22′0924 GV199.92.553

ISBN 0-906371-56-2 (UK)

Library of Congress Catalog Card Number 84-062263
ISBN 0-89886-075-X (US)

Production by
Chambers Green Limited, Tunbridge Wells, Kent

Printed and bound in Great Britain by
Butler & Tanner Ltd, Frome and London

Contents

Introduction *by Jim Perrin* — *page* 7

Nanda Devi — 15
Blank on the Map — 153
Upon that Mountain — 305
Mountains of Tartary — 455
The Mount Everest Reconnaissance Expedition 1951 — 589
Land of Tempest — 623
  Further Travels in Patagonia and Tierra del Fuego — 762
  Crossing the North Patagonian Ice-cap — 768

Appendices

I The 1935 Everest Reconnaissance (plus map) — 775
II Explorations in the Karakoram 1939 (plus map) — 781
III Eric Earle Shipton (1907–1977) by *Charles Warren* — 791
IV Selected Bibliography — 794
V Shipton's Mountaineering Record 1923–1973 — 796

Photographs in the Text

Illustrations used at the beginning of each book

Main Title: In the Nepal Himalaya. *Photo: John Cleare* — *page* 3
Nanda Devi: A view up the Rishi Gorge to Nanda Devi *Photo: Doug Scott* — 16
Blank on the Map: Glacier Camp in the Himalaya *Photo: John Cleare* — 154
Upon that Mountain: Ruwenzori summit *Photo: John Cleare* — 306
Mountains of Tartary: The Kongur massif. *Photo: John Cleare* — 456
The Mount Everest Reconnaissance Expedition 1951: The head of the Khumbu Icefall. *Expedition photo* — 590
Land of Tempest: Approaching Mount Bové. *Photo: John Earle* — 624

Illustrations between pages 128 and 129

Nanda Devi 1934: Badrinath travels; Shaksgam/Karakoram 1937

Illustrations between pages 320 and 321

Karakoram 1937 and 1939; Alpine seasons; Kamet 1931
Mount Kenya 1929–30; Everest 1933 and 1935

Illustrations between pages 576 and 577

Everest 1935; Sinkiang 1947–49; Everest Reconnaissance 1951
Cho Oyu 1952; Patagonia and Tierra del Fuego 1959–64

ACKNOWLEDGEMENTS The copyright holder and publisher wish to thank the following for help in producing this volume: Jim Perrin for his Introduction; Charles Warren for permission to republish his Alpine Journal obituary notice; John Auden, Peter Mott, Charles Warren, Scott Russell, Sir Jack Longland, Hamish Brown, Jim Perrin, Audrey Salkeld, Doug Scott, Chris Bonington, John Earle, Jane Hillmann, Janis Tetlow, Diana Drummond, John Shipton and Phylis Wint for advice and assistance on editorial matters; to photographers whose contributions have strengthened the pictures already in the Shipton collection – John Cleare, Doug Scott, Hamish Brown, John Earle, John Porter, Kurt Diemberger and Julie Tullis, Pam Morrison, Peter Mott, Scott Russell, the Royal Geographical Society, Pete Radcliffe and Leo Dickinson. All other material drawn from original books and articles and new maps and not specifically credited to being the work of expedition members and others. A debt is also due to Julian Gearing, the staffs of the RGS Map Room and General Office, John Adams, Brigadier Derek Davis and Pam Davis for sundry help and advice.

INTRODUCTION

by Jim Perrin

Early in 1930 a young planter in Kenya unexpectedly received a letter from an ex-soldier ten years his senior, who had settled in the colony after the Great War. The letter mentioned that its writer had done some climbing in the English Lake District on his last home leave, and asked advice about visiting the East African mountains. Its immediate results were a meeting between the two men, an initial jaunt up Kilimanjaro together, and the first ascent, later that year, of the West Ridge of Mount Kenya – one of the major pre-war achievements of British alpinism.

The two men were, of course, Eric Shipton and H. W. Tilman, and their chance meeting, out in the colonies at the very beginning of the decade, led to one of the most fruitful partnerships and entrancing sagas in the history of mountain exploration. Indeed, the centrality of their role in that history throughout one of its vital phases is unarguable. The chance of their acquaintance and the magnitude of their travels aside, there is another aspect of these two men which is perhaps even more remarkable. For they were both inveterate chroniclers of their climbs and journeys, and the quality of the writings so produced places them absolutely in the forefront of mountaineering and travel literature. A previous volume in this series collected together Tilman's seven mountain-travel titles. Here, for the first time under one cover, are the six mountain-travel books of Eric Shipton. (His second essay at autobiography, *That Untravelled World*, duplicated too much material to be included here.)

For the span of their contents alone, Shipton's books are noteworthy: *Nanda Devi* (1936), his first, deals with the 1934 penetration up the Rishi Gorge into the Nanda Devi sanctuary in company with Tilman, as well as the two traverses of the Badrinath – Kedarnath and Badrinath – Gangotri watersheds. From the moment of its first publication, for reasons to be examined below, it was regarded as one of the revolutionary texts of mountain literature, and it remains an enthralling story of hazardous and uncertain journeying with minimal resources through unknown country. *Blank on the Map* (1938) describes the 1937 Shaksgam survey expedition undertaken with Michael Spender, John Auden, (brothers to the poets) and Tilman – an important venture into a little-known region of the Himalayas which provided a basis for much subsequent mountaineering activity in the Karakoram. (First editions of this very rare title, reprinted here for the first time, now command fabulous prices amongst collectors.)

From 1940 to 1942 Shipton served as British Consul-General at Kashgar, in the Chinese Province of Sinkiang. During this period he completed a first volume of memoirs, entitled *Upon that Mountain*, published in 1943. This frank, vivid polemic set out his basic mountaineering creed, whilst also describing his early Alpine and Himalayan seasons, the series of climbs on Mount Kenya, and the four attempts on Everest and two survey-trips to the Karakoram in which he took part during the thirties. His next book was very different in tone. *Mountains of Tartary* (1950) is a series of light-hearted sketches of weeks or weekends seized from official consular work – in the main during his second spell of office in Kashgar – and spent on Bogdo Ola, Mustagh Ata, Chakragil (mountains which are again coming into vogue in the eighties since China's relaxation of restrictions on travel). *The Mount Everest Reconnaissance Expedition 1951* (1952) was basically a photographic volume, prefaced by a succinct and entertaining narrative about this vital piece of mountain exploration, which cleared the path for John Hunt's successful expedition to the mountain in 1953. The final title to be included in the present book is *Land of Tempest* (1963), which takes for theme the period of Shipton's life from 1958 to 1962 and includes accounts of three trips to Patagonia – on the last of which he made the first crossing of the main Patagonian ice-cap – and one to Tierra del Fuego. Two further reports of travels in Patagonia, in the form of articles from the *Alpine Journal* and two papers from *The Geographical Journal* on the orgies of peak-bagging around Everest in 1935 and Karakoram glacier-travel in 1939, are included to fill out the extant written record of his major mountain travels.

The above bald catalogue suggests the range, but captures little of the flavour, of this extraordinary man's life, the brief outline of which is as follows. He was born in Ceylon in 1907, his father a tea-planter who died before his son was three. Thereafter, Shipton, his sister and mother travelled extensively between Ceylon, India, France and England, before the family finally settled in the latter country for purposes of the children's schooling. Shipton's mountaineering career began in 1924 with holidays in Norway and Switzerland and was consolidated through four successive alpine seasons in 1925 – 1928. His first ascent of Nelion, the unclimbed twin summit of Mount Kenya, with Wyn Harris in 1929, and of the same mountain's West Ridge with Tilman the following year, brought him to the notice of the mountaineering establishment of the day and elicited an invitation to join the expedition led by Frank Smythe to Kamet, in the Garhwal region, in 1931. Shipton distinguished himself on this trip, being in the summit party on eleven of the twelve peaks climbed by the expedition, including that of Kamet itself, which at 25,447ft was the highest summit then attained. His performance in 1931 led to an invitation to join Ruttledge's 1933 Everest expedition. Thereafter the milestones slip by: Rishi Gorge 1934; Everest Reconnaissance 1935, which he led; Everest and Nanda Devi 1936; Shaksgam 1937; Everest 1938; Karakoram 1939 are the main ones amongst them, but virtually the whole decade was spent in Himalayan travel, and the extent of his exploratory achievement perhaps even now lacks full recognition.

He spent the Second World War in Government service in Sinkiang, Persia and Hungary, went back for a further spell in Kashgar from 1946 to 1948, accompanied by his wife Diana*, and was Consul-General at Kunming, in

*Who also wrote a book about the experience *The Antique Land* (Hodder and Stoughton, 1950).

Southern China, from 1949 to 1951. On his return to England he was asked to lead an expedition to reconnoitre the Southern approaches to Everest, in the course of which he and Ed Hillary first espied the eventual line of ascent up the Western Cwm to the South Col, from a vantage point on the slopes of Pumori. The following year he led a rather unsatisfactory training expedition to Cho Oyu. In the late summer of 1952, Shipton having been urged to lead a further expedition to Everest in 1953 and having accepted, the joint Himalayan Committee of the Alpine Club and the Royal Geographical Society performed an astonishing *volte-face*, appointing the competent and experienced but at that time virtually unknown Colonel John Hunt as leader, and accepting Shipton's consequent resignation.

This sorry episode effectively formed a watershed in Shipton's life. After the break-up of his marriage and loss of his post as Warden of the Outward Bound School at Eskdale, which occurred shortly after the events of 1952–53, he lived for a time in the rural seclusion of Shropshire, working as a forestry labourer. He was enticed back for a last trip to the Karakoram in 1957, and thereafter developed a new grand obsession with travel in the southernmost regions of South America, which absorbed most of the next decade in his life. Finally, in his sixties, he was a popular lecturer on cruises to such places as the Galapagos Islands, and leader of mild Himalayan treks. He died of liver cancer at the home of a friend in Wiltshire during the spring of 1977.

This, then, is the bare outline of an outstanding life. The man who lived it, through his involvement in the 1931 Kamet and 1933 Everest expeditions, had attained a considerable degree of national celebrity by the early thirties, yet at that time he was to all intents and purposes a professionless pauper and a kind of international tramp, whose possessions amounted to little more than the clothes in which he stood. There is an admirable passage in *Upon That Mountain* where Shipton recounts the dawning of a realisation that the way of life which most appealed to him perhaps presented a practical possibility. It happened on the way back to India from the North Side of Everest in 1933. In company with the geologist Lawrence Wager, he had made his way across a strip of unexplored country and over a new pass into Sikkim. Wager's influence shifted the emphasis of Shipton's interest away from the climbing of peaks to enthusiasm for a general mode of exploration – a fascination with geography itself. Twenty years later, this shift was to provide his detractors with an easy target. For the moment, his mind works over the ground thus:

> 'Why not spend the rest of my life doing this sort of thing?' There was no way of life that I liked more, the scope appeared to be unlimited, others had done it, vague plans had already begun to take shape, why not put some of them into practice? . . . The most obvious snag, of course, was lack of private means; but surely such a mundane consideration could not be decisive. In the first place I was convinced that expeditions could be run for a tithe of the cost generally considered necessary. Secondly if one could produce useful or interesting results one would surely find support . . .

When he took into account his reactions to the milieu of the large expedition, ('The small town of tents that sprung up each evening, the noise and racket of each fresh start, the sight of a huge army invading the peaceful valleys, it was all so far removed from the light, free spirit with which we were wont to approach our peaks'), then the virtue to be made of necessity was obvious, and of it was born what came to be known as the "Shipton/Tilman style of lightweight expedition". I referred above to Shipton's *Nanda Devi* as a revolutionary text, and it was just that. I doubt if there has ever been a less formulaic account of an expedition. It has a magical, fresh quality, a get-through-by-the-skin-of-your-teeth spontaneity, a candour, a clear rationale, an excited commitment, an elation about the enterprise undertaken, which no previous mountaineering book had approached. From the outset the terms are made clear: five months in the Garhwal Himalaya to tackle some of its outstanding topographical problems, 'climbing peaks when opportunity occurred', on a budget of £150 each for himself and Tilman (some of Shipton's share of which is advanced by Tilman 'against uncertain security'). The scenes throughout, from the broken-toed, frock-coated setting-out from Ranikhet to the final descent from the Sunderdhunga Col to Maiktoli, are evoked in a clear and economical style. But it is the message – the simple moral that it is possible, and in terms of response to the landscape and its peoples even desirable, to travel cheap and light, to move fast and live off the land – which is the book's revolutionary charge, and which was to make Shipton and Tilman, in the words of the American writer David Roberts, 'retroactive heroes of the avant-garde'.

Two major characteristics distinguish *Nanda Devi* and were to become hallmarks of Shipton's writing. The first of these is an intense curiosity – which remains with him, his conclusions growing more authoritative with increase of experience – about natural landforms, whether they be mountains, valleys, rivers, volcanoes or glaciers. This curiosity acts as a stimulus, a fund of energy, in his explorations, continually used as a basis, a point of reference: 'It was enthralling to disentangle the geography of the region . . . for me, the basic reason for mountaineering'.

Alongside this drive to understand the physical make-up of a landscape there operates a more reflective principle, very close to traditional nature-mysticism, which Shipton almost invariably carries off with great poise and delicacy, sure-footedly avoiding the obvious pitfalls of bathos or inflation.

> . . . we settled down on a comfortable bed of sand, and watched the approach of night transform the wild desert mountains into phantoms of soft unreality. How satisfying it was to be travelling with such simplicity. I lay awaiting the approach of sleep, watching the constellations swing across the sky. Did I sleep that night – or was I caught up for a moment into the ceaseless rhythm of space? *Blank on the Map*

A very satisfying irony lies in suggesting an affinity with mysticism of a man who claimed throughout his adult life to be an agnostic, and who would probably, even if only for the sheer joy of argument, have vigorously rejected the intimation. Perhaps his disclaimer of religious belief was like that of Simone Weill, and masked a genuine sense of divine mystery within the universe. Certainly much of the interest in Shipton's writings derives from a tension between the very practical preoccupations with physical phenomena, and a frequent lapsing into a more quietistic mode of thought. (To compound the mischief, I have to say that *Nanda Devi* puts me in mind of no other text so much as one of the late poems of that most ascetic of saints, St John of the Cross, quoted here in the translation by Roy Campbell:

The generous heart upon its quest
Will never falter, nor go slow,
But pushes on, and scorns to rest,
Wherever it's most hard to go.
It runs ahead and wearies not
But upward hurls its fierce advance
For it enjoys I know not what
That is achieved by lucky chance.

Those who knew Shipton well sound a recurrent note in their reminiscences which supports the contention that there was a mystical element to his character. It concerns a quality of detachment he possessed, and invariably fastens on a specific physical detail. The following is typical:

> He had the most marvellous blue eyes, very kindly, very amused, and very wise. But there was always a sense, when you talked with him, that somehow he was not with you, was looking right through you, searching out farther and farther horizons.

In the course of researching Shipton's biography, it was remarkable and eventually almost comical how often that impression, almost word-for-word, was repeated. Without the evidence of the text it could be taken as a mannerism, but in his books there recur time and again passages which define his response to landscape as one striving towards a mystical awareness.

In this he is very different to Tilman, his most frequent companion of the thirties, and it is interesting to compare the two men. The ten-year difference in age is for once significant, for Tilman's seniority ensured that he underwent the determining influence on his character of the First World War, and it affected him profoundly. It is what made him a master of that most serious of all forms of writing, comic irony, and it is what causes him to veer dangerously close at times to a distinct misanthropy. It explains the prelapsarian vitality with which he imbues his native characters, the neglectful portrayal of his compatriots, and the isolation which identifies his authorial persona. In his personal conduct, it provides the reason for his taciturnity, his phlegmatism and unemotional responses to situations. The vulnerability of youth, its lack of circumspection and eager commitment to affection or cause were in Tilman's case the victims of war, and the survivor, psychic and physical, of that particularly obscene war had need to be encased in adamantine.

Shipton's enthusiasms, on the other hand, operate under no such constraint. He can indulge his feelings as freely as he will, the zest and gaiety of the twenties glitters around his early activities. He commits himself freely, and as equally with a climb as a journey of exploration or to one of the many women who shared his life. A couple of comments upon him from 1931 by Frank Smythe capture the temperament of the man:

> No one who climbs with Shipton can remain pessimistic, for he imparts an imperturbability and confidence into a day's work which are in themselves a guarantee of success.

Or again, about his climbing:

> I saw Shipton's eye light up, and next instant he went at the slope with the energy of a boxer who, after months of training, sees his opponent before him.

The differences in their characters probably acted as a bond between Shipton and Tilman, and account for their sharing of some of the most ambitious undertakings of their lives. For Tilman, his own youth lost, Shipton's enthusiasm and boundless energy must have been inspiring and invigorating, whilst the fatherless Shipton may well have found that Tilman's wry, benevolent maturity fulfilled a need in him at a certain stage of his life. In mountaineering terms, the roles were reversed, and the more experienced Shipton was the leader. One very telling indication of this occurs in Tilman's diary for 30 May, 1934. After reconnoitring one of the crucial – and very tortuous – passages of the route up the Rishi Gorge, they have to hurry back to camp. The subsequent diary entry briefly states, 'Shipton's route-memory invaluable as usual, self hopeless.'

It has to be said, though, that a change occurs in Shipton's outlook, especially with regard to mountaineering, during the mid-thirties. It seems to me complex and cumulative rather than associated with specific circumstances. The influence of older companions such as Tilman and Wager would have played a part. So too, perhaps, did the relationship upon which he had embarked with Pamela Freston. But two related events could be seen as decisive in the transition from joyful mountaineering innocence to prudent experience. These were the two avalanches which Shipton witnessed on the slopes leading to the North Col of Everest during successive expeditions in 1935 and 1936. Of the first one, he had to say "I am sure that no one could have escaped from an avalanche such as that which broke away below us while we were lying peacefully on the North Col". The following year, as he and Wyn Harris were climbing up the same slope, this is what happened:

> We climbed quickly over a lovely hard surface in which one sharp kick produced a perfect foothold. About half-way up to the Col we started traversing to the left. Wyn anchored himself firmly on the lower lip of a crevasse while I led across the slope. I had almost reached the end of the rope and Wyn was starting to follow when there was a rending sound . . . a short way above me, and the whole surface of the slope I was standing on started to move slowly down towards the brink of an ice-cliff a couple of hundred feet below . . .

Wyn Harris managed to jump back into the crevasse and re-establish the belay, the snow failed to gather momentum, and Shipton survived. It was the last attempt on the mountain that year. The point is, that Shipton's faith in the material he was climbing had been undermined – just as in personal relationships, when the trust has gone the commitment is withdrawn. Shipton's heyday as a *climber* is delimited by these events. Though there are inevitably some exciting and perilous escapades after 1936 – the climb on the Dent Blanche-like peak above the Bostan Terek valley is a striking example – henceforwards, reading these books, we keep company with a much more circumspect mountaineer.

This line of reasoning inevitably leads us towards a consideration of what is generally and I think rightly regarded as one of the cruces of Shipton's life – the circumstances surrounding the choice of leadership for the 1953 expedition to Everest. It is very difficult to summarise in brief the main points of what is still a controversial topic. Even Walt Unsworth's *Everest* book, which comes nearest to being an authoritative history of the mountain, overlooked important material in its researches which throws a clearer light on some aspects of this vital area. What emerges, from close examination of relevant Himalayan Committee minutes and written submissions from its surviving members, is a bizarre tale of fudging and mudging, falsification of official minutes, unauthorized invitations, and opportunistic and desperate last-minute seizures of initiative by a particular faction. It is a perfect illustration of the cock-up rather than the conspiracy theory of history, from which little credit redounds upon the British mountaineering establishment of the time. The saddest fact about the whole sorry tale is that it appeared to place in conflict two honourable and quite innocent men – Shipton and John Hunt.

There are two basic themes to be considered. The first of these is the general climate of feeling surrounding Shipton's attitude for, and interest in, the leadership of an expedition which, even in the early stages of its planning, was subject to a jingoistic insistence that Everest must be climbed by a British party. (That this was not to be achieved for a further 22 years scarcely mattered in the event, the national attachments of the first summiteers being clearly turned to the Commonwealth's greater glory.) This climate of feeling, accepting some of Shipton's own statements at face value,* and drawing in other rather more questionable evidence, particularly that relating to the 1952 Cho Oyu expedition, where peculiar circumstances undoubtedly affected Shipton's leadership, had drifted towards the view that Shipton lacked the urgency, the thrust, the killer instinct which would be necessary to "conquer" Everest. It was immeasurably strengthened by Shipton's own submission to the Himalayan Committee meeting of 28 July, 1952, in which he expressed doubts about his suitability for the job on the following grounds: he had to consider his own career – with a wife and two young children to support, he was out of a job and needed to get one; he felt that new blood was needed to undertake the task; his strong preference was for smaller parties, lightly equipped.

At this juncture we need to pass over to a consideration of the second basic theme – the conduct of members of the Himalayan Committee over the matter of the leadership. The first point to be made is that the Committee was very weakly chaired. Because of this, the pro-Shipton faction carried the day at the meeting of July 28 and, chiefly through the efforts of Laurence Kirwan, Shipton was strongly prevailed upon to accept the leadership, the contention then resting with the matter of deputy leadership.

However, there also existed a pro-Hunt faction, headed by Basil Goodfellow and Colonel Tobin, who had both been absent from the July 28 meeting. These two men lobbied forcefully that the deputy – or assault – leadership should fall to Hunt, which would inevitably compromise Shipton, whose choice had been Charles Evans and to whom Hunt was therefore unacceptable in that role. The crucial committee meeting took place on September 11. The pro-Hunt faction was present in force, determined to reverse the decision of the previous meeting. The more ardent Shiptonians –

* In *Upon That Mountain*, for example, he had written that 'there are some, even among those who have themselves attempted to reach the summit, who nurse a secret hope that Mount Everest will never be climbed. I must confess to such feelings myself'.

most notably Kirwan and Shipton's old friend Wager – were absent. Shipton was morally compelled to offer his resignation. The rest is history, apart from a few squalid diversions, such as the subsequent falsification of this meeting's minutes by Claude Elliott, the chairman – in the words of one contemporary observer, 'as bad a chairman of committees as one could find; he was hopelessly indecisive and hesitant and was too easily swayed by anyone (like Kirwan) who held firm opinions, however wrong these might be'.

What the effect would have been upon Shipton had he led the successful expedition to Everest is a matter for conjecture. John Hunt was patently well-equipped to cope with the ensuing celebrity, and used it tirelessly in the public good. It could perhaps be thought doubtful that Shipton would have enjoyed, and responded so positively, to the inevitably massive public acclaim.

After 1953, his life went through a difficult period, but it emerged into a golden late summer of exploration in an area completely fresh to him. His Patagonian journeys of the late fifties and sixties were a harking-back in many ways to his great Karakoram travels of the thirties. They would have been rendered immensely more public and difficult and perhaps thus less satisfying to him, by the burden of international fame. Instead, he was able to slip quietly away, pursue his own bent amongst the unknown mountains and glaciers of a new wilderness. It is a myth fulfilled, a proper consummation in the life of this explorer-mystic, whose outlook and progress resonate so closely with those of Tennyson's "Ulysses", from which poem he took the motto for the first part of *Blank on the Map*, and the title for his magnificent second autobiography, *That Untravelled World*.

There is a phrase of Shipton's from this latter book which gives perfect expression to one of the great lives of our century – 'a random harvest of delight'. That is exactly what the books collected together between these covers are, in general terms. But they are also an opportunity for a new generation of readers to engage with one of the most attractive personalities the sport of mountaineering has ever produced, to keep company with his spare, lithe figure loping off into the ranges, seeking out the undiscovered country, his distant blue eyes lingering on the form of a particular peak, the passage over to an unexplored glacier. If curiosity, appreciation, aspiration and delight are a form of praise – as assuredly they are – then here is one man's testament of a lifetime spent in worship of the great world around him.

> I am a part of all that I have met;
> Yet all experience is an arch wherethrough
> Gleams that untravelled world, whose margin fades
> For ever and for ever when I move.

– It is the epitaph Shipton would have chosen for himself. No man lived out its theme more fully, nor finally more deserved its implicit tribute.

NANDA DEVI

Nanda Devi

First published by Hodder and Stoughton, 1936

Contents

Foreword *by Hugh Ruttledge* *page* 21

Part 1: Innocents from Nepal – and London

1 27
2 30
3 34
4 42

Part 2: The Secret Shrine

5 47
6 52
7 58
8 69
9 78
10 91

Part 3: The First Crossing of the Watershed

11 99
12 105

Part 4: The Second Crossing of the Watershed

13 113
14 122
15 130

Part 5: The Second Nanda Devi Venture

16 137
17 143

FOREWORD

Hugh Ruttledge

WHEN Mr. Shipton honoured me by an invitation to write a foreword to his book, I accepted with a particular sense of both privilege and opportunity; of privilege because the book is an epic of mountaineering exploration, of opportunity because so little is yet known of three aspects of Himalayan travel: the comparatively easy and inexpensive access to some of the wildest regions, the almost unlimited scope for small but thoroughly competent parties, and the amazing strength and capacity of the Sherpa porter.

I had the good fortune to serve for nearly five years in the section of the Central Himalayan chain with which this book deals. I climbed there with Sherpa, Gurkha, Bhotia and Kumaoni – as well as British – companions; and we made four attempts to enter the great Nanda Devi Basin, as better mountaineers had done before us. It is therefore with some knowledge of the facts that I acclaim the success gained by Messrs. Shipton and Tilman and their three Sherpa comrades as one of the greatest feats in mountaineering history. Not only that: it has proved beyond doubt that, in these regions at any rate, a small homogeneous party, self-contained, able to live off the country, with no weak links and ably led, can go further and do more than the elaborate expeditions which have been thought necessary for the Himalaya. What a field of adventure and enterprise this throws open to young mountaineers, now that most of the other great mountain ranges of the world are but too well known.

One word of warning is perhaps necessary: work of this kind should be undertaken only by those who have attained the highest degree of mountaineering skill, judgment and endurance. Those who read this book with understanding will realise the number of tight places this party got into, where nothing but the most brilliant technical competence could have got them out alive. It is not a game for the beginner, or for the lover of flesh-pots.

The greatest feat was the successful entry into, and departure from, the "inner sanctuary" of the Nanda Devi Basin – a place only about seventy-five miles from Almora, yet hitherto more inaccessible than the North Pole. At last men have set foot upon the slopes of the greatest mountain in the British Empire; and to them will be extended the admiration of those who have struggled and fought for it – notably Dr. T. G. Longstaff, who so nearly succeeded in 1907.

Less spectacular perhaps, but hardly less exacting, were the two great traverses of the Badrinath-Gangotri and the Badrinath-Kedarnath watershed, along lines famous in Hindu mythology. These were replete with all the misery that mountaineering in the monsoon season can entail, but the climbers have their reward in the completion of a task that was well worth accomplishment, and in the regard of good Hindus, in whose eyes this would be a pilgrimage of superabundant merit.

Mr. Shipton has paid generous and well-deserved tribute to the three Sherpa porters who accompanied him. It is no exaggeration to say that, without men of this type, climbing the higher Himalaya would be impossible. On them are based our hopes of climbing Mount Everest, and for years to come there will be none among the Himalayan peoples to equal them as mountaineers, porters, and loyal, unselfish companions. They are well on their way to become a corps of guides as famous as the men of the Alps. In time there may be others as good – there is splendid material in Kumaon, in Hunza or in Baltistan, to name a few Himalayan regions; and the humble Nepalese Dotials who served Mr. Shipton so faithfully in the Rishiganga are worth their salt. At present the Sherpa holds pride of place, and his morale and *esprit-de-corps* are tremendous assets. Given the right leaders – and they must be of the best – he is unbeatable. The description of him in this book is the most understanding and delightful that has ever been written.

The lists are now set for great deeds in the Himalayan snow-fields. Messrs. Shipton and Tilman have shown the way; let us hope that many will follow.

HUGH RUTTLEDGE

22,735 FT
23,940 FT
NANDA DEVI
25,660 FT
EAST
NANDA DEVI
24,379 FT
LONGSTAFF
1905
ICE PLATEAU
Grass
GLACIER
Camp
Camp
1ST EXPLORATION
LONGSTAFF & BRUCE
1907
BAGINI PASS
20,100 FT
Advance Base
Camp (May)
INNER SANCTUARY
2ND EXPLORATION
RUTTLEDGE
1932
SUNDERDHUNGA
COL
Exit of
Shipton Party
MAIKTOLI
22,360 FT
Grass
GLACIER
Base Camp
(September)
Camp
Grass
Herds of Thar & Bharal
HANGING
GLACIERS
INNER WALL
INNER WALL
RHAMANI GORGE
RISHI GANGA GORGE
Route — May & September
LONGSTAFF
1907
Base Camp
(May)
GRAHAM
1883
TRISULI GLACIER
TRISUL

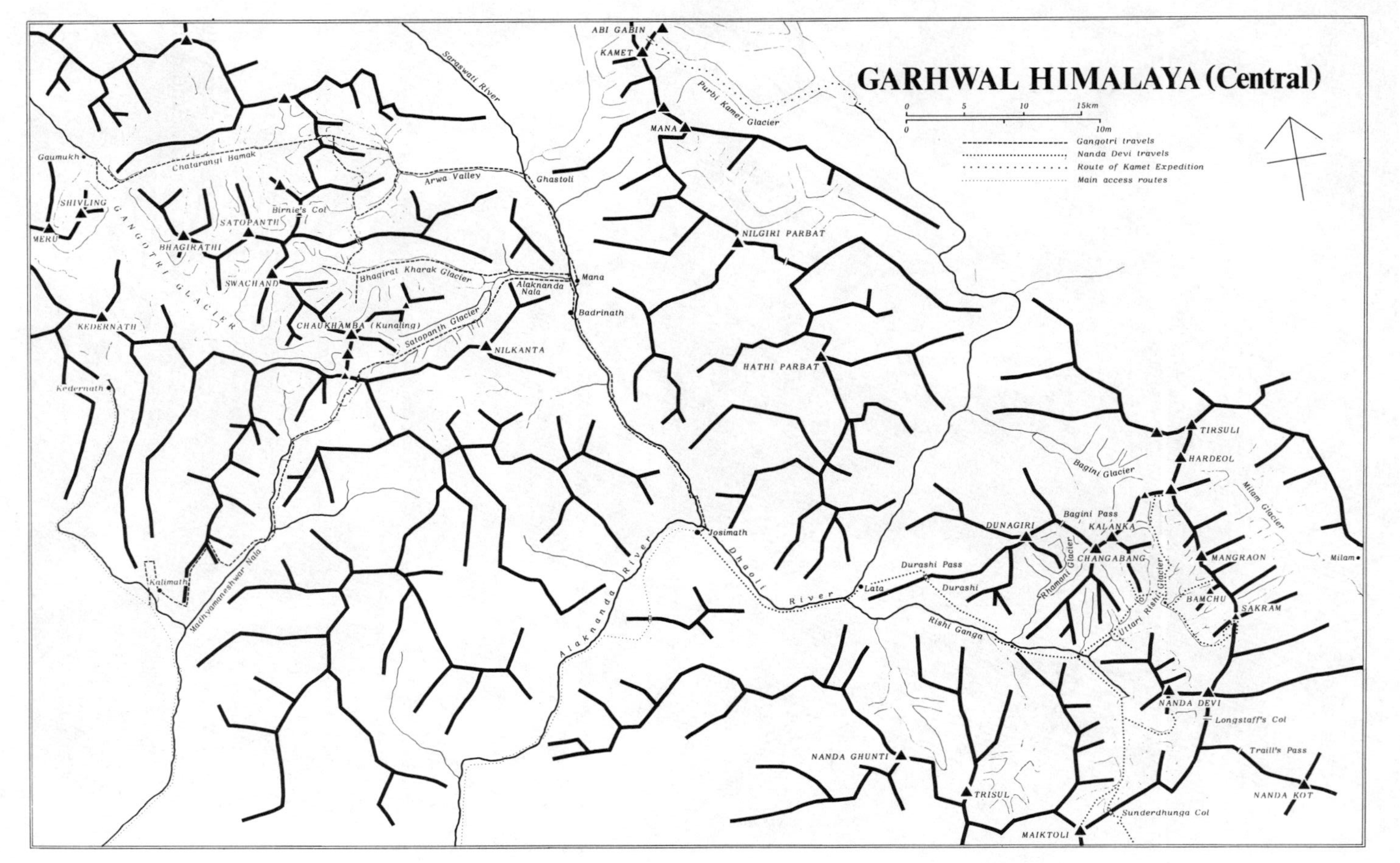

GARHWAL HIMALAYA (Central)
0
5
10
15km
0
10m
Gangotri travels
Nanda Devi travels
Route of Kamet Expedition
Main access routes
ABI GABIN
KAMET
MANA
Purbi Kamet Glacier
Saraswati River
Gaumukh
Chataranyi Bamak
Arwa Valley
Ghastoli
SHIVLING
MERU
Birnie's Col
SATOPANTH
BHAGIRATHI
GANGOTRI GLACIER
SWACHAND
Bhagirat Kharak Glacier
Alaknanda Nala
Mana
Badrinath
NILGIRI PARBAT
KEDERNATH
CHAUKHAMBA (Kunaling)
Satopanth Glacier
NILKANTA
HATHI PARBAT
Kedernath
TIRSULI
HARDEOL
Bagini Glacier
Milam Glacier
Bagini Pass
DUNAGIRI
KALANKA
CHANGABANG
MANGRAON
Milam
Josimath
Durashi Pass
Durashi
Rhamani Glacier
Uttari Rishi Glacier
BAMCHU
SAKRAM
Lata
Dhaoli River
Rishi Ganga
Kalimath
Madhyamaneshwar Nala
Alaknanda River
NANDA DEVI
Longstaff's Col
Traill's Pass
NANDA GHUNTI
TRISUL
NANDA KOT
Sunderdhunga Col
MAIKTOLI

Part 1

Innocents from Nepal – and London

CHAPTER ONE

IN the exploration of a continent the mountainous areas are generally the last strongholds of mystery to fall before the onslaught of man, be that onslaught brutal, scientific or merely inquisitive. The difficulties of transport are so great; the physical hardships so heavy; the reward so small – for glacier regions are materially useless. For these reasons then the high places of the earth remain remote and inaccessible until man, having explored all fertile regions of a particular country, finds himself dwelling under the very shadow of the mountains and becomes aware of an overwhelming desire to conquer them. This feeling doubtless owes its force partly to the attraction of the unknown and partly to the natural beauty and sublime grandeur of mountainous districts; but I like to think that it goes deeper; that the wish to explore springs from a delight in the purely æsthetic nature of the quest.

When man is conscious of the urge to explore, not all the arduous journeyings, the troubles that will beset him and the lack of material gain from his investigations will stop him. As a famous Arctic explorer remarked many years ago: "The great majority of men who visit the Arctic *do so because they want to*, a large number do so for publicity, while it is possible that one or two have gone there for purely scientific purposes."

The italics are mine. What was true of the Arctic then is equally true of the little-known mountain country of today, and of the Alps before they became "the playground of Europe". To the early explorer fighting his way across the passes of *Haute Savoie* and to people who, like myself, have come under the spell of the high Himalaya the reason for exploration remains the same – *we do so because we want to*.

It was my good fortune to visit the mighty ranges of South Central Asia, which stretch from east to west without a break for over fifteen hundred miles, as a member of F. S. Smythe's Kamet expedition in 1931. Then, for the first time, I saw mountains whose rugged splendour baffles description and whose complex structure probably renders them inaccessible even to the most advanced mountaineering technique. With this vision before me, surpassing all the wildest dreams of my early mountaineering apprenticeship, I welcomed the opportunity, some two years later, of joining the fourth expedition to Mount Everest, where I saw the harsher and less lovely aspect of the Tibetan side of the range.

The Kamet and Everest expeditions had, as their main objective, the climbing of a single lofty peak. In the one case we succeeded: in the other we failed. But on each occasion I had a mighty longing to detach myself from the big and cumbersome organisation which for some reason had been thought to be necessary for an attack on the more lofty summits of the earth, and to wander with a small, self-contained party through the labyrinth of unexplored valleys, forming our plans to suit the circumstances, climbing peaks when opportunity occurred, following up our own topographical clues and crossing passes into unknown territory. This desire held me captive even before I left the Everest Base Camp in July, 1933, and I resolved to carry out some such scheme before age, marriage or other considerations made it impossible of accomplishment.

During the winter of 1933–34 I began to form plans. The primary choice of district was not difficult. There can be few regions of the Himalaya providing topographical problems of more absorbing interest than that lying in the Almora and Garhwal districts of the United Provinces. Here there are no political obstacles (the bugbear of the Asiatic explorer) to be overcome as the region lies almost entirely in British India. Moreover, the transport of supplies and equipment to a suitable base is a simple matter, the organisation of which does not require any vast experience of the country or knowledge of the language. Brief acquaintance, while with the Kamet expedition, had given me some first-hand information on a number of problems and I felt confident that, with the modest resources at my disposal, I should be able to carry out my proposed campaign with some fair chance of achieving useful results. Therefore I plumped for Almora and Garhwal.

The question of companionship did not worry me. There were a number of people who would be quite prepared – and suitably qualified – to take part in such an enterprise, and my association with the Nepalese and Tibetan porters of the 1933 Everest expedition had convinced me that their natural, if undeveloped, mountaineering ability, their constant cheerfulness and their wonderful sense of loyalty, would make them ideal comrades. So I got into touch with Karma Paul, the Tibetan interpreter to the Everest expeditions, and requested him to send word to Angtharkay, Pasang Bhotia, and Rinzing, three men for whom I felt particular liking since they were among the eight porters who had placed our Camp VI at the enormous altitude of 27,400 feet the previous summer. Rinzing, however, was not available, and at the last moment Angtharkay brought forward his cousin, Kusang Namgir, a man of extraordinary toughness and ability.

In January '34 I had my best stroke of luck, in a letter from my old friend H. W. Tilman, who had been my companion on three expeditions to the mountains of East and Central Africa. This letter announced that, since he had long leave from Kenya, he had bought a second-hand bicycle and had ridden it across the continent alone, through Uganda, Belgian Congo and French Equatorial Territory, finally emerging on the West Coast where he sold the bicycle and boarded a cargo steamer bound for England. The letter said further that this had proved a most cheap and efficacious method of reaching home and that the writer, during his cycling travels, had existed entirely on native food, keeping pretty fit except for a few bouts of fever.

Here indeed was a kindred spirit. When I told him of my plans he at once offered to put up his share of the expenses. This, I estimated, would amount to £150 all told: that is, the whole expedition would not cost more than £300. Actually, we managed on less than that.

Our party was now complete and numbered four besides myself: Tilman, Angtharkay, Pasang and Kusang. Nobody could have had four more loyal, determined and unselfish comrades and there remained now only the choice of a main objective.

Now, nobody attempting mountain exploration in the Himalaya (or anywhere else, for that matter) can afford to miss an opportunity of discussing his plans with Dr. T. G. Longstaff. When he gave me that opportunity, therefore, I accepted with alacrity and, as a result of long discussions with him, I determined to make an attempt to force the hitherto inviolate sanctuary of the Nanda Devi Basin.

At first this seemed as if we were flying too high. Here was a mountain whose summit was the highest in the British Empire. For centuries it had inspired worship and propitiatory sacrifice as the "Blessed Goddess" of Hindu philosophers and scribes. For more than fifty years it had been the inaccessible goal of explorers who, attracted by the impregnability of its surroundings, had failed in repeated attempts to reach even its foot, the reason being that around the 25,660 foot mountain itself stretched a huge ring of peaks, more than thirty of them over 21,000 feet high, that constituted themselves unrelenting guardians of the great mountain and defeated any penetration.

And we, with light equipment, few stores, and a joint capital of £300, were setting forth to reach this goal. That we eventually succeeded was largely due to the unremitting labour of those who preceded us. To explorers in general and to mountaineers in particular, it is a well-known fact that each successive attempt at the solving of a problem makes that problem easier of solution. Few great mountains have been climbed, and few passes crossed, at first, second or even third essay. The man who eventually reaches the summit of Mount Everest will have done so, not by his own efforts alone, but over the shoulders of the pioneers – Mallory, Norton, Somervell – without whose hard-won experience he would have stood no chance. So with our own – seemingly fantastic – expedition. That measure of success met with in our enterprise, we owe primarily to those who went before us.

The days went on, passed swiftly in discussion of our base, our transport, our food – enthralling, this business of arranging an expedition that might well have been formulated on that classic statement of the great Duke of Wellington when comparing the organisation of the French tactical scheme in the

Peninsular War with that of his own. Of Napoleon's Generals he said that their plans were laid with such thoroughness that, at a single slight hitch, their whole structure was liable to collapse; whereas, if anything went wrong with his (Wellington's) less complex arrangements, all he had to do was "to tie it up with string" and so carry on . . . a moral that applies to exploration as well as to war, and is probably the reason why a small expedition, such as our own, almost invariably achieves far more than does a large and elaborate one when proportionate costs are taken into consideration.

So, on April 6th, 1934, after a short period of preparation we left Liverpool for Calcutta in the Brocklebank cargo ship *Mahsud*.

CHAPTER TWO

DURING the long hot days of the four weeks' voyage we discussed and re-discussed our plans, and made ourselves familiar with the history and geography of Garhwal; and in order to present the reader with a simple picture of the country, I cannot do better than to revert for the moment to geographical data.

"The Himalaya" is the rather loose name given to those mountains which extend, in an unbroken chain, for some fifteen hundred miles across the north of India. The word itself is a combination of two Sanskrit words, *him* meaning snow, and *alaya* abode. Modern geographers restrict the name to the range enclosed within the arms of the Indus River on the north-west, and the Brahmaputra on the south-east; but one must remember that the Karakoram and Hindu Kush ranges north and west of the Indus, and the mountains of northern Burmah and western China are all part of the same system.

Behind the chain to the north lies the plateau of Tibet at a general altitude of 15,000 feet. Here, at a point almost opposite the centre of the chain and within one hundred miles of each other, rise those two great rivers, Indus and Brahmaputra, which flow, in opposite directions to each other and parallel to the Himalaya, until they bend south and cut a way through the mountain barrier practically at its two extremities.

It might be expected, therefore, that the highest part of the Himalaya would form a watershed, but this is not so, and the Ganges, the Sutlej and numerous tributaries which between them constitute the system, rise on the north side of the axes of highest elevation. Two explanations are given of this: (a) that the rivers are gradually "cutting back" (that is, that the heads of the streams are eating their way northwards owing to the greater rainfall on the southern rather than the northern slopes); (b) that the line of drainage was formed antecedent to the elevation and has, by erosion, maintained its original course during a slow process of upheaval which is supposed to be still going on at the rate of a fraction of an inch a year.

Such geographical explanation may be dull, but it is intensely difficult to appreciate the Himalaya as it now is without indulging in these lofty speculations as to how or why. The extent of such a vast range is not easily realised, and many picture to themselves an area about the size of that of the Alps, with Everest towering in the centre and all the lesser satellites grouped round him. Some better notion may be gained if we visualise a mountain chain running from London to the Black Sea with Everest somewhere near Belgrade and Nanga Parbat somewhere near London.

Having these relative distances in mind it may be of further assistance to consider the range in its artificial or political divisions. Starting from the Indus Valley, over which looms the Nanga Parbat massif, the chain runs for two hundred miles through Kashmir, and in the same State, but across the Indus to the north, lies the parallel range of the Karakoram and Mount Godwin Austin (K2), second in height only to Everest.

Continuing south-east for another two hundred miles through a number of small States known collectively as the Simla Hill States, the range enters Garhwal. East of this it runs for nearly six hundred miles through the independent State of Nepal which contains the highest crest-line, all the southern slopes and, in its extreme north-east corner, Everest itself, the main watershed following the Nepal-Tibet border.

Two more independent States follow, Sikkim and Bhutan, which together account for another two hundred miles of the Himalaya. These States approximate in language, religion and custom to Tibet, and have both a spiritual and a temporal ruler. Finally, between Bhutan and the Brahmaputra are three hundred miles of wild and mountainous country, nominally Chinese, about which even now our knowledge is very imperfect.

The districts of British Garhwal and Almora, with which Tilman and I were chiefly concerned, lie almost in the centre of the Himalayan range and are, moreover, the only place where our border marches with that of Tibet. Garhwal has had a chequered history. In early days it was divided amongst no less than fifty-two petty chieftains, each with his own fortress, a state of affairs to which the name itself is a description, since the word *garh* means castle. Five hundred years ago the strongest chieftain brought the other fifty-one under his dominion and ruled as Prince of Garhwal, and from then down to the close of the eighteenth century there was constant warfare between his descendants and the rulers of the neigbouring State of Kumaon. But the Gurkhas of Nepal (it is worthy of note that even now Nepal, which contains at least forty-eight peaks known to exceed 25,000 feet, is strictly closed to European exploration), failing to extend their conquests in the direction of China, turned their attention to the west and overran both Garhwal and Kumaon as far west as the Sutlej. Garhwal they ruled with a rod of iron, and from this mountain stronghold they began to make raids into the plains – at the expense of subjects of the British Raj. As a consequence there followed the Nepalese War of 1814–15, which, after the usual disastrous start, finally resulted in the Gurkhas being driven back within their present boundaries. Western Garhwal was restored to its native ruler, and the rest of the State, plus its neighbour, Almora, became part of British India.

The first Commissioner was G. W. Traill, who reduced the country to order and laid a secure foundation for its future peace and prosperity. A worthy memorial to his work and the goodwill he earned as heritage for his successors, is the well-known Pass which he was the first to cross and which is named after him.

Garhwal covers about one hundred miles from east to west and some fifty from north to south. The natives are short and sturdy, and fairer in colour than the inhabitants of the plains. Blue eyes and cheeks tinged with red are not uncommon and some of the women are very beautiful although here, as in most mountainous regions, goitre is very prevalent. Approaching the Tibetan border the people are Bhotias of Tibetan origin speaking a Tibetan-Burman dialect. They have few traces of Buddhism and profess to be Hindus, but not of a strictly orthodox type. For instance, they are quite ready to eat with Tibetans, a fact which helps them considerably in their trade with that country. Indeed, they hold a monopoly of such trade and use goats and sheep to carry rice and wheat over the high passes, returning with borax, salt, and yaks' tails.

A broad outline of the topography of Garhwal is best understood by looking at the three or, if the Tehri State is included, the four great river valleys which run right up into the heart of the country, forming the trade routes and attracting populous centres. These valleys are of great depth and within ten miles of 20,000 feet snow peaks the valley floor may be but 4,000 feet above sea level and clothed in tropical vegetation.

All these rivers rise to the north of the main axis of elevation and have cut their way through the east-west range almost at right angles so that the containing walls of the valleys, on which are grouped the highest peaks, run roughly north and south. There are three such main ridges, each possessing many minor features of distinction: on the east that on which stands Nanda Devi, 25,660 feet, the highest peak in Garhwal; in the middle that of Kamet, 25,447, the second highest peak; and on the west that of the Badrinath-Kedernath group of peaks, in formation much more complex than that of the other two.

The Gori River, rising on the Tibetan border in the depression which forms the Untadhura Pass, for the first twenty miles of its course separates the eastern (or Nanda Devi) group from the tangle of snow peaks in western Nepal. Beyond this point the Gori bends away to the south-east to fix the political boundary of Nepal and concerns us no more, but its place is taken by the Pindar River which rises on the south-eastern extremities of the Nanda Devi group and, curling round it to the west, marks the termination of the regions of ice and snow in the south.

Before passing on to mention of the third river there are some interesting features to note about the valley of the Gori River, known as the Milam Valley. It forms the main highway between India and western Tibet and from it three routes lead to the Tibetan market of Gyanima and Taklakot. All involve the crossing of several high passes, the easiest of which is 16,750 feet high and can only be negotiated eight months of the year. The Bhotias have an amusing legend of the way these routes were pioneered: it seems that the first inhabitants of the Milam Valley were, like Esau, hairy – even to their tongues – and on the Gori Glacier there lived a bird of prey whose sole diet was these hairy ones. To free the people from this predatory fowl a Tibetan Lama sent his servant to kill it, and gave him as guide a man who was for ever changing his form, first into a dog at the Pass which is now called Kingribingri, then into a stag, which gave the name to the Dol Dunga Pass, then into a bear at the Topi Dunga Pass, a camel at the Unta Dhura, a tiger at the Dung Udiyar, and finally a hare at Samgoan. Thus the route to India was first shown and the bird of prey eventually killed – but not before it had eaten all the hairy ones. And the servant liked the valley so much that he expressed a desire to live in it but complained that there was no salt, so the kindly Lama took salt and sowed it like grain, with the result that there is today a salty grass on which the Bhotia flocks feed, and even yet Buddhist priests entering the valley ask for alms in the name of the Lama who sowed the salt, and Tibetans bring their herds over the border for the sake of the salty grass.

I digress. It is high time we followed the Pindar River westwards to where it flows into the Alaknanda some thirty miles away. Above this junction the Alaknanda bends to the north and receives from the north-east a large tributary, the Dhauli, whose valley lies between the Nanda Devi and the Kamet groups. At the head of this valley thirty miles further to the north is the Niti Pass, also leading to Tibet, and the river itself rises from the glaciers to the east and slightly north of Kamet. From this mountain near the Tibetan border the massif runs almost due south very nearly to the Dhauli-Alaknanda junction.

The main Alaknanda Valley which, as we saw, continues due north, separates the Kamet range from the Badrinath-Kedarnath group. The river rises near the Mana Pass and, passing under the western flanks of Kamet, receives large tributaries from the Badrinath peaks. This latter range does not extend so far south as its companion ranges but turns sharply back to the north-west, forming an acute angle in which lies the Gangotri Glacier, the largest in these parts and the source of the Bhagirathi River, the main tributary of the Ganges.

The Nanda Devi group itself, around which the interest of Tilman and myself gyrated throughout our voyage to Calcutta, presents unusual features. Imagine a main ridge running from north to south and in the southern half three arms projecting to the west. At the southern extremity a long one leads up to Trisul, 23,360 feet, and terminates ten miles to the west in Nandakna, 20,700 feet. Several miles north is a shorter arm on which is Dunagiri, 23,184 feet, and between the two lies the shortest arm of all which ends abruptly at Nanda Devi itself. From Trisul and from Dunagiri two spurs project towards each other to form the fourth side of the wall, nowhere less than 18,000 feet high, which surrounds Nanda Devi. The only breach in this formidable barrier is between these spurs where the Rishi Ganga, the river which drains the glaciers around Nanda Devi, breaks through by way of a deep gorge.

And it was by following the Rishi Ganga that we hoped to reach the shrine of the "Blessed Goddess".

CHAPTER THREE

HIMALAYAN travel is of course full of complexities. The shortness of the season during which expeditions are possible, the uncertainty of the monsoon, the danger of land-slips, endemic cholera and other diseases of the lower valleys, leeches and insect pests, extremes of heat and cold, altitude, local superstitions and the consequent difficulty in obtaining help from the natives – these are but a few of the obstacles to be overcome by the traveller.

And in the case of Nanda Devi one tremendous problem was added, the fact that the peak is encircled by a huge amphitheatre that must surely be unique. It is hard for anyone who has not studied this phenomenon at close quarters to form an adequate conception of a gigantic rampart, in places over 23,000 feet high, enclosing a bit of country itself not above the limits of dwarf trees, from the centre of which rises a stupendous peak 25,600 feet in height. Small wonder that this grim seventy mile ring of mountains had repulsed all assaults, and that the sanctuary of the inner basin had remained inviolate.

Mr. Hugh Ruttledge wrote in an article published in *The Times* of August 22nd, 1932, soon after his attempt of that year: "Nanda Devi imposes upon her votaries an admission test as yet beyond their skill and endurance; a seventy-mile barrier ring, on which stand twelve *measured* peaks over 21,000 feet high, which has no depression lower than 17,000 feet – except in the west, where the Rishi Ganga River, rising at the foot of Nanda Devi, and draining an area of some two hundred and fifty square miles of snow and ice has carved for itself what must be one of the most terrific gorges in the world. Two internal ridges, converging from north and south respectively upon this river form, as it were, the curtains of an inner sanctuary, within which the great mountain soars up to 25,600 feet. So tremendous is the aspect of the Rishi Ganga gorge that Hindu mythology described it as the last earthly home of the Seven Rishis. Here, if anywhere, their meditations might be undisturbed."

As I mentioned earlier, it was our intention to attempt to force our way up this gorge into the basin beyond. Naturally, therefore, we made an intensive study of all previous exploits of mountaineers and explorers who had tried to gain access to what Mr. Hugh Ruttledge calls, so aptly, "the inner sanctuary".

Most of the early explorers of the Nanda Devi group approached it from the east. As long ago as 1830 G. W. Traill, who was first Commissioner of Garhwal and Kumaon, ascended the Pindari Glacier and crossed a pass at its head into the Milam Valley. The object of this exploit was probably rather to find a short cut to Milam than to explore mountains. The fact that Traill suffered severely from snow-blindness was regarded by the natives as a sign that the Goddess had visited her wrath upon him and this belief had such effect that in 1855, when Adolf Schlagintweit, that remarkable Himalayan traveller, attempted to cross the range by the same route he took the precaution of making a handsome offering at the temple of Nanda Devi in Almora before he started. This inspired his coolies with much confidence and even when, on the glaciers, two of his strongest men were seized with epileptic fits, he was able to point out to the rest that it could be none of the goddess's doing and so persuade them to carry on. Later he was joined by his brother Robert, and together they explored the great Milam Glacier and crossed another pass which led them into Tibet. Travelling to the west they reached Kamet and climbed to an altitude of 22,239 feet on its Tibetan side, thus reaching the greatest height which had been so far attained.

In 1861 Traill's pass was again crossed by Colonel Edmund Smyth in the course of a memorable journey in those parts, while in 1883 Mr. T. S. Kennedy, the celebrated Alpine climber, carried out some further work on the Milam side of the range.

In that same year, on the western side of the group, was undertaken a portion of what Dr. T. G. Longstaff in 1906 described as "the greatest Himalayan expedition that has yet been made". The party was a small one and consisted of that redoubtable Himalayan explorer, W. W. Graham; the famous Swiss guide, Emil Boss, of whom Graham wrote: "One of the best mountaineers living, extremely well-educated, speaking seven languages equally fluently; a captain in the Swiss Army he is a splendid companion and I deemed myself fortunate to have his company." And lastly another first-rate guide, Ulrich Kauffmann, of Grindelwald. (Boss and Kauffmann are well remembered for their work on the Southern Alps of New Zealand for which, in conjunction with his Indian achievements, Boss received the Black Grant from the Royal Geographical Society.)

Dr. Longstaff writes (*Alpine Journal*, 1906, Vol. XXIII, pp. 203–204): "No one who reads the short and modest description of his (Graham's) Garhwal trip can fail to be fired with longing to revisit the scenes of his struggles, and no one who has not been lucky enough to have been there can realise what he went through, and what a strenuous pioneer and splendid climber he must have been. We can only lament that he did not give us as detailed an account we have since come to expect from the returning wanderer."

Graham's principal objective was to force a route up the Rishi Ganga gorge to the western base of Nanda Devi. Travel among the foothills must have been a very different proposition from what it is now, and only after several weeks of hard going did his little party reach the tiny hamlet of Rini, where the Rishi Ganga, issuing from the mouth of its lower gorge, bursts into the Dhaoli River.

"On the next day, July 6th," (he writes in *Good Words*, January, 1885) "we wished to start for Nanda Devi. As the crow flies, it was some twenty miles but, seeing the nature of the ground, we decided to allow at least a week to reach the foot of the peak. On inquiring for a guide we were told that the valley was impassable, that no sahib had ever been up it . . . etcetera, etcetera. We took most of this *cum grano*, but found, alas, that it was only too true! After getting up four miles we came to an unexpected obstacle. A glacier had once run due north from Trisul to the river; it had now retreated, leaving a bed with sheer perpendicular walls some four hundred feet in depth. We tried up and down to find a place where we could cross. Below, it fell sheer some fifteen hundred feet into the river: above, it only got deeper and deeper. It was a mighty moat of nature's own digging to guard her virgin fortresses. We gave it up and returned rather disconsolately to Rini."

After this the party moved round to the north and continued their explorations in that direction. In the course of this journey they made a determined but unsuccessful attempt to climb the giant peak of Dunagiri, which stands on the outer rim of the Nanda Devi Basin. Later they learnt from the shepherds of the Dhaoli Valley that a way was known across the ridge that formed the northern retaining wall of the Rishi Nala.

Once more they started for Nanda Devi. "On July 15th," so the record goes, "we began to make our way up the northern side of the Rishi Ganga. The climb was sufficiently steep, there being no path, and we having pouring rain the whole time. On the evening of the second day we reached a lovely little tableland called Dunassau (Durashi). The last day's route had been extremely wild, running along the southern face of the ridge, sometimes with a sheer drop to the river below – some 7,000 to 8,000 feet. Such wild rocks and broken gullies I had never met with before."

At Durashi, Graham and his companions were held up by heavy falls of snow and were deserted by most of their terror-stricken coolies. These men had been recruited from the Dhaoli Valley and shared the local superstition that their route was infested with devils. Carrying double loads, the three Europeans and the few local people who remained faithful to them, struggled on. "Our progress," writes Graham, "was very slow, partly because we had to carry fifteen loads between nine of us, partly owing to the nature of the ground, which was not only very broken and precipitous but quite *terra incognita* to the whole party . . . Guiding in its strict Alpine sense was wanted here; sharp rocky ridges ran down from the peaks on our north, and fell, with high precipices, sheer into the stream some 5,000 feet below. Occasionally we had to hang on by a tuft of grass, or a bunch of Alpine roses, and I do not exaggerate when I say that for half the total day's work hand-hold was as necessary as foot-hold. By nightfall, after twelve hours' work, we had gained some three miles in absolute distance, and this, perhaps, better than anything will give an idea of the labour involved in working along these slopes."

And after several days of this sort of work Graham writes further:

"We camped on a little space, the only one we could find which was not so steep as the rest and, after building a wall of stones to prevent us from rolling into the river, we turned in. I found, however, that sleeping at an angle of 30 degrees is not conducive to comfort. Time after time did I dream that I was rolling over the edge, and woke to find myself at the bottom of the tent on top of Boss, or *vice versa*. (We took it in turns in a most impartial manner to roll down first and made a bed for the other, who speedily followed.) On the morrow Kauffmann took the coolies back to bring up the other loads, and Boss went forward to explore the route. I lay, an interesting invalid in the tent, my foot giving me great pain, and being quite unable to wear a boot.

"Next day we worked along the spur, following Boss, who had seen a place where he thought we could cross the river. When above this we descended to it, the hill being very steep and covered with thorny jungle. Rain began again and we found ourselves on the bank of the stream shivering and waiting for Boss, who had gone after some pheasants. This little delay effectually settled our chances of crossing. The stream rose several feet in an hour, and though we tried very hard to bridge the flood, everything was washed away as soon as laid in position. Boss stood up to his knees on a slippery rock, with the water rushing by at some twenty miles an hour and worked like a horse, but it was of no avail. Once, indeed, I thought that he was gone as he slipped and nearly fell. Needless to say, to fall into that torrent would have been certain death, battered to pieces against the tremendous rocks that blocked the way. At last, soaked to the skin and very tired, we gave it up and pitched camp under an overhanging boulder.

"Next day, Kauffmann and the coolies returned to fetch up the rest of the provisions, while Boss and I worked along the river to see if we could find a crossing. About half a mile up we came to a most magnificent gorge, one of the finest specimens of water erosion ever seen. Two hundred feet above, the rocks nearly met, their smooth, black, shiny sides overhanging considerably. Through this tunnel roared and raved the torrent, here pent within very narrow limits, raging with a sound as of thunder. Yet in this fearful din and turmoil we saw a curious thing. On a tiny ledge, just above the dashing waves, a pigeon had built her nest and therein lay the two white shining eggs in perfect security: no enemy could touch them there. We carefully examined the stream up to the point where it descended the cliff in a grand fall, and found that nowhere in its present state could a crossing be effected.

"It was provoking: we were halted high under the great cliffs of Nanda Devi, which rose almost perpendicularly above us, and we could see, so near and yet so far, the spur by which we had hoped to climb. To cross, however, was out of the question with our limited appliances, and we relucantly decided to return."

They camped where they were: "Suddenly there entered Kauffmann and the shikari (hunter).

"Well, Kauffmann, when are the others coming?"

"*Hélas, Monsieur, ils sont tous partis!*"

That remark, uttered under the very shadow of the mountain for which these few men had dared so much, was the death-knell to the expedition. Yet Graham's reaction to it was wholly admirable. "It was only too true," he writes. "The coolies had evidently planned the affair and, as soon as they had got out of sight of camp, had fairly bolted. Kauffmann's face was so lugubrious that, serious as the matter was, I couldn't help bursting out into laughter. However, this settled what we had previously almost decided."

To go on without native help was impossible. Graham and his party abandoned everything that was not absolutely necessary and fought their way back down the gorge. A heart-breaking journey that must have been, unrelieved by knowledge of happenings yet in the future which were to show the true value of Graham's achievement, since further attempts to penetrate the upper gorge of the Rishi Ganga met with but small success and it was not until 1907 that any other noteworthy exploration was carried out on this side of the range.

In July, 1893, Dr. Kurt Boeckh attacked the eastern side of the range and made his way up the Milam Glacier with the idea of forcing a passage across the eastern portion of the barrier wall surrounding the Nanda Devi Basin. He had with him the Austrian guide, Hans Kerer, but when the coolies realised his intention they refused to advance and Boeckh was obliged to abandon his project before he had got very far. (Even if the coolies had agreed to accompany him it is doubtful if he would ever have been able to lead them safely over the range; such a route entailing work of a tremendously high standard of mountaineering.) Unwilling to return by the way he had come Boeckh carried out a fine journey to the north, crossing the Untadhura Pass in the middle of September and descending the very difficult gorge of the Girthi to Malari in the Dhaoli Valley.

But early in the present century, the district attracted the attention of Dr. T. G. Longstaff, whose record as a mountain explorer is assuredly in a class by itself. In 1905 he came out with the Italian guides, Alexis and Henri Brocherel, with the intention of continuing the work which Graham had started on the western side of the group. The opportunity of accompanying Mr. C. A. Sherring on a political mission into western Tibet, however, caused him to alter his plans and to spend the period before the breaking of the monsoon in exploring the valleys east of Nanda Devi. After several marches through the fern-clad cliff country of the Gori defile and up into the bare, wind-swept valley of Milam, they pitched camp on May 27th, near the hamlet of Ganaghar, on the right bank of the Gori, at a height of 11,100 feet. From here they pushed their way up the Panchu Glacier and eventually crossed a difficult snow-pass at its head. This brought them on to the Lwanl Glacier, running parallel with the Panchu and not into the Nanda Devi Basin as their map had led them to expect. They descended to the main valley for supplies and shortly afterwards returned to the Lwanl. After three days climbing they gained the Almora-Garhwal water-parting which forms at this point part of the rim of the Nanda Devi Basin and from here, for the first time in history, did man gaze down upon the glaciers at the southern foot of the great mountain.

A descent on the other side of the ridge was found to be impracticable and after an unsuccessful attempt to climb the great peak of Nanda Kot the party continued their explorations to the south and succeeded before they were overtaken by the monsoon, in crossing a pass from the head of the Salung Gadh to Baughdiar, a remarkable piece of mountaineering.

But the lure of Nanda Devi stayed and 1907 again found Dr. Longstaff in the vicinity, this time concentrating on his old plan of continuing Graham's work on the country around the Rishi Ganga. He brought with him a very strong mountaineering party, including Major (now Brigadier-General) the Hon. C. G. Bruce – the most experienced Himalayan mountaineer of his time – Mr. A. L. Mumm, and three Alpine guides, the two brothers Brocherel again and Moritz Inderbinnen of Zermatt, who had been Mumm's companion for over twenty years.

Their first objective was the Rishi Valley and examination of the lower gorge decided them to attempt Graham's route, the first part of which was known to the Tolma and Lata shepherds of the Dhaoli Valley. But they were too early in the year and found too much snow to allow them to make the passage of the Durashi Pass so they moved round to the Bagini Glacier, in the hope that if they were able to cross a certain pass at its head they would find themselves in the

Nanda Devi Basin. They made their way up the glacier on May 20th, came in sight of a gap ahead of them. "All who were bound for the pass," writes Dr. Longstaff (*Alpine Journal*, Vol. XXIV), "were heavily loaded as we had to carry Primus stoves, petroleum, cooking pots, tents, sleeping-bags, instruments, rifles and ammunition, a large supply of ropes, and provisions sufficient to last our party of eight for ten days. For, having got into the Rishi Valley, we intended to get out of it some time. In the interval we must be self-supporting. The sun was so oppressive that after tramping over the snow for five hours, we stopped, at 11 a.m. (May 21st), under the shade of some huge blocks, which formed part of an irregular medial moraine (18,300 feet).

"Instead of making for the pass directly under Changabang, we had now decided to go right up to the head of this arm of the glacier, more directly under the great easterly spur of Dunagiri. Mumm, who was not very fit, did not intend to cross the pass with us, and returned to the camp above Dunagiri (grazing ground) with Inderbinnen and Damar Sing, leaving us a party of four Europeans and four Gurkhas. He rejoined us later at Surai Thota.

"On May 22nd, we started at 4.30 a.m., but Bruce and I had very soon to stop with cold feet; and it was probable at this time that Karbir got his frost-bite. We had to rope over the last slopes, and the guides cut many steps. Our loads seemed to grow inordinately heavy, but at 10 a.m. we stood on the crest of the pass. Its height comes out at 20,100 feet, and the name Bagini Pass would most naturally belong to it. From the pass we looked down to a vast firn (snow-field), shut in by snow-clad peaks, while 3,000 feet above us on the west towered the icy crest of Dunagiri. But the descent of the south side looked so bad that we had to set about it at once. The Brocherels had brought a good supply of pitons (iron stakes) from Courmayeur, and by means of these we were able to lower our loads down the snow-draped cliffs below us. It really was a difficult bit of mountaineering, the descent of about 1,000 feet occupying over five hours; and the two Brocherels were in their element. This was a very fine performance on the part of the Gurkhas, and a striking testimony both to their inherently resolute character, and to the excellence of their military training. Remember that they were called upon to perform a feat which was quite beyond the powers of any of the local men . . . We were very glad to camp about 4 p.m. on the snow-field directly at the southern foot of the pass (18,800 feet) . . . We had fondly hoped to find ourselves on the great glaciers at the foot of Nanda Devi itself."

But on descending from the snow-field they were on, they found themselves in the Rishi Nala, at a point below that which Graham had reached in 1883. They were able to shoot some bharal (wild sheep), which provided them with sufficient food to enable them to force their way down the valley to Durashi, and so to reach their main base at Surai Thota, in the Dhaoli Valley, after nearly a fortnight of very difficult mountaineering.

Later the party came back up the Rishi Valley, and it was then that Dr. Longstaff made his famous ascent of Trisul (23,406 feet), which for twenty-three years remained the highest summit reached by man. After this he and two of the Gurkhas pushed their way further up the valley. "With considerable difficulty we reached the junction of the Rhamani torrent with the Rishi Ganga, where we crossed the latter to the northern bank by a snow-bridge (11,790 feet), as we could get no further along the southern bank, and the current was too strong for wading. Here we camped under an overhanging rock amongst the birch trees. That morning we climbed straight up to about 13,500 feet, and in the intervening 1,700 feet of cliffs between this and the Rishi Ganga, saw no practicable route up the valley, though we obtained a most wonderful view of Nanda Devi, the 'Blessed Goddess', that queen of mountains fit to rank with the Matterhorn and Ushba. I think that we were just beyond Graham's furthest point in this direction . . ." "Though no one, native or European, has yet succeeded in forcing his way up the gorge to the western base of Nanda Devi, yet I feel convinced that it is possible to do so. I can think of no more interesting or arduous task for a party composed of mountaineers, than to follow up the great glacier under the southern face of Nanda Devi, and to cross the ridge on which I camped in 1905, over into the Milam Valley. The height of the pass is about 19,000 feet, and as we stood on its crest it appeared quite possible to climb up to it from the Nanda Devi Glacier on the west. But this expedition would involve the abandonment of the base camp and all impedimenta in the Dhaoli Valley, for at least a month. The return could be made most quickly by the Untadhura Pass, and the difficult Girthi Valley to Malari, for I do not think anyone would be likely to return by the same route."

Since then, until last year, 1934, the upper gorge of the Rishi Valley was left severely alone.

During the monsoon of 1907, Dr. Longstaff proceeded to explore the Nandagini and Sunderdhunga Valleys, both of which lead up to the wall of the basin from the south. Only those who have travelled amongst the unexplored valleys of those parts in the monsoon can appreciate the appalling conditions which rendered these two reconnaissances inconclusive.

No fewer than twenty years later Dr. Longstaff returned to the Nandagini with Mr. Hugh Ruttledge, and reached the crest of the wall at its lowest point, 17,000 feet. Bad weather prevented further progress, but in any case this approach would have led them down to a point in the Rishi Nala below that reached in 1907.

In 1926 a further attempt was made to reach the great mountain from the east by a strong party, consisting of Mr. Hugh Ruttledge, Dr. Howard Somervell, who accompanied Mallory and Norton on the two highest climbs on Everest in the years 1922 and 1924, and Colonel Commandant (now Major-General) R. C. Wilson. Though the attack was not pushed home, enough was done to warrant a conclusion that the defences on this side are even more elaborate than on the south or west.

May 1932 saw Mr. Ruttledge coming again to the attack, this time with the Italian guide, Emil Rey, of Courmayeur, grandson of his famous namesake, and six of the Everest Sherpas. His plan was to attempt to cross a gap at the head of the Sunderdhunga Valley, which had been tentatively reconnoitred by Dr. Longstaff in 1907. If the gap could be crossed it must lead into the inner sanctuary of Nanda Devi.

In an article published in *The Times* (August 22nd, 1932), Mr. Ruttledge writes: "In a mood of hopeful anticipation our party, on May 25th, trudged up the narrow glacier which leads from Sunderhunga itself to the base of the wall, of which the greater part is invisible from a distance. The Sherpas cheered derisively as a little avalanche had an ineffective shot at us from the cliffs above; and raced round the last corner. One step round it, and we were brought up all standing by a sight which almost took our remaining breath away. Six thousand feet of the steepest rock and ice. '*Nom de nom*!' said Emil, while Nima* exclaimed that this looked as bad as the north-west face of Kangchenjunga in 1930. However we had come a long way to see this, so we advanced across the stony slopes to a point from which we hoped, by detailed examination, to reduce terrific appearances to milder reality. But the first impressions were accurate. Near the top of the wall, for about a mile and a half, runs a terrace of ice some 200 feet thick; in fact the lower edge of a hanging glacier. Under the pull of gravity large masses constantly break off from this terrace, and thunder down to the valley below, polishing in their fall the successive bands of limestone precipice of which the face is composed. Even supposing the precipice to be climbable, an intelligent mountaineer may be acquitted on a charge of lack of enterprise if he declines to spend at least three days and two nights under fire from this artillery. As alternative, there is a choice of three knife-edge arêtes, excessively steep, sometimes over-hanging in the middle and lower sections, on which even the eye of faith, assisted by binoculars, fails to see one single platform large enough to accommodate the most modest of climbing tents.

"The jury's verdict was unanimous; and so, with a homely vernacular *non possumus* from Emil, vanished the last hope of a straightforward approach to Nanda Devi; and the goddess keeps her secret."

Would the goddess, who had so protected herself from human intrusion throughout the centuries, reveal her secret to us, with an expedition absurd in its smallness? As we neared Calcutta both Tilman and I realised more and more the size of our task and the unlikelihood of success. But if our resources were small, we had at least the "eyes of faith" and the knowledge of the experience of our predecessors to help us to reach our goal.

*Nima Dorji, a Sherpa Porter, who had been on Everest, Kangchenjunga and Kamet.

CHAPTER FOUR

BEFORE leaving England we had arranged to send a wire to Karma Paul in Darjeeling as soon as we knew the date of our arrival in Calcutta and he was then to send our porters to meet us there, but, as Tilman and I rehearsed for the fiftieth time the programme we had so carefully mapped out and we steamed ever nearer to our goal, we grew impatient and debated the advisability of disembarking at Visagapatam, the last port of call before Calcutta, which lies three days ahead. By taking the train from Visagapatam we could save two precious days. This idea, however, had to be turned down on the score of expense and we went ashore there merely to send a wire requesting that the three Sherpas should be sent down to Calcutta, to arrive there the same day as ourselves. Although the homes of these men lay far from Darjeeling, it was there that they spent most of their time working as rickshaw coolies, and the hill-station was all they knew of civilisation. To our knowledge they had never even travelled by train before and to avoid the risk of their wandering alone in Calcutta, Karma Paul was instructed to impress upon them most strongly the necessity of not stirring a yard from the station until met by us.

These arrangements made we had a further three days in which to ponder the mischances that might befall our innocents before we met them. Another problem was whether, on the day of our arrival, we could possibly do some shopping, dispatch business at a bank, interview several people and transport half a ton of stores from the ship to the Howrah Station in time for the nine o'clock train that night. Such was our impatience to reach the mountains that the possibility of an enforced week-end in Calcutta seemed to jeopardise the success of the whole expedition.

We landed in good time on a Saturday, got the most important jobs done and then hastened to our hotel, expecting to find a telegram advising us of the dispatch of the Sherpas. Sure enough, there was the wire, but it merely said that on receipt of journey-money and an advance of pay, the men would be put in the train.

We were annoyed, to say the least! Our invective must surely have made Karma Paul's ears tingle up in Darjeeling but a little reflection showed us that the demand was perfectly reasonable and that we had been exceedingly stupid not to think of its necessity earlier. I smile even now to think of the unnecessary stew into which we worked ourselves.

Well, the money had to be sent, and quickly, or the post office would be closed until Monday, so off we raced only to find that there exists in Calcutta the most exasperating arrangement whereby the wire is handed in at one office and the money paid over at another about half a mile away. To our harassed minds it seemed that the greater part of India's three hundred million inhabitants were assembled for the purpose of sending telegrams – and that five minutes before closing time – but eventually we got the money off.

This delay was a severe blow but it was softened when we obtained permission to live on the ship over the week-end, so that our somewhat slender financial resources were not depleted by extra hotel bills. We were now "sweating" on getting away by Monday and this war-time expression most adequately describes our condition, physical and mental. Even departure on Monday was expecting a lot, because were Karma Paul on the spot to receive the wire, he would have but Sunday morning in which to round up the men, give them time to make their arrangements, and shepherd them to the train.

No further news arrived and, assuming all was well, we made our way to the Sealdah Station at seven on the Monday morning. We reached the platform when the train was already in and disgorging its passengers. I, from my previous acquaintance with the Sherpas, knew the men we were looking for, and Tilman, who had never seen a Sherpa, observed that "Three men from the wilds of Nepal, shrinking from the noise and bustle and wearing a sort of 'Bing Boys on Broadway' air, should be easy enough to spot".

When most of the crowd had passed the barriers with no sign of our men, we began to search the platform, and soon our choice was reduced to some station coolies fast asleep, a sweetmeat seller, and a one-legged beggar – whom even Tilman, inexperienced as he was, rejected as a candidate. Doubtful now, we cast our net wider, taking in all eight platforms, the booking-hall, the first, second and third-class waiting-rooms for men and women, the refreshment-rooms for Europeans, Hindus, and Mohammedans, and all other likely and unlikely places in which three affrighted innocents abroad might seek refuge from the confusion around them.

Doubt became fear. Tilman was convinced they had not come: I had more faith in Karma Paul and our luck, and began to cross-question every official I could persuade to listen to our story. It was a shade too early to get hold of any of the Directors or the General Manager, but having catechised the higher ranks – as personified by Traffic Manager and Station-Master, we descended grade by grade to humble ticket-collectors. One of these proved more observant than seemed possible – or else something passing strange had arrived by the Darjeeling Mail – for his attention had been excited by "three exotic figures", apparently from the remoter parts of Asia. Here was a gleam of light, but, on thinking matters over we realised that the exotic three (whoever they might be) were now at large in the City of Calcutta and probably untraceable.

Before enlisting the aid of the Police we decided that it would be as well to ring up our hotel to see if there were any news from Darjeeling.

"There is no telegram," came the reply, "but can you throw any light on three very rum-looking birds who drove up here in a taxi an hour ago?"

"Are they from Darjeeling?" I asked excitedly.

"Well, they seem to talk Chinese," was the answer, "and I don't know enough of the language to ask them where they come from but they are in search of two sahibs, so you had better come along and see them – and the sooner the better. They're no advertisement for my hotel!"

We drove back in silence, conflicting emotions rendering us speechless.

Swift decision followed by swift action seemed to be the habit of these three and we wondered if they would wait or set off on a wild goose-chase around the city looking for us.

They *had* waited. Not in the lounge (as we had been half afraid they would do) and they *were* our Sherpas! We found them sitting patiently in the back regions and realised immediately the true meaning of the ticket-collector's description. Indeed, "exotic" was a mild adjective. Clad in shirts and shorts, and crowned with billycock hats from under which glossy black pig-tails descended, the three were distinctive enough, but when one took into consideration that their shirts were a blinding purple in colour and that this crude shade was matched in their lips and teeth (the result of much betel-chewing) one understood how even the most myopic ticket-collector would notice them.

They greeted us gravely, apparently completely unconcerned. In the face of such oriental calm Tilman and I restrained ourselves, although our relief at finding them after our mad chase had induced a mild form of hysteria in us both, and we carefully avoided mention of the events at the station. Soon we were all down at the docks, hard at work getting our gear on shore. The astonishment of the ship's company was considerable, but the Sherpas went about their work in a matter-of-fact way, as little impressed by an eleven thousand ton ship and the busy traffic of the Hooghly as with a bullock-cart in the Darjeeling bazaar.

This attitude should not have been a surprise to either of us who were both well acquainted with African natives. When the savage sees a train or a motor car for the first time in his life he does not, as one would expect, show either excitement or fear; nor does he behave like the old lady, who, when confronted for the first time with a giraffe, said that she didn't believe it. Tilman has told me that in East Africa the inauguration of the Air Mail caused no sensation whatever. An aeroplane passing overhead was regarded merely as an excuse to stop work for a moment – if the native was not working he simply did not bother to look up! Similarly, a native boy who accompanied a friend of his to England was impressed only by the meat hanging in the English butchers' shops, and although the Sherpas have little in common with the African native they are certainly alike on this one point – their attitude to the modern amenities of civilisation.

Having somehow got all our baggage to Howrah Station we sent the Sherpas off to see the sights of Calcutta in charge of a friend's servant, a man well fitted to be their cicerone since he acted in the same capacity to the seventy porters of the German Nanga Parbat expedition. Afterwards he informed us that the Zoo alone had excited any interest!

Meantime Tilman and I went off to arrange for seats on the train and met with an unexpected difficulty. The 9 p.m. train was the Bombay Mail, which took no third-class passengers but allowed other passengers one bearer apiece; at 10 p.m. there was another train which boasted third-class accommodation but on this we could not go since all second-class seats had been reserved. Very unwillingly we decided to split our party, taking one man with us and leaving the other two to follow on the later train. Their morning's work had shown us they were not quite the simpletons we had imagined – but it was tempting providence to let them travel to an unknown destination with but a smattering of Hindustani between them. Still, the only alternative was to wait yet another day – and another day of Calcutta would have worn what small patience we had left to tatters.

As it was we did not depart without further strain on our frayed nerves, for the friend with whom we had a farewell dinner insisted that ten minutes was ample time in which to weigh, book and load our 1,000 lbs. of luggage. Personally I felt that a full hour would be all too short and endured torment (with both eyes on the clock) while he ordered beer – and yet more beer. In the end we only reached our carriage with a second or two to spare, followed by the two Sherpas who were to take the later train loudly bemoaning their lot until our friend, who was thoroughly enjoying the whirl of our departure, forcibly restrained them from climbing in beside us and promised to see them off safely at 10 o'clock.

With us travelled Angtharkay, short, sturdy and self-possessed, and despite all our arguments he flatly refused to occupy the small cupboard thoughtfully provided by the railway for bearers, and insisted upon sleeping on the floor of our compartment – much to the disgust of our fellow passengers. It was a stifling night and Angtharkay, who felt the heat, recklessly squandered his money on beakers of tea at one anna a time. Tilman and I fumed and fretted about our abandoned Sherpas, whom we were to pick up some twenty-four hours later at Bareilly so that we could all take the Kathgodam train together.

At last we steamed into Bareilly Station, ill-tempered, dusty and exhausted. Fortunately we had time to wash off the outer layer of dust, stow our baggage in the Kathgodam train and have some food before meeting the Calcutta train bearing our precious freight. We were not feeling too happy – remembering our hectic time in Calcutta. True, our friend had had the strictest instructions to tell the Sherpas to sit tight until pulled out by us, since the name Bareilly conveyed no more to them than did Bombay, but twenty-four hours of sweltering heat might well have exhausted their patience and, if they thought we had missed them, they were perfectly capable of getting out where they thought fit. Moreover, the train only stopped for ten minutes, the platform was abominably lit, and most third-class passengers were certain to be asleep.

When the train arrived our hearts descended into our boots. It seemed twice as long as any train ought to be, its carriages were of vast size, very dark and over-crowded with natives lying asleep on top of each other, all with their faces covered. Packed like sardines is a poor simile, for packing denotes order and here was chaos. To search thirty-odd "black holes of Calcutta" in a few moments was an impossible task, so I shouted orders to Tilman and Angtharkay and we all began to dash frenziedly up and down, bawling the names of our two men through the open windows. Yells of "Kusang!!" . . . "Pasang!!" rose above the hiss of the engine and the few passengers who were sufficiently awake to take any notice scrambled to their feet and eyed us askance. But all our clamour utterly failed to upset traffic arrangements and after its alloted time the train pulled out, several occupants shaking their heads from the windows as though in relief that the three madmen were being left behind.

Here was a pretty mess. Blank-faced and sore-throated we stood miserably and debated our next move. Should we go or should we camp out on Bareilly platform, giving a rendering of our bawling performance to every train from Calcutta? Just as we began to debate this dismal question a warning toot sounded from the Kathgodam train and we sprinted towards it, fearful of losing luggage as well as men.

As we ran we glanced rapidly into each carriage trying to spot our gear and, of a sudden, Tilman gripped me by the arm. There, comfortably established among their possessions and eating oranges with every evidence of serene enjoyment, were Kusang and Pasang! It seemed a pity to disturb them. We crept quietly past to our own carriage, horribly conscious that Angtharkay's account of our antics would lose nothing in the telling.

But far into the night we argued about the mystery. The most experienced traveller who had to effect a change of trains at midnight in a country whose language he did not know, might be very pleased with himself if he managed without mishap. Yet two Sherpas, neither of whom had ever travelled by rail, neither of whom even knew the name of their destination, had contrived to get out at the right station and into the right train.

Part 2

The Secret Shrine

CHAPTER FIVE

THE remainder of our journey to Kathgodam was a peaceful one. The Sherpas were (presumably) behaving themselves in their compartment and the countless irritations of the past few days faded from our minds. Our spirits rose as we left the train at last and packed ourselves and our belongings into a somewhat decrepit lorry and began the last fifty-mile stage of our road to Ranikhet, one of the loveliest of Indian hill-stations. Jolting along the broad motor-road that winds its way amongst the steep, forest-clad foothills rising abruptly from the plains, we took great gulps of the cool, pine-scented air, deliciously sweet after two days of travel in the appalling heat and dust of pre-monsoon India.

Up and up the lorry circled to Ranikhet, from the crest of whose pine-clad ridge there is to be seen a vast panorama of the Snows. The place was full of troops and all the usual pleasures of a hill-station were in full swing but these, however, were not for us, as we hoped to get away on our first march to Joshimath in two days time if all necessary arrangements could be completed.

We were lucky to find ourselves sole occupants of a spacious rest-house, where we could spread ourselves as much as we liked. We arrived at midday on May 9th, and straightaway before lunch we went down to recruit coolies. We only required a dozen men and within an hour all was settled and twelve lusty Dotials had promised to leave at once and meet us two days later at Baijnath, a little village fifty miles to the north at the end of the motor-road. These coolies were not beautiful, but they were a likely looking lot and inspired us with confidence, for we gave them a substantial advance of pay and never had the slightest doubts about their failing to keep the rendezvous!

The next thirty-six hours were very fully occupied in making preparations for departure. A ration of kit was allotted to each member of the party, and all the surplus clothing which convention had thus far imposed upon us had to be packed away and handed over for safe custody. Each man was issued with a suit of light, wind-proof material, under which he might wear quite a quantity of garments. (I may say that this "underclothing" consisted of a heterogeneous mixture collected from various friends and included long-forgotten shirts, pyjamas, tail-coats, etcetera, which I had unearthed when turning out a box-room before leaving home. Later, Kusang became firmly attached to a pair of my dress trousers, while Pasang, considering that an ancient dinner-jacket I gave him would be wasted in Garhwal, proudly carried it back to his native Tibet when the expedition was over.) Then boots – the most important item of all – had to be attended to; and finally a careful estimate of the cash which would be required over the next five months had to be worked out and the amount obtained, almost entirely in coin, from the local native bank. Since this was not a correspondent of our Calcutta bank we had been compelled to draw all our money from there in notes and travel up with them in our pockets, a proceeding we had found very wearing indeed, and we now discovered that the process of exchanging these for silver was a lengthy one owing to the many spurious rupees in circulation in India. The Sherpas willingly assisted at this business, and were far quicker at spotting duds than we were, rejecting all doubtful ones without ado. At first our feelings were hurt at seeing any money we tendered being scrutinised, rung on a stone, bitten or otherwise tested, but we soon found it paid us to do the same.

We took one large Meade tent for the Sherpas and a smaller one for ourselves. We also had a very small tent weighing about 6 lbs. in all, but we soon realised that the weight saved in carrying it was not worth the discomfort of sleeping in it! We had the usual down sleeping bags – though real eiderdown ones would have been worth the extra expense; and for the purposes of cooking above the limits of firewood, we took a small Primus stove and about four dozen "Tommy's Cookers" for use when Tilman and I were separated from the Sherpas. We had brought with us about 250 lbs. of foodstuffs to help us out while we were getting accustomed to local food (which consisted almost entirely of coarse flour) and for use at high camps. Various last-minute purchases were made in the Ranikhet bazaar and then everything had to be packed in one-man loads, 80 lbs. each, for the first stage of our journey.

In the early hours of the morning of May 11th we piled our stuff on to the waiting lorry, starting off at 7 a.m. Passing through the bazaar we suddenly remembered vegetables, lemons and eggs – and well it was that we did so. As I have mentioned before it was our aim to live on the country as far as possible, not only to save transport but because any fresh food, plain or dull though it may be, is preferable to things embalmed in tins be they ever so skilfully disguised; but though, throughout our travels, we were to find ourselves able to obtain staple foods, flour, potatoes and occasionally milk, how succulent were additional fruits, vegetables and eggs. And of these last the three dozen we bought in Ranikhet were, with one exception, the only eggs we tasted until our return.

Our lorry rolled into Baijnath at 1 o'clock and there we found our Dotials, who lost no time in making up their loads and starting for Gwaldam, the first stage of our ten-day march to Joshimath. "March," with its associations of discipline, time-tables and the hard, high road, is scarcely applicable to the next lazy, carefree days. Beyond setting a time-limit we had no set plan; and pace had, fortunately for me, to conform to that of the heavily-laden Dotials. I say fortunately, because I was, at the moment, far from fit. Besides a heavy cold and an inside the reverse of happy, I had broken a toe on the voyage out soon after leaving Aden which had not yet mended and which caused much pain. In consequence I was obliged to walk in a tennis shoe with a piece cut out of the side. On the ship this had not mattered, but in Calcutta it had looked a bit odd until we had joined forces with the Sherpas, who looked so amazing that had I gone about barefoot nobody would have noticed *me*. Even now a boot was out of the question and we discussed the hire of a pony, but in the end my journey to Joshimath was done in a pair of tennis shoes – or rather in one and a half.

So we ambled leisurely through a world of exquisite beauty. We rested when we felt inclined (which was frequently), bathed if the opportunity offered, and slept wherever seemed good to us. Until Ranikhet, Tilman and I had flattered ourselves upon our astuteness in steering three timid followers amidst the manifold difficulties and dangers of modern travel. But now that we had cast off the trammels of civilisation the boot was on the other leg, and in camp or on the march they devoted all their care to our welfare without a thought for themselves.

For the next five months we were to live and climb together, and the more we saw of the Sherpas the more we grew to like them. Porters all the time, they were also fellow mountaineers and companions, in turn playing the parts of housekeeper, cook, butler, pantryman, valet, interpreter and, on occasion, entertainer. Angtharkay was the eldest, a more sophisticated man than his brethren and possessed of Hindustani which could be understood by us and by other natives. When we had to employ them, he acted as buffer between us and the local coolies, and could generally tell us what they were thinking or feeling before they knew themselves. We could also delegate to him the very unpleasant business of bargaining, for he was a Hotspur who would "cavil on the ninth part of a hair," sometimes carrying this to excess and depriving us of a thing we really wanted rather than let us be "done." He was the soundest, too, on a mountain, both in movement and judgment, and as a route-finder we had many occasions on which to bless him.

Pasang was the most presentable of the party, taller than the other two and a bit of a dandy. He was a most graceful mover and quite brilliant on rocks, but he was exceedingly temperamental and required tactful handling. He acted as my batman – and a full-time job that was – I being the most careless of men and wont to drop my belongings all over the place. Poor Pasang was then expected to retrieve anything I suddenly asked for. Worse, he had to cope with a very bad habit of mine which was disconcerting, to say the least. No sooner was everything packed up than I would discover I *must* have something for the march, a spare woollie, a film, or a pencil. Whatever I wanted was sure to be at the very bottom of the great sack which was Pasang's load and the wretched man would have to turn it all out again. But he never seemed flustered or angered and the more work I gave him the better he liked it.

He was more Tibetan than the others and more religious. He carried a private stock of prayer-flags on which was printed the usual formula: "*Om Mane Padme Hung*" . . . "Hail, the Jewel in the Lotus Flower!" . . . and one of these would be left fluttering on the top of a pass or to mark some camp site. In addition he hoarded mysterious little squares of adhesive yellow cloth which he stuck on his face just behind the corner of each eye, (after the manner of the patches of the eighteenth-century ladies of fashion), but the meaning of these we never discovered. Another of his customs was to throw a little of his food into the air before eating in order to propitiate the spirits; a rite which I regret to say was sometimes neglected, either through stress of hunger or dissatisfaction with the way the gods were treating us in the matter of weather. He was also an inveterate builder of cairns, as were his companions, particularly Kusang, in whom this building amounted to a passion. I believe this stone-posing is a favourite devotion of all Buddhists, and they like to choose the most difficult stones and perform remarkable feats of equilibrium with them. Long practice has made them very quick and skilful, and before we had found a suitable foundation stone for our cairn, they would have built one four or five feet high, surmounted by a long slab cleverly balanced on end.

Kusang was the youngest and least experienced of the three, and I fear he was rather put upon in the way of work, just as a recruit must do the chores for an old soldier. But Kusang was a lad who thrived on work, and from the time we got into camp until the time we left, he willingly became a sort of general servant. Almost before we had our loads off, if there was any firewood to be had he would stagger in half-hidden under a great load of it, and would then trot off again to fetch water or to collect snow for melting. By the time he returned the fire would be started but if, as usually happened, it was stubborn, his were the powerful lungs that supplied most of the forced draught. This bellows business became a kind of subconscious habit, for except when his mouth was full (and he ate in the wholehearted way he did everything) he directed a gentle but persistent zephyr towards the fire from wherever he happened to be sitting, with remarkable results. Indeed, when he got his head down and blew in earnest, an almost extinct fire became a holocaust, and on a wet morning the first thing of which one became aware was the blast of Kusang's bellows and a comforting sound it was since it meant that tea would not long be delayed.

Washing-up, that bugbear of camp-life, was to Kusang a pet hobby, second only to cairn-building in his affections. To save time and trouble Tilman and I preferred to use a single plate with no washing between courses, but this Kusang seldom allowed and if, as was often the case, we were dependent on snow and the Primus for our water, his misguided enthusiasm for cleanliness in the home had to be restrained.

On the march he had a singular habit of crooning a mournful dirge, a repetition of three words and two notes, at all times and seasons. The stiffest slope or the most perilous place had no power to still him, but if we had to ford some swift, ice-cold torrent the voice would gradually die away. The habit was maddening at times and I confess to having suffered many moments when my one desire was to silence Kusang forever with an ice-axe, but in places of difficulty one liked to hear him and thus be assured that the equanimity of at least one of the party was undisturbed.

We boasted no cook, and since the food we ate called for no vast display of culinary achievement, all took a hand at preparing it in turn. If more advanced treatment than boiling was required, Angtharkay, who had a light hand with a frying pan, would take charge, and we deferred to his judgment in the all-important matter of food and its cooking, for he was something of a gourmet. Further he had an extensive knowledge of edible plants which, as will appear later, proved of great value.

The Sherpas always used a very hot sauce of some kind to help down their rice, satu, or chupatties, and carried numerous condiments tied up in bits of rag, of which chillies was the most important. They assumed our tastes were similar, and to avoid blistered mouths we kept in our own hands the delicate business of seasoning our "hoosh".

They had an ingenious system of allotting the food when divided into three approximately equal parts; two of them would take three different-sized bits of twig or grass and name one of each of them; these were then handed to the third, who did not know to whom the pieces belonged, and he placed one on each of the three portions. But they were very unselfish about food, and even when it was short were always pressing bits on each other and on us.

The making of edible chupatties is supposed to require some skill, but it is also a fairly laborious process. It devolved therefore on Kusang, and his results were not much more leathery than the professional article. It is fine exercise for the arms, and sometimes Tilman and I would take a hand, to warm ourselves and to afford the Sherpas a little harmless amusement; the sight of a chupattie in the making, curling itself round our wrists or disintegrating through too vigorous smacking, never failed to convulse them.

Their readiness to laugh was characteristic, but they had an odd sense of humour. Any minor misfortune, such as breaking a pipe or burning a hole in drying socks, would bring the house down, and once when I sat on my snow glasses and held up the result for Pasang's inspection, I thought he would have hysterics.

At one mishap which they, no doubt, considered the cream of all, they exercised commendable restraint. We were moving on very steep rock and had sat down on a narrow ledge for a rest, and taken off our sacks. Mine was put down with inexcusable carelessness and on getting up to go on, I happened to touch it with my foot, and 30 lbs. of rice, lentils, and cheese went over the edge to burst like a bomb 200 feet below. The dismay on my face, great though it was, might not have restrained them, but the fact that it was food lent gravity to the affair, and they managed to control themselves. I recovered the sack, but not the contents, and the mangled remains, spilt in all directions, proved too much for them; for a month afterwards, while it yet hung together, the sight of it always fetched a laugh.

The extent of cultivation near the villages seemed out of proportion to the few people, and herds of cows and water-buffaloes, and flocks of goats and sheep, gave promise of a fruitful land. Nevertheless flour was dispensed, if at all, by the cupful, and the livestock was apparently non-milk-producing; the hen and its product a legend; and fruit and vegetables unknown.

In these circumstances there was small scope for Angtharkay's talent for haggling, and on the rare occasions that an egg or a cup of milk appeared on the market, we were too eager to have it to worry about the price.

The scarcity of eggs was to be expected, because hens were seldom kept, but the milk shortage we never understood; the cows, so the story went, had just gone dry, the goats were all in a distant pasture, or there might be some milk tomorrow, if we did not leave too early. Flour was never on hand, each family grinding enough for the next meal and no more, and the promise of fruit was represented by a few unhappy apricot trees. With these last, I am willing to admit, the owners were generous and allowed the Sherpas to climb all over them, taking what they would without thought of payment. True, they were not giving away much, for I never saw a ripe one, but ripe or raw was of no importance to our hungry followers, and after they had finished, the trees appeared to have been attacked by a swarm of locusts.

The willingness of the villagers to supply us with anything they did happen to possess varied from place to place in a puzzling way. Sex seemed to have something to do with success or failure; if all the men were out in the fields and the village fort was held by a few old dames, stony indifference or harsh words were usually our portion. On these occasions we used to arm Angtharkay with some rupees and send him to bell the cat, and as he had pertinacity and a thick skin he seldom came away empty-handed. Kusang, though possessing a more ingratiating manner, would have wilted under the first torrent of abuse, while Pasang might have started throwing things. Most of these villages were on, or near, a "Pilgrim Route" and my theory was that the traditional hospitality ascribed to mountain villages had been soured by the importunities of the many beggars, and doubtless our appearance justified them in placing us in the same category!

CHAPTER SIX

THE first march of our ten-day programme, an afternoon one to Gwaldam, was certainly the least pleasant of any. The road had dropped perversely, as such things do, 4,000 feet since Ranikhet, and now most of this had to be made good by untrained legs on a desperately hot day. Our Dotials must have been out of work for some time as they seemed no happier than we were, and it was late in the evening before a procession of cripples crawled painfully up the last steep rise to the Forest Bungalow. This was beautifully situated on the slopes overlooking the valley of the Pindar and surrounded by abandoned tea-gardens, and once we had established ourselves on the veranda in long cane chairs and procured a vast bowl of milk, our toils were soon forgotten. Tonight we felt we had really started, and though still under a roof the link with civilisation was wearing thin.

The view beyond the Pindar which we had hoped morning would reveal, was hidden in mist and cloud which later turned to rain. Our way lay first down to the valley of the Pindar River, past many villages and well-cultivated fields. The flats near the river were irrigated and were used for growing rice, and great skill and industry was shown in the extensive terracing of the hillsides, a crop of winter wheat already being reaped. Later we left this smiling valley and turned north up a lateral branch, camping amongst some oaks on a high col in a drizzle of rain. At sundown the clouds lifted and from our vantage point 9,000 feet up we had a brief but satisfying vision of Nanda Ghunti.

We were now travelling across higher country between two main valleys, and villages were few and far between, a matter of indifference to us but of much interest to the porters who had to buy their daily rations from the hamlets we did pass. It was not always easy to find 30 or 40 lbs. of rice or of wheat flour; near the larger villages there was usually a mill turned by water, but in most of the smaller the flour was ground by hand on a flat stone, and no more done at a time than would suffice for the next meal – a really literal hand-to-mouth existence. At last, at a village called Wan, the porters got what they needed and we camped here on a little plateau above the village, under some huge Deodars.

We were now about to cross the watershed between the Pindar and Nandakganga Rivers, a long ridge, here 11,000 feet high, which leads up to the mighty Trisul ten miles away to the south-east. Our start was delayed while we waited for the Sherpas who, having only breakfasted lightly off several double-handfuls of satu, now proceeded to fill up with three of the biggest mountains of rice, plates have ever held. Two hours steady climb through shady forests of oak and chestnut brought us to the col, and from there we climbed for another 2,000 feet up a hill west of it, for the sake of the view. The lower slopes were clothed in rhododendron forest, at this altitude still in flower and presenting a beautifully varied show of colour from white to pink and deep crimson. As we gained height, passing from forest to springy turf and then to rock, the mountains which we had been glimpsing through gaps in the trees now rose before us as a distant and broken wall of dazzling whiteness. Nearly all the giants of the Central Himalaya were there to welcome us, from the Kedarnath peaks and Kamet in the north round to Trisul in the east.

Despite a fierce sun it was very cold and snow was still lying in the gullies, so we tore ourselves away from the feast of beauty and hurried back to the col, and so down into the valley to Kanol. Against this name in my diary there is the laconic entry "flies and bulls," nor is more needed, for the recollection of being driven out of the camp by the one and flying naked before the other, which attacked us as we were about to bathe, is still very vivid. But Kanol is also memorable for the opening of the first of four big "Farmhouse" Cheddars we had brought with us; this somewhat premature attack on our luxuries being brought about partly by the difficulty of buying anything, already noted, and by some concern for its health. It had somehow got into my rucksack and so drew attention to itself, and we were anxious to know what effect the damp heat of Calcutta had had on it. Great was our relief to find it had suffered no serious harm. Certainly it had wilted a little but now the cool mountain air was having as bracing an effect upon the cheese as upon us.

Next day the Nandakganga was crossed and we embarked upon a succession of ups and downs over a country almost bare of trees, in the full glare of a hot sun. Plodding up the dusty bridle-path, we met coming down a portentous cavalcade of over twenty mules, a like number of coolies, and a cloud of followers and servants, no doubt the advance-guard of some Great Personage, and we felt uneasy at the threatened meeting, because we had given up shaving since leaving Ranikhet. However it proved to be only a Forest Officer making a tour of his district, the last European we were to meet for another three months.

The magnificent forests which are such a feature of the foothills are at present safe from exploitation for timber or for paper owing to transport difficulties, the rivers being quite useless for that purpose. There is something to be said for illiteracy, and for some time India's three hundred and fifty millions and these noble forests are safe from the devastating effects of a Daily Press. The only product at present is resin, the collection of which is under the Forest Department.

We had barely recovered from the apprehension aroused by the cavalcade and the subsequent reaction, when another passing wayfarer stretched our minds once more upon the rack of anticipation. This time the trouble was caused by an old chap who sported a row of War decorations, as many of these Garhwalis do since the Garhwal Rifles, which greatly distinguished itself in Flanders and Mesopotamia, is recruited solely from them. He saluted us with vigour and we propounded our usual question about eggs and chickens, a question we now put by way of a conversational gambit rather than as a serious inquiry, but the veteran startled us by hinting that he knew where a chicken might be got. He accompanied us to the next village talking all the time, but our replies were short as we were busy arguing the respective merits of roast and boiled chicken, finally deciding in favour of the latter because we wanted to eat it that night. Arrived at the village our friend disappeared into a house to find the victim. Returning presently with an air of self-satisfaction which told us he had been successful, he proudly produced, with the flourish of a conjurer, a rather ill-nourished fledgeling whose feathers were barely visible. As a joke we thought it in rather bad taste, but we had to acquit him of that intention for when we refused to treat he became quite indignant.

The weather was now so fine and settled that every night we abandoned our stuffy tent in favour of the open, and that night we had a glorious camp on a smooth grass terrace under some pines. Shaken though we had been by the affair of the chicken, our peace and content was almost perfect as we lay round a fire of pinewood which blazed like a torch and gave off an oily smoke smelling pleasantly of turpentine. The only discordant note was provided by the Sherpas who industriously held their caps in the smoke and then suddenly clapped them on their heads, an operation which suggested, quite wrongly I believe, a very disturbing train of thought. The true explanation of this curious rite we never discovered.

In front of us now was another high ridge projecting far to the west from the slopes of Nanda Ghunti. We started early for the ascent of this, and the freshness of the morning, the oaks, the hollies, and the chestnuts, the tapping of woodpeckers and the distant note of a cuckoo, made it seem like a spring morning in England. From the col at 10,000 feet Trisul and Nanda Ghunti again showed up prominently, and then we dropped quickly down to the valley of the Bireh Ganga, and camped in a pretty dell, carpeted with big white flowers which smelt like lilies. Pleasant enough it was, but no longer reminiscent of spring at home, plagued as we were by myriads of flies and amused by a school of grey monkeys who were equally interested in us.

Early next day we crossed the river with that thirst-provoking name, the Bireh Ganga, a name, alas! and nothing more for we bathed in it in order to make quite sure. The northern slopes were steep bare hillsides up which the track wound in narrow zig-zags, and at the steepest and narrowest part we were almost swept away by a flood of goats, all carrying little saddle-bags of grain. The photo I tried to take was not a success, and several goats were nearly frightened over the cliff much to the wrath of their owner. We experienced the same difficulty in taking pictures of some of the very picturesque-looking women we passed, festooned with necklaces and strings of coins, and wearing handsome jewelled nose-rings. They either fled at sight, turned their backs on us, or covered their heads.

Looking down the Bireh Ganga, a very prominent landmark is a great scar on the hillside and below it a lake of some size. This is the mark left by the great landslip of 1893 which dammed the river and formed the Gohna Lake beneath. The lake has dwindled now; at first it was much larger and the breaking of the dam caused great havoc lower down. Still mounting we finally camped amongst some large boulders near the village of Khaliaghat. By now we should have become indifferent to rebuffs in the matter of eggs and milk, annoying as it was to go without the second-named when one could hardly throw a stone without hitting a cow, a water buffalo, or a goat. But at Khaliaghat it seems to have rankled for there is something malicious about the entry in my diary, to the effect that the peasants here were of a very low type. So far as I remember we made no anthropological investigations to establish this; certainly cases of goitre were very frequent but so they were in all the higher valleys.

Next day's march, which was to bring us to the foot of the Kuari Pass, was a long one for which we made an early start on a raw, wet morning. It was so cold that at the first halt we lit a fire and sat round it for some time, baking and eating potatoes. Later it faired up and became hot enough to make a bathe in the Kuari glen a pleasant interlude.

The approach to the Kuari was up a steep, wooded glen down which a stream rushed, by gorge and waterfall, from near the pass. After a very long and steep grind the slope began to ease off, and crossing the glen we emerged on to grass downs, bare of trees but brilliant with dwarf iris and potentillas (or red buttercups, if that is not a contradiction in terms). The tinkle of sheep bells and the plaintive notes of a shepherd's pipe drew us towards a shepherd encampment, and here we spent the night, a thousand feet below the pass. There was not the savoury pot of goat's meat and the capacious goat-skin-bag full of wine which readers of Cervantes will remember almost reconciled Sancho to a shepherd's life, but for all that we were hospitably received. Like ourselves they were bound for the pass and the little bags carried by their flocks were full of grain. This is not such a contemptible form of transport as it may sound, as each animal will carry some twenty pounds, so that a flock of a hundred, which is a small one for these parts, can move a ton of stuff. When in camp the shepherds build these bags into a wall forming an admirable wind-break and as the tree-line was not too far below to get fuel, we enjoyed a very snug billet.

The Kuari Pass was known to be a remarkably fine view point so we prayed for a fine morning and made a resolution to be up there early. Before turning in it began to rain, thus offering an excellent excuse for reconsidering this rash resolve, but we hardened our hearts and were duly rewarded. The top of the pass was reached by 7 o'clock of a clear, cold morning and we were privileged to see what must be one of the grandest mountain views in the world. As we raised our heads above the top of the pass a gigantic sweep of icy peaks confronted us, and it was difficult to refrain from gasping at the vastness of the scene. The serrated line of the Kedarnath and Badrinath peaks, Kamet, Hathi Parbat, and the great cleft of the Dhauli Valley were easily recognised, but the glittering array of snowy peaks of all shapes and sizes which filled the gaps were easier to admire and wonder at than to identify. South of the Dhauli towered the graceful Dunagiri, but a sight of Nanda Devi, so soon to be our lodestone, was denied us.

There was some snow on the pass but not enough to trouble the porters, and presently we were down again amongst pines and grassy meadows. Here we had to stop repeatedly as fresh visions of mountain beauty, framed in vistas of pines, delighted our eyes, and film after film was exposed as we endeavoured to capture them. At the first village we came to, still high above the Dhauli, we were directed along a high level route leading over the southern slopes to Joshimath. The porters who were behind followed the more usual route straight down to Tapoban in the valley, and then by the main track which ran close to the river. For them it was a long day and they did not get in till late and one, who subsequently quitted, not until the next day. We had reason to bless our high level route in spite of the temporary separation from our porters, for happening to look back at a bend in the path, we found we were looking up part of the Rishi Ganga Valley and at the pyramid-like summit of Nanda Devi floating serenely in the background. It did not look to be ten miles away but was in fact at least thirty.

We ourselves reached Joshimath at 3 o'clock and the same evening opened negotiations for porters, and porters' food, to accompany us on our attempt on the Rishi Gorge. We wanted twenty porters and about four hundred pounds of food for them, but luckily flour was not ground by hand at Joshimath or we might be there still. Some of it, however, was wanted in the form of "satu" which takes a day or two to prepare, being made by first slightly roasting the wheat or barley (or a mixture of both) in iron pans and then grinding it. The advantage of "satu" is that it requires no cooking and can be eaten dry (not recommended), moistened with cold water, or as a porridge; we found it went down best in tea with plenty of sugar, and was then very good.

The problem of porters was unexpectedly alleviated by the Dotials who, though only engaged as far as Joshimath, were now eager to remain with us. This enthusiasm was the more surprising as most of them had only just arrived after a twelve hour day, and although we painted a gloomy picture of the perils and hardships awaiting them in the Rishi (not inaccurately as it happened) nothing would shake them.

Next day was a Sunday but there was no rest for us. We began work at 6 a.m. nor did Tilman need to have his first job, the killing of a scorpion, pointed out to him. It was curled up in his bedding and very gratifying it was to see the "early bird" and the sluggard for once receiving their respective dues – it might so easily have been the other way round. Curiously enough later in the day we killed a snake close by, but these two specimens must not be taken as typical Joshimath fauna, which consists almost entirely of the more homely but equally venomous fly.

Before getting down to sorting and weighing loads we sent off one of the Sherpas to scour the surrounding country for eggs. We reasoned that as Joshimath was a considerable village on the very populous Pilgrim Route such things ought not to be beyond the bounds of possibility. It is a place of some antiquity and lies 1,500 feet above the deep gorge where the Dhauli and Alaknanda Rivers unite. The junction is called Vishnuprayag and has many sacred associations but there is nothing there save a shrine and a few huts. Joshimath itself is a long straggling village built on a projecting spur, and besides two bazaars, nearly half a mile apart, there is a hospital, a school, a post office, and one or two large houses. One of these belongs to the Rawal of the Badrinath temple who passes the winter here. The villagers' houses are solidly built of stone, with two stories and a stone roof. The living-room is on the first floor which opens out in front on to a wooden balcony, the ground floor being used as a stable, store, or shop. The timber for the houses is all cut by hand and is very massive, and on the lintels and balcony there is sometimes elaborate carving.

For all its two bazaars no one living in Joshimath could have made much of a hole in his pocket or wasted his substance on riotous living. Once or twice we succumbed to the temptations of the sweetmeat sellers, but we always found sickness intervened before a whole rupee had been spent. Nevertheless, the cost of the few things we wanted and which were obtainable was quite high enough, and the bazaar fraternity had the fine independent air assumed by the owners of seaside lodgings at the height of a good summer season.

Towards evening the scattered debris of the loads had at least begun to resolve itself into two piles, one to go with us and one to remain, and the first was even shaping itself into approximate loads. But the strain was telling, the spring balance was now, through overwork, registering several pounds with nothing on it, and we were not sorry when an interruption came.

It was the Sherpa, faint but triumphant, accompanied by the owner of three eggs. We were too pleased to argue about the very stiff price, but put them straight into a bucket of water where, to our dismay, they bobbed about merrily on the surface, obviously, by all the laws, in a fairly advanced state. Wiser men would have called the deal off but second thoughts suggested that after all eggs were eggs, and the water test, infallible as we knew in Africa, might not apply to

Indian eggs. Further than that Joshimath was 6,000 feet above the sea, and though neither of us was a physicist, we knew that altitude had queer effects on boiling water and why not on the buoyancy factor? Anyway, for better or for worse, we decided to take them, but unfortunately three into two won't go so, in a spirit worthy of Mrs. Beeton, we recklessly sank all three in an omelette, telling Angtharkay not to spare the ghee in the frying, for it has a powerful taste of its own. The result was as excellent as it was surprising and worthy of more than our somewhat sententious remarks, I observing that "the highest wisdom is not to be too wise," while all Tilman could find to say was: "*De l'audace, toujours de l'audace*." Had our heads not been in a whirl of figures relating to rations, days, and rupees (we had just counted the contents of our bag of rupees for the tenth time, to make sure we really had lost some), we might have worked out a learned thesis on "Altitude and the Specific Gravity of the Egg;" as it was we had one more unsuccessful count and turned in.

I am afraid that night we were unfeignedly glad that this delightful ten day prelude was over and that the morrow would see the beginning of more serious work, and our impatience was no doubt the reason why we did not enjoy the preliminary march to the full. At the back of our minds was regret at the apparent waste of time, regret which became more poignant as fine day succeeded fine day, for we well knew that this pre-monsoon weather was the best we should ever have. But for that we might have been content to put no limit to our wanderings in a country of such loveliness, where the air and the rivers, the flowers and the trees filled one with the joy of living.

Now, however, impatience was to be satisfied and though we should find nature in a sterner mood, there would be no carking care to prevent us echoing Petulengro's "Life is very sweet . . ."

CHAPTER SEVEN

LIGHT rain had fallen during the morning and the air was fresh and invigorating as we marched out of Joshimath along the well-made path that runs high up along the south side of the Dhaoli Valley. To the north dark precipices rose from the water's edge in a continuous sweep, to lose themselves in the clouds some thousands of feet above us. At irregular intervals these walls were cleft by narrow, ravine-like valleys, cut in the rock by streams descending from the glaciers of the great peaks above. I can never see such configuration without experiencing an almost irrepressible desire to select a valley at random and wander up into its mysterious recesses, and on such a day as this, when the clouds, darkening the upper reaches of the gorge, accentuated its apparent depth, it was hard to resist the temptation to make a drastic change of plan.

Our path, which started at Joshimath some 1,500 feet above the river, remained fairly level throughout the short day's march, and at the village of

Tapoban ran only a few feet above the floor of the valley. Here we caught up the Dotials, who had left some hours ahead of us, and a mile beyond the village, in a pleasantly wooded side-valley, we camped.

The evening was a fine one. Four miles upstream we could see the junction-point between the Rishi Nala and the main Dhaoli Valley. In the corner formed by these two valleys is a prominent forest-clad knoll called Lata afer the village at its foot. It really forms the butt end of the great western ridge of Dunagiri, and we could see at a glance that the summit of this hill must command a fine view up the Rishi Nala, a view which might well prove invaluable to us later on. It was decided, therefore, that Kusang and Angtharkay should go with the Dotials on the following day, and that Pasang, Tilman and I should climb Lata and join the others in the evening at Surai Tota, where we had made arrangements with the Bania to pick up our supplies of satu and ata.

Five a.m. saw the three of us again striding along the path by the side of the river. We moved at a good speed as we had a long day's work before us: five miles along the path, 6,500 feet of ascent and descent over the rough wooded hillside, and then some more miles of path to be accomplished before nightfall.

The morning was one of exquisite beauty. The air, cleansed and purified by the rain of the previous day, was filled with the delicate scents of the pine-woods. From behind the great ice-peaks came the beams of the newly-risen sun, in magnificent contrast to the sombre, heavily forested country about us. The trees with their drowsy limbs still wet with the dew, the song of the birds sharing with us the exaltation of the new-born day, the streams splashing down in silver waterfalls or lying dormant in deep-blue pools, all played their part in this – the second act of Nature's pageantry of dawn. A fine morning, when all consideration of time and distance was eclipsed by the pure delight in one's surroundings.

We had been going for an hour and a half when we came to a northward bend in the Dhaoli River, which marked the point where the Rishi Ganga joins it. There we paused for a moment to look into that section of the gorge up which Graham had made an attempt to force a route as far back as 1883: a gorge which has never yet been penetrated by anyone. As our object was to get into the Nanda Devi Basin, we could not afford to spend any time trying to explore this section of the Rishi Ganga. We knew of a practicable route into the middle section, and a failure to get up this lower section would cost us valuable time.

But it was interesting to have a close view of the river which, in its higher reaches, was going to play such an important part in our adventures of the next few weeks. There was less water in it than I had expected, and we became hopeful of being able to wade up it in parts where there was no other route – poor innocents that we were. I had an idea too that once the winter snows had gone from the lower mountain sides, the volume of water in the rivers would decrease considerably, and never regain its present proportions for the rest of the year. In this I was entirely wrong. In actual fact, as soon as the melting of the glacier ice sets in, after the departure of the winter snow, the rivers increase enormously in size. This I think is an impressive indication of the immense area of the glaciers in the district.

A mile beyond the mouth of the Rishi, we turned to the right and started mounting the steep slope of Lata, finding the going more complicated and strenuous than we had expected. The hillside was covered with dense undergrowth, through which it was hard work to make our way. The ground was steep, and every now and then we were faced by a little cliff which had been masked by the undergrowth. Moreover we had had no chance to make a selection of a suitable route from afar, and now we could not see far enough ahead to choose out the best line. Our pace was slow, the day waxed hot, and our throats became unpleasantly dry. Sometimes we were forced to descend a considerable way in order to avoid some overhanging cliff, which tried our tempers sorely. At 11 o'clock we arrived at the foot of a cliff of larger proportions than usual. This we saw would demand a long descent before we would be able to outflank it. Like the rawest novices we elected to try and climb the crag direct, though the upper section was screened from view. After an hour of stiff rock-climbing, we succeeded in getting down again to the spot from which we had started. More heated than ever, we started on the outflanking movement. This accomplished, we toiled upwards once more, feeling not a little humbled by the heavy weather we were making of this little knoll. Clinging on to mossy roots, which not infrequently came away from the hillside, showering earth into our mouths and down our backs, we reached at 2.30 p.m. a little bald rocky patch, which formed the summit of Lata.

A glance at the view changed our gloomy outlook on life to one of thrilling exultation. The afternoon was clear and still. All round us were scenes of grandeur, the scale of which was too vast for human conception. To the north, across the Dhaoli Valley, rose the grim turrets and delicate spires of the Hathi Parbat group, so complex in structure that we could not begin to understand its tangled topography. Eastwards was the lovely cone of Dunagiri, displaying to full advantage its beautifully proportioned curves. West of us was the Trisul range, its vast ice plateaux dazzlingly white in the torrid rays of the afternoon sun. And to the south Nanda Devi, queen of them all, held aloft her proud shapely head, her slender shoulders draped with snow-white braid.

Coming down to earth, we erected the plane-table, and worked with it for an hour. The views we had obtained of the Rishi Nala provided food for much thought.

Soon after 4 o'clock we started to descend. We got into a steep leaf-filled gully in the forest, and down this we plunged at a fine speed. I was still wearing my tennis shoes, and gave my bad toe several cracks which nearly sent me head first down the steep slope.

Since leaving the valley in the early morning, we had not come across a drop of water, nor did we find any now. The day was hot, we had been working hard, and by now were unpleasantly parched in tongue and throat. For my part this was accountable for the turn of speed which landed us on the shore of the Dhaoli River at 6 o'clock – a descent of six thousand odd feet in under two hours. To the infinite astonishment of a company of Bhotias who were camping on the shore close by, Tilman stripped and plunged into the turbulent waters of the river. I was more circumspect and performed my ablutions from a convenient boulder. Pasang, a true Tibetan, merely drank.

In the cool of the evening we marched silently up the valley. A fresh breeze blowing down from the peaks, and limbs just pleasantly tired, put me in sympathy with the subdued colouring of dusk, while I mused over the glimpse we had had into the mysterious country beyond the Rishi Ganga.

It was quite dark before we reached Surai Tota. Our camp was pitched on a flat stretch of grassland above the river, and a fine fire was blazing outside the tents. A large dish of lentils, followed by inexhaustible supplies of tea put us at peace with the world, and quite incapable of coping with a voluble flow of Hindustani from Kesar Singh,* who had awaited our arrival in the village. The night was warm, and we fell into luxurious slumber by the fireside, knowing nothing more until roused by the first beams of the morning sun.

Kesar Singh had arranged for eight Surai Tota men to come with us up the Rishi. They were to be paid at the same rate as the Dotials and receive the same rations, i.e., tea, salt, cigarettes and ata. Kesar Singh said he knew the men well, and according to him they were sure-footed, brave, strong, and absolutely reliable: in fact, it appeared that they were very paragons of virtue. The ata, it appeared, was bagged and ready; but the satu would not be ready until later in the morning. However, it was arranged that we should start on with three of the "locals" who knew the route, and the other five would follow on with the satu when it was ready. Our destination that day was a little alp known as Hyetui Kharak, situated near the upper limit of the forest, at an altitude of about 11,700 feet. The men who were coming with us assured us that they all knew the way well and, completing a touching farewell ceremony with Kesar Singh, we made our departure with his assurances that we would have no trouble from *his* men at least.

A rough track led steeply up through the forest which covered the southern side of the Dhaoli Valley, the floor of which at this point is about 7,500 feet. An hour's steady going along this track took us to the tiny village of Tolma, a charming spot built high on the steep mountain side under the shade of some gigantic conifers.

Life in these little mountain villages is delightfully simple, and the inhabitants are almost entirely self-supporting. A few stony fields, terraced out of the steep hillside by their ancestors, supply all the food they require. A flock of sheep and goats, tended in summer by the youth of the community on the high mountain pastures, provides them with wool for their clothing. This wool is spun into yarn by the men, who carry their simple apparatus about with them wherever they go, so that they can be constantly spinning, while carrying loads, tending sheep, or performing any job that does not involve the use of their hands. The yarn is then woven into cloth by the women, who sit outside their houses, manipulating complicated machines with astonishing skill. Thus all are busily employed, all are well-fed and clothed, and all are happy. Any surplus farm produce is exchanged with itinerant traders for such luxuries as salt, tobacco, etcetera.

We paused awhile to converse with some of the weavers, and to try and puzzle out how their machines worked, then continued on our ascent. Our newly enrolled Surai Tota men already seemed a bit doubtful of the way and we inquired of some ploughmen, whether or not the path to Hyetui Kharak was well

*Kesar Singh had accompanied us on the Kamet expedition and lived hereabouts.

defined. We gathered from them that we could not possibly miss it if we kept our eyes open. Nevertheless we were no sooner clear of the fields than we were floundering in dense forest, trying in vain to find the least vestige of a track. The "locals" assured us that we had just got to keep on up and we would be all right. But only when, after wading for some hours through the forest, we reached the brink of a 1,500 foot precipice, did they admit that the only two of the eight who knew the way were among those who had waited at Surai Tota for the satu! They thought that we had come too high and that the alp was somewhere below us.

It was obvious to us from Dr. Longstaff's descriptions of the country that it was still *above* us, and taking the matter of route finding into our own hands we reached the "kharak" in the middle of the afternoon. (Kharak, by the way, is a word used in these parts to mean a summer grazing ground. As the winter snows depart from the lowest of their pastures, so the shepherds and their flocks come up into occupation; later in the year they move to a still higher alp.)

The highest of these kharaks are about 14,000 feet in altitude, and are occupied for a bare two months each year. Hyetui Kharak was not yet occupied, as a quantity of snow still lingered on its higher slopes. It was a pleasant spot – a wide stretch of meadowland bordered on three sides by the forest, and we spent the remainder of the afternoon lying stretched out on the grass, dozing in the warm sunshine.

Towards dusk we began to get anxious about the non-arrival of the five satu men. Now that we had left the Dhaoli Valley, we could not afford to waste a day; for with such a large company of porters, each day spent in getting to our base in the Rishi Nala meant a large amount less food with which to carry out our work beyond. When night fell and there was still no sign of the missing five, we began to curse our folly in starting without them. We fully expected that they, like their fellows, had not the least idea of the way. However, at 8 o'clock our anxiety was relieved by their arrival.

We slept out in the open again, and were up as soon as it was light, for we knew that we were in for a hard day's work. Not far above us, at an altitude of about 12,500 feet, the forest zone ended abruptly. Above this line the snow was lying deep on the ground. This winter snow in the process of melting is vile stuff to get through. Soft and sodden, it allows one to sink in to the extent of its depth, but is sufficiently heavy to put up a formidable resistance against any forward progress.

The porters knew this as well as we did, and, as we were getting ready for an early start, the Surai Tota men came to us to say that they must have a ration of ghee before they could consent to go any further. Except for a small quantity of ghee intended for the use of the Sherpas high up, we had none to give them. But it was obvious that they had little intention of going any further, and I told them that they could do as they liked; to which they replied that they would go down and leave us! Indeed, I suspect that that had been their idea all along: to come with us as far as Hyetui Kharak, a very easy day's march from Surai Tota, to collect their pay, and clear off before they were involved in any hard work. In this they were disappointed, as of course we refused to pay them unless they fulfilled their agreement to come with us into the Rishi Nala. I would like to say here, however, that this was the only time in all our dealings with the people of this district that we were let down in any way.

The desertion of the Surai Tota men put us in a serious predicament, and threatened to wreck at the very outset our plans for the exploration of the Nanda Devi Basin. We summoned the Dotials, who were camped a hundred yards away, and explained the situation to them. Without a moment's hesitation they volunteered to carry as much as they could manage of the abandoned loads. We warned them that the going would be extremely bad, but they held to their offer, and added so much of the satu and ata to the loads which they had been carrying on the previous day, that only two loads of ata remained. These were dragged off to the forest and hidden, to be picked up on their return. Staggering under loads weighing more than eighty pounds each they cheerfully faced the steep slopes above the alp. Thus did these low-caste Dotials by their loyalty make it possible for us to go through with our plans.

These negotiations delayed our start, and it was 7.40 a.m. before we were on the move. We were making for the crest of that same ridge running down from the Dunagiri massif, whose westerly end culminated in the little peak of Lata, which we had climbed two days before. We knew that our route lay across a gap in this ridge, some 14,700 feet in height, to a grazing ground used in summer by the shepherds of Tolma and Lata, and known to them as Durashi. This kharak was not generally visited until the beginning of July, owing to the winter snow which makes the pass impossible for the transit of sheep. It was now May 24th, and the track was still buried under deep snow.

From the summit of a spur above Hyetui we got a good view of the ridge above us, and saw that there were no less than three gaps to choose from, each just as promising as the other. Moreover the ridge was serrated, and the condition of the snow made it impossible to get from one gap to another by following the crest. The only thing to do was to make a guess at which was the right one, and trust to luck.

Soon after leaving the forest we plunged into a morass of soft snow, through which we had to flog a track. At first it was not particularly deep and, keeping to the crest of a spur, the first gap was reached in a couple of hours. From here we looked down a sheer precipice of several thousand feet. We were obviously in the wrong gap, and a traverse had to be made round to the next one. Once off the spur our difficulties began. We sank first up to our knees, then up to our waists; sometimes we were floundering up to our armpits in the sodden snow. The day was fine, without a breath of wind. The blazing sun and the torrid glare from the snow produced a feeling of lassitude such as I have never experienced elsewhere except on enclosed glaciers at great altitudes.

Tilman and I took turns of twenty minutes each at the task of track making, while the others remained behind to assist the porters, whose cruel loads frequently caused them to overbalance. It was terribly hard work for them; but they stuck to it wonderfully, cheerfully chiding one another as they fell into some deep drift, from which they had to be extricated. The ground too was steep and very rough, and they avoided an accident only by their surprising skill.

It was a weary struggle and our progress seemed painfully slow. Beating with our ice-axes, kicking and stamping, we continued without pause until 2.30 p.m., when we reached the second gap, only to find that the third was the true pass. We made an attempt to get along the ridge towards it, but after some hard work we had to give this up on account of the difficulty of the climbing which made even the Dotials lose their cheerfulness. Descending a few hundred feet we reached a small rocky ledge sticking out of the snow. It was now 5 o'clock, and we decided to bivouac here for the night. We melted some snow and brewed tea; never was a drink more welcome.

The outcrop we were on was sloping steeply downwards, so we built up platforms on which to sleep. It was a commanding position, 6,000 feet above the Dhaoli River, and one from which the surrounding peaks could be seen to their best advantage.

It was a perfect evening. As I lay on my little platform, the multi-coloured afterglow of sunset spreading over the vast mountain world about me, I was filled with a deep content, untroubled either by the memory of the failures of that day, or by the prospect of further trials on the morrow. A vision of such beauty was worth a world of striving.

The last tint of sunset died, and a young moon, hanging over the ice-buttresses of the giant peak of Dunagiri, held undisputed right to shed her pale light over an enchanted world. The snowy crests stood now in superb contrast to the abysmal gloom of the valleys. Interwoven with my dreams, I was vaguely conscious of these sublime impressions throughout the night, until a new day was heralded by the first faint flush of dawn.

We made full use of the cold of the early morning, in resuming our toil through the snow, and with this ally we made more rapid progress. Now at last we were on the right route, and at 10.30 a.m. we reached the true pass. There we found a well-defined track running along the face of a steep precipice. The rocks still held a good deal of ice and snow, especially in the gullies, and much step cutting was required in order to get along the track. It was a remarkable place. The cliffs were exceedingly steep and dropped in an almost unbroken plunge for some 8,000 feet, and yet there was this narrow ledge, along which it was possible for the shepherds to take their sheep in the summer time. The length of the cliff was about half a mile.

My heart was in my mouth as I watched the Dotials coming along the track, for the ice made the passage of certain sections exceedingly delicate work. But we soon discovered that they were as sure-footed as cats, and needed very little assistance, in spite of their formidable loads. Cutting steps for prolonged periods is tiring work, but it was infinitely preferable to the heart-breaking toil of the previous day. At the further end of the terrace was a deep gully into which we had to descend for several hundred feet; when a climb up a boulder-strewn slope took us to a small gap, from which we looked down gentle grassy slopes to Durashi. The contrast could not have been more sudden and unexpected. There at our feet lay a little stretch of country, enclosed by gently rolling hills, for all the world like some quiet corner of the English Lake District. There was about it not the least suggestion of the vast ruggedness of the land from which we had just come.

The little vale of Durashi is really a hanging valley, lying high up on the northern side of the Rishi Nala. On three sides it is enclosed by these grassy hills, and on the fourth it opens out above the precipice which forms the side of the main valley. It seems to be entirely cut off from the outside world. Indeed if it were not for the cliff track, its luxuriant pastures would be inaccessible to the shepherds and their flocks. We found several stone shelters there, which were gladly occupied by the Dotials. Water and firewood were scarce and difficult of access.

In the evening we wandered down to the lower end of the valley, and looked straight down a 5,000 foot precipice into what must be one of the most fantastic gorges in the world. It has never yet been penetrated by any human being, and is believed by the locals to be the abode of demons – a superstition we were quite ready to share. The precipice was far too steep for us to be able to examine the near side of the valley, but the other side was almost grotesque in its structure. It was built up of tier upon tier of gigantic steeply inclined slabs, which culminated 10,000 feet above the river in a multitude of sharp rocky peaks set at a rakish angle. The river itself, only just visible in the depths below us, sent up a roar like that of Niagara. What a subject for an artist illustrating an old-fashioned travel book! No conception, even of Gustave Doré, could appear exaggerated beside the cliffs and turrets towering above that amazing canyon. To us the view was anything but encouraging.

The evening was overcast and we began to fear that our spell of fine weather was coming to an end. A little rain fell in the night, but we awoke to another cloudless morning. We started at 7 o'clock and climbed up to a saddle in the ridge which enclosed the head of the little Durashi glen. This ridge has been aptly named "the curtain" by Dr. Longstaff, for it is an offshoot of the main Dunagiri-Lata ridge which we had crossed the day before, and runs down at right angles into the Rishi Ganga, completely screening the upper part of that valley from Durashi. Before starting on its final plunge into the Rishi Ganga, the ridge rises to a little peak, which we called for want of a better name Durashi Peak. This was only about 600 feet above our saddle and, leaving the porters to rest awhile, Tilman and I ascended the peak with the plane-table, and spent two hours on top, studying the geography of the upper gorge and its surroundings, of which we commanded a fairly comprehensive view.

We could identify the furthest points reached by the Graham and Longstaff parties, just beyond the junction of the Rhamani Valley with the Rishi Nala, and it was about there that we proposed to put our base camp. Beyond was the untrodden section of the gorge, the key to the sanctuary of the Nanda Devi Basin. The view we got of it from here proved of the greatest value to us later.

Clouds soon began to form on the peaks around, but Nanda Devi remained clear. Indeed, this was a peculiarity of the mountain, which we came to recognise. Often when all the other peaks were obscured from view, wrapped in a dense mantle of cloud, the summit of Nanda Devi would remain clear. (This is directly contrary to general rule, for it is nearly always the big isolated rock mountains which first attract cloud, especially when they happen to be the highest in their particular district.) Now we obtained an uninterrupted view of the great southern ridge of the mountain. It was by this ridge that we entertained some slight hope of finding a practicable route to the summit, although we were not sufficiently equipped to make the attempt that year. But as we looked at the mighty upward sweep of the ridge all hope died, for the thing appeared utterly unclimbable, as indeed I still think it is.

At 10.30 a.m. we rejoined the porters on the saddle. From here we looked down some three thousand feet into a thickly wooded nala, descending from a glacier-covered south-westerly spur of Dunagiri. The nala was cut into two parts by streams which united further down. Between them, completely surrounded by a forest of tall pines, lay a beautiful strip of pasture land, known to the locals as Dibrughita. This too was used as a summer grazing ground. We were told later that nowadays it is very seldom visited by shepherds, presumably because of the difficulty of access, for the grazing must be very valuable.

The descent was steep and, owing to the loads, took a long time, but it was devoid of difficulties. Unluckily we crossed the stream in a bad place, and had considerable difficulty in getting up the other side. Later, however, we found an easy crossing, which was obviously the one used by the shepherds. It will have been noted by now that many of our difficulties at this early stage were due to our lack of local knowledge. This we had thought to provide against, by engaging Kesar Singh's friends at Surai Tota, some of whom I have no doubt knew the route well. Their desertion put us at a bad disadvantage. We had expected to have no difficulties in the matter of route-finding, at least until one march beyond Dibrughita. We were too pressed for time and food to employ any time in reconnaissance, and a false move meant hours of extra toil for ourselves and the unfortunate Dotials.

We had intended to camp on the alp, but we could not find any water there, and we were forced to go on beyond. This was disappointing, as it was undoubtedly one of the most lovely spots it had ever been my good fortune to behold. Dr. Longstaff had described it to me when I was staying with him in England, but even *his* well-known enthusiasm could not provide me with a picture to compare with the reality. Lying on the soft grass, surrounded by a luxuriant growth of wild flowers, the forest of tall stately pines bordering the alp on every side, and with only a glimpse here and there of some icy peak, it was impossible to imagine the grimly terrifying aspect of the main valley so close at hand. Tilman's remark that it was like "a horizontal oasis in a vertical desert" was one whose aptness we were afterwards to appreciate more fully.

Our camp that night was in the nala beyond Dibrughita. Close beside, a clear stream splashed its joyous way through the forest. Here the vegetation was neither dense nor oppressive, and the trees, great gnarled veterans, each possessed a striking individuality, as in a wood at home.

We had a long climb through the forest next morning to get out of the nala, and when we did so we found ourselves for the first time in the main valley of the Rishi Ganga. Looking back across the Dibrughita Nala we saw to full advantage the huge mass of "the curtain". We saw that it too was composed of gigantic steeply sloping slabs such as we had seen from Durashi on the other side of the valley. And very different it looked now from those gentle grassy slopes on which we had camped two nights before.

We now had our first taste of what moving about in the Rishi Nala was like. Having no local knowledge to guide us, we did not know whether to keep high up on the mountain side or low down, or which was the best route to take. We were then about 2,000 feet above the river, and decided to take a line at about that level. The valley-side was steep, and cut by innumerable deep gullies and cliffs. We could rarely get a clear view of the ground for more than a hundred yards ahead, and we were constantly toiling up some steep slope only to find that we had arrived at some impassable cut-off, which could only be avoided by making a long detour above or below. Tilman and I would go ahead taking different routes, and signal to the others behind to follow the better line. But even so we were continually making big mistakes, which cost us hours of needless toil. Some months later, when we came this way again with a party of porters, we had no difficulty whatever in picking out a good line, simply because we had already been over the country twice and knew it well. But on our first journey it was a worrying job, more particularly as we were in a hurry, and were relying entirely upon the good nature and steadiness of the Dotials.

At about 1 o'clock we reached a point from which we could proceed no further at our present level, and we decided to descend to the river. This was easier said than done, however, and we searched for a long while before we discovered a steep gully down which we could climb. In two places the loads had to be lowered by means of a rope. At one of these I had climbed down first, and was standing on a ledge ready to guide the loads down, when someone dislodged a rock from above, which hit me on the back of the head. It did not quite knock me out, but I was dizzy and sick for some little while afterwards. The accident was more spectacular than serious, however, as the resulting scalp wound bled with a freedom out of all proportion to the size of the cut. This elicited much tender sympathy from the Dotials, particularly from their old "Captain", and for the remainder of the day they worked with redoubled energy.

A few hundred feet above the river we got into bad bramble, through which a way had to be cut, and at 4.30 p.m. we reached the water's edge at a point about half a mile below the Trisuli Nala. We recognised it as the place at which Longstaff had crossed the river on his way to make his famous ascent of Trisul, twenty-seven years before. We decided to camp here for the night.

When we had distributed the rations and had drunk a cup of tea, Tilman and I went off to make a reconnaissance, and to try to decide on tomorrow's route before nightfall.

I had hoped to reach the junction of the Rhamani and Rishi Rivers on the following day, but we had made very poor progress that day, and the difficulties ahead appeared considerable. A number of large boulders in the river bed offered us an easy place for bridging the river. Dr. Longstaff's party had reached the Rhamani junction by crossing the river at this point; but they had been a lightly equipped party, and even so had found considerable difficulties beyond the Trisuli Nala. We had no idea whether a route along the northern bank was practicable. However, after a careful consideration of the matter, it was decided upon as being at least the more direct one. I was in a hurry, because each day that we spent in getting to our proposed base camp meant at least three days less time for the job above as, so long as the Dotials were with us, we were consuming our food supply at the rate of 32 lbs. per day.

By now the loads were appreciably lighter for, besides the food which was being consumed, we had left a dump of flour at Durashi for the use of the Dotials on their return, and here another dump was left.

We got away at about 6.30 on the morning of May 28th. After a few hundred yards we struck very bad going, but later in the morning we began to make quite satisfactory progress, though held up from time to time by small land-slips, or by fearful tangles of thorn-scrub and bramble. At midday we reached a big scar in the hillside, beyond which we could make no further progress along the river bank. We climbed up for a thousand feet or so and got on to a terrace which took us to a bend in the valley half a mile further on.

The mountain side we were on now steepened up enormously, and it looked very much as if we had reached a dead end. The porters were some way behind so, leaving his load, Tilman went off to prospect round the corner while I waited to rally the men. Now for the first time the Dotials showed signs of despondency. They said they had had enough and they wanted to leave their loads here and go back, and anyhow, they added, they would not face any more difficult or dangerous bits.

It was nearly an hour before Tilman reappeared. He reported that he had got right into a side valley which must have been the Rhamani, and that from the point he had reached it would have been a comparatively simple matter to descend to the stream but that, in getting there, he had had to traverse a tiny sloping ledge without any hand-holds to keep him in balance above a sheer precipice of several hundred feet. He did not think it fair to ask heavily laden men to go across.

We went on for a bit until we arrived at the edge of a deep gully which descended steeply to the Rishi. While Tilman and I examined the possibility of getting on to a higher line of traverse, Kusang and Angtharkay went down the gully to see if the shore of the river would help us. By now the sky had become very dark and a fierce gusty wind was blowing up the valley. It was evident that we were in for a fairly considerable storm. The Dotials huddled together, their teeth chattering.

When the two Sherpas returned with the news that they had only been able to get a hundred yards or so along the shore, we nevertheless gave the word for a general descent to the river, for it was obvious that, apart from everything else, the storm would prevent any intricate climbing on the precipitous ground in front of us. On reaching the river we set to work cutting down trees for the construction of a bridge, while the Dotials made fires on the shore and squatted round them. The actual bridging was not a difficult task with so many hands to assist, as the river was now quite low. By 5.30 p.m. the whole party was safely across.

With a good deal of persuasion we induced the Dotials to come on a little further, telling them that if they did reach the Rhamani junction that night, we would discharge them on the following morning. We told them too that it would take another two hours (though we had not ourselves the haziest notion of how long we should need). A strip of pine forest lay along the southern shore at this point, and as this was free from undergrowth and offered such excellent going, we had actually reached our goal by 6.15. A few minutes later the storm broke, and in a whirl of falling snow we pitched the tents and struggled with a reluctant fire, while the Dotials made themselves snug in a little cave beyond. We did not bother much about food that evening, as darkness had fallen before we had stowed our kit away, and the whirling snow made a mockery of all our efforts to get a fire going.

CHAPTER EIGHT

WHEN preparations for the night were complete, Pasang and I retired to the shelter of a small overhanging rock, while the others took to the tents. Until late into the night the two of us sat huddled over a fire which, after many unsuccessful attempts, we had managed to light in our shelter. Pasang had been suffering from "tummy trouble" for some time, and the heavy work of the last few days had made him feel very weak. It continued to snow heavily throughout the night, and about 1 o'clock I was woken up by Tilman, who had come up to join us, his tent having collapsed under the weight of the snow. He managed to fit some of himself under the shelter of our overhang.

The snow stopped falling in the early hours of the morning and the dawn broke on a cloudless sky. The Dotials paid us an early visit, and we gave them their well-earned pay. They said they did not like leaving us up here alone, but after a touching farewell ceremony, they took their departure. And sorry I was to see them go. They had served us well and faithfully, carrying huge loads over country where a slip would have had serious consequences. Nor should I easily forget their pleasant humour and their courtesy.

The morning was spent in moving our stuff over to the overhang which had been occupied by the Dotials, sorting things out, taking stock of food, and many other little jobs. We found that we had thirty-five days food left.

This section of the Rishi Nala is a fine example of a box-canyon, that is to say, a canyon whose sides rise perpendicularly from the water's edge. The walls of this gorge maintained a tremendous steepness and culminated in peaks of 20,000 feet. Our present altitude was 11,800 feet, and our camp was situated on a small strip of shore on the southern side of the river. The cliffs overhung the shore for about 80 feet above our heads, and afforded fine protection from the rain. In addition, the valley was running nearly east-west, and so our camp enjoyed more sun than would be supposed from the depth of the valley. One drawback to an otherwise ideal site was the lack of clean water. The Rishi was thick with a whitish glacier mud and, though there were several side-streams near by, we could not reach any of them. As we were having our evening meal one night, Angtharkay remarked that now at any rate we had milk with our tea – the milk of the great Nanda Devi!

Our camp was about two hundred yards above the point where Rhamani stream comes into the Rishi Ganga from the north. At the junction itself a huge rock had fallen across the Rishi stream, forming a natural bridge. The crossing was not easy though, and involved some delicate work, especially when crossing with loads. However, it gave us access to the northern side in our search for a route up the gorge, and later was more than useful in our retreat down the valley.

On the afternoon following our arrival, Tilman and I crossed the river to make a reconnaissance on the northern side of the gorge. A hundred feet or so above the rock-bridge we came upon Dr. Longstaff's old camp site – a level grassy platform by an overhanging rock. We climbed up the steep slopes behind it until we could command a good view of the cliffs above our base camp. It was soon evident that it would be impossible to make our way up the gorge at a low level, and that we would have to climb at least 1,200 feet before we could start traversing. We could not see how far this line would get us, but it seemed to be our only chance to get along the southern side of the valley, and it was on that side that Dr. Longstaff had told us to concentrate all our energies.

I found myself to be very nervous and shaky on the steep grass slopes and slabs on which we had to climb. This was due to the fact that I was not yet used to the immense scale of the gorge and its surroundings. Tilman suffered from the same complaint. We also had great difficulty in judging the size and angle of minor features. This made route-finding from a distance very difficult indeed, and we were continually finding ourselves in error. However, the eye gradually adjusted itself, and soon we began to move with more confidence.

That night I could hardly control my impatience to get up on to the cliffs above and start our search for a route through the upper gorge. For a long time I lay awake weighing up in my mind our chances of success. The morrow would show us much, for our reconnaissance that evening had proved to us that there, at the beginning, was but one line of possibility. Should this fail, we should be check-mated at the very outset.

Whatever may have been my enthusiasm or impatience to be up and doing on the night before, the hour for getting up always finds me with no other ambition in the world than to be permitted to lie where I am and sleep, sleep, sleep. Not so Tilman. I have never met anyone with such a complete disregard for the sublime comforts of the early morning bed. However monstrously early we might decide, the night before, to get up, he was about at least half an hour before the time. He was generally very good about it, and used to sit placidly smoking his pipe over the fire, with no more than a few mild suggestions that it might be a good idea to think about starting. Nevertheless, I always boiled (so far as my sleepy state allowed) with indignation, and thought of many crushing arguments (never uttered) why I should be allowed to sleep. Unfortunately it was easier to be a passive obstacle than an active force, and I generally got the better of the silent dispute. But on the morning of May 30th, Tilman's efforts resulted in our leaving camp at 5.20 a.m., that is to say, only twenty minutes late.

Mounting in a series of wide zig-zags, we followed the route we had worked out on the previous afternoon from the opposite side of the valley. After two hours climbing we reached the crest of a little spur which we had taken to be the start of a possible line of traverse, and beyond which we had not been able to see. The spur commanded a fine view of the upper gorge. The immediate prospect looked anything but hopeful, while some two miles further up we saw a huge dark buttress, which appeared to descend in an unbroken sweep from great heights above to the water's edge, and looked to be utterly impassable. This buttress came to be called "Pisgah", for we felt that if we could climb it we would have access to the "Promised Land" beyond.

Directly in front of us was a gully, and beyond the gully was a little terrace running steeply downwards across the face of the precipice we were on. This looked so unpromising that we decided to try it only as a last resort. We climbed the gully for a couple of hundred feet, but were soon brought up short by a line of overhanging rock, and were forced to retreat to the terrace. This led us further than we had expected and we had progressed along the face for some two hundred yards before it petered out below a great scar in the side of the valley caused by a recent landslip. There was no alternative but to climb up to the top of the scar and hope for the best. The rock was "slabby" and very rotten, and we had some unpleasant moments before we surmounted the difficulty. When we reached the top of the crag it seemed as if it would be impossible to get any further, but a search revealed a tiny flaw which enabled us to get round the next corner on to a further sloping terrace.

Our luck held throughout the morning. Above and below us the cliffs were impregnable, and had our present line of traverse failed, I think we should have had to admit defeat; but by a remarkable freak of chance the slender chain of ledges continued unbroken. The complete lack of any alternative, too, enabled us to make good progress, and our eagerness grew as we rapidly approached the gaunt cliffs of "Pisgah". Over and over again the terrace we were on would peter out in some deep cleft, and further advance would seem impossible, but on each occasion there would be a kindly fault in the rock which would enable us to climb over to the continuation of the terrace beyond. Some of the sections were very "thin", and we began to wonder if the route would be possible with loads.

All the terraces were dipping towards the east, and when we reached a point about a quarter of a mile from "Pisgah", we were only 300 feet above the river. Then came the most sensational, though not the most difficult, section of the route. In rounding a spur the terrace or ledge narrowed to a foot in width and actually overhung the river. The passage along it was exhilarating, and it was difficult to believe that a kindly providence had not placed it there to wind up that long chain of improbabilities.

On the opposite side of the river was a strip of shore which ran along the water's edge, until a bend in the river screened it from view. It was possible that if we could get across to it, it might take us past the buttress. We decided to attempt to ford the river and see. It was now 1 o'clock. We should have turned back, but I was desperately keen to "prove" the route we were on, as, if we could do that, further time need not be wasted in prospecting. We took off our lower garments and waded out into the swiftly flowing stream. The water did not reach much above our thighs, but the current was so strong that it was only with the greatest difficulty that we could retain our balance. Also the water was icy cold, and our legs soon lost all sensation. We got across; the passage was painful and unpleasant, but we considered that with due precautions it was safe enough.

The strip of shore did not lead us far and we had to make five more crossings before we were clear of the buttress, and could make our way along the southern side of the valley once more. But it was now getting late, and we had to hurry back. The river of course had to be crossed six times on the way back, making twelve crossings in all, and by the time we reached the gully at the end of the traverse, we had had enough of aquatic sports to last us for some time.

The route we had discovered was far from satisfactory. Many sections of the traverse would be extremely difficult to negotiate with loads; and a route which relied for its practicability on the state of the river was obviously bad. But in the absence of an alternative it would have to serve. Any alternative to the traverse on this side of the river was out of the question, as from what we had seen of the vast precipices of the northern side our chances over there would be remote indeed. Only freak rock formations had made the traverse possible. As for the river, I have already mentioned my reasons for believing that we need not expect a great increase in the volume of water. Also we fancied that, by exercising our ingenuity, some of the crossings could be bridged.

Therefore, after the matter had been discussed at some length, it was decided that we should start at once, relaying the loads along the route discovered that day.

Food was the factor on which all our plans depended. We now had a supply sufficient to last us for thirty-four days. The minimum we could afford to leave at our base for the retreat down the Rishi Nala was enough for three days. That left us thirty-one days for the work ahead of us. A total of 550 lbs. of food and kit had to be shifted.

There were still a good many odd jobs to be done on the morning of May 31st, and we did not get started on our first relay until 11.30. We left Pasang behind for another day's rest, as he had not yet recovered from his "tummy trouble", and we took with us a considerable quantity of light rope and iron pegs with which to construct handrails across the more difficult sections of the traverse, one of which lay just above our base. Here and there we managed to improve upon our previous route, but in the main we were obliged to stick closely to it. At first the work of carrying heavy loads over such difficult ground was exhausting, but gradually we acquired a new rhythm of movement, and the body adjusted itself to the strain imposed upon it. On these occasions my shoulders always gave me most trouble and it generally takes some time for the muscles to get set. The Sherpas support the weight of their loads by means of head bands instead of shoulder straps. This method is much the less tiring of the two, but needs considerable practice. I have tried to use a head band, but cannot manage it over difficult ground.

We decided to make our first camp above the base on the little spur from which we had got our first view of the upper part of the Rishi. It was agreed too to move all our stuff up to the first stage, before going on to the second, and so on. Thus everything was staked on our being able to get through by this route.

The next day, with Pasang to help, we started early, and by making two journeys we got everything on to the spur, where we built up a platform and pitched camp. There was a good supply of juniper fuel with which to make a fire, and we set about the preparation of that ever important item, the cup of tea. It was then discovered that the tea had somehow been left behind with the food dump at the base! I was in favour of leaving it there, but the others would not hear of that, so we drew lots to decide who should make the third journey of the day. Tilman lost and started down at once. However, I think he had the best of the bargain for, as there was still plenty of daylight left, Angtharkay, Kusang and I went off to fix ropes over the big scar at the end of the first traverse. This proved to be an exceedingly tricky job, and was complicated by the advent of a short sharp snow-storm. We returned to camp as night was falling, to find Tilman already returned, and a welcome brew of tea awaiting us.

Seven o'clock the next morning saw us descending into the gully beyond the spur, carrying between us 230 lbs. of gear. All our concentration was needed for the job, for a slip was not to be thought of. (I have often found that so long as the work does not involve complicated movements, carrying a load improves one's climbing technique. Far greater precision is needed, and one naturally abandons all superfluous movements of the body, which often more than counterbalances the weight of the load. This is one reason why a man who is used to carrying loads uphill, when deprived of his load, very often cannot climb as fast or as far as a man who is not used to carrying loads; his movements become jerky, and he finds it very difficult to adjust his rhythm to the altered conditions. Indeed, it is easier to learn to carry a load than to learn how not to carry one. The fact is very evident with the Sherpas, potentially some of the finest mountaineers in the world, but suffering from a tremendous handicap of not being able to adjust the rhythm of their movements as the weight of their loads, or altered conditions of snow, require.)

The scar caused us a lot of trouble. We could not climb the steep crumbling rocks carrying our loads. Three of us had to climb to a stance halfway up, throw a rope down and haul up each load in turn, while those below did their best to prevent it sticking half way, by means of another rope from below. This performance was then repeated on the upper section of the crag. Beyond this was a gully, to cross which the Sherpas removed their boots, so as to be more sure of their footing on the treacherous grass-covered rock.

Climbing out of the gully on the further side, we halted for a moment's rest on a small ridge beyond. While we were there, one of the loads overbalanced and crashed down into the gully some two hundred feet below us. It split open, but most fortunately got hung up on a ledge, which saved it from total destruction at the bottom of the gorge, 1,500 feet below. When we reached the battered sack, we found that some twenty pounds of lentils and rice had been lost, together with some candles. The loss of the food was most annoying, as it represented some two days of our valuable time. But the mishap might easily have been very much more serious, and it taught us to exercise greater care when handling our loads in such unusually steep country.

It was useless trying to hurry along the traverse. Each section had to be tackled with the utmost caution. It was slow work, but very far from tedious, as the job required all our attention. As we gradually became used to the gigantic depth of the ravine above which we were making our way, the early feeling of nervousness changed to one of exhilaration, a glorious feeling almost of being part of this giant creation of Nature. Towards the end of the traverse, the links became very fragile. One spot in particular caused us such trouble that it produced a fairly forceful protest from Angtharkay, and caused Kusang to pause momentarily in his monotonous flow of song. But above and below us the cliffs were smooth and sheer, and the passage could not be avoided. This section came to be known as the "Mauvais Pas", and was certainly the most hair-raising bit of the traverse. The last bit went comparatively easily, and by the middle of the afternoon we reached the river at the point where we had made our first crossing three days before. After stowing the loads under a rock, we hurriedly retreated along the traverse, and reached our camp before dark.

The dawn of June 3rd gave warning of bad weather, and it was in some anxiety that we packed up the remainder of our baggage and hastily got under way. The route was now becoming familiar, and difficulties which had cost us much time and labour before were now being tackled with the confidence and ease of familiarity. We made good time on the slabs of the scar, and the gullies which followed had lost much of their sting. But fast as we went we were still too slow for the weather. By 10 o'clock the lower valley was filled with cloud and by 11 o'clock snow was falling gently in large woolly flakes. This spurred us on to yet greater energy, as the thought of the Mauvais Pas under a covering of snow was not a pleasant one and, if we failed to get across it today, there was no knowing how long we should be held up; for it looked as if the snow had come to stay for some time.

The weight of our loads was forgotten as we raced along the little ledges of the traverse at a frantic speed. By 12 o'clock snow was falling heavily and, when we reached the Mauvais Pas, all the ledges and crannies were hidden under a thick white canopy. We removed our boots in order to be sure of our foot-holds, and proceeded with the utmost deliberation, clearing the snow from the ledges as we went. It was not easy to find places on which to anchor the rope and, though we moved one at a time, a slip would have had very serious consequences. About half way across a narrow slanting cleft had to be negotiated in order to get on to a lower ledge. This was the worst section, as one's load was apt to catch and throw one off one's balance, and my heart was in my mouth as I watched each member of the party negotiate it. The Sherpas worked with a wonderful steadiness and composure, only giving vent to their pent-up feelings when they reached the comparative security of the terrace beyond. Here we halted a moment to rub our feet and put on our boots. A wind started to blow down the valley, driving the snow into our faces as we made our way slowly across the face of the precipice, and Angtharkay suggested that we should stop where we were until the storm had blown over. A more unpleasant idea would have been difficult to conceive, though I must admit conditions had made progress not a little dangerous. By going slowly, however, and taking every precaution, we eventually reached the end of the traverse without a mishap.

Cold and wet, we huddled under the lee of the cliff rising from the little strip of shore by the water's edge. A few sodden pieces of wood lay about the beach, having been deposited there when the river was in flood. With the aid of a couple of candles and a good deal of patience we got some sort of a fire started, and "smoked ourselves" until, towards evening, the snow slackened.

On the opposite side of the river there was a wider strip of shore, on which grew a small clump of stunted birches. There was also a fair-sized cave. It was obviously the ideal base from which to tackle the final section of the upper gorge, and the sooner we got there and made ourselves snug, the better, so as soon as the snowstorm had abated we collected all the loads at the water's edge, and prepared for the crossing.

There were ten loads to be carried across. The river appeared to be slightly swollen but, as the snow had been melting as it fell, this was only to be expected. We did not anticipate that the difficulties would be much greater than they had been before.

Fastening an end of the rope to my waist and shouldering a load, I paddled up the edge of the stream, probing with my ice-axe and searching for the best place to begin the crossing. Then I started to wade slowly out into the raging waters. I soon realised that, although the river appeared only slightly higher than it had been before, it confronted us with an obstacle twice as formidable. The force of the current was terrific. As I moved a foot forward, it would be whirled sideways, and it was only by shuffling along that I could make any headway. My legs were slashed by stones swept down by the force of the river, but soon the numbing cold robbed my lower limbs of all sensation. The whirling motion of the water made me giddy, and I was hard put to it to keep my balance. In mid-stream the water was nearly up to my waist; had it been an inch higher it must have carried me away, but by a desperate effort I kept my feet. I tried to turn round, but found that the current was impossible to face, so I had to go on, and at length emerged with bleeding legs upon the opposite beach.

Tilman was a short way behind me. Being shorter, he was having an even tougher struggle. Pasang and Angtharkay were already well in the water, holding on to each other, and on to the rope which was now stretched across the river. My wits must have been numbed by the cold, for I missed the brief opportunity I had of preventing them from coming any further. Too late I realised what they were in for. Pasang was carrying a load of satu, Angtharkay had a load of clothes and bedding, which came down to his buttocks. He was very slight of build and easily the shortest of the five. When he got out towards the middle of the stream, the water was well above his waist, and it was obvious that he was prevented from being swept away only by hanging on to the rope and Pasang's firm hand, which clutched him by the arm. Soon, however, his load became water-logged, and started to drag him down. How he managed to keep his feet will always remain a mystery to me for, in spite of the help afforded him by the rope, his difficulties must have been vastly greater than my own, and I knew that I had had just as much as I could cope with. But then these Sherpas have standards of their own. As they were approaching the northern bank, however, Angtharkay actually did lose his balance and, as he went in up to his neck, I thought he was lost. But he retained his hold on the rope, and Pasang, clutching frantically at his arm, dragged him ashore. They were both rather badly shaken, but immediately set about the task of pitching camp and lighting a fire.

Tilman and I each made two more journeys across with the remaining loads (we left one bag of satu on the southern shore), and on his third trip Tilman came over with Kusang, who had been patiently holding the other end of the rope for us. This time he missed his footing and was submerged, fortunately in the shallow water near the shore. Dusk was falling as, painfully, we lugged the loads across the beach.

It was a cheerless party which sat huddled round the weakly smouldering logs under the shelter of the cave, silent save for the continuous chatter of teeth. I felt very humble indeed for having been fool enough to tackle the river in such haste. It was obvious now that a route which involved several such crossings was out of the question, and except for the fact that we had a decent camp site, we would have been much better off on the southern shore of the stream. However, one must pay for experience, and we were later to find that much was needed in dealing with these fierce glacier streams.

Tilman's pipe had been washed away out of his pocket down the river. He is a confirmed pipe-smoker, and I think that the prospect of a month without one was gloomy, to say the least. Fortunately for him, I had been travelling in Southern Tibet the previous year with Laurence Wager, who had insisted on my smoking a pipe in the evening to keep me from talking. Since then I had continued the habit, and now Tilman was able to get a smoke at the expense of an increased flow of argumentative conversation!

No rain or snow was falling next morning, but it was a dull and cheerless dawn. After an early breakfast, we walked along the little strip of shore to examine the possibility of bridging the river. A little downstream, at the point where the river entered the box-canyon, which stretched almost unbroken for the two miles separating us from our base camp, we found a place where huge boulders in the bed of the stream formed a natural foundation for a bridge. A clump of twisted birches, however, offered us poor material, and it was midday before we had spanned the river with a fragile and rickety structure. Considerable dexterity was necessary to cross the bridge, but it served our purpose so long as it was not washed away.

We now commanded both sides of the river, and it was decided that Tilman and Angtharkay should explore the possibilities of the southern side, while Pasang and I tried to get through on the northern side. I confess that when we started out on our respective jobs, I thought that if anyone got through, it would be Pasang and I; for to get past "Pisgah" on the southern side appeared to be a hopeless task.

Edging along the base of the cliffs at the water's edge, we reached another strip of sandy shore a hundred yards further upstream. From here a steeply sloping corridor led back across the face of the precipice. All the strata we had encountered in the Rishi Nala sloped from west to east in this manner, and we hoped that by following this corridor we might be able to climb on to a terrace which would at least carry us past that formidable buttress on the southern side. But the corridor became more and more difficult to follow, and finally ended in a little platform 500 feet above the river, completely isolated save for the way by which we had come. Further advance in any direction was impossible. We sat down disconsolately, and scanned the cliffs of the southern side of the gorge. High above us, like ants on a gigantic wall, we saw the other two climbing slowly upwards. Presently they started traversing horizontally, and we saw that they were making for the one point in the great buttress where, we had agreed before, lay the only slender chance of success. They reached it and disappeared from view. When after a short while they reappeared, and started up a vile-looking gully, my heart sank. It appeared that the last chance on the southern side had failed, and now it was up to Pasang and me to find a way by hook or by crook.

We descended to the river again and with great difficulty managed to make another two hundred yards upstream, before an overhanging cliff brought us to a dead stop. We tried wading, but the river was even higher than it had been on the previous evening, and we could make no headway. Then we began to search every inch of the three hundred yards we had come from our camp, in the hope of at least being able to climb out of the gloomy canyon we were in. We tried places which were obviously quite ridiculous; just as one searches under the teapot or in the coal-scuttle for a lost fountain pen when one has exhausted every likely place, and I had a similar feeling of hopelessness. But after some desperate rock-climbing, we were forced to admit defeat, and returned to camp, satisfied that at least there was no route along the northern side of the gorge.

It was a cold grey afternoon, and towards evening rain began to fall gently. The gorge wore a grim and desolate aspect, which increased my dejection as I sat in the cave, waiting for the others to return and wondering what our next move would be. If we were forced to retreat from here, we would have to abandon our attempt to penetrate into the Nanda Devi Basin, as there was no other line of possibility. As the evening wore on, we began to scan the crags of the opposite side anxiously for any sign of the others. Their delay in returning gave me some hope that they might after all have found a way; but towards dark I began to fear that an accident had occurred, for they must have realised our failure, and desperation is apt to make people run unjustifiable risks. Then all at once we spotted them, descending through the mist at a seemingly reckless speed. As they approached the river I went over to the bridge to await them. Angtharkay was in front and, as he came nearer, I could see that he was in a state of great excitement; as he balanced his way precariously over the water, above the roar of the torrent I caught the words: "Bahut achcha, sahib, bahut achcha."

When Tilman arrived, I heard from him the glad news that they had found, 1,500 feet above the river, a break in that last formidable buttress, guarding the mystic shrine of the "Blessed Goddess". From where they had stood they could see that the way was clear into the Nanda Devi Basin. The last frail link in that extraordinary chain of rock-faults, which had made it possible to make our way along the grim precipices of the gorge, had been discovered; and this meant at least a certain measure of success to our undertaking.

As I lay in the mouth of the cave after our evening meal, watching the spectral shadows hover in the ghostly clefts of the opposite wall of the gorge, and listening to the mighty boom of the torrent echoing to a great height above our heads, my feeling of despondency was changed to one of deep content.

CHAPTER NINE

THE task next morning of getting the loads back across the river over the bridge was one which required delicate handling. It was easy enough to balance across, unencumbered by any weight, but to do so with a heavy load strapped to one's back was a very different proposition. The bridge sagged unpleasantly in the middle, and, as it took the weight of the body, water swept over it. A rope stretched across the river served as an unreliable handrail. Curiously enough Kusang, normally very sure of foot and steady of head, could not face it. It was as much as he could do to get across without a load, so the rest of us each had to make several of these perilous trips. It was a painfully cold job too in the bitter morning air. But all went well, and by 9 o'clock we were across, bag and baggage, fervently hoping that this was to be our last encounter with the river.

Shouldering five of the loads, we climbed slowly up the mountain side. We encountered several difficult sections, but managed to negotiate each successfully. Twelve hundred feet above the river, we climbed on to a sloping ledge, which led us across the face of "Pisgah" buttress to the foot of the gully up which Passang and I had watched the other two making their way the previous day. Though there were one or two awkward bits, the gully was easier than it had appeared from below, and after climbing some eight hundred feet up it, we were able to escape by way of a narrow chimney, which landed us on the crest of the great ridge which had come so near to destroying our hopes. From here we could see right into the Nanda Devi Basin, though heavy rain clouds obscured all but the mighty ramparts at the base of the great peak.

A short way beyond we came upon two small caves. There was also a plentiful supply of juniper and a small spring; altogether an ideal site for a camp. So we stowed our loads away out of reach of the rain, which was now starting to fall, and romped down the 2,000 feet to the river at a break-neck speed. The second journey up the slopes carrying the remainder of the loads was a slow and tedious business; but when at length we reached the ridge once more, we were rewarded by the pleasant knowledge that for the time being we had finished with the grim austerity of that fearful gorge, and that ahead of us was a new and wonderful world to explore.

Growing in the vicinity of our new camp was a great quantity of wild rhubarb. We had found it lower down the valley, but there it had been scarce. That night we consumed a quantity which now makes me sick to remember!

Towards sunset the rain cleared off and, as we sat round our juniper fire, we witnessed a heavenly unveiling of the great peaks of the basin. First appeared the majestic head of Nanda Devi herself, frowning down upon us from an incredible height, utterly detached from the earth. One by one the white giants of the un-named ranges to the north followed suit; until at last it seemed as if the entire mountain realm stood before us bathed in the splendour of the dying sun, paying homage to the majesty of their peerless queen.

It was after 8 o'clock when we got away next morning. We cached 20 lbs. of food in the cave, together with the remainder of the rope and iron stakes we had brought for the roping up of the difficult sections of the gorge. This left us with 380 lbs. of baggage to be transported through into the basin. It was obvious from what we had seen that we could not hope to make even a rough exploration of the whole thing in the time available before our food ran out. We therefore decided to concentrate on the northern half of the basin, and to return in August, when we hoped that the main force of the monsoon would have spent itself, to explore the southern section. The distance we would be able to cover depended on the difficulty of the ground, and my previous experience of Himalayan glaciers had made me not over optimistic.

The going now became distinctly easier, and by noon we got on to the gentle grassy slopes above the junction of the two streams which came down from the main glaciers of the northern and southern sections of the basin to form the Rishi Ganga River. Half a mile below the junction, we could see a stretch of sand flats where the river broadened out, and, becoming comparatively sluggish, appeared to offer a good fording place. To cross here would save us several hours of toil, which would be necessary if we were to cross the two streams above the junction. But we sadly under-estimated the difficulties, for although we succeeded in getting across, the struggle was almost as severe as it had been in the gorge a few days before and, as there was no possibility of bridging the river at this point, a better way had to be found.

We pitched camp in a little nala formed by a stream coming down from the glaciers of the westerly rim of the basin; then, leaving Kusang to prepare our evening meal, we started out to visit the junction, and to find a better way of getting across into the northern section.

We were now actually in the inner sanctuary of the Nanda Devi Basin, and at each step I experienced that subtle thrill which anyone of imagination must feel when treading hitherto unexplored country. Each corner held some thrilling secret to be revealed for the trouble of looking. My most blissful dream as a child was to be in some such valley, free to wander where I liked, and discover for myself some hitherto unrevealed glory of Nature. Now the reality was no less wonderful than that half-forgotten dream; and of how many childish fancies can that be said, in this age of disillusionment?

Immediately above the junction of the two streams was a curious little plateau, rather resembling a giant tennis-court, which commanded a fine view up each of the rivers. About a mile and a half up the left-hand valley (facing up), we could see the snout of a great glacier. This later came to be known by us as the Main Glacier, and was formed by the ice of all the larger glaciers of the northern section. But although we had a clear view for nearly three miles up the southern stream, we could see no sign of a glacier, though the character of the stream told us that one must exist. This southern stream too contained only half as much water as the other; a clear indication that we must expect a vaster and more complicated glacier system in the section we were about to visit.

It had been decided that on the following day, while Tilman and I were at work with the plane-table, the others would go back to the previous camp for the rest of the stuff. After some discussion the Sherpas assured us that they would be able to find a way back above the junction and, as it was getting late, we decided that it was not necessary to go further that evening. On the plateau we found a quantity of wild onions, which greatly pleased the Sherpas. Beyond the junction, peacefully grazing on the gentle grassy slopes, was a small herd of bharal. We estimated the height of the junction to be about 13,100 feet.

The Sherpas were away shortly after dawn on the following morning, while Tilman and I left camp a little later on our first reconnaissance into the unknown basin. Following a ridge which came down from some of the westerly peaks, we reached at an altitude of about 15,500 feet the crest of a little shoulder, from which we obtained a good view over the lower part of the Main Glacier. I was very surprised at the type of country which lay before us. On the true left bank of the glacier the giant cliffs of Nanda Devi rose sheer and forbidding in true Himalayan style; but, bounding the glacier on the right-hand side, beyond a well-defined lateral moraine, an expanse of undulating grass-land stretched for miles, in lovely contrast with the desolation of the moraine-covered glacier. If the shepherds of the Dhaoli and Niti valleys could only get their flocks through the grim gorges of the Rishi Ganga, they would find here almost unlimited grazing. Now this pasturage is a sanctuary where thousands of wild animals live unmolested. Long may it remain so!

It was a great relief to see that when making our way up the valley we would not be confined to travel on the glacier itself; for conveying loads about on the lower reaches of a Himalayan glacier is a task which demands much time and infinite patience. The ice is generally completely covered with a thick deposit of gravel and boulders. The whole surface is rent and broken into a sea of cliffs and fissures, ridges and hollows. It is almost impossible to work out a good line beforehand, and the traveller has to worry his way through a perfect maze of obstacles. From the point we had reached we could see that by the side of the glacier there stretched gently undulating grass-land, which would provide us with excellent going for the first few miles at least.

Though the views we got were of great interest, we did not have much success with the plane-table, as there was a lot of cloud about, and we could not fix our position with any degree of certainty. Eventually, we were driven down by a shower of sleet and rain. We got back to camp at 7 o'clock, and were surprised to find that the Sherpas had not returned. When darkness fell, and there was still no sign of them, we became seriously alarmed. We were contemplating going out to search for them when from a distance we caught the sound of their voices, and presently they appeared, without loads and obviously tired. We learnt from them that they had had great difficulty in finding an alternative route above the junction of the stream, and that, being overtaken by night, had dumped their loads on the far side of the northern stream.

The next morning (June 8th), there was a great feeling of slackness, and though we got away by 7.20 a.m., we walked without much energy, stopping frequently. The ground, however, was easy and in a few hours we reached the snout of the Main Glacier.

In the afternoon, while the Sherpas went off to fetch the loads they had left on the previous day, Tilman and I climbed over the snout of the glacier, and mounted up the lower buttresses of the main peak of Nanda Devi. We climbed for some hours over rough broken rocks, and emerged at length on the crest of a sharp spur, which commanded a grand view down the Rishi Nala. We saw to its best advantage the majestic sweep of the northern cliffs of the gorge, which culminated in a formidable barrier of mountains forming the western rim of the basin. We worked for an hour with the plane-table, before a mass of evil-looking clouds blowing up from the black depths of the gorge blotted out the view, and we were driven down again, this time by a storm of hail.

Sitting round a blazing fire of juniper that night, Tilman reminded me that in the course of that afternoon we had been the first human beings to have set foot on the main peak of Nanda Devi, a point we had both neglected to observe before!

We cached a further small dump of food at the snout of the Main Glacier, when we left early next morning. We then mounted to a little moraine ledge at the side of the glacier, and soon reached the gentle grassy slopes we had seen two days before. The going could not have been pleasanter: soft springing turf with the grass still short, having only lately got rid of its burden of winter snow. And, owing to our ease of movement, we were able to give our whole attention to the enjoyment of this wonderful new world we were in. Every few hundred yards, some new feature would reveal itself – here a side valley to look up, and to speculate as to where it would lead, there some graceful ice-clad summit appearing from behind a buttress, and looking, in the newness of its form, lovelier than any of its neighbours; there again, a herd of wild mountain sheep gazing indignantly at these intruders who had violated the sanctity of their seclusion. In spite of the heavy load I was carrying, I frequently had difficulty in refraining from running in my eagerness to see round the next corner, or to get a better view of some fresh and slender spire which had just made its appearance.

Towards midday we reached the edge of a big glacier, coming in from the west. After crossing this, we came upon a beautiful lake, shut in on three sides by great mounds of moraine deposit, and on the fourth by dark, frowning cliffs. On the placid waters were reflected the icy crests of the great peaks. We had intended going further that day, but we could not resist the prospect of a camp in such surroundings.

We had previously agreed that not a moment of our time in the basin should be wasted if we could possibly help it. It was all too short as it was, and we were determined to get through as much as we could while our food lasted. Accordingly, as soon as camp had been pitched, we set off to reconnoitre the lateral glacier we had just crossed. The sky was dull and overcast, and presently snow started falling heavily. We climbed on to a ridge which bounded the glacier on the right, and followed it until we were some 2,000 feet above the lake. At 4 o'clock the snow stopped falling, and we erected the plane-table, and waited in a bitterly cold wind for the evening clearing of the mists. At half-past five our patience was rewarded. A rift appeared to the west, and framed in it was a dome of rock and ice, which could belong to only one mountain –

Changabang. There was no mistaking it. Often had I gazed at that wonderful photograph taken by Dr. Longstaff from the Bagini Pass on the opposite side: and here before us was an almost exact replica of that splendid face which Dr. Longstaff describes as "the most superbly beautiful mountain I have ever seen: its north-west face, a sheer precipice of over 5,000 feet, being composed of such pale granite that it is at first taken for snow lying on the cliffs at an impossibly steep angle." As is generally the case with such views, the mountain summit appeared as something detached from the earth, floating in the upper air at a fantastic height above our heads; and moving along swiftly in a direction opposite to that of the drifting mist.

Presently Changabang's sister-peak, Kalanka, made her appearance, and we saw that the glacier at our feet originated in a vast coombe formed by the ridge of the two peaks. Tilman suggested the name "Changalanka" for the glacier, and appeared disappointed when I expressed doubt as to whether that name would be accepted by the authorities!

Soon other summits appeared, each tinted with the fires of the dying sun, and vying with one another to tax the credibility of their puny audience. But Nature is a perfect stage-manager, and when the majesty of the vision was at its height, the curtain of cloud fell about us once more, so, with numbed fingers we packed up the plane-table, and scrambled down to camp in the gathering dusk.

From above the lake we had a view right up the main valley, along the northern base of Nanda Devi. A series of subsidiary valleys coming in from the north-eastern rim offered us a means of exploring that section, and we decided to devote the next week to that task.

The red sunset of that evening was a sure indication of better weather, and we awoke at dawn the next morning (June 10th) to a chorus of birds heralding a gloriously fine day. We ate a hasty breakfast in the frosty air and were away before the sun had reached us, carrying light loads, and having enough food with us to keep Tilman and myself in the necessities of life for three or four days. It was our intention to push as far as we could up one of the eastern valleys, and camp there while the Sherpas came down to relay the rest of the stuff up to a more suitable base. Making our way round the eastern shore of the lake we climbed over the wall of moraine deposit, and were soon worrying our way through the intricacies of a big ice-stream coming in from the north. This came to be known later as the Great North Glacier. At its junction with the Main North Glacier we found an easy route across, and within two hours of leaving camp we found ourselves in a pleasant meadow on the far side of the Great Glacier.

From here the travelling was extremely easy. A wide corridor of flat grass-land ran outside a very well-defined lateral moraine on the right bank of the Main Glacier, and we were able to stride along at a quick walk, until we were abreast of the entrance to the valley we were making for. Then we turned left and plodded up nearly 2,000 feet of slaty shingle, which had been left when the side glaciers shrank to their present dimensions.

By 2 o'clock we had got fairly into the valley and decided to camp at an altitude of about 17,500 feet. The Sherpas built a small stone wall to protect us from the wind, and left us with a promise to return in three days' time.

Later that afternoon Tilman and I went off in opposite directions to make a preliminary reconnaissance of the valley we were in, in order to be able to come to a decision as to our course of action. I took the plane-table with me. Climbing up the scree and snow-covered slope above the camp, I came, at an altitude of about 18,000 feet, to the crest of a ridge. As I did so, I saw a solitary bharal, some twenty-five yards away. He was a noble specimen, and stood so still that he might have been a stuffed beast in the Natural History Museum. We stood regarding one another for some minutes before his curiosity was satisfied, and then he stalked leisurely away and disappeared round the corner of a cliff. Most unfortunately I had left my camera in camp (as was usually the case when I happened upon something which would make a good photograph!) It was difficult to understand what brings these animals to such altitudes. Three thousand feet below was perfect grazing, and neither man nor beast to molest them. Their lives must be wonderfully care-free and one would expect them to be content to grow fat and lazy down below; instead of which they seemed to spend most of their time climbing about precipices of astonishing steepness, risking their necks on crevasse-covered glaciers, and going as far away as possible from food and comfort. Surely then they too have the capacity to appreciate the savage beauty of high mountain places, and to revel in the rhythm of practised movement over difficult ground.

I returned to camp at 5.30 to find Tilman was just back. We compared notes, and formulated a plan for the employment of our time in the valley. We decided first to attempt to reach a col at its head, which we concluded must lie on the eastern rim of the basin. From it we hoped to get a view out of the basin towards the peaks of the Nepal-Tibet border. After that we proposed to attempt to find a high level route into the next valley-system.

We consumed a dish of pemmican soup and, as the sun disappeared behind the distant ranges, we crept into our sleeping-bags, to watch the world give itself over to frozen night. We had with us our tiny bivouac tent, but we had by now got firmly into the habit of sleeping out, using the tent canvas as a blanket. This was due mainly to the discomfort of squashing ourselves into the minute space it afforded, though personally I dislike all tents and use them as little as necessity permits.

The ledge on which we were lying being high above the floor of the main valley on the north side, it commanded a superb view of the colossal northern face of the twin peaks of Nanda Devi. The two peaks were joined by a horizontal rock ridge, some two miles in length. From this ridge, the precipice fell in one unbroken sweep to the glacier which lay at its foot, 9,000 feet below the summit. The rock wall thus formed is perhaps without an equal anywhere in the world. We had recovered by now from the shock which we had experienced on coming for the first time face to face with this sight, but, as I lay there and watched the rays of the setting sun bespangle the mountain with a score of rapidly changing shades, the whole scale of height and depth appeared enhanced beyond belief.

We passed a restless night due, I suppose, to the fact that it was our first visit to that particular altitude that season. We were both wide awake at 2 a.m., though we did not want to be off much before daylight. The little streamlets about us were hard-frozen, and we spent some time melting sufficient ice for what we knew would be our last drink for many thirsty hours of toil to come. We left our bivouac just after 3.30 a.m., about a quarter of an hour before the first glimmer of dawn, and in sleepy moroseness climbed over the boulder-strewn slope to the edge of the dry ice of the glacier. Mounting on to this, we soon settled down to that gentle rhythm which alone makes early morning climbing at high altitudes bearable. For an hour and a half we plodded along in a dreamy silence, only roused every now and then when some large crevasse necessitated an altering of the course. The dry ice gave place to frozen snow, and presently one of us suggested that perhaps it was about time we put on the rope. It was then quite light and, looking back, we saw that Nanda Devi was already bathed in the warmth and splendour of the morning sun, and with this sight a modicum of enthusiasm stirred our lethargy.

The work now became intricate, and several crevasses gave us food for serious thought before we were able to cross them. At about 6.40 we were standing at the foot of a steep slope some four hundred feet below the col. Working on a short rope we started up it, and found it to be composed of a vixenish layer of hard frozen snow, covering pure ice. While the snow remained frozen it was safe enough to kick shallow steps up the incline, but directly the sun came over the col the snow would melt and form an exceedingly dangerous avalanche trap. By first cutting through the snow, and then making large steps in the ice, the slope could probably be negotiated later in the day, but it would be a prolonged and hazardous business, as the gradient was continuously steep and afforded no safeguards whatever. Moreover, the task of cutting such a staircase under the present conditions would take nearly all day. However, from the point he had reached in the course of his reconnaissance on the previous day, Tilman had seen that by climbing one of the peaks adjacent to the col, we would find an alternative route down to the lower part of the glacier we were on; and we decided, after some discussion, that we were justified in continuing the climb by relying on the snow crust alone.

This crust became thinner and thinner as we mounted, and at last we were forced into a longish bout of step-cutting in order to reach some ice-covered rocks just below the col. These too required some careful handling, before we drew ourselves up on to the knife-like crest of the ridge which formed at this point part of the eastern rim of the basin. We sat on a ledge protected from the cold wind and beat our numbed extremities back to a painful life. It was 9 o'clock. With the aid of our barometer we estimated our height at 20,300 feet.

The day was gloriously fine. The view to the east was bewildering. I had never expected to see such an extraordinary array of peaks, and we could make but a poor effort at sorting out the tangled topography. Except for Nanda Kot to the south, there was no particularly dominating feature, but as far as the eye could see there stretched a sea of glistening spires and domes, ridges and icy plateaux, in dazzling profusion and complexity, while in the distance we could discern some mighty giants, evidently belonging to the ranges of western Nepal.

At our feet, far below, we looked down into a wide valley whose glacier flowed away from us into another and much larger one, which we identified as the Milam Glacier.

We were anxious to find a way of escape from the basin in this direction, but even had there been a practicable route down to the Milam Glacier from this point, it would have been an impossible task to get our loads up the ice slopes we had just climbed.

Tilman was feeling the effects of altitude a good deal, and was suffering from the usual sickness and weakness. However, by now our retreat was cut off, and we had to go through with the traverse of a 21,000 foot peak to our north. We sat on the ledge near the col for half an hour, during which time we occupied ourselves by studying the view, forcing bits of biscuit down somewhat unwilling throats, and thawing our chilled limbs. Then we rose to tackle the eight or nine hundred feet of rock and ice which separated us from the summit of the peak. The climbing was not difficult until we got on to a sharp ice ridge which led to the summit. A cold wind was blowing, and it was a tricky job to retain one's balance in the small steps which it was necessary to cut in the crest of the ridge. This was a type of climbing which I disliked, as one had to trust to one's feet alone, and the slightest slip would be impossible to check. But it was exhilarating to see the Milam Glacier System beneath one heel and the Nanda Devi Basin beneath the other; and it is not often that these Himalayan ice ridges are even possible to climb along.

The wind was too cold and the ridge too narrow for us to stop even for a minute on the summit, and we passed straight over and continued climbing down along the ridge on the other side. Soon we were brought up by a vertical cleft in it, and we were forced to cut steps for some distance down the Milam side before we could get round this.

There now followed a very long bout of down-hill step-cutting along a ridge which never allowed any relaxation while we were on it. I felt a mighty relief when after some hours we reached a steep snow gully leading down to the tracks of the morning, and found the snow to be in a safe condition. The snow on the glacier itself was soft and we broke through several times into small crevasses. Nevertheless, we made a very rapid descent and were back in camp by the middle of the afternoon.

As I have said, Tilman had suffered severely from mountain sickness throughout the day, but I was feeling remarkably fit, considering it was the first bit of serious mountaineering that we had been engaged upon at any altitude that year. Presently I felt a considerable pain in the groin, at the top of the right leg. I thought I must have strained the leg slightly in one of the crevasses we had encountered on our descent, but I have since connected it with a mysterious fever which attacked me a few minutes later. It began with a violent attack of shivering, which caused me to pile on all my spare clothing and roll myself up in my double sleeping-bag, despite the scorching afternoon sun. My memory of the next twenty-four hours was distorted by delirium. I had a curious impression that I was lying there in the open for several days, during the whole of which time I was either trying to escape from a fierce tropical sun or from a dead Arctic cold, while the ever-changing face of Nanda Devi writhed itself into hideous grimaces. The fever lasted for about thirty-six hours and then left me as suddenly as it had come. When the Sherpas came on the morning of the 13th, I was able to hobble slowly down with them to a base which they had by now established above the junction of the Great North Glacier with the main ice-stream, and well stocked with juniper fuel collected from the area below the lake.

Having regained my senses, I was extremely annoyed at having lost two days of our valuable time in the basin. Tilman, however, had put in some good work in the meantime, and rejoined us at what came to be known as "Glacier Junction Camp", on the evening of the 13th.

The next morning we started out again, this time with provisions for only one night, for a bivouac in another of the valleys coming down from the peaks of the eastern rim. I still felt very weak, but as I was carrying no load, I managed to follow the others without delaying them too much. This new valley we found to be divided into two sections, and we decided to devote a day to the exploration of the right-hand one, if possible climbing once more on to the eastern rim, where we hoped to be in a position to make a close examination of a complicated knot of peaks to the north which had aroused our curiosity a few days before. We were still hoping too to discover a means of escape which we could use when the time came as an alternative to a retreat down the Rishi Gorge. In this we had small hope of success, however, as a strong party consisting of Mr. Ruttledge, Dr. Somervell and General Wilson, had made an abortive attempt some years previously to find a route into the basin from the Milam Glacier.

As we brewed our evening pemmican, we observed signs which promised an early change in the weather. The evening was warm and still, and our barometer was behaving in an extraordinary manner. However, we "dossed down" in the usual way, using our ridiculous little tent merely as a covering.*

I had slept for about an hour when I was awakened by soft wet snow falling on my face. The tent, an intricate tangle of sodden guy ropes, flaps and ridges, offered very poor covering, as the snow melted and lay in pools of water in the folds of the canvas, and from time to time these would empty themselves playfully down our necks. This prevented us both from sleeping until about one o'clock, when it started to freeze, and though the snow continued to fall our rest was no longer disturbed.

We awoke at 6 o'clock to a dreary morning. The snow had stopped falling, however, and we started up the glacier. Here we encountered the vile snow conditions which were to prevail throughout the summer, and this was to prove to be one of the most serious obstacles with which we had to contend. But the climbing was not difficult, and at 12.30 p.m. we reached another point on the eastern "rim", at an altitude of just about 20,000 feet. A cold wind was blowing sleet into our faces as we peered down from the crest of the narrow ridge. We caught a further glimpse of the valley which contained the Milam Glacier, but

*Since then I have come to the conclusion that for the purpose of these light bivouac camps a thin waterproof sheet would be lighter and more satisfactory than one of these small tents people have been at such pains to design of recent years. Tents with accommodation for two people and weighing 15 lbs. or more can be made to stand up against almost any conditions of weather, but I do not think a cloth has yet been discovered which, if made into a tent of much less than 8 lbs., will stand up against weather such as one must be prepared for when doing a series of bivouacs at great altitudes. Such a tent will generally collapse under a heavy weight of snow; it will be torn to shreds if exposed to a really bad blizzard, and will leak even in light rain. Under a single waterproof sheet one is at least as comfortable; it is no trouble either to pitch or to pack up, while in fine weather one need not suffer from the unbearable stuffiness of the midget tent.

beyond that all was obscured in mist. Two thousand feet of steep snow-covered rocks lay at our feet. It might have been possible to climb down, though with loads the risk of snow avalanches would have been too great. From where we stood we were able to get some slight idea of the topography of that part of the watershed, though ten minutes after we had arrived all our surroundings were blotted out and visibility was restricted to a few yards.

The descent to our bivouac took only two hours. The Sherpas were waiting for us, and, packing up the loads, we ran on down to the junction camp as fast as we could.

The present weather was obviously better suited to travel than to the mapping of intricate side valleys, and we decided that on the following day we should push as far as possible up the Great North Valley, so as to be in a position, when the weather cleared, to explore its head. Accordingly, soon after dawn we started in a northerly direction, carrying with us enough food and fuel for six days.

The morning was reasonably fine and it was not until about 10 o'clock that the more distant views became obscured. Travel in the Great North Valley we found to be very different from the easy progress we had made over the gently undulating slopes which bounded the Main Glacier, steep precipices continually forcing us on to the shattered moraine-covered surface of the ice.

We had been going for an hour or so, when Tilman, who had been lagging behind somewhat, complained that his right leg was hurting him. I suggested that he should share some of his load between the rest of us, but this he declined to do. We sat down to argue the point for a moment, when all of a sudden he began shivering, and I realised that he was starting an attack of fever similar to the one to which I had succumbed five days before. I suggested, therefore, that we should remain where we were. But Tilman would not hear of this, saying that if we did not get to a point from which I could make a useful reconnaissance on the following day, yet another twenty-four hours would be wasted. So we divided his load among the rest of us, and carried on, though how he was able to stick at it throughout a long and weary day I cannot imagine, for the work of making one's way over a badly broken moraine-covered glacier is as tiresome and exasperating a job as I know.

As I have mentioned before, it is impossible to work out a line of march over such country beforehand, and the only thing to do is to go straight ahead, and tackle the difficulties as they present themselves. A long ascent of a steep slope of boulders, poised precariously on the hard black ice, and ready at the slightest disturbance to roll down and crush one's foot; a slender ice-ridge, leading across two yawning chasms, one on either side, from which came the dull thunder of a sub-glacial stream; an ice-cliff, down which steps had to be laboriously chipped; these followed one another in monotonous succession, and led perhaps to an impasse, demanding a long, tiresome détour, perhaps to a further tangle of cliffs, ridges and towers. Here was a lake whose dark-blue waters proclaimed it to be of great depth, infinitely placid, save when some little avalanche of ice and rock, crashing down from above, whipped it to frenzy; further on, a raging torrent, rushing madly in no particular direction, barred the way. Our day's work yielded us but some three miles of progress, and we camped in a perfect wilderness of moraine débris. On arrival, Tilman collapsed into a sleeping-bag, and lay for the next thirty-six hours on a rough bed of boulders, waiting patiently for the fever to pass.

The following morning was beautifully clear, and I roused myself out of a half-frozen sleeping-bag in time to resect the position of the camp on the plane-table before the clouds came up and obscured the view. In this brief spell of clear weather I was able to get a general idea of the topography of the valley we were in, and in the gathering shadows of a snowstorm Pasang and I set off to reconnoitre the upper part of the glacier. Working our way diagonally across the ice-stream, we reached a point where the moraine débris from the left bank of the glacier met that from the right bank. The contrast between these two species of rock was very striking. That from the Kalanka side was almost white, while that from the peaks of the eastern "rim" was a dark blue-grey. At this junction we found a wide trough running up the middle of the glacier, providing an avenue of easy going. It closely resembled those glacial troughs which provide such an easy approach up the East Rongbuk Glacier on Everest.

By now it was snowing steadily, and the trough provided our only means of steering a direct course up the glacier. We made rapid progress however, and soon reached the end of the moraine-covered part. Here the trough petered out in a level stretch of ice, which provided going even more unpleasant than that which we had encountered lower down. Slush, knee-deep, covered its surface, which was scored into a maze of channels cut by twenty or more swiftly flowing glacier streams, and it was not until the middle of the afternoon that we reached an extensive lake which lay at the foot of a sheer precipice of ice-worn rock, and seen through the haze of falling snow, bore an uncanny appearance. On either side of the precipice was a confusion of ice-cliffs, which indicated two ice-falls. One, I judged, must come from an extensive ice-plateau to the north, from which the Great North Glacier derived the bulk of its strength. About the origin of the other ice-fall I could form no idea.

After a short rest on the shore of the lake, we worked round to the edge of the "plateau" ice-fall, worked out a route, and ascended some seven hundred feet above the lake. Then, as the weather showed no sign of improvement, we returned to the lake, and plodded down to camp, where we found Tilman still very weak, but better, and determined on making a move on the following morning. We discussed matters, and decided to push a camp as high as possible by the side of the ice-fall which Pasang and I had visited that day.

Snow fell gently throughout a most uncomfortable night, and despite the dreariness of the morning I was glad enough to get going. Our loads were light, as we were carrying only enough food for three men for three days, and we had with us merely the larger of the two tents. The plan was for Tilman, Pasang and myself to occupy the high camp, while Angtharkay and Kusang went down again to the one we had just left. Three is a safer number than two when travelling on extensive snow-covered glaciers as, if one man falls into a crevasse, it is extremely difficult for a single companion to pull him out.

Just before reaching the trough, we passed a curious phenomenon. We were walking along the brink of an ice-cliff about 100 feet high, and below, flowing directly towards the face of the cliff, was a large stream which, when it reached the cliff, entered by way of a tunnel in the ice. A few yards to the left it reappeared, flowing exactly in the opposite direction, until it disappeared once more into another ice channel.

The weather cleared somewhat while we were going up the glacier and, when we reached the lake, we were greeted by a gleam of sunshine which transformed the cheerless waters of yesterday into a pool of radiant loveliness in which danced the images of a thousand sparkling ice pinnacles. We saw, too, up the valley containing the second ice-fall, whose presence had puzzled me on the previous day. It was a narrow gorge-like affair, which bent round to the west and came, we concluded, from the northern foot of Kalanka. Thus its glacier came to be known as the Kalanka Glacier, and Tilman was forced to abandon his "Changalanka" jest and agree to the name "Changabang" for the glacier coming in below Junction Camp.

We sat for a while on the shore of the lake, to bask in the sun and to revel in that brief moment of beauty. Then we turned our attention to some precipitous slopes at the side of the "plateau" ice-fall. Here we became involved in some difficult climbing, which was made no easier by the snow, which soon started falling again, accompanied this time by a blustering wind.

At about 3 o'clock, at an altitude of some 18,500 feet, we started searching for a place on which to camp. The ground was continuously steep, and in the end we were forced to construct a platform on which to pitch our tent. Leaving us to complete the task, Angtharkay and Kusang went off down, climbing at top speed in order to be able to reach the lower camp before darkness cut off their retreat. They had instructions to return in three days' time.

An entry in my diary that evening reads: " . . . The wind dropped and the weather cleared, and gave us a slight idea of our surroundings. The ridge we are on seems to be covered with ice, and probably leads up to peak 113 (on our plane-table sheet). We are closer to the glacier than we thought, and above the worst bit of the ice-fall. The glacier seems to be split into two sections and the bit nearest us leads up to an extensive plateau, which does not look very far away. I suppose that is the thing to explore first; but the snow is now falling heavily again and I don't know what will happen. We have two and possibly three days' food with us. I hope we will be able to do some good in that time. We are having a spell of vile weather. I don't know if it is the monsoon or not. It does not look like it somehow. We all got very cold this afternoon, but are quite comfortable now – about 6.10 p.m. A miserable outlook, and we will soon have to be fighting our way back down the Rishi with scanty provisions.

The presence of three bodies kept the tent warm and in spite of the cramped position we all slept well, and I did not wake until Tilman struck a match at 2 a.m. to look at his watch. I cursed him roundly and went to sleep again, until he woke me again at 3.45. I know of no proceeding more dismal than the preparations for an early morning start from the chaos of an over-crowded tent. One man struggles manfully with a stove in order to provide the party with a drink of melted ice, while the others do their best to knock it over in their efforts to find some missing sock, glove or puttee. Tempers are at boiling point, and the whole business of mountain exploration seems utterly futile and ridiculous. Food in any form is repulsive, and the water, when at last it has been obtained from the ice-blocks, tastes strongly of last night's pemmican, and nearly makes one sick. This, of course, is someone else's fault for not having taken the trouble to wash the pot out the night before! Oh! for a really heavy snowstorm which would give one an indisputable excuse to get back to the only place in the world one really wants to be in – in the warmth of the recently abandoned sleeping-bag. It is stupid to start now anyway – why not wait until we see what the weather really is going to do! But at length all is ready; freezing fingers struggle for some minutes to close the complicated fastenings of the tent, and the party proceeds in silent churlishness until the sun swamps all gloom in the wonder of his early dawn.

On this particular morning, we were threading our way through a maze of ice-corridors whose walls were white, cold, dead, until all in a moment their deathly pallor was changed to a faint rose flush, faint but radiant with life and warmth.

We emerged from the badly crevassed area, and chipped our way up a steep snow slope, at the top of which we found ourselves on the ice-plateau at an altitude of over 20,000 feet. Two great ice-peaks rose in front of us. These numbered 110 and 113 on our plane-table sheet. Between them was a saddle, separated from us by a very gentle slope. We decided to make for the saddle, and from it to attempt the ascent of peak 110, which appeared very easy from where we were standing. I confess that I was vaguely hoping to find an exit from the basin by way of this saddle, though, looking back, that hope seems to have shown poor mountaineering judgment. Peak 113, seen from the plateau, was a wonderfully symmetrical pyramid of the purest ice, standing fully 1,500 feet above the saddle.

The saddle was deceptively far away and, though the snow was still fairly frozen, it took some hours of hard going to reach it. The crest of the saddle we found to be 20,500 feet. Below us to the north and west was one of the most terrific drops I have ever looked down, and it was some seconds before I could adjust the focus of my eyes to see that one could not merely step down on to the moraine-covered Bagini Glacier, 4,500 feet below. It looked as though, if a stone were dropped, it would touch nothing until it struck that glacier, up which Dr. Longstaff's party had made their way twenty-seven years before. Beyond, standing out above a belt of dark cloud, was a wonderful panorama of the Garhwal Mountains. Close at hand on the extreme left rose the slender spire of Dunagiri, whose delicate structure of ice-ridges has presented such formidable barriers to her votaries. Beyond, in the distance, the graceful head of Nilkanta stood in superb contrast to the massive shoulders of the Badrinath group, some of whose secrets we were to be privileged to reveal. Then came my first Himalayan acquaintance, Kamet, ruling despotically over his colony of peaks of the Tibetan borderland; then the untrodden glaciers of Hathi Parbat; and lastly to the north a wondrous mass of mountains of all shapes and sizes, still unnamed and unmeasured.

The wind was too cold to stand for long admiring the view, and we started up the slopes of peak 110. The snow was soft and powdery, and it was exhausting work making a trail. Tilman had not yet recovered from his fever, which was not surprising, considering that he had only risen from his bed of sickness on the previous morning. He seated himself in a shallow crevasse, which was sheltered from the wind and exposed to the warm sun, and told us to carry on and see what we could do with the peak. Pasang and I laboured on for an hour, through snow into which we sank up to our hips. In that time we made some 300 feet of height, and I decided that we would stand no chance of getting to the top, and regretfully abandoned the attempt. From where we had got to, however, there seemed to be no technical difficulties between us and the summit. It was evident too that the good weather would not survive many hours.

When we regained the plateau, we found the snow in a vile condition. As we got lower down, we were out of the wind, and the heat and glare were intense, and the labour of flogging a trail was a hearbreaking one. But we were in no particular hurry, and every now and then we sat down to gaze at the glorious view over the Nanda Devi Basin which our position commanded. The valleys were filled with great banks of woolly storm clouds, and the peaks of the eastern rim and the twin peaks themselves showed up in splendid isolation, which helped us to get a general idea of their relative size and position.

Once, while we were preparing to glissade down a very steep slope of about thirty feet into a crevasse, Pasang started off before we were ready, and, misjudging the length of the rope, both Tilman and I were pulled head first after him. The landing was soft and the fall was not long enough to have any serious consequences, but the incident was an annoying one, as it was a bad mountaineering error caused by pure carelessness. The badly crevassed section of the glacier required delicate handling, as the complicated system of snow bridges, which had been hard-frozen and secure in the morning, were now very unsafe, and we were constantly breaking through and hearing that ominous tinkling sound of icicles falling into the frozen depths of the crevasses below us. We reached our camp without further mishap, just as the usual afternoon snowstorm made its appearance, and spent the remainder of the day brewing and consuming vast quantities of tea and strenuously debating the subject of our next move.

CHAPTER TEN

WE had been keen to climb peak 110 primarily in order to be able to get a comprehensive view of the complicated topography to the north. Our reverse had merely stimulated that desire. Probably a more useful alternative for the morrow would be to continue the exploration of the ice-plateau in that direction. By doing this, if the weather were reasonably fine, we would be bound to see much of interest, whereas if we failed on the peak again, it would be a day of our most valuable time in this unknown country wasted. However, from what I had seen, the peak looked easy and eventually its blandishments won the day.

Pasang had had about enough on the previous day, and at 4 a.m. on the 20th Tilman and I left camp, heading once more for the ice-plateau. We suffered all the usual early morning torments, but were more than adequately compensated by the splendour of the dawn over the Nanda Devi Basin. Having our tracks of the previous day to follow, we climbed at a great pace, and reached our highest point of the previous day while our mountain world was still frozen; but beyond this we were faced with quite unexpected difficulties. A slope of dangerous snow, through which steps had to be cut into the ice below, led us, after some hours of hard work, into a long snow-filled corridor, running across the face of the mountain between high walls of ice. The snow had been swept into the corridor from the ice-slopes above, and was deep and soft. We sank in up to our waists as we beat our way along. We could not see where the corridor was leading us, but it was soon obvious that if we did not escape from it soon, we would have neither time nor energy to go any further. After half an hour or so, I saw a narrow vertical crack or "chimney" in the wall nearest the mountain. I started up it and, by putting my feet against one wall of the "chimney", and my back against the other (a method familiar to all rock climbers) I could make slow progress. But we were now at an altitude of nearly 22,000 feet, and I had not got many feet up the "chimney" before I was gasping like a fish out of water. Also the ice, of course, did not offer much friction to either boot or back, and the tendency to slip was very great. The air in the cleft was deathly cold, and in spite of my exertions my extremities soon lost all sensation. It was not long before I was bitterly regretting my folly in having tackled so severe a climb at such an altitude. The top of the cleft resisted my efforts so sternly that when, eventually, I emerged on to the steep ice-slope above, I sat there faint and sick for several minutes before I could summon up sufficient self-control to take in the rope as Tilman climbed up the "chimney". If it had been cold for me it was far worse for poor Tilman, who had had to wait below while I was wrestling with the "chimney".

When, after ten minutes' rest, we started up the ice-slope, we were both very shaky. The slope was steep and covered with three inches of slush, which made the job of chipping steps a difficult one. Higher up conditions became worse, and we soon realised that our struggle with the ice-chimney had left us too weak for the labour of hacking a safe pathway up ice of such a texture. Also the work called for absolute steadiness, as a slip on the part of either of us would have been impossible to check, and must have resulted in disaster, and we were both too tired to be able to guarantee safe movement. Again we had to admit defeat and turn back. Of course, if we had had time to spend on the job, we would have been able to make a bivouac in one of the crevasses nearby, and so eventually to hack our way up those relentless slopes. But we had come here primarily to explore the Nanda Devi Basin, and we could not afford the two days which would be necessary for a serious attack on peak 110.

The descent to the plateau called for unremitting care, and I was mightily relieved when we got clear of those vicious ice-slopes.

Our second reverse on this peak was another clear demonstration of the tendency to under-estimate mountaineering difficulties in the Himalaya.

After a close observation of the mountain, we had expected to have no serious difficulty in climbing it, and yet we had twice failed to do so. Our camp was only 18,500 feet high, and 4,500 feet is a lot to have to do in a day at that altitude, but this was not the reason for our defeat. In time, when these mountains become more familiar, a great many of their difficulties will be looked upon with less respect; but one wonders if mountaineering technique will ever reach so high a standard as to allow men to climb the more formidable giants of this vast range.

When we reached the camp we found all three Sherpas waiting for us. After slaking a raging glacier thirst, we packed up the tents and sleeping-bags, and hurried on down.

When we reached Great North Glacier, we found that the streams were enormously swollen. There had been a terrific increase in the rate of melting of the surface ice. I imagined that this was a sure sign that the monsoon was at hand, and we became seriously worried about the state of the rivers below.

After an undisturbed night in the open, I awoke at sunrise on June 21st to the song of many birds, which, strangely enough, seemed to be just as numerous far up in these barren moraine-filled valleys as amongst the pastures lower down. At 6.30 on this brilliant morning, while the Sherpas packed up the camp preparatory to going down, Tilman and I started up the glacier once more. We had a busy and interesting morning working with our plane-table at various points about the glacier, and in the afternoon, when the storm clouds had once more re-asserted themselves over the country, we ran at a great speed down the Great North Glacier to Junction Camp. When we reached the main valley, we found that a wonderful change had taken place in the short week we had been away. To a great height the mountain sides were a brilliant green with young grass. Our camp, lovely before, was now set in a garden of wild flowers, whose gay colouring framed the pools and new-born streams, contrasting deliciously with the harsh ruggedness of the higher glacier regions from which we had just come.

That evening we took stock of our food, and found that we had sufficient for only three more days. The weather was very unsettled, and it was evident that the monsoon was at hand. This was surprising, as we had not expected it until after the first week in July. Tilman was suffering from a severe pain in his foot, for which he could not account. There was still much minor exploratory work to be done in the northern section of the basin; this we could not hope to complete.

On the 22nd we took a light camp into yet another side valley leading towards the eastern "rim", and Tilman and I spent that night at an altitude of 18,100 feet, while the Sherpas returned to Junction Camp. We slept as usual in the open, and that evening, after a sharp hail-storm, we experienced again that vision of divine beauty which is, I suppose, the chief object of the strange pilgrimages which men make to the less accessible regions of the earth. It does not come to one at any particular place or time, and may elude the hunter over hundreds of miles of arctic waste or on countless mountain summits, to be found only on rare occasions, when the mind is unexpectedly attuned to the realisation of a delicate perfection of form and colour.

Before us, rising out of a misty shadow-lake of deepest purple, stood the twin summits of Nanda Devi, exquisitely proportioned and twice girdled by strands of white nimbus. This was backed by a liquid indigo, changing to mauve as it approached the south-west, where the icy pyramid of Trisul stood in ghostly attendance. Then, after passing through every degree of shade and texture, the colour died, leaving the moon to shed her silver light over a scene of ravishing loveliness, and to revive within me childish fancies, too easily forgotten in the materialism of maturer years.

We had intended to attempt, on the following day, the ascent of an attractive peak of some 21,500 feet, above our camp. Tilman's foot, however, appeared to be getting worse, and it was deemed wise that he should rest it in preparation for the heavy work which our retreat down the Rishi Nala would involve. Without his early-morning energy to assist me I found it more difficult than ever to summon up the strength of mind necessary to extricate sleepy limbs from the warmth of my sleeping-bag; particularly as the morning was dull and cheerless. Vanished were all the lofty enthusiasms of the previous evening, eclipsed by the hateful obligation of having to expose swollen lips and sore hands to the damp cold. Leaving the bivouac at 7.20 a.m. I crossed Glacier No. 5 on dry ice and climbed up the ridge which divides that valley from the Great North Valley, reaching a height of some 20,000 feet. Although the sky was overcast, the clouds stood well above the peaks and from my perch I obtained the most comprehensive view I had yet seen of the northern section of the basin, and spent an interesting and instructive hour filling in minor detail on the plane-table sheet. Towards 1 o'clock a bitter wind started blowing from the east, and snow fell. I made an unpleasant but quick descent to the Great North Glacier and reached Junction Camp at 4.30 p.m. to find Tilman and the Sherpas already arrived with our high camp kit. Tilman's foot was now badly swollen, and had caused him intense pain on the descent. It was now apparent that the trouble was a carbuncle on the upper surface of the foot.

On June 24th, while the others moved the camp across the Great North Glacier to the side of the lake, I had a long walk up the side of the Main Glacier, principally with the object of sketching the features on the northern face of Nanda Devi. The going was easy and pleasant along the level grass-land beside the glacier. It rained steadily most of the day and although my attention was constantly occupied by flowers, lakes, and herds of bharal, I was able to see very little of topographical interest and returned down the valley earlier than I had intended, reaching camp at 4.20 p.m.

I had hoped that by cutting our rations down slightly we might have time to explore the head of the Changabang Glacier, but it was now evident that the monsoon had broken and that we could not hope for more clear weather. Also we were far from sure how long the return journey would take us and one of the party was lame. We decided, therefore, to begin our retreat at once. And lucky it was that we had no great temptation to stay on in the basin, for our food dumps proved inadequate as it was!

A heavy mist hung over its grey waters as we said good-bye to the lake which had greeted us more than a fortnight before with so much sparkling life. We started very early and had reached the snout of the Main Glacier by midday, to find our fears regarding the state of the rivers only too well founded. The one issuing from the Main Glacier was now a raging torrent, despite the fact that the ground over which it was flowing for the first half mile of its course was relatively flat, and to ford it seemed at first to be a hopeless proposition. Moreover, the alternative of crossing the glacier above its snout and getting to the opposite side of the river in that way was out of the question, owing to a formidable line of overhanging cliffs thereabouts. For a moment our position looked serious, and I began to visualise the unpleasant consequences of having our retreat cut off. We waded out in several places, only to find each time that we could not stand up to the force of the current. After repeated attempts we were standing disconsolately at the water's edge when Pasang suggested a line which appeared to me to be at least as bad as the rest. However, he seized me by the hand, and I was led into the water's edge with a sinking heart. We immersed our lower halves in the seething turmoil, and advanced slowly. One of us moved forward a few inches supported by the other, then he would stand firm while the other moved, and so on. The rushing water made me giddy, and I knew that the least mistake would put us in a false position, from which there would be no hope of recovery. When the water touched my waist I knew that I had reached my limit, and any increase of pressure must sweep me off my feet. Pasang was splendid; never did he relax his concentration on himself or me for a fraction of a second. At length, after what seemed an age, the depth of the water began to lessen, and we bounded out on the other side, Pasang, who had done much more than his share of the "supporting", letting out wild cries of joy.

With the help of a rope stretched across the river, the others got over without mishap, though Angtharkay had an extremely bad time of it and required much support from the other two. Our relief at getting across without mishap was shared by the Sherpas, who danced with delight. But there was no time to waste in celebration, and we started down at full speed towards the junction of the northern and southern streams. To reach it we had to cross a spur coming down from Nanda Devi, and here we became involved in some difficult rock-climbing. However, at 3 o'clock we reached the southern stream just above the junction. After a short search, we were fortunate enough to find a place where the river, running over a stretch of mud flats, was very sluggish and, though the water was deep, we managed to get across without further unpleasant adventures. We found a nest, hereabouts, with three grey-blue eggs belonging, we supposed, to snow-pigeons. These birds were very common in the basin.

We climbed diagonally up the steep slope beyond the river, heading in a south-westerly direction until, about a thousand feet above the junction, we came upon a little grassy shelf with a spring of clear water. Here we settled down for the night, deliciously conscious that a heavy day's work had taken us clear of two serious difficulties, and that we were now well on our way to the Rishi Nala. But as we sat round our blazing fire of juniper wood in the gathering dusk, watching the heavy rain-clouds float lazily over the rolling moors of the basin, my content was marred by a feeling of sadness at having to leave so soon this country, which had provided us with a deep and lasting happiness, and whose beautiful secrets it had been our privilege to explore.

June 26th was a terrific day. During an early breakfast we caught a last fleeting glimpse of Nanda Devi's mighty head through a rift in the heavy monsoon clouds which hung over us. Then we started off towards the west, moving across the steep grassy slopes at a breathless pace which never slackened throughout the morning, and by midday we reached the little cave in which we had camped on June 5th. The Sherpas were as anxious as we were for speed, and I think that the mind of each of us was on the "flesh pots" of the Dhaoli Valley. But this was not the only reason, for the supplies of food left in the dumps were meagre and did not allow for any hitch which might easily occur on the return journey, on account of the early breaking of the monsoon.

Most of us were feeling fairly fit, but Tilman was rendered very lame by the carbuncle on his foot. He insisted, however, in carrying his share of the loads, and never breathed a word of complaint, though the furious pace over such difficult country must have caused him very considerable pain. We halted at our old camp for about twenty minutes, in order to eat a cup-full of satu mixed with cold water. The scramble from there down the very steep slope of 2,000 feet to the river took us two hours on account of the awkwardness of the loads. The river was many feet higher than when we had made its acquaintance before, and of course our little bridge had been swept away. On we went through the afternoon, and darkness found us encamped in a little clump of silver birch beyond the dreaded "Mauvais Pas".

I passed the night in a tiny recess between two boulders, and throughout the first half of it a thunderstorm raged above the gorge. The boulders provided inadequate shelter from the heavy rain which accompanied the storm, and I got very wet. The scene, however, was one not easily to be forgotten. Lightning flashes played continuously upon the grim precipices about me, while the fleecy rain clouds, entwining themselves about ridge and gully, accentuated their already stupendous size. Echoes of the thunder and hissing of rain provided fitting accompaniment.

The next morning, in thick mist and steadily falling rain, we continued our way along the delicate traverses which constituted the only practicable route across the gaunt precipices forming the southern wall of the canyon. The long tedious task of discovering the way and relaying our loads along it had made us familiar with almost every yard of the route, so that in spite of the bad visibility we were now experiencing, we made no mistakes. We were assisted too by the cairns which we had built at various points, and at 1 o'clock that afternoon we reached our base camp on the shore of the river we had left nearly a month ago. We had all been looking forward to a good square meal, but on arrival we found that by some mistake we had left only half the quantity of food which we had intended leaving, and that we now had sufficient only for three more days. This allowed for no contingencies, and there was no time to lose.

Below our base camp we had a choice of several routes. Dr. Longstaff had made his way to this point along the southern slopes of the valley, but he had encountered considerable difficulties, and with our loads and in such weather we would certainly take two and possibly three days to reach the place where he had bridged the Rishi Ganga. The route by which we had come with the Dotials was out of the question, owing to the impossibility of crossing the river in its present state where we had crossed it before. The only alternative then was to cross by the natural bridge to which I have referred before, ascend the Rhamani Nala until we found a place where we could cross it, and try to get on to the high line of traverse which Dr. Longstaff's party had taken after they had crossed the

Bagini Pass in 1907. So shortly after 4 o'clock that afternoon Pasang and I set off to investigate the possibility of this alternative.

We crossed the river by the natural bridge, which Pasang had not seen before. He was delighted, and seemed to think that it solved our last remaining problem. In gently falling rain we climbed up a difficult cliff to Longstaff's old camp site, some two hundred feet above the Rishi. From here we edged our way along a narrow shelf which gave us access to the Rhamani stream, but at a point where the river, issuing from a deep-cut ravine, descended in a series of waterfalls, and offered no hope of a crossing. We retraced our steps, and in some anxiety scrambled up along the steep rhododendron-covered slopes above the ravine, whose smooth unbroken walls overhung the river. We were forced to climb some fifteen hundred feet up before we found another break in these walls, and were able to get down to the river again. This time, however, we found ourselves at a fairly level stretch between two waterfalls, and decided after some discussion that the crossing could be attempted at this point. It was now getting late, and we had to get back quickly if we were to avoid being benighted, but I would have given much to have been able to continue our investigation of that remarkable gorge.

At the base camp we deposited our plane-table, some lengths of rope, candles, "Tommy's cookers" and a few items of clothing, to be picked up when we returned in August for the exploration of the southern section of the basin. This lightened our loads somewhat, and on the following morning we were back at the crossing place by 10 o'clock. We got over without much difficulty, and climbed a further five hundred feet up on the other side. This brought us on to a prominent ridge, from which we had a clear view down the Rishi Nala. Fortunately visibility remained good until 3 o'clock, by which time we had covered about a mile and a half on a fairly horizontal line. Then mist enveloped us, and for the next two hours, in pouring rain, we floundered helplessly about the intricate hillside until we came upon a spacious cave, where we decided to spend the night. There was a quantity of juniper growing nearby, and we were soon drying our sodden gear by a blazing fire.

The weather was still bad when we awoke next morning, and we did not get started until 8 o'clock. Groping our way through heavy mist, we got on to exceedingly difficult ground, and by 11 o'clock we had covered only a quarter of a mile. However, soon after this the weather cleared, and we found ourselves close to the terrace from which we had descended to the river nearly five weeks before. On reaching this we were on familiar ground once more and made such excellent progress that by the middle of the afternoon we were running down the pine-clad slopes to Dibrughita – "the horizontal oasis in a vertical desert". The alp was more beautiful than ever – a vast meadow of lush grass interwoven with forget-me-nots, deep red potentillas, large blue gentians, and flowers of a dozen other varieties, while the stately army of tall dark pines stood in a wide circle as if guarding this little shrine from the demons of the Rishi Gorge.

Our troubles were now over, and as we lay on the damp ground in the gently falling rain before an immense log fire, we basked in contentment undisturbed by sordid considerations of time, distance, and food.

A long slog up the steep slopes of the "curtain" ridge the next day (June

30th), took us to Durashi, where we found that the shepherds from Lata village had been installed for about ten days. These were the first human beings, besides ourselves, that we had seen since discharging the Dotials on May 29th, and our arrival startled them considerably. However, we managed to persuade them that we were not the mythical devils of the upper gorge, and they supplied us with quantities of goat's milk, which I thought at the time was the finest drink I had ever had. It must have strengthened us considerably too, for on the following morning, we made astonishingly quick time up to the Durashi Pass. I had been hoping that some snow would still remain in the gullies, as this would have enabled us to glissade some of the way down to Tolma, but except for a few patches here and there it had practically all gone. We decided to descend diagonally to the Lata village, instead of going down to Surai Tota. We had not much idea of the way, but before we had gone far we struck a sheep track which led us through an intricate network of cliffs in the forest, and soon blossomed out into a sizable path, down which we ran recklessly. Kusang lagged behind to gather considerable quantities of wild strawberries. He gave me all he had picked, and when I asked the reason for his generosity, he said that he had damaged his knee and that eating strawberries would make it worse! I failed to see the connection, but did not argue the point too strongly. We reached Lata village just before 4 o'clock, and immediately set about trying to persuade the inhabitants to sell us some food. We were bitterly disappointed, for the net result of our scrounging was a few unripe apricots and a cup-full of flour. There were no chickens, and therefore no eggs. There were cows, but no milk, and the last year had been a bad one for grain and, with the next harvest still so far off, the villagers could not afford to part with their flour. It was evident that the land of plenty was not yet reached, and we tightened our belts with a grim resolve to reach Joshimath the next day.

That evening we paid a social visit to the village, which we found in a great state of excitement on account of the arrival of an itinerant trader. His wares consisted of a miscellaneous assortment of buttons, matches, jews' harps, soap, etcetera, for which the villagers were eagerly exchanging the grain which had been refused us earlier in the day, though we had offered money some five times the value of the ridiculous trinkets supplied by the pedlar. We could not find out how he disposed of the grain, but it must have been a slow and precarious method of livelihood.

Early next morning, a large section of the village turned out to see us depart and acocmpanied us for some distance in order to see that we got on to the right path. It was a tedious march and we all felt very lethargic, the cause being, no doubt, our enforced underfeeding for the past few days. In the pouring rain we sped down the Dhaoli Valley practically without a stop. Each of us, I suppose, was thinking of hot tea and lots of food; but to a passer-by (if there had been such a phenomenon) we must surely have resembled the demons of the Rishi to whom we had been likened by the shepherds at Durashi. Early in the evening we entered Joshimath, exactly six weeks after leaving it.

Part 3

The First Crossing of the Watershed (Badrinath – Gaumukh)

CHAPTER ELEVEN

WE had over-estimated the joys of Joshimath. After three or four days of idleness and over-eating we were quite ready for a move to the north, where we fondly hoped we might be beyond the reach of the monsoon. We were bound for the Kedarnath-Badrinath group of mountains which are of great topographical interest since in them lie the sources of three of the main affluents of the Ganges, the rivers Bhagirathi, Mandakini, and Alaknanda, and close to these sources are the well-known temples of Gangotri, Kedarnath and Badrinath.

Our object in wishing to visit these was to cross the range which forms the watershed between the Alaknanda and the Bhagirathi, and so to link up the two chief sources of the Ganges. The range was but twenty miles north of Joshimath and it seemed very likely that there we should escape the influence of the monsoon and enjoy fine weather. (This theory was sound enough – in theory; but like most it did not work out in practice and we found that we were in the same predicament as if we had gone to see the English Lakes in the hope of avoiding a wet summer in the south.)

We knew that in 1912 Mr. C. F. Meade and his two Swiss guides had gone from Badrinath up the Bhagat Kharak Glacier, climbed the ridge at its head, and looked down on the Gangotri Glacier. They did not descend on the other side, but they thought the pass was practicable, and it was our intention to find and cross this pass and thereby not only cross the range, but also explore the unknown head of the Gangotri Glacier.

But there is more than geographical interest in this district. It is believed to be the home of the gods of Hindu mythology, and every feature of the landscape is sanctified by some legend and is traditionally memorable.

It seemed that from earliest Vedic records (Hindu writings), the geography of the mountainous regions sheltering the Ganges sources was well-known. In those distant times when men still worshipped the elements, a region which saw the birth of great rivers and greater storms was naturally regarded with awe; and so, when the worship of the elements was supplanted by the worship of gods, it began to be revered as their home.

The learned and the pious were drawn there for meditation and adoration, and hill and valley, peak and waterfall, came to be associated with particular gods and embellished by stories of their lives. Indeed, in the Hindu legend of the creation, Brahma, Siva and Vishnu assumed the form of mountains. When Brahma desired to create the earth he began by assuming the visible form of Vishnu, the whole universe being covered with water on which floated that god, resting on a bed supported by a serpent. From his navel sprang a lotus from which issued Brahma; from his ears issued two Daityas (or, when transferred to an earthly sphere, Dasyus, the aboriginal black race as opposed to the fair Aryan), who attacked Brahma; and Vishnu and Brahma fought with them for five thousand years until Vishnu finally killed them and from their marrows made the world.

Vishnu then assumed the form of a tortoise and raised the earth out of the water and asked Brahma to create all that the world was of earth, sky, and heaven; divided the earth into nine parts and created wind and sound and time; past, present, and future; work and desire, and anger; from the last-named Siva was created as making the third of the great trinity, Brahma the creator, Vishnu the preserver, and Siva the destroyer.

The story then goes on that during the terrestrial reign of one Prithu, all plants perished by reason of his tyranny, which so angered him that he determined to destroy the earth. The earth sought pardon, and begged the king to remove the mountains which prevented the spread of vegetation. Prithu uprooted the mountains and heaped them on top of each other, but then from the earth proceeded to milk all plants and vegetables. Other gods and demons followed his example and milked the earth of all its virtues, who then fled to Brahma to complain of this everlasting milking. Brahma took her to Vishnu, who made the following promise: "Soon the head of Brahma will fall upon thee" (at Brahm Kapal a great rock in the river at Badrinath); "Siva will come to sit upon the mountains of Tankara" (at Jageswar in Kumaon); "Bhagirath Raja shall bring down Ganga" (Ganges) "to thee. Then I myself will come in my dwarf incarnation and all the world will know that Vishnu has descended on thee. Then thy pains shall be removed and the mountains cease to afflict thee with their load, for I shall be Himalaya; Siva will be Kailas" (a mountain in Tibet north of Kumaon); "Brahma will be Vindhyachal and thus the load of the mountains shall be removed."

But the earth asked "Why do you come in the form of mountains and not in your own form?" and Vishnu answered: "The pleasure that exists in mountains is greater than that of animate beings, for they feel no heat, nor cold, nor pain, nor anger, nor fear, nor pleasure. We three gods as mountains will reside in the earth for the benefit of mankind." (An answer which mountaineers would do well to learn in order to baffle the all-to-frequent inquiry of why they climb mountains, for it leaves the questioner no wiser than before, yet it has an authority sufficiently impressive to silence him!)

Thus Himachal, the Snow Mountains, were invested with sanctity, but the holy of holies is Mount Kailas, in Tibet, and the sources of the Ganges and the mountains which surround it, and here are the ancient temples of Badrinath, Kedarnath, and Gangotri. They are all reached by roads having a common origin at Hardwar, another holy city which marks the place where the Ganges debouches from the hills on to the plains. The three temples are within a circle of twenty miles radius, but between each rises a twenty-thousand-feet ridge of snow and ice, and to pass from one to the other pilgrims must retrace their steps for more than one hundred miles, so to outflank this great barrier.

Kedarnath was particularly associated with the worship of Siva, whose adventures there are definitely not of the kind associated with the life of that grim and terrifying god, the very apotheosis of lust and cruelty. The legend is that the god took refuge here when pursued by the Pandavas (a tribe of the Dasyus whom we have already met) by assuming the form of a buffalo and diving into the ground for safety. Unluckily he left his hinder parts exposed on the surface, and there is still a mountain here which is supposed to resemble in shape the hindquarters of a buffalo and is now an object of adoration.

These high-spirited Pandavas were effectually subdued later, and when told that their power had left them and that they should begin to think on heaven, it was to the Himalaya they retired. The account of their departure is most moving, a pathetic touch being that of the dog who, I suppose, had taken a too prominent part in the buffalo hunt. We read that, "Yudishthira, their ruler, then took off his earrings and necklace, and all the jewels from his fingers and arms, and all his royal raiment; and he and his brethren, and their [*sic*] wife Draupadi, clothed themselves after the manner of devotees in vestments made of the bark of trees. And the five brethren threw the fire of their domestic sacrifices and cookery into the Ganges and went forth from the city following each other. First walked Yudishthira, then Bhima, then Ayuna, then Nakula, then Sahdeva, then Draupadi, and then a dog. And they went through the country of Banga towards the rising sun; and after passing through many lands they reached the Himalaya Mountain, and there they died one after the other and were transported to the heaven of Indra."

Close to Kedarnath on the north, but reached by a different road, is Gangotri. There is a celebrated temple here and close by is Gaumukh, the Cow's Mouth, which should have proved an even greater attraction, but from what we saw and what I have heard since, is visited by only a few. This is the snout of the Gangotri Glacier, fifteen very rough miles above the Temple, and the sacred source – or rather the most sacred, for there are others – of Mother Ganges. Apparently when the world was young and man was in a state of innocence the Ganges rose at Benares, so that it was an easy matter for believers to visit it. As the earth increased in years and wickedness, the source retreated successively to Hardwar, Barahat, and now to Gaumukh, whither the long and arduous pilgrimage may atone in some measure for the sins of a more vicious age.

In the temple at Gangotri are two images representing the Ganges and the Bhagirathi, and below in the river bed are three basins where the pilgrims bathe. One of these is dedicated to Brahma, one to Vishnu, and one to Siva, and the water of these basins will not only cleanse away all past sins, but ensure eternal happiness in the world to come. It is almost as efficacious if taken away – and returning pilgrims may then hope to get back some of their expenses! The water is drawn under the inspection of a Brahman and by him sealed for a small consideration, and when carried down to the plains it realises a high price. The mighty Ganges is here only about fifty feet across and at Gaumukh perhaps half of that, but in the summer when the snows are melting the current is very fierce.

Such are the interesting legends attached to the Kedarnath-Badrinath country and, the flesh-pots of Joshimath having so quickly palled, we were glad to begin drawing up food lists and to engage the necessary coolies. Unfortunately our eight deserters from Surai Tota had so blackened our characters that we had great difficulty in finding anyone else, but at last we collected six coolies, and two days' march along what is called the "Pilgrim Road" brought us to Badrinath on July 11th. At a village on our way up we stopped to sample some exciting-looking sweetmeats and were led to believe that all the inhabitants were positively clamouring for work as coolies. Now our six were only coming – and that reluctantly – as far as Badrinath with us and we wanted eight to come on to the Bhagat Kharak Glacier, so we promised to give eight villagers the work and received in return an ardent promise that we could rely on them presenting themselves next day in Badrinath at dawn.

This was excellent, and on the 12th we were up at 5 o'clock and had all the loads in readiness, but when 8 o'clock came and there was still no sign of any porter, we began sending out into the highways and byways of Badrinath for recruits. By 9 o'clock we had five men and we then moved over to the bazaar, where we sat, with what small patience we could muster, beside the three extra loads until men could be found for them. Every man in the bazaar joined in the search – which meant that no spare man could be found, but two hours later our complement was somehow made up and we gave the word to start. By then, of course, the first five had drifted off to see their friends or to buy food, but we were assured they would follow. So in ones, two and threes did we straggle out of Badrinath – a distressing sight to an orderly-minded man.

But our fellow-marchers were as happy-go-lucky as ourselves. They had started from Hardwar, a journey of some thirty days from Badrinath and were for the most part townsmen or peasants from the plains; the former in "dandies", or walking before a plodding coolie carrying their baggage: the latter walking – without the coolie. For the majority baggage was not a serious hindrance as a brass bowl for food and a pilgrim's staff was generally enough. One additional thing was carried by all, whatever their station in life. This was an umbrella. Indeed, the almost universal use of this very European article was most striking, and I must admit that the umbrella was a highly incongruous adjunct when borne aloft by a hardy shepherd of the hills, clad in a long, blanket-like coat of homespun fastened across his chest by a metal skewer and chain for want of a button; but seemingly he was sensible enough to prefer dryness to a picturesque appearance.

The pilgrims were of both sexes, and we inclined to believe there were more women than men. Many of the former, could they afford it, were carried in a basket or a "dandy". The basket was high, narrow and cylindrical, not much bigger than a dirty-linen basket, and was hitched to the coolie's back, he carrying a T-shaped staff to support its weight when at rest. The passenger sat facing the rear with only his head showing, and the many we passed appeared to be asleep, with handkerchiefs over their faces to keep off the flies. The "dandy" was rather like a sedan chair without any sides and was carried by four coolies, thus making it a very expensive mode of transport. Slung at each end from a pole which rests on the bearers' shoulders, it was so arranged that they might walk in echelon, and not side by side. The passenger is literally and metaphorically "in the hands" of his carriers, as the following story shows.

Tradition relates that the ruling family of Kumaon, at that time the Katyuris, had their origin here. There is a story about the last Katyuri Rajah which illustrates the steep contours of this country more vividly than can any descriptive writing. Rajah Dham, the last of his line, ruled so tyrannically that he went in fear of his life. In such circumstances the usual safeguard is to wear an extra steel waistcoat or to change the cook, but in this case the Rajah took the precaution of having iron rings fastened to the shoulders of his dandy-bearers. The poles passed through these rings, and so it was impossible for the bearers to drop their royal burden over a cliff without themselves accompanying it. But no one is secure against desperate men, and when oppression grew intolerable, four men were found ready to sacrifice themselves for the sake of their country, who flung themselves off the road, with the Rajah, to their deaths.

The profane like to recount a more recent tradition which also shows how the country lends itself to the arranging of "accidents", but puts the dandy-bearers in a less pleasing light. The pilgrim season is short: it starts in May and none leave Hardwar after the end of August, and so like other seasonal workers the dandy-men try to make the most of it. It is the custom to contract for transport and pay in advance, but if the dandy-men went the whole way, they could at the best make only two full journeys. They therefore hit on the happy plan of tipping their passenger over any convenient cliff into the river, many marches short of Badrinath, and hastening back for a fresh load. They argued that the arrangement satisfied both parties, the pilgrim bathed in the sacred waters as he had desired, and the coolies could earn twice as much in the season. The practice died out with the coming of the British raj, who probably regarded it as a too free interpretation of the contract.

The pilgrims, so we have been told, found the fruition of all earthly desire in a visit to their sacred places, the shrine of Vishnu at Badrinath, the Panch-Sila, the Five Rocks and their respective pools which encircle the throne of Vishnu, and what is called "The Holy Circle of Badrinath", which includes a tract of country from the shrine of Kanwa to the peak of Nanda Devi, on the summit of which is supposed to be a lake, the abode of Vishnu himself. Their day's stage was usually about nine miles and at each halt they found accommodation in long, low sheds open in front to the road and surrounded on the remaining three sides by stone walls supporting a grass roof. The floor was of beaten earth which received daily a fresh wash of mud or clay and along the roadside were a dozen or more little circular fireplaces, also of clay, spaced at four-feet intervals. There were also shops, at which the pilgrims might buy their food and fuel, the purchase of which entitled them to a free night's lodging. Some of these rest-houses were provided with big thatched-reed sleeping mats, but there was no other furniture. Certainly everything looked very clean (owing probably to the frequent washing with yellow clay) but, fortunately perhaps, we were never called upon to put this supposed cleanliness to the test.

The Government, having made the "Pilgrim Road", a well-engineered bridle-track seven to ten feet wide and maintained by the P.W.D. of India, were rightly concerned about the health of the pilgrims, for an outbreak of cholera at any of the rest-houses would be most serious. The greatest difficulty was sanitation, and therefore inspectors were employed along the route to see that at least the most rudimentary regulations were carried out. At most of the villages, too, pipe-lines had been laid down to bring drinking-water from high up the hillsides, where the chances of contamination were less. Even despite these precautions dysentery and, in the lower valleys, malaria took toll of the pilgrims, many of whom, weakened by unaccustomed effort and the cold, were in no condition to resist an attack. We were told that at Badrinath alone that year there had been thirty deaths – but as probably there had been some thirty thousand pilgrims this did not strike us as being an alarming proportion. Besides, more than a few of them were most likely caused by weakness and starvation, since many of the poorer classes start out with little or no money and are soon reduced to begging their way – no easy task in such a sparsely populated district. Doubtless such a method answered well enough for the professional beggar (for whom India is renowned). He had only to pass through a bazaar and thrust his bowl under the noses of unfortunate shopkeepers to have a handful of rice or ata put into it. In this walk of life a disgusting appearance is a positive asset, and I have never once seen the most repulsive-looking individual turned away empty-handed. At Badrinath itself the Temple authorities dispense every day quantities of free food: at mid-day a great bowl of cooked rice is carted into the main street and anyone who asks may be filled.

We were much puzzled by the complete apathy which most of them betrayed. Here was no "Happy Band of Pilgrims", but a procession of woebegone miseries that reminded us of refugees, driven from their homes by an invader. None seemed to derive any pleasure from the performance of a duty which to them meant the principal thing in life, or from the glorious scenery through which this duty led them. One and all went along with downcast head, bestowing no glance upon the grandeur of the hills and deigning but a sour look at passers-by. Possibly, of course, this latter was reserved for ourselves – the outcasts and unbelievers defiling holy ground. (After all, a European on the road to Mecca during the pilgrim season would be lucky to receive nothing more harmful than angry looks.)

But these Hindus were not so fanatical in such matters as the Mohammedans, and on several occasions we found them pleased to show us their temples, so we came to the conclusion that a possible cause of their indifference lay in their awe and fear of mountains. To nearly all of them rocks, hills, snow and ice, were things outside their previous experience and, as we told ourselves, we had not to go so very far back to find similar emotions in our own forefathers. Whether their faces showed these we cannot tell, but what they felt they have very clearly expressed, as, for example, in the writing of Defoe in his *Tours*: "Here we entered Westmorland, a country eminent for being the wildest, most barren, and frightful of any that I have passed over in England, or even Wales itself. . . . Nor were these Hills high and formidable only, but they had a kind of an unhospitable terror in them. . . . But 'tis of no advantage to represent Horror as the character of a Country, in the middle of all the frightful Appearances to the right and left." And a writer of yet later date describing an ascent of homely Saddleback seems to be even more moved, though he does omit the capitals: ". . . views so tremendous and appalling that few persons have sufficient resolution to experience the emotions which those awful scenes inspire."

In addition we had to remember that every rock or pool was supposedly the abode of some god, so that a fearful and downcast air on the part of the supplicant were understandable. In very truth, these pilgrims might exclaim with Kim: "Surely the gods live here. This is no place for men!"

CHAPTER TWELVE

INTERESTED though we were in the behaviour of the pilgrims, the country ahead was yet more interesting, and soon we left the last pilgrims behind, for only a few go much beyond Badrinath.

Three miles from Badrinath we passed through the village of Mana, the last inhabited village on the road to the Mana Pass into Tibet. Its site was picturesque, overlooking the mouth of a terrific gorge and backed by a bleak hillside studded with prodigious boulders, some of which had rolled down, thus completely spanning the ravine. Here the low huts, roofed with rough flat stones, appeared to grow like some fungus out of the landscape, and here the Alaknanda Valley bent abruptly to the west and three miles up gave birth to a river at the adjoining snouts of the Bhagat Kharak and the Satopanth glaciers. But contrary to expectations our pilgrims did not visit this source: instead, they resorted to a place called Bhasudhara, about a mile short of the glaciers. Here, in truth, was the spot where "the slender thread of the Lotus flower falls from the foot of Vishnu", a spot far more fitted to witness the birth of the sacred Ganges than the desolate, moraine-covered ice of the Bhagat Kharak. Almost as soon as one rounded the bend at Mana the eye was drawn, without conscious volition, to a narrow white ribbon of water outlined against a wall of reddish rock at whose feet was a grassy alp. Here the water, cascading from some hidden glacier, dissolved at the bottom into a fine mist with which the wind sported, and so sprinkled a rude shrine and the pilgrims who bowed before it.

This part of the Alaknanda above Mana was a favourite resort for those who wished to commune alone and to practise austerities. We came upon several living the lives of hermits in caves and under sheltering boulders – an existence pleasant enough during the summer months, away from the flies and smells of

Badrinath, and sustained by the milk of the goats which were herded here in great numbers. (In winter, no doubt, these folk descended to a kindlier climate as did the entire population of Badrinath, since from November to May their temple is shut.)

But a far more interesting ascetic than the hermits of the Bhasudhara was a Professor Ram Serikh Singh, known to all in the district as "the Master". We had met him first in Badrinath, whither he came every year, not to stay in the town but to withdraw, with a single attendant, to a tent pitched on a green alp in the shadow of the beautiful Nilkanta. There, in the midst of scenery grand and inspiring, he passed his time in reading and meditation. Deeply learned in Hindu religion and in philosophy, and also in the traditions of these mountain regions, his learning had not been gained from books alone since he was a lover of mountain-travel and had journeyed extensively, even to Mount Kailas in Tibet, which lay some hundred miles to the north-east and was of the greatest sanctity to both Hindu and Tibetan. We spent many delightful hours with "the Master" in his wild and secluded valley, and the memory of them is among the fondest of our travels. His genial countenance and robust figure had at once a resemblance to Mr. Pickwick and to Friar Tuck. Sitting talking in his tent, or poring over a map with his spectacles athwart his nose, his likeness to the former predominated; outside on hillside or road, sturdy of frame, his thick gown girdled at the waist, a mighty staff in his hand, he recalled a favourite picture of Robin Hood's trusted companion. That there is no portrait of "the Master" in these pages is what we call "our fault". He, however, out of the depths of his philosophy, refers to it as Providential (in the strictest meaning of that word). Before setting out to visit him at his camp we constantly reminded each other about a camera, hoping that he would permit us to photograph him – and in the end, both of us inevitably forgot it! When we told him of this omission of commission he displayed great satisfaction, laughingly told us that never had he had his photograph taken, and saw, in this last narrow escape, the directing hand of some Higher Power determined to protect his immunity.

But it is high time we left "the Master" and the "Pilgrim Road" and concentrated upon our reconnaissance of the Kedarnath-Badrinath group!

Our stay in the village of Mana was lengthened by our inability to collect our still scattered followers. But having at last mustered them all, we crossed the grim gorge of the Saraswati by a natural rock bridge and followed the Alaknanda Valley westwards. The valley was pleasantly open and was the grazing ground for all the Mana herds and flocks, and the abode of many anchorites engaged in meditation and the practice of austerities. Had there been juniper wood as well as grass we would have liked it better, for we had no wish to vie with the anchorites in mortifying the flesh. When we camped that night one mile short of the Bhagat Kharak Glacier all hands had to range far and wide to collect enough pitiful little twigs to boil a kettle. Just across the river, tantalisingly close, was a little birch spinney but it might as well have been fifty miles away.

Before reaching the glacier we had to ford a side stream of which we had been warned at Mana and advised to go up it for a mile before attempting to cross. After the Rishi it looked fairly harmless, as indeed it was if taken in the right place, and we scorned to be driven by it two miles out of our way. While we were looking for an easy place the Sherpas tried a line of their own, and Pasang got into serious difficulties. He lost his footing and went right under, but luckily for him his load came free (we again noticed the merit of head-straps), and he was pulled ashore, bruised and badly shaken and minus his ice-axe. The load, containing his own and my kit and bedding, went bobbing downstream, on the way to Calcutta and the sea, and in trying to stop it, Tilman's ice-axe fell a victim to the hungry river. The load grounded lower down on some shallows but the axes were never recovered, and from now on the Sherpas had to use sticks which later proved a serious handicap.

The moraine on the north side of the glacier made a fair path, and two days later we camped at 16,000 feet near the head of the glacier and sent the local coolies back. The glacier was about seven miles long and as soon as we rounded a bend in it half way up we could see there was no pass at the head; there were, however, four subsidiary glaciers flowing in from a south-westerly direction so our hopes were by no means extinguished. The first of these, close to the head of the main glacier was disposed of before camp was pitched, for I went round the corner to look for a better camp site and saw, with disgust, a most forbidding cirque of cliffs at the head.

From the camp we climbed a small peak (19,000 feet), from where we saw enough to rule out a second possible pass, and we also obtained a good view of the northern bounding wall of the Bhagat Kharak, which was to prove useful to us later. We then made a traverse of our peak and came down a new way, in the course of which Tilman made the discovery that glissading on steep ice was too rapid, even in these fast-moving times, and we reverted to slow but safe step-cutting.

Our camp on the ice was not very home-like so we moved it across to a grassy flat on the north side where conditions were pleasant, and where we were well placed for a fresh move, the necessity for which was now looming ahead of us. A walk up the third glacier confirmed our fears, and after much heart-searching we decided the fourth was best left alone. We had caught a glimpse of the col at the head of this on the way up and it seemed to offer some hope, but the approach to the glacier was up a steep and difficult ice-fall which, moreover, was raked by avalanches from the tremendous north face of Kunaling, the giant of this range, some 23,400 feet. The roar of an intermittent bombardment of this glacier from the slopes of Kunaling was ever in our ears.

(Since returning to England we have learnt that it was up here that Mr. Meade went, but he got on to the glacier by some route which avoided the ice-fall and the avalanche-swept area.)

Defeated in the Bhagat Kharak we fell back on a fresh plan. In 1931 the Kamet expedition had gone up the Arwa, a valley system north of the Bhagat Kharak, and in one of its branches had found a pass which obviously led to the Gangotri side of the range, although it was not completely crossed. We therefore decided to cross first to the Arwa and, if our food allowed, to attempt to find a way over the great Gangotri Glacier.

So on July 18th we started relaying loads (including a quantity of juniper wood) to the top of the 20,000 feet ridge beween us and the Arwa. The direction we wanted to take was due north but the only place by which the ridge could be crossed lay well to the east of north, and we were reluctantly driven farther from the watershed. In four days we established a camp on the ridge, where we stayed two days while Tilman and I climbed a peak of about 21,500 feet. It was an interesting ridge climb, but the pleasure we expected, and in fact received, from it was secondary to getting the hang of the geography of the Arwa glaciers on to which we were about to descend. In this object we were disappointed, for the weather which earlier was so good that we flattered ourselves we had outrun the monsoon, now broke up, and snow, rain, and mist were our daily portion.

But our two-day halt here enabled us to eat some of the weight out of our loads and when we started the descent we were just able to carry everything in one shift – everything except our juniper which we abandoned regretfully. The descent was not as exhilarating as descents should be; indeed, soft snow and heavy loads made it purgatorial. We towed the loads behind us like sledges, lowered them in front of us, or sent them rolling down under their own steam; any method rather than carrying them which only sank us deeper and deeper in the snow. At last, after passing at great speed under some hanging glaciers, where the Sherpas called loudly and effectively upon their gods, we reached dry glacier; the first of the Arwa branches which we called "A".

The sun had come out and now blazed down on us as if bent on making up for past deficiences, and we spread ourselves and the loads out to dry. The Sherpas stretched themselves like lizards on rocks, bottom upwards, for they were over partial to sitting glissades and suffered accordingly. We had dropped over three thousand five hundred feet from the pass and the barometer now registered only 16,200 feet, though it was surprising it could register anything at all after the treatment the load in which it travelled had received. Pasang and Tilman had a little joke of their own about that barometer. When he saw us consulting it so earnestly he often asked Tilman what its name was, and upon being told "Shaitán" (Satan) he seemed to appreciate the name and thereafter took an affectionate interest in "Shaitán's" welfare.

The glacier on which we were camped was three-quarters of a mile wide and the watershed was now two miles west of us, but there was no crossing it here and we had to go still further north. On the opposite side of our glacier two subsidiary glaciers flowed down from the north, and of these we chose the westernmost for our route to the next branch of the Arwa.

The col at the head of this was about 18,000 feet and the approach to it not difficult. We left a small dump of food at our camp on "A" glacier, went up to the col and crossed it, and in the afternoon camped on the "névé" of what we called "B" glacier at 17,000 feet. From here we could see where our pass lay, still two miles north and two thousand feet higher, and the condition of the snow had up till now been so bad that we began to despair of reaching it. Soon after making camp it began to rain and as we had omitted to pitch the tents door to door and there was only the one "Primus", the party of five assembled in one tent to advise and assist in the cooking, thereby raising a very satisfactory "fug".

The rain turned to snow in the night and the morning was overcast, but by

8.30 we were ploughing slowly to the north with the watershed now close on our left hand. Had there been any drying power in the sickly sun which leered at us out of a big halo, sure presage of foul weather, Tilman would have made a passionate appeal for a later start. It was his privilege to carry the tents and he preferred them dry, the extra weight being a consideration but not nearly so objectionable as the water which seeped through on to his back.

That virtue is its own reward we were beginning to learn, for in the matter of early starts we found there was no other. At whatever hour in the day we were afoot the snow crust would never bear our weight, and we sank to our knees or waists as much at dawn as at midday. To-day we encountered an exceptionally bad patch in which we wallowed to the point of exhaustion, but as we neared the col conditions improved and by midday we gained the top (19,500 feet).* A desultory snowstorm prevented us seeing much but it was very noticeable how, as we came north, the hills assumed a more Tibetan aspect; the rock being reddish and loose, the slopes more gentle, and the tops flatter.

Below us a steep, loose gully led down for three hundred feet to a small glacier. The bottom of the gully was iced, and below the *bergschrund* gaped hospitably. We descended one at a time in order to avoid the danger of loose stones. On the icy bit Pasang parted company with his load which headed straight for the abyss, but fortunately jumped it and was fielded by myself on the far side. Long-suffering "Shaitán" had had yet another narrow escape!

The glacier we were now on was badly crevassed and to Tilman, who was in front, it seemed to fulfil somebody's definition of a sieve, "a lot of holes held together by wire". He duly fell into one but his load got wedged and held him up very comfortably. Pasang, the next man, was unaware of this and before Tilman could explain matters had nearly pulled him in two with the rope, thinking, not unnaturally, that he was dangling over space. For the next fortnight every deep breath fetched a groan from poor Tilman's battered ribs, the burden of their groaning being "Save me from my friends".

Above a deep ice-fall we forsook the glacier for a scree slope and were soon at the bottom on another much bigger glacier, fortunately "dry", and flowing due west. We camped on some rocks in the middle of this and now the snow which had fallen fitfully all day, stopped for a moment. There, looking down the glacier, we saw in the distance the wall of another valley crossing it at right angles, unmistakably the Gangotri. This was a cheering sight – moreover we now had water at hand instead of snow to melt, and one of us, gifted with a strong imagination, conceived the happy idea of mixing raisins in the dough for our "chupatties" – and so in great content to bed.

Again it snowed all night and was still at it in the morning, so we stayed in bed singing doleful songs which presently had the desired effect, for the snow stopped. Dumping two days' food here we started down the glacier, doing the first mile on "dry" ice very quickly. Then we got into a jumble of moraine and spent the next two hours clambering in and out of great hollows. Finally we won clear and got on to a smooth lateral moraine on the right bank, and soon the

*The cols and glaciers of the Arwa are mapped in detail on p.280 of *Kamet Conquered*. Although *Abode of Snow* states that they used Birnie's Col, this is probably incorrect – an easier pass to the north providing the route. (Editor)

sight of a few flowers gladdened our ice-weary eyes. We made five miles that day in spite of a long, luxurious halt at midday, when the sun came out and we basked and dried our sodden loads. The colours in this valley were most striking, for besides the vivid patches of green provided by the grass there were bold splashes of red, blue, and white rock. As yet we had found no juniper but we promised ourselves a fire next day.

We camped that night in a pleasant alp only two miles from the Gangotri ice-stream, but our friendly moraine had petered out and the going promised to be rough. For once we woke to a fine morning (July 27th) and looking out of the open tent-flap we saw a sight which fairly made us spring from our bags. West across the Gangotri floated, high up, a silvery spire, graceful as that of Salisbury, and sparkling in the early sun.[1] It seemed poised in mid-air, for the base on which it rested was momentarily hidden and revealed by the mists writhing upwards from the valley.

By 10 o'clock we reached the junction of our unknown "X" glacier[2] and the Gangotri, and we halted on a friendly alp to discuss our next move, watched by an inquisitive herd of bharal from the cliffs behind. We had imagined that the glacier which we had come down would join the Gangotri five miles above the snout, and we were now, at a guess, ten miles from the head. We much wanted to visit both, the head because no one had seen it, and the snout because many had. We felt that to come to the Gangotri Glacier and not see Gaumukh, the Cow's Mouth, the birthplace of Mother Ganges, would be like going to Cairo without seeing the Pyramids; at least one of us felt this but the other was not so sure, and an interesting debate began as to whether sightseers and trippers (which we were in danger of becoming) were to be emulated or despised. Before the question was put, the debate being still in progress, the clearing mist revealed a river not three miles away, a sight which altered things considerably for it meant we could go down to Gaumukh and back in the day. We camped where we were and unashamedly set forth as trippers.

We made our pilgrimage to Gaumukh from the wrong direction, and if the merit acquired is proportionate to the energy expended, ours must have been great. There was no lateral moraine on our side and we toiled by devious ways through chaotic hills and valleys of ice strewn with gigantic boulders, the short two and a half miles taking us a long two hours. On the way we passed the mouth of a valley lying parallel to the glacier we had descended, but there was no indication of it on our map and this omission gave us a feeling of quite unmerited superiority to map-makers in general and the author of this map in particular. We ought to have blessed him for giving us something to correct, whereas we made lofty and scornful remarks about slipshod work; but in less exalted moments we did appreciate at their true worth the labour and skill which had gone to the making of a map that was never meant for mountaineers.

Drab though the scene was, like the tongue of any glacier, it was impossible to be unmoved at sight of the turbid flood rushing from a black ice cave under the towering wall of ice which marked the end of the Gangotri Glacier, and to reflect that here, where it was a bare thirty feet wide, the Ganges began a journey of fifteen hundred miles to the Bay of Bengal into which it poured

[1] Probably Shivling [2] The Chaturangi Glacier (Editor)

through many mouths, one alone full twenty miles wide. When one further reflected that from sea to source it was regarded with veneration by more than two hundred million human beings who, in life, believe that to bathe in it is to be cleansed from sin, and at death ask no more but that their ashes may be cast upon its waters, one had a combination of stupendous spiritual and physical marvels which could hardly be equalled elsewhere in the world.

Not wishing to acquire a double dose of merit, we returned by an easier way on the south side of the glacier where, beyond a high moraine, were grassy flats brilliant with flowers and watered by meandering streams. Opposite to our camp we recrossed the mile-wide glacier and the Sherpas welcomed us with a cheerful juniper fire and a dish of wild rhubarb, not quite equal in flavour to that of the Rishi Ganga, but rare and refreshing for all that.

We had left dumps of food on the way for the return journey but we still had two days' food in hand, and the question was what we should now do. Our tripper instincts being satisfied, the explorer instinct was asserting itself. We wanted to traverse the whole length of the Gangotri Glacier, but with only two days at our disposal we could not get far. As we were discussing alternatives inspiration came to us, borne perhaps on the wings of the wild rhubarb, and such was the attractiveness of this fresh plan that we decided to return to Badrinath forthwith to put it into execution.

On July 28th we started back up "X" glacier and two days later camped at the foot of the small glacier leading to the pass; the weather was clearer than when we came down and we could now sketch in the many lateral branches. Mindful of the loose stones in the gully we made an early start on the 29th and went up to the pass as fast as we could in order to tackle the gully while it was yet frozen up. Tilman, as last man, was in the best position for feeling the results of and criticising careless movements on the part of the others, but thanks to our early start, and the Sherpas' Agag-like tread, we reached the top without shifting a stone. On the other side snow conditions were now better and we pushed on past our old camp and straight down "B" glacier, for instead of crossing the second pass back to "A" glacier and our food dump, we had decided to go round by the Arwa Valley and camp at the foot of "A" glacier, retrieving our food next day.

By the time we were clear of "B" glacier and heading down the valley the weather became very thick and we had some difficulty in locating the snout of "A". At last we came to a stream issuing from a glacier, and assuming it was "A" we camped. Next morning Angtharkay and Pasang started early up the glacier, which we devoutly hoped might be the right one, though any doubts we had we kept to ourselves. They found the dump, but did not get back till afternoon, by which time it was raining, so we declared our half-holiday a whole one.

We now held all streams, of whatever size, in the greatest respect and to avoid having anything to do with the one by which we were camped, we went up to the glacier and crossed on the ice. In these uncongenial surroundings we were surprised to meet a large flock of goats going up the valley, and it is to be assumed the shepherds knew where they were going for as yet we had not seen a blade of grass, and even a Tibetan goat would jib at a stone and water diet.

The nearer we approached to home the worse became the weather, as it had in the Rishi, and a searching wind blew up the valley, bringing with it a cold rain. We huddled in the lee of a boulder to brew the last of our tea and then, pushing on, we got on to the track which came down from the Mana Pass. Here we met a Tibetan and two women living in a tent which was remarkable for its superior ventilation, and with them the Sherpas had a long chat. In appearances there was not much to choose between our party and the Tibetan; of both it was true to say that they were without visible means of support. But it seemed that they were the less destitute and they presented the Sherpas with a handful of twigs. I was struck by the kindliness of this gesture, for it was no more than that, the twigs hardly sufficing for tinder, let alone a fire. In this, however, I was under a misapprehension, because when I mentioned it to the Sherpas I was told that the gift was tea!

We carried on till 5 o'clock, getting wetter and colder, hopefully expecting to find some juniper wood, but at last we resigned ourselves to the bleak prospect of one more fireless night which a brew of the Tibetan's firewood did something to ameliorate.

Next day, August 2nd, we crossed the upper end of the same remarkable Saraswati gorge whose lower end we had crossed on the way out. It ran for half a mile to the mouth of the Alaknanda Valley like a gigantic slit, and was but a few yards across at the top, while the river roared through, heard but not seen, two or three hundred feet beneath. The track crossed it here, as below, by a natural rock bridge and passing through the village of Mana we were presently in Badrinath and busy with letters and preparations for our next venture.

Part 4

The Second Crossing of the Watershed (Badrinath – Kedarnath)

CHAPTER THIRTEEN

TWO days' rest enabled us to explore Badrinath and its surroundings more fully. On our first view of the town itself we had been greatly disappointed as, upon breasting the last steep rise from Joshimath, our minds filled with the severe grandeur of the country through which we had passed, we looked down on a hideous huddle of tin huts and were grieved by the thoughtlessness of man in introducing such ugliness to the mountains. The roll on the drum, which welcomed all incoming pilgrims and had its length and loudness nicely adjusted to the stranger's probable generosity, was an added irritation and the temple itself did nothing to modify our first impressions. It was of no great height and so hemmed in by houses that little could be seen until close up to it, while even the façade, upon which there was some really fine carving, had a ramshackle appearance.

But on our second visit, when we viewed the temple from the far side of the river, we realised better the extraordinary atmosphere of the place and the lure that had drawn men to it throughout the ages. For at Badrinath, Krishna, probably the best beloved of all Hindu gods and one of nine incarnations of Vishnu (a tenth is expected in the future) was supposed to have "practiced austerities", as the saying goes. Since "he stood here for one hundred years on one foot, with arms aloft, subsisting on air, with his outer garments thrown off and his body emaciated and with veins swollen," and since but one of his exploits was to lift a huge mountain on one finger to shelter some milkmaids from the wrath of Indra, the god of the skies and rain, we felt that "austerities" was an understatement to say the least.

On the bank opposite the temple was a bathing pool fed by a hot spring, with steps leading down from it to the leaping, icy waters of the Alaknanda, where a ring-bolt was sunk in the rock so that the pilgrim might cling to it while undergoing his ceremonial bath. By this baptism and by worship by Badrinath a man might obtain whatever he desired and all sins of former births were cleansed if the deity was supplicated through the priest. A legend proving the efficacy of this relates how one Janami Jaya slew eighteen Brahmans (whether rivals for or guardians of the lady we are not told), in order to possess a beautiful girl whom he met out hunting. Even for this enormity a visit to Badrinath was sufficient atonement! When one remembers that the Rawal or priest here, and at Kedarnath and other important centres, is usually a Brahman from southern India of the Vaishnava sect, and that he is assisted by a secretary or clerk who is also from these parts, the above story seems all the more remarkable.

The origin of this custom of a Brahman priest seemed very remote, but apparently, at one time the ancient religion was supplanted by Buddhism until there arose the reformer, one Sankara, a native of Mysore. The century in which he lived is doubtful but is thought to be about the eighth A.D., and he was particularly active in Nepal and Kumaon, where he drove out the Buddhists and unbelievers and restored the ancient faith. He displaced the Buddhist priests of Badrinath and Kedarnath and in their places introduced priests from the Dhakin and Mysore. Everywhere through his followers he preached the efficacy of pilgrimage to the holy shrines, and there is no doubt that the consequent – and lasting – influx of orthodox pilgrims prevented Kumaon from a second relapse into Buddhism.

Brahmans, the priestly caste, are thus seen to be very powerful, but in many proverbial sayings the lower castes have published their defects. The most glaring seems to be an eye for the main chance, as hinted at in the saying: "Brahmans and vultures spy out corpses"; while in another instance we see a case of diamond cut diamond or two of a trade when we are told: "The Brahman blessed the barber and the barber showed his glass."

But these legends, if believed in and acted upon wholesale, might lead to results which would tax the forgiving powers of even the Badrinath deities, and to offset this there is another little story which inculcates more desirable conduct. A wealthy trader who had ten sons was told to go to Badrinath with his family and his property, there to give all his possessions to the Brahmans and to make his home, thus securing his admission to Paradise. But while living there his wife (who seemingly had her own views as to property) lost a valuable ivory ring, and the sages then told her that as penance for this duplicity in holding back a valuable article, the family must once more do the round of thc "tirthas" or places of pilgrimage. When this had been accomplished and they were back in Badrinath, the elephant whose tusk had provided the ivory for the ring suddenly appeared and conveyed the whole family at once to the paradise of Vishnu.

Of men brought up on such traditional tales, none who believed could resist the promises of desires fulfilled and past misdeeds forgotten, and at some period in their lives the majority of Hindus visit one or more of the holy shrines. Judging by the swarms of pilgrims met with on the road and in the town most of them had chosen Badrinath.

Among the many legends of these parts believed to have been founded on fact is a story that, many hundred years ago, there was no high priest of the

Kedarnath Temple, and that the high priest of Badrinath used to hold services in the temples of both places on the same day. The shortest known route between the two temples was well over one hundred miles, and over a high mountain pass at that. Tradition has it that a quick way across the watershed was known to the priests of those days. But although the natives believe that the two places are only two and a half miles apart, in actual fact, the distance is some twenty-four miles as the crow flies.

Our observations from the Bhagat Kharak had suggested to us that if a pass could be found from the head of the Satopanth, it would lead us into the Kedarnath Valley system. If this proved to be the case, we should stand very little chance of getting down on the other side, owing to the immense depth of the valley there. However, a view from the crest of the watershed would solve for us many interesting problems.

We had intended to return to the Rishi Ganga about August 10th, and August had already come round. But by now we were thoroughly absorbed in the manifold problems of this range, and to have come away without investigating the head of the Satopanth Glacier would have left our task only half finished.

We did not have the same difficulty as before in collecting men to accompany us, but on the morning of our departure, the porters, despite an early appearance, had neglected to have any food before they left their homes three miles away. Consequently we had to fume for a full hour while they made good this oversight – an unpropitious start!

A dense mantle of cloud still hung over the peaks, as we began to plod up the valley towards Mana and, remembering our little *contretemps* with the Bhasudhara River of a few weeks earlier, we kept this time to the southern bank of the Alaknanda. This provided us with only a narrow walking space under great perspiring, mossy cliffs, down whose black sides streamed a thousand tiny waterfalls, but luckily there was quite a presentable sheep track which allowed our attention to wander from the main business of getting along to the enjoyment of impressive scenery about us, and, a mile or so further on, the valley widened out and provided a stretch of moderately flat grass-land.

Suddenly, with a shout of joy, the Sherpas dumped down their loads and set to work collecting some small, light-blue berries which grew in great quantities amongst the grass. They brought us handfuls of these with great enthusiasm, saying that the berries were considered a delicacy in Sola Kombu, where they came from. On tasting them we found that they had a flavour remarkably like that of tooth-paste, and were certainly pleasanter to look upon than to eat.

At 3 o'clock we came to a small isolated wood of birch and rhododendron about half a mile below the snout of the glacier. We had seen this from the opposite side and had looked forward with relish to the luxury of a blazing camp-fire. But by now it had started to rain again and the locals were still a long way behind. Before we could get the tents pitched we were wet through. There was no dry wood at hand and it was an hour or so before we had sufficient fire to brew some tea, and that only by dint of continuous blowing on the part of

Kusang. The rain having cheated us out of a blissful lounge before blazing embers we retired to our leaky tents with an unpleasant foreboding of what was in store for us higher up.

Awakening to the song of birds and the exhilarating freshness of a perfect morning, our spirits rose and eclipsed the gloom of the night before. Our meal of satu and tea completed, we were content to sit and dry ourselves and our tents in the slanting rays of the morning sun.

It was with an effort that we packed up and started up the boulder-strewn valley. We found that the locals had spent the night in a nearby cave in company with some shepherds, who when we passed their shelter appeared to have not the least intention of stirring themselves for some time to come. What a delightfully carefree life they must lead, requiring nothing but the bare necessities of life, living always up in this wonderland of Nature, with little to worry about and nothing to hurry about; knowing nothing of the filth and squalor of our modern civilisation!

Shortly after leaving camp we came to the corner of the Satopanth Valley and turning half left we made our way along the grass slopes at the sides of the glacial moraine. The slackness of the morning remained with us and we made frequent halts to gaze up at the huge ice-clad precipices about us.

Soon we came in sight of the head of the glacier, still many miles away, and were able to get an uninterrupted view of the gap we hoped to cross. From now on little else interested us and we talked of nothing but the "col". Was it practicable even from this side? Where would it lead us? Back on to the great Gangotri Glacier? Or over the range to Kedarnath? We argued that point over and over again. I felt most convinced that if we succeeded in reaching its crest we would see a great snow-field descending gently before us, turning northwards and forming eventually the Gangotri ice-stream which we had reached a few weeks before. Tilman on the other hand held the other view, that the main Gangotri-Kedarnath watershed was to the north of us and that if we succeeded in crossing the gap we would find ourselves amongst the Kedarnath valleys. The discussion waxed heated in spite of Tilman's common-sense suggestion that we should wait and see.

As was the case on the Bhagat Kharak Glacier our chief concern now was how far we could go up the glacier before our supply of firewood ended. We could not expect the locals to spend a night above the limit of firewood, though we could transport sufficient for one night. So we had to aim at pitching our camp as near as possible at the upper limits of the dwarf juniper. As the valley ascended at a very gentle angle this line was by no means easy to gauge.

The going was easy and we made rapid progress, walking on the crest of a kindly lateral moraine which ran for miles down the southern end of the Satopanth Glacier.

Late in the day we came upon a lateral glacier flowing into the main ice-stream from the south. This glacier was fed almost entirely by ice-avalanches falling from the ice-cliffs of Nilkanta, and in the angle formed by the junction we found an alp whose attractions as a camp site were irresistible. So we spread ourselves out in the sun and basked until the chill of evening sent us to our sleeping-bags. Mine that night was squeezed in between two rocks, a position which was more suitable for contemplation of the infinite than for sleep.

The Mana shepherds occasionally brought their sheep far up these moraine-covered glaciers, and we came across a great many piles of stones hung with prayer flags as in Tibet. These prayer flags were simply bits of rag on which were written prayers. Each flap was supposed to emit one repetition of the prayer written thereon, and consequently on a windy day the hanger of a flag could get through many thousands of prayers in the course of a few hours.

(A similar, and, I should judge, a more effective praying-machine is the prayer-wheel which is commonly used in Tibet. This consists of a drum wrapped round with paper on which are written countless thousands of prayers. Each revolution of the drum emits one repetition of all the prayers written on it. The large prayer-wheels are worked by water power and must get through sufficient praying in one week to insure for each member of the village a high place in the hereafter.)

The going now became very rough as we had to cross a succession of side glaciers, each bringing down on its surface a perfect wilderness of boulders. This meant the usual wearisome performance. Toiling up a long slope of large stones balanced precariously on the ice, balancing along an edge above a yawning crevasse, jumping from a boulder or slithering down some icy slope beyond.

At about 2 o'clock on August 7th we reached a point at which the moraine-covered surface of the main glacier gave place to bare ice only half a mile or so from the cliffs which enclosed the Satopanth Glacier. Across the valley we recognized our old friend Kunaling*, from this side presenting a very much more formidable appearance.

We decided that this was the best point from which to launch our attack on the gap, and dismissing the Mana men, we pitched our tents just before a strong wind descended on us from across the ice.

Shortly after an ominous dawn on the following morning we shouldered our heavy loads and tramped slowly across the ice in the direction of the col.

It appeared to us that there was not much choice of route. A steep ice-fall descending direct from the col seemed to be the only way. The line of rock cliffs which bounded it on the left appeared far too steep in its lower section to offer much chance even of getting a footing on them from the glacier. The ice-fall did not look too difficult, though it was certainly very broken in its upper section. So it was towards the ice-fall that we turned.

Over the level stretch of ice we made quick time, but when the angle steepened up our heavy loads made themselves felt and the straps bit cruelly into our shoulders. It was a sultry, windless morning and we were oppressed by an intense lassitude. The ice was bare of snow and steps had to be chipped, though the angle was quite moderate. Our pace became painfully slow.

Soon the ice became broken and complicated, and we came to a section where climbing with a load on one's back was impossible. The leader had to cut steps up the rickety piece of ice and haul the loads after him. The section was only some thirty feet high, but it cost us a good hour to negotiate, and from here the climbing needed the utmost care and called for much step cutting.

*The peak referred to is probably Chaukhamba – the highest in the Gangotri area. (Editor)

However, it had the advantage of taking our minds off our sore shoulders and aching thighs.

We climbed steadily for some hours, making long detours to avoid crevasses and ice-cliffs and we were within a thousand feet of the crest of the gap when we were brought up by a yawning chasm whose bottom was lost to view, hundreds of feet down the icy depths below us. Dumping our loads, we hunted this way and that, but could find no place which offered the slightest chance of crossing this formidable obstacle.

This was a bitter disappointment. After all that weary toil we had but one thousand feet to go to learn the solution of the riddle which had been occupying our minds for so long.

We descended for a few hundred feet when it occurred to us that we might be able to find a way off the ice on to the upper part of the rock cliffs to the south. Dumping our loads once more, we worked our way over towards the edge of the ice-fall. Reaching it we saw that just below us was a point at which we could get on to the rocks immediately above the steep section below. We could not see how far the rocks would take us, but it was worth trying, and with fresh hope we returned to our loads and pitched camp in the midst of the tangled mass of the ice-fall.

By now it was snowing heavily, and our small tents soon resembled chips off the great ice-blocks which surrounded them. Night fell to the accompaniment of an almost continuous roar of ice-avalanches from the great cliffs of Kunaling above us, and into the early hours of the morning the thunder of falling ice continued. Though our position was quite safe, being well protected by the crevasses and ice-cliffs about us, several times during the night I was brought to a sitting position, trembling, as some particularly large avalanche fell close at hand.

Snow fell gently all the while, and was still falling when we awoke to a grey and unpromising dawn. In consequence of this we made a later start than we had intended. The tents were wet and the loads were heavier in consequence.

Through the mist we could see only a small section of the face of rock above us. Several of the gullies showed signs of recent stone falls and the rock was damp and slippery. When we reached it, however, we found that the angle was easier than it had appeared from below and we mounted at quite satisfactory speed, hurrying here and there when we were obliged to cross one or other of the stone-swept gullies.

Higher up the mist became really thick and we had to grope our way up the rock face – through the still gently-falling snow as if blind-fold.

On the previous day Tilman had fallen and injured another of his ribs, and climbing under such a heavy load as he was obliged to carry caused him considerable pain.

The route-finding now became complicated and we had to trust mainly to a sense of direction. Ridge, gully and rock-facet followed one another in monotonous series, until after a step round an awkward corner we found ourselves at the base of a blunt ice-ridge which we had seen from below.

Chipping small steps in the ice we mounted to the crest of the ridge. From here we caught a glimpse below us of the ice-fall in which we had camped. We followed the crest along until it landed us on what appeared to be a great ice-plateau. The mist was still thick about us and we could only guess at the direction to be followed. We plodded on for half an hour and then halted and pitched the tents.

Our height was 18,400 feet and we calculated that we must be just about on the crest of the col.

Snow was still falling lightly and a southerly wind was blowing. All five of us crowded into one of the tents and sat huddled up waiting for the Primus stove to melt some ice and heat the water sufficiently to make tea. But the Primus had sprung a leak somewhere and had to be pumped up continuously. We waited for two hours before the water was sufficiently warm to absorb any colour from the tea-leaves, and we began to realise that if we were to have a prolonged sojourn on the glaciers we would not have enough fuel for anything but the simple production of water.

That night we were content with a cup of tepid pemmican soup before we turned into our sleeping-bags. At dusk it started to freeze very hard and we became more hopeful about the weather.

Our cheerless camp had done nothing to damp our excitement at having reached the col, and we could hardly curb our impatience for the view which would tell us where the col was leading us.

I still held to the theory that we were at the mysterious head of the Gangotri Glacier. The level stretch of ice over which we had come seemed to indicate the head of a long, gently-flowing glacier. Shortly after dark there was a momentary clearing of the mists above us and we caught the sight of the great buttresses of Kunaling to north of us and those of another, unnamed peak to the south. But in front, a great sea of cloud still withheld from us the secret of our whereabouts.

I spent much of the long, cold night praying fervently for a fine morning, which the frost gave me good reason to expect.

I was disappointed, however, and when I looked out of the tent door at dawn it was into the same "pea-soup" as on the night before.

After a cup of warm satu, Tilman and I left the camp and started off in a south-westerly direction to reconnoitre.

The surface of snow we were on soon began to fall away in front of us in an ever steepening curve. Shortly after leaving camp we were jumping over and threading our way through a network of small crevasses, and we had not gone far before we were brought up short by a vertical drop of about one hundred and fifty feet. Beyond this a great tangle of ice-cliffs showed us that we were on the brink of an ice-fall.

It was useless to attempt to find a way through it with a visibility of only fifty yards, and we sat down on the edge of the cliff and waited. The outlook was pretty hopeless as the glacier was narrow at this point and the ice-cliffs seemed to stretch the whole width.

We had been waiting for half an hour when all of a sudden the fog rolled away from below us, and we found ourselves looking down into the immense depths of a cloud-filled valley at our feet. The glacier we were on descended in a steep ice-fall for about a thousand feet, then flattened out into a fairly level stretch of ice before it heeled over for its final colossal plunge into the gloom of the gorge six thousand feet below us.

This was obviously not the Gangotri ice-stream, which at its snout, some twenty miles from here, is 13,000 feet high. Tilman had been right and we were looking down into the Kedarnath Valley system, from the "pass" said to have been known to the ancient high priest of Badrinath.

Our little problem was solved, but the grim aspect of the ice-falls below us offered little hope for our succeeding in our project of finding a direct route between the two temples.

After some search we were able to trace a route through the first ice-fall. We hurried back to the camp, reaching it just as Angtharkay and Kusang were starting out to look for us, fearing that we might have come to grief in a crevasse.

Packing up the tents we shouldered our loads once more and made our way down towards the ice-fall. By now the clouds had enveloped us again and we had a difficult job to find the route we had traced through the maze of ice-cliffs and crevasses of which the ice-fall was made up.

In and out of great ice-corridors, past towers and turrets of all shapes and sizes, we worried our way; balancing across slender ice-bridges, which spanned gaping crevasses whose icy depths seemed illimitable; toiling up some bulge which obstructed our path and clinging our way down the slippery banks of its further side.

At length we found ourselves on the flat stretch of ice we had seen from above. Going to its further edge we halted for a few moments to gaze down upon the head of the second and very formidable ice-fall. It was appallingly steep, and for a long time we could not see any way of attacking it which offered the slightest hope of success.

Immediately in front was a sheer drop of some hundreds of feet to the head of the ice-fall itself.

After a careful examination it occurred to us that it might be possible to descend the ice-fall for some distance on its right-hand side, and then force a way off on to the cliffs which bounded it in that direction. Beyond this we could not see, but these cliffs appeared to fall away vertically to the valley still some five thousand feet below.

We worked over to the right and descended for some time before we were brought up by an impassable crevasse. Search as we would we could not find a way of descending a yard further or of reaching the rocks to our right; so very slowly we toiled our weary way back to the level section where we sat for some minutes sucking lumps of ice in vain attempt to assuage a burning thirst.

By this time the weather had cleared somewhat and as we made our way over to the left-hand side of the glacier we saw that by traversing along an ice ledge under some evil-looking seracs we might get down five hundred feet below the level section. Beyond this the glacier disappeared from view on account of the steepness of the angle.

We started to traverse below the seracs and the Sherpas as usual burst into their monotonous praying chant, evidently beseeching the demons of the ice world not to throw things at us.

Hurrying across the débris of a recent fall, we found ourselves at the brink of the glacier's final downward plunge. So steep was it indeed that we thought that we must be standing on the upper part of a hanging glacier.

We dumped our loads on the ice and set off down on what seemed to be an utterly futile errand. But it was the last chance, and we thought we might as well finally prove the thing to be impossible so as to be able, later, to find comfort in that fact. Also the Sherpas, for some reason, were almost frantically keen to get down, and would not admit that the thing could not be done. Whether this attitude of theirs was an outcome of their extreme loyalty to us, or whether they were taking a personal interest in the exploration I cannot say. But in any case it was typical of the fine spirit of these men that, from the time we had left the Satopanth Glacier, they seemed willing to go almost to any lengths to get over that pass. Their loyalty to the expedition did not cause them merely to carry out our instructions; they understood our aims and did everything in their power to see that we realised them.

With these allies we hope, one day, to reach the summit of Mount Everest; without them we would have little hope of doing so.

I have often found that towards the end of a long, tiring day's mountaineering one gets a sudden rejuvenation, particularly when faced with a problem of unusual severity . It was certainly the case this evening and we set about that ice-fall as if our lives depended upon our getting down.

The work was intricate and needed delicate handling as a slip would have had serious consequences. The further we advanced the steeper became the ice until further downward progress on the glacier itself became an impossiblity.

We worked our way over to the left until we came to the left-hand edge of the ice-fall. Standing on a small promontory we looked down a sheer drop of some two hundred feet into a steep gully which separated the ice-fall from the rock cliffs bounding it on that side. We saw that if we could reach the floor of the gully we might be able to work our way down between the ice and the rock. But the two-hundred foot drop at our feet appeared quite impossible. Tilman and I sat down feeling that we had reached the end of our tether.

But Pasang and Angtharkay refused to admit defeat and asked to be allowed to try the wall below us. We consented; and they roped up on a short rope and gave us an exhibition of calm, surefooted climbing whose equal it has rarely been my fortune to witness.

After some twenty minutes they were back with us admitting that the face below was too much even for them. But Angtharkay's blood was up and no sooner had he recovered his breath than he started traversing to the left and soon disappeared from view behind an ugly ice bulge.

Minutes passed as we waited with bated breath. Then, crash! a great chunk of ice hurtled down and smashed itself into a thousand pieces on the floor of the gully, sending up along the cliffs a rolling echo. I think my heart missed several beats before a shout from Angtharkay assured us that all was well. Presently his head appeared from behind the ice bulge, and we saw that his face wore a broad grin.

He informed us that he had found a ledge from which it might be possible to lower our loads and ourselves.

With this hope we raced up our steps back to the loads. It was beginning to get dark and we had yet to find a suitable camp site and get ourselves fixed for the night. To have attempted to get down into the gully that night would have been too much to expect of them. Also, lower down, the gully was overhung by some ice-cliffs and it would be dangerous to pass under these at any other time than the morning.

I spent most of the night tossing about our uncomfortable perch, though it was not so much the discomfort of my bed as excitement which kept me awake.

CHAPTER FOURTEEN

WE had decided not to bother about food or drink in the morning, and as soon as it was light we were packing up the tents and getting ready to start. It was a fine morning and for the first time we were able to get a view down into the valley we were making for, the upper part of which was now only two thousand feet below us.

A level stretch of glacier some three miles long ended in what looked like a pleasantly wooded valley. About a mile below the glacier there seemed to be a bit of a "cut-off", and below that dark vegetation stretched away as far as the eye could see. This we took to be pine forest, while far beneath we could see patches of light green interspersed amongst the forest.

Two days marching at the most, we thought, would take us through this pleasant looking country to some habitation. Also it seemed reasonable to suppose that we would strike a forest path or game track and be able to cover, if necessary, some twelves miles a day. We knew that it could be no very great distance from the snout of the glacier to the great Kedarnath pilgrim route.

Working along Angtharkay's ledge, clinging close to the cold clammy walls of glacier ice, we reached the little platform from which we were to lower ourselves and our kit. It was an unpleasant place, enclosed on all sides by walls of sickly green ice, and it required but the slightest slip to send one crashing into the depths below, while the most careful handling was needed to save the loads from a similar fate.

Pasang was lowered down into the gully and he stood there ready to receive the baggage. It was painful work. The rope, wet from contact with the snow on the previous day, was now frozen stiff and cut cruelly into our numb fingers.

It took us two hours of hard work before we were safely assembled on the floor of the gully, and it was with feelings of some relief that we turned our backs upon the scene of our labours.

Now the climbing became more straight-forward and for the first time since leaving the Satopanth Glacier we were able to dispense with the rope. Hurrying over the section threatened from above by the ice-cliffs we were soon able to break out of the gully to the left where the angle of the cliffs eased off about a thousand feet above the level stretch of glacier in the valley. This we managed to reach by means of an intricate zig-zag course down the intervening slopes.

After a few moments "breather" we raced down the glacier at top speed, leaping the crevasses in our stride. We were full of pleasant anticipation of a camp in some grassy meadow below the glacier. We were doomed to disappointment. For on leaving the glacier we found ourselves immersed in a tangle of sappy, green vegetation about eight feet high through which we had to hack our way. So thick was it, that we could not see where we were going and all we could do was to stumble on blindly.

We cleared a small space and sat down for a meal, after which we flogged our way on in the hope of finding a better camping place before nightfall. By now it had started raining and the contact with the sodden undergrowth soaked us to the skin. In addition to this the floor of the valley was made up of large boulders which were completely screened by the undergrowth, and at every few steps one stumbled into some pot-hole between the rocks. Brambles soon made their appearance and added to our difficulties.

Late in the evening, after some two hours of this work, we reached the edge of the great cut-off which we had seen from above. This proved to be a sheer drop of some one thousand two hundred feet in the floor of the valley. There was no time to look for a way down the gaunt crags and we had to make shift for the night. After an hour's work we had cleared a muddy space underneath a boulder and collected some sodden stumps of juniper with which to make a fire.

Squatting huddled up under the boulder which afforded scant protection from the rain, vainly trying to dry our sodden garments before the smouldering logs, we discussed our position. Our supply of food was beginning to run low and we had no idea how far we would have to go before we reached the first habitation where we could obtain more supplies with which to carry on. If the going had been good, there would have been little doubt that we could force our way through, however pressed we were for food. But our experience since leaving the glacier had given us an unpleasant taste of what we must expect lower down. The precipice below us might prove to be impassable or cost us much of our valuable time; and with time went food.

Again: what of the side-streams which we must meet further down the valley? By now we had considerable respect for this form of obstacle, which we knew could not only hold us up but completely block our way.

The only alternative was to struggle back up the ice-fall and over the pass back to Badrinath. The matter had to be decided here and now, for as it was, we would have to go all out to get back over the pass before our food and fuel ran out altogether.

The prospect of retracing our steps and committing ourselves once more to the icy slopes we had just left, did not appeal to us in the least. Moreover, the weather showed no signs of improvement and we might quite well be held up by a fall of new snow on the pass.

Starvation high up on the glacier, besides being more unpleasant, would be very much harder to fight against than it would be in a forest, where at least we would be able to make a fire. On the other hand, in going down we were taking a step into the unknown. The difficulties of the forest might easily take us some weeks to overcome, though, of course, we might strike some sort of a path tomorrow, or the next day. It was a difficult problem on which to make a decision, and we sat discussing it long into the night before retiring to our damp sleeping-bags.

On visualising the position over again I think undoubtedly the wisest plan would have been to go back up the ice, and several times during the week which followed, we sincerely wished we had done so. I am afraid that the fact that we wanted to make the complete crossing of this most intriguing range weighed too heavily on us all, and the downward course was decided upon.

The rain had stopped by the morning and we optimistically delayed our departure in order to get some of the water out of the tents and sleeping-bags. That this was a mere waste of time we were soon to realise. However, it gave us time to look around and decide on the best course of action for attacking our immediate problem, the descent of the thousand foot cut-off.

It was an impressive affair. The river, here of quite sizable dimensions, disappeared underground for a short distance above the bank of the precipice and issued forth in a great waterspout to crash down into the depths below. Owing to this we were able to get from one side of the valley to the other without difficulty and could choose either side down which to make our descent.

A short examination of the left-hand side of the valley convinced us that there was no practicable route to be found there, and so, striking camp, we committed ourselves to a search on the right-hand side. Here we fought our way for a quarter of a mile up and along the side of the valley and then began to descend. Clinging on to handfuls of matted undergrowth we clambered down, cursing our loads the while for their insistence on slipping sideways and often nearly dragging us down with them.

Soon we came to a vertical cliff whose rocky sides were too steep to hold any scrub, but whose cracks and crevices were filled with damp earth and moss. Balancing ourselves precariously above this we lowered Angtharkay, the lightest member of the party, on a rope, until he was able to get a footing on a grassy ledge below. Our loads followed in a similar manner. Then, tying two lengths of rope together and doubling them over a convenient juniper root, we slid down to join Angtharkay on his perch below.

Fortunately the side of the valley on which we were was made up of a series of terraces, which were not too widely separated from each other, and by repeating the process described above we eventually reached the densely forested floor of the valley.

Under the spread of the giant forest trees the undergrowth was not so thick and, walking for once in a normal attitude, we made fairly good progress until we reached the upper limit of bamboo. There, at least, was help against the exhaustion of our meagre food supply, and at 1 o'clock we called a halt and set about gathering a goodly quantity of the small soft cylinders which form the edible portion of the bamboo shoots. This, and the fact that lately we had not been battling through bramble scrub, put us in better spirits, and we almost forgot to call down curses on the rain which had by now started to fall again.

The bamboo was certainly our ally and was later to prove our salvation, but it was not an unmitigated blessing. Really dense bamboo provides an obstacle second only to thickly matted bramble, and when the valley narrowed and we were forced up on to its steep sides, the bamboo jungle reduced us once more to our weary hack, hacking of a way.

The almost impenetrable density of the jungle down by the river forced us to climb up the steep sides of the valley until we were about fifteen hundred feet above the stream. There we found ourselves in a zone of tall straight plants about nine feet high. The plants were crowned with a spray of most beautiful blue flowers, in shape rather like snapdragons. The growth was as dense as that of a good stand of corn, and, viewed from above, the general effect closely resembled a forest of English bluebells.

Through these lovely blue flowers we waded for three hours, each taking it in turns to go ahead and flog a path with our ice-axes.

Constantly throughout the day we came across fresh spoor which provided ample evidence that large numbers of bears inhabited the forest we were in. These animals, though not wantonly vindictive, possess very poor senses of sight and hearing and should one stumble upon them by accident they are liable to attack through sheer fright. The Sherpas were very alarmed at seeing the tracks of these beasts, and kept up a continuous shouting to give warning of our approach. They were very anxious too that the party should keep well together.

At about 5 o'clock the ground in front of us began to fall away steeply and, from the change in the tone of the river's roaring, we realised that we were approaching a sizeable side stream, coming down from the peaks of the Satopanth range. Pressing on through the forest we soon arrived at the edge of a ravine from whose unseen depths the thunder of a mighty torrent reached our ears. Looking up to the right we could see the turbulent white river booming its way down towards the gorge.

Here was a problem the seriousness of which we were not slow to recognise, for, if we could find no way of crossing the stream in front of us, we would be in a sorry plight, as now it was too late to think of a return across the pass by which we had come.

Going to the edge we examined the cliffs below us and saw at once that a direct descent into the ravine was out of the question. Moreover, even if we could get across thereabouts, it would be impossible to scale the sheer walls which formed the opposite side of the gorge.

Two alternatives were open to us. Either we could go down to the junction of this torrent with the main river, or we could follow the stream towards its source in the hope of being able to cross it higher up.

We could see that, above the junction, the stream issued from the confines of the ravine and ran for some twenty yards between moderately sloping banks before emptying itself into the main waterway. But here the stream was very broad and there appeared to be but small chance of bridging it at this point. On close scrutiny of the cliffs above the ravine, however, it seemed to us that there was one point where the opposing walls of rock met high above the level of the water.

At first I was sceptical about this and declared it to be an optical illusion produced by a bend in the river; for, although we had seen many such natural bridges during our travels in this amazing country, such formations are rare.

But after studying it for some minutes, I agreed with others that it was indeed a natural bridge.

To reach it, however, would involve a climb of some two thousand feet, over difficult ground, and we decided to pitch camp as soon as we found any water. This was not an easy matter and we had climbed a long way up towards the "bridge" before we came to a small trickling spring shortly before dark. We were lucky in finding a nice level space on which to camp, and, after pitching the tents and collecting a vast quantity of firewood, we settled down to an evening which for sheer enjoyment would take a lot of beating, despite the fact that five yards from the camp was a bear's lair. Luckily its recent occupant kept well clear of the vicinity during our occupation of the camp.

Growing close at hand we found small clumps of forest fungus, which the Sherpas declared to be edible. We collected a large quantity, but each piece was subjected to a searching scrutiny by Angtharkay, and, for some obscure reason, more than seventy-five per cent were rejected. However, in solidity they made up for what they lacked in taste, and, together with the bamboo shoots, the remainder provided us with a square meal. And this was more than welcome, for on unpacking our sacks we found that what remained of our satu was soaking wet and was rapidly going bad; this in spite of the fact that it had been carefully packed in canvas bags.

Indeed, by now almost all our kit was water-logged an we resigned ourselves to living in a state of perpetual wetness.

By now the rain had slackened, and after Kusang had blown the sodden logs for an hour or so we sat before a blazing fire. But though it blazed and needed no further encouragement, Kusang continued to blow late into the night. Tilman conjured up a pleasant picture when he remarked that should Kusang happen upon a house on fire, while others were fighting the flames, he would be unable to resist the tempation of blowing on them!

Lying on a soft, sodden bed of leaves we basked in the glow of the fire. Warm now and, for once, not hungry, we allowed our tobacco smoke to drug us into forgetfulness of the worry which had seemed so acute throughout the long day.

It is astonishing how quickly warmth and a well-satisfied belly will change one's outlook. We were too happy to question whether the bamboo and mushrooms would remain with us all the way along, or whether kindly nature had provided natural bridges over all the side streams which would cross our path. Considering that we had had the "cut-off" to negotiate that morning our estimated distance of a mile and a half did not seem bad. Later we came to look upon a mile and a half as good progresss for a day's labour! Meantime we lay peacefully in a half-doze, watching the firelight flickering on the great gnarled branches above us and making weird play with their shadows.

It was raining more heavily than usual when we shouldered our loads next morning and toiled on and up through the forest. Soon we came to dense bramble and began once more the tedious job of fighting our way through it. Our water-logged kit made our loads doubly heavy, weighing us down and causing us to overbalance as we bent and twisted to rid ourselves of the clinging thorns. Soon a dense mist descended upon us and we had to grope along the ever-steepening side of the nala with only a hazy notion of where we were going. Every now and then a steep-sided gully would bar the way and we would have to scramble up some hundreds of feet before we could find a place at which we could cross it.

After some hours of this, the mist cleared and we saw that we were near to the place where we thought we had seen the natural bridge spanning the gorge. Immediately we realised that we had been mistaken, and that the supposed "bridge" had indeed been an optical illusion!

Leaving our loads where we halted, we clambered on through the still heavily falling rain towards the stream. The rocks were steep and very slippery and we had to exercise extreme caution, for a slip would have deposited any one of us in the turbulent waters of the torrent some hundreds of feet below.

At length we reached a point from which we could command an uninterrupted view of the stream for some considerable distance above and below us. Below us the cliffs dropped sheer to the water's edge, while above, the river, descending in a series of waterfalls, did not permit the faintest hope either of fording or of bridging the stream.

We held a hurried consultation. Either we could go down to the junction in the small hope of bridging the torrent down there or we could work on upstream on the chance of finding better things above the point to which we could see. The Sherpas were very much against going down to the junction. On the other hand, to have gone up even to the spot to which we could see would have involved the best part of a day's climbing, and then what chance would we have had of finding a place to cross up there? Fording was out of the question and higher up we would find no trees with which to build a bridge. Much as I respected the judgment of the Sherpas, which in country of this sort had usually proved sounder than my own, at that moment I just could not face, on such a slender chance, the toil which the upward course would involve.

It was decided, therefore, that we should return to last night's camp site, leave our loads there, go down to the junction to examine the possibilities of bridging the stream, and return to the old camp for the night. This latter prospect was the one bright patch in a gloomy outlook.

We returned to our loads and made our way slowly back down the bramble-covered slopes, reaching our old camp at about 3.30. While Kusang blew upon the seemingly dead embers of the morning's fire we stood shivering in our soaking garments and reviewed our position. This certainly appeared unpleasant enough, for, if we failed to get across at the junction, two more days at least would be wasted before we could hope to find a way across on the higher route, and probably more, if indeed we could manage it at all. The work involved in getting along was heavy, and without food it would be well-nigh impossible.

At 4 o'clock, after swallowing some tepid tea, we raced off down towards the junction, leaving Kusang to build the fire and prepare a meal of the few bits of fungus which still grew near the camp. We were some eight hundred feet above the junction of the two rivers, but sliding down on the sodden carpet of leaves which formed the floor of the forest we reached it in a few minutes. That is to say we reached a point about a hundred feet above it, for the only way we could get down to the stream itself was by way of a steep gully. From a rock above we surveyed the stream as it issued from the mouth of the ravine. The water was obviously much above its normal level, and carried with it great quantities of mud. In the short stretch between the mouth of the ravine and the actual junction there was only one point which offered the slighest possibility of our constructing a bridge. There two rocks stood up well above the surging water, one close to either bank. If we could balance a tree trunk on these two rocks so that it lay across the stream, we could lay other trees diagonally across it and so make a sufficiently sound structure to enable us to cross. But from above, the rocks appeared much too far apart for us to be able to do this.

We climbed down the gully to the water's edge and, measuring the distance across roughly by means of a rope, we came to the conclusion that the thing must be attempted, then reascending the gully we selected some suitable pines which most luckily happened to be growing in small numbers hereabouts.

As it was growing dark we climbed the steep slope back to camp at a pace set by Pasang which left us with aching lungs and thudding hearts. And so we camped in exactly the same position as on the previous night, but with so much less food, considerably less confidence in our ability to cross the stream and with our sleeping-bags wetter than ever. As we ate our vegetarian meal, therefore, we lacked much of the content that had been with us twenty-four hours earlier.

The dawn of August 14th saw us sliding once more down the leafy slopes, albeit with more caution than previously by reason of our heavy packs. Dumping our loads at the water's edge, and noting thankfully that the stream was no more swollen than on the previous evening, we clambered back up the gully and set to work on the trees which we had marked the night before.

Pasang gave us a fine display with his kukri and after a few minutes the first tree crashed to the ground. Stripping it of its branches we dragged it to the edge and, heaving it to an upright position, tipped it into the gully, down which it crashed its way to the water's edge. Angtharkay and I then descended the gully to make the necessary preparations while the others worked above.

In a surprisingly short time three more trees had arrived at the edge of the stream and Tilman and the other Sherpas began to climb down the gully. Angtharkay and I were engaged in building a rock platform at the water's edge, when all at once there was a crash and looking up I saw a huge boulder hurtling down. The others seemed to be well to the side of the gully and I resumed my work thinking how lucky it was that they had not been lower down where the route lay in the actual floor of the gully.

A few moments later, chancing to look up, I saw Pasang leaning against one of the walls of the gully some way above me. His face was very pale and he was trembling. I scrambled up to him and found that the boulder had hit him a glancing blow on the left arm and left foot. It had even torn the lacing from his boot.

Helping him down to the foot of the gully I examined the damaged members. The arm, though temporarily useless to him seemed only to be badly bruised. His foot was very badly swollen and he could not move his toes. It looked as if one of the small bones on the top of the foot had been broken.

It was a nasty blow to us all, though I could not help being devoutly

1 Eric Shipton and H. W. Tilman leaving England for Nanda Devi in 1934.

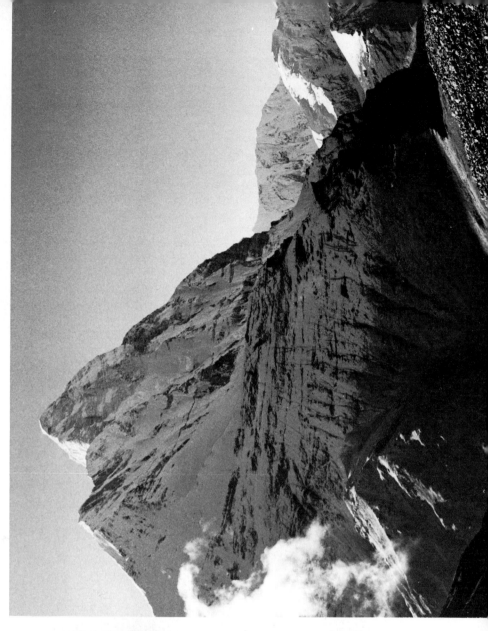

3 (right) Nanda Devi from the north. The cliffs of the southern rim of the Sanctuary can be seen on the right. *Photo: Hamish Brown*

4 (above) A difficult section on the path through the Upper Rishi Gorge.

(above left) Peaks on
eastern rim of the
ctuary – l to r:
Damla, Bamchu
Sakram (with
minent ice-ridge)
to: Hamish Brown

below left) The
0 ft. cliffs on the
hern flanks of the
Peak of Nanda Devi.

above) Peaks ringing
northern end of the
ctuary seen from
h of Trisul –
ngabang, Kalanka,
deol and Pt 6992, the
r peak was
mpted twice by
ton and Tilman.

bottom right) The
der camp in the
boo forest –
ng, Angtharkay
Pasang are
aring a meal of
rooms and bamboo
ts.

The 1937 Shaksgam Expedition

Preparations at Srinagar

10 (top left) Shipton consulting with Sir Peter and Lady Clutterbuck.

11 (centre left) Shipton, Lady Clutterbuck, Spender and Tilman enjoying afternoon tea.

12 (lower left) Preparing pack animals at the Woyil Bridge.

13 (right) The Uli Biaho Tower from the Trango Glacier – a celebrated photograph that first appeared in *Upon That Mountain* and inspired later generations of climbers.

14 15 Two views of the Sarpo Laggo Pass with the porters nearing the highest point, where most of them dumped their loads and returned to the valley.

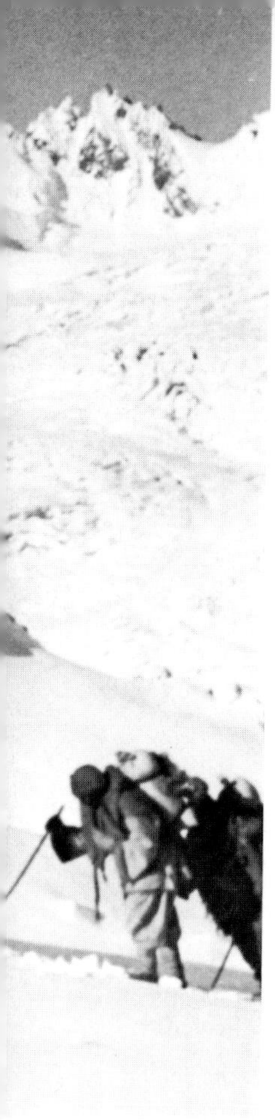

16 (above) A rock peak near the head of the Trango Glacier.

17 (below) The expedition base camp near the Shaksgam Valley.

18 19 In the Aghil Range: looking back up the Shaksgam Valley from the Aghil Pass (above); in the Surukwat Valley (below). *Photos: Kurt Diemberger/Julie Tullis*

20 (right) The North Face of K2 from the K2 Glacier.

21 (above) The North Face of the 'The Fangs' (Skamri Peaks) from the Skamri (Crevasse) Glacier.

22 (below left) Skyang Kangri from a 21,000 ft. peak north of K2. 23 (below right) The head of the Crevasse Glacier. The Ogre can be

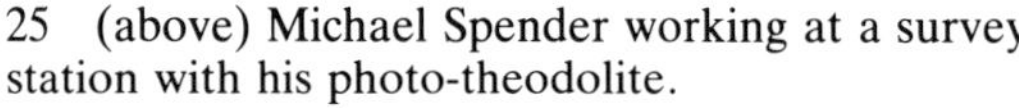

25 (above) Michael Spender working at a survey station with his photo-theodolite.

26 (top right) A view south-west from a spur above the Nobande Sobande Glacier. The Latok Peaks and The Ogre (right) dominate the sky-line.

27 (bottom right) The South Face of 'The Fangs' from the Drenmang Glacier – curiously reminiscent of the northern flank (see photo 21)

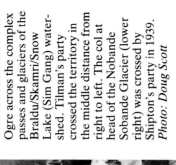

28 (left) A view from the summit of The Ogre across the complex passes and glaciers of the Braldu/Skamri/Snow Lake (Sim Gang) watershed. Tilman's party crossed the territory in the middle distance from right to left. The col at head of the Nobande Sobande Glacier (lower right) was crossed by Shipton's party in 1939. *Photo: Doug Scott*

29 (far left) A peak on the Snow Lake/Braldu watershed.

30 (near left) Sen Tensing and Ila heading west across Snow Lake.

thankful for his lucky escape, for had he been a foot or two further on the boulder would have hit his head and would have crushed it like an egg; for the rock weighed a good two hundred-weight.

After treating Pasang's wounds as best we might we set to work once more on our task of bridging the stream. We tied the end of a climbing rope round the top of the longest tree trunk, and placing its butt on the rock platform we had built, we heaved it up to a vertical position. Then taking careful aim we let it fall out across the stream. The top of the log hit the rock on the other side and bounded off into the stream to be swept off by the current. Hanging on to the rope for all we were worth we played it into the side.

Having strengthened the structure of the rock platform, we repeated the process with a similar result, but at the third essay the tip of the log remained balance precariously on the slimy edge of the rock opposite us. We then placed another shorter pole diagonally across the first. This scarcely reached the rocks on the other side.

On this flimsy structure Tilman, with a rope fastened to his waist, started to balance across the raging torrent. We stood watching him with bated breath as, inch by inch, he crept along the swaying poles. It was obvious that he *must* not either slip or upset the balance of the poles, while the further he went the more difficult was his task owing to the thinning of the tree trunks towards the top and the consequently greater sag of the poles. But at length, with what looked like a cross between a leap and a fall, he landed on the other side. We sent up a cheer which was drowned by the roar of the river.

After Tilman had performed this feat the rest was easy, and with all four poles laid across and lashed together with strips of bark, and a rope stretched across as a hand rail we had a bridge over which we could transport the loads without further difficulty. It was now about 10.30 a.m. and we halted for about half an hour on the further side of the river, partly to give Pasang more time to recover from his shock and partly to distribute his load between us. Of course Kusang and Angtharkay insisted upon adding the lion's share of Pasang's load to their own, which made their packs of water-sodden gear quite enormous.

We followed the bank of the main stream down for a few hundred yards and were then forced by cliffs to climb high up into the forest. Here the going was very bad indeed. The side of the valley was exceedingly steep and we had to hang on to the undergrowth above to prevent ourselves sliding down into the undergrowth below while we hacked our way through. At times it took us as much as an hour to cover twenty-five yards.

At first I went ahead with the kukri in order to cut a passage through. It was gruelling work and my shoulders, already burdened by my load, began to ache fiercely. We soon found that except in a few places we could get along faster without the cutting.

The rain was coming down in torrents, but (while on the march) except for making our loads heavier, it could no longer increase our discomfort.

At about 3 o'clock a small side stream, which had cut deeply into the side of the valley, caused us some trouble and by 4.30 p.m., being by a small spring of water, we decided that we had had enough and began to prepare for the night.

This was no easy job. There was no place level enough to pitch a tent on, and we had to dig with an ice-axe into the slope for a long time before we could construct a suitable platform. In the pouring rain it was out of the question to make a fire in the open. Here again the woodcraft of the Sherpas was equal to the occasion. Cutting great quantities of bamboo they set to work to construct a shelter under which to make a fire.

These various jobs kept us busy and warm until dusk. Meanwhile poor Pasang sat huddled under the lee of a tree-stump, shivering with cold – the picture of misery. And small wonder, for his struggle with the undergrowth on that steep slope must have been cruel, and now he was incapable of lending a useful hand.

At length, the shelter finished, we huddled under its scant protection. With numbed fingers (we were still at an altitude of 9,500 feet) we struck match after match. (It was fortunate that we had got a good supply of these stored away in sheep-skin gloves!) In this manner we had got rid of two boxes and had started on the third before we succeeded in lighting a piece of rag steeped in paraffin. Once this was accomplished we soon had a fire going. We found that dead bamboo, however wet it may be, catches fire very easily and makes most excellent kindling. Indeed, without it, in such rain as we were experiencing it would have been impossible to light a fire at all. Thus the bamboo plant was providing us with house, fire and food; and without it our lot would have been a sorry one indeed.

Stripping ourselves of our sodden garments we lay naked before the fire while boiling a large pot full of shoot. With a modicum of "ghee" added after the water had been drained off, these were served and eaten as one would eat asparagus. Indeed Tilman's imaginative palate detected some slight resemblance to that delicacy. Unfortunately we had found no more fungus, and our meal failed sadly to satisfy our all too robust appetites.

It had been the busiest day of a hectic week, and I fell asleep without much difficulty only to be roused by Tilman in what seemed a few moments to find it daylight once more.

CHAPTER FIFTEEN

SO tired were we that the morning was already well advanced before we woke. Hurriedly packing our loads, we left our lonely little shelter to engage once more in fierce strife with the tangled vegetation. While amongst big trees the undergrowth was fairly sparse, but where the trees were small of spread or few and far between, there did the brambles grow in profusion, their large thorns clinging and tearing at our clothes, hands and faces as we kicked, flogged and pushed our way through them.

Here and there the valley was broken and rocky. Such a place could provide a formidable obstacle, for, fighting one's way along, one would be brought up suddenly at the edge of a cliff and a long weary ascent would have to be made before a way was found round it. Further on maybe, one would fall into one of many booby-traps in the form of a deep pit filled with bramble and thus disguised better than any man-made game trap. Down one would crash for ten or fifteen feet with load on top.

But it was the gullies which we came to dread most, for here, on account of some old land slip, or the rocky bed of an ancient stream, there were no trees to keep the lesser vegetation in check, and the brambles ran riot.

There was very little variety. At first, struggling to the crest of a ridge full of hope of better things "round the corner", we felt disappointed when we saw before us yet "another —— gully!" Later we got resigned to it and accepted what came without comment.

Five hundred feet up we went and then five hundred feet down; now to avoid some impassable cut-off, now in the hope of better going above or below as the case might be. Generally speaking we kept between fifteen hundred and two thousand feet above the river.

At 1 o'clock we made a brief halt and at 3 o'clock we came to the edge of a steep lateral valley. Through the falling rain we could see two moderate-sized streams coming down the valley in a series of waterfalls, and uniting just before they flowed into the main river far below. Separating the two streams was a high ridge.

Scrambling down a steep slope we reached the first stream and, crossing it without much difficulty, we climbed the ridge beyond. For some while we could see no way of crossing the second stream. The water was coming down with tremendous force and the bank beyond rose in an unbroken line of slimy cliff.

Following the ridge along, however, we soon came to a place where a large tree trunk spanned the torrent. In order to reach this we had to prop a small pine up against it, and clamber up this improvised ladder until we could swing ourselves on to the broad back of the giant – no easy task with our loads.

The further side of the valley provided a steep climb at the top of which, for the first time in some days, we found ourselves on a stretch of level ground. Moreover, owing to the gigantic spread of the branches overhead there was little or no undergrowth. It was now 5.30 p.m. and the temptation to spend the night in this delectable spot was too great. The only snag was the lack of a stream. This difficulty was overcome by spreading the tents on the ground and it was not long before we had sufficient water for our modest culinary needs. During the whole of our sojourn in the forest the torrential rain hardly ever slackened.

The net result of our day's labours in actual distance we reckoned to be one mile. Our altitude was now about 10,000 feet. We had two reasons for keeping so high: one, the fact that the valley was steeper and more broken nearer the river, or so it had seemed from our distant views; two, our fear of getting out of the bamboo zone. (On most tropical mountain ranges there is a narrow belt of altitude where bamboo grows in the forest.) If the bamboo were to fail us our plight would be serious indeed.

An entry in my brief diary for this day is fairly representative of the tone of the rest and runs: ". . . Pasang is no better. The job is becoming very tedious;

always wet, not enough food, and can't see where the —— we are going. . . ."

Pasang was bearing his lot with great courage. He was hard put to keep up with us, even though he was carrying no load, and the frequent stumbles into pot-holes must have caused him agony.

The procedure on this evening was the same as before and we had a difficult task to get our various jobs done before nightfall. There was water to collect, firewood to gather and cut and the shelter to build before we could light a fire, strip off our clinging garments and huddle round its insufficient heat.

The level stretch on which we camped enabled us to make good progress next morning for a bare two hundred yards, before we plunged once more into a gully where the going was worse than any we had struck so far. For two hours we made hardly any progress at all, and when we had succeeded in forcing our way across that gully we found ourselves in another almost as bad as the first. At 1 o'clock we halted for a quarter of an hour on the crest of a ridge. Looking back we caught a glimpse through the rain-mist of the ridge where we had camped the night before – about one-third of a mile away. Late in the afternoon we came to a cliff of open rock up which we had to climb in order to continue our traverse along the side of the valley. In two places the climbing was too difficult to be done with loads and these had to be left behind to be hauled up after us.

The weather cleared slightly and from the top of the crag we got our first real view down the valley. A mile away we saw two large patches of grass-land, a strangely welcome sight. We saw too that we were about to descend into a side valley from the bottom of which the boom of a river reached our ears.

We had dropped a good thousand feet before we reached the water, and at about 5.30 p.m. we started looking for a camp site. Presently we espied a large overhanging rock which would provide us with shelter and an ideal place to camp. We were some ten yards from it when a large black bear emerged from the darkness of the cave. Angtharkay, who was in front, dropped his load and made as if to run for it. But the bear was in an even greater hurry and ambled off into the forest without a sound. However, we had to alter our ideas of a camp site for the Sherpas refused to remain in the vicinity of the cave.

That evening we found that the bears were our rivals, not only in the selection of suitable camp sites, but for that all important commodity, the bamboo shoot. Wherever we went we found that the bears had been there before us and ravished the supplies. We had to search far and wide before we could collect enough even for a frugal meal.

Nevertheless, it was in a more cheerful frame of mind that we sat before the blazing furnace which Pasang had made. This, I think, was wholly due to the fact that for once we were not being rained upon and could hang our things before the fire to dry. For it had been a long hard day and we had no reason to be pleased with our progress. We decided that if we did not strike something soon we would have to leave our loads behind and push on without them.

The next morning the stream provided us with no small problem until we found another friendly tree trunk spanning it. The going now became decidedly better and we made such excellent headway that by midday we had reached the first of the two patches of open grass-land. The grass was thick and tall, but, oh! what a relief to emerge for a while from the oppression of the forest. Rain had fallen early as usual, but now it stopped for a space and we actually saw an anæmic sun appear. Perched upon a rock we basked awhile in the feeble rays.

Our respite was short-lived and being forced down again into the forest we found ourselves once more immersed in bramble, the rain falling more heavily than ever.

At 3.30 p.m. we came to a cave which bore the signs of previous human habitation, and hunting about, the Sherpas declared that they had found a track. This latter proved to be a mere figment of the imagination however, though the evidence in the cave certainly made things seem more hopeful.

We continued on our way until 5.45 p.m. and arriving at a small stream decided to halt for the night. By now the bamboo was very scarce and, search as we could, we could find no more than a few pieces for our supper. Darkness fell before we were prepared for it and we passed an uncomfortable night in a small cave high up in the face of a small crag.

The next morning was a most unpleasant one. The going was just as bad as it had ever been and I began to experience that nasty feeling of faintness caused by hunger and heavy work together. So it went on, hour after hour, in and out of those pitiless gullies, flogging every inch of the way.

At 1 o'clock, suddenly, dramatically and without warning, came relief from our worries.

We had found our tedious way across a gully, resembling in appearance many of its fellows, and clambering up a steep slope had breasted the ridge beyond. The point marked a slight bend in the main valley. In front of us stretched an open grassy hillside. A mile down the valley on the opposite side we saw two fields of standing crops. Leading from these down to the water's edge was a path, ample evidence that the village from which the fields were worked was on our side of the valley.

At first we could not believe our eyes, then with one accord we gave expression to our feelings of joy and relief with a prolonged and lusty cheer.

Two hundred yards beyond the fields a large river joined the one which we had followed for the last week. This we knew to be the Madmaheswa in whose valley was the remote Hindu temple of that name.

Even Pasang's foot seemed to have recovered somewhat as we sped joyously along the steep grass slopes. For two hours we kept up a breathless pace when, mounting a spur beyond, we saw far below us a tiny hamlet consisting of some four oblong buildings. When we first spied it we felt like castaways who had at last sighted land. The Sherpas were if anything more relieved than we were, for it was only in the last day or two that the unpleasant possibilities of our position had begun to dawn on them. It was a suitable moment for an oration on our part, but all Tilman could say, mindful evidently of late descents into some Lakeland dale, was "We shall be down in time for tea"; while I merely stuttered: "Thank heaven for that!" We hurried on rejoicing, the Sherpas yelling with delight when we met a herd of cows, and so frightening the man in charge of them that he took to his heels.

There were but three houses in the village and, when we arrived, only two old women out of whom we could get nothing but a cucumber. It was still raining hard so we billeted ourselves in a barn which some goats kindly vacated for us, and waited on events. Presently a greybeard appeared with some apricots which went the way of the cucumber, and when we had got it into his head that we wanted some real food, he brought along some flour. He was not slow to realise how sore was our need, for only after prolonged haggling did we get four pounds of it in exchange for an empty bottle and one rupee; the bottle representing the actual price, and the rupee a souvenir of the occasion, for it would be of no use to him.

We slept well that night, unmindful of bugs and fleas, but we paid dearly for it as many days elapsed before the last flea evacuated our sleeping-bags.

It was pleasant to be once more on a track, but as we got down the valley villages became more numerous and tracks led in all directions. We kept getting off our road and none of the villagers seemed anxious to put us right. At 5 o'clock we were still three long miles from the place we were making for and, as usual, were drenched to the skin, so at the next village we parked ourselves in the one dry spot under a balcony, and started a fire.

Our reception here was frigid, and the woman of the house flatly refused us the use of an empty room which opened off where we were sitting, and added insult to injury by ostentatiously locking the door. The Sherpas got annoyed at this lack of hospitality, and Pasang had to be restrained from coming to blows with some of the villagers who had gathered to hear the old lady's apparently vivid description of our manners and appearance. But after peace had been restored the owner of a nearby house took pity on us, and offered us the use of his balcony where we had a comfortable night.

As no one was robbed during the night the atmosphere next morning was more friendly, and we opened negotiations for two men to accompany us as porters for we were tired of losing our way, and still more tired of carrying heavy loads. Their indecision would have been amusing had it not been so annoying, for we were impatient to start. After a long wrangle over rates of pay and finally seeming agreement, the men would calmly announce they were not coming, and the whole business started over again. Patience was at last rewarded, and two of the more enterprising recklessly consented to cast in their lot with us for at least one day.

By the time we reached Kalimath, the place we had hoped to reach the day before, it was raining harder than ever and even the inhabitants were heard to complain of the weather. We had now got to something more than a village; there was a temple and, at that moment of more interest to us, a shop. Sheepskins were spread for us and tea made, and hoping for a few luxuries we held an informal stock-taking. First we got hold of some almonds which were good, and then we found some jaggary (lumps of raw sugar), excellent if one was not averse to eating one's obligatory peck of dirt at one sitting. We had been without sugar for a week so we bought two pounds of it, and Tilman, who suffered from a sweet tooth, seized the biggest lump. After only a couple of bites he rose hastily, and showing all the symptoms of violent nausea rushed outside – he had eaten a piece of soap! After this we were more careful but it was difficult to distinguish the soap from the sugar without biting it.

Late that afternoon we got on to the "Pilgrim Road" leading to Kedarnath and were greatly tempted to turn in that direction, but we had already spent too long on this journey and, turning our backs on it regretfully, we headed south. A long day ended at Okhimath where there was a hospital, a bazaar, and an important temple. As usual now, food was uppermost in our minds and we made straight for the bazaar to get the taste of soap out of our mouths. While sitting there the doctor and the clerk of the temple (a Madrassi) came along and took us over to it. Here we were given tea, a room and beds were prepared for us, and the clerk lent us some of his clothes, as of course all our kit was still wringing wet. Meanwhile he and the doctor plied us with questions about our journey, the news of which had apparently gone before us, and were eager to hear about this legendary pass to Badrinath, the crossing of which had invested our party with some merit, the temple authorities treating us as honoured guests, and the doctor doing what he could for Pasang's foot which was still giving him considerable pain.

The temple buildings were arranged round a courtyard in which stood the shrine, and our room opened off this yard. It served the purpose of the village green and was full of gossipping men and playing children, who with one accord adjourned to our room to have a look, filling it to overflowing. It was several hours before they left us to ourselves.

Our quarters were all that could be wished, but the temple precincts were a bit noisy at night what with praying and ringing of bells, and the dawn of another day was heralded (we thought prematurely) by rolling of drums. When it came to making a start our local men refused to go any further and we had to send out for volunteers. The first to answer the call blenched visibly at the sight of the heavy load which Angtharkay had thoughtfully got ready for him, and incontinently fled. At last we persuaded a sturdy, cheerful little man with an alarmingly large goitre to come with us, and our kind host saw us several miles on our way.

As we were toiling up the long ascent to the village which was our next stage, we had a very pleasant meeting with an old native officer who was going up to Kedarnath with his family. He and Tilman exchanged reminiscences about the War and Neuve Chapelle (the mud and wet had left more impression on him than the bullets), and his fine, open manner and obvious pleasure at our success were very charming. The village was grandly situated only a few hundred feet below a ten thousand foot pass, but the bad weather we were still experiencing deprived us of a view back to the Kedarnath peaks which we much wanted to see.

Five miles of descent through forests of oak and sycamore brought us to a small village where we joined a group of returning dandy-bearers who were sitting round the hut of the village milkman and baker. We got this worthy to boil us up a great bowl of flour, milk, and sugar, and the result was a fine, filling batter pudding. Fortunately the road was still downhill and with this weighty cargo on board we were hard put to check our momentum.

That evening a very violent storm made the thought of our tent so unalluring that we prepared to risk a pilgrim doss-house. Just as we were settling down, one having authority came along and opened for us the Dharmsala, a sort of village meeting-hall. He was an ex-havildar of the Garhwal Rifles with eight years war service, who besides making us comfortable insisted on bringing us presents of milk, ghee, rice, and pickled mangoes.

Our cash resources now began to worry us considerably. A whip round amongst the five of us produced exactly seven rupees and we still had to buy food for the four remaining days to Joshimath, so it was clear we should have to eschew luxuries. We might have raised the wind by becoming strolling players, for Kusang could juggle with three stones and Tilman and I had a varied repertoire of hymns, but on the whole we thought it would be more dignified to try what our credit would do at Chamoli, the first important place we came to on the "Pilgrim Road". Arrived there we went to the postmaster, who having communicated on the "buzzer" with his colleague at Joshimath, readily advanced us some money.

Chamoli is under four thousand feet above the sea and the heat is almost tropical; after dinner that night we sat outside the bungalow in long chairs talking with the Tahsildar, a local magistrate. He was very interested in Yog and pronounced the theory that Christ, many years of whose life are unaccounted for, had spent part of this time in India studying Yog.

At our next stopping place, Pipalkoti, there was a little stone-paved square in the centre of the village, and round this the bazaar was ranged. While waiting for our men we sat here with one of the shopkeepers discussing tea and politics. The all-important question for him was not Dominion Status but whether Pipalkoti should have its post office back or not, and he showed a touching faith in our power and influence as Englishmen to right all wrongs. Apparently through some delinquency on the part of the postmaster, the village had been deprived of its post office, which was now placed in a much smaller village three miles away. Our public-spirited friend had been battling manfully to restore the lost prestige of his village, as a file of letters a foot thick well showed; and though we could afford him only sympathy he was determined to spill his last drop of ink in the cause.

On the last march to Josimath we had an interesting encounter with the young Prince of Nepal who was returning from a pilgrimage to Badrinath. He was a boy of about ten, spoke very good English, and was travelling on foot. Unfortunately our Sherpas were a long way behind so that we missed seeing what took place at the meeting of a Prince and his subjects.

And so on August 26th, once more to Joshimath to get ready for our final campaign.

Part 5

The Second Nanda Devi Venture

CHAPTER SIXTEEN

On August 27th we began hurried preparations for our second Nanda Devi venture. We had, by good fortune and the experience of those who had gone before us, met with far more success than we had deserved in the first penetration of the basin which I have already described. But, greatly interested as we were in the Badrinath Kedarnath topography, the major task of exploring the Nanda Devi Basin was yet unfinished.

Now that the monsoon had abated somewhat there was no time to waste and Angtharkay was despatched with instructions to recruit fifteen men from the Mana Valley and to return with them as soon as possible. Meanwhile we were busy working out our ration lists, collecting food, packing up and planning our last little campaign.

Pasang's foot was by no means healed, and I expressed some doubt as to whether we would be able to take him with us. But the mere suggestion that he should be left behind hurt him so desperately that I had not the heart to insist and weakly agreed that, as it was two weeks since the accident and he was no longer feeling pain, he could come along.

The rest of the party, although there was much work to be done, were glad enough of the respite from marching, and a newly arrived batch of letters and papers provided Tilman and myself with a certain amount of recreation, although through these we learnt for the first time and with profound sadness of the terrible disaster which had overtaken the German expedition to Nanga Parbat early in July, when four Europeans had perished together with six of our gallant Sherpa comrades from the 1933 Everest expedition. We thought it wiser to keep this news from our three men, and it was an unpleasant ordeal when, some six weeks later, we broke it to them, for nowhere can be found a more warm-hearted friendship than amongst these great little men of the Himalaya.

Late on the night of August 29th Angtharkay arrived with as tough a squad of men as we could have wished for, amongst whom I recognised several whose aquaintance I had made on the Kamet expedition in 1931. He brought too kind messages of congratulation from His Holiness the Rawal and other of our friends in Badrinath. We were particularly gratified to receive a message from "Master" Ram Serikh Singh who, on hearing of Angtharkay's arrival had rushed down from his camp in the lovely valley below Nikanta to hear our news. Later I had the pleasure of receiving a long and charming letter from him in the course of which he says: " . . . When you and Tilman Sahib started from Badrinath to explore the Badri-Kedar snowy ranges the rains began to fall, and they were not only heavy but record rains. I have never experienced such heavy and continuous rain for the several years of my residence in this part of the Himalaya. I was expecting you to return without success. When nothing was heard of you I expected that both you and your porters must have perished in the snow. They were anxious days for me. But when I received your letter in my camp from Joshimath with the news of your unique success I hurried down to Badrinath to send a message of my heartfelt congratulations to you and Tilman Sahib . . ."

We managed to get away just before noon the following day. The weather was bad and we experienced heavy rain as we marched once more up the Dhaoli Valley. After our recent experiences we were anxious about our food supply getting wet. As usual it consisted mainly of flour in the form either of ata or satu. At Tapoban, where we spent that night, we came across a thermal spring. Near its source the water was so hot that one could hardly bear to immerse one's hand. The Sherpas have very great faith in the benefits to be derived from these springs and even Pasang was persuaded, contrary to his Tibetan custom, to have a bath.

Our next day's march took us to Lata, where we billeted in an ancient barn, innocent of roof. We hoped that we would now be able to obtain some food from the inhabitants so as not to have to broach our new stores until we were well on our way; however, as usual, nothing very substantial was forthcoming. Two cucumbers and some potatoes were brought to us by an old woman. When we asked her how much she wanted for them she burst into tears and replied that as her child had recently died she would rather that we did not pay her. We failed to see the connection, but could not induce her to take any money. However, a gift of matches so delighted her that she seemed to forget her late bereavement. An old man actually brought three eggs for which he demanded eight annas (9d.) each. We told him that we could not possibly pay such a ridiculous price, but when he started to go away with the eggs I panicked and gave him the money without further discussion. At that moment an egg seemed an almost priceless luxury.

We were told that at Tolma rice was obtainable, and Kusang volunteered to start very early next morning and go with one of the Mana men to purchase the rice and catch up the rest of us in the evening by taking a short cut from Tolma. We agreed to buy the rice on condition that there were no complaints later about the weight of the loads.

The weather was fine during the morning and we had a most pleasant march along a well-defined path amongst the tall sombre pines of the forest through which we had raced exactly two months before. Now we were not spurred on by the pangs of hunger and we were going uphill instead of down; so we had time to linger in the shady glades of the lovely, open forest. It was a long pull up however as Lata was under 7,500 feet and the little alp of Lata Kharak which we were making for was nearly 13,000 feet.

We pitched camp at the upper limits of the forest just in time to bundle the loads of food inside the tents as a heavy rain storm burst upon us. But it did not last long, and after it had cleared away we collected great masses of rhododendron firewood, and were soon sitting round blazing fires, I for my part lost in wonder at the sight of the ranges across the valley, flooded in that unbelievable blue light which occasionally follows a heavy evening shower in the hills. From far down in the forest there came a faint shout which was at once answered by the full strength of the party, after which the job of guiding the wanderers was taken in turn and shrill whistles broke the silence of the forest at intervals of a minute or so. Kusang and his companion eventually turned up long after dark and after what must have been a very hard day. They had secured a maund (80 lbs.) of rice, the arrival of which was greeted with great jubilation.

The rain came on again and continued to fall throughout the night, with the result that we had some difficulty in getting the men started next morning and did not leave before 9 o'clock. By then the rain had stopped but a damp mist enveloped the mountain side and a cold wind beat in our faces. This seemed to have a good effect on the coolies, who displayed a remarkable turn of speed. We managed to hit off the sheep-track which led us once again over the scene of the exhausting labours of our first visit in May. It was interesting to pick out old landmarks – here a ridge to reach which had cost us half a day of weary flogging; there a gully into which we had floundered up to our armpits. Now we were swinging along a well-defined path at the rate of miles an hour. We passed a short way above our old bivouac place, and pointed out to the Bhotias the little platform on which we had passed the night; how different it looked from that little island of rock which we remembered so well!

When still in thick mist we reached the Durashi Pass, the Sherpas, led by Kusang, insisted on building an enormous cairn for old times sake. On this they deposited various tattered garments which had hitherto clung miraculously to their bodies. Pasang sacrificed his hat in order to create a huge joke by placing it on top of the edifice and leaving it there. I think he would have abandoned his boots if he had thought that it would make a better jest!

The Bhotias were mightily impressed by the sheep-track which ran from here across the face of the cliffs to Durashi, as indeed anyone must be who sees it for the first time. We found some juniper growing in some of the steep gullies, and remembering the scarcity of firewood at Durashi we gathered great quantities so that the party resembled a small army of itinerant bushes. When we reached the alp, we found that a new lot of shepherds had taken the place of those we had met before. With their tall, strong frames, flowing hair and handsome, weather-beaten features, their appearance harmonised wonderfully with the prodigious splendour of their surroundings. They told us that the weather was becoming too cold for their flocks and that they were starting their retreat to the Dhaoli Valley on the following day. This retreat must have meant a long anxious job for them, as most of the new-born lambs were still too small to walk far, and there were hundreds of these little creatures to be carried over the difficult ground which led to the Durashi Pass. Indeed, it was difficult to imagine how they hoped to achieve the passage without a considerable loss. Their dogs were beautiful animals and had wonderful control over the sheep.

The morning of September 3rd was gloriously fine and the view from the "Curtain" ridge appeared to make a deep impression on the Bhotias, who demanded a detailed explanation of the topography. They were very thrilled to see a distant view of their own mountains, the Badrinath and Kamet ranges, and started a heated debate amongst themselves as to the identity of certain features. But it was the sight of the graceful curves of their Blessed Goddess, Nanda Devi, as she stood framed between the dark walls of the upper gorge which most excited their admiration. Several of them asked to be allowed to remain with us until we had finished our travels. What an extraordinarily nice lot they were! Always cheerful, they kept up a constant stream of good-humoured back-chat amongst themselves. They had not, of course, to undergo the hardships which the Dotials had suffered on our first journey, but before very long I came to have considerable respect for them as cragsmen, while their every-ready wit and carefree laughter will remain as one of my pleasantest memories. They and the Sherpas came to be the very best of friends and I think there was a measure of genuine regret when the time came for the Bhotias to leave us. In camp in the forest beyond Dibrughita that evening they treated us to a concert of part songs which reminded me very much of those of the Welsh singers. After this one of their number produced a book which was apparently written in Nepali from which he read laboriously to the Sherpas.

During the next few days, as we traversed once more high up on the flanks of the Rishi Nala, we were able to appreciate the tremendous advantage of possessing local knowledge when travelling over difficult country. Across places which had previously cost us hours of anxious toil we were now able to lead our party safely in half the time. We found, however, a great many landslips had occurred in our absence, and that portions of the country were quite considerably altered. The rains must have been terrific. Small, steep-sided nalas, normally dry, and with very little collecting capacity, showed signs of having had as much as seven feet of water coming down them. We soon realised that the delay which had been caused by our experiences on the Satopanth Pass had been a blessing in disguise, for the Rishi Nala would have been no place to be in during such weather as we experienced in the forests of the Kedarnath valleys.

In order to preserve our rapidly disintegrating climbing boots, we wore rubber-soled shoes on this journey. They slipped about horribly on the damp grass and earth-covered rocks and made the traversing along narrow ledges a most unpleasant business. On one occasion Tilman did slip and for a moment I thought he was lost as he swayed on the brink of a dreadful drop.

From Dibrughita we followed the high level route by which we had returned in June. On September 5th we crossed the Rhamani, one thousand five hundred feet above its junction with the Rishi. The stream was still in spate and we experienced some difficulty in getting across. Most of the Bhotias were very frightened of being swept away and left the task of getting the loads across mainly to two young "tigers" each of whom made some half a dozen crossings. One old man flatly refused to wade into the stream and was eventually carried across. Later it transpired that he was the "egg wallah" who had achieved a certain amount of fame on the Kamet expedition in 1931, by being washed away in a river in the Alaknanda Valley, only I had not recognised him. That evening we reached our old base camp at the entrance of the upper gorge. At one period during the monsoon everything had been flooded, though as we had walled in the belongings which we had left we found that they were still intact. There were several things which we did not require, but we soon came to wish that we had pitched them into the river as the Bhotias spent most of the night noisily dividing the spoil.

As we knew every inch of the route through the upper part of the gorge we decided to take ten of the Bhotias on with us, while the rest returned. Huge segments of the cliffs had broken away and it was very lucky for us that none of the vital sections of the route had been touched. One landslip might well have rendered the gorge impassable, though it is possible that it might have the reverse effect. The men climbed splendidly and on the evening of September 8th we pitched camp some miles up the main valley of the southern section of the basin. The Bhotias were astonished at the country. Such enormous areas of splendid pasturage and no one was able to get their flocks through to graze it! Pasang said he would like to bring a few yaks through into the basin and live there in peace for the rest of his life!

Our camp was situated near the junction of the two main glaciers of the southern section, and promised to serve as a useful base for our work. Besides the exploration of the country to the south of Nanda Devi we meant to reconnoitre the southern ridges of the mountain to see if we could find a practicable route to the summit. But our chief ambition was to force our way out of the basin either to the south or to the east, for besides not wishing to return by the way we had come, Dr. Longstaff's words, "I can think of no more interesting or arduous task for a party composed of mountaineers than to follow up the great glaciers under the southern face of Nanda Devi and to cross the ridge on which I camped in 1905 into the Milam Valley," had fired our imaginations.

Our activities in the southern section were governed largely by this ambition. We had two possible alternatives. One was the col reached by Dr. Longstaff from the Lwanl Glacier on the Milam side, the other was the depression on the southern "rim" by which Mr. Ruttledge and his guide Emile Rey had tried to gain access to the basin in 1932. Both these ways were likely to prove extremely difficult, but we were inclined to favour the former proposition as Longstaff had proved the practicability of the further side of the Lwanl Col by climbing it from that direction, whereas from what we had heard of Ruttledge's col it seemed very doubtful whether a reasonably safe route could be found down the southern face even if we succeeded in reaching its crest from the north.

It was mainly then with the object of obtaining a clear view of the unknown side of the Lwanl Col that on September 9th Tilman, Angtharkay and I, after bidding farewell to the Bhotias, left camp heading in an easterly direction. We crossed the stream to the northern side of the valley by means of a snow bridge formed by a huge avalanche cone which had fallen from the cliffs of Nanda Devi. Presently, as we made our way along a moraine ledge under these cliffs, we were alarmed by the ominous whirr of falling stones accompanied by some shrill whistles, and, looking up, we saw a number of bharal high up among the crags above us. Never have I seen a more extraordinary display of rock climbing. The cliffs on which these animals were scrambling about looked from where we were to be utterly unclimbable; and yet here were four-legged creatures, young and old, running about on them as if they were horizontal instead of being almost vertical. Later we found out that owing to the inward dip of the rock strata the cliffs of this side of the mountain are not so difficult as they appear. Nevertheless, although I had often watched chamois in the Alps, I never before believed that these animals could move about on rock faces of such appalling steepness. I do not imagine that such agile climbers would be so careless as to knock stones down by accident and I strongly suspected that they were bombarding us purposely and probably enjoying a good laugh at our obvious alarm as the stones shattered themselves unpleasantly close to us.

Soon we got on to the big glacier flowing from the west under the southern face of Nanda Devi, and crossed it diagonally to its left bank, where we found a well-defined lateral moraine along which we could make good progress. We had gone for some miles before we rounded a corner and came in sight of the head of the glacier. There was a lot of cloud obscuring the peaks, but after we had waited for half an hour or so we got a brief and distant view of the col. What we saw made us somewhat uneasy. From the col itself a steep ice or snow gully descended for about two thousand feet to the head of the glacier. If the gully consisted of good snow throughout its length it would not be difficult to climb it even if it were steep. But from where we stood it appeared to us to be composed of ice, particularly in its upper part. If this proved to be the case the task of cutting steps all the way up it, at the same time carrying loads of 50 lbs. and being responsible for the safety of the Sherpas, who would be carrying at least 70 lbs., was one which neither of us was very keen to face; for on steep hard ice it is almost impossible to check a bad slip, while there is nothing easier than to make one. Moreover, several deep ruts in the gully and piles of débris below indicated that the route was swept by stone falls, while the rocks on either side of the gully did not appear to offer a satisfactory alternative. Our view, however, was too fleeting and too distant to be at all satisfactory or conclusive, but we saw enough to make us decide to examine the possibilities of the Sunderdhunga Col, as Ruttledge has named the depression on the southern "rim", before making a serious attempt to force a route up the grim precipices of the south-eastern wall.

Across the glacier from where we stood the great southern ridge of the main peak swept up into the drifting clouds at an appalling angle. I could not repress a shudder as I looked at its great glistening flanks and reflected that it had been our intention to look for a route up it. The lower section was hidden from view;

but higher up the icy cliffs mounted without a break to support the majestic head of the virgin goddess, near ten thousand feet above us. I do not remember even remarking upon the apparent inaccessibility of the ridge, and I began to hope that we had proved the mountain to be unclimbable.

We returned to camp in the evening by way of the left bank of the glacier. The Bhotias had taken their departure and Pasang and Kusang, having performed their numerous duties about the camp, were busily engaged as usual with their intricate coiffure. As they wore their hair long it was in constant need of attention, and long continued practice had taught them much which would make many a Paris hairdresser sit up and take notice. Sometimes a long and richly ornamental pigtail was allowed to hang down the back; sometimes it was wound round and round the head; on other occasions the hair was bunched coquettishly behind the ears. A parting, when such was worn, was ruled with the most scrupulous accuracy. This evening I watched, fascinated, while Kusang (he did not know I was looking) ran a short stump of pencil up his nose and over his forehead to make sure that his parting ran exactly down the middle of his head. He repeated the process over and over again before he was satisfied, squinting the while so grotesquely that I began to wonder if his smiling eyes would ever be the same again.

CHAPTER SEVENTEEN

ON the morning of September 10th we were greeted by a warm sun. As it was the first we had experienced for nearly two months we were tempted to bask in its kindly rays for some time before embarking upon the more serious work of the day. We decided to go up the great glacier which we had seen coming in from the south, at the head of which we suspected the Sunderdhunga Col must lie. We intended to camp near the head of the glacier, push a camp on to the crest of the col if that were possible and spend some days examining the ice-cliffs on the southern side in the hope of being able to find a way down. If we were successful we could return to continue our work in the basin for as long as our food lasted, in the comfortable knowledge that an escape over the rampart was possible. If we failed we would have to make an attempt on the great ice-gully leading up to Longstaff's col. We started, carrying heavy loads, and were content to take things gently. By the time we got into a position which would command a view of the glacier the clouds had come up from the south and we could get no idea of the type of country for which we were making. The going was good on the dry ice of the glacier and we made steady progress, passing one or two remarkably fine specimens of "glacier tables". These somewhat surprising phenomena are caused by a large slab of rock falling on to the surface of the glacier and protecting the section of ice on which it has fallen from the rays of the sun, so that as the rest of the glacier melts the slab is left perched upon a pedestal of ice which it has protected. In the case of smaller rocks the process is reversed, the stone becoming heated by the sun and sinking into the ice instead of being left perched above it.

Soon after midday a bitter wind blew up from the south and sweeping across the glacier drove hail and sleet into our faces. This caused us to put on a spurt and before we camped we were a great deal further up the glacier than we had expected to go that day. With difficulty we erected the tents and got the Primus going. The wind dropped towards sunset, and chancing to look out of the tent I saw that the clouds had retreated down the valley leaving the peaks to the south clear. We saw that we were near the head of a very wide glacier-filled valley from which gentle ice-slopes rose to a broad saddle which we knew must be the Sunderdhunga Col. To its right was a massive ice-peak. This we concluded must be the triangulated peak, 22,360 feet, which is such a conspicuous landmark when seen from the south, and which is known by the Survey of India as East Trisul*. The delicious purity of the summit snows, tinged as they were by delicate rays of the setting sun, filled me with desire for a closer acquaintance with the peak. Moreover, unlike most of the peaks in the vicinity, there was an obviously practicable route to the summit, and the prospect of a view from such an elevated point in this wonderland was irresistible. Arguments against the present plan were not difficult to find. The col was easily accessible from this side and in order to find out whether a descent on the south was practicable or not, one would have to go down several thousand feet of very difficult ice, and once one had done that, one would probably be disinclined to climb back again. So it was decided to cut out the reconnaissance, and make a full-dress attempt when our work in the basin had been completed.

We passed a very cold night and in consequence did not emerge from our tents until the sun was well up. Carrying one tent, bedding for three and food and fuel enough for three days, we started in the direction of the ice-peak. The weather remained fine all day, and as hour after hour we threaded our way laboriously through a badly-crevassed area which stretched for a long way up the mountain side, the heat and the glare from the newly-fallen snow was almost unbearable. We aimed at getting our camp up to 20,000 feet. Tilman had been feeling very unfit all day, and in the afternoon when we were at an altitude of about 19,000 he decided not to go any further, and suggested, most unselfishly, that Kusang should stay up at the camp in his place and attempt the peak with Angtharkay and myself, while he went down with Pasang. I, too, was not feeling in very good form, and was suffering from a bad attack of that mysterious complaint loosely known as "glacier lassitude", so that I was glad when 500 feet higher up we came upon an excellent camping site in a crevasse.

With three of us crammed into a two-man tent, we settled down to a most uncomfortable night. Lack of space did not permit independent movement and when one man wished to turn over the others had to turn too, in order that each should fit spoon-wise into the curves of the other. The Sherpas thought this a tremendous joke and as far as I could make out simply laughed themselves to sleep. I suppose I must lack much of that priceless gift – a sense of humour, for I could see in the situation very little to laugh at, with the consequence that I lay long into the night hiding my head and trying to decide which of my companions snored the loudest.

I roused them at 4 a.m. and after a great deal of struggling we contrived to melt ourselves a drink and wrap our shivering bodies in all the clothing which we could extract from the tangled mess inside the tent. Boots then had to be thawed out and forced after a frightful struggle on to feet which had apparently swollen overnight. Soon after 5 o'clock we issued reluctantly out into the bitter morning air.

It is curious how the Sherpas, when they have no loads to carry, seem to lose all power of controlled, rhythmic movement which is such a vital necessity in mountaineering and particularly at considerable altitudes. Their steps become jerky and impulsive, they rush along for a few minutes and then sit down, with the result that they soon become exhausted. All that their life of mountain wandering has taught them about the best methods of walking uphill seems to be lost and they are like raw novices who are amongst the mountains for the first time in their lives.

Today this was very evident and before we had been climbing an hour the party was feeling very sorry for itself. Higher up, too, the snow conditions became bad and the work of kicking steps extremely laborious. We began to feel as we had felt at a considerably higher altitude on Everest the year before. We started off by going for an hour without a halt, then the hour was shortened to half an hour, half an hour to twenty minutes, twenty minutes to a quarter of an hour, and at length we would subside gasping into the soft bed of snow after only ten minutes' struggle. But the morning was fine and as we lay there, we gazed out over a scene of ever-increasing grandeur until even the gigantic southern face of Nanda Devi became dwarfed by the mere extent of the panorama.

I can never hope to see a finer mountain view: the Badrinath peaks, Kamet, the Kosa group, Dunagiri and the great peaks of the northern part of the Nanda Devi Basin – all mountains amongst which we had been travelling for the past four months, served merely as a foil to set off the stupendous ranges lying beyond Milam and across the borders of western Nepal. What a field of exploration lay there – the heritage of some future generation.

Only one frame of mind is possible when working one's way up bad snow at high altitudes. One must shut out from one's mind all but the immediate task of making the next step. To start fretting about the slowness of one's progress or about the time it is going to take to reach the goal would render the whole business unbearable. On a larger scale, this frame of mind, the firm concentration on immediate necessities, made possible those terrible months of sledging through the blizzards of the Antarctic.

As we approached the summit the wind, which had been unpleasant in the early morning, now became very strong indeed and it was the fear of frost-bite which spurred what little energy we had left. My hope of seeing something of the southern side of the watershed was disappointed, for when we reached the summit ridge we looked down into a boiling cauldron of cloud a few feet below us. This was rising rapidly and soon enveloped us. However, we did get one brief glimpse down to the little Simm Saga range which lay at our feet; and also into the head of the Sunderdhunga Valley which we were so hoping to reach. What we saw went a long way to quenching that hope for there seemed to be very little break in the 10,000 feet of precipice which lay between us and the grassy floor of the valley below. I had refrained from taking any photographs on the way up in order to preserve the exposures for the summit. But before my numbed fingers would open and set the camera we were wrapped in a dense cloak of cloud, and we passed the remainder of our stay on the top clapping our hands and banging our feet about in an attempt to restore rapidly diminishing circulation. Then we bustled off the summit and embarked upon a descent which proved to be almost as trying as the ascent. On reaching the camp we packed up the tent and sleeping-bags, and in spite of the loads we had now to carry, we shot down over the lower ice-slopes at a tremendous speed, paying little respect to the crevasses which had caused us so much trouble on the previous day. Tilman greeted us with apparently unlimited tea. He had put in a useful day's work with the plane-table and had succeeded in fixing several important points about the glacier.

On the following day we went down to our base and, leaving a dump of flour there just sufficient to enable us to beat a retreat down the Rishi Ganga in the event of our failing to escape from the basin to the east or south, we carried the remainder of our stuff to a pleasant little alp a couple of miles up the left bank of the main glacier. By now we had been able to make a fairly lengthy examination of the southern aspect of Nanda Devi. We had seen a curious diagonal spur running down in a south-easterly direction from about half-way up the main south ridge. This appeared to be accessible in its lower section and it seemed to us that we might be able to work our way for some distance along it. We decided to attempt to do this in order to get a comprehensive view of the southern section of the basin, though it did not even occur to me that we might also find a practicable route to the summit.

The morning of September 14th was brilliantly fine, and we started early carrying with us the usual light camp and enough food for Tilman (who was now recovered) and myself for two or three days. We crossed the main glacier and made our way again along the valley which lay at the foot of the great black buttresses of the southern ridge, fixing our position on the plane-table as we went and taking shots to distant landmarks. We camped that night by a pool of crystal clear water, on a lawn of close-cropped grass over which snowy eidelweiss grew in profusion.

It was an hour after dawn the following morning before we got away. It seemed as if the last remnants of the monsoon had departed. The glacier was silent, bound under the iron grip of frost; and we joyously sped over its desolate stony surface. Forty minutes of hard going took us to the foot of the black precipices which girdle the base of the great southern ridge. Here we found that the rock was well broken but firm and that the strata sloped in our favour which made the climbing a great deal easier than we had anticipated. Within an hour of leaving the glacier we had reached the crest of the diagonal spur which we had seen from a distance. This was as far as we expected to get and we sat down contentedly in the warm sunlight and gazed lazily at our unique surroundings.

We saw that the spur we were on, coming down from the main southern ridge of Nanda Devi, formed a gigantic glacier cirque. In front of us across a deep valley rose a stupendous ice-wall which formed the southern face of the twin peaks. We were too close and, for all our 18,500 feet, far too low to get anything but a very fore-shortened view of the face and it was a long while before the colossal scale began to impress itself upon my imagination. The ice-wall was fringed on top by a band of rock forming the actual summits of the twin peaks and the two mile ridge connecting them. By now the sun had been shining on this band for some hours and had already started to dislodge masses of rock, which set up an almost continuous moan as they hurtled through the air towards us, yet so great was the distance of the peaks above us that throughout the day we did not detect a single of these avalanches which must have involved several hundreds of tons of rock. The whole effect was very uncanny.

As it was such a brilliantly fine day and as yet quite early we decided that we would investigate the possibilities of climbing further up the spur. A virtual tower rising straight out of the ridge blocked a way along the crest, but we soon found that we could traverse along under the tower on its eastern side and climb diagonally towards a gap in the ridge beyond. This we reached in a couple of hours without much difficulty, and were surprised to find that here again the inward sloping strata made progress comparatively easy. By now we were about nineteen thousand feet high and beginning to get really excited. We had already overcome the apparently inaccessible lower part of the ridge and were still going strong. Was it possible that we had discovered the one key to the innermost defences of this amazing mountain? Of course, we would not be in a position to make an attempt on the summit but to have discovered the way was sufficient to work us into quite a frenzy of excitement. Up and up we went without finding any place which gave us more than a moment's hesitation. Our pace was slow by reason of the fact that the rocks were still under a deep covering of monsoon snow, but our progress was steady enough. The higher we got the more fully could we appreciate the immensity of the glacier cirque on the rim of which we were climbing.

We climbed on until about 2.30 p.m. when we halted and decided that we had come far enough. We estimated our height at close on twenty-one thousand feet. The ridge was certainly showing signs of becoming more difficult but for the next few hundred feet there did not appear to be any insuperable obstacle and we came to the definite conclusion that if a well-equipped party were to spend a couple of weeks over the job that there was a good chance that the ridge could be followed to the summit. It would be no easy task and the party would have to be supremely fit and competent. Prolonged siege tactics (which are so much the fashion in the Himalayas nowadays) would be too dangerous to be justifiable, since this method would involve too many men in the upper camps, and if it were overtaken by bad weather high up such a party would be in a very serious plight. In high mountains, mobility is the keynote of efficiency and safety, and it is for this reason that I find it hard to believe that a large, heavily organised expedition will ever achieve success on Everest.

We were now sufficiently high to get a true idea of the immensity of our surroundings, and even though I had been living for months amid perpendicularity on a huge scale I suffered from a feeling of panic which resembled the delirium of a fevered mind.

Our slow rate of descent was evidence that we had climbed too fast earlier in the day and night was falling as we made our way back across the glacier after yet another unforgettable day.

The morning of September 16th was spent mainly in plane-tabling, on the slopes above the camp, and in making further examination of "Longstaff's Col". This more detailed study confirmed our first impressions that an ascent of the couloir with heavy loads would be too difficult and dangerous a job. We could not, however, tell for certain as so much depended upon whether the gully was composed of snow or ice. By now we had become really worked up about our chances of being able to force an exit over one of these gaps. In doing so, we would make a complete crossing of the range, thus linking up with the explorations of those who had attacked the rampart from the south and east; we would see for ourselves those valleys, which though not unexplored, we knew to be of surpassing loveliness; and the last phase of our quest would be through country new to us. If we were to fail we would be forced to retreat once more down the Rishi Nala, and from Joshimath to journey back by the way we had come, thus missing a rare and glorious climax to our little season of perfect happiness.

When we returned to camp early in the afternoon we found that the Sherpas had come up and were busily engaged in their hobby of building cairns. Packing up, we ran off down the glacier, reaching our little green alp before sundown, here to spend one more night lying in the open, dozing in the light of the half moon and waking to watch the rosy light of dawn steal gently down the east-turned face of the "Blessed Goddess".

The week which followed has left with me a richer and more varied stock of impressions than any other I can recall. We started up the glacier to the south that morning, staggering under the weight of very heavy loads. I was feeling lazy and lagged behind the others, sitting down often to gaze at each new aspect of the peaks around me. Once I found myself by a deep pool in the ice of the glacier, and stayed as if hypnotised by the reflections on the placid blue surface of the water. It was irresistible. I threw off my clothes, plunged in and swam for some seconds under water along the glistening walls of ice. The day ended in camp far up the glacier, under the icy cirque standing at its head.

A frigid night was followed by an even colder dawn and we were hurried along in spite of our cruel loads by the bitter morning breeze. The snow was iron-hard, and as the slope steepened the already burdened shoulders of the leader would ache painfully as he chipped steps, while those behind were frozen with inaction. The arrival of the sun changed all this and we were soon stamping a way, and sinking up to our knees at every step, while a fierce glare scorched our faces unbearably. Several large crevasses caused us some trouble, but we worked at full pressure and at 11.15 a.m. we reached the crest of the "col". We found that this consisted of an extensive snow plateau which sloped gently towards the south, so that we were obliged to descend some five hundred feet before we could get any view of the southern precipices on which all our thoughts were concentrated. From the edge of the plateau we could look down into the cloud-filled Sunderdhunga Valley up which, as I mentioned earlier, Hugh Ruttledge and his guide, Emile Rey, had come in 1932 to attempt to gain access into the Nanda Devi Basin. In order to save the reader the trouble of referring back to that incident it may not be out of place to requote here, Mr. Ruttledge's description published in *The Times* of August 22nd, 1932, of the obstacle which now faced us:

"In a mood of hopeful anticipation our party, on May 25th, trudged up the narrow glacier which leads from Sunderdhunga itself to the base of the wall, of which the greater part has been invisible from a distance. The Sherpas cheered derisively as a little avalanche had an ineffective shot at us from the cliffs above; and raced round the last corner. One step round it, and we were brought up all standing by a sight which almost took our remaining breath away. Six thousand feet of the steepest rock and ice. 'Nom de nom,' said Emile, while Nima exclaimed that this looked as bad as the north-west face of Kangchenjunga in 1930. However, we had come a long way to see this, so we advanced across the stony slopes to a point from which we hoped, by detailed examination, to reduce terrific appearance to milder reality. But the first impressions were accurate. Near the top of the wall, for about a mile and a half, runs a terrace of ice some two hundred feet thick; in fact, the lower edge of a hanging glacier. Under the pull of gravity large masses constantly break off from this terrace and thunder down to the valley below, polishing in their fall the successive bands of limestone precipice of which the face is composed. Even supposing the precipice to be climbable, an intelligent mountaineer may be acquitted on a charge of lack of enterprise if he declines to spend at least three days and two nights under fire from this artillery. An alternative is the choice of three knife-edge arêtes, excessively steep, sometimes overhanging in their middle and lower sections, on which even the eye of faith, assisted by binoculars, fails to see a single platform large enough to accommodate the most modest of climbing tents."

We dumped our loads in the snow and set about our task immediately. Remembering Ruttledge's description we decided that our best chance of success was to get on to one of the three rock arêtes or ridges, for though they were referred to as being "excessively steep", at least their crests would be safe from the bombardment of ice-avalanches. The clouds had now come up from below and our view was very restricted. After working over to the left for some distance, however, we came to the edge of a tremendously steep gully from which came an incessant rattle of stone falls. Beyond we could make out a dark mass which we concluded was the first of the rock arêtes. After hunting about for some time we found that in order to reach the arête we would be forced to run the gauntlet of the rock falls in the gully. As these were coming down at very short intervals the chances of our getting across without some member of the party being killed was very small, and the risk was quite unjustifiable. So that was that.

The ice-fall below us plunged out of sight. We returned to our loads and worked over to the right. In about twenty minutes we were brought up short and found that we were standing on the edge of the ice-terrace overhanging six thousand feet of polished limestone. It was a wonderful sight. Every now and then enormous masses of ice would break away from the cliffs we were standing on and crash with a fearful roar into the cloudy depths below. After satisfying ourselves that there was not the slightest hope in this direction we waited for some while to watch this unusual scene. It is not often that one gets a chance of watching a display of ice-avalanches from so close, and rarer still to see them breaking away from the very cliffs on which one is standing.

We returned disconsolately to our loads for a meal at 2.30 p.m. A cup of tea and satu put new heart into the party and we set off to tackle the last line of possibility. This was the ice-fall which lay immediately below us and which separated the ice-terrace from the rock arêtes. A few feet of twisted and riven ice was all that we could see: beyond this the ice-fall plunged out of sight into the whirling mists which filled the depths below. It was useless to attempt to work out a line of attack from above and all we could do was to go straight at it and worry our way down by the tedious processes of trial and error. We had plenty of food with us, however, and we could afford to take our time. As long as we kept fairly well out of the line of bombardment from the ice-cliffs of the terrace and avoided a slip we could carry on for several days if necessary.

Soon we found ourselves on ice more torn and complicated and more frighteningly steep even than that which we had tackled six weeks before on the southern side of our Satopanth Pass. It was exceedingly strenuous work trying line after line without success, but as the evening wore on our energy seemed to increase, probably from a growing feeling of desperation. A series of slender ice-ledges suspended over space by some conjuring trick of Nature would lead us downwards to the brink of an impassable chasm. Then a wearisome retreat back by the way we had come to try a new and perhaps equally futile chance. The further we went the more involved became the precipitous maze we were in, until my head began to whirl and I began to think we should neither find our way on or back. By dark, however, we had managed to get some hundreds of feet down and we crept into our sleeping-bags in a slightly more hopeful frame of mind.

The night was an extremely cold one and we decided not to start before the sun was up on the following morning as our clothes had become sodden in the soft snow of the previous day and an early start would almost certainly have resulted in frost-bite. This decision gave us a moment of leisure in which to watch a sunrise whose beauty far surpassed any I had seen before. In the right and left foreground were the icy walls, steep-sided and grim, enclosing the head of the Maiktoli Valley; in front beyond the brink of the ice-ledge on which we were camped, and immensely far below was a lake of vivid colour at the bottom of which we could see the Sunderdhunga River coiling like a silver water snake, flowing away into the placid cloud-sea which stretched without a break over the plains of India.

The day was one of heavy toil, over-packed with thrills. Hour after hour we puzzled and hacked our way down; sometimes lowering our loads and ourselves on the rope down an ice-cliff, at others chipping laboriously across the steep face of a tower or along a knife-edged crest, always in constant dread of finding ourselves completely cut off. The bitter cold of the early morning changed towards midday to a fierce heat and glare which robbed us of much of our strength and energy. Our heavy loads hindered every movement and threatened to throw us off our balance. But we were all absorbed in our task, and worked on through the day without pause.

Evening found us working on dry ice three thousand feet down. Beside us to our right was a prominent rock ridge, which, though lying immediately below the higher line of hanging glaciers, offered us a heaven-sent alternative if only we could reach it. We cut steps to the edge of the glacier and from there we looked down a sixty-foot ice-cliff into a steep slabby gully. The gully was evidently a path for ice-avalanches, but it was narrow and once in it we could run across in a couple of minutes. By chipping away the ice in a large circle we soon fashioned a bollard. Round this we fastened a rope, down which we slid, recovering the rope from the ice-bollard without difficulty. A short race across the gully with hearts in our mouths took us to a little ledge under the overhanging walls of the ridge, which offered a convenient and well-protected site for a camp. No sooner had we got the tents pitched than there came a fearful roar from above and for fully a minute a cascade of huge ice-blocks crashed down the gully, sending up a spray of ice-dust, while a number of ice-splinters landed harmlessly on the tents.

The day, begun with the sight of a dawn fair beyond description and crowded with so much vivid life, closed with us stretched luxuriously on our ledge, perched high up amongst the precipitous glaciers of one of the grandest of mountain cirques. Lightning flickered somewhere to the east; the distant thunder was almost indistinguishable from the growl of the avalanches. Mists floating stealthily in and out of the corries about us, forming and dissolving as if at will. Far to the south the placid sea of monsoon cloud still stretched over the plains, and the silvery light of a full moon lent to the scene an appearance of infinite depth.

Three thousand feet of precipice still remained to be descended and this took us nearly the whole of the following day. Frequently we had to rope down the more difficult sections. On one of these occasions one of the sacks came open; most of the contents fell out, bounced once and hummed out of sight. In the afternoon we were enveloped in mist and had considerable difficulty in groping our way downwards; but Antharkay distinguished himself by a really brilliant piece of route-finding and in the evening we reached a collection of rude stone shelters, used by shepherds, and known as Maiktoli. The shepherds had departed some weeks before.

The high mountains were now showing signs of approaching winter, a sharp reminder that our season of freedom and perfect happiness was at an end. But the marches which followed have left their quota of memories. A struggle to find an exit from the grim gorge in the upper Sunderdhunga Valley into which we had blundered in a heavy mist; our last encounter with a swollen mountain river; an enormous feast on wild raspberries and Himalayan blackberries lower down the valley; the generous hospitality of the first villagers we met, and the sweetness of their honey; the sparkling sunlit mornings, as one lay, sleepily watching the smoke of a distant wood fire mounting straight up into the clear air; a dawn on the distant ice-clad giants, whose presence we had just left.

Return to civilisation was hard, but, in the sanctuary of the Blessed Goddess we had found the lasting peace which is the reward of those who seek to know high mountain places.

BLANK ON THE MAP

Blank on the Map

First published by Hodder and Stoughton Limited, 1938

Contents

Foreword *by T. G. Longstaff* *page* 159

1 How an Expedition Begins 161
2 Of the Real Value of Climbing 166
3 Sherpas and Sahibs 169
4 Local Colour 174
5 The Passes of the Great Karakoram 182
6 Trouble with the "Hungry Hundred" 192
7 Mutiny on the Hanging Glacier 200
8 Loads Across the Watershed 205
9 Finding the Aghil Pass 210
10 Finding the Zug Shaksgam River 217
11 In Unexplored Zug Shaksgam 224
12 K2 233
13 The Crevasse Glacier 241
14 Survey and Adventures 248
15 Panmah Journey *by J. B. Auden* 256
16 Legends *by H. W. Tilman* 259
17 Which Way Out? 276
18 Conversation Piece 284
19 Marching Back 291
20 How an Expedition Ends 297

Maps
Central Karakoram – principal glaciers, peaks and passes 158
The Approach to the Karakoram 175
Aghil Explorations 216
Tilman's Journey 258
Journey of Shipton and Spender 280

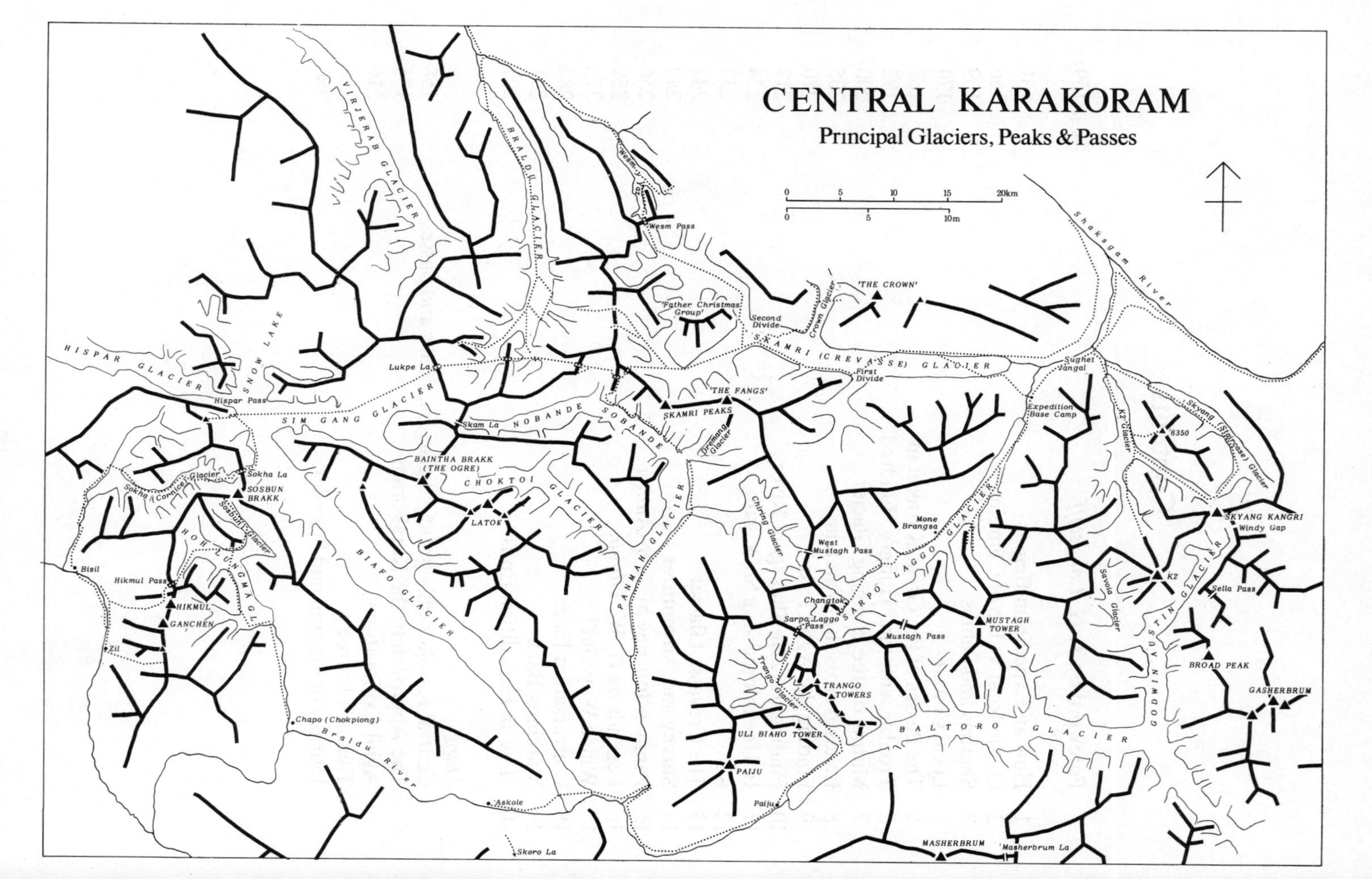

CENTRAL KARAKORAM
Principal Glaciers, Peaks & Passes
0 5 10 15 20km
0 5 10m
Shaksgam River
'THE CROWN'
Crown Glacier
Second Divide
'Father Christmas' Group'
Wesm Pass
SKAMRI (CREVASSE) GLACIER
First Divide
Sughet Jangal
Expedition Base Camp
K2 Glacier
Skyang (Staircase) Glacier
6350
SKYANG KANGRI
Windy Gap
K2
Savoia Glacier
Sella Pass
GODWIN AUSTIN GLACIER
BROAD PEAK
GASHERBRUM
VIRJERAB GLACIER
BRALDU GLACIER
HISPAR GLACIER
SNOW LAKE
Hispar Pass
Lukpe La
SIM GANG GLACIER
Skam La
NOBANDE SOBANDE
SKAMRI PEAKS
'THE FANGS'
Dremong Glacier
BAINTHA BRAKK (THE OGRE)
CHOKTOI GLACIER
LATOK
PANMAH GLACIER
Chiring Glacier
West Mustagh Pass
Mone Brangsa
SARPO LAGGO GLACIER
Changtok
Sarpo Laggo Pass
Mustagh Pass
MUSTAGH TOWER
TRANGO TOWERS
Trango Glacier
ULI BIAHO TOWER
PAIJU
Paiju
BALTORO GLACIER
MASHERBRUM
Masherbrum La
Sokha La
SOSBUN BRAKK
Sokha (Cornice) Glacier
Sosbun Glacier
HOH LUNGMA GL.
Bisil
Hikmul Pass
HIKMUL
GANCHEN
Zil
BIAFO GLACIER
Chapo (Chokpiong)
Braldu River
Askole
Skoro La

FOREWORD

T. G. Longstaff

MOUNTAINEERS usually seek the Himalaya in the hope of adding the ascent of some great peak to their experiences in the Alps or the Caucasus. But the exciting vastness and variety of the two-thousand-mile buttress of High Asia present conditions so different from anything which they have experienced in other ranges that their energies are often diverted from the climbing of peaks to the exploration of the unknown ridges and valleys which entice them on every hand. My own first climbing expedition to the Himalaya inevitably developed into a trek of nearly a thousand miles: I could not bring myself to waste time over second attempts on the same peak: there was too much to see and too many fascinating problems to be solved.

After notable ascents in Europe and Africa the author of this book made four long journeys in the Himalaya. With his old companion Tilman he has again this year tackled Everest, on whose grim slopes he reached 28,000 feet in 1933. The first to unveil the Sanctuary of Nanda Devi, he has achieved some thirty new peaks and passes in the eastern and western Himalaya. Last year he turned far to the north-west, to the solitudes of the Karakoram, and in the present volume he appears essentially as an explorer, subordinating the climbing of peaks to his main objective of filling in a great blank on the map.

Nowadays would-be explorers are more and more forced to seek high latitudes or high altitudes. In these empty regions achievement is limited by the number of days' food the traveller can carry: success in both cases depends on a very special technique of travel. Today probably a majority of young explorers are dog-drivers or mountaineers. The days of the unveiling of continents are over: in almost all other regions of the world the tracks of an explorer will cross and recross those of former travellers.

But the mountaineer, whose training is so much longer than that required for any other form of travel, must further equip himself as a surveyor. For, as the actual area of the unknown shrinks, so rises the standard of accuracy and detail expected in his mapping. At once he is beset by new difficulties. His man-power must carry tentage, sleeping-bags, food and fuel for a sufficiently long time to complete his survey work. Therefore his instrumental equipment must be of the lightest consonant with accuracy. It is equally essential that this method of survey be as rapid as possible, in order to lessen the food he must carry. For several years past, officials of the Royal Geographical Society, working with mountain surveyors and instrument makers, have been elaborating a very light theodolite combined with a small camera. An efficient instrument has now been evolved, and it has fallen to Spender, the leading surveyor of Shipton's party, to demonstrate its use by mountaineers in difficult country for filling gaps which could not be covered by his own more rigid survey. He worked out his results at Dehra Dun under the critical eye of Brigadier Clinton Lewis, the Surveyor-General of India, than whom there is no higher authority. One of the most inaccessible white patches on the map of the Karakoram is now filled in: the case for the new method is proven: but we badly need some generous benefactor who will give us a stereoplotter so that future photographic material can be quickly worked out in London.

It is to be feared that few readers of Shipton's modest account will quite realize all that is implied by the remarkable success of this expedition. The combined party has surveyed 1,800 square miles of one of the most difficult mountain fastnesses in the world; and Auden has revealed its geological structure. With a reversion to the practice of a generation ago, the venture was organized and financed with an avoidance of publicity and with an economy quite unusual to-day. Sums ten times as large have often been spent on expeditions which brought back one-tenth of the results obtained by Shipton and his companions. He knows the secret of counting men before means. Equipment you can buy. Individual qualifications you cannot buy. The personal attainments of the individual members of an exploring party are more important than the funds at their disposal. This is the heartening message of Shipton's book.

T.G.L.

THE ATHENÆUM

'. . . all experience is an arch where thro'
Gleams that untravell'd world, whose margin fades
For ever and for ever when I move.'
Ulysses – Alfred, Lord Tennyson

CHAPTER ONE

How an Expedition Begins

A fascinating way of spending a few hours of leisure is to sit down with a paper and pencil and work out in minute detail the preparations for an expedition into unexplored country. The fact that there is very little chance of carrying out the project matters little. These dream expeditions can be staged in any corner of the world. I have imagined them in the forbidden mountains of Nepal, and in the wind-swept ice peaks of Tierra del Fuego, and across the Antarctic continent.

On the 1936 Everest expedition, during the tedious hours of a snow-storm on the East Rongbuk glacier, lying in my sleeping-bag, I discussed a detailed scheme with Noel Humphreys for the exploration of the remote snow range above the dense, steamy forests in the centre of New Guinea. The plan was to charter a dhow from a Dutch port on the south coast and sail to the southern extremity of the island; then to land with sufficient food and equipment to last one and a half years, and to relay the loads for three hundred miles, following a high ridge, above the fever swamps, that we hoped would lead to the snow range. We contemplated taking a dozen Sherpa porters with us to carry the loads inland and to help us to live in the hostile country, and eventually to take part in the climbing. Lest the Sherpas should be homesick so far from their country, for so long, we even considered allowing them to take their wives; and we discussed the possibility of planting crops in the foot-hills to help us to live in the interior.

I often amuse myself by making a list of these imaginary expeditions in order of their attractiveness. Sometimes one heads the list, sometimes another. Always one plan is uppermost in my mind, until circumstances determine which shall be attempted.

Talking like this with John Morris, on the way down from Base Camp to Rongbuk, after the 1936 Everest expedition, he asked me if I had ever considered his pet plan of a journey from Hunza to Leh by way of the Shaksgam river. During the march back across Tibet there was plenty of time to discuss this project, and to weigh its possibilities. By the time we reached India it so far headed my list of plans as to exclude the thought of all others.

The Shaksgam river lies somewhere on the undemarcated frontiers of Chinese Turkestan, Hunza and Kashmir. It was necessary to obtain permission from the Government of India to take a party into that area. At the end of July I went to Simla to explain the project to the authorities. Some months later permission was granted. In August, while waiting for the start of a survey expedition to the Nanda Devi basin, I stayed with Bunty and Norman Odling in their lovely home in Kalimpong – a haven for so many travellers; during this pleasant interlude, with the aid of all the existing maps of the Karakoram, I made myself familiar with the geography of that range, studying the various routes, the costs involved, and the difficulties inherent in each plan of approach. Eventually I decided that instead of making the suggested journey it would be more valuable to establish a base in the middle of the Shaksgam area, with sufficient food to last three and a half months, and to make exploratory excursions from there in all directions.

At this stage my plans were necessarily vague, but I was fascinated by the idea of penetrating into the little-known region of the Karakoram. As I studied the maps, one thing about them captured my imagination. The ridges and valleys which led up from Baltistan became increasingly high and steep as they merged into the maze of peaks and glaciers of the Karakoram, and then suddenly ended in an empty blank space. Across this blank space was written one challenging word, "Unexplored". The area is dominated by K2, the second highest mountain in the world, and is bounded on the south by the main Asiatic watershed.

The southern side of this range has been visited by many explorers and mountaineers who have partially surveyed its vast glaciers. But it is the northern side of this great watershed which has proved so difficult of access. The country is inhospitable and uninhabited, and no traveller can stay long in its remote valleys. These are deep and narrow with precipitous rocky sides. The unbridged rivers, fed by the huge glaciers, tend to flood to an enormous depth during the summer months when the ice is melting, and are then quite unfordable.

The first explorer of this part of the Karakoram was Sir Francis Younghusband, then a Lieutenant in the Dragoons. In 1887, at the end of his great journey across Asia, from Peking to India, he crossed the Aghil range, by what has since come to be known as the Aghil pass. This range lies to the north of the Karakoram. On the southern side of the pass he discovered a river which his men called the Shaksgam. From there he ascended the Sarpo Laggo glacier and crossed the main Karakoram range by way of the Mustagh pass. His account of this remarkable feat will be quoted later in this book.

Two years later he again crossed the Aghil pass to the Shaksgam river, which he followed upstream for a considerable distance. He then tried to enter the mountain country to the south-west; but failing to make his way up a great glacier, called by him the Crevasse glacier, he followed, in the late autumn, the lower reaches of the Shaksgam and so reached the Shimshal pass, which lies at the north-western extremity of this area.

Since then other travellers have visited various parts of this region. In 1926 Colonel Kenneth Mason led an expedition, financed by the Survey of India, to the Shaksgam. His object was to cross from the Karakoram pass, which lies at the eastern extremity of the Aghil range, to the head waters of the Shaksgam. From there he intended to work downstream so as to connect up with Younghusband's route, and to fix the geographical position of the Shaksgam river and of the Aghil pass. His way was barred by a great glacier, which, coming down from the northern slopes of the Teram Kangri range, dammed the Shaksgam river. The ice was so appallingly broken that it was quite impossible for the expedition to cross the glacier and to continue its progress down the river. Mason named the glacier the Kyagar. His party went up into the Aghil range and explored its eastern section. There they were faced by the great difficulties of travelling in an entirely uninhabited area. In August they found another great river, which at first they imagined to be the Shaksgam itself. They failed to follow it down-stream owing to the enormous volume of water which was racing through its gorges. But they went far enough upstream to realize that this river was not the Shaksgam. So Mason named it the Zug – or false – Shaksgam. The lateness of the season forced the party to leave the problem of its course unsolved.

In 1929 a party from H. R. H. the Duke of Spoleto's expedition crossed the Mustagh pass into the Shaksgam valley, and followed it up to the Kyagar glacier. The work accomplished by this party will be mentioned in a later chapter.

In 1935 Dr. and Mrs. Visser, who have made three remarkable expeditions in the Karakoram, followed Mason's route and succeeded in crossing the Kyagar glacier and in mapping the great glaciers coming down from the Gasherbrum peaks on the main watershed. They were prevented from going farther down the river by the summer floods.

But to the west and north-west of the areas visited by these explorers there still remained vast regions of unknown country of absorbing interest to the mountaineer and to the geographer. It was the exploration of a portion of this area that was the main object of my expedition.

We had three principal interests. First, the section that lies between the Sarpo Laggo valley and the Shimshal pass, bounded on the north by the Shaksgam river, an area of about 1,000 square miles. Younghusband had touched the fringe of this country when he tried to ascend the Crevasse glacier. Second, the glacier system lying to the north and north-west of K2. Third, the portion of the Aghil range, west of that explored by Mason's expedition. The two outstanding problems of this last area were to find the lower reaches and outlet of the Zug Shaksgam river, and to fix the geographical position of the

Aghil pass. As 1937 was the fiftieth anniversary of Sir Francis Younghusband's famous journey, we had an additional incentive to visit this pass. So far as we knew no European had been there since Younghusband's second crossing in 1889.

The first thing to be decided was how to tackle the problem of getting to the Shaksgam. Apart from attempting to reach it from China, three alternatives were open to us: first, to cross from the Karakoram pass to the head waters of the Shaksgam and make our way down over the difficult glacier trunks which had defeated Mason's party in 1926; second, to cross the Shimshal pass early in the spring, and force a route up the lower gorge of the Shaksgam before the river became too high; and third, to cross the main Karakoram range from the Baltoro glacier. The first two alternatives would probably have involved considerable difficulties with the river even early in the year, and would have rendered us liable to be cut off by the summer floods until late in the autumn. Besides this, the journey either to the Shimshal or to the Karakoram pass is very long and costly, particularly early in the year when the routes are not officially open. The difficulties involved by the third alternative, the crossing of the main Karakoram range, were of a purely mountaineering character, and though we were likely to have considerable trouble in getting several tons of stores and equipment over a difficult glacier pass early in the year, I chose this route.

Our rough plan of campaign then was this: to reach the Baltoro glacier by the end of May; to cross the watershed with sufficient food to last the party for one hundred days after reaching its base below the snout of the Sarpo Laggo glacier; leaving a dump there, to cross the Shaksgam and spend as much time in the Aghil range as possible without being cut off by the summer floods; to return to the Sarpo Laggo about the middle of July and to spend the remaining two months working on our other two objectives, the Crevasse glacier region and the area to the north of K2.

The chief difficulty which had to be faced in working out details of this plan was the fact that once across the main Karakoram range the party would have to be entirely self-supporting for the whole period of its stay there – nearly three and a half months. This, and the enormous expense of transporting each effective load across the watershed, necessitated the rigorous exclusion of every ounce of equipment which could possibly be dispensed with, and very careful rationing; and again, the exclusion of all delicacies which did not carry the maximum food value, or which interfered with a properly balanced diet.

The next matter that had to be decided was the all-important question of the composition of the party. I had originally asked H. W. Tilman to join me in the proposed journey from Hunza to Leh through the Shaksgam valley, and had intended that the party should consist of only the two of us, and four or five Sherpa porters. Tilman and I hold the same views about expeditions. We have evolved a technique for light travel which has met with some success in the mountains of East and Central Africa, as well as in the Himalaya.

When, instead of making the journey, I decided to work from a base, it was obvious that by increasing the size of the party I could hope to bring back more valuable results. I therefore decided to take a surveyor to work near the base and form a nucleus of accurate mapping to which we could attach our long, less detailed exploration. It was likely to be a difficult task to begin such a survey.

Only one fixed point, the peak of K2, would be visible, and it might be necessary to determine the position of the map astronomically. Also a good deal of ingenuity would be required to cut down the loads of survey equipment to a practicable number. The man best suited to the job was Michael Spender, and I was lucky enough to enrol him as a member of the party. Spender had learnt his work in Switzerland and Germany. He had been the surveyor attached to the Barrier Reef expedition in 1928-29; he had taken part in two Danish expeditions to Greenland; and had been with me as surveyor on the 1935 Reconnaissance expedition to Mount Everest. He is a rapid and precise worker and has the ability to adjust his mind to unexpected circumstances. I also invited John Auden, of the Geological Survey of India, to join the party, to assist in the exploratory work and to carry out as much geological investigation as possible. Auden has done a good deal of climbing in Europe and had travelled widely in the Himalaya in the course of his work. In 1933 he had made an expedition to the Biafo glacier, beyond Askole, and his first-hand knowledge of the route and the people was a great assistance; he was a valuable asset to the party.

I decided to recruit seven Sherpa porters from Darjeeling. This was very expensive, for not only had we to pay their wages for the whole period of their absence from their homes, regardless of whether they were working or not, but also they had to be brought by rail right across India from Darjeeling to Srinagar. In fact, the expense of their inclusion in the party amounted to one-fifth of the entire cost of the expedition; but it was well worthwhile. They more than justified the expense and without their support we would have accomplished little. During the expedition I frequently regretted that I had not brought double the number of Sherpas.

There are good and bad among the Sherpas as among all other people, and not an unusually large proportion of good. It is necessary, therefore, to select the men who are to play so important a part in an expedition, with very great care, or one is liable to be badly let down. If one can find a Sherpa whose judgment can be relied upon absolutely, it is a good plan to entrust him with the task of choosing his own companions, for no one can know the Sherpas as well as they know themselves.

I was fortunate in having such a man in Angtharkay, who had previously been my companion on five Himalayan expeditions. As usual he thoroughly justified my trust in him, and brought with him a batch of men as tough and loyal, and as full of humour as himself. Owing to a generous contribution to the funds of the expedition we were able to engage four men from Baltistan for the whole journey. This brought our numbers up to fifteen: four Europeans, seven Sherpas and, later, four Baltis.

I estimated that the cost of the expedition, including three return passages to India (Auden joined from Calcutta) would amount to £855. With no private means it was necessary to rely on the support of scientific societies to raise this money. The Royal Geographical Society, the Survey of India and the Royal Society took an interest in the project and contributed generously towards the funds. In actual fact the whole cost of the expedition was less than my estimate by a few pounds.

CHAPTER TWO

Of the Real Value of Climbing

THOSE days in London, before we had even packed our rucksacks, were very strenuous. There were formal permissions to be set in order, supplies to be bought, passages to be booked, and a mass of detail to be attended to that seemed to have little relation to the life we would lead in the mountains. Was all this effort worthwhile? Why should we go to such lengths to plunge ourselves into a life of discomfort and privation? To me it is worthwhile because of what it leads to. Every time I start an expedition I feel that I am getting back to a way of living which is now lost.

With a wistfulness, perhaps a little tinged with sentimentality, I think of the leisurely days of a few hundred years ago, before life was so mad a rush, before the countryside was spoiled by droves of people, and beauty itself exploited as a commercial proposition.

It is true that the very act of looking back seems to touch the past with gold. Probably the "good old days" were hard and uncomfortable, but they did foster individuality. Life had then an essential quality of reality which now we seem to have lost. We have become so accustomed to having everyday life made easy for us, that our energies are not absorbed in the art of living, but run riot in a craving for sensation. Individuality is swamped in the mass emotion of hurrying mobs of people whose thoughts are dragooned by the ready-made ideas of shallow press articles.

So many human activities have lost their power to refresh the spirit because people tend to do things for the wrong reasons – for publicity, for sensationalism, for money, or because it is the fashion to do them. A wrong attitude, based on an unreal sense of values, poisons our recreations no less than the more serious aspects of living. Reality should be the essential factor in sport as in life. Any other basic aim endangers the right attitude of mind without which there can be no real happiness nor the full enjoyment of any activity.

A man who is really keen about sailing is in the first place attracted by the sea with all its problems, hardships and beauties – by the very form of life which the sea offers. He sails because sailing teaches him the art of living in the environment which he loves. It gives him a larger, clearer view of the problems and difficulties of his craft; and so he comes to a realization of the true æsthetic value of the sea.

In the same way the skier wishes to become part of the country of snow-laden firs and winter mountains which means so much to him. He finds in his sport a way of identifying himself with this enchanting world. He cannot easily achieve this in the competitive social atmosphere of a crowded winter sports resort. He must go to the higher mountains, or to the silent forests of Norway. So it is with the fisherman and his lakes and rivers; and with the big-game hunter and his jungles; and with the mountaineer and his peaks and glaciers.

But directly people allow the element of competition to rule their activities, and care more for trophies, or record-breaking, or acclamation, than for a real understanding of their craft, or even if they are content with short cuts to proficiency and superficial knowledge, they are in danger of losing the touchstone of genuine values which alone makes anything worthwhile.

The tendency nowadays to be artificial instead of genuine, and superficial instead of thorough, is caused partly by everyone being in such a hurry, and partly by things being made too easy for us. If a man has money to spend and feels that it would be exciting to go and shoot big game in East Africa, all he need do is to go to a travel agency and book his passage in a luxury liner. When he arrives, he engages the services of a "white hunter", relies on that man's marksmanship and knowledge of the bush, and returns a few months later with a number of tall stories and several crates of trophies. But he has not lived the real life of a hunter; nor has he made the experience a part of his own life. He has taken an easy short cut to vicarious adventure. The mountaineer who goes to the Alps for a season's climbing, with a desire to climb more peaks than other men, and by more difficult routes, misses the real value of the experience – the love of mountains for their own sake. The real purpose of climbing, and of any other sport, should be to transmute it into a way of living, however temporary, in an environment which appeals to the individual.

Often when I have been climbing in the Alps I have thought how enthralling it must have been to see the Alps as De Saussure saw them, before they had been civilized out of their wild unspoiled beauty and tamed into a social asset. A hundred and fifty years ago men went to the Alps to investigate the phenomena of mountains. The result of their quest was the birth of the sciences of geology and glaciology, and the study of the rarefication of the atmosphere at high altitudes, together with its effect upon the human body and upon plants. But in addition to all these discoveries, De Saussure and his companions found in mountains not only the grim hostility which tradition had ascribed to them, but also infinite beauty, peace and solitude, and a recreation of spirit of which they had not dreamed. And just as hundreds of years before sailors had learned to love the sea though it confronted them with dangers and hardships, so these scientists and pioneer travellers came to love the mountains in spite of, or perhaps because of, their severity.

We, to-day, envy them the access they had to that unknown mountain world, and the unspoiled culture of its people. But even now the Alps themselves are potentially what they were, if only a man goes to them in the right spirit. Hilaire Belloc, in our own day, saw the Alps by the grace of his shaping imagination, as "peak and field and needle of intense ice, remote, remote from the world".

But it is useless to long for the past. We cannot put back the clock of Time. We cannot set out with Columbus and experience the thrill of finding

America, nor sail with Captain Cook in search of the mythical continent of the South Pacific. We cannot share the mounting excitement of the men who first crossed the high pass from Zermatt to Breuil and saw Italy below them, and above them the curving spire of the unclimbed Matterhorn. Now, whether we like it or not, the Matterhorn is surrounded by hotels, and if we climb it we have the help of fixed ropes and the security of other men's experience.

But the greater mountain ranges of the world are still surprisingly little known. We now have the opportunity to see the Himalaya as De Saussure saw the Alps a hundred and fifty years ago. Its peaks and valleys are unexplored. Its people are leading natural lives, instead of feverishly exploiting their country for profit of doubtful value. The Himalaya provides an even greater field of opportunity than the Alps gave to De Saussure. It is so vast a range that it embraces many countries and different types of people. The peaks and glaciers present such difficulties to the pioneer that exploring them calls for a higher standard of mountaineering skill than at present exists.

Let us approach this great heritage in the right spirit, not impelled by ambition. Let us study its people and their culture. Let us explore its vast tangle of mountains and glaciers, penetrating the deep sunless gorges to find the hidden beauty which lies beyond, crossing unknown passes which lead us from one region of mystery to another. Let us climb peaks by all means, because their beauty attracts us; not because others have failed, nor because the summits stand 28, 000 feet above the sea, nor in patriotic fervour for the honour of the nation, nor for cheap publicity. Let us approach the peaks with humility; and, having found the way to them for ourselves, learn to solve their problems. Let us not attack them with an army, announcing on the wireless to a sensation-loving world the news of our departure and the progress of our subsequent advance.

But it is not yet time to climb these great mountains. With so much of the vast Himalaya still a blank on the map, our first privilege is to explore rather than to climb. In two hundred years, when the Himalaya are known, then we may enjoy the range by climbing its peaks. In two thousand years time, when all the peaks are climbed, we shall look for more difficult routes by which to climb them, to recapture the feel of adventure, and perhaps to demonstrate our modern superiority!

It is unfortunately just as possible to go to the Himalaya, as to the Alps, with the wrong attitude of mind. Whether people realize that mountaineering is an inspiration, or condemn it as an insane risk of human life, it is obvious that its value lies in the motives of the climber. The ascent of Everest, like any other human endeavour, is only to be judged by the spirit in which it is attempted.

There is something fine in the desire to test human endurance against the deadening power of altitude, the difficulties of steep ice and rock, and the searching rigours of intense cold and wind; but the greatest value of the art of climbing, with its perfect co-ordination of mind and muscle, is that it teaches man a way of living in the beauty and solitude of high remote places.

And so – despite all the turmoil – the preparations of an expedition are for me so full of excitement that the irritation and delays only increase my longing to be off.

The voyage out to India was an interlude between a life and a life. We arrived at Bombay on April 22nd.

CHAPTER THREE

Sherpas and Sahibs

OUR first camp was on the railway platform at Rawalpindi. Tilman, Spender and I arrived there at 5 a.m. on the morning of April 26th. I was not very popular with my companions, as I had travelled from Karachi in complete luxury in a gleaming white-and-chromium special coach, whereas they had slept – or rather failed to sleep – on the dirty floor of a crowded second-class carriage. My exalted circumstances were due to "friends at court". On the strength of a slender introduction to Government House, I had been thrust into the luxurious comfort of a private saloon. My host welcomed me with the greatest kindness. The next morning, after a deliciously comfortable night in an air-conditioned bedroom, followed by a bath and a sumptuous breakfast, I emerged immaculate – having honoured the occasion with my best suit – and strolled along the platform of a wayside halt. I encountered two soot-blackened ruffians, their unshaven faces streaming with grimy sweat, their tired eyes regarding me with incredulous loathing. I could just recognize them as Tilman and Spender. I asked them how they had slept, and made some remark about it being surprisingly cool in the Sind desert for the time of year. Their effort at self-control would probably have broken down if the guard's whistle had not, at that moment, sent us hurrying back to our respective coaches. For the rest of the journey I kept a lofty distance.

We had arranged for our seven Sherpas to meet us at Rawalpindi. Auden was responsible for arranging to send them from Darjeeling and had told us when they would leave there. Time-tables had led us to expect their arrival at 8 a.m. on the 26th. I have had a good deal of experience of sending Sherpas across India, and have come to realize that they do not always keep to the schedules laid down by the railway organizers for the convenience of ordinary mortals. So when the eight o'clock train had disgorged its noisy mob and we could see no sign of our men, I was not discouraged. We settled down to a routine of meeting each train that came into Rawalpindi from an easterly direction. The station authorities soon began to take friendly interest in our activities. They joined heartily in the spirit of the game and wired to their colleagues down the line instructing them to search all trains for pigtailed passengers.

When evening came and there was still no sign of the missing men, we became tired of the monotony of station platforms and began to suspect that something was wrong. At ten o'clock we abandoned our vigil and went to sleep. I was roused at 3 a.m. by the station-master, who was in a great state of excitement. The Sherpas had arrived suddenly out of the blue. Going along the platform I was met by a bellow of greeting from Angtharkay and his followers. I am not usually conscious at 3 a.m. of any emotion except intense irritation, but the sight of the little group of grinning faces and the sound of their excited chatter penetrated my jaundiced soul, and persuaded me that after all there are some things worth being woken for.

We had chartered a lorry for which we had been persuaded to pay far too much. At 5.30 a.m. we loaded it with our baggage, squashed in somehow ourselves, and started on the two hundred mile drive to Srinagar. The Sherpas were in splendid spirits. They laughed and sang and fought with one another. It was difficult to believe that they had spent the last three nights and days on the wooden seats of a third-class carriage, chugging over the narrow-gauge lines of the cross-country route between Darjeeling and Rawalpindi, in the unaccustomed heat of the plains.

A long day in an Indian lorry is not a pleasant experience. In fact there are few hardships that I find more trying. We were delayed for several hours on the Kashmir frontier by the exasperating indecision of the customs officials; but by nightfall we reached Baramula, on the edge of the great plateau of Kashmir. We finished the journey to Srinagar on a brilliant frosty morning. The mists were rising from the green meadows; beyond them curved the placid hills, still white with winter snow. Lines of willows traced the course of lazy streams fringed with broad ribbons of mauve and white iris, a drift of colour above their stiff spear-shaped leaves. The cool air, bright with sunlight, welcomed us to the strange loveliness of this fabled land.

Srinagar was to be the starting-point of the expedition, and we spent a busy week there completing our arrangements. The last few days before the actual start of an expedition are usually rushed, muddled and uncomfortable. Tempers are strained, and one eventually sets out with the frantic feeling that something vital has been forgotten. But our week in Srinagar was a welcome exception to this rule. We were the guests of Sir Peter and Lady Clutterbuck, who smoothed out all our difficulties. Large tents had been pitched on their lawn for us, and we had the secluded peace of their garden in which to make our preparations. Our host and hostess were endlessly kind to us, and their help was invaluable. Whenever there was a lull in our work we found that they had planned some pleasant distraction for us. The Sherpas, too, had the time of their lives. They looked so fat and happy that we began to have serious doubts whether we should ever induce them to leave such luxurious living.

But it is time I introduced the Sherpas. Angtharkay I have already mentioned. He is a man of rare qualities, which make him outstandingly the best of all the Sherpas I have known. He is a lovable person, modest and completely sincere, with an infectious gaiety of spirit. There were six others: Sonam Tensing, known always as Sen Tensing, fat and jovial, with an engaging grin and a deep bass voice, with which he chanted religious incantations most of the day and night; Lobsang, serious, shy and slightly cynical, who regarded our activities with puzzled condescension; Ila, small, vivacious and shyly humorous; Lhakpa Tensing, wild and strong, who lived for laughter and nonsense and hard work; Angtensing, young in mind and behaviour; Nukku, slow in the uptake, but tough and strong as a mule. A fine band of men, both as friends and as servants.

Six expeditions to the Himalaya had convinced me of the tremendous advantage which a light mobile party has over the cumbersome organizations which have too frequently been employed for climbing and exploration in that part of the world. To my mind, the first essential of efficiency in planning and carrying out such an enterprise is to avoid taking any item of equipment not strictly necessary, and to see that every man in the party has his own particular job and that no one is redundant. In determining what clothes and equipment are necessary for the safeguard of health and efficiency and what items are superfluous one must rely on actual experience. One man, for instance, may find that he needs four sweaters to keep him warm at high altitudes; another may find that he is comfortable with two – should he take four, he is burdening the expedition unnecessarily. Some men can sleep without a pillow, others find this impossible. Some men wear out their socks more quickly than others do and must therefore take a larger supply. But in the case of equipment, one can generalize more freely. The most important items are sleeping-bags, boots, tents and rope, and these must be the very best procurable. The most suitable sleeping-bags are made of eiderdown, covered with silk fabric.

Here is a list of the personal kit allowance for each of the European members of the party, which we estimated as sufficient for a five months' expedition:

- 1 sleeping bag
- 1 rubber ground mat (2 ft. × 3 ft.)
- 1 windproof suit
- 2 pairs long woollen pants
- 3 sweaters
- 9 pairs socks
- 2 shirts (Tilman only took one)
- 1 pair shorts
- 1 pair pyjama trousers (these are used as a spare pair of trousers and to sleep in)
- 2 pairs fingerless woollen gloves
- 1 Balaclava helmet
- 2 pairs snow glasses
- 1 pair ankle puttees
- 1 pair climbing boots
- 1 pair gym shoes
- Camera and films
- Ice-axe
- Tobacco

All these can be packed easily into one large rucksack, and the ice-axe makes a good walking-stick for the march. Four or five aluminium cooking pots are needed for the whole party. For meals no one needs more than a tin mug, a tin plate, a spoon and a pen-knife. If a plate is lost, it is easy for two men to share. It is a mistake to add to the total weight by taking spare utensils.

It is far better to improvise than to take too much. For instance, when the remnants of my bootlaces were so knotted that they could no longer be used, I have often cut long strips of cloth from the ration bags, which have been just as effective. Should some of the spoons be lost, new ones can be fashioned out of bits of wood. Flat stones will serve for plates, and from the start a sharp twig makes an effective fork. If one's only pair of windproof trousers is wrecked on a jagged rock, and there is no more ration-bag cloth available as a patch, a piece of canvas out of the floor of a tent will serve to stop the draught. Every Sherpa can always produce a needle and cotton literally out of his hat.

I have found that such amenities as paraffin lamps are not necessary, for the party usually goes to bed with the sun. A glacier lantern, and a reasonable supply of candles for it, must of course be taken for early morning starts, and in case of the party being benighted. Soap is a refinement that one soon forgets; like so many other essentials of the civilized world, it is not missed in a primitive life. A tea-pot is an entirely unnecessary gadget of civilization, for the best tea in the world is made by throwing a handful of tea-leaves into boiling water. For cooking above the altitude where wood-fuel is found, a Primus is the most efficient stove. The rationing and carrying of paraffin oil, for a long period, is a very difficult problem: it is impossible to predict how long the party will remain above fuel-level, and containers are apt to leak when they have been roughly handled for several months. It is not advisable to risk running short of matches, for they are essential to the party's existence, and are light and easy to carry. Only experience can teach one the rate at which such items as matches and oil will be used. It is important to make a note of this, at the time, for future reference.

When travelling through inhabited districts it is best to rely on food which the natives can supply. A healthy man can easily accustom himself to the native diet of any country. More care is needed in provisioning the party when living in uninhabited regions; but this, too, is easy enough when there is some means of communication with the outside world, as is generally the case when a party is attempting to climb one of the great peaks of the Himalaya. For this reason, little thought has been given by Himalayan travellers to the question of rationing as it is understood in the Arctic, where the uninhabited areas are so vast that an exploring party is often cut off from supplies for many months.

As I have explained in chapter one, we had planned to be beyond the reach of supplies for a period of about four months. It was therefore necessary to base our provisions on the various rations which Arctic explorers have so carefully tabulated. It was, of course, advisable to make certain alterations to suit the different altitude conditions. I have found that fats are not easily digested at high altitudes; we therefore took a greater proportion of carbohydrates than is usually found in an Arctic diet, and in order to provide the same amount of calories we were obliged to take slightly greater bulk.

Our daily ration for each European member of the party was as follows:

Pemmican, 4 ounces.
Butter, 2 ounces.
Flour, rice and tsampa, 10 ounces.
Dried skimmed milk, 2 ounces.
Sugar, 8 ounces.
New Army Emergency Ration, 1 ounce.
Oats, 2 ounces.
Cheese, 3 ounces.

Total weight of food per man per day, two pounds.

Pemmican is a highly nutritious but dismally unpalatable meat extract in the form of paste. The new Army Emergency Ration looks rather like coarse chocolate, but I believe has some meat extract mixed with the chocolate.

Tsampa is roasted flour, a most convenient form of food used by the people of the Himalaya and throughout Central Asia.[1] Skimmed milk was taken rather than full cream milk, because of its higher protein content. Vitamins A and D were provided for by Crook's Halibut Liver Oil, Vitamin C by Hoffman La Roche a-scorbic acid tablets, and Vitamin B by dried yeast. We took a .375 rifle in the hope of supplementing this diet occasionally with fresh meat.

In accordance with their usual fare, the porters' rations were somewhat different from ours, and consisted of a much higher percentage of flour and tsampa. We also took with us tea, salt and curry powder, but these were not strictly rationed.

All the principal items of equipment had been brought from England, but we purchased cooking and eating utensils and minor domestic necessities in the bazaar in Srinagar. The Sherpas took a leading part in our shopping expeditions. They would not allow us to buy anything which they considered to be expensive. They know all the arts of bargaining, and regard it as a sacred duty. We spent hours in the bazaar comparing the relative weights of various makes of spoons, plates and mugs, and debating whether each member of the party should be allowed a knife, or whether one knife was enough for two of us. Tilman was strongly opposed to our taking plates, insisting that one could eat everything out of a mug. I maintained that if we happened to be eating curry and rice and drinking tea at the same time, it would be nicer to have them served in separate receptacles.

When we had decided exactly what was to be bought, the actual purchase of each article was left to the Sherpas, who played one shopkeeper against the next, in masterly style, until they had achieved rock-bottom prices.

We ordered, among other things, about a hundred canvas bags to hold the flour which was to be taken from the last villages which we should pass. It was essential that the flour should be kept dry, so we bought a tarpaulin to spread over the stores at night.

Our stuff had finally to be sorted out and made up into loads suitable for transport. To save weight, we packed everything in sacks, instead of wooden boxes. For the first few marches we were to use pack-ponies, and we interviewed a series of contractors, each desperately eager to secure our custom.

Meanwhile Spender was busy adjusting his survey instruments, and trying to reduce their weight to my rigid specifications. Auden arrived from Calcutta on May 2nd already equipped with a full-grown beard, which he had acquired in his recent geological survey in the Garhwal Himalaya, and clung to through the social occasions of a three weeks' stay in Calcutta. He had brought business-like crates of equipment, which Tilman and I viewed with dismay and rejected without discussion, substituting instead one large rucksack, to which he resigned himself without much protest.

One of our chief difficulties was to forecast accurately the amount of money which would be required during the actual expedition. Most of the money had to be taken in silver, which weighs a surprising amount. We took a thousand rupees with us from Srinagar and arranged to collect a further three thousand from the

[1] The word "tsampa" is Tibetan, its Urdu equivalent being "satu".

Government Treasury at Skardu, which was a fortnight's march on our way.

All our arrangements were completed by May 5th and at noon on that day we packed our loads and the Sherpas into a lorry and sent them off to Woyil Bridge, where the motor road ends. Sir Peter and Lady Clutterbuck, and my mother who had been staying with them, motored us there, and gave us a farewell picnic lunch, which we were often to remember in the lean days ahead.

CHAPTER FOUR

Local Colour

THE vale of Kashmir is a wide plain, with many lakes, 5,000 feet above sea-level. It is ringed by mountains rising to 15,000 and 17,000 feet. To the north and east the various passes across these mountains are closed to traffic in the winter months by heavy snow, and it is difficult to reach Ladakh, Baltistan and Gilgit. These passes are not usually declared open officially until June; but it is possible, by travelling at night, to cross them without much danger of avalanches earlier in the spring. Our way led from the Vale of Kashmir, up the Sind valley and over the Zoji La (11,500 feet) into Ladakh.

For the first two marches, May 5th and 6th, the valley was wide and well cultivated. The days were hot, and a gusty wind blew clouds of dust into our faces. We were not in a mood to enjoy life. We were out of training. We trudged petulantly along with parched throats, stiff muscles and blistered feet. The world seemed dry, harsh and unfriendly. But the marches were short and ended pleasantly in the comforts of a rest-house and countless mugs of tea. It was chilly in the evenings, and we sat round splendid log fires, feasting on hot buttered toast. Lady Clutterbuck had given us a hamper filled with delicious fruit and English bread and cakes, luxuries from which we were soon to be parted. But the days of strict rationing were still far ahead, and every night Angtharkay fed us royally on soup, roast chicken, vegetables and potatoes. Spender had smuggled two pounds of coffee into his load. He had a real flair for coffee-making; I have never tasted better.

On the 7th we passed through a narrow gorge, choked with an immense quantity of avalanche debris – rocks, twisted tree trunks and cones of snow, a proof of the danger of these upper valleys in the winter months. This ravine led us into the open Alpine valley of Sonamarg. Drifts of snow still lay on its lower slopes, and where the grass showed it was sodden and dead. It was too early for the spring flowers. We spent a dismal rainy afternoon in the empty village. We paid for our ten pack-ponies and sent them back, as there was too much snow ahead for pony transport. Coolies had come up from below to take their place.

Our start the next morning was delayed by the usual pandemonium among the coolies, each man struggling to find the lightest load. But the upper valley was sunlit and peaceful. The morning light slanted across the pines, giving them

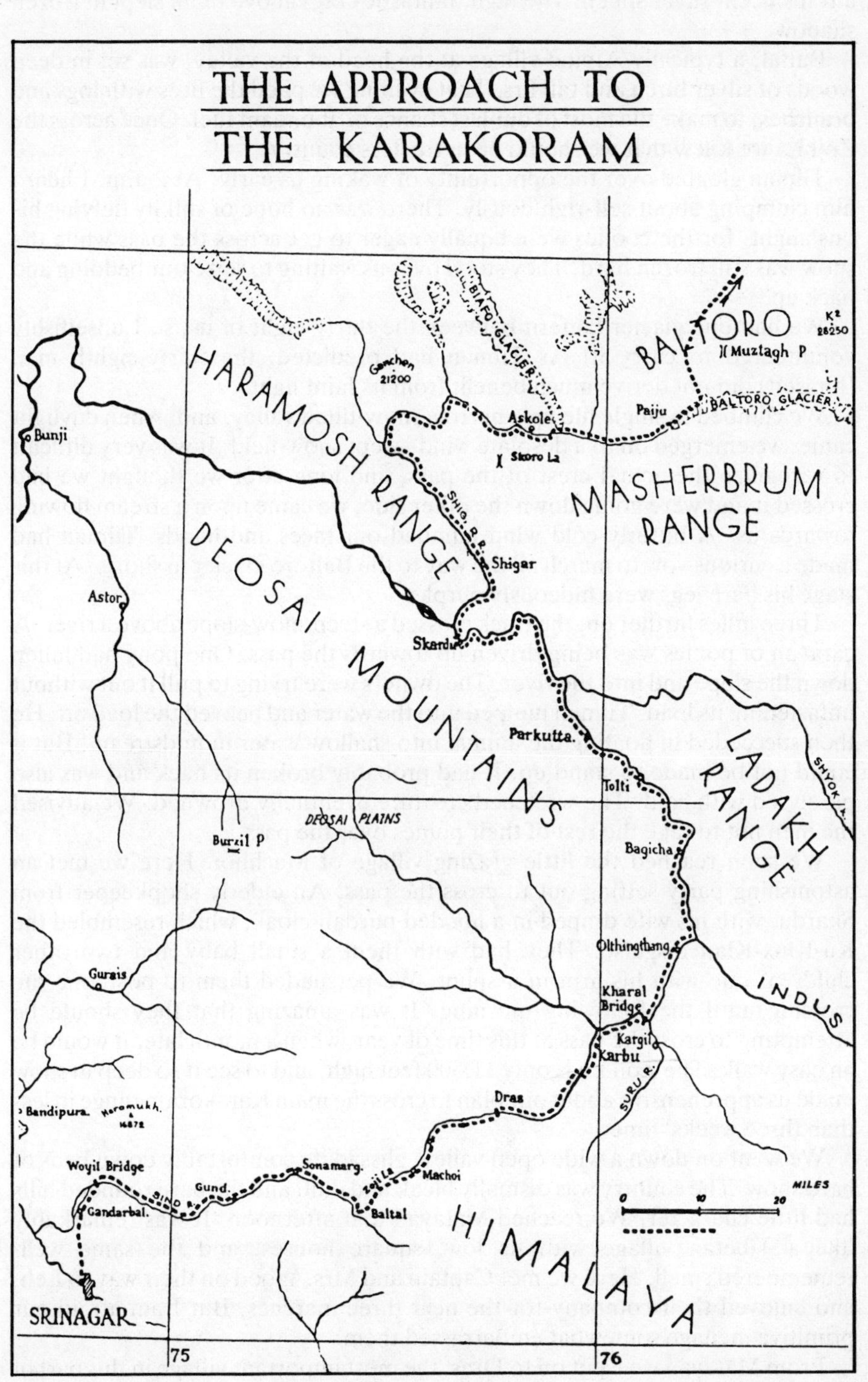
THE APPROACH TO
THE KARAKORAM
HARAMOSH RANGE
DEOSAI MOUNTAINS
MASHERBRUM RANGE
LADAKH RANGE
HIMALAYA
BALTORO
BIAFO GLACIER
BALTORO GLACIER
K2
28250
Muztagh P
Ganchen
21200
Paiju
Askole
Skoro La
SHIGAR R.
Bunji
Astor
Shigar
Skardu
Parkutta
Tolti
SHYOK R.
DEOSAI PLAINS
Burzil P
Bagicha
Olthingthang
Kharal
Bridge
Kargil
Karbu
INDUS
SURU R.
Dras
Gurais
Bandipura
Haramukh
16872
Woyil Bridge
Gund.
SIND R.
Gandarbal.
Sonamarg.
ZOJI LA
Machoi
Baltal
MILES
0
10
20
SRINAGAR
75
76

a translucent silver sheen. The high, fantastic crags above them slept in frozen shadow.

Baltal, a typically Alpine village at the head of the valley, was set in deep woods of silver birch and tall firs. That evening we piled the fires with logs and branches, to make the most of our last chance of abundant fuel. Once across the Zoji La we knew that we should be in treeless country.

Tilman gloated over the opportunity of waking us early. At 2 a.m. I heard him clumping about self-righteously. There was no hope of sulkily defying his onslaught, for the coolies were equally eager to get across the pass while the snow was still frozen hard. They stood over us waiting to seize our bedding and pack up.

We had one glacier lantern between the thirty-eight of us, so I unselfishly volunteered to carry it! As Tilman had predicted, the thirty-eighth man (himself) did not derive much benefit from its faint light.

We climbed in single file up a narrow snow-filled valley, and, when daylight came, we emerged on to a desolate wind-swept snow-field. It was very difficult to recognize the actual crest of the pass, and long after we thought we had crossed it and were going down the other side, we came upon a stream flowing towards us. A bitterly cold wind numbed our faces and hands. Tilman had made a curious vow to march all the way to the Baltoro glacier in shorts. At this stage his bare legs were hideously purple.

Three miles farther on, the track crossed a steep snow-slope above a river. A caravan of ponies was being driven up towards the pass. One pony had fallen down the slope and into the river. The owners were trying to pull it out without unfastening its load. Tilman jumped into the water and heaved the load off. He then succeeded in floating the animal into shallow water in midstream. But it could not be made to stand up. It had probably broken its back and was also paralysed with cold. The wretched creature eventually drowned. We advised the men not to take the rest of their ponies over the pass.

We soon reached the little grazing village of Machhoi. Here we met an astonishing party setting out to cross the pass. An elderly shopkeeper from Skardu, with his wife draped in a hooded purdah-cloak, which resembled the Ku-Klux-Klan disguise. They had with them a small baby and two other children, one with his arm in a splint. We persuaded them to postpone the crossing until the following morning. It was amazing that they should be attempting to cross the pass at this time of year, when a month later it would be an easy walk. The Zoji La is only 11,500 feet high, and to see it so deep in snow made us apprehensive about our plan to cross the main Karakoram range in less than three weeks' time.

We went on down a wide open valley, glissading comfortably down beds of hard snow. The country was dismally bleak and dull, and the bare rounded hills had little character. We reached Matayan that afternoon. It was remarkably like a Tibetan village with its low, square houses, and the same well-remembered smell. Here we met Captain and Mrs. Wood on their way to Leh, and enjoyed their company for the next three marches. But I am afraid our primitive ménage somewhat embarrassed them.

From Matayan we went on to Dras, the most important village in this part of the world. There we tried to buy eggs and a sheep, but Angtharkay said they were too expensive. He was adamant about this, so our fare was leaner than usual. Everyone in Dras who gave us the slightest assistance, or even spoke to us demanded "baksheesh". This is an unpleasant characteristic of the villages on any route by which Europeans journey. It is largely due to the thoughtlessness of travellers. It is so easy to be the "pukka sahib" and to dole out money to all and sundry, but so degrading for everyone concerned.

Below Dras, we had a long march of twenty-two miles to Karbu. The country became more rugged and we entered a deep-cut valley. It was a hot, tiring day, and we were glad to reach the cool shade of the irrigated village.

The next day, May 12th, I started early and walked ahead of the others, thoroughly enjoying the cool morning air. After several miles, I halted on the sandy shore of the river. I was surrounded by steep cliffs, utterly barren, but across the river was a village in a mist of pink apricot blossom, its terraces of young corn climbing the hillside in steps of vivid green. It was like finding a corner of Kentish spring set in the midst of the arid crags of Aden. In this lovely place I waited for the rest of the party. We lazed in the sun and bathed, forgetting the time, and continued our march reluctantly in the heat of the day. In the middle of the afternoon we reached Kharal bridge, which spans the Dras river at its confluence with the Suru river, and marks the junction of the Leh and Skardu routes. There is no village at this point, but three miles away, along the Leh road, lies the important town of Kargil. We camped on a hot dusty shelf near the bridge. Angtharkay and Lhakpa Tensing went on to Kargil to see what they could buy. They returned in the evening with three chickens, two dozen eggs, two pounds of meat and a bottle of arak. They had drunk a whole bottle of this intoxicating brew, but, in spite of this, they did not think much of Kargil, though they were full of stories of the Coronation Day celebrations in this remote town. We drank to the occasion, and when the arak was finished our surroundings looked somehow less depressing.

From Kharal bridge we followed the course of the Suru river down through its barren rocky ravines. Every few miles we came to the startling contrast of irrigated villages, with their cascading terraces of young crops, shaded by spreading trees in new leaf, feathery against the light. The fruit-blossom here was over, but the tumbling streams were bordered with purple iris. This surprisingly swift change was due to the lower altitude, for only the previous day, at the first of these enchanting villages, the fruit trees had spread a cloak of blossom over the hillside. Between these villages, our path led down through a succession of ravines. It was sometimes carved out of the face of a vertical cliff, overhanging the Suru hundreds of feet below. The oily river slid silently through this strange country with sinister strength. From time to time it plunged over rapids, with a roar that echoed for miles up the valley.

We went on through increasing heat, glare and desolation. Every afternoon we camped in a pleasant oasis. It was good to wash away the dust of the march in clear streams, and to forget the day's heat, lounging in shady meadows. Stripping to bathe at Olthingthang I dropped my watch and broke the spring. My diary's comment reads: "Bloody nuisance! But I suppose I shall get as used to being without it as I have got used to having no trousers to change into." This prophecy proved remarkably correct, and I spent the next five months without giving a thought to my loss.

We reached the Indus on May 14th, having followed a network of rivers from the tiny beginning of one of them in a mountain stream on the Zoji La, till we saw them pour finally into the Indus in a mighty force of water. To follow any river throughout its course is strangely fascinating to me.

For some curious reason, the Indus is destined from its very source to flow through desert for the whole of its journey to the Arabian sea. A few miles away from the Indus valley there is often fertile country, but the river itself seems to create arid desolation wherever it goes, except where human ingenuity has irrigated its banks into fertility.

It follows a peculiarly difficult route, and seems to delight in carving a way through the highest mountain barriers. It rises on the north side of the main Himalayan range, only a short way from the source of the Brahmaputra, and is at once attracted, as if by a magnet, to the great peaks of the Karakoram. When it approaches Nanga Parbat it alters its course towards it, and cuts its way through a maze of obstacles to reach the Sind desert.

Following the Indus downstream, we passed river terraces many hundreds of feet above us – indications of the river's course in former times, before it had cut down to its present level.

Tilman used to bathe several times a day, though the rest of us found the water too cold, and therefore maintained that it was a bad thing to do, though sometimes even I was tempted to have a dip. Once we passed a splendid waterfall plunging over a great overhanging cliff two hundred feet high. It fell on to a circle of huge boulders, throwing up clouds of spray which watered a little green meadow below. Tilman and I stripped off our clothes, and climbed on to the boulders, while the spray beat up into our faces. It was very cold. The sun was diffused through a silver mist, and a brilliant rainbow formed round each of us, expanding and contracting in the drifting spray. It was a wonderful sight. After a pause to recover my breath and bask in the hot sun, I returned to explore the enchanting caves behind the waterfall. They were filled with moss and ferns, and beads of spray clustered everywhere like dew. Each drop reflected the colours of my personal rainbow as I moved.

We used to make a long halt each day, about noon, at one of the villages through which we passed. Those ahead would choose the halting-place. When the whole party had forgathered, we always lit a fire in the shade of the apricot trees and scrambled as many eggs as the village could provide. No one ever had the forethought to bring any utensils, so we always had to rely on the villagers for a cooking pot, and we ate out of this, to the vast amusement of the natives, with spoons made from bits of wood. In spite of these halts, or perhaps because of them, we never succeeded in accomplishing the daily march without a great deal of effort. We usually arrived at our destination thoroughly weary and footsore, complaining bitterly about the length of the march. Tilman declared dejectedly that we would certainly be turned out of any self-respecting hiking club in England. But I found solace in the fact that mountaineers are notoriously bad walkers. Frequently in the hot afternoons we suffered a good deal from thirst. This was particularly bad when we had succumbed to the temptation of drinking from a spring early in the day. During these thirsty hours, when we were marching over long waterless stretches, we would walk sullenly along, thinking of beer, and feeling that nothing else in the world mattered. But ten seconds after arriving at a spring, beer meant nothing, and we would not have gone a hundred yards to get it.

At every village and all along the route the natives were helpful and friendly, and one of my most pleasant memories of the journey was our daily contact with them. At Tolti, a large settlement with many square miles of terraced cultivation, we were honoured by a visit from the local Rajah. A sticky conversation was helped out by a few cigarettes that Spender had brought from Port Said, and ended by the Rajah's servant asking to see our rifle. We assembled it laboriously, but he insisted on seeing it shoot. We obliged, and blazed off into the air. But this did not satisfy him, and someone was sent to put up a bit of paper as a target, at about two hundred yards' range. Tilman was entrusted with the task of upholding our prestige. He had never fired the rifle before, and shot too high, completely missing the target. We were reluctant to waste more ammunition, but the Rajah's servant insisted on trying his skill. He had obviously never fired a rifle before, and he clutched it in a most haphazard manner, holding it loosely, with the butt in the middle of his chest. While he was aiming, we took the hurried precaution of making everyone stand well behind the firing line. He tugged at the trigger. The recoil nearly knocked him over, but the target was blown to bits! Inspired by this triumph, the Rajah then suggested that we should take on the local team at polo. But fearing further humiliation, we made specious excuses, and he departed with his retinue.

Polo is the national sport in this part of the world. All the larger villages have a polo ground, usually bounded by stone walls. A queer variety of the game is played, with no chukkers, and no change of ponies. The game does not end till one side or the other has scored nine goals – and not always then. It starts by the captain of one side galloping madly down the field and throwing the ball in where he feels inclined, usually just in time for him to hit a neat goal. If a Rajah is playing he is usually accompanied on to the field by the local band! Brighter polo perhaps, but I am not sorry that we decided to let discretion be the better part of valour.

The last march into Skardu, the capital of Baltistan, was twenty-one miles, mostly over sand flats, which made tiring going. We arrived there, after fourteen marches from Srinagar, on May 18th. Skardu is situated in a broad alluvial plain, at the junction of the Shigar river with the Indus. We had decided to halt for a day in Skardu, as we still had many things to settle. In the evening, we called on the Thasildar, the administrator in charge of the district. He was extremely helpful, and gave us much valuable information about transport and supplies. He advised us not to buy our flour in Skardu, but to rely on getting it in Askole, the last village through which we should pass, five stages farther on. He explained that as there had been a famine in Askole the people there would be only too willing to sell us all the flour we needed at very cheap rates. We did not quite follow this curious reasoning, and wondered whether he perhaps had a grudge against the local flour merchant! But as the plan would save us the enormous expense of transporting two tons of flour from Skardu to Askole, we decided to rely on his statement. He sent a chaprassi (orderly) ahead to see that the difficult route to Askole was open.

The next morning, we celebrated the rest day by lazing in bed till 7.30. But there was very little else in the day that was restful. Letters had to be written, for this was the last place from which we could post them, and our last purchases and final arrangements had to be planned. We bought 250 lbs. of sugar, 500 lbs. of tsampa, 280 lbs. of rice, 40 lbs. of ghi (clarified butter used for cooking), 40 lbs. of salt, and 12 gallons of paraffin oil for the Primus stoves. We also bought several thousand coolie cigarettes for the porters. We went with the Thasildar to collect the three thousand rupees which we had paid to the Kashmir Government in Srinagar, to be handed over to us in Skardu. The Treasury was heavily guarded, presumably from a mob of loafers who sat and chatted amicably with the guards, and who helped us to count the money and to detect bad rupees. We had tea with the Thasildar and discussed the administrative problems of the district. His secretary stood behind him swotting flies and joining enthusiastically in the conversation. The local doctor called on us in the evening. He said that he had recently vaccinated 30,000 people in the neighbourhood and wanted to add us to his victims.

The Thasildar had asked us to employ men from some villages near Skardu. They were a fine looking crowd and we agreed to sign on seventeen of them. Our transport column had now expanded to sixteen ponies. These and all the rest of our stuff had now to be transported across the Indus. The Thasildar accompanied us down to the shore, where we found the ferry arriving with a large cargo from Shigar. It was a big wooden barge of rough solid build, propelled and navigated by two huge oars astern, three crooked punt poles and half-dozen paddles. When it had disgorged its cargo, it had to be towed for several hundred yards upstream before we could embark. It would only hold eight ponies and half our kit, and we had to do the journey in two relays. The Sherpas were in a great state of excitement as we cast off, shouting wildly and bombarding those on shore with dried dung. They then seized the paddles and wielded them furiously in the wrong direction. However, as the craft relied for its progress mostly on the oars and the poles, their efforts did not hinder us much, and soon they abandoned paddling for the better sport of splashing each other with water. We were carried downstream by the current at an alarming rate, and seemed to make very little progress across the river. However, we eventually stuck in the mud on the opposite side and landed our belongings. Then the barge had to be dragged laboriously upstream through the shallow water before it was pushed out into the swirling river again. It took about three hours to get the whole party across.

In the afternoon we marched over hot sand flats to Shigar, bathing on the way. We camped on the dusty polo ground, and were so thirsty that we spent hours combing the bazaar for drink, but only succeeded in raising half a bottle of arak, which was deplorably inadequate.

Before leaving Shigar the next morning, we bought a large quantity of locally-woven blankets at five rupees each, for the coolies whom we were to take from Askole. It was another twenty-mile march to Yuno, the next halting-place, but the first half of it was very delightful, along a shady lane, the air fresh with the smell of green corn. We made a long halt at midday for a more than usually excellent lunch of scrambled eggs, dozens of them, and stewed apricots. The export of dried apricots is a considerable industry in Baltistan, and we were told that they send quantities to England. They are exceptionally sweet, and quite unlike the usual loofah-like atrocities in grocers' shops. The kernels, too, are delicious, with a delicate almond flavour.

As we went up the Shigar valley, we found that the people were a depressingly weedy crowd. We began to wonder if, at Askole, we would find men strong enough for the severe task of carrying loads over the main range. Most of the people we saw were afflicted with enormous goitres. The Skardu men, who by now had caught us up, looked magnificent in comparison. Some of the Skardu coolies were really fine creatures, tall, blue-eyed and well built.

At Yuno, we had to camp on a tiny, dusty terrace with no water near at hand. Angtensing and I went a long way up the hill to find an irrigation channel, and we opened a dam to let the water flow towards our camp. Before we had completed our task, we were attacked by an irate farmer, brandishing a spade and swearing unintelligible oaths. He drove us off, and rectified the damage we had done, so that we had to search elsewhere for water.

At the end of the next day's march to Dusso we had to cross the Shigar river, which was here a foaming torrent. The voyage had to be undertaken on rafts, each made of twenty sheepskin bladders lashed together, and strengthened by strips of wood. Four men paddled each raft with sticks that had no blade to them. It was a terrifying experience to entrust our lives and our belongings to such ridiculously frail craft, on a racing river with ugly rapids in sight ahead. The most alarming moment occurred when the crew downed sticks to blow up the leaking bladders! There were two rafts working, and they both had to make four complete journeys before all our stuff was across the river. It was an anxious time, and I felt very relieved when the last load arrived safely. We could not, of course, get the ponies on to the raft, and from here we had to rely entirely on coolie transport. We required forty-five men, and these had been collected by the Skardu Thasildar's chaprassi, who was waiting for us at Dusso. There was an aquamarine mine at this village, which Auden went to investigate.

The last two marches to Askole lead over very difficult country. The route has frequently to be altered according to the state of the river. Sometimes long detours are necessary to avoid an impassable gorge, and in places rickety ladders propped against the rock solve the problem of a vertical precipice. More alarming still are the rope bridges across the river. These are made of three strands of thick rope, constructed in the shape of a V, with one rope for one's feet, and the other two ropes as hand-rails. We managed to avoid these horrors by performing a delicate rock traverse across water-polished cliffs. The coolies negotiated the rocks with surprising skill, though they were each carrying sixty-pound loads.

Tilman, who returned by this route, was obliged to cross the rope bridges, as the river was flooded and he could not traverse the cliff. He gave me a vivid description of their perils, and said that Sen Tensing, who was with him, turned pale with fright.

As we went up the valley we noticed a greater number of cretins and deaf-mutes among the inhabitants, a state of affairs due, I suppose, to inter-breeding in this isolated district.

The last week had brought us rainy weather, which became worse as we approached the high mountains. With so much moisture it seemed strange that the country was so arid.

About four miles from Askole we came upon a sulphur spring. Tilman and I wallowed in its deep pools of hot water. It was rather like bathing in soda-water, for the sulphur bubbles hissed on the surface as we moved. Our ablutions were disturbed by the arrival of some Balti maidens, who giggled at our evident embarrassment.

A short way farther on we came to a village which was in a state of pandemonium. A battle was raging between the villagers and the Sherpas. It transpired that one of the Skardu men had damaged the tin of ghi that he was carrying. The Sherpas had remonstrated with him, and the argument had ended in a fight, in which the villagers had sided with the Skardu man. We managed to restore peace, but two hundred yards beyond the village we found the blubbering figure of the culprit. He sobbed more violently as we approached, and displayed the wounds that he had received from one of the Sherpas. We pointed out that he was nearly twice the size of his assailant. We eventually managed to console him by promising to inquire into the whole affair when we reached Askole. He followed us, bursting into tears whenever we met anyone, or overtook one of the coolies. The matter was settled later by reprimanding the Sherpas, and compensating the injured man. But the incident did not improve our relations with the Balti villagers, whose goodwill was of such importance to us during the next few weeks.

CHAPTER FIVE

The Passes of the Great Karakoram

WE had now arrived at the most critical stage of the expedition. Everything depended on our being able to transport our equipment and about one and a half tons of food across the main Karakoram range into the Shaksgam valley. But besides this food, which was calculated to keep the party alive for three and a half months, we had to take with us food for the men who were carrying our stuff, and then food for those who had to carry that food. Not only had these men to be fed while they were with us, but they had also to be catered for on their return journey to Askole. It was the old problem which has to be faced whenever a journey is being planned through country where there are no supplies, and where everything has to be carried: a party cannot travel for many days without the carriers being burdened with so much of their own food that they cannot carry anything else. In this respect a man is a very inefficient beast of burden, for he eats more in proportion to his carrying-power than any of his four-legged rivals.

We estimated that the crossing from Askole to the Shaksgam could be made in eleven stages. Although the route had not been used by the people of Baltistan or Turkestan for a very long time, the Mustagh pass had been crossed twice by Europeans, whose accounts of their journeys we had to guide us in making our plans. This, of course, was a great assistance, and made our task comparatively straightforward.

In 1887, Younghusband, at the end of his famous Trans-Asiastic journey, crossed the Mustagh pass, from the Shaksgam river into Baltistan. Before leaving Yarkand, the last town through which he passed in Turkestan, he received a letter from Mr. (now Sir Charles) Bell urging him to attempt the former direct route to Baltistan, over the main range of the Karakoram, by way of the Mustagh pass. This route had never been explored by Europeans, though its existence had been reported to the early explorers of the south side of the range. Younghusband found that a large number of Baltis – about two thousand – was settled in the Yarkand district. Several of these men were willing to accompany him. One of them, a native of Askole, whose name was Wali, said that he had come to Yarkand over the Mustagh pass many years before. He assured Younghusband that he had not forgotten the way, and undertook to guide the party.

They left Yarkand on September 8th, 1887, and were obliged to take three weeks' supply of food with them, enough for the whole journey. They followed the course of the Yarkand river and reached the Shaksgam by way of the Aghil pass. The ascent of the Sarpo Laggo glacier and the actual crossing of the Mustagh pass, was an astonishing climax at the end of Younghusband's great journey from Pekin to India. It is best described in his own words:

"When we ascended the valley of the Sarpo Laggo stream, towards the Mustagh pass, we came to a point where the valley was blocked by what appeared to be enormous heaps of broken stones and fragments of rock . . . On coming up to the heaps, I found that they were masses of solid ice, merely covered over on the surface with a thin layer of this rocky debris, which served to conceal the surface of the ice immediately beneath. And my dismay can be imagined when, on ascending one of the highest of the mounds, I found that they were but the end of a series which extended without interruption for many miles up the valley to the snows at the foot of the pass. We were, in fact, at the extremity of an immense glacier. This was the first time I had actually been on a glacier, and I had never realized till now how huge and continuous a mass of ice it is."

The astonishing fact that Younghusband had at that time no mountaineering experience and had never been on a glacier, makes his achievement even more remarkable.

"To take a caravan of ponies up a glacier like this," Younghusband goes on, "seemed to me an utter impossibility. The guides thought so too, and I decided upon sending the ponies round by the Karakoram pass to Leh, and going on myself over the Mustagh pass with a couple of men. This would have been a risky proceeding, for if we did not find our way over the pass we should have scarcely enough provisions with us to last till we could return to an inhabited place again. Supplies altogether were running short, and the longer we took in reaching the pass, the harder we should fare if we did not succeed in getting over it. But while I was deciding upon sending the ponies back, the caravan men were gallantly leading them up the glacier. I rejoined the men, and we all helped the ponies along as well as we could; hauling at them in front, pushing behind, and sometimes unloading and carrying the loads up the stone-covered mounds of ice ourselves. But it was terribly hard and trying work for the animals . . . We had only advanced a few hundred yards, and there were from fifteen to twenty miles of glacier ahead. I therefore halted the ponies for the day, and went on with a couple of men to reconnoitre. We fortunately found, in between the glacier and the mountain-side, a narrow stretch of less impracticable ground, along which it would be possible to take the ponies. This we marked out, and returned to our bivouac after dark . . .

"At daybreak on the following morning we started again, leading the ponies up the route we had marked out; but a mile from the point where our previous exploration had ended we were confronted by another great glacier flowing down from the left. We now had a glacier on one side of us, mountains on the other, and a second glacier right across our front. At this time my last remaining pair of boots were completely worn out, and my feet so sore from the bruises they received on the glacier I could scarcely bear to put them to the ground . . .

"We were in a sea of ice. There was now little of the rocky moraine stuff with which the ice of the glacier had been covered in its lower part, and we looked out on a vast river of pure white ice, broken up into myriads of sharp needle-like points. Snowy mountains rose above us on either hand . . . and rising forbiddingly before us was the cold icy range we should have to cross . . .

"That night we held a council of war as to which of the two Mustagh passes we should attack. There are two passes, known as the Mustagh, which cross the range. One, to the east, that is to our left as we were ascending the glacier, is known as the Old Mustagh pass, and was in use in former days, till the advance of ice upon it made it so difficult that a new one was sought for, and what is known as the New Mustagh pass, some ten miles farther west along the range, had been discovered. It was over this latter pass that the guides hoped to conduct our party. They said that even ponies had been taken across it by means of ropes and by making rough bridges across the crevasses. No European had crossed either of them, but Colonel Godwin-Austen, in 1862, reached the southern foot of the new pass in the course of his survey of Baltistan. The New Mustagh pass seemed the more promising of the two, and I therefore decided upon sending two men on the following morning to reconnoitre it and report upon its practicability.

"At the first streak of daylight the reconnoitrers set out, and the remainder of us afterwards followed with the ponies along the route which we had explored on the previous day. We took the ponies up the glacier without any serious difficulty, and in the evening halted close up to the head of the glacier. At dusk the two men who had been sent out to reconnoitre the new pass returned, to say that the ice had so accumulated on it that it would be now quite impossible to take ponies over, and that it would be difficult even for men to cross it. The plan which they now suggested was to leave the ponies behind, and cross the range by the Old Mustagh pass, push on to Askole, the first village on the south side of the range, and from there send back men with supplies for the ponies and the men with them, sufficient to enable the caravan to reach Shahidula, on the usual trade route between Yarkand and Kashmir. This was evidently all we could do. We could not take the ponies any farther, and we could not send them back as they were, for we had nearly run out of supplies, and Shahidula, the nearest point at which fresh supplies could be obtained, was one hundred and eighty miles distant. All now depended upon our being able to cross the pass. If we were not able to, we should have to march this one hundred and eighty miles back through the mountains with only three or four days' supplies to support us. We might certainly have eaten the ponies, so would not actually have starved; but we should have had a hard struggle for it, and there would still have been the range to cross at another point.

"Matters were therefore approaching a very critical stage, and that was an anxious night for me. I often recall it, and think of our little bivouac in the snow at the foot of the range we had to overcome."

This statement of Younghusband's problem clearly illustrates why it is that the pioneer in any mountaineering or exploring venture meets with difficulties enormously greater than any his successors have to face.

"Next morning," the narrative continues, "while it was yet dark, Wali, the guide, awoke us. We each had a drink of tea and some bread, and then we started off to attack the pass. The ponies, with nearly all the baggage, were left behind under the charge of Liu-san, the Chinaman, and some of the older men . . . The ascent to the pass was easy but trying, for we were now not far from 19,000 feet above sea-level, and at that height, walking uphill through deep snow, one quickly becomes exhausted. We could only take a dozen or twenty steps at a time, and we would then bend over on our sticks and pant as if we had been running hard uphill. We were tantalized, too, by the apparent nearness of the pass. Everything here was on a gigantic scale, and what seemed to be not more than an hour's walk from the camp was in fact a six-hours' climb. It was nearly midday when we reached the top of the pass . . . There was nothing but a sheer precipice, and those first few moments on the summit of the Mustagh pass were full of intense anxiety to me. If we could but get over, the crowning success of my expedition would be gained. But the thing seemed to me simply an impossibility. I had had no experience of Alpine climbing, and I had no ice-axes or other mountaineering appliances with me. I had not even any proper boots. All I had for foot-gear were some native boots of soft leather, without nails and without heels – mere leather stockings, in fact – which gave no sort of grip upon an icy surface. How, then, I should ever be able to get down the icy slopes and rocky precipes I now saw before me I could not think; and if it had rested with me alone, the probability is we never should have got over the pass at all.

"What, however, saved our party was my holding my tongue. I kept quite silent as I looked over the pass, and waited to hear what the men had to say about it. They, meanwhile, were looking at me, and, imagining that an Englishman never went back from an enterprise he had once started on, took it as a matter of course that, as I gave no order to go back, I meant to go on. So they set about their preparations for the descent. We had brought an ordinary pick-axe with us, and Wali went on ahead with this, while the rest of us followed one by one behind him, each hanging on to a rope tied round Wali's waist to support him in case he slipped while hewing steps across the ice-slope. This slope was of hard ice, very steep, and, thirty yards or so below the line we took, ended in an ice-fall, which again terminated far beneath in the head of a glacier at the foot of the pass. Wali, with his pick-axe, hewed a way step by step across the ice-slope, so as to reach the rocky cliff by which we should have to descend on to the glacier below. We slowly edged across the slope after him, but it was hard to keep cool and steady. From where we stood we could see nothing over the end of the slope but the glacier many hundreds of feet below us . . . We were standing on a slope as steep as the roof of a house. We had no ice-axes with which to anchor ourselves or give us support; and though I tied handkerchiefs, and the men bits of leather and cloth, round the insteps of our smooth native boots to give us a little grip on the slippery ice, I could not help feeling that if any one of us had lost his foothold, the rest of us would never have been able to hold him up with the rope, and that in all likelihood the whole party would have been carried away and plunged into the abyss below. Outwardly I kept as cool and cheerful as I could, but inwardly I shuddered at each fresh step I took . . .

"At last we reached the far side of the slope, and found ourselves on a projecting piece of rock protruding through the ice. Here we could rest, but only with the prospect of still further difficulties before us. We were at the head of the rocky precipice, the face of which we should have to descend to reach the ice-slopes which extended to the glacier at the foot of the pass . . . The cliff we had now to descend was an almost sheer precipice: its only saving feature was that it was rough and rugged, and so afforded some little hold for our hands and feet. Yet even then we seldom got a hold for the whole hand or whole foot. All we generally found was a little ledge, upon which we could grip with the tips of the fingers or side of the foot . . . There was a constant dread, too, that fragments of these ledges might give way with the weight upon them; for the rock was very crumbly, as it generally is when exposed to severe frosts, and once I heard a shout from above, as a huge piece of rock which had been detached came crashing past me, and as nearly as possible hit two of the men who had already got half-way down.

"We reached the bottom of the cliff without accident, and then found ourselves at the head of a long ice-slope extending down to the glacier below. Protruding through the ice were three pieces of rock, which would serve us as successive halting-places, and we determined upon taking a line which led by them. We had brought with us every scrap of rope that could be spared from the ponies' gear, and we tied these and all the men's turbans and waist-cloths together into one long rope, by which we let a man down the ice-slope on to the first projecting rock. As he went down he cut steps, and when he had reached the rock we tied the upper end of the rope firmly on to a rock above, and then one by one we came down the slope, hanging on to the rope and making use of the steps which had been cut. This was, therefore, a comparatively easy part of the descent, but one man was as nearly as possible lost. He slipped, fell over on his back, and came sliding down the slope at a frightful pace. Luckily, however, he still managed to keep hold of the rope with one hand, and so kept himself from dashing over the ice-fall at the side of the slope; but when he reached the rock his hand was almost bared of skin, and he was shivering with fright. Wali, however, gave him a sound rating for being so careless, and on the next stage made him do all the hardest part of the work . . .

"At last, just as the sun set, we reached the glacier at the foot of the pass. We were in safety once more. The tension was over, and the last and greatest obstacle in my journey had been surmounted. Those moments when I stood at the foot of the pass are long to be remembered by me – moments of intense relief, and of deep gratitude for the success that had been granted. Such feelings as mine were now cannot be described in words, but they are known to everyone who has had his heart set on one great object and has accomplished it. I took one last look at the pass, never before or since seen by a European, and then we started away down the glacier to find some bare spot on which to lay our rugs and rest."

Not content with this staggering achievement, Younghusband set out two days after his arrival at Askole to investigate the problem of the New Mustagh pass.

"I would now willingly have had a rest," he says, "but . . . I set out to try the other Mustagh pass – what is called the New Mustagh pass. It was depressing, just as I had reached the first village on the Indian side, to have to turn my back on India; but I did not like to leave this pass untried, and with a party of men from Askole we set out on the second day after our arrival to explore it . . .

"As I now had some new foot-gear, we were able to push along rapidly up the Punmah glacier. But on the third day from Askole . . . we were brought to a standstill. At this point the glacier flowing down from the New Mustagh pass joins the Punmah glacier, and we were competely 'cornered' between the two glaciers. To reach the pass we should have had to cross the glacier flowing down from it; but this we found it impossible to do, for just at this point there had evidently been an immense ice-slip on to the glacier, and gigantic blocks of ice were tumbled about one on the top of the other, in a way which made it perfectly impossible to get any footing at all on the glacier. So we turned round and faced for Askole once more."

Since Younghusband's journey the Mustagh pass has been crossed once by a European. This was in 1929 when the Italian expedition, led by H.R.H. the Duke of Spoleto, working on the Baltoro glacier, sent a party, which included Professor Desio, across the pass to explore the upper reaches of the Shaksgam valley. Although they had their main base on the Baltoro glacier, and only required to take with them about a month's provisions, this strong party of mountaineers experienced considerable difficulty in getting their coolies over the pass.

On his return journey Desio went up to the head of the Sarpo Laggo glacier, where he reached a saddle from which he looked down into the Trango glacier, which is one of the lower tributaries of the Baltoro. Later he went up the Trango glacier from the south and reported that the saddle was practicable from that side as well.

This pass, discovered by Desio, seemed to us an attractive alternative to the Mustagh. But no pass can be considered proved until it has actually been crossed, and as so much depended on our being able to get over the range easily and quickly, we could not afford to run any avoidable risk. However, we deferred the important decision as to which of the two routes we should attempt until we reached the Baltoro glacier.

Before continuing with my narrative I should like to discuss briefly the causes of the abandonment of these ancient routes across the passes of the high Karakoram. In the passage quoted in this chapter from Sir Francis Younghusband's book, there are several allusions to this question. He also refers to it in the letter which he wrote to his father in 1887 describing his crossing of the Mustagh pass:

"On ascending towards the Mustagh pass my real difficulties began. Since my guides had crossed, an immense glacier had advanced, completely blocking up the valley with ice and immense boulders."

In each case the suggestion is that the increase in the size of the glaciers is the principal reason for the disuse of the passes into Yarkand. This theory agrees with the view, stated many years before, of Godwin-Austen, who was the first man to do any detailed scientific work in the district. He states in his paper, "On the Glaciers of the Mustakh Range" (Royal Geographical Society, 1864), that when he visited the district in 1861, the main Mustagh pass was already closed, "owing to the great increase of snow and ice", and an alternative route had been found (the New Mustagh pass). He mentions that in his time ponies and yaks were frequently brought over the new pass from Yarkand. While he was camping on the Panmah glacier in August of 1861, four men came over the pass from Yarkand. They were Baltis who had emigrated to Turkestan some years before. They had experienced much difficulty on the actual pass.

In discussing the question in his paper, Godwin-Austen says:

"I have often been struck by the indications of considerable amounts of change of temperature within what we may call our own times . . . Many passes which were used even in the time of Rajah Ahmed, Shah of Skardo, are now closed. The road to Yarkund over the Baltoro glacier, which before his time was known as the Mustakh, has by the increase of the ice near the pass become quite impracticable. The men of the Braldoh valley were accordingly ordered to search for another route, which they found in the present pass, at the head of the Panmah glacier above Chiring. Again, the Jusserpo La can now be crossed only on foot whereas in former times ponies could be taken over it. The pass at the head of the Hoh Loombah is now never used, though there is a tradition that it was once a pass; no one, however, of the present generation that I could hear of had ever crossed it. Certain large glaciers have advanced, such as that at Arundu, of which the old men assured me that in their young days the terminal cliff was one and a half miles distant from the village. Mr. Vigne says, 'It was a considerable distance'; it is now only about four hundred yards. A like increase has taken place at Panmah, where within the last six years the old road has been completely covered by the ice and moraine, and where Mahomed, my guide, told me the old camping ground was, now lies a quarter of a mile under the ice:

the overthrown trees and bushes plainly testified to the recent advance which this mass had made; this evidence was equally well seen along the side of the Arundu glacier."

In the same paper, however, Godwin-Austen mentions the decrease in the size of the main glaciers of the Karakoram. This apparent discrepancy is supported by present geological opinion, which holds that there are cycles in the increase and decrease of these glaciers, not necessarily simultaneous in the case of all glaciers of the district. John Auden, the geologist of our expedition, in his appendix to the paper I read to the Royal Geographical Society on January 10th, 1938, says:

"All of us were impressed by the recent decrease in thickness of the Sarpo Laggo and Crevasse glaciers near their snouts. That these glaciers are subject to periodic changes is suggested by historical records, since at different times they have been easy and difficult of access. The Nobande Sobande branch of the Panmah was inaccessible to Younghusband in 1887 beyond Skinmang. It was so smooth and uncrevassed in 1929 that Desio was able to ski up to its head. In 1937 it was again highly broken up."

In 1892, Conway, discussing the Nushik La, a pass lying between Skardu and the Hispar glacier, says: "The pass was believed not to present any extraordinary difficulties, and even cattle were stated to have been taken over it. Of late years, however, the natives admit that they have rarely crossed it, if at all. They state that the road became buried in snow, and that it ceased to exist as a practicable route from their point of view." The natives' explanation was corroborated by Godwin-Austen and subsequently by Major Cunningham, who both found this pass to be corniced with an overhanging wave of snow, leading to a difficult snow-slope below. Neither of them crossed the pass, though Cunningham attempted it. Bruce and Eckenstein, members of Conway's party, experienced a good deal of difficulty in crossing this pass in 1892.

Colonel Schomberg in his book *Unknown Karakoram*, which describes his expedition to the Shimshal district in 1934, agrees with the theory that the ancient routes have become impracticable because of increased glaciation. He adds that in his opinion the change is exceptional and comparatively recent. He writes:

"From what I have seen of the glaciers of this region, and have gleaned from the large volume of tradition, I am certain that the extensive glaciation is recent, at a hazard not more than about one hundred years old. Before then, the accumulation of ice and snow did not prevent people from crossing to and fro from Baltistan to Hunza and Nagir, and certainly into several parts of the Mustagh valley . . . I think, moreover, that the time is coming, but it will not be for some decades, when these routes will be again open, provided, of course, increased glaciation does not take place. There is no reason why it should, as judging from past history the great increase in the glaciers was definitely exceptional."

But though Younghusband, Schomberg, and the other explorers all agree that the old passes have become impracticable because of the increased glaciation, it is probable, in my opinion, that this theory is incorrect, and that the present blocking of the passes is in most cases due to the disintegration of the glaciers: not to increased glaciation, but to the breaking up of the ice. In the earlier days there may have been easy snow-covered ice-slopes leading up to the passes, which in the gradual deterioration of the glaciers have become jagged, steep and impassable.

It should be remembered that the local reports on which the explorers have founded their theories, are those of untrained observers, who having encountered greater difficulty with the ice on the passes, assumed as a matter of course that there was more ice than before. Whereas, in my experience, glaciers which are in a rapid state of decay present many more obstacles than are met with on the smooth surfaces of actively growing glaciers. The decaying condition of the Sarpo Laggo glacier, which will be described later in my narrative, illustrates this theory. It was on the lower reaches of this glacier that the decay was most evident. And it was this condition that caused so much difficulty both to Younghusband in 1887 and to ourselves fifty years later.

In spite of this I do not question the fact that there has recently been an increase in some of the glaciers, and the passages quoted from Godwin-Austen's paper, read to the Royal Geographical Society in 1884, give definite proof of this. Later in the same paper he says, "As we skirted the Kero Loombah glacier, evident signs that it was now on the increase were constantly to be seen in the masses of upturned and broken turf."

Also, we ourselves found an astonishing increase in the side glacier which barred our way down to Mone Brangsa. This glacier had been reported by Desio, in 1929, to be an insignificant ice-stream, but by 1937 we found that it was a formidable obstacle.

With so much conflicting data it is extremely difficult to assert the correct solution of the problem. But personally, I do not think that the main reason for the closing of the passes is due to the increase of the ice. But whatever the reason, it is certain that these passes across the main range of the Karakoram were used extensively in former times by native travellers going from Baltistan into Yarkand, and are now completely impracticable for native transport. Of course the disuse may be due to other causes besides the difficulty of snow and ice conditions. Schomberg suggests that there is no incentive now for trade between Baltistan and Shimshal. For the Shimshalis can now get all they require from Hunza, owing to the development of the Hunza valley in the last century, without having to cross any difficult country to obtain supplies. This, however, does not explain the cessation of trade between Baltistan and Turkestan across the Mustagh pass, nor between Hunza and Baltistan across the Hispar pass.

Another theory is put forward by Godwin-Austen, who suggests that the old routes were abandoned because they were frequented by robbers. He says that the former route over the Hispar pass was given up because of the danger of these raids, and an alternative route was adopted, which seemed to be free from the menace of attack by bandits. This route must presumably have been up the Crevasse glacier which we explored. But in my opinion it is almost unbelievable that this route was ever used, for its length would have been enormous and its difficulties considerable.

But whatever the reason for the present disuse of the passes, it is a noteworthy fact that travellers nowadays not only find that the passes are closed, but they have great difficulty in getting any information about the former existence of the routes across them.

It would be valuable historically to send an expedition into this country to try and trace the remains of old routes and disused habitations, and to determine the migratory history of the primitive people of these remote districts.

CHAPTER SIX

Trouble with the "Hungry Hundred"

WHEN we arrived at Askole on May 24th, we sent for the Lambadar and the headmen of the neighbouring villages and opened negotiations with them for the recruiting of one hundred men, and the collecting of 4,000 lbs. flour. There seemed to be no difficulty about the latter; we were assured that almost any quantity was available. The Thasildar of Skardu had been right about this, though whether his reason was the correct one we did not discover. The question of porters was more delicate, and had to be handled with great care. At first it was assumed that we were simply going up the Baltoro glacier and coming down again, so for some time we talked at cross purposes. When at last it dawned on them that we intended to cross the range, their faces fell, and they told us that no one would consent to come with us. They said that it had only once been done, and then by a really well-equipped party; poverty-stricken novices like ourselves would certainly perish if we attempted anything so foolhardy. In any case, they said, it was far too early in the year, and it was impossible even to reach the higher pastures. At first this looked like a serious set-back, but after some hours of diplomatic argument we managed to convince them that we were not so incompetent as we looked, and that we were willing to pay well for any help we received. They left us with a promise that they would collect the men and give the matter further consideration in the morning.

Early next day the male population turned up in force. This was a hopeful sign, but we soon found that everyone was strongly opposed to our project. We had to go through all the previous day's preamble again, with the added disadvantage that now we were trying to change the mind of a multitude, who all talked at once. Moreover, most of them could not understand what we said. The Thasildar's chaprassi worked hard on our side, hinting that if the headman did not help us too, their unfriendliness would be regarded with disfavour by the authorities in Skardu. The seventeen men we had brought from Skardu were also useful allies. They despised the Askole men and were glad of an opportunity to show their superiority. Besides, they realized that if the Askole men were not forthcoming, the expedition would have to be abandoned, and they would lose the chance of the well paid job for which they had come so far. The part played by the Sherpas in the dispute was of doubtful value to us, and I kept them as much as possible in the background. They believe in force rather than tact when dealing with a situation of this kind, though later, when the party was actually on the move, they displayed surprising skill in diplomacy.

Quite suddenly, after hours of apparently hopeless argument, we found that everyone was clamouring to come with us. Whether it was the blandishments of the chaprassi, or the scorn of the Skardu men, or our promise of very large bonuses which turned the scales in our favour, or perhaps the fear that, with such a large number of men they might find themselves left out of a good thing – I do not know. But the change was dramatic, and it was some little time before I realized what was happening. The men caused such an uproar in their eagerness to have their names written down that it was a long time before we could restore order. On the whole they were a poor looking lot and most of them had large goitres. Even with so many candidates to choose from, it was a difficult task to select enough who looked as if they were capable of carrying loads over a high pass. I had written down about fifty names when the headmen of some distant villages came and implored me to wait until the following morning when their men would come to offer their services.

We made a final effort to reduce the weight of our equipment loads. Every object came under dispute. Spender had to cling hard to the less vital items of his survey equipment, and Auden nearly lost his geological hammer. The rifle caused heated discussion; two of us were in favour of leaving it, the other two said that it should be taken. The disappointment of the Sherpas at the mere suggestion of leaving it decided the question. We imposed a limit of thirty-five pounds each on our personal equipment and bedding. This had to include sleeping-bag, rubber ground sheet, books, tobacco, cameras and film, and all spare clothing. Spender cut his tobacco allowance down to one pipeful a day in order to take with him Tolstoy's *War and Peace* and Forster's *A Passage to India*. These were a great boon to us in our few bouts of bad weather, though Tilman and I felt ourselves morally obliged to pay with tobacco for the luxury of reading. The Sherpas have a remarkable way of adding to their personal belongings on their way through a country. Before leaving Srinagar we had issued them with a strict ration of kit and had seen to it that everything else was left behind. Now their bedding sacks weighed twice as much as they had weighed at the start. They were bursting with an amazing assortment of junk: wooden spoons, packets of snuff and spices, electric torches, nails, filthy rags, and other treasures which they were reluctant to leave behind.

Throughout the day the flour kept arriving in small consignments of a few pounds. This was packed in the green canvas bags which we had brought with us, and weighed up in 60 lb. loads. Every now and again a fierce shower of rain interrupted proceedings and everything had to be bundled under the tarpaulin or into the tents. Much time, too, was spent administering our usual remedies of Epsom salts and boracic lotion to the sick and ailing. The result of this was that we had a busy day doing very little. The last few loads of flour were packed and weighed after dark by the light of a candle, which was constantly extinguished by raindrops. Dinner that night was a memorable feast. Angtharkay excelled himself with a favourite Tibetan dish of mutton boiled with spaghetti. The spaghetti we had made ourselves with flour, eggs and milk according to a recipe which I had learnt from a friend's Italian cook.

Spender and Auden left fairly early on the morning of the 26th of May. They were going ahead so as to have time to make a large-scale map of the snout of the Biafo glacier, which almost blocks the main valley about five miles beyond

Askole. The Biafo glacier is one of the giant ice-streams of the Karakoram, and rises near the Hispar pass about thirty miles north of Askole. Very little scientific work has been done on these great glaciers, which present numberless geological problems. Auden had examined the Biafo in 1933 and was anxious to see what changes had taken place at the snout of the glacier since then.

Tilman and I spent a frenzied morning surrounded by heaving and shouting humanity. All the villages in the neighbourhood were now amply represented. The little field in which we were camped was as packed with people as a tube train in the rush hour, all clamouring for our attention. After an hour or so we succeeded in establishing some sort of order. We began by sorting out the men we had signed on the previous day. This was no easy task, for they only seemed to have about half a dozen names between them. These were served up to us in various combinations, so that a section of one of the lists we were making appeared something like this:

Ali Mohamad	Ali Mohamad Khan
Khan Mohamad	Mohamad Ali
Ali	Mohamad.

Matters were made more difficult by the nepotism of the various headmen and those who had already been signed on. They pleaded with us to take their various sons, cousins, fathers and nephews. Also some of the suppliers of our flour threatened to take it back unless their families were chosen. During all these chaotic negotiations it drizzled steadily, wetting our clothes and our baggage, wrecking our tempers and soaking the scraps of paper on which we were trying to write the names of the coolies.

When at last we had extracted the hundred chosen men from the mob, we made up the loads and sent them off in batches of ten, writing opposite each name what the man was carrying. When they had all gone we found that there were four loads left over. The mob made a rush at these and we had some difficulty in rescuing our possessions from scores of tugging hands. But it was very gratifying to see such enthusiasm and we began to take a more optimistic view of the situation. We paid out large sums of money for the food we had received and the rent of the land on which we had camped, said good-bye to our friend the chaprassi and the headmen of the villages, and started on our way at 1.15 p.m. Among our caravan was a sheep which we had bought. We had put one of the Baltis in charge of it. It was very reluctant to walk, either because it had overeaten or was homesick; soon its stubbornness prevailed and the Balti carried it slung across his shoulders.

The rain had stopped by now, but great banks of grey mist hung low above our heads, and the valley, once we had left the irrigated fields behind, was depressingly barren and bleak. It was difficult to understand how the hillsides could remain so bare of vegetation when they were subject to such long periods of damp, cloudy weather. Presumably the reason is that the clouds deposit all their moisture on the high mountains, and that below a certain level there is very little precipitation. This also accounts for the enormous size of the glaciers. Before we reached the Biafo glacier, we saw on the opposite side of the valley an isolated patch of cultivation. A lonely clump of apricot trees reminded us that we had left behind the comfort and fecundity of the inhabited world. I wondered wistfully when we should see our next trees. Tilman replied dryly that it would probably be the same trees in a week's time!

Two hours of easy going took us to the side of the Biafo glacier. It thrusts its great boulder-strewn tongue down into the main valley, carrying with it the rubbish which falls from the great peaks standing above the upper reaches of the glacier. A dirty stream issuing from a black cavern in its side forced us to climb on to the ice and work our way over its dreary undulations, cutting up steep, muddy slopes and hopping from one unsteady boulder to another. We had left the Askole coolies a long way behind by now. The Skardu men, on the other hand, seemed to be determined to show their superiority by keeping ahead of us. They went really well on the glacier, moving with skill and agility. We came down off the ice on to some sand flats which lie between the snout of the glacier and the main river. It was a splendid place for a survey base and we expected to find Spender and Auden encamped there. But we did not see them and went on beyond the glacier to a shepherd's shelter, known as Korofon.

The rest of the coolies arrived at about a quarter to seven. The issuing of food took a very long time. Their ration was two pounds of ata per man, and they insisted on it being served out in small lots of four or eight pounds, instead of clubbing together and taking it away in sackfuls. It was weighed out in scarves, handkerchiefs, blankets, coat-sleeves and trouser-legs. Often the receptacle burst open and the contents were scattered on the ground. We had not eaten anything since our somewhat scanty breakfast and when our work was over we supped ravenously on the remainder of the spaghetti and some cheese-rind soup.

A coolie brought in a letter from Spender and Auden the next morning, reporting their progress, and I sent word back telling them to catch us up at Paiju, a couple of miles below the snout of the Baltoro glacier, by the evening of the 28th. We left Korofon at eight o'clock. A serious obstacle in the day's march was the river flowing down from the Panmah glacier system. It is bridged several miles upstream where its gorge is narrow. But the route to the bridge involves a big detour, and we hoped that, as it was early in the year, it might be possible to avoid this by fording the river lower down. Flowing over gravel flats in the main valley, the river was diverted into several channels, and with care in the choice of a route, it was not difficult to get across. But the water was terribly cold, and caused us agony each time we waded into it. The porters came across without much fuss. The Baltis are good at crossing rivers, far better than the Sherpas. Certainly they need to be, for the rivers of the Karakoram are the most dangerous and the most difficult to deal with that I have ever met. Sen Tensing, quite shamefacedly, bribed one of the Skardu men to carry him across, and came in for a good deal of jeering from the other Sherpas. Neither party divulged the extent of the bribe.

It was another dismal day. We got very cold waiting about at the river crossing. The rain held off until we had pitched camp at a place called Badumal, and then swept down on us in a steady drizzle. We were very depressed that evening. It looked as if an enormous quantity of fresh snow had fallen above 13,000 feet during the last week of bad weather. We knew that the spirit of the Baltis, already considerably chastened since the start, would not stand many camps in the snow. It would be impossible to take them far through deep snow, quite apart from the risk of avalanches; and in bad conditions there was no knowing how long it would take to reach either of the passes. If, on top of all this, we were to work in heavy mist and falling snow it was doubtful if we would be able to urge the men much beyond the snout of the Baltoro glacier. We had quite made up our minds that we should have to relay the loads across the pass ourselves, but the question was how far it would be necessary to induce the Baltis to come before it was worth even attempting to do this. We could not afford to send the men home to wait until later in the year. For one thing, it would have cost too much; and for another, we could not postpone our crossing of the Shaksgam river until much later than the middle of June. To cheer ourselves up we began to discuss many attractive plans. We contemplated an attempt to climb K2, or Masherbrum. Another tempting possibility was the exploration of the unmapped country to the south of the Baltoro glacier.

It rained most of the night, and was pouring down heavily when we finished our breakfast next morning. A slight clearing at nine o'clock induced us to start, but then the downpour came on more heavily than ever. I was very worried lest the flour should get wet. Some of it had to last us for nearly four months, and it would have entirely upset our calculations if it had gone bad. However, there was not much to be done, except to trust to the waterproof quality of the canvas bags, and to try and persuade the men to sacrifice their blankets to keep the flour dry. They did not much like the idea of going along one behind the other covered over with the tarpaulin, like a Roman Testudo. But soon the rain stopped, and the sun peered weakly through the clouds.

The first part of the march was over gravel flats. The coolies went maddeningly slowly over this easy ground, stopping to rest their loads on their sticks every fifty yards. Farther on, the river ran against the cliffs on our side of the valley, and forced us to climb a long way up the steep hillside. There were two really difficult places to negotiate, where only one man could move at a time. We reached Paiju at about four o'clock. Here we found wide stretches of meadow-land, wooded with willow thickets, beneath which there was a number of shepherd's huts and sheep-folds. It was an unexpectedly pleasant spot.

Tilman had complained of feeling shivery that morning, and when we got into camp he retired to bed with fairly high fever. Spender and Auden came in about five, and showed me a neatly drawn detailed map of the Biafo snout. They had met with difficulties crossing the Panmah stream that morning, and Spender had been completely submerged. After the usual brew of tea which always celebrates the arrival of a party in camp, Auden and I climbed a knoll in order to get a view of the Baltoro glacier that might help us to decide which of the two passes to attempt. We could see nothing that could influence that decision, but with the beginnings of the routes in front of us, we could visualize more clearly the scale of things we had seen on the map.

We identified Desio's Trango valley and were able to make a good guess at the position of the Mustagh glacier. It was a country of bold granite spires and huge rock precipices. Had we not known that the passes existed, nothing would have persuaded us to go up the Baltoro glacier in search of a way across the range. From the accounts of those who had visited the Mustagh pass, it was clear that it was not easy on the Baltoro side. With all this new snow about, it would probably be quite impossible to reach the pass so early in the year. On the other hand, the saddle which Professor Desio had reported as situated between the Trango and the Sarpo Laggo glaciers was described as being easy of access. Also the route across this part of the range appeared on the map to be a good deal shorter. But the fact that no one had ever crossed Desio's saddle had a bad moral effect on the Baltis. They knew that the Italian party had been up the Trango glacier, and they assumed that they had returned because they had failed to find a pass at its head. What worried them more, however, was the fear that if we managed to cross the pass, we should find ourselves in a country from which we could not return. They could not believe that we knew where we were going. At length after still further discussion, the fun of making a new way across the range weighted the evenly balanced scales in favour of the Trango route.

That night the meadows of Paiju looked enchanting in the flickering light of six huge camp fires which blazed beneath the willow branches. We sat by each fire in turn and chatted with the Baltis. The Skardu men sang with splendid strength and rhythm. We stayed in their circle for a long time to lend our feeble support. Later the party warmed up to some spirited dancing.

Tilman's temperature was still 102 degrees next morning, and Sen Tensing, too, was down with a similar fever. We were faced with rather a difficult problem. Obviously they could not start marching up the Baltoro glacier immediately. But we could not afford to wait with this huge party of porters. Apart from the money it was costing to employ them, we were consuming over two hundred pounds of food a day. It was too early yet to make any sort of diagnosis of the fevers. They might subside in twenty-four hours, but they were more likely to go on for two or three days at least, and a decision had to be made at once. Auden most unselfishly volunteered to wait at Paiju with Tilman and Sen Tensing. It was decided that Spender and I should go on with the main party and attempt to get the loads across the pass. If we failed, it would take us several weeks to relay the stuff over ourselves, and Auden would easily be able to get in touch with us on the Trango glacier. If we managed to get the porters across, Spender could begin his survey on the other side of the range, and, if necessary, I could come back to deal with any situation which might have arisen. Meanwhile, two Baltis were to wait with Auden. If the sick men recovered within the next three or four days the party was to follow us up. If they were delayed more than four days Auden was to send word up to us. If the fever developed into anything serious, which necessitated sending the patients down, or sending to Skardu for help, no word was to be sent up to us. It was agreed that if we received no news within nine days of leaving Paiju I was to start back. It was an unsatisfactory arrangement, but probably the best we could make.

All this took some time to arrange, and it was late before we got our army on the move. It took us an hour to reach the glacier. We mounted on to it by way of a steep gully between the ice and the rock wall at the side of the glacier. A fierce wind was blowing down the valley. This dislodged stones from the crags above our heads, which made the ascent of the gully rather dangerous. Angtharkay said he saw some ibex joining in the fun of bombarding us; but this may have been imagination. Half a mile farther on we came to the first tributary glacier – the Uli Biaho – coming from the north. It is almost entirely free from moraine deposit, and appears to mount on to the Baltoro. The clean ice was very broken, and though it was easy enough for us to cross, we had to cut a tremendous number of steps for the Baltis, who were wearing skin boots which slipped on the ice. Beyond this point, we climbed up to a remarkable corridor, running between the ice and the great overhanging granite cliffs which tower above the glacier. Though the corridor was, in places, so narrow that it was difficult for a man to squeeze himself through, its floor was flat, and provided us with wonderful going. It had obviously been formed by a glacial stream which had found itself a new course.

The corridor opened out into a large triangular courtyard which was roofed by a slanting buttress. A number of juniper trees grew on the rocky walls, their great gnarled roots wedged in the fissures. A trickle of clear water ran over the sandy floor. Here was the ideal site for a camp, offering shelter, abundant fuel, and good water. The altitude of this place was 12,600 feet. Though it was only the middle of the afternoon we decided to stop for the night. The longer we were able to keep the Baltis really comfortable and warm, the longer their spirit would hold, and the farther they would come with us. A large quantity of wood was collected. This was to be carried up with us for use in the higher camps. Some wood had already been brought from Paiju, as we had not expected to find any juniper on the northern side of the Baltoro. Ten loads of ata had already been consumed and some food had been left at Paiju, so that at least a dozen men were now available for carrying wood. The Baltis spent a long evening baking sufficient bread to last them for the next few days, so that they should have less cooking to do at the higher camps. They have a very simple and efficient method of bread-making. The flour is kneaded into a stiff dough, which is rolled into fat round loaves, about seven inches across and one inch deep, and then baked in the red-hot ashes of the fire. The result, when treated by Balti hands is excellent, and later nearly all our bread was made in this way. But the Sherpas could never master the art to our satisfaction.

At sunset, I walked out on to the Baltoro glacier. It was a beautiful evening. Only small wisps of cloud remained, interlaced among the innumerable rock spires. There was a promise of better weather. I sat for a while on a mound of moraine debris, two hundred feet high and tried to grasp the scale of my surroundings. The enormous size of these glaciers, compared with those on Mount Everest and in Sikkim and Garhwal, made me feel as bewildered as when I first went to the Himalaya after being used to Alpine mountains.

We made the most of our last unrestricted camp fires. Half a dozen furnaces blazed with such fury that it was impossible to go anywhere near them. The Baltis were in high spirits, and each group vied in song with the next. The Sherpas, too, added to the tumult with their tuneless dirges. The crags above echoed this boisterous medley of sound. The Baltis enthusiastically promised to go as fast and as far as they could on the following day, though we realized that the promise would lack determination when morning came. We hoped that day to reach a point on the Trango glacier from which we could see the route to the pass, for we did not want to waste any time in reconnoitring.

There was a heavy frost that night, and a consequent reluctance to start early on the following day. But we got the party moving by seven, and by eight we were complaining of the heat of the morning sun. We soon realized our mistake in succumbing to the temptation of the "ideal camp site". We could have gone at least two hours farther on the previous day and would still have found plenty of juniper fuel. Moreover, the Baltis were marching with their usual slow reluctance, and it was obvious that we were not going as far, that day, as we had hoped. After a mile or so of excellent going we turned a corner into the Trango valley. We kept to the true right bank of the glacier until we were forced by a difficult ice-fall on to the glacier itself. At noon we halted for a meal. We had intended to give the men an hour's rest. But it was very nearly an hour after we had stopped that the last stragglers of the party, pursued by torrents of abuse from Lobsang and Angtharkay, arrived at the halting-place. These men also required an hour's rest. In the meantime, a sudden storm had blotted out the sun, and it was snowing. A freezing wind swept down the glacier. The Baltis huddled together in little groups under their blankets, and looked as if they had no wish but to die where they sat. At length we persuaded the Skardu men to start, but as we remained behind to try and urge the others forward, the Skardu contingent sat down again fifty yards away. The only thing we could do was to go ahead and leave the Sherpas to deal with the stragglers. It was a long anxious business coaxing our "Hungry Hundred" over the desolate intricacies of the glacier. The ice was very broken, and it was not easy in such weather to find a way through. Often we had to retrace our steps, which did not increase the confidence of the coolies.

We did not succeed in reaching the point from which Professor Desio had seen the pass. We were far from certain up which of the side valleys it lay. But we found a good place for a camp. It was a little grassy plain formed by the corner of a steep side glacier flowing into the main ice-stream, at an altitude of about 14,000 feet. It was a pleasant surprise to find that, in spite of the recent weeks of bad weather, most of the winter snow had already gone from the level glacier at this altitude.

Shortly after we had decided to camp, it started to snow, and soon our tents, loads and bundles of firewood looked like a picture on a Christmas card. It was unusually cold for snow to be falling so heavily. This gave us a faint hope that the bad weather would not last much longer. Otherwise the outlook seemed pretty hopeless. Spender amused himself by describing in detail what May 30th should look like in England. I had not seen it for nearly ten years. But as he talked I remembered beech leaves, in the late spring, frail, almost transparent against the light; and in the woods, the pale green fronds of young bracken uncurling; everywhere flowers opening and sap rising towards the full life of summer. In actual fact, it would probably have resembled more closely the dreary scene outside!

CHAPTER SEVEN

Mutiny on the Hanging-Glacier

THE bad weather brought out the worst trait of the Baltis. When conditions were bad they seemed to be entirely incapable of looking after themselves. They crumpled up where they stood and refused to do anything towards making themselves comfortable or protecting themselves from the weather. It was surprising to find this failing in people whose livelihood depended so much on their ability to use difficult country to the best advantage, and whose forefathers were in the habit of making arduous journeys across these glaciers. Much of their lives must have been spent in the open, herding their flocks in high mountain pastures, and yet they seemed to be ignorant of the simplest notions of outdoor comfort: camping in the most protected places, building walls for shelter, crowding together for mutual protection and making use of rock overhangs. But I must admit they were tough, and put up with more cold and discomfort than I had expected they would endure. We spent a busy and exasperating evening trying to make them work in order to improve their unpleasant circumstances. The trouble was that they were thoroughly dispirited by the weather and our evident ignorance of the country through which we were leading them. We made a dump of six loads of ata for the Baltis' return journey, and two loads of wood were burnt. So we discharged eight of the weakest men. Thirty asked to be included in this discarded party!

It was clear that if the bad weather lasted into the next day, or we had any difficulty in finding the way, there would be a wholesale desertion.

At sunset on May 30th the weather cleared and it began to freeze very hard. We dined off boiled rice, washed down with mugs of excellent mutton broth. Unfortunately, Angtharkay had seasoned the soup with curry according to his own taste. This caused us acute agony, and our faces poured with sweat.

I woke next morning to find the mouth of my sleeping-bag crusted with the usual coating of ice, caused by the freezing of moisture from my breath. The first task of the day was to bring back life to the apparently frozen bodies of the Baltis. This done, we drank a cup of tea with tsampa, and then supervised the packing of the loads. There was a good deal of fuss, because someone had stolen some of the firewood for the higher camps. Of course no one would confess to the crime; not that it would have helped much if they had.

Our luck was in, for the day was brilliantly fine. Down the valley, across the Baltoro glacier, rose the mighty ice spire of Masherbrum, framed by the clear-cut walls of the Trango. On the opposite side of the glacier, towering six or eight thousand feet above our heads, were immense columns of granite supporting graceful summits, so remotely inaccessible that they seemed hardly to be part of the same colossal structure. The flanks of these peaks were frosted over with ice and powder snow sparkling like a million diamonds in the morning sunlight.

After two hours of easy going up the Trango glacier we reached the first large tributary coming down from the main watershed. We supposed that it was at the head of this that we should find the pass. But we were by no means certain, and, with the porters on the verge of mutiny, we could not risk taking them up the wrong glacier. So, leaving the party below the junction, Spender and I went ahead to reconnoitre. Soon we were up to our knees in soft snow. When we had turned the corner into the side valley, we found that it curved to the left. We could not see round this bend. As far as we could see, a rock precipice, crowned by a hanging glacier, walled in the upper part of the valley. But, in order to get a clear view of the head of the glacier, where we hoped the pass lay, we had either to go to the bend, which would involve several miles of trudging through soft snow, or to climb a steep ridge immediately above us, till we were high enough to see round the bend. We decided to climb the ridge. The snow was soft and very deep. We flogged our way up for many hours, without seeing the view we wanted. It was exhausting work floundering up to our hips in soft snow, while the sun, reflected from the surface with redoubled strength, scorched our faces and parched our tongues. We poured with sweat as we toiled upwards. It seemed crazy to think that a few hours ago our feet and hands had been numb with cold. But I have been hotter on the ice-slopes of the North Col on Everest, at an altitude of 22,000 feet, in glaring sun, than ever in the plains of India in May.

At about 17,000 feet the ridge that we were climbing became difficult and dangerous. The higher we got, and the more our view extended, the less likely it seemed that there would be a route from the head of the glacier. I went ahead, in a despairing effort to make certain of this. But soon I reached a steep rock buttress which I could not negotiate with reasonable safety, owing to the deep snow on its ledges. I sat at the foot of this, feeling crushed by a sense of futility and frustration. When we had left the coolies that morning, we had no idea that we should have to spend the entire day in reconnoitring the valley. We had imagined that within half an hour of leaving them, we should know definitely whether or not the pass was at the head of the first glacier. Now, not only had the day been wasted, but we were still uncertain where the pass lay. If it were not at the top of this glacier, the chances of our getting the coolies to the next glacier, in such bad snow, seemed hopeless. Their morale, already so nearly broken, would not stand much more hardship, and their supply of fuel would soon be finished. Unless we could find the pass quickly, and get to it easily, we were beaten.

From where I sat, though I could see enough to be almost certain that there was no feasible pass at the head of the glacier we were reconnoitring, yet there was still some of it that I could not see. In my despairing mood I was tempted to put all my faith in the slender possiblity that the unseen part hid the pass, and I contemplated taking the whole party up there on this frail chance.

Still undecided, I began to descend. A small avalanche slid away below me, and I was able to glissade down its track to rejoin Spender, whom I found also dejectedly contemplating the problem of our next move. We climbed down from the ridge together, and trudged wearily back to the place where we had left the coolies. We arrived at half-past four, exhausted and thoroughly depressed. The coolies sensed our mood and realized that we had met with a reverse.

After a short rest, we roused ourselves to deal with our various tasks. A further batch of men had to be discharged, boots, snow-glasses and rations had to be distributed. Such incredible confusion ensued that all our other problems were dwarfed into insignificance. Everyone shouted at once. No one listened to what was said. Occasionally blows were exchanged between the coolies themselves. A hundred angry men surrounded us, all yelling and cursing and getting in each other's way. The Sherpas struggled nobly to help us to deal with this ugly crisis. Large numbers of the Baltis again demanded to be discharged. It was a long time before the matter could be settled. When all the items of equipment had been amply distributed, there was a clamour of protest. Some had no glasses; some no warm clothes; some no gloves; some no boots; some no blankets; some had sore eyes; some had boils; and everyone had too much to say. No one thought of making himself as comfortable as possible for the night. When darkness fell the mob was still arguing and had made no attempt to dig out platforms of rock from under the snow on which to sleep. The Sherpas had to show them how to do this. At last, with the stars, came peace and soup and rice, and sufficient quiet to discuss again the tangle of bleak plans.

The next morning, June 1st, the weather was still fine and clear. We started very early, so as to cover as much ground as possible while the snow was frozen hard. We were pleasantly surprised to find perfect snow conditions. The going was so good that we decided to take the party up the main glacier to the next side valley, instead of attempting to find a way up the first valley which we had unsuccessfully reconnoitred the previous day. The hard snow and clear frosty air seemed to improve the temper of the Baltis. I went ahead very fast, with the Skardu men not far behind.

We had now reached a point where the moraine-covered surface of the glacier gave place to clear ice. As the glacier was very broad and open to long periods of daily sun, most of the winter snow had already left the surface of the ice. We made astonishingly swift progress and reached the next side glacier in a few hours. We cut steps up a steep ice-fall at the bottom of this side glacier, which led to a rock shelf. Ahead of us was a glacier descending in a precipitously steep ice-fall. At first we thought that we were again faced by an impasse, but when we reached the rock shelf we found that another glacier, farther to the right, led up to an easy col. It was still only 9.30. We debated whether we should make straight for the col; but although the Skardu men had already arrived, some of the other Baltis lagged a long way behind, and by the time they reached us the hot sun was rapidly melting the deep snow ahead. If we took the coolies on through this, and failed to reach the col, we should lose our present advantageous position. It would be impossible to camp with the Baltis anywhere above the shelf. It seemed more prudent to stop where we were, and not to attempt to reach the col till the following morning.

Tantalizing though it was to waste the whole of the rest of the day when we appeared to be within easy reach of the col, we made the decision to camp on the shelf at 17,000 feet. It was a bleak and exposed place, and when the Askole men realized that they were expected to spend the night on it, a mob of them bombarded us with clamorous demands to be sent down at once. Eventually we discharged eight men who departed promptly, strung together with a rope made of yak hair.

We wrestled with the usual jobs in the fierce noon-day sun; we dug through the snow to the rock to make platforms for the men to sleep on; we even had to take off their boots ourselves, and put them in the sun to dry. Some of the men to whom we had issued snow-glasses on the previous day offered to sell us the spare pairs which they had scrounged, to issue to those who had none. At three o'clock ominous clouds and a biting wind blew up, and it was soon bitterly cold. We feared a change in the weather and began to regret our decision to wait here until the following day. Bad weather at this stage would have been disastrous.

That evening we broached our supply of Danish pemmican. We finished a whole tin between the two of us, with the result that I felt horribly sick all night, for it is most indigestible, and it is necessary to accustom oneself to it gradually. At midnight the wind increased and the cold became more intense. I was very worried about the Baltis who were not really equipped for such severe conditions. But they did not seem any the worse for it, and made a surprisingly early start in the morning. To our relief, the fine weather still held.

For the first 700 feet the snow was as hard as iron, then suddenly the conditions changed and we sank into deep powder snow which was covered over with a vicious crust that broke at every step. The very hard work of stamping a track was shared by the Sherpas, and we reached the col (about 18,000 feet) before 9 a.m. To our dismay we found that the col was not the crest of the pass we were seeking. Beyond, more than a mile away, across a curving basin of snow, we could see another col a few hundred feet higher. This was a devastating discovery. In order to encourage the Baltis, we had assured them that the first col was our objective. Before they arrived we plunged down in the basin and waded through the soft snow until we were half-way across. The basin proved to be the top of the hanging glacier terrace which we had seen at the head of the first side glacier on the previous day. The Skardu men followed without any protests, and we hoped that the others would come at least as far as this, if only to get their pay. Angtensing and Ila went on to stamp a trail up to the higher col. We sat in the snow for a long time, waiting for the rest of the coolies to appear over the crest of the first col. When at last they got there, they sat down in the snow. It looked as if nothing would ever move them. We yelled at them till we were hoarse trying to make them come over to us. But nothing happened. At last we sent Angtharkay back to try and induce them to follow. Eventually most of them came on.

By the time they joined us it was midday, and it was quite evident that, with the exception of the Skardu men and two of the others, they were determined not to go a step farther. Many of them complained of mountain sickness; and some of these lay in the snow, holding their heads and groaning. Of the whole number, only seventeen were fit and willing to go on. The rest had to be paid off at once and sent back. So, on top of a hanging glacier terrace, in the torrid heat of the afternoon, we solemnly sat down and counted out great piles of rupees. The usual uproar, despite the mountain sickness, was as vehement as ever.

We watched the retreating army safely over the col. When they had gone we made a huge stack of most of their deserted loads, and staggered along with as much as we could possibly carry. Although a track had been stamped through the deep snow, it was gruelling work, and we were thankful when, after two hours of it, we reached the second col, and stood at last on the Central Asiatic divide.[1]

It was a thrilling moment; and all the exasperation and worry of the last few days slid away from our minds. To the north, the Sarpo Laggo glacier curved down towards the desolate rust-coloured ranges of Chinese Turkestan. This was our first view into the country which we had come so far to see. There is something fascinating about these great continental watersheds, which divide the rivers of two such vast areas, so entirely different in character. Our contemplation of the momentous significance of the pass was cut short by the usual afternoon flurry of bad weather. The icy wind made us glad of the shelter of some rocks which jutted out of the snow.

We had intended to camp on the crest of the pass and to spend the next day bringing up all the loads. But there was not room to camp, as the ridge was too sharp. The first rocks at the side of the Sarpo Laggo glacier did not look so very far away, and we expected to have ample time to reach them before dark. The descent on the northern side of the pass was very steep. We lowered the loads by the simple method of rolling them down the snow-slope: finding that the powdery snow was inclined to avalanche, we fixed some ropes, down which the party slid in safety.

When we reached the level glacier, we were disappointed to find that the snow conditions were even worse than they had been on the other side of the range. By this time we were all very tired. The Baltis wanted to sleep where they were. Spender and I were inclined to agree with them. But the Sherpas urged us to push on until we found rock to lie on and water to drink. We plodded wearily along through the soft snow, sinking up to our knees at every step. The straps of our heavy loads bit painfully into our shoulders, and the rocks we had noticed never seemed to get any nearer. When at last we reached

[1] The height of this col is 5,685 metres (18,650 feet).

them they were inadequate and comfortless – a most unsuitable site for what was to be a lengthy stay. But at least there was plenty of water, and we were too tired to bother about anything else. It had been a long and strenuous day, and we had eaten very little food. Sleep tempted us more than supper; we were too weary to eat. We crawled into our sleeping-bags, contented that at least some of the party were on the right side of the pass.

CHAPTER EIGHT

Loads across the Watershed

THE next day Spender and I stayed in camp to make preparations for the start of the survey. The Sherpas and the seventeen remaining Baltis went back to the dump in the snow basin and brought another batch of loads across the pass into camp. Early on the morning of June 4th, soon after Spender had left camp to climb to his first survey station, Auden arrived with his two Baltis. They brought the welcome news that Tilman and Sen Tensing were somewhat better and were following slowly. I sent a Sherpa and two Baltis back to help them. Auden had come through from Paiju at a tremendous pace, and was very tired.

Although a great number of loads was still on the other side of the pass, I decided to take a relay from our present camp down the glacier, so that the less rigorous conditions of lower altitudes would give the men I took with me a welcome rest. They were cheered by the prospect of an off-day when we got down there. Leaving Auden in camp, I set off down the glacier with the Baltis and three Sherpas. We took with us as much as we could carry. Below the camp, snow conditions improved and in just over an hour we reached a grassy glade by the side of the glacier, known as Changtok. Here we found traces of Professor Desio's camp; possibly some of these were the remains of Younghusband's halt at this place, for it is indeed the only suitable base on the north side of the Mustagh pass.

We also found relics of much earlier date, which indicated that Changtok was an important halting-place on that remarkable ancient route which connected Baltistan and Yarkand. It was difficult to visualize the significance of this place in those days. We could not tell whether the stone circles and the remains of stone buildings marked the site of a permanent caravanserai, or a grazing ground, or whether it had only been used by occasional parties of local adventurers. It is difficult to imagine that they could ever have used the route for regular trading. In any case, the pass we had just crossed for the first time, now to be called the Sarpo Laggo pass, would have been a much easier route than the Mustagh pass with its difficult precipice, though the latter is supposed to have been used by these ancient travellers.

On the grassy slopes we found the whitened bones of large animals. These were probably the skeletons of wild asses, though it is said that ponies were taken over these passes in olden days. This I find very hard to believe, and Younghusband's experiences in failing to get ponies across the Mustagh pass supports my doubts. Scattered about we saw a number of bharal horns (a bharal is a mountain sheep), and the droppings of some very large birds, which we afterwards found to be a kind of snow-cock.

Changtok was a lovely place, surrounded by vast, curving, open glaciers. It was sheer delight to see grass again, and though it was too early for the spring flowers, the grass had the scent and feel of life. A few small birds were already here; their gay singing made the place an island of spring set in a waste of snow and ice. Clear streams lingered in limpid pools which mirrored the surrounding snow peaks. But we could not stay. I was anxious to reach Mone Brangsa, which was several miles farther down the glacier. There I hoped we should find some scrub which could be used for fuel. We had Desio's compass sketch map to guide us, and we knew that his party had camped at Mone Brangsa.

It was easy walking at the side of the glacier, with only a few difficult stretches to check our progress. Half-way down we came to a clear blue lake. From its shores we could see, far away to the south-east, the famous peak which the early explorers of the Baltoro glacier had named the Mustagh Tower. Beyond the lake, half a mile before we reached the place marked on Desio's map as Mone Brangsa, we were surprised to find that a large side glacier barred our way. Desio, when he had sketched this map in 1929, showed this glacier as ending a long way above the floor of the main valley. Since then it had evidently made an astonishingly rapid advance, and was now a considerable tributary of the Sarpo Laggo glacier, joining it in a tangled confusion of ice pinnacles. Desio's photograph of the place confirmed the fact of this remarkable change.

It was a formidable obstacle. We could not cross it, for its sides were vertical, and we were obliged to make a big detour on to the main glacier. This took many hours, and it was nearly dark before the whole party reached Mone Brangsa. It was a disappointing camping-place: a stony trough, bare and ugly, shut in by untidy scree-slopes and piles of moraine rubbish. No distant peaks could be seen. Nothing relieved the dreary monotony. There was no grass. The only vegetation was a bare wiry plant, like dead heather, which clung to the barren rocks. This provided us with firewood of a sort, but in order to keep it burning, the fire had to be blown continuously. A Sherpa's lungs are better than any bellows, but even so it was a difficult job to coax a blaze out of the stubborn fuel.

The next morning we slept late, until the sun poured into the deep valley. After breakfast we lazed in its warmth. My morning peace was shattered by the arrival of two snow-cock, which perched screeching near the camp, and strutted about protesting indignantly against our intrusion. The Sherpas were wildly excited, exclaiming that the gods had sent us the best meat in the world. They insisted that I should shoot our visitors. There was a wild rush for the rifle, which was packed in its case. By the time our fumbling, eager fingers had put it together, the birds had begun to suspect us of evil intentions. Before we were ready to launch the attack, they had flown away and perched somewhere in the crags above us, squawking their provocative taunts out of sight. This challenge was too much for Angtharkay, who insisted that he and I should stalk them. I felt forced to go, though I fully realized the stupidity of pursuing two birds in a maze of precipitous crags, with a .375 rifle which I had never tested and which would probably blow them to pieces if by any remote chance I managed to hit them. We sweated a long way up a scree-slope, scarcely daring to breathe as we approached the crags in which we thought the birds were hidden. An occasional gobbling sound led us on from crag to crag, while we performed terrifying feats of rock gymnastics which we would not have dared to contemplate in cold blood. Eventually, as we paused on a dizzy ledge, we heard the birds' mocking challenge floating across from the far side of a wide ravine. Angtharkay saluted their cunning with a farewell grin, which broadened into a bellow of laughter as he caught sight of me, clinging precariously to the sheer face of the crag, with unlaced boots over which bulged the torn remnants of my pyjama trousers, the tail of my shirt flapping in the breeze.

Auden arrived in the late afternoon, having had some difficulty in finding the camp. After our early evening meal, the birds were located again by a party collecting fuel. In spite of my protests Angtharkay induced me to renew the chase. He led me up a steep, scree-slope at a terrific pace, which gave me outrageous indigestion after my huge meal of rice. I remembered repentently that I had been one of those who voted against leaving the rifle at Askole. This time we actually succeeded in getting within twenty-five yards of one of the birds. I was panting heavily with the exertion of the climb. This, coupled with the unfortunate fact that I used the three hundred yards' sight, caused me to miss badly. We returned to camp empty-handed to face the jibes of the disappointed party. Next morning I restored my self-esteem with a little range practice, which proved, to my satisfaction at least, that the rifle was throwing high and to the right.

We all returned to Changtok on June 6th where we found Spender encamped. He had made a good beginning in his survey work during the last three days of fine weather. From the upper part of the glacier the great peak of K2 was clearly visible. It was the only fixed point which could be seen from anywhere in the district, and the whole of the survey had to be based on it. Using a Wild theodolite, subtense-bar, and plane-table, he had laid out a base and fixed the relative positions of a large number of prominent peaks in the district, which formed a network of fixed points for a plane-table survey. This process was repeated at intervals throughout the season, in order to keep a check on the plane-table work, and to renew the circle of distant fixed points. Azimuth determinations fixed the map with relation to K2. (An Azimuth is an exact bearing to a point, and is generally determined astronomically.) Spender also made observations for latitude from time to time.

Leaving Spender to continue his work at Changtok, we went on the same afternoon to the upper camp, where we spent an uncomfortable night in that inhospitable spot. Early the following morning we set out to fetch the last remaining loads from the dump on the other side of the pass. By this time there was a well-trodden track over the upper part of the glacier, and after two and a half hours of steady going we reached the top of the pass. On the other side we saw Tilman and his two Sherpas toiling up the steep slope which led from the snow basin. It was a great relief to see them, though we noticed that Tilman was moving with evident difficulty.

While our porters went down to the dump to collect the loads, Auden and I climbed a prominent rock spur above the pass to observe a round of angles with the theodolite. The climb proved to be much more difficult than we had expected, and a biting wind whipped the snow into our faces as we struggled with the survey work on the summit.[1] When we got back to the pass again, Tilman had arrived. He told us that at his last camp he had been ill again with another attack of fever which had not yet left him. We escorted him slowly down to the camp. He was very weak and was obliged to halt every few yards to rest.

The porters arrived at about five o'clock, staggering under the weight of enormous loads. After vehement persuasion, I managed to induce the Baltis to proceed as far as Changtok that evening. I was anxious to do this so that the whole party and all the loads could reach Changtok the following day. The porters had already done a strenuous day's work, and the seventeen Baltis were reluctant to do any more. But as an inducement I offered them treble pay for the day and the prospect of a pleasant camp site. The Sherpas, of course, came with me cheerfully, without any of these bribes. In fact they took a prominent part in urging the unwilling Baltis along. Tilman was too ill to go any farther that day, so he remained in the upper camp with Auden and Sen Tensing.

The bad weather of the day had quietened into a tranquil evening. The last of the daylight lingered in the sky and touched the ice with delicate opal colours. Dusk was falling as we reached the first glades of Changtok. We lay down there to sleep on soft cushions of grass; the hollow where we camped was brimmed with peace.

This place was more than a mile above Spender's camp, and the next morning, while the rest of the party fetched the remaining loads from the upper camp, Angtharkay, Nukku and I relayed the loads from the hollow to the place from which Spender was working. Auden and Tilman joined us later in the day. Tilman was still very ill, but fortunately he had time to recuperate in this delightful spot, while we were relaying all the loads down to Mone Brangsa.

This relay work was tedious. We had hoped that, having left the hardships of the high glacier camps, the Baltis would be more contented and would work more willingly. But two days later our strength was further reduced by the departure of five more Baltis, who suddenly refused to work any more. We paid them in full and sent them away without our blessing. This desertion lengthened the time necessary for transporting our loads to Suget Jangal, which lies about six miles below the snout of the Sarpo Laggo glacier. It was the place we had selected for our main base.

It was now nearly the middle of June, and before long the summer melting of the glaciers would make the Shaksgam river unfordable. If we were to attempt our proposed expedition to the Aghil range, which lies to the north of the Shaksgam river, it was imperative to get there quickly. We therefore decided to leave a big dump of loads at Mone Brangsa, and to take with us only the

[1] The height of this point is 5,748 metres (18,860 feet).

equipment and food which we would require for three weeks' exploration in the Aghil range. Even so, two relays were still necessary, as our party had to be fed during the next week while we approached the Shaksgam river. But this slow progress gave Spender time to complete his survey of the ranges surrounding the Sarpo Laggo glacier.

By June 10th all the loads were at Mone Brangsa. On the 11th we took as much as we could carry farther down the glacier. As we descended, the valley became more dreary and desolate. There was no life. It seemed as if nothing living had ever moved there. Mysterious hollow sounds rumbled from the glacier, and the melancholy clatter of falling stones echoed weirdly from the bleak crags. Though the cliffs were steep and menacing, there was nothing grand or shapely in the muddle of the graceless flanks – only crumbling decay. It was hard to get along, as the walls of the valley rose abruptly above the glacier, and we were obliged to work our way laboriously over the torn debris-covered surface of the ice.

As we went farther down the glacier our admiration for Younghusband's achievement increased. To have attempted such a difficult route at the end of his tremendous journey, having already travelled for many days through uninhabited country, nearly at the end of his resources, must have called for rare courage.

We only covered three miles before camping again in this dismal valley. On the next day the second relay of loads was brought down to this dump. On the thirteenth we had a long day. Though we started early, it was 2.30 before we reached the snout of the glacier. It was a relief to be able to walk freely again after days of scrambling over boulders, leaping across chasms, fording rivers, and chipping steps up ice-slopes, always uncertain of finding a way through. We had hoped to reach Suget Jangal that day, but after marching rapidly for two hours over the river flats below the glacier, we decided to camp, still about three miles from our objective. In this place we found plenty of fuel and water. The position of the camp was strategically suitable as a main base. For although it was a full day's march away from the junction of the Sarpo Laggo river and the Shaksgam, it had the advantage of being within carrying distance of Mone Brangsa. Also the site commanded a fine view of the Crevasse glacier, and into the vast area of unexplored country beyond, which was our main objective.

Our immediate objective, however, was the usual brew of tea; and as we swallowed great mugfuls of it, we discussed the unnamed peaks which we saw at the head of the Crevasse glacier. The most distant of these formed a circle of snow domes. It was intriguing to speculate how far off they were. None of us could agree. Tilman's estimate was fifteen miles, but Auden was convinced that they were quite forty miles away. We had one of our usual bets on this question. The stake for all our bets was a meal at Simpson's. Though since our return none of us seems to have had enough spare cash to honour his debts. Auden's estimate was the more accurate, for Spender measured the distance the next day, and found that the peaks were quite thirty miles from our base camp.

In the evening Spender and I wandered down the valley to see if we could find the extensive oasis which Younghusband's men had called Suget Jangal. It was too far away to reach it before dark, but from some rising ground we saw the place in the distance, a dark patch of trees which stretched like a shadow across the bleached gravel flats of the valley. As we turned to go back to camp we looked again up the Crevasse glacier and saw, in the far distance, a superb mountain, shaped like a trident, piercing the sunset sky. I felt stirred by a compelling impatience to find out how high it was, and where it stood. I longed to set out at once into such enticing country. At that moment it seemed exasperating to think that six weeks must pass before we could start the journey up the Crevasse glacier. The once fascinating problem of the Aghil range seemed to fade into insignificance before the urge of this immediate desire. Also I dreaded the possibility of floods in the Shaksgam river cutting us off from the chance of carrying out this plan. We returned to camp and ate our supper by the faint light of a young moon.

That evening was for me one of the greatest moments of the expedition. Warmed by the unaccustomed luxury of a blazing fire, its leaping flames fed with unstinted wood, I felt that after long days of toil and disappointment we had at last arrived. East and west of us stretched an unexplored section, eighty miles long, of the greatest watershed in the world. To the north, close at hand, across the Shaksgam river, was the Aghil range, with its romantic associations and unknown peaks and valleys. To share all this, I had with me three companions as keen as myself, supported by seven of the most stout-hearted retainers in the world. We had food enough to keep us alive for three months in this place of my dreams, and the health and experience to meet the opportunity. I wanted nothing more.

CHAPTER NINE

Finding the Aghil Pass

ON June the 14th the Baltis and four of the Sherpas started at dawn and spent a long day bringing the rest of the loads down from the lower Sarpo Laggo glacier camp. Spender laid out a survey base on the gravel flats which stretched for miles around our camp, and fixed the position of all the distant peaks in view; Auden was busy with his geological work. Tilman, Angtharkay, Lhakpa Tensing and I set off down the valley taking the rifle with us. After an hour's quick walking we reached the long stretch of meadow-land and willow groves referred to by Younghusband as Suget Jangal. It was a delightful place of clear springs, shade and soft green turf. It was deserted except for a few hares playing on the grass, which scuttled under cover as we approached, and some small birds singing in the willows. Everywhere there were tracks of wild asses (kyang), and a great number of bharal horns littered the ground.

We lay for a while on the grass and then climbed up the hillside for about 1,500 feet, until we stood on the crest of a ridge which divides the

Sarpo Laggo valley from another big valley which descends from the north face of K2. Far away to the south-east we could see some of the great ice peaks of the main water-shed which cluster round the head of the Baltoro glacier. K2 itself was hidden by a corner of the valley. For want of a better name this valley had been called the K2 nullah.[1] Our position on the ridge commanded a fine view down the Shaksgam river and far up into the unknown ranges of the Crevasse glacier. We quite forgot to hunt for game and discussed excitedly the various aspects of the view. Suddenly a herd of about a dozen bharal ran out from a hollow below us, not fifty yards away. They hesitated for a moment, then plunged over a shoulder into the K2 nullah. Angtharkay and I followed, climbing gingerly over each section of rising ground and peering into the gully beyond. We stalked for nearly two hours before we found the animals again grazing peacefully on the hillside at a hundred yards' range. It seemed criminal to kill them, and when it came to the point I felt very reluctant to shoot. But the chance of adding to our scanty rations outweighed my scruples and I shot two of the creatures. The Sherpas were in a great state of excitement. They shouldered the dead animals and trotted back along the steep hillside under the great weight of meat, laughing and shouting as they went.

While I was walking back across the flats, I saw something standing alone by the river. It was some way off, and the shimmer caused by the hot afteroon sun on the gravel made it difficult to distinguish what it was. I thought it must be Spender working with his plane-table. Then I saw that it was coming towards me. When it drew nearer, I realized that it was a wild ass. It came up to within fifteen yards of me and stood switching its tail about and staring at me. When I turned round to go on it followed me, stopping when I stopped and walking when I walked, rather like an obedient dog. However, it lagged behind as I approached the camp and kept a respectful distance away.

That night we had a feast of rice and meat, and then sat round the fire feeling bloatedly contented. The Baltis were Mohammedans, and would not join in the meal as their religion forbade them to eat meat that had been killed by someone of another faith. It was a beautiful starry night, and Spender made some astronomical observations to determine our latitude and the exact bearing to the peaks that he had fixed.

As I have explained in an earlier chapter, we had brought enough food down from Mone Brangsa to enable us to carry out our projects across the Shaksgam river, in the Aghil range. We had not allowed more than three weeks' supplies, firstly, because we could not carry more without the tedious business of relaying, and secondly, because July 10th was the latest date on which we could be reasonably certain of being able to cross back over the Shaksgam before the summer floods, which are caused by the intensive melting of the glaciers. Even so, we would be running some risk of being cut off, and in order to save time, we had planned to take all seventeen Baltis up the Shaksgam as far as the foot of the Aghil pass, to avoid any relaying of loads.

[1] Nullah is the English spelling of the Hindustani word "nala" meaning valley or stream bed.

While Spender and Auden were continuing their scientific work, Tilman and I spent a busy morning weighing and checking the food, and making detailed plans for our movements during the next three weeks. We had promised to give the men a day's rest, and the Baltis slept peacefully during the morning. But, in the afternoon, they announced with determination that they did not propose to accompany us any farther. We argued with them, pleaded and bribed, pointing out that we were only asking them to come on for another two days over flat, easy country, But nothing would shake their determination to go back straight away. So we paid them their money, and they departed that evening. We sent Angtharkay and Nukku to escort them for part of their journey. Only four Baltis remained with us; these were the four who had undertaken, from the beginning, to stay with us as long as we required them. They were: Mancho, tall and gaunt, with a huge beak-like nose; Mahamad Hussain, elderly and philosphical, an amazingly daring climber on rotten rock, known always to us as Buddha; and Mahadi and Hussain, inseparable friends, who had followed us from Parkutta, a village in the Indus valley. These men greatly increased our carrying strength, and they served us well, particularly in the valley below the snow-line. While we were travelling over glaciers or crossing high passes, however, they became very depressed, and caused us a great deal of trouble.

The departure of the rest of the Baltis and the temporary absence of two of the Sherpas weakened our position considerably. We cut down the weight of our equipment loads still farther, and also left some of the survey instruments and all the money at our base. Even so, and with all the men carrying seventy or eighty pounds each, we could not move everything that was necessary. On June 16th, Tilman and Auden went to the junction, with the four Sherpas and the four Baltis, carrying as much as they could manage. Spender, Angtensing and I spent the day relaying to Suget Jangal all the loads that were left. The other four Sherpas returned there from the junction in the evening. Sen Tensing was very ill with a recurrence of his fever, and the next day we had to leave him behind in this delightful spot to recover, and to await the return of Angtharkay and Nukku. We left a small dump of food for him, and while the others were carrying the rest of the loads to the junction, Spender and I spent the day doing a series of high survey stations on the ridge above the entrance of the K2 nullah. It was fascinating work getting to know the features of the country and speculating how the individual pieces would fit into the whole intriguing puzzle which new country always presents. We crossed the mouth of the K2 nullah and marched to the junction in the late afternoon. We found Tilman in his tent, down with fever. He had been ill since the previous evening. Auden had taken the Baltis with a relay of loads seven miles up the Shaksgam. He had sent the men back, and was camping there alone, in order to have a clear day for his geological work. Near our camp, at the junction of the two rivers, there was a number of old huts and some oval-shaped rings which looked like graves. These puzzling relics of former habitation seemed to accentuate the isolation of the country.

The next morning Tilman's temperature was down, and though he felt very shaky, he was able to come with us. The Shaksgam valley was a weird place, shut in on both sides by gaunt limestone cliffs, slashed across with twisted streaks of yellow, red and black strata, which gave them the strange, bizarre appearance of a camouflaged ship. The bottom of the valley was composed of sand and gravel flats, often half a mile wide. Over these the river flowed; sometimes concentrated into one great body of water as it swirled round a bend in the valley; sometimes split up into a dozen streams which sprawled their independent courses across the flats, for ever changing their pattern. As long as it was possible to keep to the valley floor our progress was easy and quick. But every now and again the river hurled itself against the cliffs on our side of the valley, and forced us, either to attempt a fording, which would have been very difficult in most places, or to look for a route along the face of the crags. Spread out at long intervals along the valley we found curious clumps of tall vegetation which grew, for no apparent reason, out of the sand. The main river was turbid, but at each side of it clear streams flowed through a chain of deep green and blue pools, close under the crags. Steep glacier-filled corries split the sides of the valley, and we looked up them to a profusion of Dolomite spires.

Angtharkay and Nukku caught us up on the evening of the 18th. They had come all the way from the Sarpo Laggo glacier, and had brought with them Sen Tensing, who had now recovered.

Beyond our camp of June 18th–19th, the river flowed for a long way against the cliffs. A narrow ledge, a few feet above the water, helped us to overcome this obstacle, though in places its continuity was interrupted, and we had to negotiate some awkward steps. After this, for the next few miles, we were able to walk along the gravel flats.

Our problem now was how to find the valley which led to the Aghil pass. We had Younghusband's description of it to guide us, but as there were a great many narrow side valleys, all with much the same characteristics, it was not an easy task to choose the right one. The only important tributary coming down from the Aghil range was wide and open, and we could see up it for many miles. It seemed to be the obvious valley to choose as an approach to the interior of the range, and Desio had shown it on his map as descending from the Aghil pass, but it did not resemble in any way the one described by Younghusband. The difficulties of the cliffs on the southern side of the main valley prevented us from climbing high enough to get a view that was of any use to us.

Farther up, the valley became more open, and the river, spread over the whole of its width, offered a good fording-place. Angtensing and I led the way across the stream, holding on to each other for mutual support. We very nearly came to grief. Angtensing was swept off his feet, and I had great difficulty in holding him up until he had recovered enough to struggle ashore. He and his load of survey instruments escaped with nothing more serious than a wetting. After this we humbly followed the lead of the Baltis, who knew far more about this hazardous business than any of us, and faced the torrents with surprising nonchalance. But the experience was quite unpleasant enough to serve as a warning to us to keep a very close watch on the increase of the rivers of the Aghil range, and not to prolong our stay on the northern side of the Shaksgam until it became quite unfordable.

A remarkable feature of the country through which we were travelling was the ancient river terraces that lined the sides of the valleys. These terraces were roughly level on top and cut vertically at their outer edges as if by a sharp knife. Sometimes the cliff so formed was only twenty feet high, sometimes it stood as much as a thousand feet above the present level of the river. In some places the terraces were no more than inconspicuous fringes clinging to the sides of a valley; in others they covered almost its entire floor, leaving only a narrow canyon for the river. They were composed of a mass of boulders and pebbles in a matrix of sand, and, being uncemented, were very friable – a structure known to geologists as *conglomerate*. It is difficult to visualize the conditions in which these deposits were laid down, and to understand the extraordinary changes that must have taken place to produce the present phenomenon. A rejuvenation of the whole mountain mass seems to be the only way to account for the rivers having suddenly cut into the wide beds of gravel which they have built for themselves.

The river terraces and their conglomerate cliffs play a most important part in travel through this country. The cliffs are absolutely perpendicular, and it is impossible to climb them if they are high. It is possible to go for many miles along a valley without finding a place where one can climb out. Similarly, though a terrace will make an excellent highway, comfortably remote from interference from the river, it is often difficult to descend from it. Often, too, terraces are slashed across by ravines, cut by side streams to such a depth that they are quite impassable. When an unfordable river runs through a narrow canyon of high conglomerate cliffs it is generally an insuperable obstacle. Although the tops of these terraces occasionally provide a path, their cliffs confront the traveller with difficulties second only to the problem of crossing the swift, quickly-flooding rivers.

Soon after we had crossed the Shaksgam to its northern side, we were stopped by the river running against a conglomerate cliff, three hundred feet high. In order to avoid recrossing the river we climbed a steep gully. We had a good deal of difficulty, and it took us nearly two hours to get the party on to the terrace. We soon regretted this move, for the terrace was cut by a number of ravines, and progress was slow. We could not get down to the valley floor again, and when at last we reached the valley, which we had chosen to ascend in our search for the Aghil pass, we found ourselves stopped by a chasm cut by the very stream that we wanted to reach. Tilman and I tried to get round the end of the cut-off by climbing along the cliffs above the terrace. We got on to an old glacial till, in which we chipped steps, but became involved in horrible difficulties, and had to give up our attempt. We then joined the Sherpas, who were engaged in trying an even more desperate-looking manoeuvre. Eventually we succeeded in lowering our loads into the ravine and climbing down ourselves, on rounded boulders jutting out of the face of the cliff. Several great chunks of the wall fell away as we were doing this and crashed with an alarming roar. We climbed up the bottom of the ravine for a few hundred yards, and emerged on to a terrace at the mouth of our valley. Here we pitched camp. All this trouble had been caused by our choosing the wrong place to cross the Shaksgam.

Near the camp we found some more remains of stone buildings, which gave us a comforting clue that we were still on the ancient route, and that we had been lucky in our somewhat blind choice of the valley. Even with this evidence we were far from sure of the way to the pass, and debated whether we should send parties to reconnoitre some of the other valleys as well. But as we had such a very short time at our disposal for our various jobs, we decided to put all our eggs into one basket and rely on our first choice being the right one. Our plan was to find the pass and, using it as a central dump and meeting-place, to disperse the party in various directions with all the food that was available. The view from our camp was very fine. We were on the northern side of a sweeping curve of the Shaksgam river. To the south-west we looked down the desolate gorge up which we had come. To the south-south-east, upstream, we could see twenty miles of the river's course, interrupted here and there by the mighty, pinnacled glaciers coming down from the Teram Kangri and Gasherbrum ranges. Farther to the east was a range of magnificent peaks, which, we supposed, lay between us and Mason's Zug Shaksgam. Opposite us, to the south, towering Dolomite peaks formed a barrier to the unexplored northern glaciers of K2.

We started on the morning of June 20th in a great state of excitement. So much depended on whether we would find the pass at the head of the inconspicuous valley on which we were pinning our faith. We had left dumps of food along our route for the return journey, so we were no longer so heavily laden. We passed through a narrow defile into an open rocky basin. Beyond, the valley divided; the eastern section seemed to be surrounded by great granite precipices; the western branch, descending from the north, held out promise of better things and we started up it, encouraged by the discovery of more traces of human occupation; we even found a nail. The going was very easy, and, a great deal sooner than we expected, we stepped on to the crest of the divide. It was, unquestionably, the Aghil pass. To the north the ground fell away in a gentle slope to a placid tarn. Beyond, across a deep valley, was a range of gently rounded, snow-capped peaks, so typical of the mountains of Central Asia. This was the valley of the Surukwat river, by which Younghusband had approached the pass, and the peaks were those of the northern part of the Aghil range. West of us were the limestone peaks of the Shaksgam, standing like sentinels above this remarkable pass. A keen wind blew from the north, driving sleet into our faces, and snow was falling on the neighbouring peaks. It was too cold to sit for long on the pass, but neither the wind nor the bleakness of the scene could spoil our first experience of the view which Younghusband had seen with the same excitement fifty years before.

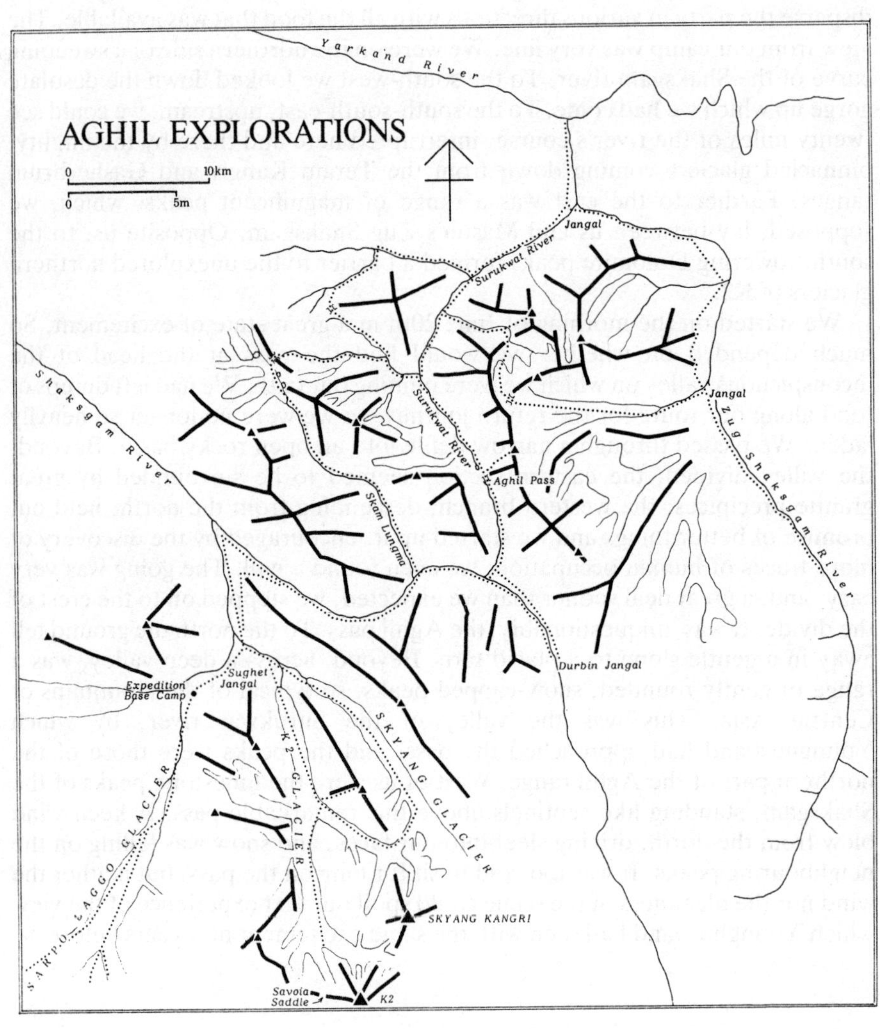
AGHIL EXPLORATIONS
0 10km
0 5m
Yarkand River
Jangal
Surukwat River
Jangal
Zug Shaksgam River
Shaksgam River
Surukwat River
Aghil Pass
Skam Lungma
Durbin Jangal
Sughet Jangal
Expedition Base Camp
K2 GLACIER
SKYANG GLACIER
SARPO LAGGO GLACIER
SKYANG KANGRI
Savoia Saddle
K2

CHAPTER TEN

Finding the Zug Shaksgam River

WE camped above the lake and took stock of our food supplies. We found that we had enough to last us for fifteen days. As we had left dumps for the return journey to the Sarpo Laggo, all the supplies that we had with us could be used in the Aghil range. It was decided that Spender should work in the vicinity of the pass. Having fixed its position in latitude, and in relation to K2, he was to make a detailed survey of as wide an area as possible. He was allotted four Sherpas and one Balti to help him with his work. Auden, with Lhakpa Tensing and Mahadi, was to traverse the range to the Yarkand river, continuing his geological studies. Afterwards he was to explore towards the west and attempt to force a new route across the range to the Shaksgam. Tilman and I were to work over to the east to try and find the Zug Shaksgam river.

We were surprised to find that the ground was littered with a great quantity of yak dung. Evidently the pastures round our camp were used extensively as grazing grounds, presumably by the people living on the banks of the Yarkand river. Yak dung makes excellent fuel and it was a great relief to find it, for there was no wood of any sort in the vicinity, and, although we had brought with us a certain amount of paraffin, the problem of fuel had been worrying us.

That evening, Angtharkay and I walked down the valley in search of game. The gentle grass slopes above the lake were covered with mauve primulas, a lovely splash of colour in the evening light. At first we could see no sign of life. I was searching the valley through binoculars when suddenly Angtharkay clutched my arm excitedly and pointed to an apparently barren hillside. I could see nothing but boulders. Then it seemed to me that the whole hillside was moving slowly upwards, and I realized that I was looking at an enormous herd of bharal. We went on down the valley until we were out of sight and then climbed up and made a big detour, using what cover we could find. The stalk was very successful and we got close to the herd, but in the fading light I missed every shot and we returned empty-handed to camp, after dark.

The weather had improved and the next morning was fine. The Aghil pass had a quite different appearance in the warm sunlight which danced on the rippled surface of the lake. We said good-bye to Auden, who was leaving us for twelve days, and he went off down the valley with his two men. Spender was busy with the preparations for his survey. Tilman and I had decided to climb a peak to the east of the pass in the hope of seeing into the country towards the Zug Shaksgam river to get a better idea of our problem. The peak looked so easy that we stupidly decided not to take a rope. For the first 3,000 feet we climbed at a steady pace, first over boulders, then over easy rock, and then kicking steps in the firm snow. Gradually the ground became more complicated, and soon we were climbing along a sharp arête of really awkward rock. An enormous load of winter snow, which had not yet melted and so had created the illusion of simplicity from below, made climbing exceedingly difficult. Each hold had first to be cleared of snow before it could be used, and we had to chip the ice out of the vertical cracks before it was possible to wedge arms and legs securely. Our fingers became numbed by continual contact with the snow, so that when a hold had been made it was difficult to grip it. We climbed close together, one man supporting the other with his ice-axe while the snow was flogged away from the rock. As the pitches succeeded one another with increasing difficulty, we cursed our folly at not having brought a rope. As usual in such circumstances, we overcame several obstacles before we realized what was happening, and our subsequent reluctance to turn back was due more to a dislike of going over this dangerous ground again than to a desire to reach the top. After an exciting climb, we emerged on to a plateau covered with soft snow, in which we sank up to our hips. It took us another two hours of hard work to climb to a snow dome which was the summit of the mountain. There was a violent wind blowing, and on the way up Tilman had lost his hat, which floated down to one of the glaciers to the east. It was 4.30 when we reached the top. We estimated its altitude to be about 20,200 feet.

The view was magnificent, but we had not time to contemplate it, and the wind had robbed us of the inclination to do so. Earlier in the day, while we were on the easy lower slopes, we had watched the great peaks of the Karakoram mount above their lower satellites as we climbed, and had marvelled at the beautiful symmetry of K2 soaring above the rest. Now our view was too vast to comprehend, in the uncomfortable ten minutes that we spent on the summit. I tried to memorize the form of the country to the east, which we had come to see, but it was far too complicated, and I could not disentangle its intricacies. All we could gather was that a wide system of glaciers flowed towards the east into a deep river basin, and that a high ridge of peaks separated it from the valley of the Surukwat. We took a complete round of photographs and started to descend. We followed a snow gully down from the summit. It became very steep and icy lower down, but was a good deal easier than the rock ridge that we had been on earlier in the day. We finished the descent with some swift glissades which brought us back to camp before dark.

Spender left the camp soon after five the next morning to do a high survey station above the pass. Tilman and I lazed in bed until the sun reached the valley and warmed the tent. After our reconnaissance of the day before we had decided to follow down the Surukwat river to the north, to go up the first big side valley coming from the east, and to look for a pass at its head to the glacier system that we had seen. We hoped that in this way we would be able to reach the Zug Shaksgam river.

Tilman, Angtharkay, Lobsang, Mancho, Buddha and I started at nine o'clock. We took with us a light photo-theodolite, the rifle and enough food to last us for twelve days. We marched rapidly over the grassy meadows below the lake. Three miles down we came to a recently used shepherd's encampment, consisting of three strongly built pens and a curious erection of long willow poles. We found a well-constructed fireplace and a complicated wooden implement, the use of which we could not understand. It was a pity that the place was not occupied, for if it had been we should have learnt something about the present inhabitants of the range. We were most anxious, too, to find out if any of the ancient routes across the ranges were known to the people of the Yarkand at the present day, and if so, what possible significance they could have.

The Sherpas were very excited at our discovery, and evidently felt themselves to be approaching the luxury of a civilized metropolis. They said that, even if we did not find a village a few miles farther down, this place was sure to be occupied when we returned. I am afraid that they were destined to be disappointed. I do not know when these mountain pastures are used, but from what we learned later in Shimshal, I suspect that it is during some months of the winter. The Baltis were not enthusiastic at the idea of meeting anyone. They said that the people on this side of the range were a race of giants and were not friendly towards intruders. This was probably a legend from the days of banditry in these parts.

Two miles farther on, we came to the junction of three streams which formed the Surukwat river. The other two came from the mountains to the west, which made a barrier of vertical precipices in that direction. We lunched by a spring, resting on a green bed of chives, which made a savoury addition to our bread and cheese. Below this point, the valley became dreary and unattractive. The river ran steeply down through a narrow canyon and we were forced to climb high up on the side of the valley. Rounding a corner, we looked down on a series of immense river terraces through which the stream had cut a gorge three hundred feet deep. It was easy walking along the flat top of one of these terraces and we soon came to the first big tributary valley on the east. We were fortunate enough to find a narrow gully by which we could climb down from the terrace, and we camped by a clump of wild rose bushes at the foot of the side valley. We found some rhubarb growing there, so we called the valley Kharkul Lungpa (Balti for Rhubarb Valley). The rhubarb stewed was excellent, but it required more than our ration of sugar to make it sweet.

By timing ourselves over each section of the march and taking a compass reading whenever we changed direction, we were able to plot, with reasonable precision, our position relative to the Aghil pass.

The weather was set fine and we did not bother to pitch tents. My night, which started with that delicious sensation of dozing in the moonlight, was disturbed by lice. We had found some of these creatures in our clothes a few days before, and though we adopted drastic measures to get rid of them, alternately boiling and freezing our shirts, we could not check the increase of their numbers. It is the first time that I have ever been troubled with lice in the Himalaya. Presumably we caught them from the Baltis, though they never seemed to be bothered by them. But I found that one soon became almost immune to their irritation; weeks later I used to take as many as a hundred at a time out of my shirt without having been worried unduly. In the end, garments were de-loused simply as a means of passing the time during bad weather!

We started up the Kharkul Lungpa at eight o'clock next morning. It took us in a direction about ten degrees south of east. We halted at the end of each hour for a short rest. At about half-past ten, Tilman went down with yet another bout of fever. It seems probable from the symptoms that these recurrent attacks were caused by an infection of malaria which he may have picked up during our march up the Indus valley. After some discussion, it was decided that I should leave him behind with one of the Baltis, provided with a tent and food enough for four days and the rifle, while I went on with the rest of the party to explore the head of the valley.

Farther up I found that the valley divided into two branches, one containing a fair-sized glacier coming down from some high peaks on the right, and a narrow nullah filled with shale on the left. It was difficult to know which to choose, as one seemed to lead too far to the south of our general line, and the other too far to the north. I chose the left hand, or northern branch, as it appeared to be the easier of the two. We toiled for many hours up slate scree, with our heavy loads and reached a col, about 18,000 feet high, at the head of the nullah. I was disappointed to find that it led into another big tributary of the Surukwat. It was possible to descend into this valley, at the head of which there seemed to be another col which would take us farther to the east; but I decided to go back and try my luck with the southern branch of the Kharkul Lungpa. I set up the theodolite, and took a round of photographs and angles of all the conspicuous points I could see. In this way, when Spender had fixed some of the points which I observed to the west, the position of my station could also be plotted, and the country drawn in from the photographs. I got a fine view northwards across the Yarkand river to the mountains of the Kuen Lun range in Sinkiang. We ran down the shale nullah at a tremendous speed, and reached the main Kharkul Lungpa at about half-past eight. It had been a disappointing day, but a very interesting one. The country was exceedingly complicated and I realized the truth of what Mason had told me: that the Aghil range followed none of the normal rules of mountain topography.

I sent Mancho down with a note to Tilman next morning, and Angtharkay and I started very early to reconnoitre the southern branch of the valley. We climbed on to the glacier, which proved to be a great deal longer than we had expected. Higher up the snow was soft and progress was slow and laborious. The glacier had its origin in a complicated mass of peaks to the south. At its head there was a col leading over to the south-west, while to the east, in the direction we had planned to take, there was a steep and broken ice-fall. The prospects looked so unpromising that I nearly gave it up, but I thought that I might as well climb to a high point to get a clearer idea of the country. A rock rib, covered in deep powder snow, led us up by the side of the ice-fall, and at one o'clock we reached the crest of a ridge about 19,000 feet high. On the other side I was delighted to see a glacier flowing gently down towards the east. It was tantalizing to have to wait for another day before we could cross this exciting pass, and to be obliged to toil all the way up to it again. But it was a great relief to have found it, and I returned to camp thoroughly pleased with the day's work.

When we got back we found that Tilman had arrived. His fever had not lasted twenty-four hours, and it proved to be the last attack of the series.

Angtharkay and I had eaten nothing since our breakfast tea and tsampa, so we were ravenously hungry, and spent the rest of the evening eating, and drinking mug after mug of tea.

We were away by seven o'clock on June 25th. The Baltis went extraordinarily well considering how much they disliked the idea of crossing a high glacier pass. When we got on to the snow, it transpired that they had left their snow-glasses behind at the dump in the Sarpo Laggo valley. I made substitutes with little discs of cardboard with a tiny slit in each. They could not see much, and later suffered a certain amount of eye-strain, but it prevented them from getting snow-blindness. Our tracks of the previous day made things a great deal easier than they had been before. Also the sky was overcast during the morning and we did not suffer much from the oppressive lassitude which is so great a trial on Himalayan glaciers. Tilman was, of course, still feeling weak, but this hardly seemed to affect his pace.

We reached the pass at 1.15 and sent the porters on down the glacier to the east, while Tilman and I did a survey station on a rocky point above the pass. The weather had cleared and we got a good round of angles and photographs. We also had time to study the country to the east. We gave temporary names to some of the peaks and made sketches of them to help us to identify them later. The whole job took about two hours and when it was finished we packed up the instruments and followed in the tracks of the porters. We ran easily down the smooth surface of the glacier for two miles, when broken ice forced us to climb on to steep rocks on the left bank. Farther on, after we had overtaken the porters, we climbed on to the glacier again and worked our way over the ice, until we reached a place where the glacier plunged down in a precipitous ice-fall for a thousand feet. To the left of this we found a scree-filled gully, which we ran down in a few minutes to a wide, grassy trough, or *ablation valley*, formed between the high lateral moraine of the glacier and the flanks of the main valley. We were following a large ice-stream which would have been regarded as a major glacier in the Eastern or Central Himalaya, though of course it did not compare with the main glaciers of the Karakoram range. It was joined by several big tributaries from the south. We had not expected to find such extensive glaciation in the Aghil range.

The trough offered us easy walking and we followed it at a good pace until darkness forced us to camp. Some dried moss growing on the rocks provided us with scanty fuel, but we supplemented it with our Primus, and used some of our precious store of paraffin to cook our meal of tea and pemmican and tsampa. We estimated our height to be about 16,000 feet.

The ablation valley was a godsend, and on June the 26th we hurried swiftly down it, past some very complicated sections of the glacier, where forests of ice pinnacles would have delayed us for many hours.

When we reached the end of the glacier our difficulties began. The river entered a narrow conglomerate gorge, and ran from one side of it to the other with such merciless frequency that we were never able to follow one bank for more than a few hundred yards at a time. Fortunately, as it was still fairly early in the day, the river was not flooded, and though crossing it was an unpleasant business it was not really dangerous. By wading through the stream from side to side, we were able to keep to the floor of the gorge. This was fortunate as I do not think that it would have been possible to climb along its precipitous sides. I had a severe headache all day, due, no doubt, to a touch of sun-stroke.

As we were most anxious to reach the end of the valley that day, we could not afford to stop for a rest, because the afternoon floods might at any moment prevent us from continuing. We had seen from the glacier that the gorge joined a big valley running roughly from south-east to north-west. It took far longer than we had expected to reach this valley, and when we were still a mile away from it we realized that the river had become too dangerous to ford again. But by then our gorge had widened slightly and we were able, with a good deal of difficulty, to climb for another half-mile, high up along its right flank. Then we dropped down to the river again, and camped in a little jungle of birch and wild roses. It was wonderful to have ample fuel again and we brewed many pints of tea. The late afternoon sun beat down on us, and the heat in the narrow airless gorge was terrific. The sand on the shore of the river was so scorched that we could not sit on it with comfort. I spread a sleeping-bag over some rose bushes, crept under it for shade, took a large dose of aspirin, and slept.

Tilman went on down the valley to reconnoitre, and, by the time I woke, he had returned. He had reached the big valley after some difficult rock-climbing. He found that it contained a large river, fully as big as the Shaksgam. This was good news, for it seemed likely that this really was the Zug Shaksgam, for which we were searching. To his surprise, on a well-wooded spit of land at the junction of the two rivers, he had found a collection of stone huts. There was no possibility of grazing in the vicinity and the huts must have marked a regular halting-place on some route. But where the route could lead and from whence it came we could not imagine. It was an intriguing problem that we wished we had enough time to solve. A thorough investigation of the question would be an interesting piece of work, but it would take many months to accomplish.

Early next morning, we went down to the junction. The stream in our gorge was quite low, but in spite of that we were forced to do an unpleasant piece of rock-climbing to get down. We cooked breakfast at the huts and discussed our next move. Below the junction, the river entered a gorge which looked quite impassable, but the huts suggested that a route through it must exist. We assumed from the direction in which it was flowing that the river, whatever it was, must flow either into the Surukwat or direct into the Yarkand. We decided to try and follow it down and to make our way back to the Aghil pass from its junction with either of these rivers. But we had enough food to last us for seven more days and we were anxious to prove whether this river really was Mason's Zug Shaksgam; so we decided to spend two days exploring upstream in the hope of reaching a point from which we could see into Mason's country. We sent Angtharkay and Mancho to look for a route through the gorge while the rest of us started upstream. Each party took food enough for one night and we agreed to return to the huts on the following evening. We dumped all our spare food and equipment there; as we did not require tents or stores or warm clothing we had very little to carry and were able to travel at a great speed.

We fancied that we had found a track leading up the valley from the dump, but it did not take us far, and before long we were obliged to do a very hazardous climb up a conglomerate cliff. I thought the risk was quite unjustifiable at the time, for I could see nothing to prevent the whole face of the cliff tumbling down on top of us. It seemed that if one stone were dislodged the whole structure must collapse. Buddha was a tower of strength; he led up these places with absolute confidence, climbing like a young chamois, and pulling us up after him. It occurred to me afterwards that his serenity was in reality his Mohammedan fatalism. If one relied completely on divine providence to hold the rocks in place, the climbing was not unduly difficult! And Buddha was in all things a philosopher. However, I am glad that I did not analyse his daring at the time or I should have been even more frightened on those conglomerate cliffs than I actually was during the climb. After we had reached the top in safety, we walked for two miles along a river terrace and came to an oasis watered by a spring. At first it looked like a village of fertile orchards and fields, but when we reached it we found that the vegetation, though varied and very dense, was wild, and there was no sign of former cultivation. There was, however, a number of old stone huts with skilfully built, dome-shaped roofs. It was obvious that with a little irrigation these river terraces could be made fertile; but we could not see any trace of an attempt to do this, and the purpose of the huts remains a mystery.

A short way beyond this place, we came to another large tributary coming from the west. We supposed that it drained the glacier system that we had looked down upon from the peak above the Aghil pass on June 21st. From the size of the stream it looked as if these glaciers were even larger than those which we had recently descended. It was still early and we crossed without difficulty. Several more ravines cutting across the terrace by side streams caused us some trouble. After that, the valley opened out surprisingly, its sheer sides became gentle slopes and the terraces diminished to a manageable size. By evening, we had come a long way, and the character of the country suggested that we were approaching the most westerly point reached by Mason in 1926. We camped by a spring of clear water which rippled away in a tiny stream, edged with emerald banks of grass and chives, patterned with flowers. For wood we found an ample supply of the same aromatic plant that we had found in the Sarpo Laggo. After a supper of pemmican and boiled chives, we settled down on a comfortable bed of sand, and watched the approach of night transform the wild desert mountains into phantoms of soft unreality. How satisfying it was to be travelling with such simplicity. I lay watching the constellations swing across the sky. Did I sleep that night – or was I caught up for a moment into the ceaseless rhythm of space?

CHAPTER ELEVEN

In Unexplored Zug Shaksgam

TILMAN roused us at 2.45 a.m. for we had a long day before us. We breakfasted off salted tea and bread which Buddha had baked for us on the previous evening. We started marching up the valley again, with Lobsang carrying the survey equipment. Buddha was left behind to resume his interrupted sleep. A waning moon floated in the cloudless sky and lit our way across rough ground, scored by countless stream furrows. We were making for a high spur which stood above the inside of a sweeping bend in the valley. As soon as we started climbing, we became involved in a maze of steep, conglomerate gullies, a strange and lovely setting for that enchanting moment when moonlight merges into early dawn.

With the full light of day, we stood high above another big tributary flowing south-west from a group of tapering ice peaks. These resembled the peaks that we had seen from the southern side of the Aghil pass, and were probably in the same group. We were strongly tempted to change our plans and to explore this valley for a pass which would take us back into the Shaksgam. But the solution of the problem of the Zug Shaksgam was more important. We had to descend a long way to cross the side valley and to climb up the other side to the spur we were making for. We reached its summit at half-past six. The view from the top proved quite definitely that we were in the valley of the Zug Shaksgam. We were only five miles below Mason's farthest camp in this direction, and the features on the limits of his map were easily recognizable. We set up the theodolite and took a round of angles and photographs. Then, sending Lobsang straight back with the survey load, Tilman and I ran down about 3,000 feet to the river. We walked two miles farther up the valley to get a clearer view of its upper reaches, where it flows due north. The river itself at this point flowed over a broad bed. It was split up into many streams and might have been fordable.

We did not get back to camp until noon. Our little spring had dried up during the morning, which was disappointing as we had been looking forward to a long drink of its clear water. We ate the last of the food, which consisted of one round of bread each, and then started off down the valley. We went as hard as we could, for we were all anxious to reach the dump that night and did not like the prospect of spending a hungry night. Having been over the ground before made a great deal of difference, as we knew just where to find a way across the difficult ravines. We might easily have arrived at the dump before dark, but at four-thirty, when we reached the big tributary that we had crossed the day before, we found that the river was so swollen that there was not the slightest chance of crossing it. We had rather expected this disaster, but we did not meet it quite so philosophically as Buddha, who simply curled up on the bank and went to sleep. The situation seemed to appeal to a perverted Sherpa sense of humour, for Lobsang made a lump of mud to look like a loaf of Balti bread and solemnly handed it to me. There was no difficulty in getting the party away early next morning, and crossing the river with ease, we reached the dump by half-past seven. We ate last night's dinner and this morning's breakfast in one, and had started on lunch before our hunger was satisfied.

Angtharkay and Mancho had returned from their reconnaissance. They reported that the gorge was quite impossible from the very start. They seemed to have had a hair-raising time trying line after line before they gave it up. Certainly that report corresponded with what we had seen of the gorge from above and we should probably never have thought of attempting to find a way through it had it not been for the huts. Angtharkay and Mancho had climbed a very long way up the side of the valley and Angtharkay said that he thought it would be possible to get over into another valley which might take us back into the Zug Shaksgam below the gorge. Mancho, however, did not think much of the idea, and strongly advised us to recross the pass by which we had come while there was food enough to do so. We decided to pin our faith on Angtharkay's judgment. We packed up the loads, and at eleven o'clock, guided by Angtharkay, started climbing the precipitous side of the nullah. It was very hard work, as our loads were still fairly heavy. We climbed about 4,000 feet on to a sharp ridge which commanded a superb view of the Zug Shaksgam valley. Here we halted long enough to do a survey station, and then traversed across to another ridge, from which we looked down a steep nullah into the side valley that Angtharkay had mentioned. We slid down the nullah on frozen scree until we came to a trickle of water. There we camped on little platforms dug out of the slope. I was very tired and fell asleep at once.

The next morning Tilman, Angtharkay and I climbed a rocky peak to the north, while the others went on down the nullah, with instructions to wait for us when they reached the valley below. There was a thick haze over everything and we had to wait for a long time for it to clear sufficiently before we could observe to the more distant points or take any photographs. We did not finish the work until eleven. Then, in order to save time, we started climbing down a steep gully to the north, which descended directly to the valley that we hoped to reach. At first it was easy, but lower down we became involved in very delicate work on rotten rock before we reached the valley nearly 5,000 feet below. The theodolite nearly came to grief. It was dropped ten feet on to a ledge while the load of survey equipment was being lowered over a difficult place. Tilman, who was not very fond of the theodolite, and was standing where it landed, showed great self-restraint in not encouraging it to fall the rest of the way.

When we reached the valley we walked up it for half a mile and found the other three waiting for us in a grove of bushes at the foot of their nullah. At half-past three, after a meal, we started down towards the Zug Shaksgam. Soon we came to a place where an overhanging wall of rock forced us to cross to the other side. Although the stream was muddy and swollen, it did not appear to be a serious obstacle. But we under-estimated both its volume and the angle at which it was flowing. Tilman started across and very soon got into difficulties. When he had nearly reached the far side he was swept off his feet, and was carried, load and all, about ten yards down before he could haul himself on to the bank. His leg was bleeding freely and he had lost his ice-axe. But in spite of this I did not take the river very seriously and thought that with reasonable precautions it was perfectly safe. I threw a rope across to Tilman, and together we held it taut across the torrent. Lobsang and Angtharkay waded out into the stream, hanging on to the rope. In a moment Angtharkay was knocked over. Lobsang made a desperate effort to hold on to him, but Angtharkay was wrenched from his grasp by the force of water, and was carried down, battered against the rocks in midstream as he went. Twice he managed to stop himself, but was dragged on by the pressure of water on his sodden load. We could do nothing, for if we had let go of the rope, Lobsang, who was hanging on to it for all he was worth, would have been swept away too. It was horrible to stand there watching Angtharkay being pounded to death without being able to do anything to help him. Each time he was flung against a rock I thought he would be stunned, and every moment I expected to see his head disappear for the last time. He was approaching a steeper drop in the river bed, when, by an amazing chance, he was caught up on a large rock sticking out of the water. Lobsang had got across to the other side by now, and I was able to run down the bank and help the Baltis to get hold of Angtharkay and haul him ashore. His load was so heavy from the weight of the water in it that it took two of us to lift it on to the bank. Happily Angtharkay was not seriously hurt. His body was very bruised and he was completely exhausted. It was some time before he could move, but when we had taken off all his clothes and wrapped him in a sleeping-bag by a fire, he soon recovered. I was acutely aware that my own stupidity had very nearly caused his death.

Of course we made no attempt to join Tilman and Lobsang, nor to get them back to our side of the stream. We corresponded by throwing notes, packed in a snow-glass case, across to each other, for we could not make ourselves heard above the roar of the torrent. Having exchanged cooking utensils and food by hauling them over the river on the rope, each party settled down for the night. After all the fine weather we had been having, we did not think of sending tents across to the others. Nor did we pitch them ourselves, and went to sleep, as usual, in the open. At about ten o'clock it started to rain heavily. With a good deal of trouble we managed to erect a tent in the dark, though it was impossible to get one across to the others. I spent a sleepless night wondering if, in this bad weather, the river would subside sufficiently for us to get across. The rain soon turned to snow, which was still falling when the dawn broke.

As soon as it was light enough to see, we started packing up our stuff. In the excitement of the previous evening we had left everything strewn round our makeshift camp. Now it was all buried in snow and we had great difficulty in collecting our possessions. My boots were on the wrong side of the river, as I had thrown them across before our troubles had begun. It was very painful walking about in the snow in bare feet. To my great relief the river was no longer dangerous. The raging torrent of muddy water had subsided into a clear stream, so shallow that the water hardly reached our knees. Tilman and

Lobsang had spent a miserable night, without a tent, in the snow; they were wet through. We found Angtharkay's ice-axe stuck in a crevice in the river bed, but we did not recover Tilman's axe, though we searched for a long time.

While we were sorting ourselves out and re-distributing the loads, we heard a series of sharp reports among the crags above, followed by an ominous whirring sound. A cannonade of boulders, that had been loosened from the cliffs, crashed into the valley a short way below the place where Tilman had been sleeping. This was a prelude to a continuous bombardment all the way down the valley. I have never before seen such a number of rock-falls. We had continually to be on the look-out, ready to take cover when we saw them coming, for, owing to the noise of the stream in the narrow gorge, we could not always hear them. Both sides of the valley were extremely steep, and we had to cross the river repeatedly from side to side. But it was now so small that it caused us no trouble. It was hard to realize that it was this same stream which had nearly caused a tragic disaster on the previous day.

We reached the Zug Shaksgam at about nine o'clock, after we had been going for two and a half hours. We lit three enormous fires in a clump of birch trees near the junction to dry our waterlogged kit and to cook our breakfast. While this was being done, Tilman and I went on to reconnoitre the ground. We found that we had rejoined the Zug Shaksgam valley just below the point where the river emerged from a narrow gorge; probably the same one that Angtharkay had reconnoitred on June 27th. From here it flowed over wide sand flats and was split up into a number of streams. But the cliffs on either side were very steep, and, as the river ran from side to side of the valley, it was not likely that we would have an easy journey down it. We went up to the mouth of the gorge. It was a most impressive chasm, with precipices of clear-cut rock rising perpendicularly from the floor of the valley for thousands of feet. When we returned to the porters we found a splendid breakfast of tea, cheese and hot bread ready for us. Our kit, too, was dry, and after we had fed and smoked a pipe we started down the valley feeling greatly refreshed.

All went well for about a mile. Then, as we had expected, the river flowed up against the cliffs on our side of the valley for about a hundred yards. The Baltis were determined to get round the obstacle, and performed some appallingly hazardous feats of climbing on the conglomerate cliffs overhanging the river. We did not follow them, and they soon abandoned what was obviously a completely futile attempt. Re-tracing our steps for a few hundred yards, we started up a steep gully of congealed mud. We climbed fast for four hours without a halt, chipping steps in the mud and soft rock as we went; it was very steep and smooth and it would have been difficult to check a serious slip.

When we had climbed about 4,000 feet the slope eased off and we crossed to a sharp ridge which bounded the gully on our right. From there we started a gradually descending traverse over steep slopes of scree. This took us for several miles at a fine speed and landed us on a wide river terrace which stood high above the river. By this manœvre we had rounded a big bend in the Zug Shaksgam valley which was now running due west, and we were delighted to see that it joined a valley six miles away which was obviously the Surukwat. But our difficulties were by no means over. The terrace that we were on was cleft by a ravine fully five hundred feet deep. There was no chance of climbing down to the floor of the main valley to avoid it. When we had succeeded in getting across this obstacle we were confronted with more steep mud slopes in which we had occasionally to cut steps. Tilman had damaged his heel in his struggle with the river the day before, and found this traversing painful, particularly as he had no ice-axe to assist his balance.

Two more difficult ravines were crossed before we reached a continuation of the terrace along which we could walk freely. It was already six o'clock and we began to think about camping. But since leaving the river that morning we had found no water. We hunted for a way down from the terrace, but everywhere conglomerate cliffs, hundreds of feet high, prevented us from descending to the floor of the valley, and we were forced to continue along this high-level route. A storm was brewing down the valley, and a violent, gusty wind swept against us. We came to another deep rift into which we descended, laboriously hewing steps in the soft, crumbling rocks, while the wind did its best to tear us from the cliffs. More perpendicular conglomerates faced us on the other side. But we were dealing with these villainous-looking cliffs with more confidence now. This was due probably to the reckless energy that so often comes to a party at the end of a long and exhausting day. But whatever the origin of this spurt, we were for once climbing with more dash than the Baltis, and even old Buddha was glad of a pull on the rope.

On reaching the terrace once more, we had a discussion as to whether to go on or to resign ourselves to a waterless, and consequently foodless, night. Our strenuous efforts during the last nine hours had made us very parched and the prospect of a night without water was not attractive, but, on the other hand, it was already eight o'clock and would soon be getting dark. Most of us were in favour of stopping, but Angtharkay's indignation at the idea seemed to outweigh the fact that he was in the minority, and we went on. Several small ravines split the terrace that we were on, but none of these caused us much trouble. Angtharkay followed one of these gullies in the hope of finding a way down to the river, but it ended abruptly, high up on the wall of the terrace. We raced on over rough ground in the gathering dusk. Half an hour later, as the Baltis were some way behind, I tried another of these ravines. I left Tilman and Angtharkay with my load at the top, and plunged down into the gully on scree. The ravine narrowed until the walls met over my head. I passed through a dark tunnel into a cavern lit from above by a ghostly green light. Beyond this the passage was so narrow that it was quite difficult to squeeze through. The corridor seemed to go on for ever, and I thought I should never reach the end of it, but eventually I emerged on to the wide sand flats of the river. I ran back as fast as I could for it was becoming almost too dark to see. Soon I came to a place where the passage divided, and I could not remember which of the two branches I had come down. So I waited there and shouted. It was a long time before I heard any reply, and when it came the voice sounded far away but directly above my head. Tilman had walked along the top of the ravine and was shouting down to me. I could not make out what he said, nor whether he understood what I was trying to tell him. There was a long, perplexing silence before I heard the clink of ice-axes coming down the ravine.

By the time we reached the sand flats it was quite dark. We felt our way along, spread out in order to find a pool of water. Frequently we stumbled over bits of driftwood, which we collected for fuel. Presently Angtharkay, who was on the extreme left of our line, found water immediately under the cliffs of the terrace. We closed in on him and pitched camp. The storm had spent its energy elsewhere, and we were left in peace to eat and drink and fall asleep beside a blazing fire.

Our task was now completed. We still had two days' food in hand, and all we had to do was to make our way up the Surukwat river to the Aghil pass. Half a mile beyond our camp there was an extensive jungle of tall bushes and grassy meadows which stretched as far as the junction of the Surukwat and the Zug Shaksgam. From there, only two miles to the north, we could see the place where these rivers joined the Yarkand. We marched up the Surukwat in drizzling rain, sometimes walking on the sand flats of the river, sometimes along low terraces. At frequent intervals we came upon traces of habitation. Some of these remains were on the very brink of conglomerate cliffs, and were occasionally cut in half by the edge. They could not originally have been built in such a position, and though the denudation of these terraces is comparatively rapid, the remains were certainly very old.

As a result of the last few days of strenuous activity, we were all feeling rather lethargic, now that the excitement of finding our way through difficult country was over. But we covered the ground quickly, as it was easy and straightforward. The river was an insignificant stream and could be crossed and recrossed at will. Farther up the valley we noticed a number of recent footprints in the sand, and were not surprised, when we reached the Kharkul Lungpa that evening, to find Spender's party encamped there. We had intended to spend the night there ourselves, but we had seen a herd of bharal on the hillside beyond, and in stalking the animals we had passed right under their camp without seeing it. We were creeping cautiously along when we were startled by a shout from behind, which sent the bharal galloping out of sight. Tilman and Angtharkay went on in pursuit, while the rest of us returned to Spender's camp.

The reunion was a great event; the Sherpas and Baltis enjoyed it as much as we did. It was exciting to hear the other party's news and to compare notes. Spender had made full use of the ten days of fine weather which had followed our arrival at the Aghil pass. He had accomplished an astonishing amount of work. Having completed the important task of fixing the geographical position of the pass, he had extended his survey to the north, and had mapped, in great detail, an area of about two hundred and fifty square miles, as well as fixing the position of many of the more distant peaks of the range. Besides the value of his map, this survey made a splendid base on which to attach our rough theodolite survey and Auden's compass work. It was a great pity that we had so short a time to work in this enthralling range; but it had been a memorable fortnight of rare freedom and interest. We had all thoroughly enjoyed ourselves and were reluctant to abandon this country for the more cramped and complicated life of high glacier exploration.

It started to rain very heavily soon after we arrived. Tilman and Angtharkay returned, soaked to the skin, without having seen the bharal again. It rained hard all night, but the morning of July 3rd was fine, and Spender did a high survey station before breakfast, while the others carried the loads on up the Surukwat to the shepherd's encampment that we had found three miles below the pass. Angtharkay and I set out in search of game. We had a long day's stalking, and managed to secure two bharal, to the delight of all, except the Baltis. When the others had arrived at the shepherd's huts, they had found a note from Auden, that had been sent up the day before from the Shaksgam valley, where he was engaged in some geological work. It was good to hear from him, though he did not tell us much of what he had been doing. He was very concerned about the state of the river which, he said, was covering almost the entire floor of the valley. This was most disturbing news.

I had promised to take one of the Baltis shooting in the morning, for they said that as long as an animal's throat was cut by one of them immediately it had been shot, they would be able to eat it without breaking their religious laws. Buddha and I set out soon after dawn. He was not much help, and, when eventually we spotted a herd, he got so excited that I had to hold on to him to prevent him from dashing up the hill after them. He became almost uncontrollable during the stalk, but, in spite of his antics, we succeeded in getting within reasonable distance of the herd without their seeing us. I missed my first shot; Buddha dashed wildly out in front of me, and I had to fire over his head. Eventually, I got three of the unfortunate creatures, and the Baltis were thoroughly satisfied. But all this extra meat, though it kept the men in good heart, and provided us with a welcome change, did not seem to make very much difference to the length of time that our rations lasted. When we got back to camp we found that Spender, who had been surveying on the opposite side of the valley, had watched our strange manœuvres inverted close-up, through the telescope of his theodolite, and had been hopelessly mystified by our curious behaviour.

After breakfast, we packed up and started towards the pass. The porters were carrying enormous loads of meat. The Baltis halted repeatedly to make a fire of yak dung and to cook some tit-bit.

The grass banks above the lake were now covered with pink, blue and mauve flowers – sloping meadows of colour. I had become very attached to this place, and was most reluctant to leave. But one day I shall go back there, prepared for a long stay, to gain a real knowledge of the range.

From the pass, it was a pleasant run down to our last camp in the Shaksgam valley. On his way down, Spender found a camping-ground, where there was a dead horse. This was proof that the pass had been used recently, though for what possible reason we could not imagine. We were relieved to find that the Shaksgam river had sunk to its previous level. Presumably the recent cloudy weather had been a check on the melting of the great glaciers which flow into it, though it was clear that the subsidence was temporary, and that it would not be long before all the rivers would rise to their normal summer level. The Shaksgam would then become unfordable until the late autumn. At the camp we found a note from Auden, written in verse, telling us that his party had finished its supply of food and had taken advantage of the opportune fall of the river to return to Suget Jangal. The enjoyment of an unlimited supply of meat that evening was spoilt by the lack of salt. We had run short some days before, and our desire for it had become a craving. Having never been without salt before for any length of time, I had not realized what an extremely important item of diet it is. But now I could understand why countries had become depopulated because of the lack of it.

Spender climbed 3,000 feet up the side of the valley on the morning of July 5th, while we lay in bed discussing plans until he returned at 11.30. He had seen traces of camping-grounds which suggested that there was an old route going up the Shaksgam valley. We wondered if this could possibly have any connection with the remains that we had found in the Zug Shaksgam, and seriously considered spending several days in looking for a pass which would connect the two rivers. But we decided that it would be tempting providence not to cross the Shaksgam while the river was low. This we did without much difficulty, and camped in a jungle on the other side.

On July 6th I was roused at 5.30 by a large plateful of fried liver thrust at me by Tilman. At that hour of the morning I found it rather repulsive.

We walked a long way up the Shaksgam valley that day for survey purposes. From opposite the place that Younghusband had called Durbin Jangal, we looked up a wide side valley to a snow saddle at its head. We fancied that this saddle might lead over into the last of the tributary valleys that we had crossed in the Zug Shaksgam. We had to ford the stream several times on our way up the valley. In the afternoon we climbed 1,500 feet up, but rain-clouds prevented us from seeing much and a biting wind soon sent us down. The return to camp, that evening, was an unpleasant business. A surprisingly ferocious wind whirled sleet into our faces. We got thoroughly drenched in fording the rivers, and the wind intensified the painful numbness that accompanies these aquatic sports in glacier rivers.

The next morning we started down the Shaksgam. Spender surveyed as we went, and it took us two days to reach Suget Jangal in the Sarpo Laggo valley. There we found Auden, Lhakpa Tensing and Mahadi. Auden had been employing the fine intervals of the last few days in geological work in the neighbourhood, while the two porters had been up to Mone Brangsa to fetch more food. We were two days overdue, and Auden had been concerned about us. He and his men had just set out in search of us, when they saw us coming over the col between the Shaksgam and Sarpo Laggo valleys.

Suget Jangal was a perfect resting-place, for it had a quality of serene peace, rare in this country of stern severity. Some tall shrubs which grew beside the shallow blue pools were now covered with pink blossom. The song of small birds, the splash of a brook which welled from a crystal spring, the young hares running shyly across the meadows, all welcomed us, and we lay on glades of soft green grass, half hidden in shady caverns of willow branches.

When Auden had left us on the 21st June with Lhakpa and Mahadi, he had descended the Surukwat to a camp six miles above its confluence with the Yarkand river. He left Mahadi in charge of the tent and continued with Lhakpa towards the Yarkand river. After travelling four miles they found a much larger river, almost the size of the Shaksgam, joining the Surukwat from the east. It seemed clear that this would prove to be the Zug Shaksgam. The water was chocolate in colour, a fact which agreed with Mason's account of the higher reaches of the river. Mason had been reluctant to assume that the Zug Shaksgam joined the Yarkand river. The only possible place for such a confluence would have been together with the Surukwat near Bazar Dara. There was some evidence to show that this was unlikely. Wood's 1914 survey showed admittedly a river joining the Surukwat only three miles from the Yarkand river, but the height of its confluence with the Surukwat was given as 12,550 feet, and it was shown to fall very steeply from the mountains to the south. Spender has shown that this height was probably a misprint, since the rest of Wood's heights are only 300 feet too high, while this is 1,300 feet in error. Had Mason known that his river could fall to 11,270 feet before joining the Yarkand, and had he realized that the topography of the river joining the Surukwat was incorrect, he would probably have assumed, as the present expedition has shown to be the case, that this latter was the valley of the Zug Shaksgam. The difficulty of gradient in supposing that the Zug Shaksgam joined the Yarkand thus did not really exist.

Another two and a half miles brought Auden and Lhakpa to the flat gravel terrace of the Yarkand river, sticking out of which were small hill outcrops of slate. While eating lunch on one of these hills, Lhakpa noticed many figures appearing from the west. Knowing the fears of the Baltis about robbers, and impressed by Younghusband's accounts of his two journeys in Central Asia, both of them felt slightly apprehensive. The field-glasses resolved these figures into two men and a herd of yak. Lhakpa was sure that the men would be armed, and was in favour of moving quickly back to their camp. However, they walked towards the herd, which seemed to become smaller and smaller the closer it approached. Eventually two small Yarkandi boys and a flock of goats appeared over the brow of a gravel ridge. The boys were quite unconcerned until the camera was taken out of the rucksack, but were comforted by being given two boxes of matches. Lhakpa tried Nepali and Tibetan on them, but they gave no intelligible reply.

Auden and Lhakpa then returned to their camp, alarming Mahadi by telling him that a band of robbers was on its way up the Surukwat. They then went back to the junction of the east and west Surukwat rivers, which have a height of about 13,700 feet. It was here that Younghusband's guides were undecided in 1887 about the route up to the Aghil pass. Auden and Lhakpa climbed a rock peak 17,950 feet in height (peak 5,462 metres of Spender's survey) in order to see if there was any route over the Aghil, leading out from the west Surukwat. Only one col appeared to be easy, and they crossed this two days later,[1] on June 27th, after first ascending a peak of 19,000 feet in order to obtain a round of compass bearings. The weather was perfect, and the view from this peak towards K2, twenty-six miles distant, was magnificent. The descent of the south-west side of the col turned out to be difficult, since the scree, which was at an average angle of about 50 degrees, was so cemented with ice that it proved very resistant to step-cutting, and necessitated delicate balancing with heavy loads. Mahadi had evidently profited during his two off-days by eating more than his share of the food, and for the remaining five days they had to live on

[1]The height of this col is about 18,200 feet.

short rations. After making a compass sketch map of the complicated glacier system at the foot of the col, they descended over the gravel flats of a wide and barren valley for ten miles down to its confluence with the Shaksgam. This valley, for which Auden suggests the name Skam Lungpa,[2] on account of its barren nature, proved to be that erroneously shown in the Italian map as leading up to the Aghil pass. They then ascended the Shaksgam to a point three miles south of Durbin Jangal, where, in two places, they discovered interesting fossils. The weather got worse on June 30th, and, by the time their food supply was exhausted on the morning of July 3rd, the Shaksgam had again become fordable. They reached the dump-camp in the Sarpo Laggo on July 4th, crossing from the Shaksgam to the Sarpo Laggo by the 14,200 feet col previously used by Desio.

CHAPTER TWELVE

K2

WE did not spend long in luxurious idleness at Suget Jangal. The very next day, July 9th, we again split up into groups, each with a separate task. Seven porters, under the charge of Angtharkay, were sent up the Sarpo Laggo glacier to Mone Brangsa to relay all the loads that had been left there down to the junction of the Sarpo Laggo and Crevasse glacier valleys. I estimated that this would take a week, and our plans were arrangd to coincide with this. Spender, with Angtensing and Nukka to help him, was to accompany the porters up the glacier, and from a suitable base he was to explore and survey the country to the east, between the Sarpo Laggo glacier and the main watershed. Auden, Tilman and I, with Lhakpa Tensing and Ila, were to spend a week exploring the glaciers rising about the northern flanks of K2, and to connect up with the Duke of Abruzzi's surveys at the head of the Baltoro glacier, and those that Spender had planned.

The other two parties left Suget Jangal in the morning, carrying a large supply of fuel. Tilman and Auden and Lhakpa went with them to our main dump, three miles away, to fetch food, warm clothes, spare films and tobacco that had been left there. Ila and I spent a declicious morning lazing on the grass in the hot sun. Later we attended to various domestic jobs, such as airing sleeping-bags, washing and mending clothes, until the others returned. We packed up and started after lunch; this required a considerable effort of will.

We followed the same route that we had taken when we had been hunting bharal nearly four weeks before. On the way I visited a nest that I had seen on that occasion, and found that the young birds had flown. We crossed the high ridge into the K2 nullah, contoured along a thousand feet above the stream, and camped when we came to a deep gully containing a trickle of water.

[2]Balti for barren valley.

We climbed 2,500 feet the next morning, to a rocky point about 16,300 feet high. It commanded a view up the K2 glacier to a wonderful circle of ice peaks in the country ahead of us. In the opposite direction we could see an enormous distance to the west, far up the Crevasse glacier. The weather was clear and still and we stayed for a long time, taking a wide round of angles and photographs, and discussing lazily the many questions that are raised by any view into unexplored country. Not far below us on a little saddle there was a herd of bharal, grazing peacefully on a meagre pasture. The descent to camp took us only a few minutes of swift scree-running.

After a short halt for a meal of tsampa and tea, followed by a pipe, we packed up and climbed down to the valley, carrying a supply of firewood besides our usual loads. When we reached the snout of the glacier, we climbed into a corridor between the ice and the valley-side, which served us as a road for several miles. We camped late that evening by a small lake in the ablation valley above the glacier.

By way of contrast with the peace and sunshine of the previous day, it was snowing when we woke on July 11th, and we could not see far. We kept to the true left side of the valley for half a mile, and then crossed the glacier. It did not take us more than an hour to do this, which was good going, for the glacier was nearly a mile wide and its surface consisted of the usual tortuous wilderness of moraine-covered ice. On the previous day we had seen a peak, about 20,700 feet high, which stood well detached from the main range of giants to the south. Its summit would obviously command a superb view of the whole district, and we decided to spend two days in attempting to climb it. We pushed on another mile or so up the true right flank of the glacier and halted on a flat shelf at the foot of a small side nullah. It had stopped snowing and the weather had showed signs of a sudden improvement. So, after a meal of bread and cheese, we started up the nullah towards the peak carrying equipment for a light camp for the three of us and food for two days. Bearing to the right, we climbed up an easy slope for 3,000 feet and camped on a ridge at an altitude of 17,700 feet. The Sherpas descended to the dump by the glacier, with instructions to spend the next day bringing firewood up there from below. The view from the ridge was very fine. The great peaks of the K2 massif were beginning to stand up in their true perspective, and the glaciers looked like gracefully sweeping trains at their feet. The camp made a splendid survey station, but being on the ridge it had one disadvantage – that there was no water at hand. Snow had to be melted for cooking and drinking purposes, which always takes more than twice as much time and fuel. We were using a Primus stove for cooking. On the way up, Auden had been feeling ill. He did not eat any supper for evening, and he had a bad night.

By sunset the sky was clear. Only torn ribbons of mist swathed the mountains to the south, their soft colour giving promise of fine weather. The delicately carved flutings of the snow peaks flushed with the same coral glow before the ghostly grey of night enveloped this lofty world of ice.

I woke as the sun touched the summit of K2. The glaciers below us were still sleeping in frozen darkness. We heated some tea and tsampa. Auden was running a temperature and stayed in his sleeping-bag, while Tilman and I climbed sleepily on to the ridge. It was a cloudless morning. We mounted quickly along the ridge over snow-covered rocks. Higher up, in spite of an intensely cold night, the snow was very bad, and when, after climbing for two hours, we reached a sloping glacier plateau, we began to sink in up to our hips. It was surprising to find such bad conditions, for it was already nearly the middle of July and the weather in June had been more than usually fine. We began to wonder if in these parts the snow ever consolidates in the normal way. But in spite of the very hard work, we climbed quickly, and three hours after leaving camp we reached a bergschrund at the foot of the final pyramid of the peak, only 400 feet below the top. There we had a short rest to eat a chunk of "emergency ration". I took off my boots to thaw my feet in the sun, as they had lost all feeling. Meanwhile Tilman cut steps across the bergschrund and up the slope above. We found this to be a great deal more difficult than we had expected. It consisted of hard ice, set at an exceedingly steep angle and covered with about nine inches of powder snow. At each step the snow had first to be cleared away before we could cut into the ice. It was terribly hard work and we advanced ridiculously slowly. We took the lead in turns of about twenty minutes each, while the man behind anchored the rope as best he could and speculated what to do in the event of a slip. We were climbing in a wide gully coming down from a ridge which led along the skyline to the top.

After we had been cutting for about two and a half hours, I was about fifteen feet below the crest of the ridge when I missed my stroke and hit myself violently on the knees with the pick of my axe. This made me feel very sick, and Tilman had to cut the rest of the way to the ridge. We had hoped that when we reached this the rest of the climb would be comparatively simple. But the ridge was very narrow and was crowned by a snow cornice which curved like a breaking wave over a terrifying drop on the other side. It led to a square tower of rock which formed the summit of the peak. The top was so close that we could have thrown a stone on to it. But the prospect of the ridge and the tower was so alarming that we nearly abandoned the climb. Tilman led along the ridge flogging away the cornice as he went. After some exceedingly delicate work he reached the rocks. As he took in the rope I followed along the ridge and we climbed together on to a little platform. This was the first place where we could rest since we had left the bergschrund, and we had a bite of food before tackling the final pitch. It was my turn to take the lead and I did not much like the look of it. But it was not quite as bad as it appeared, and in short time we were sitting astride a sharp rock which formed the summit.

The view from the top was astonishing; well worth the trouble and difficulties of the climb. To the south were the colossal northern faces of K2 and other peaks of the main watershed, a breath-taking panorama of sweeping ridges, lofty summits and hanging glacier terraces, dazzling in the midday sun. For a stretch of fifty miles, the Aghil range filled our northern horizon. We could trace the course of the Shaksgam valley almost from its source to its junction with the Yarkand river; while across the Aghil pass we could see far into the barren ranges of Turkestan. To the west were the peaks of the Crevasse glacier, whose intricacies were to occupy our attention during the next two months. Among these mountains "The Fangs" stood out clearly, and another beautiful rock peak which came to be known as The Crown. Beyond these, to the south-west, peak after peak rose in jagged profusion of rock spires.

Immediately below us to the east, between the peak we had climbed and the southern wall of the Shaksgam valley, we were surprised to see another ice-stream, nearly as big as the K2 glacier. It rose at the foot of K2's massive neighbour, Staircase peak, and the river which issued from it flowed into the K2 nullah through a narrow gorge. We called it the Staircase glacier. Staircase peak has now, by a decision of the official Karakoram Names Committee, been called Skyang Kangri.

In spite of all the fascination of this gigantic panorama, we did not stop long on the summit, for a cold wind was blowing and there was too little room for comfort. We slid down a doubled rope from the summit tower. This is a method frequently used when climbing down difficult places and usually it saves a lot of time. But we had arranged the rope carelessly, and when we had tried to recover it we found that it had jammed in a crack. We struggled with it for a long time without success, and I was just about to repeat the climb up the tower when it yielded to a final tug. The ice-slope was much more difficult to descend than to ascend. Our steps had been obliterated by snow sliding down from the above. Tilman went first, while I gave him what support I could from above, I followed when he had gone the whole length of our eighty-foot rope. But it was impossible to anchor one's axe in the ice owing to the powder snow on top, and we both had to work with the greatest possible care to avoid a slip which would have been disastrous. When Tilman had only got fifty feet to go, the step I was standing in gave way. Leaning heavily on my axe, I managed to break into a standing glissade, and to keep my feet, though I went down past Tilman at a tremendous speed, and shot over the bergschrund into the soft snow below it. Tilman followed my example, and we stood at last on the glacier, having taken seven hours to go up and to come down the last 400 feet of the peak. The remaining 2,000 feet to camp was pleasantly easy.

We found that Auden was no better, but he was anxious to go to the lower camp and started down ahead of us. After a meal of tsampa and sugar, washed down with melted snow, we followed. Though we were both tired, we were obliged to carry heavy loads. But the descent was mostly down easy scree and we reached the lower camp at eight o'clock, to find the two Sherpas waiting for us with tea and hot bread and a thick brew of pemmican. It had been a glorious day and I was very sorry that Auden had not been able to share it with us.

We were lucky to have had such perfect weather for the climb, for snow was again falling when we woke on July 13th. It was pleasant to have an excuse to lie late in bed. But my morning peace was disturbed. Breakfast was served unnecessarily early, and while I was trying sleepily to deal with a plateful of watery porridge, I upset the whole lot into my sleeping-bag.

Auden's fever still persisted, and it was decided that he should stay where he was for the next two days, while Tilman and I went up to the head of the glacier, to reach the great north face of K2, which promised to be something very remarkable. We took both Sherpas with us and sent one of them back to Auden from our next camp. This was at the foot of a great rock ridge which screened the upper part of the glacier from view. On the way we had to cross the only tributary of the K2 glacier coming from the east. It showed signs of recent and substantial decrease in size. Our camp was on a little grassy alp, covered with flowers and set in a wilderness of black boulders. The weather had cleared by the evening, and we climbed a thousand feet on to the rock ridge to reconnoitre the upper part of the glacier and to do a survey station.

It was snowing again early next morning, but this time without much determination, and soon rifts in the clouds gave us hope of better things. Tilman's watch had finally succumbed to the rough treatment it had received while crossing rivers, and when the sky was overcast we had no means of telling the time. I do not think it had been light for long when we started. Ila came with us, carrying the theodolite. We climbed obliquely up to the rock ridge and crossed it over a low shoulder. Heavy mists hung in the upper glacier basin. Above them the summit of K2 appeared, floating at an incredible height above our heads. While Tilman went on, I waited with Ila on the ridge for nearly an hour in the hope that the mists might clear enough for me to photograph the whole north face. The pattern of cloud was constantly changing as it drifted across the mountain, revealing for a moment some new ridge or corrie in its gigantic structure and altering its apparent shape. But though we waited a long time this shifting drapery of cloud still clung to the mountain, and we had to leave the ridge without a clear view of the stupendous north face.

We ran diagonally down scree-slopes to the glacier and walked easily along by the side of the ice. But before we had covered a mile we were stopped by cliffs rising sheer above the side of the glacier. Tilman was sitting disconsolately on a ledge wondering what to do. The ice was broken up into a complicated maze of those serrated pinnacles which are a common feature on the glaciers of the northern side of the main watershed both in the Karakorams and in the vicinity of Mount Everest.

These northern glaciers are nearly always divided into four distinct zones. Firstly, there is the upper *névé*, or snow basin, from which the glacier rises. Then follows a section of smooth ice, free from a covering of permanent snow and morine deposits. Below this the ice-stream merges gradually into the pinnacled zone. Farther down the pinnacles increase in size and decrease in numbers, until a few isolated towers are left standing out of the lower section of the glacier, which is so covered with gravel and boulders that very little ice can be seen.

It is an interesting fact that these pinnacles very rarely occur on the glaciers of the southern side of the watershed, whereas the middle section of those on the northern side of the range are always pinnacled to a remarkable extent. I have never heard a satisfactory explanation of the phenomenon. On the large glaciers, moraine-covered troughs, caused by the junction of tributary ice-streams, run down through the pinnacled areas. Such a trough provides an easy route up this difficult section of glacier. But if it is necessary to cross from side to side one is forced into a labyrinth of pinnacles. We now had the choice of climbing four miles along difficult cliffs, or crossing a few hundred yards of pinnacled ice into a trough where we might expect to find reasonably easy going. There was some difference of opinion as to which course we should take, but after much discussion we decided to try and reach the trough. We were soon immersed in the usual blind maze of narrow corridors enclosed by smooth walls of ice as much as 150 feet high. It was difficult to maintain a sense of direction and impossible to work out a route for more than a few yards ahead. No corridor led far without interruption. Sometimes the way was blocked by a cul-de-sac, sometimes by a vividly blue lake, with sheer sides, unfathomably deep. Occasionally it was possible to surmount these obstacles by chipping steps laboriously up the ice walls. More often we were forced to go back and try another route – balancing along the crest of a knife-edged ridge, sliding down on a rope over a vertical cliff, squeezing through a tiny opening into a slit of a gorge, or jumping over a chasm, with a river thundering in the unseen depths below. Except for the appalling length of time that it takes to cover any distance, the work of finding a way through these pinnacles is very fascinating. The ice scenery is most beautiful. It is like being in a deserted city built to satisfy the whims of a fantastic imagination. The shapely church spires are supported by slender buttresses of translucent crystal; the walls of the streets are carved with intricate tracery, and the alleyways are spanned by delicately balanced arches and fragile bridges – all of ice.

When eventually we reached the trough it was past midday. We left Ila to wait for our return, and hurried on over moraine-covered ice between the rows of high pinnacles. After an hour we reached the smooth ice of the upper part of the glacier, and were able to travel more swiftly. As we went, the valley gradually opened into a great cirque at the foot of the north face of K2. In the midst of this, on a wide plain of ice, I halted, while Tilman went on to collect a specimen of rock from the mountain.

The afternoon was fine, and nothing interrupted my view of the great amphitheatre about me. The cliffs and ridges of K2 rose out of the glacier in one stupendous sweep to the summit of the mountain, 12,000 feet above. The sight was beyond my comprehension, and I sat gazing at it, with a kind of timid fascination, watching wreaths of mist creep in and out of corries utterly remote. I saw ice avalanches, weighing perhaps hundreds of tons, break off from a hanging glacier, nearly two miles above my head; the ice was ground to a fine powder and drifted away in the breeze long before it reached the foot of the precipice, nor did any sound reach my ears.

To the right of K2 lay the famous Savoia saddle which had been reached twenty-eight years before by the Duke of Abruzzi from the Baltoro glacier. It presented a formidable appearance from this side. To the left of K2 was a bewildering mass of peaks and glaciers whose existence I had not suspected. Sitting alone gazing at the cirque forming the head of the K2 glacier was an experience I shall not forget; no mountain scene has impressed me more deeply.

It was an hour before Tilman returned, and we hurried back down the glacier, for it was late in the afternoon and we had a long way to go. By the time we reached Ila, the weather had made a sudden change for the worse. Great billows of cloud were rolling over the peaks from the south and a cold blustering wind blew up the glacier. Before everything was blotted out, we managed to erect the theodolite, to fix our position and to take angles to some important points at the head of the glacier. Instead of crossing to the side of the glacier at once, we went several miles down the trough, hoping to find an easy way through when the pinnacles had thinned out. We had passed below our camp before we found a hopeful line. We tried several passages, but each was filled with an impassable lake. It began to look as if we should have to spend the night without food in the middle of the glacier. At length, just before dark, one of us hit on a possible route, and we climbed through to the side of the glacier. The long pull up from there to our camp was a severe penance at the end of a long day.

The weather had broken badly. We went down, in steadily falling snow, on the morning of July 15th, to Auden's camp. His fever had gone, but he was still rather weak. Ila and I accompanied him slowly down the glacier to our first camp in the K2 nullah. In spite of the weather, which was becoming worse, Tilman went with Lhakpa Tensing up the eastern tributary of the K2 glacier with the intention of crossing a saddle at the head of it into the Staircase glacier basin which had interested us so much when we saw it from the top of the peak we climbed.

It snowed all night and did not stop until eight o'clock the following morning. The snow was lying thick upon the ground when we started traversing round the hillside toward Suget Jangal. As it was still early in the day, and we had not far to go, we did not bother to put on snow-glasses. When we got round the corner out of the K2 nullah, we saw a herd of a dozen bharal. They had seen us and were running away up the hill. Ila and I dumped our loads and followed them, while Auden went on down to Suget Jangal. The animals had disappeared from view, but it was easy to follow their tracks in the snow. We climbed for several thousand feet, creeping cautiously over each bit of the convexly sloping ground expecting to find the bharal on the other side. It was an exhilarating chase, and, with the cries of innumerable snow pheasant echoing across the hillside, reminded me pleasantly of following game over winter snow in Europe. I was enjoying it so much that I quite forgot that we had left our snow-glasses in our loads.

The bharal led us over some very difficult country, and we did not see them again until the middle of the afternoon. I shot one, and, while Ila dragged it down to the main valley, I returned to our loads and carried them down to Suget Jangal. Auden was not there, and, having skinned the bharal, we were just about to start on to the main dump as dusk was falling, when he arrived. He had been to the dump, but had found no one there, nor any food. He had seen a camp across the Sarpo Laggo river, about a mile away, but he could not attract attention. Also the river was in flood and he could not cross.

We settled down on the grass before a blazing fire, and cooked a mixed grill of liver, heart and kidneys which would have satisfied the most fastidious epicure. The weather had cleared; we sat talking, and feeding the flames with dead willow branches until eleven o'clock, under a moonlit sky flecked with soft fleecy clouds. I congratulated myself on having escaped the usual dreaded penalty of spending a day amongst snow without snow-glasses. But, as I got into my sleeping-bag, I began to feel some slight discomfort. At first I thought it was the smoke from the fire that was making my eyes smart. However, in a few minutes the pain increased so much that I found it impossible to sleep. It felt as though the inside of my eyelids had been lacerated and then filled with sand. Any movement of the eyelid over the eye aggravated the pain. The continual flow of tears made it difficult to keep my eyes open for long without blinking. The muscular quivering caused by closing my eyes gently was extremely unpleasant. I found that the only way of obtaining any slight relief was to hold my eyelashes down with my fingers. In the morning I found that Ila had been suffering in the same way. It was not a severe attack of snow-blindness, and though neither of us could see very well, we were able to walk over the sand flats to the dump.

When we got there, we saw someone on the other side of the river trying to attract our attention by waving a coat. He walked downstream, evidently indicating the way to a possible crossing-place. Having left a note for Tilman at the dump, we followed. We went a long way down before we came to the crossing-place. Even at this early hour it was by no means easy to ford the Sarpo Laggo river, which, a month previously, had not given us a thought, even late in the afternoon.

Spender came out to meet us, and conducted us back to a comfortable camp, where both the other parties were waiting for us with all the loads that had been left at Mone Brangsa early in June. Spender had completed the mapping of the glaciers to the east of the Sarpo Laggo. It was very interesting to compare and fit together the results of our respective explorations.

Ila and I spent the rest of the day bathing our eyes in a saturated solution of sugar and water, an ineffective remedy prescribed by Angtensing.

The next morning Tilman arrived. He had managed to reach the Staircase glacier and to follow it down. In the bad weather he had seen very little, but it was an interesting trip, and his compass bearings have been a help in plotting that section of the map.

CHAPTER THIRTEEN

The Crevasse Glacier

WE could now give our whole attention to the problem of getting supplies up the Crevasse glacier into the ranges to the west. Looking back, now that their geography is known, it is difficult to recapture our feelings while we were working out plans from the slender data that was then available, but I well remember, long before the expedition started, poring for hours over the existing maps of that part of the Karakoram, and trying to visualize the probable lie of the ranges and glaciers in the unknown regions that we were now about to penetrate.

We knew that it lay immediately to the north of that remarkable knot of mountains which gives rise to several of the largest glaciers in the whole range. Among these were the Hispar, Biafo, Virjerab and Panmah. In 1892, Martin Conway ascended the Hispar glacier and crossed the Hispar pass at its head. In describing the view from there, he wrote (*Climbing in the Himalayas*, page 378): "Before us lay a basin or lake of snow. From the midst . . . rose a series of mountain islands, white like snow that buried their bases, and there were endless bays and straits as of white water nestling amongst them." Later he referred to the phenomenon as the "Snow Lake", though how much more importance he intended to be attached to the name I do not know. He was not able to explore it, but from there he descended into the Biafo glacier, which he followed down to Askole.

Dr. and Mrs. Bullock Workman, who ascended from the Biafo to the Hispar pass in 1899, used Conway's name for the great basin that they saw from the

Hispar pass, retaining the capital letters. By degrees the Snow Lake developed a great importance in geographical speculation. In fact it was recently expected that there might exist a vast ice-cap, such as was unknown in the Himalaya, and from which flowed, besides the Biafo, a number of glaciers whose sources were unexplored. Certainly the area of three hundred square miles mentioned by Conway suggested something of the sort.

In the account, read to the Royal Geographical Society, of his expedition to the Shimshal area in 1925, Dr. Visser expressed the view that the Virjerab glacier had its origin in the Snow Lake. It had also been suggested that the Crevasse glacier rose in this fabled ice-cap, and also a great ice-stream, that Younghusband had seen in 1889, flowing towards the Shimshal pass. The lower reaches of this glacier had been visited by Colonel Schomberg in 1934, and called by him the Braldu glacier.

In 1933, Gregory and Auden had made an expedition up the Biafo glacier with the object of investigating the Snow Lake, but circumstances prevented them from reaching it. So, in 1937, our knowledge of the area was limited to the reports of Conway and the Workmans who, in 1908, had again seen, but not explored, the Snow Lake.

The idea that the Crevasse glacier would lead us on to this strange ice-cap was an intriguing one. By carrying a fortnight's food up the glacier and travelling as quickly as possible, and given good weather, we could no doubt have solved the problem of its source. But in the first place we wanted to be able to survey the glacier, its tributaries and the surrounding ranges, as accurately as possible; secondly, we wanted to be in a position to make a thorough exploration of the country at its head, and to attempt to clear up the problem of the sources and all these great glaciers, and to fix their geographical position; and thirdly, it would be a waste of time to be compelled to return by the way we had come, and we hoped to finish the expedition by descending, either to Shimshal or to Hunza, or to some place as remotely distant from our starting-point. So I had decided that when we finished our work in the Aghil range and on the northern glaciers of K2, we should start up the Crevasse glacier, carrying all the supplies that were left.

A stock-taking on the morning of July 18th showed that we had 1,500 lbs. of food; enough to last for another fifty-four days. In addition to this we had 700 lbs. of equipment and packing; three journeys were necessary to move everything forward to each camp on the glacier. As time went on, our food supplies would become lighter, and we would be able to reduce the number of relays to two. Even so, I estimated that it would probably take us a month to get everything within striking distance of the head of the glacier. But time would not be wasted by this slow rate of progress, as there would be more than enough exploration and survey work to be done on the way.

Travelling over difficult glacier country, when it is necessary to work from a base which is entirely out of reach of any outside assistance, presents a very different problem from that of an expedition for which some sort of transport and supplies, however bad, are available. I found, as I had expected, that cutting ourselves off from such support, for a period of more than three months, threw a considerable strain on the party.

As Spender had fixed our position, we knew roughly the direction that we had to follow to reach the country surrounding the Snow Lake. But whether we could keep going in that direction depended upon where the glacier led us. The views that we had seen up the Crevasse glacier from the heights above the Sarpo Laggo valley showed us that our course would, at first, lie due west. Ten miles up, however, the valley split into several branches, each filled with a very large ice-stream. We called their point of junction the First Divide. From that distance it was difficult to see which was the principal glacier, and we would not forecast the direction of our route beyond the First Divide.

Our main worry was fuel. We had brought twelve gallons of paraffin with us. So far, we had been very lucky in finding wood, and we had used the Primus stoves a great deal less than we had expected. But the containers in which the fuel was carried had been badly battered in transport, and more than half of the oil had leaked away. We now had less than five gallons and even that was leaking. It is difficult to estimate how much oil will be used by a party when it is working beyond reach of wood fuel, as so much depends on conditions. But only a small proportion of the food that we had with us could be eaten without being cooked, and although we might never be compelled to melt snow for drinking purposes, we could not exist for long without fuel. Much depended upon how far up the glacier we should find wood, for we could not afford the time to transport it for any great distance.

On July 18th, the morning after Auden and I arrived, we sent seven men, under the charge of Angtharkay, to make the first dump on the Crevasse glacier. I told them to choose for themselves the best route, and to go as far as they could. The rest of us spent a busy day doing our various jobs. Our camp was in a little sandy bay at the corner formed by the junction of the Sarpo Laggo and the Crevasse glacier valleys. Near by there was a large collection of huts. In one of these we found the remains of a quite recent fire. The Baltis were as puzzled as we were and could offer no explanation of this extraordinary discovery.

Angtharkay's party was very late in getting back. The sun was setting when we saw them coming across the mile of river flats which separated us from the snout of the glacier. They appeared to be moving very slowly, and with the aid of field-glasses we saw that they were dragging something between them. In the dusk we could not make our whether there were six or seven of them, and we feared that there had been an accident. But, as they approached, their cheery shouting reassured us, and when they arrived we found that the object that they were pulling along was a fox that they had managed to capture on the glacier. The poor creature was very frightened and made vicious attacks on anyone who went close to it. We photographed the animal and set it free, and it ran off amid roars of cheering from the Sherpas. Angtharkay reported that the going on the glacier had been difficult, but they seemed to have covered quite a lot of ground, and he said there was plenty of fuel above the dump.

After supper that evening Spender took advantage of the weather to make some more astronomical observations for Azimuth while I booked his angles, lying in a warm sleeping-bag. Unfortunately the Wild theodolite had been seriously damaged and he had to work with the smaller Watts instrument, which was not accurate enough for a latitude observation. This place became known as Azimuth Camp.

The next day, Spender, Tilman and all the porters carried loads to Dump I. Spender stayed up there alone to survey while the others came back in the evening. Auden stayed in camp with a recurrence of his fever, and I spent a most enjoyable day hunting bharal in the hills behind. The weather was perfect, and as I climbed to a great height I had some wonderful views of the surrounding country. I found a herd and shot two very good heads. When Tilman returned in the evening he told me that Spender had fixed the position of Dump I on his plane-table and found it to be five miles west of Azimuth Camp. This was surprisingly good progress, even though a mile of the way was over gravel flats. I began to hope that we might reach the head of the glacier very much more quickly than I had expected.

The carrying of the last relay to Dump I was complicated by the new supply of meat that had resulted from my hunt. However, the meat so cheered the Sherpas that they did not mind how much they had to carry, nor how far they had to go. There was keen competition amongst them to make up the biggest pack, and it was regarded as riotously funny when the load was so heavy that its carrier collapsed under its weight. The Baltis regarded this frivolity with mournful resignation. They were never able to understand the buffoonery of the Sherpas. But in justice to them in this case, it must be admitted that they could not benefit from the extra meat on account of their religious scruples.

It had been decided that Auden should go down the Shaksgam with Mancho and Buddha to continue the survey and his geological work in that direction. We left a fortnight's food with him and arranged that his party should catch us up while we were working up the Crevasse glacier. Then we went, with all the remaining loads, to Dump I, which we reached on the evening of July 20th.

On July 21st, while I was helping Spender with the survey among the mountains of the north, Tilman conducted another carrying-forward to Dump II. He managed to get on to a moraine shelf running along the northern bank of the glacier, and succeeded in going four miles before depositing the loads. I had not expected to be able to put the dumps more than two miles apart on the lower, broken part of the glacier, so this rate of progress was extremely satisfactory. Another relay was carried up the next day, and on July 23rd we camped at Dump II with all the loads.

From Dump II on July 24th we were able to reconnoitre the confusion of glaciers at the First Divide. There was no doubt as to which of the branches we should follow. To the south, a gigantic fan of ice-falls descended from the vertical cliffs of the main watershed, and united into one ice-stream, which joined the main glacier in a jumble of pinnacles. Even if our route had lain in this direction, it would have been practically impossible to get far up these broken ice-falls. A mile or so further up a big tributary came in from the north. As it seemed to flow roughly from the direction of the Crown, we called it the Crown glacier. We were surprised at its size, for it came from the range of mountains dividing the Crevasse glacier from the Shaksgam valley, and we had not expected to find any very extensive glaciation there. The main valley, we were pleased to find continued on a bearing only ten degrees north of west. Ten miles farther up there was another confluence of glaciers. We called this the Second Divide.

The junction of the pinnacled Crown glacier prevented any further progress up the northern flanks of the Crevasse glacier. On July 25th, while Tilman and Spender were surveying, I set out with the men to cross the glacier, carrying the first relay of loads for Dump III. We had not gone far before we got into trouble. Our way was barred by a wide stream flowing down the glacier. It had cut a deep trough in the ice, through which it slid with such velocity that there was not a chance of fording it, and it was far too wide to jump. We followed it up for some way until we got involved in the pinnacles of the Crown glacier. At length we came to a place where the stream was spanned by a remarkable bridge. In order to get across this, we had first to climb through a tunnel in the ice and cut steps spirally upwards, while the torrent thundered through the enclosed canyon fifty feet below. It was a sensational and very beautiful place. The exit at the top of the tunnel was made by a somewhat dangerous step from one ice cornice to another. Having been granted such a dramatic and unexpected way out of our difficulties, I thought there would be no further trouble in reaching the other side of the glacier. But soon we were held up by a smaller stream, and, when it seemed that we were almost across the glacier, another big river confronted us. For five hours we hunted for a way of getting over this obstacle. First we explored downstream until we could get no farther; then we went up until we became entangled in a network of pinnacles amongst which we were continually losing ourselves and our companions, and even the river itself. At length Angtharkay and I found an ice bridge, and reached it by cutting steps down a steep slope and sliding down a rope over an ice cliff. But although we could cross the bridge, it led us into a cave twenty feet high, from which there was no exit.

Meanwhile Sen Tensing had found a place where the near wall of the canyon overhung the river, and he thought he could jump across to an ice cliff on the opposite side. It was a formidable distance, with only a tiny ledge on the other side on which to land, while below there was a nasty drop into the torrent at the bottom of the ravine. I should not like to have undertaken the jump myself, but Sen Tensing insisted that he could do it. We tied a rope to him and he started to make elaborate preparations. When it came to the point, he did not like the prospect, and kept walking to the brink and back again. Angtharkay was doubled up with laughter at Sen Tensing's mounting nervousness and discomfiture. Though the victim had my full sympathy, it certainly was very funny to watch, and I had some difficulty in maintaining an air of grave concern. But at least he hurled himself across the abyss and landed on the ledge on the opposite wall. He swayed backwards for a second and I thought he must fall; but he recovered his balance and clung to the ledge. From there he was able to climb to the top of the wall.

We worked downstream until we found a suitable place for a rope bridge. A treble strand of rope was fixed from a high ice bollard on our side of the river to a point lower down on the opposite bank. We used for a runner a piece of bent wood that was carried by one of the Baltis instead of an ice-axe, and the loads were easily hauled across the river by Sen Tensing. It had been my intention to leave them there and to return to camp by the way we had come, as by now it was late in the afternoon. But we could not get Sen Tensing back across the river as we could not haul uphill across the bridge. So I decided that Angtharkay and I should join him, and, while the others went back, we would look for a route much lower down the glacier. We entrusted ourselves to the flimsy contraption and were hauled across. Neither of us was very successful in concealing his alarm, but Sen Tensing displayed admirable generosity and restraint!

We stacked the loads, waved good-bye to the others, and set off down the glacier, taking a tin of pemmican with us against the probability of being benighted. We soon discovered that we were on a narrow tongue of ice with a river on either side, gradually converging towards each other, so that we should soon be forced to cross one of them. It also transpired that Sen Tensing had sprained his ankle in his heroic leap and he could not get along very fast. Angtharkay and I went ahead, looking for a new way across either of the rivers. The one on our right was the smaller of the two, but it was out of the question to think of fording it. We found a place from which we could do a downward leap of about fifteen feet, on to the farther bank, but it was a difficult landing and unlikely that Sen Tensing could manage it on one foot. Eventually we were cut off by the confluence of the two rivers. Here, luckily, there was an unexpected way out of the difficulty. Two ice pinnacles, leaning out from the opposite banks of the right-hand stream, almost touched one another. I chipped steps to the top of one and from it jumped over to the other. The distance from one to the other was small, but the pinnacles were so slender, and they were leaning at such a dizzy angle, that I was afraid that one of them would collapse under my weight. However, we all three got across safely.

From this place we reached a high ridge of moraine which had been swept right across the main glacier by the big ice-stream coming in from the south. Angtharkay and I went ahead again, as fast as we could, to find a route before it became too dark to see. We built small cairns every hundred yards or so, to guide Sen Tensing. We encountered no more difficulties, and reached camp before eight o'clock. The other porters had got in nearly two hours before us. We had now found a good way across the glacier, but I cursed my stupidity for not having spotted the difficulties of the other route before having embarked upon it. This had wasted much time and a great deal of energy. However, to make up for it, Spender and Tilman had done a very successful day's work.

For the next two days a thick haze made visibility so bad that survey was impossible. But during this time the rest of the baggage was carried up to Dump III, which was established three and a half miles farther up, on the southern side of the glacier. Also the loads that I had left by the river were rescued and brought along, so that on the evening of July 27th everything was at Dump III. We were now twelve and a half miles west of Azimuth camp, and we had been working up the glacier for only ten days. As we were already over the most difficult part, and we expected soon to get on to smooth ice, the position was very satisfactory.

On July 28th, Tilman and I, with the porters, all carrying big loads, pushed forward towards the Second Divide. For the first two miles the way was complicated and difficult, but we were able to keep to the moraine at the side of the ice, and so to avoid the worst of the pinnacled section of the glacier. Beyond this we found wide troughs of smooth ice in which we were able to walk at a considerable speed. As we approached it, we saw that the Second Divide formed the junction of two huge ice-streams of equal width, one flowing from the north-west and the other from the south-west.

It is difficult to think of suitable names for geographical features in unexplored country. But from the explorer's point of view it is better to give unsuitable names than to give no names at all. It is irritating and confusing, for instance, to speak of 'The glacier coming in two miles below Dump III', 'The peak we climbed the day so-and-so was ill', or 'The valley that puzzled us when we were doing our first station in the Shaksgam'. Generally the first name suggested, however unsuitable it may be, comes to stay. In this way, to the annoyance of scientific societies and survey departments, important features of newly explored country come to be known by such frivolous names as Cockeyed peak and Lousy valley, and occasionally by names that would hardly pass the censor.

In a moment of exasperation, I called the range of high peaks, lying between the two glaciers beyond the Second Divide the "Father Christmas" group. The name was adopted by my companions without comment, and it soon lost its ridiculous sound. The northern branch became known as the "Father Christmas glacier", and the highest peak of the group was "Father Christmas". The southern branch was regarded as the main Crevasse glacier, for no better reason than that we thought our ultimate route would lie up it.

We succeeded in establishing Dump IV at the inside bend of the Main glacier, between an ice-fall and steep rock cliffs. There was a division of opinion as to the actual site of the camp. We had to choose between a stretch of soft sand that had been deposited at the foot of the cliffs by a glacial stream, and the broken surface of the ice where a platform would have to be cut. There was no doubt about which would be the more comfortable place, but most of us thought that the sand flat was in danger of being bombarded by stones from the very rotten crags above. The sybarites in the party ridiculed this idea, and despite their minority they had their way. We returned to Dump III in bad weather. We paid later for the foolish choice of this camp site.

We were so well in advance of our schedule that we decided to strengthen our position by bringing up wood from farther down the glacier. This job occupied July 29th and 30th. On July 31st, Spender, Tilman and I went up to occupy Dump IV, and on August 1st, the porters brought all the remaining loads to that camp. Also Auden arrived with his Baltis at this opportune moment. At each dump we had left him a sketch map and detailed instructions of how to get to the next. In this way he found no difficulty in following us up the glacier when he had finished his work in the Shaksgam valley.

CHAPTER FOURTEEN

Survey and Adventures

APART from the insecurity of the camp site, Dump IV was an ideal base from which to reconnoitre the various possibilities that were now taking shape. Spender's survey showed how the lower part of the Crevasse glacier system fitted into the blank space that we were exploring, and we were able to calculate, with some degree of accuracy, our position in relation to the mapped country on the southern side of the main range. Even allowing for a considerable discrepancy in these neighbouring surveys, most of which were known to be very unreliable, it was clear that we must be approaching that high network of watersheds in which the Snow Lake was supposed to lie.

The dullness of relaying all this food up the glacier had been relieved by the excitement of speculating where the glacier would lead us. But our impatience had increased as we approached the upper basin. Now at last we were in a position, still with many weeks' food at our disposal, to make a prolonged exploration of this exciting country, and to indulge in that most absorbing of all forms of mountaineering – the search for passes which lead from one unknown region to another.

But there was a very large field to be covered, and so many alternative plans, that it was hard to choose between them. For this reason, we decided to split up into three self-contained parties, each with its separate objective. The main survey party, consisting of Spender and myself and five Sherpas, was to concentrate on making its way to the north-west. If possible, we were to try to find a route into the Braldu glacier system and follow it down to the country that had been traversed by Younghusband, and later by Schomberg, to the north of the Shimshal pass. In comparison with the rest of the Karakoram, this region was extremely inaccessible, and it was important to take the opportunity of exploring it thoroughly. Tilman, with two Sherpas, was to find the Snow Lake, and having explored it, to work his way back to Skardu, across the little known ranges to the south-west of the Hispar pass. Auden, who had to get back early, was to try to find a pass that would take him into the Panmah glacier, or failing that, he would accompany Tilman and make his way down the Biafo glacier, from the Snow Lake. He was to take the four Baltis with him.

Whether it would be possible to achieve any of these ambitious plans, or whether we would be forced, by the difficulties of the country, to retreat ignominiously down the Crevasse glacier, was our chief concern. And it was enough to cause us some anxiety, for, although we were in an unusually strong position as regards food, it had to be remembered that very few passages had been made across the main ranges of the Karakoram.

A reconnaissance from a high ridge above Dump IV, on August 1st, helped us to decide upon our immediate plans, and gave us a superb view of the north face of "The Fangs" which swept upwards for 5,000 feet from a vast glacier basin, in a beautiful glistening arc, curving up to the summit ridge like the crest of a gigantic wave, frozen as it was about to break. Both the "Father Christmas glacier" and the Main glacier bent round to the west again, and were lost to view several miles north and south of the Second Divide.

On August 2nd, Auden, Tilman and I, with Ila and Angtharkay, took a light camp up the Main glacier, intending to make a rapid reconnaissance of its head, and to look for a way of starting our respective journeys. Meanwhile Spender, with the rest of the porters, went up the "Father Christmas glacier" to extend his survey in that direction; for it seemed less likely that we would find a route so far north, so it was best to take this opportunity of mapping the area.

Progress was so easy on the smooth ice of the Main glacier that we must have kept up an average speed of nearly two miles an hour. Strewn all over the surface of the glacier we found a large number of dead birds, some just skeletons, some still with all their plumage. They mostly belonged to the duck family, though I found one big bird with legs longer than my arm. This phenomenon was not confined to the Crevasse glacier. We found these fozen birds in the upper basins of most of the big glaciers that we visited in this part of the range. Presumably they had perished during migratory flights, though it is hard to understand why they should choose such difficult routes from Central Asia to India, when there are many lower passes over which they could fly across the main range. As a reason for this it has been suggested that the ancestors of these birds began their flights before the present range existed, and, as the mountains rose gradually out of the plains, the birds, instead of flying round the new obstacle, preferred to fly over it. But it seems to me that this is carrying the reputed conservatism of birds too far.

I asked Auden how deep he thought the ice might be at this point on the glacier. He surprised me by saying that it was probably at least two thousand feet thick. It seemed hardly credible that if two Eiffel Towers were placed vertically on top of each other on the bed of the glacier, the topmost one would not appear above the surface of the ice.

In a remarkably short time, we reached the point where the Main glacier bent round at a sharp angle to the west. We camped at this corner in a wide hollow, partly filled by five small lakes. In the evening we climbed several hundred feet above the camp to a sharp ridge of disintegrating marble that formed the actual corner of the valley. The weather, which had been bad all day, cleared at sunset, revealing a splendid view of the upper part of the glacier, which ran up at an easy angle to a snow basin enclosed by sharp peaks. We saw no less than four saddles leading over the watershed formed by these peaks. Each of these saddles lay at the head of a small tributary glacier, and was accessible from this side. We took compass bearings to these saddles and made a guess at their distance so as to be able to plot their rough position on our chart. The gathering dusk put an end to our work, though the sky was still luminous with the soft colours of evening. In my mind was a curious mingling of peace and impatient excitement.

That night I dreamt that Angtharkay and I succeeded in crossing a pass which led down to a glacier flowing between beautiful woodlands. At the snout of the glacier we met an Englishman, who invited us to a cocktail party at his house. Angtharkay was opposed to this idea, as he said it was late in the afternoon and we would be benighted on our way back. However, I was weak-minded, and we went into a crowded drawing-room for a "quick one". I asked where we were, and my host replied, "Braldu of course, didn't you know?" We took a taxi back up the glacier to the foot of the pass, but even so we were too late, and night had fallen before we got back to the camp. The dream had a grain of prophetic truth.

In spite of the fine evening, it started to snow lightly before we slept, and had not ceased when we awoke next morning. But we started early, and soon there was a temporary lull in the falling snow. We had numbered the saddles that we had seen the night before from right to left, beginning with the one farthest up the glacier. I had elected to explore No. 2 saddle with Angtharkay, as my calculations of its position had suggested that it would lead in the right direction for my purpose. The others were bound for No. 3 saddle, which was farther to the south and a great deal higher.

The two parties kept together for an hour and a half, and then our ways separated. We passed some fairly large tributaries coming down from the "Father Christmas" group, which probably connected with the country that Spender was surveying. Angtharkay and I kept going steadily for another three hours before we made a brief halt. After that the weather changed for the worse. Visibility was restricted to a few yards and snow was falling heavily. But we had seen the ground ahead of us, and with a compass we had no difficulty in keeping our course. When we reached the saddle (about 19,000 feet) we were met by a violent wind, which doubled us up and lashed our faces with hard, fozen snow. The only hope of seeing anything seemed to be to cross the saddle; there was a chance that we might find shelter from the bitterly cold wind on the far side. But a few cautious steps forward took us on to a very steep ice-slope, of unknown depth and covered with a thick deposit of fresh snow. We waited for a few minutes, but I got so cold that I started cutting steps down the slope into an inferno of whirling snow and mist. Once we had started we had to go on, taking the work in turn. I could not make up my mind which was the more unpleasant job: the infinitely laborious task of cutting steps through deep snow into the ice, blinded by the strong upward swirl of frozen particles, or standing above trying to brace one's body against the possibility of a slip, while the wind did its best to blow one over, and froze one's limbs into useless numbness. We had no idea whether the bottom of the slope was twenty feet below us or two thousand. The work seemed to go on interminably, and I was about to give it up when we reached a bergschrund, below which we could see a gentle snow-slope. We crossed the bergschrund in a swift sitting glissade.

It was 1.30 by Angtharkay's watch, which kept fairly good time, providing it was wound up every six hours. A slight rift in the clouds gave us a vague view into a deep and complicated valley system below us. To the south, a great wall of peaks stretched away for a long distance. This meant we couldn't be above the Panmah glacier, while the void below did not suggest the proximity of the Snow Lake.

We made our way down through soft snow, and before long we emerged below the clouds. We found that we were in the upper basin of a small glacier which was one of many flowing from an immense cirque, which in its turn was obviously the head of a large glacier system. The main glacier could not be seen, but there were indications that it flowed in a northerly direction. The view to the north was blocked by a high rock ridge running west from the watershed we had just crossed. It was high time to turn back, but the temptation to see over this ridge was too great, and we made towards it as quickly as we could. Angtharkay entered into the spirit of the hunt with his usual enthusiasm, and led the way across steep ice-slopes. It was slow work and we took a long time to reach the foot of the ridge. We climbed to the top of a rock pinnacle, and saw below a great glacier flowing away to the north. Judging from its position, direction and size, there could be no doubt that this was the Braldu glacier, and from where we stood it would be easy to reach it. For me it was an exciting discovery, as it gave us access to the ranges of the Shimshal pass.

I drew a sketch map and took a round of compass bearings. Then we started back, hurrying as much as possible. We were both tired, and although the track was already made, it took us nearly two hours to reach the bergschrund at the foot of the pass. We had a lot of trouble in crossing it to reach the ice-slope above. There we found that our steps had been obliterated by the driving snow; and had to be recut. I thought that we should never reach the pass, but it was easier to cut steps uphill, and by now the blizzard had ceased.

By the time we had regained the pass, the mountains to the west were clear, though great masses of storm-cloud still hid the high peaks. The view was magnificent, but very perplexing, and there was not time to try to understand it. I managed to identify the saddle that the other party had been aiming for, and saw that it also led into the Braldu basin, though a tremendous ice cliff on its north-west side made it impossible to cross. I had been lucky in my choice; from what I had seen it was plain that there was no route over Saddle No. 1. The peaks on the other side of the Braldu basin looked a tremendous distance away, and there was no sign of the ice-cap that we had expected to find.

It was doubtful if we could reach the camp before it was too dark to see; everything depended upon the state of the snow on the glacier. It was a relief to be going gently downhill, and we ran madly along. At first the snow was good, but soon we came to a very bad patch, and as we floundered slowly across it, we realized that we were going to be beaten by the oncoming darkness. However, the conditions soon improved, and we swung down over the hard surface with a peaceful sense of unreality induced by physical fatigue and by the fading evening light. But the innumerable crevasses that crossed our path were real enough and were becoming increasingly difficult to see. I fell up to my head in one of these, and heard the ominous tinkle of icicles as they fell into the void below my feet. A welcome drink from a glacier lake refreshed us. It was another fine evening, and after night had fallen there was still enough light to grope our way along.

The ice became smoother, and we stepped out with more confidence. As we approached the corner we heard a shout from someone who had evidently come to look for us. Suddenly I felt the ground give way from under my feet and found myself falling through space. It seemed an age before a tug came from the rope, and I had time to wonder whether it really was tied round my waist! But at length my fall was checked with a sudden jerk; it felt as if the rope had nearly cut me in two. It was difficult to judge how far I had fallen. The ragged patch of starlit sky, at the top of the hole through which I had dropped, looked very far above me. I found that the crevasse was just narrow enough for me to get my feet against one ice wall and my back against the other. By this method, known to climbers as *chimney-ing*, I climbed up for a short way. But I soon became exhausted, for it is no easy matter to obtain sufficient friction on ice to *chimney* between vertical walls. In the dark I thrust my foot against an icicle that gave way, and I fell again, this time into a deep lake at the bottom of the crevasse. I tried to find some purchase below the surface of the water, but could find nothing but loose bits of ice floating about. I was becoming very cold, and there was not much time to waste before numbness would make action impossible. I found an ice bollard jutting out of one of the walls, a few feet above the water. I managed to get my left arm over this, and, with some help from the rope, to hoist myself out of the water. The bollard did not feel very safe and I was afraid that it would collapse; by this time I had little strength left for further efforts.

When only two men are travelling together on a glacier – a stupid practice at the best of times – it is wise for the man behind to carry a spare length of rope. Fortunately Angtharkay was doing this. I shouted to him to send down an end with a loop tied in it. At first I could not make him hear, and it seemed a long time before the rope came dangling down. Having found it in the dark, I slipped my foot into the loop, and, using it as a stirrup, stood in it. Angtharkay then pulled in the slack of my waist rope. It was rather difficult to make him understand which rope to make fast and which to pull in, but eventually I was brought to the surface of the glacier, and climbed out of the crevasse. I sat gasping on the ice while Angtharkay banged and rubbed my limbs, which had lost all feeling. In his excitement Angtharkay put one foot down the crevasse and very nearly fell in himself. I had lost my ice-axe.

The incident was a well-deserved lesson; firstly, for being so rash as to get benighted; secondly, for travelling over an unknown glacier with only one companion; and thirdly, having taken that risk, for not having made certain that he had a full understanding of the "stirrup rope" method of getting a companion out of a crevasse. I was lucky to have got off so lightly.

We groped our way on to the corner. Here we met the other three on their way up to search for us. Apparently it had been Tilman whose shouts we had heard just before I fell into the crevasse. Angtharkay had shouted back rather incoherently, and Tilman had gathered that something was wrong. Not knowing what was the matter, he returned to camp to fetch the others, and to bring spare clothing, food and ropes. We all went down to the camp together. I stripped off my water-logged clothes and was soon in my sleeping-bag with hot tea and a pipe.

The other three reported a completely blank day. They had reached their col, which was 19,500 feet high, at about midday. It was blowing a gale and snowing heavily. As far as they could see, there was no chance of getting down the other side, and there was only a narrow corniced snow ridge to sit on and wait for a possible clearing. So they gave it up and returned to camp, expecting to find us already there. When by evening we still had not returned, they became anxious, and Tilman had climbed to our view point of the previous evening to look for us. As it turned out, their failure to see anything from their col did not matter, as we had been able to settle the question of its farther side.

Next morning, the other three went off to explore Saddle No. 4. Angtharkay and I stayed in our sleeping-bags. It was a fine day, but I had no regrets at my laziness, for I was tired and more than satisfied with the previous day's work. Also I had a pain in my back, a souvenir of my adventure in the crevasse. I slept most of the morning and, in the afternoon, I lay in the sun and read copies of the Calcutta *Statesman* four months old, that Auden had brought for wrapping up geological specimens. I derived as much enjoyment from them as if they had been that morning's issue. Angtharkay washed his long hair with great care, then he oiled it and twisted it up into a neat plait, which he wound round his head. He loves to do this,in the sunshine, whenever he has any spare time.

The other party returned in the evening after a successful day. They had reached the saddle which was 18,000 feet high. From the top they looked down into what they at once recognized to be the basin of the Nobande Sobande glacier, which is the principal tributary of the Panmah glacier on the southern side of the main watershed. These glaciers had been explored by Professor Desio, of the Duke of Spoleto's expedition, in 1929. Crossing a small tributary glacier on the other side of the col, Tilman, Auden and Ila had climbed on to another col about 18,100 feet high. From there the view to the west was very extensive. They looked for a great distance along the main continental watershed, which, as we had now discovered, separated the Braldu and the Nobande Sobande basins. Far beyond they saw a range of pinnacled rock peaks, which must lie, they supposed, near the head of the Biafo glacier and the Snow Lake. This view enabled them to make tentative plans.

The reconnaisance of routes from the head of the Crevasse glacier had taken less time than we anticipated. In spite of the fine weather, which persisted on August 5th, we retreated to Dump IV, though we regretted having to waste the day by going down the glacier instead of breaking new ground. Tilman, Auden and Ila, taking with them a light camp and food for three days, went on to investigate the Crown glacier, the source of which we had not yet placed. The next day Angtharkay and I went up the "Father Christmas glacier" to find Spender and to hear his report of the country he had been surveying. We had trouble in crossing some surface streams which had cut deep troughs in the ice, and a line of ice pinnacles at the junction of the two glaciers delayed us. But on the "Father Christmas glacier" we walked up a medial moraine that was as smooth as a high road. We met Nukku coming down with a note from Spender, and he conducted us far up the glacier to Spender's base, which we reached that evening. Spender had been luckier than we in the timing of his work.

He had employed the two days of bad weather, August 2nd and 3rd, in marching up the glacier. The three succeeding days had been perfect and he had accomplished an amazing amount of work. He had completed no less than three high stations on each of these days. In this way he had not only mapped in detail the whole of the "Father Christmas glacier" system, but he had fixed the position of many distant peaks which had come into view. What was more, he had discovered a route to the north, over a comparatively easy pass, into a deep valley running east and west, which he supposed to be a tributary of the Braldu glacier. After discussing the question in detail, we decided that it would be more profitable to attempt this route than to cross the pass that I had discovered into the upper basin of the Braldu glacier. The difficult ice-slope on the other side of my pass, and the extraordinary simplicity of travel on the "Father Christmas glacier", were additional arguments in favour of this plan.

That night the fine spell broke, and on August 7th, leaving behind a small depot of stores, we returned to Dump IV in rain and falling snow. We got very wet and had difficulty in cooking our evening meal. We sat up late; I was just dozing off to sleep at about ten o'clock when a boulder, falling from above with a series of sharp retorts, set my nerves tingling. This was followed, ten minutes later, by louder crashes near the camp. Obviously something had to be done. It was snowing steadily and the night was warm. If it were to freeze later, an enormous mass of rock would probably be dislodged, and might wipe out the whole camp. But it was pitch dark, and the glacier lantern was somewhere outside in a dump of loads that was buried in snow. The candles that we burned in our tents would not stay alight for a second in heavily falling snow. I was discussing the situation with Spender when there was a prolonged and deafening roar, which became louder and louder, and was accompanied by the whirring sound of flying splinters. This culminated in a noise like a clap of thunder within a few yards of the tent, which was followed by absolute silence. It was difficult to believe that none of the camp had been hit, but after a moment of frozen suspense I heard shouts and laughter from the Sherpas whose tent was twenty yards away. This bombshell had the effect of bringing the whole party to its feet, except for the Baltis, who did not seem unduly disturbed, and were quite indignant when we dragged them out from under their blankets. It was a long, cold business shifting our tents and sleeping-bags on to the ice hummocks out of range of the bombardment. We got very wet. It was impossible, in the dark, to cut platforms, but somehow we succeeded in erecting the tents with sufficient floor-space for everyone to lie down.

When dawn broke we found that a foot of snow had fallen, and it was still coming down in large soft flakes. At midday, when there was still no improvement in the weather, we began to get rather worried about the other party. It would be difficult to get through pinnacled ice with all this new snow, and by now their food and fuel would be nearly finished. Visibility was practically nil, and until it improved it was no use setting out to look for them. At about three o'clock it stopped snowing and diffused sunlight filtered through the clouds. We were preparing to start down the glacier when we suddenly saw the others approaching the camp. They were all very tired, having covered a lot of difficult ground during the last three days. They had obtained sufficient data for Spender to be able to place the Crown glacier, which was twelve miles long, on the map. This helped us considerably in our subsequent attempt to unravel the intricacies of the mountains lying between us and the Shaksgam.

It started snowing again in the evening and continued heavily all night.

Although it cleared up at about ten o'clock the next morning and became brilliantly fine, there was too much snow for us to move up the glacier, and we were confined to the camp for another day of inactivity. It was an annoying waste of time, but when we considered that it was the first time that we had been seriously held up by bad weather during the whole season, we could not complain.

There is a good deal of talking during these occasional days of forced idleness. I recorded in my diary a list of subjects of conversation on a similar occasion: Organ playing compared with engine driving (Spender was a bit of an expert at both); national characteristics; farming at home and in Africa; art and literature for love or money; life in Berlin and Vienna; winter in Norway; food (always the most enchanting of subjects); why men go to sea; civilized and primitive culture; Tolstoy – from which to strategy and luck in war; sensitiveness and callousness; asceticism and indulgence; that dinner we had in Paris on the way out; and so back to food – with special emphasis on dripping!

On August 10th Tilman and Auden started on their journeys. Tilman had with him Ila and Sen Tensing, and took food enough for twenty-three days. Auden had the four Baltis, and took food to last for a fortnight. Spender and I, and two of our Sherpas, accompanied them to our camp up the Main glacier, while Angtharkay, Lobsang and Nukku started relaying our thirty days' food up the "Father Christmas glacier". Travel on the upper glaciers was very different from what it had been a few days before. Now, in the deep new snow, we had to work hard for every yard of progress. At the upper camp we said good-bye to Auden and Tilman, whom we did not expect to see again until we got back to England.

CHAPTER FIFTEEN

Panmah Journey

by J. B. Auden

MY last view of Tilman and the two Sherpas was on August 15th through the theodolite telescope from a survey station at 17,300 feet. They were black specks on the top of the Faith col. The day was fine and, as the two Baltis whom I had sent on the 12th to reconnoitre a route had reported that there was an easy way down to the Nobande Sobande, I did not hurry, but lazed by the theodolite admiring the view and thinking of arriving back in England after nearly four years' absence. But our feet were wet, and at midday we started our descent to the main glacier. It was out of the question to go down the ice-fall of the side glacier, but the Baltis had stated that there was a gully on the west side. This gully unfortunately led down to a precipice, necessitating a horizontal traverse before descending with the rope some couloirs in the limestone cliffs. The Nobande Sobande was reached at sunset, and we saw to our dismay that it was far more crevassed and broken up than had been apparent from above. The Primus stove had always been a failure, and as it would not light at all on the night of the 11th, I had already thrown it away to lighten our loads, and had given the paraffin to Tilman. We therefore spent our second night without hot food.

The next day we tried to get on to the main glacier, a short distance above our camp, but were held up thirty yards from the edge by blocks of tumbled ice. There was only one ice-axe between the five of us, so that it was not possible to split up into two reconnoitring parties. An unsuccessful attempt was then made to cross the side glacier leading down from the 18,000-col, after which the main glacier was penetrated by a route just below the camp. After several hours amongst an intricate system of small valleys in the ice we had advanced about 600 yards into the Nobande Sobande, but crevasses had so split up the glacier into isolated wedges and towers that further advance was barred. It was now about three o'clock and despondency was setting in. It would have been possible to return next morning up the cliffs by which we had come down, cross the 18,000-col glacier above its ice-fall, descend to the Nobande Sobande from the east side, but by so doing two days' rations would be used up, without having gone more than half a mile towards Askole. We climbed a certain way up the mountain-side to get a revised bird's-eye view of the crevasse system cutting the col glacier late in the evening. There was a little dry grass here, but not enough to cook a hot meal. Hussain was diligent with his prayers, and Allah was invoked throughout the night.

The next day we kept to the left wall of the Nobande Sobande, sometimes along an ablation valley, and sometimes, where the ice pressed against the rock wall, traversing along the cliffs above. The first flowers were seen just west of the Drenmang glacier. Mahadi put some in his hat and began singing at the prospect of an early release from his hardships. He became more subdued when we reached the Drenmang. The broken ice of the Nobande Sobande lay against the valley wall and appeared to offer no route. I climbed about 1,500 feet hoping to find a gully descending to the Drenmang, but all the gullies ended in difficult couloirs. On returning to the others, I gave Mahadi and Hussain my ice-axe and sent them to explore an alternative route. Two hours went by, and once again imagination invented the worst disasters. But they returned radiant and covered with mud. They had found a route through tunnels in the ice where the highly broken-up margin of the glacier joined on to the cliff, and had cut steps in all the difficult places. We had to hurry, since the ice the whole way along this route was discharging its boulders in the evening sun. Once on the Drenmang glacier the going was easy, and we reached the moraine on the south-east side whilst it was just light enough to see grass, flowers and wood in plenty. We at once lit a fire and had our first warm food since breakfast with Tilman sixty hours before.

The next day was perfect. While I went up at dawn to a station 15,230 feet in height with the theodolite, the Baltis roasted some fresh satu from our stock of flour. From Drenmang to Skinmang our route was over a grass-covered hillside. About one and a half miles from Skinmang and at least 800 feet above the glacier we found a well-built cairn. Desio shows no itinerary on his map through this place, and it is probable that the cairn had been put up by Baltis, at a time when the Nobande Sobande presented fewer difficulties than now. After crossing the Skinmang glacier*, we descended another five miles, following a bear track down an ablation valley and being occasionally bombarded by boulders dropped from the overhanging ice. Camp was pitched at the foot of the Eriole valley by flowering rose bushes.

Five minutes after crossing a ravine entering the Dumordo valley by the snout of the Panmah glacier, a mud-flow swept down, carrying with it immense boulders. I had often read of these flows, known as *swas* in the Punjab, and knew abstractly of the size of the boulders that are moved. But here was an actual demonstration, for one of the boulders must have weighed about 120 tons. The Baltis considered this escape to be one more proof that God exists and was favourably disposed.

The rest of the journey to Srinagar via the Skoro La and Deosai plains saw the fulfilment of long anticipated pleasures. Tobacco and eggs at Askole, apricots at Skoro, over three months' mail at Skardu, the grassy uplands of Deosai, and silver birch above Birzil. I arrived at Bandipura on September 3rd and was welcomed by a letter from Lady Clutterbuck and a hamper of food. She had sent her car, which took me the next day to the trees and shady lawns of Srinagar.

* This appears to refer to the Chiring Glacier. *Editor*

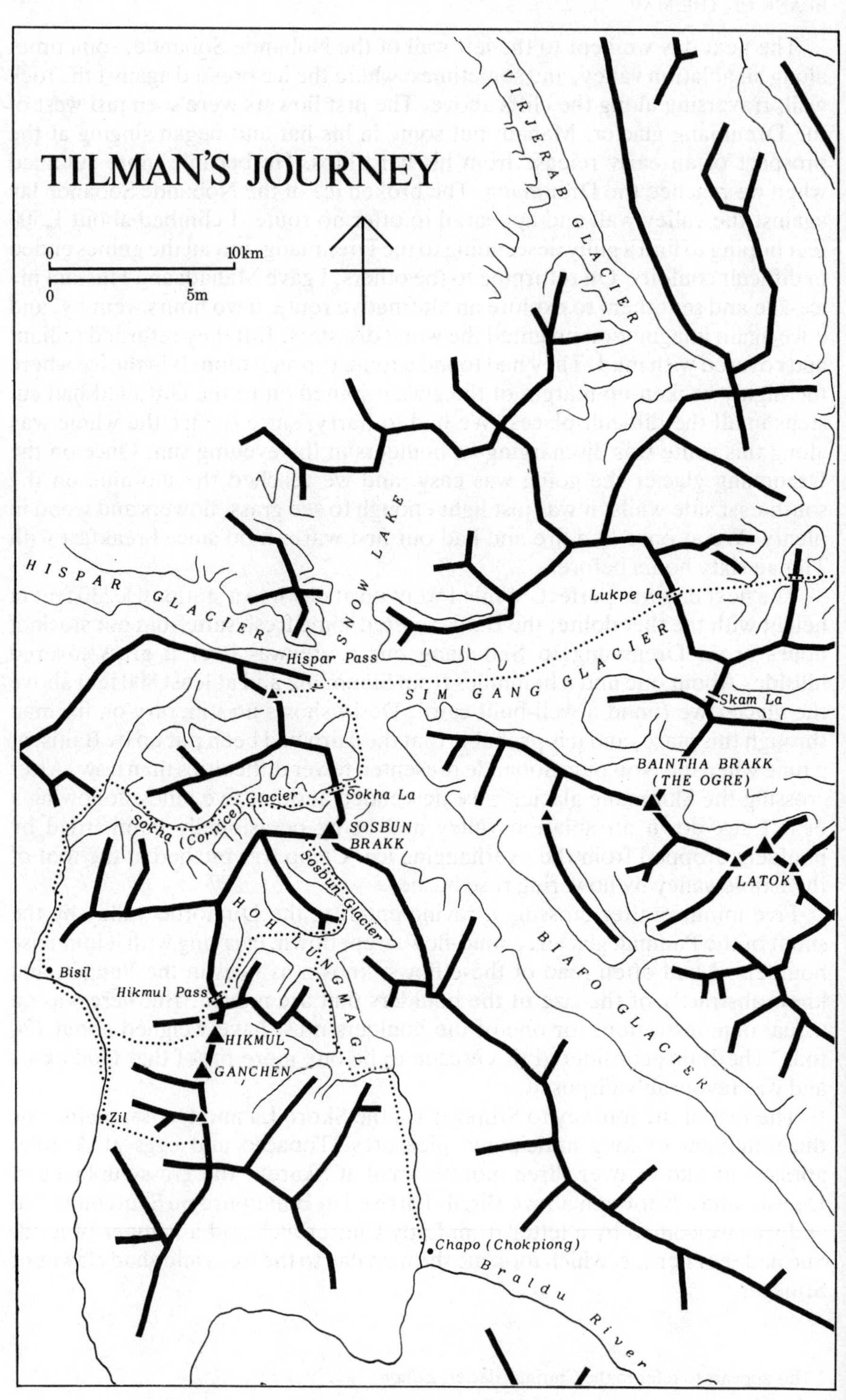
TILMAN'S JOURNEY
0
10km
0
5m
VIRJERAB GLACIER
HISPAR GLACIER
SNOW LAKE
Lukpe La
SIM GANG GLACIER
Hispar Pass
Skam La
BAINTHA BRAKK
(THE OGRE)
Sokha (Cornice) Glacier
Sokha La
SOSBUN
BRAKK
Sosbun Glacier
LATOK
HOH LUNGMA GL
BIAFO GLACIER
Bisil
Hikmul Pass
HIKMUL
GANCHEN
Zil
Chapo (Chokpiong)
Braldu River

CHAPTER SIXTEEN

Legends

by H. W. Tilman

AUGUST 11th was another glorious day. Auden, with the four Baltis, myself, and my Sherpas, went up to the col that we had reconnoitred on August 4th. I dumped my loads on the far side and returned, while Auden, after doing a theodolite station on top, camped on the other side of the pass. The food for twenty-two days which my party was carrying, and our equipment, made up loads too heavy for the two Sherpas and myself, so we had to relay. Meanwhile Shipton and Spender were finishing the survey of the Crevasse glacier. On the 12th I left them at a station on my way to the col, or pass, as it had now become. Crossing quickly we found Auden's camp and a note, and at the same time saw his party moving down the glacier ahead of us. We joined forces and dropped down on to another tributary glacier lying north-west; having gone a little way up it, we camped on the ice.

Opposite was another short glacier leading to a col on the Nobande-Braldu watershed which we had already marked down as worth a visit. However, next day, we went above this col, by climbing an easy peak (18,770 feet) overlooking it from the west. From the top there was a remarkable view, but Auden was ungrateful, because there was no concrete bed, or its equivalent, for the legs of the wretched theodolite, and the sky was rapidly clouding over. He explained at some length, and with great warmth, that readings taken as the theodolite sank slowly into the snow might be accepted by nit-wits like myself, but certainly by nobody else, and that some observations should have been made lower down, when the visibility was good.

Stunned though I was by this verbal storm, it was impossible not to enjoy the view which I, at any rate, had come for, and which was all the better for not being looked at upside down through the telescope of a theodolite. We could see the Ogre (23,900 feet), a triangulated peak whose position relative to the Biafo had always been a puzzle, Kanjut peak (25,460 feet), a great area of the upper Braldu, the Crown peak, the Drenmang, Chiring, upper Panmah, and Nobande Sobande glaciers, together with a confused jumble of peaks to the south, amongst which the mighty Masherbrum was alone distinguishable. From here I could see a route to the west across the two main arms of the Braldu. If there were a pass from the westernmost, it must lead either to the Biafo or the Virjerab; I hoped and believed it would lead to the former, but anyhow I made up my mind to try it.

The next day we all went up the glacier leading to the same col which later was called Faith pass. Auden turned aside to geologize, while I pushed on to the col with the two Sherpas and one Balti, all laden. This glacier was as badly crevassed as any I have seen, and the price of safety, as of liberty, was eternal vigilance. Approaching the col, the weather, which had been threatening, developed into a blizzard. We struggled on, hardly knowing the top when we reached it, dumped the loads there, and started back. In the driving snow it was difficult to keep even an approximate direction, and when the snow froze on our glasses it would have been impossible to see a haystack at a yard, let alone the half-concealed crevasses through which we had to thread our way. Removing my glasses every few yards, I led on, expecting every instant to be engulfed. Nothing happened. We got clear without putting a foot through; perhaps a benign Providence watches over the blind as well as the drunk.

The following day, August 15th, we separated, Auden making for the Panmah with the four recalcitrant Baltis; the two Sherpas and I for Faith pass and the Braldu. It was a brilliant morning, our tracks of yesterday were in places faintly recognizable, but in spite of that I fell into two crevasses in quick succession. The Sherpas held me, but in one my snow-glasses were swept off as my head went through the snow. My luck was in, for they were caught on a ledge. I was lowered to the ledge and managed to retrieve them.

Somewhat shaken by these untoward happenings, which made us marvel still more that we had escaped disaster under the unfavourable conditions of the previous day, we pushed slowly on to the dump on the col. Because of our small fuel reserve, we had exercised such strict economy since starting to use the Primus four days ago, that we had cooked nothing but tea and pemmican. The Sherpas at this inopportune moment complained of hunger and suggested opening a tin of pemmican to eat raw. Sen Tensing thought we ought to camp and make a real meal. Neither of these motions could be accepted by the Chair, and, having pointed out a distant rock outcrop by a glacier lake as our objective, I turned to find a way down.

Once down on the glacier, which was a tributary of the Braldu, we pressed on without stopping, camping finally at the appointed place on one of the main arms of the Braldu. The rocky spur on which we wanted to camp was rather high above the lake, and the question was whether to camp coldly on snow close to the water, or warmly on rock some distance from it. As I should not have to fetch the water, and also had a casting vote, we went to the rocks. That evening we made some satu on the Primus, and Sen Tensing's face assumed a less lugubrious look.

Sen Tensing was rather a character. He had attached himself to the Everest reconnaissance party in 1935 on the East Rongbuk glacier at Camp II, having turned up, unannounced, from Sola Khumbu in Nepal. He was so pleased with the clothes we gave him, or rather his appearance in them, that he never again took them off. Down in the valley under a blazing sun, miles from any snow, Sen Tensing could be seen fully attired in a windproof suit, gloves, glasses, boots, puttees, and Balaclava helmet, ready apparently to battle with some imminent and terrific blizzard. So fond was he of dressing the part of the complete mountaineer that I dubbed him the Foreign Sportsman, and the name stuck.

He is as broad as long and somewhat stout, very willing, cheerful, and talkative, full of his own importance, and by no means regardless of his own comfort and general well-being. For instance, at this very camp, I found that he had made himself an extra sleeping-bag out of the canvas food-bags that had been emptied and discarded from time to time. Most of us had collected one or two, but the Foreign Sportsman had "won" six, cut them up and sewn them into a sleeping-sack. Having got over his earlier passion for looking like the complete mountaineer, he now no longer wears the clothes he receives at the beginning of an expedition, but keeps them for sale or barter, and appears dressed like a country gentleman. This year he favoured a grey flannel suit with thick white stockings worn outside the trousers. He is for ever chanting interminable Tibetan prayers – at least the patience with which the other Sherpas suffered this chanting led us to suppose they were prayers and not smutty songs. He reads and writes Tibetan characters, and manages to do rather less than his share of the menial work without protest from the others; this, taken in conjunction with the prayer-chanting, leads us to suppose him an unfrocked Lama.

The following day I decided to risk a reconnaissance instead of first bringing the remaining loads down from the col. The dawn was not promising, so there was the risk of not seeing anything and thus wasting a day. Moreover, most of our food was still lying on the col, and I, no less than the Foreign Sportsman, was haunted by the thought that a prolonged spell of bad weather might prevent us from reaching it.

However, all went well. Starting very early while the snow was crisp, we followed a tributary glacier to the west, crossed the low but steep col at its head which took us down to the other main arm of the Braldu, crossed that, and made for a low snow ridge three miles away to the west. So wide was the saddle on this ridge that we had to go on for half a mile down a swelling convex slope before we could see anything below. There was much cloud about and more was rolling up, but we were in time to see and recognize the strikingly bold peaks of the Biafo west wall and the end of what the Workmans called the B15 ridge, all of which we had looked at so often in their photographs. With our eyes on the lowering clouds we hurried back, afraid of being caught by a storm similar to that of two days ago. No storm came, and by evening the weather looked more promising.

But it was snowing briskly when we left early on the 17th to fetch the loads, and visibility was poor. The crevasses on this tributary glacier were comparatively few, but there were enough to make us wish to avoid groping our way back in a blizzard. Conditions on top of the col and over the Panmah side were similar to those of the earlier storm, but once we started back the weather improved, and fitful gleams of sunshine brightened our return.

All we ever learnt about this Karakoram weather was that it is unpredictable. I remember on the Crevasse glacier, on the fifth day of a very fine spell, a sun halo was observed, and all our weather prophets tumbled over each other in haste to predict a change. Two more fine days followed, while the evening of the third appeared so settled that the prophets now spoke contemptuously of sun haloes and promised more fine weather. It was not surprising, therefore, that we woke the next morning to find it raining and blowing hard. It proved to be one of the only three really bad days we had. I say "really" bad, though it was merely unpleasant – but there appear to be two sorts of bad weather – ordinary bad weather and surveyor's. Any day that is not clear, cloudless, still and warm, is for them "bad" weather.

I hoped this would be our last relay. We had eaten 40 lbs. of food, a few odds and ends could be jettisoned, and by carrying very big loads, everything could be moved in one shift. When we arrived back I got the Sherpas to build the father and mother of all cairns which, before we left, I crowned with a tin containing a note. I had to climb the cairn to reach the top. It was likely that the pass which the main body were to cross would take them into the Braldu a long way down; they would have to come to the head for survey purposes, and I hoped they would spot our cairn, as in fact they did.

The promise of a clear night was this time realized. At dawn, mist spread up from the Braldu, but to the west, whence most of our weather came, it remained clear, and at 8 a.m., when we sat on the half-way col (Hope pass), it was brilliantly fine. The Sherpas were carrying 75 lbs. each and myself 50 lbs., but we got safely down over the bergschrund and began the long plod, going very slowly, the snow rapidly softening.

The wide saddle (Charity pass) was reached at 1 p.m. There was not a cloud anywhere, so it was much easier to recognize the familiar land-marks of the Workmans' photographs. Unmistakably conspicuous was the Ogre, which was now seen to lie on the eastern end of the so-called B15 ridge, which itself formed the southern boundary of a long eastern tributary of the Snow Lake itself. This now lay below us, and it was already clear that it was a large *névé* field, the upper basin of the Biafo.

The descent was easy except when we got caught in some desperately soft patches of snow, but we soon set foot on dry land, on what might truly be called the shore of the Snow Lake, and camped about 3.30 p.m. Another blazing hot day followed. We left the camp standing and walking across the *névé* field to the south wall, a distance of about four miles. Two feeder glaciers, besides the one that we had descended, flow in from the east; one leads apparently to the Nobande Sobande where the watershed seemed difficult to cross, and the other and more southerly to the Choktoi, the pass to which looked very easy. This latter feeder is about three miles long, and its south wall is the remarkably high, precipitous, straight ridge carrying the Ogre, the peak almost overlooking the col. Some nine miles in length, this ridge terminates where the Snow Lake ends and the main Biafo begins its south-easterly course.

While contouring round the foot of the ridge between these two feeder glaciers, we saw in the snow the tracks of an Abominable Snowman. They were eight inches in diameter, eighteen inches apart, almost circular, without sign of toe or heel. They were three or four days old, so melting must have altered the outline. The most remarkable thing was that they were in a straight line one behind the other, with no "stagger" right or left, like a bird's spoor. A four-footed animal walking slowly puts its hind foot in the track of its forefoot, but there is always some mark of overlapping, nor are the tracks immediately in front of each other. However many-legged it was, the beast or bird was heavy, the tracks being nearly a foot deep. We followed them for a mile, when they disappeared on some rock. The tracks came from a glacier pool where the animal had evidently drunk, and the next day we picked up the same spoor on the north side of Snow Lake.

The Sherpas judged them to belong to the smaller type of Snowman, or Yeti, as they call them, of which there are apparently two varieties: the smaller, whose spoor we were following, which feeds on men, while his larger brother confines himself to a diet of yaks. My remark that no one had been here for nearly thirty years and that he must be devilish hungry did not amuse the Sherpas as much as I expected! The jest was considered ill-timed, as perhaps it was, the three of us standing forlorn and alone in a great expanse of snow, looking at the strange tracks like so many Robinson Crusoes.

I have no explanation to offer, and, if I had, respect for ancient tradition would keep me silent. They were not the tracks of one of the many species of bears which seem to haunt the Himalaya, either Isabillinus, Pruinosus, or "Bruinosus"; for naturalists, like stamp collectors, are keen on variety. There was no game of any kind, nor grass, within fifteen miles, and the nearest village was forty miles away. A few days later, lower down in the Cornice glacier valley, bear-tracks were common and were recognized as such by the Sherpas and myself. A one-legged, carnivorous bird, weighing perhaps a ton, might make similar tracks, but it seems unnecessary to search for a new species when we have a perfectly satisfactory one at hand in the form of the Abominable Snowman – new perhaps to science but old in legend. All respecters of tradition must have noticed with surprise and regret how a certain great newspaper allowed the hospitality of its columns to be used, or rather abused, by the iconoclasts for a determined attack upon the very existence of the Abominable Snowman. No great harm, however, was done. Bear-tracks (species not agreed) were in the course of a column and a half successfully proved to be made by bears; wolves and otters were found to make tracks after their kind, and when the dust had settled the Abominable Snowman remained to continue his evasive, mysterious, terrifying existence, unruffled as the snows he treads, unmoved as the mountains amongst which he dwells, uncaught, unspecified, and not unhonoured.

On the 20th we struck camp and crossed the Snow Lake to the west, walking first on *névé* and then on bare ice. The descent was almost imperceptible. The area of this nearly flat eastern basin of the Biafo I should put at about six miles by three; at the most twenty square miles instead of three hundred. It is a disappointingly small area for such a grandiose name, and though one might wish secretly to find the first impressions of earlier and better travellers confirmed, a discrepancy of that size is difficult to overlook.

Another strange feature that had caused a good deal of dispute among geographers was the Workmans' Cornice glacier. According to these explorers they had found a glacier which had no outlet, being completely surrounded by mountains. This remarkable glacier lay in the angle formed by the Hispar south wall and by the Biafo west wall, and although never actually reached, yet it had been observed from all sides. Sir Martin Conway denied the physical possibility of an enclosed glacier, on the ground that for thousands of years snow must have been pouring into it, and that either the resulting ice would have piled up and over-flowed the barrier wall, or melted and found an outlet as water. The Workmans retorted that they had observed correctly, and appealed to the *argumentum ad hominem* – Sir Martin Conway "not having seen the glacier in question nor its barriers" – leaving the controversy to be renewed by us after a lapse of nearly thirty years. Shipton and Spender had derided the idea of a completely enclosed glacier, while Auden and I supported the Doctor and Mrs. Workman – more, perhaps, from chivalrous motives than for any scientific reason. So upon me lay the task of establishing (I hoped) the truth of the Workmans' assertion and of confounding the scientific sceptics – a consummation always desirable, if seldom attainable.

Five miles from our camp of August 20th we reached the main Biafo glacier. To our right we looked up a northern extension of it to the watershed of what must be either the Virjerab or Khurdopin glaciers. Facing us to the west was the gentle rise to the Hispar pass some three miles away, while on our left the main Biafo glacier flowed in a broad stream to the south-west. We crossed it here, where it is, perhaps, two miles in width, and camped on some rocks at the foot of the western wall just below the point where this bends to form the southern wall of the Hispar glacier. On the way over we noticed a deep gash cut in this great wall, some two miles below the spot where we pitched our camp. It looked somewhat like a col shown on one of the Workmans' photographs, which now proved to be close to camp. I had studied this photograph hopefully, but the col itself proved to be quite impracticable. Lying between this impassable col and our camp was a short tributary glacier leading to a high saddle and to a snow peak, from which it seemed likely that a view of what lay behind the west wall could be obtained. Somewhere behind the wall lay the Workmans' Cornice glacier, on which we meant to set foot.

We tackled the peak next day. Having left camp very early, we presently became involved in the intricacies of a difficult ice-fall. When at length found, the route was amusing, passing through a tunnel under a mammoth block of cold, blue ice, and beneath beautiful but dangerously unstable *séracs* which were just beginning to catch and reflect the light of the rising sun – a fact which made one mentally resolve to return by another route if that were possible. A mile beyond, another and steeper ice-fall held us up until overcome at last by means of a series of snow bridges, which no reasonable man would have contemplated had there been an alternative crossing.

From the snow plateau above we gained a footing on the peak which "went" pleasantly enough until within about 200 feet from the top, when our ridge became icy, and narrowed to what climbers like to describe as a knife-edge. It is an expressive term, but the knife-edges of some, probably my own, are blunter than those of others. There ought to be some kind of definition for those knife-edge ridges, those ice walls, and overhanging rocks, which are climbed with such distressing ease and fequency. However, we left this particular knife-edge ridge alone. There was some excuse for this faint-heartedness – one of the soles of my boots was flapping loose, and to my mind the Foreign Sportsman and Ila climbed with too much abandon to be desirable companions on such a place.

We descended to the plateau and ascended the saddle whence another ridge of our peak beckoned invitingly. On closer inspection it proved more formidable than the first, but from a short way up we got a reasonable view.

Immediately below, at the bottom of a deep chasm, was a glacier flowing south-west, to be joined after a short distance by two other valleys. We could not see into them, but they obviously contained glaciers flowing from the Biafo west wall. Beyond the glacier was a tumbled sea of peaks that would have defied the topographical sense of a homing pigeon. The head of the glacier abutted against the Hispar south wall, and a remarkable feature was the grass and juniper wood which we could see growing in the valley unusually close to its head. To our ice-weary eyes the vision was tantalizing, and prospect of reaching wood so quickly fired the Sherpas with a mighty longing to get down to it. It was clear that the glacier was either the Cornice glacier itself or a branch of it. There was no way down to it from the saddle, and a descent from the Hispar wall looked doubtful, so before investigating that, we decided to try another low col we had noticed further along the Biafo wall, which very probably led to one of the two tributary glaciers whose presence we guessed. It would be far more satisfactory to enter the Cornice glacier at its head and follow it down, or better still remain imprisoned in its fastnesses, than merely to view it from afar, as the Workmans had done, or to search for its outlet.

For our return on so hot an afternoon it seemed wise, if possible, to avoid the two ice-falls. The attempt was unsuccessful. After a long snow trudge we came to an impasse, and after thus wasting an hour and much energy, found ourselves trusting once more to the precarious bridges of the steep ice-fall, which were weakened now by the hot sun. This mistake rather lessened the allure of new routes, and although the next ice-fall could have been avoided by a long climb, when I put the proposal to the Sherpas, pointing out the increasing risks from the *séracs* and the ice tunnel, they replied that my imaginary perils would be passed in a few minutes while the climb might take hours – a very unsound argument but one with which, at the time, I heartily agreed.

On August 22nd we went down the Biafo to reconnoitre the gap in the west wall. There was no approach by any side glacier, for it was simply a deep notch cut in the high, precipitous rock ridge which bounds the Biafo on that side. To reach it we had to climb up a long avalanche cone of ice debris directly beneath the hanging glacier from which this had fallen. Frequent creaks and groans seemed to portend another fall. There was little difficulty in gaining the col, perhaps seven or eight hundred feet above the Biafo, but at first glance the chances of getting down the other side looked exceedingly slim. The unknown glacier, whose surface was bare ice, lay nearly 2,000 feet below, shut in by tremendous cliffs. After about a mile it disappeared out of sight round a corner, but I was confident that this was the glacier on which the Workmans had looked from the Sosbun and Hoh Lungma cols, and, moreover, that it joined the glacier we had seen the day before from the peak. We stood on a narrow gap between two frowning rock walls. On our right only 100 feet of smooth rock separated us from a negotiable slope of snow below, but we could not climb down, nor was there anchorage for an abseil, even if we had sufficient rope. On the left a narrow corridor of snow dropped steeply to end in a snow wall above an ice-fall, but after studying the wall for some time we detected a break in its defences. Some grass which we could see just above the corner drew us like a loadstone; we felt that the Cornice glacier was as good as reached, and that the ice-fall must be difficult indeed to stop us.

While we were walking back to camp, a white, filmy look in the sky indicated the end of another fine spell. Dawn of the 23rd was thick and snow was falling lightly. We packed up and hurried down the glacier, having some difficulty in locating our col in the gathering mist. The fractured ice above groaned ominously as we panted up the ice debris, sweating profusely with the fear of its falling and with the haste we made to get clear before it did. The sweat fogged our glasses so that we stopped often to wipe them, and though this made us realize the foolishness of hurrying, yet it was difficult to move slowly under the threats of immediate extinction from above. That day the narrow gap was a forbidding spot. Mist drove across it and swirled about the great, gaunt cliffs which lowered blackly at us as though grudging our passage. We built a cairn before descending into the mists, and by midday we were looking back at it from the Cornice glacier. I had tried to impress upon the Sherpas the peculiarities of this glacier – that no river issued from it – that presently we should come to a blank wall and find ourselves entirely shut in by mountains. They listened politely but incredulously, evidently entertaining more respect for my imagination than my veracity. Their belief in the strange behaviour of the glacier was no greater than mine in the man-eating propensities of the Yeti.

As we rounded the first corner, the mist turned to rain, and we pressed on in search of the wood that we were confident we should soon find. On the abrupt cliffs of the north side – the south-facing wall – grass grew wherever it could cling, and presently we camped in a little meadow, lying at the foot of a crag, where there were flowers, birds, the hum of insects, and much spoor of bharal; all commonplace things, but giving unbounded pleasure to us after five long weeks of glacier travel. Down the valley a high ridge, seen dimly through the rain, appeared to block the way, but if I ever had indulged any hopes that the glacier might outrage natural laws, the rapidity of its fall dispelled them. Nevertheless our situation was not without charm. We could sing that night as we used to sing in France, trundling across country in a troop train to some unknown destination: "We don't know where we're going, but we're on the way".

After our usual breakfast of tea and satu, eaten by a less usual wood fire, we continued down the north bank, our direction lying slightly north of west. To our starved senses the vegetation seemed tropically lush; in the moraine trough were rose bushes, and juniper, while long grass covered the hillside to a height of several hundred feet. Traces of bear and buck abounded. Five or six miles from our pass we came to a slightly bigger glacier flowing south-west, and in the corner between the two glaciers was an old unused grazing camp, a sight which greatly excited us, as traces of human life in wild country always did. We crossed the mile-wide glacier, finding on the far side a path and recent signs of cattle. I was sure that this was the glacier we saw from the peak, but to make certain I went up it for a mile. The vegetation here was equally profuse. On the hillside grassy bays ran up for 500 feet above the ice, and there were even a few birch trees growing within two or three miles of the Hispar watershed. I reached a point far enough up to see the peak on which we had failed, but the short glacier which must lie below it on the south was still hidden.

After I rejoined the Sherpas we followed down the right bank, passing great logs of juniper which made me long to camp and start a fire. After a fortnight without wood, I felt quite guilty at passing all this fuel without adding some to our loads, forgetting that we were going down the glacier and not up. Two miles on we reached the snout of the glacier and a grazing village of tumble-down stone huts. Conversation with the inhabitants was not easy, but we managed to get a few eggs and learnt that the village from which the shepherds came was Bisil in the main Basha valley. We could now identify the nullah we were in as that marked on the map as the Kushuchun Lungma. It is difficult to understand how the Workmans failed to suspect some connection between the large stream issuing from this nullah and their Cornice glacier, when they affirmed so positively that it had no outlet. In a drab world it would be refreshing to report the discovery of a glacier flowing uphill, or even of one which did not flow at all. It gives me no pleasure, therefore, to have to affirm that this glacier behaved as others do. To many – scholmasters and parents, editors and politicians, for instance – correcting the mistakes of others is a congenial task. As it is more usual for me to give than to receive opportunities for performing this pleasant duty, I ought to have rejoiced, but I can honestly say that to tramp down the Cornice glacier, hoping every moment to reach an impasse and finding none, was as sorry a business as any that has fallen to my lot.

The path down the nullah was rough, and having crossed the river by a snow bed, we began casting about for a camp site still some miles short of the main valley. One promising site had to be abandoned because the sparkling spring which first attracted us proved to be impregnated with sulphur.

Early next morning we dropped down to Bisil, but before reaching the village we stopped to admire a beautiful, pointed snow peak to the south-east which I identified on the map, wrongly as it happened, as Ganchen (21,100 feet). From that distance it looked climbable, as most peaks do, and I set my heart on it. From the village itself two more snow peaks on the same ridge, but farther north, came into view. The northernmost appeared to be the highest of the three and was called Ganchen by the men of Bisil. Later, viewing the range from the opposite side, I thought the second peak the higher – which agreed with the Workmans, who had named that Ganchen.

There can be no more delightful village at which to arrive after four months in uninhabited wilderness than Bisil. Yellowing wheat fields, pale pink buckwheat, shady walnuts and stately poplars gladdened my eyes, and in the centre of the village a stone tank fed by a bubbling hot sulphur spring waited to refresh my body. Though I was watched by the whole astonished populace, man, woman, and child, I lost no time in undressing, but before I was ready to leap into this heavenly tank a curious conversation took place between the Sherpas and the village headman. "How many are there in your party?" the headman asked. "We porters and a Sahib." "Yes, I see, but" (looking hard at me) "where is the Sahib?" This pleased the Sherpas immensely, and I kept the thing going by assuring the headman that the Sahib was a bit tired but would arrive shortly.

Flour, eggs and potatoes were forthcoming, also some apples, which, though watery, woolly, and everything an apple should not be, tasted to me, at that moment, like a Cox's. The Basha valley with its pleasant villages was a scene of peace, made beautiful by the changing greens and yellows of the ripening crops. We were, of course, the subject of much curiosity because no one could understand by what route we had come.

Six miles down, at a village called Zil, we struck up the hillside to the left in the direction of our peak. The elevation of the valley is only about 9,000 feet, so there was clearly some stiff climbing in front of us to get within striking distance of a 21,000-foot peak rising so close to the valley; nor would it be easy, now that we were so close underneath it, to find the best line of approach. When we had climbed high enough to dislike the idea of turning back, we discovered that the nullah we were making for was closed at its head by a high rock ridge, apparently cutting us off from the peak. Above us was a grazing village, to which we climbed disconsolately, and there we camped. What our next move should be I had no notion, but at any rate the hundreds of cows, yaks, goats, and sheep grazing on the hillside assured us of a drink of milk. We got our milk and with it some information, the locals assuring us that the forbidding rock curtain at the nullah head could be climbed easily. They had no name for the fine peak close above, radiantly lit by the last rays of the setting sun, though it surely must have impressed itself upon their imaginations, if they had any. They had never heard of Ganchen, but paradoxically, the man who did all the talking, knew all the principal cities of India.

In the morning, leaving Sen Tensing to guard our few possessions, Ila and I set out to reconnoitre. After a climb of about 3,000 feet we reached the foot of the rock ridge and found it scored with a number of easy gullies invisible from below. Having selected one of these we had no difficulty in reaching the top, some 4,000 feet above camp. Only a few hundred feet below, on the other side, was the meeting-place of two small glaciers descending from our pointed peak and from the next peak to the north, Ganchen of the map. There was a high, but apparently possible col on the ridge south of Ganchen, but neither peak could be climbed either from there or from the glaciers. Descending 1,000 feet and climbing another gully, we looked into a nullah on the south. From there, too, our peak was inaccessible, so I decided to curb ambition and try the col. We had to get back to Askole, but to go round by the valley was dull, whereas if we crossed this Ganchen range we should find ourselves in the Hoh Lungma valley, whence we could climb one of the Workmans' cols and thus make sure that the glacier they saw was the same as that which we had traversed. The possibility that somehow we had mislaid the Cornice glacier had just occurred to me, so I determined to make sure. Opponents of the "enclosed glacier" school, of which, as I have said, I was a warm supporter, would no doubt have derided me for clutching thus at straws.

Sitting perched on the ridge in warm sunshine, debating these matters of high policy, we saw an old grey-bearded ibex stroll unsuspectingly beneath us within spitting distance. Ila, of course, wanted to hurl a volley of stones; any moving animal, whether ten or a hundred yards away, seems to excite the stone-throwing proclivities of the Sherpas.

We got back about 4 p.m., to find the village unoccupied except for one old man and a boy. I feared that the Foreign Sportsman had somehow been the cause of this wholesale exodus, but was relieved to find they had merely gone down to the valley to work in the fields for the day. They returned at dusk and all gathered round our fire; with them was the much-travelled ex-bearer who had already entertained us with his travels from Bombay to Rangoon. The subject he unfailingly returned to was his last master, whom he called a "bhot-baksheesh-deni-wallah sahib", which is to say, a very open-handed gent. The hint, however, was not taken, and I gave him no opportunities for invidious comparisons. Like the headman of Bisil, he, too, on first seeing us, had asked where the Sahib was, but in this case the mistake was more reasonable, because it is conceivable that the sahibs he saw in Bombay, Calcutta and Rangoon were less shaggy and better dressed than I was.

On one or two occasions earlier in the year Shipton and I had almost come to the conclusion, directly contrary to that of the text-books, that time spent in reconnaissance is always wasted, but if you do choose to waste (or save) time by reconnoitring a route it is not at all a bad plan to follow it. However, Ila and I thought better and decided that by crossing the ridge, which divided us from the glaciers, much farther north we should save ourselves some steep climbing. So next day we traversed gently upwards for a mile and a half, gained the ridge at a reasonable height, and then looked down a most unmanageable drop, which, had we attempted it, would have brought us into the nullah at a point several thousand feet below the glacier we were trying to reach. Comment was unnecessary, even inadvisable. Sorrowfully retracing our steps to the gully of yesterday, we toiled up it with our heavy loads, dropped down the other side, and camped on grass just above the glacier descending from the pointed peak. It was a pleasant camp, with fresh water, enough wood for cooking, and a great view, comprising most of the Hispar peaks including Kanjut (25,460 feet) and one which might have been Dasto Ghil (25,868 feet)*. From the ridge above camp we had seen in the far distance the huge white mass of Nanga Parbat.

Next day, the 25th, we started for the col, fully laden. Quickly crossing the first glacier, we reached the other descending from the south slopes of Ganchen and our col. The surface was bare ice, and in spite of the gentle slope, the Sherpas had difficulty in standing. Arriving at the foot of the long and steeper rise to the col, we halted to take stock. The route seemed easy, the angle perhaps 30 degrees, but it was either bare of snow or thinly coated with what had once been snow but was now turned to slush by the midday sun. At first it was not bad and I hoped that we should be able to keep our feet without cutting steps, but when deeply committed, with the angle gradually steepening, I began to realize that we should have to cut the whole way. On the easy slopes near the bottom the Sherpas disdained a rope until the Foreign Sportsman slipped and slid down pretty violently for some way before coming to rest on a shelf just above a crevasse. The Sherpas were not happy on the ice, nor was I. Their boots had few nails left in them and mine even less. On my left boot only the inner sole remained.

Only the Foreign Sportsman's dignity was hurt. We gathered him up and his

* This peak is now called Disteghil Sar. *Editor*

belongings, put on the rope and climbed slowly on through an ice-fall, cutting steps the whole time. Twice we had to haul the loads after us, up steep ice-pitches, but about 3 a.m., when my arms were rather tired, the slope eased off, enabling us to rest and have some food. Still hoping to reach the col, we carried on until 6 p.m., when we camped; the col looked close enough, but we were the best part of 1,000 feet below it.

Prolonged step-cutting with a load is very chastening, so next morning I decided to go up to the col for a look before taking the camp up. We had to cut nearly all the way, and at last when we stuck our heads over the top at 9 a.m. a glance showed us that it was hopeless to try to get down the other side. A very remarkable view slightly tempered this keen disappointment, for it is not often possible to see two such mountains as K2 and Nanga Parbat at the same time. All the Baltoro giants were there, the Ogre too, the Chogo Lungma glacier, and the peaks of the Hispar. Immediately below, a glacier led north-east to the Hoh Lungma, whose wide valley we could plainly see.

On returning to camp we began looking for another way down; none of us much liked the look of the ascent. After some search, we concluded that the only alternative was a rather sketchy route by some rock on the south side of the ice-fall; we decided to try it. Before packing up we made another journey to the col to take a photograph, as I had stupidly left my camera behind the first time. The Sherpas philosophically accepted the double journey imposed by my carelessness.

Our new route began well. There was not much step-cutting and the rocks were easy, but below the half-way mark it was less accommodating. I was inspecting a gully, so loose that I devoutly hoped we should not have to use it, when I brought down a rock which nearly pinned me by the leg. On beating a hasty but cautious retreat, the Foreign Sportsman, who was supposed to be safeguarding me from above, let loose a small avalanche of rocks, one of which caught in the rope and almost dragged me off. However, he managed to support the rock from his end while I feverishly untied and severed my connection with this new and unwelcome addition to the party. Finally, we avoided the gully by an abseil and the rest was easy.

This repulse only made me the more determined to get over this ridge between us and the Hoh Lungma, and to spend a month over it rather than go tamely round by the valley. I decided to go back up the Basha valley to Bisil and then to strike up one of the nullahs there. This move would bring us on to the range near Ganchen, so that besides searching for a pass we could have a look at the peak.

Our camp was in a nullah leading directly down to the village of Zil, but we took an unconscionable time reaching it next morning. We spent several hours locked in a fierce struggle with some stubborn bush which was so thick that we could not even fall through it, though it grew on a steep slope. At Zil we had some food, but the difficulty was water, for although irrigation channels led everywhere, they were full of silt and useless for drinking. Fruit was the best substitute, so the Foreign Sportsman went off to buy apricots, and presently returned in triumph with a hatful on which he had squandered half an anna. I thought they were dear at that price because they were all green, and the

Sherpas had my share as well. The villages through which we had passed a few days ago made no attempt to conceal their astonishment at our return. We had come from nowhere and were now on the way back; perhaps they thought us disembodied spirits doomed to perambulate the Basha valley, like the Flying Dutchman, to the end of time.

Every nullah we passed was examined briefly and discarded. To select the right one, with so many to choose from was a difficult problem; we could not see far up any of them, and the locals seemed to know as little about them as ourselves. It was another brilliant day; every day had been fine since the rain on the Cornice glacier; the heat in the bottom of the deep valley was tropical. We passed many streams, but all were the colour and consistency of Turkish coffee.

We camped a mile short of Bisil, near a small village which provided eggs and a few potatoes, and the next day I sent the Foreign Sportsman to Bisil to see what he could get. The Sherpas were "tough" that night and slept out, or perhaps they found the tent too stuffy even for them. Except for the night on snow I had been sleeping out since leaving the Cornice glacier, partly because I enjoyed it and partly because of the Foreign Sportsman. He is not a good sleeping companion – singing far into the night is his least offensive habit. The previous night, although I was lying some distance from the tent, I had to ask him to sing under his breath.

The whole of next morning was occupied playing "Sister Anne", Ila and I taking the name-part alternatively, but at 1 p.m. the Foreign Sportsman returned from Bisil where he had spent the morning and three rupees. For this we got 15 lbs. of flour, 2 lbs. of potatoes, two dozen eggs, an ounce or two of salt, and (displayed with pride) a hatful of green apples. The waste of time was even more annoying than this ineradicable preference for unripe fruit, and we began to rush violently up a steep path under a grilling sun in a mood even sourer than apples.

In the course of a couple of hours the path took us to a grazing alp, but above it ended in a gully. A trickle of water, coming down, encouraged us to climb until at length the trickle ceased, darkness came on, and we camped at the spot where the water failed, on the steep, rocky bank of the gully. It was an unaccommodating site and we had to dig three separate shelves for ourselves and one for the fire. The Foreign Sportsman atoned for his morning's work by digging a particularly large and luxurious grave for me.

The path had vanished completely, and this was the more astonishing because last evening I had seen a few cows grazing high above this point. I stuck to the gully while the Sherpas chased an ephemeral path which took them into a nullah blocked at the top by the high, smooth snout of a glacier. They were forced to rejoin me, and another 1,500 feet of climbing brought us out on to the glacier well above the snout. South-east were the two big snow peaks; the northernmost called Hikmul by the Workmans, and the other Ganchen. Straight ahead to the east was another glacier descending from a col on the ridge of Hikmul, which looked as if it might "go". Crossing the first glacier we came suddenly to a steep drop of seven or eight hundred feet, at the bottom of which flowed yet another glacier from the western slopes of Hikmul. These two glaciers joined. It is annoying to lose height during an ascent, but there was no help for it, so down we went and camped on moraine by a small lake. A dull, cold afternoon presaged the end of one more fine spell.

The only flour we had left now was the 15 lbs. bought at Bisil, so I reduced our flour ration from 2 lbs. to 1 lb. per man, to make it last five days. In addition we ate 1 lb. of pemmican daily between the three of us, and a little satu.

On the following day, September 2nd, we went up to look at the col. There was a fairly straightforward route on bare ice most of the way, and the short slope to the col was of good, hard snow. As we were beginning to discover, this was rare so late in the season, for most of the slopes were of bare ice. My first glance down the other side to a tributary glacier of the Hoh Lungma was not reassuring, and a more leisurely inspection confirmed the view that it was an exceedingly nasty place. A steep and very loose gully led to a snow-slope which ended in a gaping bergschrund. The upper lip of the schrund was an ice cliff which could be seen only imperfectly, but it was clear that to overcome the difficulty we should have to employ roping-down tactics. Such methods usually take a long time, and in this case would have to be carried out while exposed to rock-falls which the gully apparently dispensed with some prodigality, for the snow-slope below was littered with dirt and stones. The judgment of the Sherpas does not usually err on the side of rashness, but in this case I think they failed to see the bergschrund, the ice cliff, and all that it implied, because they seemed as keen to try this interesting route as I was loath to risk it.

Farther north was another glacier tributary of the Hoh Lungma; the two were separated by a narrow ridge, so we retreated from the col and moved round the low glacier cirque to the north. From here we climbed to another col, cutting huge bucket steps hopefully on the way, in the belief that we should want them next day. The descent to the northerly glacier looked more practicable, but at the top was a difficult bit of ice-glazed rock, on which I spent some time preparing it for the morrow. The glacier below led north-east and joined the Hoh Lungma much farther north than the other, a point which was rather to our advantage if we wanted to reach the head of that glacier. The thoughts of the Foreign Sportsman, however, were directed more to the lower end of the glacier and the valley, and he suggested that much time would be saved if, having got down, we then crossed the narrow dividing ridge back to the glacier we had first seen. It was difficult to treat this suggestion kindly because, apart from the fact that we were not going home yet, the ridge in question was the sort of place one climbs only in nightmares.

We were back in camp by 1 p.m., so after some food the Foreign Sportsman and I went up the glacier which flowed beneath the western slopes of Hikmul. This peak I had inspected closely, deciding that it was not for such a weak party as ours. At the head of the glacier, however, a low col seemed to give access to the slightly easier Ganchen. A trudge of two miles up the glacier brought us to the col only to find a sheer drop of several hundred feet cutting us off effectually from the peak. As, from the col, Hikmul looked even less inviting, I decided to cross to the Hoh Lungma without further delay.

We started early on September 3rd in mist and snow. Snow had fallen in the night, so that even the great bucket steps that I had cut on the approach to the col took some time to find. On top a bitter wind chilled the Sherpas, who waited patiently while I recut the steps down the bad bit to a rock rib. Having rejoined them on top, I lowered them down and then the loads. We then picked a careful way down 700 feet of loose snow-covered rock, crossed a bergschrund by an ice bridge, and, without a pause, hurried down a much crevassed glacier to its junction with the Hoh Lungma which we reached about noon.

Relying on the old map, I had assumed, perhaps unwarrantably, that we were on the Evi Gans glacier, and was prepared for a walk of some eight miles up the Hoh Lungma before reaching the col at its head, from which the Workmans had looked down upon the Cornice glacier. But to my great surprise, on turning the corner, we found that the Hoh Lungma ended in a pinnacled rock cirque a bare half-mile from where we stood. Two miles farther down it was joined by a big glacier from the east, and thinking that this was the Hoh Lungma and that the short, wide arm on which we stood had been ignored by the map-makers, we went down to it. Proceeding up this glacier, which began to trend north, we camped on the bend.

Whether we were on the Hoh Lungma or Sosbun glacier, the map led me to expect a march of seven or eight miles to reach the head. Allowing a day to get up, another day to climb the col and return, on the third day we must make with all speed for the nearest village because our remaining two days' food would then be finished.

Starting next day with a one-night camp and reconciled to a day of glacier travel, we had not gone more than two miles before it became evident that the head of the glacier was not far away, for a mile farther on there was a sharp bend to the north-east, after which it ended abruptly in an unpromising rock wall crowned with jagged towers. There seemed to be little hope of climbing this wall, but leaving our loads we pressed on, and as we advanced the head of the glacier gradually opened up, revealing a low snow col on the extreme right of the rock wall. We had still about two miles to cover, but the glacier (which I still thought was the Hoh Lungma) was a gentlemanly one with neither crevasses nor streams to hinder us.

We soon reached the foot of the col, now about 500 feet above us, and began climbing the slope which, though not very steep, was icy. A third of the way up was a wide and deep bergschrund, fortunately bridged, whence we cut diagonally to the left. Fully conscious of this yawning receptacle below, and of the Foreign Sportsman's carefree methods, I cut the steps very big and safe. It took a long time, but at length the final step was cut, the few feet of rock wall crowning the top scaled, and we were gazing at a most unexpected sight. At the bottom of a 2,000-foot cliff, so sheer that we could drop a stone on to it, lay the head of the Cornice glacier, and across the void, barely a mile away, was the col which we had crossed from the Biafo a fortnight ago. I had expected to look on to the Cornice glacier, but from a point very much farther west. The explanation was, of course, that the glacier we had ascended was the Sosbun and not the Hoh Lungma. Anyhow, from one point of view it was a very satisfying conclusion, and that very startling topographical phenomenon, an entirely enclosed glacier, had gone the way of the Lost City of Atlantis and the Loch Ness Monster.

We descended, picked up our loads, and returned to camp. With the unexpected saving of this day the food situation was easier, so we indulged in a mild orgy of chapattis.

Starting at 6 a.m. on September 5th, we crossed back to the right bank of what we now knew was the Hoh Lungma. The crossing of a glacier sounds very easy on paper, but in the Himalaya it is not to be undertaken lightly. The opposite side of a glacier always looks easier than the side one is negotiating, and though it looks close it seldom takes less than an hour to reach – an hour miserably spent climbing out of one hollow in order to get into another. Four miles down, we had to cross the combined glaciers descending from the Ganchen group, and on the moraine, on the far side, we met a shepherd with a dog looking for three lost sheep. He was neither startled nor curious, but promptly asked us for "baksheesh". We might have been lifelong residents of the Hoh Lungma. It was gratifying to be recognized as a sahib, but it was disappointing to find the hardy hillman differing so little from men of the plains and the city.

In the course of the afternoon we reached the first village, Chokpiong, where we had camped on the way up in May. It was, I remembered, remarkable for a toothless but vociferous lambadar,[1] an unusual number of cretins who gibbered at us, horrible goitres, and dirt. They were all still there, and next morning I was not sorry to see the last of Chokpiong and the sad numbers of goitrous, eye-infected morons. The principal idiot sat by our fire half the night mowing at us, and was the first of a long string of similar admirers who visited us before we were up.

From here to Askole the way is long, tedious, and difficult; the difficulties centred in the two rope bridges by which we crossed and recrossed the Braldu river. On the march up, these bridges were avoided by a short rock traverse along the north bank, but now the river was too high to permit this, and the bridges had to be faced. The first of these was the less trying of the two because it was well made, and we had the assistance of a local man who crossed backwards facing us, partly, I suppose, to give us something slightly less frightening to look at than the river, and also to spread the handrails when necessary. These bridges are merely three thick fibre ropes; the centre one, which is for the feet, hangs a little below the two handrails. At the anchorage at either end these three ropes are wide apart and on the same level, but farther out the foot-rope hangs at a more or less convenient distance below the other two, which are then close together and have to be kept apart with two sticks. Even so they are much too close to be comfortable for a man carrying a load. The whole bridge sags so badly that there is a steep hill at each end. Every few feet the three cables are secured in their relative positions by a connecting rope, and fifty feet below the flimsy structure the dirty grey waters of the river roar through the ravine with a cold fury horrible to contemplate.

To watch a Balti on one of these bridges is a lesson in confidence. He rests his hands lightly on the handrails and walks boldly and quickly across. Not so the novice, who clutches frantically at everything within reach and fearfully shuffles each foot forward a few inches at a time. It would be less trying if one could get a real "Thank God" hold of the handrails, but these miserable things,

[1]Lambadar – the officially appointed head man of a village.

while not thick enough to inspire confidence, are far too thick to grip properly, so that if a foot did slip off, one would not have a dog's chance. I was surprised to find that the Sherpas liked these atrocities as little as I did, for I imagined they must have used them in their own country. They assured me that this was their first experience, and, watching the Foreign Sportsman, I thought at times that it was going to be his last. His caution was almost excessive. He attended to the placing of each hand and foot as though climbing very difficult rock, and by the time he got over, his face was a pale saffron.

The second bridge was much worse, because it had a permanent cant sideways as well as a very deep sag, nor had we any Balti to encourage us. The most ticklish part, the "mauvais pas", is where you have to get over the stick which keeps the handrails apart. The stick is, of course, at the same height as the rail, which means that you have to balance on one leg, hoist the other high enough to clear the stick, and then bring the first after it. This manoeuvre is performed twice.

But this was our last adventure, and from Askole we returned to Skardu by a shorter route over the Skoro La, which was now open, and, journeying across the Deosai Plains, we reached Srinagar at the end of September.

CHAPTER SEVENTEEN

Which Way Out?

WHILE Tilman and Auden were starting on their interesting journeys, connecting up the mountain ranges surrounding the Crevasse glacier with the partly explored, though very little known, country to the south of the main watershed, Spender and I were continuing to reap the benefit of the abundant supplies that we had brought so laboriously from our Sarpo Laggo base. Three fine days of intensive work enabled Spender to complete the survey of the upper Crevasse glacier, and to fix the position of remote ranges on the Panmah-Biafo-Braldu watersheds. I had intended to employ the time by climbing some of the peaks on the main divide, but I found the survey so absorbing that I escorted Spender to his stations to help him to reach them and to give him what assistance I could in the survey work. It was enthralling to disentangle the geography of the region, to arrange the peaks and valleys and glaciers in their true perspective, and gradually to learn to know them with an intimacy and understanding that, for me, is the basic reason for mountaineering.

Again we were lucky with the weather, for it kept fine until this part of the survey was finished. Angtharkay's party had worked hard, and when we got back to the Second Divide we found that they had relayed nearly all the loads to a dump at the foot of a side glacier leading to Spender's pass. We ascended the "Father Christmas glacier" in a blizzard, and by the evening of August 15th everything was in readiness at that dump.

The head of the "Father Christmas glacier" was enclosed by precipitous peaks, and there seemed to be no possibility of forcing a route across them. But a narrow tributary glacier, flowing in from the north, offered the unexpected line of escape that Spender had discovered. His reconnaissance had made it possible for us to reach the col in bad weather, and on August 16th, in spite of wind and snow, we carried the first batch of loads up to it. We made a dump on top of the pass, and looked for a moment into the ravine where we hoped to find a route, but we were driven back by a bitter gale.

I felt rather like a schoolboy, at last beginning a holiday full of exciting possibilities which had first begun to take shape months before, but which, as the term dragged on with maddening slowness, had receded to an unattainable but infinitely enticing dream. The Shimshal pass, the people of the lower Braldu valley, and the unknown ranges that surrounded it, had been discussed by us for so long, that it seemed impossible that we should ever get there. Now at last we were on the threshold of this region, ready to cross its passes and to grope our way through its unmapped valleys.

August 17th was another day of bad weather. We trudged up the side glacier again, carrying the remainder of the loads. Though in fact we made much better time than on the previous day, we seemed to be going irritatingly slowly. It was extremely cold on the pass, and the visibility was poor. On the other side of the pass, we found a fairly steep slope of soft, deep snow. At the bottom, this slope ran into a flat snow plateau which extended for several hundred yards before the glacier entered a steep gorge. We hurled all the loads recklessly over the edge and slid down the slope after them. We then tried dragging the loads behind us, but the snow was too deep and soon we had to abandon this method. We had intended to take half the loads down to a suitable camping-place, and to return the following day for the rest; but the Sherpas disliked the prospect of struggling back uphill through the deep snow as much as we did, and after much rearrangement we managed to take the whole lot. The Sherpas were then carrying *over 130 lbs. each*.

Lower down, the glacier became very badly crevassed. A thick covering of new snow made it exceedingly difficult to detect the crevasses. My adventure of a fortnight before had made me very cautious, particularly as it would have been extremely dangerous if one of the Sherpas had fallen when carrying such a tremendous load. I prodded the snow in front of me with my ice-axe at every step; my slow progress was very tiresome for the Sherpas, for it was almost as difficult for them to stand still as to walk forward, being so heavily laden. At length we reached a place where the glacier plunged down for nearly 1,000 feet over a sheer ice-fall. We camped on moraine just above this point.

In the evening the heavy mists cleared from below and we went to the brink of the ice-fall to reconnoitre. We soon saw that it was impossible to climb down the chaos of contorted ice cliffs that fell in a sheer precipice, gashed by a network of black fissures. But fortunately a slender gully, which contrived somehow to run unbroken between the glacier and the sheer crags which bounded it on the right, offered us a heaven-sent way out of the difficulty. Below the ice-fall, the glacier was joined by another in a confusion of pinnacles. Below the junction, the ice-stream ran in a north-westerly direction, and to our amazement, seemed to end about three miles farther down. Below this, we had a thrilling glimpse of grass and bushes. But we were worried about the direction of the lower valley. At first it seemed that it swung round in a right-angled bend to the north-east. This was not at all to our liking, for, although we still had three weeks' food, the country was difficult and we could not afford to be led far out of our course.

Though, next morning, the sky was overcast, there were signs that it might clear. So, while a relay of loads was being carried down the gully, Spender, Angtensing and I climbed a peak lying to the east. Bad snow conditions made the climb laborious and dangerous, but we reached the summit (19,000 feet) at half-past nine. The weather had become beautifully fine and windless, so that we got a clear view of our immediate surroundings, and Spender worked for nearly two hours with his plane-table. We saw, to our relief, that we were mistaken about the valley below us, and that, below the snout of the glacier, it continued to run in a north-westerly direction. We saw the whole of the glacier that joined our glacier from the east; but the country beyond to the north and east, was terribly complicated, and we decided to go up this glacier to spend a short time exploring in that direction. This decision required considerable resolution, for we were very impatient to find out where our valley would eventually lead; and the green grass and bushes that we had seen lured us to lower altitudes.

When we returned to camp, we found that the Sherpas were already back. The gully had not belied its promise and had taken them quickly and safely down past the twisted cliffs of the ice-fall. We packed up and started down immediately. At the junction of the two glaciers we made a dump, and then, taking with us sufficient for a light camp, we started up the valley to the east in the late afternoon. For nearly two hours we worked up badly crevassed ice which threatened to stop us, but after that things became easier and we were able to camp as far up the glacier as we wished. It was a beautiful, peaceful evening, and from where we lay we could see for many miles down the valley to a far-off range of placid rounded mountains which were a restful contrast to the rugged country piled around us. Spender called the highest of these the Jökul, which is the word used for the ice-capped volcanic cones of Iceland.

It was a bitterly cold night, followed by an even colder dawn. We struggled petulantly with the leathery chapattis that were provided for breakfast and with our boots that were frozen in impossible shapes, and started with Nukku and Lhakpa Tensing, at 6.30. I had a severe stomach ache which was not improved by the biting wind which blew down the glacier. I climbed in a doubled-up posture until we got into the sun. With the warmth my belly ceased to ache and I was able to climb upright and enjoy the brilliant morning.

The slope was easy and we climbed as fast as we could, racing against the clouds that we imagined would soon blot out the view. Four thousand feet above the camp, at an altitude of more than 20,000 feet, we reached a sharp ridge, surmounted by a heavy cornice that overhung a tremendous precipice to the north. We cut an aperture in the cornice and set up the plane-table on a precarious rock platform. Spender and I trod delicately between the legs of the tripod, trying not to disturb its balance nor lose our own, while Lhakpa Tensing held the umbrella above the instruments, and Nukku sat below holding the ropes attached to each of us, like a showman controlling the antics of a group of marionettes. I should explain that the umbrella, peculiar though it may look on a mountain, is a necessary adjunct to the survey equipment. Spender used a neat lady's parasol with an elegant blue ribbon loop, that he had obtained from Messrs. Marks & Spencer for 3s. 11d. It looked somewhat incongruous held by a grimy hand, shading a bearded, sun-scorched face.

From this high station we looked down on to the head of the Crown glacier, and were able to disentangle much of the country towards the Shaksgam river. But it was the distant views that compelled our attention. Many of the peaks that we had been amongst a month earlier, including K2, The Crown and "The Fangs", were to be seen. To the west, the great peaks of the Kanjut range and Dasto Ghil, provided us with new food for discussion, and a fresh vision of the incredible size and majesty of the Karakorams. North-west of us were the snow domes of the Shimshal mountains, and beyond them stretched range after range into the blue distance of Kashgar and the Hindu Kush. The wind of the early morning had died and, when the work was finished, we sat for some hours trying to understand this limitless tangle of country. Then we plunged down at a thrilling speed over snow and scree to the camp.

Angtharkay's culinary genius had produced a lunch of sandwiches of toasted cheese-rind and curry powder between large soggy chapattis. While we were munching these the camp was packed up, and we then ran down the glacier in high spirits. Most of the new snow had melted from the ice, which simplified the passage of the crevassed section. We picked up more loads at the dump and camped a mile down the lower glacier, in a narrow rocky passage which ran for several miles like a street between high walls of ice. The crystal turrets glowed with the soft colours reflected from the evening sky, and after dusk shone like silver in the brilliance of a full moon.

The next day, August 20th, we reached grass and flowers and wood-fuel, and camped on "dry land" for the first time after a month of glacier travel. This seemed to mark a further stage in the complex experience of this slow journey.

Four Sherpas went back to the dump on August 21st to fetch the remainder of the loads. Spender spent the day surveying high up on the valley sides, while Angtharkay and I went in search of game. My stupidity in spurning some animals with poor heads lost us an opportunity that never recurred, of securing plentiful meat. But it was a day full of the delicious freedom of movement that had been denied us during our sojourn on the glaciers. In the evening we succeeded in shooting a couple of snow-cock. With a rifle it is necessary to stalk these creatures and to shoot them sitting. This method might not meet with approval in some circles, but it provided us with a memorable meal.

The next day we managed to shift all the loads at once, though some of the Sherpas had to carry over a hundred pounds each. We tried to follow the course of the river, but soon it entered a narrow ravine and we were forced to leave it. Ancient river terraces, whose cliffs rose several thousand feet above the present river level, cut by side streams into grotesque canyons, caused us endless trouble, as they had done in the Aghil range. We were obliged to climb higher and higher in our search for a route, and before long we lost sight of the river. Although we were gradually evolving a technique for dealing with the obstacles presented by these conglomerate deposits, it was still a frightening business negotiating them with a heavily laden party. For two days we made lamentably little progress. At length the terraces became so broken that it was almost impossible to make any headway. We climbed down a long and difficult gully, and on the evening of August 23rd we camped on the shore of the river. The weather was bad during this time, and, as there had been no sun to melt the snow, the river was so reduced in volume that we found that we could make our way along the bottom of the gorge by wading through it. At eleven o'clock on August 24th we reached the end of the valley and walked out on to the wide gravel flats, which we at once recognized to be part of the Braldu valley. Immediately to the south was the great moraine-covered snout of the Braldu glacier, and we realized that the valley we had come down was the one mentioned by Colonel Schomberg in his book *Unknown Karakoram*, and called by him Wesm-i-Dur. At the junction of the two valleys we found the sheep-fold and huts that he had reported. They were in good repair. The Sherpas were in a great state of excitement and examined the buildings with a

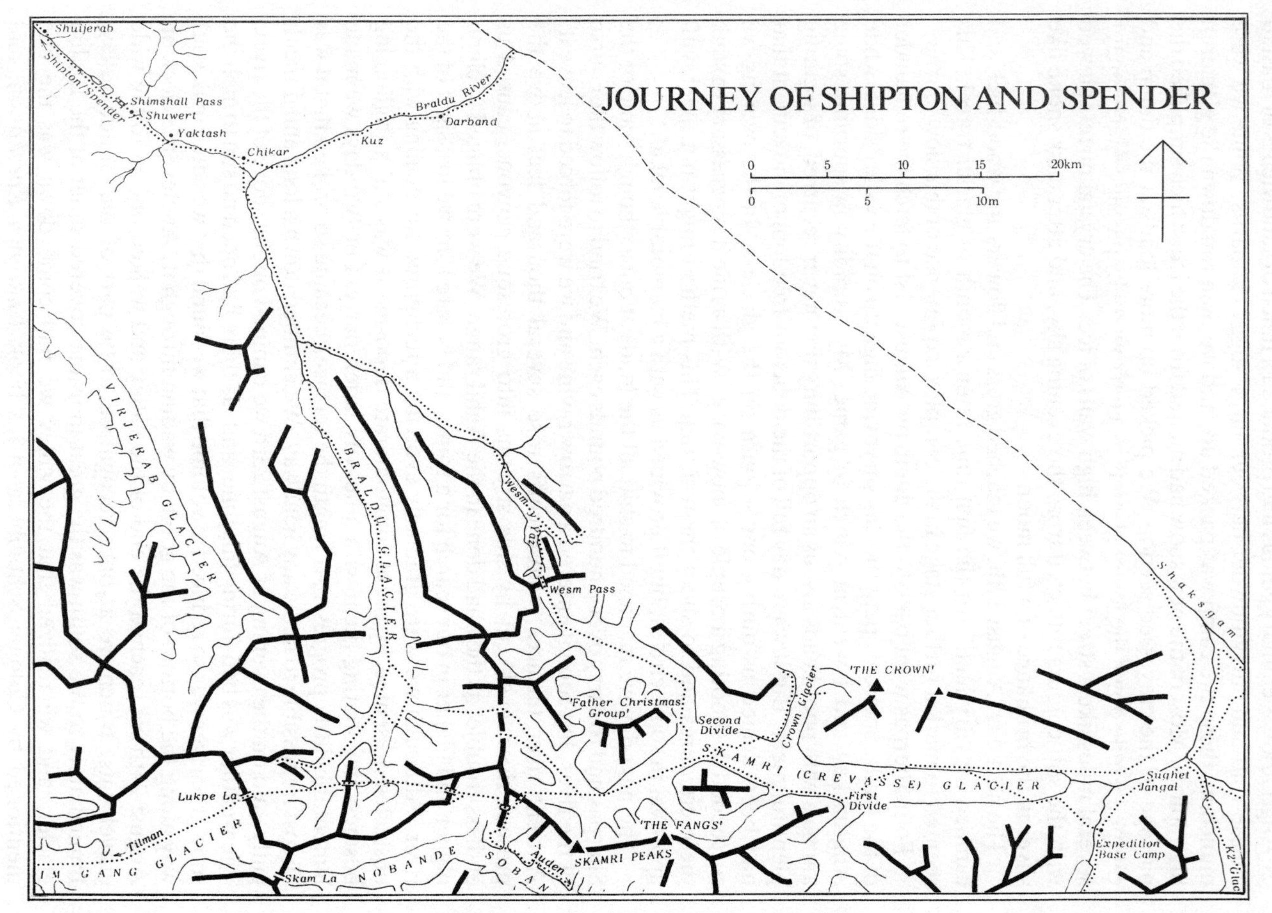

JOURNEY OF SHIPTON AND SPENDER
0 5 10 15 20km
0 5 10m
Shuijerab
Shipton/Spender
Shimshall Pass
Shuwert
Yaktash
Chikar
Kuz
Braldu River
Darband
VIRJERAB GLACIER
BRALDU GLACIER
Wesm-y-Yaz
Wesm Pass
Shaksgam
'THE CROWN'
Crown Glacier
'Father Christmas' Group'
Second Divide
SKAMRI (CREVASSE) GLACIER
First Divide
Sughet Jangal
Expedition Base Camp
K2 Glac
'THE FANGS'
SKAMRI PEAKS
Auden
Lukpe La
Tilman
IM GANG GLACIER
Skam La
NOBANDE SOBAN

professional interest to see whether there were signs of recent occupation.

I have often wondered exactly what the Sherpas think during these long journeys in uninhabited mountain ranges so far from their own homes. On earlier expeditions they often seemed worried, but now they accepted the situation with philosophical resignation, and displayed a touching confidence in our ability to find the way to inhabited country before the food ran out.

August 25th was an off-day. Spender, as usual, employed it in intensive survey work, while the Sherpas settled down to a long session of a strange game called Barachu. Always popular, this pastime had, during the last month, become an obsession, and every moment of the day, when the party was not actually on the march, there was a game in progress. It is a kind of Ludo, played with a pair of dice and a collection of stones and match-sticks. Though I have often played, I have never been able fully to understand the rules, which may be the reason why I have never won! The game requires a strong voice and a quick wit. The dice cup must be slammed down with as much force as possible, while the player either screams a cat-call or gabbles a mystic incantation, according to the state of the game. When the cup is lifted from the dice it is important to move the pieces before anyone has time to question the action. Little attention is paid to the actual fall of the dice.

We had enough food left to last us for another sixteen days, but there was still a great deal of work to be done. The most important job was the exploration and mapping of the Braldu glacier, which was the only great glacier in this part of the main Asiatic watershed that was still unexplored. In order to round off the survey, too, it was important that it should be carried right down the Braldu valley to join up with the lower Shaksgam river, and also up to the Shimshal pass, whose exact geographical position was still unknown. We had hoped that there would be time to go into the unknown ranges to the north-west. In fact, we would both gladly have spent the whole winter in these parts, but I had agreed to join the 1938 Everest expedition and had to get back before the passes to Kashmir were closed for the winter. Two minor considerations were the state of the party's boots, which were now practically useless, and the possibility of not being able to obtain fresh supplies of food. But without the other obligation these difficulties could doubtless have been overcome, and there was a very strong temptation to continue our life in this interesting country. However, we consoled ourselves with the reflection that we had at least learned to understand some of its problems, and that we might some day be privileged to return to use that knowledge.

We started up the Braldu glacier with food enough for eight days. If we were to finish the job we would have to travel with all possible speed, and to be blessed with a spell of fine weather. The lower part of the glacier was the usual wilderness of broken moraine-covered ice. On the way over this we passed a very remarkable ice arch, which must once have formed part of a tunnel cut by a glacier stream. In spite of the rough going we succeeded in covering six miles on August 26th, and camped that evening on a beautiful grassy alp on the western flank of the glacier, just below its pinnacled section.

Recent bharal spoor enticed Angtharkay and me into a hunt before breakfast the following morning, while Spender was plane-tabling. We found a place where a herd had spent the previous night. From there we tracked the animals for miles over difficult country, expecting each moment to find them feeding in a nullah. After four hours we discovered that a pack of six wild dogs was stalking the same herd. In the confusion that resulted the bharal escaped unharmed, and we returned to camp still breakfastless, and digusted at having wasted most of the morning.

We got into difficulties farther up the glacier, but in the middle of the afternoon we reached a corridor leading through the pinnacles for several miles, without interruption, so that by nightfall we found that we had covered another five miles, and were approaching the smooth ice of the upper part of the glacier. On August 28th we camped in the middle of the vast glacier basin into which Angtharkay and I had descended on August 3rd. We had come up the glacier a great deal more quickly than we had dared to hope.

During the next three days the weather was perfect, and we wasted none of our precious time. Angtharkay, Lhakpa and I reached a high saddle at the head of a branch glacier on the west. It was not situated on the main watershed as I had hoped, but from it we were able to climb a small peak (about 19,000 feet high) for a round of photographs and compass bearings. Again I was able to see the great peaks of the K2 range, and this time my view extended past the Mustagh Tower to Masherbrum and the pinnacles of the lower Baltoro glacier, whose acquaintance we had made in May. Conway's Ogre and its sculptured satellites were now close at hand, and, seen from this angle, they looked more than ever astonishing. But all this was of small interest compared with the fascinating newness of the world we were in.

While surveying on the glacier to the south, Spender saw, through his telescopic alidade, a large cairn. We sent two Sherpas to investigate this, and found that it had been built by Tilman's party to mark the site of one of their camps. There was a letter in it, telling us of their movements up till August 18th and of their discovery of a route to the Snow Lake.

The Braldu glacier proved to be a large ice-stream with a great number of branches in its upper part. The heads of some of these branches were twenty-two miles from the snout of the main glacier. The basin of the Braldu abuts on those of the Virjerab, Biafo, Nobande Sobande and Crevasse glaciers, and its bounding walls form a considerable part of the main Asiatic watershed. With the help of his survey of the head of the Crevasse glacier, and the fine weather, Spender succeeded in completing a detailed survey of this basin in the very short time that remained, but he had to work at high pressure to achieve this.

A forced march enabled us to reach the shepherd's huts below the snout of the Braldu glacier on the evening of September 1st, with our job done. On the way down Angtharkay had shot two snow-cock, a gratifying result of the rifle instruction that I had been giving him. A sumptuous dish of roast fowl and rice made a fitting feast of celebration at the end of a strenuous week of work and deep enjoyment.

We started down the following morning, making for a point, about six miles away, where the Braldu valley made a right-angled bend to the east and was joined by the stream coming down from the Shimshal pass which lay to the north-west. We were all in a state of suppressed excitement, as we expected, that very day to make contact with some sort of habitation. But for three miles Spender and I lost interest in this intriguing prospect, being absorbed in an argument about the ethics of Empire. The debate was only temporarily checked when my opponent fell head first into a muddy side stream.

The river which flowed down the valley was an alarming size, certainly a great deal bigger than the Shaksgam when we had last seen it. We were uncomfortably aware that in order to reach the nullah leading to the Shimshal pass we would be obliged to cross the Braldu river. Lower down, flowing over gravel flats nearly a mile wide, it broke up into five or six streams. I decided to attempt the crossing here, for it was still early, and later in the day, even if we found a better fording-place, the river would probably be greatly swollen. I started alone, and crossed the first stream fairly easily. But I failed to cross the second one direct and went a long way down before I could negotiate it. The third was a desperate struggle, and I emerged on the other side feeling very cold, humiliated and alone. The idea of going back was so unpleasant that I felt prepared to go to great lengths to get over the fourth stream.

A bitter wind started to blow down the valley bringing with it clouds of dust. I tested the next stream in several places by throwing boulders into it, but each time I heard the ominous dull sound produced by deep water. My better judgment prevailed at last and I turned to face the return journey. The third stream gave me a very bad time on the way back, as my numbed limbs were not easy to control. The mad, merciless rush of water, surging giddily round one, trying with ceaseless uneven thrusts to throw one over, is the most frightening thing I know. Near the side, I fell into a deep pocket, but fortunately it was in a slight back-water and I was able to scramble out. At length I got back to the rest of the party, having made a complete fool of myself.

When I had changed into dry clothes and restored life to my legs, we continued on our way. Just before the corner of the valley the river spread out, nearly covering the gravel flats. On the other side we could see trees and grass. We recognized this as the grazing ground marked Chikar on Schomberg's map. In spite of my lesson, we decided to try to cross the river again.

It was here that we evolved a simple but effective technique for crossing these rivers. One man is tied to the end of a long rope; the rest of the party anchor the rope at a point upstream, preferably above the outside of a bend. Leaning, if necessary, his full weight on the rope, the first man then advances through the water swinging pendulum-wise on the rope. Except for the last man, the rest of the party carrying the bulk of the loads have the safeguard of a rope stretched at right angles across the river, as well as the pendulum rope. The last man crosses in the same way as the first, though this time with the others holding him from a point farther up the opposite bank. The support of the pendulum rope enables one to withstand the force of the water to an astonishing extent.

In this way, we got across the streams without an accident, and reached a lovely oasis of willow thickets and meadows. We found a number of stone huts and signs of old cultivation. We were disappointed to find no evidence of recent occupation. But the sight of glades, the smell of growing things, and the song of many birds filled us with a great joy. The grass was gay with flowers, despite the lateness of the season. The most common and most lovely of these was a little blue flower, with a tall stalk, which closed its petals at dusk and when the weather became cold or stormy.

The evening and a huge wood fire brought peace, and we slept on luxurious beds of deep grass.

CHAPTER EIGHTEEN

Conversation Piece

I woke on September 3rd with a delicious sense of comfort and well-being, and, lying on my soft bed of grass, with the willow branches swaying above my head, lazily watched the dawn break over the storm-clouds which now filled the valley of the Braldu. It was a great temptation to indulge in this new luxury.

In spite of the unpromising weather, Spender decided to attempt the high station on the Jökul, which we had planned from above, and with a great effort we managed to get away at 7.15. Angtharkay and I took the rifle with us in the hope of being able to relieve the food situation. As we climbed, the weather became worse. All the country we had hoped to see was hidden by cloud, and a bitter wind harried us. It was obvious that a high station would be of no value, and after climbing for 2,000 feet, Spender stopped to do some range finding to points down the Lower Braldu valley. Angtharkay and I found some spoor a fortnight old and followed it over into a big glacier nullah. The ground was difficult and I had a good deal of trouble in moving about over it because of the deplorable state of my boots. Higher up, the wind was very fierce and made things so unpleasant that we abandoned the hunt, and returned down an impressive gorge, soon after midday.

Coming round the corner of a willow thicket, we saw a horseman riding away from our camp. The idea crossed my mind that the camp had been raided, but when the man saw us he dismounted, came over to us, and shook us cordially by the hand. He was the first human being outside our party whom we had seen for nearly three and a half months. It was at once evident that we had no common language. Angtharkay tried Tibetan and Nepali, which were as useless as my Hindustani and English. The subject of food was uppermost in our minds and it was an easy matter to communicate this to him. He indicated that he had none to spare, but made it clear that he wished to be friendly with us. He then remounted and rode off towards the river. When we reached camp, I learnt from Spender about the arrival of our visitor. He appeared from across the river and had come right up to the camp before he saw it. The discovery appeared to give him a shock and he tried to bolt. Lhakpa, however, managed to get hold of him and somehow persuaded him that we had no evil designs. He consented to come and have some tea in the camp. Though for us the arrival of a stranger was an exciting event, the other three Sherpas, being engrossed in a long session of Barachu, hardly noticed it, and from the depths of the willow jungle came the sound of the slapping of the dice-cup and loud appeals to the God of Chance. This must have puzzled our guest a good deal, but he was very polite about it, and joined in a sign conversation with Spender and Lhakpa. It appeared that he had come from down the valley where he and others were engaged in working a salt deposit. Why he had left the rest of his party on the other side of the river we could not discover, but he took his leave saying that he was going to fetch them. We watched him cross the river, which for a man on horseback held no terrors. We continued to observe his activities through field-glasses when we reached the other side.

Besides him we could see three men and four yaks. After much fuss, they shifted their loads to a sheep-pen and came across, riding on the yaks and the horse. It was entertaining to watch them coaxing the animals into the swift stream and hunting for the places where the water was most broken. When they arrived, after a round of formal introductions, we settled down with Lhakpa and Angtharkay to a lengthy conference. During this the Barachu continued uninterrupted. Not even talk of food, the main subject of discussion, drew the players from their game. Conversation was difficult and laborious, as we had first to establish a system of conventional signs which were mutually understood. Lhakpa had a few words of Turki, but these did not take us far. However, our friends were intelligent and had a great sense of humour, so that things went better than might have been expected. It appeared that flour was not obtainable this side of Shimshal – four days' march away – but that sheep and butter could be got more readily. Our friends agreed that one of their party should ride across the Shimshal pass as fast as he could and bring back some of these provisions. But they first demanded that we should write our names on a bit of paper. I wrote our two names and was then told to write those of our Sherpas. This done I had to add their own names: Dildorbik, the old man who had first visited us and who seemed to be in charge of the party, Mohi Bacha, Mohamad Ali and Sour. Then I had to state, in any language I pleased, whence we had come and where we proposed to go. We could not understand the reason for all this, but we were obliged to comply with their wishes. The precious document was then wrapped very carefully in a bit of cloth, unwrapped and wrapped up again and then entrusted to the youngest member of their party, who was to be the messenger. We paid the price of one sheep, six rupees, as security. This sum was counted half a dozen times by each of them, which incidentally taught us how to count up to six in Shimshali. The youth then mounted the horse and departed, encouraged by the promise that he would be rewarded with one of our empty flour-bags, if he returned in two days. The idea of two days was conveyed in our sign language by placing the palms of the hands together in an attitude of prayer and then twice laying one's head on them, to indicate sleep. This primitive transaction took quite two hours to complete.

The other three Shimshalis deposited their few belongings in one of the huts and joined us round our fire. The conversation which followed was much more difficult than it had been before. It is easy enough to capture a man's sympathy and understanding when discussing affairs of the stomach, but it is a different thing to keep the party going with small talk when neither side can understand a word the other says. Nor was it easy to learn much about their country. However, we began to compile a small vocabulary of their words, and by the time we had been in the valley a week we had learnt something of their culture.

Darkness put an end to the Barachu, which had been in progress since morning, and the three players joined the circle. We cooked and ate our supper of pemmican and rice, but we did not invite the Shimshalis to join us. A dinner invitation is one of the easiest things to put across without the help of a common language – if one has enough food! But we were uncomfortably aware that our supplies were dwindling and that shortage of food was likely to curtail our work before we had completed all that we had planned. So Western hospitality went by the board; but it was comforting to remember that they probably thought we were Chinese! Besides, we imagined that they were well provided with the usual dirty but plentiful Shimshali food. They sat silently round us in a circle and watched us eat. We thought that they eyed our heaped plates rather hungrily; but perhaps rice, and even pemmican, look wildly exciting if one seldom sees them! When the meal was over two of them left; apparently to cook their own food. Soon they came back to borrow one of our cooking pots, and later returned to ask for some curry powder. After a long time they came to summon Dildorbik. We accompanied them to their hut, as this appeared to be the correct procedure, and we hoped that politeness might atone a little for not having asked them to share our dinner. On the floor we saw one cold round of leathery bread, leaning unappetizingly against our smoke-blackened cooking pot, in which they had heated a little water and coloured it with curry powder. Someone suggested hopefully that this might only be the *hors d'œuvres*, but we soon discovered that it was their complete menu, and that they had eaten nothing since the previous night. They were positively cheerful about it; as if the curry powder had transformed bread and hot water into an extra special debauch! We reluctantly upheld the hospitable traditions of the British Empire and supplied them with some flour. But we felt that they had given us a lesson in the real meaning of "travelling light". Even those of us who have a reputation for "toughness" make far too much fuss about the danger of running short of food.

Our belated hospitality had finally dispelled the Shimshali's mistrust of us, and next morning Dildorbik offered to show us some game, if two of the Sherpas would help with the transport of the salt which they had dumped on the other side of the river. One of the yaks, being a young one, was given an off-day. Lobsang, Nukku and two Shimshalis mounted the other three yaks and the cavalcade set out, looking rather like a party of holiday-makers nervously embarking on a donkey-ride at Margate. The rousing send-off that we gave them made the Sherpas look painfully self-conscious and nearly caused a disastrous stampede among the yaks. Angtharkay, Dildorbik and I forded the stream coming from the Shimshal pass and climbed the steep hillside beyond, in search of meat. Before we had gone far, the old man made Angtharkay exchange his black coat for my buff-coloured sweater, so as not to be too conspicuous. We traversed into a big side valley, at the foot of which was a collection of huts and sheep-pens. The valley was filled with wonderful pasturage which would support many thousand head of sheep. We spotted a herd of bharal on a ridge 3,000 feet above us. Dildorbik urged us to remain in hiding until the animals came down to feed and drink. In a deep ravine he curled up and went to sleep, while we shivered through some dull hours of waiting. This proved to be the wrong policy, for instead of coming down towards us, as we had hoped, the herd went off down the other side of the ridge. We spent the rest of the day hunting for them among the crags without success. However, before we returned to camp Angtharkay secured a hare with a remarkable shot. Spender had put in a useful day's work surveying the valley. His measurement of the distance to the Braldu-Shaksgam junction showed that both Younghusband and Colonel Schomberg had greatly underestimated the length of this valley.

That evening, from the warmth of our camp-fire, we watched a mighty storm raging over the peaks of the Braldu glacier. But the next morning was cloudless and still. Shafts of sunlight filtered through the willows, and bits of thistledown and cobwebs floated in the frosty air. Spender left early in order to get a high station on the Jökul, while I went to have a look at the valley with Mohi Bacha and Sour. We kept to the left bank of the river and passed through many oases of lush grass and willow clumps like the one where we had camped. Hundreds of birds flitted in and out of the thickets; the most common of these was the hoopoo, with its quaint lolloping flight. We also saw many different kinds of water-birds near the clear river pools.

At each of these oases I found clusters of huts, and my guides showed me water-mills for grinding corn, and various contrivances for making butter and cheese. I was told that these places were only inhabited in the winter, when they were used as grazing grounds by the people of Shimshal. The season was not due to begin for another month. This explained the mystery which had been puzzling us since we had arrived in the valley. It is an unusual state of affairs to find winter migration to higher pastures. Presumably it is due to the smaller precipitation on the northern side of the watershed. It would be most interesting to travel in these parts in mid-winter. The occupation of these high valleys would probably make it possible to live off the country to an unusual extent. Rivers would not present the almost insoluble problem which they do in the summer. With the help of skis one might be able to undertake long journeys into the unexplored glacier regions.

The Shimshalis were most instructive and attentive. Whenever we stopped they took off their coats for me to sit on, and they were quite unnecessarily helpful whenever we came to the slightest difficulty on the route. They were extremely eager to explain everything about the country. It exasperated poor Mohi Bacha that we could not converse more easily. He kept holding his tongue and tugging it, in a gesture of despair at its impotence!

We got back to camp in the late afternoon, to find things in a great state of excitement. Spender's party was back, and the youth had returned with two sheep and some butter. He had brought with him two more Shimshalis, who had come mainly out of curiosity. We spent a merry evening feasting off liver and blood sausage. The latter is a very favourite dish of the Sherpas, and they gorged themselves preposterously. This gory delicacy is made by stuffing the entrails of the animal with a mixture of blood and tsampa. Conversation with the Shimshalis was now becoming much easier. Lhakpa Tensing was our most successful linguist. He had been very assiduous in making a list of words and their meanings, which he wrote laboriously on a dirty scrap of paper, in Tibetan characters. He looked rather like a tourist abroad grappling with some difficult situation with the aid of Hugo's "All you want in France". He had made wonderful progress in the last two days.

The next day we lazed in the sunshine until late in the morning. We had arranged to make a journey, with Dildorbik as our guide, down to the junction of the Braldu river with the Shaksgam. We were just about to start when a small army was seen approaching down the hill. Three of the party rode ponies and wore smart frock coats and bright pink shirts. The visitors proved to be the Lambadar of Shimshal and his party. The Lambadar was now in residence at Shuijerab, a grazing village just at the other side of the Shimshal pass, and on hearing news of us from our messenger had brought a strong force with him, presumably to exterminate us if we were enemies and to honour us if we were friends. The party had come from Shuijerab that morning, and must have started very early. I went out to greet the Lambadar, and as I shook him by the hand he addressed me in some language that I could not understand. I replied in Hindustani, which did not seem to mean anything to him. Blankets were spread on the ground, and we all sat down to wrestle with a difficult interview. The Shimshalis were now in huge force. I again addressed the Lambadar in Hindustani; whereupon he expressed great surprise, and speaking that language very badly and with evident difficulty, asked in amazement if we were Indians. When we told him that we were "Angrezi" (English), he displayed violent emotion – probably relief. The assembled multitude leapt up for an orgy of strenuous handshaking. I am sure that they had thought we were Chinamen, and that the language in which the Lambadar had first addressed me was Turki. Probably the messenger's description of the Sherpas and their pigtails had led them to that conclusion. We now got on splendidly and were able to learn all that we wanted to know about the lower Braldu valley and the route across the pass to Shimshal. The Lambadar took great interest in our recent journey, and expressed polite amazement at our intrepidity and hardihood. The Sherpas produced a particularly filthy brew of tea, with which our guests struggled for some time before good manners gave place to nausea, and they handed it on to their followers. I thought that the session would go on all day, but the Lambadar cut the proceedings to an almost European brevity by taking his leave, again addressing me in Turki to make quite certain that we were not playing him false. The Shimshali party went over to the huts and had a meal. Presently a plateful of apples arrived. Of all possible gifts this was the most welcome. We returned the compliment with one of our ropes, apologizing at the same time for our impoverished condition, which we put down to the difficulties of our journey. This, of course, brought forth a further flood of compliments. We asked our friend if he would send down to Shimshal for flour and any other form of food he could get. For our proposed trip down the valley he provided us with two ponies and his two pink-shirted attendants. We were also given two yaks for our equipment, so that nobody should have to carry loads. Angtharkay's digestion had not survived last night's feast, and now he was suffering for his greed. We left him behind with Lhakpa and set out at noon.

The river had gone down tremendously since we had last forded it, and with the ponies and yaks to help, it caused us no trouble. When we reached the other side we rode ahead, with the two pink-shirted gentlemen in attendance. The three Sherpas followed driving the two yaks – a reminder of home, which they much enjoyed. We were making for a place called Darband, which we imagined was where Dildorbik's party had been extracting their salt.

The way led through a country of vivid contrasts. The gaunt flanks of the valley and the barren gravel flats made a sombre and forbidding background to sloping lawns of delicate green. These meadows were astir with life amongst the bleak sterility of the surrounding crags; and the springs of clear water which danced through them were sun-flecked and gay compared with the turgid, muddy river that slid down the valley below. As in the Aghil range, it seemed to me that, with a little ingenuity, a great deal more of the valley could be irrigated into fertility and made to support a permanent population.

At four o'clock, we reached a grazing ground known as Sar-i-Laksh, and our guides told us that we were nearing Darband. We left one of the pink shirts here to wait for the yaks and rode on over the next rise. From the crest of the hill we saw ahead of us a round stone tower. When we reached it we found that it was part of a long rampart built above a ravine. In fact it defended the only approach to the upper part of the valley. As the other side of the main stream was bounded by a vertical cliff, anyone coming up the gorge would find the way barred by the rampart. In the middle of this there was a great wooden gate barricaded by a heavy beam. It was a great surprise to come upon this relic of former wars, and to find it still in a perfect state of preservation. There were two towers in the rampart. We were taken into one of them, very like a chamber in the turret of a Norman castle, with small windows overlooking the ravine, through which the defenders could shoot arrows against an attacking force. Our guide demonstrated how the archers used these slits, and also produced for our inspection an incredibly ancient matchlock gun. There was evidence that the gun was still used, for hanging from the beams was a bharal skin, and joints of dried meat. On a shelf were stored balls of fermenting yak-milk cheese. We tasted these but found them too sour to be appetizing. We did not discover to whom all this belonged; there was no sign of life in the place, save for a solitary yak grazing on the far side of the ravine. We were then taken through a trap-door on to the roof of the tower. In its low walls were more narrow slits. Looking down across these ancient battlements, and over the grim gorge beyond, gave us a vivid sense of the present mediæval state of Central Asia. We returned to camp at Sar-i-Laksh, our guide having first carefully barred the gateway in the fortress, as if expecting a night attack.

The next morning, while Spender climbed to a high station from which to survey this part of the Braldu valley, I rode down the valley, with one of the pink shirts, whose name was Abdulla. He looked very like a brigand chief in his short riding-boots of rough brown hide, with off-white plus-fours bagging over them. His costume was completed by a frock coat, and a round woollen hat perched jauntily on the side of his head. We let ourselves through "the gateway to Central Asia", and led our ponies across the gorge by a precipitous path. We then rode on down the valley, over a wilderness of boulders, which is evidently part of the ancient terminal moraine of the Braldu glacier. Above this the river flows over gravel flats, below, it falls into a spectacular canyon, whose vertical rock walls are so close together that in one place the narrow gap is spanned, 200 feet above the torrent, by a flimsy wooden bridge, not more than five yards long. It felt weirdly exciting to be riding down this sinister ravine, towards the Shaksgam, with my barbaric retainer.

In about an hour we reached a grove of tall willows, growing in a grassy swamp. Here we found one of the salt diggings. My guide demonstrated the method of salt extraction. A large pit is dug and filled with water, and the salt-bearing earth is churned about in the pit until it becomes a saturated solution of salt and mud. The mud is allowed to settle. Meanwhile in a long trench a fire is made, small V-shaped vessels of slate and clay are placed across it, and filled with the salt solution. The water is evaporated by the heat, and the salt is left behind in long bricks.

There is a Tibetan proverb which says: "If your horse cannot carry you uphill, it is no horse; if you do not lead it downhill, you are no man," but the latter half of the statement does not seem to hold good in these parts, for we rode down the most precipitous places, and our sure-footed ponies did not turn one hair of their shaggy heads.

Towards the junction of the Braldu and the Shaksgam the country became grimly forbidding. Vast masses of black scree welled from tiny fissures in the pale limestone cliffs. To the north the view was blocked by the mountainous desolation of the Aghil range, vividly striped by broad wavering bands of black and yellow strata. An intensely green oasis on the other side accentuated the rugged austerity of the scene. We rode along the shingle flats at the junction of the two rivers and turned eastwards, following the Shaksgam for a mile up its gorge. Great bleached boulders bore witness to the river's higher channel in former years.

We ate our lunch imprisoned in the depths of this gloomy canyon. Then I climbed 2,000 feet up its precipitous side, and from there could see the river as far as its junction with the Oprang. My view upstream was restricted to a few miles. It seemed to me that it would be possible for a lightly-laden climbing party to force a route up this gorge, without having to ford the river, which, except in mid-winter, cannot be crossed. The rocks up which I was climbing were covered in clay, which tended to peel off and made me very scared. Queer cactus-like plants clung to the crannies, and added to the nightmare quality of the place.

When I had rejoined my companion, we rode back to the junction and retraced our steps back up the Braldu valley. We lingered for a while among the willows. The afternoon sunlight slanted through their swaying branches, and made patterns of light on the grass. The cool air was murmurous with the sound of the stream and the rustle of leaves. And yet only a few yards away we were surrounded by stark desolation.

We reached camp late that evening to find that Spender had done a good day's work on the hills above the fort. Early the next day we rode back up the valley through the lush meadows of Karmush and Kuz, where pools of transparent jade held the morning sunlight. Spender stayed behind to complete his survey of the valley, while Abdulla and I rode ahead. We had some good gallops across the sandy flats, and finished up on the other side of the river, racing each other back to camp through the meadows of Chikar. An exciting finish was greeted by a rousing cheer from Angtharkay and a group of Shimshalis.

I lazed the golden afternoon away, drinking innumerable pints of tea.

CHAPTER NINETEEN

Marching Back

WE started on the first stage of our homeward journey soon after seven o'clock the next day, with three Shimshalis carrying our loads. Dildorbik, Abdulla, Spender and I rode ponies. They took us at a fine pace up the steep hillside. In this way, we avoided the gorge above Chikar and reached the upper valley. The country here reminded me of the approach to so many Tibetan passes, except for the great Dolomite spires which stood like watch towers above the gently undulating ground. Two hours' riding brought us to the junction of three flat valleys. We halted here and lit a fire of yak dung and waited an hour for the porters to arrive. The views in every direction across this plain were magnificent. The limestone peaks to the south-west rose sheer out of flat glacier beds and looked twice their height. In contrast to these, the Jökul peaks, to the north, showed their gently rounded ice-caps. When the porters arrived, Spender did a station and Angtharkay cooked some meat pies over the smoky yak-dung fire. We rode on to a village called Shuwert, Abdulla leading some breakneck gallops over uncertain country. His clothes, especially his boots, had the real Cossack look about them, and his reckless speed and wild cries would have been rewarded with volleys of applause at the Cossack display at Olympia.

Shuwert was quite a large place of about four dozen houses. At this time it was quite deserted. A surprisingly large glacier, rising in the country behind the Jökul peaks, fed the main stream of the valley up which we had come. The Shimshal pass itself lay to the left of this on a mass of ancient moraine material. It formed such a gentle and indefinite curve, that as I rode up to it I found it hard to believe that it really was the pass that was such an important link in the main Asiatic watershed, which we had explored through eighty miles of rugged intricacy. Our companions were fully aware of the significance of the pass, and kept repeating what we already knew, that the water on one side flowed into India, while that on the other side made its way into Turkestan, later to be lost in the deserts of Central Asia.

I sat for a long time on the crest of the pass, caught up in the magic of the view. Away to the south-east many of the peaks with which we had been so familiar during the past month, and to which we had given such strange names as "Flat-Iron", "Father Christmas" and "The Fangs", rose up as if to give a last friendly salute before receding into the past with other expedition memories. My contentment was shadowed with regret.

Below the pass on the other side was a great blue lake, a square mile or more in area. Beside this was an extensive plain known as Maidan Abdulla Khan. Across this I was made to race against Abdulla and Dildorbik. But for the fact that Abdulla's hat blew off half-way across I would have come in a very bad last, though they had given me the biggest and strongest mount. Soon we came upon large herds of yak and sheep, and heard the melodious calls of shepherd children. Then a steep descent took us suddenly out of this charming world into the steep-sided barren valley of Shuijerab. Our friend the Lambadar came across the bridge to meet me, accompanied by an enormous retinue of villagers. They brought with them apples and apricots, from Shimshal, and a vast bowl of curdled milk on which I fed while exchanging compliments and platitudes. This went on for some hours, until a combination of food and the hot afternoon made me commit the social error of dozing. The situation was relieved by the arrival of Spender, who had put in a terrific day's work winding up the survey and fixing the geographical position of the Shimshal pass.

At sunset, we made a conducted tour of the village, which was then a busy hive of activity, in which the women and children played the chief parts. The women greeted us in their usual manner by waving their hands round above their heads. The huge pens were filled to overflowing with sheep and goats. We watched some infants supervising with extraordinary skill the herding of the enormous flocks. There were innumerable lambs, each of which had to be placed by its mother. The children worked until long after nightfall, settling the disputes and attending the bleating complaints of the sheep.

The following morning we made a late start, owing to the lengthy business of giving presents to our hosts. Also the Lambadar made strong efforts to dissuade us from leaving. The reasons given were various and disconnected, and most of them we could not understand. His excessive hospitality led him to refuse to provide us with men to carry our loads in order to induce us to stop another day. However, when we demonstrated that we were quite capable of carrying all our kit ourselves, he yielded, and men were forthcoming, and refused to allow us even to carry light rucksacks. We made fruitless efforts to photograph some of the rather picturesque women of the village. As in other parts of Central Asia, they were terrified of the camera, and could not be induced, even by their men-folk, to submit to the ordeal. But they, in company with the whole village, turned out to see us off. I was particularly sorry to say good-bye to our old friend Dildorbik, who was a most delightful character.

The Sherpas got on extraordinarily well with these people. They shared the same boyish sense of humour and love of the ridiculous. After a very short acquaintance they were playing the fool with one another, as if they had been friends all their lives. On the march below Shuijerab, they were continually putting stones in each other's loads, having weight-lifting matches and splashing one another with water as they crossed the streams, quite regardless of how long they had been marching, or how much they had to carry.

The going was easy at first, as we kept to the floor of the valley. But soon the river began to cut its way through limestone and conglomerates and disappeared far below, while we continued along the hillside, keeping on top of one of the ancient river terraces. These terraces were more imposing than anything we had seen on the northern side of the watershed, and formed country of which it is difficult to give an adequate description. Evening brought us to the edge of the most fantastic ravine carved out of these alluvial deposits by a side stream. Angtharkay remarked, with some truth, that had we encountered it in unexplored country it would have presented an unsurmountable obstacle. As it was, a stairway had been engineered through it with astonishing skill, and it was an easy matter to descend the 1,500 feet into this fearsome gorge. When this path was first constructed I do not know; it may have been perhaps two hundred years ago. The pioneers of the route must have had remarkable determination, for anything less promising than the way they had chosen would be hard to imagine. Half-way down we passed through a wooden doorway without a door, which was built into the cliff. It appeared to serve no purpose but to add to the eeriness of the ravine. I am inclined to believe, however, that it was an artistic expression on the part of the path-builder. We camped at the bottom of the chasm and built a huge bonfire, that lit up the extravagant pinnacles and gullies which towered 1,000 feet above our heads. Below, the stream thundered through a bottle-neck so narrow that it must almost be possible to touch both sides at once. It then plunged in a waterfall to the main river below.

On September 11th, we were faced with a long day's work, which included the crossing of two high passes. Although we were now only about five miles from Shimshal, the gorge below us was so bad that not even the ingenuity of the natives, with hundreds of years at their disposal, had been able to construct a way through while the river was at its summer level. In mid-winter it is possible to get through the gorge by walking along the river bed itself, but now we were forced to take a circuitous route over the Shach Mirr and Zard-i-Gar passes and into the Shipodin nullah, which joins the main valley below the gorge. We started the day with a long climb out of the ravine. This took us back on to the river terrace, and level going for a short way, until we had to plunge down into the next side nullah. From here a steady climb of about 3,000 feet took us to the first pass, from which we looked across another ravine to the second, 1,000 feet higher. We found it most interesting to see how the natives dealt with this terrific country. We had so often been faced in the last few months with the problem of making our own route over this type of ground. The day was cloudy, which prevented us from seeing the wonderful view of the great peaks of this part of the Karakoram, which these passes must command. However, I thoroughly enjoyed the journey through the gorges, without the worry of finding a way. But by the time we had climbed 2,500 feet to the next pass, we had done quite enough uphill work for one day, and were glad to run swiftly down a steep scree-slope into the broad, open Shipodin valley. We camped here at five o'clock in a threatening snowstorm, which deposited most of its venom on the crags above us.

The morning of the 12th was brilliantly fine. The great peaks across the Shimshal valley, including the Kanjuts and Dasto Ghil, which stood over 25,000 feet high, were ethereal in the early morning light. Before we were up, a large troop of men, horses and yaks was seen coming down the valley towards us. To our great astonishment, the new arrivals turned out to be our friends from Shuijerab, including the Lambadar himself and Abdulla. They had left the village on the previous morning, and must have travelled at a tremendous speed in order to overtake us. We could not understand the reason for their journey, but we imagined that it was connected with us. They had probably discussed the situation after we had left, and come to the conclusion that we must be kept under friendly arrest, until word had been received from the Mir of Hunza, to whom news of our arrival had been sent as soon as they had heard of us in Shuijerab. The messenger who took this news was still under the impression that we were a party of Chinese. We all went down together through a steep gorge to the main valley. The Lambadar hurried along with Spender and me, and became very fussed when by some scree-running, I got a long way ahead.

When we reached the main valley, we saw Shimshal a mile or so farther downstream, on the other side of the river. It was a gladdening sight, after the bleakness of the conglomerate gorges, to see the village climbing the hillside in terrace upon terrace of green and gold. The river was spanned by a rope bridge, grouped at both ends of which a large gathering was awaiting our arrival. Before we reached the bridge we were met by our old friend Mohi Bacha, bringing with him a great quantity of apricots and some excellent cakes. He seemed delighted to see us again, and insisted that we should sit down and eat his food there and then, before facing the perils of the rope bridge.

This type of rope bridge consists of several strands of yak hide wound together into a single cable and slung across the river on two tree-trunks, which are built into great piles of boulders. A horse-shoe shaped wooden runner is placed over the rope. The two ends of the runner are tied together and pulled across the river with a load, human or otherwise, attached to it. I have crossed these bridges in Tibet without using the runner, but the friction caused by the contact of one's legs on the rope, throws a far greater strain on the arms than that produced by climbing a rope hand over hand without using one's feet. There is considerable danger therefore of dropping into the river from sheer exhaustion. Tied to the runner, however, it is not difficult for an active man to pull himself across with his hands. The rope bridge at Shimshal was about 200 feet long. While our loads were being hauled across, the yaks and horses of the Lambadar's party were driven into the river and made to swim to the other side. They were carried several hundred yards downstream by the force of the current before they could reach thc opposite bank. Before we were allowed to try our skill on the rope bridge several exhibition crossings were made by the natives. The cable was very knotted, which, in spite of assistance from the other side, added greatly to the work of pulling oneself across. The Sherpas put up a bad show, which caused a good deal of merriment among the Shimshalis. The best thing about these rope bridges from the Sherpas' point of view is that they offer a splendid opportunity of playing a joke on the man who is making the crossing. He is, of course, quite helpless, and a few well-aimed stones thrown into the water below will soak him to the skin. This pastime, it seemed, had never occurred to the Shimshalis, but they were so delighted with it that I fear it is now an established custom that may cause embarrassment to future travellers.

We were greeted on the farther side of the river by what must have been nearly the entire male and infant population of Shimshal. When I had been unstrapped from the bridge. I was immediately taken in charge by an elderly man, who could speak Hindustani fast and fluently. He was evidently an ex-servant of Europeans and had fallen on bad times. We learnt afterwards that he had been banished to Shimshal for some crime or series of crimes. It appeared that he relied for his living upon the charity of the natives. From the moment I landed, he started talking and continued without a pause for the next two hours. He talked so fast that we could understand little of what he said. Fortunately he did not attempt to ask any questions, and we were able to survive the verbal torrent without hurting his feelings. When we reached the village, he conducted us to a grand house which had been appointed for our use, and showed us our apartments with a flourish, while the Lambadar, our true host, stood somewhat mournfully in the background. It was a magnificent place, richly ornamented with carpets and brass. At first we thought we were being shown over a temple, but this notion was expelled when our garrulous friend showed us an alcove where we were to take our baths. We did not disillusion him by mentioning that we had been many months without a bath and did not propose to have one now. A number of ancient matchlock muskets, swords and stringed instruments decorated the walls. The Sherpas at once made themselves at home, strumming on the guitars and playing soldiers with the muskets. It caused them endless amusement to drill each other and march about as if on sentry-go. I suppose that they had seen this going on in Darjeeling, and regarded it as one of the more entertaining of the pointless activities of the British Raj!

As many people as possible squeezed into the place and squatted round, watching us gorge ourselves immoderately with all the good things that were brought. Apples, apricots, apricot kernels, cake and fried potatoes. Our arrival must have been a considerable hindrance to the work of the village. At length we were left in peace, and spent a happy afternoon lounging and over-eating under the novelty of a roof.

In the evening we were taken by the Lambadar and the ex-butler for a tour of the village and its orchards and fields. The world was very lovely, with the gold of the ripe corn and the early autumn colours of the thorn trees framing the deep green of the apple and apricot orchards and the slender Lombardy poplars. The air was filled with the peace and mellow beauty which autumn brings to these high mountain valleys. The people were busy with their various harvest jobs, reaping, threshing and stacking. We were surprised to see the dashing Abdulla engaged on one of these domestic tasks. He was solemnly driving a line of yaks slowly round and round on a bed of corn, a primitive method of threshing. Abdulla as the industrious husbandman, was hard to reconcile with our last memory of him galloping madly down the valley. We were introduced to Abdulla's ancient father, and we spent a long time chatting to other cronies of the village. There we found the ex-butler most useful, for he was able to translate the old men's stories of former times, and their answers to our questions about their country. The Lambadar pressed us to further over-indulgence in his orchards.

In all our dealings with the Shimshalis, we met with kindness, courtesy and good humour. In this we were agreeably surprised, as we had not been led to expect these qualities. The community of Shimshal is remarkable for its isolation and independence of support from the outside world. Very few of the Shimshalis go out of their valley. From any direction their country is difficult of access, but they have sufficient arable land and grazing to support a much larger population than exists at the present day. They grow barley, wheat and peas, the flour of which, with cheese, butter and curd is their staple food. They have no tea, sugar or tobacco, and they do not grow many vegetables. They are a strong and healthy race; far superior in this respect to the people of Askole. We were surprised to find a complete absence of goitre among them. They weave all that is necessary to clothe themselves. They pay tribute and taxes in kind to the Mir of Hunza, who exercises jurisdiction over them. The control of the Mir, however, is somewhat laxly enforced. Of the founding of Shimshal, Colonel Schomberg writes in his interesting book *Unknown Karakoram*:

"Eleven generations ago (perhaps three hundred years) a certain Mamu Singh, a Yeshkun or peasant of the Shinaka race from the valley of Chaprot in the Gilgit district, came with his wife and settled in this valley. His wife always disliked her husband, but she loathed him when he brought her from the comparative comfort of Chaprot to live in this cold and isolated place. She never called him anything else but Shum, which means dog in the Shina tongue – for the subservience of Eastern women is largely a Western fiction – and the village was called Shimshal. When I asked what Shal meant the elders said briefly 'God knows'. In our maps the place is called Shingshal, and the people never refer to their village or themselves except as Shimshal or Shimshalis – so I suppose that, not for the first time, the Western traveller has been too ingenious and too learned. I have often asked them about this point, and never once have I found them agree with the pronunciation of the European pundits and map-mongers. Shum had one son called Shir, who in turn had three sons, Bakhti, Wali and Boki. Both Shir and his sons married Wakhi women from Gulmit, Ghulkin, and the neighbouring villages in the Guhyal district of Hunza. The men were positive that there was no Balti and no Hunza strain in them, but I am quite certain that they are wrong, and that there is a very large admixture of Balti blood."

They are a happy community leading an ideal existence in magnificent surroundings. The country is sufficiently difficult, and conditions sufficiently severe, to foster in the people that hardihood without which it seems to me impossible for mankind to be content.

CHAPTER TWENTY

How an Expedition Ends

WE returned over the fields lit by the glow of an ominous sunset. We found, when we got back, that two Hunza men had arrived with orders from the Mir to escort us down. It transpired that the bit of paper, bearing our names which we had given to Dildorbik's party at Chikar on the occasion of our first meeting, had been carried by an express runner to the Mir's palace, who then communicated the news to the Political Agent in Gilgit, who fortunately recognized our names and asked that we should be given every assistance. So these two men had been sent up to take charge of the two sahibs. When they saw us they stood for a long time in solemn silence with an expression of utter disgust on their faces. In spite of their huge drooping moustaches, which intensified their appearance of gloom, they reminded me irresistibly of Tweedledum and Tweedledee. It was easy to see what was going on in their minds. There had been some dreadful mistake. They had been ordered by the omniscient *Sircar* (government) not only to serve two of the illustrious heaven-born, but to be their guides and protectors. In these remote parts the glamour of the White Man's prestige is still undimmed. At their home they had exaggerated the importance of their mission, and all the way up they had basked in the happy expectation of reflected glory. Now they were faced with stark disillusionment. Here were two ragamuffins who surely could never have had anything to do with sahibdom. There was, quite obviously, nothing "white" about them. Their clothes were dirty and ragged, their unwashed faces could hardly be seen through a tangle of unkempt hair and matted beard. But orders were orders, and there was nothing for it but to carry out the unsavoury task.

That night the Lambadar entertained us to a musical evening. Some surprisingly good talent was revealed with the fiddle, guitar and flute. There was also some clever dancing. The show was kept going until very late. A huge wood fire blazed in the centre of the room. The house was packed to capacity and the air was stifling. I was lying on a bed which had been produced from somewhere, and again disgraced myself by falling asleep during the performance.

The sunset's foreboding was accurate, and we awoke to a dismal morning. I was still in my sleeping-bag when the Lambadar came to pay a call, escorted by a large number of villagers, who could not proceed with their harvest jobs because of the rain. It was a serious thing for them, and an atmosphere of general depression prevailed. After breakfast, I presided – merely as a figure-head – over a vast council which had gathered together in order to decide what we should pay for the many presents we had received, and what tips should be given to the various people who had, in some way involved themselves in our visit. It appeared, for instance, that the rope bridge had been moved from its old place when news of our impending visit had come through. This apparently useless job had employed sixteen men for two days. Then there were the men who claimed to have brought the news of our arrival, first from Chikar to Shuijerab, then from Shuijerab to Shimshal. Also there were the brothers of those who had relayed – unasked – the tidings to Hunza, and the farmers who had supplied the food for last night's party, most of which, incidentally, had been consumed by the villagers. Many other payments were decided upon by the Committee but in general hubbub I was too bewildered to decide upon the justice of the claims. Taking advantage of a lull in the uproar, caused, I suppose, by a temporary lapse of imagination, I managed to exercise a chairman's authority and bring the proceedings to a close, before our money-bags were quite emptied. Soon after ten o'clock, we set out in the rain, accompanied by the entire population. They left the convoy in small groups, and as each party detached itself, we halted for a round of handshakes, and expressions of friendliness. These grew longer and more emotional as the gathering became smaller, and those taking their leave were more closely connected with our visit. At last only Abdulla remained. He was about to bid us a sad farewell, when we heard the sound of much shouting, and a figure appeared, running towards us from the village. This turned out to be Mohi Bacha, who must have overslept himself and had failed to put in an appearance at our departure. He seemed to be quite beside himself with grief. He was wearing a pair of snow-goggles, in order, I like to think, to hide his tears. At length words failed him, and we went on alone down the dismal, wind-swept valley. Tweedledum and Tweedledee preferred not to be seen in our company and had taken a path some way to the left of our route; but as the valley narrowed and we walked as fast as they did, they were forced to put up with our repulsive presence. I made repeated efforts to break down the barrier of their aloofness, and at last succeeded in forcing a smile out of one of them. After this our friendship gradually ripened. The way led us across the Mulunguti glacier. On this, our technique of glissading down steep ice-slopes so impressed our escort, that by the time we reached the other side they were willing to believe that perhaps our beggarly appearance maligned our true worth, and we became on terms of rib-poking familiarity.

After leaving Shimshal we had plunged once more into a desolation of conglomerate cliffs, which made us realize more strongly the extraordinary isolation of the community we had just left. But every now and then we came upon patches of jungle clinging unexpectedly to the ravines or spread out along the gravel flats of the river. These thickets were now ablaze with autumn colours, and were unbelievably beautiful. The latter part of the day's march was along the gravel flats. In one place the river ran against the cliffs on one side, and we had to wade for a short stretch. But we were lucky in being able to do so, for as an alternative we would have had to perform a long and difficult climb, probably in the dark. By nightfall we reached an isolated hut known as Lashkar. Judging by the number of prayer-flags hung round the hut, we supposed that the place must have some religious significance. Certainly there seemed to be no other reason for the building to be there, as the site was bleak and uncomfortable, and appeared to be in danger of bombardment from falling stones. However, at the invitation of our guides, we made use of the hut, which was equipped with a fireplace and brass cooking pots.

Angtharkay has always had an instinctive dislike for anyone on any expedition who is neither sahib nor porter. In his view, only three grades of humans should be included in a party. Firstly, there is the sahib, who is there to be satisfied. Secondly, there is the Sherpa, without whom no expedition could achieve its pointless objective; and lastly, there is the local porter, a greatly inferior being, whom, unfortunately, it is necessary to employ when the party has more luggage than can be carried by the sahibs and Sherpas. Anyone who does not fulfil one or other of these rôles is superfluous. Moreover, he is generally there to usurp the most dignified function of the Sherpa: namely, to look after the comfort and well-being of the sahib. From the outset Angtharkay resented the presence of Tweedledum and Tweedledee, and had made several efforts to persuade me not to have them. He could not understand that it would not be polite to refuse their assistance. During supper, Angtharkay, resenting Tweedledum's concern for our comfort, was seized by a fit of jealousy, and told the Hunza men that we were quite capable of finding our own way down the valley, and that it was quite unnecessary for them to be there. Poor Tweedledum was deeply hurt. With tears in his eyes he rose to his feet, packed up his few belongings, and ordering his companion to follow, stalked out into the night intending, I imagine, never to see us again. With a great deal of difficulty I managed to get him back and partly to repair his wounded feelings explained that without his help, not only would we fail to get down the valley, but even if we did, we would inevitably fall a prey to the wolves of civilization.

The recent rain had caused a danger of falling stones, and the next morning we had to make a long detour to avoid a bad place, where there was a continuous cannonade. After this the river entered more fearsome gorge-country. The path took us 4,000 feet up the valley side over surprisingly difficult ground. The man who first found and colonized Shimshal must have had amazing determination. But as we toiled up the interminable zigzags of the path, my admiration for him was not unmixed with sympathy for his wife's loathing of him. At length we reached the crest of a sharp ridge from which we looked down on to the Monhill glacier, which rises in a group of 24,000 and 25,000-foot mountains, culminating in the magnificent peak of Dasto Ghil (25,868 feet). We made our way down to the main valley again, crossing the Monhill gorge by a ridiculously flimsy bridge spanning an alarming drop. The main river had then to be crossed by a similar bridge, which bounced and swayed horribly above the booming turmoil of the water. Across this was a wilderness of water-polished boulders lying at the bottom of the huge desolate valley. The place was known as Karun-i-Ben, and marked the spot where the river entered another gorge. Like the one above Shimshal, the natives consider this gorge to be impassable except in mid-winter, when it is possible to make a way up the river bed itself. In the winter of 1892, during one of his remarkable exploratory journeys in these parts, Sir George Cockeril made his way up this route, but I am unaware that any other European has traversed the gorge.

It was very tantalizing. Only five miles separated us from the flesh-pots of the Hunza valley, but in order to reach them, we would have to climb 8,000 feet up a steep, waterless slope to the Karun Pir pass, which would lead us out of the Shimshal valley to the north. The idea of doing the climb in a single day did not appeal to us much, particularly as the men were still carrying heavy loads. But to camp half-way up without fuel or water was an even less attractive notion. Angtharkay suggested an acceptable compromise; to do half the climb by moonlight and finish it off in the morning.

Karun-i-Ben is about 8,800 feet high. This was the lowest we had been since leaving the valley of the Indus in May. It was now three o'clock in the afternoon; the sun glared down from a cloudless sky; the stifling heat danced over the rocks and crags till they were too hot to touch. The heat was reflected into the stagnant air of the gorge, making the temperature and our tempers soar uncomfortably. We collected the few plants that somehow contrived to grow among the rocks, and were able with this fuel to cook our usual meal of bread and tea. We drank great quantities of tea in preparation for the thirsty hours to come. The place we were in was very like the delightful illustration of the "dismal and desolate valley" up which the Beaver and the Butcher ventured in their search for the Snark.

My stomach was now suffering from the inevitable result of continuous fruit-eating, and I did not view the prospect of severe physical effort with relish. But I succeeded in performing a remarkably quick and complete cure by a remedy which does not seem to have occurred to the medical profession – eating a lot more fruit.

At six, an hour before dark, we packed up and plunged into the tangle of conglomerate gullies at the start of the climb. The cliffs formed by the remains of the ancient river terraces were a stupendous size, extending, in this part of the valley, as much as 3,000 feet above the present level of the river. It was a very beautiful evening. As we made our way through these ghostly relics of a former geological age, the clouds rolled away from the mountains of the Dasto Ghil range. While we climbed we were able to watch their glaciers flush in the snow of the setting sun. Later, when the glow had died, they sparkled like gigantic diamond drops in the moonlight. Inspired, no doubt, by the glories of our surroundings, Tweedles Dum and Dee began to rhapsodize about the opulence of their own country which we were about to visit. On reaching the first village in the Hunza valley (Morkhun), which was Tweedledum's home town, we should, they assured us, lack nothing. Every kind of fruit and vegetable known to agriculture grew there in profusion; all the spices and sweetmeats of the East were to be bought at the shops; an abundant supply of eggs, chickens, butter, milk and honey was to be had for the asking; the houses were built and furnished with princely luxury. This eulogy at first annoyed us; it shattered the enchantment of the moonlight. We were climbing in a dreamlike world, lost in its magic, and we had no thought of anything so mundane as bodily comfort. A climb in the early part of a moonlit night is an ethereal experience, for some reason very different from the ordinary departures of early morning. But even the most entranced mood sinks to earth when one is hungry and tired, and as aching thighs and empty stomachs took a larger share of our attention, the chant of the Tweedles in praise of the luxuries of the promised land assumed the importance of an enticing menu.

When we had climbed 4,000 feet we reached a sheep-fold built under the lee of a huge boulder. We slept in this until shortly before dawn, when we resumed the climb. The morning was disappointing. The perfect weather of the night before had promised a dawn view of the great sweep of country which our bivouac must command, but by daybreak the sky was overcast. Huge piled clouds, charged with rain, hid the great peaks of the Hispar watershed. Long tongues of mist rose from the valleys. Far away to the south loomed a gigantic mountain mass, wreathed with a wide swathe of cloud, its lower slopes lit by pale sunlight. At first we imagined that this was Nanga Parbat. But I think we must have been mistaken, and more probably it was Rakaposhi. As we approached the pass, the Tweedles became more and more excited, and chided us and the porters for our leisurely pace. Before reaching the crest we halted for about an hour in order to let the stragglers of the party catch up. This was more than Tweedledee could stand. He suggested that he should go ahead to the grazing village of Boibar, in order to warn the villagers and prepare the fatted calf. There had been great competition between the two Hunza men to carry the rifle. Tweedledee, who had been playing with the bolt during the halt, insisted upon taking the rifle ahead with him now – presumably in order to create a sensation in Boibar. Tweedledum agreed to this on the understanding that he should be allowed to carry it into his own village on the following day. We gave Tweedledee twenty minutes start and then followed him over the pass. The slopes on the other side were covered in deep snow. Down this we exhibited a turn of speed which amazed Tweedledum, who nearly broke his neck trying to keep up with us. I was following in the deep sunk tracks of Tweedledee when I happened to see a silvery object sticking up out of the snow. I picked it up and found that it was the rifle bolt. I put it in my pocket and said nothing about it.

Below the level of the snow we found ourselves in an entrancing grassy glen. Its sides were covered with juniper trees, and its smooth meadows were a strange contrast to the rugged barrenness of the other side of the pass. We lay for a long time by a spring of clear water before running on down through the richly coloured glades. On the way we met poor Tweedledee, rushing up the hill in a frantic state of mind. He had made his triumphal entry in Boibar only to find that the rifle was without its bolt! After his first torrent of frenzied chatter I managed to ask what was wrong. The poor man was in a desperate state, quite ready, I think, to cut his throat, if the Sherpas did not do it for him. Things were becoming serious when I casually took the bolt from my pocket and started playing with it, as if I had not understood what was the cause of the trouble. Tweedledum and the Sherpas laughed riotously. But Tweedledee, with a look of injured dignity, took the bolt from me and hurried down the hill again.

The village of Boibar was drowsily lazing through a still autumn afternoon, and our arrival awoke only a mild interest. Its setting was typically Alpine; unlike the vast scale of most Himalayan valleys, it had the charm of littleness. The gently sloping meadows were dotted with toy trees, and curved upwards to a miniature peak at the head of the valley. This mountain stood as high above the village as the Matterhorn above Zermatt, but after the stupendous scale of the mountains of the main range this new world seemed comfortingly small.

The next morning we were aroused by the Tweedles long before dawn, and hurried our departure in excited anticipation. Two hours hard going would take us down to the main valley, where we would feast on the promised luxuries of Tweedledum's saga. We started breakfastless. No leathery chapattis or un-sweetened tea must be allowed to dull the keen edge of our appetite. As we ran down the valley we hardly noticed the clear blue and gold of the early morning, nor the aromatic scent of the junipers tingling in the frosty air. Our expectant stomachs governed our emotions, and as we raced along we thought only of scrambled eggs, roast potatoes and butter, fat juicy chickens, green vegetables, roast mutton, and fruit, and sweetened tea.

When we emerged from a deep gorge we found ourselves in the main valley, with the promised village just ahead. Our excitement was curbed by a faint apprehension, the village looked too ordinary to produce the succulent dishes of our dreams. It was. Tweedledum conducted us to a squalid stable, and sat us down on a couple of bug-ridden blankets, and left us to wait with gloomy misgivings. He returned half an hour later, empty-handed, and told us that we had only to say the word and anything we desired would be brought to us. Realizing from his expression that something was amiss, we precluded our demands with a modest request for milk. But he reluctantly confessed that there were no cows in the village. Eggs then? All the hens had died. Mutton? But the sheep were still in the higher pastures. Vegetables? Sugar? Our host pretended not to hear. Despairingly we asked him what he could produce. His gloomy countenance brightened as he repeated his boast: "Anything you want."

I diffidently suggested potatoes. "Potatoes; but of course, as many as we liked."

After another long delay these were brought and boiled. We washed them down with our own un-sweetened milk-less tea, to an accompaniment of Tweedledum's fruitlessly hospitable offers. We made no further requests, but assured our host that we had all that we required. When our sparse meal was finished, in our embarrassment we paid far too much for it. We said good-bye to Tweedledum, who, looking like a balloon pricked by a pin, sadly intimated that his period of usefulness had come to an end. Poor Tweedledum! He had not wittingly deceived us. His behaviour was typically oriental. He saw things not as they were, but as he wished they were. His promises had not been deliberate lies, but the result of a desire to tell us the things we most wanted to hear.

The journey back to Srinagar took nearly three weeks. It was the most varied and the most interesting which I have made through the populated districts of the Himalaya. One by one the approaching land-marks of civilization absorbed us, and we lounged through the marches with an increasing sense of relaxation and well-being. The road was rough, which generally helps us to foster good fellowship among those who use it, and we seldom met a traveller without learning his intimate history and the reason for his journey. An astonishing variety of people use this road, which is the main route from India to Kashgar and Russian Turkestan. Spender and I were generally taken for poor Russians. No one would believe that we were English, and, later, we found it simpler to say that we were Shimshalis. The size of the party would flunctuate from day to day as we joined up with other caravans or left them behind.

As we went, the villages had more and more good things to offer us, and by the time we reached Hunza our visions of abundance were realized at last. Here, as guests of the Mir, we stayed for a day and indulged in a feast of fruit. We reclined on beds, like Roman Emperors, round a table six feet long by four feet wide, which was piled to a depth of two feet with peaches, apricots, pears, apples, melons, grapes and walnuts. In the intervals of fruit-eating we were shown something of this strange and beautiful place, with its miles of intensively cultivated terraces, and its ancient forts and palaces.

Below Hunza, a great landslide had occurred a few days before. This dammed the river, which, when the dam burst, swept away the road and caused much havoc, somewhat impeding our journey to Gilgit.

Gilgit marked an important stage in our return. We were delightfully entertained there by Major and Mrs. Cropper. From them we heard a summary of events of the outside world during the past five months. The bus strike they had forgotten; Spain was still sunk in its inferno of civil war, with no hope of the end in sight; piracy in the Mediterranean was complicating European affairs; the Sino-Japanese war was a new horror. The world seemed an even blacker and madder place than when we had left it. We thought regretfully of the tranquil, beautiful seclusion of Shimshal.

It was here that we learned of the terrible tragedy which had overtaken our friends on Nanga Parbat in June.

From Gilgit our way led to the valley of the Indus, which we followed for some miles of its desert course, past the glistening flanks of Nanga Parbat. The Burzil pass, bleak and treeless, led us into the entrancing valley of Gurais. Here autumn's colours of orange and scarlet and gold burnt like little tongues of flame against the sombre green of the pines. There were tumbling streams, so lovely after the muddy glacier torrents of the high mountains, with here and there still, deep pools, brilliantly reflecting small bushes with pointed crimson leaves. Once more our path lead upwards, and one evening, at the end of a long day's march of twenty-five miles, we stood on the crest of the last pass. From above the pines, we looked down upon the whole vale of Kashmir, spread like a map below. Overhead the sky was flecked with coral sunset clouds. We stayed for a moment. Then we ran down the hill as the red-gold sunset faded from the snows of Haramuk, leaving them ghostly white in the blue dusk. Light ebbed from the sky, and the pines were black against the stars.

The next day we were welcomed back to Srinagar, and realized the full meaning of true hospitality, which gives comfort and rest and makes no demands. Kashmir was a delicious interlude in which to harvest a store of memories and arrange them in perspective for later delight.

Distance has no need to lend enchantment, although it seems to lessen the difficulties and soften the hardships; for the supreme value of the expedition centred in an experience of real freedom rounded off with the peace and content of an arduous job of work completed and enjoyed.

UPON THAT MOUNTAIN

Upon That Mountain

First published by Hodder and Stoughton Limited, 1943

Contents

Foreword *by Geoffrey Winthrop Young* *page* 311

1 The Approach 315
2 The Alps 324
3 First Climbs on Mount Kenya 335
4 Mount Kenya – the West Ridge of Batian 350
5 Mountains of the Moon 364
6 Everest, 1933 – 1 369
7 Everest, 1933 – 2 382
8 Large Expeditions 394
9 Small Expeditions 399
10 Nanda Devi 408
11 Everest, 1935, 1936, 1938 421
12 Shaksgam – 1 436
13 Shaksgam – 2 445
14 Karakoram, 1939 451

Maps and diagrams
Mount Kenya 339
Mount Kenya – diagrams of Shipton's routes 344
Mount Everest – northern approaches 427

FOREWORD

by Geoffrey Winthrop Young

THE outbreak of war overtook Eric Shipton beyond the frontiers of India. His long and self-reliant experience of peoples, places and tongues qualified him for war work of a responsible kind. He returned last winter for a few weeks, writing this book upon the journey; he married, surveyed the home field, left to his wife the publication of the book in the intervals of her own work in the A.T.S., and again disappeared, upon a distant, responsible charge. The adventures, and this their fashion of issue, seem to me equally characteristic of the man; and it is a peculiar pleasure that their richness of suggestion for the future of mountain exploration should be appearing during my own presidency of the Alpine Club, the parent of all mountain associations. For, as it has been the nursery of the finest of adventurous traditions, so also the Club should continue to show itself the guardian of the new training for fitness of body and spirit which our own hills, no less than distant ranges, will be offering to oncoming generations.

Twice in a lifetime we have seen war – indefensible in itself – eliciting from commonplace or uncultivated men and boys and girls qualities of heroism and acts of supreme self-sacrifice, and educating in the majority of those who by chance survived its dangers a new and finer moral and social conscience. And twice we have had to face the realisation – not agreeable to the educational minded – that our accepted ways of training the young in peace years have been defective; and that they will go on being so, until we have discovered how to stress qualities of chivalry, self-reliance and generosity, and how to soft-pedal their opposites, without having to wait for some periodic purge of war to educate those whom it does not destroy.

Only a contact with realities, realities of endurance, of uncertainty and of service, can train character; and in our early years they must be realities so modified as to test but not overtest immaturity. There is no such reality in the competition of games, or of examination. It can be found only in contests of uncertain issue, and progressive severity, with opposing natural forces: either with other human beings in destructive warfare, or with the elements, waves and winds and height and space. Even during this war we have reflected; and we have begun to retrace our steps in the revival of our one-time splendid sea training. Sea schools, and not only for the future sailors, are one answer to our problem. Another is to be found in this book, in the story of the discipline and spiritual self-realisation which are to be found on the ascent of the Hill Difficulty and in the sojourn among hostile spaces.

Eric Shipton stands in the forefront of our present-day explorers. Since boyhood he has been an adventurer, and since boyhood a rebellious intelligence has held him back from all conventional openings and steered him inevitably into the single positive alternative – the life of a pioneer. He has refused to accept traditional methods even in exploration, and he has gone far towards perfecting a new technique of toughening by travel. Happily, he is also an illuminating writer, and I have for long placed his "Nanda Devi", the first penetration into the sanctuary of that glorious mountain, among the best books of adventure known to me. In the present volume he relates his whole Odyssey from a fortunate boyhood, when even in school holidays he was free to wander far afield, to the week when news of the war found him in the Shaksgam valleys.

In each of his chapters, or stages, we can now see that he set himself to solve some special explorer's problem: how, for instance, to mountaineer for long and far at little cost, and without the majestic cumbrousness of preceding Himalayan tradition; how to inure the human body to hardship and perpetual rains under tropical conditions, until an absolute fitness is attained, at which point the capacity to enjoy beauty or strangeness begins to function again independently of physical discomfort; how, without large provisioning, to live off a barren or glacial land, even if it means competing with the local bears for the seasonal bamboo-shoot to avert starvation; how again, where even bamboo-shoots are wanting, to carry provisioning enough oneself, even though it meant a schism between the Shipton and the Tilman schools – whether a second shirt is or is not a superfluity for a three months' rude travel; how again to evade the restrictions of time hitherto imposed by the coming of the monsoon; and again how – but the solution in this case was postponed by the war – to fortify an explorer so that he may be able to continue his work irrespective of the coming of winter and its additional severities among glacial ranges. He traverses new ground, also, when he is treating of the management of temper and mood under primitive conditions; a vital but formerly unmentionable condition of success, which I ventured first to approach, in writing of mountaineering, after the last world war had dissipated some little of our dangerous Victorian reticence.

Eric Shipton is picturing for us, in effect, a transition to which he has been contributing: the ending of one epoch in mountain exploration and the beginning of a new epoch, in which such venturing may well be within reach of all, regardless of the size of a bank balance, and in which such determined courses may even be insisted upon as essential to a training for any form of leadership. He gives us also the answer to another question, of how a post-war generation will be able to accumulate even the lesser funds needed for the new method of exploration. For the principles governing all such adventure, and directing the process of preparing for it, are the same, whether we are setting out as experienced travellers without hoarded pounds for Turkestan, or tramping as boys, upon our hoarded shillings, into the – to us – equally unknown and wonderful hill spaces of Wales or Cumberland or Scotland. Weather, hunger, weariness, loss of route or of temper or of nerve, are to be our opponents in either case, and our own spirit is to become the disciplined ally, whose measure we have first to take and then to mend, until it can serve us as a fit and happy leader.

Like most of us, Eric Shipton started his adventure from two impulses: the one, the urge to try himself out against the unknown; the other, the passion to reach "neverendingness", to be free of that inevitable "other side" which bore so heavily upon Richard Jefferies' *Bevis*. Like many of us, too, he was first inspired by Whymper's writings to look for this realisation among mountains; and like R. L. Stevenson – and again like a number of us – he began with a solitary wandering in France . We can follow his expeditions, almost unaware of the twofold progress we are sharing, until we find ourselves echoing his own dictum, that "it is not the approach that matters, but the attitude of mind", and we realise suddenly the inner meaning and the true end of his – as of all – good physical adventuring. It is not long since the restless spirit of a disillusioned younger Europe was acclaiming the frantic feats of young Fascists and Nazis upon northern Alpine rock walls and in contempt of all known Himalayan risks. It would be hard to imagine a wider divergence, in the method and nature of the undertaking, in the spirit of the doing and in the ultimate effect upon the performer, than that between the stories of those single despairing stunts, to force some self-reassurance from death or from notoriety, and these memories of austere and perilous journeys, pursued in seclusion, and achieving as between the adventurer and his surroundings an always heightened sense of the humour, the beauty and the deeper, harder values of a life lived under natural conditions. I remember Gino Watkins, a forerunner in the art of exploration as a higher art of living, saying that he would prefer to live among Eskimos in the Arctic, but that returns to civilised ways were necessary, as contrast, in order to be able to retain a detached judgment and to renew a deliberate choice. Eric Shipton reinforces this view. Culture and our civilised arts are there to discover to us the apparent values of this or that fashion of living. But, in order to be able to live, in actual conduct, up to these standards, and to develop in accordance with them, we have to undergo real and hard experience. The outcome for us, whether we match our forces with nearer hill and lake and coast, or further glacier, desert and ocean, is to be our escape from hearsay, from wishful book-worlds and from wilful creeds, and our achievement of a lively and ennobling inward adventure, by means of a series of inspiriting outward conflicts and travels.

CHAPTER ONE

"In the calm darkness of the moonless nights,
In the lone glare of day, the snows descend
Upon that mountain; none beholds them there,
Nor when the flakes burn in the sinking sun
Or the star beams dart through them."
Shelley (Lines from *Mont Blanc*, 1816.)

The Approach

EVERY child, I suppose, spends a large proportion of its time in a day-dream about trees, or engines, or the sea, or horses, or Central Africa, or some other subject that has captured its imagination. Unfortunately these longings are seldom expressed and are generally submerged by the weight of conventional upbringing and education, but sometimes sufficient remains to have a decisive effect upon later life.

My earliest recollections are of day-dreams about strange countries. My adventures in these places were not very startling, but everything had a quality of endlessness – the rivers went on for ever, the mountains were infinitely high, and the country always changing. My great delight at the seaside was to put a bottle or a piece of pumice into the sea and watch it float away, or on a windy day to throw a rag into the air to be blown away. I used to imagine these objects travelling on for ever, and I went with them. I am glad that nobody pointed out that my bottles and pumice would be washed up a few hundred yards farther along the beach, or that my rags would soon be swept into a dustbin.

I was lucky, as I had plenty to stimulate my imagination, for I was never in one place for long, and spent much of my time travelling about in Ceylon and Southern India with frequent voyages between Europe and the East. To an adult these journeys measured in an exact number of geographical miles, or in days and hours, become rather monotonous. I found them immensely exciting, and often finished them in a state of exhaustion. Having no precise conception of time and distance, they confirmed my notion of a boundless world. The train winding towards the sandy tip of India at Dhanushkodi, and chugging noisily through the jungle clad gorges of up-country Ceylon and the Nilgiris; an early morning of strange scents, travelling swiftly by coconut palms and paddy fields; Stromboli belching fire and smoke; a whale spouting far in the wake of the ship – these were some of the impressions that kept alive the blissful day-dreams during the later dreary years of preparatory school routine, and successfully removed all chance of mastering Latin syntax.

Then came those old-fashioned books of natural history that dealt courageously with The Universe, illustrating it with quaint engravings of strange rock formations in the Hartz Mountains, the Mammoth Caves in Kentucky, the Aurora Borealis, and eruption of Mount Etna; always with little men, armed with long staves, looking on as though they themselves were responsible for the phenomena. But none of these things was a part of the school curriculum. They could find no expression; and never for a moment did it occur to me that interest in such things might suggest a line of approach when considering the awful question, "What will I do when I grown up?" The choice of a profession seemed to be limited to the Army, the Church, Doctoring, or an office (whatever that meant). At the time none of these seemed very attractive, but seeing no alternatives I avoided the question as much as possible. Explorers were only mythical beings that one read about, and scientists were men of vast intellect who would certainly have had no difficulty in learning Kennedy's Latin Primer by heart. So my all absorbing interests were relegated to the classification of "a hobby" – hardly even that since I could do nothing about it.

Any particular set of tastes can find expression in a variety of ways, and most people who know what they want have a large choice of routes along which they can pursue the same objective. If at an early age I had been taught to handle and navigate a small boat, I think I should have derived as much satisfaction from sailing as I have from climbing; the sea would have absorbed my interest and enthusiasm in the same way that mountains have done. The two pursuits offer the same opportunities for personal identification with natural phenomena – both demand a thorough knowledge of the elements concerned and skill in dealing with them; both provide an unlimited outlet for physical energy and a capacity for aesthetic enjoyment; both open up a vast field of possibility, each has its great tradition of adventure, each has its history, though while the history of sailing is as old as that of the human race, the history of mountaineering covers only the last hundred and fifty years.

But instead of learning to sail, I read Edward Whymper's "Travels Among the Great Andes of the Equator". The author is better known for his "Scrambles Amongst the Alps", but this came later in my education. On his Andes trip Whymper set out, with two Alpine guides, to study natural phenomena at high altitudes. He approached his task with that extraordinary diversity of interest which was a quality of travellers of the nineteenth century. He described his adventures with delightful simplicity, and illustrated them with countless engravings. How much more satisfactory are those engravings than the modern photograph! I have not read the book again, but I still have the most vivid impressions of it: the climbing of Chimborazo; the illustration of the be-goggled climbers, with enormous mercurial barometers on their backs, flogging their way through deep snow towards the summit, while below was the dramatic caption, "We were then twenty thousand feet high" – to reach twenty thousand feet on a mountain seemed to me an achievement with which I would die happily; the night spent on the summit of Cotopaxi, looking down into the inferno of the active crater; the yarn about thousands of tons of eyeless fish erupted by the volcano from subterranean rivers that never saw the light; the frontispiece depicting the party struggling to erect their tent in a blizzard – "The whirling snow mocked our efforts." This book focused my attention upon mountains and my dreams upon mountain travel. It was obviously a field with unlimited scope for adventure and strange experience. I read everything I could lay my hands on about mountains.

Soon after this I spent an Easter holiday with my mother and sister in the Pyrenees. It was thrilling to see that the things I had read about really did exist: the thundering torrents, the great rock gorges with glistening, sweating flanks, the dark pine forests that guarded the approaches to the wonderland of everlasting ice and snow beyond, the great peaks infinitely remote and inaccessible and with all the strange feeling of mystery and hidden treasure. One wonderful day we went to some caves and sailed in a boat down a subterranean river overhung by fantastic stalactites. The journey took about two hours, as far as I can remember, and carried us clean through a mountain. On another occasion we went to see the Cirque de Gavarnie, which had been the subject of an illustration in one of my Universe books.

Yes, there was no question about it, mountains offered all that the heart could desire. Once I saw a party of climbers with ice-axes and rope. I regarded them with reverence and awe. I was a bit worried about this climbing business. Obviously, it seemed, one must climb if one were to have anything to do with mountains. I had experienced a tremendous thrill scrambling up a rough mountain slope, which suffered little by the disillusionment of my rapid exhaustion. But real climbing involved hanging by finger nails over giddy drops. I was frightened of drops, and could not bear to look over the edge of a high building or even to stand on a high balcony with only a flimsy iron railing between me and the street below. But the attraction of mountains was so strong that even this fear assumed a kind of fascination.

But how did one set about climbing? I had met no one who was remotely interested in that sort of thing. Mountaineering obviously did not form part of the more serious life, in preparation for which I was spending so many dreary hours and days trying to get some sense out of meaningless Latin text books. Whymper had gone to the Alps as an artist for some London newspaper, Tyndall as a scientific professor, but I was just an inky-fingered schoolboy. My holidays had all been arranged for me, and I did not conceive the notion of going off to the mountains on my own. It is curious at that age how shy one is of talking about one's passions, particularly when those passions are evidently outlandish and not shared by normal people. It was particularly strange in my case, for I would certainly have received a sympathetic hearing at home. But the set formulæ of examination and athletic education did nothing to encourage originality of interest and outlook.

However, Providence was remarkably kind, and sent a Norwegian lad named Gustav Sommerfelt of about my own age, to my school. He came in the Easter term preceding my visit to the Pyrenees, and was due to go back to Norway after the summer term. Early in the summer term he proposed that I should go to Norway with him to spend as much of the holidays as we could afford in the Jotunheimen, the highest mountains in Norway, and the rest of the time in a hut that his parents owned in the forests farther to the south. The proposal took my breath away and it was a long time before I could bring myself to believe in its possibility. There must be a snag somewhere. Such a thing was just too good to be true. What about the passage to Norway, surely that must cost the Earth? But no, the father of my remarkable friend knew a man who had something to do with shipping, and he could easily fix us up with a free passage on a cargo boat.

The weeks of that term were the longest I have ever known. I could talk and think of nothing else but the Jotunheimen, and day by day Gustav's descriptions of the country increased my excitement. It appeared that we were to carry everything on our backs and just push off by ourselves into the mountains with nothing to govern our movements except a map and compass and our own fancy. It was going to be the most wonderful thing that had ever happened. But behind all this exultation was an awful dread. Would something happen to crush with one blow all these heavenly plans? A broken limb, the measles, a decision to keep Gustav in England for another term; it seemed impossible that all those weeks could go by without providing some such disaster. But these fearful speculations were confined to the hours of "work". Leisure hours were devoted to blissful discussion of plans, when nothing but the one glorious certainty of our project was allowed to obtrude. Then suddenly everything crashed. Gustav came to me with a long face and announced that he had strained his heart, and had been ordered to rest for an indefinite period. Of course it had to be like that. I had known all along that such castles in the air could not really turn out to be built on solid foundations. The bitterness of the disappointment swamped me, and it never occurred to me that the idea was still there and could surely be put into practice somehow. However, the diagnosis had either been wrong or Gustav's heart made a remarkable recovery, for he was soon pronounced fit again.

The sailings of Norwegian cargo ships were admirably timed. This one necessitated leaving school a whole day early, and provided us with an excuse that even a headmaster would accept. A day, moreover, was composed of 24 hours, or 1,440 minutes, which ever way you look at it.

At last it arrived. The end of term was always an occasion of wild excitement, just as the last day of the holidays was one of profound gloom, but never had I felt such mad joy as on the last morning of that particular summer term. Sitting in the train, I pointed out to Gustav the highest point of the Chiltern Hills, and we laughed heartily at the idea that these ridiculous little bumps should even be called hills. We could afford to laugh, for we were both experienced mountain travellers – he in the wild mountains of Norway, and I with my great experience in the Pyrenees.

We spent one night in London. I had a delicious feeling of superiority which always preceded and followed my early mountain adventures. I was genuinely sorry for all those silly people at the theatre that evening who were not sharing our enterprise, and I hoped that they would find something to compensate them for their sad misfortune. The next day we travelled to a place called Blyth in Northumberland. I was in a fever lest our ship had left without us. But after a long search among grimy docks we found her lying passively in a cloud of coal dust, and with no evident intention of moving. Indeed, we had to wait for 24 hours before we set sail, and I began to revise my opinion of the excellence of

Norwegian time-tables. Also the appearance of the ship itself was a bit depressing. She was of the type that one imagines for ever fastened to the quay-side, idly loading and unloading some mysterious cargo. But the warmth of our welcome by the captain and crew soon put us in better spirits.

We were given comfortable berths in the sick-bay. Most appropriately as it turned out. I am not as a rule worried by rough seas, but on this occasion I had been introduced to that brown Norwegian cheese known as Mesost. It is very sweet. I thought it was great stuff, and spent much of my 24 hours in Blyth eating it. The result of my gluttony was twofold: though the sea was not unduly rough I was very ill, and I have never been able to eat Mesost since. Gustav was ill too, which mitigated my sufferings a little. But some three mornings later we awoke to find ourselves moving smoothly up the Christiania Fjord (as it was called in those days) with the rocky pine-clad shores of the promised land close at hand. We left our ship at Fredrikstad and went by train to Christiania (Oslo), where we spent two days buying boots and eating enormous quantities of strawberries and cream. Strawberries in Christiania were remarkably cheap: I have never understood why.

On the night before we left the capital, Gustav gave me lessons in oiling boots and packing a rucksack. The latter task was a most serious affair, and appeared to require as expert a hand as packing valuable glass. I was made to do it over and over again before my efforts would pass muster. I am afraid that like so much of my education this lesson had no lasting effect, and in all the years that I have packed rucksacks since that early initiation, my only method has been to take the things as they came to hand and to ram them down with as much force as was necessary to get them all in; and when mere arm power failed to produce sufficient compression, feet generally did the trick.

The main trouble about those rucksacks was their weight. But this was only forced upon my notice later, and even then it did not occur to me that it was largely due to all the unnecessary things we carried. I simply accepted the idea that a spare pair of trousers, pyjamas, and a change of underclothing and shoes were necessities, and tried to forget my aching, untrained shoulders. We even took washing materials, which in view of my later ideas of "travelling light" seems incredible. Soap was the first of the civilised amenities that I learnt to dispense with. Indeed, my sister still maintains that the only reason I climb is that it provides me with an opportunity to avoid washing.

Our journey to the Jotunheimen was first by train through endless rocky pine forests, and then by bus climbing up and up above the trees, through wide valleys of rough grass and boulders, to Bygdin at the end of the road. The next day the real adventure began. It was a sad anti-climax to those months of eager anticipation. After half an hour my shoulders began to ache from the drag of the rucksack straps. It rained in torrents, and I was soon wet through and very cold. I could only see a few hundred yards in any direction, and what I could see was bleak and dismal. My enthusiasm for mountains evaporated, and I could only think of the end of the day's march and wonder how much farther we had to go. I did not dare to complain, and plodded wearily behind my companion in morose silence. But soon I was to discover that the pain and weariness of physical effort are quickly forgotten in a glow of retrospective warmth, and even before we had entered the rest house at the end of our first day's march my spirits had revived. A fire and a huge meal restored to mountains their lost enchantment.

Our trip to the Jotunheimen was a simple walking tour, and we did not attempt any serious mountaineering. But I think on the whole it justified my high expectations. After a few days my stiffness and fatigue left me, and I was able to take an intelligent interest in the country and in the thrilling business of identifying it with our large-scale map. I even became resigned to the weight of my rucksack, though I never really liked carrying a load, and my shoulders still ached. The mountains were very different from those I had seen in the Pyrenees. They were smaller and rounder, and the peaks seemed to be less aloof and mysterious. There were none of those tremendous forest-filled gorges. But the country had a different kind of fascination; a grand desolation and an endless breadth. Walking on and on from place to place through an ever changing scene was a most satisfying experience. Sometimes we stopped for a day to climb an easy peak. These days were all the better because I could leave my hated load behind. One day Gustav was ill and stayed in bed, while I walked to the head of the valley we were in. Here I found a glacier which came down from a hidden world of ice peaks. In a state of glorious excitement I started to walk up by the side of the glacier, and before long I was forced to get on to the ice itself. But soon I was brought up short on the brink of a crevasse. I had read about these sinister monsters, and I was suitably scared, so I decided not to proceed any farther with my exploration of the glacier. It was very tantalising, but my disappointment and my fright only increased the delicious mystery of the region above. Later on we joined another party with a guide to cross a glacier pass. For this we had to be roped together.

We finished our holiday with two weeks at the Sommerfelt family hut in the forest of Hardanger, where we spent our days idly pulling pink-fleshed trout out of the lake, eating them and discussing our mountain journey. The weather in the Jotunheimen was almost always bad. We had cursed it heartily, but it had not upset our plans. Besides, bad weather in mountains, though it generally puts a stop to serious climbing, does not spoil the mountains themselves. In fact, I have come nearer to being bored with mountain scenery during a long spell of cloudless weather than I ever have in rain and mist.

That trip to Norway opened the door to all sorts of wonderful possibilities. One had only to look at the map of Europe to sow the seeds of some new project. In those days it was not mountaineering as such that attracted me. I did not think much about climbing except as a means of seeing mountains. No, it was all the strange and wonderful things about the mountains themselves, as described by Whymper and Tyndall and now seen by myself. But the most fascinating of all these phenomena was volcanoes. I bought all the books I could find on the subject. Some of these plunged me into a sea of geological and physical technicalities that I did not understand, but most of them were by nineteenth-century scientists who told a simple story of fantastic events, and provided nice easy explanations.

So, most of all, I wanted to go and look at volcanoes. For a long time I thought about Iceland, but unfortunately no Icelander turned up at school, and

31 'The Ogre' (Baintha Brakk) from the western side of Snow Lake.

32 33 Shipton's and Tilman's indefatigable Sherpa partners – Angtharkay (left) and Sen Tensing ('Foreign Sportsman').

34 The pass (Sokha La) in the West Biafo Wall that Tilman used to reach the controversial 'Cornice' (Sokha) Glacier. *Photo: Don Morrison*

35 (above) A view up the Sokha (Cornice) Glacier. The Sokha La is off picture to the right.

36 (left) A rocky cirque on the south side of the Sokha Glacier.

37 (bottom left) Peaks of the Sokha/Sosbun watershed from the Sosbun Glacier. The South Face of Sosbun Brakk is in the centre.

These photos were taken by Peter Mott during the 1939 Expedition. In 1937 Tilman called the main glacier stream in Photo 37 the Hoh Lungma Glacier, and the branch on the right the Sosbun.

(above) The head of the Braldu Glacier
ɔking south-west to the peaks along the
.ow Lake watershed.

(left) A view down the Biafo Glacier
ɔm a camp at its junction with the Sim Gang
acier.

(top right) A huge ice-arch on Braldu
acier.

(bottom right) Michael Spender in
ȝs after three months in the field.

The 1939 Karakoram Expedition:

42 (top) A panoramic view across Snow Lake to the south and west from Khurdopin Pass.

43 (above) A view east from the camp on Hispar Pass showing the Sim Gang Glacier section of Snow Lake with the icy walls of The Ogre on the right and Bobisghir on the left.

44 (near right) Peter Mott surveying from above Snow Lake. 45 (far right) A crevasse on the edge of Snow Lake below Khurdopin Pass.

46 (above) The Choktoi Glacier basin flanked by the Latok Peaks and The Ogre (right). Shipton and Fountaine crossed cols at the head of the valley (off picture, right of The Ogre) to return to Snow Lake.

49 Shipton with his mother and Elie Richard (centre right) in the Dauphiné in 1926.

48 (above right) Rock-climbing on the Terrace Wall Variant, Tryfan, North Wales in 1928.

50 (below left) Shipton on the Aiguille Mummery.

51 52 (above right) Gilbert Peaker and Jack Longland (top). On the boat to Kenya, 1929.

53 (right) Shipton and Lewa approaching the summit of Kamet (25,447 ft.) in 1931.

55 (below left) Nelion from the summit of Batian. Mackinder's first ascent route reached the col ('Gate of Mists') by a line up the Diamond Glacier on the right. *Photo: John Cleare* 56 (inset) Shipton and Wyn Harris on the summit of Nelion in 1929.
57 (right) Batian from Point Piggott. This splendid vantage point enabled Shipton and Tilman to make an advance assessment of the difficulties of the West Ridge which faces the camera.

Rongbuk Glacier curves round from the left into the cwm below the North Col. The route took the summit/shaded rib in the centre of the face.

59 (below left) A telephoto of the North-East Ridge and North Face of Everest from the summit of Khartaphu, a 23,000 ft. peak first climbed by Shipton and Edwin Kempson in 1935. The pre-war route follows the spur rising from the bottom right and thence across the upper slopes towards the summit. The heavy, unconsolidated snow conditions seen here frustrated all the attempts in the late 'thirties.

60 (right) Frank Smythe and Shipton after their 1933 attempt.

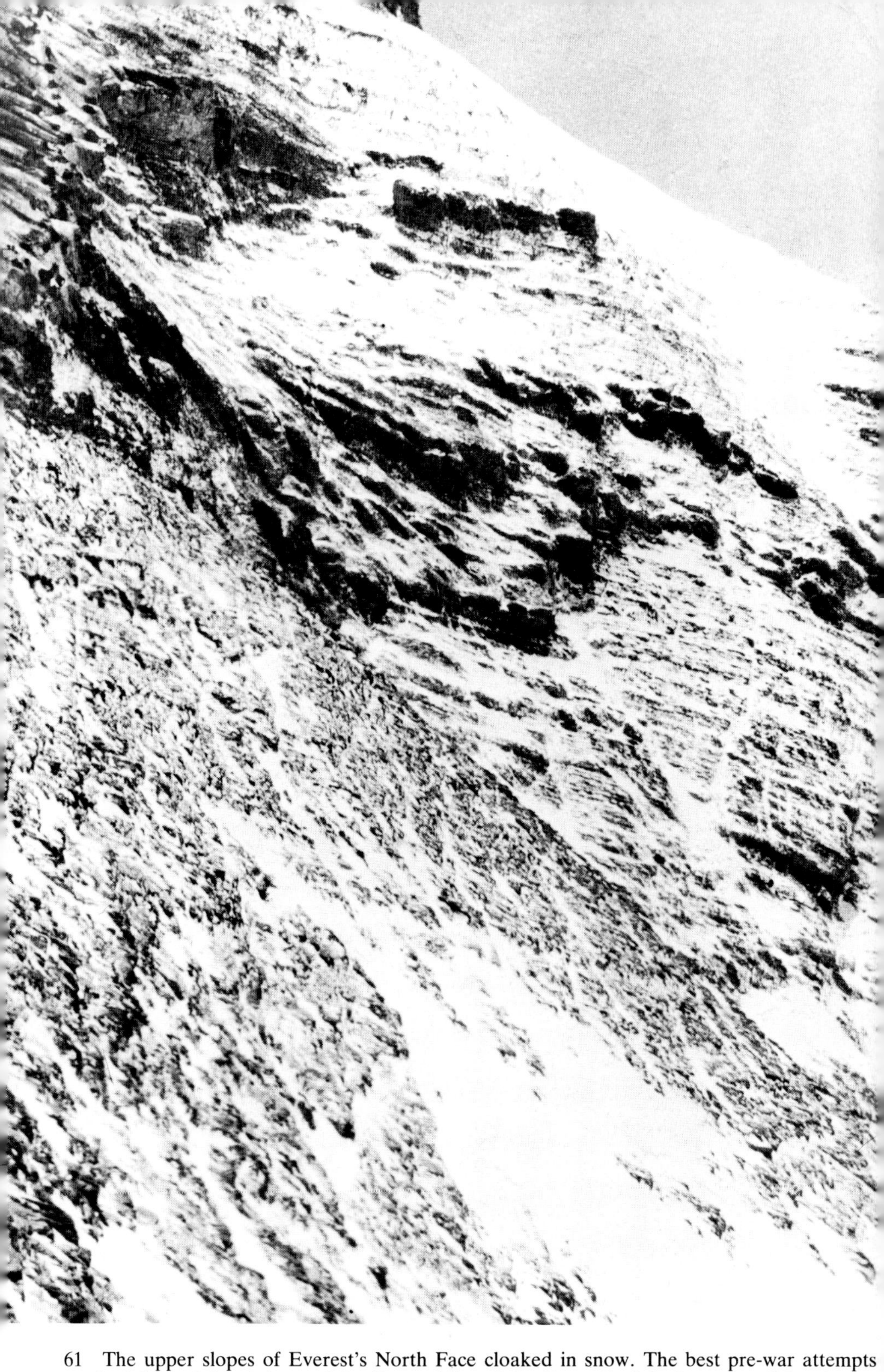

61 The upper slopes of Everest's North Face cloaked in snow. The best pre-war attempts reached the rock bands beyond the diagonal line of the Great Couloir. In unconsolidated snow these slopes are very dangerous, but Reinhold Messner's solo ascent in 1982 and that of the Australian climbers in 1984 proved that in adequate snow conditions rapid progress is possible.

the difficulties of getting to that country by myself seemed to be insuperable. The extinct volcanoes of central France presented me with a poor alternative. Here things were easier. The journey was easy; the exchange made it far cheaper to travel in France than to take any sort of a holiday in England, and my mother had an old friend called M. Chalus who lived in Clermont-Ferrand and who offered to provide a companion for me, thereby overcoming the quite unreasonable objection to my going alone. Moreover French, unlike Icelandic, was part of my school curriculum, and therefore provided a more effective weapon of persuasion. Once I had made up my mind to go, there was no "poor alternative" about it, and the Auvergne appeared to be the most alluring place in Europe. In achieving this rôle it was greatly assisted by engravings in my Volcano books. My prospective companion somehow disgraced himself in the eyes of his family, and as a punishment was forbidden to take a summer holiday that year. I was sorry for my unknown colleague, but deep down I was truly thankful, for it seemed unlikely that a stray Frenchman would have shared my passion for gazing at extinct volcanoes. Besides, it was good to feel entirely free. It required little argument to overcome the objection to my going alone. I owe a great deal to my mother's broad-minded attitude towards my activities.

But these plans were for the following summer, and in the meantime I quite unexpectedly started climbing. My sister and I were taken to Adelboden in Switzerland for winter sports. Rising above the village was a mountain called the Gross Lohner, 10,000 feet high. I had spotted it on the map, and, before I left England, I was consumed with a longing to climb it. But I knew enough to realise that mid-winter was not the right time for climbing mountains. Fortunately that year there was no snow in the lower valleys for ski-ing, and I managed to persuade five other people in the hotel to share with me the expense of two guides and attempt to climb the Gross Lohner.

It was the most thrilling experience I had ever known. For once the event was even better than the anticipation of it. We spent the night in a snow-bound hut below the Wildstrubel and started several hours before dawn the next morning. The climb was not difficult, but in winter conditions difficult enough to impress me. We were roped together; there was some step cutting to be done by the guides, and we wore snow goggles just like the pictures in Whymper's book. I was tremendously impressed by the lovely easy movements of the guides on difficult ground, by their power and self-confidence, and I longed to emulate them. The day was fine and the view from the summit was magnificent. I do not think that wide views of mountains in winter can compare with those in summer; the mountains look untidy and crowded together, and the lovely contrast between green valleys and white peaks is lacking. But the view from the top of the Gross Lohner was good enough for me. The guides pointed out the Matterhorn and Weisshorn of the distant Pennines and the nearer giants of the Oberland. Then the descent: the slow cautious movements down the steep upper face; the sudden freedom when the difficulties were passed; the joyous plunge down long snow slopes to the trees; the tired, happy plod along the forest paths. I felt when I got back to the hotel that all my senses had been sharpened and my whole outlook changed by the crowded experiences of the last 24 hours. In the Gross Lohner I now had a priceless possession. I bought a big picture of the mountain, looking in its mantle of winter snow as fine as any Himalayan giant, and hung it in my room at home.

There were two more climbs that holiday; one, alone with a guide up a gaunt rock spine, where I discovered that looking down a vertical drop from an exposed rock ledge was not half as bad as I had feared; the other with two French experts who had climbed the Matterhorn.

The Easter holidays were spent in northern Italy, where I saw another aspect of the Alps and managed to get a little more climbing by making a hazardous expedition to Monte della Disgrazia. So by the time the next summer holidays came round my attitude towards mountains had undergone a considerable change. The desire to explore them had found a practical expresion in the sport or art of mountaineering, and this new-found passion was soon to eclipse for many years the wider view. I had not, I am glad to say, lost interest in the Auvergne, but school summer holidays are long and there would be plenty of time to visit the Dauphiné Alps as well. Life was very full.

In Clermont, I was treated by the Chalus as a member of the family. Indeed, I found it hard to get away. When eventually I managed to persuade them to let me go, my kind host rushed off to the tourist bureau and booked me a seat in the Mont Dore bus. I had considerable difficulty in persuading him that I proposed to walk. At first he regarded it as a joke, but when he saw that I was serious he became very perturbed. After the generous treatment I had received I was most reluctant to upset these kind people, but what could I do? Many of the most interesting old volcanoes lay between Clermont and Mont Dore, and my plan had been to walk slowly over them and to linger in the places that took my fancy. I might, of course, have started in the Mont Dore bus and left it when I was well out of Clermont. But this would certainly have led to complications, and I thought it best to have the matter out there and then. I do not think I convinced them of my sanity, but at length they acquiesced with eloquent shrugs. However, I evidently repaid them for their anxiety by providing a story which was recounted and embroidered for many years.

There is a lot to be said for travelling alone. Contact with the country and the people is more intimate, and the traveller has only himself to consider in his day to day plans, and in the satisfaction of his whims. I was very young, and the whole thing seemed a tremendous adventure. At first I was rather lonely and felt very foolish tramping along a main road with an enormous pack on my back while cars flashed by, blinding me with their dust. But when I got into wilder country and learnt to seek my food and rest in peasant cottages, I began to feel more at home, and there was too much to occupy my attention and too much to do, to notice that I was alone. Anyone who has read Stevenson will understand the charm of that country, certainly a great deal better than I can ever describe it. I had not at the time read his famous "Travels", or I might have been tempted to take a companion to carry my load. This was still ridiculously heavy, and caused me much pain and grief.

This journey took place a very long time ago, and as I did not keep a diary most of the details of times and place-names and the exact sequence of events are forgotten. I have sometimes tried to keep a diary, but writing down the events of the day has always seemed rather silly at the time, and it is not until long after that the little mundane entries can do their work of romantic reconstruction. Never having had much of an eye for the future, my occasional efforts at diary writing have rarely survived the first few days of an expedition. But though the details are gone the essence of the experience remains, and can be vividly reproduced in thought and feeling.

So far as I can remember I walked for about three weeks in the Auvergne and the Cevennes, generally along the smaller roads, sometimes across the mountains. There is no better way of getting to know country than by walking over it, and I had a delicious feeling almost of personal possession, such as I had already felt for my first Alpine peaks, and which comes from a true understanding of the country. It was not, in fact, the long unbroken sensation of glorious enjoyment that it seems now in memory. My load dragged as unpleasantly as ever; I was often hot and painfully thirsty; I developed enormous blisters on my feet; a strained Achilles tendon was rubbed mercilessly by my boot; once I was rather frighteningly lost in the mist amongst some wild mountains. But I became so absorbed in my adventure that I hardly thought about the more spectacular Dauphiné plans, and towards the end I was tempted to continue my wanderings in central France for the whole of the holidays. I found I could live quite comfortably on ten francs a day, which at the rate of exchange then prevailing, amounted to about 1s. 3d. At first I made few friends, being much too shy to display my school French more than was absolutely necessary. However, this mood soon passed, and presently I was conversing happily with anyone I met. Once I met a Greek at an inn and travelled with him in a punt through the wonderful gorges of the river Tarn.

Eventually I returned to Clermont by a different route. M. Chalus was away in Paris and the only occupants of the house were his mother who was over eighty, and her nun companion. These two ladies were profoundly shocked by my disreputable appearance, grimy, sun-scorched and tattered. I had not realised my beggarly appearance, or I doubt if I should have had the courage to enter that select and spotless establishment. But I soon discovered that their concern was for my apparent discomfort and not for the impropriety of entertaining a tramp. I was plunged into a hot bath, provided with endless luxuries and petted and pampered in a most delicious manner. After basking in their heart-warming hospitality for a day or two I set out for the Dauphiné and the high mountains.

This then was my approach to the hills. It was a devious and round-about route that led by a series of accidents to a passion that has had a decisive influence upon my life. Some start climbing because their fathers before them have climbed, others because of tutors or friends. These ways of introduction have many advantages. I prefer my own line, as the next man will prefer his. But in any field of human activity it is not the road of approach that matters, but the attitude of mind; for whatever changes time and experience may bring, whatever conceits or failures, something of the early feeling will always remain. Best of all is the eager humility of a child.

CHAPTER TWO

The Alps

IT is impossible of course to provide an entirely satisfactory explanation for any recreation. The predominant motive in any human activity varies according to the temperament of the individual. Mountaineering provides good exercise in pleasant surroundings, a sense of satisfaction in overcoming difficulties, the joy, akin to dancing, of controlled rhythmic movement, a stimulating contact with danger, a wealth of beautiful scenery and a release from the tiresome restrictions of modern life. The expert likes to practise or display his skill. Some confess to having been drawn to climbing by a physical inferiority complex engendered by their failure at school to hit a ball straight and far. These motives are probably sufficient in themselves, and they certainly form the basis of many other sports. But in the deep devotion to any form of active endeavour there is generally something else we seek. In the case of mountaineering it is a kind of personal identification with the hills themselves, which comes of intimate understanding and strenuous contest and which brings with it a wealth of philosophical content. Above all, in my view, the attraction lies in the memory of those rare moments of intellectual ecstasy which occur perhaps on a mountain summit, perhaps on a glacier at dawn or in a lovely moonlit bivouac, and which appear to be the result of a happy coincidence in the rhythm of mind and scene. These moments are not of course peculiar to mountaineering; they may be realised in deserts, on the sea and elsewhere. Such exaltation of feeling is achieved more often, I imagine, and in more normal circumstances by the mind of the creative artist, but for ordinary folk it would seem that it is more readily found in close contact with nature.

Mountaineering is an art in the same sense that sailing is an art, or horsemanship, or big-game hunting. The thorough mastery of each of these crafts requires a combination of technical skill, knowledge and experience. It is possible to become proficient at handling a boat on the Norfolk broads and yet to know nothing of sailing in its wider aspects of navigation and deep-sea travel, to ride well without becoming an expert horseman or to shoot a tiger and remain ignorant of jungle lore. Many people, owing to circumstance or inclination, are content with such superficial contact. In the same way the experience of climbing behind guides on well known ground is very far from being the whole art of mountaineering.

The sport of climbing as we now know it began somewhere in the middle of the nineteenth century. Mountains were climbed long before that, but then motives appear to have resembled more closely those attributed by the general public to the would-be scientific purpose. It was not until about the 1850's that people started to go to the high Alps for sport and recreation. At first of course their objective was the climbing of the great peaks by the easiest way they could find and the crossing of high passes. Later, as the number of unclimbed peaks diminished and mountaineering technique developed, interest began to centre less on the summits themselves and more on the great faces and ridges of the mountains. To-day not only all the peaks of the Alps, but nearly all the faces and ridges, too, have been climbed, and the mountaineer in search of new conquests must look to the more distant ranges, in some of which the field is practically unlimited.

But for all that, the Alps still provide as good climbing as can be found in any other range in the world. Certainly there is nowhere that offers such a good training ground for mountaineers. The reason for this lies in the combination of three factors; variety, accessibility and expert tuition. Almost any kind of climbing can be found there, from the rock pinnacles of the Dolomites to the great ice precipices of Mont Blanc. The mountains themselves are so easily accessible and so well provided with hotels and huts that most of one's time there can be spent actually climbing. Moreover the size of the peaks is exactly right from the climber's point of view; anyone, with say, a fortnight's holiday can go to a hut and, if he is energetic enough, can do a dozen climbs in the time. It is obvious then that the opportunities for practice and training are far greater than those offered by the Himalayas, for example, where it may take weeks to get to the foot of a mountain, besides the laborious business of establishing high camps and the unpleasant effects of rarefied atmosphere. Finally, expert guides are to be found in almost ever district of the Alps; this and the large number of people who climb there set a very high standard of performance.

There are only two satisfactory ways for the novice to start mountaineering. One is to be taught the rudiments by an expert amateur; the other is to engage a professional guide. In many ways the former is the more satisfactory method,. A guide is too often interested only in the business of getting the climb done; it is difficult for an inexperienced amateur to assert himself and he is very liable to remain a mere passenger. Usually, too, the guide is climbing on ground with which he is thoroughly familiar, and for him the element of exploration, which is one of the most serious and the most attractive aspects of mountain craft, does not enter into the problem.

In the early days of mountaineering when the Alps were comparatively little known, these objections to guides did not exist to the same extent, and the relations between guide and employer were much less professional. This is probably one reason why the pioneers were content for so long to climb with guides; they themselves had an important function in the team, and were not treated as so much baggage to be got up the mountain and down again with the least possible delay. But it is not so easy to understand why the guide continued so long to be regarded as indispensable. For a time guideless climbers were regarded as reckless heretics who were bound sooner or later to come to a sticky end. There seemed to be something mystic about a guide's powers. Accidents, when they occurred to guideless parties were frowned upon as a result of folly, when they happened to guides they were attributed to events beyond human control. Certainly a guide's local knowledge is a considerable safeguard, but to insist upon local knowledge being present in all climbing parties would be to set such limits to the scope of mountaineering as to rob it of most of its charm. Of course this prejudice against guideless climbing was bound eventually to die. It was gradually recognised not only that an amateur could master the whole of his craft, but that he must strive to do so if he were to taste all its joys.

The average Alpine guide has his limitations. When a man has climbed all his life in the same district he will acquire sureness on his particular peaks, and will tend to rely upon his memory for the ground that he has covered so often. His instinct for finding his way in new country remains undeveloped. A peak that is climbed for the second time presents only a small proportion of the difficulties that were met on the first occasion; if one were to climb it fifty times the procedure would become almost automatic; many of one's mountaineering faculties would be lulled to sleep. Handicapped though he is by the lack of continuous lifelong training, the experienced amateur has this one great advantage over the average guide, by far the majority of his climbing is on ground that is new to him, so that his experience of dealing with new situations is constantly growing, and his capacity for mountain exploration is developed alongside his capacity for mountain climbing. Moreover, different types of mountains require various modifications in technique. For example, anyone who has spent all his time climbing on the sound granite of the Chamonix Aiguilles would probably be at a loss on the friable rock of the Dauphiné, and a climber in the Dauphiné has little opportunity to acquire the gymnastic skill required on the Aiguilles. Many good guides have disappointed their employers when taken out of their native districts.

But this criticism does not apply to the really great guides – and there are and have been many such – who will always be a step or two ahead of the best amateur in most branches of their craft. In mountaineering as in everything else it is the professional who reaches the highest peaks of perfection. For this reason, whether the beginnings are made with amateurs or professionals, the experience of climbing with a first-class guide is an important part of the education of a mountaineer.

Knowing no one who was interested in climbing I had no alternative but to start with guides. My early reading had been confined to the work of the pioneers, and in consequence it never occurred to me that big mountains could be climbed without guides. I imagined that my career as a mountaineer would be severely limited by the amount of cash I could scrape together for their hire. I had acquired a copy of Abraham's "Swiss Mountain Climbs" which set out in depressing detail the official tariffs for the great peaks, the study of which acted as a constant check to my ambitions. I did not see how I could ever aspire to more than a few minor climbs. But the prospect of climbing any mountain made me wild with joy, and even to wander about the valleys and look at the peaks I had read about would be thrilling enough.

I was sorry to leave the Auvergne where I had enjoyed such delicious freedom and adventure. But when I found myself in the train bound for the Alps my regrets were swamped by a mounting excitement. My plans were vague and I had very little idea what I was going to do. The obvious thing seemed to be to make for La Bérarde, which lies in the heart of the highest mountains of the Dauphiné, and I had intended to walk there from Grenoble. I stopped in a pension in Grenoble to give my still painful Achilles tendon a few more days to recover. My time there was divided between watching the local lads trying to climb a pole at the Exposition, wishing I had the moral courage to try myself, and gazing at the windows of the tourist bureaux. Here I saw pictures of wonderful peaks with names straight out of Whymper's book. Mont Pelvoux, Les Ecrins, La Meije. This was too much. Here I was wasting my time dallying on the threshold of Paradise. I packed my rucksack and boarded a bus for La Bérarde.

It was a dismal morning. Rain had been falling for days and leaden clouds covered all the peaks. My fellow passengers were making a day trip to La Bérarde. Their talk was gloomy. Never had there been such a summer. The sun had not appeared for weeks. The higher valleys were not really worth visiting for one could never see more than a few hundred yards; but one had to do something with a holiday. I was incautious enough to remark that I was going to stop in La Bérarde in the hope of climbing. The idea appealed to that lugubrious sense of humour peculiar to the French, and I became the butt of sarcastic witticisms.

But when we reached St. Christoph the clouds were retreating up the mountain sides. Presently a window opened and framed a sharp white peak which seemed to be hanging almost directly overhead; it glistened like a great diamond. Then another appeared and another, and at last sunlight filled the valley. I could not have asked for a better introduction to the summer Alps.

We made a long halt at Les Etages, a tiny hamlet a few miles below La Bérarde, while our driver refreshed himself, and his passengers photographed one another. At the inn I enquired for a guide and was promptly introduced to a bandy-legged little man named Elie Richard. Yes, he would act as my guide. It had been a terrible summer, very little climbing had been possible in August and now the peaks were heavily laden with new snow. But we would climb, and from now on it would be fine. He seemed to be as keen as I was to get going and announced that on the very next day we would climb the Pic Coolidge, which despite its 12,000 feet was not difficult. After that the new snow would settle and we would go after bigger game. This all sounded too good to be true. I broached the question of finance by explaining that I had very little money to spend. But this obstacle was brushed aside as lightly as the weather and the new snow. He would charge me 60 francs (then about 7s.) a day, we would climb every day if I wished, we would live in huts which cost nothing and the cost of our bread would not amount to much. It was settled then; Richard would be at La Bérarde, with a spare ice-axe for me, at one o'clock the next morning. I climbed back into the bus with a joyous heart.

I found pleasant company at La Bérarde. There were very few people staying in the small hotel, and they were all climbers. Everyone was friendly. We sat together at one table and the talk was all of mountains. The others seemed very expert and talked of their lofty ambitions which could not be attempted until many days of fine weather had settled the new snow. I felt very raw and shy, but I basked blissfully in the company of the gods. In the evening some of them invited me to go for a walk with them up the valley. All the clouds had gone, I learnt the names of the peaks in view and we watched the sunset glow touch the western face of the Ailefroide.

The ten days that followed were beyond my wildest expectations. Hitherto I had looked upon the climbing of mountains as isolated experiences, and I had not conceived the idea of linking them together into a continuous mountaineering journey by travelling from place to place over the ranges and even by crossing the peaks themselves. Elie was as good as his word, we used every day, and his optimism about the weather was amply justified. Every day we crossed a high pass or climbed a peak, and each night was spent in fresh surroundings. From each new summit we looked across the scene of our previous wanderings, and beyond over great ranges of unlimited promise. I found this new view of mountains profoundly impressive.

The climbs we did were not difficult, but I was not disappointed by that; indeed I was rather relieved, and anyway I found them fully satisfying. I was pleased to discover that the art of mountaineering consisted, not in getting into difficulties as I had once supposed, but rather in avoiding danger. There were all sorts of little things to learn which later became matters of commonplace routine in thought and action: the hot sun loosens rocks that have been split off but held in place by frost, so that a gully which is safe in the early morning may become a death trap later in the day; new snow lying on old is liable to avalanche; the rope which links the members of a climbing party, if properly handled, is a very real safeguard, and is not merely intended to provide the comforting thought "If I fall they all fall with me." The height of the peaks was sufficient proof that they were real mountains, and I was very gratified by the memory of Whymper's dramatic descriptions of the first ascent of Les Ecrins. I had yet to learn that following a guide up a well trodden peak was a very different matter from discovering a route up an unclimbed mountain.

There were many things I did not like about climbing, and there were brief periods of bitter disappointment: being woken at 1 a.m. from a deep sleep of real physical fatigue, and having to turn out into a cold hard world of stale bread and boots and cracking lips – it is not easy to break with sleep in one's 'teens, and it was many years before I became resigned to that grim business of the midnight start; the endless trudge up a slope of soft snow with nothing to divert the attention from aching thighs and a raging thirst; moments of clumsy fear that made me feel supremely helpless and foolish. But all these things vanished in the ecstasy of gaining the summit, and in the retrospective view of the day. Besides, even then I must have realised that contrast sharpened appreciation: the sudden rush of life that came with the dawn after the dead monotony of the night approach; a cup of water collected from a rock outcrop at the top of the snow slope; the gradual achievement of rhythmic mastery over steep unstable rock.

The end of the ten days was also the end of my holiday, as well as the end of my purse. But my mind was too full of the unexpected successs of my first real Alpine season and the glorious possibilities that it opened for the future, to leave any room for regrets. Even my rucksack felt light as I swung down the road towards Grenoble.

When still at school it is easy to achieve singleness of mind. The problems of having to make a living are still remote, and in spite of the warning of elders, life continues to revolve round a new-found passion. The shock of finding that it cannot always remain the only important thing is severe, but the illusion is good while it lasts, and perhaps it contributes a measure of peace in after life. I had found in mountaineering a fulfilment of all my early longings; I had no doubt about it. Looking at pictures of the Alps I experienced such a wild surge of feeling and memory that I could not understand why everyone did not want to climb. I supposed that it was either because they could not get to the mountains or because they had not discovered them as I had; I longed to talk about the Alps but I also wanted to keep it as a jealously guarded secret.

After that first season, time was divided into two categories: the summer holidays and the ten months between them that unfortunately had to be lived through as well. A stupid and ungrateful attitude, particularly as the winter holidays between included, among other good things, a Christmas spent in Gustav's hut in the Norwegian forests and an exploration of the volcanoes of Teneriffe, both of which were thrilling experiences.

My second Alpine season was again spent in the Dauphiné. The value of the franc had dropped to 240 to the pound. Elie was still willing to climb with me for 60 francs a day, and the use of the huts was free so long as one was a member of the French Alpine Club, which could be joined by anyone for the payment of a very small sum. We lived nearly all the time in huts.

The high Dauphiné is barren country, with narrow rocky valleys in which there are few trees and little pasture land. Scenically it cannot compare with most of the Swiss Alps, but its grim austerity has a great fascination. From the mountaineering point of view, too, it has many advantages, and it would be hard to find a place better adapted for learning the game. There is an extraordinary profusion of peaks, the large majority of which are rarely visited. We climbed twenty that season and on only two or three occasions did we meet another party on a mountain. In those days Elie was a "Guide de Deuxième Classe", and was anxious to be promoted to the first rank. So with this in view he was very keen to get to know as many peaks as he could; and far from having to be urged to work for his 60 francs, it was often that he forced the pace. Much of the ground that we covered was new to him, and I soon found myself sharing in the problems of finding the way and of deciding which routes were safe and which were not. As before we traversed the peaks from one valley to another, and before long I began to have that exciting feel of connected knowledge of country.

A thing that surprised me about climbing in the Alps (and indeed which still rather surprises me on looking back) was the number of long days one did. Most of our climbs that year took anything from twelve to sixteen hours. We would do four such days consecutively, then a morning off with a three or four hour walk to a hut in the afternoon, followed by another four long days in succession. I remember feeling very tired at night, so that my whole body ached when I lay down, and the early morning starts were hateful; but the fatigue of one day never lasted long into the next, and my appetite for food was prodigious. Off days were occasionally forced on us by the weather, but very rarely. I hated them, and it was a long time before I acquired the philosophy that could find pleasure in a day of rest in the valley.

It would be a mistake, I think, to begin climbing in one of the famous centres like Zermatt or Chamonix. For one thing the peaks are so well known, and the various routes up them are tabulated in such detail that one might easily get the wrong impression of mountaineering. Each climb would seem like a set piece in which one was forced by convention to stick to a rigid series of steps, each with a name and a history. In a less frequented district there is a sense of freedom of choice, and it is easy to imagine that the route one takes has never been climbed before. This presents mountaineering in a totally different light, and as first impressions are important it is better that this exploratory aspect of the game should predominate at first. Also to begin by climbing famous peaks might lead to a scornful attitude towards lesser ranges, and to despise any mountain is a cardinal error both of philosophy and practice. It is wrong to suppose that because a mountain is in a well-known district and is itself famous, it necessarily provides good climbing. From the mountain point of view there is no finer mountain in the Alps than La Meije in the Dauphiné, and a traverse of, say, Les Bans is every bit as good a climb as, for example, a traverse of the much more famous Zinal Rothhorn.

Elie Richard was an excellent companion and his desire to climb little-known peaks from unusual directions suited me admirably. I owe a great deal to his friendly interest and encouragement. He was not at the time a really first-rate guide, having had no experience outside his native Dauphiné, but I should say that in temperament and ability he had the makings of one, though he was very shy and modest. The next summer I was fortunate enough to climb on some of the Zermatt peaks with Théophile Theytaz, who was a very much more forceful character.

It is impossible to climb for long without meeting other climbers, and when those contacts came I found a new source of joy in talking of mountains with understanding. This also suggested the exciting possibility of climbing without guides, which was strengthened by an Easter holiday of rock climbing in the English Lake district.

To those who wonder at the reason for mountaineering, this rock climbing on British mountains must seem quite incomprehensible. Its object is not to reach the top of mountains but to climb up some particular part of a precipice. A cliff three hundred yards long by a couple of hundred feet high may have as many as fifty routes up it each bearing a name, such as "Eagle's Nest Ridge" or "Great Gully", and each classified according to an accepted standard of difficulty. It is a fascinating sport; there are those who prefer it to Alpine climbing, and of course it provides excellent practice in rock climbing. But rock climbing is only a small part of a wider art. Climbing on British crags is to mountaineering as yachting on the Norfolk Broads is to sailing.

Just as the relative smallness of Alpine mountains enables one to tackle far harder climbs than would be possible on the great peaks of the Himalaya, so the standard of rock climbing difficulty on Welsh or Lake District crags is a good deal higher than is normally met with on Alpine climbs. It is a highly specialised and a restricted technique. When I started climbing in the Lakes I was extremely frightened and not a little humiliated. The climbs that were dismissed by the initiated as easy, struck me as formidable. Seeing a nice easy grass slope a few yards to the side while I was spread-eagled on a giddy precipice seemed to increase my discomfiture ten fold, and I began to wonder if I really liked mountaineering after all. Like most things it was simply a question of adjustment to environment. After a time I found the knack of easy poise and with it came a sense of security and a great exhilaration.

A day on the Lakeland fells is a joy second to none. In driving rain or in rare sunshine, it is the same clean, good country of soft, rich colour. The climbing gives a spice of adventure, and objective interest; like all good sport its real function is to provide a medium for experience, through changing moods, of the country itself. Not least of the day's delights is the evening spent in good company at a farm house, satisfying a mighty hunger with an endless Cumberland tea.

That Easter I climbed mostly with George Peaker (at least I thought his name was George and when our friendship had ripened I always called him that; he never bothered to correct me and it was not until ten years later that I discovered that it was not really his name). He was an experienced rock climber, though at the time he had not climbed much in the Alps. He nursed me through my initiation into Lakeland climbing. I had a great admiration for his imperturbable temperament. In moments of crisis he always spoke with absolute calm, using precise, well chosen phrases as if he were engaged in an after-dinner discussion. I remember one occasion particularly, when he was leading up a steep wall, slashed by an icy wind-driven rain. He remained for some considerable time clinging to small slippery holds near the top of the wall apparently unable to get any further. Then he looked down at me over his shoulder and announced that he was going to fall off. This he proceeded to do, but it did not matter much as he had taken the precaution of tying himself to the top of the wall.

The following summer we went to the Alps together. George was a lecturer in mathematics, so that his long summer holiday coincided with my own. We had decided to start in the Graian Alps, and, by crossing peaks and passes, to wander from there in whatever direction seemed good at the time. Climbing without a guide seemed a great undertaking. I felt as though I were rediscovering all the delights I had found in previous years and many more besides. The new responsibility of decision and action, the feeling of self-reliance, the modest triumphs shared by a companion of equal standing and similar outlook sharpened the whole field of sensibility and deepened delight.

Our first experience was not a happy one. We arrived at Pralognan in the morning, after a sleepless night in the train, and set out heavily laden for a hut in the afternoon. Before long it started to rain in torrents, we missed the way and darkness found us lost on the hillside. Soaked through and tired we spent a long shivering night huddled together in a sheep pen and retreated to Pralognan the next day crushed and dejected. But after that the weather was gloriously fine – day after day, week after week hardly a cloud appeared in the sky and we never halted for a rest.

It is a further advantage of the lesser ranges of the Alps that they enjoy far better weather than their more lofty neighbours. All this time a continuous series of storms was raging over the peaks of the Mont Blanc group only a short way to the north. When we went there later we met friends who had spent their entire holidays waiting in the valleys for an improvement in the weather.

When we had climbed or traversed the more attractive peaks of the Graian Alps we crossed the frontier into Italy and climbed in the Gran Paradiso group. We got into a lot of unnecessary difficulties, due to bad judgement, and we often paid the penalty of being caught by night high up on the mountain side, though somehow we alway succeeded in worrying through, and never, after that first occasion, had to spend the entire night out. We learnt slowly by our mistakes.

From the Paradiso we worked our way to the north and crossed the Mont Blanc range to Chamonix. We had intended to stay there, but the stormy weather seemed as if it were set for the whole season; so after some minor climbs we took a bus to the Dauphiné, where we continued our interrupted adventures.

Mountaineering used to be regarded as a rich man's game. If you stay at big hotels in the famous Swiss resorts, and climb with first class guides it certainly is. But there are ways of doing a mountaineering holiday which make climbing as inexpensive as any sport. From England the chief cost is getting to the Alps, but the third class fare does not amount to very much. Once there it is possible to live entirely in huts, which in many parts of the French Alps costs nothing. In my experience one gets so hungry that the simplest food is completely satisfying. I think I sometimes overdid the economising in food. In those days I knew nothing of balanced diets, and once or twice at the end of the season I suffered from boils, which were no doubt due to some diet deficiency. But a well-balanced diet costs little more than an ill-balanced diet, and it is only a question of care.

Many young continental climbers who could not afford the railway fare used to bicycle to the Alps. They had their counterparts in the north of England and in Scotland. A friend of mine met a young but experienced American climber at the Hörnli hut below the Matterhorn, who had brought himself a return steerage passage from New York to Antwerp. There he purchased a second-hand push-bike and rode it to the Alps. He could not afford even the price of the Swiss huts and was content to sleep outside. He ate nothing but bread. Sometimes he found a companion to climb with, when he did not he climbed alone. My friend who was also in need of a companion joined forces with him. When they parted the American cheerfully mounted his bicycle with only six Swiss francs in his pocket besides the return half of his steamer ticket.

But apart from these extreme cases, forced by necessity, there is much to be gained by this frugality. To my mind a large measure of the charm of mountaineering lies in its simplicity; a rope, an ice-axe, dark glasses and nailed boots are all the special equipment that is needed; the object is uncomplicated; the rest lies in the physical, mental and æsthetic contact of the climber with his mountains. The simpler the approach the easier it is to achieve a synthesis. At least that is the only way in which I can explain the feeling I have so often experienced on large and luxuriously equipped Himalayan expeditions, and on rare occasions when I have climbed from a big hotel, a feeling of having lost touch with the essence of the life I was subconsciously seeking.

My last season in the Alps was the best of all. Again I had Peaker as a companion and this time we were joined by H. M. Kelly, who was famous for his remarkable achievements on English rocks. We started with three weeks in the Zermatt valley. It was one of those seasons that one dreams about, and during the whole of our time there we were never troubled even by the threat of bad weather. It seemed to me almost a crime to waste any of it, though sometimes we were forced by exhaustion (or, more likely, laziness) to take a day off. But in the three weeks we managed to do eight of the classic climbs. The two I enjoyed most of these were the West ridge of the Dent Blanche, and the Zmutt ridge of the Matterhorn which is the finest approach to that lovely mountain. I had climbed it before with two guides and two other amateurs, but in spite of this I missed the way on the upper part and forced our party to climb a new and a somewhat spectacular chimney. I had some excuse for this mistake, for on the previous occasion the mountain had been sheathed in ice and it had taken us exactly twenty-four hours of continuous going to climb up the Zmutt ridge and down the north-east or Swiss ridge. This year we descended by the Italian ridge which is chiefly a matter of sliding down fixed ropes. When we reached the hut at the foot of the ridge, George and I wanted to go on down to the valley, as we had very little food with us. But Kelly refused, saying that he would rather go hungry than be arrested by the Italian police on a charge of espionage, which had recently been the fate of several unfortunate climbers who had strayed across the frontier.

Although our programme that year was a good deal more ambitious than it had been before, we never encountered serious difficulties. Increased experience, of course, had something to do with this, but I am certain that it was partly due to the fact that it is so much easier to find the way about well-known mountains, though with the exception of the Zmutt ridge all climbs we did were new to us. I regard this as evidence of my contention that in some respects the smaller ranges of the Alps provide a more complete training in mountaineering.

From the Zermatt mountains we made our way slowly along what is known as the High level Route to Chamonix stopping to climb on the way. We had hoped that Kelly would come with us to Chamonix, and we were looking forward to watching him display his rock-climbing genius by leading us up some of the more spectacular granite faces. But unfortunately he had to return to England at the end of our three weeks in Zermatt.

It is doubtful if there is any place in the world that can rival Chamonix as a climbing centre. The flawless granite of the Aiguilles offers almost unlimited scope for the rock climber, the bigger peaks provide ice- as well as rock-climbing of a high order, while the great southern faces and ridges of Mont Blanc, their scale unique in the Alps, are not far away. But Chamonix itself is a horrible place. It combines everything ugly and vulgar in modern "tourism"; vast hotels sprout in unsightly clusters, charabancs roar through the streets, every kind of cheapjack is there to exploit the mountains. Unfortunately these horrors of mass touristdom are not confined to the main valley. In the height of the season the mountain huts overflow with trippers, many of whom having no intention of climbing, create an intolerable hubbub which continues far into the night, and they generally leave the huts in a state of filth and disorder. Even among the climbers there is an atmosphere of fevered competition. It is fairly easy to forget these things when one has some great adventure in prospect, but even in my brief acquaintance with the district I found myself longing for the peace of the Dauphiné or the quiet dignity of Zermatt, and I made a resolution never to return there after I had tasted some of the superb fare that its mountains offer.

Our first climb that year on the peaks of the Mont Blanc range was the traverse of the Grépon. By then we had reached a high pitch of fitness, and the feel of rough clean granite under toe and finger and the swift glides down the long *rappel* line were tremendously exhilarating. It is a remarkable climb, for although one is constantly poised over a sheer drop of thousands of feet, one has a feeling of perfect, almost careless security that I have never felt on any other mountain of similar difficulty. It was a day of supreme physical enjoyment. Then came the traverse of the two Drus, climbing up the Petit Dru and crossing from there over the summit of its taller brother. This was a much more serious proposition and its enjoyment of a more sombre kind.

Later we joined forces with Jack Longland and George Trevelyan, and climbed with them on the Rochefort Ridge and on Mont Blanc, where the weather spoilt our plan to climb one of the great southern ridges. Then the others went home. Having now no studies to return to, I snatched another week of this, my last Alpine season, and spent it on and around the Aiguille Verte, in company with Graham Macphee.

I left the Alps with a heavy sense that I was breaking with an episode in my life that would not be repeated. If I had been able to foresee something of what the next twelve years would bring I should not have been depressed. But in a way I was right. The Alps for all their limitations, their sophistication, their spoiling, have some qualities that I have not found in other ranges. It is difficult to describe these qualities exactly, but they are due I fancy to tradition, to the higher culture of the native inhabitants, to the easy friendships made and to the wonderful variety of scene small enough in scale to be easily appreciated and large enough to be wholly satisfying.

But the memory of my Alpine seasons has another importance to me, for they represent my first real contact with great mountains. Though experience has its own rewards – a wider view, a fuller understanding, a more sober and perhaps a deeper passion – inevitably something is left behind. We can never quite recapture the feelings of early youth; the mystery that lay behind each peak, and in the deep cloud-filled valleys at dawn; the wild joy that made one want to claw the ground that was part of this miracle. Oh yes, I continued to grow just as excited as each new vista appeared on my mountaineering horizon, but I suppose the other feeling was akin to those childish fancies that sometimes reappear in after life as a fleeting moment of absolute happiness.

CHAPTER THREE

First Climbs on Mount Kenya

In my experience the problem of what to do in life was not made any easier by those who were entrusted with my education. Looking back, it seems most odd that never once in all the years that I was at school was there any general discussion about careers. As presumably the main object of going to school is to prepare for after life, it surely would have been very easy and relevant to organise lectures or discussions designed to give boys a broad view of the enormous variety of occupations open to men of average intelligence? Of course many boys were destined from birth to follow their fathers' careers, but even these would have benefited by glimpses of a wider horizon. Often and often in after life I have come across people doing jobs that I had never dreamed of before, and which would have thrilled me had I been told about them at school. I suppose the reason for this extraordinary omission is that so many school masters had themselves such a restricted view. Spending all their time working to a rigid curriculum, the passing of examinations by their pupils gradually became the whole object of their working life. I recognise the importance of being made to learn things that one does not like, but surely it was not good to give the young mind the impression that all education was a form of mental gymnastics. For example, I used to find geometry rather fun, and, when I still had the naïve idea that what I was being taught might have some practical value, I asked what geometry was for. The only answer I ever got was that it taught one how to think and to solve problems. If, instead, I had been told the simple fact that the word was derived from the Greek *ge*, the earth, and *metron*, a measure, and that the meaningless triangles that I was asked to juggle with formed the basis of geographical exploration, astronomy and navigation, the subject would immediately have assumed a thrilling romance, and, what is more, it would have been directly connected in my mind with the things that most appealed to me.

My experience in this connection may have been unfortunate, but it was by no means unique; many of my friends who went to different schools confess to a similar experience, and complain that when they had completed their school education they had not the remotest idea of what they wanted to do. Moreover I do not think that this curiously detached attitude towards education was confined to schools. It had been intended that I should go to one of the great universities. I was tepid about the idea myself, for I had developed a dislike for the very thought of educational establishments. However, the prospect of three extra seasons in the Alps was a considerable incentive, and by dint of an enormous mental effort, I succeeded in cramming sufficient Latin into my head to pass (at my second attempt) the necessary entrance examination. In due course I went to be interviewed by the Master of my prospective College. When I was asked what subject I proposed to take when I came up to the university, I replied, somewhat diffidently, that I wanted to take Geology – diffidently, because I still regarded such things as having no reality in the hard world of work. The answer to my suggestion confirmed my fears. "What on Earth do you want to do with Geology. There is no opening there unless you eventually get a first and become a lecturer in the subject." *A first, a lecturer* – I, who could not even learn a couple of books of Horace by heart! I felt that I was being laughed at. In fact I am sure I was not, and that my adviser was quite sincere and only trying to be helpful, but I certainly did not feel like arguing the matter. I listened meekly to suggestions that I should take Classics or Law, and left the room in a state of profound depression. "O Lord," I thought, "even here I won't be able to escape from Kennedy's Latin Primer," with which I had been struggling for ten years.

That interview was largely responsible for my decision not to go to University after all. Now it seems a spineless decision, and that I was remarkably lacking in determination. But at that age one is not always wise. In actual fact of course there were enormous opportunities open to a man who had specialised in any one of the natural sciences, but in those days I had never heard of the Geological Survey of India, oil prospecting, marine biological stations, the exploration ship *Discovery II* which has been working almost continuously in the Antarctic during the last two decades, manned by young specialists in almost every branch of natural science.

Farming in East Africa sounded a good sort of life, one which offered reasonable freedom of scope, not only for making a living but for wider interests as well. Moreover the map showed me that there were some high mountains at hand. I did not suppose that these would offer much in the way of climbing, and I pictured the ascent as being a matter of hacking a way through jungle to a gently sloping ice-cap on top. Somehow I had acquired the extraordinary notion that the Alps were the only mountains in the world that could offer real mountaineering, but I still felt that all mountains were good mountains, and I hoped that the interest that East African peaks lacked in technical difficulty they would provide in unexplored ground. I had read something about the Ruwenzori range, which lies between Uganda and the Belgian Congo, and I knew that this at any rate was one of the most fascinating parts of the world. Accordingly I set out for Uganda with the intention of settling there for the rest of my life.

As luck would have it the place I went to first with the object of learning my job was only about twenty miles from the foot of Mount Kenya. The evening on which I arrived at my first Kenya home was cloudy. But when I came out of my bungalow early the next morning I was met by a sight that made by heart leap. I stood on a ridge and looked through a break in the trees over wide plains, still dim in the early light. The whole northern horizon was filled with a gigantic cone of purple mist. The cone was capped by a band of cloud. Above this band, utterly detached from the Earth, appeared a pyramid of rock and ice, beautifully proportioned, hard and clear against the sky. The sun, not yet risen to my view, had already touched the peak, throwing ridge and corrie into sharp relief, lighting here and there a sparkling gem of ice.

On my way through Nairobi from the coast I had called upon Dr. J. D. Melhuish who had made several attempts to climb Mount Kenya. He had shown me his magnificent collection of photographs and had told me much about the mountain, altering all my preconceived ideas. It was obviously a mountain that would stand comparison with any I had seen in the Alps. I was expecting something good, but the exquisite loveliness of that sunlit peak, floating high above a still sleeping world of tropical colour was far beyond anything I could have imagined.

Mount Kenya is an ancient volcano. It rises from a relatively flat tableland, the general level of which is about 4,500 feet above the sea. The base of the mountain is about seventy miles in circumference. From this it rises at a gentle slope to a wide ring of peaks which are the shattered remnants of the crater. In the centre of these, at the apex of the great cone, rises the main peak crowned by twin summits, and draped with fifteen glaciers. This central peak is composed of a kind of granite, a non-volcanic rock, which, when the volcano was active, had been forced up from below and choked the main pipe. The softer volcanic rocks of the crater gradually weathered away and left this hard plug or core standing thousands of feet above the present level of the ancient crater. The summit of the peak is 17,040 feet above sea level and is the second highest in Africa.

The mountain was first seen by a European, Ludwig Kraph, in 1849. Towards the close of the century the explorers Count Teleki (1889), Professor Gregory (1893) and Georg Kolb (1896) made their way through the forests that cover the lower slopes of the mountain, and reached the glaciers at the foot of the main peak. In 1899 Sir Halford Mackinder climbed the peak with two Alpine guides, the brothers César and Joseph Brocherel. The story of his expedition (recorded in the Geographical Journal of May, 1900) is a great one. In those days the country was very wild and little known. The party had frequent encounters with unfriendly tribes and the piercing of the great forests was a long and laborious task. More than once they were forced to retreat for fresh supplies and their journey to the glaciers took several months. After some reverses, Mackinder and his guides reached a small and very steep glacier coming down from the gap between the twin peaks. The ice was so hard that they named it the Diamond Glacier. After what appears to have been a somewhat desperate struggle they reached the gap, which they named the Gate of the Mist, and from here they climbed to the summit of the higher peak. Mackinder named the two peaks Batian and Nelion, after two famous Masai chiefs. Batian is slightly the higher.

For nearly thirty years after this, the highest peak had remained unclimbed, though repeated attempts were made, notably by Dr. Arthur Melhuish, and Major E. A. T. Dutton, the author of the very charming book "Kenya Mountain". The summit of Nelion remained untrodden.

It was indeed a splendid prospect, and I could hardly bear to contemplate the months that must elapse before I could move towards this glistening prize. But it was wonderful to be able to look at it each day. It was generally clear in the morning, until about nine o'clock when the swiftly forming clouds clustered round the peaks and extended far down the great volcanic cone. In the evening the clouds would dissolve and the peaks would unveil. I looked forward each day to that time, and wondered just how the daily miracle would be revealed. Sometimes the two tips of the twin peaks would appear above the cloud mass – incredibly high they seemed; sometimes the lower glacier skirts would come first into view, grey and cold under the dark pall; sometimes a window would open and show a section of flying buttress and deep ice-filled couloir, steep and forbidding; sometimes the western clouds would break before the southern, and the peaks would emerge already bathed in the sunset glow, shreds of rose-coloured mist clinging to their sides. Each evening, week after week, it was different, though I had learnt to know every detail of ridge and corrie. After a while the rains broke and the peaks remained hidden for weeks at a time. Those were dull days.

Arriving on an East African farm with an ice-axe, climbing boots and several hundred feet of rope seemed for some reason rather ridiculous. At first I managed to conceal these clumsy implements in my baggage, but soon the house servants discovered them and my secret leaked out. My enthusiasm for the mountain became a standing joke and I found few sympathisers among my neighbours. But there was quite a number of kindred spirits in the Colony. Among these was P. Wyn Harris, of the Kenya Civil Service. I knew him well by repute as he had been a prominent member of the Cambridge University Mountaineering Club, and I had been told by several of his friends to look him up. He had already made one attempt to climb Kenya the previous year. Most luckily he was due for home leave at just about the time that I could decently apply for a short holiday. We arranged to join forces for three weeks before his ship sailed.

Besides Harris there was my old friend Gustav Sommerfelt, the Norwegian, who had also come to settle in Kenya. Though he had not done any mountaineering in the full sense, he was very tough and athletic and a splendid companion for such a project. He jumped at my suggestion that he should join us.

After months of gazing at the peak I had almost come to regard it as something unreal, and I found it hard to believe in our plans. I was haunted by the old feeling that something must go wrong to upset anything so perfect. Sure enough it did. One day in the jungle I fell from a cliff into the fork of a tree and broke my ankle. This seemed a bit unanswerable at first, but the ankle mended after a fashion. Then a telegram came from Wyn to say that he could not get away after all, owing to some tribal disturbance in his district. However at the last moment another telegram arrived to say that all was well.

The three of us met in Nairobi. We had about three weeks before us, the limit being set partly by the length of Gustav's and my holidays, but mainly by the date on which Wyn had to reach Mombasa to catch his ship. Three weeks was enough time in which to make a strong attempt on the peak and get back, providing everything worked smoothly. But it allowed very little time for reconnoitring routes, for bad weather and for failures. So, to give ourselves a chance of success, we could not afford to waste time on our journey to the mountain, and up to the foot of the peak. We hired a lorry with a native driver to take us to Chugoria, a little village in the forests at the foot of the mountain. Innumerable delays occurred, due chiefly to Wyn having to report at the secretariat and the congenital inability of our driver to realise the need for haste. Following the practice of his kind he waited the entire morning while we were busy with our several chores, then when at last the lorry was loaded and all appeared ready he decided to fill up with petrol, an operation which required the partial unloading of our carefully packed goods. This done he disappeared for what, judging by the time it took, must have been a veritable banquet. However by two o'clock in the afternoon we were clattering out of Nairobi along one of its typical corrugated roads.

It is only 150 miles from Nairobi to Chugoria along one of the main roads leading to the Northern Frontier Province. But in those days even the main roads of Kenya were not always easy to negotiate, particularly in a lorry hired for its cheapness rather than its mobility. But we made fair speed, and we only had one tyre burst and one ordinary puncture – remarkable luck considering that on each of the wheels patches of inner tube were visible. By nightfall we were well into the forests that skirt the southern base of the mountain. Our

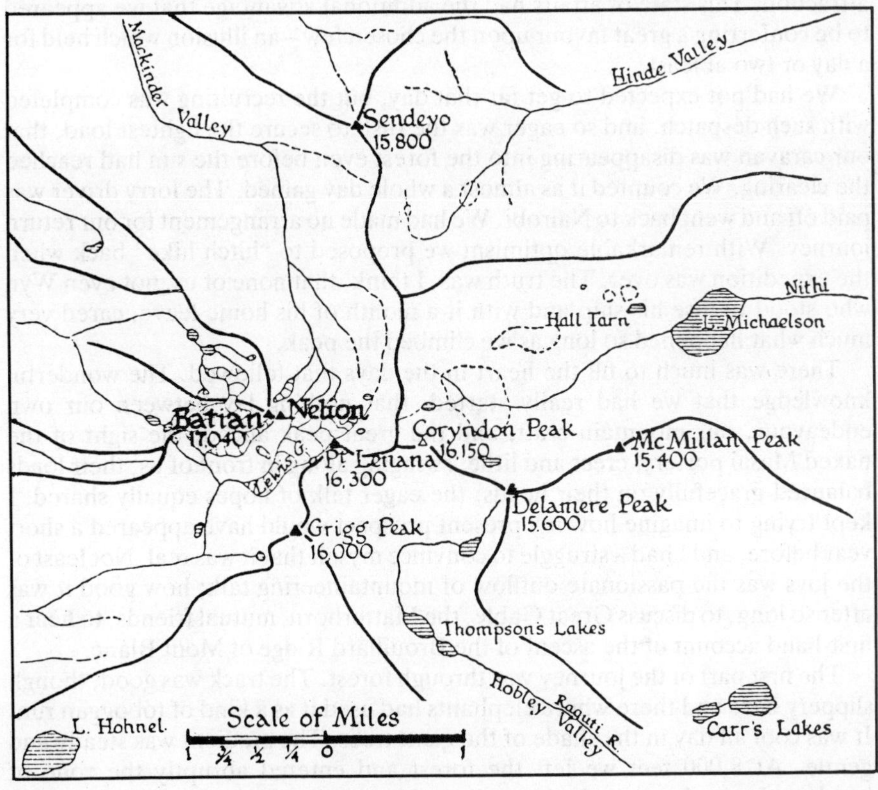

driver stopped with the intention of spending the night by the side of the road. A pal of his, he said, had been attacked by elephants while travelling along this road at night not so long ago, the lorry had been wrecked and the driver killed, and it was not his intention to share the same fate. He could not be made to see that we would be much more vulnerable to attack by the side of the road than moving along it, and for some time he refused to budge. For our part, elephants or no elephants, we were determined to get to Chugoria before morning. We were three to one, and supported by the omnipotent ten shilling note we eventually succeeded in winning the argument.

Chugoria lies about four miles up a side track to the north of the main road. We had some trouble in finding this track in the dark and it was past midnight when we reached our destination, where we found a comfortable billet in a mud hut. Our arrival was adequately anounced by the noise of the lorry and at dawn a large number of Masai villagers collected to welcome and inspect us. This suited us admirably as our next concern was the recruiting of porters for our *Safari* up the mountain. Our offer of a shilling a day was greeted with such enthusiasm that we were able to select fifteen of the most likely looking warriors from scores of eager volunteers. I fancy that the gorgeous blankets we had brought for distribution among those who came with us were the real attraction. This state of affairs had the additional advantage that we appeared to be conferring a great favour upon the chosen few – an illusion which held for a day or two at least.

We had not expected to get far that day, but the recruiting was completed with such despatch, and so eager was the rush to secure the lightest load, that our caravan was disappearing into the forest even before the sun had reached the clearing. We counted it as almost a whole day gained. The lorry driver was paid off and went back to Nairobi. We had made no arrangement for our return journey. With remarkable optimism we proposed to "hitch hike" back when the expedition was over. The truth was, I think, that none of us, not even Wyn who stood to lose his ship and with it a month of his home leave, cared very much what happened so long as we climbed the peak.

There was much to fill the heart in the days that followed. The wonderful knowledge that we had really started, that nothing lay between our own endeavour, our mountain craft, and the great peak ahead; the sight of the naked Masai porters, erect and lithe, swinging along in front of us, their loads balanced gracefully on their heads; the eager talk of hopes equally shared. I kept trying to imagine how my present prospect would have appeared a short year before, and I had a struggle to convince myself that it was real. Not least of the joys was the passionate outflow of mountaineering talk; how good it was after so long, to discuss Great Gable, the Matterhorn, mutual friends, to hear a first-hand account of the ascent of the Brouillard Ridge of Mont Blanc.

The first part of the journey was through forest. The track was good, though slippery here and there where elephants had used it as a kind of toboggan run. It was cool all day in the shade of the giant trees. The gradient was steady and gentle. At 8,000 feet we left the forest and entered abruptly the zone of bamboo. In the forest we had seen little of our more distant surroundings, but among the bamboos our view was even more restricted. We might have been walking between walls of matting. But for the track it would have been an incredibly laborious job to hack a way through. At 10,000 feet the bamboo gave place to giant heath and presently we emerged into spacious park land. It would be difficult to imagine a more lovely spot. Many great trees, exiles from the forest, stood in grand solitude or in shady woods. Here, in place of the wild tangle of monkey rope and tropical creeper, they were draped with wisps of moss and lichen. There were clumps of tall bamboo, of giant heath, no longer engaged in their mad struggle for the predominance of their species, but content in the more temperate climate to live as friendly neighbours. The grass was tall and green.

In this idyllic place a Nairobi business man, Mr. Ernest Carr, had built a comfortable wooden hut for the use of all who came. At this time the hut was occupied by Miss Vivienne de Watteville, who is well known for her adventurous African journeys made in the company of her father. She was stopping here for several months engaged in writing a book about her travels. It seemed unkind to disturb her peace, but she welcomed us with charming hospitality, and gave us a dinner that would have done justice to any English home. We would certainly have been tempted to prolong our stay, had we been less impatient to reach the glaciers. Our hostess promised to pay us a visit while we were there.

Above the hut the country was open downland, covered with thick tufted grass. Our way led up a wide ridge. It was a relief to be free from the confinement of the forest. The view in every direction was magnificent and ever wider as we mounted the flank of the vast cone. To our left was the deep ravine of the Gorges valley, holding the dark waters of a lake and dominated by a tremendous precipice and huge, fantastic spires. Below us was the wide belt of forest beyond which the plains stretched away towards the horizon, lost in the distance of infinite space.

Though Mount Kenya lies astride the equator we were already in the region of night frosts. Our porters thought they had gone quite far enough, and we had considerable difficulty in inducing them to face the morning stars. But they were cheerful people and easy to handle, and once they were warmed with exercise they went very well. They had long hair done up in a bun and dyed red. It never seemed to require attention and remained as neatly dressed at the end as at the start. Their great delight was to set a giant groundsel tree alight and to cluster round the warm glow. These curious plants, and the giant lobelias, are peculiar to the mountains of equatorial Africa. They grow in profusion at altitudes of eleven to fourteen thousand feet. They stand about twelve feet high on stems so soft and pulpy that it is quite easy to push the whole tree over. They look quite dead and rotten except for a cabbage-like growth at the very top. As this dies it is replaced by another and the dead leaves form a thatch below. The lobelia grows as a single feathery cone about six feet high.

Once we were above the forest and bamboo, the north-east faces of the twin peaks were in view, and so long as they remained clear of cloud most of our attention was concentrated upon them. Mackinder's ascent had been made from the south-east, and all subsequent attempts had been made from that direction. But after a careful study with the aid of field glasses it seemed to us that a route up the north-east face of Batian might be practicable. The lower part was screened by the surrounding mountains but we decided to gamble some of our precious days on an attempt from this side. As we drew nearer our optimism grew, and with it our impatience to get to grips with the peak. At last we reached a high saddle on the main axis of the mountain. From here, across the head of the Mackinder valley, we could see the whole wall from top to bottom. The face of Nelion appeared smooth, vertical and utterly unclimbable, but the face of Batian, though very steep, was broken by a network of ledges and gullies. The lower part, which before had been hidden from us, was certainly easier than the upper half, that our previous study had pronounced practicable. The faces of the two peaks were divided by a dark gully that plunged in one frightful sweep from the Gate of the Mist. No, there was no alternative, but we did not want one. Our mood of optimism had changed to one of complete certainty. Nothing but a heavy snowstorm, we felt, could now defeat us; and surely the weather which had held for so long, would not change before tomorrow.

It was still before noon when we reached the ridge. Wyn and I left Gustav to pitch our tent, pay off half the porters and send the other half back to the upper limit of giant groundsel, while we rushed off to reconnoitre the route. Plunging down a thousand feet of scree slopes, and skirting under two small glaciers, we reached the foot of the face. We were thrilled to find that the rock was as firm and clean cut as Chamonix granite. It was difficult, but though we climbed a long way up we found nothing to damp our confidence. We returned to camp just before dark with bursting lungs and high spirits. By the next evening, after a glorious climb, the summit of Batian would have been reached for the second time in history, and after a lapse of thirty years.

It was a cold, uncomfortable night and I slept badly, though this was due largely to sheer excitement. But at last it was time to start cooking our breakfast of porridge and bacon, and as soon as it was light the three of us were running down the scree towards the foot of the peak. As we had to move one at a time, with three on the rope, our progress was slower than it had been the day before, but it was steady enough and it seemed that we had plenty of time. Above the point that we had reached before, matters continued to be satisfactory for a while. But gradually the climbing became more difficult. Each new step demanded a more determined effort. Gully, ice slope and ridge were mastered ever more slowly and we began to get worried about the time. At last we reached a great slab, about two hundred feet below the summit ridge.

The slab was smooth and offered only tiny finger and toe holds. It was not excessively steep, but above it was a great bulge which ran the whole width of the face and ended in the gloomy overhanging gully under the Gate of the Mist. We had seen this bulge through field glasses from our camp, but we had greatly underestimated its size. Moreover it had appeared to be split by a vertical crack, but this turned out to be no more than a shallow groove as smooth as the rest and overhanging in its lower portion. It did not take us long to recognise that we had arrived at a hopeless impasse; but we continued to gaze at it in silence, each hoping that the other would find some miraculous solution, each waiting for the other to pronounce the verdict he knew only too well.

I do not remember who had the courage to sound the retreat, but whoever it was it was none too soon. During the next few hours the surge of my disappointment was checked by the urgent necessity of getting off the face before nightfall. But it welled up again with yet greater bitterness as we stumbled and toiled up the long scree slopes in the dark. We were all very tired when we reached camp and several mugs of tea brewed on the Primus from melted snow was all we could face for supper.

We felt better in the morning. Our defeat on the north-east face had been complete and decisive. We were not tempted to try again, and so had no awkward decision to make. We still had five clear days before we need move down. Conditions were still perfect, all snow was hard, safe snow, all rock faces were clean. For failure we could blame nothing but our lack of skill and the intrinsic difficulties of the peak. If our confidence was shaken our enthusiasm was, if possible, keener and our goal more desirable than before.

The eastern side of Nelion is nearly vertical, but about half way down a sharp ridge abuts against the face, and leads down to a high saddle dividing a sharp little peak, known as Point Thompson, from Nelion. Through this peak the ridge continues in an easterly direction and climbs to the glacier-capped Point Lenana. At Point Lenana the ridge divides, one branch running north, to form the watershed on which we were camped, others, less well defined, fall away to the south and east. The north side of the ridge between Nelion and Lenana forms the head of the great Mackinder valley, while on its southern side lies the Lewis glacier, the largest ice-stream on Mount Kenya.

Early that morning the remaining porters arrived from below as they had been instructed. Our next task was to move our camp round Point Lenana to the side of the Lewis glacier. It was a tiresome journey. We had to carry loads ourselves, and the way was across steep slopes of shifting boulders. From the start we were enveloped in thick cloud, so that our view was restricted to a few hundred yards. But it was not difficult to find the way as all we had to do was to maintain the same altitude at which we started and keep on traversing. Also Wyn had been to the Lewis glacier a year before, and when we got close to our objective he was able to recognise the ground. His previous attempt to climb the peak had been frustrated by a heavy snowfall, and by his companion collapsing with paratyphoid while they were at their high camp.

We arrived at the side of the Lewis glacier at about midday, and pitched our tent by a small frozen lake. It had often been visited before, and was known as the Curling Pond or Skating Lake, the indefatigable Melhuish having practised both these sports on it. Mr. Carr had also built a small hut there, but it had been wrecked by storms and only scattered debris remained.

The weather was still thick when we arrived, but I knew the south-east aspect of the peaks well from photographs. From this side Nelion dominates the picture. It has the appearance of a blunt obelisk supported by two sharp buttresses. One of these forms the upper part of the east ridge, already mentioned, and the other runs up from the south and joins Nelion to a sharp rock spire known as Point John. The south ridge meets the face of Nelion about half way up from the glacier. From the Curling Pond only the very top of Batian can be seen appearing over the south ridge.

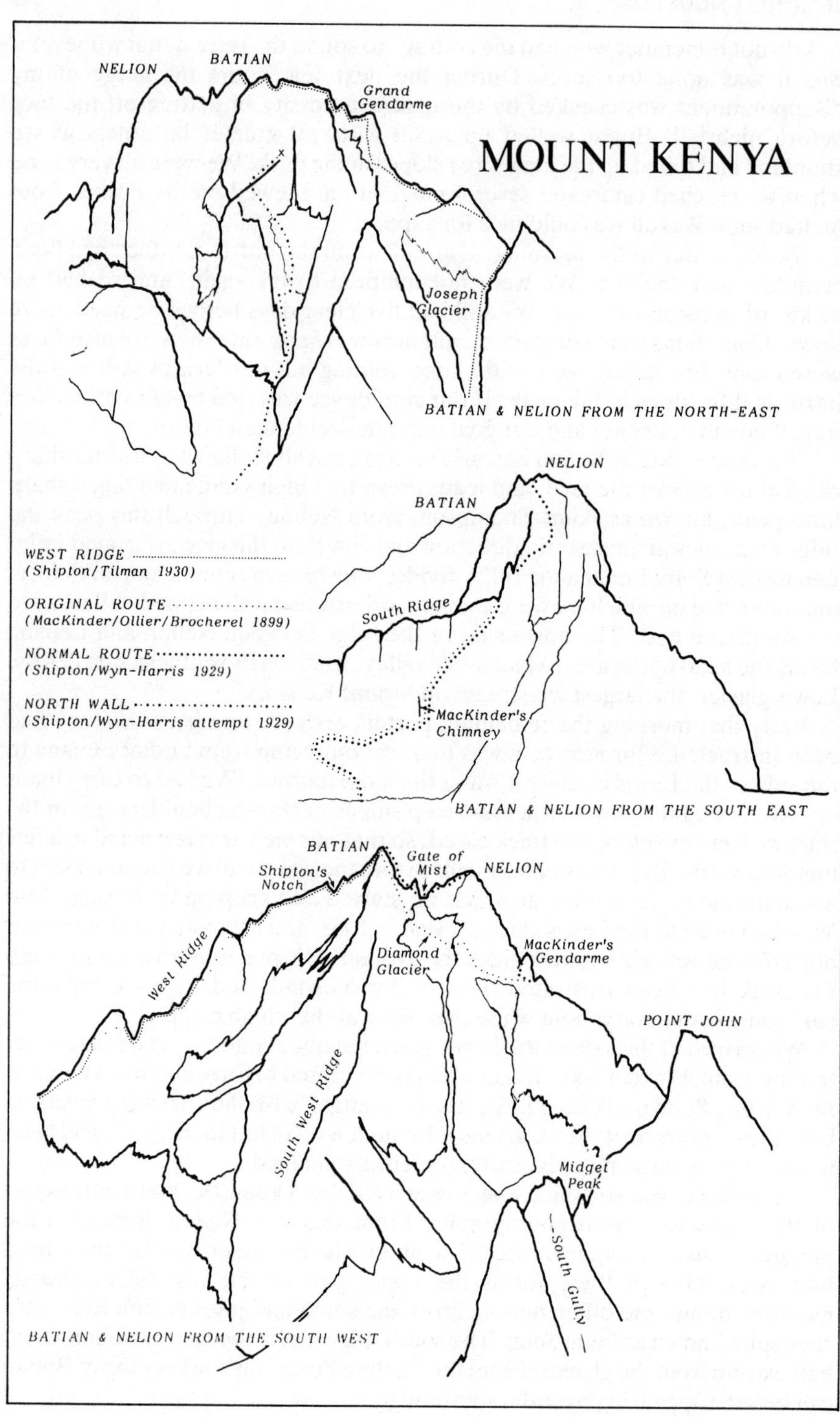
MOUNT KENYA
NELION
BATIAN
Grand Gendarme
Joseph Glacier
BATIAN & NELION FROM THE NORTH-EAST
WEST RIDGE
(Shipton/Tilman 1930)
ORIGINAL ROUTE
(MacKinder/Ollier/Brocherel 1899)
NORMAL ROUTE
(Shipton/Wyn-Harris 1929)
NORTH WALL
(Shipton/Wyn-Harris attempt 1929)
NELION
BATIAN
South Ridge
MacKinder's Chimney
BATIAN & NELION FROM THE SOUTH EAST
BATIAN
Gate of Mist
NELION
Shipton's Notch
West Ridge
Diamond Glacier
MacKinder's Gendarme
POINT JOHN
South West Ridge
Midget Peak
South Gully
BATIAN & NELION FROM THE SOUTH WEST

By the time we had pitched our tent and sent the porters back to their lower camp and had eaten some lunch, the clouds began to lift and we could see across the glacier to the lower part of the peak. Wyn and I set off across the glacier to reconnoitre. The alternatives were few. The east ridge looked exceedingly difficult in its lower portion; half way up it was broken by a sharp cleft from which descended an ugly-looking couloir, and the rock face above its junction appeared sheer and smooth. The narrow part of the face of Nelion lying between the two ridges was very steep, and did not seem to offer much chance of success. This left only the southern ridge, which was easy to reach and appeared to be quite straightforward as far as it went, except for a small notch about half way up. It would at least give access to the upper part of the peak and we believed that, from its junction with the face of Nelion, Mackinder and his guides had reached the Diamond glacier. So it was on the southern ridge that we pinned our hopes.

The surface of the Lewis glacier was composed of bare ice, in which hundreds of locusts were imbedded. There had been a plague of locusts in Kenya during the previous year, and these must have been carried up by the wind. Crevasses were few and small, and we did not bother to put on the rope until we reached the other side. We found the rock here was as sound and clean as it had been on the north-east face, and we climbed quickly to the ridge.

Just before we reached it we came across a ladder. This was a surprising discovery, and it brought back a pleasant recollection of those early Alpine prints which depict fantastic glaciers on which dozens of little men are seen carrying ladders with which to surmount the crevasses and ice cliffs. We learnt later that this ladder had been left there by Dutton and Melhuish. We were by no means disposed to laugh at their idea.

From the crest of the south ridge we looked down upon the Darwin glacier lying below the south face of the twin peaks. The clouds were steadily lifting. The ridge was easy at first, but soon it became sharp and serrated like the edge of a huge saw. We soon reached the notch that we had seen from below. One glance across it through the thinning mist was enough to shatter our hopes again. It was easy enough to get down from our side on to the narrow level terrace that formed the floor of the notch, but we could see no way of getting up or round the opposite side. This was a thin vertical buttress, smooth like the prow of a ship; at both sides of its base it overhung. Again the verdict was distressingly simple.

Until then I do not think that I had seriously entertained the idea that we should not reach the summit. Before the expedition had started all the gloomy forebodings of my friends, all their statements that the peaks were unclimbable (many of them did not believe that Batian had ever been climbed, though of course they had no justification for their disbelief) had fallen on deaf ears, and had only increased my determination to prove them wrong. Some of the people I had met had themselves been up to the glaciers and had seen the peaks at close quarters so that they knew much more about it than I did. Melhuish was the only man I had met who had actually attempted the peaks. He, of course, knew that Batian had been climbed and rightly assumed that it could be climbed again.

Wyn had encountered the same cynical attitude, and had felt as I did. Our reverse on the north-east face had been a salutary check to our over-confidence, but our failure to reach even the upper end of the south ridge, where the real difficulties, it seemed, would only begin, was a much more severe blow and it left us feeling rather hopeless.

It was now about six o'clock. The mists were clearing rapidly, as I had so often seen them from the farm more than forty miles away. I wondered if anyone were watching from there now. For us, in the midst of the scene, a part of it, it was profoundly impressive. First Point John appeared as we were nearly level with its summit, an island in a restless sea of soft pink and grey. Then, all about us were spires and wild buttresses, floating, moving; and above, infinitely high, the rocky dome of Batian. The level rays of the sun had broken through. We looked towards the east and saw there a great circle of rainbow colours, sharp and clear, framing our own dark silhouettes. It was the Spectre of the Brocken – the only one I have ever seen. Mountains have many ways of rewarding us for our pilgrimage, and often bestow their richest treasures when least expected. For my part, all disappointment, all care for the future were drowned in the great joy of living that moment. We climbed slowly down the ridge and crossed the glacier back to camp.

In my experience, the lofty thoughts, the enthusiasms and good intentions of the night before seldom survive the early interruption of sleep, the hateful business of making and eating an early breakfast, the sullen struggle with frozen boots. The next morning was no exception. I could think of nothing but the futility of renewing our efforts to climb this confounded peak. But yet it had to be done, there was no way out. Anyway in a few hours I would be back again to resume my blessed slumbers.

Gustav had slept badly, and had a headache, so he stopped in bed. Wyn and I slouched across the glacier and sorted ourselves out on the other side. It was still very early and very cold. The peak was black and hard against a clear sky. Our only hope now was straight up the face of Nelion between the junction of the south and east ridges. I gazed up at it in dreamy bewilderment, without the faintest idea of how to start. But a fiery spark seemed to have kindled in Wyn during our short halt, and as soon as we had roped together he led off up the rocks with such energy and decision that he might have been an Alpine guide climbing a familiar peak. First up a gully to the left, then to the right along a broken terrace under a smooth wall – this was fine, I began to come to life. But it was too good to last. Our terrace ended abruptly against a vertical rib, and there was still no sign of a breach in the wall above us. Descending a little, Wyn disappeared round and below the obstructing rib, while I belayed the rope and prepared for the worst. The rope went out slowly, and I waited. Then came a wild cry from round the corner. I thought Wyn had fallen off, and braced myself to receive the jerk. But instead came an excited "All right, come on!" When I joined him on a square platform I saw the cause of the excitement. A steep and narrow gully led up from the platform, and down it dangled a rope, white with age. It could only have been put there by Mackinder's party; no one since had succeeded in getting so far up the face. Though the rope was too frail to use, the discovery was a tremendous encouragement.

Wyn had found the way, and it was now my turn to take a hand. I led off up the gully and, after struggling for some time below the overhang, at last succeeded in reaching a firm hand-hold away to the right and swung myself, breathless, above the obstacle, where I pulled in the rope for Wyn to follow. The gully was certainly the key to the lower part of the face, and after some straightforward climbing we reached the place where the south ridge abuts against the upper wall of Nelion.

Flushed with our success we sat down to reflect. It seemed amazing to find ourselves here after the hopelessness of the early morning. The day was still young and fortune appeared to be on our side. The sky was clear and the rocks were warming in the sun. We looked out over a vast sea of billowy white clouds, gently rising. They would envelop us before long. To the south, above the clouds, stood a great dome of shining ice. That was strange. We knew there was no peak of that shape and size in the Kenya massif. Yet there it was clear against the blue sky, and it seemed quite close to us. Then suddenly we realised it was Kilimanjaro, the highest mountain in Africa, 250 miles away. The atmosphere over East Africa is remarkably clear. I do not think I have seen mountains at that distance anywhere else.

But we could not spend long enjoying the view, and we had almost at once to turn our attention to the immediate prospect. This was far from encouraging, and our spirits soon clouded. It must have been from here that Mackinder's party had reached the Diamond glacier, and here too that they had been forced to bivouac after their successful but prolonged struggle with it. Above and to the left the great cliffs of Nelion bulged over steep white slabs that fell away to the Darwin glacier. Along the top of these slabs there was a possible line of traverse. But it was an ugly-looking place, and the rocks were plastered with ice. Even if it were possible to climb along the slabs in these conditions, which was very doubtful, we would then be faced with the Diamond glacier. We decided to try to climb the face of Nelion direct. It did not look very promising, but it was the only alternative to those ice-covered slabs.

We climbed to a little recess at the end of the ridge. Behind this was a smooth wall some 60 feet high. But in its lower part there were some tiny holds, and balancing on these I started climbing, hoping to find more holds higher up. But before I had got 15 feet up they petered out. I managed to make a little progress to the left, but without gaining height, and there I clung until my fingers and feet were aching painfully. Working my way back above the recess I tried to the right and here found a narrow sloping hedge that led round a corner out of sight. It was an airy place above a sheer drop whose depth I did not bother to estimate. But before I had got far round the corner I found a shallow crack which split the surface of the wall above me. It was obviously the only line of possibility and I took it, though I was not at all happy. The crack was not wide enough to wedge my foot in it, and the only holds were smooth and sloping outwards. My progress was painfully slow, but soon the prospect of beating a retreat was even more repugnant than climbing on up. At length I reached the top of the crack and found myself on a fairly wide platform above the wall. I felt rather ashamed of myself for wasting so much time on a fool's errand.

But Wyn, when he joined me on the platform, was jubilant, though what there was in our situation to be pleased about I could not see. For the next hundred feet or so the ground was certainly easier, but above that the upper cliffs of Nelion frowned over us in a fearsome overhang, which, even in my somewhat desperate frame of mind, I could not imagine myself attempting.

We climbed on until we were directly under the overhang. From here a wide gully ran steeply down to the right and plunged out of sight. By climbing a little way down this it seemed that we could cross to the buttress on the other side, which formed our skyline in that direction. But if we could get round this it would only bring us out on to the terrific precipice of the eastern face of Nelion. However it was the only way, and Wyn led off down and across the gully. The full length of the rope was stretched taut across the gully before he found a suitable stand and I could join him. Then we climbed diagonally up the buttress. Before it disappeared round the corner, I looked back and saw that we were already above the overhanging part of the southern face of Nelion. We crossed the crest of the buttress, expecting to be faced with a smooth perpendicular cliff. Instead, to our incredulous delight we found that easy broken rocks led on upwards. We could not see the summit, but it was clear that we were above the great wall of the east face and that there was nothing now to stop us. This sudden change from hopelessness to the certainty of success was among the most thrilling experiences I have known. There followed only a swift joyous scramble and we were there, on the hitherto untrodden summit of Nelion.

By now the cloud was all about us, though we could still see the Lewis glacier below. Gustav had been watching the summit through field glasses. He saw us now and let out a tremendous shout which came faintly to our ears. Across the gap, filled with swirling mist, we could see dimly the rocky dome of Batian.

After a short rest we started down the ridge towards the Gate of the Mist. Our first attempt to reach it failed, but by cutting steps down a hard snow slope on the northern side of the ridge we turned an overhanging pinnacle and got down to the floor of the gap. Thence we reached the summit of Batian.

In climbing a peak, or a ridge, or a mountain face for the first time, the anxiety of finding the way, not knowing where each step is going to lead or how far to press home the attempt upon each difficult section, the ever-present fear of being placed in a false position from which there is no retreat, the nagging time factor, all these things enormously exaggerate the actual difficulties of the climb. Wyn and I were so impressed by our ascent of Nelion that we were seriously worried about our ability to get down by the way we had come. We actually contemplated cutting our way down the Diamond glacier and crossing the ice-covered slabs which, only that morning, we had dismissed as impracticable.

I have since repeated the climb several times, and each time I was more amazed, not only that we should have thought of such a desperate alternative, but that we should have regarded the ascent of Nelion as so very difficult. Each step became so engraved on my memory that it seemed commonplace and perfectly straightforward. Even the crack in the 60-foot wall, that had turned out to be the key to the upper part of the mountain, was no longer formidable. This experience of repeating a climb, the first ascent of which I had made myself showed me very clearly how it was that mountains in the Alps, which had resisted the attacks of the pioneers for so long and had appeared to them such desperate ventures, should come to be regarded as quite easy. To a lesser extent, too, this illustrates the main difference between "guided" and "guideless" climbing in the Alps.

Most fortunately for us, Wyn and I resisted the "temptation" of going down the Diamond glacier, and, with a good deal of anxiety about the time, we climbed down into the Gate of the Mist again and recrossed the summit of Nelion. Most of the way down from there Wyn occupied the more responsible position of rearguard. My job of finding the way was easy. We avoided the crack by roping down the 60-foot wall. I felt better when the upper half of the mountain was behind us, and I let my mind dwell upon the glorious knowledge that the peaks had been climbed.

For all our misgivings the climb was perfectly timed, and we reached the foot of the peak as the clouds were breaking in the evening light. We made our way across the glacier in the soft glow of the setting sun. I was tired and utterly happy.

Two days later we repeated the ascent of the twin peaks, this time with Gustav. I must confess that neither Wyn nor I were very keen on the idea, but we were well rewarded by enjoying much that in the excitement of the first ascent we had failed to appreciate. When we returned that evening we found that Miss de Watteville had come up with three of her porters to the Skating Lake, as she had promised. We had intended to go down the next day, but her visit provided us with a welcome excuse to allow ourselves just one more day, and the next morning the four of us set off down the Lewis glacier. The sky and the peak remained free from cloud all day, a rare occurrence on Mount Kenya, and one which, in my experience, usually heralded a storm.

We walked round the foot of Point John, and from there climbed to a rocky gap that gave us a splendid view across the Darwin glacier to the southern face of the peaks, crowned by the Diamond glacier. It is pleasant after a climb to have leisure to trace from afar the scenes of recent adventures. Above our gap to the west stood a rock peak, as slender and graceful as the spire of Salisbury Cathedral. Later this came to be known as Midget Peak, and was to be the scene of an unpleasantly exciting adventure.

We went on down to the Lewis glacier and crossed the valley of the Tyndall glacier to Two Tarn Col. Here we spent a blissful hour basking in the sun and gazing up at the great western face of Batian. The principal features of this face are two hanging glaciers. These treated us to a wonderful display of ice avalanches.

That night there was a heavy snowstorm. It is remarkable how satisfactory bad weather can be when it comes at the end of a successful climbing season. The otherwise dismal scene outside our tent next morning seemed to provide a perfect climax. We had intended to carry our things down, but before we had struck camp our porters appeared through the mist and falling snow. It was a gallant gesture, for they were not equipped for such conditions. Miss de Watteville's men had stayed up at the Skating Lake.

Walking down hill was delightfully easy, and we reached the hut above the forest by evening. A huge meal was followed by a most remarkable rum punch for which our resourceful hostess had all the necessary ingredients. The next morning we said good-bye to her, and plunged down into the forest. After even so short a time in the sterile world of ice, it was a glorious feeling to be amongst trees again. When we reached Chugoria we waited for two days camped by the side of the road. Poor Wyn began to despair of reaching the coast in time to catch his ship. But on the third day a lorry belonging to a Dutch *padre* came along and gave us a lift into Nairobi, where we arrived in time but with none to spare.

CHAPTER FOUR

Mount Kenya – the West Ridge of Batian

KENYA Colony was a land of wonderful variety and great promise. But so far the promise has not been fulfilled. Of the large number of people – Britons, Danes, Russians, Dutch, Swedes, Norwegians, Germans – that went there after the last war to make their homes, probably the majority found only disillusionment. It was not that these people were not prepared to work or that their one idea was to "get rich quick"; this was a belief that originated in the malicious and quite misleading publicity to which the colony was subjected in the 1920's. Most of the settlers were honest, hard-working folk whose object it was to build this new and beautiful land into a prosperous and developed country.

Undoubtedly the colony was over-capitalised; banks tumbled over each other in their rush to open branches in all the small towns and to advance huge sums to the farmers, large grocery and drapery stores were opened, grand hotels sprouted amongst the low corrugated iron roofs of Nairobi. These parasites lived on the capital rather than the income of the farmers, and when this was exhausted, or the farmers became too wise to fall for their blandishments, they had to close down. Though this did a good deal of harm, the real trouble was that no one knew what to grow or how best to grow it. This is no new problem in a young country, but it was aggravated by a great wave of optimism, for which the government publicity department was largely responsible, and which induced otherwise level-headed people to sink all they possessed in what were at best very doubtful projects. For example, it was found that flax grew well in some districts. The price of flax at the time was £300 per ton which would certainly show a very handsome profit. Farmers put all their land under flax and raised enormous overdrafts at the bank to install the machinery necessary for dealing with the raw product. Then without warning, and almost overnight, the price of flax dropped to £20 or £30 per ton. The crops were not worth reaping at that price, the land became valueless and the farmer was faced with a debt that he could not hope to settle. Again, coffee had been grown with some success in Kiambu and Nyeri; therefore it was assumed that coffee could be grown in other parts of the colony and farmers with good land on the slopes of Mount Elgon and in the Ushin Gishu planted it. Coffee was then fetching £100 or £130 per ton. When the coffee trees were young they appeared to flourish and everyone became excited and planted coffee. But when after five years the trees reached maturity and should have begun to produce their beans, they assumed a woe-begone appearance and produced nothing, no matter with what manurial delicacies they were fed, how much they were petted and pampered, shaded and irrigated. But you do not abandon five or six years work without a struggle and it was twice that time before people could be induced to realise that they had failed. A few were more lucky and actually succeeded in producing regular annual crops, only to find that the bottom had dropped out of the market. Although there were millions of people in Europe who had to use maize and other things with which to make synthetic coffee, the genuine article could not be sold. Thousands of tons of Brazilian coffee were dumped every year into the sea in an endeavour to induce the middle-men to raise their offers. It may be noted too that although the producer was getting a fifth of his former price, if he were lucky enough to sell at all, the well-do-do English housewife who could afford to buy coffee paid exactly the same price for this expensive luxury as she had paid before.

Flax, coffee, maize, dairy farming, sheep, pyrethrum, fruit, sisal – they were all tried, occasionally with success, usually without. Strange diseases attacked crops and livestock, plagues of locusts, never seen before within living memory, laid waste the land, the rains failed. No, it was not easy to make a living against these odds; everything was too experimental, too little was known.

But for all that it was a good life, full of interest and variety, and there was a great sense of freedom. Each day's work showed a concrete result in so much land cleared or ploughed, a drain dug, trees planted, a wall built – too few occupations in our modern world yield this satisfaction. One was always engaged in some experiment, thinking out new schemes, discussing them with neighbours, visiting other districts at week-ends where friends were engaged in some totally different undertaking – breeding polo ponies for the Indian market, or forestry. Some people spent months exploring the deserts of Turkana and the shores of Lake Rudolf in search of gold, while their partners ran the farms; others secured government contracts to build roads or bridges near their land; others again set up as "white hunters" and made a good living by conducting wealthy tourists who had come out to shoot big game.

Although there was always plenty of work to do, some seasons were not so busy as others. One could generally manage to get away for a short holiday once or even twice a year. There was an infinite number of things to do, and if one kept away from the big towns these holidays cost very little. I spent all mine on the mountains. Wyn had been sent to an inaccessible spot near Lake Rudolf, and Gustav and I were now working on the same farm and could not get away together. But it was not difficult to find people with whom to climb. Nearly a year after that first expedition I went to Mount Kenya again with Pat Russell. I wanted to explore the north-west approaches to the peaks, but a week of our time was wasted by my being laid up with an attack of fever. When I had recovered we had time only to work round to the south-east and climb the peak by our old route, though we managed to climb Point John as well.

Early in 1930 I had a letter from H. W. Tilman, who had been given my address by Melhuish. This turned out to be a most fortunate contact and we were destined to share many mountain ventures together. At that time Tilman had not done much climbing, having only started during his last home leave in the Lake district. But I have met few people so admirably adapted to it both physically and temperamentally. He was very strong and tough, he had a natural aptitude for moving about difficult country, I have never known him rattled, and he had a remarkable ability to put up with – even a liking for – unpleasant conditions. He said very little, too little I thought, but, like many quiet people, when he did speak he was generally worth listening to. As a companion the qualities I liked best were his tremendous sense of humour and his constant readiness to embark upon any project. When I first knew him he was a recluse, and, to my way of thinking, too anti-pathetic towards the softer forms of human pleasure, such as novel reading, cinemas or any form of social intercourse. Most of our occasional quarrels arose, I think, from our disagreement on these matters. Though still at school when the last war began he had served nearly four years of it in France as a gunner in a battery commanded by Major (now Lt.-General) Norton of Everest fame, and had won the Military Cross and bar. He came out to settle in Kenya soon after the last war and had spent most of his spare time hunting elephants and other big game.

Our first trip together was to Kilimanjaro. It was a most interesting journey, through the great game reserve south of Nairobi and across the Tanganyika border to Moshi, near the southern foot of the mountain. Like Mount Kenya, Kilimanjaro is an old volcano. It has two main peaks, Kibo, the higher, and Mawenzi. Though Kibo (19,000 ft.) is nearly three thousand feet higher than Kenya, there are no real difficulties in the ascent. We must have gone there at the wrong season for we struck continuously bad weather and reached the top of Kibo only after a hard struggle through masses of soft snow. To see better in the bad visibility we removed our snow-glasses and suffered for it a few hours later with a mild dose of snow blindness. This is a most painful affliction; it feels rather as though the insides of one's eyelids have been lacerated and then filled with sand. When we had recovered we climbed Mawenzi, which, in those conditions, presented us with quite a tough proposition.

Some six months later Tilman and I joined forces again, this time with a more serious ambition of traversing the twin peaks of Mount Kenya by climbing Batian from the north-west and descending by our old route to the Lewis glacier. I was then living in Turbo near the borders of Kenya and Uganda, and Tilman lived in Sotik, south towards Victoria Nyanza. We met at Nukuru and motored in Tilman's car via Nairobi to Nanyuki near the western foot of the mountain. Motoring in Kenya in those days was an uncertain business, and one generally set out in the expectation of spending a considerable portion of the day digging the car out of a morass, for which the equipment of shovels and crow-bars was as necessary as the supply of petrol and oil. In some places, even on the main roads it was fatal to go where other cars had been and so slip into their deep rutted tracks. Each car had to plough a furrow of its own if it were to stand a chance of getting through. Things, I believe, have changed since then, and now metalled causeways span those uncharted seas of black cotton soil.

Unlike Chugoria which was in a native reserve, Nanyuki was in a European settled district. The surrounding country was a wide open prairie lying between Mount Kenya and the Aberdare Mountains. The farmers of the district went in mostly for cattle. Nanyuki itself was a typical Kenya township of tin roofs, shapeless and unlovely. It had the usual small and sprawling hotel, the Silverbeck, run by a retired Naval officer, Commander Hook. These small hotels were a very pleasant feature of Kenya, and were to be found at remarkably frequent intervals along the roads through the settled districts. They were generally spotlessly clean, most efficiently run and the food was excellent. They combined the friendly unpretentiousness of an English inn with a service that left little to be desired. They were miles ahead of anything I have ever met with in India.

It was said that the bar at the Silverbeck had been built across the Equator, though geodesists would no doubt deny that such an exact determination of latitude was possible. However, it appears that the legend was popularly believed, for a famous chess match had been played on it between representatives of the Northern and Southern Hemispheres, each sitting on his respective side of the Equator.

Raymond Hook, the brother of the Commander, combined farming with professional big-game hunting – a remarkably pleasant way of life. He had kindly undertaken to arrange for out modest requirements of pack ponies and drivers for the journey to our base near the head of the Mackinder valley.

Having completed the 250 miles from Nuruku to Nanyuki in a single day without a hitch, we proceeded to get firmly stuck in the mud between the Silberbeck and Raymond Hook's farm, about four miles to the east. As it was getting dark we abandoned the car and walked the rest of the way. We returned the next morning to salvage the vehicle and its most precious load, with the result that we did not start with our small caravan until two o'clock in the afternoon.

I do not think that the route up the mountain from Nanyuki is as attractive as that from Chugoria. That may be partly because I saw the eastern route first, but the forest on the western side is not so magnificent, and there is nothing to compare with that wonderful belt of parkland which on the other side divides the zone of giant heath from the open downs above. But the Nanyuki route is nevertheless very lovely.

We camped the first night in a grassy glade on the outskirts of the forest. I always enjoyed the first camp. One felt so deliciously free, stretched luxuriously on the soft grass in front of a blazing fire that flickered on the dark clumps of jungle, listening to the strange night noises. All the senses seemed to be sharpened by the contrast with one's normal surroundings, just as they were on returning to the forest from the glaciers. Early the next morning as we were eating our breakfast we were startled by a fearful trumpeting close behind us. Perhaps I should say I was startled, for Tilman exhibited no more than a mild interest. Looking round I saw an elephant. We had no means of defending ourselves, but the beast appeared to share Tilman's nonchalance, and to my relief he turned and trundled off into the forest. An African elephant is an impressive sight in its natural surroundings. Later in the day we were fortunate enough to see some rhinoceroses, prehistoric-looking creatures, again to my relief going in the opposite direction.

The forests were full of strange creatures. One of the most interesting, I thought, was the honey-bird. He would follow you about all day flitting from branch to branch above your head, singing all the time. In this way he would try to induce you to follow him, for then he would lead you to a bee-hive. You were then under a gentleman's agreement to smoke out the bees, take your share of the honey and leave him the rest. I never had time to try the experiment but I have it on good authority that it is perfectly true. The Wanderobo carry the tale further. They say that if you do not leave the honey-bird a sufficient share of the loot, when next you meet he will lead you to a snake.

The Wanderobo are a tribe of forest dwellers in Kenya. They are a somewhat mysterious people, very shy, and rarely show themselves unless they have reason to know that you are friendly and have a supply of tobacco to trade for money. They are nomads, living entirely by hunting, of which they are probably among the greatest human exponents, and, presumably, by following honey-birds.

Our way led diagonally up the northern side of the mountain, and so into the Mackinder valley. When we reached the upper part of the valley we found a cave, a mile or so from the northern foot of Batian and about 14,000 feet above sea level. It offered us a most excellent base camp. Being just about at the upper level of giant groundsel it was amply supplied with fuel and a great improvement upon our bleak, comfortless camp by the Skating Lake. The floor of the cave was swampy, but by draining it, drying it with a huge bonfire built at the mouth of the cave, and laying down a carpet of grass and groundsel leaves, we made a very pleasant home for ourselves. We sent the ponies and their drivers down with instructions to return after ten days. I had brought a Wagishu tractor driver, named Masede, from the farm in Turbo. He stayed at the cave with us, where we spent a happy time sleeping and eating until our food ran out.

We spent the first day climbing two sharp granite pinnacles on the ridge forming the western side of the valley. Besides a lot of fun, these peaks provided us with a most comprehensive view of the northern aspect of Batian. I know no mountain in the Alps, with the possible exception of Mont Blanc, that presents such a superb complexity of ridges and faces as the twin peaks of Mount Kenya – a complexity that would delight the heart of any mountaineer. Each feature is clear-cut and definite, none is superfluous to the whole lovely structure. It would take many years of climbing holidays to explore them all, and each would involve a high standard of mountaineering.

From the summit of Batian a sharp, serrated ridge runs north. After some distance it divides and plunges down in two main buttresses, one towards the north-east, the other to the west. The north-east ridge forms the northern boundary of the wall up which we had made our first attempt to climb the peaks, nearly two years before. The west ridge is, to my mind, the finest feature on the whole mountain, though perhaps I am prejudiced. From its junction with the north-east ridge it descends in a series of sweeping steps, each larger than the one above, until the ridge takes its greatest plunge in what I unimaginatively named the Grand Gendarme. From the foot of this the ridge rises to a pinnacle – the Petit Gendarme – and then drops to its lowest point, a snowy saddle dividing Batian from a massive peak known as Point Piggot. Point Piggot is really a continuation of the west ridge which gradually curls south to enclose the basin of the Tyndall glacier, and sinks finally to the grassy slopes of Two Tarn Col.

Planning a climb is a fascinating occupation. In some respects it is even more fun than the climb itself, though of course it would lose most of its charm without the knowledge that the plan would be put into operation. The imagination is free to wander over the entire gigantic scene, to dance on the toes of fancy up sunlit rock and shining silver crest, to shudder in warm security at precipitous ice gullies and airy crags, to trace link by link the slender chain of possibility.

The triangular face between the two main ridges was guarded by a hanging glacier terrace, from which the risk of ice avalanches precluded any prolonged operations on the steep polished slopes below. The north-east ridge was supported by two massive buttresses, smooth and steep, and divided by a straight, deep cleft. For all its forbidding grandeur the west ridge seemed to offer the best hope of success. It was very long and complicated and there was much that we could not judge from a distance, many links that had to be taken for granted.

The first thing to do was to get a closer view of the lower part, which might give us an insight into the all important time factor and the nature of the ice and snow and rock of which the ridge was built. So the next day we set out for the high saddle between the Petit Gendarme and Point Piggot.

It took us most of the morning and a lot of hard work to reach it. Crossing a low gap in the western wall of the Mackinder valley we climbed down to the lower edge of a great circular sheet of ice that sloped steeply down from the foot of the main peaks. This phenomenon goes by the name of Joseph glacier, after one of Mackinder's Alpine guides. Brother César has been immortalised by a similar slab of ice farther to the east. Immortalised is perhaps hardly the right word, for I fancy all the glaciers of Mount Kenya are dying. Indeed it is a mystery how they contrive to maintain themselves on their present meagre diet of snow. Situated directly on the Equator they have no winter in which to recuperate their strength. In the Himalayas, which at their nearest point are a very long way from the tropics, isolated peaks of 17,000 feet are not usually festooned with hanging glaciers. The daily cloud cap over Kenya no doubt affords some protection to the ice. Admittedly I have taken pains to visit the mountain when I was most likely to meet with fine weather, but I have been there at several different seasons and have observed it during the whole of one "rains", and I confess that I am puzzled to reconcile the appearance and disposition of the glaciers with the small quantity of snow that appears to fall on the mountain. But then I have never been quite satisfied with the accepted explanations of glacial phenomena, and still cling to a sneaking belief that they are just put there by some beneficent power for the delectation (or grief) of mountaineers.

We spent a long time cutting steps up the Joseph glacier to a steep snow and ice gully that led to the saddle. Here we had to negotiate a bergschrund (a kind of crevasse that divides the main body of the glacier from the steeper ice or rock above). Above this a lot more step cutting was required, and by the time we reached the saddle we were dismally conscious that we had undertaken a very tough proposition. Nor was the immediate prospect above us in any way reassuring. By now the upper part of the peak was hidden by cloud. The Petit Gendarme frowned down upon us like an ogre that resented our intrusion. If it had been his scalp that we were after we might still have been over-awed, but he was only an incident on the great ridge, the first of a long series of obstacles. A direct assault seemed to be out of the question and we must outflank him. This we could only do by climbing diagonally up a very steep slope to the right. Whether this slope was composed of ice or snow we could not tell from where we stood. It was a matter of considerable importance, for if it were ice, cutting steps up it would involve a good day's work to reach the ridge behind the Petit Gendarme. Above and beyond we could see the vertical flanks of the Grand Gendarme thrusting up into the clouds.

We sat down on a rock shelf to reflect, our legs dangling over the Tyndall glacier several hundred feet below. It was a grand view. Across the way was the great west face of Batian, so close that we might have been hanging from a balloon before its ice-scarred ramparts. We were about level with the lower of the two hanging glacier terraces; the lace fringe of the upper terrace was just visible through the cloud. These monsters were silent now, which was a pity, for here we had front seats in the dress-circle from which such an avalanche display as we had seen from Two Tarn Col would have been a fine spectacle. To our right the ridge mounted in a series of jagged spires towards Point Piggot, to our left –, we averted our eyes; we had learnt as much of the west ridge as we could digest in one lesson. The stage was set and to-morrow the chosen day.

How I hated Tilman in the early morning. Not only on that expedition, but through all the years we have been together. He never slept like an ordinary person. Whatever time we agreed to awake, long before that time (how long I never knew) he would slide from his sleeping bag and start stirring his silly porridge over the Primus stove. I used gradually to become aware of this irritating noise and would bury my head in silent rage against the preposterous injustice of being woken half an hour too soon. When his filthy brew was ready he would say "Show a leg", or some such imbecile remark. In moments of triumph on the top of a peak I have gone so far as to admit that our presence there was due in large measure to this quality of Tilman's, but in the dark hours before dawn such an admission of virtue in my companion has never touched the fringe of my consciousness.

The next morning was no exception. I remembered that it was my birthday, which seemed to make matters worse. We issued from our lovely warm cave soon after three o'clock, leaving Masede in full possession, and plodded slowly up the side of the valley in the bright moonlight.

I began to feel more human when we reached the Joseph glacier. We supplemented the light of the moon with that of a candle lantern and climbed rapidly. Our steps of the previous day, large and comfortable, were still intact. Hours of toil now sped beneath us with an effortless rhythm of hip and ankle joints, as we climbed towards the dawn. Daylight was flooding in upon us as we crossed the bergschrund. Half way up the gully above, we branched to the left so as to reach the ridge beyond a small but difficult section east of the saddle. In this manœuvre we were delayed by some difficult climbing on ice-covered rocks, but even so we reached the crest below the Petit Gendarme with the whole day before us. And what a day! Crisp, sparkling, intoxicating. I have never known more complete physical well-being. The western face of Batian caught the full light of the newly risen sun, and every lovely detail of ice fretwork and powerful granite column was hard and clear.

Though what we could see of the west ridge towering above us looked no less formidable than before, we were now in a very different frame of mind, and we paused barely a minute. But the slope under the Petit Gendarme soon began to exercise a sobering effect. It turned out to be composed of hard ice covered by a layer, not more than an inch or two thick, of frozen crystalline snow. It was exceedingly steep and ended below in a sheer drop to the Tyndall glacier. While we were both on the slope together a slip on the part of either of us would have been almost impossible to hold, since we were traversing diagonally across it. It was possible, by kicking small toeholds into the hard layer of snow and by sticking the blade of the axe in for a hand rail, to climb up and along the slope with reasonable security. But this security would only remain so long as the snow held firm. The slope was still in shadow, but an hour or so after the sun had climbed above Point Piggot the snow would begin to melt and would no longer offer any hold. The proper procedure would have been to cut steps through the snow into the ice below, but this would have taken nearly all day, and we were still at the very beginning of the climb. This is a common problem in mountaineering, and each case must be judged by the circumstances. We must have a line of retreat in the event of failure higher up, particularly as that event was very probable. Cutting steps downhill, besides being very slow and exhausting, is apt to be a hazardous business when prolonged for many hours on so exposed a slope without any sort of anchorage. In this case I was fairly confident that we could climb over the top of the Petit Gendarme from behind and rope down its western side. Even if this line of retreat failed, we could always wait until the following morning and come down the slope when it was again frozen. So we decided to risk it and to use the snow layer covering the ice.

Even so it was a long job. In some places, near rock outcrops, the snow was too thin to provide any foothold, and steps had to be cut in the hard blue ice. It took us several hours to regain the crest of the ridge behind the Petit Gendarme. We halted for five minutes to eat some chocolate and look about us. The peak was already covered in cloud. It was obvious that we could not get very far unless things improved, and at first sight there did not seem to be very much chance of that. For a short distance the ridge was fairly easy, but then it rose up like a mighty wave, several hundred feet of vertical and unbroken rock. It was hopeless to think of climbing this direct, and the only chance was to look for a way of turning it on the left. We traversed out on to the north face and reached a gully that led directly upwards. Here the climbing was more straightforward, and except in a few places we could both move up together. We could never see very far ahead, and had little idea where we were getting to. Suddenly after about an hour and a half we reached the crest of the main ridge again, and were delighted to find that we were standing on top of the Grand Gendarme. This was a very welcome surprise, and our hopes began to revive, until we came to examine the next obstacle.

This appeared to us as a red pinnacle, but it was, in fact, a step in the ridge similar to the Grand Gendarme on a much smaller scale. It was extremely steep and was undercut at its base. This time there was no chance of getting round the obstacle. To the right there was a giddy drop to the hanging glaciers of the west face; to the left the scoop at the base of the pinnacle ran downwards in a groove towards the centre of the narrowing north face, overhung by a continuous line of ice-polished slabs.

There was a good ledge below the pinnacle, and by standing on Tilman's shoulders I could just reach two finger holds. Hanging on these, and with a final kick off from Tilman's head, I managed to swing myself up to grasp a hold higher up and also to find some purchase for my feet to relieve the strain on my arms. After an exhausting struggle I established myself above the overhang. Then followed some very delicate work. The wall of the pinnacle was nearly vertical, and the holds were only just large enough to accommodate a boot nail. But the rock was perfect, and at first the holds, though few, were well spaced. Half-way up, however, there was an extremely nasty bit. It involved a long stride from one nail to another with nothing but a few rough excrescences for the hands with which to maintain my changing centre of balance. I contemplated this stride for a long time, before cautiously swinging my right foot to the upper hold. It felt so unpleasant that I hastily brought my foot back again for further contemplation. After repeating this faint-hearted operation about half a dozen times, and prompted largely by my increasing distaste for the present position of my left foot which was beginning to hurt, I gradually transferred my weight to the right foot, which to my intense relief did not slip, and by clawing at the face of the rock managed to hoist myself into an upright position.

Fortunately, after this the holds, although still small, became more profuse. But by now there was a new source of anxiety. The rope between us was clearly not going to be long enough to enable me to reach the top of the pinnacle. It was no use Tilman unroping, for he could not possibly get up the lower overhanging bit without a pull from above. There was a little recess below the top, and I just reached it as the rope came taut between us. In this I wedged myself sufficiently tightly to support his full weight. I hauled up the ice-axes and the rucksacks and sent the end of the rope down again. In spite of my pulling, Tilman had a much more severe struggle than I had experienced. When he had succeeded I climbed quickly to the top of the pinnacle where I got into a really strong position. The rest was easy.

Nothing provides such a strong incentive to struggle on up at all costs as the memory of a really severe pitch below, and from now on we were infused with a pleasant sense of abandon. Time was our chief anxiety, and we hurried upwards as fast as we could. The steps that followed were difficult, but not nearly so bad as the red pinnacle which we had just surmounted. They grew smaller and smaller until at last we reached the junction of the north-east and the west ridges.

It was an exciting moment as we turned south to look along the final ridge leading to the summit. It is impossible to tell from below how difficult such a ridge is likely to prove. We had seen that it was long and serrated, and that the steepness of the west and north-east faces on either side of it would oblige us to stick to the crest. Much depended upon the width of this crest. We could not see far along it through the mist, and so the issue remained in doubt. At any rate, the short length of ridge that we could see, though very narrow and broken, was not hopeless. We started clambering along it, sometimes balancing along the top, sometimes sitting astride and sometimes swinging along the crest with our hands while our feet sought purchase on the wall below.

It was a splendid situation, thrust up infinitely high, isolated by the mist from all save this slender crest of granite along which we *must* find a way, the thrilling knowledge that the mighty west ridge was below us, mind and muscle set to a high pitch of rhythmic co-ordination. I have rarely enjoyed anything more. Somewhere down in the grey depths to the left was the great bulge of rock that had defeated us nearly two years before. To the right, below our feet, was a white glow, the upper hanging-glacier terrace of the west face. The rock was superb, as hard and strong as the granite of the Chamonix Aiguilles.

We reached a gap about 30 feet deep, and roped down into it. Our boats had already been effectively burnt, and there was no time to bother about cutting off our retreat still further. One after another pinnacles loomed into view, greatly magnified by the mist. One after another we set about the new problem that each presented, always expecting it to be the last. I soon lost count; the ridge seemed to go on for ever; but we were going with it, and that was the main thing. Surely nothing could stop us now.

At last, in place of the sharp pinnacle we had come to expect, a huge, dark-grey mass loomed ahead of us. A few steps cut in the icy floor of a gully, a breathless scramble up easy rocks, and we were there beside our little cairn on the summit of Batian.

It was half-past four. There was no chance of getting down before nightfall, but no consideration of that sort could stem the flood of my joy and, let it be admitted, relief. I do not know what Tilman thought about it. He did not know the way down the south-east face. If he imagined it to involve climbing of a standard similar to that which we had just done he must have had some misgivings, though characteristically he expressed none.

There was no view to look at, and so, after swallowing a tin each of some meat essence, we began the descent. The rocks on the south side of Batian were plastered with snow, which delayed us. But we made up time between the Gate of the Mist and the top of Nelion which we crossed without a pause, and plunged down into the gully beyond. In our haste Tilman slipped and lost his ice-axe which vanished out of sight in a single bound. After that we were more careful. It was getting dark as we reached the top of the 60-foot wall above the head of the south ridge, and night had fallen by the time we had pulled the rope after us at the foot of the wall.

It was here that I began to feel very sick. I imagine that the tin of meat essence I had eaten on the summit was bad. But an hour or so later I was sick, and after that I felt more philosophical about it.

The clouds had not cleared at dusk in their customary manner, and it looked as though we should have to stop where we were until the morning. It was already very cold, and the prospect was not welcome. But later, breaks began to appear in the mist, the moon came out and there was enough light to enable us to climb on down slowly. I felt very tired and the phantom moonlight, the shadowy forms of ridge and pinnacle, the wisps of silvered mist, the radiant expanse of the Lewis glacier plunging into soundless depths below induced a sense of exquisite fantasy. I experienced that curious feeling, not uncommon in such circumstances, that there was an additional member of the party – three of us instead of two.

It was not very difficult nor even laborious, dropping from ledge to ledge. I remembered every step of the way, and had no difficulty in finding it. We had some trouble in negotiating the chimney where we had found Mackinder's rope, but once below that the rest was easy. When we reached the Lewis glacier we started plodding up towards the saddle between Point Lenana and Point Thompson. But this demanded more physical effort than we had bargained for, so we altered course and made for the hut by the side of the Skating Lake. Here we huddled over some bits of timber that we managed to ignite, and waited for the dawn. The rest did us good, and we reached the saddle before the sun was up. From there back to our cave in the Mackinder valley was mostly downhill, but it seemed a very long way.

Masede was pleased to see us, but he was not greatly concerned. It is no longer possible to surprise the East African negro by the inexplicable follies of the White Man. For our part we were in no mood for conversation. We got into our sleeping bags, a 10-lb Cheddar cheese and a bottle of pickled onions between us, and ate and ate until we fell asleep. We awoke in the evening and ate again, and then slept until late the following morning.

I still regard the traverse of the twin peaks of Mount Kenya as one of the most enjoyable climbs I have ever had – a perfect and wholly satisfying episode, shared with an ideal companion.

We still had nearly a week left. The weather held, and we climbed several more peaks. One of these was Point Piggot, which gave us a superb view of the west face of Batian. The sky remained clear most of the day, and we lay for a long time on the summit basking in the sun and gazing contentedly across at the west ridge. Another long day was spent walking all the way round the foot of the central peaks. Immediately below one of the glaciers we found the skeleton of a wild buffalo, which had evidently broken its leg by slipping between the great boulders that formed the slope. Others had been found before, and it would be interesting to know why these creatures should wish to stray from the pleasant country below. It cannot be to escape from the heat, and the glacial regions offer them nothing to feed on but lichen. There was the skeleton of a leopard near the summit of Kilimanjaro.

Our last climb provided an adventure which came too near to disaster to be pleasant. We set out to climb the lovely, slender spire of Midget Peak. We had examined it in passing on our journey round the peaks, and it seemed to us that it might be possible. It would certainly provide rock climbing of a high standard, but on clean granite there is no knowing what you can do until you try. To get to the peak we had once more to cross the high saddle near Lanana and go down the Lewis glacier past Point John. The clouds came up in the usual way, and apart from the fact that the two previous days had been brilliantly fine, there was nothing to suggest that we were in for a spell of bad weather. Once on the peak the climbing, which was difficult and exposed, occupied all our attention. About two-thirds of the way up we found ourselves in a sort of cave the only exit from which was by way of a narrow, slightly sloping ledge that jutted over a considerable overhang. There was no handhold, and it was simply a matter of standing on the ledge and edging along it. It was only about three yards long, and led to a comfortable platform. Above this there was a steep and narrow gully.

After some more hard climbing we reached the summit. We were sitting there feeling rather pleased with ourselves when snow started to fall in large, soft flakes. This was a nasty shock. What had been pleasantly difficult on the way up would be decidedly unpleasant on the way down with the holds covered in snow. We hurried off the summit and began climbing down as fast as we could. The rock was still reasonably dry when we reached the top of the narrow gully. Here there was a large rock bollard. While I hitched the rope round this and paid it out, Tilman climbed on down the gully and soon disappeared from view. The rope continued to go out for a while, then it stopped and I guessed that he had reached the beginning of the sloping edge. Suddenly there was a sickening jerk, and the rope stretched down the gully as taut as a wire hawser from a dragging ship. I waited for a moment hoping to get some instructions as to whether I should hold fast or lower away, but nothing happened. I shouted, but could get no reply.

What was I to do? Possibly the wisest thing would have been to make the rope fast and to climb down the gully to investigate the situation. But it is not good to leave an unconscious man dangling in mid-air for long, as he might easily suffocate. Of course I could not be sure that he was dangling, but judging by the strain on the rope and my memory of the cliff below it seemed very probable. It was quite impossible to haul him up owing to the friction of the rope against the rock; and in any case if he were dangling he would have got stuck under the overhang. The only alternative then was to lower away and hope for the best. Foot by foot the rope went out, and still no slackening of the strain. So far all the weight was taken by the bollard, but soon the rope was finished, and there was nothing for it but to take it off the bollard. Here I made a stupid mistake. I should have done this while there was still sufficient rope to put over my shoulder. I thought of it too late, and of course I could not pull the rope back again. So, instead of taking the strain from my shoulder, I had to start climbing down with it dragging from my waist. Now the friction of the rope against the rock was my ally, acting as it did as a slight brake to the downward movement. On the other hand, whenever I bent I could not straighten myself again except by stepping downwards, and I had to think out my movements very carefully. Fortunately the gully was very narrow, and I could brace my arms against either wall.

To my great relief, before I had gone very far down the gully, the strain lifted, which meant that Tilman had come to rest on a ledge. I hurried on down to the platform below the gully, and looked over the edge. He was sitting on a ledge looking up at me. I thought he looked a bit queer, though he answered my questions rationally. He seemed to be unhurt. I discovered afterwards that he was still only half conscious, and had not the least idea of where he was. I asked him if there was a way on down from where he was sitting. I could not see because of the overhang. He said there was a way, and I decided to join him.

By climbing a little way down to the right I reached a place from which the doubled rope would reach the ledge below. Then hitching it over a bollard I slid down it. To my dismay, when I reached it I found that Tilman's ledge was quite isolated, and that there was no possible means of getting on down. The next ledge below was far beyond the range of our rope. The only thing to do was to climb back again up the rope.

Tilman was recovering rapidly. I do not know when he started remembering things again, but I believe it was not for quite a while after this. To this day he cannot remember anything that happened between his slip and our safe arrival in the cave beyond the sloping ledge. How he contrived to climb up the rope to the platform above, I cannot imagine. At the best of times a climbing rope is not very easy to swarm up, as it is too thin; now our fingers were cold and the rope was wet from its contact with the snow. I found it about as much as I could do. However, we were beginning to get somewhat desperate, and that can account for a lot.

Back on the platform we still had to cross the sloping ledge which now had a thick layer of snow on it. It was impossible to climb carefully along it as one's foot would certainly have slipped. There was only one way to deal with it. Firmly belayed by Tilman against the possibility of a repetition of the *contretemps* we had just experienced, I placed one foot as far out on the ledge as I could reach, and, with a combination of a spring and a dive, I leapt forward. The manœuvre succeeded, and I landed sprawling on the lip of the cave beyond. Tilman repeated the performance, and the worst of our troubles were over.

By now all the ledges and cracks in the rock were deep in snow, and climbing in the ordinary sense was impossible. We could only proceed by a series of *rappels*. This is a method of "roping down" which has been referred to before. It is a simple dodge employed either to save time or to get down an otherwise unclimbable place. The rope is doubled and fixed to a rock bollard (if there is none available, an iron spike hammered into a crack in the rock will serve) and the two ends are allowed to dangle evenly down. By letting the rope slide between the legs and over one shoulder, by holding the upper part of the rope with one hand and the lower part with the other, and by steadying oneself with one's feet against the rock it is possible to slip comfortably without much muscular effort. So as to retrieve the rope when one is at the bottom, it is generally necessary to pass it through a separate sling which is itself attached to the bollard, then, by pulling one end, and with reasonable care, the rope slips through the sling and is recovered. The slings are generally made by cutting a short length (varying according to the size of the bollard) from the main rope.

I forget how many *rappels* we did that day, but by the time we reached the foot of the peak our rope, which had started as a 120-foot length, was reduced to about 40 feet.

Large soft snow-flakes were still falling steadily as we trudged slowly up the Lewis glacier through the deep, new snow. I did not know how Tilman felt, but I was mighty glad to be on firm ground again. It was dark by the time we reached our cave.

The next morning it had stopped snowing and I took Masede up to show him a glacier at close quarters. He was politely interested, but what he was really curious to know was how much the Government would pay us for our activities of the last ten days. He just would not believe me when I told him that we had done it for our own amusement and that the Government would not pay us a cent for all our hard work. Like a skilful barrister he kept trying to trap me into an admission, and it began to rankle that he could not prove me a liar. However, on our way back through Nairobi I happened to go to lunch with Major Dutton at Government House. When I came out Masede met me with a smirk on his face. It was quite clear to him that I had gone there to collect our money. In face of such evidence it was useless for me to argue further, and so long as I knew him he never again believed anything I said.

CHAPTER FIVE

Mountains of the Moon

WHETHER Ruwenzori, Kenya, Kilimanjaro or the group of volcanoes of Kivu are Ptolemy's "Mountains of the Moon", is an open question. Nor is it of great importance, for the ancient tradition of the Nile rising in a system of lakes fed by snow mountains, though true, seems to have been more in the nature of a lucky guess than a result of actual geographical observation. However, as Ruwenzori alone fulfils the ancient tradition, it has come to be labelled with that romantic title. Its mystery, invisibility and remoteness, surrounded by thousands of miles of tropical swamp and vegetation, and the fact that, unlike its rivals, it is a *range* of non-volcanic mountains, perhaps make it the more worthy of the distinction. The origin of the name Ruwenzori is very doubtful, and it is not used by any local natives in speaking of the mountain range.

Nevertheless, it is remarkable that the ancients should have believed in the existence of these snow mountains, as it was not until 1888, some thirty years after the discovery of the Victoria Nile by Speke, that Stanley discovered the existence of snow mountains in Central Africa; this despite the fact that many explorers had been travelling for a number of years in the neighbourhood of the range, and Stanley had himself camped for months at its foot without so much as suspecting the existence of vast glacier-covered mountains. To those who have experienced Ruwenzori weather, this is not so surprising!

During the next eighteen years various attempts were made to penetrate to the glaciers, but it was not until 1906 that a large expedition led by H.R.H. the Duke of the Abruzzi explored the peaks and glaciers of the range and reached the summits of the highest peaks.

In 1926, G. N. Humphreys led two remarkable expeditions, during which he explored much new country to the north of the range, and carried out some very good work amongst the peaks. During the second expedition he reached the summits of Margherita and Alexandra for the first time since the Duke's expedition.

In spite of the opening of good motor roads through Uganda to Fort Portal and beyond to the foothills of Ruwenzori, very few Europeans ever penetrated far into the mountains, and, since 1926, the ascent of the high peaks had not been repeated. In recent years Humphreys had explored much of the country, but there was a great deal still to be discovered. Tilman and I had decided to go to Ruwenzori at the earliest opportunity. Our interest was centred mainly upon the high peaks, for we had not yet realised that fascination of unexplored valleys.

In 1931 I was invited to join Smythe's expedition to Kamet, and it was not until early in 1932 that we had the chance of further African ventures. We travelled the five hundred miles from Turbo in Kenya to the foot of the mountains in Tilman's car. We had no difficulty whatsoever in collecting porters to establish us. Our requirements were very small as we proposed to establish any high-level camps ourselves. We started with twelve porters, and one man cut a path through the forest. All porters' food had, of course, to be taken with us.

The porters were of the Bakonju tribe, who live on the lower slopes of the range. They were delightful people, with a ready grin, even in adverse circumstances, and they were generally cheerful and willing. One of their chief characteristics was the way they balanced up and down formidable slopes, or from one tree trunk to another, with 50- lb. loads on their heads – a feat to be envied by even the most practised mountaineer.

Three marches took us to the forest. It was difficult going as the vegetation was everywhere dense and perpetually wet. Sometimes we went for half an hour at a time without touching the ground, walking over thickly-matted branches. The sides of the valley were steep and broken, and progress was infinitely laborious. We found rock shelters at frequent intervals; these were very useful as camping sites, for it was always raining. In the evening, sitting before a fire, sheltered from the rain, it was good to watch the clouds driven wildly about the craggy foothills of the range, or clinging to the gullies in the enormous rock precipices; to listen to the roar of a hundred torrents; and, after dark, to see the flickering of lightning towards the high peaks. One afternoon, while still in the forests, the weather cleared, and we saw the great ice peaks of Stanley and Speke – a startling sight indeed, seen from such very tropical surroundings. It is easy to realise with what excitement those early explorers first set eyes on these snow peaks after travelling for many months through the swamps of Central Africa.

At an altitude of about 10,000 feet we came to very strange country. A fantastic tangle of rotting vegetation – giant groundsel, lobelia and giant heath – all thickly covered in moss. Moss was everywhere; we waded feet deep in it and walked through tunnels of it. The very air seemed to be tinged with an eerie green light. All the streams were hushed and a strange silence reigned.

Two more days were spent in reaching the Bujuku Lake, at the foot of the Scott-Elliott Pass, where we made our base camp in a cave. Moving about in the high valleys was exasperating. We were either in swamp, groundsel forest, or struggling through a vile growth known as "helichrysum", which is a sort of juniper growing to a height of about seven feet, and so dense as to be at times impenetrable. The giant groundsels found on Mount Kenya grow singly and far apart. In the Ruwenzori they grow close together in dense forests, their rotten trunks lying about in a thick tangle on the ground. These, though stout, were rarely strong enough to bear our full weight, so that when we stepped on them they snapped helplessly in mid-air. Apart from the great labour needed to make any headway, it was almost impossible to go more than a few yards in any direction without getting wet to the hips – even if it did not happen to be raining or snowing. Again, above the limit of the helichrysum the rocks were covered with thick moss, which peeled off as soon as any weight was placed on it. This rendered any but the simplest approaches very dangerous.

But when all is said, Ruwenzori, like our Lakeland, would lose a great deal of its beauty, mystery and charm were it deprived of its continuous cloud and damp. Nor did we go there for comfort or freedom of movement.

We discharged two porters en route, and from the Bujuku camp we sent down another five. The remaining six were installed in a cave, and waited there with food and fires until we returned down the mountain. We went on alone with a light bivouac camp to the glaciers of Mount Stanley. All the time we were in thick mist and, with our heavy packs our progress was slow for we became involved in many difficulties by not being able to see more than a few yards ahead. Eventually, however, we reached the plateau of the Stanley glacier and, by accident rather than by design, camped right on the summit of the main divide. Though when we stopped we had no idea where we were.

At sunset that evening the mists cleared, and we looked straight down to the Congo. In the foreground was a sheer precipice of broken glacier, from which angry clouds strove to detach themselves. Beyond, like a hazy map beneath us, stretched the plains of the Congo across which the Semliki River coiled like a silver snake. To the south was the huge expanse of Lake Edward. The whole scene was flooded in the deepest blue – a blue so vivid that it coloured everything around us, becoming more and more intense the farther one gazed over the Congo, until swallowed up in a blazing sunset.

For the next twenty-four hours it snowed almost continuously. The following morning we set out in the vain hope of finding our way about the glaciers, but we spent a fruitless day losing ourselves in snow flurries, as our tracks were immediately blotted out by the driving snow. However, late in the evening, we managed to reach the foot of the south ridge of Alexandra. The next day, January 19th, we climbed the ridge to the summit of that peak. There was one difficult cornice to be overcome and a fair amount of step cutting on the ridge. This, I believe, was the route taken by the Duke of Abruzzi's party. We found a cairn on the summit. The mist cleared for a few moments while we were on the top, but we could see very little.

We were four and a half days on the glacier. There was a high wind most of the time, and snow fell all night and most of the day. But each evening at sunset the weather cleared for a moment and gave us superb views over the Congo. On the 20th we became hopelessly involved in a maze of crevasses while attempting to reach the east ridge of Margherita. At last, on the 21st, after repeated efforts, we managed to strike it at a point where the cornice was small, and could be cut through without great difficulty. From there we had little trouble in making the third ascent of the highest peak of Ruwenzori.

The snow and ice formations on these peaks are remarkable. Strong, cold winds, blowing newly fallen snow against any irregularity, produce the most fantastic shapes and forms. Practically no melting seems to take place, and gigantic cornices are formed. The snow surfaces have a very curious feathery appearance which is most beautiful.

When our food was finished we started an undignified descent to our base. We slid and slithered on moss- and lichen-covered rocks, and spent most of the time sitting down heavily on the ground. Our packs were far heavier than they had been when we left our base camp, owing to the fact that tent, sleeping-bags and all our kit were water-logged. But our real troubles began when we got amongst the helichrysum and rotting giant groundsel. At last, floundering through swamp and black mire, we reached the luxury of our cave by the Bujuku Lake.

We allowed ourselves a whole day to recuperate from this battering and to dry our sodden garments and bedding. It was a mystery to me how the porters continued to keep a fire going, still more to light it in that perpetual wet. But it did not seem to present any problem to them and two furnaces raged day and night at the mouth of the cave.

The Bakonjus of Ruwenzori have a remarkable method of carrying fire about with them. Straw, thatched tightly in the shape of a cigar about 18 inches long forms a receptacle in which the fire lies dormant. They carry these curious objects strapped to their shoulders and when they want a light they just take off the end of the cigar and blow. It is said that fire can be carried in this way for a month without renewal.

We set out for Mount Speke in thick weather on January 23rd, and after a further tussle with swamp and drenching vegetation, reached a glacier. A short clearing enabled us to see that we were almost directly above the Stuhlmann Pass. We climbed to the crest of a ridge and followed it to the summit of Vittorio Emmanuele Peak without encountering any mountaineering difficulties. There was a biting wind and we were wet to the waist. We waited for three hours hoping for a view, stamping about in a vain attempt to keep the circulation moving in our legs. At about 1.30 p.m. the mists lifted for a short time. We raced along the long ridge to the north, and, after crossing three intervening peaks, reached the unnamed peak which was climbed by Humphreys in 1926. It is the highest point of Mount Speke.

One of our principal objects was to force a route direct from the Bujuku valley to the highest peaks of Mount Baker. With this in view, we left our camp at dawn on January 24th. We had hoped to make the attempt direct from the Scott-Elliott pass, but the vicious ice-clad slabs and ice-filled cracks and gullies of the ridge above the pass looked impossible, so we decided to attempt the face about half a mile farther down the valley. The lower part of the face was covered in thick moss and lichen, and required extreme care. Above this the steep rocks were covered with ice and snow which, together with the rottenness of the rock, produced an exasperatingly false appearance of simplicity. It was difficult in the thick mist to make a good choice of route. After some hours of this sort of climbing we were faced by a formidable line of overhangs guarding this side of the east ridge of Baker. But after several attempts we overcame these and gained the ridge at 11 a.m.

Turning to the west, we followed a long easy ridge leading over several minor peaks to Semple Peak, which we reached at about 1 p.m. From there we turned south and climbed to the summit of King Edward Peak, the highest point of Mount Baker.

Shortly before reaching the summit, the whole range of high peaks cleared and we had a superb view of Mount Stanley. Having been surrounded by impenetrable fog for many days, the effect of such a sudden and complete clearing was indescribably wonderful; it felt as though a great load had been removed from one's mind. Subjects of considerable speculation and heated argument suddenly became clear. Our flounderings amongst the glaciers of Mount Stanley were at once revealed, and it was difficult to understand why we should ever have been at a loss to know where to go; though no doubt we would have been in exactly the same state of perplexity had we found ourselves again on the Stanley glacier wrapped in cloud.

With the sudden clear weather we decided to complete the traverse of Baker, disregarding the painful prospect of the weary return to the Bujuku valley by way of the Scott-Elliott Pass. We allowed ourselves about half an hour's rest on King Edward Peak, to examine our first real view of the range as a whole. Far below, the valleys, now bathed in sunlight, looked mild and beautiful, and we almost forgot our struggles amongst their vile vegetation and swamp. Their intense green contrasted superbly with the crags surrounding them. Here and there deep blue lakes nestled in emerald beds. The neighbouring ice peaks, with the fantastic shapes of the twin peaks of Mount Stanley, completed this wonderful scene. Boiling masses of cloud still hung over the lower valleys.

The descent south towards Freshfield Pass was easy, though we had to be careful as the snow was inclined to avalanche. About half-way down the ridge we turned west and descended the steep glacier, on which there was a layer of unstable snow covering the ice. Once off the glacier we again encountered rocks with a treacherous coating of moss. At first it was so sparse as to be hardly perceptible, which made it the more dangerous, as our feet were apt unaccountably to slip off the most secure ledges. This direct descent was something of a step in the dark as we could not see what was below us. Lower down when we reached the upper line of the helichrysum, we became involved in a series of difficult crags. There the helichrysum in part atoned for its previous behaviour, as without its assistance the crags would have been impassable and a return to the summit ridge unavoidable – a matter of many hours' toil. Even as it was, the descent of the line of crags, which we were lucky enough to strike in the only feasible place, proved a difficult struggle, during which Tilman lost his watch and I succeeded in spraining my right shoulder. We reached the valley close by a small lake, and then toiled wearily towards the Scott-Elliott Pass. When at last we reached its foot, we were delighted to find that the vegetation gave place to scree, up which we could walk in a normal position. The clouds had long since enveloped us again, and we were fortunate in reaching the pass at a point from which a descent could be made on either side. Most of the way down was through a narrow gully, at the foot of which we were exasperated to find more giant groundsel and helichrysum. During the descent Tilman suffered the further loss of his camera. It was getting dark when we reached the Bujuku valley once more, and we spent a long time before reaching camp, floundering knee-deep in vile-smelling black mud by the lake.

Long into the night we sat before a blazing fire of groundsel wood in our cave and in turn forgave this plant some of its atrocities, taking back a few of the unmentionable names we had called it. Even when damp (which is always) it makes excellent firewood.

On the following day we started back. Progess was almost as bad as on the ascent, except that there was no cutting to be done. But the porters were anxious to reach their homes, and consented, with some persuasion, to a double march each day.

Climbing on Ruwenzori was a memorable experience, and well worth the discomfort and the exasperating toil. When at length we left the rain-forest it felt as though we had emerged from a world of fantasy, where nothing was real but only a wild and lovely flight of imagination. I think perhaps the range is unique. It is well named "Mountains of the Moon".

CHAPTER SIX

Everest, 1933 – 1

DURING the nineteen-twenties and thirties the repeated attempts to climb Mount Everest bulked large in the thoughts of mountaineers. The idea of climbing the mountain was a natural one for those interested in such things, and it is probable that the project had been considered ever since 1852 when the height of Mount Everest was computed, showing it to be the highest known peak in the world. From the nineties of the last century several definite plans for the exploration of the mountain were formulated. But Mount Everest lies on the borders of Nepal and Tibet and both these countries are for the most part closed to foreign travellers. It was not found possible to overcome these political barriers and the plans came to nothing.

However in 1920 Sir Charles Bell, who was a personal friend of the Dalai Lama, visited Lhasa and succeeded in obtaining the permission of the Tibetan Government for an expedition to approach Mount Everest through their country. The Royal Geographical Society and the Alpine Club jointly undertook the organisation of an expedition, a Mount Everest Committee was formed from these two bodies, and in the spring of 1921 the first Mount Everest Expedition was sent out under the leadership of Lieutenant-Colonel C. K. Howard-Bury.

This was undoubtedly one of the finest exploratory expeditions of the century. Its main objects were to explore the approaches to the mountain, to find a route by which it could be climbed, and to collect as much scientific data as possible in the fields of physiology, zoology, botany and geology. For these purposes experts were selected, and when the expedition reached its field it was divided, as all well-regulated expeditions should be, into self-contained parties each engaged upon its particular task. In this way a tremendous amount of ground was covered. The surveyors mapped 13,000 square miles of unexplored country, some of it in great detail, some more roughly, and the scientists brought back a mass of valuable results. The expedition was conducted with admirable economy and efficiency.

Mallory and Bullock were entrusted with the task of reconnoitring the mountain, and of finding a route by which it would be possible to climb it. It had been seen from a distance that the only hopeful line of approach was from the north. They made their way up the Rongbuk glacier, so called from the monastery of that name. The upper basin of this glacier was found to lie directly under the north face of Everest. To climb straight up this face, which rose in one continuous sweep of 10,000 feet above the level of the glacier, was out of the question. The face was bounded by two main ridges which joined at the summit. One ran down to the north-west and the other to the north-east. Both of these obviously presented great difficulties, but from about half way along the north-east ridge a subsidiary spur ran down to the north to a high saddle between Everest and a peak which came to be known as the North Peak or, translated into Tibetan, Chang Tse. The saddle was called the North Col, or Chang La. This north-east spur provided the only easy route to the upper part of the mountain. The problem then was to reach the North Col at its foot. It was possible to do so from the Rongbuk glacier, but Mallory judged that the route was too difficult to be undertaken with laden porters, and if possible an alternative must be found from the east.

Four miles above the snout of the Rongbuk glacier an inconspicuous defile enters the main valley from the east. Farther up, this broadens out into a wide glacier combe which curls round the spurs of the North Peak and has its origin below the north-eastern face of Everest. It offers a perfectly easy route to the eastern foot of the North Col. But Mallory attached no significance to this valley, and only discovered his mistake when, after many weeks of arduous travel, he reached its head by crossing a 22,000-feet pass from the distant Kharta Valley. By this time winter was approaching, but he and his companions succeeded in reaching the North Col, and so set foot on Mount Everest for the first time.

The following year, 1922, another expedition was sent out, this time under the leadership of Brigadier-General the Hon. C. G. Bruce. It was a very different type of expedition from the first one. The way had been found, and the job now was to climb the mountain. For a mountaineer this was a thrilling enough task though it lacked the wide horizons of a journey through unknown country. Little was known about climbing at great altitudes. The highest point that had ever been reached on a mountain was 24,600 feet – on Bride Peak in the Karakoram by the Duke of Abruzzi. Many scientists believed that it would be impossible to climb much higher without an artificial supply of oxygen.

The 1922 party consisted mainly of expert mountaineers, though there were a few scientists and transport officers attached. The party was equipped with a number of portable oxygen apparatuses for use above the North Col. But there was considerable dissension among its members concerning the use of oxygen. One group held that their task was to climb the mountain by their own unaided efforts, and that to use an artificial means of breathing in the rarefied atmosphere at high altitudes would be to overcome by unfair means Everest's principal weapon of defence. The opposing school of thought argued that their instructions had been to climb the mountain by every available means; that they were mountaineers and therefore principally interested in the mountaineering difficulties; that, in fact, the climbing of Mount Everest was not just a stunt to see whether their lungs could or could not sustain life at an atmospheric pressure of 10 inches of mercury, but an interesting piece of geographical and mountaineering exploration. They pointed out, moreover, that the term "unaided efforts" was meaningless. Were not ice-axes and ropes aids? Would moral principle forbid the use of thermos flasks? If science could produce oxygen in tabloid form instead of in heavy, cumbersome cylinders, would it then be acceptable to the purists?

But apart from this moral aspect of the case it is by no means certain that the use of oxygen as it has hitherto been provided is, in fact, an aid to climbing Mount Everest. In the first place the apparatus weighs about 35 lbs., which is an awkward burden to carry on one's back while climbing over difficult ground. Then, any sort of mask over the face produces a feeling of claustrophobia, and must impede the climber's sense of balance and his general efficiency. Again the oxygen contained in such an apparatus only lasts for about eight hours, and it is probable that the sudden cutting off of the supply when one has become used to it would produce a state of collapse. There is also the possibility of a breakdown in the working of the apparatus. No one has yet produced a satisfactory answer to the objections by actual demonstration, and the debate continues.

It was thought that the best time of year for an attempt on the mountain was between the middle of May and the middle of June. Before that period Tibet is swept by violent northerly gales which make life very unpleasant and would render climbing, or even existence, on the exposed north face of Everest quite impossible. In June the warm, moisture-laden monsoon winds would start blowing up from the south, and though life at high altitudes might be more comfortable, masses of snow would be deposited on the mountain which would make climbing very difficult, if not impossible.

The 1922 expedition established its Base Camp (16,800 feet) in April, a mile or so below the snout of the Rongbuk glacier, and from there started working slowly up the glacier by establishing a series of camps. Camp I (17,700 feet) was put at the entrance of the valley branching off to the east. The glacier contained in this valley came to be known as the East Rongbuk glacier. Camp II (19,800 feet) was placed about four miles up this glacier, and Camp III at an altitude of 21,000 feet in the upper basin, and in full view of the North Col. Camp IV was on the North Col, some 23,000 feet above sea level. Thus far, the same procedure has been followed more or less by all the subsequent expeditions. The camp on the North Col has formed a sort of advanced base from which the real climb begins.

In 1922 two climbs were made above the North Col. Mallory, Norton, Somervell and Morshead established their Camp V on the north-east spur at an altitude of 24,500 feet. Morshead was suffering severely from exposure, and had to remain behind there while the other three climbed on up the spur and reached an altitude of 26,985 feet. (I have never understood why this figure is always quoted with such precision. In the first place no height on Everest can be estimated with greater accuracy than to the nearest 50 or 100 feet; secondly, even this degree of accuracy could only be achieved by theodolite observations from a dozen miles away, and such precise identification from this distance of the spot reached would hardly be possible.) The second attempt was made by Finch and J. G. Bruce using the oxygen apparatus. They put their Camp V at 25,000 feet, and after weathering a storm, succeeded in climbing to 27,300 feet.

Both these parties suffered very severely from the cold and the deadening effects of altitude. As far as they had gone they had encountered no great mountaineering difficulties, and the sloping, tile-like rocks forming the upper part of the mountain presented a foreshortened effect, and led them to suppose that the rest of the way would be similarly devoid of serious obstacles. It was thought that the altitude, the severe cold and the wind constituted the real problem. In this they were very much mistaken.

After their tremendous effort, all those who took part in these two climbs returned in a state of great exhaustion, several of them suffering from frost-bite and badly dilated hearts. By the time a further attempt could be organised the monsoon had broken. In attempting to reach the North Col again the party was involved in an avalanche, and seven of their Sherpa porters were killed.

Two years later, in 1924, another expedition went out, again under the leadership of General Bruce. Unfortunately Bruce became ill and had to retire. However, Norton, who had played such a distinguished part in the 1922 attempt, took his place as leader. With the lessons learned on the previous expedition, the party were confident of success. It had been proved that men could spend more than one night at 25,000 feet. It seemed reasonable to suppose that it would be possible to climb to 29,000 feet. It was clear that the chief problem was to put a camp considerably higher than Camp V had been placed before, and this would necessitate porters spending the night at Camp V and carrying yet another camp farther up the mountain. It would be no small task to induce them to do this.

In May a series of terrible storms overtook the party while they were engaged in the task of establishing Camp IV. A party of porters was marooned on the North Col for several days, and, only after the most desperate efforts by the climbers were they rescued. "Desperate efforts" are not made above 22,000 feet without great exhaustion, from which it is not possible wholly to recover without a prolonged rest at a very much lower altitude. So, by the time the weather improved, the strength of the climbers was seriously impaired.

On June 1st, Mallory and J. G. Bruce set out from the North Col for the first attempt. They established Camp V at 25,900 feet, and spent the night there with their porters. But they were met by a hurricane and forced to return. Norton and Somervell took their place at Camp V with a fresh lot of porters, with whom they succeeded in establishing Camp VI near the place where the north-east spur abuts against the north face at a height of 26,800 feet. The next day they set out for their final attempt on the summit. Somervell had to give up before Norton, who continued alone to a point estimated at about 28,100 feet, before he was forced, partly by exhaustion and partly by the difficulty of the ground, to abandon the attempt.

A few days later Mallory and Irvine came up the north-east spur for one more attempt, this time with oxygen. They set out from Camp VI on a fine, calm morning (June 8th) and never returned. What happened to them we can only guess. We should all like to think that they reached the summit and that they died on the way down, but I for one consider that to be improbable. On the day of their attempt Odell came up to Camp VI in support and returned to Camp V in the evening, as there was not room for three to spend the night at the upper camp. He came up again later and found Camp VI still empty. Though he scoured the mountain side above he could find no trace of the missing climbers.

Taken together and told in detail, the story of these first three expeditions to Mount Everest is an inspiring one that cannot fail to move even those who can see no reason for wishing to climb the highest mountain in the world. From almost every point of view it was sad that they were not crowned with the success they so richly deserved. Not only would this have rounded off a fine epic of mountaineering, but, in my opinion it would have induced a healthier outlook towards Himalayan exploration in the years that followed. I say "almost every point of view" because there are some, even among those who have themselves attempted to reach the summit, who nurse a secret hope that Everest will never be climbed. I must confess to such feelings myself.

Ten years is an epoch of almost infinite length when it spans one's 'teens and early twenties. I was still at my preparatory school when the first Mount Everest Expedition took place, and not being in the habit of reading *The Times*, it passed me by unnoticed. As a result of this I came to regard the three expeditions as ancient history, something that had always been discussed, like Scott's journey to the South Pole, or the Spanish Armada. There was always a good deal of talk about the attempt being renewed, but I was not very well up in those circles, and as the talk never seemed to come to anything it appeared that the idea was buried in the past. I regarded participation in one of these expeditions as an impossible dream upon which it was not good to dwell for long, since it made me feel that nothing else in the world was worthwhile.

One day in the autumn of 1932 while I was peacefully occupied with problems of manure, soil erosion and farm politics, I received a note from a neighbour who had a wireless set, saying that he had just heard that Lhasa had consented to allow another expedition to go to Mount Everest, and that this was being organised under the leadership of Mr. Hugh Ruttledge, and would set out early the following year. This news was deeply disturbing, and a storm that carried away a long job of terracing that I had completed passed almost unnoticed. It seemed that I might have some claim for consideration, and I could think of nothing else. I had an Irishman staying with me at the time who became almost as excited about it as I was, and certainly a good deal more optimistic about my chances. But as the days passed and nothing further happened I tried to resign myself to disappointment.

A little time later, however, when I was returning home from a job at the other end of the farm, I was met by my friend brandishing a bit of pink paper. This turned out to be a telegram which read "mount everest committee invite you join expedition subject medical approval please reply goodenough".

Admiral Sir William Goodenough was at that time President of the Royal Geographical Society. To save time, and mistaking Sir William's name for a kind of code word, my enthusiastic friend had sent the telegraph boy back with the cryptic reply "Goodenough–Shipton". I managed however to intercept the message.

The need to collect equipment seemed to provide sufficient excuse for coming home, and I secured a third-class passage on a German ship sailing from Mombasa on 1st November, and reached England on 1st December. Wyn Harris, who had also been invited, came home a little later. Seven of us sailed for India towards the end of January, 1933: Hugh Ruttledge, C. G. Crawford, L. R. Wager, J. L. Longland, T. A. Brocklebank, Wyn and myself. We travelled First Class P. & O., which I found a pleasant contrast to my voyage of a few weeks before. Of the other seven members of the expedition Frank Smythe and Raymond Greene came out on a later ship, Hugh Boustead came to India from the Sudan where he was commanding the Camel Corps, and W. McLean, the second medical officer, from Jerusalem. Shebbeare, who had been transport officer with the 1924 expedition, Bill Birnie and George Wood-Johnson were already in India.

We had two main occupations on the voyage out. One was to learn Khaskra, a language spoken by the Sherpas. For this we had a teacher in Crawford, who had been in the I.C.S. for twelve years in North-East India, in a Gurkha regiment in the last war, and a member of the 1922 Everest Expedition. I am afraid we were reluctant and most inept pupils. As far as I remember, Longland was the only one who learnt enough to be of any use. Ruttledge, of course, spoke Urdu fluently, which was far more use than a smattering of Khaskra, Wyn conversed happily in Swahili which certainly seemed to be as effective as anything else, and Wager remained content with English.

Our second occupation was much more congenial: an endless discussion of how the mountain should be climbed. As far as the North Col it was all fairly plain sailing, and we had only to follow the practice of our predecessors and to organise the transport of sufficient supplies and equipment to stock the three glacier camps and Camp IV on the North Col. Though of course this task was of fundamental importance, its accomplishment was a matter of straightforward organisation and much hard work, mainly on the part of the porters.

The first real problem was the establishment of the high camps. It was clear that we must aim at getting a camp considerably nearer to the summit than Camp VI had been placed in 1924. Would it be possible to do this with only two camps above the North Col? Camp V, at 25,500 feet, was already a tremendous carry from the North Col, and could not be placed very much higher. But to attempt to establish a third camp above the Col would involve serious difficulties. In the first place it would mean increasing the size of Camp V enormously, to accommodate the extra number of porters necessary to carry the food and equipment for those porters who would have to sleep at Camp VI which would itself have to be very much bigger. It was by no means certain that a platform could be found wide enough to accommodate either of these enlarged camps. This difficulty might be partly overcome by a system of relay, but it would not be easy to find many porters to go far above the North Col, and it was most unlikely that more than a very few could be induced to make the trip twice. Again, would any of them be willing to stay the night at Camp VI and carry still higher? Norton and Somervell had experienced the greatest difficulty in persuading them to go above Camp V after the exhaustion and discomfort of a night spent there. Also the longer any individual party spent above the North Col the greater the risk of encountering a storm which would force them to retreat, probably in a state of such exhaustion as to render them incapable of further effort.

The next question was the route to be followed, and this matter was debated over a large photograph of the north face of the mountain. After the 1924 expedition, it was realised that the climbing on the upper part of the mountain was not so easy as had at first been supposed. Between the North Col and the top of the north-east spur there were, in good conditions, no real difficulties. The upper 2,000 feet of the mountain was built of three horizontal bands or strata. The first of these, composed of a light-coloured rock, was about 800 feet thick and lay between 27,200 feet and 28,000 feet above sea level. This was known as the "Yellow Band". Above this was a stratum of dark rock called the "Black Band"; on this again was superimposed another layer which formed the summit cap or "Final Pyramid". The surface of the Yellow Band was composed of a series of overlapping slabs set at a fairly steep angle and sloping outwards like the tiles of a roof. The surface of the Black Band was considerably steeper, and, as the rock strata were also tilted towards the north, they formed a series of overhangs. The Final Pyramid, though steep, was more broken and appeared to offer several relatively easy routes.

From the purely mountaineering standpoint, then, the crux of the climb was clearly to get past the Black Band. At first sight the obvious route to follow from the head of the north-east spur seemed to be along the crest of the main north-east ridge. This could be seen in profile from the Base Camp, and its general angle was very gentle. But ridges, and particularly Himalayan ridges, are apt to be deceptive and often turn out to be knife-sharp. Climbing along such a knife-edged crest is a slow and laborious business, and any serrature might present a formidable obstacle. Also, by the intersection of the north-east ridge, and the Black Band two steps were formed. The "First Step" did not appear to be very formidable, but the "Second Step" was vertical, and its height was estimated at some 200 feet. A third objection to the ridge route was the fact that the climber would be exposed to the full force of the wind, which, if at all violent, might blow him clean off the mountain.

The alternative to following the crest of the north-east ridge was to traverse diagonally across to the head of a conspicuous gully that ran down the north face from a point below the Black Band, a few hundred yards beyond the Second Step. This gully was known as the Great Couloir. It was flanked on the west by a prominent ridge which formed the only breach in the wall of the Black Band. Norton had chosen this route and had reached the Great Couloir, but had failed to cross it, largely on account of physical exhaustion, but partly, too, because of the treacherous nature of the tiled slabs over which he was climbing. Mallory had favoured the ridge route, and his views were supported by the rock-climbing experts of our party, of whom Longland was the recognised ace.

The question of weather we took very much for granted. The original hypothesis had been confirmed by the experiences of the 1922 and 1924 expeditions, and it appeared that we could count on a break of at least a fortnight between the end of the spring gales in May and the beginning of the monsoon precipitation in June. The great thing to avoid was the exhaustion of the party's strength by battling against the early blizzards.

The real bone of contention was how long the climbers should stay at high altitudes. The opposing factors were "Acclimatisation" and "Deterioration", and as we had very little data from which to argue the debate waxed exceeding fierce. It was recognised that men could only climb to great altitudes by allowing their bodies gradually to acclimatise themselves to conditions of low atmospheric pressure and lack of oxygen. If a man is lifted rapidly from sea-level to a great height he will lose consciousness at altitudes varying, in normal cases, between 20,000 and 22,000 feet. The experiment is easy to make in a decompression chamber, and has been done hundreds of times. A peculiar thing is that the patient does not realise that he lost consciousness, and often hotly denies it when he is brought back to normal conditions. The best method of convincing him that he did in fact "pass out" is to make him write while the experiment is conducted.

This difficulty is quite easy to overcome in flying, by supplying the airman with oxygen. But it is clearly impossible to supply all the members of a climbing party with oxygen all the time, and whether or not oxygen is used as an aid in the final assault, some degree of acclimatisation is obviously necessary. The question is, how much? For although the lungs, blood and heart have the power to adjust themselves to a reasonable lack of oxygen, above a certain altitude the body begins to lose strength very rapidly. These two processes are going on at one and the same time, and the problem is to strike the optimum mean between them. What then is the altitude at which this physical deterioration begins; how long does it take a man fully to acclimatise to a given altitude; how quickly will he deteriorate at that altitude? Unfortunately no definite answer can be found to these questions, except perhaps the first. Each individual varies in his reactions to altitude; one man acclimatises quickly, another slowly, some deteriorate more rapidly than others; I have known men with robust constitutions who have failed altogether to acclimatise even to quite moderate elevations. The whole process appears to be analagous to sea-sickness about which predictions are impossible. Indeed one of the party advanced the ingenious theory that bad sailors acclimatised quickly, though I suspect that the only evidence he had to support it was his own dislike for rough seas.

Obviously upon the conclusion adopted on this weighty matter rested the whole question of tactics to be followed in the attempts to climb Mount Everest; and we had lamentably little to go on. Those in favour of long acclimatisation made much of the experience of Odell in 1924. He had gone very badly at first, but when at last he did acclimatise he accomplished some remarkable feats. From this slender evidence it was assumed that all slow acclimatisers would go well later. On Kamet two years before, on the other hand, although we had talked a lot about acclimatisation, actually we had gone from the Base Camp at 15,000 feet to the summit at 25,450 feet in a fortnight, which was considerably quicker than the quickest of the plans for attempting Everest. Nor had we had the advantage of a long journey across the high Tibetan plateau. We had not suffered seriously from the altitude while climbing the peak, though on the other hand in that short time we found, when we arrived back at the Base Camp, that we had suffered considerable physical deterioration.

It seemed odd to be discussing earnestly such problems as these as we sat deep in deck chairs, listening to the gentle swish of the sea, a cool drink within reach and with the comfortable prospect of a large lunch and a sleep to follow. In these circumstances gasping toil, blizzards and the like were hard to visualise in true perspective. No one, I think, doubted for a moment that we would succeed. Indeed it was solemnly debated whether, in the most probable event of the first "assault party" reaching the top, it would be permissible for others subsequently to climb the mountain.

Three very pleasant weeks were divided between Darjeeling and Kalimpong; we spent busy days recruiting porters and sorting out, numbering and arranging in 80-lb. loads, suitable for animal transport, an enormous mass of stores that had been sent out from England. The real starting point was Kalimpong, and here we enjoyed the perfect hospitality of Mr. and Mrs. Odling in their delightful home. We left there in two parties; the first on March 3rd and the second a week later. There were seven of us in the first party. Our departure must have been very amusing to watch. We were given a tremendous send-off by the 600 children of Dr. Graham's St. Andrew's Homes. Our ponies, which were very fresh, entered into the spirit of the thing, and, scared by the noise of the cheers, charged off down the road at a breakneck speed, entirely out of control. Every hundred yards or so we were ambushed by a batch of yelling children which maddened our ponies still more. Most of us had very little idea of how to ride. Wager led the field clinging grimly to his pony's neck. He tore round the wrong corner, and the rest of us followed, crashing down towards the forest-filled valley where we seemed destined to meet an ignominious end. Eventually we succeeded in pulling up, though how I never knew. Our return to the right road provided something of an anti-climax.

The march from Kalimpong to the Rongbuk valley took us some six weeks. It can be done in considerably less, but in the first place we were in no hurry and had purposely left early so that we could take it in easy stages; in the second place the formidable number of transport animals (between three and four hundred) required to carry all our baggage caused some delay. The same animals could not be taken right through and they had frequently to be changed. It was no easy job for the authorities of the small towns through which we passed to produce enough yaks or donkeys. For the first eight stages the way was through pleasantly wooded foothills and over the 14,000 feet Natu La into the Chumbi valley in Tibet. Before crossing the border we halted for a few days by a little lake at a place called Tsomgo. Beyond the Chumbi valley we halted again to allow the main body to catch up. After that we left the trees behind and climbed up on to the great tableland of Tibet.

From here, most of us had expected to encounter severe conditions. For the first two days our expectations were realised. The temperature dropped to 36 deg. of frost and a continuous gale blew from the north-west. But after that the weather was so mild and pleasant that soon some of us began to wonder if we had come to the right place. The only hardship we had to bear was the dust, which was at times rather unpleasant. Apart from that nothing could have been more delightful than riding along at a comfortable speed of about fifteen miles a day through that lovely land. Tibet is a very beautiful country – at least the part of it through which we were travelling; rather bleak perhaps in the early spring, but even that was mitigated by the clear, blue sky, the sharp detail of the distant ranges and the lovely colouring of the nearer hills. To the south was the sparkling white barrier of the great Himalayan range. The peaks themselves did not look their best owing to the gradual lift of the plateau towards a nearer range of rounded mountains, but they formed a lovely background to the wide, frozen rivers and lakes, teeming with Brahmini duck and bar-headed geese. The large majority of us had never been to Tibet before, and we found the people with their strange way of life, their art and architecture a source of constant interest and delight.

Each of us had a large Whymper tent to himself, and a big marquee served as a mess tent. We had not yet had time to become irritable or tired of each other, and, with the wide diversity of professions in the party, the talk was good and varied. This was spoilt at times by a natural tendency to talk shop. To a layman it would have seemed amazing that, in a simple matter like the climbing of a mountain, we could have found so much to argue about. Each of us had his own pet theory on every aspect of the problem and aired it with monotonous regularity and lamentable disregard for opposing points of view. I was certainly one of the worst offenders in this respect, and despite my frequent resolves to conduct myself in a more gentlemanly fashion, I could never refrain from joining the fray. But we were saved from serious dissension by the wise and balanced judgment of our leader, who refused to be drawn into taking sides.

We were all rather ridiculously self-conscious about our acclimatisation. The average altitude of the plateau over which we were travelling was about 13,000 feet and several of the passes we crossed were 18,000 feet high. We used anxiously to count our heart beats and watch our breathing, while the doctors examined the reaction of our blood-pressures and counted the red corpuscles in our blood. All this tended to produce a state of hypochondria and a sense of rivalry, which Ruttledge did his best to discourage. His was no easy task with such a large party of mountaineers – temperamental and individualistic creatures at the best of times – each passionately keen to justify his selection, and we owed a great deal to his sympathetic understanding. On the whole we kept our sense of proportion remarkably well, on the march out anyway. Crawford's acute sense of the ridiculous kept us from taking ourselves too seriously; Greene's remarkable gift for anecdote was always fresh – I never grew tired of listening to him; Shebbeare's deep knowledge of natural history was a constant source of delight; each contributed something. I have very pleasant memories of that march.

At each of the big towns we were entertained by the Dzongpen, the administrative head of the district. From these parties we often emerged in a pleasantly intoxicated condition, as it was impossible to refuse the large quantities of Chang provided by our hosts. Chang is the Tibetan equivalent of beer. It is brewed from barley, has a greyish-white appearance, an acid taste and varies greatly in quality and potency. Good Chang is an excellent drink. I also developed a great liking for Tibetan tea. This is made from Chinese brick tea and is properly prepared in a large bamboo churn, with the addition of butter and salt. The butter is not generally rancid as is popularly supposed. The tea has a soft, delicate flavour, and is remarkably refreshing; badly made it is disgusting. Our contact with the Tibetan people was made easy and pleasant by our Tibetan interpreter, Karma Paul.

We arrived at Rongbuk on April 16th. The next morning was occupied with the ceremony of receiving the blessing of the Abbot of the Rongbuk Monastery. This old man was a great character. He was then close on seventy years of age, had a tremendous sense of humour and he took a kindly interest in our project. The blessing ceremony consisted in each of us bowing before the Abbot in turn, receiving a sharp tap on the head from his mace and repeating after him "Om Mani Padmi Hum" (Hail, the jewel in the Lotus). Most of us had to repeat the formula several times before we got it right, to the great amusement of the Abbot. We were each given a little packet of pills to take when we felt in need of spiritual sustenance. The Sherpas conducted themselves with far greater dignity and *savoir-faire* than we did. The same afternoon we went four miles farther up the valley where we established the Base Camp, which was to be our haven of rest, our coveted metropolis, for nearly three months.

The Rongbuk valley is a grim and desolate place, a waste of stones shut in from all pleasant prospects, flanked by shapeless, disintegrating walls of rock. Its upper end is dominated by the huge mass of Everest. Seen from the top of the surrounding peaks, this northern face of the mountain has a fine simplicity of design and a certain grandeur, though even then it cannot compare with the magnificent architecture of the eastern and southern aspects. But from the Base Camp it appears stunted and deformed, a mere continuation of the graceless forms about it.

The features of the upper part of the north face were so well known to us from our prolonged study of photographs that it seemed as though we had been looking at it most of our lives. But it was exciting to see at last all the obstacles we had discussed so endlessly – the Second Step, the Great Couloir, the Yellow Band. We spent hours gazing at them through a powerful astronomical telescope. It was tiresome to reflect that many weeks must still elapse before any of us could make their close acquaintance.

Before the arrival of the monsoon, the north face of Everest is, for the most part, swept clear of snow by the violence of the northerly winds. Very little melting appears to take place at great altitudes, and, but for these winds, which probably blow more or less continuously throughout the winter, the snow would accumulate to a great depth, the pressure of its weight would form ice and the north face of Everest would be covered by a glacier sheet resembling those on its far steeper eastern and southern slopes. The mountain might then be much easier to climb.

The establishment of the lower camps was a leisurely business. In the first place we were in no hurry, because the severity of the conditions would forbid operations on the mountain for several weeks; secondly, slow progress was necessary for our acclimatisation, and thirdly, we had so much stuff to transport up the glacier that even with our vast army of porters (forty-six more joined us later from Solu Khombu which brought our total strength up to about one hundred and seventy), many relays were necessary to establish each camp. The distances between these were fairly even, and it took about three or four hours of very easy going to go up from one to the next, and about half that time coming down. The porters carried 40 lbs. each; we carried nothing, the theory being that we must conserve our energy for higher up. Though it is a debatable point, there is certainly something in this argument. At high altitudes (in my opinion above 21,000 feet) the wastage of muscle tissue is so rapid that it is well to start with a fairly large reserve of flesh. A man highly trained in the athletic sense is liable to be worn down much more quickly than one less finely drawn. On the other hand we had too little to do. We fell over each other in our efforts to secure the few jobs that were going. It is not enough to say that a man of intelligence should find sufficient interest in his surroundings, in reading or in playing chess. We were all intensely keen about the expedition and could not be expected to remain satisfied with a purely waiting rôle, particularly knowing as we did that only a very small proportion of the party could be chosen to go high. On the whole people were remarkably good about disguising their feelings, but that did not remove the feelings themselves. We made a great show of reconnoitring the route and "escorting" parties of porters; but no one but a blind man could have failed to find his way up the East Rongbuk glacier, there were no more difficulties than one would expect to encounter in a country walk at home and the porters certainly needed no escorting.

One of the most tiresome things about an Everest Expedition was the amount of time one had to spend in bed. It was not usual to spend more than six hours on a job, so that the day's work was generally done by three o'clock. In the spring, at any of the lower camps the sun would disappear at about four o'clock; it was too cold to sit outside after that, so from four o'clock until about nine o'clock the next morning was spent in our sleeping-bags. That was in good weather; on the frequent days of bad weather we usually spent twenty-four hours in bed.

In 1933 it was all new to us and interesting. When we were not engaged in walking from one camp to another we climbed up the sides of the valley for practice and to get a wider view of our surroundings. But our main pre-occupation was in keeping ourselves reasonably fit. This was no easy matter for we were constantly assailed by influenza and throat troubles. It has been the same on each of the four occasions that I have been to Everest. It appeared that the party became infected on the march across Tibet, and that the lowered resistance of the individual, due to altitude, made it impossible to throw off the disease once above the Base Camp. This bugbear contributed largely to our general weakness which was a potent factor in our failure to reach the summit. The valiant efforts of the doctors had little effect. We consumed enormous quantities of antiseptic tablets and were forever gargling and douching our noses. Already, at the Base Camp, several members of the party had been ill,

Wyn Harris and Wager with 'flu and Crawford with bronchitis. Nor were the Sherpas exempt. Ondi developed double pneumonia, for the treatment of which the oxygen supply came in handy. We all had our troubles in varying degree. I lost my voice completely for six weeks, which, though a considerable boon to my companions, was certainly a handicap to me.

The glaciers on the northern side of Mount Everest were different from any I had seen before. They were divided into four distinct zones. Firstly there was the usual upper *névé*, or snow basin, from which the glacier rises. Then followed a section of smooth ice, free from a covering of permanent snow or moraine deposits. Below this the ice-stream merged gradually into a forest of fantastic pinnacles of all shapes and sizes. Some of these pinnacles have been measured and found to stand more than 300 feet high, though usually they do not exceed 100 feet. Farther down they increased in size and decreased in numbers, until a few isolated towers were left standing out of the lower section of the glacier, which was so covered with gravel and boulders that very little ice could be seen. Moraine-covered troughs, caused by the junction of tributary ice-streams, ran down through the pinnacled areas, and provided easy roads up the glacier. I have never heard a satisfactory explanation of why these pinnacles occur. Camp II on the East Rongbuk glacier was situated in this zone which was very beautiful.

CHAPTER SEVEN

Everest 1933 – 2

THE work of carrying loads up from the Base Camp began on April 19th and on May 2nd we established and occupied Camp III in the upper basin of the East Rongbuk glacier at a height of 21,000 feet. We were now in full view of the North Col. At last we were confronted with a real mountaineering proposition which would require some concentration of energy and skill. The prospect was a good one. Pleasant and intensely interesting though the journey had been, most of us I imagine had been keyed up by the anticipation of the toughest climbing of our lives. So far it had all been make-believe, and it was difficult to avoid the question, "When are we going to be called upon to do a job of work; when will we have something really to bite on?"

The eastern slopes of the North Col are composed of steep broken glacier and rise about 1,500 feet from the level of ice below to the crest of the col. As the glacier is moving slowly downwards the slopes present a different appearance from year to year. Our task then was to find a way up them, to make a ladder of large, safe steps to fix ropes to serve as hand rails all over the difficult sections, so that it would be possible for laden porters to pass up and down with ease and safety.

We started the work almost at once. It was about an hour's walk from Camp III to the foot of the steep slopes below the Col. The ice of the upper basin had been swept clear of snow by the wind. It was rather like walking on an ice-skating rink and required some little practice to avoid sitting down heavily. But fortunately the slopes above were composed of hard snow, for it would have been a tremendously laborious task to cut steps all the way up in hard ice, and also very difficult to fix the ropes. As it was it was very hard work. Even at that height any physical exertion left one gasping for breath. We took turns of about twenty minutes each at cutting the steps. Even that seemed an eternity and it was a great relief to be told that the time was up. We climbed about a third of the way up to the Col on the first day.

There followed days of storm and wind which rendered work impossible. Below, we had experienced fairly severe conditions, but Camp III was much more exposed to the weather, which deteriorated a good deal during the fortnight after our arrival there. I gathered from the Sherpas who had been with the 1924 Expedition that the conditions were very similar to those experienced in that year. But we had an additional item of equipment, which added enormously to our comfort and rendered us impervious to the buffeting of the wind. This was a large, double-skinned, dome-shaped tent of a type that had been used by Watkins in the Arctic. It had a circular floor about 15 feet in diameter, and was built round a bamboo frame, the outer skin fitting over the frame while the inner skin hung from it, so that there was an air space about a foot wide between the two. It was difficult to erect, but once up it was as snug as a well-built log hut.

As soon as there was a lull in the wind, we resumed work on the slopes below the Col. We found that the steps we had already cut had been swept away, and that not a trace of them remained. So as to take advantage of brief periods of fine weather, we put a camp (III A) at the foot of the slopes. This was a bleak and comfortless spot, and even more exposed to the wind than Camp III, which was situated on rocks close under the cliffs of the North Peak. The new camp was pitched on hard, smooth ice on which it was difficult to anchor the tents. One night, during a particularly violent storm, one of them broke loose from its moorings causing a certain amount of excitement. But the new position was a great help, and from it we were able to make progress. But our advance was very slow, and as we set out day after day I began to wonder if we should ever reach the Col. The most difficult part was about half way up. This consisted of an ice wall about 20 feet high, topped by a very steep ice slope. We had a lot of fun getting up it, and succeeded largely owing to a fine lead by Smythe. We hung a rope ladder down it for subsequent use.

At last, by the 15th of May, the road of steps and fixed ropes was complete, and we established Camp IV on an ice ledge, some 20 feet wide, about 200 feet below the crest of the Col. The ledge was formed by the lower lip of a great crevasse, the upper lip of which, 40 feet above, almost overhung the ledge. The camp was well sheltered and quite comfortable, the only disadvantage being the danger of small snow avalanches falling from above.

For the next four days the storm was continuous, and we could do nothing but lie in our sleeping-bags. Nor was any communication possible with the camps below. But on the evening of the 19th, the wind dropped and Smythe and I climbed up the last 200 feet. Apart from the ice wall this was by far the steepest part of the North Col slopes. When we reached the narrow crest of the Col we were met by a most glorious view to the west, over range after range of giant peaks, draped by dark cloud banners, wild and shattered by the gale. The mighty scene was partly lit by an angry red glow, and rose from a misty shadow-lake of deep indigo that often appears among high mountains in the evening after a storm.

The next day Wyn Harris, Birnie and Boustead started up with ten porters, intending to reach 25,500 feet to choose a site for Camp V. But they were forced to retreat from 24,500 owing to the wind. Actually there was some difference of opinion about the wisdom of this decision, and a hot-tempered argument raged most of the succeeding night, by the end of which the subject under debate had become rather confused. Nerves were already frayed, and we were all liable to lose our tempers at the slighest provocation, and to take our silly grievances sorely to heart. This seems to be a common manifestation of the effects of life at high altitudes. In our case it was undoubtedly aggravated by the rough handling we had received from the weather, and by having been forced to spend so much of our time during the past month cooped up in a tent with too little to do and too much to anticipate. Being unable to speak above a whisper, I found it difficult to quarrel with anyone, and it would have been too exhausting to attempt to pull my opponent's beard. Had I been psycho-analysed at the time, I would no doubt have been found to be suffering from some fierce repressions.

We were very comfortable at Camp IV. Cooking and breathing soon produced a pleasant fug in the tents: we had large double eiderdown sleeping-bags, and our snow beds were soon made to conform with the shapes of our bodies. The crevasse provided a convenient latrine, though it required a strong effort of will to emerge from the tent. It was only at the upper camps that the cold compelled us to use a bed-pan in the form of a biscuit box. So long as we did not have to do anything, the time passed pleasantly enough. Lethargy of mind and body was the chief trial. Once one got going it was not so bad, but the prospect of toil was hateful. At the higher camps, of course, this lethargy increased tenfold.

Eating, however, was the serious problem, and one which, to my mind, did not receive nearly enough attention. This was entirely the fault of the individual, for we had more than enough food, and its quality and variety could not have been better. The trouble is that at such an altitude the appetite is jaded, and unless a man forces himself to eat regular and sufficient meals he does not consume anything like enough to maintain his strength. Melting a saucepan full of snow for water and bringing it to the boil took so long that people tended to delude themselves that they had eaten a hearty meal. Over and over again I saw men starting for a long and exhausting day's work on the mountain with only a cup of cocoa and a biscuit or two inside them; the cold and the wind discouraged eating during the climb, and they were generally too tired to eat anything much when they returned. This state of affairs contributed largely towards the rapid physical deterioration of the party. There was endless talk about rations, and certainly these were carefully and efficiently planned beforehand; but in actual practice we ate whatever we wanted and whenever we felt inclined. Sweets were the easiest kind of food to swallow, but it is doubtful if haphazard sweet-eating is as beneficial as the taking of regular substantial meals, which it certainly discourages. In most cold climates people develop a craving for fat, which has a higher calorific value than any other food. Unfortunately at high altitudes fat of any kind is particulary repugnant.

On the 21st May, Smythe and I climbed some 1,500 feet above the North Col for exercise. We both felt extremely fit, and without undue effort we maintained an average speed of 1,000 feet an hour, which would not have been a bad performance had we been at sea-level. Individuals differ very widely in their physical reactions to the effects of high altitudes; some vomit a great deal, some suffer from blinding headaches, some cannot sleep, while others can hardly keep awake, some gasp and pant even when at rest. I used not to suffer much from any of these maladies; my particular trouble was physical lethargy which grew progressively more intense the longer I remained at a high altitude. For example, in 1933 I made three climbs up the north-east spur above the North Col. On the first occasion, after six nights at Camp IV (about 23,000 feet), I felt very strong, and as though I could go on indefinitely; the second time, after eight hours at Camp IV, I was weaker, though I still went fairly well; on the third occasion, after two nights spent at

Camp V (25,700 feet) and twelve at Camp IV, I only reached Camp V, for my second sojourn there, after a hard struggle. Smythe and I reacted to the effects of altitude in very much the same manner, though in 1933 he deteriorated considerably less quickly than I did. For men with no previous Himalayan experience, and considering that they had spent a whole fortnight laid up at the Base Camp while the rest of us were working slowly up the glacier, Wager and Wyn Harris acclimatised remarkably quickly. Longland was slow in adjusting himself, which made his subsequent performance all the more remarkable. Crawford and Brocklebank were at their best when it was too late for further attempts on the mountain, and thus were robbed of the chance of going high, though they spent weeks of the monotonous but vital work keeping the North Col route open.

Weather conditions now appeared to have reached that state of comparative quiet that we had expected just before the arrival of the monsoon. Wireless messages received at the Base Camp spoke of an exceptionally early monsoon in Ceylon and its rapid spread over India. This news was confirmed by the appearance of great banks of cloud from the south which, however, were still far below us. Obviously the critical moment had arrived. On the 22nd of May, Birnie, Boustead, Greene and Wyn Harris, with twenty porters carrying 12 lbs. each, established Camp V at 25,700 feet. The plan was for these four climbers and eight of the porters to stop the night at Camp V and to carry Camp VI as high as possible on the following day; Birnie and Boustead would then return to Camp V with the porters, while Wyn Harris and Greene would stop at Camp VI and attempt to climb the mountain by the "ridge route". Meanwhile Smythe and I would follow up to Camp V on the 23rd, take the place of the first party at Camp VI on the 24th, and make our attempt on the summit on the 25th, choosing our route in the light of the experiences of the first pair. Greene unfortunately strained his heart during the climb to Camp V, and his place was taken by Wager who had accompanied the party for exercise.

It was hard to believe that the time for the supreme test had arrived. Waiting at the North Col on the 22nd of May, I felt as I imagine an athlete must feel just before the boat-race, Marathon or boxing contest for which he has been training for months. It was difficult to keep one's mind from the nagging questions, "Will the weather hold long enough to give us a decent chance?" "How will I react to the extreme exhaustion that must inevitably accompany the final effort?" "What is the climbing really like on that upper part?" "For all our previous optimism, is it, in fact, possible to climb to or even to live at 29,000 feet?" Three more days, seventy-two hours!

It was a great relief when, the next morning, the moment to start arrived. We had the whole day before us, and there was no need to hurry. The basis of all mountaineering is the conservation of energy by the three fundamental principles – rhythmic movement, balance and precise placing of the feet. As far as possible, steps should be short so that upward motion appears as a gentle sway from the hips rather than a strong thrust by thigh muscles. It is better to use a small nail-hold at a convenient distance than a large foot-hold involving a long stride. If a long stride is necessary, the balance must be adjusted by lateral pressure by the hand or ice-axe. A practised mountaineer is, of course, in the habit of observing these principles even on the simplest ground; his ability to maintain them on difficult and complicated terrain determines in large measaure his quality as a climber. Nowhere is perfection of technique so important as at high altitudes where the slightest effort takes heavy toll of the climber's reserves of strength; nowhere is it more difficult to achieve.

Above the North Col we were met by a strong wind, which increased in violence as we climbed. I have no idea what the temperature was. On the glacier below a minimum of 20 deg. F. was observed. I doubt if we experienced less than that on the upper part of the mountain. Judged by winter temperatures in the Arctic or Antarctic, such cold is not considered severe. But at great altitudes it is a very different matter. Due to lack of oxygen, the various functions of heart, lungs and circulation are most inefficient, lost heat is difficult to restore, and there is danger of frost-bite even at freezing point, particularly when there is a wind blowing: one has constantly to watch for its symptoms. If a foot loses feeling it is wise to stop to remove one's boot and bang and rub it to life again. This is one of the greatest difficulties we have had in dealing with the Sherpas at high altitudes; it was most difficult to induce them to take these precautions.

We were not altogether surprised, when at about four o'clock we reached Camp V, to find that the whole party was still there. Though by now the wind had dropped, it had been even more fierce at Camp V than it had been below, and it had been impossible to move on up the ridge. There was no room for two more at Camp V, and, though we offered to go down again, it was decided that Smythe and I should change places with Wyn Harris and Wager, in the hope of being able to push on up the mountain the next day.

The site of Camp V was composed of two platforms, one about 4 feet above the other. Each was sufficiently large to accommodate two "Meade" tents pitched end on. The tents themselves were about 6 feet 6 inches long by 4 feet wide by 4 feet high, made of light canvas and weighed about 16 lbs. each. The "Meade" tent is really a smaller edition of the "Whymper", and is named after the well-known mountaineer C. F. Meade – I have asked him why, but he could not enlighten me.

I doubt if anyone would claim to enjoy life at high altitudes – enjoy, that is, in the ordinary sense of the word. There is a certain grim satisfaction to be derived from struggling on upwards, however slowly; but the bulk of one's time is necessarily spent in the extreme squalor of a high camp, when even this solace is lacking. Smoking is impossible; eating tends to make one vomit; the necessity of reducing weight to a bare minimum forbids the importation of literature beyond that supplied by the labels on tins of food; sardine oil, condensed milk and treacle spill themselves all over the place; except for the briefest moments, during which one is not usually in a mood for æsthetic enjoyment, there is nothing to look at but the bleak confusion inside the tent and the scaly, bearded countenance of one's companion – fortunately the noise of the wind usually drowns the sound of his stuffy breathing; worst of all is the feeling of complete helplessness and inability to deal with any emergency that might arise. I used to try to console myself with the thought that a year ago I would have been thrilled by the very idea of taking part in our present adventure, a prospect that had then seemed like an impossible dream; but altitude has the same effect upon the mind as upon the body, one's intellect becomes dull and unresponsive, and my only desire was to finish the wretched job and to get down to a more reasonable clime – with strong emphasis on the latter part of the programme. I found that I could sleep pretty well, providing I was reasonably comfortable, but the slighest irritation, such as a jagged rock sticking into my back was enormously exaggerated, as it is when one is suffering from a high fever. At Camp V we had a fairly comfortable place to lie on.

All that night and most of next day a blizzard raged, and it was impossible to move either up or down. Fine snow driven in through the thin canvas of the tent, covered everything inside and filtered in through the opening of our sleeping-bags. Being on the crest of a ridge we received the full force of the gale. There was a continuous and mighty roar, and it seemed that the tents could not possibly stand up to such a hammering. At one point one of the guy ropes of our tent broke loose. Smythe struggled outside to deal with the situation, while I had the soft job of acting as ballast inside to hold the tent down. Smythe was only out for a couple of minutes, but when he returned we spent hours rubbing ahd thumping his limbs to restore the circulation.

On the evening of the 24th the wind dropped, and there was a great calm. We opened the tent flap and looked out. Such cloud as there was, was far below us. The magnificence of the view penetrated even my jaded brain. The summit, greatly foreshortened, seemed close above us. Smythe and I discussed seriously whether it would not be better after all to make our attempt from Camp V. We were still fairly active, and all this delay at high altitudes was certainly doing us no good. Anyway, there was no need to decide yet; we could start out with Birnie and Boustead and the porters who would be going up to establish Camp VI, and judge our condition then. That we could have discussed such a hopeless proposition shows how we were feeling.

But while we were preparing to start next morning, the gale began to blow again. Standing outside the tents the icy wind made us feel supremely helpless and foolish. The others had spent three nights at Camp V; already the Sherpas were nearly exhausted by the storm, and some of them were frostbitten. Had the weather been calm it is doubtful if they would have been able to go far; any advance under the present conditions was out of the question. Nor could we ask the porters to stay at Camp V yet another day and night, even if we had been willing to do so ourselves. There was nothing for it but to retreat to the North Col. It was a bitter blow, for all the time we were losing strength, and none of us could hope to be really fit for another attempt.

In the meantime a good deal of snow had fallen on the North Col, and Camp IV was in danger of being buried by a snow avalanche. The following day, the 26th May, was spent moving the tents and stores to the crest of the Col, while Ruttledge, Greene, Crawford and Brocklebank escorted the exhausted porters down to Camp III. Some of them were very weak, and required assistance over every step of the descent.

Birnie who was chiefly responsible for handling the porters, now had a difficult job in finding more men who were fit and willing to go up the ridge for the all important task of establishing Camp VI. He was helped a great deal in this by the remarkable courage and loyalty displayed by two of the old gang, Angtharkay and Kipa, who volunteered to go up again. It must be remembered that the Sherpas could not be expected to have the same feeling about the job that we had. These two had already done as much as could reasonably be expected of them. Their example was an inspiration to the other porters – and to us.

On the 28th May, Birnie, Longland, Wager and Wyn Harris went up to Camp V, with the eight porters. Smythe and I followed on the 29th. This time there was less wind than there had been before. We reached Camp V after five hours' climbing, and we were relieved to find that things had gone according to plan. Birnie was there in sole occupation. For the next few days his was the thankless job of remaining at Camp V in support of the parties attempting the summit. During the afternoon the gale returned with something of its old violence, and we were much relieved when Longland and the porters arrived from above. They had fought a tremendous struggle with the blizzard during the last two hours. Two of the porters were almost exhausted, and Longland had a difficult job in getting them down. Poor, gallant Kipa was in a bad way. It was already clear that he was out of his mind. For a long time he remained firmly convinced that he was dead. In consequence it was most difficult to persuade him to move, for, as he argued with perfect logic, dead men could not walk, even down hill. Even when, after several weeks it dawned on him that he was, in fact, alive, he still clung to his original hypothesis and attributed his phenomenal recovery to Green's magic. Such temporary madness or hallucination is not uncommon at high altitudes.

Longland brought us the splendid news that Camp VI had been established at 27,400 feet; 600 feet higher than it had been placed in 1924, and only 1,600 feet below the summit. This was a magnificent achievement on the part of the porters and those that were leading them. Their feat gave us a fine chance of climbing the mountain. Wyn Harris and Wager were now at Camp VI, and would start the next morning on their attempt to reach the summit.

By now the force of the gale had slackened, and after we had provided them with a mug of tea each, Longland and six of the porters went on down to the North Col. The other two porters stayed the night with us.

The next morning was beautifully fine. Not a breath of wind disturbed the stillness, no cloud obscured a single detail of the vast panorama beneath us. To the east was a fantastic tangle of ice and jagged rock, each fold a mighty peak, now dwarfed to insignificance; to the north the desert ranges of Tibet, calm and soft, stretched away into the violet distance. The sun was well up before Smythe and I left Camp V. In spite of a fairly good night I felt far from well. I was suffering from slight diarrhœa which accentuated the weakness due to the phsical deterioration that was now becoming only too apparent. Every movement was a great effort, and I found myself counting each step and wondering when I could decently suggest a halt. At first the climbing was fairly difficult over a series of outward sloping buttresses, but after a while it became easier. We followed the ridge until, in a little hollow, we found the remains of the 1924 Camp VI – a few broken and bleached tent poles with some tattered wisps of canvas clinging to them. From there we traversed diagonally across the face of the mountain, climbing slowly up towards the Yellow Band.

The climbing was very easy, and it was possible while moving along to examine the features of the upper part of the mountain. The Second Step looked very impressive. It now appeared almost end-on, and I saw that on its southern side there was a steep ice slope. Suddenly I noticed two dots, one above the other, on this slope. The day was so still that Smythe, who was about 10 yards in front, heard my excited whisper, "There go Wyn and Wagers on the Second Step." We sat down to watch. Yes, they were moving, but very slowly, probably cutting steps in the ice. But after a while we were not quite so sure; we got up and went on. After a quarter of an hour the dots did not appear to have moved, and we gradually realised that they were rocks sticking out of the ice. When we came closer we saw that they were a great deal larger than human beings. For all our knowedge of the features gleaned from photographs and distant study, we were greatly surprised by the scale of things up there; certainly everything was very much bigger than I had imagined. Longland had described the position of Camp VI, and as we approached we had no difficulty in spotting it – a little dark patch against the yellow limestone.

Before reaching the foot of the Yellow Band we had a prolonged struggle, first with a short ice slope which required stepcutting, then in powder snow into which we sank to our knees. I thought we would never get through it. That was followed by 200 feet of difficult rock climbing, each sloping ledge laden with snow. I found this less unpleasant; to have a technical difficulty to grapple with, which required delicate balance rather than dull plodding, was somehow stimulating. All the same, we were both very thankful when we crawled into the tiny tent that was Camp VI. I believe it was somewhere about one o'clock.

Camp VI was no luxury establishment. A tiny recess at the head of a gully and some loose stones had enabled the others to build a rough platform, perhaps three feet wide, on which to pitch the tent. The platform sloped downwards, and one side of the tent hung over the edge, forming a pocket. But at least it provided somewhere to lie down. After a rest we set about the task of melting a saucepan of snow. At the other camps we had used Primus stoves, but these did not work above a certain altitude, and at Camp VI we used little tins of solid fuel known as Tommy Cookers. Even these were most inefficient at that height, and it took us an hour to provide two miserable cups of tepid water slightly coloured with tea. Then we brewed some more against the return of Wager and Wyn Harris.

They arrived about the middle of the afternoon, showing every evidence of the tremendous effort they had made. They had tried to reach the ridge just below the Second Step but had met a continuous line of overhanging rock, so they had traversed along below the Black Band, and had reached the Great Couloir. This they had managed to cross, but had found the rocks on the other side laden with powder snow, which about 12.30 had forced them to abandon the struggle. How far this decision had been induced by sheer exhaustion and how much by the difficulty of the ground, on which the slightest slip must have been fatal to both, it is difficult to determine. Wager has since told me that he has found it impossible to assess the real position in which they found themselves. At that altitude mental processes are so sluggish and inefficient that it is most difficult to retain a clear memory of what has actually occurred. In any case their decision was absolutely right; there was not the slightest chance of their reaching the summit and to have persisted much farther would most probably have involved them in disaster.

Just below the crest of the north-east ridge they had found an ice-axe. This can only have belonged to Mallory or Irvine and throws some small light upon their fate. It seems probable that they fell from the place where the axe was found. It may be that one of them slipped, the other put down his axe to brace himself against the jerk of the rope but was dragged down. Certainly the axe cannot have fallen, for had that happened, there was nothing to prevent it from bounding down at least to the foot of the Yellow Band.

I had gone so badly that day that I offered to change places with one of the others, and let him try again with Smythe. But they had both had more than enough. Wager was gasping for breath in a most alarming manner and Wyn looked terribly tired. So after a short rest and a cup of our home-brewed nectar they went on down to Camp V.

That night and the one which followed were by far the worst that I had spent on the mountain. I had the lower berth and kept on rolling off the ledge into the pocket formed by the tent floor. Smythe spent the time rolling on top of me. From sheer self-preservation, to prevent myself from being suffocated, I had to kick him with my knee or jab him with my elbow. This I did over and over gain, hoping vaguely that the action would not reveal the temper that was undoubtedly behind the blows. I did not sleep at all and I do no think Smythe fared much better. Several hours before dawn we gave up the unequal struggle and started to prepare for the climb.

But before it was light snow started to fall, and presently a strong wind was driving the flakes against the side of the tent. It was no use thinking of starting in those conditions, and there was nothing for it but to resign ourselves to spending the day at Camp VI. I think we both realised then that our slender chance of reaching the summit had now vanished. In the first place the snow that was falling would, at the lowest estimate, increase the difficulties enormously; secondly, our physical deterioration due to lack of oxygen, sleep and appetite must now be very rapid. Indeed we were worried, so far as we were capable of worrying about anything, by the question of how long it was possible to live at 27,400 feet. Would the danger line be apparent? or would one suddenly find oneself inapable of moving? or perhaps just die in one's sleep? Nobody had ever tried the experiment of a prolonged sojourn at such an altitude.

It was a dreary day. The wind dropped in the afternoon. Looking out of the little window at the back of the tent, we could see the summit. Very little of the intervening ground was visible, and it looked ridiculously close. Well, 1,600 feet was not far; without the powder snow on the rocks and in sea-level conditions one could climb it comfortably in an hour! An ambition of a lifetime and we were too weak to reach out to grasp it! Fortunately our dulled intellects lessened the sting of this thought, but it was sharp enough.

The next night was a repetition of the first, tossing, kicking, panting. At about three o'clock in the morning we started melting some snow, to make a brew of something – Café-au-Lait I believe it was called, though everything tasted much the same. Thawing our boots was the longest job; they were like lumps of rock. We had intended taking them to bed with us to keep them soft, but, like so many good resolutions made below, this had not been done. But by holding them over candle flames we managed to make the uppers sufficiently pliable, and, with a tremendous effort, to force our feet, already incased in four or five pairs of socks, into them. For the rest we each wore two pairs of long woollen pants, seven sweaters and a loosely-fitting windproof with a hood that went over a balaclava helmet. Our hands were protected by one pair of thick woollen mits covered with a pair of sheep-skin gauntlets. I felt about as suitably equipped for delicate rock climbing as a fully rigged deep-sea diver for dancing a tango. It was quiet outside and we waited for the dawn.

It must have been about 7.30 when we started. It was a fine morning, though bitterly cold. I had a stomach ache and felt as weak as a kitten. We started climbing diagonally up towards the head of the Great Couloir, taking the lead in turns of about a quarter of an hour each. The ground was not exactly difficult nor particularly steep. But it was rather like being on the tiles of a roof; one had to rely largely on the friction of boot-nails on the shelving ledges. A slip might have been difficult to check. The more exposed parts of the Yellow Band had been swept clear of snow by the wind, but in the little gullies and cracks there were deep deposits of powder snow which obscured all foothold. We were not climbing quickly, but our progress was steady and fast enough. After about two hours I began to feel sick and it appeared to me that I was approaching the end of my tether. In such a condition I would certainly have been no use to Smythe in an emergency; also it was a firm rule among us that one simply must not go on until one collapsed altogether, as that would have placed one's companion in a most awkward position. So I decided to stop and let Smythe go on alone.

By now it was fairly warm in the sun. I sat down and watched Smythe making his way slowly along the slabs and wondered if I might follow him at my own pace. But then it occurred to me that, seeing me coming, he might wait for me, so I relucantly gave up the idea, and afer waiting a little longer started back to Camp VI.

It was about 1.30 when Smythe returned. He had reached the Great Couloir, but had found masses of new snow on the rocks beyond and had been compelled to return from much the same place that the previous party had reached. The height at this point was estimated at 28,100 feet. The altitude of all the major features on the north face of Mount Everest had been determined (to within a hundred feet or so) by theodolite observations from below, and it is from these computations that we were able to judge with reasonable accuracy the height of any point on the upper part of the face. The readings on an aneroid barometer at that altitude would be hopelessly inaccurate.

Smythe was so exhausted by his effort that he was reluctant to move farther down that day. To give him a chance of a good night's sleep, and also to relieve the anxiety of the unfortunate Birnie, it was decided that I should go down to Camp V and that Smythe should come all the way down to the North Col on the following day. With the tent to himself and two sets of sleeping-bags he would be fairly comfortable. I left Camp VI at 2.30. By now we were enveloped in cloud. To avoid the difficult pitch below the camp I traversed along towards the north-east shoulder as the other descending parties had done. For some distance the way was along a sloping terrace that provided fairly easy going, but near the north-east shoulder, the terrace petered out into steep rocks that were now laden with powder snow. At one point I nearly came to grief by lowering myself on to a ledge of snow which promptly slipped away and left me hanging by my fingers.

I had scarcely reached the easier rocks below when I was met by a tremendous blast of wind. I have never known anything like the suddenness of those Everest storms. They arrived out of perfect stillness, without any warning, and at the full height of their power. This was the fiercest gale I had encountered on the mountain – at any rate while out of shelter. I found it impossible to stand up against it even for a moment, and all I could do was to cower against a rock with my back to the wind. Luckily this did not maintain is maximum velocity for long and after a time I was able to proceed in short rushes. But presently I found that I had lost all sense of direction. The cloud was thick and I could see no more than a few yards ahead of me. It was no use going on down, for if I missed the top of the north-east spur I should get myself into a hopeles mess. I sat down helplessly and waited. For those who wish to achieve complete philosophical detachment, there is perhaps something to recommend life at high altitudes. The mind appears to be quite incapable of strong emotion of any sort. To be lost on a mountain side in such circumstances would normally be an unpleasantly exciting experience to the calmest of men. I found it neither unpleasant nor exciting, and was blissfully resigned to whatever the fates chose to do with me. I have no idea how long I waited, but eventually a sharp spire appeared through the driving mist and snow. I remembered having seen this before and made towards it. Presently a window opened, and far below I saw the summit of the North Peak, a rock in a storm-tossed sea. Soon I reached the little hollow of the 1924 Camp VI which provided a welcome refuge from the storm.

I almost enjoyed the rest of the descent to Camp V. I felt gloriously careless as I bumped and slithered down from ledge to ledge; the wind provided a mad confusion that matched my state of mind. When I arrived I found that Birnie had made a tremendous brew of hot liquid; I think it was tea, but whatever it was it was excellent. He, poor chap, was very weak. He had spent longer above the North Col than any of us, his feet were frost-bitten and the altitude had taken a severe toll of his strength. He had had none of the interest of the attempts on the summit; only a long, lonely vigil and anxiety. But I found his cheerfulness even more warming than his tea. It was nearly dark before I had the strength of mind to go out into the storm again to collect a sleeping-bag from the other tent. I found this to be full of snow and though I tried for a quarter of an hour, my fingers were so lifeless that I could not undo the fastenings. I tried to tear the canvas open with no more success, and finally I gave it up. Birnie gave me half his sleeping-bag and we spent a miserable night huddled together in a tent half filled with snow, listening to the crazy raving of the storm. This had partly spent itself by morning and when the sun was up we made our way slowly down to the North Col.

Here we found Longland and McLean. While the former went off up the ridge to meet Smythe, the latter ministered to our needs. The large dome tent which we were now housed seemed to us the height of luxury and spacious comfort. McLean insisted on our relaxing completely, while he undid our boots, massaged our limbs and provided endless supplies of food and drink. Smythe came in some hours later.

It took us a very long time to get down from the North Col the next day. Immediately after we had started, McLean became ill. He could hardly walk and had to be nursed carefully down the slopes. When we reached the bottom we found that a party had been sent up from Camp III to meet us with tea. When we had assembled to drink this I suddenly found that I was suffering from aphasia and could not articulate words properly. For example if I wished to say, "Give me a cup of tea" I would say something entirely different – may be "tram-car, cat, put". It was a most aggravating situation and reminded me of the fate of the banker in "The Hunting of the Snark", though I was spared the more spectacular symptoms of his malady. As in my normal speech I was still confined to whispering, my peculiar complaint did not attract attention at first. But I could not conceal it for long and I had to suffer the pitying looks of my companions who were obviously thinking, "Poor old Eric, now he's gone bats". In actual fact I was perfectly clear-headed; I could even visualise the words I wanted to say, but my tongue just refused to perform the required movements. At length, from sheer exasperation I got up and ran off down the glacier so fast that I arrived at Camp III a long time before any of the others. There however my case was even worse, for everyone was naturally eager to hear news of our attempt, while all I could do was to talk drivel. Poor Ruttledge was most concerned at having another lunatic on his hands. The cause of my complaint was attributed either to sunstroke or to the blizzard. I think it was a form of migraine, a theory that is supported by the blinding headache from which I suffered throughout that night. However I was well again in the morning.

The whole party retreated down the glacier quickly or slowly, each according to his physical condition. Birnie had to be carried most of the way, and McLean required the support of a strong arm. The Base Camp was now very different from the bleak comfortless place we had left seven weeks before. It was still no beauty spot, but there was grass, the soft, warm smell of earth and growing things, blue poppies brought the sky to earth and primulas peeped from behind the rocks. After a week of delicious rest and luxury we returned up the glacier to Camp III, in the high expectation of renewing our attempt on the mountain. But it soon became obvious that this was impossible. The monsoon had broken and though it was much warmer and more comfortable than before, the slopes of the North Col were too dangerous, and masses of snow had fallen on the upper part of Everest.

Before retreating again some of us visited the Rapiu La, the saddle at the foot of the north-east ridge of Everest, and climbed a small peak above it. From the top we had a view that could not be imagined by those who have not seen the fantastic country that lies to the south-east of Mount Everest – the colossal ramparts that join Everest with Lhotse, the delicately fluted ridges of purest ice, a hundred peaks of exquisite form, deep, wooded valleys; what a contrast to the bare, unlovely slopes of rubble about the East Rongbuk glacier!

CHAPTER EIGHT

Large Expeditions

In 1933 I formed a deep conviction of the fallacy of tackling Mount Everest with such a huge organisation. In the first place no expedition had in practice launched more than two attempts on the summit; it was agreed that the best number for an attempt was two, therefore it seemed improbable that in any expedition more than four men would be required to make the actual attempts. Why then should a party consist of fourteen climbers? It was argued that there must be reserves in case some of the climbers went sick. But in no case had a man, who was known to be capable of climbing to great altitudes and who had been relied upon to take part in the final climb, actually succumbed to sickness before the attempt. It seemed clear, then, that this risk was insignificant compared with the enormous chances against any one expedition finding the mountain in a climbable condition. Reserves yes, but not three reserves to every one man who was expected to go high. Again, this question of sickness should surely be regarded against a background of individual experience. In all the dozens of expeditions and climbing holidays that I have done I do not recall a single occasion on which sickness of any member of the party has prevented us from reaching our objective. I believe that most climbers can say the same, or at any rate will agree that such a misfortune is a rare occurrence. Further, when a man is sent on a important job during which he has to live, perhaps for years, in a bad climate the appointment is not duplicated in case he goes sick. Why, then, this extraordinary expectation of disease and accident on an Everest expedition? I refer of course to the approach and not to the final attempt on the summit.

Another reason given for the inclusion of a large number of Europeans in the party was the alleged necessity of having experts to deal with the problems of transport. This may or may not be true of a giant expedition; I have never had the job of running one. But it is certainly not the case with an expedition of moderate size. The organisation of transport to Mount Everest is peculiarly easy – a far simpler matter than in any other part of the Himalayas that I know. Animal transport can be used all the way to the Base Camp and even beyond; the passport issued by the authorities in Lhasa includes an order to all Tibetan officials along the route to supply the transport required, a luxury that I have met nowhere else; supplies of fodder can be obtained all along the route; on the wide, open plains of Tibet, over which lies the majority of the way, one is blissfully free from the danger of landslides, a constant menace in other parts of the Himalayas, which may cut the road for weeks; the Tibetan interpreter deals efficiently with the problem of language and the settling of minor disputes. The rest is a simple division sum: the weight of each load into the total weight of baggage to be transported equals the number of animals required.

Opinions vary considerably regarding the optimum size of expeditions. I once asked my friend Dr. Humphreys for his views on the matter. He replied firmly and without hesitation "Three constitutes a large expedition, a party of one may be considered a small expedition". I did not propose anything so drastic for an attempt on Mount Everest, though I have always thought that a party of three climbers would stand almost as good a chance as any large number. The kind of expedition that I visualised was one consisting of six European members all with considerable Alpine experience and all with a proved capacity for going high, and about thirty carefully selected and specially trained Sherpa porters. I advocated a considerable reduction in the quantity of stores and equipment taken per head, and the total expenditure of somewhere between £2,500 and £3,000, as against £12,000 which was the average cost of each of the previous expeditions (except for the first "Reconnaissance").

Such an expedition would have the advantage of mobility, with a consequent lessening of the risk of a breakdown in lines of communication. Even at the enormously reduced cost, each porter could be provided with much better and more carefully selected equipment. The climbers would get to know the porters individually in a way that was quite impossible when there were 170 of them; this would lead to a greater mutual understanding and trust. The chances of theft of equipment would be greatly reduced. With a huge caravan of three or four thousand animals, varying from powerful yaks to tiny donkeys, which inevitably become spread out over miles of country, it is exceedingly difficult to prevent looting, and vital equipment is as liable to be stolen as are superfluous stores. In 1933 a considerable number of porters' boots were lost in this way; had the theft been larger than it actually was it might have resulted in the complete breakdown of the expedition. Also the provision of a small number of animals would not disrupt the normal life of the country, which is one of the principal objections of the Tibetan officials to Everest expeditions.

But it was mainly on psychological grounds that I was opposed to large expeditions. It is vitally important that no member of a party should at any time feel that he is superfluous, or that he is simply there in case someone else breaks down. Such a state of affairs imposes an intolerable strain on everyone, and is bound to lead to friction and a consequent loss of efficiency. This matter is easily overlooked by a leader who has all the interest of the organisation and is constantly busy with his plans. On a scientific expedition each man is, or should be, absorbed in his particular line of research; the party can easily be split up into self-contained units each with its special task and responsibility. But when the sole object of a venture is to reach the top of a particular mountain, the problem is entirely different. It is merely tactless to remind a man that he is lucky to be there at all, and that there are hundreds of equally good climbers at home who would be only too glad to take his place. You cannot argue an expedition into running smoothly, nor avoid a competitive feeling by appealing for the "team spirit". The strongest mountaineering party is one in which each member has implicit confidence in all his companions, recognises their vital importance in the common effort and feels himself to have an equally indispensable part to play. This ideal is no less important to a Himalayan expedition than on an Alpine peak. To my mind it can only be achieved with a relatively small, closely knit party. Only then can you talk (if you must) about "team spirit". How is it possible, when at least 50 per cent. of the members are destined to remain in reserve, to avoid a feeling of competition? Only a saint could expunge from deep down in his soul all hope of another man falling sick, that he might take his place. How different from the joyous partnership we have known on other climbs!

For my part I loathed the crowds and the fuss that were inseparable from a large expedition. I always had the ridiculous feeling that I was taking part in a Cook's tour or a school treat, and I wanted to go away and hide myself. Of course this did not apply to the few days or weeks when one is actually doing a hard job of work, but unfortunately such spells occupied a very small proportion of the whole time. The small town of tents that sprang up each evening, the noise and racket of each fresh start, the sight of a huge army invading the peaceful valleys, it was all so far removed from the light, free spirit with which we were wont to approach our peaks. And I believe that spirit plays an important part in the success of any mountaineering venture. Remove, then, the impression that one is engaged in a vast enterprise upon which the eyes of the world are focused, realise that one is setting out to climb a mountain, higher perhaps, but fundamentally no different from other mountains, and one will add greatly to one's chances of success, and, more important still, enjoyment.

Then there is the question of finance. The argument here, as I understood it, was that money for an Everest expedition was easy to raise, so why not spend it if it would help? In the first place the mere spending of money does not in itself increase the efficiency of an expedition; indeed it can, only too easily, be a source of weakness by cluttering up the works with a lot of superfluous junk and obscuring the really important issues. For example it would be of more value to supply all the porters with precisely the same equipment – dome-tents, boots, sleeping-bags – as that used by climbers, than to transport cases of champagne and other luxuries all the way from London to Rongbuk. Secondly, if the money must be spent, there are many profitable ways of doing it. For the difference in cost between a large expedition and one of moderate size, no fewer than a dozen expeditions could be sent to other parts of the Himalayas. These, if properly run, could have a direct bearing upon the main problem of climbing Mount Everest, and could be undertaken during the years when political permission to enter Tibet was not forthcoming. There are hundreds of young mountaineers who would give anything for a chance to go to the Himalayas. How much easier would be the work of the Mount Everest selection committees if some of them could be given that chance. Again, the climbing of Mount Everest is as much a physiological as a mountaineering problem. We are lamentably ignorant of the real effects of high altitudes upon the human body, or of the means by which these may be countered. Physiologists have been working for years upon these problems; they have been handicapped by lack of opportunities and subjects for their experiments. It would be possible for a small party of trained physiologists and climbers to camp for a month on the summit of Kamet. The results of their experiments would be as valuable to science as to those who wish to climb the lofty peaks of the Himalaya.

Finally, the disadvantage of large expeditions lay in the fact that the necessity of raising big funds made it difficult to control publicity. The expeditions became invested with a glamour foreign to the fundamental simplicity of the game. It was quite natural that mountaineers should wish to climb the highest peak in the world, or at least be interested in the project. But unfortunately Everest's supremacy among mountains appealed to the popular imagination of a record-breaking age, and gradually the expeditions began to receive a press publicity out of all proportion to the value of the undertaking, and certainly out of keeping with what used to be regarded as "the best traditions of mountaineering". It was claimed that the enterprise symbolised the spirit of modern youth, and that its success would represent a triumph of humanity over Nature. In fact, of course, the first part of the venture was an intensely interesting piece of geographical exploration, and the second an absorbing mountaineering problem – no more, no less; both were on the same plane as any similar project.

I knew a man with a strong claim for a place on the expedition, who said that he wanted to climb Everest so as to make a big name for himself, which would enable him to use his influence in the cause of world peace. A worthy ambition no doubt, but surely it would have been more profitable to devote his energies to the study of political economy rather than to proving himself a mountaineer with an exceptionally large lung capacity, or whatever it is that enables a man to climb to great altitudes. This is one example among many of an extraordinary distortion of values which has its roots in the opening of a short-cut to fame. Were it not so laughable it might well be resented by those who find in mountaineering a deep æsthetic pleasure.

It was perhaps difficult for those actually engaged in the expeditions not to be carried away by this flood of notoriety, and it needed a good deal of sober introspection to trace the origin of the nasty taste that began to appear in the mouths of the more sensitive. But I think that the feeling of a large section of mountaineers was summed up by the remark that a friend of mine (not himself a member of the expeditions) once made: "For heaven's sake climb the wretched thing and let us get back to real mountaineering." It seemed a pity that so simple a project should have led to such a feeling.

One of the most unfortunate effects of the Mount Everest expeditions was their influence upon Himalayan mountaineering. In consequence of their elaborate scale, it came to be thought impossible to achieve anything in the Himalayas without an enormous and costly organisation. Many of the expeditions – Italian, German, French, international – which followed the early attempts to climb Everest, were run with an extravagance that made the

Everest expeditions appear modest by comparison. Fantastic equipment was evolved, dynamite brought to blow away obstacles, aeroplanes used for dumping supplies on the mountain, all the delicacies known to culinary art were provided to sustain the exhausted climbers, whole populations were uprooted from their homes to carry this stuff up the glaciers – with the consequent risk of famine the following year due to the neglect of agriculture. Needless to say these tactics met with very little success, and not one of the peaks attacked with such ferocity was climbed. But the sad thing was that the lessons taught by the great pioneers of Himalayan exploration – Longstaff, Conway, Kellas, Godwin Austin, Freshfield, the Schlagintweits – who achieved so much by the simple but hardy application of their art, were forgotten or ignored.

It is perhaps unfair to blame this cult of mighty Himalayan campaigns entirely on the Everest expeditions, but from talks I have had with the organisers of one of these foreign expeditions, in which I tried in vain to persuade them to adopt a less elaborate plan, I am sure that they based their ideas largely upon the Everest precedent.

These observations are made in no unfriendly spirit, and I hope that they will be regarded as constructive criticism. It was sincerely believed that the job could best be tackled by employing all the resources that money could buy. There are still those who hold this view, though I am narrow-minded enough to believe that they cannot have themselves experienced the enormous moral and material advantages of the small compact expedition. One day men will again turn their eyes towards the Himalayas; I hope that then this other point of view will be kept in mind.

When all is said, the Mount Everest expeditions have been a good adventure, and I think that most of those who were lucky enough to take part in them have gained much by the experience. For my part, much as I disapprove of large expeditions, I would not have foregone a single friendship that I made in 1933.

CHAPTER NINE

Small Expeditions

ONE cannot wander far from the normal trade and tourist routes without being impressed by the enormous area of the earth's surface still unexplored. It is a pleasant discovery to make. The superficial observer is too apt to suppose that, because the South Pole has been reached, the mysteries of the Antarctic Continent are all revealed, or to imagine that if Everest were climbed then there would be nothing more to discover in the Himalayas. In fact, of course, the journey to the Pole disclosed no more than a thin strip of country on either side of the route followed; the climbing of Everest would tell us nothing that we do not already know about the earth's surface. Certainly there are no more continents to be found; it is doubtful if we will ever see falls more magnificent than Victoria and Niagara; lost civilisations beyond the ranges exist only in the imagination of romantic novelists. But the detailed exploration of the world is very far from complete; huge areas are still untrodden by the foot of man, unmapped and unknown; a school atlas will show with dotted lines that many of the mighty rivers of Asia are unexplored in their upper reaches; within the last twenty years the largest glacier known to exist outside the polar regions was discovered. Besides, geographical exploration means more than the discovery and survey of country; even a well-mapped area may be *terra incognita* to the botanist, the geologist, the zoologist, the archæologist. There is no end to it. Start, with a spark of interest, to look into the matter, and your head will soon begin to reel with the mass of fascinating problems crying out for investigation. It is a virulent bug, this desire to see what lies round the next corner. An energetic life-time spent in the pursuit will leave you as far from complete satisfaction as you were at the start.

Mountain climbing has its roots in mountain exploration, and it is not unnatural that in little-known ranges the mountaineer should tend to revert to the basis of his pursuit. It would be difficult for anyone with an interest in strange country to go all the way to Mount Everest without feeling some desire to leave the route and wander off into the labyrinth of unmapped ranges that stretch away on every side. On the way back to India in 1933, Wager and I left the main party and made our way across a small strip of unexplored country to the south, and crossed into Sikkim by a new pass. My chief interest was in climbing peaks. Wager, on the other hand, as a geologist, had a wider view. He had already tasted the joys of serious exploration in Greenland, and his main enthusiasm was for the country itself. Though I disputed the matter hotly at the time, I gradually became converted to his way of thinking. Something of my early feeling for mountains began to revive.

Then the thought occurred to me, "Why not spend the rest of my life doing this sort of thing?" There was no way of life that I liked more, the scope appeared to be unlimited, others had done it, vague plans had already begun to take shape, why not put some of them into practice? It was a disturbing idea, one which caused me much heart searching and many sleepless nights. The most obvious snag, of course, was lack of private means; but surely such a mundane consideration could not be decisive. In the first place I was convinced that expeditions could be run for the tithe of the cost generally considered necessary. Secondly if one could produce useful or interesting results one would surely find support; and as experience grew, so too would the quality of the results. No, lack of money must not be allowed to interfere. The fact that I had no training in any particular branch of science was a more serious obstacle. But might not this defect be remedied as one went along, or in spare time between expeditions? Also there is much to be said against the organiser of a scientific expedition being himself a specialist; firstly because he would tend to take a narrow view of the work of the expedition, and secondly because the running of an expedition is in itself nearly a whole-time job. For I did not expect to have to hunt alone – I anticipated no difficulty in finding men willing to join me on an attractive project.

I do not know how much I fought the temptation. I certainly suffered qualms of conscience, but they were due more to the mere prospect of such exquisite self-indulgence than to the fear of the consequences of abandoning the search for an assured future, provision for old age and other worthy ambitions. I had always rather deplored the notion that one must sacrifice the active years of one's life to the dignity and comfort of old age. Also the less conservative of my monitors assured me that things had a way of panning out so long as one knew what one wanted. So the decision was taken, albeit with a faint heart.

Beginnings must be small. I could hardly expect much backing at first, and it looked as though my theories regarding small expeditions would receive a pretty severe test. Of the dozens of fascinating projects that presented themselves, the one that appeared to suit my purpose most admirably was the exploration of that remarkable geographical phenomenon, the Nanda Devi basin. First, because there were no political obstacles to be overcome, and secondly, I had already had experience on the Kamet expedition of that part of the Himalayas. I first became interested in the problem after hearing Ruttledge talk about it. He had made four attempts to enter the basin, and had given me an enthusiastic description of them, and a vivid picture of the strange sanctuary. The spark was rekindled by a conversation with Dr. Longstaff.

Here was a famous peak, 25,660 feet high, completely surrounded by such a formidable mountain barrier that no one had been able to penetrate to the country lying at its foot. The only breach in this barrier was on its western side, where the Rishi Ganga river had carved a tremendous gorge some twenty miles long. Since W. W. Graham and his two Swiss guides, Emil Boss and Ulrich Kauffmann, had tried to force their way up the gorge in 1883, repeated attempts had been made by explorers to reach the sanctuary. Every angle of approach had been tried without success. Dr. Longstaff, with his usual generous enthusiasm for the projects of younger men, advised me to try the gorge once again. Although he himself had tried to find a way up it, he had not been able to press home his attempt, but he was convinced that there was a way.

At first it looked as though it might be difficult to find anyone who would fall in with my apparently heretical ideas of extreme frugality. Most fortunately, however, Tilman arrived in England at just the right moment. I had a letter from him announcing that, after indulging in a little gold-mining in Kakamega, he had bought a push-bike and had ridden it right across Africa to the west coast where he had picked up a cargo ship which had brought him home. He asked me to go with him to climb in the Lake District for a week or two. I replied with the counter proposal that he should come with me to the Himalayas for seven months. He agreed that this was the better plan, and came to London immediately to discuss my project.

I also asked Dr. Humphreys to come. He had wide experience of mountain exploration in Africa, and was a great believer in travelling light. Besides being a doctor, he was an expert surveyor and botanist. He was tremendously keen on the idea, but unfortunately, just before I asked him he had undertaken to lead an expedition to the Arctic. But his sympathetic advice and encouragement were invaluable. Our "expedition" was lamentably short of scientific qualification, though we did manage to acquire some small knowledge of survey.

Money, of course, was our first concern. Try as I would, I could not bring my estimates to below £150 each, if we were to allow ourselves the rather important luxury of three Sherpa porters, and spend the whole season in the field. I had managed to raise a little money by the distasteful business of lecturing during the winter, but not as much as that. Tilman, however, in spite of his gold-mining was rather more affluent, and he thought he could put up his share. The chief item of the budget was the passage to India. The cheapest return fare by passenger steamer was £50. The romantic notion of working one's passage is difficult to put into practice, for few ship's masters are willing to sign on hands who have every intention of deserting half way through the voyage. Tilman's idea of bicycling to India was turned down. For some weeks the issue hung in the balance. In the meantime I went off to lecture in Norway. When I came back I found that Tilman had fixed up return passages by cargo steamer for £30 each return from Liverpool to Calcutta, including our modest baggage. This put the project just about within our grasp, though even then Tilman had to advance some of my share against uncertain security.

We set sail on the 6th of April, 1934. The voyage took a month. We had nothing much to do, but the tedium was lightened by the extremely pleasant company of the ship's officers. We had collected all the available literature about Nanda Devi, and before long we knew the whole story by heart. I taught Tilman what little Urdu I knew, and then we spent a weary hour each morning supplementing this from Hugo. We passed a considerable part of each day throwing a medicine-ball at each other and skipping. In spite of this we became so liverish that by the time we reached Aden we felt compelled to supplement the ship's food with extra fruit. In its purchase I nearly succeeded in ruining the finances of the expedition. All the cash we had with us was one £5 note, which had rashly been entrusted to my care. After some difficulty we found a local financier who was willing to provide us with change. This consisted mostly of shillings and sixpenny pieces which took a long time to count. It was very hot, and we were hard pressed on all sides by shouting pedlars, all eager to take their share of our wealth. When the count was complete, and our pockets and hands were laden with silver, our banker not unnaturally demanded his £5 note. This had vanished. In a frenzy I emptied each pocket in turn, spilling coins all over the place; it was nowhere to be found. Then suddenly I noticed a screwed-up bit of white paper reposing in a basket of oranges. To my intense relief, and the chagrin of the slow-witted owner of the basket, this turned out to be the missing note.

The only other incident of importance during the voyage happened a few days later, when I broke a toe by jumping onto an awning that had been rigged up to provide a swimming-bath. However, the purser performed a painful but successful operation, and in time the toe resumed its normal appearance.

Before leaving England I had arranged with Karma Paul to engage the services of three of the Sherpas who had been with us on Everest the previous year – Angtharkay, Pasang and Kusang – and to send them down from Darjeeling to meet us in Calcutta. At Vizagapatam we sent him a wire informing him of the date of our arrival, but we had to wait for two days before the Sherpas appeared. Our budget contained no provision for hotel bills, but fortunately the captain of our ship was kind enough to allow us to remain on board.

The journey from Calcutta to Kathgodam took thirty-six hours – the hottest I have ever known. I suffered from a raging thirst, but Tilman was a stern task-master and would not allow me to squander our slender reserves on tea or soda water. Every piece we spent had to be accounted for in a little note-book, and each day's expenditure was carefully scrutinised. My discomfort was increased by watching Angtharkay, who travelled in our compartment, quaffing cup after cup of tea at every halt. I had not quite the face to sponge upon him, and bore my torment in silence. The last fifty miles of our journey to Ranikhet were completed by lorry, and at last we had relief from our suffering as we took deep gulps of cool, pine-scented air, deliciously sweet after the appalling heat and dust of pre-monsoon India.

We reached Ranikhet at about noon on the 9th of May, and put up at the government rest-house. A day and a half was sufficient to complete our simple preparations. We had worked out everything beforehand and knew exactly what we wanted. Within a couple of hours of our arrival we had engaged twelve Dhotial coolies to carry for us across the foothills, and had sent them off to meet us at Baijnath, the terminus of the road, fifty miles farther on. Then each of us was issued with his allowance of kit, which consisted of a suit of light, windproof material, sweaters, woollen pants, a woollen helmet, puttees, socks, a double sleeping-bag, a pair of climbing boots and an ice-axe. Survey instruments, cameras, ropes, two small Meade tents, Primus stoves, two tins of kerosene oil, candles, lanterns, matches and the food we had brought out from England were packed into 80 lb. loads. We collected from the local bank the money we would want for the next five or six months, most of it in silver. A lorry was chartered to take us and our baggage to Baijnath. The surplus clothing which convention had thus far imposed upon us was packed away and deposited with the secretary of the local club. All was set by the evening of the 10th, and we started early on the morning of the 11th.

It all seemed too easy. I had been told so often before leaving England that my budget was ridiculously inadequate, and that though we might reach Ranikhet we would certainly not get much farther; there had been so much talked and written about the vast amount of organisation required for an expedition, that I had begun to suspect that there must be some hidden snag. There was no snag. These widespread beliefs were simply founded upon a confusion between necessity and luxury; this great bug-bear of cost and organisation was largely due to the attempt to carry the amenities of civilisation into wild places. In most parts of the world travel is as simple or as complex as you care to make it. As it was, in our ignorance, we had brought many things that we could well have done without. On the other hand there was not a single item of equipment or food which we needed and had not brought; nothing that in the smallest degree could have aided us in the achievement of our plans, or increased our enjoyment.

The Dhotials were waiting for us when we arrived at Baijnath at about noon. Without any fuss they shouldered their loads and started on the first stage of the march. Their regulation load is 80 lbs., 20 lbs. more than the usual load carried by Himalayan porters. Like the Sherpas they support the weight with a head-strap; indeed this seems to be the method employed by most of the best load carriers throughout the world. I have tried it myself but without much success, though I could see that if one acquired the knack it would be very much less tiring than the usual shoulder-strap method.

Though it was only about ten miles, I found that first march a great trial. I was suffering from the usual complaint of newcomers to the Indian hills, known as "hill diarrhœa" and which is due either to mica in the water or to a chill induced by the change of climate. My broken toe was still painful, and I had to wear a tennis-shoe with the toe-cap cut off. Baijnath was only about 2,000 feet above sea-level, and it was a very hot, sultry afternoon. It was uphill nearly all the way. The path was dusty and I suffered from a fearful thirst. In the evening we reached Gwaldam, 7,000 feet up on a wooded ridge overlooking the deep valley of the Pindar River, cool and lovely. I satisfied my only desire – to drink and drink and drink. Instead of any supper I took a huge dose of castor-oil.

It was a typical start and I have made many such. But two or three days of easy marching produced a wonderful change. Fatigue and stiffness left us; feet were no longer sore; having left behind the filth of semi-civilisation we could drink freely from frequent springs; we marched in the cool of the morning and lazed in the shade of the oak and pine woods during the heat of the day; we became fit and gloriously alive. The weather was perfect, the country magnificent. Our way led over ridge after ridge of forest-clad hills; not the oppressive rain-forest of the Eastern Himalayas, but gentle wooded slopes interspersed with grassy glades, moss and bracken and splashing streams. The rhododendrons were in bloom, and many kinds of Alpine flowers. Above were the sparkling white peaks of Trisul and Nanda Ghunti. The soft music of running water, the murmur of a light breeze in the trees, the summer note of the cuckoo, these were the sounds we awoke to each morning. With such a small party, we could camp far from the dusty villages, wherever we chose. We rarely bothered to pitch a tent, but lay, instead, on a luxurious bed of deep grass, beside a huge log fire. We lived with a sense of perfect freedom and deep physical and mental well-being. We wanted nothing.

Our food was very simple. It consisted mainly of flour, rice and ghee (clarified butter) which we bought as we went along. We had brought various luxuries to supplement these; sugar, tea, lentils, a number of 10-lb. Cheddar cheeses sewn up in cloth, and some tins of pemmican. Except for the pemmican we rarely tasted meat. Tilman favoured a vegetarian diet, largely because he had recently had most of his teeth knocked out by a fall from a horse while steeplechasing, and I was quite willing to fall into line. For the first few days I found our diet a bit hard, but as I became fit my appetite grew and I ate my meals with great relish. I certainly found this simple fare far more satisfying than a diet of tinned food, which soon becomes dead and tasteless. There cannot have been much wrong with our diet for we never lacked energy. The supply of Vitamin "C" presents no problem anywhere in the Himalayas for it is always easy to find edible plants such as chives and wild rhubarb.

The bulk of our time was spent in uninhabited country, and for this we collected supplies of flour from the last village through which we passed. And here was yet another advantage of travelling light. For our small party we rarely experienced any difficulty in obtaining food for several weeks. Most of the flour was converted into tsampa by the simple process of roasting it. Tsampa is almost universally used in the high regions of Central Asia, particularly by travellers in Tibet and by shepherds grazing their flocks in the mountains beyond the reach of fuel. Its great virtue lies in the fact that it can be kept almost indefinitely without going bad, and it can be eaten without any further cooking. Our breakfast generally consisted of tsampa mixed in mugs of tea, for supper it was usually boiled into a thick porridge with a sauce of lentils strongly seasoned with chillies and other spices.

The simplest method of working out the amount of food required for a given period is to allow two pounds per man per day, and to divide the total suitably between the various commodities available. Then with a small spring-balance it is easy at any time to take stock of the food situation. I have nearly always found this way infallible; for months at a stretch one is rarely out more than a day or two either way. For us the task of estimating the food we needed was a matter of a few minutes' work with pencil and note-book. It went something like this:–

Food for five men for six weeks:
$42 \times 5 \times 2 = 420$ lbs.

	lbs.
Flour	210
Rice	60
Ghee	40
Cheese	30
Pemmican	10
Sugar	40
Lentils	30
	420

Such things as tea, salt and spices were not included in this weight, and were calculated separately. Provided most of the food is dry, two pounds a day is liberal allowance, and men can do hard physical work on quite a lot less for short periods. The normal Arctic sledging ration is something like 27 ozs., but it contains a very high proportion of fat. In the Himalayas fat is difficult to procure locally, expensive to import, awkward to carry and very indigestible at high altitudes. Fresh meat does not keep long, and is wasteful in weight as it contains a high proportion of water and bone. Tinned meat is also very wasteful in weight. Dried meat, similar to the original Canadian pemmican, is better than the modern tinned pemmican, but it is not easy to procure and is very expensive. The great advantage of a carbohydrate diet in the Himalayas are that it can most easily be procured locally and that it can be carried in sacks. But it is necessary to supplement it with a small proportion of fat and some form of protein, though most Asiatics seem to be able to get along very well without these additions.

The word "march" with its associations of discipline and routine seemed scarcely applicable to that blissful saunter over the foot-hills. Beyond setting a time-limit, we had no fixed plan. The distance we covered each day was limited by the pace of the heavily laden Dhotials, and it rarely amounted to more than three or four hours walking, which even in our untrained condition was not very tiring and gave us plenty of time to bathe in pools, to climb a hill for a more extensive view or to practise rock climbing on boulders. One of the things that I enjoyed most was the opportunity of getting to know the Sherpas intimately, which was impossible on either of the two previous Himalayan expeditions I had known. Sharing with them the same life, the same camp fire, the same food and, later, the burden of load-carrying, we soon came to regard them as fellow mountaineers rather than servants and they felt with us the excitement of anticipation and the joy of success. We were admitted to their endless jokes and their occasional philosophical talk. We relied upon their judgment as much as upon our own.

Much has been written about the Sherpa, and he certainly deserves the praise he has been given. Besides a natural mountaineering skill, toughness and an ability to carry heavy loads, which are shared by most hill people, the peculiar qualities that make him such an admirable companion on an expedition are his inexhaustible humour and love of nonsense, his individuality, his great sense of loyalty, his willingness and ability not only to undertake but to seek out a job that needs doing and a pride that does not turn easily to sophistication. His trust in his employers is, I think, an acquired rather than a natural virtue, and I have known it to break down.

But for all their lovable qualities, it is as well to remember that there are good and bad among the Sherpas as among all other people, and not an unusually large proportion of good. This fact has very often been overlooked. Many expeditions coming out from Europe, have sent word to Darjeeling to order so many Sherpas to be sent to meet them at their particular starting point, just as one might order pack-mules. Often they have received very inferior material, either raw lads with no real mountaineering experience or the riff-raff of the Darjeeling bazaar. These unfortunates have then been called upon to tackle severe climbing propositions and to undertake responsibility that was wholly beyond their capacity, sometimes with disastrous results. Even among the good Sherpas each man has his own peculiar characteristics. One may be a superb load-carrier, and very agile on difficult ground, but lacking in intelligence; another may be intelligent and reliable in normal circumstances, but very highly strung and liable to break down under stress; another may be a born leader and a bad mountaineer, another only able to give his best under the influence of a strong personality among his companions. There is no end to the variety of these combinations. The Sherpas are essentially individualists, and they do not take kindly to mechanical discipline.

Mrs. Townend, the Secretary of the Eastern Section of the Himalayan Club, has done a great deal towards the organisation of the Sherpas. Every man who has taken part in serious expeditions has been given a little book in which is entered his past record together with a note written by each of his employers. But this cannot be expected to act as a wholly reliable guide. The leader of an expedition employing hundreds of men cannot have much insight into the character of each of them; further, anyone with experiences of references will realise that employers are not always honest in what they write; moreover a man who has performed a prodigious feat of endurance in 1924 might be a drunken sot by 1934. When employing Sherpas on an expedition involving serious mountaineering, or long periods when any kind of crisis may arise, one is not justified in asking any one of them to undertake responsibility without a pretty shrewd knowledge of his physical and moral capacity. This may seem a heavy demand from someone without previous experience of the Himalayas. But actually, so long as not more than, say, half a dozen Sherpas are employed, it is not difficult to get to know them well if one is prepared to take the trouble. The first thing, of course, is to obtain as much really reliable information about them as possible before starting, and not merely to accept a few eulogistic references; then to make a point of becoming on intimate terms with them on the march; and then to study them closely in the early stages of the climb. The personal element is by far the most important on any climbing or exploratory expedition. In difficult circumstances, the presence of one weak member in the party is a far more serious handicap than any lack of equipment.

If possible, it is a good plan to find one good Sherpa, whose judgment is absolutely reliable, and to give him a large share in the choice of his companions. In this I may have been exceptionally lucky, and admittedly I have based the theory largely on one outstanding example.

The development of the Sherpas has a long way to go before even the best of them become guides in any way comparable with those of the Alps. Personally, much as I like and admire them, I cannot envisage this. Their environment and their temperament are so totally different; the Himalayas are so vast and the opportunities for practice of really difficult mountaineering so rare, that they can never achieve anything like the same standard of technical excellence as a first-rate Alpine guide. But for unselfish loyalty, for strength and endurance, for sureness of foot and steadiness of head, for resourcefulness in all kinds of conditions, and as delightful companions, the best of them are unbeatable.

It was more by luck than by good management that Tilman and I had such a remarkably good trio in 1934. Pasang I knew fairly well as he had acted as my private servant during the march across Tibet in 1933. He was tall and slim, with fine, aristocratic Mongolian features. He was really a Bhotia (Tibetan) from Shigatse, but there is so much intermingling between the Sherpas and Bhotias that I think of them all as Sherpas, who, in fact, have formed the large majority of the men employed by expeditions. The Sherpas proper came from two districts, Sola and Khumbu in the north-east corner of Nepal, though many of them have recently migrated there from Tibet. Pasang was highly-strung and temperamental, sometimes absurdly sentimental and often moody. When he was on form nothing could stop him, when depressed he required tactful handling. Luckily on this occasion he had two very steady companions, which helped to maintain a balance. He was a beautiful mover on difficult ground, and consequently rather a brilliant rock-climber. He had been among the eight who carried Camp VI to 27,000 feet on the 1933 Mount Everest Expedition.

I had chosen Angtharkay for his remarkably fine performance in weathering the storm at Camp V and then volunteering to carry to Camp VI. Beyond that I knew nothing about him. He was small even for a Sherpa, but very well built. We soon learned to value his rare qualities, qualities which made him outstandingly the best of all the Sherpas I have known. He had a shrewd judgment both of men and of situations, and was absolutely steady in any crisis. He was a most lovable person, modest, unselfish and completely sincere, with an infectious gaiety of spirit. He has been with me on all my subsequent journeys to the Himalayas, and to him I owe a large measure of their success and much of my enjoyment.

I had intended to have another Camp VI man, Rinzing, to complete the party, but he was engaged elsewhere and Angtharkay had brought Kusang in his place. The latter had joined the 1933 Expedition from Sola Khumbu, but as he had only been employed on the glacier, I do not remember having seen him. He was by far the youngest of the trio, and very raw. He hardly spoke any Urdu. He was not remarkable for his intelligence, but he was very strong, quite imperturbable, and, under Angtharkay's leadership, absolutely reliable. To us it seemed that he was rather put upon in the matter of work. But the performance of domestic chores seemed to be his chief delight, and he was never idle – tending to the fire, fetching wood, scrubbing pots and plates, darning socks, greasing boots, washing clothes. In spite of our strict censorship of his personal belongings, he somehow contrived to smuggle with him some cakes of soap. When occasion demanded he could carry a prodigious load, and he always took more than anyone else.

One of the most delightful things about the Sherpas is their extraordinary sense of comradeship. During the six months we were together, I never once detected the slightest sign of dissension among our three. There are few Europeans who can live in close proximity to each other for long without an occasional quarrel or divergence of opinion. Often, on the numerous occasions when I was irritable and quarrelsome, I was made to feel thoroughly ashamed of myself by the example of the Sherpas. This quality of theirs is due largely, I imagine, to their robust sense of humour. It hardly ever failed. Each enjoyed jokes against himself as delightedly as those which he perpetrated. Two of them would conceal a heavy rock in the load of the third, and when, after an exhausting climb, this was discovered, all three would be convulsed with mirth. I do not consider it a compliment that they did not try out this one on us, though I was glad they did not. They were forever laughing and chatting together as though they had just met after a prolonged absence.

Nine leisurely days took us from Gwaldam, across the Kuari Pass, with its magnificent views of the great peaks of the Central Himalayas, to the valley of the Dhauli River at its junction with the Rishi.

CHAPTER TEN

Nanda Devi

LOVELY though our ten-day march across the foot-hills had been, we were glad when it came to an end. We had been speculating for so long upon the nature of our curious problem that we were most anxious to get to grips with it. The idea of this stupendous gorge that had guarded for so long the secret shrine of Nanda Devi was fascinating, and filled us with a pleasant mixture of eager anticipation and fear for what we should find. The unbroken series of fine days too, had worried us, for although we had the whole summer before us, we knew that once the monsoon broke towards the end of June our chances of success would vanish; and we wished not merely to reach the sanctuary but to explore it.

The gorge of the Rishi Ganga, about twenty miles long, is divided into three sections. The lowest of these is so formidable that no one has yet succeeded in forcing a way through. Graham and his guides tried in 1883, but they were forced to retreat after they had covered some four miles. Later however they out-flanked this section of the gorge by crossing a pass to the north and following a track used by the local shepherds. In this way they succeeded in reaching a point some sixteen miles up the valley before they were forced to abandon their attempt. In May, 1907, Longstaff, Bruce, Mumm and their three Alpine guides attempted this route again, but the pass was still blocked by winter snow. Rather than waste time waiting for this to clear they explored the country still farther to the north. They found their way up the Bagini glacier which flowed down from the peaks forming the north-western "rim" of the Nanda Devi basin. From the head of the glacier they crossed a very difficult pass (Bagini Pass), about 20,000 feet high, which they hoped would lead them into the basin. They found instead that it led them into a valley (Rhamani) which curled round to the south and joined the Rishi Ganga at about the point that Graham had reached. After making their famous ascent of Trisul, Longstaff and his guides tried to find a way along the northern side of the upper gorge. They failed, however, and had not sufficient food with them to explore the southern side. But Longstaff was convinced that there was a way and had advised us to concentrate all our efforts on this southern side.

In this way we had an enormous advantage over our predecessors. All the preliminary work had been done, and the problem was fined down to a single line of possibility. Nor were we likely to be tempted from the gorge by the hope of discovering another entrance to the basin. In the first place repeated attempts had been made from every side to find a way in, and secondly it would have taken us many weeks to make our way round to the north, east or south sides of the amphitheatre.

Our first objective, then, was to reach the junction of the Rhamani and Rishi rivers with sufficient food to give us time to find a way through the upper gorge, and, if we were successful, to explore the country beyond. It was not much past the middle of May, and we knew that masses of snow would still be lying on the pass we must cross into the middle section of the Rishi Ganga. But to have waited for this to clear would have left us with too little time before the arrival of the monsoon. We had intended to engage eighteen men in the Dhauli valley to accompany us as far as the Rhamani junction, who would then leave us there and return. These men, as well as providing local knowledge, would be more adept at travelling over difficult country than the Dhotials who earned their livelihood by carrying loads along well-made paths in comparatively civilised country. But ten of the Dhotials were so tremendously keen to come on with us that we agreed and decided only to take eight local men. This was a lucky decision, for after the first day the local men deserted us. This produced a serious crisis, and the situation was only retrieved by the gallant Dhotials who agreed to carry most of the abandoned loads as well as their own. I am sure they had no idea what they were in for, and many times in the days that followed they refused to go any farther. Moreover, our obvious lack of knowledge of the country made it difficult to inspire them with confidence. However, the prospect of receiving the wages of the deserters in addition to their own turned the scale in our favour.

For the best part of two days we fought our way through soft snow up to our knees, our waists and occasionally up to our armpits. Tilman and I, lightly laden, went ahead to flog the trail, while the others struggled along behind with their enormous loads. Twice, after exhausting effort, we reached a saddle which we hoped was the pass, only to find a sheer drop of several thousand feet on the other side. The third time we were lucky.

Once in the valley beyond the pass we descended below the spring snow-line, and life was more comfortable. But the huge scale of the country made route-finding very difficult, and over and over again we reached an impasse and were forced to retreat to try another line. This was terribly disheartening for the Dhotials, but they stuck to it splendidly. As we went, their loads became lighter by the amount of food that was eaten, and by the dumps of tsampa which we left each day for their return journey.

It was a most magnificent place. The southern side of the valley was built up of tier upon tier of gigantic, steeply inclined slabs, which culminated 10,000 feet above the river in a multitude of sharp rock spires set at a rakish angle, while beyond them stood great ice peaks. The northern side, along which we were travelling, was broken up into a series of glens. Some of these contained little alps, each a fairy garden of birch and pine trees, deep grass and drifts of flowers, aflame with colour, each secluded from the savage world outside by precipice and crag.

Unfortunately we had little "time to stand and stare", for now we had a fresh reason for haste. The Dhotials had to be fed, and each day we spent in getting to the Rhamani junction meant that we would have three days' less food for the work beyond. We were by no means certain of inducing them to go as far. As we advanced, "the valley grew narrow and narrower still", and its sides became steeper and steeper. The Dhotials liked the look of it not at all. Their protests became stronger and more difficult to overcome. Mercifully the weather held; a single day of mist, rain or snow would have stopped us, and we would have been faced with the laborious task of relaying the loads the rest of the way to our base by ourselves. Actually, in spite of our many mistakes and setbacks and by driving the unfortunate Dhotials through all the daylight hours, we covered the distance in the time allotted – six days from the Dhauli River – and arrived at the Rhamani junction by nightfall on the 28th of May. To emphasise our good fortune, a storm which had been brewing for some time past, broke five minutes before we had found a suitable site for our base camp, and heavy snow fell throughout the night.

The next morning we paid the Dhotials the reward they had so richly deserved, and parted with them on the best of terms. They expressed reluctance at leaving us alone in such a fearsome spot, and we for our part were very sorry to see them go, for they had served us well, and we had become very fond of them.

I have never been able to decide whether, in mountain exploration, it is the prospect of tackling an unsolved problem or the performance of the task itself, or the retrospective enjoyment of successful effort which affords the greatest amount of pleasure. Each provides emotions so widely different; each has its particular limiting factor – restless uncertainly, fear and fatigue, or regret for an enchanting problem that is no more. Certainly no situation has provided me with greater happiness than that in which we found ourselves at the mouth of the upper gorge of the Rishi Ganga. Four miles of canyon, one of the mightiest in the world, separated us from the untrodden country beyond. We had sufficient food to last us for five weeks. Whether we succeeded or failed, nothing but a bad accident could deprive us of some of the best weeks of our lives.

Our base camp was on a narrow strip of shore, covered with birch jungle, on the southern side of the river. The cliffs, undercut by the action of water, provided us with a snug cave. It was a very pleasant spot for temporary residence; though the lack of sunlight, the sense of confinement and the thunder of the river, amplified by echo, might have become irksome had we been forced to stay there long. The immediate prospect was far from encouraging. A few yards beyond the strip of shore the river issued from a perfect box-canyon, whose vertical sides were smooth and almost unbroken. However, a little gully above the camp enabled us to climb beyond the overhanging cliffs to easier ground. Two thousand feet above the river we reached the first of a series of broken terraces which ran along the side of the gorge.

It took us nine days to find a way and to relay our food and equipment through the remaining four miles of the gorge. It was exhilarating work, for until the last moment the issue was in doubt, and each section of our route appeared to rely for its practicability upon the slender chance of a rock fault. Apart from the immense scale of the precipices, the weight of our loads precluded any really difficult climbing, except in short vertical sections where the baggage could be hauled up on the rope. The last mile of the gorge looked so unpromising that we tried to force our way up the river bed itself by zig-zagging from side to side. This attempt provided our most exciting adventure, as the force of the current was terrific. It was perhaps fortunate that it did not succeed, for later, as the ice of the glaciers started to melt more rapidly, the river became very swollen, and we would certainly not have succeeded in getting back that way. Defeated there, Pasang and I then tried to find a way along the northern side of the gorge, while Tilman and Angtharkay explored the remainder of the southern side. We failed to make any headway, but the other two discovered the last frail link of the chain, and we entered the Nanda Devi basin with enough food for three weeks.

We set about our task of exploring the basin with a feeling of great exultation. After the confinement of the gorge, the freedom of movement about wide open country was a delicious contrast. The exquisite joy that any mountaineer must experience in treading new ground lent a special charm to everything we did and saw; even our clumsy toil with the plane-table yielded deep satisfaction as a form of self-expression. It was glorious country; gentle moorland grazed by herds of bharal (wild sheep), and in places gay with Alpine flowers; small lakes that reflected the surrounding mountains; deep lateral valleys holding glaciers, enclosed by a hundred magnificent peaks of clean, strong granite or glistening ice and snow. Out of the centre of the basin rose the wonderful spire of Nanda Devi, 13,000 feet above its base, peerless among mountains, always changing and ever more lovely with each new aspect, each fresh effect of colour and cloud.

Three weeks was not long enough to explore the whole of the basin, so we decided to concentrate upon the northern half, and to return to survey the southern half in September when the monsoon should be over. This plan had an additional advantage, as we wished to find another way out, over one of the ranges that formed the "rim" of the basin; to have done so now would have interfered with our programme for the monsoon season in the Badrinath range to the north. We had many more fine days than bad, and the weather seldom hindered us. We rarely bothered to pitch a tent as we found it so much pleasanter to sleep in the open, even at our higher camps. It seemed somehow to provide a continuity between rest and action, to deepen the sense of harmony between ourselves and our surroundings, which even the thin canvas walls of a tent can destroy. In the lower parts of the basin there was a plentiful supply of juniper wood, and there we had the luxury of huge camp fires. Higher up we had to be more economical though we generally managed to carry some wood up with us so as to avoid using a stove. Though we were concerned mainly with exploring and mapping the country, we were able to combine this with some mountaineering on the higher peaks. We reached three saddles on the western and northern "rim" of the basin, each more than 20,000 feet high. We climbed a peak of 21,000 feet, and made an unsuccessful attempt to climb another of about 23,000 feet. On each occasion we had wonderful views of the basin itself and over the great ranges outside it.

The monsoon came gradually towards the end of June, and its arrival coincided with the exhaustion of our food supplies. Meagre dumps had been left at various places in the Rishi Ganga. We returned down the gorge in torrential rain; tussles with the swollen waters of the river and of side streams provided the main excitement. The gorge was even more impressive in foul weather than in fair. Particularly I remember one night of heavy storm. I was snugly wedged in a little recess between two boulders listening comfortably to the hiss of the rain outside, and to the thunder which, echoing along miles of crag, maintained an almost unbroken roll. Lightning flickered continuously upon the grim precipices and upon cloud banners entwined about buttress and corrie. The sense of fantasy was heightened by the semi-consciousness of a fitful sleep. At one moment it seemed that I was perched on an eagle's nest above an infernal cauldron of infinite depth, at another that I was floating with the mist, myself a part of an unearthly tempest.

July and August were spent in exploring the range of mountains which forms the watershed between the three main sources of the Ganges. It is a country full of romantic legend. Most of this is rather difficult to follow without a deep study of Hindu mythology, but mountain legend is always fascinating. Our chief object was to link up the three main affluents of the Ganges, the rivers Alaknanda, Bhagirathi and Mandakini, by passes leading across the range direct from one to another.

The determination of the actual source of a great river is often a matter of conjecture, since the choice may lie between streams with various claims to the title. First there is the traditional source, ascribed by ancient history or local legend. An example of this kind is to be found in Ptolemy's remarkable statement that the Nile was born of two small, bottomless wells situated in the

"Mountains of the Moon" – a statement made nearly two thousand years before any recorded visit to the upper reaches of the Nile. Dr. Humphreys discovered in Ruwenzori two tiny lakes of immense depth which gave rise to a stream which formed part of the head-waters of the great river. Some Hindu mythology ascribes the source of the Ganges to a beautiful waterfall which forms a tiny tributary of the Alaknanda river. Modern geography demands a more concrete claim: the stream which rises the farthest in a direct line from the river's mouth; the stream whose waters travel the greatest distance; the source that supplies the greatest volume of water.

There is nothing in my experience more fascinating than finding and crossing an unknown pass across a mountain range. The more important the watershed, geographically speaking, the more satisfying is the achievement, but even the crossing of a minor pass can be an exciting experience. To my mind it is mountaineering at its best, for it combines in even measure so many branches of the craft: accurate appreciation of the country as a whole, judgement of difficulty, anticipation of unknown factors, technical skill and disposal of resources. Then there is the eager speculation upon the difficulties of the other side, the thrilling moment when these are revealed and the enchanting descent into the new world beyond. The view, too, from a pass is often much more satisfying than that from a high peak, for, though less comprehensive, it reveals the surroundings more in their true perspective: the mountains are not dwarfed, and there is not the same mass of jumbled detail.

Our first plan was to cross the range from Badrinath to the Gangotri glacier, the largest in the Central Himalayas, to explore its unknown upper reaches and to work our way down to the source of the Bhagirathi at its foot. In 1912, C. F. Meade and his two Alpine guides had reached the watershed from the Bhagat Kharak glacier, but they had not descended to the other side of the range. This was therefore the obvious way of approach. But when we reached its foot we judged that the route to Meade's saddle was in danger of being swept by ice avalanches from the peaks above. In this I think we were mistaken. However, as there seemed to be no alternative route across the main watershed from the upper basin of the Bhagat Kharak, we crossed a series of passes to the north. This led us eventually into the glacier system above the Arwa valley, where we had spent a fortnight after climbing Kamet, three years before. From there we crossed the main watershed and descended a long tributary which joined the Gangotri glacier only two or three miles above its snout. We went on down to the source of the river, and then returned over the range to Badrinath.

These activities occupied us during most of July, and at the beginning of August we started on the second half of our monsoon programme. This proved to be considerably more exacting than the other. Our plan was to cross the range, this time from Badrinath to Kedarnath, another famous Hindu shrine. No route was known to exist across the range between these two places, but among the many legends of the country was a story that many hundred years ago there was no high priest of Kedarnath Temple, and that the high priest of Badrinath used to hold services in the temples of both places on the same day. The tradition of the Lost Pass is a common one in mountains of Central Asia.

From the head of the Satopanth glacier we reached a saddle, 18,400 feet high, on the crest of the main watershed. We arrived there in thick mist and falling snow, but on the following morning there was a brief clearing which revealed a discouraging view of the other side. The glacier forming our saddle descended in a steep ice-fall for about a thousand feet, then it flattened out into a fairly level stretch of ice before heeling over for a final tremendous plunge into the blue depths of a gorge 6,000 feet beneath us. We began to have a healthy respect for our reverend predecessor.

After some search we managed to find a way down through the first ice-fall on to the terrace. But the next part of the problem was much more formidable. The angle of the ice below increased steadily, and it soon appeared that we were on the upper part of a hanging glacier. We worked over to the right and descended for a few hundred feet before we were brought up by an impassable crevasse. Then we tried on the left, and on the following morning succeeded in roping down into a narrow gully between the ice and the containing rock wall of the glacier.

The forest-filled valley below appeared very enticing from the icy steep above, but when eventually we reached it we soon changed our opinion. The undergrowth in the forest was so dense and the sides of the valley so steep that we could rarely cover more than a mile a day. Side streams, too, caused us a lot of trouble, for they were generally at the bottom of deep ravines and always in spate. One of these held us up for two days before we found a place at which we could bridge it. It rained incessantly and with considerable vigour, so that our loads soon became waterlogged. This precipitated a crisis in the food situation. We had already spent longer over the job than we had anticipated, and now our small supply of tsampa had become as sodden as everything else, despite the fact that it was packed in canvas bags. It went bad, and we suffered such acute stomach-ache when we ate it in this condition that we jettisoned the remainder. To add to our troubles, a falling rock hit Pasang on the foot and, I think, broke a small bone, so that he could only just get along without a load, and from then on was no more than a passenger.

The main concern of the Sherpas was their fear of bears. Having no experience of Himalayan bears, Tilman and I were able to take the menace more calmly. Actually we only encountered one of the creatures at close quarters, and he ambled off as soon as we came upon him round a corner. That we did not meet more was probably due to the din the Sherpas made as we went along, designed to scare them away, for their spoor was everywhere. But the bears were a nuisance in that they were our rivals in the difficult matter of feeding.

We owed our salvation, or at least the fact that we did not land ourselves in a considerably worse mess, largely to the woodcraft of the Sherpas. First and foremost they provided us with food by their knowledge of edible plants. Our staple diet was bamboo shoots. This delicacy only occurs in its edible form for a short season of the year, and it was fortunate for us that it was then in season. The shoots were anything up to 8 feet long, but only an inch or so below each notch was edible. However, except where a hungry bear had forestalled us, it was fairly easy to collect a pot-full of the little green cylinders, which, boiled, constituted our evening meal. It was quite a good dish; with a little imagination, not unlike asparagus. But, though the shoots could also be eaten raw as we went along, they were insubstantial food to sustain the long hours of heavy physical labour that our progress demanded. Once we found a fairly large quantity of an edible forest fungus. Boiled, it had the negative taste of overstewed meat, but it was pleasantly satisfying.

Each night Angtharkay and Kusang displayed considerable skill in constructing a bamboo shelter under which we could light a fire. On the first night this appeared to me an impossible undertaking, but it was not beyond the ingenuity of the Sherpas. By pounding some sodden sticks of dead bamboo with a stone, and holding the pulp over a series of lighted matches it eventually took the flame. This was fed by more dead bamboo until there was a sufficient blaze to dry and ignite logs of wood, and in a couple of hours we would have a good fire. Fortunately we had a large supply of matches that had been safely stowed in a pair of sheep-skin gauntlets. We halted at about five o'clock each evening so as to give ourselves time to construct a platform if necessary, to build the shelter and light a fire under it and to collect bamboo shoots and fuel. After that we would strip off our sodden garments and roast our naked bodies by the fire until we went to sleep.

The work during the day was rather exasperating. An endless succession of rocky, bramble-filled gullies made the going exceedingly slow and laborious, so that frequently it took us an hour to cover 25 yards. In some places a cliff or ravine would force us to climb many hundreds of feet. We had to maintain our altitude so as to avoid getting out of bamboo zone. But in other places the going was good, and the day's toil generally yielded about a mile of progress.

Apart from the problem of food, which was worrying, it was not on the whole an unpleasant experience; the days were full of vital interest, the nights warm and comfortable, and the forest was wild and beautiful. Anyway, whatever discomforts and anxieties were our portion, these were amply repaid when at length we reached a tiny hamlet consisting of three houses and some fields. The hamlet provided us with a dry billet in a barn, four pounds of flour, a cucumber, some dry apricots and the happy knowledge that our struggle with the forest was at an end and that a well-worn path would lead on down the valley to the Kedarnath pilgrim route.

In September we went up the Rishi Ganga again. The difference between this and our previous journey was even more striking than the difference between the first and second ascents of a peak, for the size of the valley had laid more emphasis upon the problem of finding a route than upon actual difficulties. We had covered the ground so often in the process of relaying loads and knew so exactly what lay round each corner and how long each section would take, that now it was hard to believe that we had experienced any difficulty on the first occasion. For once I was keeping a day to day diary, and it was interesting to read over the entries made on the first occasion. This time we were only two days getting through the upper part of the gorge from the Rhamani junction, and we took local men with us right through into the Nanda Devi basin before we discharged tham and sent them back. By then the monsoon was spent and we had a long spell of fine weather.

The geography of the southern section of the basin was simple and our rough plane-table survey of it did not take long. First we set out to climb a peak (since named Maiktoli), 22,320 feet high, and situated on the southern "rim" of the basin. We pitched a camp at 20,000 feet, but just before we reached this point Tilman became ill with "mountain sickness" and had to return with Pasang. The following day, Kusang, Angtharkay and I climbed the peak from which we had a most magnificent view. Even the gigantic southern face of Nanda Devi was dwarfed by the very extent of the panorama. The Badrinath peaks, Kamet, the Kosa group, Dunagiri and the great peaks of the northern part of the Nanda Devi basin, all mountains amongst which we had been travelling for the past four months, served merely as a foil to set off the stupendous ranges lying beyond Milam and across the borders of western Nepal. What a wonderful field of exploration lay there – the heritage of some future generation.

Tilman, for all his strength and mountaineering competence, appeared to be quite unable to acclimatise to high altitudes. It seemed that his ceiling was about twenty or twenty-one thousand feet, and on the several occasions when we went above that altitude he became ill. Though he was supremely fit, he was no better in this respect at the end of the season than he was at the beginning.

One of the chief interests on our second visit to the basin, was to find a route by which Nanda Devi could be climbed. The northern side, which we had seen on our first visit, was utterly impregnable and the great western ridge scarcely less so. This left two alternatives; firstly an ascent of the east peak of the mountain from the south, and thence along the crest of a tremendous curtain of rock, two miles long, to the main peak; secondly a route up the great south ridge of the main peak. The former we ruled out owing to its immense length, and to the appearance of the connecting ridge, which was serrated and probably knife-sharp, and which maintained an altitude of some 24,000 feet throughout. But the south ridge, though formidable, was by no means hopeless. It swept up in a great curve from the floor of the basin at about 17,000 feet to the summit, 25,660 feet. Though steep it maintained a fairly uniform angle and was broad enough to allow the choice of alternative routes up its difficult sections. Its great advantage was that there was no long and complicated approach, and that its base was within easy reach of juniper fuel so that it could be reached by porters without special high-altitude equipment.

With only two tents, one Primus stove and very little kerosene, our boots full of holes and now almost devoid of nails, we were obviously in no position to make a serious attempt to climb Nanda Devi. But we could at least climb some way up the ridge and get a pretty good idea of the nature of the difficulties. We camped near its foot on a little alp covered with grass and snowy edelweiss, and on the following day climbed some three thousand feet up the ridge. We would have had time to go farther, but Tilman again felt the effects of the altitude and began to vomit. But we had gone far enough to see that the ridge was practicable. We had encountered no serious difficulties, and though there might be plenty ahead, the uniform angle of the ridge and its width made it unlikely that any of these would prove to be insurmountable by a thoroughly competent party. It would be no easy task, and in my judgment, not one for a large, heavily organised expedition. But what a prize! There is no finer mountain in the world. Its graceful beauty from every aspect was a source of inspiration and wonder as the Matterhorn had been to Alpine mountaineers in the middle of the nineteenth century. And what finer setting than a hitherto inviolate sanctuary?

Finally we set about the achievement of our long cherished ambition, to find an exit from the basin over some portion of its "rim". The southern segment offered us two alternatives. One was a saddle reached by Longstaff and his guides in 1905 in their attempt to reach the basin from the east, the other was a depression on the southern "rim", which Ruttledge and his guide Emile Rey had attempted in 1932. Both these ways were likely to prove extremely difficult. At first we were inclined to favour "Longstaff's Col", for he had proved the practicability of its farther side by climbing it from that direction; also it was the lower of the two. But its western aspect looked so formidable that we decided to attempt the Sunderdhunga Col, as the southern saddle was called. We had seen that we could reach it easily from the north, but Ruttledge's description* of its southern aspect was far from encouraging: "Six thousand feet of the steepest rock and ice . . . Near the top of the wall, for about a mile and a half, runs a terrace of ice some two hundred feet thick; in fact the lower edge of a hanging glacier. Under the pull of gravity large masses constantly break off from this terrace and thunder down into the valley below, polishing in their fall the successive bands of limestone precipice of which the face is composed. Even supposing the precipice to be climbable, an excellent mountaineer may be acquitted on a charge of lack of enterprise if he declines to spend at least three days and two nights under fire from this artillery. An alternative is the choice of three knife-edge arêtes, excessively steep in their middle and lower sections, on which even the eye of faith, assisted by binoculars, fails to see a single platform large enough to accommodate the most modest of climbing tents."

I had seen something of this precipice from the summit of Maiktoli which stood immediately above the saddle, and the view confirmed Ruttledge's description. But it is a very different matter to get down such a place carrying a small quantity of food, and to force a way up it with the prospect of being cut off for weeks from further supplies. We should be able to move much more rapidly over the danger areas, and to rope down ice-cliffs and other obstacles that might otherwise have been impossible or very difficult to climb; though of course we should be handicapped in the choice of a route. Anyway, we decided to give it a trial, and leaving a dump of food in the basin against our probable failure, made our way to the saddle.

We reached it one morning and spent the rest of the day trying, in bad visibility, to find a point from which to start the descent. First we tried to reach the rock arêtes or ridges that Ruttledge had referred to as being out of range of the ice avalanches from the hanging-glacier terrace. We could see the top of the first one through the mist on our left, but we could not reach it. Then we tried to the right but were brought up short on the brink of the ice terrace overhanging the ice-polished limestone cliffs that plunged out of sight. It was a fine spectacle. Every now and then enormous masses of ice would break away from the cliffs on which we were standing and crash with a thunderous roar into the

* *The Times*, August 22nd, 1932.

cloudy depths below. It is not often that one has the opportunity of watching a display of ice avalanches from so close, and rarer still to see them breaking away from the very cliffs on which one is standing.

Our only alternative now was a narrow ice-fall lying between the terrace and the three arêtes, and of which we could see no more than a few feet of twisted and riven ice. There was nothing to do but to go straight for it and worry our way down by a tedious process of trial and error. However, we had plenty of food with us, and so long as we could keep out of the line of bombardment from the terrace we could afford to take several days over the job if necessary. It was strenuous work trying line after line without success, but as the evening wore on our energy seemed to increase – a phenomenon I have often noticed in mountaineering. A series of slender ice-bridges suspended over space by some conjuring trick of nature would lead us downwards to the brink of an impassable chasm. Then a wearisome retreat by the way we had come, to try a new and perhaps equally futile chance. The farther we went the more complex became the precipitous maze we were in.

The next morning we waited until the sun was up before starting again, as our clothes had become sodden in the soft snow of the previous day and an early start would probably have resulted in frost-bite. It was a most lovely dawn. In the right and left foreground were the icy walls, steep-sided and grim, enclosing the head of the Maiktoli Valley; in front, beyond the brink of the ice ledge on which we were camped, and immensely far below, was a lake of vivid colour, at the bottom of which we could see the Sunderdhunga River coiling like a silver water-snake, away into a placid cloud-sea which stretched without a break over the foothills and the plains of India.

The day was one of vivid life and heavy toil. Hour after hour we puzzled and hacked our way down, lowering our loads and ourselves on the rope down an ice cliff, chipping laboriously across the steep face of a tower or along a knife-edged crest, sometimes hopeful and sometimes despairing. The ice-fall stood out in high relief from the mountain-side, so that we were fairly well protected from the ice avalanches, which started falling again in the heat of the afternoon. Evening found us working on dry ice three thousand feet down, and it was becoming increasingly clear that we must soon find a way off the glacier which evidently overhung at its base. Beside us to our right was a prominent rock ridge, which, though lying immediately below the higher line of hanging glaciers, offered us a heaven-sent alternative if only we could reach it. We cut steps to the edge of the glacier and from there we looked down a sixty-foot ice-cliff into a steep gully of polished slabs. It was obviously a path for ice-avalanches, but it was narrow and once in it we could cross to the farther side in a couple of minutes. By chipping away the ice in a circle we fashioned a bollard from which we roped down the wall into the gully. A short race across it took us to a little ledge under an overhang on the ridge, which offered a convenient and well-protected site for a camp. No sooner had we pitched the tents than there came a mighty roar from above and for fully a minute a cascade of huge ice blocks crashed down the gully sending up a spray of ice dust, while a number of ice splinters landed harmlessly on the tents.

The day, begun with the sight of a dawn beautiful beyond description and crowded with lively experience, closed with us stretched luxuriously on our ledge, perched high up amongst the precipitous glaciers of one of the grandest of mountain cirques. Lightning flickered somewhere in the east; the distant thunder was almost indistinguishable from the growl of avalanches. Mists floated stealthily in and out of corries above us forming and dissolving in an ever-changing pattern. Far to the south a placid sea of cloud still stretched over the foot-hills, and the silvery light of a full moon lent to the scene an appearance of infinite depth. It was our last high camp that year, for by the evening of the following day we had reached the foot of the precipice and we slept that night on grassy meadow-land.

Our exit from the sanctuary by way of the Sunderdhunga Col provided a fitting climax to our season of joyous freedom and high mountain adventure – the best five months that either of us had known. We considered the idea of setting out on some new project, but autumn was already well advanced, boots were ragged and funds running low; the break had to be faced sometime, and the perfection of the whole might be spoilt by some minor or uncompleted venture. So we set our course for home.

The march back added a rich store of memories: a struggle to find an exit from the grim gorge in the upper Sunderdhunga valley, into which we had blundered in a heavy mist; our last encounter with a swollen mountain torrent; an enormous feast of wild raspberries and Himalayan blackberries lower down the valley; the generous hospitality of the first villagers we met, and the sweetness of their honey; the sparkling sunlit mornings as we lay sleepily watching the smoke of some distant wood fire mounting straight up into the clear air above the pine forest; a dawn on the distant ice-clad giants whose presence we had just left.

Our venture had met with more success than we had anticipated, and it was sufficient unto itself. But it had a splendid sequel. Two years later, in 1936, a party composed of four British and four American mountaineers came out to climb Nanda Devi. Unfortunately for me I was engaged elsewhere that summer and could not join them, but Tilman was among the party. They agreed among themselves to have no leader, but Tilman with his recent experience naturally played a prominent part in the business of organisation and in the difficult task of reaching the foot of the mountain. He went out to India some months ahead of the others, and after preliminary training in Sikkim, he made the journey to the Rishi Ganga, and, with the help of seven Sherpas and some local men carried the bulk of the expedition's stores and equipment through the gorge. Then he returned to Ranikhet in time to meet his companions. They had a difficult time getting up the gorge again owing to torrential rain, but at length they succeeded in establishing their base camp at the foot of the south ridge of Nanda Devi. Once on the mountain six of the seven Sherpas they had brought proved useless and remained below. This was no one's fault, because the Everest Expedition that had gone out earlier had taken nearly all the good men. The seventh Sherpa, Pasang Kikuli, had a severe attack of snow-blindness at the start and was completely incapacitated. So the entire work of carrying the loads up that formidable ridge, on which five camps were established, fell on the climbers. This in itself made their performance unique in the annals of Himalayan mountaineering. Tilman had seen to it that nothing but the barest essentials were taken.

In a climb of this sort the credit for success is shared by each member of the party. Each step of the way calls for a high standard of mountaineering skill and judgment, and the man who reaches the summit owes his achievement as much to the competence of his companions as to his own. Tilman, in a most astonishing manner, found his high-altitude form. This may have been partly due to the psychological result of his responsible position, though I suspect that sheer strength of will had something to do with it. But whatever the cause it enabled him to share with Odell the exquisite pleasure of reaching the summit of that wonderful peak.

In my opinion the climbing of Nanda Devi is the finest mountaineering achievement ever performed in the Himalayas. It was certainly a brilliant example of a light expedition. More daring and desperate feats have been performed and perhaps greater skill displayed, as for example, in the Bavarian attempt to climb Kangchenjanga; but after all success counts a lot. Incidentally Nanda Devi, being some two hundred feet higher than Kamet, is still the highest mountain ever climbed.

Not content with that, Tilman, Houston and Pasang Kikuli, later crossed Longstaff's Col over the eastern rim of the Nanda Devi basin.

After returning from the Everest Expedition that year, I was invited to accompany Major Osmaston of the Survey of India who had been detailed to make a photographic survey of the Nanda Devi basin. We met the party (except Tilman and Houston) in the lower part of the Rishi Ganga on their way out. Peter Lloyd and Graham Brown were a couple of days ahead of the others, and it was from them that we heard the news of the climb. I had met Lloyd many times in the Alps in the twenties, and it was a delightful reminder of old days to see his tattered figure coming towards me and to ask the familiar question, "Well, did you get up?" Yes, I felt a pang of envy. But it was grand to hear that Tilman had reached the summit.

And there were a hundred other compensations: to revisit the sanctuary and climb again on the surrounding mountains; a swift attempt on the great peak of Dunagiri; the second crossing of the Bagini Pass; the exploration of the beautiful Rinti Nala and the crossing of a pass at its head; to wander among the forests and glaciers south-west of Trisul enchanted by the exquisite autumn colouring, the brilliant monal pheasants rocketing up into the clear, frosty air of late November, the hillsides of long, golden grass moving in the wind . . . Oh! but there is no end to it. No life-time is long enough to absorb the wonder of that country.

CHAPTER ELEVEN

Everest 1935, 1936, 1938

It soon became apparent that Mount Everest was the most immediate barrier to the enchanting plans that had begun to crowd upon my imagination. Having once taken a share in the attempts to climb the mountain, it was hard to stand aside. Although the problem now appeared one of restricted scope, it was no less fascinating. Any one year might yield the right conditions for an unhampered climb up that last, thousand-foot pyramid of rock upon which so much eager speculation had been lavished. It was like a gambler's throw, in which a year of wide opportunity in untrodden fields was staked against the chance of a week of fine weather and snow-free rock. In those days it was not realised how slender was that chance. In 1933 we thought that we had been unlucky with the weather; but never again was it to treat us so well.

When we returned to England in the winter of 1934, Tilman and I set to work at once upon plans for our next venture. He, too, had abandoned himself to a life of self-indulgent freedom. Our plans were well advanced and a grant of money had been obtained, when, early in 1935, permission came for another attempt upon Mount Everest. This time the permission covered two years, 1935 and 1936. It was considered too late to organise a full-dress attempt upon the mountain in 1935, but the Mount Everest Committee invited me to take out a reconnaissance expedition in 1935 prior to the main attempt in 1936, which was again to be led by Ruttledge.

The objects of the 1935 expedition were to try out new men and to give them some preliminary training in high altitude mountaineering, to examine snow and weather conditions on the mountain during the monsoon and to investigate the possibility of climbing it during that season, to experiment with equipment and food, to obtain further data regarding acclimatisation, to train a nucleus of high-altitude porters, and to carry out a sterio-photogrametric survey of the glaciers lying to the north of Mount Everest and of as much of the surrounding country as possible.

At first Tilman did not like the idea of abandoning our plans – I think the idea of travelling with a large party oppressed him – but after a little discussion he waived his objections. Two things attracted me to the scheme: the prospect of being free for several months to wander among the peaks and valleys surrounding Everest, which had not been possible on the 1933 expedition, secondly the opportunity which it offered to demonstrate the possibility of running an expedition at little cost and the advantages of the light over the heavy organisation.

Besides myself, six others were invited to join the party: Edwin Kempson, who had had very wide experience of Alpine mountaineering both in winter and summer; Charles Warren, a doctor with some Himalayan and much Alpine experience; L. V. Bryant, one of the best-known New Zealand climbers; Edmond Wigram, a medical student who had done a lot of climbing in the Alps; Tilman and Michael Spender. Chief among Spender's wide interests was the introduction of sterio-photogrametric methods of survey into England. He had studied the subject for two years in Switzerland and Germany, had taken part in a long scientific expedition on the Barrier Reef and in two Danish expeditions to Greenland, and had worked for some years at the Geodetic Institute in Copenhagen. I budgeted for a total cost of £1,400 – or £200 per head – including travelling expenses to and from India.

We left Darjeeling in May and travelled up the Tista Valley, crossing from Sikkim into Tibet by way of the Kongra La. Our caravan consisted of thirty-five transport animals – seven of which were carrying Spender's delicate apparatus – fifteen Sherpas, Karma Paul the interpreter, and ourselves. From the Kongra La, instead of joining the old route by way of Kampa Dzong, Tengkye and Shekar, we kept south, along the foot of the main range to Sar. We were in no great hurry and had decided to devote a little of our time to the exploration of the Nyonno Ri range which lies to the north of the great Arun Gorge. For this we made our base at Sar where we were most hospitably received by the Dzongpen. We did not reach Rongbuk until about the 6th of July.

While on the march we lived largely off the country. Mutton was easy to procure, though at first the sheep were rather thin. We cooked the meat in pressure cookers and the result was a great success. Where transport presents no problem and fuel is scarce these gadgets are well worth their weight; they overcome in twenty minutes the resistance of even the toughest meat. We could generally get potatoes and onions, though until later in the summer other vegetables were not obtainable. However we had brought out dried vegetables from England, and these provided us with quite a good substitute. Eggs were always plentiful in the villages, and though many of them were rather stale we consumed enormous quantities. Our record was 140 in a single day between four of us, and many times our combined party of seven put away more than a hundred. Tilman could bake an excellent loaf with the local flour and the dried yeast which we had brought as a supply of Vitamin B. Excellent butter made from yak's milk was always available. So food presented no problem while we were in inhabited parts of Tibet; appetites were healthy and no one was inclined to be fussy about lack of variety.

Food for life at high altitudes was a more serious question. I had developed an exaggerated antipathy towards tinned food, largely as a result of two expeditions on which it had been used almost exclusively. There is no doubt that food embalmed in tins, however cunningly, lacks some essential quality, and when one is fed on nothing else one very soon becomes heartily sick of even the most elaborate delicacies. I believe that to be one of the reasons why we had found it so hard to eat enough at high altitudes in 1933. That year I had been given the job of running the commissariat. At first everyone was loud in praise of the fare, and I was always having to emerge from the mess tent to open another tin of this or that to satisfy rapacious appetites. Long before we had reached the Base Camp this enthusiasm had died down; before the expedition had run half its course the complaints against the food were bitter and endless, and to these I had lent strong support. Actually the quality of the tinned food could hardly have been improved; we had every conceivable variety – half a dozen different kinds of breakfast food, bacon, ham, beef, mutton, chicken, lobster, crab, salmon, herrings, cod-roes, asparagus, caviare, foie gras, smoked salmon, sausages, many kinds of cheese, a dozen varieties of biscuit, jam, marmalade, honey, treacle, tinned and preserved fruit galore, plain, nut-milk and fancy chocolates, sweets, toffee, tinned peas, beans, spaghetti – I cannot think of anything that we did not have. And it was supplied in such quantities that, rather than transport what was left all the way back from the Base Camp we threw away scores of cases of provisions. And yet, one and all, we agreed that the food was wholly unsatisfying. It seemed to me that the conclusion was obvious – and it was amply confirmed by my subsequent experience. But it was by no means universally accepted, and the majority were inclined to blame the firms that had supplied the food.

In 1935 I went rather too far the other way: it was bad policy to force people who were quite unused to rough food to make such a sudden and complete break with their normal diet. Taken in moderation, tinned food undoubtedly has its uses, particularly when – as on Mount Everest – transport presents no particular problem. But it should be used to supplement fresh, salted or dried food, rather than as the main diet. A perfectly simple compromise is possible on an Everest expedition. If, for example, the party were kept on a diet of fresh food supplemented with untinned ham, bacon and cheese until it reached a point well beyond the Base Camp, such things as tinned brisket of beef and chicken's breasts would then provide a most welcome change of which people would not tire, at least during the critical weeks of the actual climb. I would dispense altogether with caviare, lobster, crab and the like. These are no doubt very delicious when eaten in suitable surroundings, properly served, washed down with the appropriate wine and followed by a comfortable cigar; but I find that they lose all their charm when eaten as a mangled mess out of a battered tin on which someone has probably cut his finger.

I had made a fairly close study of this problem of diet during the previous winter. Dr. Zilva of the Lister Institute had very kindly devoted a good deal of time to helping me to devise a suitable diet. I induced each man to keep a simple chart of his daily food consumption so that one could see at a glance how far he was conforming to the balance and quantity prescribed. For the first few weeks, even at the quite moderate altitudes of the East Rongbuk glacier, no one succeeded in consuming more than 1,500 calories a day. This was very far short of the 4,000 calories advocated by Zilva – I doubt if anyone ever approached this figure while we were on the glaciers. However I think the charts succeeded in their main purpose which was to make people watch their feeding and force themselves to eat when otherwise they might have been too lazy or preoccupied to do so. Certainly the party displayed a very satisfactory output of energy throughout the expedition.

We left Karma Paul to amuse himself at Rongbuk and to organise foraging parties to collect a stock of eggs, butter and sheep from the north, and while

Spender was busy with his work the rest of us went up the East Rongbuk glacier. Conditions were much more pleasant than when I had been there before, and having had some previous training on the Nyonno Ri mountains we climbed from Rongbuk to Camp III in three days.

About three hundred yards above Camp III we found the body of Maurice Wilson, who had attempted to climb Mount Everest alone the previous year and about whom nothing more had been heard. From a diary which we found on his body and from subsequent enquiries we were able to piece together his curious story. He was a man of about thirty-seven and had served in France during the last war. He had developed a theory that if a man were to go without food for three weeks he would reach a stage of semi-consciousness on the borderland of life and death, when his physical mind would establish direct communication with his soul. When he emerged from this state he would be cleansed of all bodily and spiritual ills; he would be as a new-born child but with the benefit of the experience of his previous life, and with greatly increased physical and spiritual strength. Wilson had fanatical faith in his theory. He believed moreover that he had seen a vision in which he had received divine instruction to preach the doctrine to mankind. Somehow the word "Everest" had featured in the vision, and he thought that it was intended to indicate the means by which he could achieve his purpose. Obviously if he succeeded in reaching the summit of Mount Everest single-handed, the feat would cause no small stir, and his theory would receive wide publicity.

He knew nothing whatever about mountaineering. At the time, however, the Houston Everest Flight was receiving considerable press publicity. Presumably this gave him the idea that if he were to fly a plane as high as he could and crash it on the side of the mountain he would be able to climb the rest of the way to the summit and return on foot. So with this object in view he learnt to fly, bought a small aeroplane and set out for India. At Cairo he was stopped and turned back by the authorities. But eventually he reached Purnea in India where his machine was confiscated. He went to Darjeeling where he stayed for four months, training himself and making secret preparations for his journey to Mount Everest. He got in touch with some of the Sherpas who had been with us the year before and they agreed to smuggle him through Sikkim and into Tibet. He then covered up his tracks by paying for his room at the hotel six months in advance so that he could keep it locked with his things inside, and gave it out that he had been invited by a friend to go on a tiger shoot. It was some time before the authorities discovered that he was missing.

In the meantime, by wearing a disguise and travelling at night he had succeeded in passing through Sikkim and into Tibet. There he travelled more openly, but with practically no baggage and by avoiding the big places he and his three Sherpa companions attracted no attention. When they arrived at Rongbuk he told the abbot of the monastery that he was a member of the 1933 expedition and induced him to hand over a few small items of equipment that we had left there. He had evidently made a good impression upon the old man, who, when we visited the monastery in 1935 talked to us a great deal about him. He left the Sherpas at Rongbuk and started up the glacier alone with the complete conviction that he would reach the summit in three or four days. He had with him a small shaving mirror with which he proposed to heliograph to those at Rongbuk from the summit, so as to provide proof that he had actually reached it. He was used to starving himself and intended to live on a small quantity of rice water. It was early in April and he encountered the usual spring gales on the East Rongbuk glacier. He appears to have reached a point somewhere about Camp II before he was forced to retreat, exhausted.

After a fortnight's rest he set out again, this time with the Sherpas. They reached Camp III and the Sherpas showed him a dump of food which we had left about half a mile beyond, and which contained all kinds of luxuries such as chocolate, Ovaltine, sardines, baked beans and biscuits, with which he was delighted. He left the Sherpas at Camp III and went on alone. He had evidently expected to find intact the steps which we had cut in the slopes below the North Col, and he was bitterly disappointed to find nothing but bare wind-swept ice and snow. Though he had an ice-axe, he did not know how to use it and could make little headway up the slopes. He camped alone on the rocks near the dump and set out day after day to renew his fruitless attempts to reach the Col. Though he had plenty of food, he was gradually weakened by the severe conditions. This was clear from the entries in his diary, which became shorter and less coherent towards the end. But he would not give up and still clung to his faith in divine inspiration. The last entry was on the 31st May, 1934. He died in his sleep, lying in his small tent. This had been smashed by storms, and all the fragments, except the guy-lines which were attached to boulders, had been swept away.

The Sherpas said they had waited a month for him at Camp III. This is clearly untrue for they would certainly have visited the food-dump from time to time and would have found the body. We had two of the men with us in 1935, but one had been attached to Spender's party and the other had been sent down to fetch some stuff from Camp II on the day that we found the body. We buried it in a crevasse.

It had been generally supposed that it would be useless to attempt Mount Everest during the monsoon. But there was little practical evidence to support this belief. Before 1933 complete faith had been placed in the advent of a fine spell during the few weeks immediately preceding the arrival of the monsoon, and the exploration of further possibilities was thought unnecessary. This faith however was somewhat shaken by our experience in 1933. Some people expressed the opinion that the monsoon season would offer a better chance of success than the late spring. These ideas were, I believe, based largely upon experiences in the Karakoram and those of the Bavarians on Kanchenjunga in 1929 and 1931. One of our jobs in 1935 was to investigate the matter.

There were two factors: the risk of avalanches on the slopes below the North Col and the condition of the snow on the upper part of the mountain. Regarding the former we had little evidence, and of the latter we had none. In 1922 a disastrous avalanche had overtaken the party attempting to reach the North Col in June. In June 1933, Crawford and Brocklebank had reported that the slopes were dangerous (Crawford had himself been involved in the 1922 avalanche). On the other hand in 1921 the North Col had been reached safely in September; but with all respect to Mallory's skill as a mountaineer this may have been due more to luck than to good judgment. In the Alps the study of snow conditions has been reduced to an exact science, but we are still very ignorant about Himalayan snow. It was believed that the dangerous conditions prevailing on the North Col in June were caused by the wind blowing the newly fallen snow from the west side of the Col and depositing it at a low temperature on the eastern slopes, thus producing what is known as "wind-slab", one of the most vicious of all conditions of mountain snow. But it seemed reasonable to suppose that these causes might not be operative later in the summer.

When we arrived there towards the middle of July, 1935, we examined the slopes below the North Col with extreme care. Kempson had had wide experience of winter mountaineering, in the Alps, and by now I had seen a good deal of Himalayan snow conditions. We could find nothing wrong with the slopes. With ten Sherpas it took us three easy days to establish a camp on the crest of the col. On the first of these days we had a slight contretemps with the Sherpas. They had evidently been shaken by the discovery of Wilson's body and regarded it as a bad omen. So half way up to the Col they refused to go any further. However a heart to heart talk in camp that evening set the matter right and after that we had no more trouble.

Warren, Kempson and I and eight Sherpas occupied the camp on the North Col with enough food to last us for at least sixteen days. We intended to push on up the mountain at least to 27,000 feet to see what the conditions were like up there. Actually we were in a position to make a strong attempt on the summit if these had proved to be good. The whole of the north face was plastered with snow and very little rock was showing. At lower levels the heat of the sun and the cold nights would have combined in a short time to pack the snow and provide a splendid surface up which one could climb without difficulty. The weather for the past fortnight had been very fine. But it was thought that practically no melting takes place above about 26,000 feet, and that except where it is subjected to great pressure the snow remains powdery. It was our object to prove or disprove this theory. We had seen in 1933 how difficult it was to climb those upper slabs with even a slight covering of powder snow; a blanket of this substance covering the whole face to a depth of perhaps eight or ten feet would present an impassable obstacle. If on the other hand the snow were to consolidate in the normal manner, the mountain would be a great deal easier to climb during the monsoon than at any other season.

The weather deteriorated and we waited for four days on the North Col. One day we climbed some way up the north-east spur for exercise, but it seemed unwise to establish the higher camps until the weather improved. At length we decided to retreat to Camp III and to wait until the bad spell had spent itself. We had the whole summer before us and it would be best to preserve our condition. So we left tents and stores on the Col and started down. We were disconcerted to find that 200 feet below the crest of the Col the entire surface of the slope had slipped away for a distance of a quarter of a mile and to a depth of six feet. The resulting avalanche had crashed down on to the glacier below. The snow that we had examined with such care, about which we had been quite satisfied and over which we had been blithely working for three days had been completely rotten.

The term "justifiable risk" is used a good deal by mountaineers, particularly when discussing fatal accidents. It is meant to imply that degree of predictable danger to which, according to the general body of mountaineering opinion, a party is entitled to expose itself. But obviously each man must determine his own standard, and there must be a tacit agreement on the matter among the members of any climbing party. Opinions vary widely according to temperament, between those who regard mountaineering as an exact science whose rules must never be broken and the "death or glory" attitude of the climbers of the north face of the Eiger. Particular circumstances, too, will exercise an influence; for example, one is likely to accept a narrower margin of safety on the final pyramid of Mount Everest than during a holiday climb on the

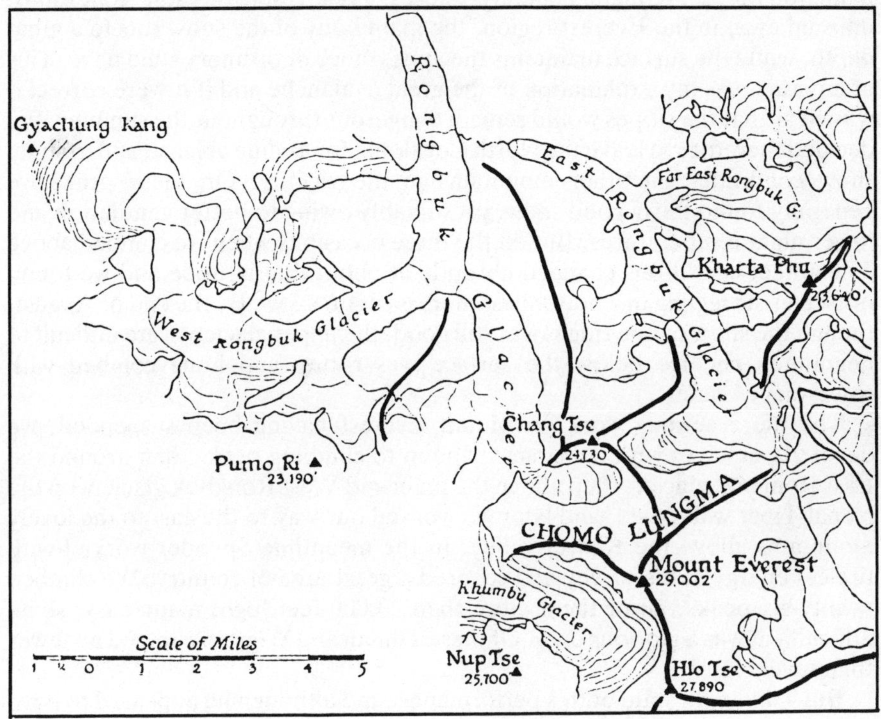

Matterhorn. There can be few mountaineers who have not at some time run the gauntlet of some obvious danger for the achievement of a particularly enticing goal. Most of us have done it more times than we can remember. But in making a route up a great Himalayan peak the position is altogether different. Each section of the route has to be traversed not once but many times, and generally by slow, heavily laden men, many of whom are not trained to act correctly in a moment of crisis. One may pass beneath a tottering serac nine times, to be buried by it on the tenth. A competent mountaineer involved in a snow avalanche can often save himself by going through the motions of swimming on his back, but even without an awkward load strapped to his back a Sherpa porter is unlikely to have the presence of mind to do this. I am sure that no one could have escaped from an avalanche such as that which broke away below us while we were lying peacefully on the North Col.

Two things were clear: first that the slopes below the North Col were not safe, and secondly that we were not competent to judge snow conditions at that particular time and place. I am quite satisfied that the avalanche was not caused by "wind-slab". The eastern slopes of the North Col form a semi-circular basin, unusually well protected from the wind. The mid-day sun in July, only six degrees from the vertical, beats down with tremendous force upon the stagnant air of this blinding-white cauldron. On occasion I have suffered more from the heat on the snow slopes of the North Col, at 22,500 feet, than I ever have on the plains of India. At night it barely freezes. As a result of these conditions, unusual even in the Everest region, the main body of the snow rots to a great depth, while the surface maintains the appearance of ordinary solid névé. This at any rate was my explanation of the great avalanche and if it were correct it was clear that the slopes would remain dangerous throughout the summer. We decided therefore to leave the North Col alone, for a while at least, and to study snow conditions on other mountains in the vicinity. On these peaks we generally found fairly good snow, presumably owing to better ventilation and lower night temperatures. But on the three occasions when we climbed above 23,000 feet conditions changed abruptly at about that altitude and we found ourselves struggling in a bottomless morass of soft snow. By the end of August, though the snow on the ridges was still good, the upper glaciers were difficult to negotiate. The ice below the surface was rotten and honeycombed with reservoirs of water.

The more serious work on Mount Everest having been suspended, we devoted ourselves with delicious abandon to climbing peaks, first around the East Rongbuk glacier, then above the main and West Rongbuk glaciers on the Nepal-Tibet watershed, and later we worked our way to the east to the lovely mountains above the Kharta valley. In the meantime Spender worked with tireless energy at his survey and covered a great area of country. We climbed twenty-six peaks, all of them more than 20,000 feet high, many easy, some difficult – it was a glorious orgy. Of these Tilman and Wigram climbed no fewer than seventeen.[1]

But Tilman, in spite of this performance, and although he appeared to have raised his ceiling to perhaps 23,000 feet, was still unable to acclimatise himself to these altitudes. Even to reach 23,000 feet appeared to require an enormous effort; and, as late as the end of August after he had already climbed many high peaks, he became very ill, while he, Wigram and I were making an abortive attempt to climb the North Peak. Bryant took even less kindly to high altitudes. His troubles had begun before we had crossed into Tibet and he became ill again in the Nyonno Ri range. When we reached the East Rongbuk glacier he vomited almost continuously for ten days and could not keep down any solid food. In August he recovered a bit and was able to climb peaks of nearly 22,000 feet. I climbed alone with him for a fortnight above the West Rongbuk glacier: I

1 Shipton's original account of this expedition is reprinted as Appendix 1 (page 777).

have never had a more delightful companion – cheerful, humorous and supremely competent. It seemed a tragedy that two men so eminently suited, both temperamentally and technically, to take part in the attempt on Mount Everest, should be debarred from doing so by a slight physical peculiarity. Though they were both bitterly disappointed, neither of them questioned my inevitable decision. Tilman's attitude may be judged from the fact that, later, he subscribed towards the funds of the 1936 expedition in which he was to take no part, although he had other plans of his own. Nothing could have been a more fitting reward than his remarkable achievement on Nanda Devi.

I would have liked to continue with our travels throughout the winter, for besides the intense interest of exploring those ranges there were many questions regarding conditions at high altitudes during the winter months that required (and still require) an answer. But I had promised to return to England to assist in the preparations for the expedition of the following year.

EVEREST 1936

The 1936 Everest Expedition was a bitter disappointment. Camp IV was established on the North Col early in May, but continuous bad weather compelled us to retreat. After a brief rest at Camp I we returned to Camp III. But we were soon forced to realise the almost unbelievable fact that the monsoon was already established. We waited there for some days as though hoping for a miracle. From sheer exasperation Wyn Harris and I set out to climb the North Col. It was a ridiculous thing to do, but we were feeling rather desperate. A strong wind had been blowing from the west for many days, sweeping great masses of newly fallen snow over the col and depositing it on the eastern slopes; there had been heavy night frosts; ideal conditions for the formation of "wind-slab". We climbed quickly over a lovely hard surface in which one sharp kick produced a perfect foot-hold. About half way up to the Col we started traversing to the left. Wyn anchored himself firmly on the lower lip of a crevasse while I led across the slope. I had almost reached the end of the rope and Wyn was starting to follow when there was a rending sound – "rrumph" – a short way above me, and the whole surface of the slope I was standing on started to move slowly down like a descending escalator towards the brink of an ice cliff a couple of hundred feet below. Wyn managed to dive back into his crevasse and to drive his ice-axe in to the head and twist the rope round it. I collapsed on to my back and started to perform the frog-like motions prescribed by the text-books, though this was obviously not going to help me much if I were carried over the ice cliff. My principal feeling was one of irritation at having been caught in such an obvious trap. Before it had travelled far the slope began to break up into great blocks. Presently the rope became taut between my waist and Wyn's axe, my swimming was arrested, the blocks began to pile up on top of me and it seemed clear that either I or the rope must break in two. However, before either of these events occurred the avalanche miraculously stopped. It is probable that Wyn's quick action had saved the situation. The slope was not particularly steep, the avalanche had not developed much momentum and the fact that it stopped at that critical instant suggests that the modicum of support afforded by my body held up by the rope was sufficient to arrest it. I was completely winded by the pressure of the rope round my waist, but otherwise unhurt. Having extricated ourselves we went slowly down to the glacier where we met Ruttledge hurrying up with a rescue party. He and the others had watched our inglorious performance through field-glasses from Camp III and were not unnaturally alarmed by it.

Except for a tentative examination of the western approaches of the North Col from the main Rongbuk glacier there were no further activities on Mount Everest that year.

EVEREST 1938

There was another attempt in 1938. This time it was decided to send out a smaller expedition, and Tilman was placed in charge. He decided on a party of seven climbers and budgeted for a total expenditure of £3,000. The weather in 1938 was almost an exact replica of that experienced in 1936. By flogging a way through deep snow in the upper Lachen valley we reached Rongbuk earlier than ever before. With a team of thirty Sherpas, we laid the usual dumps up the glacier and established Camp III about the 20th of April. The usual spring gales were blowing on the mountain and there was every sign that we had struck a "normal season". It was clear that until the gales abated there was nothing to be gained by pushing on up the mountain, and everything might be lost. We supposed that our chance would come during the last ten days of May and the first half of June. On this assumption we had a clear month to spare and it was agreed that this could best be employed by improving the health of the party. Every member was suffering in a greater or less degree from the usual coughs, colds and influenza. It was decided therefore to leave the bulk of the stores and equipment at Camp III, and, travelling as lightly as possible, to cross the 22,000-foot Lhakpa La. Then after spending a week or ten days of rest and fat living in the pine forests of the lower Kharta Valley we would return to Camp III about the middle of May. We had already been up the North Col slopes and had found the route to be comparatively easy. Our acclimatisation would last and we would have the enormous advantage of being thoroughly fit and free from bronchial troubles which had always been a great bugbear on Everest. Physiologically the decision was thoroughly sound and the plan is well worth the consideration of future parties. We started to put it into effect on April 26th.

L'homme propose, Dieu dispose. Monsoon conditions were established on the mountain by May 3rd, and from that date the north face presented the appearance of a sugar cake that had been our despair in previous years. To avoid any further adventures with "wind-slab" avalanches we retreated to Camp I and from there made our way up the main Rongbuk glacier to the western foot of the North Col. We succeeded in reaching the Col from that side, and in establishing Camp IV, but I doubt if the performance was justifiable in the existing conditions. The narrow combe which led to the foot of the slopes was menaced by avalanches both from the south-east face of the North Peak and from the north face of Everest; a big avalanche had come down from the latter a few days earlier and we camped amidst its debris. The slope leading to the col was of tremendous length, continuously exposed and very steep. Except upon the upper three hundred feet, a layer of snow about three feet deep had recently slipped away, leaving a surface of bare ice. Though this was solid enough, it provided no safe anchorage throughout its entire length, and a slip by one of the heavily laden porters would have been almost impossible to hold. To my mind there is no question about the wisdom of Mallory's judgement in rejecting the route.

But we were lucky. The whole expedition reached the Col without mishap. It was the beginning of June; we had sufficient resources in men and material on the North Col for three or even four leisurely attempts upon the summit; the weather was pleasant; we were all very fit. The only fly in the ointment – a pretty sizeable one – was the deep blanket of snow that covered the whole north face from head to foot. Still, there was a slender chance that the scientific prophets were wrong and that soon we would find ourselves kicking steps up the dreaded Black Band in good firm snow. We became quite optimistic.

Tilman, Lloyd, Smythe and I went up the north-east spur with about fifteen Sherpas and established Camp V at our old site, at 25,700 feet. Lloyd used oxygen. It was the first time that the much discussed apparatus had received a practical trial on the mountain since 1924. The going, though harder than it had been in 1933, was not altogether discouraging. Smythe and I remained at Camp V with eight Sherpas, while Tilman and Lloyd returned to the North Col with the rest. We stayed for two nights at Camp V owing to a strong wind on the intervening day, and started on up the spur on the second morning.

Above Camp V the conditions rapidly deteriorated. Everything was buried deep in soft, feathery snow into which we sank up to our hips. Little buttresses fifteen feet high, that before had caused us scarcely a moment's hesitation now presented us with really difficult climbing. On one of these I became badly stuck and wasted a lot of time until Smythe found an alternative route. It was terribly heavy work, even for the porters who had merely to follow in the trail we had flogged. It was 4.30 p.m. before we reached the foot of the Yellow Band a little way beyond and directly above the head of the north-east spur. It was high time to stop, so as to give the Sherpas time to return to Camp V before dark. Two of them had collapsed a little lower down, and while a platform was being built and our tent pitched two others went down to retrieve their loads. The only concern of the Sherpas was to put our camp high enough to give us a chance of reaching the summit. Frequently they asked us if we had gone far enough. But they were all terribly tired. Even had there been time it would have been quite impossible to pitch a tent anywhere on the Yellow Band.

The height of our camp was about 27,200 feet. It was considerably more comfortable than our Camp VI of 1933 had been, and we slept very well. We were free from throat troubles and had deteriorated physically very little compared with our state five years before. Nevertheless we experienced the well- remembered feeling of helplessness, of being only half alive.

We started the next morning before the sun had reached the camp and plunged immediately into a morass of powder snow below the Yellow Band. Soon our extremities had lost all feeling and we returned to the camp and waited until about nine o'clock when there was more warmth in the sun. Then we set off again with the intention of reaching the crest of the north-east ridge, now only three hundred feet above us. A direct line was impossible and we climbed diagonally up to the right. The conditions were absolutely hopeless. There was no sign that the snow had consolidated anywhere. An hour's exhausting toil yielded no more than half a rope's length of progress. Nor was this by any means the most potent factor. Had it been simply a matter of ploughing a way through many feet of soft snow, we might somehow have contrived to get a large party up to Camp VI and, by working continuously in a series of shifts for a week, to force a way along to the top. But in those conditions the smallest movement even on the moderately steep rocks of the Yellow Band was excessively dangerous. It was the knowledge that we were climbing beyond all reasonable limits of safety that induced us to abandon the attempt. Even if we had been able to reach the Black Band, to have climbed its difficult rocks would have been as impossible as it would have been suicidal to attempt it. We were now completely convinced that when it is covered by its blanket of monsoon snow, the upper part of the north face of Mount Everest is absolutely unclimbable. From where we were, near the top of the north-east shoulder, the peak looked very impressive and very frightening.

We returned to Camp V where we met Tilman and Lloyd on their way up for the second attempt. We were anxious that they should continue, so as to corroborate our evidence. They could make no more impression on the rocks of the Yellow Band than we had. Lloyd used oxygen all the way from the North Col to Camp VI and on their short climb above. He said that he derived a good deal of benefit from it, but Tilman was going well and the difference in their performance was not sufficient to be in any way conclusive.

We had intended to descend from the North Col by the western route, but Ondi became ill and Pasang, who had also accompanied us to Camp VI, had become paralysed all down his right side. It was obviously impossible to get these two men down by the way we had come, so we were forced to risk a descent by the eastern slopes. Poor Pasang had to be lowered all the way on the end of a rope, or dragged along the horizontal traverses like a sack of coals. He could neither speak nor move. Some months later he recovered his speech and could hobble about, but the paralysis unfortunately proved to be a permanent affliction.

One day Mount Everest will be climbed; of that there can be little doubt. It may be achieved at the next attempt; there may be another twenty failures. From the evidence we have at present it would appear that success will demand a combination of circumstances which in the very nature of the conflicting components is not common. In the spring, northerly gales render climbing on the north face practically impossible. These gales are neutralised by the advent of the monsoon currents blowing up from the south. The monsoon however deposits powder snow upon the mountain which again renders the steep upper rocks unclimbable. This snow neither melts nor consolidates, and the only agent which clears it away is the north wind. We have always relied upon a short period of quiet weather immediately preceding the monsoon precipitation. But was it reasonable to assume that such a period is the rule? Our experiences in

1933, 1936 and 1938 would certainly suggest that this is not the case. From an examination of photographs taken during the attempts in 1922 I should say that there was far too much snow on the rocks to have permitted a crossing of the Black Band. Only once, then, in June, 1924, has the upper part of the mountain been found in a condition which offered any real chance of success. Unfortunately the climbers were then already too exhausted to take full advantage of their opportunity. Nevertheless I believe that the pre-monsoon period is the only possible one.

But there are those who hold that the winter (November, I think, is the month advocated) is the right time for attempting to climb Mount Everest. As far as I know this view is not shared by anyone who has climbed high on the mountain. The risk of frost-bite even in June is deadly at that great elevation. The noon altitude of the sun over Mount Everest in November is only about 43 degrees, which means that the rocks on the north face would be in shadow for all but a very few hours of the day, and it is doubtful if sunlight ever reaches the upper part of the Great Couloir during the winter months. The cold would be intense, far worse than anything that we have hitherto experienced up there; the slightest breeze would inevitably result in severe frost-bite. All the Sherpas with whom I have discussed the matter are agreed that October and November are months of heavy wind during which they experience great hardship in crossing the passes from Nepal to Tibet. However it would be foolish to dogmatise. The mountain should certainly be attempted in the winter by those who believe in the plan, so long as they have a clear understanding of what they are up against and are determined not to allow their disappointment to get the better of their sense of proportion, which is very liable to happen on Everest. Actually we had intended in 1938 to stay there throughout the winter, so as to examine the conditions. But we evolved another plan which unfortunately did not materialise.

I believe that the best way of tackling the job would be to obtain from the Tibetan Government permission covering five consecutive years in which to run a series of small expeditions. Each should include four mountaineers with wide Alpine as well as high-altitude experience; its main object would be to attempt the mountain in the usual pre-monsoon period, but it would also have secondary scientific objectives, among which physiological research might well take pride of place. Such a series would not be expensive to run, as the bulk of the equipment could be dumped at Rongbuk on the first occasion for use of the subsequent expeditions. It would not be necessary to have the same party each time, though it would be as well for one man to remain in charge during the whole period, so as to co-ordinate the scientific work and to accumulate first-hand experience of conditions on the mountain. It is probable that at least one of the five consecutive years would provide the fairly late monsoon which appears to be a necessary condition for that period of calm weather and snow-free rocks experienced in 1924. Four thoroughly competent climbers with proved ability to go high would be ample to take full advantage of such an opportunity. In addition, with careful organisation, an ambitious programme of valuable scientific work could be undertaken. Winter conditions on the mountain could also be investigated.

With regard to the tactical plan to be adopted on the upper part of the mountain, I am convinced that it is a mistake to keep men for too long on and above the North Col. I believe that in 1933 too much emphasis was laid upon acclimatisation. Admittedly many of us were forced to live above the North Col for longer than had been intended; but the whole policy had been one of slow advance. When we returned to the Base Camp we were terribly emaciated. It was a standing joke that we looked like a collection of famine-stricken refugees. In 1938 we were far fitter both while on the mountain and when we returned. For this reason alone I should be opposed to attempting to establish a third camp above the North Col, and there are many other strong objections. It has been amply shown that the establishment of two high camps can be a simple and rapid operation. No doubt a better site could be found for Camp VI than that used in 1933. I believe that under good conditions the porters could carry from Camp V to the foot of the First Step where Wager and Wyn Harris found a good place for a camp. From there to the Couloir is a very short distance. If in good conditions the climbers could not reach the summit from such a camp it is doubtful if they could ever do so.

The wide interest which the Mount Everest Expeditions aroused among the non-climbing public, the great confidence of each successive expedition in its ability to reach the summit and the fact that several parties have been forced to turn back when success was apparently almost within their grasp, have caused a good deal of perplexity and perhaps have made the repeated failures seem rather foolish. To see the matter in its true perspective it is well to remember that in spite of all the attempts that have been made during the last sixty years upon the giants of the Himalayas by climbers of many nations, not a single mountain of 26,000 feet has yet been climbed. Most prominent among these attempts were the repeated, desperate and sometimes disastrous German efforts to climb Kangchenjunga and Nanga Parbat. There were no fewer than five German expeditions to Nanga Parbat in the nineteen-thirties. On the first of these in 1932, the climbers appeared to come so close to their goal that when I discussed the prospects of the second attempt in 1934 with the leader he appeared to regard its success almost as a foregone conclusion, in much the same way as we had assessed our chances on Everest in 1933. It would seem almost as though there were a cordon drawn round the upper part of these great peaks beyond which no man may go. The truth of course lies in the fact that, at altitudes of 25,000 feet and beyond, the effects of low atmospheric pressure upon the human body are so severe that really difficult mountaineering is impossible and the consequences even of a mild storm may be deadly, that nothing but the most perfect conditions of weather and snow offers the slightest chance of success, and that on the last lap of the climb no party is in a position to choose its day.

In this connection it is not irrelevant to reflect upon the countless attempts to climb the Matterhorn before the summit was finally reached in 1865 – attempts by the best mountaineers, amateur and professional, of the day. Compare the two problems. The Matterhorn could be attempted on any day in each successive summer; attempts upon the summit of Everest have been launched on, at the most, two days of a few arbitrarily chosen years. The upper part of the Matterhorn could be reached in a single day from a comfortable hotel in the valley so that the same party could set out day after day to attempt the climb, gaining personal knowledge and experience of the problem with each successive effort; no man has yet succeeded in making more than one attempt upon the summit of Everest in any one year – few have tried more than once in a lifetime. Climbing on the Matterhorn is an experience of supreme mental and physical enjoyment; life on the upper part of Everest is a heavy, lifeless struggle. The actual climbing on the Matterhorn is no more difficult than that on the last two thousand feet of Everest. Today the Matterhorn is regarded as an easy climb for a competent party in reasonably good conditions. And yet year after year it resisted all the efforts of the pioneers to climb it; many proclaimed it to be unclimbable. It was certainly not that these men were incompetent. The reason must be sought in that peculiar, intangible difficulty presented by the first ascent of any peak, to which reference has been made in an earlier chapter. How much more should we expect this factor to play a part in the defence of the great peaks of the Himalayas!

No, it is not remarkable that Everest did not yield to the first few attempts; indeed, it would have been very surprising and not a little sad if it had, for that is not the way of great mountains. Perhaps we had become a little arrogant with our fine new technique of ice-claw and rubber slipper, our age of easy mechanical conquest. We had forgotten that the mountain still holds the master card, that it will grant success only in its own good time. Why else does mountaineering retain its deep fascination?

It is possible, even probable, that in time men will look back with wonder at our feeble efforts, unable to account for our repeated failure, while they themselves are grappling with far more formidable problems. If we are still alive we shall no doubt mumble fiercely in our grey beards in a desperate effort to justify our weakness. But if we are wise we shall reflect with deep gratitude that we seized our mountaineering heritage, and will take pleasure in watching younger men enjoy theirs.

CHAPTER TWELVE

Shaksgam – I

THE great mountain ranges of Central Asia merge so imperceptibly into one another that it is difficult for the ordinary traveller not to regard them as one stupendous mass extending from the middle basin of the Yangtse-kiang in the east to the Hindu Kush and even beyond into Persia – a continuous stretch of three thousand miles. Though possibly the conception is geologically unsound, I have always thought of the division of this mountain mass into separate ranges as analogous, on a vastly greater scale, to the groups into which the Alps are divided; each has its peculiar structure and each its climatic conditions, which provide the whole with such an infinite variety of scene and environment.

But in the case of the mountains of Central Asia the appreciation of this division is rendered more difficult, sometimes by the startling contrasts which occur within a single group and sometimes by the great similarity between one range and its neighbour. For example, Mount Everest rises on its various sides from almost every conceivable kind of mountain country; rounded hills and valleys, utterly barren and desolate; pleasant grassy moorland flanked by gentle Alpine peaks; wide sheets of slightly undulating glacier resembling Arctic ice-cap country; mighty peaks of fluted ice standing above dense tropical rain-forests; deep, sunless gorges – all this within a radius of some twenty miles. On the other hand, there is little difference scenically between the Western Himalayas and the Hindu Kush or between the Pamirs and the Kuen Lun.

There is so much exploratory work to be done in these ranges that once one has become involved in the game there seems to be no end to it. Moreover, each expedition suggests half a dozen other equally attractive plans, every one of which clamours for attention. I had hoped that Tilman and I might soon be able to break away from the influence of this strong attraction and chance our arm in the mountain ranges of Alaska, or in the southern Andes, or in the Sierra de Merida of Venezuela, or in the strange mountains of New Guinea. But with the widening of our Central Asian horizon these plans receded into the more distant future. Obviously there were some things that we must do first, before we could claim even a passing acquaintance with our present field. One of these was a journey in the Karakoram, the greatest concentration of lofty peaks in the world. Here, it seemed from all accounts, nature had spread herself on a truly titanic scale. I was told by Longstaff and Bruce that I would never believe in the existence of such country until I had seen it for myself.

Sheer size by itself is no attraction, though it often enhances the value of other characteristics. For example, I have never been very impresed by the

10,000 feet of precipice forming the north face of Mount Everest, though the wonderful architecture of the south-eastern combe of that mountain owes much of its beauty to its immensity. St. Paul's is beautiful in itself, but an exact model on half the scale would not be nearly so impressive. I find the Eiffel Tower neither impressive nor beautiful.

For some reason I had the impression that the country in the Karakoram was bleak, desolate and colourless; a gigantic stretch of unrelieved austerity, devoid of the soft contrast that I find so essential for the full enjoyment of great peaks; the valleys destitute of trees and grass and flowers, the mountains supported by bare desert hills. So it was not without some misgivings that I decided to go there in 1937. Besides, the more I studied the geography of the country, the more doubtful I became whether the technique for light travel that we had evolved for work in the Himalayas could possibly be applied on the vast glaciers of the Karakoram which were on a scale altogether different from anything I had ever seen, and in country where we would be cut off for many months from any habitation. I was most agreeably surprised when I got there to find that none of these gloomy forebodings was justified.

The most interesting of the many unexplored areas of the Karakoram was that lying in the basin of the Shaksgam river, on the northern side of the main range and somewhere on the undemarcated frontiers of Hunza and Ladakh and the Chinese province of Sinkiang. The first explorer to penetrate this part of the Karakoram was Sir Francis Younghusband. In 1887, at the end of his great journey across Asia, from Peking to India, he crossed the Aghil range by what has since come to be known as the Aghil pass. On the southern side of this pass he discovered a river which his men called the Shaksgam. From there he ascended the Sarpo Laggo glacier and crossed the main Karakoram range by way of the Mustagh pass to the Baltoro glacier.

Two years later he again crossed the Aghil pass to the Shaksgam river, which he followed up-stream for some distance. Then he tried to enter the country to the south-west; but failing to make his way up a great glacier, which he named the Crevasse glacier, he made his way, in the late autumn, down the Shaksgam valley, and so reached the Shimshal pass which lies at the north-western extremity of this area.

The next expedition to visit the region was the one led, in 1926, by Colonel Kenneth Mason and financed by the Survey of India. Mason's object was to cross from the Karakoram pass, which lies at the eastern extremity of the Aghil range, to the headwaters of the Shaksgam. From there he intended to work downstream so as to connect up with Younghusband's route, and to fix the geographical position of the Shaksgam river and the Aghil pass. His way was barred by a large glacier, which, coming down from the northern slopes of the Teram Kangri range, dammed the Shaksgam river. The ice was so appallingly broken that it was quite impossible for the expedition to cross the glacier and to continue its progress down the river. Mason named the glacier the Kyagar. His party travelled north into the Aghil range and explored its eastern section. There they were faced by the great difficulties of spending, in an entirely uninhabited area, the long time that detailed scientific work demands. In August they found another large river, which at first they imagined to be the

Shaksgam itself. They were not able to follow it downstream owing to the enormous volume of water that was racing through its gorges. But they went far enough upstream to realise that the river was not the Shaksgam. Mason named it the Zug – or false – Shaksgam. He was compelled to leave the problem of its course unsolved.

In 1929 a party of H.R.H. the Duke of Spoleto's expedition crossed the Mustagh pass into the Shaksgam valley and followed it upstream beyond the point reached by Younghusband.

In 1935 the Dutch explorers, Dr. and Mrs. Visser, whose expeditions in the Karakoram have accomplished such a remarkable amount of work, followed Mason's route and succeeded in crossing the Kyagar and in mapping the great glaciers coming down from the Gasherbrum peaks on the main watershed. They were prevented from going farther down the river by the summer floods.

To the west and north-west of the areas visited by these explorers there was still a very large region of unknown country full of interesting geographical problems. It was the exploration of a portion of this area that was our main object in 1937. We had three principal interests. First, the section that lay between the Sarpo Laggo valley and the Shimshal pass, bounded on the north by the Shaksgam river, an area of about 1,000 square miles. Second, the glacier system lying to the north of K2. Third, the portion of the Aghil range west of that explored by Mason's expedition. The two outstanding problems in this area were to find the lower reaches and outlet of the Zug Shaksgam river, and to fix the geographical position of the Aghil pass which had not been revisited by any European traveller since Younghusband's second crossing in 1889.

The most formidable problem in travelling in the uninhabited regions of the Karakoram is that presented by the rivers. After mid-summer the ice of the great glaciers begins to melt in earnest. When this happens the rivers swell enormously and remain continuously in spate until late in the autumn. In this condition they are quite impossible to ford, while the width of the riverbeds precludes the possibility of bridging, even if timber were available. A party that has crossed one of these rivers, say, in June, and has not recrossed it by the time the floods arrive will have its retreat cut off for perhaps four months.

The bursting of the "Shyok dam" several years ago is a good illustration of the colossal scale of the glacial phenomena in the Karakoram. A subsidiary glacier had advanced across the bed of the Shyok river near its source, thus damming the stream. In time, the weight of the water collected behind the dam burst the ice barrier. Besides causing havoc throughout the length of the upper Indus, the bursting of the dam caused disastrous floods in the plains of the Punjab some six hundred miles away. Similar catastrophes on a smaller scale are common in those parts.

The passes from India to the basin of the upper Indus remain closed until the early summer. This and the winter snow on the far more formidable barrier of the Karakoram range made it virtually impossible for an expedition to reach the Shaksgam early enough to allow a reasonable amount of work to be accomplished before the floods started. Fortunately the bulk of our work lay to the south of the river, though if we were lucky we might snatch three weeks or a month in the Aghil range to the north.

Clearly our best plan was to establish a base somewhere in the middle of the area, so that we would be independent of outside help for the whole period of our stay there, and transport difficulties, once the work was begun, would cause the minimum of delay. The next question was how to achieve this plan. Apart from trying to reach the Shaksgam from China, which would have taken too long even if the political situation in Sinkiang had permitted it, there were three alternatives open to us: first, to cross from the Karakoram pass to the head waters of the Shaksgam and make our way down over the difficult glacier trunks which had defeated Mason's party in 1926; second, to cross the Shimshal pass and force our way up the lower gorge of the Shaksgam before the river became too high: and third, to cross the main Karakoram range from the Baltoro glacier. The first two alternatives would probably have involved considerable difficulties with the river even early in the year, and we might easily have been cut off before reaching a suitable base. Besides this the journey either to the Shimshal or to the Karakoram pass would have been very long and costly, particularly as early in the year as we would have had to tackle it. The third route was much more direct; moreover, the difficulties involved were of a purely mountaineering character, and though we were likely to have considerable trouble in transporting several tons of stores and equipment over a difficult glacier pass early in the year, this route seemed to offer the best chances of success.

The party had to be small, but not so small as to prevent us from taking adequate advantage of our opportunities. Above all, every man must be willing, whatever his other duties, to undertake his full share of load-carrying. Tilman was as keen as ever. Spender was the best man I knew to take charge of the survey, and I was very lucky in getting him to come with us again. Unfortunately the necessity of limiting our baggage to the barest essentials made it impossible for him to undertake any sterio-photogrametric work, and we had to resort to less elaborate methods. I also invited John Auden of the Geological Survey of India to accompany the expedition, and his department kindly seconded him for the purpose. Auden had done a good deal of climbing in Europe and had travelled widely in the Himalayas in the course of his work. In 1933 he had made an expedition to the Biafo glacier in the Karakoram and his knowledge of the first part of our route and of the people was a very great help. Seven Sherpas were engaged. I entrusted their selection to Angtharkay, and his choice proved admirable.

The question of finance was easier than it had been before. I estimated that the total cost of the expedition, including three return passages to India (Auden joined us from Calcutta) would amount to £855. The Royal Geographical Society, the Survey of India and the Royal Society each contributed generously towards the funds.

We assembled in Srinagar at the end of April. I had heard so much about the wonders of Kashmir that I was prepared to be disappointed. I expected to find a place in no way superior to the other Indian hill stations I had seen, and hideously disfigured by the horrors of excessive tourist traffic; in fact a kind of Himalayan Chamonix. I was wrong. The vale of Kashmir is a lovely place. With its wide plains completely surrounded by mountains, its great lakes and placid rivers, its floating gardens, the strange, colourful life of its river-dwelling inhabitants, the peaceful sense of its isolation, the variety and soft friendliness of the side valleys it is quite unlike anything else I have seen. Even the racket of its exploited capital is remarkably unobtrusive, at least to the casual visitor. Admittedly we saw it through rose-tinted glasses, for we were the happy guests of Sir Peter and Lady Clutterbuck, whose kindness and hospitality made our work of preparation in Srinagar a most delightful experience.

The passes leading out of Kashmir to the north are not officially open until June; but by travelling at night it is possible to take a caravan of porters over them a good deal earlier in the year without undue risk from avalanches. We started up the Sind valley from Gangarbal with a caravan of twelve pack-ponies on the 5th of May. We changed to porter transport before reaching the foot of the Zoji La, which we crossed on the 9th. The pass marked a sudden change of scene. In the Sind valley we had been amongst pinewoods and pleasant meadows, above which stood shapely rock peaks draped with little glaciers of clean, blue ice; it was like an Alpine valley in the spring. Once across the pass, we found ourselves in bleak, colourless country of bare, shapeless hills, rendered more dreary by the untidy remains of winter snow. I thought that this was a gloomy foretaste of what we were in for during the whole season. But as we followed the rivers down into the maze of gorges forming the basin of the Indus, the country changed again. The steep mountain sides were still utterly barren, but the deep, twisting valleys and their sleek, powerful rivers had character and a grim beauty. Every few miles we came upon a stretch of intensive cultivation perched upon an ancient river terrace, and irrigated by the hardy ingenuity of the local population. The apricot trees were in full blossom, a pink mist above the fields of young corn climbing the hillside in steps of vivid green. It was like coming upon a corner of Kentish spring in the midst of the barren crags of Aden. Sometimes these belts of cultivation continued unbroken for several miles, and there our way would lie through shady orchards, the path flanked by broad ribbons of mauve and white iris. It was utterly unlike any country I had seen before, though typical of nearly all the great river valleys of the Western Himalayas and the Karakoram. I never lost my early delight in its bold contrast and extravagant grandeur. Later we found that many of the side nullahs, so stark and rugged where they joined the main valleys, held in their upper reaches little fairy combes of pinewood and flower-filled meadows.

After a fortnight we reached Skardu, the capital of Baltistan. From there we crossed the Indus by an ancient ferry, and made our way to the north along the Shigar river. The main stream of the Indus marks the boundary between the Himalayas and the Karakoram, though it seemed to me that the division was somewhat artificial. Five more days took us to Askole, the last outpost of habitation in Baltistan. The last two marches were over very difficult country. The route had frequently to be altered according to the state of the river. Sometimes long detours were necessary to avoid an impassable gorge, and in places rickety ladders propped against the rock solved the problem presented by a vertical precipice. More alarming still were the rope bridges across the river. These were made of three strands of thick rope, slung in the shape of a V, with one rope for one's feet, while the other two ropes served as hand-rails.

Many a hardened mountaineer has been known to blench while passing over these frail contraptions, swaying giddily over the raging flood. Most of the Sherpas were terrified of them, though each laughed immoderately at the craven performance of his fellows.

With our arrival at Askole we had reached the most critical stage of the expedition. Immediately ahead was the mighty barrier of the main Karakoram range, and everything depended on our being able to transport our equipment and about one and a half tons of food across it to the Shaksgam valley beyond. But besides this food, which was calculated to keep the party alive for three and a half months, we had to take with us food for the men who were carrying it, and also food for those who had to carry the porter's food. And not only had these men to be fed while they were with us, but they had also to be catered for on their return journey to Askole. It was the old problem which has to be faced whenever a journey is planned through country where no supplies are available, and where everything has to be carried: a party cannot travel for many days without the carriers being burdened with so much of their own food that they cannot carry anything else. In this respect a man is a very inefficient beast of burden, for he eats more in proportion to his carrying power than any of his four-legged rivals.

Until the middle of the nineteenth century there were a number of passes leading direct across the range from Baltistan to Hunza and to Sinkiang, which were used by travellers, traders and small bandit armies. But since then these passes have all been abandoned, and although we know from the records of early European explorers that they were in fact used by the native peoples, their existence is merely legendary as far as the present-day population is concerned. It is not quite clear why they fell into disuse, though it was probably due to a combination of several causes, one of which was the great changes which have taken place in the glaciers. Whatever the reason, it is now a difficult matter to persuade the Baltis to venture far above their normal summer grazing grounds.

Two of these passes led from Askole to Yarkand by way of the Shaksgam river. They were known as the Old and the New Mustagh passes. Of these only the Old Mustagh pass had been crossed by Europeans, once in 1887 by Younghusband and again in 1929 by the party detached from the Duke of Spoleto's expedition, under Professor Desio. From their accounts it appeared that the Old Mustagh pass was very difficult, and it seemed unlikely that it would be possible for us to cross it so early in the year and with so much baggage. The route over the New Mustagh pass was unknown and probably much longer. However, Desio had reported the probable existence of a practicable saddle west of the Old Mustagh pass, and we decided to gamble on that.

When we arrived at Askole on the 24th of May we opened negotiations with the local headmen for the recruiting of porters, and the collecting of 4,000 pounds of flour. There was no difficulty about the latter, and for the next thirty-six hours a steady stream of flour came to our camp carried in sheepskin bags. It was then transferred to canvas bags we had brought for the purpose and was weighed up into sixty-pound loads.

The question of porters was much more delicate and had to be handled with considerable care. The inhabitants of the valley of Askole, for all their remoteness, were more accustomed to expeditions than those of any other part of the Karakoram. At first sight that fact might appear as an advantage; but this was very far from the case. Most of the expeditions had been bound for the head of the Baltoro glacier, which involved for the porters a straightforward journey with very little hardship. Several of the enterprises, notably the 1929 Italian Expedition, the 1934 International Expedition led by Professor Dyhrenfurth, and the French attempt to climb Gasherbrum in 1936, were run on a huge scale, quite regardless of cost. Upwards of six hundred men were employed. The porters were paid fabulous wages besides acquiring all kinds of perquisites and loot from abandoned equipment and stores. Naturally, the men of the Askole valley soon came to regard expeditions as heaven-sent opportunities of making small fortunes with very little trouble to themselves. Moreover, they had formed very definite ideas as to what an expedition should look like, and to them our Spartan outfit appeared laughable. We could neither inspire confidence by our appearance nor tempt with a bottomless purse. We had every reason to resent the methods of our plutocratic predecessors.

At first it was assumed that we were merely going up the Baltoro glacier, and things seemed to be going well. But when it dawned on the populace that something very much more arduous was expected of them we met with blank refusal. However, after many hours of apparently hopeless argument, we succeeded in winning them over, and quite suddenly we found that the entire multitude was clamouring to be enrolled. Our dramatic change of fortune was presumably due to the realisation of a few of the more thoughtful spirits that we would not employ the whole population and that they had better take what they could get while the going was good. Once a few had changed their attitude the rest followed with the speed of an avalanche. But so long as we retained our connection with the Baltis we were for ever hearing invidious comparisons between the bounty of the "Dook Sahib" and our poverty.

We had reduced our equipment to the barest minimum, but even so we required a hundred local men. Of these about one-third were to carry the food and equipment to be used in the Shaksgam, the rest were needed to carry food which they ate themselves. We had brought seventeen men from Skardu. These were invaluable, for they were not imbued with the big ideas of the Askole men and were prepared to do a job of work in return for their pay. Moreover, they tended to despise the others and usually sided with us in the innumerable disputes and strikes that occurred when conditions became uncomfortable; or at least they remained neutral and so broke the otherwise united front against us. We had decided to retain four of them for the whole period of our stay, so as to increase the carrying power of our small party.

We set out from Askole soon after noon on May 26th. On the third day we reached Paiju, a pleasant patch of willow jungle near the snout of the Baltoro glacier. The weather was bad and our prospects looked gloomy. Everything depended upon our getting the loads across the range with the least possible delay. It would obviously be impossible to cross an unknown pass with such a large caravan in bad weather. Also it was clear that a great deal of new snow was falling on the high mountains to add to the masses of unmelted winter snow. Matters were still further complicated when Tilman and one of the Sherpas, Sen Tensing, became ill with fever. After much deliberation it was decided that they should remain at Paiju with Auden and two porters, while Spender and I and the other Sherpas went on with the main body. We could not afford to wait, for the whole caravan was now consuming 220 lb. of food a day.

The next few miles of our way led up the Baltoro. The size of the glacier was prodigious compared with those on Mount Everest and in Sikkim and Garhwal. It rose somewhere beyond our range of vision in a knot of giant peaks culminating in K2, the second highest mountain in the world. It was flanked throughout its course by countless spires, immense columns of granite standing six or eight thousand feet above their bases, supporting graceful summits, so remotely inaccessible that they seemed hardly to be part of the same colossal structure. Had we not known of the existence of the Mustagh pass and the saddle described by Desio, nothing would have persuaded us to look in this fantastic country for a way across the range.

After another day we turned to the north and entered the narrow valley of a tributary glacier known as the Trango. For a time the weather continued to be bad and snow fell. In these conditions the Baltis seemed to be entirely incapable of looking after themselves. They crumpled up at the end of the day's march and refused to do anything towards making themselves comfortable or protecting themselves from the weather. It was surprising to find this failing in people whose livelihood depended so much on their ability to use difficult country to the best advantage, and whose forefathers were accustomed to making arduous journeys across the glaciers. Much of their lives must have been spent in the open, herding their flocks in high mountain pastures, and yet they seemed to be ignorant of the simplest notions of outdoor comfort: camping in the most protected places, building walls for shelter, crowding together for mutual protection and making use of rock overhangs. But I must admit they were tough, and put up with more cold and discomfort than I had expected them to endure. Fortunately the weather changed at the critical moment, and we were able to avoid the disaster of a complete collapse before we had even found the pass.

The fact that no one had ever crossed Desio's saddle also had a bad moral effect upon the Baltis. They knew that the Italian party had been up the Trango glacier, and they assumed that they had returned because they had failed to find a pass at its head. We could not maintain for long the pretence that we knew the way, and each mistake made them more certain of our incompetence. Nor could we tell them how long it would take to reach the pass. What seemed to worry them most, however, was the fear that if we managed to cross the pass we would find ourselves in a country from which we could not return.

Farther up, the remains of the winter snow was leg-deep upon the glacier, and it only stayed firm until about the middle of the morning; after that the going was terribly laborious. We wasted most of one day reconnoitring a route up a valley which ended in a semi-circle of precipice crowned by a hanging-glacier terrace. But at length we found a glacier rising gently to a saddle which we imagined must lie on the crest of the main watershed. By then the spirit of the Baltis was almost broken. For some days all except the seventeen Skardu men had been clamouring to be allowed to return. They certainly had plenty to complain about; the nights were bitterly cold, the camps, on little rock platforms dug out from beneath the snow, were bleak and comfortless and such fuel as we had been able to bring from below was most inadequate. Luckily the good weather held, and by pointing to the saddle and promising them that if they could reach it we would ask nothing more of them, we managed to persuade the men to stick it for just one more day. But when, the next morning, we reached the saddle we found to our dismay that it was not the crest of the pass we were seeking. Beyond, more than a mile away across a curving basin of snow, we saw another col a few hundred feet higher. The Askole men were still some way below, and before they had a chance to share this devastating discovery we plunged down into the basin and waded through soft snow until we were half-way across. The Skardu men followed without protest. The basin proved to be the top of the hanging-glacier terrace which we had seen at the head of the valley we had reconnoitred. Eventually most of the Askole men arrived, but it was clear that we could not induce them to go a step farther. They lay in the snow, holding their heads and groaning, though the altitude was only about 18,000 feet. Only the Skardu men were willing to come on with us. We paid off the rest, and after watching them safely back over the first saddle, we made a dump of their abandoned loads. Then we struggled with as much as we could carry. The second saddle proved to be the true pass, and soon after nightfall that evening we camped on a little rock outcrop in the upper basin of the Sarpo Laggo glacier, on the northern side of the main continental watershed.

The next few days were occupied in rescuing the remainder of the loads from the hanging-glacier terrace, and in bringing them across the pass. Then, while Spender began his survey, we started to relay the baggage down the glacier. In the meantime Tilman, Auden, Sen Tensing and their two porters arrived. The invalids had recovered from their fever, but they were still very weak and it had been a hard struggle to drag themselves across the pass. On the 14th of June we reached broad gravel flats below the Sarpo Laggo glacier, and here we established our main base, nine miles south of the Shaksgam river. Most of the Skardu men returned from there and left the fifteen of us – four Europeans, seven Sherpas and four Baltis – to our own devices.

In spite of the many vicissitudes, we had accomplished the journey over the range almost according to schedule. That evening I experienced a sense of profound relief, of delicious freedom and of happy expectation of good things in store. Warmed by the unaccustomed luxury of a blazing fire, its leaping flames fed with unstinted wood, untroubled by the cares of the preceding weeks, we could reflect upon the entrancing prospects of our position. East and west of us stretched an unexplored section, eighty miles long, of the greatest watershed in the world. To the north, close at hand, across the Shaksgam river, was the Aghil range, with its unknown peaks and valleys. We had food enough to last us for nearly three and a half months, and a party equipped and strong enough to meet the opportunity.

CHAPTER THIRTEEN

Shaksgam – 2

ONE of the most acute problems of expedition life is the difficulty of preserving harmony among the members of a party. In the sentimental days before the last war there was a tendency to hide or to gloss over this ugly factor in the otherwise romantic accounts of expeditions. But sufficient of the inner history of the classic expeditions has leaked out to show that they suffered at least as much from this particular form of human fraility as their humble successors. To-day the bugbear is widely, though by no means universally, admitted.

All manner of things, great and small, are liable to promote discord. Garrulity is notoriously hard to bear; silence can be no less trying. Even an unconscious display of virtue can be as intolerable as any vice, gentlemanly poise as hasty temper, efficiency as clumsiness, knowledge as ignorance, energy as sloth. In conditions of boredom or of nervous strain one is quick to resent the way a man drinks his soup or wears his hat, or the silly manner in which his beard had grown, or a thousand other trifles that in normal circumstances would pass unnoticed. When one is on short rations it generally seems that one's companion has secured the larger portion of a meal; and he invariably occupies more than his share of the tent. Disagreement about the route is a common cause of open hostility. On occasions when this has occurred and we have each gone our own way, I have found myself hoping that my opponent will fall down a crevasse rather than that he should get there first. I remember once that someone became very angry when I playfully threw an egg at his face; it was not that there was at the time any scarcity of eggs, nor was the egg particularly bad. There is no limit to people's unreasonableness. I know several travellers, most delightful people, who admit quite frankly that they cannot stand having a companion on their journey. Very wisely they travel alone. Others, of course, are equally incapable of enduring their own exclusive company for long, though they quarrel with all who share it.

Admission of this universal weakness is the first step towards combating the evil. For only then can one recognise the phenomenon when it shows its ugly head, or see it retrospectively in its true light. Sometimes even at the time one can appreciate its comic side. But acceptance does not solve the problem, and the personal relations between the individual members of an expedition can, more than any other single factor, make or mar the success of the enterprise.

It is extremely hard to predict which men will get on with each other, though I suppose most of us imagine that we have a clear idea of the kind of people we can or cannot live with. Our particular likes and dislikes may or may not reflect our own characteristics. For example, I do not find self-centred people specially hard to bear; far worse, to my mind, is a man who continually talks platitudes. But this does not imply that I am not selfish myself, nor that I do not think always in clichés. I often find that I get on well with men who are given to making wild statements providing they support them with intelligent argument. I consider that people who never say anything unless they are perfectly sure of their ground become most irritating. But even for individuals there is no rule. Certainly few people will agree upon what constitutes the ideal companion.

It would be difficult to find two people less alike in their intellectual make-up then Tilman and Spender. Yet I regard each in his way as the best companion I could wish for. Their own relationship was a curious one. Neither appeared to take the other particularly seriously, though I detected a strong mutual esteem. Far more inflammable was the contact between the two scientists, and it was generally prudent to keep them separated as much as possible. This was odd in a way because each was untiring in his co-operation in the work of the other. Perhaps it was because they both had unusually hearty appetites, or perhaps because both had brothers who were celebrated poets. I find that scientists often are rather intolerant of one another.

But though without direct experiment it is almost impossible to tell which men can tolerate each other's company, there are certain conditions that can and must be observed when organising an expedition. The first essential, as I have said elsewhere, is that every man should feel that he has an important part to play. Nothing is more conducive to bloody-mindedness than the feeling, even for a short time, that one is superfluous or redundant. It is surprising how quick people are to feel this. For this reason the expedition should be divided as much as possible into small, self-contained units, each with its special task and responsibility. On an exploratory expedition the advantages of this method are obvious. But it is remarkable how much better men like each other after a few weeks' absence. The prospect of meeting "old so-and-so's" party to-morrow, of hearing an account of his adventures and of recounting one's own, rarely fails to have a most stimulating and refreshing effect. The illusion of brotherly love may be short-lived, but it is well worth while.

The second essential condition for the achievement of harmony is interest. Each man must be capable of deriving a deep satisfaction from some aspect of his environment and of sustaining his enthusiasm. It is a capacity that can only be discovered by experience. It does not necessarily demand the pursuit of scientific study or even a hobby. Some men appear to derive a strong philosophical satisfaction from dragging a sledge across miles of arctic snow, or from mere existence in strange conditions. Many people have an intangible though profound feeling for certain types of country, and can be completely content doing any job which takes them into such places. Presumably for most mountaineers such a feeling for mountain country is their principal reason for climbing.

Thirdly, it is important that all the members of a party should be in agreement about the general policy and conduct of the expedition. I have suffered agonies of ennui and self-righteous disgust on an expedition that has appeared to me too large and clumsy, and I have made myself an infernal nuisance in consequence. No doubt the protagonist of large expeditions would be equally unhappy with the light expeditions that delight my heart.

In my opinion far too much emphasis has been laid on leadership in connection with mountaineering and exploratory expeditions, for this led to an exaggerated notion of the importance of the leader and the difficulty of his task. How often does one hear the word "brilliant" applied in this connection, when in fact all that was called for was the exercise of a little tact and common sense? In ordinary mountaineering the man who has had most experience on the particular type of ground to be covered generally assumes tacit charge of the party; the more evenly experience and skill are distributed among the members, the less obvious is this assumption of charge. Anyone who tries to play the dictator in the lower valleys is likely to become very unpopular. As far as possible the same principle should be applied in the whole conduct of an expedition. A leader should make his position as inconspicuous as he can, and he should certainly avoid the appearance of taking his responsibilities too seriously. His primary task is the selection of his party. In the field his main function is to see that every man is placed in a position which gives him the widest scope for his particular job and for the use of his own initiative. Heavy military discipline, obviously necessary when vast armies are involved, is wholly out of place when dealing with a handful of carefully selected and thoroughly competent specialists. When it ceases to be laughable, it becomes intolerably irksome.

Travel in unexplored country is a curious mixture of freedom and cramping self-discipline, of careless abandon and rigid time schedule. Free from all the tiresome restraints of normal life, encircled by a boundless horizon, one is all the more a slave to the elementary considerations of time and distance, food and warmth, weather and season. The simple life is simple only in that it deals with direct fundamental things.

It was already the middle of June when we reached our base in the Sarpo Laggo valley. In less than a month the Aghil range would be almost encircled by an impassable barrier of flood, leaving only one line of escape, eastward, through a tremendous tangle of unexplored mountains to the country mapped by Mason's expedition, itself many weeks' journey from the nearest habitation. To be caught beyond the Shaksgam by the summer floods would almost certainly be disastrous, for we could hardly survive there until the following winter when the melting of the glaciers would slacken and the rivers shrink. Days were precious and we had no time to waste in relaying supplies. Thus an automatic limit was set to our work in the Aghil range, for without relaying we could only carry with us enough food for three weeks.

The valley of the Shaksgam river was a weird place, shut in on both sides by great limestone cliffs, slashed across with twisted streaks of yellow, red and black strata which gave them a bizarre appearance. The bottom of the valley was composed of gravel and sand flats, often as much as a mile wide. Over these the river flowed, sometimes concentrated into one great body of water as it swirled round a bend in the valley, sometimes split up into a dozen streams which sprawled their independent courses across the flats. Spread out at intervals along the valley we found jungles of grass, willow and tamarisk, natural counterparts of the cultivated oases of the Indus valley. The main river was turoid, but, on each side of it, clear streams flowed through a chain of deep green and blue pools. Steep, glacier-filled corries split the vertical sides of the main valley, forming narrow openings into a dark forest of Dolomite spires.

At the foot of one such cleft we found a collection of ancient stone shelters which gave us a clue to the route through a narrow defile to the Aghil pass. Here we came upon a sudden change of scene. A wide grassy valley carpeted with drifts of mauve primulas, sloped gently away to the north, cradling a placid lake and backed by the rounded ice-caps of the Kuen Lun. Looking back across the Shaksgam valley, framed by vertical rock walls, we could see the full splendours of the Karakoram, rising to the mighty cone of K2.

The party was divided into three parts, and for a fortnight of perfect weather we worked upon our several tasks. Spender stayed in the vicinity of the pass, to fix its position and to map in detail two hundred square miles of the surrounding country. Auden journeyed north to the Yarkand river, and then worked his way back across the range by another route. Tilman and I went eastwards to find the Zug Shaksgam. We started by climbing a 20,000 foot peak, then we found a high pass across which we travelled to the basin of the river. It was already too swollen for us to attempt a crossing, but we were able to follow it up-stream until we were certain that it was in fact the Zug Shaksgam, and down-stream through deep canyons to its junction with the Yarkand. The country through which we travelled was extremely difficult and our short weeks were over-crowded with toil and interest, though the glaciers were relatively small and we were never beyond easy reach of fuel. This and the fine weather gave us a sense of freedom, for we were able to travel from dawn until nightfall, lying down to sleep wherever we happened to be. In the wide valleys north of the Aghil range, as in those of the Sarpo Laggo, we found enormous herds of wild sheep and countless snow-cock. Elsewhere that year, we met with foxes, wild asses and small mountain wolves. When we had time to stalk them, the wild sheep provided us with poor sport but a welcome change of diet.

The expedition reunited in a pleasant jungle in the Sarpo Laggo valley on July 8th. The following day Spender went off to complete the survey of the intricate system of glaciers coming down from the main Karakoram range west of K2, while Auden, Tilman and I set out to explore the country lying immediately to the north of the great mountain. From the summit of a peak 21,000 feet high, on a calm and cloudless day, our senses sharpened by a difficult climb, we looked into the heart of this wild and lovely region. Later we stood for one unforgettable hour in the midst of a wide amphitheatre at the foot of the north face of K2. A single buttress, straight and slender, rose from the level icy floor of the cirque in one prodigious sweep of twelve thousand feet to the gleaming summit dome. We watched avalanches, involving perhaps hundreds of tons of ice, break from a hanging glacier nearly two miles above our heads. Long before the ice reached the foot of the precipice it was ground to a fine powder, slowly to vanish in a misty spray. Nor did any sound reach our ears.

When, towards the close of the last century, Sir Martin Conway travelled from the Hunza valley, up the Hispar glacier and across the Hispar pass at its head, he came upon a large basin of ice and snow. He named this the "Snow Lake", and although he did not explore it, he estimated its area at three hundred square miles. Since then it had only been seen once, by the Workmans, who, following Conway's route, also did not explore the region. Something of a legend had grown up around the "Snow Lake", which gave rise to a good deal of geographical speculation. It was suggested, for example, that it might form an ice-cap of a kind unknown outside arctic regions, in which many of the vast glaciers of the Karakoram had their origin. Its southern fringes, traversed by Conway and the Workmans, represented the limit of exploration in this part of the Karakoram, so that the map of the main continental watershed faded into the unknown with this intriguing enigma.

From our base in the Sarpo Laggo we looked to the west up a mighty ice-stream which stretched away into a jagged horizon of far distant peaks. This was the Crevasse glacier up which, in 1889, Younghusband had tried to make his way in search of the Shimshal pass. On its lower reaches he had encountered a forest of ice pinnacles, so complicated that he had abandoned his attempt. From the size of the glacier and its general direction we calculated that one of its upper branches might lead us, if not into the "Snow Lake", at least to its vicinity.

With food sufficient for nearly two months we started to work our way up the Crevasse glacier. It was a laborious task for the way was intricate and hard to travel, and though the Sherpas carried as much as 120 lbs. each, our loads were more than we could transport in a single journey. But our slow progress enabled Spender to make a detailed map of the country through which we passed. After a fortnight of steady work we had penetrated the region of ice pinnacles and reached a point some twenty miles up the glacier. Beyond this the ice was smooth and easy to travel. The glacier divided into a number of branches. We went forward in several lightly laden detachments to explore the range ahead of us and to search for passes that would lead us into whatever country lay beyond.

After another ten days we had learned sufficient to enable us to form further plans. We had found many routes, each leading in a different direction, each with intriguing possibilities. To make the best use of our unique position we decided thenceforward to work in three independent parties, each with its separate objective to be pursued as circumstances and the nature of the country dictated. We did not meet again until we returned to England.

Auden and the four Baltis crossed a pass which took them to the south into the Panmah glacier system, and thence to Askole. Tilman and two Sherpas set off to the west in search of the "Snow Lake". Abandoning all but the barest necessities, they crossed a long series of passes, eighteen or nineteen thousand feet high, until they found the great basin, crossed it and connected Conway's explorations with our own. Finally they broke through the great rock wall to the south of the Hispar pass into the fertile valleys near Arandu in Baltistan. Meanwhile Spender and I, with the five remaining Sherpas carrying the heavy survey equipment, struck north, and, after wandering for a month through a maze of ranges reached habitation in the remote valleys of Shimshal.

It is hard to compare the experiences of life or to assess their relative value.

Each is influenced by the mental impression left by its forerunners; none can stand quite alone. With each new view our standards alter, with each fresh endeavour our interests change. I cannot say which mountain venture or which mountain scene has afforded the deepest delight. Certainly no experience of mine has been fuller, no undertaking more richly rewarded than those few months among the unknown mountains beyond the crest of the Karakoram. The vast scale of the country, its complete isolation from any source of help or supply, demanded all our ingenuity and a wide range of mountaineering technique. Striving to traverse and understand such a world, and thus to absorb something of its peace and strength, was at once our task and our reward.

Our time was all too short, and we were sorely tempted to extend it into the winter. For with each phase of our journey new problems crowded in upon us. It was hard indeed to call a halt. But I had promised Tilman to return to England to help with the preparations for the 1938 Everest Expedition, and I had to remain content with a resolve to come back some day to this land of boundless promise with unlimited time before me.

The first people we met were salt-gatherers in the valleys beyond the Shimshal pass. Our sudden descent from an unknown country caused some consternation among these folk, who took us for a band of Chinese marauders. It was with difficulty that we reassured them, and when they had called up armed reinforcements we were escorted in a state of friendly arrest across the pass to Shimshal, where we succeeded in convincing the headman of our nationality and our innocent intentions.

There can be no denying that one of the great pleasures of an expedition lies in the return to normal things. This fact indicates no lack of appreciation of the life involved, no lessening of its value. It is a natural delight in contrast, in rest after toil, in soft living after austerity. I know few joys more poignant than the relaxation of walking along a path after months of mountaineering travel; there are few pleasures sweeter than the sight of abundant fertility, of flocks and fields and orchards, after the desolate splendour of high places.

Our journey back to Srinagar took four weeks. It was the most varied and the most impressive that I had then experienced in the inhabited regions of high Asia. First there was the passage through the monstrous gorge of conglomerate cliffs below Shimshal, astonishing and terrifying even to our practised eyes; then the slow climb up the moonlit precipice, parched and bare, to escape from its infernal depths to the crest of a pass eight thousand feet above; the descent on the other side into a gentle land of meadow and pinewood where we slaked raging thirsts and cushioned our tired limbs in beds of deep grass. Our way led through Hunza, that principality straight from the pages of legend with surely the most fantastic setting in the world; here, as guests of the old Mir, we reclined on couches in the shade of the palace garden, eating luscious grapes and pears and peaches and melons from an inexhaustible supply.

There is a peculiar quality about the western ranges of Central Asia, that I have since come to appreciate more fully, though I am no better able to account for or describe it. It is an atmosphere created, I fancy, partly by the country, its fantastic natural phenomena, its vastness and arid severity, and partly by the people, their vivid mode of living, their habit of wide travel, their kinship with the western world, perhaps too their proximity to the cradle of civilisation. These two attributes of weird environment and peaceful culture blend together in an unusual harmony which makes travel in this region an unforgettable experience.

CHAPTER FOURTEEN

Karakoram, 1939

THE vague plans that I had so timidly formulated in 1933 were developing with the most gratifying smoothness. The horizons of the "untravelled world" had widened with each step along the enchanting road of exploration. The fascination of new country had deepened with each fresh experience. Each expedition, however successful in the achievement of its main purpose, left behind it a ragged fringe of unsatisfied desire which formed the nucleus of some new and more ambitious venture. I was constantly debating in my mind new ways of approach and better methods of travel and of living in uninhabited country, and I was continually aware of fresh and exciting possibilities. Luckily the question of finance had presented no great problem and I found it easier to raise money for expeditions of wider scope.

A severe limit has always been imposed upon expeditions in the high Himalayas by the shortness of the summer season and by the difficulty of crossing the southern passes until the winter snows have melted. These factors have restricted the actual work of an expedition to three or four months in the remoter districts and enormously increased its cost. I had often resented this limitation and had resolved at the first opportunity to break down the seasonal barrier. By providing suitable equipment, and arranging for the disposition of the expedition at points where they would be least affected by the rigours of winter and spring, it seemed that it would be possible to do useful and well-coordinated work throughout the year. Besides the enormous extension of opportunity and freedom of movement that such a plan would offer, one would gain a totally different view point and a far more intimate contact with the country that one was seeking to discover, by a leisurely and uninterrupted sojourn in it through all the seasons.

It is curious how time is affected by familiarity. The Kamet expedition, my first in the Himalayas, had lasted less than three months. It had seemed an eternity, as though I had spent half my life travelling among those vast and lovely valleys. Later, double that time seemed sadly insufficient, and I felt that I could not claim a real understanding of such places until I had lived a full year in their solitudes.

The frequently recurring expeditions to Mount Everest had made it impossible for me to embark upon this attractive experiment. In 1939, however, the opportunity came. The most obvious choice of country was the

Karakoram, since its problems and its fascination were so fresh in my mind. The Shaksgam expedition of 1937 had fulfilled its main purpose in the fixing and detailed mapping of the country surrounding the Aghil Pass and the great glacier system lying immediately to the north of the main Karakoram watershed between K2 and the Shimshal pass. There still remained much of the Aghil range to be explored, as well as the mountains stretching to the north-east of the Shimshal pass across the Oprang river, before the map of the main features of the Great Karakoram could be completed. From the experience I had gained in 1937 it was clear to me that the task would best be tackled during the winter, when the river, instead of presenting the traveller with impassable barriers, might even be used as high roads by which to penetrate into the heart of the unexplored regions. I mentioned my plans to the Surveyor-General of India when I was in Calcutta in 1938, and he replied that he was anxious to straighten out the topographical confusion which existed in that part of the main range surrounding the basins of the Hispar, Biafo and Panmah glaciers. This was an obvious prelude to my winter plans. I submitted detailed proposals to the Surveyor-General, who at once offered me full support and encouragement.

This, then, was the outline of my plan. The party would consist of four Europeans equipped to spend some sixteen months in the field. We would spend the summer of 1939 in the region of the Hispar-Biafo watershed. The principal task here would be to make an accurate triangulation not only for the mapping of this country, but also to form a basis for our winter work. The winter of 1939–40 was to be spent in the country to the east of the Shimshal pass. As this was beyond the main range, the snow precipitation would be light. It would be extremely cold, but we would be provided with special arctic equipment, and I was not unduly worried on that score. During the spring of 1940 we would attempt a journey from Shimshal to Leh via the Shaksgam river, for which I proposed to acquire a small herd of yaks to be used both for transport and as a source of food supply. In the summer of 1940 I hoped to travel from Leh to the source of the Indus exploring the unknown Aling Kangri range on the way. Thence – well, who could tell?

Alas! the end of this way of life was at hand, and most of the lovely plans came to nothing. It was clear to most people that war must come sooner or later. But to me it seemed that little purpose would be served by anticipating it; and one hoped that it would be later rather than sooner. In any case, it did not seem to matter whether one were in the East or in Europe when the storm came. Spender and Tilman, whom I had hoped to have with me, thought differently. Spender had a scientific job of considerable importance: Tilman, who was on the reserve list of officers, did not wish to be away for so long. He went instead for a short trip to the mountains of Assam.

However, to share my plans I had excellent companions. Scott Russell, a practised mountaineer, came to help in the exploration, to make detailed botanical collections and surveys, and to continue some physiological researches which he had been making into the effect of cold climates upon plant growth. Eadric Fountaine came as doctor and general help, and also to make zoological collections, and to study certain medical and ethnological aspects of the people of Shimshal. Peter Mott came as chief surveyor. All these three had had experience of Arctic work, which would have been invaluable in the execution of our winter plans. The Surveyor-General lent the expedition the services of two Indian surveyors, Fazal Ellahi, who had already made a considerable reputation by his mountain surveys and his resource in difficult circumstances, and Inayat Khan. Nine Sherpas, under my old friend Angtharkay, were engaged. The expedition was financed by grants of money from the Royal Geographical Society, the Royal Society, the Percy Sladen Fund, the British Museum and the Royal Botanic Gardens, Kew. Mr R. W. Lloyd and Mr A. Courtauld also most kindly contributed towards the funds of the expedition.

We set off across the passes to Gilgit in the middle of June, and once again enjoyed the gentle progress through entrancing foothill valleys which is the prelude to all Himalayan expeditions. We crossed the Tragbal and the Kamri passes on fine mornings. The remains of the winter snow was still on the ground, and the huge cone of Nanga Parbat stood clear in the sparkling air. In the sunlit woods of the Gurais we forgot the ugly turmoil of the world we had left behind. In the lower valleys of the Indus basin the fruit was already ripe, and every few miles we stopped to gorge ourselves with mulberries and apricots.

From Gilgit we travelled on past the giant peak of Rakaposhi, which rose from a belt of pinewoods in the gorge of the Hunza river in one colossal sweep of twenty thousand feet. It presents one of the most stupendous mountain faces in the world. At Nagir we were received with great courtesy by the old Mir who entertained us with exhibitions of polo and dancing. We began our work on July 3rd. The party was divided into several groups, each with its allotted task – some to explore and map the giant glaciers of the Nagir district, some to work on the triangulation, some to cross the Nushik La to Baltistan in the south and some to establish a dump of food up the Hispar glacier at the foot of the Hispar pass. The glaciers of this region were flanked by wide ablation valleys formed by ancient lateral moraines, which offered easy and pleasant roads for travel. They were filled with willows and rose thickets and wild flowers. In July the roses were in full bloom and for miles along the glacier great banks of their gay blossom lined the ablation valleys. Our camping grounds were meadows carpeted with flowers of every colour.

Early in August the party reunited at a rendezvous on the Hispar glacier. While Fazal Ellahi was making a detailed plane-table map of the Hispar glacier and Mott was carrying forward his triangulation we relayed supplies across the Hispar pass, which formed a huge ice-plateau, to the "Snow Lake". Again the party was divided up, the better to cover the enormous area of country we had set ourselves to explore before winter set in. Fazal Ellahi worked from a base on the "Snow Lake". It was his task to survey this and then to work his way slowly down the Biafo glacier, which has a total length of some forty miles. Mott and Russell crossed a difficult pass to the south-west, and I did not see the former again until we met at Gilgit two months later. Fountaine and I made our way down the Biafo and then east to the Panmah, where we spent a busy three weeks mapping. In September we separated and each made his way by new passes back into the Snow Lake. Fountaine then set off on a long journey up the Chogo Lungma glacier and over a pass at its head, which led him eventually back to Gilgit.

I had arranged to meet Russell at a rendezvous on the "Snow Lake". I arrived first and waited for a few days of heavy snow-storm. Late one afternoon his party was seen approaching through the mist. I went out with Angtharkay to meet him. The approach to our camp was guarded by an intricate network of crevasses. With a deep covering of fresh snow it was a laborious and delicate task threading our way through this area, and the two parties approached each other slowly. When at last we were within earshot, Russell shouted out the shattering news that England was at war with Germany. He had heard it on the tiny wireless receiving set that we had brought to get time signals for our astronomical work.

It was a strange, dreamlike experience hearing such news in those surroundings. I felt for the moment as though one of the crevasses had opened and that I was dropping into a bottomless pit. I passed the news on to Angtharkay, and for a timeless moment we stood motionless. Then we went on to meet the other party, relieved them of some of their loads and made our way slowly back to camp, where I listened to such details as Russell was able to give. It was no dream, but a grim reality. I suppose we must have been expecting it, but that did not seem to lessen the shock. It was hard to realise the meaning of the disaster. Perhaps even now the London where we had planned this very venture was a chaos of destruction and terror. How fantastic, how supremely ridiculous it seemed in our remote and lovely world of snow and ice.

As if to point the contrast the mists cleared and for a moment the glacier was bathed in a sunset glow reflected from the high peaks. The great granite spires of the Biafo stood black against a deep blue sky. At least this mountain world, to which I owed so much of life and happiness, would stand above the ruin of human hopes, the heritage of a saner generation of men.

He is lucky who, in the full tide of life, has experienced a measure of the active environment that he most desires. In these days of upheaval and violent change, when the basic values of to-day are the vain and shattered dreams of to-morrow, there is much to be said for a philosophy which aims at living a full life while the opportunity offers. There are few treasures of more lasting worth than the experiences of a way of life that is in itself wholly satisfying. Such, after all, are the only possessions of which no fate, no cosmic catastrophe can deprive us; nothing can alter the fact if for one moment in eternity we have really lived.

MOUNTAINS OF TARTARY

Mountains of Tartary

First published by Hodder and Stoughton Limited, 1950

Contents

1	Introductory	*page* 461
2	Hunza-Kashgar-Tashkent	463
3	Bostan Terek-A Glissade	476
4	Political Background	486
5	Karakoram Journey	490
6	The Arch	508
7	Muztagh Ata	516
8	Uch Tash	529
9	Urumchi and the Heavenly Pool	543
10	Bodgo Ola – 1	553
11	Bodgo Ola – 2	564
12	Chakragil; and Hunza again	575

Maps

General map of Sinkiang and adjoining territories 460
Bogdo Ola 563
Chakragil 579

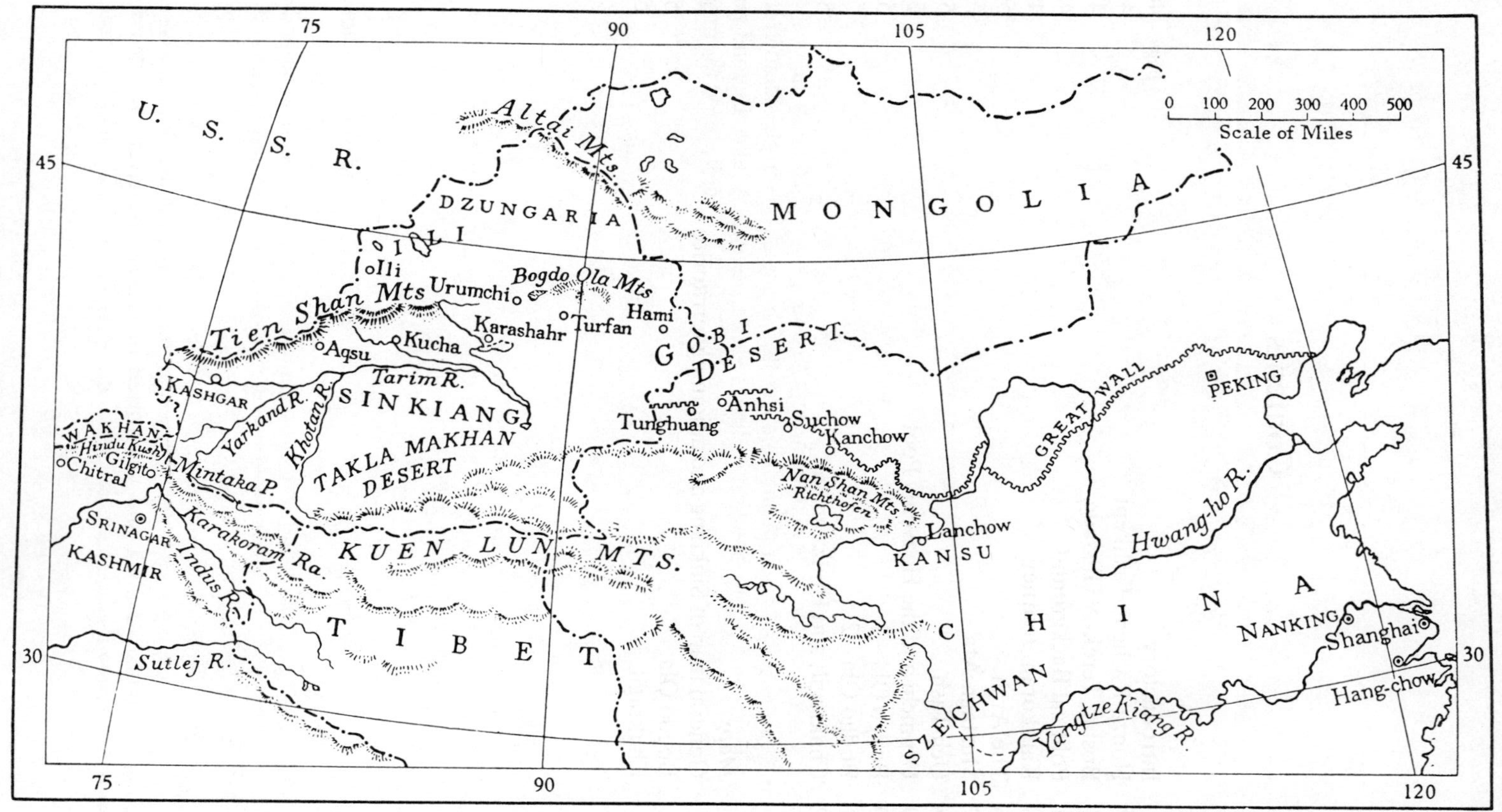
U. S. S. R.
MONGOLIA
Altai Mts
DZUNGARIA
ILI
Ili
Tien Shan Mts
Urumchi
Bogdo Ola Mts
Hami
Turfan
Karashahr
Kucha
Aqsu
Tarim R.
GOBI DESERT
KASHGAR
Yarkand R.
Khotan R.
SINKIANG
TAKLA MAKHAN DESERT
WAKHAN
Hindu Kush
Gilgit
Chitral
Mintaka P.
SRINAGAR
KASHMIR
Karakoram Ra.
Indus R.
KUEN LUN MTS.
TIBET
Sutlej R.
Tunghuang
Anhsi
Suchow
Kanchow
Nan Shan Mts
Richthofen
Lanchow
KANSU
GREAT WALL
PEKING
Hwang-ho R.
CHINA
NANKING
Shanghai
Hang-chow
SZECHWAN
Yangtze Kiang R.
0 100 200 300 400 500
Scale of Miles
75
90
105
120
45
30

CHAPTER ONE

Introductory

I was returning to Kashgar after a week-end in the mountains, hunting ibex. I had spent Sunday night by a spring in the foot-hills twenty-five miles to the north-west, and had started alone just before dawn. My pony knew the track well and set off at a brisk trot, though I could see nothing but the outline of the cliffs above me, black against the stars. With the first grey light he broke into a rhythmic canter, which he kept up for an hour or more. The wind was keen against my face; but I was very sleepy and a bit stiff after the exertions of the previous day. The steep sides of the valley paled to a ghostly hue. They were utterly barren; riven and pitted by dark, cavernous nullahs. The clatter of the pony's hooves echoed hollow, as though it were the only sound that had ever disturbed the silence of this dead world.

At a sharp turn the valley ended abruptly, and we emerged upon flat desert, sloping gently to the great plain. This was flooded in deep purple shadow; the desert appeared to sink beneath it, like a shore beneath a lake. Beyond and above the purple shadow, near or infinitely far I could not tell, stood the great ice-mountains: the rounded dome of Kungur,[1] the twin spires of Chakragil,[2] the granite peaks of Bostan Terek, and scores more unnamed. They were very white and sharp against the light-blue sky, from which the stars had lately faded. Sleep and stiffness were swept away in a sudden wave of ecstasy. I urged the pony to a gallop. As we raced along, the ice-mountains, one after another along their huge arc, flushed pink and then kindled to a burning gold. Gradually, as the rays of the rising sun struck across it, the purple shadow dissolved, and from it emerged, first a small group of poplars, then what seemed to be a dark forest beyond.

At the edge of the oasis my pony drew up, his coat steaming. The Turki inn-keeper came out to greet us. It had become quite a regular practice, my arrival at his tiny inn early on Monday morning. He had tea ready and some bundles of dried lucerne for my pony. A carpet was already spread for me on the mud floor of the verandah, where half a dozen other travellers lay asleep, wrapped in their padded coats. My host woke them with his chatter, and they stared at me, first with sleepy petulance, then with round-eyed curiosity. They obviously thought I was Russian. The inn-keeper soon put them wise.

I paid my host a paltry 40,000 Chinese dollars. My pony was led reluctantly from his unfinished meal and we trotted on across the river. We had still another twelve miles or so to go. The sun was now well up. The fields of young

[1]Subsequently spelt Qungur (*World Atlas of Mountaineering*) and Kongur (present official name).
[2]H. W. Tilman spells this Chakra Aghil in *China to Chitral*. The Shipton version is more common.

rice sparkled in its slanting rays. It was all so green. Thick clusters of wild iris lined the path. The peasants were already at work. Judging by their raucous songs, they seemed to find life as exhilarating as I did. Soon we reached a broad, dusty highway, flanked by willows and poplars. Here I had plenty of company. But the riders going my way were in no hurry, and, as I sped by, we had time for no more than a brief greeting: "*Salaam Alaikum, yakshi kelde ma?*" At intervals along the road there were villages with stalls laden with small brown loaves or melons. On we went, past a Chinese barracks with a guard outside, past an ancient milestone in the form of a great mud pyramid, along the edge of a high loess cliff overlooking a marsh, where, in the winter, I used to go for snipe, till at length the great walls of Kashgar appeared through the trees. At half-past eight we entered the Consulate compound, in nice time for breakfast, for which I was more than ready.

That is one of the most characteristic of my memories of Kashgar; at least so far as the country itself is concerned. There were, of course, other aspects of my life during the four years that I spent there; but this book is not concerned with these. It deals mostly with visits to some of the various mountain ranges surrounding the Tarim Basin.

I discovered long ago that there are many ways of enjoying mountain country. Not even the most enthusiastic Alpine mountaineer would claim that climbing difficult ridges and faces is the only one. Certainly to the critics who denounce his sport as a vulgar display of a useless and artificial skill on a sort of glorified greasy pole, he can with justice reply that mountaineering provides an understanding of mountains and a variety of æsthetic and emotional experience without which he could never achieve a full appreciation of his enjoyment. Experience of a more sombre kind is found in the struggle to reach the summit of a great Himalayan peak; it is unique, perhaps, and certainly well worth while, but so circumscribed that, in my view, a little goes a long way. Mountain exploration, on the other hand, offers limitless scope, and is without doubt the most fascinating occupation I know.

But there is much to be said for a simple mountain journey, whose object, unencumbered with the burden of detailed map-making or scientific observation, is just to get from one place to another. Central Asia provides, *par excellence*, the type of country for journeys of this kind and, of all our little expeditions from Kashgar, I enjoyed these the most. Though many of them were over ground already covered by Stein and Hedin and other travellers, it was easy, even at a week-end, to penetrate unexplored country. Unfortunately, such journeys, however rewarding in themselves, are much harder to describe than quests of discovery or conquest. For, in the absence of any climax or special adventure, unless the writer happens to be a Stevenson or a Doughty, a monotonous repetition of scenic eulogy is apt to result from his efforts to convey his enjoyment, or long, boring descriptions of topographical detail from the necessity of presenting some sort of coherent narrative

For this reason I have been tempted to give undue prominence to the few mountain-climbing ventures in which I indulged, at the expense of the straightforward journeys which were more typical of my contact with those mountain ranges. In the main, these climbing ventures were unsuccessful. This was due largely to bad management and lack of recent practice, partly to bad luck, but mainly to lack of adequate time for reconnaissance, acclimatization and preparation on the spot; for great mountains, however simple, do not readily yield to the first impetuous rush. But the climbs were no less enjoyable for their lack of success – or so I like to think.

It was not my intention to discuss the history, the social and economic life, or the political problems of the country. I have, however, with some misgivings, included one short chapter designed to explain the political background to my experiences. To those who, like myself, are profoundly bored with the politics of a remote land, I recommend skipping that chapter.

Some of the chapters were written while I was still in Kashgar, the rest in moments of ennui and nostalgic recollection, some time later in Yunnan.

CHAPTER TWO

Hunza – Kashgar – Tashkent

1

In 1937, with two companions, I had spent several months exploring some thousands of square miles of country on the undemarcated frontier of China and India, on the nothern side of the Karakoram. It was my first acquaintance with the vast land of mountain-desert and mountain-oasis, so utterly different in form and scale from the parts of the Himalaya that I had visited. As is usually the case in detailed exploration among great mountains, the scope of our travel was severely limited – in time by the seasons, in distance by the labour of moving unaided by animal transport over steep and difficult country. After the months of toil that had gone into its making, our map, when printed on a scale of 1 inch=4 miles, seemed ridiculously small in relation to the stupendous mountain vistas I remembered, an absurdly simple solution to the topographical problems we had puzzled over for so long. But, better than any diary, any album full of photogaphs, it had the power to re-create in imagination every phase of the experience.

As I look at it now I can recall vividly the feelings with which, during the whole of that summer, I gazed northward to the barren mountains of the Kuen Lun, which for us represented an impossible barrier to an intriguing and very desirable land. Even if the flooding of the Shaksgam had not threatened to cut off our retreat, we could not have travelled beyond the uninhabited regions of the Aghil Range without the certainty of being captured and thrown into a Chinese prison. For at that time Sinkiang was more inaccessible to the Western traveller than it had been for half a century, more inaccessible than Tibet, and scarcely less so than Outer Mongolia. And it seemed, by the way affairs were shaping in Central Asia, that the Iron Curtain had been dropped beyond the Karakoram finally and for ever. Like small boys gazing over a fence into a forbidden park, this rigid political barrier greatly enhanced the enchantment of the remote country, where, compared with the small compass of our horizon, distances were prodigious and where vast areas were still unexplored. I came to regard Sinkiang as one of those places where I could travel only in imagination. Had I been told then that for four years its strange landscape was to become as familiar to me as England, I should have dismissed the notion as fantastic.

But three years later, when, with the outbreak of war, I had abandoned all hope of ever going to Central Asia, when I was applying my mind, with little success, to learning to be an army officer, I was suddenly taken out of that environment and, in August 1940, sent to Kashgar as Consul-General. In those days one had grown accustomed to refrain from looking far ahead. The fact that the Consulate had for the past couple of years suffered frequent and prolonged boycott; that British subjects (Indian traders) had been suffering severe and calculated maltreatment; that I could hardly expect a pleasant time and would certainly not be free to travel; the strong possibility that Russia, whose influence in that remote spot was then paramount, would enter the war against us – none of these considerations did much to damp my enthusiasm at the prospect of six weeks' trek through the Karakoram, across the great Asiatic watershed and over the Pamirs to the Tarim Basin beyond.

The first half of the journey, from Srinagar to Gilgit and through the Hunza gorges for ten marches beyond, I already knew well. But I could never have enough of it. Hunza is the most spectacular country I have ever seen. For a hundred and fifty miles the caravan route follows along the great gorge of the Hunza River, through the very heart of the greatest concentration of high mountains in the world. The whole way the river is closely flanked by peaks more than twenty thousand feet high. The first of the giants is Rakaposhi, whose northern face rises straight out of the river-bed at 6,000 feet, first through forested slopes, up steep glacier corries to the great ice-buttresses which support its lovely snow summit (25,550 feet), nearly twenty thousand feet above. A large part of the caravan road is carved out of the sheer sides of the gorge, but every few miles there is a village oasis of terraced fields, fruit trees, briars, willows and poplars, vivid green in spring and summer, aflame with red and gold in autumn. Where the gorge widens out around Baltit, the capital, these villages merge into a great area of intensive cultivation, perhaps forty square miles in extent. Above stand the vast rock walls of the Kanjut Peaks, whose summits, individually unnamed, rise to 24,000 feet. It is difficult to describe this fantastic principality without indulging in superlatives. Both to look at and in character the people are worthy of the unique settings of their country. We like to romanticize about mountain people; and certainly some have produced as fine types as can be found anywhere. But they are so often marred by a high proportion of goitred and cretinous people. The Hunzas are remarkably free from this affliction. Indeed, I have heard it said that there is less sickness, disease and malformity in Hunza in proportion to the size of the population than anywhere else on earth. Their passion for polo is evidence of their splendid horsemanship; as natural mountaineers it would be hard to find their peers. They are proud, loyal, brave and open-hearted. They certainly lack subtlety, but they are not less likeable for that.

My caravan was a large one, for besides the ponies carrying my own baggage and stores for two years, two Indian clerks were travelling with me. I had brought as servants two Sherpas, Lhakpa Tenzing and Rinzing, who had been with me on several Himalayan expeditions. We crossed the Mintaka Pass (15,600 feet), on the frontier, in a snowstorm. Beyond the pass the country changed suddenly and completely. The great gorges and huge mountains of the Karakoram gave place to rounded hills and grassy, U-shaped valleys, with only a few, comparatively small glaciated peaks. We spent our first night in Sinkiang, unmolested, in the pleasant valley at the northern foot of the pass. The next morning, after we had gone a few miles down the valley, we met a platoon of mounted Chinese soldiers under the charge of a young officer. The latter was quite polite, but he told me that we must halt where we were. I showed him our papers, which, of course, included diplomatic visas issued by the Chinese Consul-General in Calcutta. However, these did not interest him much and he said we must wait until he got permission from higher authority to let us through. I asked how long this would take and he replied that he hoped to get a reply within a week. We spent most of the rest of the day arguing the toss. But it was quite useless, and, wondering how far I would be allowed to explore the surrounding mountains, I resigned myself to a long wait.

However, the officer evidently reconsidered his decision overnight and early the next morning he informed us that we were to proceed with an armed escort. We marched for thirty miles and as it was geting dark we reached the wide open valley known as the Taghdumbash Pamir. We started again very early the next morning, but before we had gone more than five miles we reached a large, gaunt fort at a place called Dafdar. We were ordered to halt half a mile from the fort and told not to move until we received further instructions. I expected the commander of the garrison to come out to see me, or at least to be summoned to his presence. But we waited all day in vain, and towards evening we pitched camp. The next morning I rode over to the fort with the intention of paying a call, and finding out the form. As I approached the great mud walls and the large, six-pointed red star painted over the entrance, three soldiers appeared on top of the parapet and waved me back. At first I took no notice and continued riding towards the entrance. The soldiers shouted angrily and finally aimed their rifles at me. I took this gentle hint and returned to camp. In spite of this depressing treatment, I found infinite satisfaction in being in this strange and beautiful land. Far away to the north I could see the great ice-dome of Mustagh Ata. Some fine granite peaks flanked the wide valley on the west. The great distances, the clear, cold air, the intense blue of the sky, the bare, rounded hills that coloured so vividly in the evening light – it all reminded me very much of the plateau of Tibet.

On the third day two officers and some soldiers came over to our camp, made a thorough search of our baggage, making us open all our cases of stores, and told us to be ready to start early the following morning. With another armed escort we marched thirty-five miles and arrived at

Tashkurghan late in the evening. We were herded into a filthy serai, pack-ponies and all, and an armed guard placed at the entrance to see that none of us emerged. There we were kept for another three days. We were not allowed out for any purpose, except to answer calls of nature, and then we were escorted by one of the sentries, presumably to check that our stated reason was genuine. I requested permission to call on the local magistrate, but this was ignored. Eventually one morning a number of policemen with red stars in their caps turned up and started to search our belongings. I had thought that the examination at Dafdar had been thorough, but it was a mere cursory glance compared with this. All the boxes of stores had, of course, to be opened again; all garments were turned inside out and linings were felt with the utmost care; the clothes we were wearing were subjected to an equally rigorous search; a statement of my bank account was studied minutely (at least that was in the right colour!). Whatever was the nature of the contraband that they hoped to find, it must have been capable of being carried in extremely small pieces – opium, perhaps, or vile imperialist propaganda in tabloid form. I had with me a simple route-map. This was taken to be studied, presumably by higher and more expert authorities. Fortunately, none of the party had brought any incriminating articles so diligently sought, and on the following morning we were told that we could proceed with our journey to Kashgar.

All this was not quite the kind of welcome that might reasonably be expected by the accredited representative of a friendly country. But I was not at all surprised, though it served as a salutary reminder of the kind of treatment that we could look for during our stay in Kashgar. It was clearly not worth raising any objections then, and though I submitted a formal protest when I reached Kashgar, I did not receive, nor did I expect, any apology. The Indians, Sirdar Raza Ali and Qazi Gulam Sarwar, behaved with admirable restraint and good-humour, which won my lasting regard and was a great encouragement for the future.

It was a wonderful relief to be on the move again. To my amazement I found that no armed guard had been attached to our party. For some time I expected to see mounted policemen or soldiers chasing after us. But when we left the wide valley of the Taghdumbash and made our way up the narrow little gorge into the mountains of the Kungur-Mustagh Ata massif, I felt sure that I was to be left in peace and freedom to enjoy the last ten days of the journey. Wanting to get as far as possible from the unpleasant memory of Tashkurghan, we made a long march that day, in spite of a fairly late start. It was evening when we reached the 13,500-foot Chichilik Pass, which has two summits, with a wide, undulating plateau between. This was already deep in snow. I was riding alone, well ahead of the caravan. As I crossed the second pass, the sun had sunk below the mountains behind me. The snow was coloured by the reflected evening light. Suddenly two snow leopards walked out from behind a buttress of rock not fifty yards ahead of me. They paused for a moment and looked at me, then ambled on across the snow, apparently quite unconcerned. It was the first time I had seen these beautiful creatures. In that wild and lovely setting it was a most moving experience.

I rode on until long after dark before reaching the little grazing-ground of Tarbashi, where there were two Kirghiz *akois* (dome-shaped felt tents).[1] It was nearly eleven o'clock before all the caravan arrived. The Kirghiz gave us a warm welcome, provided us with food and milk and insisted that we spent the night in one of the *akois*. This was my first encounter with these mountain nomads, for although we had seen many of them south of Tashkurghan, we would not have been permitted to visit their *akois*, and they would have been much too frightened to have any intercourse with us. Each day that followed was as delightful as the last; each night we spent in an *akoi* with a Kirghiz family who gave us the impression that they were really pleased to see us and could not do enough for us. After crossing two more steep passes, we made our way down a valley, forty miles long, which took us gently down towards the plains. As we went, the mountains on either side became less steep and high. Near the foot of the valley we came to a series of villages, with square, flat-roofed mud-houses, terraced, irrigated fields and poplars, not unlike those in the upper Hunza Valley that we had left nearly three weeks before. We spent a night at one of these, in a house built around a square courtyard, with a high verandah, where we ate and slept, looking on to it. In the courtyard I was intrigued to see a large wooden cartwheel in the process of construction. Having travelled for so long among high mountains I had become so unaccustomed to the idea of wheeled traffic that I had quite forgotten that I would presently be coming to a country where it could be used.

The next day we emerged at last from the mountains. The valley widened out like an estuary of a river flowing into the sea. The river meandered over flat, stony ground and finally disappeared underground. We rode out into the desert. There was a thick dust haze over the country; the mountains behind became ghostly shapes and soon disappeared altogether. The march across this stretch of desert was an interlude between two worlds. The day before, as for many weeks past, we had been travelling through wild mountain country, with rushing torrents, huge rock precipices and lofty snow-peaks as the chief landmarks of our march. That evening we reached one of the great oases of the Tarim Basin: mile upon mile of flat, cultivated fields, divided by avenues of poplars, dusty paths, walled orchards, canals and sluggish streams flanked by willows; thickly populated, intimate country, yet strangely unlike anything I had ever seen. We reached Yangi Hisar as it was getting dark and put up in a caravan serai on the edge of the town.

This distance from Yangi Hisar to Kashgar is forty-three miles. I decided to ride ahead and cover it in a single day, while the rest of the caravan took the prescribed two. I started at dawn, and as my pony was tired after the journey I took it gently, so that it was dark before I reached Kashgar. In that time I was able to absorb much of the curious atmosphere of the country. There was still a dust haze, and though it was lighter than on the day before, I could not see the mountains which I knew to be away to my left. The sun, when it rose above the haze which had made it look like a squashed orange, was warm. Indeed, at noon and in the early afternoon it was almost oppressively hot, though it was already October, and the glare from the white, dusty road was

[1] See page 525

trying. Most of the time I was in cultivated country; the fields were largely under plough, though in some, crops of maize and millet were still standing. From time to time I crossed a strip of desert, flat, stony ground, with tamarisk scrub, occasionally broken with high sand-dunes; but I was never out of sight of an oasis, marked on the horizon by a line of poplars. In a way it was dull, monotonous country, but it had a peculiar enchantment which I could not define, and which it never quite lost even when it became familiar. Perhaps it owed some of its appeal to the fact that, though it was a fertile land supporting a prosperous community, nowhere was there any trace of Western culture to distort its ancient, indigenous grace. But though, nowadays, that is rare, it is not unique; and Southern Sinkiang has a quality that is unique in my experience.

At the small town of Tazghun, half-way between Yangi Hisar and Kashgar, it was market-day. As I approached it, I became swept up in an ever-increasing throng of people coming into the market from the surrounding villages. Most of them were riding and carrying their goods on donkeys; but there were also gaily-coloured "Peking carts" drawn by ponies, ox-drawn wagons and strings of camels. It was a cheerful procession. Everyone seemed to be talking and singing at the tops of their voices, oblivious of the choking dust. They were surprisingly well-dressed in long, padded coats, black leather riding-boots and embroidered skull-caps, black and white or brightly coloured. Very few were ragged. Some of the older men wore white turbans, denoting that they had made the pilgrimage to Mecca. Many of the women, who also wore padded coats and riding-boots, were veiled with dark-blue material.

It was evening when I rode past Yangi Shahr, the New or Chinese City of Kashgar. The light of the declining sun seemed somehow to be absorbed into the great mud walls that were all I could see of the town. I had still six miles to go. Though I was tired and stiff, I hadn't the heart to urge my pony into a trot. But it was pleasant riding slowly along in the gathering dusk. The wide, green bed of the Kashgar River was on my right, a line of loess cliffs beyond. It was long after dark when I reached Kashgar and I had a good deal of difficulty in finding the Consulate. It had been a long final day to the journey from India, but it had given me a fascinating introduction to the country where I was to spend the next two years – a rather lonely and very exasperating two years, unfortunately, but not without its compensations.

2

In broad outline the geography of Southern Sinkiang is simple. It consists of the Tarim Basin, a vast oval-shaped plain almost completely surrounded by high mountain ranges; the Kuen Lun on the south and south-east, the Pamirs on the south-west and west, merging into the Tien Shan which, running in an arc, nine hundred miles long, forms the northern rim of the Basin, and separates it from Northern Sinkiang. The rivers draining from these mountains, though many of them are fed from some of the largest snow-fields outside Polar regions, can do no more than irrigate a narrow fringe of country, resulting in a circular chain of oases nearly two thousand miles long, before they disappear into the arid interior of the Basin, which consists of the formidable Takla Makan Desert. When in 1937 we were battling with the flood of waters of the Shaksgam, itself a mere tributary of the Yarkand River, it was difficult to believe that they would eventually be dissipated in this way. The majority of the streams disappear even before they reach the plains, though they add to the water-supply in the form of springs.

These glacier-fed rivers are the life-blood of Southern Sinkiang. For, though the precipitation of moisture in the high mountains is heavy, the rainfall in the plains is negligible (in Kashgar, for example, the average is about two and a half inches a year), and agriculture is entirely dependent on irrigation. The archæological researches of the late Sir Aurel Stein have shown that in ancient times great cities existed far out in what is now complete desert. From this it can be inferred that the extent of the oases was many times greater than it is today. Evidence that the desert is still encroaching is not difficult to find. Unless the present climatic trends are altered, it looks as though the plains of Southern Sinkiang will eventually become uninhabitable. But the process is far too slow to concern the present inhabitants of the country; and in any case our scientists and statesmen between them will probably have achieved the same result over the entire planet long before the desiccation of the Tarim Basin is complete. For the present population of the country the area under cultivation is adequate; and with improved methods of water conservation it could certainly be very greatly increased.

The people of the oases are mostly Turki; they are closely akin in race and language to the Ottoman Turkish. Their standard of living is comparatively high. With a plentiful supply of water from the mountains they make an easy livelihood from the fertile loess soil. Indeed, if one believes that progress is the key to human happiness, it may be that their life is a bit too easy. The most primitive methods of agriculture and irrigation suffice. Serious failure of crops because of drought or pestilence is almost unknown. The climate is not severe, and owing to the lack of rain the simplest mud-walled, flat-roofed houses are all that is required to withstand the weather. As a result, the people are placid and easy-going. Like most people who make an easy living from the land, they want more than anything else to be left alone. It is their unfortunate geographical positon that has caused the centuries of strife which make up their turbulent history.

Kashgar, which lies at the western extremity of the great circle of oases surrounding the Takla Makan, is typical of the towns of Southern Sinkiang. The main part of the town is surrounded by a massive wall about fifty feet high, though it has overflowed the boundaries of the wall in a cluster of suburbs. The streets are narrow, though not unduly squalid. They are lined with the shops of metal-workers, potters, cloth-merchants, caterers, bakers and fruit-sellers. In the centre there is a large market-square and a mosque with a dome of blue tiles. An old Chinese temple stands high above the rest of the town, in curious contrast to the indigenous architecture.

I can best give an impression of the country around Kashgar by describing the scene which I saw for the first time the next morning from the terrace of the British Consulate-General; and, as I discovered later, the description can be applied, with minor modifications, to almost any oasis in Southern Sinkiang. From a high bluff shaded by tall chenar trees, I look across the stretch of fields to the river. The lanes between the fields are flanked by willows. A constant stream of people passes along them: bearded men in turbans and heavy, padded coats, young men in brightly coloured skull-caps, singing lustily, women in tent-like purdah garments. They are nearly all riding donkeys, for the Turkis never walk if they can possibly avoid it. Occasionally a camel caravan appears, lumbering slowly along with a deep clang of bells. The camels are strung together in a long line and always led by a donkey. To the left, across a sunken road, there is another bluff slightly lower than ours, so that I can look down into a walled orchard of peach and apricot trees, and occasionally watch my neighbour, a rich man apparently, entertaining his friends with feast and music.

Across the river there is a line of buff-coloured loess cliffs upon which there are clusters of flat-roofed mud-houses, almost indistinguishable from the cliffs. Beyond, fields and orchards, willows and poplars, stretch away to the edge of the oasis. In the background the desert rises gently to a line of yellow hills, fluted and scored like the "Bad Lands" of Arizona. If the air is clear, I can see, through a gap in the hills, far away to the north, the western ranges of the Tien Shan. But on most days the view is restricted by a dust haze like a slightly foggy day at home, and I cannot see beyond the edge of the oasis, above five miles away.

This dust haze is a peculiar and rather unpleasant feature of Southern Sinkiang. I have never met anything quite like it elsewhere. I presume it is in part due to the unusual form and the geographical situation of the Tarim Basin, but I have seen no convincing explanation of its physical causes. Although there are wind-storms, they are not unusually frequent or persistant, and I have found that, in Kashgar at any rate, they usually precede a period of good visibility, while the dust haze is usually accompanied by a period of still weather. Again, in my experience, there is no time of year when clear periods are more likely to occur than at any other. On the average throughout the year there are perhaps two clear days in ten; but it would give a truer idea of the (very irregular) rhythm to say that three weeks of dust haze is followed by four or five days of clear air. Perhaps, for the foreign resident in Kashgar who cares for such things, the dust haze has one advantage: it certainly heightens the almost dramatic effect of the astonishing panorama that is revealed when it rolls away – the towering rock mountains far away to the north-east and north-west, the smaller desert hills that give distant perspective to the scene, the huge ice-peaks of the Pamirs that stand in a great, glistening arc to the south and south-west. Perhaps if one saw this every day, one would get used to it, I could never quite believe that I should.

In the winter the Kashgar scene is often drab and colourless. There are no evergreens and scarcely any grass. Everything is brown and grey. The rice-fields are frozen. There are sheets of ice along either side of the wide, meandering river. Vapour rises from it into the frosty air. Flights of mallard, pochard and grey geese whirl back and forth in search of some unfrozen spring where they can feed. It seldom snows. About the middle of March a misty green appears on the willows. Then comes the fruit blossom in scattered drifts of pink and white. In April the lucerne appears in the fields and the young wheat, and, with the trees in new leaf, the whole country is swept by a flood of green. So sudden is the change that only two or three weeks seem to have separated deep, arid winter from the fullness of summer. The fig trees and grape vines are dug from the ground where they have been buried for protection from the frost. About the middle of May some of the fruit begins to ripen. First apricots, then, in continuous series, strawberries, (only in the Consulate garden), mulberries, cherries, nectarines, figs, peaches and grapes; pears and apples, too, but they are indifferent. Most important of all are the melons; for the melons of Southern Sinkiang are, I think, the finest in the world. There are certainly none to compare with them in the Middle East or in India; while even the Hami *gwa*, famous throughout China, are not so good as those of the Southern oases. I counted twenty-six varieties. Some have a maximum girth of more than four feet. They play a very imporant part in the lives of the people. Melon stalls serve as wayside cafés where the thirsty traveller can refresh himself by paying a few cents for a juicy slice. In a market there seem to be almost as many melon-sellers as the vendors of all the other commodities put together. It you call at a Turki house, the first thing you are offered is a slice of melon. Traders carry them for many days' journey up into the mountains to exchange with the Kirghiz nomads for butter, meat and skins. A man can make a very comfortable living by cultivating a few acres of melons, though when the fruit is ripening (between July and October, according to the variety), he and his family must spend the nights in the fields to prevent theft. To get the best prices, he must store the melons for sale in winter and early spring, so that, except for about three months, they are procurable the whole year round.

Yes, Kashgar was a pleasant place to live in; for anyone with a taste for travel, with a sense of geography and with a spark of curiosity about people and their ways there can be few places in the world more satisfying. Though that great scourge of modern civilization, the internal-combustion engine, had, alas, made its appearance in Southern Sinkiang a few years before, it was still a rarity, and still confined to the immediate environs of Kashgar and to the two main arterial highways, to Urumchi and to Khotan. All other journeys had to be done with pony or camel caravan or on foot, which are the only methods of travel that can provide a sense of intimacy with, and understanding of, the country. Despite the political influences at work, the people still pursued their ancient way of life; they and their country were as yet almost untouched by contact with the West. Although during my first two years there I was able to travel very little and to explore not at all; although the hostility, the boycotts and the general frustration were at times hard to bear, I was sorry to leave.

3

I travelled out by way of Soviet Turkestan and Persia. I was given an armed escort as far as the frontier at Irkestam. During the past few months the attitude of the local authorities towards our Consulate and towards Indian traders had undergone a remarkable change, and I was now treated with great friendliness and courtesy. By a curious chance the officer in charge of my escort was the one who had met me at Lup Gas the day after I had crossed the Mintaka Pass just over two years before. He appeared rather sheepish when I showed my recognition, but we soon laughed it off and became great friends. At Irkestam I was handed some Soviet currency which had been sent for me from Moscow. Beyond the frontier there was a first-class motor-road. I was travelling in a decrepit Russian lorry, driven by a delightful young Russian who talked hard all the time, heedless of the fact that I hardly understood a word he said. The scenery on this part of the journey was magnificent and I bitterly regretted that I could see it only from the cramped cab of the lorry. We were going down an immensely wide valley, to the south of which there was a vast panorama of ice-mountains of the Trans Alai Range. The road then crossed an 11,000-foot pass and descended steeply to the Feighana Plain. On the third day we reached Osh. Here I was placed under the charge of a charming girl who took me in a luxurious limousine to Andijan. We travelled at high speed along a broad tarmac road through fertile, cotton-growing country. At Andijan I boarded the night train for Tashkent. This swift, almost violent, transition from the slow tempo and medieval atmosphere of Sinkiang to the bustle and crowded turmoil of modern industrial life was fantastic. For a time I was in a daze, hardly able to take in half I saw.

Early the next morning I reached Tashkent. It was raining and the place looked dismal. I was met at the station by a seedy-looking individual who spoke to me in French. He told me that there would be a train on to Krasnavodsk soon, but no one could say quite when, and in the meantime a room had been reserved for me at an hotel, to which he escorted me. It was clearly the hotel-de-luxe of Tashkent; a relic of Tsarist times. It had the form of a good Continental hotel, with a wide staircase leading up from a spacious hall, but everything was in a state of advanced decay. My bedroom on the first floor was evidently the best in the place. It was a large, high-ceilinged room with french windows leading onto a balcony overlooking the street. The furnishings also dated from Tsarist times and obviously had not been renovated since. A vast gilt-framed mirror, with a great crack diagonally across it, occupied most of one wall, above a marble mantelpiece on which there were some coloured china ornaments. For the rest there was an iron bedstead, an upright, singularly uneasy chair, a hard settee and a dilapidated carpet. The following day I was moved to a mean room at the back, nearer to the evil-smelling lavatory. This was the worst thing about the hotel. None of the flushing systems in the half-dozen cubicles worked, nor had they done so, apparently, for some years. Nor was there anyone whose job it was to make good this deficiency by cleaning them out. The resulting filth and stench were indescribable.

I stayed in Tashkent for four days. Hitherto I had been quite impressed with my first brief glimpse of Soviet Turkestan. Osh had had an appearance of well-ordered prosperity. The country between there and Andijan looked well organized and well cultivated. I was very disappointed in Tashkent. In Kashgar, one of the most common Soviet propaganda posters was a somewhat impressionistic representation of Tashkent; rather like a glorified edition of those fantastically palatial factories pictured in the advertisements of biscuit manufacturers. It showed spacious boulevards, flanked by wide stretches of parkland, leading up to superb modern buildings. The streets certainly were wide; there were tramways and there was a not-unpleasant little park where one could sit in the sun and gaze at large busts of Lenin and Stalin. But the place was terribly drab; there was nowhere the charm of an old Asiatic town, nor anything of the efficient comfort of a modern city. There was nothing to relieve the monotony of the square concrete and plaster buildings, which were all shabby, while many revealed their active decomposition by great cracks in the walls.

Beyond the ordinary curiosity aroused by a new country, and one normally so inaccessible to a Western traveller, I found little to interest me in Tashkent and nothing to admire. But two things struck me most forcibly. One was the very high proportion of the million or so inhabitants who seemed to be European Russians. Certainly it was not always possible in their uniform European clothing to tell whether the people I saw were European or Asiatic, but even allowing for that, the number of the former was most striking. The other was the quite remarkable poverty of the food. I had only that provided by my hotel to go on, but judging by the crowds of non-residents that assembled in the restaurant at mealtimes, it can hardly have been considered much below the average. The only dish I ever succeeded in obtaining in the restaurant was a thin vegetable – and occasionally meat – stew and bread. The bread was very dark brown and tasted of coarse brown cardboard, which seemed to stick in one's throat. Sometimes the kind chambermaid in charge of my room brought me a couple of eggs, but I gathered these were not normally provided. Russia had been at war for little more than a year.

Each evening my French-speaking friend came to pay me a brief visit to tell me that the time of my train had not yet been announced. At length, one morning he came with the news that the train was approaching and would leave at noon. He took me to the station in a car. On the way he pressed into my hand a parcel, furtively, as though it were opium; it contained two white-bread rolls. The train pulled out about about half-past two . It had come from Moscow, which it had left a week before, and was crowded with troops bound for Krasnavodsk, on the Caspian Sea, and thence, I gathered, for the Caucasus front. I was provided with a fairly comfortable upper berth in one of the officers' carriages. The troops travelled on wooden seats in squalid, badly sprung trucks and they bore the marks of their week's journey.

The railway, which had been built in Tsarist times, was still a single-tracked affair, with sidings at regular intervals to allow the trains to pass each other.

Troop trains were evidently of low priority, for ours never seemed to have the right-of-way and always drew into the siding to wait for oncoming trains to pass. The reason for this was that the supply route up the Volga having been cut by the German advance to Stalingrad, the urgently needed oil supplies were being sent by this roundabout route to the northern fronts. We passed about a dozen oil-trains a day. Our progress was thus exceedingly slow, and it took three days to cover the 850 miles from Tashkent to Ashkabad, my destination; an average of about twelve miles an hour. The way passed by Samarkand and Bukhara, but from the train I saw nothing of these romantic-sounding places, for they both lay some miles from the railway. The journey, from the scenic point of view, was intensely dull. Almost the whole way there was nothing to be seen but stony desert, featureless and dead flat; no living creature was to be seen and scarcely any human habitation, save an occasional mud-village clustered round a station. I was even denied the mild excitement of seeing the Oxus, for we crossed it at night. The frequent halts, however, had one advantage; one could avoid using the lavatory, which, after a momentary inspection, I did; it was in the same repulsive condition as that in my Tashkent hotel. There was a restaurant car on the forward part of the train, where twice a day a watery vegetable stew and "cardboard" bread was served. On the third day there was a sudden violent rush towards the restaurant car. My compartment mates generously explained the cause of the excitement, thus enabling me to secure a place in the forefront of the rush and a plate of meat stew.

The monotony of the journey was relieved by my travelling companions, who were most friendly and hospitable, as Russians always are when they are not being official. At first their interest in me appeared mainly due to the fact that I was expected to know the exact date of the opening of the Second Front. But when it became evident that I was not to be induced to disclose military secrets, and under the mellowing effects of vodka, supplies of which were replenished at each halt, intercourse became more convivial, though no more intelligible, and the time passed pleasantly enough in song and simple card-games. A young officer in the next compartment spoke excellent English. He found me out on the morning after we left Tashkent and thereafter took me under his benevolent protection. He was a tremendous talker and I was surprised by the openness with which he discussed political problems. By the second day he had become irresistibly attracted by my Rolex wrist-watch. He kept bringing the conversation round to the subject of watches. Watches, he said, were impossible to obtain in Russia. How could one fight a war without a watch? He had heard that they were plentiful in India where I was going. I resolutely ignored the hints. It was not that I minded his having my watch, but I hate being without one on a journey, and I still had a long way to go. At length he was forced into the open and made me an offer for it of two thousand roubles (about £44 at the official rate of exchange). The money would have been quite useless to me, for there was little I could buy with it, and I could not take it out of the country nor change it into foreign currency. I protested that it was a very old watch and that I did not expect it go for much longer. However, nothing but a rude refusal would have deflected him from his purpose, and at last I yielded, and exchanged my beloved watch for a couple of bottles of vodka, in which we drank to the eternal friendship between our two countries.

At Ashkabad I bade farewell to my kind companions, a particularly fond one to my English-speaking friend. I was not met, and had to make my way to the hotel by myself, lugging a hugely expanded suitcase. The distance seemed about two miles, but as I had great difficulty in finding the place, it may, in fact, have been less. I made several abortive enquiries (of the "stranger-here-myself" type), but at length happened upon an English-speaking Pole who took me along with marked enthusiasm. Thereafter he became a persistent, though somewhat secretive, visitor. After a bit I began to suspect that some motive other than the charm of my company lay behind this display of *bonhomie*. Towards the end of my stay, when we were alone together behind carefully closed doors, he unburdened his long and heartbreaking story. He was by trade a film-producer who had been uprooted from his home in Poland at the beginning of the war, suffered terrible privations with his wife and small children and had somehow (I forget exactly how) landed up, still with his family, in this remote spot, where naturally he did not find much scope for his vocation. He sought my help to get him out. Of course, there was nothing I could do for him beyond promising to visit his brother who was living in Kensington and pass on the news of his whereabouts and the story of his odyssey. This I did. Another frequent, and at first somewhat surprising visitor, was my English-speaking officer friend from the train. He turned up the morning after I had arrived, when I was thinking of him as tossing on the Caspian Sea. He explained casually that he was an engineer and had something to do with the railway. I suppose he had just forgotten to tell me that he too was getting off at Ashkabad; or perhaps it had something to do with the watch transaction. However, I was delighted to see him and my time again passed pleasantly enough, drinking vodka and talking.

Ashkabad I found to be built on much the same lines as Tashkent, but it was a comparatively small place without the noise, bustle and crowds, so that on the whole it was no more drab and depressing than, say, Toulouse after the German occupation. Moreover, close at hand were the mountains of the Persian frontier, whose shapes and colours, though not especially exciting in themselves, provided a great relief from the intolerable flatness of the country over which I had lately been travelling. Typical, I imagine, of most of the towns of Soviet Turkestan, the centre of Ashkabad was marked by a vast parade – or meeting – ground presided over by an elegant concrete rostrum or saluting-base. Apparently the absence or obstruction of public conveniences presented as big a problem to the local populace as they had to me, for on closer inspection I found that not only the ground immediately surrounding it but the spacious steps and platform of the rostrum itself were covered deeply with deposits of evil-smelling filth.

I stayed two nights in Ashkabad, and then late on the third I was given a place on one of a convoy of lorries, and was taken to the Russian frontier post about ten miles away. Here my baggage was given a cursory examination, I surrendered the remainder of my roubles, and waited for dawn, when I got a lift on another lorry to a tiny village a few miles on the Persian side of the frontier. From here to Meshed I had to hitch-hike. There should have been no lack of traffic on this part of the road, as it was one of the lesser arteries in the already active "Supplies to Russia" system. My main problem was money; not a problem exactly, for I had none. I had brought some food with me from Kashgar, but for transport I had to rely upon the goodwill of the Persian lorry-drivers. After waiting a day in the village, I got a lift down to Kuchan, and after thirty-six hours there, another to Meshed.

At Meshed I had two days of ease and luxury at the British Consulate-General. The Consul-General, Mr. C. P. (now Sir Clarmont) Skrine, had been one of my predecessors in Kashgar. He himself was unfortunately away in India at the time, but Mrs. Skrine welcomed me with very great kindness. She had been with her husband in Kashgar in the palmy days of the early 'twenties and had loved every moment of it; so that I was able to indulge in that very rare luxury for a returning traveller – unlimited talk with a sympathetic audience about the subject which is nearest his heart. Under her expert guidance, too, I saw a lot of Meshed, including a private view of the famous Blue Mosque.

The remainder of my way to India consisted of three days by lorry to Zahidan, and thirty-six hours in the weekly train from Zahidan to Quetta. In many ways it had been an interesting journey from Kashgar, and I would not have missed it. But had it been my only experience of travel across the great spaces of Central Asia, I would have been sadly disillusioned. Fortunately, I had done enough to realize that even today most travel in Central Asia must be done by less banal methods.

CHAPTER THREE

Bostan Terek – A Glissade

THERE are those, I believe, who imagine that the number of unexplored and unclimbed mountains is fast running out; that given reasonably peaceful conditons, quicker and cheaper transport, in a generation or so, half a century at most, all the peaks of the world will have been scaled, and that, even in the more remote ranges, mountaineers wishing to tread new ground will have to "invent" new ways of approach. That must indeed be a gloomy prospect. But I defy even the most pessimistic mountaineer to travel far in the highlands of Central Asia and still to hold that view. He may come to wonder, as I have often wondered, whether in a century and a half of mountaineering, one-tenth of the summits of the world have as yet been reached.

For the first thirty years of this century, the huge panorama of ice-mountains seen from Ranikhet contained only one peak (Trisul) that had been climbed. Those mountains are the most easily accessible in the Himalaya. Imagine, if you can, several hundred such ranges. One of them I can see from the roof of my house in Kashgar. From here on a clear day I can count a score of peaks without name, without position on any map, unmeasured. Not amorphous desert hills that no one can want to climb anyway; not the 25,000-foot giants that would demand the tiresome organization of "high camps" and "assault parties"; not "aiguilles", "nordends" or subsidiary summits (I could use the word hundreds if I included those). They are peaks of Alpine stature and form, each rising from its own system of glacier valleys and supported by its own complex of granite face and ice-ridge. Any one of them could be climbed by a competent party, after due reconnaissance and failure, from a camp barely above the pine forest. Many of them would offer problems as attractive as any in the Alps. Yet I doubt whether by the end of the twentieth century much more will be known about these peaks, in climbing terms, than is known today. Not because of "iron curtains"; not because they lie far from the offices and homes of those interested in these matters; but simply because of the vastness of the field for new mountaineering adventure of which they form so small a part.

It may well be objected that the existence of such a field is scant consolation to those whose brief holidays confine them to overcrowded Alpine peaks. But, even so, it is well for them to contemplate this wider background, to realize that the future of mountaineering does not consist only in the unending development of gymnastic technique, and that though the advance of modern means of transport may shrink the world to lamentably small proportions, it should also continue, for a very long time to come, to open an ever-expanding field of mountaineering enterprise. Let us not waste our sympathy on posterity; there will be enough for them as there is for us.

On even the most familiar journeys in this part of the world, unexplored ranges are such a commonplace, so much the order of the marching day, that to cross a side-stream whose source is known usually calls for excited comment; a peak distinguished with a name stands like a lighthouse in a limitless sea. This is enchanting, no doubt, but over-familiarity with these conditions has, I find, one unfortunate and rather disconcerting result. I appear to have lost a good deal of my interest in climbing mountains. Not entirely; but much of the rapturous enthusiasm seems to have gone. I recall, for example, my intense eagerness to make the second ascent of Mount Kenya, which for some months was a ruling passion of my life, and with some sadness contrast it with the nonchalance with which I gaze at a view of half a dozen peaks, greater in height, equally beautiful in form. I am not alone in this. I have often remarked, for example, how little members of the Mount Everest expeditions used to avail themselves of the opportunity, for many of them unique, of climbing virgin peaks around the Base Camp or in Sikkim. The excuse was rarely valid that the exhaustion of high climbing or lack of time prevented them. Everest has all too seldom allowed us to exhaust ourselves on her higher reaches; few, surely, have calculated their time with such precision as to have to deny themselves an extra week, even if as much were needed.

How, then, are we to explain this away? Is it an ugly reflection upon the purity of our motive? Is the fame of a mountain a necessary part of the stimulus that makes us wish to climb it? Must we be able to point out our conquest to an appreciative audience and say "I climbed that"? Do we wonder, even subconsciously, what is the use of climbing one of a range of a thousand mountains that nobody has even heard of? I have tried to account for this disturbing tendency in myself by the reflection that mountain-climbing has its roots in a desire to explore; that given the genuine article, the substitute loses much of its allure. There is a good deal of truth in this, but the explanation is far from being entirely satisfactory. It cannot be claimed that much exploration was done on the later Everest expeditions. It does not account for the fact that in my present mood I would undoubtedly be more stirred by a view of the Peuterey Ridge than by a ridge of twice the size of an unknown mountain. Nor does it explain my acute feelings of envy when I read a friend's account of his ascent of the Guggi Route or of the Viereselgrat. Such things should be paltry beside my own opportunities, if not my exploits. But they often seem a great deal more desirable. I have wondered if this is not due to my advancing years; whether I am not becoming an armchair mountaineer, ready to envy but not to act. But I think I can honestly (if eagerly) reject this explanation. For I am satisfied that were I to visit the Alps again, my enthusiasm for climbing peaks would be little or no less than it was twenty years ago. Unfortunately, in that period I have only had one brief opportunity of putting the speculation to the test. I found, in those days, infinite satisfaction in being once more in country, every inch of which was accurately mapped, the smallest buttress named. I set out to climb a third-rate mountain as eagerly as though it had been my first expedition with rope and axe.

It seems, then, that we must look for some deeper reason for the failure of these unknown mountains to attract us to their remote and lonely summits; for we must at all costs avoid the indictment of a competitive spirit. An analogy might perhaps be allowed in the case of rock-climbing. Does the Lakeland expert gaze with longing at the great rock walls of the Lauterbrunnen Valley as he passes them in the train? Would he be consumed by an irrestistible desire to force his way up one of an infinite number of possible routes on a twenty-mile-long precipice flanking the path up the Hunza Valley? Would he not be overcome by a feeling of cold futility if he tried? Like most analogies it exaggerates the case; and, of course, it will be argued that while there are great peaks to be climbed, one does not bother with minor buttresses, that, in fact, as mountain-climbing is a substitute for mountain exploration, so cliff-climbing is a substitute for mountain-climbing. This, too, may be allowed, but again I find it an unsatisfactory explanation. There *is* some quality about a buttress on Scafell that urges us to climb it, which is lacking in a cliff that is less well-known by reason of the very profusion of precipices in which it is set. So, I find, it is with mountains themselves. Some kind of intimacy, either personal or historical, seems to be necessary, without which we are oppressed by an overwhelming sense of loneliness and awed by the insignificance of our achievement.

The best way to cure a mountaineer of such unhealthy introspection is to deny him access to the mountains. Until my first tour in Kashgar, I had never been in a position of being able to gaze month after month at mountains with little or no prospect of reaching them. It was not an unmitigated torment. There was so much joy and solace in just looking at them in their never-ending variety of cloud and colour setting, that I certainly would not have wished them away. The memory that there had been periods in my life when I was completely satisfied by physical contact with great peaks was an enormous help in curbing regret and in preventing it from spoiling the contemplation of that remarkable view.

Even so, there were times when the craving to reach the mountains was almost intolerable. For in those days in Kashgar I was living in a police state. Moreover, I and my fellow-nationals were lucky enough to be fulfilling that important political rôle performed by the Jews under Hitler and by the bourgeoisie during the French Revolution. A scapegoat is apparently necessary to a dictatorship, at least in its earlier years. Later, of course, the species is liable to become extinct through failure of the authorities to observe even the most elementary rules of game preservation, and the ruling clique must seek or invent some external object for its righteous abuse. The excellent band of Swedish missionaries who had done such fine work here for the best part of half a century and had won the universal respect and liking of the local population, being more vulnerable to attack, had succumbed a couple of years before. The Indian traders clung to life with unreasonable tenacity, and we stayed to support them. Between us we served their purpose. Any official or private individual whom the authorities found it convenient to remove, was at once found to have been friendly with, or spying for, the British Consulate-General. I discovered later that our sinister influence had spread far and wide: in distant cities that no Indian trader or member of our staff had visited for a quarter of a century; among Kirghiz tribesmen in remote mountain valleys, who had never set eyes upon our humble establishment. The resulting boycott was tiresome, but I found it easy to bear compared to the confinement to a ten-mile radius in the midst of this country of such boundless opportunity.

At length, after nearly a year, I could stand it no longer, and I decided to slink away in secret to the nearest mountains. At the time I attributed the success of my plan to my cleverness in its execution. I later discovered that, a thousand miles away in the Provincial capital, forces were at work which were to result in a complete political *volte-face*, and which ended for a time that ugly spell of totalitarian rule. But for this, I am more than doubtful whether I would have achieved my innocent design. However that may be, I left Kashgar before dawn one morning in September in a covered country cart, together with Lhakpa Tenzing and a Hunza servant, and after two long days' travel reached the Kirghiz settlement of Bostan Terek, sixty miles to the west.

The first day's march was through the south-westward extension of the Kashgar oasis, along dusty country roads, flanked by willows, irrigation channels and fields, to Opal. This I thought was the danger-point, and though we passed through the bazaar in the dusk, I was fully expecting to be challenged and asked for our papers. However, we got through without a hitch, spent the night at the edge of the oasis, and were off again by dawn the next morning. Once out in the desert beyond Opal I breathed a sigh of relief, for I then felt fairly safe from pursuit. It was a long, hot, waterless march, utterly motononous, over gently rising ground, rocky and scored by innumerable dry water-courses. But the mountains were in view, and though we seemed to be moving infinitely slowly, they were gradually getting nearer. Though we could see Bostan Terek the whole time, it was not easy to find the track, and once off it the going was terribly rough for our clumsy cart. We were still five or six miles from our destination when night fell. Luckily we found a spring of water and, as there was plenty of dry tamarisk wood, we made a pleasant camp. We reached Bostan Terek early on the third morning.

We were sure of a friendly reception, for the Swedish missionaries had made a summer resort in the valley, to which they had come in relays each year. I knew that they had been very well liked, and that I would benefit from a reflection of that popularity; but, even so, I was not prepared for the warmth of the welcome we received. Every family seemed to vie with each other to entertain us. If their hospitality had not been so charmingly simple and genuine, it might have been embarrassing. They seemed to think that our arrival heralded a return to the good old days. We spent the remainder of the morning drinking milk in various *akois* and talking to our hosts. It was wonderful to be away from the atmosphere of fear and suspicion, that in those days ruled in the large oases. I spent the afternoon shooting chikor (hill partridge) of which there were thousands in the foot-hills nearby. I shot some dozens without any difficulty and distributed them to our hosts.

Bostan Terek is one of the eastern valleys of the Kashgar Range, a northerly continuation of the Pamirs. The river flowing down it from the glaciers at its head disappears when it leaves the foot-hills, under the thirty-mile-wide band of coarse alluvial deposits which we had just crossed. The water emerges again in springs, helps to irrigate the Opal oasis and eventually flows into the Yarkand River. At the foot of the valley there is enough water for the cultivation of quite a wide area of fields, where the Kirghiz grow wheat and barley. Like most of the Kirghiz of these parts they are semi-nomadic grazing their flocks on the high pastures during the summer and living at the foot of the valley in winter. I have often wondered why these semi-nomads, who always inhabit the same valley, continue to live in *akois,* moving them from the arable land to the various levels of pasture and back again according to the season. It would be easy enough for them to build stone and timber houses at each place, which would far outlast their frail tents, and save the continual transport back and forth. They have told me that they dislike houses as they are difficult to keep clean and are apt to become vermin-ridden.

The following day Lhakpa and I set off up the valley, together with two Kirghiz and a couple of yaks we had hired to carry our baggage. After we had passed through the cultivated area, we climbed up onto the wide, grassy ridge of an ancient moraine. To the left, across the gorge cut by the river, the southern flank of the valley was covered with fir forest for several miles, until it merged into sheer granite cliffs. Beyond, the valley floor climbed in a series of wide, grassy terraces into the heart of the ice-mountains. We camped in a pleasant little hollow by a spring at a height of about thirteen thousand feet.

From there, during the following week, Lhakpa and I did a series of climbs of varying difficulty. I had brought my dog, Khombu, with me. We had, of course, to leave him tied up when we set off each morning, telling the Kirghiz to let him free when we had been gone an hour. Each evening as we came off the glaciers we would start shouting and he would come up to meet us.

It was a perfect place for a climbing holiday. A short way above our camp the valley opened out into a wide circle of granite peaks between 17,000 feet and 18,500 feet high. Several glaciers draining from these met in the centre and flowed a short way down the main valley. The highest peak was a lovely twin-headed one which formed a prominent landmark in the view from Kashgar. I had hoped to attempt it after we had got into some sort of training on the smaller mountains. It looked very difficult indeed. It was built of a remarkable complexity of sharp granite ridges divided by steep ice-couloirs and hanging glaciers. Each day we studied it from a new angle, hoping to find some way through its formidable defences. But each aspect looked more forbidding than the last, and at length I decided reluctantly to abandon any idea of attempting it. We had neither the time nor the facilities for exploring the western aspect of the mountain, and the standard of climbing involved in an attempt on any route on the eastern side was obviously higher than anything we were likely to reach on this visit.

The second-highest peak in the group was also a very fine one, which resembled the Dent Blanche seen from the upper Zinal valley. The side of it facing the cirque was a granite precipice standing some four thousand feet sheer above the glacier. But just beyond a high col on the main watershed I had caught a profile glimpse of a face in its upper part which seemed to offer a possible route. The lower part was hidden behind the col. So on the sixth day, after we had done several climbs, we set out to reconnoitre.

The way to the col led through a glacier bay shut in by the great rock walls of the highest and the second-highest peaks, and thence up a long snow-couloir. As we were making our way up the glacier bay there was an eclipse of the sun. At this point it was not a total eclipse (the edge of the belt of totality was about a hundred miles to the north), but it was sufficiently complete to produce a weird effect of deep twilight. We reached the col before noon. From it we saw the whole of the face of our mountain. The lower part was an easy snow-slope which we could reach without any difficulty by climbing a couple of hundred feet down beyond the col. The upper part consisted of a band of broken rocks split by a very steep snow- or ice-couloir. Above the rocks an ice-dome formed the summit of the mountain. To reach it from our camp would involve a climb of more than five thousand feet. But the difficult section was comparatively small. Much depended upon the quality of the snow on the lower part of the face.

We started the next morning just before dawn. Like each of its predecessors, it was a lovely day. Although as soon as the sun rose we were in its light, it was very cold and the snow remained frozen hard all the way up to the col. We made much better time than on the previous day. But on the face of the mountain beyond the col the snow deteriorated extraordinarily quickly, and before we had gone a thousand feet up we were sinking in well above our knees. This was an unpleasant surprise, for after at least a week of fine weather, and probably much longer, I could see no reason for such a depth of soft snow. The slow, upward struggle consumed hours of time, with almost imperceptible results.

As we approached on the rocks, the slope became steeper and the snow firmer. We had intended to climb the couloir which split the rock face, but as we came nearer to it we saw that it was composed of hard, blue ice. It was tremendously steep and it would have taken us at least six hours to cut steps to the top of it. As it was already nearly one o'clock by the time we reached the foot of the rocks, this was clearly out of the question. The rocks themselves did not look too difficult. We chose a line and started to climb them. Here we met with our third disappointment. The rocks were completely rotten, coated with ice and a great deal steeper than they had appeared from below. It was the kind of ground, common on broken, ice-covered rocks, where it appears that if one can only overcome the next ten feet it will be much easier and where this appearance always turns out to be wrong. We climbed some way up a nasty little gully and were defeated by a slippery scoop, only ten feet high, at its top. With great difficulty we traversed across to a rib to the left. Here we found that the rock was firmer and comparatively free from ice. I decided that we should give the rib a trial and if we failed to climb it we should abandon the attempt.

After a couple of pitches the rib steepened a lot and the climbing became very difficult. But by then we were only a hundred feet below the base of the ice-dome forming the summit. I led off in a determined attempt to reach it, supposing that the difficulties would then be over. I had already conceived the idea of glissading down the ice-couloir as an alternative to climbing down the rocks. Though it was steep and narrow and composed entirely of ice, there was a perfect run out at the bottom and providing we kept our feet we could not come to any harm. The idea appealed to me so much that I pressed my efforts on the upper part of the rib a good deal farther than I ought to have done. I climbed very slowly. It was difficult all the way and there was absolutely no stance, let alone a belay to which I could bring Lhakpa. I had almost reached the ice when the rope came taut behind me. I could not possibly have held Lhakpa, who in any case said, very wisely, that in the circumstances he would rather not follow. I had either to retreat or unrope and go on to the top, perform my wild glissade and then return to fetch Lhakpa, who fortunately was in a comfortable position. The prospect of climbing down the way I had come was so abhorrent that I decided on the latter course.

I unroped and threw down the end, thus effectively burning my boats. I then climbed the remaining few feet to the top of the rocks. Here to my dismay I found that my difficulties were by no means over. The base of the ice-dome was flush with the top of the rocks and there was no ledge between the two. Moreover, for the first four feet the ice was vertical, before it gradually began to slope back. At the top of the rib there was one foot-hold, flat but only large enough to take the sole of one boot. With infinite caution, by a sort of "mantelpiece" movement, I managed, after two attempts, to stand with my left foot on this. It was a horrible position, for at first there was nothing to hold on to, and the bulge of the ice seemed to be pushing me outwards off my balance. I remember wondering how many times I would bounce if I fell, before reaching the snow-slope below. I swung my axe above my head and dug the pick into the ice. That helped matters, but it was not a permanent relief and I had to face the unpleasant task of cutting a step in the ice. Fortunately, immediately to my right, the face of the ice, though still vertical, receded in conformity with the contour of the rock, which allowed me to swing my axe much more freely than would otherwise have been the case. First I cut a handhold well above the four-foot vertical section, and then, holding on to this with my gloved left hand, began work on the step. It was very laborious; for the step had to be large, as it would be awkward to step into it, and also knee-room had to be fashioned above. After every dozen or so strokes I had to rest my right arm. Also my left foot was getting very tired and I had often to relieve the pressure on it by anchoring my axe in the ice-slope above and leaning on it and the hand-hold. I must have worked on that step for well over half an hour before I was satisfied with it. I had cut it too high for convenience and had a struggle to get on to it. But once there, the relief was intense. The weight at last off my left foot, I could lean forward over the ice-bulge. The second and third steps were easy to make, and after that I was standing squarely on the ice-slope above. Soon, as the angle eased off, there was a covering of firm snow on the ice, and presently I could stop cutting and kick steps instead. I almost ran up the last slope, and five minutes later I reached the top of the mountain.

It was a quarter-past four. The air was calm, and the sun was still quite warm. I was still feeling the blissful relief of no longer being plastered against the ice-bulge. To this was now added the thrill of reaching the summit, of which I had several times during the day almost abandoned hope, and which latterly had become merely a way of escape. For a moment I almost forgot the unpleasant prospect of the glissade to which I was now committed. I would like to have sat for an hour studying the view. But I could not afford more than ten minutes; as it was, there was no chance of getting back to camp before dark. To the south, the peaks of the Kungur and Chakragil massifs were clear. But the best part of the view was to the north where stood the highest mountain of the Bostan Terek group. I was only a little lower than its twin summits, and its clean-cut, sweeping ridges stood out, magnificently defined in the slanting sunlight. I had no camera with me. In those days in Sinkiang cameras were strictly forbidden and it would have been asking for trouble to carry one.

It was nearly half-past four by the time I started the descent. I walked a little way along the wide summit ridge, and then started diagonally down to the right until I was immediately above the ice-couloir. A shout came from below and, looking down, I saw that Lhakpa had already climbed down to the snow-slope below the rocks. I cut a few steps down until I could get a clear view of the whole length of the couloir. It was dead straight, but very narrow in its middle section. It was essential that I should start exactly above this narrow part, for, once started, I could not possibly control the direction of my glissade. I cut a large platform from which to start, and stood for a few minutes contemplating the prospect with a sinking heart. It was much more frightening than I had expected. The ice was tremendously steep; Lhakpa and the blessed snow-slope looked miles away down; though the length of the couloir was not more than a few hundred feet; the two crags projecting from its sides half-way down allowed distressingly little room for error. However, there was nothing for it but to take the plunge, and the sooner I did so, the sooner I would get it over. It was at least, very simple; all I had to do was to keep my head, keep my legs and my body absolutely rigid, and hang on to my ice-axe for all I was worth. I leant hard back with my right hand almost on the ferrule of the axe (even so I seemed to be standing almost upright) and let my feet slip out of the step. The next moment I seemed to be falling through space with hardly any contact on the ice. The rushing wind caught my breath, but at the same time I felt as if I were shouting at the top of my voice. It seemed endless; but I was dimly aware of the rock promontories rushing up towards me, and then past me, one on either side. I had no time to realize that my aim through the narrow section had been true before a wave of snow rushed up and blinded me. Then after a while I felt my pace slacken. I dug my heels in, came to a halt and sank down on the snow, completely winded.

For the second time in about an hour I experienced a glorious sense of relief. The summit had been reached and the somewhat unorthodox descent of the only difficult part achieved. Nothing remained but a long but easy downward journey in the soft evening light. While I lay on the snow-slope recovering my breath, Lhakpa came across to join me. My hat had disappeared. I made no attempt to look for it. We roped up and plunged on down the slope. The slight rise from the foot of the face to the col demanded unwelcome effort, but the snow in the couloir beyond was sufficiently firm for a gentle glissade. Darkness fell as we were making our way over the rough, moraine-covered lower glacier. But soon we had the camp-fire to guide us. Khombu came up to meet us in answer to our shouts. The Kirghiz, bless them, had a pot of boiling water ready for us, and tea was soon made.

The next day we went down and camped by the river below the fir forest on the southern side of the valley. There, in delightful contrast to the peaks and glaciers, we spent our last three days, hunting ram chikor.

These remarkable birds are widely distributed in the high mountains of Central Asia. I have found them in the Mount Everest region, all over the Karakorams, in the Pamirs and in the Tien Shan, at altitudes varying from 9,000 feet to 17,000 feet. Their taste in local environment seems to be equally catholic. In early spring I have found them high up on the tops of mountains covered by a deep mantle of snow, with no bare ground to be seen for miles around; in the summer I have found them living in pine forest; I have met with them many miles up great glaciers and amongst barren mountains where water is very hard to find. They are large grey birds, sometimes as big as a small turkey. Their flesh is delicious. Hunting them with a shot-gun is, I find, even better sport than hunting ibex or *ovis poli*.

At dawn their echoing call, a long ascending note, can be heard high up on the mountain-side. It is the most thrilling sound I know; it seems somehow to express perfectly the wild grandeur of the country in which they live. Even with the call as a guide, it is generally difficult to locate them from a distance;

and the first essential in hunting them is to spot them before they are aware of your presence. Except in the mating season, they keep together in flocks of twenty, thirty, or even more. They are difficult to stalk because one of their number usually sits perched on a rock commanding the surrounding mountain-side while the others are feeding, ready to give warning of an approaching enemy. When they are startled into flight or wish to fly to another grazing-ground, they launch themselves into a steep downward glide, thus gaining tremendous speed, which carries them in a sort of pendulum swing across the valley without any apparent wing movement. The beginning of the flight is nearly always accompanied by a shrill, gobbling cry.

It is no use attempting to shoot them on the wing, for they are always in steep country, high above the valley floor, and even if you were lucky enough to hit one, the speed of its flight would carry the dead bird such a distance that it would be almost impossible to find. The problem, then, with a shotgun, is to get within thirty yards of them before they take off. It would be easier, of course, to shoot them with a rifle, but that is liable to ruin most of the flesh. If they are approached from above, they invariably take off as soon as they are disturbed and it is almost impossible to get a shot at them. But if they see you coming from below, they start running up-hill and usually do not launch into flight until within range. I have found that, when I am fresh and in good training, I can, by going all out, run up-hill a little faster than they can. But at that speed, after a few hundred feet, I can no longer gain on them. My stalks were rarely so successful that I could get within range of them unobserved, and they usually ended with a long up-hill chase which left me so winded that I often failed to hit the birds even if I got near enough. The best that I generally hoped for was to get so close before exposing myself that an upwards dash of only two or three hundred feet would put me within range.

But sometimes the chase would go on for thousands of feet. For even when, as often happened, the birds spotted me a long way below and started their upward trek, all was not lost. If I could contrive to disappear again from their view they would loiter, thus enabling me to gain on them without exhausting myself by climbing too fast. The difficulty, then, was to keep on their track and still remain hidden. Lhakpa would co-operate from far below indicating their whereabouts with wild and usually unintelligible gesticulations.

In the matter of rock-climbing the ram chikor could always beat me, for they could flutter from ledge to ledge far faster than I could climb. So when they got on to cliffs I would have to try and outflank them, which often led to some very interesting mountaineering problems.

In all the scores of ram chikor stalks I have done, I doubt if more than one in ten has been successful. But whatever the result, they have always provided wonderful sport. On this occasion I was either exceptionally fit or, more likely, the birds were unusually fat and lazy after a whole summer of good eating, for in the three days I succeeded in shooting no fewer than six.

CHAPTER FOUR

Political Background

BEFORE considering recent events in Sinkiang it is as well to reflect upon its history during the present century. From this the salient fact emerges that from the foundation of the Chinese Republic until 1942 there was virtually no Central Government control over the Province. In the general confusion that followed the revolution in China in 1911 Yang Tseng-hsin came over from Kansu where he had held the post of Governor, and took complete charge of the Province. For the next seventeen years he ruled with absolute authority, taking no orders from the Central Government and submitting to no foreign influence. The weakness of the Central Government and events in Russia made it easy for him to retain his independence. What was remarkable was the way in which he established and held firm control throughout the Province. He rarely left his capital in Urumchi and, so far as I know, never visited the great southern oases. Yet he managed largely to prevent the establishment of local tyranny, to restrain corruption within reasonable limits and to avoid serious unrest throughout the whole vast area. It was an era of peace and prosperity which many of the older inhabitants think of as a golden age. For Indian traders this was certainly so.

How long Yang could have maintained this admirable state of affairs in the face of increasing external pressure is a matter for speculation, for in 1928 he was murdered. By whose agency, it was never fully established. He was succeeded by Chin Shu-jen, who unfortunately lacked both his character and his political sagacity, with the result that the Province soon relapsed into a state of turbulence which, in the early 'thirties, crystallized into a three-cornered civil war. The leaders of the opposing factions were: (i) the Tungan general Ma Chung-ying, who invaded the province from Kansu and for a time controlled the whole of South Sinkiang; (ii) General Chang, the commander of Chin's army who had control of the Ili district, and (iii) General Sheng Shih-t'sai, Chang's second-in-command, who seized Urumchi. In the meantime, Chin had fled. There is some evidence that, at first, all three factions received Soviet support. Later, however, it was Sheng Shih-t'sai who was selected as the most promising and with strong support in the shape of aeroplanes and other modern weapons he succeeded in defeating his rivals. Chang committed suicide, Ma, after holding out for some time in the Kashgar district, finally disappeared into Soviet territory. The establishment in 1933 of Sheng Shih-t'sai as Tupan or Governor of the Province was known as the "Great April Revolution", the anniversary of which was celebrated each year throughout the Province until 1942.

From 1933 until 1942 Sinkiang was dominated by Soviet influence. Early resistance by Ma in Kashgar and by the Amir of Khotan, and the Tungan Rebellion which gained temporary success in the south in 1937, provided the only serious opposition. To what extent Sheng was a mere puppet of the Soviet, or to what extent he controlled the affairs of the Province, one can only guess. The fact remains that during that period Sinkiang became a police state on the Soviet model: all outside influence other than Russian was rigorously excluded; no order of the Central Government was obeyed unless it happened to be convenient; Russian civil, military and scientific advisers were employed throughout the Province; trade with the Soviet Union expanded, all trade with India and with Central China was stopped; Islam was ridiculed in the schools, though its teaching was not actually prohibited; the Chinese national emblem was replaced by a six-pointed red star (the Soviet star has five points) on public buildings, flags and the badges of officials; all foreign missionaries were expelled; Indian traders were persecuted, maltreated and deported in large numbers, often in cruel circumstances; the British Consulate-General in Kashgar suffered a rigid boycott.

In 1940–41 it seemed almost certain that Sinkiang would at last become absorbed into Russian Turkestan, an event foretold by Lord Curzon as long ago as 1901. Towards the end of 1942, however, Sheng Shih-t'sai, presumably taking advantage of Russia's preoccupation elsewhere, performed a remarkable *volte-face*. He placed himself under the orders of the Kuomintang, and arrested a large number of his former subordinates. The Russians withdrew, leaving Sinkiang under the effective rule of the Chinese Central Government for the first time since the foundation of the Republic.

The Chinese were still heavily engaged with the Japanese war and they were naturally slow to consolidate their position. Nothing very much seems to have happened until 1944, when Sheng Shih-t'sai was relieved of his post. On 7th November of that year a rebellion broke out in Ili and quickly spread to the two nothern districts of Chugachak and Altai. It was, of course, ostensibly a nationalist uprising, but there seems to be little doubt that the rebels received considerable help from outside. They quickly overwhelmed the Chinese garrisons and massacred a large number of Chinese civilians. They marched on Urumchi, and it seemed as though nothing would prevent them from capturing the capital and achieving their declared intention of setting up a "Republic of Eastern Turkestan" comprising the whole province. The Soviet Ambassador in Nanking offered the services of the Soviet Consul-General in Urumchi as a mediator to arrange a settlement between the rebels and the Chinese. The Central Government accepted this offer and sent General Chang Chih-chung, commander of the North-west Mobile Headquarters, to Urumchi to act as governor and to conclude peace with the rebels. An eleven-point agreement was signed (January 1946) by both parties. It provided, among other things, for a considerable measure of self-government for the native population, popular elections of local officials and for a reduction in the number of Chinese troops in Sinkiang. A coalition government was formed, but there was discord between the two parties and tension developed.

In the meantime, in the autumn of 1945, another revolt broke out, this time among the nomad populaton of Sarikol on the south-western frontier of the Province. There is no doubt that a considerable number of the so-called rebels came from across the border, or that the arms and ammunition for the revolt came from the same source. Most of the small Chinese garrisons were quickly annihiliated; some fled to Gilgit. The "rebels" advanced to the plains, threatened Kashgar, captured Kaghilik and invested Yarkand. The position of the Chinese was extremely critical; indeed, it would almost certainly have been untenable if the rebels had had the support of the Turki population of the oases. It is significant that they obtained no help from this quarter, and that the Chinese forces, which at the time were very weak, were able to drive them back to the mountains and a year later to regain control of Sarikol. While the rebels were in control of the mountain regions they slaughtered and drove off a large number of cattle, sheep and horses belonging to their nomad brothers (Kirghiz and Tajik). About this time, too, Aksu was attacked and portions of the Urumchi-Kashgar highway occupied from across the Tien Shan.

By the end of 1946 there was an uneasy peace throughout the Province. In the north each side accused the other of failure to honour its obligations under the agreement, until in the summer of 1947 the representatives of the Ili faction left the capital and returned to Ili, declaring that they would not co-operate with the Provincial Government until their demands were met. In the south there was a great deal of anti-Chinese agitation instigated by communists and nationalist extremists, probably a very small minority. In the meantime large numbers of troops and a considerable quantity of arms and equipment arrived from Central China, and with these the Chinese strengthened their garrisons in seven out of ten districts of the Province, to an unprecedented extent. The arrest of a small number of agitators in the south effectively silenced opposition, while in Urumchi and the north-east the Chinese obtained the support of the Khasaks, under their leader Usman, who had quarrelled with the Ili faction.

But by the autumn of 1947 the rift was complete between the Ili faction, who controlled the "Three Areas" (Ili, Chuguchak and Altai), and the Chinese. Notes continued to pass between the leaders of the former and General Chang Chih-chung. The Ili faction took the line that they did not wish to secede from China, and that if only the Chinese would implement their obligations under the agreement of January 1946 they would willingly resume their co-operation in the government of the Province. The Chinese for their part maintained that they had in fact fulfilled all their obligations, that it was the Ili faction who had failed to honour theirs and that it was necessary to maintain a strong Chinese garrison to keep the peace so long as the Ili faction and their supporters in the rest of the Province continued to ferment trouble.

There was no trade and hardly any communication between the "Three Areas" and the rest of the Province. This imposed a severe burden upon the economy of the Province, for, although the south was self-supporting in food, the Urumchi district formerly relied for grain upon the Ili district and was now obliged to import its requirements from Kansu and Szechwan. Nearly all the mineral resources hitherto discovered were in the "Three Areas", whence the wolfram and other products were now exported to the Soviet Union.

Despite all these upsets, China had a fair opportunity of winning the goodwill and loyalty of the native people of the remaining seven districts, and of restoring a measure of prosperity and, above all, peace to this unfortunate land. Southern Sinkiang, comprising all the great oases around the Takla Makan, is very fertile, well watered from the glaciers of the Tien Shan, Kuen Lun and Pamirs, and under-populated. Left alone, the people could supply themselves with abundant food; with suitable encouragement, they could produce a substantial grain surplus. Like most agricultural people in similar circumstances, they desire more than anything to be left in peace, a condition they have rarely experienced owing to their unfortunate geographical position. Despite the cries of the nationalist, most of those who thought at all realized that they could not be completely independent of both China and Russia. Ten years of Sheng Shih-t'sai's Soviet-dominated rule gave them a taste of a method of government which they did not like. A small measure of independence, a modicum of social justice, a little less corruption, a genuine effort to improve the educational and medical services, however small its results, would have won whole-hearted and almost universal support. But by the end of 1948 unbiased observers would have agreed that the Chinese were failing. It must be admitted that they were handicapped by circumstances which may have made their task impossible. The civil war in Central China weakened the confidence of the people and the morale of the officials; economic conditions in the outside world made it impossible to obtain either the technical help or the tools, even for the most elementary development; the currency inflation which after 1942 closely followed that of Central China, though it troubled the agricultural population comparatively little, made it difficult to launch constructive enterprises and encouraged competitive corruption. As already mentioned, the Ili rebellion, which could not fairly be blamed upon the Chinese, and the subsequent separation of the "Three Areas" from the rest of the Province imposed a severe economic burden and constituted a running political sore. General Chang Chih-chung and many of his able team of senior officers appeared to make a genuine effort to overcome these difficulties and to establish a fair and progressive government. In May 1947, Mahsud Sabri, a Turki, was appointed Governor of the Province; most of the local administrative posts were filled by natives, even though they were often little more than puppets of the local Chinese military commanders. But the Chinese were bad colonizers: with their traditional method of governing minorities by absorbing them, their contempt for what they considered to be inferior races and creeds, backed as it usually was by no evident superiority, their total lack of interest in their work and the country they were working in (there were very few who had bothered to learn the local language, even after a residence of twenty years), their remarkable lack of any civic sense, they were hardly likely to succeed without a rigid dictatorship backed by force and efficiency.

Already in the spring of 1948 there was mounting dissatisfaction. The rising spiral of graft; the burden of the large Chinese army garrisoned in the

Province, together with the marriage of Moslem girls with Chinese soldiers; to a smaller extent the complete lack of medical services and economic development and the poverty of education: these were its principal causes.

Such was Sinkiang as I knew it. Now, for better or for worse, a new era has begun, which will certainly change profoundly the pattern of life in that curious, medieval land.

CHAPTER FIVE

Karakoram Journey

MY second term in Kashgar materialized as suddenly as the first; entirely unexpected and unsolicited. I was in Vienna early in May 1946 when a telegram arrived asking me to take up the appointment again. I had completely lost touch with the situation in Sinkiang, and as I hurried home to learn some more about it and to discuss the proposition with my wife, I was filled with conflicting emotions. The prospect of the journey across the Karakoram and the Pamirs, the thought of being connected again with that strange and lovely land, consumed me with the same tingling excitement as I had felt when planning my first Alpine seasons and when I received the invitation to join my first Himalayan Expedition. On the other hand, the memory of the frustration and sinister hostility I had met with before had a sobering effect. I wondered, too, whether it was fair to ask my wife, for all her love for mountains and strange country, to undertake a prolonged spell of such loneliness and isolation.

The information I got from the India Office was far from promising. The Ili rebellion had thrown Sinkiang into a state of confusion. The so-called "Kirghiz Revolt" in Sarikol had cut both routes between India and Kashgar for the past nine months, and the rebels had advanced to the oases south of Kashgar. Michael Gillet, who had succeeded me in Kashgar in 1942, had been due to leave the previous summer, and though his successor had managed to get through just ahead of the trouble in Sarikol, he himself had been marooned in Kashgar for another winter. He was known to have left for Urumchi in March to travel out by way of Central China, but nothing was known of his present whereabouts. Nor was there any up-to-date information regarding the situation in Kashgar. Indeed, the outlook was so gloomy that before discussing it with my wife I had almost decided to turn down the offer. She, however, would not hear of my doing so, and we decided to go, whatever the situation. What was perhaps even more remarkable was her readiness to leave our nine-month-old-son behind in a nursery school. He was a bit too young to enjoy the Karakoram passes.

In the midde of June, Gillett arrived in London by air from Central China, which he had succeeded in reaching a short while before. Although his account of the situation in Sinkiang was somewhat reassuring, he was not very encouraging about the prospect of our getting there. Sarikol (Tashkurghan), it seemed, was still in the hands of the rebels, who had extended their operations eastwards to cut the route across the Karakoram Pass from Ladakh. No one seemed to think much of the prospect of obtaining Soviet visas to enable us to travel by way of Tashkent. However, we supposed that if the worst came to the worst, we would be able to get in from Central China as Gillett had got out. We sailed for India from Southampton on 26th July, hoping that by the time we reached Delhi there would be sufficient information available there to enable us to make a decision.

I believe that in travel our feeling for places is influenced very largely by the means of approach. It is one of the curses of modern forms of travel that they deny the traveller the chance to make a slow, progressive mental adjustment to his changing environment, which, in my view, is as necessary to the full appreciation of the place to which he is going as it is to his understanding of the geographical implications of the intervening distance. The faster the means of transportation, the stronger this adverse influence. Thus a journey by air halfway round the world, not only reduces the hemisphere to a series of chromium-plated waiting-rooms and irritating customs officials, but leaves one with a sense of unreality, of flatness, which robs any destination of much of its charm. Whereas even a journey by train, say from Northern India to Ceylon, is slow enough, the change of scene sufficiently gradual, to allow at least a measure of the adaptation necessary for full sensitivity of perception.

Exactly why this should be so I cannot explain. Certainly one would hardly expect an airman alighting upon the summit of a Himalayan peak (if such a thing ever becomes possible) to have the same feelings about it as a mountaineer who has climbed there. But it might be supposed that a sudden change of environment as, say, between London and Peking, should sharpen rather than dull the appreciation of the traveller. I remember once, on the Kamet Expedition, one of my companions said what a pity it was that our return to the flesh-pots would be so gradual that by the time we reached London our appetite for good food and wine, our appreciation of the comforts of civilization, would be so blunted that we would no longer relish them. At the time I agreed with him; but I have since learnt that he was wrong. It is, in fact, only by a gradual return to civilized amenities that one can savour each to the full, or fully enjoy them all.

Whatever the reason, I am sure that my intense enjoyment of Sinkiang and the vivid impression it left upon my mind were due, in no small measure, to the influence of the long journey from India. Not entirely, of course; one would be dull indeed to feel nothing of the subtle charm of its medieval atmosphere, its peculiar beauty, even if one had gone there in a jet-liner. But without the preliminary experience of weeks of travel with pony or camel caravan across those great ranges, the long absorption in those wide horizons, it would have been harder to throw off all mental contact with the modern world and so to achieve complete receptivity. I was very anxious, therefore, that we should not miss this journey. The approach from Central China would certainly be slow enough, but much of it would have been by mechanized transport.

There are two routes from India to Kashgar. In point of time there is little to choose between them; both involve a march of six or seven weeks from Kashmir, first across the Himalaya, then across the Karakoram range and, finally, across the Kuen Lun or the Pamirs. The western route through Gilgit and Hunza is the one usually taken by travellers. For small caravans it is certainly the easier of the two; the passes are lower and there is some sort of habitation to be found nearly all the way. But the bulk of the trade goes by way of the ancient trade-route, eastward through Ladakh and then north across the Karakoram Pass to Yarkand and Khotan. This is mainly because supplies of fodder for the pack-animals are more plentiful in Ladakh than in Hunza; partly, too, because it would be impossible to take camels along the narrow ledges across the precipices of the Hunza Gorge. It is one of the longest and certainly one of the most remarkable caravan trade-routes in the world. There are two passes of eighteen thousand feet to be crossed and several more of sixteen and seventeen thousand feet. For much of the way the traveller meets with no human habitation of any kind.

When we reached Delhi on 10th August we were disconcerted to find that nothing more was known there of the situation in Sinkiang or of conditons on the trade-routes than the little we had learnt in London. The diplomatic courier service between Gilgit and the Kashgar Consulate was, of course, still closed, and it was assumed that the country to the south of Yarkand and Khotan was still in the hands of the "Kirghiz bandits" as they were officially called. The atmosphere at the Secretariat was depressing. The Calcutta riots were then at their height, and it was feared that similar trouble might break out in Delhi at any moment. All departments of the Government were beset by a mass of problems that clamoured for solution in that delicate period between the end of the war and the granting of independence. Government officials were oppressed by uncertainty regarding their own futures. It was hardly surprising that the question of how to get a Consul to the remotest of all their posts did not seem to be one of prime importance. Someone suggested that a Chinese aircraft might be chartered to take us from Shanghai to Urumchi. I had, of course, to acquiesce, though I did so with a sinking heart. Fortunately, for some reason or other, the proposal was found to be impracticable.

After we had been there for a few days, however, a telegram came from the British Joint Commissioner in Ladakh saying that a caravan of Turki traders had left Leh for Khotan. We decided to follow this bold lead and attempt to travel by that route. At least, by the time we reached Leh, in a month's time, we might hope for some definite news about conditons beyond the ranges. With profound thankfulness, but feeling thoroughly jaded, we left Delhi, its heat and its fevered atmosphere on 20th August and reached Srinagar in Kashmir two days later. We hired a houseboat and allowed ourselves a week in which to prepare for the journey. It was a busy time, but the work was familiar and congenial and we had leisure enough to enjoy the balm of our lovely surroundings.

A new Consulate doctor, Allan Mersh, had been appointed to succeed Doctor Binns, whose relief was long overdue; he, the new first clerk

Rafaqatullah Khan, and a new compounder, Mohammed Shah, were to accompany us on the journey. It was arranged that they should travel two days behind us as far as Leh, to facilitate transport arrangements.

On our arrival at Bombay I had sent a telegram to Lhakpa's young brother, Gyalgen, in Darjeeling asking him to come to Kashgar. He had accepted and had reached Delhi the day before we had left, after some hazardous adventures in the Calcutta riots. Lhakpa, whom I had left in Kashgar in 1942, was still there. Gyalgen had been with us on Everest in 1938 and also on my 1939 Karakoram expedition. Another contact we had made in Delhi was with my old Hunza servant, Amir Ali, who had left Kashgar some years before to come to India. In the mysterious manner of Asiatic servants, he had learnt of my reappointment to Kashgar, and, having decided to come with me, I found him on my first morning in Delhi, waiting for me at the entrance of the External Affairs Department.

Our arrangements were completed on 29th August, and on the following day we went to Sonamarg. We camped in a delightful alp surrounded by fir forest in one of the side-valleys, and spent two pleasant days climbing about the surrounding mountains. On 1st September, our caravan assembled and we set out the following morning on the two weeks' march to Leh.

For anyone with a normally sybaritic turn of mind there is, I find, a melancholy complexion about the start of an expedition or a long caravan journey that is difficult at first to combat. With whatever eagerness we may have anticipated it, however much we had craved release from the tiresome restrictions and conventions of normal life, when it comes to the point, the final irrevocable break with these very conditions bears a sombre aspect. There are so many small things that we take for granted and scarcely notice until, suddenly, they are no longer there. A pint of beer, so easily bought and so lightly appreciated; the comfort of beds, of regular, well-served meals; fresh milk with our tea; access to books, newspapers, letters; the fun of meeting friends – it is always a bit of a shock to find that they have all gone. If it were for the period of a short holiday we would not give the matter another thought, we might even derive a certain masochistic pleasure from their absence. But saying goodbye to them for months, to some of them for years, is a different matter. Only the evening before we had left Srinagar we had dined and danced on the deck of the *Blue Bird*, a houseboat-restaurant run by a Russian who supplied exquisitely cooked Slavonic dishes and excellent wine. Tonight our jaded palates would be at the mercy of Gyalgen's primitive cuisine. It was a sober thought that a month hence we would still be plodding along, in conditions still more austere, little more than half our journey accomplished. A heavy rainstorm overtook us as we reached Baltal that afternoon. It cleared at sundown. Far away to the west, above the shifting cloud that half-filled the forested valley, a line of lofty peaks was etched in deep blue against a brilliant sky. Somehow this lovely sight merely lent poignancy to our doleful mood.

Fortunately, this nostalgic depression does not last long, though at the time I never seem to be able to remember that. As the routine of the march takes a firm hold, so we become quickly absorbed in it. As our feet become hardened to the road, our seats to the saddle, our stomachs to camp fare, we begin to pay more attention to our surroundings. As the memory of civilized comforts recedes, new animal pleasures take their place with greater and yet greater zest: the freshness of the morning air, the prodigious appetite at the breakfast halt, the sweetness of spring water after a thirsty stretch, the bliss of relaxation at the end of the day's march.

On this preliminary march to Leh it was particularly easy to make the adjustment. There were rest-houses at every stage, and abundant supplies of fruit, vegetables, eggs and meat; sometimes even fresh milk. A wide, comfortable path made walking easy; milestones kept us informed of our progress and of how much more was required of us that day. Beyond the Zoji La there was an excellent system of transport for touring officials. Word of our coming had been sent ahead, and at each halt the village headman was responsible for supplying a fresh set of pack-animals on the day required. Prices were fixed and there was no haggling. The muleteers, anxious to get their job done, were willing to start as early as we liked and to travel as fast as they could. Each morning we rose at half-past five, drank a cup of tea, and started walking at six o'clock, leaving Gyalgen and Amir Ali to pack up and get the new caravan under way. Gyalgen, mounted on a pony, with the breakfast things packed in a saddle-bag, would catch us up. Between nine and ten, a good half of the day's march done, we would choose some pleasant spot for a halt of two hours. While we were eating our elaborate breakfast of porridge, fried eggs, toast and marmalade and tea, the caravan would pass us, and so reach the next halting-place before us. Most of the daily stages were eighteen miles long; none was more than twenty-two miles. There was little else but pleasure in this luxurious form of travel.

At Baltal we left the forested mountains behind us and saw no more until the following March, when we visited Bostan Terek. For across the Zoji La, we entered the barren ranges of the Indus valley basin. At first the country seemed harsh and bleak after the soft valleys of the Vale of Kashmir, but we were not long in discovering its particular, less obvious charm. I had crossed the Zoji La in 1937 on the Shaksgam Expedition, and knew the route as far as Kargil, whence we had then turned north into Baltistan instead of south-east into Ladakh. Kargil was a typical Balti town. Our first march beyond it was a long one; we passed no important villages and, having dallied on the way, we arrived at Mulbekh late in the evening. It was as though we had stepped straight into Tibet. White- and red-faced buildings, with slightly inward-sloping walls, climbed the hill-side from the wide, fertile valley. Monasteries, gaunt and severe, but incredibly lovely in the evening light, stood upon lofty crags, as though they had grown out of the living rock. There were chortens and "mani" walls along the path. In feature, in speech and in dress, the people were Tibetan.

The Tibetan culture of Ladakh is one of its chief delights. As in Tibet proper, the architecture is in the same perfect harmony with the landscape; the inhabitants have the same attractive characteristics. Whether it is that a religion moulds the character of a people, or whether the native character of the people fashions the religion of their adoption, is a question over which there is much diversity of opinion. If it be the former, then there is certainly much to be said for Tibetan Buddhism. On entering Ladakh we were immediately struck by the cheerfulness of the people, the charming courtesy and friendliness, devoid of all sense of servility, of apprehensive reticence, on the part of men, women and children alike. There was about the country an atmosphere of peace, of mental and material prosperity, of essential goodwill which, after post-war Europe and the passionate turbulence of India, was gently intoxicating.

The way from Mulbekh led over a steep pass to Lamayuru, an oasis of terraced fields and willows cupped in a deep fold of barren mountains, and dominated by the massive walls of the monastery built flush with the sheer cliff upon which it stood. From there we descended into a deep and gloomy canyon, and so emerged into the valley of the River Indus at Khalatse, still three days' march from Leh. The Indus Valley here presents the same appearance of stupendous desolation as everywhere else along its mountain course. As elsewhere, its desolation is relieved, at intervals of half a dozen or so miles, by areas of intensive cultivation. The villages are usually set near the mouth of small, steep, tributary streams, which provide wide alluvial fans on which the terraced fields are built and water easily diverted into irrigation channels. The water of the parent river is rarely used, as it is too difficult to "lift" to the level of the fields. Though Khalatse and the villages beyond were more than nine thousand five hundred feet above sea-level, we found there abundant fruit – apricots, apples and lemons; walnuts, too, were just ripening on the massive trees shading the village streets.

Near Leh, the Indus Valley widens out. The southern flank, freed for once from overshadowing precipice, lifts gently to the distant snow-peaks of the Zaskar Range. For once there is natural verdure along the banks of the great river, which flows with unwonted placidity between green meadows and willow thickets. Here, on 15th September, we found a large deputation of traders who had come out to meet us. We were provided with spirited ponies and escorted swiftly over six miles of sloping desert to Leh, where we found, somewhat to our embarrassment, that a pompous reception had been arranged for us. Our arrival apparently was welcomed as a sure sign that the profitable trade-route to Yarkand and Kashgar was at last to be reopened. A heavy burden of responsibility seemed to have descended upon our incompetent shoulders.

Leh is the junction of several important trade-routes; from Kashmir, from Kulu, from Gartok and the Tibetan Plateau, from Chinese Turkestan. Like other such junctions in Central Asia, its bazaar is the meeting-place of many races: Turkis, Baltis, Kashmiris, Tibetans, Hindus from the United Provinces, Moslems from the North West Frontier. These heterogeneous throngs, their rich and diverse cargoes, their busy affairs, have had little visible effect upon the placid life and the distinctive culture of the native people. Leh, the capital, for all its commercial importance, is still one of the most typical towns of Ladakh. It is set in a deep recess of the Indus Valley, a wide bay in the mountains, whose floor slopes gently up from the river, now some six miles away. Dominating the town are the monasteries and the huge palace of the old kings of Ladakh; surrounding it are the fields, claimed by irrigation out of the desert land, and groves of willow and poplar; at 11,500 feet above sea-level it is too high for fruit trees. The wide view over to the Zaskar Range adds immeasurably to the sense of peace which surrounds it. There had been wars and strife, and, alas, there have been since, but we found it hard to imagine that the tranquillity of this remote and lovely place could ever be disturbed.

The British Joint Commissioner for Ladakh, who was in residence only during the summer months, had already returned to Srinagar. We had the small Residency and its garden to ourselves. It was pleasant for a spell to live in comfortably furnished rooms and to dine at a table laid with glass and silver. We stayed for a week to prepare for the serious part of the journey.

Of the various trade-routes radiating from Leh, by far the most lucrative was that which led north to Yarkand and Khotan. Silk, felt and rugs came from there; in exchange went a vast assortment of manufactured goods and trinkets. During most of the thirties the embargo imposed by Sheng Shi-t'sai's regime upon trade with "imperialist reactionaries" had kept the route closed to traffic. But nearly a decade of hardship and disappointment did not kill the initiative of the traders; and not long after the *volte-face* in Urumchi in 1942–43 caravans again started out across the ancient passes. Then came the "Sarikol revolt" of 1945, and again the route was virtually closed, this time by the presence of hostile forces across it. No one yet knew what was happening on the other side of the ranges. At the end of July a party of bolder spirits had ventured forth, but the majority of the caravan leaders had chosen to wait, though most of them were by now running seriously short of money and supplies. The entire carrying trade was in those days perfomed by men from Yarkand and Khotan. So when we reached Leh, we found a large number of these Turki traders awaiting our arrival in the naïve belief that our official presence would protect them from the ravages of the "bandits" and ensure a safe passage for their caravans. We had no difficulty therefore in joining up with one of these caravans and hiring as many animals as we required. We even induced them to agree to travel a great deal faster than was customary, and after going over the route again and again we planned a series of stages which would enable us to perform the journey from Leh to Yarkand inside a month. For it was already late in the year and I was anxious to reach Kashgar in time to allow those we were relieving to get back across the passes before winter set in.

The Doctor, Rafaqatullah Khan and Mohammed Shah arrived two days behind us. Rather to our dismay Mohammed Shah had brought his wife, travelling in strict purdah, and two small children.

We had plenty to do during this week in Leh; repacking our belongings from boxes that had already proved unequal to the rigours of animal transport; laying in fresh stores; buying vast and evil-smelling sheepskin coats and hats against the cold. There were numerous conferences with representatives of the trading community, who had various proposals to make for the development of trade. At least once a day I received a call from a pathetic company of Chinese soldiers, headed by a captain, who a year or so before had escaped to Gilgit from the massacre in Sarikol, and had lately come to Leh in the hope of finding a safe way back to their country. They begged to be taken under our protection. But in spite of all these activities, we found time in the evenings to wander about and see something of Leh.

By the afternoon of 20th September all was ready for our departure on the following day. At four o'clock I received an urgent telegram from the Government of India. It stated that a message had been received by Chinese radio from the Consul-General in Kashgar to the effect that the caravan that had left Leh at the end of July had been attacked by "bandits" north of the Karakoram Pass and robbed of both their baggage and their animals. The message recommended most strongly that I should not attempt to travel by that route, but go instead to Gilgit in the hope of travelling through Sarikol. It also said that Dr. Binns and his wife and two children had left Yarkand towards the end of August on their way to Leh in the belief that the route was now safe; and nothing had been heard of them since.

This news put us in an awkward dilemma. It would take us at least three weeks' hard travelling to go from Leh to Gilgit, and perhaps a week to arrange transport for the journey. It was most improbable that we would be able to obtain pack-animals in Gilgit to take us from there to Kashgar, and even if we could it might take us weeks to do so. The journey from Gilgit to Kashgar would take at least another month, so that we would be lucky to get there much before the end of December. Presumably Kashgar had reason to advise me to attempt the Sarikol route, but it seemed that if the "bandits" were operating as far west at the Karakoram Pass, Sarikol, their original base of operations, would be even more dangerous, particularly when the rigours of winter forced them back to more habitable regions. This, too, suggested a potent argument in favour of the Karakoram route. The country beyond the Karakoram Pass was so severe, so totally lacking in grazing and other amenities to support even the tough Kirghiz nomads, that the "bandits" could not remain there indefinitely and there seemed to be a reasonable chance that we could slip through without meeting them, even if they were still molesting the district. Finally, we had already paid some ten thousand rupees to our caravan leaders, and they had already spent most, if not all, of it on fodder and merchandise. It seemed unfair to demand the money back, to say nothing of the "face" we would lose by doing so, and, indeed, by displaying our concern at the news.

On the other hand, to be attacked by bandits in such a place, even if they confined their activities to looting, might have serious consequences. For such a party as ours, to be deprived for example, of pack-animals at 16,000 feet in the middle of October, in country without a stick of fuel, several weeks' march from the nearest habitation, with scores of river crossings, impassable on foot, would be a situation not unlike that of mariners deprived in mid-ocean of their ship. Even the Turki caravan men could hardly be relied upon to walk far carrying loads, to say nothing of the compounder's wife and small children. The "bandits" might be more or less lenient, according to their own plight, though it would certainly be to their advantage to prevent victims from getting through to report their whereabouts and strength. However, it was comforting to reflect that presumably at least some of the unfortunate caravan in question had been allowed to get through or we would not have received the news.

The first thing to do was to talk the matter over with the leaders of our caravan, who, after all, in the matter of property stood to lose a good deal more than we; a fact behind which we might conveniently shelter our pride. We held a solemn conference in the drawing-room of the Residency. The Turkis heard the news with disconcerting calm. They said they would be willing to travel by the Gilgit route if supplies of fodder could be arranged (which was doubtful); but on the whole they thought that there would be less chance of avoiding the "bandits" in Sarikol than across the Karakoram Pass, where the severity of the country, particularly in October, would prevent them from lying in wait for long. But they made it quite clear that they considered it up to me to decide, and that in any case their fate was in the hands of Allah. Such nonchalance might have been comforting, even though it was no guarantee of stoical behaviour in face of an actual crisis; but I was sorry to have the burden of decision thus flung back at me.

I considered the possibility of travelling by a new route far to the west, but it would have been largely through virtually unexplored country, and, even if the caravan men had been willing to try it, which they were not, it would have been altogether too hazardous at that time of year. It happened that Colonel Schomberg had just arrived back in Leh from an exploratory journey in that region. He reported that conditions were already terribly severe on the high plateaux. He agreed that we were more likely to run into trouble in Sarikol than across the Karakoram Pass; indeed, he took a gloomy view of the whole situation and was inclined to think we should return to Delhi.

However, amid all these conflicting considerations, one thing was clear; we could hardly leave the region without finding out what had become of the Binns family. If they had run into trouble, they might be struggling on towards Leh, in desperate need of help. We decided, then, to go forward with the whole caravan as far as Panamik, five days' march away and the last inhabited place on the southern side of the ranges. If all had gone well with them, they should have reached Panamik before we could get there. If not, I planned to leave the rest of the caravan there and go on with a light party by double marches in search of them. The adoption of this plan was a great relief, for although if we ultimately decided to abandon the Karakoram route we would then have to bring the caravan all the way back, thus wasting more precious weeks, at least this final decision was postponed, and action took the place of vacillation.

Consideration of all the many alternatives took a long time and we did not leave Leh until two days later than we had planned. The first obstacle to be crossed was the Khardung Pass, variously estimated on maps at 17,500 feet and 18,200 feet high. It lies in the centre of the cirque of mountains surrounding Leh, and is clearly visible from there. Though the first march was a short one, it impressed upon us the realization that we had left behind the well-ordered comforts of the march to Leh. Despite their two days' grace, the caravan men apparently still had much business to transact; or it may have been reluctance to drag themselves away from the flesh-pots of Leh. Whatever the reason they went on delaying our departure until in a fit of undignified rage I fined them fifty rupees, which I gave to some delighted children among the fascinated crowd assembled in the marketplace, and threatened to levy another fifty rupees for every quarter of an hour of further delay. This had the desired effect and the caravan was clattering out of Leh long before the first levy was due. The result was that we did not reach our camping-place, a bleak spot, some 14,000 feet high, at the foot of the pass, until after dark, with all the consequent confusion and misery that implies. This reluctance to start on the day's march proved to be a chronic debility of the Turkis, and during the month that followed it remained an unresolved bone of contention between them and ourselves, and resulted in many late and comfortless camps.

There was a well-graded, zigzag path up the southern side of the Khardung Pass, and despite a late start we were assembled on its snowy crest at eleven o'clock next morning; most of the party suffering from headaches and nausea. Far away to the north, in country with which we were soon to become familiar, we could see the 25,000-foot Saser peaks. The descent from the pass on the northern side was difficult, and the first 500 feet took our caravan about three hours to accomplish. There was virtually no path and the way led over a very steep slope of boulders, close up against the flank of a glacier. The ponies were relieved of their loads, which had to be manhandled over the worst bits, but even so the unfortunate animals slipped and slithered on the icy surface between the boulders in such a way that I expected at any moment to see one of them go crashing down the slope. We did not have anything like enough men to control them. However, we got down without a mishap and once in the valley below, the orderly line of march was resumed. Again we did not get in until after dark, but this time we had relatively comfortable quarters in a caravan-serai in the village of Khardung.

Thence the way led down through a narrow gorge, utterly barren except along its narrow floor, where dense willow and tamarisk jungle flanked a stream of sparkling rapids and clear, still pools; and so out on to the huge gravel- and sand-flats of the Shyok River. The Shyok is a tributary of the Indus, which it joins a hundred miles to the west. Like other great rivers of the Karakoram, it flows its wandering course through a trough many miles wide. Almost more than any other feature, these river valleys have impressed upon my imagination the prodigious scale of the ranges which have produced them. For here distance can be realized better than upon the mountains themselves, where movement is restricted and views too wide to be measured by the eye. Here, marching hour after hour, one seems scarcely to move relative to the opposite side of the valley; a buttress by which one has camped is still clearly visible the following evening after a day's long journey.

After a day's march down the Shyok we entered the Nubra Valley, which is almost as large as the former and joins it at such an acute angle that our course was scarcely deflected by entering it. The Nubra River has its origin in, and derives almost all its water from, the Siachen Glacier, which was discovered by Dr. Longstaff in 1909 and, fifty miles long, was thought, until the discovery of the Fedchenko Glacier in the Russian Pamirs in 1926, to be the greatest ice-stream outside Polar regions. Every few miles we passed through villages surrounded by wide areas of irrigated fields. Like those in the Indus Valley, these villages were all situated on alluvial fans at the mouths of side-streams; for, although the precipitation of moisture over the range as a whole must be enormous to maintain the great glaciers, rain- and snow-fall in the lower valleys is negligible and without these glacial streams, cultivation, and thus habitation, would be impossible. Another feature, resulting, I imagine, from the curious fact that precipitation is confined to the vicinity of the high mountains, is the extraordinary form of these side-valleys. Owing to the absence of lateral erosion in their lower reaches, the rivers enter the main valley through slender canyons carved slit-like out of its precipitous flanks. Higher up, these narrow passages gradually expand into wide, open valleys of rich pasture before they finally merge onto the great glacier plateaux above.

We reached Panamik, the last village of any size up the Nubra, on 27th September. To our intense relief we found that Dr. Binns and his family had arrived. They had reached Panamik on the very same day, and were enjoying the exquisite luxury of being once more in inhabited country, in comparative warmth and comfort, among trees and fields, after weeks of harsh and lonely travel. We listened eagerly to their news. Their caravan had been attacked and fired upon in one of the valleys north of the Karakoram Pass. Although they had not heard of the plunder of the unfortunate trading caravan, they naturally supposed that their assailants were a party of the famous "Kirghiz rebels" or "bandits". They dismounted hurriedly and took cover behind boulders, waved a white handkerchief in token of submission and waited until the shooting stopped and the attackers came up to claim their booty. The shooting continued for a quarter of an hour. Fortunately this was somewhat wild, there were no casualties and none of their animals was hit. When the "enemy" arrived they found that they were a body of Chinese troops who had been sent to the area in search of the "bandits" and had mistaken the caravan for their quarry. The officer-in-charge made scant apology for his mistake and they were left to proceed with their journey.

The Chinese had had some excuse for shooting first and asking questions after. On our way to Panamik we had been overtaken by a special messenger from Leh bringing further news from Kashgar relayed by telegram from Delhi. It had informed us that a body of Chinese troops had been sent (presumably before that encountered by Dr. Binns) to deal with the "bandits", that they had encountered them and had been defeated, losing most of their number. It was reassuring to know that action was being taken against the marauders. Even though it appeared not to have been very successful hitherto, it seemed unlikely that they would remain in the district until stronger forces arrived. So, though with some misgivings, we decided to continue on our journey.

The next day's march took us some sixteen miles farther up the Nubra

Valley, to the foot of one of those slit-like side-valleys already mentioned. It would be difficult to imagine a less likely looking place for the continuation of the great trade-route to Chinese Turkestan. It was manifestly impossible to get up the gorge, its floor wholly occupied by a thundering river, its sheer walls almost touching each other a thousand feet above. To the right of its mouth the great precipices continued perpendicular and unbroken; to the left was a vast slab of smooth rock, two thousand feet high, very steep and, apparently from below, not offering a foothold for a goat. As we gazed up at it, however, we gradually detected a tiny black line moving, ant-like, across the slab about halfway up. This was one of the caravans of ponies and camels that had now joined us in our journey, and had made an earlier start from Panamik. It looked like some fantastic conjuring trick, until we realized that a wonderfully well-engineered path had been constructed zigzag up this remarkable place, to turn the gorge and permit access to the valley beyond. From below, this path was almost invisible owing to the steep tilt of the rock.

So far as I know, no one has traced in detail the history of this great trade-route; if this is so, it is probably owing to lack of available information concerning the early pioneers. I had hoped, before writing this book, to attempt to do so, for it would be a fascinating study; or, at least, to make a synthesis of what has been written about it. Unfortunately I have not had the opportunity, nor access to the necessary books. It is difficult to imagine the hardships, the adventures, the repeated failures experienced, many centuries ago, by the original pioneers of the route, in quest of trade or conquest, before they succeeded in finding a way through the labyrinth of gorges, the innumerable blind alleys and across the awful solitude of seemingly endless ranges. In all probability it was not one party of explorers but many, who, during the centuries before the establishment of regular trade, had to find the route for themselves, without any guidance save for the vague knowledge that it had been done. For, unlike the sea pioneers, these explorers probably left no detailed record of their journeys, and certainly no charts to guide their successors. Climbing the Matterhorn today, it is hard to appreciate the difficulties and doubts that beset the minds of Whymper and his contemporaries, or, sailing round the Horn, to imagine the terrors it held for the early navigators. So with this trade-route; though the physical conditions of travel are precisely the same as they were a thousand years ago, though there has been little improvement in the "road", familiarity with the way has removed all but the purely objective difficulties and hazards: the problem of keeping the pack-animals alive, blizzards on the great passes, cold, the fording of the rivers, and, in their season, bandits. It is possible, I suppose, even for the new-comer to perform the journey and to notice nothing but the tedium of the marches and the stark discomfort of the country. But to anyone with any geographical sense it must be at least a profoundly impressive experience.

From the top of the great rock slab, more than two thousand feet above the valley floor, we looked back down the Nubra to the isolated patches of trees and cultivation which represented the last signs of permanent habitation we were to see for almost three weeks until we reached the first oases of the

Tarim Basin. Then, crossing a shoulder, we were swallowed up in the desolate gorge beyond. By the evening of the second day from Panamik we reached a wide confluence of open valleys surrounded by great ice-peaks, up to twenty-four thousand feet, with many glaciers descending towards us from the saddles between them. On one of these saddles lay the Saser Pass, 17,480 feet high, the next major obstacle in the way. Again it was nearly dark before we started to pitch camp and, as we were above 15,000 feet and a sharp wind was blowing down from the glaciers, it was cold work. We did not descend below that altitude for the next ten days.

The crossing of the Saser Pass is, in many ways, the most exacting part of the whole journey; certainly for the ponies. In foul weather it is apt to be a hazardous business, and I should hate to be caught in a blizzard with a caravan of ponies high up on the glaciers. On the northward journey, with the animals still fresh and well fed, it is not so bad, but on the journey from Turkestan it comes near the end, when the animals are usually very weak from fatigue, hunger and exposure. This last effort often proves fatal to them even in fine weather, and in the valley leading up to the Pass we first encountered the dismal line of corpses, bleached skeletons and heaps of bones which formed a continuous trail for hundreds of miles until we reached the first oasis beyond the ranges. Indeed, on this account it would be hardly possible to lose the way, and in the absence of any path when we were not marching with the caravan we often found ourselves following this grim trail. Of course, it represents the relics of many decades of caravans. It has been estimated that an average of 15 per cent. of the ponies and camels perish on each journey. Considering the difficulties of the route and the natural temptation to the traders to overload their animals with merchandise at the expense of fodder, I am surprised that the death-rate is so low.

We started comparatively early the next morning. The weather was clear and still. For the first two hours the going was easy along the broad floor of the valley, until we came up against a great semicircle of glaciers at its head. The lower part of the glaciers consisted of a series of ice-cliffs separated by steep ice-falls. The only way through was to the left, up a narrow corridor of moraine, consisting mainly of large boulders, pressed hard up against the precipices of a rock peak. It was the kind of ground on which one spends a large proportion of the time on any mountaineering expedition, but over which I should never before have dreamed of taking pack-animals. It was steep, there was not the least vestige of a path, nor any chance of making one between the boulders, on which the ponies' hooves scraped and slithered agonizingly in their efforts to gain and keep a purchase with trembling, bleeding legs. It was terribly slow work, as each pony required individual attention and there was only one man to every eight animals. As we struggled to get the unfortunate creatures up that moraine, ground so very familiar to me in different circumstances, I had repeatedly to remind myself that I was not on an expedition engaged in a desperate attempt to get pack-transport to a high base camp on a mountain or into a piece of unexplored country, but that I was performing a necessary journey along a regular trade-route to take up a government appointment.

At length we got past the zone of ice-falls and the angle of the glacier to our right became sufficiently gentle for us to take to the ice. Then for the next few miles the going was fairly easy. The ice was hummocky, but no snow lay on it and there were very few crevasses; deep ravines had been cut by surface streams, but these lay more or less parallel with the line of march and caused little inconvenience. The pass itself was on a wide ice-field, so gently rounded that it was difficult to tell when we had reached the actual crest. Beyond, the ice heeled over to form the glaciers on the far side, gradually steepening until, after another two or three miles, we were forced to find a way off it to the left. Thence we descended a small cwm, which led us once more into the valley of the Shyok, 160 miles up-stream from the place where we had crossed it before.

Near the headwaters of the Shyok River is the site of the famous Shyok Ice Dam. This is a typical example of a phenomenon which is fairly common in the Karakoram Range, and its fame is due to the terrible destruction it has caused. Such a dam is formed by a large glacier advancing across a major river valley until the ice presses up against the cliffs on the opposite side. The river thus obstructed forms a great reservoir behind the ice-barrier. When the glacier starts to retreat, perhaps after many years, the barrier is weakened and may burst, releasing the pent-up water in a tremendous flood. The Shyok Dam has formed and burst several times during the past century. Some idea of the immense volume of water involved is shown by the fact that villages were destroyed hundreds of miles below the dam, throughout the course of the Shyok and far down the Indus below the junction, and that floods were caused in the plains of the Punjab some eight hundred miles away as the river flows. The last occasion was in 1929. Warning had been given of the impending catastrophe by travellers and explorers.

The site of the dam was little more than a dozen miles above the point where we reached the Shyok River. I was very anxious to visit it, partly to satisfy my own curiosity and partly so that I could furnish a report upon the state of the glacier and whether the dam had formed again or was likely to do so in the near future; for it had not been visited for a good many years. Our route, however, lay straight across the Shyok and up a nullah into the mountains on the opposite side. So I arranged for the caravan to make a short march on the following day, and set off at six o'clock up the river, together with the Doctor and Gyalgen, mounted on the three best ponies. Our progress was a good deal slower than I had expected. In the first place, we had to ford the river many times, and though by now this had sunk almost to its winter-level, the current was very strong and we had to search carefully for places where it could be crossed. Then, the valley floor was mostly composed either of boulders or of soft sand into which the ponies sank deep, so that we could rarely get them into a trot. Again, there were frequent spurs and outcrops of rock which were difficult to cross.

The valley was fascinating; I think it was the weirdest place I have ever seen. To the right, for mile upon mile, precipices rose straight out of the river-bed for several thousand feet. These were rent by slender, vertical clefts which sometimes united in depth so as to carve gigantic monoliths, isolated from the main face. The vast walls were slashed across with bizarre colours, like some monstrous oil-painting. To the left the mountains stood well back from the valley. From them, over the steep intervening ground, came a series of glaciers of that peculiar pinnacled formation found to the north of Mount Everest and on the northern side of the Karakoram. The pinnacles, a dazzling white, looked like columns of a ghostly army advancing upon the bastions across the valley. I have never before seen a great river valley so completely sterile, so utterly devoid of any form of vegetation. It was the kind of valley one might expect to find in the exotic landscape of a dead planet. There was no cloud in the sky; the brilliant blue above sharpened every outline, every contrast of shadow and colour. The air was very still. The hiss and boom of the river echoed far up the cliffs; but here and there, by some trick of acoustics, we found ourselves in a pocket of absolute silence. At about two-thirds of the distance we reached a glacier which descended to the floor of the valley. By climbing a small bluff to the side we could see right to its head, which was enclosed by a magnificent cirque of ice-peaks, 22,000 to 24,000 feet high. The sight of their sublime, ordered grandeur was a relief after the grotesque structures, the chaotic desolation of the valley.

It was one o'clock before we reached the site of the Shyok Dam. The glacier, which came down a wide tributary valley from the west, sprawled across the main valley in a tumultuous jumble of ice. But the most advanced ice-cliffs were two or three hundred yards from the cliffs on the opposite side. Moreover, so far as I could judge from the formation of the ice, the glacier was "retreating"; that is to say, the terminal ice was melting faster than the advance of the main body of the glacier could reinforce it. The "advance" and "retreat" of a glacier is normally determined by the excess or deficiency of the snowfall in its collecting basin. In a district where the snowfall is usually just sufficient to maintain the extent of the glaciation, a glacier will "advance" following a cycle of exceptionally heavy precipitation, and "retreat" after a cycle of exceptional drought. But the glaciers of the Karakoram, some at least, behave in a very odd fashion, for which there is as yet, so far as I know, no plausible explanation. I know of several cases where a tributary glacier has been "advancing" rapidly while its neighbour, a couple of miles away, with the same aspect and with a collecting basin in an adjacent corrie of similar size, has been "retreating".

We had no time to spend on a close investigation of the dam, so, after taking a set of photographs, we started back as fast as we could go. We made much better time on the return journey owing to our knowledge of the way and of the best places to ford the river, and at half-past five we reached the little side-valley opposite to our camp of the previous night. It was a narrow gorge flanked by vertical cliffs, but it had a flat, sandy floor and contained only a small stream, so that we could travel at a good speed. After we had gone along it for several miles, the tracks in the sand suddenly ceased. There was an inconspicuous crack in the right-hand wall of the gorge, but at first I could not believe that the way lay there. In the first place, it seemed impossible that it could lead anywhere but into the bowels of the mountain; secondly, it did not look wide enough to admit a pony, let alone a camel.

However, the evidence of the tracks was irrefutable; so, dismounting, we led the ponies into it. Inside, the crack, or chimney as it would be called in climbing parlance, became a steep gully, so narrow that in several places the pack-animals must have had to be unloaded to get through between the vertical walls. Again it seemed incredible that we were on a trade-route, and that anyone could have bothered in the first place to search for a route in such an unlikely-looking place. But after half an hour of scrambling we suddenly emerged into a great, open valley, several miles wide, running between two ranges of rocky peaks. The contrast was astonishing, and, but for the tracks and the skeleton trail we might have been at a loss to know which way to turn. The surface was perfect and we coaxed our tired ponies into a canter. It was getting dark when we reached the caravan, encamped below the crest of a gentle pass.

For the next ten days we travelled through the most forbidding country I have ever seen. By now we were far from the great ice-peaks of the Karakoram, and it was only occasionally, crossing a pass or a high plateau, that we saw them in the distance. Their absence increased the appearance of wild desolation in our surroundings. For ice-peaks have shape and majesty; the purity of their outline and their commanding presence dwarf, and so largely obscure, the barren surroundings from which they may rise. Here there was nothing to distract the eye from the stony wastes, the interminable scree slopes, the vast ruins of rock; mountain skeletons, huge, but without form or identity. Considering the great elevation, there was a remarkable absence of glaciation. We passed some glaciers, hideously deformed, blackened with rubbish, coiled like repulsive serpents in their sunless chasms. But in this savage wilderness there was often exquisite beauty; particularly in the early morning and in the evening when the slanting sunlight brought out the delicate colouring in the rocks and subdued the austere landscape to match the simplicity of celestial space.

For three days the way led through gorges, and our view was restricted to our grim surroundings. Then we climbed up on to a wide, flat plateau, 17,000 feet high, known as Depsang; a waterless stony desert, above the rim of which the ice giants of the Siachen appeared shimmering and detached from the earth in a kind of mirage. All this time we were blessed with perfect weather, and, what was more important, there was little or no wind. So during the day we were warm enough, though it was very cold at night; at sun-down we used to creep into our sleeping-bags, fully dressed except for our boots, and remain there until the sun was up next morning. It was difficult to estimate distances, but I suppose we normally covered from twenty to twenty-five miles a day, and, occasionally, about thirty, which was as much as the pack-animals could do at that altitude. From the Depsang plateau we descended about a thousand feet to a river known as the Chip Chap, which is the longest head-stream of the Shyok. Crossing this, we entered a valley which led to the Karakoram Pass.

We crossed the Pass, and so from India into Sinkiang, on 6th October. For all its 18,250 feet, and despite its position on the crest of the main watershed of the greatest range on earth, it was a curiously unimpressive affair. It consisted of a gentle, rounded gap, one of many, in the flank of a rounded valley; to our jaded eyes, considerably less spectacular than Sty Head or Pen-y-Pass. When we reached the top, we saw a large caravan approaching up the slope on the other side. This was a welcome sight, for we were now within a day's march of the area where the bandits had been operating, and the presence of the caravan presumably meant that the route was now reasonably safe from this menace. The caravan men were quite as delighted to meet us, for they were unprovided with the necessary visas to enter India. They implored me to give them letters of recommendation to the authorities in Leh. In the circumstances, I had not the heart to refuse. Somehow the idea of requiring a visa to cross this howling wilderness seemed absurdly incongruous, and though it was part of my business to enforce this piece of modern barbarism, the rules of hospitality which generally govern the behaviour of people living and travelling in desert places seemed to demand some concession.

We were now in the upper basin of the Yarkand River, and for several days we made our way down this great water-course. Here our main preoccupation was in crossing from side to side of the river, as it flung itself, first against one wall of its valley, then against the other. During the course of one day we had to ford the river as many as thirty times. Even at this time of year it was quite an alarming business as one's pony, with belly submerged, struggled to maintain a footing on the shifting boulders against the powerful current, whose swirl made one giddy to look at; or perhaps worse still to watch the staggering pack-ponies, with great "bow waves" beating up against our precious belongings on their flanks. In July and August the river is usually quite unfordable, even for camels. One night we spent with a company of Chinese soldiers who had been sent up from Khotan on anti-bandit operations. Farther down the valley, when we had reached the moderate elevation of 12,000 feet, we found little jungles of tamarisk and driftwood washed down by the summer floods which provided us with the novel luxury of camp-fires. We were now barely a week's march away from the basin of the Zug Shaksgam that I had been exploring nine years before, and I spent much of my time speculating how the various side-valleys to the south fitted in with our survey of that well-remembered country.

One morning we left the valley of the Yarkand River for a narrow gorge which led up to the 16,500-foot Yangi Dawan. The gorge was very difficult for the pack-ponies. They kept slipping into crevices or getting themselves and their loads wedged between great boulders and the vertical walls of the gorge, thus causing a traffic block behind them until they could be extricated. The caravan men had been particularly slow in getting away that morning, and it soon became obvious that we would not be able to cross the Pass before nightfall as we had planned. The weather had broken, and when in the late afternoon we eventually emerged from the gorge it started to snow heavily. I had intended to force the caravan on over the Pass even if it took us half the night, in the hope that this would at last teach the men the folly of starting late in the morning. But eventually the sight of the unfortunate compounder's wife sitting with pathetic resignation on her pony, and the thought of probable further casualties among the animals (we had lost two), softened my bad-tempered resolve, and I agreed, with ill grace, to stop for the night a little way below the crest of the Pass. It was a bleak, comfortless spot among the boulders, and once again we were without fuel for our evening meal. I was somewhat mollified by hearing, close at hand, the evening chuckle of ram chikor. While the camp was being pitched, I managed, after an easy stalk under cover of the gathering dusk and the falling snow, to shoot one of these magnificent birds, which gave us promise of a welcome change from tinned food for the next two days.

Beyond the Yangi Dawan we began to feel that we had left the severities of the high range behind. The mountains, though lower, were no less barren and rugged, and some of the gorges just as grim, but in the valleys we found, here and there, delightful willow groves along the river banks, and sometimes wide stretches of pasture, while the climate became so balmy that we shed at least our outer garments before turning in at night. On 16th October we crossed the last pass, a mere 10,000 feet, and on the 17th we found ourselves marching down a hot, waterless valley between low desert hills which formed the last northward spurs of the range. We reached its end and saw, across a stretch of dazzling sand, a dark line of poplars, the first oasis of the Tarim Basin. Two hours later we were lying in the shade of a willow hedge beside a bubbling stream, eating melon after delicious melon, and bunch after bunch of sweet, seedless grapes, as though our thirst and our greed would never be satisfied, while Mohammed Kurban, the caravan leader, was engaged in the tortuous negotiations of an Oriental customs post.

The main part of the journey was over. The past seven weeks, which, because of their full and varied life, had at the time seemed so long, now contracted and telescoped into a single unit of experience. There had been no great hardship, for we had had plenty of food, and were adequately clothed and equipped against the cold. Indeed, once we had accepted the conditions of travel, the time and distance involved, we had found in the simplicity of our daily routine a feeling of peace and of well-being such as perhaps no other form of travel can give. But the slow, plodding progress through a gradually changing scene, the hundreds of miles of uninhabited country, the lonely camps which gave us a sense of kinship with the stark magnificence of our surroundings, had caused us to shed the mental habit of our former life and left us acutely sensitive to the impressions of our new environment.

I had thought that I remembered that country well; I had certainly thought about it enough; but I was astonished at the force with which half-forgotten memories returned: the strange moonlit feel of the landscape induced by sunlight diffused through the dust haze; the way the shadows melted into the mud walls of the houses; the unsubstantial appearance of the loess cliffs; a hundred sensations of sight and sound and smell, too intermingled for distinct analysis. Most of us, I suppose, experience something of the same surprise returning to England after a long spell abroad. However much we may have thought about it, there are still so many things we have forgotten; the greenness of the fields, the scent of a box hedge, the special colour of winter woods, the size of the sheep and cows, the freshness of the air, or the peculiar, rather exciting smell of the Underground Railway.

CHAPTER SIX

The Arch

SOME twenty-five miles west-north-west of Kashgar is a small range of jagged rock-peaks. From Kashgar it does not look very impressive, as it is seen end on and is partly obscured by a featureless mass of desert hills. But from the north or south the range, which for want of a better name we called the Tushuk Tagh (Cave Mountains), is seen to consist of scores of bold pinnacles stretching in long ranks from east to west. The highest peaks are probably about 11,000 feet.

While I was travelling from Kashgar to Tashkent in 1942, I saw from Min-yol (twenty-five miles west of Kashgar) that one of the peaks was pierced by a hole which appeared to extend from a couple of hundred feet below its summit almost down to its base. From a distance of ten miles it was difficult to form an idea of the size of this gigantic archway, but I estimated that the vault could hardly be less than a thousand feet high.

It was not until several years later that I had an opportunity of attempting to investigate this remarkable phenomenon. Greatly under-estimating the difficulty of the task, my wife and I set out from Kashgar one week-end in January 1947 with this object in view. We took with us our two Sherpas, Lhakpa and Gyalgen. A few miles east of Min-yol we turned off the road and made our way up a broad water-course which led us in the direction of the highest peaks. The Arch, now clearly in view, was among them. For several miles we made our way across a boulder-strewn desert which sloped gently down from the foot of the range. It was one of those days, rare in Turkestan, when the air was crystal clear and the great ice-peaks of the Kashgar Range could be seen in every detail.

Reaching the foot of the range, we climbed a small spur to prospect for a route. From here we could see that the range was divided into two distinct zones. The first was a region of foot-hills composed of shale and sandstone strata which dipped to the north at a general angle of about fifty degrees. Beyond the foot-hills rose the perpendicular rampart of the main peaks, whose clean-cut sides showed, so far as we could see from where we stood, no sign of stratification. A deep canyon ran up into the heart of the foot-hills and we could see that it had several branches. It was obvious, too, that this canyon was only one of a large number of similar passages which, with their branches, split the foot-hills into an intricate labyrinth of gorges. Each of the narrow clefts in the jagged skyline, by which the peaks of the main range were separated from each other, probably represented the continuation of one of the main canyons. The Arch was no longer visible, but we could make a fairly accurate guess at its general direction. Noting that we must take an early branch to the left to maintain this direction, we started up the canyon. It was rather like plunging into a maze after a brief, bird's-eye view.

For a short distance, a broad, flat floor wound between cliffs cut square out of level alluvial deposits. As we entered the foot-hills, the gorge narrowed abruptly, the walls rose to a height of several hundred feet above us, often sheer and sometimes overhanging. The strata, composed of alternating beds of sandstone and shale and variously metamorphosed examples of each, stood out in extravagant relief, dipping at a high and uniform angle. The whole structure appeared alarmingly unstable; an appearance amply confirmed by the frequent masses of landslip debris with which the gorge was choked. The gorge was dry, except here and there where ice, clinging to the walls, marked the position of springs.

We turned up the first branch passage to the left. It was steep, and choked with debris; so steep, indeed, that after a couple of hours' scrambling we found ourselves only a hundred feet below the crest of its confining walls and it showed signs of ending in a fan of shallow cwms. We climbed to the brittle crest of a ridge to see where we were. The surrounding country presented a remarkable appearance. It seemed as though we were standing in the midst of a stormy sea, its crested waves poised to break over the plains to the south. The "wave" on which we stood was one among thousands, each indistinguishable from the rest. The island peaks of the main range appeared no closer; of the Arch there was no sign. To our right we looked down into a deep canyon, which was obviously a continuation of the one we had started up, or a major tributary of it. It had curved round to the north-west since we had left it and now seemed to lead in exactly the right direction. We had obviously been too hasty in our decision to abandon it for its promising but feeble tributary.

When the direction of these valleys was at right angles to the strike of the strata, their sides were almost vertical and frequently overhanging. Although this was their general direction, their sinuous courses placed some portions of them parallel to the strike. The south slope of the valley then followed the angle of dip, often right to the top of the flanking wall. This was the case where we had emerged and we had little difficulty in finding a route down into the canyon. The view which we had seen from the crest of the ridge, though spectacular, was depressing and we realized that we could not hope to reach the foot of the main peaks that day. However, we had time to prospect a bit farther, and we followed up the canyon for another hour or so. On the whole there was no difficulty in doing this, but there was a frequent tendency for bands of comparatively hard strata, less easily eroded than the rest, to form overhanging curtains across our path. Eventually, just as we reached our self-imposed time-limit, we were confronted by one such curtain over which it was impossible to climb. But here again we were lucky in that it occurred at a place where it was possible to climb out of the bottom of the gorge and along one of its flanks. So we returned to Kashgar confident that we had not yet been baffled by this line of approach.

About a month later we decided to devote another weekend to the problem of reaching the Arch. This time we camped in the mouth of the canyon. We had left Kashgar in a severe dust-storm which continued throughout the journey. Fortunately, the wind was from the north-west and eventually it blew the usual dust haze away, so that by Sunday morning the air was again clear. We breakfasted in the early light and watched the dawn break over the ranges to the south. Framed by the walls of the canyon, Kungur and the great ice-saddle of Chakragil gradually emerged, flooded in the soft sunlight, from the liquid purple shadows of the plains.

We reached the overhanging curtain in little more than two hours and had no difficulty in climbing round it. Beyond, the going was again easy and such glimpses as we had of the peaks showed that we were getting appreciably nearer to them. But soon the floor of the gorge began to steepen; the valley split repeatedly into several branches and it was difficult to decide which to follow. In any case it seemed clear that they would soon peter out and deposit us again like flotsam on an isolated crest in the sea of foot-hills. But this time we emerged on a fairly wide gravel plateau, so far as we had seen, a unique feature in that landscape. At first we naïvely hoped that it might lead us without further trouble to the foot of the peaks, which now seemed much closer. They were a remarkably fine array, rising in smooth unbroken sweeps of prodigious steepness, three or four thousand feet above their foot-hills.

We had not walked more than two hundred yards along the gently sloping plateau before we were brought up on the brink of a sheer drop, down which we looked into the gloomy recesses of another canyon. From its size, structure and direction, it was obviously the main valley of a system entirely separate from the one which we had left; it drained to a point some way farther along the range to the west. At the point where we overlooked it, it was joined by a large tributary canyon which bounded our tableland on the north. It was obvious that before we could progress another yard toward our objective we must climb down into this new system. There was no feasible way of doing this from where we were and we made our way along the brink of the tributary canyon. Soon the tableland gave place to the usual series of wave-like ridges which made progress very laborious. It was a long time before we reached a point from which we could climb down into the gorge.

It was already getting late, so my wife and Lhakpa waited on the ridge while Gyalgen and I climbed down into the canyon as fast as we could. We were now very close to the foot of the main peaks and could see the point where the tributary canyon disappeared into one of the slit-like ravines that split the main massif. But I could not yet see of what rock the peaks were composed. Their smooth faces and the apparent absence of stratification suggested a massive limestone, though the boulders in the gorges contained a large proportion of crystalline rock as well as of limestone. We made our way down to the junction and turned up the main canyon. Here we found thickets of tamarisk, briars and coarse grass, watered by a stream which was only partly frozen. We raced along the almost level floor. But before we had gone for half an hour from the junction the walls of the canyon converged above us and we entered a circular cavern. The floor was covered with a sheet of ice; at the far end a frozen waterfall, about sixteen feet high, hung from a V-shaped cleft which represented the continuation of the gorge. Supported by Gyalgen on its lower portion I cut steps up the waterfall, climbed through the cleft and emerged on to a second recess, also floored with ice, but this time open to the sky. A second frozen waterfall a good deal higher than the first confronted me. I did not attempt to climb it, and doubt if I could have done so if I had tried. A jutting stratum of rock which formed part of the roof of the lower recess, sloped back along the wall of the canyon at the prevalent angle of about fifty degrees. It was formed of hard conglomerate and was easy to climb. It took me right to the top of the 300-foot wall and once more I looked across that incredible tangle of sharp ridges that formed the foot-hills. There was no obvious way of climbing on towards the peaks nor of regaining the floor of the canyon above the second waterfall, but I did not make a thorough search as it was already an hour later than the time I had decided to turn back.

It was the middle of April when we made a third attempt to find the Arch. This time we went to the village of Min-yol, where we consulted the local population. In my experience, Asiatic peasants are usually quite uninterested in the natural phenomena around their homes, unless they happen to have some economic significance; the most majestic mountain is left unnamed; the advance of a glacier will pass unnoticed unless it should happen to destroy their houses or encroach upon their grazing-grounds. We were surprised to find, therefore, that the villagers of Min-yol took the keenest interest in the Arch. They and their fathers before them had explored the labyrinth of gorges that led through the foot-hills usually in quest of game, but often, during the perennial revolutions and civil wars that sweep this unfortunate country, when it provided them with welcome refuge from the storm. Never had anyone seen the Arch from close to, let alone reached it. Its curious disappearance as soon as one reached the foot-hills had long been remarked upon, and some of the more adventurous spirits had even set out to find it. The circumstance was fertile for legend. It was said that somewhere among the lofty pinnacles there was a beautiful garden of flowers and fruit trees, inaccessible to the ordinary mortal.

It had occurred to us that the Arch might prove to be an optical illusion. But we had studied it very carefully with a telescope, from various points along the road and from a distance of twenty-five miles to the south, and were positive that it did exist. Moreover, we had seen a similar, though less spectacular, arch above the Artush plain at the eastern end of the range. We had no difficulty in persuading two of the villagers to join in our quest, though they were quite confident that it would not succeed. One of them, Usman Akhun by name, was obviously the J. A. Carrel of the village. He had a splendid physique and self-assurance of an Alpine guide.

We set out across the desert to the north. This time the weather was more normal, and a thick dust haze obscured the mountains until we were within a mile of the foot-hills. Then the peaks began to appear in ghostly outline; there once again was the Arch. We entered a canyon which at first I thought was the one that Gyalgen and I had reached on the previous occasion. But it soon became obvious that it belonged to a different system, probably the next to the west. We camped about two miles up the gorge, and set out again next morning at a quarter-past seven. We soon came across fresh tracks of ibex, which had descended from their crags for their morning drink at the intermittent springs on the floor of the canyon. We would certainly have surprised some of the creatures had it not been for the loud and continuous chatter of our guides echoing far up the surrounding cliffs. After about an hour, still following the game-tracks, we turned up a steep side-nullah to the right, intending to continue the exploration of the main canyon later. Very soon the nullah ended in a little cwm surrounded by vertical cliffs. A small terrace ran diagonally across the right-hand wall. We climbed this to the outer edge of the cwm, and round the corner we found that it continued across a big south-facing buttress. It was an impressive place and commanded a fine view over the foot-hills. There were large deposits of ibex droppings, and here and there those of ram chikor. Soon after we had turned the corner, two of these birds came sailing over our heads from the opposite side of the main canyon. We made our way along the terrace for about half a mile, hoping to find some way round the vertical cliffs above. Eventually, however, it petered out high above a system of gorges, which was evidently the one which Gyalgen and I had reached on the previous occasion. There seemed to be no way of getting down into this from where we stood, so we began to retrace our steps.

A couple of hundred yards back along the terrace the wall above was cleft by a crack which, higher up, widened into a chimney which in turn ended under an overhanging block. A suggestion of mine that we might try to climb this cleft was turned down peremptorily by Usman Akhun, who had hitherto nursed the party along like a guide with a bunch of incompetent tourists. I ignored his protests, however, and tying myself on to the end of our 100-foot rope, started to climb the crack. This was obviously regarded as a piece of gross impertinence and but for Gyalgen I think Usman would have pulled me down again. The chimney was not particularly difficult and just as I had run out the length of the rope I reached a wide recess below the overhang. Usman Akhun's blood was up. He removed his boots and started up after me. He was a good climber on slabs, being quite fearless and very agile; but though he managed the lower crack the idea of backing up a chimney was evidently new to him. He struggled valiantly for some time before he was forced to bury his pride and clutch the rope. By this he managed to haul himself up to the recess, where he arrived, winded and obviously impressed.

It was decided that the others would remain on the terrace and await our return. We did not expect that to be long delayed. The overhanging block was pierced by a hole, through which we climbed and so emerged at the top of the cliff. Following the uniform structure of the foot-hills the ground beyond dipped steeply down into a wide notch, beyond which was another formidable cliff. But by following the exposed strata diagonally to the right we climbed down about four hundred feet to the floor of the canyon beyond. Here I found that we had at last penetrated through the foot-hill zone and were right up against the walls of the main massif. I was astonished to find that these cliffs, which stretched to almost vertical sweeps for thousands of feet above our heads, were composed entirely of conglomerate. Although, looking at the smooth faces of the peaks as a whole, there appeared no sign of any bedding planes, examination of the sides of the ravines by which they were cleft showed that the strata dipped to the north more or less in conformity with that of the foot-hills.

We made our way along the canyon. The floor where we reached it was about ten yards wide. Presently it plunged into the vertical wall of the main massif. Here it had a maximum width of about three yards, though often it was so narrow that we had to edge along sideways. For a long way the floor was flat and though it was often deeply covered with snow we could get along rapidly. Usually the skyline above us was so narrow that we could see nothing but the ravine; but sometimes it widened sufficiently to enable us to see, far above, a great amphitheatre of peaks that we were entering. It was obvious that this fantastic passage could not go on indefinitely without interruption. After surmounting two small steps in the floor, we reached a third, about twenty feet high. I managed to chimney up this and went on alone. About a hundred yards farther on the walls of the ravine began to close above me, the light faded and I was soon in complete darkness. Eventually my groping hands came up against a cold slippery surface. I struck a match and saw that a great column of ice descending from the darkness above marked the end of the ravine; at least, so far as I was concerned, for I did not contemplate climbing the vertical ice in the dark. I estimated that I reached a point directly below the wall of the amphitheatre.

When I got back to Usman he showed me, with some display of excitement, a number of dead leaves which he had found on the floor of the ravine. He evidently regarded them as indisputable proof of the existence of the legendary fruit gardens, and he preserved them carefully in his hat. We made our way back along the ravine until we reached the point where it widened out at the junction of the main massif and the foot-hill zone. From here we followed another passage, which climbed steeply along the line of junction to the west and led us into a wide cwm filled with tall grass and briar trees. As we emerged into the cwm, we startled a pair of ibex, which bounded up a sloping ledge to the left and stood gazing down at us, silhouetted against the sky. Beyond the cwm a line of overhanging cliffs once more barred our way and effectively disposed of yet one more line of approach.

It was now high time to retreat. Usman was strongly opposed to going back by the way we had come as he did not like the idea of climbing down the chimney. He had no faith in the rope. He argued that we could find a way of traversing across to the terrace where we had left the rest of the party. I was rather doubtful, but the possibility of avoiding some upward climbing was attractive: we had been going extremely fast and I had become uncomfortably parched. A little way below the point where we had entered the canyon we managed to climb on to a ledge which looked as if it might serve our purpose. For some way all went well; but then it began to narrow rapidly and soon it ended above a twelve-foot drop to a parallel ledge below. Usman proceeded to jump down this without much apparent consideration either of the unpleasant landing or of the consequences of thus cutting off our retreat. I was shamed into following suit, though I would very much have preferred to turn back. Our new ledge took us on for barely a hundred yards before it too ended. This time the drop to the next ledge was more like fifty feet. I was relieved that my companion showed no inclination to leap down this, though at first there was no obvious way of climbing down, nor was there any means of *abseiling*. I began to feel rather foolish, until a few yards back along the ledge we discovered a diagonal scoop down which it was possible to climb. We rejoined our companions on the terrace at about half-past two, about four hours after leaving them for a tentative reconnaissance up the chimney. The melon, without which no one in this country is suitably equipped for travel and which is a very passable substitute for a pint of beer, tasted uncommonly sweet.

We had now seen and heard enough to realize that the chances of reaching the Arch from the south were extremely slight. We had already had several views of the range from among the foot-hills of the Tien Shan to the north, but had seen no sign of the Arch. Nor had any of the Kirghiz nomads of that district from whom we had made enquiries ever heard of it. Nevertheless, we decided to explore the range from that direction, and some weeks later we camped among its northern foot-hills. The weather was stormy. A good deal of rain had fallen and we had some doubts about the wisdom of penetrating those unstable gorges when the hills were wet. Fortunately, we found that, owing to the continued northerly dip of the strata, the canyons did not develop until the hard conglomerate of the main range had been reached. This, too, made the approach considerably easier. Wide water-courses led gently up through low hills to the very foot of the peaks.

But a close view of the range was far from promising. Individually the peaks were not so spectacular as they had been from the south. But from here, there seemed to be several parallel ranges, each with countless jagged summits. It was easy to see why the Arch was not visible from the north. The shape of the skyline bore no resemblance to the one we had seen from the south, which we had taken particular care to memorize. We could not now be certain even which was the highest peak of the range, which had seemed so obvious from there. The maze of ravines by which the range was split was correspondingly complex. It looked as though we would have to devote many more long week-ends to a systematic exploration before we could hope to find a way through to the Arch.

We chose a point on the crest of the range which seemed most likely to correspond to the place where we had seen the Arch, and selected a ravine that seemed most likely to lead in the direction of that point. We were immediately swallowed up in the twisting labyrinth, where we had no choice of direction save where our chosen passage-way divided. The walls and spires above us, though composed of the same hard conglomerate, were quite different in appearance from those we had seen on the south side of the main range. In place of the smooth, almost polished surfaces, the faces here were deeply pitted and honeycombed so that the peaks often resembled gigantic beehives; some were carved into remarkable fretwork patterns; all were excessively steep.

The going was considerably easier than anything we had met on the south side of the range. Mostly the floor of the canyon sloped gently upwards and when it was interrupted by steps, these were comparatively low and easy to climb. This difference was, of course, again due to the northerly dip of the strata. We were making height steadily, and we began to hope that at least we might reach the watershed and be able to look down into the amazing country to the south. A variety of large shrubs grew among the mounds of scree, particularly at the valley junctions, and higher up we were surprised to find a number of small firs. The floor of the ravine was generally about twelve feet wide, though for short stretches it would narrow to about two feet.

At last, emerging from one of these clefts, we were confronted with a sight that made us gasp with surprise and excitement. The gorge widened into a valley which ended a quarter of a mile away in a grassy slope leading to a U-shaped col. Above and beyond the col stood a curtain of rock, pierced by a graceful arch. Through the arch we could see nothing but the clouds of a stormy sky. This sudden end of our search was almost an anticlimax. My wife remarked upon the amazing chance that had led us to choose exactly the right canyon, and at each branch the right alternative so that we came direct to our objective at the first essay. I preferred to think of it as the result of sound mountaineering instinct! We hurried up to the col. There was nothing of an anticlimax about the Arch itself, or the view beyond.

Before we reached the col we had seen only a very small portion of the Arch; now the whole vast structure opened before us. On the other side of the col the ground dropped vertically into a profound abyss, so narrow in its lower portion that its floor was for the most part invisible. The Arch was about a hundred and fifty feet from where we stood, a quarter of its height above us, three quarters below. Its supports, beautifully curved in their upper portion, smooth and vertical below and for a long way down, stood out in sharp relief from the sides of the canyon with which they eventually merged. It was impossible to estimate its total height, but I do not believe that this was far short of a thousand feet. Its span was about one-sixth of its height. The canyon was no ordinary product of fluvial erosion. It looked more like a rift caused by some titanic earthquake. And yet the vast blocks by which it was enclosed had a strange symmetry; for all the incredible confusion of the whole, each feature was clean-cut, sweeping and without blemish; below the walls were some slender buttresses slanting this way and that, quite irrelevant but smoothly curved. It was like some wild design of modern sculpture. A mile away the canyon was blocked by a massive tower of similar form. Probably this was one of the line of peaks whose outer edge we had reached from the south. To pass it on either side or in either direction looked impossible.

A cold wind blew and for the most part the sky was overcast, though an occasional shaft of sun would light up part of the strange scene before us. With some difficulty we climbed a small peak above the col, from which we saw beyond the canyon into another, scarcely less remarkable than its neighbour.

The next morning, before starting back to Kashgar, we followed another gorge, and again, though with considerably more difficulty, succeeded in reaching the watershed at a minor peak, some 10,500 feet high. The storm had passed, and though the wind was still strong, the air was very clear. The same terrific rockscape lay to the south at our feet, again enclosed by an outer line of towers. Beyond stood the great peaks of the Pamirs looking incredibly high and sharp. Northward, across a wide expanse of desert hills, red and gold, the western ranges of the Tien Shan were arranged in a vast arc, mauve below, dazzling white above in their mantle of freshly fallen snow.

CHAPTER SEVEN

Muztagh Ata

THE literal meaning of "Muztagh Ata" is "Ice-mountain Father". It is said that the mountain received its name in the following way: When Sven Hedin asked one of the Kirghiz nomads in the district what it was called, he received the polite reply: "It is called 'Muztagh', Father." I was told this by one of the former Swedish missionaries in Kashgar, who may have got it either from Hedin himself or from a member of one of his later expeditions. I cannot vouch for the story and I am not even sure whether it was Sven Hedin who was originally responsible for the adoption of the name. However, it is not an improbable explanation of the fact that no inhabitant of Sinkiang with whom I have discussed the matter has ever heard of the name Muztagh Ata. On the other hand, every ice-mountain or range of mountains that I have approached in South Sinkiang is known to the people in its vicinity as Muztagh. As applied to mountains, such names as Kungur and Chakragil, so well known to European travellers, are quite unknown locally. Usually, too, the nearest grazing-grounds to the glaciers of a particular range are known locally as Muztagh. The result has been the adoption by western geographers of the name Muztagh for at least four of the major peaks of Central Asia and for scores of rivers and grazing-grounds. There have been determined attempts by some influential geographers to change the name of the Karakoram Range to "Muztagh". I am glad that these were resisted successfully. The name Muztagh is in danger of becoming a bit overworked, while the name Karakoram, however unsuitable (it means "Black Rock"), has a fine classial ring to it.

For a long time it was thought that Muztagh Ata was the highest mountain in this part of Central Asia. Sven Hedin makes much of this supposed supremacy in his many flowery passages. "Mus-tagh-ata", he writes (*Through Asia*, page 221, published in 1899), "the loftiest mountain in the Pamirs, towers up to the height of 25,600 feet . . . The unchallenged pre-eminence of Mus-tagh-ata over the peaks which cluster around it is proved by its name, which means 'Father of the Ice Mountains'." I find it puzzling to account for this confident assumption. A few miles to the north, though entirely detached from it, there lies the huge massif of Kungur. Standing between the two, it is difficult to see how anyone could question the superiority of the latter in height. Even assuming a strong prejudice in favour of the former, it is impossible to account for the use of the phrase "unchallenged pre-eminence", a phrase, moreover, that has not merely been allowed to slip out in the exuberance of descriptive emotion; it is reinforced over and over again in succeeding chapters by the expression of similar sentiments. Apart from the obvious height of several of the peaks of the Kungur massif, the quite exceptional extent of its glaciation would inform any experienced observer that Kungur was among the highest mountains of the world. One possible explanation of the mistake is suggested by the height quoted by Hedin, 25,600 feet. Kungur, whose height is now accepted at about 25,200 feet, must have been observed and its height computed by many travellers in the plains of Kashgar during the nineteenth century. Anyone who asked from the natives what the mountain was called would naturally be given the name "Muztagh". But to accept this explanation merely confronts one with a question still more baffling. How anyone who has seen Muztagh Ata could ever mistake Kungur for the same mountain is quite beyond comprehension. Aside from the fact that they lie twenty-five miles apart, Kungur is a part of a range comparable with Kangchenjunga, while Muztagh Ata is an isolated peak somewhat resembling a volcanic cone in appearance.

A rare opportunity came my way in the summer of 1947. Bill Tilman joined the Swiss Expedition to attempt Rakaposhi, and I managed to persuade him to come up and visit us in Kashgar before returning home. The Chinese Government kindly granted him a visa to do so. The war had interrupted an excellent habit we had formed during the 'thirties of travelling together. As the years lengthened towards a decade, I had begun to suppose that the thread had been irrevocably broken, and that this easy and profitable partnership belonged only to the past. The prospect of renewing it, even for a brief spell, in a field of such unlimited scope was very exciting. I did not even need to take more than a few days' holiday. I had several just reasons for visiting Sarikol. The various alternative routes to that place led past a hundred unclimbed peaks and a score of unexplored valleys. In Sinkiang a consul is still in the happy position of having to tour much of his district on horseback; even a short tour takes several weeks to complete, so that a few days spent wandering off the route is neither here nor there. It is easy to combine a modicum of business with a great deal of pleasure. We arranged to meet at Tashkurghan on 6th August.

My wife, Gyalgen and I left Kashgar on 28th July. Three days before, I had a severe attack of influenza from which I had barely recovered by the time we reached Tashkurghan. This was a bad beginning. We travelled by the eastern route, by way of Yangi Hisar and the Chichilik Pass, reaching Tashkurghan on 5th August. I had not been there since the occasion of my first arrival in Sinkiang, seven years before, and the place held unpleasant memories for me. Our reception this time was in striking contrast. As soon as we emerged from the mountains we were met by Fatih Ali Khan, the supervisor of our diplomatic courier service to Gilgit, together with all the chief civil and military officials of the place, with whom he was on the best of terms. We were provided with fresh ponies and rode with this impressive escort for the last dozen miles to Tashkurghan, where we were received with lavish hospitality.

Bill arrived on the following day as arranged. We had a dozen alternative plans to choose from. There were, for example, two extremely attractive peaks, twenty or twenty-one thousand feet high, both within ten miles of Tashkurghan. They were made of solid gneiss, decorated with finely chiselled ice-âretes and precipitous ice-falls; to climb either would clearly call for all the mountaineering skill that remained to us after so many lean years. We could thread our way back to the north through the Shiwakte group, connecting up some of its unexplored valleys by passes yet to be found. There was the unexplored valley which apparently leads right up into the heart of the Muztagh Ata massif from the south. The east face of Kungur has not yet been seen by Western eyes.

Our choice was unimaginative, and actuated, I think, by second-rate motives. We both had a sneaking desire to see how we would react to high altitudes after an interval of nine years; we both, I suspect, nursed a secret hope to achieve an easy and spectacular triumph. The western route to Kashgar passes close under the western side of Muztagh Ata. This side of the mountain had been explored by Sven Hedin and it was obvious that there was the probability here of a fairly easy route to the top. We ignored a lesson that we had learnt a dozen years before; that to climb a mountain for its height and fame alone is infinitely less rewarding than to attempt a peak whose form has charmed, or to cast a new light upon an attractive mountain range. We agreed that Muztagh Ata from the west had little to recommend it either in interest or beauty; but we chose it first from among a score of others.

But there was a second item on our programme. Two or three marches north of Muztagh Ata, at the point where it plunges into the Gez defile, the western route to Kashgar passes close to the southern side of Chakragil. Though a mere twenty-two thousand feet, Chakragil forms one of the most beautiful sections of the tremendous panorama of snow mountains seen from Kashgar. During two years of exasperating confinement I had drawn solace from the contemplation of its fluted ice-ridges, glistening in the early morning sun, floating high above dark storm-clouds or silhouetted against the evening sky. With Kungur and the others, it greeted me when I returned four years later. I had the exquisite excitement of introducing it to my wife, and it had formed a background of our morning walks, winter duck-shoots and week-end expeditions. We had paid it a brief visit the previous May, and had camped for three days among the pine forests and the wide grassy alps at its northern foot. Now there was the chance of getting on intimate terms with this lovely mountain by attempting to climb it from the south.

We left Tashkurghan on 8th August accompanied by a large cavalcade of civil and military officials belonging to the post. As usual it was taken as an occasion for a wild display of horsemanship in which we took as little part as our mounts would allow. Beyond the five miles which etiquette required our hosts to accompany us, our escort was reduced to two armed Tajik policemen and two junior civil officials. They were sent for our protection and guidance by the Commandant and the Magistrate. These escorts were one of the bugbears of our official tours in Sinkiang and we used to spend much of our time trying to avoid them. The simple policemen or soldiers were fairly innocuous as a rule and could generally be induced to adapt themselves to our primitive taste in travel. But the civil officials were very tiresome. In the first place, they regarded all journeys as evils to be got over as soon as possible. They tried, usually successfully, to exercise dictatorial powers over our every action; they chose our halting-places during the march; there was a fuss every time we decided to walk rather than ride; they stubbornly opposed our choice of camping-sites and forced us to impose upon local hospitality; any divergence from the regular route was, of course, bitterly resented.

There had been a thick dust haze over the country for the past two days, and as we made our way up the wide Tagharma valley we saw little of our surroundings. The dust haze often persists for weeks at a time, even among the high mountains, and can utterly ruin the enjoyment of a journey. It is far more exasperating than bad weather, which, though it may obscure the hills and interfere with plans, rarely reduces the scene to one of such monotony and, indeed, often provides some of the most spectacular views. However, the haze had disappeared by the morning of the 9th, and as we made our way round the south-western flanks of the Muztagh Ata massif the mountains were clear.

The quarter-inch map, No. 42 N. of the Survey of India, marks two points, 22,956 feet and 22,240 feet, on a long ridge running gently down to the south from the summit of Muztagh Ata. Actually these two points are entirely separate peaks, isolated from the main mountain and from each other by gaps several thousand feet deep. There is a similar col between Muztagh Ata (24,388 feet) and a northern summit which is indicated on the map by a 24,000-foot contour ring. From each of these two summits a broad, unbroken ridge descends to the west, separated by a deep trough containing the Yambulak Glacier. On his first and second attempts on Muztagh Ata in 1894, Sven Hedin chose the northern of these two ridges. This is surprising, because, although it is the easier of the two, the descent to the col from the northern summit would be a laborious business, while to climb to the main summit from the col would, even by modern standards, be very difficult, if not impossible. On the second occasion, Hedin estimated the highest point he reached at 20,600 feet.

For his third attempt Hedin chose the other ridge, that comes down from the main peak. He reached a height of 18,500 feet. "Evening was coming on," he writes, "and I was again constrained to beat a retreat, for it would have been useless to wait till the next day and then try to find another passage" (through the crevasses). "It was plainly impossible to venture upon Mus-tagh-ata from this side without special appliances, which were not at our disposal. Above us towered the loftiest summit of the mountain, and down its precipitous sides glided the eternal ice, streaming in part to the collecting basin of the glacier; and where declivities were convex and the ice-mantle was checked by the relief of the underlying ground, it built itself up into veritable terraces, walls, towers and solid blocks of enormous dimensions. To get past these seemed, so far as we could judge from the spot where we stood, altogether beyond the reach of human power." The ice may have changed a great deal in the last fifty years; even so, I am inclined to think that this last sentence was a considerable exaggeration. Nevertheless, it is not surprising that he did not persist, seeing that he had not even a rope. The remarkable thing is that he attempted the mountain at all "without special appliances".

He made a fourth attempt (16th August, 1894), this time reverting to the northern ridge which leads to the northern or lower peak. He camped at the highest point he had reached before (20,600 feet), but did not proceed farther on account of a strong wind. In July 1900 Sir Aurel Stein ascended this same ridge to 20,000 feet. On the previous day his two Hunza "guides" had reconnoitred the ridge to a point about 1,500 feet higher and had found the way barred by a difficult notch.

We made a longer march than we had intended on 9th August, and for a very unusual reason; our transport ponies went so fast and so far ahead of us that we could not catch them up in time to prevent them crossing the Ulugh Rabat Pass, which we had intended to cross the following day. We followed wearily behind and reached the Pass about sunset. A great mass of dark cloud, streaked with deep crimson, hung over the Kongur massif, beneath which the lower fringes of its vast ice-cap showed cold and gloomy. The rest of the world was flooded in a delicate mauve light. We camped in the wide alluvial plain beyond the Pass.

We were now due west of Muztagh Ata and in full view of the mountain, so that we could lay our plans for climbing it. Without much hesitation we chose the ridge forming the southern flank of the Yam-bulak Glacier, and leading direct to the summit. The alternative was the parallel ridge leading to the minor northerly peak. Before we had seen the western side of the mountain, I had assumed, from Hedin's description, that this would be the best route to follow, partly because it seemed to offer the possibility of using local transport up to a considerable height and partly because it avoided the tangled ice-fall of which he had given such a lurid account. But one look at the face of the mountain over-looking the northern peak was enough to dispel this idea.

The next morning we moved up to a grazing-ground known as Yam-bulak, near the foot of the mountain. Most of the Kirghiz had already moved down to lower pastures, but one family remained. They had intended to go down the following day, but they kindly volunteered to stay while we were there to supply us with milk, cream and butter. The Kirghiz, of course, had little interest in the rapidly inflating Chinese currency. For this reason we used always to travel with a sufficient supply of tea, cloth, rice-soap and mirrors to distribute among them. Not that they ever expected any payment for their liberal hospitality, and they were always overcome with a gratitude out of all proportion to the value of the gifts. We managed to get rid of our escort, who, seeing that we could not be shaken from our incomprehensible intention of going up on to the glacier, shrugged their shoulders and left us with evident relief.

Our hosts provided us with a yak and a driver. We hoped that the beast would carry our loads to a point on the ridge, about 17,500 feet high, where the rock disappeared under the ice and where we proposed to put our first camp. Sven Hedin had taken yaks to considerable heights on the mountain on each of his attempts. He had never had any trouble with them except when he took them on to the ice. Load-carrying was our principal worry. I had not done any since 1939; Gyalgen had done very little during the last few years and none at all for more than a year; Bill had had some practice that summer, but nothing like enough to get back to a reasonable degree of proficiency. Going unladen to 17,500 feet would certainly be a great help, though we did not relish the prospect of carrying all our stuff beyond that unaided, particularly if the snow proved to be bad. We had no spare boots, so that we could not recruit local help for work on the ice; but even if we had, I do not think we could have induced any of the Kirghiz to come with us. In all, allowing for bad snow conditions, we planned to have three camps on the mountain to get us within striking distance of the summit.

We started from Yam-bulak at eight o'clock the next morning (11th). My wife came with us and we also took a Turki youth, Roza Beg, whom we had brought from Kashgar, so as to accompany her on the way back from our first camp. About an hour's walk to the south took us to the Yambulak Glacier. It was very broken and be-pinnacled throughout most of its length, particularly in its lower reaches, so that to cross the valley we had to keep below its snout. From there, another hour's easy climbing took us to the foot of the ridge, at about 15,000 feet.

The ridge was a very broad affair and throughout most of its length offered a variety of routes. For the first 2,500 feet it presented a rock slope set at an ideal angle, divided by two deep gullies which contained ice on their upper portions. Once on the mountain we had no means of gauging our height except for Hedin's estimate of the point where the rock of the ridge disappeared under the ice. We were very careful to note our climbing time, so as to reach as accurate an estimate as possible of our vertical progress by dead reckoning. We climbed steadily at a good 1,500 feet an hour, for spells of half an hour each. From the outset the yak made very heavy weather of it, despite energetic exhortations by Gyalgen, Roza Beg and the driver. By the time we had completed our second half-hour spell, we had left them far behind, out of sight. We waited for an hour, and then Bill and I went down to see what was happening. We found that the yak had given up about five hundred feet below, and the driver was lying on his face gasping out the information that he himself was dying. Evidently yaks are not what they were in Sven Hedin's day. We divided up the loads and plodded back up the slope, whereupon the driver revised his plans and set off down at a brisk speed. My wife insisted on carrying some of the baggage, which noble gesture I did not resist too strongly.

At about a quarter-past three we reached the end of the rocks. My wife and Roza Beg went down, while we pitched our tent and brewed tea. Later in the evening, Bill and I went forward to reconnoitre. The rock disappeared immediately under a moderately steep ice-slope which obscured the view of the mountain beyond. We cut steps to the top of this, from where we could see the next couple of thousand feet. We were confronted by a wide ice-fall, not particularly steep, but so broken that we were doubtful if we could find a route through it. On the extreme right there was a high ice-ridge, easy and unbroken, which ran down to a point opposite to where we were standing. If we could reach it we could avoid the ice-fall altogether. But to do so we would have to climb a very steep ice-couloir about three hundred feet high. The ice was obviously very hard and it would involve several hours of cutting. Also the couloir sloped up from the edge of a high precipice above the Chattumak Glacier, which bounded the ridge to the south. It would be an unpleasant place to negotiate with loads, and there was not time that evening to prepare the way. So we decided to have a closer look at the ice-fall. We climbed on for about eight hundred feet. The ice-sheet covering the ridge formed, along its northern edge, a hanging glacier above the Yam-bulak Glacier. This presumably accounted for the fact that it was split by an unusually large number of crevasses running both up and down the slope and across it. Though the thin covering of snow was very hard, we had a certain amount of trouble in finding a safe route, for it was difficult to avoid both being on the same crevasse at the same time. This intricate structure was reflected in the ice-fall above, which made it remarkably complicated. However, it was wide enough to offer a considerable choice of routes, and although we still could not be certain of finding a way through, we returned to camp having decided to take the chance. On the way back we found two heads of *ovis poli* embedded in the ice.

We started the next morning at a quarter-past seven. We found a way through the ice-fall without any loss of time, though we had to do a certain amount of step-cutting. Beyond, for the next two hours, the route-finding continued to be fairly difficult, and, though we met with no serious obstacle, it would have been very difficult indeed to find the way back in thick weather. At about half-past eleven we reached a conspicuous hollow which we had seen from below, and beyond which the route was perfectly straightforward. Thus far the snow conditions had been perfect and we had made very good time; so good, indeed, that we decided, there and then, to have only one more camp instead of two as we had originally planned.

Beyond the hollow we ran into soft snow and the going became more laborious. By tradition, Gyalgen was carrying the largest share of the load, while Bill and I took it in turns to kick steps. But Gyalgen showed signs of tiring, and as we now hoped to attempt the summit from the next camp, we lightened his load by dumping some of the surplus food and kerosene. At half-past three we decided that we had done enough, and pitched camp. While the evening meal was brewing we reviewed our decision to attempt the summit from there. We estimated our height to be at least 20,500 feet, though we had no means of checking it. This left us with rather less than 4,000 feet to climb, which did not seem excessive, given reasonably good snow conditions. We assumed that the soft snow we had lately encountered was the result of melting; by starting at six o'clock we could count on at least four hours of frozen snow. The climbing was devoid of difficulty and we could surely count on making at least 800 feet an hour. The weather was good, though it seemed to me that there were cloud signs suggesting a change. I confess that the idea of taking up another camp, with all the toil and paraphernalia involved, seemed like breaking a butterfly on a wheel. Bill agreed, though, I think, with less conviction. We settled down fairly comfortably to the long frozen night.

We started brewing tea long before dawn on 13th August. Bill had a bad headache and was obviously not feeling well. Five a.m. is not a good time for making decisions; morally, as well as physically, human beings are at their lowest ebb. It is clear now that we should have reversed our decision of the day before, spent a comparatively easy day taking our camp higher and giving Bill time to recover. Certainly I did suggest it, but probably without enough force, and Bill, being Bill, was not going to agree to it lightly. He had had a headache the morning before, which had disappeared, as such headaches often do, when we had emerged from the stuffy tent. I thought the same might happen again. Whether Bill thought so too, I do not know.

It was beginning to get light by half-past five. We were off by a quarter-past six. The snow was excellent and we climbed a good thousand feet in the first hour. Then things began to go wrong. The snow suddenly deteriorated. It had a thin crust on top which would not hold our full weight but which demanded a sharp kick to penetrate, while in the soft snow below we sank more than a foot; quite one of the most laborious kinds of snow in which to make a trail. This by itself, although disappointing, was not a serious factor, nor was it wholly unexpected. At extreme altitudes there is so little melting during the day that the surface snow does not readily consolidate. In the Everest district, for example, we had found that the monsoon deposits always remained soft above an altitude of 23,000 feet. Two attempts I have made to climb the North Peak have been frustrated by this factor. Muztagh Ata is ten degrees north of Everest, and it seemed reasonable to expect similar conditions at a much lower altitude, though our experience of the day before had been reassuring. However, we could go on for at least eight hours more before turning back, and, unless the snow became very much worse, it seemed inconceivable that we could not climb the remaining three thousand feet in that time. The serious trouble was that Bill's condition did not improve. He could follow in the tracks, but could not lead.

The weather was very clear, but there was a strong wind blowing from the south across the ridge. At first it did not seem to be very fierce or unusually cold, but it must have been peculiarly penetrating, for whenever I paused for a rest I started to shiver as violently as if I had been standing naked in a wind after a cold plunge. Admittedly I had no wind-proof trousers, but I was wearing thick, long, Shetland pants, and four sweaters, while the skirt of my wind-proof smock came down almost to my knees. Gyalgen was the only one of us who kept tolerably warm; he was wearing one of the padded suits worn by the Kashgar Turkis in winter. Bill and I later agreed that we had never been so cold before while actually climbing. The sun reached us at about eight o'clock, but it seemed to give no warmth, either then or at noon. Though the ridge was several hundred yards wide, it was now smooth and the surface of the snow provided no irregularity behind which we could shelter. We could not stop for a moment to rest, so we plugged on, as much in a race to get warm as to make height.

The next misfortune occurred when it transpired, at about nine o'clock, that Gyalgen also was not feeling well and declined my invitation to take a turn at flogging the trail. Why, at that point, we did not turn back, I find it difficult to explain. It was certainly entirely my fault and I can only summon the lame excuse of cold-befuddled wits to mitigate my stupidity. I think my reasoning, such as it was, was something like this: that it was now too late to return, collect the spare food and kerosene which we had dumped the previous day and then to move our camp higher that day; that as, apart from the cold, I was feeling very well, it was a pity not to use at least the morning by stamping a trail which we could follow with much less effort the next day; that soon we would be warmed by the sun and would be able to sit down and contemplate the situation; and, finally, that the good weather would not hold. This line of thought later changed imperceptibly into the feeling, shared more wholeheartedly by my companions, that we must be getting so close to the summit that we might as well go on and finish the job.

I can recall nothing of the next three or four hours except dull, plodding monotony and intense cold. We were prevented by the width of the ridge from seeing the other peaks of the massif by which we might have been able to gauge our upward progress. We avoided going to the left for fear of getting too close to the edge of the ice-cliff overhanging the Yam-bulak Glacier, while to the right the ground was somewhat crevassed. The snow neither improved nor deteriorated; the force of the wind neither increased nor slackened; the sun seemed to become no warmer. Early in the afternoon a small, swiftly moving cloud attached itself to the ridge a few hundred feet above us. This seemed to show that we were getting very close to the top, and I now had very little doubt that we would reach it.

By about half-past two we had reached a point where the slope eased off into what was obviously the summit dome. We reckoned that we must be at least 24,000 feet high, for, apart from the change in the slope, we had now been climbing steadily for more than eight hours, the first of which had been at a very good pace. This estimate was, I think, confirmed by the views of the mountain we had later from the north. But having seen the peak only from the west, we had no idea of the extent of the summit plateau. It was now a question of distance rather than height, and we were depressed by the thought that we might have to go trudging on for hours before finding the highest point in this wide expanse of snow. And yet we might find ourselves suddenly upon it. We decided to give it another hour. But at half-past three we were still not on the highest point, though we can have been only a very few feet below it. With a mixture of relief and bitter reluctance, we agreed to abandon the struggle.

When we started down, I realized for the first time that I was very tired indeed. I had once or twice to call on the others to halt, and once I vomited. But we reached camp in such good time that one more regret, that we had not persisted for just half an hour longer, was added to our contrition. When I removed my boots I found that the toes of my left foot were very obviously frost-bitten. This was most unexpected, for although I had been so cold all day I had not noticeably suffered from cold feet, and I had imagined that I could feel my toes by moving them about in the boots. The boots were old; they had let in the water the day before, and that morning I had noticed that the insides were coated with a layer of ice. But I had put on three dry pairs of thick camel-hair socks. Before this unpleasant discovery, we had been discussing carrying our camp up a couple of thousand feet higher the next day, and from there paying a more leisurely and decisive visit to the summit dome. But my frost-bitten foot put this idea out of count.

We waited for the sun to reach us before starting down the next morning. We stopped to make a brew of jam soup at the site of our first camp, and reached the foot of the ridge in the middle of the afternoon. We could not face humping the loads across to Yam-bulak, so we dumped them under a rock and went on, with the object of sending ponies back for them. But we saw a flock of sheep grazing near by and Gyalgen thought it prudent to stay to guard the loads until the ponies arrived. He did not get in until after dark and was so exhausted that he could not even drink a cup of tea.

The condition of my foot precluded the possibility of attempting to climb Chakragil. Bill might have tried it with Gyalgen, but, typically, he was more concerned that I should get back to Kashgar as soon as possible to have my foot treated. Both he and Gyalgen had had their toes touched by frost, and Bill had at least one sleepless night as a result; but, beyond a blackening of the tips of the toes, they suffered no lasting effects. Our Kirghiz hosts insisted on wrapping my foot in a poultice of cheese mixed with ash from their yak-dung fire. This is the universally accepted remedy for frostbite in these parts. Unfortunately, I cannot testify as to its effectiveness, for, being a man of little faith, I abandoned it after the first day in favour of Sulphonamide.

We went down to the main valley and rested for a day at Subashi, a large Kirghiz settlement, consisting of scores of *akois*. "*Akoi*" is the Turki word (it means literally "white house") for the dome-shaped tent used by all the nomads of Turkestan and Mongolia.[1] (I have not seen it in Southern Tibet.) It consists of a light, skeleton frame of wood, covered with a jacket of felt. *Akois* vary a good deal in size and appearance, according to the prosperity of the owners. Normally they have a floor diameter of about fifteen feet and are about nine feet high. The richer ones are decorated with gaily embroidered felts. The fire is laid on the centre of the floor, and there is a hole in the apex of the tent through which the smoke (most of it) escapes. In heavy rain or snow the hole can be covered by a sheath of felt operated from the outside; then, of course, most of the smoke remains inside. Piles of rugs are stacked all round the walls. A small portion of the *akoi* is screened off for the domestic activities of the women. The inmates sit cross-legged round the fire, and sleep with their feet towards the centre and their heads towards the circumference like the spokes of a wheel. A medium-sized *akoi* can accommodate a dozen people. It is a very comfortable form of dwelling; there is no draught and even in the coldest weather it is kept pleasantly warm inside. It can be assembled or taken down in about an hour and can be carried by one camel or two ponies.

At Subashi we stayed with the Beg (or head-man) in his luxurious and very ornate *akoi*. We spent the day talking to our host and an endless stream of visitors who crowded into the tent, and consumed great quantities of milk and

[1] Tilman refers to Akois as Yorts in *Two Mountains and a River* and *China to Chitral*

cream. Dinner, which was shared by all who could squeeze into the tent, consisted mainly of great chunks of mutton which were boiled in a vast cauldron and handed round on large steaming platters. There was also a kind of pastry cake, made of flour and cream, which took two hours to prepare; it was delicious, but very rich.

The Kirghiz have a Mongolian appearance, in contrast to the Aryan features of the Turkis. When one has their confidence, they are a most friendly and hospitable people. They lead a free and varied life, moving with their great herds of sheep, goats, yaks and camels from pasture to pasture (usually within the same valley basin), according to the seasons. They make occasional journeys to the oases of the plains to trade their sheep, skins and butter for flour, salt and other needs. Like all nomads of Central Asia, they are splendid horsemen, for, of course, riding is an indispensable part of their lives. Their mode of living precludes real squalor, while their work is free from much of the drudgery of agricultural toil. There is, I suppose, a tendency to over-idyllize the simple life; but if contentment, physical well-being and a means of livelihood which tends to promote individual dignity and self-reliance together consitute a yardstick by which to measure standards of living, then, certainly, that of the Kirghiz is high in relation to the majority of human beings.

Early the next morning we rode swiftly down the wide, grassy valley to the Kara Kul, seven miles away, where we spent another idle day. We chose a flat promontory on the western shore of the lake and settled down to enjoy one of the finest views in Central Asia. It was a clear, still day, and the glassy surface of the lake, four or five square miles in extent, was very blue. We were at the centre of a complete semicircle of ice-mountains with a radius of about twenty miles. To the north and north-east there was an uninterrupted view of the Kungur massif, with its two 25,000-foot peaks, so laden with ice that throughout its length there was hardly any rock to be seen. To the east there was a long line of peaks of the Shiwakte group. The huge mass of Muztagh Ata filled the southern arc; from here, at last, it showed us a form and character consistent with its size. Wide grassy valleys, intersected by rounded hills, filled in the middle distance. Flights of geese and duck passed over the lake. In the late afternoon we rode over to the northern lake of Basik-Kul, set in a deep hollow in red and yellow hills and fringed with meadowland of vivid green. We returned to camp in time to watch the sunset colours kindle upon the great cirque of ice-peaks.

The next day we marched on to the north down the Karatash Jilga. Immediately after leaving the region of the lakes, the valley becomes barren and forbidding, in sharp contrast to the soft, undulating country that we had been travelling through almost all the way from Tashkurghan. Bursting its way over the wide barrier of ancient moraine deposits, which mark the former extension of the great ice-sheet covering Kungur, the river plunges down into a conglomerate ravine. The flooded river forced us to follow a route high up on the west side of the valley, and we did not reach Bulun-Kul, where there was a Chinese military post, until late in the evening. The commander of the small garrison had died that day. A week before, the bolt of his rifle had burst back into his face while he was shooting *ovis poli*, and had penetrated his skull. My wife, who had spent much of her time while we were on Muztagh Ata ministering to sick Kirghiz who came to her from far and wide, had received a deputation from the garrison asking for medicine for the unfortunate man. Misunderstanding what was said, and in any case quite unequipped to deal with such an emergency, especially at a distance of thirty miles from the patient, she had sent a piece of Elastoplast and some Dettol. This had been accepted by the emissaries with full confidence in an immediate cure.

The lake of Bulun-Kul has almost completely disappeared and its bed is now covered with grass. Immediately north there is a large sandy plain, six miles long and a mile and a half wide, marking the site of another recent lake. This had obviously been formed by the damming back of the waters of the pre-existing Gez and Kara-tash Rivers by the comparatively recent rise of the Chakragil-Kungur massif about them. The resulting formation of the remarkable Gez defile is similar to that of the Arun and other Himalayan gorges. If the modern theory regarding the recent rise of the Himalayas be accepted, cannot the rise of the Kashgar Range (Chakragil, Kungur, Muztagh Ata) also be explained as the readjustment of isostatic equilibrium resulting from the erosion of the Pamir plateau? The drying up of the lake seems to indicate that the cutting action of the combined rivers is now at least keeping pace with the rise of the mountains. It has also resulted in a remarkable feature of the landscape. The country around the entrance of the *Gez* Defile is subjected to exceptionally violent windstorms, which seem to blow up the defile itself. Since the drying of the lake-bed enormous quantities of sand have been blown from it up on to the hills which flank it on the west, completely filling all the nullahs and forming immense dunes which bury the hill-sides for a thousand feet above the floor of the valley. The dunes look remarkably like the undulating and broken snow-slopes on, say, the northern side of Mont Blanc. It would be interesting to know when these dunes began to form. I can find no reference to them by Hedin or Stein, who visited the area in 1894 and 1900 respectively (I have no access to the account of Stein's later journey), and I cannot believe that they could have been passed unnoticed. Moreover, the 1925 edition of the Survey of India map No. 42 N. which was compiled in this area from Stein's survey, marks the lake-bed in question as a swamp; it also shows the area of the Bulun-Kul Lake as about two square miles, while, as I have said, this lake has now almost entirely disappeared.

We were prevented by the volume of water in the river from travelling down through the Gez Defile, which would have taken us back to Kashgar by way of Tashmalik in four days. Instead, we had to make a long detour to the north-west so as to cross the Kashgar Range by way of the Ulughart Pass. From Bulun-Kul we followed the Gez River upstream for two days, along the southern flanks of the Range. Chakragil was beautifully clear, and we saw that there was a possible route to the summit from this side. It was extremely galling to have to pass it by, and once more I experienced an agony of regret for my stupidity and my carelessness in getting my foot frost-bitten. The valley was wide and green, and interspersed with lakes and swamps inhabited at this time of year by a great number and variety of wild fowl which had migrated from the plains in the spring. It was well populated, too, by large Kirghiz settlements, and we made frequent halts during the day's march to refresh ourselves with milk and curds. Bill aptly described our progress as "*akoi* crawling".

Since leaving Tashkurghan, except for two riding-ponies that we had brought from Kashgar, we had been getting the transport we needed as we went along; an arrangement to be avoided if possible. At Kunti-imes, which we reached on 19th August, our Kirghiz hosts were most reluctant to provide us with the animals we needed to cross the Ulugh-art Pass, which is 16,600 feet high, and difficult for pack-animals. At length, however, after a great deal of argument they produced five ponies and two donkeys (travelling officially, one was compelled to carry a disgusting amount of baggage), with three boys to tend them, none of whom, it transpired later, had been over the Pass before. We were assured that, although the way was long and hard, the Pass could be crossed in a single day from Kunti-imes. In attempting to do this, we let ourselves in for a great deal of trouble.

We started early on the 20th, and were by no means indolent. Throughout the morning we climbed steeply, and by noon we reached the crest of a preliminary pass. From here we had a fine view of Mount Stalin (known to our fathers as Mount Kaufmann), the highest peak of the Trans Alai, a hundred miles away to the north-west. Descending from this first pass, we made our way up a long, desolate, stony valley, adorned with several side-glaciers, until we reached the snout of a big ice-stream coming down from the main watershed. The path then wound its way high up along the steep mountain-side above the glacier, making long detours into deep, precipitous nullahs, cut by glacier torrents. Some of these were very difficult to cross, as they were now dangerously swollen by the melting ice under the afternoon sun. Although the Ulugh-art Pass could be seen from a long way off, these detours made it impossible to tell how long it would take to reach it. Nor, of course, could we get any help from the three boys. Had we known it would take us so long, we would have camped on some flat ground before reaching the glacier, and crossed the Pass the following day. Once we had climbed up on to the steep slopes above the glacier, there was no place on which to make a reasonably comfortable camp; so we pressed on in the hope of getting across before dark. But it was seven o'clock before we reached the foot of the final slope leading to the Pass. The caravan had straggled badly and some of the animals were a long way behind. The leading ponies were still some four hundred feet below the Pass when the light began to fade. The slope was very steep and the exhausted creatures were making painfully slow progress. It became obvious that it would be quite dark before they could all reach the top; and we had no idea what the other side was like. There was nothing for it but to return to the foot of the slope and spend the night in a makeshift camp beside the glacier.

The night was fine, fortunately, but very cold. The next morning my pony died before he had gone, unloaded, a couple of hundred feet up the slope. He was a large strong animal and had given no sign of undue fatigue the day before, but he had been bred in the plains and was not used to high altitudes. This disaster had a bad effect on the morale of the Kirghiz, who declared that their five ponies would also die before reaching the Pass. They insisted on sending them back with one of the youths, leaving us to transport our baggage as best we could with the two donkeys and what man-power we could muster; for our own second pony was now so weak that it could carry nothing. The entire day was spent relaying the loads across the Pass, a laborious operation in which I could take no active part. The next day we managed to make another five miles down the valley on the other side of the watershed.

A mile or so up a side-valley from this point there was a small Kirghiz settlement marked on Stein's map with the discouraging name of Yamen (Bad) Serai. We sent Gyalgen to lay our sad case before the inhabitants and to try to hire from them four yaks to take us to Yolchi Moinak at the northern foot of the range. This was evidently a tactical mistake; it would probably have been better if my wife had gone with him to inspire confidence. For, though he was unarmed and alone, the Kirghiz mistook Gyalgen for an official come to commandeer some of their flocks. Before this dread invader the male population fled into the mountains, taking with them the faster animals and leaving the women and children and the sheep to his mercy. Gyalgen followed them for a weary day and at length managed to persuade them of his innocent intentions. Even so, he could not induce any of them to come with us; instead, they handed over a herd of a dozen yaks, including three calves, telling him that he might take them to Yolchi Moinak and leave them with the Kirghiz there. Normally the yak is a fairly docile creature, but these seemed to resent being ordered about by strangers. It was only after a prolonged struggle and many abortive attempts that we succeeded in loading our belongings on to the backs of the four least pugnacious beasts and set off slowly down the valley. Gyalgen had had a good deal of experience of the art of yak-driving, and we reached Yolchi Moinak without further misadventure. Here we managed to hire two camels to take us across the thirty miles of waterless desert between the foot-hills and the Opal oasis, where, once more in a land of plenty, our troubles were at an end.

CHAPTER EIGHT

Uch Tash

1

ACCESS to the high mountains was restricted to a very few months in the year. But the lower mountains to the north, which were accessible for very much longer, provided an unlimited field for travel and minor exploration. Unfortunately, any journey in that direction meant approaching the Soviet frontier and, although they never said as much, the local authorities were not very happy about our going there lest we should run into any trouble. I had assiduously cultivated a reputation for being a keen huntsman, which provided a plausible reason for our otherwise inexplicable passion for travelling in these wild places. However, I generally considered it best to say nothing about our trips in this direction so as to absolve the authorities of responsibility which would otherwise have impelled them to provide us with an armed guard, always a tiresome burden both to us and the Kirghiz with whom we used to stay. But this policy had the great drawback that we were liable to run into trouble with small frontier posts that we went near. It was essential to have with us a Kirghiz from the district, who could establish contact with the nomad tribes and explain our identity. Once, my failure to take this precaution led to infinite trouble.

On our frequent week-end trips to the mountains north of Kashgar, we established a close friendship with a delightful family of Kirghiz at a tiny mountain hamlet called Suget. Whenever we went there, we were welcomed as members of the family. The son of the house, Mohammed Khurban, was a very skilful and enthusiastic hunter and our week-ends there usually had as their main objective the stalking of ibex and ram chikor, which was an interesting occupation in itself and provided us with long and glorious days in those remote and very lovely hills. With the ibex we usually succeeded; with the ram chikor we nearly always failed. But I had an ulterior motive with Khurban, which was to entice him to come with us on our journeys. He was quite willing, when we promised him some hunting. Gyalgen was oddly jealous of Khurban, who, was in far better physical condition for moving about the hills, and he protested that the Kirghiz would be useless to us when we took him out of his district.

To the north-west of the Min Yol Range there was a large triangle of country which, so far as I know, was unexplored by Western travellers. It was bounded on the north-west by the Soviet frontier and comprised nearly a hundred miles of the extreme western end of the Tien Shan. The mountains, which were not glaciated, did not appear to exceed seventeen thousand feet in height, and I supposed that it would be possible to travel through the area in the spring. From Ulug Chat, a village about one hundred and twenty miles west of Kashgar along the Irkestam road, there was a wide valley, known as Uch Tash, running up in a north-easterly direction into the heart of the mountains. It was so large that it seemed probable that its basin must drain a considerable proportion of the area. In the early spring of 1948, shortly before my wife left Kashgar to return to England, she and I, Doctor Allan Mersh, Gyalgen and Khurban made an attempt to explore this valley. On 27th February we sent our ponies, unloaded, to a place called Uksalur, eighty miles along the Irkestam road, which was as far as we could take our Ford lorry, in which we followed ourselves a couple of days later. From here we hoped to travel due north and cross a range of mountains into the Uch Tash Valley. In this way we hoped, first, to cut short the journey to the Uch Tash Valley by two or three days and, secondly, to avoid contact with the police-post at Ulug Chat. We then proposed to travel to the head of the Uch Tash Valley, where we hoped to find a pass leading eastward to the country to the south of the frontier pass of Turugart, which we had visited the previous year, and so back to Kashgar.

At Uksalur, a grazing-ground inhabited by semi-nomadic Kirghiz, we were told that, although there was a pass across the range to the north, it was quite impossible at this time of year, as the snow was still lying shoulder-deep upon the mountains. I found this hard to believe, as the country to the north appeared completely arid and not a vestige of snow was to be seen on the southern flanks of the range. However, the Kirghiz were so emphatic, that we decided to change our plan and go on to Ulug Chat, which we reached at noon on 5th March after two days' march. Fortunately, the commander of the police-post, a Turki, turned out to be an old friend of ours to whom we had once given a tweny-five-mile lift into Kashgar. After a little persuasion, he agreed to allow us to travel up the Uch Tash Valley. He told us, however, that we would not be able to get far, as thc upper part of the valley was still blocked by great masses of snow and ice. He urged us to come back in June, when, he said, the upper valley was very beautiful, miles of meadows waist-deep in flowers, and enormous herds of ibex and *ovis poli* grazing on the high mountain pastures.

We marched for two days up the Uch Tash. In the first part, the floor of the valley was composed of wide stretches of grassland, over which the river meandered through a chain of deep, clear pools. A dozen miles up, we reached a zone of dense jungle, interspersed with patches of swamp which were inhabited by a large number and variety of water-fowl. At first, villages were fairly frequent; higher up, these gave place to collections of *akois* situated farther and farther apart. Eventually, after we had passed though a great limestone gorge, at about forty miles from the entrance of the valley we reached an encampment known as Karakchi, set at the junction of many valleys. We were told by the inhabitants that at this time of year there was no habitation farther up the valleys. Certainly the country was beginning to look rather bleak and cold, though so far there was no sign of the great masses of snow we had been led to expect. However, we decided to stay for two days at Karakchi and explore the surrounding country. The Kirghiz told us that there was a route up one of the valleys running to the south-east, which led over the high range to the south to a place called Karanglik on the Irkestam road some thirty-six miles west of Kashgar. There was another up one of the valleys to the east, which led over a pass at its head to Toyan, a grazing-ground to the south of the Turugart Pass. In normal conditions both Karanglik and Toyan were three days' march away, but both routes were now quite impassable.

On the first day, while my wife was enjoying a rest after the strenuous marching we had done, Mersh, Khurban and I, with one of the local Kirghiz, rode some distance up the valley to the south-east. Before we had gone more than half a dozen miles, there was a remarkably sudden change in conditions. The flanks of the valley were covered to a great depth in snow, while the bed was overlaid with hard, slippery ice. Travelling in these northern ranges in the summer, we had encountered frequent heavy rainstorms. Now we had further evidence of the extraordinary difference in the climate of these mountains from that of the waterless desert flanking the Tarim Basin, not thirty miles to the south. On both sides of the valley we saw hundreds of both ibex and *ovis poli*, the largest herds of these creatures that I have ever seen. The former were all on the northern flank of the valley and the latter on the southern.

As we went, the valley became steadily narrower, and with every mile the depth of the snow on its sides increased. After a while the icy bed over which we had been riding became covered with soft snow, which was soon so deep that it was impossible for the ponies to go any farther. We had been approaching a massif of fine limestone peaks which were by far the highest in the district, and which I supposed must lie on the axis of the range forming the southern watershed of the Uch Tash valley system.

By now, Khurban, who had also been sceptical, and I were quite convinced that the upper valleys in this region were inaccessible at this time of year. We turned back and retraced our steps for about a mile down the valley. Then, leaving the ponies tethered, we set off up a nullah in the northern flank of the valley in search of ibex. I would have preferred to go after the *poli*, but the snow on the southern flank was far deeper than on the northern. As it was, the going was extremely hard work and after a while the Doctor decided to remain below with the ponies. I asked him to take them to the foot of the next side-nullah, down where we expected to find the game. But we soon spotted a herd in the upper part of the nullah we were in. It was a difficult business to approach them. Providing we kept to the crest of ridges, the snow was relatively shallow, but as soon as we left them to find cover, we were floundering up to our waists. However, after a two-hour stalk I managed to shoot an ibex with a very fine head. While the two Kirghiz were carrying it down, I went ahead down to the main valley to bring the ponies back. Two hundred yards below the foot of the nullah I came upon saddlery and bits of harness scattered over the snow, which was stained with blood. Half a mile farther on I found the Doctor leading one of the ponies, trying to approach a second, while a third, a mare, stripped of harness and saddlery, was floundering in the snow a little way up the side of the valley. The fourth had bolted down the valley and was nowhere to be seen. Apparently, soon after the Doctor had started to lead them down the valley, a fight had started over the mare, and the resulting stampede had been quite impossible for one man to control. Poor Mersh had been trying to retrieve the situation ever since. Between us we managed to capture the three ponies we could see and to recover most of the jettisoned harness. By the time we returned to the foot of the nullah, the Kirghiz had arrived with the dead ibex. It was already past six o'clock and less than an hour's daylight remained. Leaving one pony with them, the Doctor and I rode off down the valley as fast as the slippery surface would allow. It was almost dark before we caught up with the missing pony. Its passions cooled, we had no difficulty in catching it. We tethered it to a rock, where it could not be missed, and rode on in the gathering darkness, which, but for the starlight and the whiteness of the snow, soon became complete. The route, which had been easy enough in daylight with a guide to lead us, was now anything but straightforward. In several places it led along narrow snow-covered ledges on the side of the valley to avoid some impassable defile or cliff. But I soon discovered that my pony, which I had brought from Kashgar, apparently remembered every step of the way. Several times, when I thought that we had gone wrong and I tried to coax him on to another line, he refused to budge until I abandoned the struggle and gave him his head; then he went on with perfect confidence. It was ten o'clock before we reached the cluster of *akois* at Karakchi. We sent two men back to help the Kirghiz, who arrived with their precious burden of meat an hour later.

The next day, while the Doctor went shooting chikor in the vicinity of the camp, Khurban and I, with another of the local Kirghiz, rode up the valley running to the east. For the second day in succession, it was beautifully fine; these were the only two fine days we had during the whole journey. The valley was more open than the one we had followed the previous day and the sides less steep. The early sun sparkled on the ice-fringed river and upon the billowy surface of snow which stretched away on either hand. It would have been perfect country for skis. After riding for about three hours, at a point where the river disappeared under a great depth of snow, we tethered the ponies and began to climb the northern flank of the valley. Although it was laborious work, by following a gentle ridge we managed to keep in snow which was no more than knee-deep, and in another three hours we reached a little peak on the crest overlooking the next valley to the north. It was a splendid view-point and we sat there for a long time while the Kirghiz explained the local topography, pointing out the routes to the passes leading over to Toyan and Karakchi and to another which led across the Soviet frontier. From here the whole range appeared as a vast, wavy sea of snow, and, except for the knot of limestone peaks to the south, I could distinguish no familiar object.

While we were sitting there, I was astonished to hear the familiar call of ram chikor, and soon we saw a dozen of them half a mile along the ridge to the west. It was difficult to imagine what could have brought them so far up into that barren waste of snow; so far as I could see, there was not a scrap of grazing for many miles around. Khurban at once seized the shot-gun, which he had insisted on bringing as well as the rifle, and set off in pursuit, while I sat lazily watching his stalk, which, though skilfully executed, ended as usual in the birds flying off just before he could get within range. On the way back Khurban and I between us shot three ibex, which provided a very acceptable gift to our hosts in Karakchi.

We had, of course, to resign ourselves to returning to Kashgar by the way we had come. The weather deteriorated the very next day, but, except for an occasional flurry, the snow held off until after we had reached the end of the Uch Tash Valley. Nearly all the way from Ulug Chat to Uksalur it snowed gently, though it was not heavy enough to obscure the track or to cause us any serious inconvenience. But on the night we reached Uksalur, 12th March, it snowed very heavily. On the morning of the 13th, a dense mist enveloped the country, and although it had stopped snowing, we found that a foot of new snow covered the ground. None of the local Kirghiz was willing to come with us to show us the way. They assured us, with the bland confidence of all country people who have known their surroundings all their lives, that even in these conditions we could not fail to find our way. We did not share their confidence, but we were reluctant to wait, for we had already been away longer than we had intended and there was no means of telling how long these conditions would persist, even if no more snow fell.

We started at eight o'clock. As we had expected, the route was extremely difficult to find. It crossed an interminable series of steep-sided nullahs, each closely resembling the last. Sometimes it would go straight across; sometimes it would follow the nullah for a long way up or down to reach an accessible exit. Although our helpless flounderings in deep drifts between boulders made it quickly obvious when we had missed the route, it was always surprisingly difficult to find it again, and having found it to divine its direction. We all went on foot so as to stamp a trail for the ponies, and by exercising extreme care we maintained contact with the path for three hours. But somewhere around eleven o'clock we went seriously astray. We spread out and cast about in every direction without finding the elusive path. Although by now the mists had lifted and visibility had been thus extended to about half a mile, none of us could recognize a single object in the landscape. The whole aspect of the country was, of course, totally different under this deep covering of snow; also it was far too broken and difficult for us to march on a compass bearing. Even the physical labour of searching for the path was most exhausting, and it would have been impossible for the ponies to go far without it. At length, soon after noon, we had to admit that we were lost. I was just formulating a somewhat desperate plan of trying to make our way down the nullah to the valley of the Kizil Su, where perhaps there was less snow, as an alternative to following our tracks back to Uksalur, when two horsemen emerged from the mist and rode across the nullah three hundred yards below. We shouted to them, but they would not stop. However, they were going in the right direction and all we had to do was to follow their tracks. By six o'clock that evening we had reached ground so much lower that much of it was already uncovered and the route was clearly visible. That night we found shelter in a deserted hut by a stream. By making two more very long marches, we reached Kashgar on the 15th March.

2

Two months later I had an opportunity of making another visit to the basin of the Uch Tash. I only had ten days at my disposal, but I hoped that by travelling fast and carrying our small requirements in saddle-bags instead of on pack-ponies we would have ample time to reach Karakchi from the east, thus establishing the link across the ranges from that direction. I was very anxious, among other things, to see the wonderful flower-covered alps that the local Kirghiz, as well as the policeman at Ulug Chat, had described. It was still rather early in the year, but in Kashgar it was already full summer and I supposed that something of spring must by now have come to these comparatively low ranges. In any case, it was the last chance I was likely to get. I had discussed with Khurban a probable line of approach to the Uch Tash Valley, westward from his home at Suget. He was familiar with the first two marches and with the local Begs in the district.

I sent a tough young Turki, who went by the pet name of Kapak, and who often came with us on our journeys, to Suget to warn Khurban of our coming. Gyalgen and I followed a few days later on 12th May. I was dismayed to find that Khurban was away from home, having gone off, shortly before Kapak had arrived, on some business of his own. This was a disaster, for not only had I been relying on him to show me the first part of this hypothetical route, but, vastly more important, to introduce me and explain my innocent purpose to the tribesmen we met. And there was no other able-bodied young man in this tiny hamlet to take his place. Khurban's relatives were very upset at my disappointment and suggested sending an ancient uncle to help us on our way. But, after some discussion, the latter wisely thought better of the offer. I thought seriously of abandoning the expedition, but the temptation was too strong and I decided to go on alone with Gyalgen and Kapak, and hope for the best.

A strong north-westerly wind blew during the night and by morning the thick dust haze that had hung over the country for the past two weeks had cleared away. When we set out at seven o'clock, the air was beautifully clear and the outlines of the distant mountains were sharply defined. It was a most remarkable landscape, even in this country of strange forms and colours, and it never failed to fascinate me, whether it was half-hidden by the misty gloom of the dust haze, or dark and forbidding under lowering storm-cloud, or, as on this morning, clear and vast, lit by the soft light of the early sun. The wide horizon was formed by a sinuous ring of mountains enclosing what must in recent geological times have formed a great gulf of the inland sea. Its floor, broken by steep rocky "islands" and now scored into a labyrinth of ridges and canyons, which exposed the horizontal bedding planes, was for the most part grey, but splashed here and there with great sweeps of vivid colour. Our way led close by a curious outcrop of volcanic hills, which from a distance looked remarkably like a line of crimson sponge-cakes, over which black chocolate sauce had been carelessly poured. To our left was the range of mountains which we had so often explored in search of game.

We crossed this range by a deep gap known as the Bai Kurut Dawan, and descended to the great gorge of the Chakmak River, which had its origin on the main divide of the Tien Shan, near the Turugart Dawan. At the little village of Bai Kurut at the foot of the pass, we met a young man who had once received treatment at our Consulate dispensary. He insisted on entertaining us to a meal in his *akoi*. It was now eleven o'clock, and having had no breakfast that morning we were not reluctant to accept. From Bai Kurut I had hoped to travel due west out of the Chakmak Valley and across a pass direct to the next major valley in that direction. I had seen the lower part of the river draining this valley. Khurban had referred to it as the Uruk, and had told me that it flowed from the north-west. We had agreed that its head must lie very close to the Uch Tash, and that from there it would be an easy matter to find a pass leading over to the latter. But our host and his friends assured me that there was no way of getting out of the Chakmak Gorge immediately to the west, and that the quickest way of getting to the Uruk Valley was to go up the river until we came to the first tributary on the left. I was reluctant to go far in that direction, for two reasons. First, the farther north we went, the longer and more complicated the crossing between the two valleys would become. Secondly, about seventeen miles up the gorge was the Chinese post of

Chakmak Karaul. Travelling in that district the previous summer, my wife and I had become embroiled with the commander of this post, fortunately on our way back, and although he had been perfectly friendly, I realized that if he came to know of my presence his hospitality would severely restrict my travels. However, there seemed to be nothing for it and we went off up the gorge.

We had ridden for about ten miles, crossing and recrossing the turbulent river as it swung from side to side of the gorge, before we reached a prominent side-valley coming in from the west. It had been an exasperating and rather profitless day; but now at last, at five o'clock, we entered new country and spirits rose. It was a delightful grassy valley, in pleasant contrast to the grim gorge we had just left. But my enjoyment of the country and the soft evening light was short-lived. The wind had been blowing strongly throughout the afternoon, and before we had gone more than a couple of miles up the new valley it increased to a gale. Clouds of fine sand came sweeping down the valley and struck against our faces with stinging force, and for short periods blotted out visibility so completely that we had to stop until the gust subsided. Farther on we passed some Kirghiz settlements, where we found that the people had removed the felt covering from their *akois* to decrease the wind-resistance and prevent them from being blown away. They sat with their backs to the wind hanging on to the frames and patiently waiting for the gale to subside. At about seven o'clock we reached a fork in the valley. On a wide stretch of grassland between the two rivers there was a substantial stone building, and in this, with considerable relief, we took refuge from the storm.

The place belonged to the local Beg. He welcomed us warmly, and did not seem for a moment to question our identity. He gave us a room to sleep in and soon produced a steaming meal of "sucash". Moreover, he was most encouraging about the route. He told us that we could reach Uch Tash in two days; the first across a high pass called the Kara Bel Dawan to the Uruk Jilga, the second, over an easy saddle at its head. He agreed to send a man with us across the Kara Bel to a place called Assan Tolmak, where another man would escort us onwards. All this sounded very satisfactory and I went to sleep with a feeling of peace and pleasurable anticipation. This was heightened the next morning when, soon after dawn, we started up the left-hand fork of the valley. The morning was fine and still. The valley was flanked by smoothly curved grass slopes, topped by fine limestone crags, from which the enchanting call of ram chikor floated down on the cool sunlit air. We saw a herd of ibex on a crag high above us, standing motionless against the sky. The valley was short and at its head we could see the pass, a U-shaped gap between steep rock walls. Only one disquieting thought disturbed this delightful prospect. Our long northerly trek up the Chakmak River had taken us uncomfortably close to Chakmak Karaul. It seemed to me very probable that the commander of the post would get wind of us, and send some men to bring us back, if only to explain ourselves and our movements. At best this would cause a delay of two days, which I could not spare. So throughout the morning, while we plodded slowly up the long steep slopes towards the pass, I kept glancing apprehensively back down the valley, expecting to see a couple of galloping horsemen approaching. I felt quite illogically relieved when we reached the pass and began to descend the other side.

The view beyond the pass revealed an intricate complex of steep, narrow valleys all draining towards the south. Three miles down we reached Assan Tolmak, which consisted of a single *akoi*. The owner emerged from it, looking scared, but when he had received an explanation from our guide and a number of small presents from us, his expression lightened. We were ushered into the tent and plied with curds and cream, while our host bubbled over with geniality. He said he would gladly send his son with us to show us the way. He agreed that we could easily reach Uch Tash the following day if we started at once; first, we must go a short way down to the main Uruk Jilga, then follow it up-stream to its head, whence a gentle pass would lead us to our goal. No mention was made of any difficulties such as snow-blocked valleys, lack of grazing or any other of the obstacles of which we were soon to hear so much.

Paying off our first guide, we went on down the valley. Its general direction was somewhat east of south and it was far longer than I had expected. When we had covered another seven miles, I estimated that we had reached a point opposite, and only a short distance across the mountains from, Bai Kurut in the Chakmak Valley. Our new guide agreed that we could have crossed over from there in a few hours. Our detour had cost us a long day's superfluous travel. When at last we reached the Uruk Jilga, he announced that he would come no farther as there were no settlements up the valley and therefore nowhere for him to spend the night. I was convinced that this was untrue, but he was adamant. We could probably have forced him to come on, with the threat of a complaint to the Beg. But we had hitherto been received with such friendliness that I thought we could dispense with his services, which were valuable, not so much as a guide, but as a guarantor of our goodwill. In this I made a fatal mistake, which soon became apparent.

It was obvious from the size of the river that we had a very long way to go before reaching the head of the Uruk Jilga. But the general direction of the valley, slightly north of west, was satisfactory, for if this were maintained, I reckoned it must lead us to the country in the vicinity of Karakchi. Before we had gone more than a couple of miles, we met a party of Kirghiz evidently returning from a hunting expedition, for they had portions of ibex carcass slung across their saddles. They seemed oddly scared of us, and when we explained who we were they obviously did not believe us. They assured us that the route up the valley led nowhere and that there were no further settlements in that direction. They were clearly determined to be as unhelpful as possible, so we bade them good-bye and continued on our way. Whereupon they rode after us and said that one of their number would come with us to the next village, blandly ignoring their recent denial of its existence. Their purpose was evidently to keep an eye on us, but we thanked them for their kindness and started once more with our new companion.

All this gave me an unpleasant foreboding of trouble to come. But it was a glorious evening, and the valley was very beautiful. It was wide and grassy; great peaks and ridges stood above it, made of a limestone so white that the snow, which lay deep in the upper corries, was almost indistinguishable from the rock. So, cantering over the soft green turf towards the declining sun, I forgot all else in the exquisite loveliness of the place. Whatever the outcome of our journey, whether we reached our goal or not, the experience of this moment was reward enough.

At about half-past seven we reached a group of four *akois* where we stopped for the night. Though convention demanded that we should be invited indoors, our reception was chilly. The atmosphere was warmed somewhat by a generous gift of rice, soap and tea, but this did not establish our identity, which was obviously suspect. Nor did our liberality win us the slightest encouragement: the pass over to Uch Tash (whose existence was, however, admitted) was many days' journey beyond the farthest settlement in the valley; the country was bleak and desolate, without water or grazing or fuel; up there we would find the snow waist-deep; and even if we succeeded in forcing our way over to Uch Tash, which was highly improbable, we would find it uninhabited and would die from want and exposure. The most that we could achieve was a promise that one of our hosts would come with us to the farthest settlement in the valley.

We started at half-past six the next morning. In a narrow defile a couple of miles on, we saw a herd of ibex on the crags some two hundred feet above the river. Our new companion showed considerable excitement, which I found encouraging, for hitherto he and his friends had been careful to display nothing but polite scorn. Hoping to complete the breakdown of this icy barrier with a supply of meat and the promise of more to come, and to gain favour and prestige which would certainly be transmitted to our future contacts, I dismounted and took aim at a large buck that stood gazing down on us. But I had carelessly neglected to clean the bolt of my rifle after the dust storm of two days before; it was choked with grit and clicked ineffectively as I pressed the trigger. I tried again without success, and by the time I had taken out the bolt and cleaned it the whole herd had disappeared. It may well be that this incident sealed the fate of our expedition; for by it we lost face we could ill afford and which we had no chance to recover.

Beyond the defile we passed an old fort with a rampart built across the valley. The general direction of the latter changed to north-north-west, which was less satisfactory from our point of view. The limestone gave place to shale and slate, and in consequence the mountains were less attractive. At frequent intervals we passed small settlements of two or three *akois*, each with large flocks of sheep grazing on the ample pasturage. We met several travellers coming down the valley; from each we asked for information about the route. Some said it was four days' journey to the head of the valley, others said two; some said they knew nothing about it, others declared that no route existed.

At half-past eleven we reached a village, which our guide assured us was the last. We stopped to enlist help, and, as was the local custom, we entered one of the *akois*, sat down and made ourselves at home. The whole male population of the village followed suit and the usual tedious conference began: Who were we? Where were we going and why? But English Consuls don't come into the mountains for *tamasha* (the word is used in Turkestan for all forms of frivolity, from a theatrical performance to a short country walk).

"On the contrary, all Englishmen like to go to the mountains for *tamasha*." This was obviously not believed. As usual, I tried to interest them in a free supply of meat. They admitted that there were large herds of ibex and *poli* up the valley. "Why not come with me, then? I have come mainly for shooting and have plenty of ammunition, but I do not want the meat." This was a tactical error and drew the obvious retort, "Why, then, do you want to shoot?" "I want to get the horns." "But we can give you as many as you like." To explain that it did not count unless I had shot the animal myself was obviously useless, particularly as it was a matter about which I was myself far from clear. I abandoned the struggle. My main objection to going on alone, apart from the valuable time we would lose by searching for the right pass, was the fact that, with the valley leading in its present direction, there was danger of our straying across the frontier, which would almost certainly have disastrous consequences. However, we could at least go to the head of the valley and see how the land lay.

"Well, come or not as you like," I told them. "We are going over to Uch Tash to shoot *keek* (ibex). We would be grateful if you would tell us about the route." They replied that it was impossible to go farther up the valley; the snow was waist-deep and even if we survived, our ponies would certainly perish. Thus we talked in circles for about two hours. We were about to take our leave and move on when a large cavalcade arrived, headed by the Beg of the upper Uruk, and including, I noticed, most of the men we had met and questioned that morning. Courtesy demanded that we should stay and explain ourselves to the Beg, and the tedious conversation was repeated. As politely as possible I signified my disappointment at the unhelpful reception we had met with. Whereupon the Beg said that if we would come with him to his place a short way down the valley, he would show us an easy way from there to Karak-chi; it was only two days' journey and he would either come with us himself or send a man as guide. I was far from sure that he meant what he said, but I could hardly refuse his offer after all that talk, and we set off down the valley again at a steady canter, accompanied by the Beg and a large retinue. On and on we rode, into the evening, until at length we reached a place near the fort, only a few miles from our starting-point that morning. We crowded into the Beg's *akoi*, and a meal was prepared by his women-folk from rice provided by us and meat by our host. After which I retired to my little mountain-tent, with the assurance that all would be ready for an early start the next morning.

I woke at dawn to find that an inch of snow had fallen. As I expected, the Beg and his companions used this circumstance as an excuse for going back on his promise. I pointed out that the day was very fine and that at this time of year all the new snow would be gone in a couple of hours. They retorted that though there was little in the valley, higher up in the mountains we would find that it had fallen to a depth of several feet. This was obviously untrue, and after some argument I ordered my horses to be saddled, informed our hosts that we would revert to our original plan, bade them a somewhat curt good-bye and rode off up the valley once more. Soon, however, they overtook us, full of apologies and assurances that their promises would be implemented.

By now I had abandoned hope of reaching Uch Tash; a journey in any direction from here would be interesting; so I decided to yield with good grace.

A surly, sour-faced individual was appointed our guide. It was difficult to make him speak, and nothing would induce him to smile. He led us up a small steep nullah to a low gap in the mountains to the west. From here we had a sweeping view westward over a wide, open valley system to a cluster of fine peaks very much higher than the rest of the mountains in the district. I was fairly sure that it was the same massif that we had seen to the south of Karakchi whose whereabouts relative to our surroundings I could now visualize with reasonable clarity for the first time since we had left Suget. It was closer than I had expected and my hopes of reaching it began to revive. The air was still beautifully clear and the sun shone dazzlingly on the new snow. But a mass of black cloud was developing in the south-west, which threatened bad weather.

We rode down the other side of the gap and soon reached the floor of a valley as wide, and containing a river almost as large, as the Uruk. At the point where we reached it, there were two *akois*. Our guide handed us over to the owner, who readily agreed to take his place. We rode on up the valley in a north-westerly direction and in an hour and a half reached another group of *akois* where we halted for a meal. Here, for the first time for several days, we received a really friendly welcome and, what was more, ungrudging information about the route. If the snow conditions on the pass were good, we were told, it was possible to reach Karakchi in a single day from there. But it was a difficult pass and so dangerous in bad weather that many Kirghiz had lost their lives on it. No one had crossed it that year, so they did not know what the snow was like, but if the weather held we could probably manage it. The most encouraging thing was that our new escort resolutely declined to hand over his charge to our hosts, declaring that he knew the way well and would get us across the pass if it were possible. I could have hugged him.

We started again at one o'clock. The weather was beginning to look decidedly threatening and a cold, blustering wind blew in our faces. In spite of this, I felt more cheerful and more able to lose myself in the interest of my surroundings than I had for days. The mountains looked bleak and unfriendly, and there was a considerable depth of snow lying on the slopes, particularly the north-facing slopes, a couple of thousand feet above us. But the valley itself was attractive; there were frequent green meadows and great quantities of juniper which offered the prospect of a pleasant camp and good grazing for the ponies. Some of the juniper bushes were like small fir trees. I was surprised to find such luxuriant growth of this plant, for in the neighbouring valleys it had been sparse or non-existent. We saw several large herds of ibex, but no *poli*.

By five o'clock it began to look as though we had reached the upper limit of the juniper, and when we came to a small grassy side-nullah, well protected from the wind and watered by a clear stream, I decided to camp. A fire was quickly lit and water set to boil, and while Kapak and the Kirghiz remained behind to deal with the ponies and pitch camp, Gyalgen and I went up the nullah to collect juniper fuel. I took my rifle in case I should get a shot at an ibex, for we had been over-generous in distributing our food, and our supplies were beginning to run low. We went about half a mile, round a right-angled bend in the nullah, and so were out of sight of the camp. We climbed a little way up the hill-side and worked for about half an hour. Then we started back, each with a large load of firewood.

Suddenly we saw five mounted men, obviously Chinese soldiers, riding up the nullah towards us. My heart sank. As they approached, they deployed so as to surround us. One man dismounted and aimed his rifle at us. We tried to appear as unconcerned as possible and walked towards him with our innocent burdens. But our demonstration failed in its effect. Our adversary, now twenty yards away, was extremely excited and made it quite clear that he would shoot if we did not alter our policy. I flung down my load and put up my hands in the approved style. But Gyalgen was evidently ignorant of this convention, and continued, under his massive stack of juniper, to shout plaintively, "Englis, Englis." I roared at him to follow my example, but he either did not hear, or thought he knew better how to deal with Chinese soldiery. For one horrible moment I expected to see him shot. He was a few yards ahead of me and I ran to overtake him. This diverted the attention of the soldier to me (a result I had by no means intended) and he swung his rifle in my direction. Then I remembered that I had my rifle slung across my back, and though this was clearly the best place for it from the point of view of the soldier, it occurred to me that its presence might be causing him offence. On the other hand, it also occurred to me that if I started to remove it he might regard this as an act of aggression. However, the *status quo* was obviously unsatisfactory, so, as casually as possible, I turned my back on him, unslung the offending piece and dropped it, with profound relief, upon the ground. This had the desired effect. The soldier lowered his rifle and stopped shouting his threats.

By this time the rest of the troop had closed in, and a very young officer appeared on the scene. My explanation of my identity was obviously not believed. We were searched; the innocent contents of my pockets (glare glasses, a pipe, etc.) were removed and we were escorted back to the camp. Here I was amused to find the Beg of the Uruk Valley and three of his friends, including our sour-faced guide of that morning. They looked rather sheepish and ignored my friendly greeting. I was now able to produce my passport and a Chinese visiting-card. The young officer examined these, blushed and said, "I am velly solly," which I soon found was the extent of his knowledge of English. Tea was ready, cigarettes were passed round and we sat down to a friendly chat.

It transpired that the post at Chakmak had, after all, got wind of our suspicious presence in the neighbourhood, and had sent word of it to the officer in charge of the district at Kizil Oi, on the Irkestam road, fifty miles west of Kashgar. The Beg of the Uruk Valley had also sent a messenger, travelling day and night to Kizil Oi, reporting our whereabouts. It was now clear that his main purpose had been to delay us as much as possible; in this, his admirable balance of diplomacy and obstruction had succeeded pretty effectively. It was interesting that our repeated assertions that I was the

British Consul-General from Kashgar on pleasure bent were so completely disbelieved that it had not even been mentioned as a possibility in the reports that got through. These had stated categorically that we were Russians. The Kirghiz whom we had met had not, of course, been able to read my papers. On receipt of definite information as to our whereabouts from the Beg, the Commander at Kizil Oi had sent out a "flying squad" to capture us. None of them had been in that district before, but the Beg and his friends had followed us over from the Uruk Valley so as to meet and guide them and to be in at the kill. The whole operation had been carried out most efficiently, and showed remarkable co-operation between the Chinese Army and the Kirghiz nomads of the district. The young lieutenant later claimed that he and his men had travelled 300 li (100 miles) that day. Though that was an over-estimate, they had certainly done well. He was most courteous and friendly, and showed not the slightest annoyance at the trouble I had caused.

I was so relieved by the peaceful outcome of the encounter, whose ugly possibilities I had perhaps been inclined to exaggerate ten minutes before, that I almost forgot my disappointment at this obvious frustration of my plans. The lieutenant had been sent from Kizil Oi to capture me, and it was clear that, even now that he knew who I was, he could not allow me to go on without orders from his commanding officer. We avoided the subject for some time, and then I suggested that I should remain where I was for the night so as to go shooting the next morning, for I hoped at least to visit the pass. But even this he was reluctant to permit, and I was clearly not in a position to press my request. Though it was getting very late, Chinese manners forbade any hurrying over these negotiations. For my part, I continued to nurse the forlorn hope that the lateness of the hour might induce the lieutenant to relent and allow me to stay where I was for the night. It was a quarter-past seven before we had packed up our kit and started down the valley towards the small Kirghiz settlement where we had exchanged guides that morning and where the soldiers had dumped their food and other belongings on their way up.

It was an exhilarating ride. The dark storm-clouds, which still hung above, had wide rifts in the west which allowed the rays of the setting sun to strike up beneath them, casting a weird reflected light upon the vivid green of the valley and the grim mountains above it. The air was fresh and invigorating. For an hour, before it became too dark, we raced one another at a breakneck speed, which seemed to me quite crazy considering the roughness of the ground, and which the soldiers' ponies maintained with remarkable vigour after their very long day. After dark it rained. I amused myself by riding ahead to watch again the sureness with which my pony picked out the route. A young moon, shining through the cloud, was little help. We reached the *akois* at a quarter-past ten, though Gyalgen and Kapak, who had the bulk of our baggage on their ponies, did not get in until midnight. The women of the *akois* prepared a meal from flour and meat brought by the soldiers. The lieutenant and his men were cheerful and very friendly, but the Beg and his pals, bitterly disappointed, I fancy, by the turn of events, were silent and rather morose.

The following day we made a long march down the valley and reached Kizil

Oi in the evening. I found that I had met the colonel in charge of the post before; he greeted me with great cordiality. Later, he administered a gentle and well-deserved rebuke for my having wandered off towards the frontier without having notified him; but he brushed aside my apology by making it appear that he was at fault for having spoilt my trip. He insisted on my staying with him for at least two nights so that I could visit some oil-wells that were being worked in the hills to the south. My host slept, ate and worked in a mud-plastered room, furnished with only a wooden table and chair and a rough wooden bed. Another bed was put in for me. The colonel apparently spent his spare time teaching himself English from a couple of very bad phrase books; and on both nights I was there we sat up till after midnight while I went through the books with him. By the end of that time we had practically rewritten them.

For the trip to the oil-wells I was provided with an excellent mount with a high cossack saddle, and accompanied by my friend the young lieutenant and two Turki soldiers. As none of them had been there before, we missed the way and spent most of the day riding at great speed through a labyrinth of those fantastic gorges by which most of the desert hills surrounding the Tarim Basin are honeycombed. We reached our objective in the middle of the afternoon, though it turned out, after all, to be only a couple of hours' ride from Kizil Oi. The oil, which was mostly in the form of a solidified pitch, was dug out of deep grottoes in the sides of a nullah. It was carried on donkeys to Kizil Oi, where it was refined in primitive distillers into kerosene, the daily production of which amounted to about five gallons.

We left Kizil Oi at dawn the following day, 19th May. My pony, well fed and refreshed by his rest, was in good form and covered the fifty-odd miles to Kashgar by two o'clock that afternoon. Gyalgen and Kapak followed in a more leisurely fashion and got in twenty-four hours later.

CHAPTER NINE

Urumchi and the Heavenly Pool

THE provincial capital, Urumchi, lies about a thousand miles by road to the east-north-east of Kashgar. Until 1935 the only means of communication between the two cities was by cart or by pony or camel caravan. The journey took normally about two months each way. During the last fifteen years a very rough motor-road has gradually been developed, and now quite a number of lorries ply between the two places. Travelling fast one can cover the distance in about a week; Chinese lorries often take as much as a month. However, the bulk of the traffic is by the old method; even the mail still goes by cart, though by a relay system, and travelling continuously day and night, it takes only three weeks.

Throughout my first tour in Kashgar I tried persistently to obtain permission to visit Urumchi, as there were many matters that I wished to discuss with the Provincial Government. I met with equally persistent refusal until, in the summer of 1942, I asked once more to go there to meet my successor, Michael Gillett, who was coming from Central China to relieve me, and to bring him back with me to Kashgar. To my surprise my request was granted. Hitherto, each refusal had been accompanied by the monotonously reiterated excuse that the Tupan was indisposed, and would therefore not be able to receive me in a manner fitting for the representative of a friendly Power. In my ignorance, though partly because I had long grown tired of looking for signs of a change of heart, I at first assumed that this unexpected success was due simply to my new lines of approach. But the lengths to which the local authorities went to facilitate my journey, and the unwonted cordiality with which I was received by the officials in the various towns on the way, soon gave me an inkling that there was something more to it than that.

We started on 28th July, travelling in the Ford V-8 30-cwt. lorry which had been brought to Kashgar by Sir Eric Teichman on his journey across Central Asia from Peking in 1935. Gillett was due to reach Urumchi about the end of July; not wishing to keep him waiting, I set out to perform the journey as quickly as possible. At least that was the reason for my haste given to the local authorities, and with which I tried to persuade myself. My real reasons were selfish. I had hitherto regarded a long journey by lorry as the worst form of purgatory to be met with in the more common methods of travel. To my mind there were only two tolerable ways of tackling the ordeal. Either one must grit one's teeth and drive as fast and as far each day as the machine and the human frame would stand, in order to get the business over as soon as possible; or one should loiter sufficiently long at each halt (several days at least) to recover mentally and physically from the racket and discomfort of each stage. In the circumstances the latter method would have taken too long, so I chose the former. Actually I have always derived very great enjoyment from my journeys to and from Urumchi. The country along the route is so spectacular, so varied and so strange that not even the hideous discomfort of motor-travel could wholly spoil its enchantment. Of course, it was a great help to be in command of the vehicle in which I was travelling; to be able to start punctually at the time planned, to be able to choose the halting-places along the route, and above all to be able to sit for the bulk of the time behind the steering-wheel, the only tolerably comfortable seat on any lorry.

The old caravan road, of course, followed the line of oases fringing the northern edge of the Takla Makan Desert. So does the "motor-road", except for the first two hundred miles where it follows a line some ten miles north of the oases, along the desert close under the foot-hills of the Tien Shan. Actually, in 1942, although the construction of a motor-road had been started in places, it was nowhere possible to use it, and except for this first two-hundred-mile stretch, where the stones had been swept to the side of the way, we followed the country roads of the old caravan route.

We left Kashgar at four a.m. For the first ten miles we drove northward, until we had crossed the gap in the line of desert hills in that direction. Then we turned east, and for the rest of the day we ran across gently sloping desert, close under the steep, barren foot-hills. Sometimes these presented an aspect of towering precipices, vividly coloured by alternating strata of green, red and yellow sandstone. The surface of the track was quite good except for the fact that every two hundred yards or so it was intersected by the deep ditch of a dry water-course. These required very careful negotiating in bottom gear, so that we could never get up any speed. The heat and glare reflected from the desert were unrelenting. We halted an hour for lunch, and for five minutes every hour and a half to fill the radiator. At seven o'clock in the evening, when we had covered 185 miles, we reached a stream containing the first water we had passed for 135 miles. We camped there for the night and started again at dawn.

Immediately after crossing the stream we ran into soft sand, into which the lorry sank to the axles. The only means of progressing was by laying planks for the rear wheels to run over. We had brought these planks against this contingency which occurred many times during the journey. In this way we covered the next three hundred yards in about an hour, after which the surface became fairly firm again. We now joined the line of oases, and followed these, driving along the rough country roads, to Aksu, which we reached at eleven o'clock. I had intended to get to Bai, about a hundred miles farther on, that day; but the authorities in Aksu had been warned of our coming and they insisted on our staying there for the rest of the day and for the night. We were entertained to a sumptuous feast, and plied with brandy and rice-wine in such quantities that I could scarcely maintain any semblance of dignity, and which gave me cause, the next morning, to regret the otherwise welcome change in the political atmosphere.

Aksu is the largest and most fertile oasis in Southern Sinkiang. There is much greater luxuriance of vegetation than in Kashgar or Yarkand; the willows grow to twice the size; there are wide areas of scrub, pools and waterways.

We left in the early dawn the next day. We had to wake the night-watchman to open the massive wooden gates of the city to let us out. The road ran north for eight miles to Kona Shahr, the city of tombs. A white mist blanketed the rice-fields, from which the trees loomed in spectral shapes. Night still clung to the loess cliffs which towered above us on our right. Straight ahead, floating above the mists, yet with their capture of the earliest light the only clearly defined objects in view, were the great ice-peaks of the Central Tien Shan. I had not seen them before.

Thirty miles farther on, beyond the oasis of Jam, we entered a broad belt of tamarisk and desert poplar, a veritable forest. I have since travelled through this in the late autumn; it was like passing through a forest of flame, for the desert poplars were then slender cones of untarnished gold, and the tamarisk tumbling fountains of crimson. Beyond, we crossed a wide river, shallow, but unbridged and with a bed of soft, clinging mud. Then followed a forty-five-mile stretch of parched hills, with steep climbs up and down through narrow, twisting canyons and across three passes. At two points along this stretch there were springs of sweet water, where lonely inns catered for the needs of the animal caravans. The track was very rough, which restricted our speed to an average of some ten miles an hour. From the third pass we looked down upon the oasis of Yaka Arik, the first of a continuous string, stretching through the town of Bai, for the next sixty miles.

So it went: stark desert, flat or rugged, alternating with fertile oasis or tamarisk jungle; on the right the grim emptiness of the Takla Makan always near; on the left the Celestial Mountains, and here and there a rare vision of lofty snow-peaks.

We reached Karashahr, some seven hundred miles from Kashgar, on the afternoon of the fifth day. Thus far the towns and villages had been similar to those on the southern side of the Takla Makan, in that their population is mainly Turki. Karashahr, being the centre of the Kalmuk tribes, is predominantly Mongol. The town is built on a swiftly flowing river, as wide as the Rhine at Coblenz, which we crossed by ferry. A few miles farther south, the river flows into the lake of Bagrach Kol, which is fifty miles long by about ten wide. The lake appears to be the breeding-ground of great numbers of ducks and geese. Its exit flows through a narrow gorge by the side of the road in a deep, clear stream which has sufficient volume to carry it across two hundred miles of flat desert to the mysterious Lop Nor.

From Karashahr the road runs for 140 miles up and over a range of barren mountains, a south-easterly offshoot of the Tien Shan, to the rim of that extraordinary basin known as the Turfan Depression, one of the most remarkable geological features in the world. Though it lies in the very centre of the great land-mass of Eurasia, and is thus the farthest point on the earth's surface from the sea, parts of its floor are a thousand feet below sea-level. From the 6,000-foot pass on the southern rim, the road plunged down through a steep gorge. Here we had to work hard with a crow-bar to clear a way through masses of rock debris which had fallen from the cliffs and blocked the road at frequent intervals. Since then another route has been found down a gorge with more stable sides. We emerged from the gorge in the late afternoon onto a wide shelf of desert, formed by gigantic alluvial fans, sloping down to the floor of the basin. Below us was an opaque mass of dust, like a cloud-sea but without its sharp definition of outline. Above this, curving away to our left and right, the walls of the vast crater were now clearly defined. Across it, to the north, the glaciers of Bogdo Ola glistened in the slanting sunlight. Then we ran down into the dust-fog and the mountains disappeared. We reached the Toqsun oasis on the floor of the Depression as night was falling.

In the summer the heat in the Turfan Depression is terrific. Many of the inhabitants have had cellars constructed beneath their houses to escape from it. A fierce wind develops every day about noon as the floor of the Depression becomes heated. It blows incessantly throughout the afternoon and evening, sweeping up great clouds of dust. Here in the winter it never freezes; and it is a strange experience to come from the frigid regions surrounding the basin – from Tapanchen, for example, a bare fifty miles away, where the normal winter temperature is far below zero Fahrenheit – to this warm and sun-baked land. As in the Tarim Basin, it hardly ever rains. The rivers from the surrounding mountains mostly disappear into the wide desert slopes which skirt them, so that the inhabitants of the Depression have to rely largely upon water pumped from wells and laboriously constructed subterranean aqueducts.

From Toqsun the road climbs once more to the north, across sloping desert into stark, arid foot-hills. Crossing these by way of a steep pass it descends suddenly into an enchanting valley filled with dense willow jungle, and watered by a lovely, clear river. This it follows for a dozen miles, and so across the main divide to the fertile plains of Tapanchen. Beyond the pass the whole character of the country changes. The deserts, the arid mountain ranges, the rich, irrigated oases of South Sinkiang, give place to the wide steppe-land of Dzungaria or North Sinkiang. The dust haze, which for eight days out of ten spoils the view in the south, is almost entirely absent in the north, where on most days the clear, often rain-washed air enables one to see for a hundred miles in any direction. With this change of scene there is, too, a great change in the character and culture of the people. Han Chinese and Tungans form a high proportion of the population. Their influence is everywhere to be seen, in the towns and villages and on the farms. The Khasaks, in their colourful robes and head-dresses, usually mounted on their stocky steppe ponies, are much more in evidence than are their nomadic counterparts, the Kirghiz, in the south.

We reached Urumchi at noon on the seventh day, thereby, I was told, beating the previous record for the journey by some five days. Word of our approach had been telegraphed from Toqsun, and in a willow grove five miles outside the town we found a large deputation, including Gillett and the heads of the various Provincial Government departments, gathered for my reception. After this ceremony, Gillett and I were driven into the city in the Tupan's limousine. We were comfortably housed in a suite of rooms in the Foreign Affairs Department. There was no British or American Consulate in Urumchi in those days. After two years of isolation from European society, I had an insatiable appetite for talk. The flood now burst on the head of poor Gillett. He bore with me kindly tolerance, though he had sometimes to drive me from his room in the early hours of the morning in order to get some sleep.

Urumchi is not an attractive place. A bazaar of unspeakable squalor surrounds the walled city. Inside the wall the streets are cleaner, the buildings are fairly well constructed and a number of modern shops lend a superficial air of metropolitan prosperity. But, as is usually the case when a modicum of Western culture is imported to an Eastern town, it has lost all character. Urumchi is treeless; it is begrimed by the soot of the coal which is dug from mines a short way off; in the winter it is utterly bleak; in the spring the melting snow turns its streets into quagmires; in the summer dust and smells predominate. It has, however, one saving grace: it is easy to get out of the town into most attractive country. The river-beds are flanked by wide stretches of woodland, interspersed with occasional lakes and reed-swamps. Most of the surrounding country consists of undulating downland covered with coarse grass and small scrub. Once out on this, either on foot or on horseback, one is soon out of sight of the drab ugliness of the town. To the south and south-west the distant view is filled by a fine sweep of mountains forming the eastern ranges of the Tien Shan. Though many of the peaks are ice-covered they are of no great height; but their arrangement presents a splendid sense of space and distance. Their foot-hills, a few hours' journey away, are covered with thick fir forest. To the east the downs sweep upwards and soon merge into the great mass of the Bogdo Ola Range.

Bogdo Ola has the charm of isolation. Though it is really an easterly extension of the Tien Shan, it is separated by the deep and wide gap between the Turfan Depression and Urumchi. The range is ridged by a score of bold granite peaks arranged in a line from west to east. Two of these are so much higher and more massive than the rest that from a distance they completely dominate the scene. Seen together it is difficult to tell which of the two is the higher. Neither has been accurately measured, and the various estimates that have been made of the altitude of the highest point of the range are wildly divergent. *The Times Atlas* marks it as 22,770 feet. Doctor Grœber, the geologist of Merzbacher's Tien Shan Expedition, who visited the range in 1903 and made a rough map of the area, puts the height of the western mountain at 6,500 metres (21,626 feet). The Survey of India map, *Highlands of Tibet and Surrounding Regions,* marks no high peaks in the area. The western mountain is generally regarded as the highest of the range, though this is probably due to the fact that from Urumchi it is the dominating feature of the whole landscape, while its rival cannot be seen at all.

Gillett and I had expected to stay in the capital together for about a fortnight, while I completed my business with the Provincial Government. We were well entertained, and provided with a limousine to drive about in; in the afternoons we were taken out to bathe in some hot springs near by; and on most evenings we were taken to see either Chinese opera or a Russian picture at the "Anti-Imperialist Cinema". At the opera one evening an interesting event occurred. A savage warrior on the stage was executing a violent war-dance with a gigantic spear. As he was whirling the weapon above him, the wooden head became detached from the shaft, flew through the air and struck a girl sitting in the front row of the circle full in the face. Blood gushed from the wound and she slumped over the rail. The audience, who had hitherto paid little apparent attention to the performance, were delighted; they roared with laughter and applause, and although the dance continued as though nothing had happened, all eyes were focused upon the unfortunate girl until she was removed.

Despite these diversions we were not anxious to prolong our stay in the capital. But for some reason, which at the time we did not quite appreciate, our hosts were most reluctant to let us go. Gillett had acquainted them with my peculiar taste for mountains, and when we began to show signs of becoming restive they invited us to visit a sacred lake, known as T'ien Shih (Heavenly Pool), high up in one of the northern valleys of the Bogdo Ola Range. We could not return to Kashgar in any case until our hosts were ready for us to go, so we accepted the invitation eagerly. I had not for a moment imagined that I would have either the time or the opportunity to do any mountaineering and, though I had brought Lhakpa with me, I had left ropes, ice-axes and climbing-boots behind in Kashgar. However, the idea of a trek into these little-known mountains was very welcome, even though the official nature of the trip meant that we would be burdened with a large armed escort. Two minor officials of the Foreign Affairs Office were also detailed to accompany us.

The expedition set out in two decrepit lorries bound for Fukang, a small town forty miles along the northern highway from Urumchi to Hami. From Urumchi, Bogdo Ola does not show to advantage. The rounded foot-hills forming the end of the range screen the ice-peaks, and only the very apex of the high western mountain can be seen. But from a point some twenty miles along the Hami road the whole of its great northern flank came into view. With its hanging glaciers and its steep ice-couloirs leading up to the long summit ridge, it was a very impressive sight.

At Fukang we sat for several hours with the magistrate and the local police officer drinking tea and talking polite platitudes while pack-transport and riding-ponies were being arranged. At length, after the usual prolonged argument with the magistrate as to whether or not we should spend the night with him, we set off towards the mountain. We soon reached the foot-hills, made our way up a wooded valley and halted for the night in a pleasant spot. Beyond, the valley narrowed to a gorge. We were told that the lake was only about a dozen miles away but that the gorge was impassable at this time of year owing to the summer floods. The alternative was to make a long detour to the west. We started at six o'clock the next morning, crossed a series of bare, rounded ridges and descended again to another valley, thickly wooded with deciduous trees. A few miles farther up this valley we turned up a steep side nullah to the left and were soon amongst fir forest.

The weather, which had been fine in the morning, turned cloudy and threatening in the afternoon. By evening we were still climbing up through the forest, and the pass by which we were to cross over to the lake was still a long way off. Gillett and I were in favour of camping in the forest, but our Chinese companions were strongly opposed to this plan, having little faith in the ability of the small mountain tents we had brought with us to protect us from the weather. It was eight o'clock when we reached the pass. Beyond, we looked down over a wide basin flanked on all sides by steep, fir-covered mountains. Heavy rain-clouds overhung the lake, and hid it from view. A short way below the pass there was a wide, grassy shelf, breaking the downward sweep of the forest. On it I was relieved to see three or four *akois*. We were soon sitting comfortably round a fire on rich carpets, drinking large bowls of *kumis* (fermented mare's milk).

The *akois* of the Khasaks are almost identical with those of the Kirghiz, and, of course, their way of life is very similar. I have found that they are a good deal less hospitable and friendly; though, as with the Kirghiz, one's reception varies considerably from place to place, and it is perhaps unfair to judge from my limited experience of the Khasaks. But it is generally accepted that they are more truculent and less amenable to control, and their suspicion of strangers is only to be expected. The Chinese appear to have a considerable respect for them. On this occasion, however, their hospitality left nothing to be desired. The customary sheep was killed in our honour. Usually I struggled hard to avoid this ceremony, and more often than not I succeed. But as guests of the Government we could not protest too loudly. Moreover, our escort had to be fed and they would certainly not have foregone an orgy of meat to which they considered themselves entitled, and which for them was certainly the only mitigating feature of this otherwise intolerable journey.

The next morning we awoke to find everything shrouded in dense mist. I climbed up through the forest and on to the ridge that we had crossed the previous day. I had not gone far before it started to drizzle. After two years in South Sinkiang, where it hardly ever rains, the fresh, damp smell of the forest was sheer delight. Soon I emerged, at the upper limit of the firs, upon steep, grassy slopes. A slender granite pinnacle, cleft from top to bottom, stood upon the crest of the ridge. Rounding this, I disturbed a covey of ram chikor; they plunged, screeching, down into the mist. I sat for a while wrapped in a blanket of silence. From time to time the clouds opened, once revealing, far below, the dark waters of the lake. I returned to the camp, and, about eleven o'clock, we all went on down through the forest. It was raining more heavily, and by the time we reached the lake we were thoroughly wet. A short way above the shore we came to an old Taoist monastery where we secured comfortable lodging.

The next morning was brilliantly fine. Coming out of the monastery, we saw the whole of the lake for the first time. It was about two miles long by a mile wide. The surface of the water was calm and very blue. The eastern shore was overhung by precipitous slopes, dark in the shadow of the rising sun. The western shore, fringed with firs, and the gentler slopes above it were bathed in sunlight. From the farther end of the lake a U-shaped valley ran up towards a curved line of ice-peaks. Of the big mountains, only the ice-dome forming the summit was visible. The scene had all the attributes of the conventional Alpine landscape – the lake, the forested slopes, the ice-peaks at the head of the valley, the dark gorges cutting into the lofty precipices. We might have been a thousand miles, instead of a bare twenty, from the vast, barren steppes of Central Asia. It is a quality peculiar to high mountains and perhaps one of their chief attractions, this paramount insistence upon the immediate environment, which isolates so completely in space and time and excludes all outside influence.

Gillett and I set off along a rough path by the side of the lake. Winding round innumerable inlets, climbing steeply over rocky headlands, it took us about an hour and a half to reach the farther end. From there we went a few miles up the valley coming down from the peaks. I was very anxious to get a close view of the big mountain. At the time, of course, I did not suppose that I would ever have the opportunity of an attempt to climb it, but the distant views of it from the Turfan Depression and from the north had been very tantalizing. Gillett, too, was keen to prolong our stay in this delightful country. From the monastery we could see a high rock pyramid, with a small glacier on its eastern slopes. It appeared to lie immediately in front of the big mountain, and to be accessible from a camp in the valley. When we returned to the monastery that evening we announced to the Chinese officials that we wished to spend two or three days in the valley beyond the lake. Their faces fell and a prolonged argument ensued. Though, of course, their real reason for objecting was the fact that they wished to get back to Urumchi as soon as possible, they tried to dissuade us by emphasizing the grave risk we would run of an attack by the wild and unruly Khasak tribes, and the appalling discomforts we would suffer. However, Gillett's command of Chinese and his powers of persuasion won the day, and they agreed to allow us to go with a small armed escort.

The next day we went back past the end of the lake and spent the night at a small Khasak encampment at the foot of a large tributary valley coming down from the east. At four o'clock the following morning, an hour before dawn, Gillett, Lhakpa and I started climbing towards the rock pyramid. We had considerably under-estimated its height, for, although we climbed steadily and with little pause, it was half-past two in the afternoon before we reached the top.

It was a splendid view-point. The morning had been very fine, but by now clouds had formed. These, however, only partly hid the ice-peaks and enhanced their height and splendour. The north face of Bogdo itself was revealed as a long rampart of steep ice-fall and hanging glacier, divided by a series of rock- and ice-ridges sweeping up to three summits, evenly spaced on a crest some two miles long. The eastern-most summit was the highest, and consisted of a magnificent ice-dome. A large glacier flowed along the foot of the wall. Throughout the whole length of the face I could see no practicable line of ascent. On the eastern skyline, however, a steep rock ridge descended from the ice-dome to a high col between the main mountain and a small pointed peak. This col was accessible from the glacier below, and it appeared that the rock ridge might be climbable. But I remember thinking that if I ever had the opportunity of attempting to climb the peak I would certainly explore the southern approaches before making a serious effort from the north.

We sat for an hour on the summit of the rock pyramid studying the view, while new aspects of it were constantly revealed from behind the drifting cloud. We heard the clatter of stones a short way below us to the west and peeping over the edge in that direction, we saw a herd of fifteen ibex not thirty yards away. We must have been sitting very silently, for they were quite unaware of our presence. The way down seemed even longer than the way up, and it was dark before we reached the camp, thoroughly tired after a long and delightful day.

Our brief visit to Bogdo Ola had been an unexpected and exciting experience. Having studied only the Survey of India map I had, stupidly no doubt, hardly suspected the existence of this range of great ice-peaks, let alone its nature. The very denial of a close acquaintanceship sharpened my appreciation, though it accentuated in the years that followed the curious sense of unreality that I feel for all Central Asian country when I am not there.

It was the middle of September before Gillett and I were able to leave Urumchi. On the eve of our departure we were given a farewell banquet, a formidable affair at which some two hundred people were present. A military band was stationed at one end of the large banqueting-hall; at the other end a small round table was set for the guests and the presiding host. Unfortunately the Tupan himself was "indisposed", and his place was taken by Mr. P'eng his deputy. There were six guests: a visiting Minister of the Central Government, my Soviet colleague and his Vice-Consul, Gillett and myself and my secretary, Mr. Chu. The remainder of the two hundred sat at long tables stretching the length of the room.

There was an order in force at the time forbidding the consumption of alcohol by Government officials. Unfortunately it did not extend to guests; so that whereas at the long tables nothing was drunk but water, at our table the only liquid available was Russian brandy. Each of the chief officials toasted us in turn, and each demanded "Kan Pei" (bottoms up), blandly ignoring the inequality of the contract. In face of such unfair odds, I determined, with unreasonable bravado, to accept each challenge. After the first few toasts, my colleague, who was sitting on my right, and I, made a solemn undertaking, in the name of the friendship which would henceforth always bind our two countries, to support each other through the ordeal. But presently I noticed that he was prudently emptying most of the contents of his glass on to the floor prior to each toast, and it seemed clear that he would have to do most of the supporting.

By the fifteenth course I was feeling on top of the world and quite impervious to the effects of alcohol. Indeed, I was looking forward keenly to discharging my part in the evening's entertainment, the thought of which had earlier spoilt my appetite. But at about the time when Mr. P'eng rose to make his speech of welcome, I began to feel very ill. I must have looked at least as bad as I felt, for Mr. P'eng, a kindly gentleman, interrupted his speech to say that if Mr. Shipton wished to go out for a breath of fresh air he was welcome to do so. But with the foolish arrogance common to those in my condition, I rejected his invitation. About this time I noticed that my left-hand neighbour, the minister, had passed out and was lying across the table, peacefully asleep.

Circumstances had placed me in the position of principal guest, and it was my task to reply to Mr. P'eng's speech. I controlled my nausea with the aid of some more brandy, and Mr. Chu and I rose to our feet. I had planned my speech carefully that afternoon. So far as I remember it was intended to open with some apposite remarks about Central Asia being the cradle of mankind. I plunged straight into my subject and announced: "The dawn of civilization." This profound remark was translated into Chinese by Mr. Chu and thence into Russian by a Russian translator, and I clearly had the engrossed attention of my audience. I repeated with great weight, "The Dawn of civilization." Mr. Chu, doubtless taking this for a rhetorical gambit, again translated it into Chinese, whence it was again rendered into Russian. When I repeated the phrase a third time Mr. Chu reminded me that he had already translated it twice. I replied hotly, "Well, say it again." This he did and I sat down amid great applause.

Soon after this we moved to one of the long tables. Here I remember sitting opposite to my colleague, listening with powerful concentration while he lectured me upon the vital importance of co-operation between Britain and Russia. The next thing I remember is walking down the garden path on Mr.

P'eng's arm. I am told that I had made a steady passage along the hall and down the great curling stairway, even keeping time to the regimental march which the band had struck up to speed the departing guests, all of whom were in a state as mellow as any host could desire.

In November 1947 my wife and I were in Urumchi and we paid a hurried visit to the Heavenly Pool. This time we were able to go straight up the gorge. The trees were bare and the river small and clear. Large numbers of chikor had come down to the valley to glean the tiny fields and to escape from the autumn snows. Six miles up, the gorge contracted to a steep, narrow canyon, through which the river poured in a booming cataract. The path climbed steeply to a wide, grassy cwm above the canyon. At the far end there was a gentle slope of fir forest, beneath which the river flowed through a subterranean exit from the lake. The winter snows had been late in coming to the plains, but up here it already lay deep in the forest. We reached the shore towards sunset; a pink light was reflected from the mountains beyond on to the surface of the lake. It was very silent. We spent the night in the monastery, and the next day climbed through the snow-laden forest to a rocky crest, two or three thousand feet above the lake.

CHAPTER TEN

Bogdo Ola – 1

WHEN Tilman left Kashgar in September 1947 he said that he would like to return the following year if that were possible. During the winter I devised an ambitious programme for the following summer, which not only fascinated me but induced Tilman to overcome considerable difficulties in order to pay me a second visit. My contract expired in July 1948, and as the Kashgar Consulate-General was then to be handed over to the Governments of India and Pakistan, it seemed probable that I would be relieved of my post by mid-August at the latest. I had to go to Urumchi again in June and I suggested that if Tilman could meet me there, having travelled by way of Central China, I could probably spare some time for a trip to Bogdo Ola. After that we would travel back to Kashgar together, possibly visiting the Central Tien Shan on the way. After I had handed over charge of the Consulate in August, I proposed that we should travel to India together by a new route. One of the possibilities I had in mind was a journey involving two hundred miles of continuous glacier travel. Starting from Shimshal in Hunza, we would make our way up the Khurdopin Glacier and over a pass to the "Snow Lake" that Scott Russell and I had discovered in 1939, then over to the Panmah Glacier by a pass that Fountaine and I had found in the same year, then over to the "New Mustagh" Pass to the Sarpo Laggo and the "Old Mustagh" Pass to the

Baltoro, up that glacier and across to the Siachen Glacier by a pass yet to be discovered, and finally down that great glacier to Ladakh. The second possibility I had in mind was a journey south from Khotan to investigate a piece of unknown country in the Kuen Lun, south and east of a great 23,800-foot mountain called Muztagh. From there we would travel along the undemarcated border of Tibet and across country recently explored by Colonel Schomberg to Leh. It was certainly an interesting programme, but, in the circumstances, not too ambitious if things had worked out as I had expected. Unfortunately, they did not.

Our meeting in Urumchi was much delayed. Tilman arrived there by lorry from Lanchow on 6th July. Before leaving Kashgar I had received a message from the Government of India informing me that my Indian successor would be coming to Urumchi about the end of July, and suggesting that I should wait there for him and drive him back to Kashgar in the Consulate lorry. This poor old machine was by now very decrepit; indeed, it would certainly have been superannuated long ago had it been possible to replace it. I handed it over to the workshops of the Provincial Transport Department in Urumchi to have some major repairs done, and hoped for the best. By the time Tilman arrived I had nothing further to keep me in Urumchi. I had hoped to pay a visit to Ili, but this was politically impossible, and I was free to spend nearly three weeks on Bogdo Ola. While we were in Urumchi we stayed with Mr. and Mrs. Hall Paxton, the U.S. Consul and his wife, whose delightful hospitality my wife and I had enjoyed the previous winter.

Before leaving England, Tilman had searched the library of the Royal Geographical Society for such scant material as existed relating to Bogdo Ola. The most interesting thing he found was Doctor Grœber's sketch-map, and he brought some photostat copies of it with him. The altitude given for the glacier that I had seen flowing across the foot of the North Face of the peaks was 11,000 feet, while the summit of the highest peak was given at 21,300 feet. This meant a vertical rise of ten thousand feet of very difficult climbing, a feat rarely attempted by the strongest expeditions. However, according to the calculations made on Sven Hedin's Expedition in the early 'thirties the mountain was only about eighteen thousand feet. This would mean that the North Face stood a bare seven thousand feet above the glacier, and this, though formidable enough, was a totally different proposition. It was difficult to understand how Grœber had made an error of more than three thousand feet in his estimate, but we were inclined to accept the height given by Hedin's party, for though they had not apparently been so close to the mountain as Grœber, they had been doing geodetic work which necessitated some fairly accurate triangulation.

Tilman and I had been used for so long to conditions in the Himalaya that it was difficult to adjust ourselves to the idea that a mountain of eighteen thousand feet could present a really tough proposition. For there, partly because of the height of the snow-line and partly because of the great elevation of the main mass, peaks of eighteen thousand feet could never be regarded as more than minor heights. Our base camp on Everest had been 16,800 feet, that on Kamet 15,500 feet; the Karakoram Pass was 18,200 feet, and even on

Mustagh Ata our first camp had been 17,000 feet high. We had continually to remind ourselves that, though we were still in Central Asia, our latitude (44 degrees) was equal to the southern ranges of the Alps, and a long way north of the Caucasus. Although I had made a study of the mountain from close range, I could form very little idea of its difficulty. All that I could predict with reasonable certainty was that the rock would be good and that the climbing would be of a high order.

I had brought Lhakpa with me from Kashgar. But in the years he had spent there performing his sedentary duties he had grown fat, and it seemed unlikely that he would be much use to us on the higher reaches of the mountain either as a load carrier or as a climber. But, however out of condition, he was always a good man to have on an expedition – keen, intelligent and resourceful. To help us with the carrying of the higher camps I had brought a young Hunza man named Agasha from Misgar, who had a remarkable reputation as a hunter of *ovis poli*. He certainly appeared tough and active enough, and he had never before been anywhere but in rugged mountain country or below an elevation of eight or ten thousand feet. The journey to Urumchi was the first time he had ever been in a motor-car, and when we had started, the staff of the Consulate had pulled his leg mercilessly – telling him that he was expected to ride it like a horse or that it would explode if he rode with his back to the engine. My Chinese secretary aptly named him Hill Billy.

We left Urumchi on 9th July. Bob Dreesen, the American Vice-Consul, accompanied us for the first two days. We took with us enough food for three weeks, some of which I had brought from Kashgar, though the Paxtons, with characteristic generosity, had invited us to take whatever we wanted from their well-stocked store-room. We had my two battered old "Meade" tents, two Primus stoves, two lengths of nylon rope, and a pair each of rubber-soled climbing boots of Swiss make that Tilman had brought out from home. These were equipped with devices designed for keeping the boots dry in wet snow, one of the most serious problems in climbing at high altitudes. They consisted of skin spats, which were supposed to fit closely over the uppers of the boots. However, we never succeeded in attaching them securely to the boots, and soon abandoned them.

The Mayor of Urumchi had promised me to send instructions in advance to the magistrate of Fukang to arrange for pack-transport to take us up to and beyond the Heavenly Pool. But when we reached Fukang at about eleven o'clock, we found that the magistrate had received no such instructions. However, he was very helpful, and after a good deal of talk it was arranged that we would go on as far as possible in the lorry and that he would collect the pack-animals from the surrounding villages and send them up to us that afternoon. Our anxiety to get out of the bleak, comfortless rooms which characterize Chinese *yamens* and up into the hills was such that, though with some misgivings, we decided to take him at his word. Two local policemen, armed with rifles, were attached to our party. Both were old friends who had come with me the previous autumn and who were apparently so pleased with the tips I had given them that they were keen to come again. They did not realize what was in store for them. We forced the lorry as far as possible, and in the early afternoon settled down in a charming, wooded valley to await, with growing anxiety, the arrival of the pack-transport. When night was falling and we had given up hope, the animals arrived.

The next morning we packed up in the dawn light and were off by six o'clock. We went up the gorge again, and though it was summer we encountered no great difficulty with the river. The air was cool and invigorating. Three hours' steady walking, first through the deciduous woods which filled the lower valley, then through the fir forest, took us to the lake. The sky was clear and the water was still and very blue. We built a fire of pinewood and cooked a breakfast of porridge, fried eggs, toast and tea. Tilman and Dreesen swam in the lake. We basked on the grassy shore until the ponies arrived. There was a large, clumsy rowing-boat which we borrowed and rowed ourselves to the other end of the lake, while the ponies went round by the rocky path. It took us just over an hour, while the ponies took two hours and a half. We went on up the main valley to the place where Gillett and I had camped, and then turned up the large tributary valley to the left. The path followed a steep rocky torrent for two miles and then began to zigzag up the southern flank of the valley through dense fir forest. At about six o'clock we came to a small Khasak encampment just at the upper limit of the trees, and we stopped here for the night. It was a fine position: steep grass slopes behind were crowned by a cirque of crags, from which the long, echoing cries of ram chikor could be heard; in front, the forest plunged down into a deep gorge; beyond, the lower foot-hills melted into a haze which overhung the plains. It seemed incredible that we were only a day and a half's journey from Urumchi and its evil-smelling squalor. The indefatigable Dreesen, determined to make the most of his long week-end, set off in vain pursuit of ram chikor. Bill and I lounged luxuriously by the fire in one of the Khasak tents, drinking tea and smoking until supper was ready. Later that evening the local Khasak Beg turned up, having heard of our arrival. He was a large arrogant man, not particularly friendly. But we had brought a letter of introduction to him from an influential Khasak woman in Urumchi, and he agreed somewhat reluctantly to do what he could to help us.

The next morning Dreesen left very early, as he intended to get back to Urumchi that evening. Bill and I made a late start, accompanied by the Beg and a small retinue of Khasaks. An hour farther up the valley we stopped to collect juniper roots from a patch which the Khasaks told us was the last we should find. A short way beyond, the valley made a right-angled bend to the south. At the corner there was another small Khasak encampment, their highest grazing-ground in this part of the range. The Beg and his friends left us here.

We now found ourselves in bleak, desolate country. Although it was nearly mid-July and though we were at an altitude of no more than ten thousand feet, summer had not yet reached this broad flat-bottomed valley. The ground was still sodden from the newly melted winter snow. Indeed, there were large beds of it still unmelted. The grass and spring flowers had not yet appeared from the muddy soil. The valley was flanked by shapeless rocky peaks, skirted by long scree slopes and smooth, lozenge-shaped glaciers. A cold, blustering wind blew in our faces, and mounting thunder-clouds in the south threatened a storm. The ponies were painfully slow over the swampy ground and the morale of the drivers was evaporating fast. We were making for a rounded saddle at the head of the valley, which we knew from Grœber's sketch-map lay on the main watershed of the range and close to the North Face of Bogdo, which was still hidden from our view. We had planned to put our base camp just on the other side of the saddle. By the time we reached the head of the valley and started up the final slope, it appeared that the storm was just about to break. The slope was gradual but covered with huge boulders, so that the going was very difficult for the ponies. The drivers were most reluctant to go any farther, but somehow we managed to induce them to do so. At last, at about three o'clock, we reached the rounded crest of the saddle. The view on the other side was terrific. A short way beyond, and some three hundred feet below us, there was a wide sweep of glacier. Beyond this, towering up into a dark mass of cloud, stood the huge granite ridges of the mountain, separated from each other by steep ice-couloirs and hanging glaciers. Here and there a window opened in the cloud above, revealing an extension of one of the ridges, and giving an impression of prodigious height and steepness.

Miraculously, the storm held off. We ran down the slope beyond the saddle until we came to a place that was reasonably level, and set to at once with ice-axes to clear space for the tents. These were ready by the time the ponies arrived. We had just got the tents pitched and most of the baggage stowed away under cover when the storm burst with a deluge of rain. The ponies and their drivers started back at once, together with one of the policemen; the other chose to stay with us, sharing a tent with Lhakpa and Agasha. Lhakpa was feeling far from well. He had suffered from a severe headache during the march, as well as from shortness of breath; now he felt shivery and complained of a pain in the chest as well. It seemed incredible that this veteran Sherpa, however soft he had become, should be suffering from such a bad attack of "altitude" at a mere eleven thousand feet, and though his temperature was normal, we feared that he was sickening for something considerably more serious.

Another cause for concern was the behaviour of the Primus stoves. We could not get them to burn properly. After a struggle we would achieve an even blue flame, and we would settle back with a sigh of relief. But after a minute or so they would begin to gasp like men fighting for breath; then they would burst into flame, filling the tent with black smoke and covering everything with greasy, black soot. Then the laborious process of heating and coaxing would begin all over again. Certainly the stoves were very old and battered; they had been used on Everest in the 'thirties; but Primus stoves do not usually suffer from age, and I have never known mere battering to put them out of action. More likely the cause of the trouble lay in the indigestible quality of the Urumchi kerosene. After two hours of unremitting toil we succeeded in brewing a potful of lukewarm tea. This was discouraging, for in our higher camps we would be entirely dependent on the Primuses, and, moreover, would have to melt snow for water. Producing water from snow takes at least as long as boiling the water when produced.

In the meantime, the rain had turned to a cold and equally drenching sleet. The tents leaked and our sleeping-bags became wet, while an unaccountable accumulation of mud infiltrated from outside. It was one of those occasions when it seems that the price to be paid in misery and frustration for the doubtful pleasure of climbing mountains is altogether too high. Travel these remote ranges by all means, but confine your camps to the meadows or the forested slopes! Climb peaks perhaps, but go to the Alps for the purpose, where you can enjoy the sound of the weather from the warm security of a hut, and if it is still bad tomorrow, a pleasant swinging walk through mist and dripping pines is all that separates you from a well-cooked meal and mulled wine! The evening closed in on us and it became too dark to read; the holed tent let in too much wind to keep a candle alight. We ate with no relish the cold contents of a tin, and settled down to eleven hours of fitful sleep.

At six o'clock the next morning the wind had dropped. We peeped out of the tent at a cloudless sky. Very little snow had fallen. Agasha managed to get a fire going and we cooked breakfast. This, according to our old custom, consisted of tsampa and well-sugared tea. Tsampa appears to be unknown in these parts of Turkestan, but we had prepared a supply of it before leaving Urumchi. By the time breakfast was over, the sun had reached us and we spread our sodden belongings to dry. Lhakpa was no better; but he was no worse and we decided to keep him with us for another day. At half-past eight we started out, taking Agasha with us.

The geography of this part of the range is remarkable. A well-defined axis of high peaks runs for some ten miles due west from the highest summit. The main mountain (which we had come to refer to as Bogdo) has a crest nearly two miles long on which there are three summits – the highest at the eastern end, the lowest at the western end, though the difference in height between the two is probably not more than a couple of hundred feet. A wide glacier flows westward along the foot of the North Face of this mountain and terminates at the western end of the face. As the eastern and northern boundaries of the glacier are formed by low, scree-covered hills, almost all its ice comes from the steep corries and hanging glaciers of the North Face of Bogdo. The river issuing from the snout of the glacier, instead of flowing down the northern side of the range, turns abruptly to the south and flows clean through the main axis of high peaks through a narrow defile. Another strange feature of the glacier, as we discovered later, is a great tongue of ice near its head, which has broken through the hills to the north. Here, therefore, is an unusual phenomenon of a glacier situated in a normal cirque, yet draining down the two opposite sides of the range. I wished that we had had a competent geologist with us to account for that great defile through which the bulk of the water drained. The idea of headward erosion through those massive granite walls, which formed the peaks of the main axis of the range, was inconceivable; nor could I detect signs of "river capture" on the northern side. It seemed then that here, as is apparently the case with so many formations in the Himalaya, the alignment of the river must have existed before the high peaks.

The going on the glacier was easy; there were very few crevasses and most of the winter snow had gone, leaving a surface of bare, smooth ice. So, as we went, we had plenty of time to study the mountain. The opinion that I had formed several years before about the North Face was confirmed. All the ridges looked terribly difficult, and although on some of them each individual section might have been climbable without loads, they were far too long to tackle without establishing several camps along them, and that would have meant carrying heavy loads up some of the most difficult parts. All the couloirs between the ridges were guarded by hanging glaciers, so that, apart from their steepness and length, it would have been suicidal to attempt to climb them. The only hope of climbing the mountain from this side was the rock ridge which ran down direct from the highest peak in a north-easterly direction to a high col separating the main mountain from a small pointed peak at the head of the glacier. A steep ice-fall led down from the col to the glacier, and though it was very crevassed, it looked as though it would be possible to work up it and to carry a camp to the col. Whatever the height of the col it did not look to be more than two or three thousand feet below the summit. The ridge itself stood out in profile against the sky. It was bisected by a prominent notch, but above and below this it appeared to be set at a uniform angle, so far as we could judge it, of about fifty-five degrees. This is not excessively steep, even if maintained for three thousand feet, provided the rock is good, clear of snow and sufficiently broken.

Our object that day was to make a more detailed study of the North-east Ridge. For this purpose the high col, besides being too far away for our untrained state, would have been too close under the ridge to have provided us with a comprehensive view of it. So we climbed to a lower saddle at the head of the main glacier and to the left of the Small Pointed Peak. From this, we made our way up along a jagged rock ridge to the north-east, away from the mountain until we were high enough to see the North-east Ridge. We were startled by its appearance. It looked far steeper and more forbidding than before. This in itself meant nothing, for it is impossible to judge the angle of a ridge when looking at it end on, as we were now doing. Also the ridge was broad, which would afford sufficient choice of routes. But every ledge and crack on the rocks was laden with a mass of snow, evidently the remains of the winter deposits. We could now see the eastern face of the Small Pointed Peak. Here, too, the rocks were covered with a deep mantle of snow, and though they were nothing like so steep as the North-east Ridge, they would be very hard to climb in these conditions. It was quite clear that it would take many days – even weeks – of hot sun before it would be possible to tackle the North-east Ridge. After this disappointing discovery, we climbed down to the glacier and returned to camp.

That evening it started to snow again, and continued throughout the night and most of the next day; not heavily, but enough to make it impossible to do any useful exploration. During the day the snow turned to rain. Agasha spent a long day hunting ibex, but though he saw a herd in the distance, he could not get close enough for a shot. Bill and I lay in our sleeping-bags discussing plans. We did not agree. Bill thought that as soon as possible we should take a camp up to the High Col and decide definitely whether or not the North-east

Ridge was climbable. I considered that before doing anything else we should make a thorough reconnaissance of the mountain. I argued that, with snow conditions as they were, it was unlikely that we could come to any definite conclusion about the North-east Ridge, and that taking a camp to the High Col would therefore be a waste of time; that we might find an easy or, at any rate, an obviously easier route on the southern side; that snow conditions on the southern side would certainly be that much better than on the northern; and that even if we failed to find an alternative route, a week or so spent in wide reconnaissance would provide us with much-needed training, and allow time for the melting of the snow on the North-east Ridge, to which we could then turn with the stimulating conviction that it was the only route. I suppose I argued more forcibly, for Bill, though still not convinced, eventually agreed to adopt my plan.

In the middle of the afternoon it stopped raining and we went to examine the route through the Great Defile. We made our way round the snout of the glacier. The river issuing from this was remarkably small considering the great volume of ice that it drained. This was further evidence that the real summer melting had scarcely begun on the north side of the mountain, though the sun was well past the solstice. In the very throat of the Defile we found a big lake. Gigantic granite walls swept up on either side, forming a cup, breached on its farther side by a great cleft which was the narrowest part of the Defile. About two thousand feet above the lake, the walls disappeared into cloud. To the right a hanging glacier loomed out of the mist. Great blocks of ice had recently fallen from this into the lake. As we made our way round the eastern shore, which was composed of vast granite blocks interspersed with grassy meadows, a pair of Brahmini duck flew out from behind a rocky promontory and circled, screeching, above the lake. Beyond the lake the valley plunged steeply down through the Defile and then, a bare mile away, widened out between rounded grassy slopes on the southern side of the range. Though in the gloomy evening light we could not see any sign of habitation, it was clear that we would not have far to go to reach the first Khasak encampments.

In the meantime, Lhakpa was still ill and obviously not improving. We decided that when the pony-men visited us, which we expected them to do with a load of fuel on the following day, we would send him down to the Khasak camp just above the forest, where he would be warmer, more comfortable and supplied with plenty of milk. His illness was our first real misfortune, for though we had not relied on him to take part in the climbing or load-carrying, he was necessary to us as a sheet-anchor for our base camps and for negotiating with the Khasaks, particulary as the morale of the policeman would not stand much more of this bleak and cheerless life. Also, his absence proved a constant source of worry and restricted the range of our travels.

The next day, 14th July, it was fine again. Our first task was to move camp, in several relays, to a large, overhanging boulder a quarter of a mile away, near the lateral moraine of the glacier. Though the boulder gave little shelter to the tents, it provided an excellent kitchen where we could store the wood in a dry place, make a fire and cook, even when it was raining. The move was completed by nine o'clock, and Bill and I set out on our next reconnaissance. The object of this was to cross over to the eastern side of the mountain and to see what lay beyond the North-east Ridge and the High Col. We crossed the col we had reached two days before, descended a glacier on the other side and crossed another ridge coming down from the Small Pointed Peak. We then found ourselves in the eastern cwm of the mountain. It was an impressive affair, formed by the narrow, triangular face of the mountain and bounded on the right by the North-east Ridge, the High Col and the Small Pointed Peak, and on the left by a long ridge running eastward from the summit of the mountain. Before we could get a clear view of the cwm, we had to climb a tangled ice-fall, making our way through a maze of crevasses and ice-cliffs to a flat glacier plateau forming the upper floor of the cwm. From this side the mountain looked tremendously steep and forbidding. The High Col was flanked by some three thousand feet of utterly unclimbable ice and rock. The North-east Ridge itself looked really formidable. The main feature of the face of the mountain was a great ice-couloir of prodigious steepness, topped by what looked like a great overhang. But the East Ridge seemed to offer some hope, if we only could reach it. It was very long; it was obviously narrow and corniced; but its crest, except for its final sweep to the summit, led upwards at a gentle angle. Away to the east it looked accessible from this side, but the approach was up a steep face of ice which was overhung by the great cornices of the ridge. Again I considered that we should explore the southern side of the mountain before committing ourselves to such a venture. This time Bill agreed with me, though he still hankered after a close-up view of the North-east Ridge.

We saw that the East Ridge was a continuation of the main axis of the range. It formed a high curtain, nowhere less than 15,000 feet, running through several minor peaks and connecting Bogdo with its unnamed eastern rival. We came to refer to the latter as "The Six Thousander", as Grœber had guessed its height as 6,000 metres (19,686 feet). It was a splendid peak.

Having seen all that there was to be seen of the Eastern Cwm, we made our way back down the ice-fall. The journey back to camp was laborious, as the snow on the eastern glaciers had melted in the hot afternoon sun and we sank into it up to our knees.

When we reached camp, we found that the two pony men had arrived with two ponies and a load of wood. Had it not been for Lhakpa, we would have moved down to the gorge through the Defile that evening, and as things turned out it would have been much better if we had done so. But we thought we had better send him back to where we knew he would be comfortable; so he went off, with instructions to send the ponies back as soon as possible on the following day, and also, if possible, to send a yak as well, as we were doubtful if the ponies would be able to negotiate the very rough going through the gorge. Bill set off early in the morning with the object of going as far as possible round the southern side of the mountain so as to look for the best line of approach. I was to await the arrival of the ponies and then bring them and all the baggage through the Defile into the grassy valley beyond, where Bill would meet me. I expected the ponies to arrive by eleven o'clock and I spent a pleasant morning climbing about the hills above the glacier, from which I had superb views of the North Face of the mountain. The ponies did not arrive until three o'clock in the afternoon. I was relieved to see that they were accompanied by a yak. It took me an hour to get the camp packed and loaded on to the animals. I was just about to start when I saw Bill returning up the valley. He had gone without any food, having expected to meet us at about two o'clock. But he was too full of news, which he recounted as we went, to show any annoyance.

He had descended to the valley below the Defile and had found himself at the junction of a wide tributary valley coming in from the east. Here he met some Khasaks herding large flocks of sheep. They had greeted him very coldly. He went up the tributary valley, which curled round to the north, and he soon found that it had its origin in a great rock cirque which formed the south-west sector of Bogdo. It was bounded on the right by what was evidently the main South Ridge of the mountain. He had a clear view of the ridge, and after careful examination came to the conclusion that there was a perfectly sound route up it. The only question that remained was whether it led up to the main summit ridge and, if so, at which point they joined. From where Bill stood it appeared to culminate in a snow-peak so close to the main summit ridge that it seemed reasonable to suppose that there was a fairly easy link between the two. Also, he was able to identify the Western and Central Peaks of the mountain away to the left, so he assumed that the South Ridge was joined either to the highest eastern summit or to the col between that and the Central Peak. It certainly looked as though he had found the key to climbing the mountain.

As it was still early in the day, Bill climbed, in another two hours, to a col about eleven thousand feet high at the foot of the South Ridge, from which he looked down to a big ice-stream which had its origin in the cwm formed by the south-eastern segment of the mountain. The existence of such a large glacier in this quarter might have warned us that the South Ridge probably did not connect with the eastern summit, but neither of us made this deduction. When Bill returned to the valley junction, he found that the shepherds had been joined by another man who carried a rifle. He was quite obviously hostile. He threatened Bill with his weapon and demanded his coat. However, Bill ignored him and walked on. Some time later, when he had reached the lake, he heard a shout behind him, and, looking round, saw the man two hundred yards behind, aiming his rifle and signalling to him to stop. Again Bill took no notice and the man disappeared.

It was very slow-going with the animals and when we reached the lake we decided to camp on its shore. We chose a delightful spot: a little grassy patch covered with wild flowers, and with a view of the lake between two great granite blocks. Later, the moon came out from behind the eastern portal of the Defile, its light sparkling on the dark waters of the lake and gleaming on the hanging glacier and the steep ice-ridges on the other side of the cirque. Behind us the vast cliffs of Bogdo were jet velvet-black by contrast.

Again it was a slow and laborious business getting the animals down through the rocky Defile the next morning, and it was ten o'clock before we reached the meadows below. The shepherds were there. With the policeman to explain our identity, they were more friendly and undertook to supply us with milk, butter and fuel. They said that they had taken Bill for a Russian, but that they were glad now that they had not shot him. Bill thanked them for this expression of friendship, and after reminding them of their promise of supplies, we went on up the tributary valley and camped just below the point where the pasture gave place to barren scree. We were in full view of the South Ridge and Bill explained the route he had traced on the previous day. It

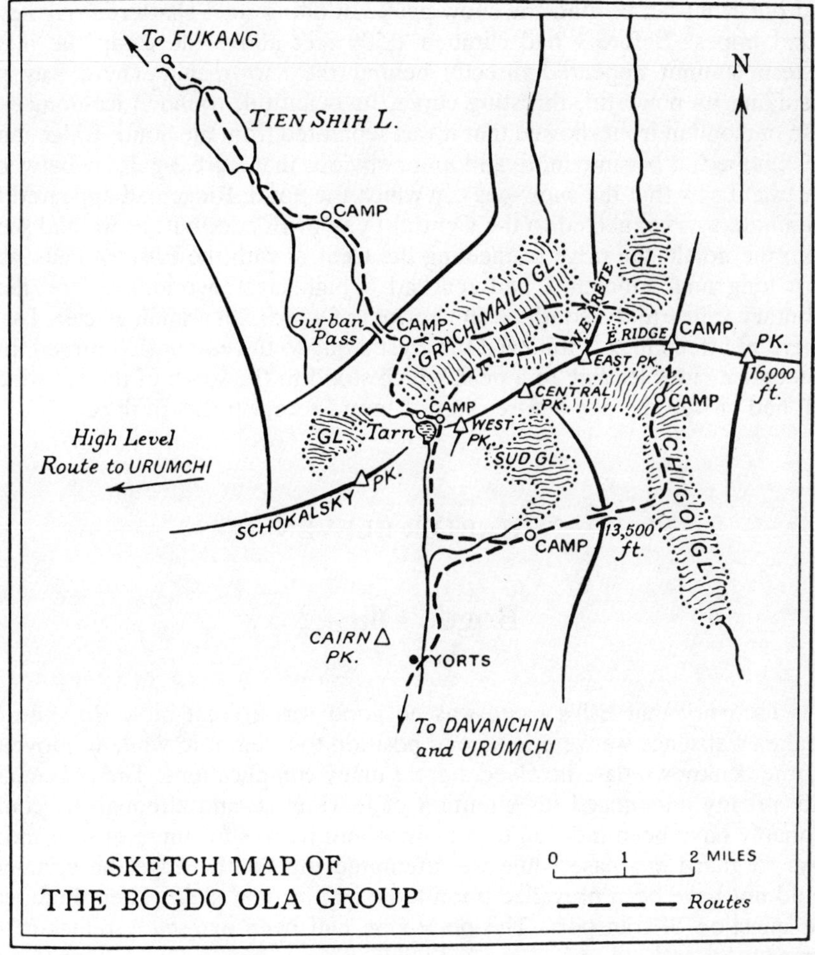

BOGDO OLA

certainly looked quite feasible. From the glacier that filled the upper part of the valley there was a wide snow-couloir running up two or three thousand feet to the crest of the ridge. Near the top of this, we would put our first camp. Then came a section of ridge which was narrow and serrated, but even if we could not climb along its crest, it would not be too difficult to traverse below it. It ended at a buttress three or four hundred feet high, which, though steep, offered a wide choice of routes, both on rock and ice. Above this, an easy snow-slope led to the top of the snow-peak which was the highest point of the South Ridge visible from here. We proposed to put our second and highest camp at the foot of the buttress.

That afternoon I climbed two or three thousand feet up the southern flank of our valley to see the South Ridge in better perspective and if possible to find out what lay beyond the snow-peak. In doing so, I shattered our new-found hopes. Before I had climbed 1,500 feet above the camp the main eastern summit appeared directly behind the snow-peak. There was no mistaking its powerful, thrusting curve, its beautiful, rounded ice-dome. A wisp of cloud in front showed that it was separated from the South Ridge, and as I climbed, it became more and more obvious that a great gulf lay between the two. I saw that the snow-peak in which the South Ridge had appeared to culminate was connected to the Central Peak of Bogdo, but, as we had seen from the north, the ridge connecting the Central with the Eastern Peak was very long and difficult. I had reached a high crest overlooking the next tributary valley to the south, at the bottom of which, on a small glacier, I saw a herd of fifteen ibex. I followed the crest along to the east until it turned into a steep ice-ridge leading to a peak which stood to the south of the col which Bill had visited the day before. Here I found recent tracks of ibex.

CHAPTER ELEVEN

Bogdo Ola – 2

MY discovery that Bill's route was no good was a great blow. In spite of Lhakpa's absence we were in a good position to attempt it, while to move to another unknown base involved a great many complications. The policeman had already announced his intention of leaving us, and although he could probably have been induced to remain where he was for three or four more days to guard our base while we attempted the South Ridge, he certainly could not have been prevailed upon to go any farther afield. Then there was the question of transport. The pony-men had been extremely reluctant to come so far and we had persuaded them to do so only by promising to pay them off and send them back the next day. The local Khasaks had told us that it was impossible to get animals over the col to the south-eastern side of the mountain and, of course, they would not supply any to attempt what they knew to be impossible. Nor would they agree to act as porters. We could, of course, take a light camp over ourselves, but besides the fact that this would put us in a weak position to attempt any route we might find, we did not trust the local Khasaks to refrain from stealing what we left behind. Once the policeman had gone, we had no means of negotiating with them. Still another point was our reluctance to get too far out of touch with Lhakpa. He had sent a note with the pony-men saying that he was feeling better, but he was still sick. Bill suggested that we might at least attempt the Central Peak by way of his route up the South Ridge. But this would use up so much of our available time and resources that it would put any attempt on the Eastern Peak out of count, and I think we both felt that we would rather fail in an attempt to reach the highest summit than climb the lesser.

However, these problems could be postponed for at least another day. We could explore the south-eastern segment of the mountain from where we were. This would no doubt include the southern side of the great East Ridge which we had seen from the north. If we could prove that there was no feasible route up the mountain from there, the question of moving to a new base would not arise and we would have no choice but to turn our energies and place all our hopes upon the North-east Ridge. So, early the next day (17th), having discharged the pony-men but persuaded the policeman to stay with us a few days longer, we crossed the col at the foot of the South Ridge. We took Agasha with us. It was a laborious climb of about two thousand feet, mostly over scree, to the top, and a delightful run down, also over scree, for two thousand feet on the other side. This took us to the side of a wide glacier which flowed due south between steep rock walls. There was a good deal of cloud about and most of the peaks at the head of the valley were obscured. But we could see what we took to be the lowest part of the East Ridge, a sort of wide col between Bogdo and the "Six Thousander". There was a perfectly straightforward route to its crest.

It looked as though the clouds would lift; so we crossed the glacier, climbed to the top of a rocky knoll on the other side and waited. The cloud lifted slowly and by one o'clock a substantial portion of the East Ridge was clear. It was long and led over a small peak, beyond which it dropped to a col that we could not see. But it looked easy enough to carry loads along. The upper part of the glacier was invisible from where we stood, as there was a sharp left-hand turn in the main valley. Beyond this lay the South-eastern Cwm of the mountain, and from it the glacier issued in the form of an ice-fall, through a narrow defile. In the afternoon we went on up the glacier and eventually succeeded in getting a view into the South-eastern Cwm. It was in the form of a huge quadrangle bounded on the left by the South Ridge, which, at the snow-peak, bent round to the west and connected direct with the Central Peak of Bogdo; in front, by the long ridge connecting the Central and Eastern Peaks, and on the right by the East Ridge. The walls of the cwm were tremendously steep and nowhere less than four or five thousand feet high. As we turned back down the glacier, the Eastern Peak came out from the clouds. From where we stood, the upper part of the East Ridge was very foreshortened and largely screened by the lower part. But judging by what we could see and from our memory of what we had seen from the Eastern Cwm we came to the conclusion that it was well worth attempting, and anyway more promising than the North-east Ridge.

Earlier in the day Agasha had complained of a pain in his stomach. This had got worse and he made very heavy weather of the climb back up to the col. He refused to eat anything that evening and the next morning he lay in the tent groaning. This was another bad set-back. When we had left Urumchi, three weeks had seemed a generous allowance of time. We had taken things fairly easily at first, the best policy while becoming adjusted to the altitude and mountain exercise. We had not exactly frittered away our time, yet half was already gone. We could doubtless have done better by concentrating more determindly upon a thorough reconnaissance of the mountain before forming any conclusions about a route. But, as Bill said, it is so difficult to make up your mind about a route until you have rubbed your nose in it. Again, we should have spent at least one of the next two days in trying to reach the crest of the East Ridge from our present camp. I think we could have done it in a very long day, and it would have given us a clearer idea of what the ridge was really like. Perhaps we had lost some of the ability for making the right decisions that we had acquired in our long expeditions before the war. As it was we spent two days in useless discussion and negotiation with the Khasaks over the problem of getting our baggage across the col. Certainly we had the excuse that the weather was bad, and a day and a half of light rain damped our zeal for action. We went down to the Khasak encampment in the valley below to try to induce them to take us over to the big glacier by a roundabout route, but we got no satisfactory answer from them. The Beg was away and they could do nothing until he returned. Agasha's illness complicated matters still further, for besides robbing us of his carrying-power, we felt we ought to stay with him in case he took a turn for the worse.

On the afternoon of the 19th, the weather cleared. The sun came out and warmed our spirits, Agasha was a bit better, and although he would not be fit for heavy work for several days, we felt justified in leaving him behind. We had just decided to start relaying loads up to the col, when the Khasak who had been bringing us a daily supply of milk arrived. He had always been more friendly than the rest, and when we told him of our decision he said he would bring his two yaks up the next morning and these would at least carry the loads to the col. That evening, to our great joy, Lhakpa arrived. He seemed to have quite recovered and said he was ready to come with us. Things were looking up.

The next morning the milkman and his two yaks came at nine o'clock and we were off by half-past nine. It was a difficult job getting the yaks up the scree, but they managed it and we reached the col by midday. It was not fair to ask our friend to bring the yaks down the other side, as he could not have got them up again alone. But he volunteered to leave them on the col and help us to carry the loads down to the glacier, which we reached by one o'clock. We had lunch, and then the three of us divided up the loads and made our way very slowly up the glacier. Our equipment was by no means light and we were carrying provisions and fuel for a week. The route from the glacier to the lowest part of the East Ridge was up an ice-slope about three-thousand feet high, its lower half steep and bare, its upper half comparatively gentle and snow-covered. There was a rock ridge running for about seven hundred feet up the side of the ice-slope. We climbed about three hundred feet up this and pitched our tent, at about six o'clock, on a wide ledge. While I was in the tent getting the Primus going, Bill stood outside looking up at the peak, only the upper part of which was visible, its ridges thrown into sharp relief by the light of the setting sun. Suddenly Bill said: "Eric, we're bats. The upper part of that ridge is bloody awful." But he admitted that perhaps it was not fair to judge from that very foreshortened view. We debated whether or not we should abandon the attempt while we still had time and supplies enough to go back to the north side of the mountain and try the North-east Ridge. But we were both most reluctant to go back now that we had come so far, and we decided to go on and hope for the best: after all, some trick of the evening light might have exaggerated the steepness and narrowness of that upper section of the ridge. Of course, we should have gone up to reconnoitre. We could have gone a long way without loads and, as we found later, we had only to go to the lowest part of the ridge to see all we needed. But the weather was now brilliantly fine and from our previous experience we did not expect it to remain fine very long.

We cooked and ate a huge brew of macaroni and pemmican, and settled down to a comfortable night. We started cooking breakfast before five the next morning, and had packed up the camp and were away by six. We expected to reach the ridge quite easily that day, and our early start was designed so that we should get over at least some of the upper snow-slope while it was still hard. We climbed to the end of the rock ridge and embarked upon the ice. This was rough and we expected to be able to climb it with a minimum of step-cutting. But I think we had under-estimated the steepness of the slope, for with our heavy loads we found it necessary to cut steps the whole way. It was very laborious work and our progress was painfully slow. After a couple of hours, we speeded things up by changing our tactics. The leader went ahead without a load, cutting tiny nicks in the ice, until the rope was taut. Then he would cut a large stance, haul up one of the loads and help the second man to climb up the nicks by a pull on the rope. Then he went ahead again while the second brought the third man up. It is extraordinary how quickly the time passes in such work. At first, when we were still in the shadow of the East Ridge, it was painfully cold waiting for the steps to be cut. No sooner had the sun reached us than we became unpleasantly hot. I kept trying to estimate the number of rope-lengths which remained before we reached the easier ground above; each time that we had completed the estimated number we seemed to be exactly the same distance from the top of the steep part of the slope. Lhakpa was not feeling at all well. Bill and I shared the cutting, but, even so, standing for hours on a steep ice-slope with a heavy load on your back is a great deal more exhausting than climbing continuously up-hill.

At about half-past two we reached a point where the slope began to ease off and we decided to send Lhakpa back. I lowered him down on the end of our two ropes joined together, going some way down the slope myself until he reached easier ground. While we went on working, we watched him down to the glacier. He would easily cross the col before nightfall. While we were still on bare ice it was awkward work dealing with the three loads, as we were constantly in danger of letting one of them slip. Presently, however, we got onto soft snow, into which we sank up to our hips. Then it was just a question of flogging a track. We made such slow progress that at four o'clock we gave it up, dug a platform out of the slope and pitched the tent. We were still about fifteen hundred feet below the crest of the ridge. A very hard day's work had brought us about twelve hundred feet up the slope. We felt tired and frustrated. If we had made such heavy weather of a comparatively straightforward section of the climb, what hope had we of getting up that long East Ridge with no one to help us with the load-carrying? However, the Primus behaved well, we had found a rivulet of water by digging down to the ice and tea was soon ready. We ate great hunks of bread (which Bill had baked two days before) and jam. Lying snugly in our sleeping-bags sipping mugs of hot, sweet tea, the frustration and fatigue of the day was gradually replaced by a feeling of great contentment. The evening was calm. We could see the whole of the South-eastern Cwm and its immense retaining walls; the sun sank behind the ridge between the Central and the Eastern Peaks, lighting its ice-crest with a nimbus of burning gold; the glacier below was drowned in blue shadow. The snow about us froze, and apart from an occasional sharp report from the ice below, the silence was complete.

We decided the next morning to carry up the loads in relays. We started early, and the snow was frozen so hard that we had to give a sharp kick to obtain purchase on it. In an hour we reached a bergschrund three hundred feet below the crest of the ridge. Emptying our rucksacks there, we glissaded back to fetch the remaining loads, which we carried past the bergschrund and up a steep snow-slope to the ridge. The crest was of ice, narrow and heavily corniced on the northern side. We reached it at an outcrop of rock.

One glance along the ridge to Bogdo dashed what hopes we might still have nursed of being able to climb it. Although there was a small peak on the ridge between us and the main mountain, there was a slight northerly bend in the ridge which enabled us to see most of its length. The section running over the small peak was very narrow and crowned by a heavy snow cornice the whole way. This would have made it impossible to keep to the crest. The northern flank was composed of ice, impossibly steep. The southern flank was broken by a series of rock buttresses, each one of which would have been difficult to traverse; the prospect of doing so with loads did not appeal to us. On the other side of the small peak there was a fairly deep depression where we had hoped to put our next camp. Beyond this there was an exceedingly steep ridge, perhaps four hundred feet high, which appeared to be composed of hard ice. Beyond this, again, there was another long narrow section, while the final pyramid of the peak looked formidable. We did not have to study it long before coming to the conclusion that it was not for us to attempt to climb the East Ridge.

I have always been of the opinion that the art of mountaineering, in the perhaps limited sense of climbing difficult mountain-sides, can be learnt only in the Alps or some similar comparatively small and much-frequented range. In the first place, in the Alps the length of the climbs are such that they can mostly be done in a day, while huts and other facilities enable a man to spend a very long proportion of his time actually climbing difficult snow, ice and rock. Given fine weather, there is no reason why, in say, a month, he should not do some twenty climbs, each twelve or fifteen hours in length, so that at the end of that time he has acquired an immense amount of technical practice and experience. Secondly, the great number of mountaineers who visit the Alps, the fact that a number of experts can, year after year, specialize on one mountain face or on a group of peaks, and also the easy accessibility of the mountains – all these factors have naturally resulted in an exceedingly high standard of performance. And however modest a climber's ambitions, his standards are almost bound to be improved by the raising of the general level: climbs that twenty years ago were tackled only by the most daring experts are today undertaken by very mediocre performers. Thirdly, the fact that the climbs are so well known, documented and classified, deprives the mountain of one of its most formidable defences, the unknown; so that, apart from the factors of changing weather and snow conditions, a climber can concentrate almost entirely on the purely technical difficulties. This again, of course, provides him with greatly increased facilities for improving his technique and, even more important, of measuring his skill against an accepted standard of excellence.

In the greater and comparatively unknown ranges, the case is just the reverse. The great distances involved, the long glacier approaches, the slow, laborious business of establishing camps and of reconnoitring, result in only a tiny proportion of the time being spent actually climbing in the Alpine sense. The fact that heavy loads have to be carried a long way up the mountain, the physical disabilities resulting from altitude, the disastrous consequences which threaten from bad weather, these so often make it impossible to accept the challenge of a difficult ridge or face. The emphasis, therefore, is always upon the avoidance of difficulty, and one very rarely allows oneself to be committed to a spell of many hours of really hard climbing, which is commonplace in an Alpine season. With so many new mountains to tackle, climbs are hardly ever repeated, so that a comparison of standards is almost impossible. Lastly, perhaps the most important element of all, the fact that each upward step is on new ground, each ridge of unmeasured length, each slope of unknown steepness, absorbs so much of the climber's attention and his nerve that he cannot give the whole of himself to grapple with sheer technical difficulty.

Thus a man might spend a lifetime climbing in the Himalaya and never acquire the skill, the experience or the judgment needed to tackle a really difficult mountain (in the Alpine sense of the word "difficult"), which a few good seasons in the Alps would give him. I have always said that if I had to choose, for an Everest Expedition, between a man who had had a thorough training in the Alps and one who had only climbed in the Himalaya, even though his experience there had been great, I should, other things being equal of course, unhesitatingly choose the former.

Unfortunately, all skills need practice if they are to be retained. Just as the athlete will lose his speed, dexterity and strength without practising his sport, so the Alpine mountaineer may lose, not only his gymnastic agility on difficult rock, but that instinctive power to distinguish between danger and difficulty, that confident poise on a knife-edged arête, the acute judgement of difficulties ahead of him, that automatic adroitness in handling the rope and axe, that toughness of nerve that can withstand long hours of delicate movement over, say, precipitous, ice-covered rock, which in some degree must form part of his stock-in-trade. Thus, as it is almost impossible to learn the art of mountaineering in the Himalaya, so, by climbing exclusively in the Himalaya for a long period, one tends to lose the art one may have learned. I do not deny that there is a vast amount that one learns in the Himalaya that one cannot possibly learn in the Alps, but here I am discussing mountaineering in the strictly limited Alpine sense of climbing difficult ice, rock and snow.

In the summer of 1948 it was exactly twenty years since I had climbed in the Alps. Bill's case was certainly no better. Tackling the problems with which we were faced in the mountain ranges of Central Asia, exploring, crossing unknown passes, climbing or attempting to climb great peaks, we had not been greatly hindered by any deterioration in our technical ability, though I had always been aware of it as a fact. Faced with a proposition like Bogdo, it was painfully obvious. Neither of us had tackled so difficult a climb since we had climbed the West Ridge of Mount Kenya in 1930. Whether, placed in the same position but endowed with our 1930 form, we would have succeeded in climbing the East Ridge of Bogdo I cannot say. We would certainly have tried, and I believe we would have done it. Bill was inclined to attribute our failure to age; I found our physical ability to carry loads and to work on the mountain-side sufficient evidence to the contrary.

Even now I suppose we could have turned back and gone all out for an attempt on the North-east Ridge. It was half-past ten, 22nd July. We could have got the loads back down to the glacier before dark, spent the next day relaying them back across the col and with luck induced our Khasak friend to lend us his yaks to take a camp back to the north side of the mountain on the 24th. If the weather held, we might just have had time and supplies to carry a camp up to the High Col and to attempt the North-east Ridge. I am not sorry that we stayed where we were. It was a glorious position on the ridge, and our camp there was one of the best I have ever experienced.

We fetched the remaining loads from below the bergschrund, dug an ice-platform out of the crest of the ridge up against the rock outcrop and pitched the tent on it. We brewed tea from the ice-chips we had cut from the ridge, ate a large meal and then lay basking in the sun, our legs dangling over the edge. The view was grand. The western section was filled with an intricate pattern of superb ice-ridges and precipices which formed both the Eastern and South-eastern Cwms, culminating in a slender pyramid of ice which, as seen from here, was the summit of the highest peak of Bogdo. Across the Eastern Cwm we could see the outline of the North-east Ridge, running straight and steep from the summit down to the High Col. To the south, across the plain of Tapanchen, were the mountains of Eastern Tien Shan. To the north we could see down a wide valley to the steppes of Dzungaria, featureless as a wide expanse of ocean. To the east, the ridge, sharp and corniced, swept up to a snow-peak.

A haze hung over the Turfan Depression to the south-east. Looking at it reminded me of our remarkable position, sitting up there at 15,000 feet on an icy crest and within sight of that great hollow in the earth's surface, where the inhabitants must now be sweltering in torrid heat. I wondered if its proximity to the mountain produced any freaks of weather. We were very soon to experience one.

At about half-past four a wind started to blow from the north, and we retired to the tent and started to prepare the evening meal. By half-past five the wind had increased to an extraordinary violence. Looking out of the tent, we saw the sun sinking behind the highest peak of Bogdo. All along the East Ridge a huge wave of ice-particles was breaking over the crest, like spray across a breakwater, lit to a golden brilliance by the sun. Similar waves were sweeping over the Central and Eastern Peaks, forming long, swiftly moving plumes. For a short while the wind became a hurricane, the tent floor heaved under us, and it felt as if we were being swept away. One of the guy-ropes snapped, and one end of the tent collapsed upon our heads, flapping madly. Then came a brief lull, accompanied by a curious hissing noise, as clouds of ice-particles rained down upon the tent. One of us struggled outside to repair the broken guy-rope and to fasten the others more securely. This operation was barely completed before the next blast was upon us with a noise like a cannonade. Each blast seemed more violent than the last and more prolonged. We lay in our sleeping-bags, braced up against the sides of the tent, each clinging to one of the poles in the hope of relieving the strain on the guy-ropes. It seemed impossible that the tent would not be ripped to pieces, and we fully expected to have to ride out the storm lying in the open in our sleeping-bags. So during the next lull we put on all our sweaters, gloves and balaclava helmets, and put our boots inside our bags. We discovered later that the wind was being diverted by the steep northern flank of the ridge so that its main force was in an upward direction, and was thus not fully concentrated upon the tent. All the same the tent was getting a terrific hammering, and the fact that none of the stitching gave way was a fine tribute to the workmanship that had gone into its construction. Night fell and there was no slackening in the violence of the storm. Each brief lull was accompanied by a shower of ice-dust, each blast by a tremendous booming noise which seemed to shake the whole ridge. So it went on for hour after hour. I did not expect to sleep, and lay with my head buried in my bag with my arms stretched up and my hands clutching the tent-pole. Once it became evident that the tent was not going to be torn to pieces or lifted bodily off the ridge, I began to derive a good deal of enjoyment out of the noise of the storm, which I think was more violent than any I had experienced on Everest. Indeed, the noise seemed to have a soporific effect, which I have often found to be the case with violent thunder-storms, and in spite of the wild jolting of the tent I fell into a desultory sleep.

The storm was still raging at dawn the next morning, but its violence was declining and by eight o'clock we were able to get the Primus going and to cook breakfast. We decided to spend the day climbing the snow-peak on the ridge to the east. By ten o'clock the wind had slackened enough to allow us to start, and before we had been going for an hour it was quite calm. It was a delightful climb. The ridge was long; it was not particularly difficult and the snow was perfect, but it was narrow and heavily corniced so that we had to keep our wits about us. From the top (16,500 feet), the view of Bogdo was really magnificent, while in the other direction the ice-ridge continued over another peak about the same height as our own to another wide col, beyond which stood the massive "Six Thousander". We returned to our camp at four o'clock. We had thought of staying another night there and possibly making our way along the ridge towards Bogdo the next day. But while we were brewing tea the wind started to blow exactly as it had done the previous night, and it soon became clear that it would develop into another storm. We quickly decided that one was enough, and set about packing up the camp. It was nearly six o'clock when we started down, and it was already almost impossible to stand on the crest of the ridge. A few feet down on the lee side the air was still, and as we climbed down we could enjoy to the full the sight of the great golden plumes flying from the tops of the peaks, and the deepening colours of evening. We seemed to be descending into a sea of Mediterranean blue, transparent in the shallows immediately below, opaque beyond. We reached the camp beyond the col the following afternoon.

On the 25th we went down to the Khasak encampment. The Beg had returned. He was a charming old man, extremely friendly and hospitable. The other Khasaks, following his example, warmed to us and we had a very pleasant evening with them. On the 26th we climbed a sharp rock peak, about five thousand feet above the valley. Its corries were filled with small, steep glaciers, and it provided an amusing climb. The day was fine and still. We spent two hours lounging on the summit, from which, as it was quite isolated from the main range, there was a splendid view. Away to the west we saw a score of peaks belonging to the eastern ranges of the Tien Shan, every one of them as spectacular as Bogdo itself. The region is virtually unknown. It would provide a glorious field for exploration and mountaineering.

Soon after we had returned to the encampment that evening, two Tungans turned up. It appeared that they were the owners of all the flocks in the valley, the Khasaks herding them, using the milk and wool and presumably taking some percentage of the profit resulting from the increase in the flocks. It seemed a curious form of capitalism. We had found the same system among the Kirghiz in the Pamirs and Western Tien Shan, where the owners were often Turkis from the plains. But I was even more surprised to find it among the Khasaks who are such a particularly tough and independent people. And how had it survived the numerous civil wars and revolutions of recent decades and the period of Soviet domination over the Province? Surely during those times it would have been easy for the Khasaks to break away from their alien masters and to assume ownership of the flocks themselves, even if in peaceful times they failed to win economic independence. It appeared as though there must be some advantage to the Khasaks in the system, though it is difficult to see where it lay. It was evident that our hosts had no affection for the visitors. The atmosphere in the tent that evening was strained. The previous evening the Khasaks had been gay and talkative, now they were silent and rather morose. The Tungans were an unpleasant-looking pair.

The next day we hired some ponies from the Khasaks and travelled on down the valley. There is no fir forest on the southern side of the range, though lower down, the valleys are filled with thickets of willow and other deciduous trees. We reached the main highway between Turfan and Urumchi, where we had no difficulty in getting a lift on a lorry to the capital.

When we reached Urumchi we found that the new British Consul had arrived, but there was no sign of my Indian successor. It appeared that he could not be expected for several months yet and there was nothing for it but for me to return to Kashgar. But when we went to get the old Ford lorry out of the workshops it was discovered that there was a crack in one of the cylinders which it would take at least a week to repair. There was nothing for me to do in Urumchi during that time. I would have liked to pay a visit to Ili, but that area had been politically separated from the rest of the Province for more than a year and it was virtually impossible to go there. The weather was cloudless. The North-east Ridge of Bogdo stood out against the clear blue sky, a stabbing reminder of our failure even to attempt the only reasonable route to the summit. The ridge would surely by now be clear of winter snow and in perfect condition. Dreesen talked of spending the week-end going up to visit our Khasak friends on the southern side of the mountain. The temptation was too great. In a week we would just have time, if the weather held, to make an attempt on the ridge and get back to Urumchi. On Saturday we set out in the American Consulate lorry, followed the Turfan road for about thirty miles and turned up a rough path leading to the valley we had come down. We managed to get the lorry a long way up. On Sunday, while we were marching up the valley, the weather broke, and for the next three days it snowed heavily on the mountain, though very little rain fell in the valley below. Bill and I, Lhakpa and Agasha went on and camped by the lake in the defile below the big north glacier. A few hundred feet above, the great rock precipices were completely white with the newly fallen snow.

By the morning of the fourth day the weather had cleared a bit, but by then so much snow had fallen on the mountain that it was obvious that it would be impossible to attempt the North-east Ridge for a long time to come, even if the weather remained perfectly fine. However, we wanted to make certain, so we went up the glacier and started to climb the ridge leading to the Small Pointed Peak. As we had expected, even here nearly a foot of new snow covered the rocks. With a good deal of difficulty we reached a point about 15,000 feet, a little way below the High Col. The ridges of the main mountain were festooned with great masses of new snow. There was a great deal of cloud, but for a time after we had reached our highest point it cleared and we had an excellent view of the North-east Ridge. We were a great deal closer to it than ever before. We came to the definite conclusion that in good conditions it could be climbed, and in a single day from the High Col.

I must confess that I had rather hoped we should decide otherwise, for now I knew that we should always think of Bogdo with a slight feeling of regret. If we had planned otherwise than we did, if we had reconnoitred the East Ridge before committing ourselves to it, if we had not wasted so much time in the beginning, we might – indeed, I think we would – have reached the top of that very lovely mountain.

How much of the pleasure of mountaineering lies in all the varied experience of the Attempt; how much depends upon the garnish of Success? It is a philosophical question that most climbers would find hard to answer honestly. We like to think that success is not essential to our maximum enjoyment, which should derive from our knowledge and experience of mountains. The men who eventually reach the top of Everest will not know the mountain as Mallory knew it. Had we in the beginning tried the North-east Ridge and succeeded, we should not have experienced Bogdo as we did. But where is the man whose enjoyment is not slightly shadowed by the memory of failure, particulary when it was due to his fault?

Our greatest compensation came at the end, and there were moments during the next three days when I really believed that I was glad the snow had frustrated this last attempt. We decided that evening to send Agasha down by the way we had come, taking with him tents, stoves and other surplus baggage, while Bill, Lhakpa and I, carrying only our sleeping-bags and a minimum of food, went westward, keeping as near as possible to the main axis of the range. The journey took us two and a half days. It was one of the most delightful walks I have ever had. In a small way, it had the charm of exploration. It had all the variety that we could have wished.

We started at dawn and climbed in two hours to a little glacier col to the west. From here we looked down into a grassy cwm, half-encircled by ice-mountains, which formed the head of the main valley of the Heavenly Pool. On the floor of the cwm there was a small lake, by the shore of which we saw a herd of about twenty ibex grazing. On the slopes, as in all the upper valleys of the range, there were a great number and variety of alpine flowers. Half a mile below the lake, coming over a grassy mound, we stumbled on another large herd of ibex. They were lying on the ground, the nearest only fifteen yards from us. We crossed above the head of a dark, forested gorge which led down to the Heavenly Pool, and climbed up to a gap in the next ridge running north from the peaks of the main axis. So we went on throughout the day, crossing cols, I forget how many, and keeping close under the long line of ice-peaks. At about five o'clock we halted for the night on a grassy bank by a stream which came from a small glacier. We found plenty of yak dung for a fire. After cooking and eating our supper, we lay in our sleeping-bags and watched the evening colours fade on the peaks until they were black against the stars.

We started again at dawn, climbed up past the shoulder of the last of the ice-peaks and reached the crest of a broad hog's-back which was the westward extension of the axis of the range. Except for a few basalt towers, it was level and delightfully easy to walk along. On either hand, the view was uninterrupted. It was most exhilarating to go for mile after mile along this strange isolated ridge, eight thousand feet above the plains. To the south the mountains of the Tien Shan were clear, their height exaggerated by a wide plain between us and them and by our own height above it. Soon after noon we reached the end of the ridge and found ouselves at the hub of half a dozen deep valleys radiating outwards. Though we were high enough above them to trace the course of each, their tributaries seemed to intermingle in a confusing maze. Each was filled with dense fir forest, which reached to a point some two thousand feet below us. We sat for an hour debating which we should choose, reluctant to descend from our lofty eminence. Then we climbed down a rocky gully, disturbing a covey of ram chikor. The gully became a nullah, filled with brambles and scrub, already tinted with the reds and golds of autumn; the gorge opened into a great valley, sombre under dense fir forest except where the river still sparkled in the sunlight and in the occasional grassy clearings. At one of these, at four o'clock, we stopped for half an hour to drink milk in a Khasak tent. By now there was a wide pathway, with bridges where it crossed the river, and walking became a relaxation. A couple of hours later we began to emerge into the foothills; the fir forest had ceased and we were in a valley filled with willow and briar thickets, flanked by low hills covered with tall grass and scrub. It was very beautiful in the golden evening light, but the river had disappeared underground and the prospect of a waterless, and therefore foodless, night almost spoilt its enchantment. It was nine o'clock and quite dark before we reached another Khasak encampment.

Our hosts were very friendly and, besides plying us with milk and cream and cooking our food, they agreed to lend us three ponies and to send a man to show us the way. We started again as soon as it was light. A tiny path led out of the valley and across an intricate pattern of hills and nullahs, until, after about three hours, we reached open downland. My pony was more energetic than the others or I urged it with more effect, for I got well ahead, travelling at a fast trot and occasionally cantering. Between the rounded downs, the wide fertile valleys cultivated by Tungan farmers were filled with golden wheat. The harvest had just begun. It was beautiful country, but I suppose it was partly the contrast with the scenes of the last two days, in themselves so wonderfully varied, that lent to it a special enchantment. The forested spurs of Bogdo Ola were now far up to the left. The ice-peaks were just coming into view.

CHAPTER TWELVE

Chakragil; and Hunza again

I arrived back in Kashgar with Tilman on 24th August. Even if I had been able to leave immediately, it was already much too late for us to embark upon the glacier journey from Shimshal to Panamik. As it was, besides having various matters to attend to before handing over my charge, I had to await instructions from the Governments of India and Pakistan, and this would have made our departure too late even for the alternative journey I had planned, that south from Khotan across the Kuen Lun to Leh. Moreover, by that time Ladakh had become a battle-ground, and it seemed likely that we would not be able to travel through. But although we had to abandon these fascinating plans, there was time before the winter set in for one more mountain venture. There was no lack of choice. For my part I favoured either another journey to Uch Tash country to the north-east or an exploration of the still unknown valleys coming down from the North Face of Kungur. Bill, on the other hand, hankered after climbing a great peak; and none was more attractive than Chakragil. It would have taken too long to get round to the southern side of this mountain which we had seen to be climbable, and as I could not get away immediately, we agreed to a compromise. He would spend a week or ten days reconnoitring the North Ridge of Chakragil and come back to report. If he found a possible route, we would return to try it; if not, we would go to the Kungur valleys. He set out at the end of August, taking Mersh with him.

I had paid a brief visit to the northern side of Chakragil with my wife in May 1947, when we camped for three days close to the foot of the mountain in a valley of extraordinary beauty. Our camp, at 8,500 feet, was set in a grassy glade surrounded by tall firs. The forested slopes of the valley ended abruptly in bare, sweating precipices of rock, cleft by dark ravines, and surmounted by snowy peaks. Lofty waterfalls cascaded down the cliffs; sometimes they were caught by the wind and diffused into waving curtains of spray. There were seven in all, though not all were visible from the camp; some must have been six or seven hundred feet high. The precipices formed a rough frame for the great peaks at the head of the valley. A few hundred yards from our camp was the snout of a glacier, which appeared almost jet-black against the green firs. The glacier was only two or three miles long. Its head lay immediately beneath a cirque, 12,000 feet high, of terraced and fluted ice, which formed the North Face of the two peaks of Chakragil.

A remarkable feature of the glacier was the abnormal size of the ablation valleys at its sides. Standing on one of them, we could see nothing of the glacier, which was screened by the huge grass-covered lateral moraine. This produced the curious illusion that the gigantic ice-precipices of Chakragil rose straight out of the luxuriant grass of the meadows on the floor of the ablation valley. Though it was too early in the year for them to be at their best, there were already masses of wild flowers on the meadows. The fir forest extended a mile or more above the snout of the glacier. Seen from above, the glacier had the curious appearance of being confined in a narrow, built-up trough, running down the centre of a grassy and forested valley.

There was no possibility of climbing that stupendous North Face of the peaks. But running northward from the higher of the two summits there was a great ridge which in its lower reaches formed the western side of the valley we were in. It had seemed to me that if we could get a camp on to the crest of this ridge it would be possible to climb it to the summit of the mountain. I could see no way of reaching the ridge from this side, and I had no time then to explore the opposite side. To do this was now Bill's object.

If we were to attempt to climb Chakragil, which is just over twenty-two thousand feet high, it would greatly increase our chances of success if we had with us a third man to help us to carry the loads to our high camps. Besides this, I am strongly opposed to a party of two climbing for long on crevassed glaciers if

The Shipton/Tilman preference for fast-moving uncomplicated expeditions found expression in the 1935 and 1938 Everest projects:

62 (above) Members of the 1935 Reconnaissance Expedition. Edwin Kempson (left), Tilman, Shipton, Dan Bryant, Charles Warren, Michael Spender and Edmond Wigram.

63 (left) Setting out to Everest in 1938. Noel Odell, Bip Pares (the illustrator of Shipton's early books) and her husband, Charles Warren, Shipton and Peter Oliver (right).

64 (below) The fracture line of the huge slab avalanche that swept the slopes below North Col in 1935.

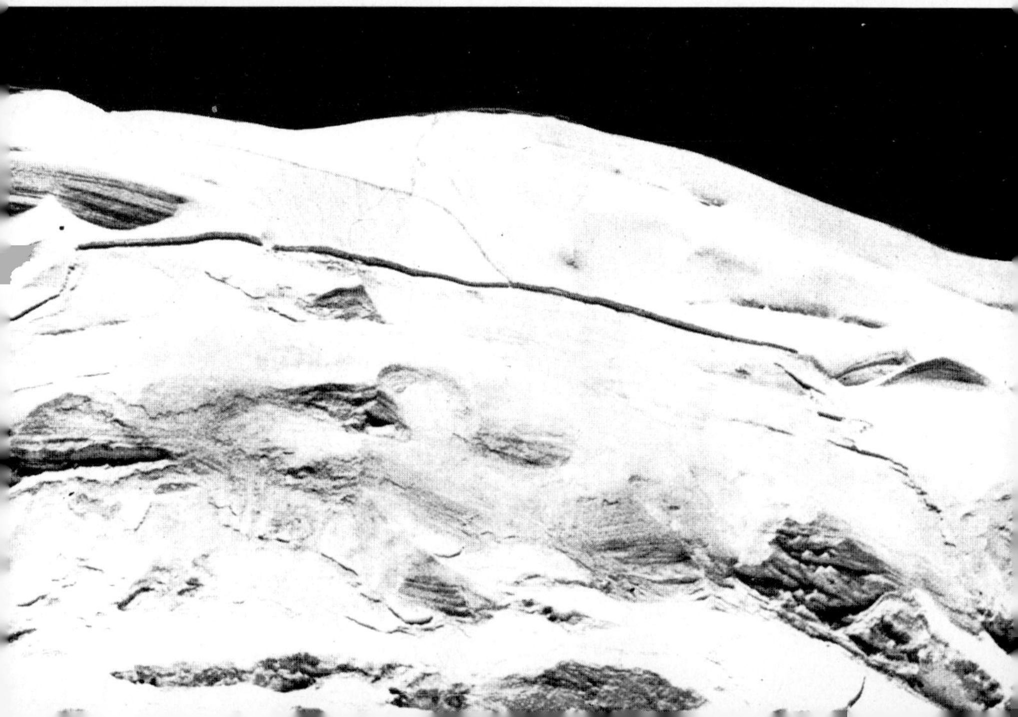

↓ Mallory

935 Shipton's party
ied out a study of
w conditions on
rest and climbed
nty-six peaks:

(above) A telephoto
verest's upper
es showing the
cult ground between
sites of Camp 6 and
summit.

(left) Kharta
ngri (23,000 ft.), one
he beautiful peaks
bed by members of
expedition (Charles
rren and Edwin
npson).

68 (right) Shipton
Dan Bryant climbed
peaks of the
gtren group (the
n peak seen in the
photo) from where
y were able to
ss some of the
blems of Everest's
st Ridge, the
umbu Icefall and
Western Cwm.

69 The Tushuk Tagh range (c.11,000 ft.) near Kashgar, showing the complex canyon systems leading through the foothills.

70 71 72 Three views in the depths of the range, with the Arch seen from the north.

73 (above) A Kasak encampment with two yorts (akois).

74 (left) Usman Akhun who joined the quest for the Arch '. . . he had the self-assurance of an alpine guide.'

75 Chakragil (22,070 ft.) from the high point reached on the North Ridge (17,000 ft.).

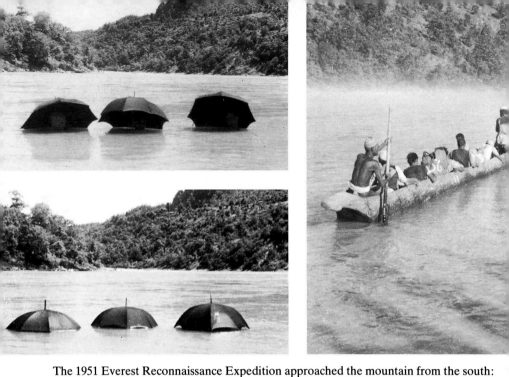

The 1951 Everest Reconnaissance Expedition approached the mountain from the south:
76 77 78 (above) A bathe before crossing the Arun River in a huge dugout canoe

79 (below) The first comprehensive view of the Western Cwm, from the slopes of Pumori.
80 (above right) The Khumbu Icefall – 'riven with cracks that seemed to threaten collapse'.

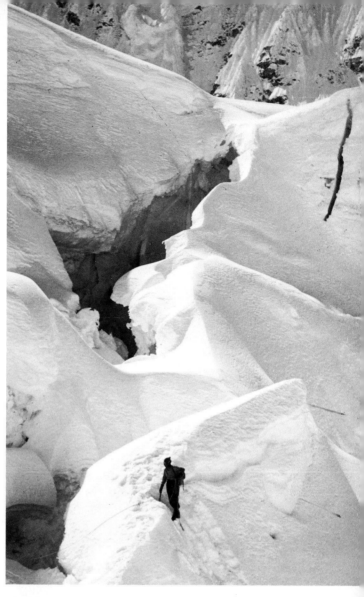

(below right) The team:
o right – Shipton,
ray, Bourdillon,
liford (standing);
d and Hillary (seated).

82 83 Menlungste (23, 560 ft.), the unclimbed p
west of Everest 'we were in a vaste amphitheatre in the centre of which stood the most lovely peak of pale granite'. On the glacier below this peak Shipton's party found fresh tracks providing evidence of the existence of the Yeti (inset).

The 1952 Cho Oyu Expedition:

84 (top) Cho Oyu from Nangpa La. The attempt was made on the snowy rib in front of the shadowy distant face. Chinese territory is on the left.

85 (left) A peak above the Teshi Lakpa Pass that was virtually climbed by Shipton, Gregory and Evans.

86 (above) George Lowe and Ed Hillary.

rations in
onia:

top left)
Onelli Glacier with
lving off the cliffs
iiles away. Several
es later the tidal
from this swept
each.

below left)
agonian glacier
contorted to
l the seasonal
grain.

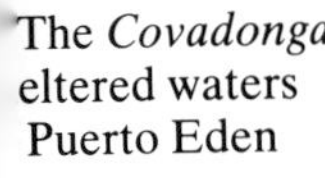

The *Covadonga*
eltered waters
Puerto Eden

A section of
oulin (water
) sliced and
ed to a vertical
tion by the
on of the Seno
o Glacier

An Alacaluf
an hut, 'like
imitive version
n Asian yort'.

The South Patagonian Ice-cap Journey 1961: 92 (above) Shipton carrying sledge sections on the Jorge Montt Glacier. The Canal Baker is in the background. 93 (top right) The mists clear to reveal the first mountains. 94 (bottom right) Marangunic and García with the sledge near the head of the Viedma Glacier.

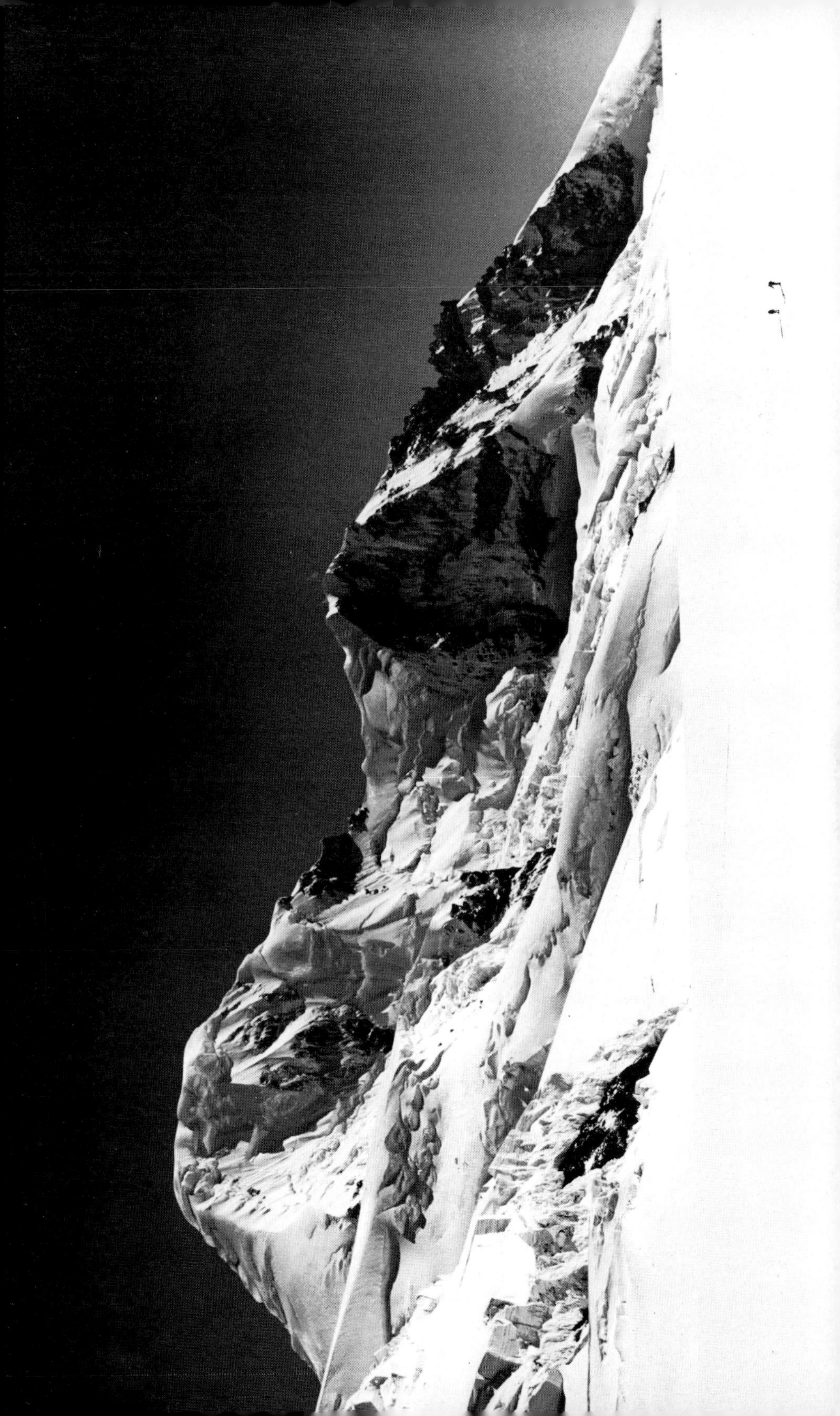

96 (above) A view north from the summit of Cerro Don Bosco. The South Patagonian Ice-cap is flanked by the Moreno range (left) and the Fitzroy group (right).

The North Patagonian Ice-cap Journey, 1964:

101 (far left) An unnamed peak towering 4,500 ft. above the ice-cap.

102 (left) Approaching Cerro Arenales

103 Miguel Gomez on the airbed raft used

it can be avoided, particularly when carrying heavy loads. If one man falls into a bad crevasse so that he is dangling on the rope, it may be extremely difficult, if not impossible, for a single companion to get him out; with a third man to help, the task is a very great deal easier. The problem was, who to take with us. After his two years of comparatively sedentary life in Kashgar, I very much doubted whether Gyalgen was up to it. We had been disappointed with Agasha's performance on Bogdo. I had intended to get hold of my Kirghiz friend, Khurban, and ask him to come with us; he, at least, would be in first-rate physical condition; he was a good climber and used to carrying loads.

While Bill was away, I went for a week-end hunting *ovis poli* in the hills west of Minyol. Lhakpa, Kapak and I were in camp by a spring on the Saturday evening when a party of three Kirghiz turned up. They were on their way to Kashgar from the west and they stopped with us for the night. While we were having supper, one of them, named Mahmud, a small wiry man of thirty or so, asked me if I would like him to come with me the next day. He knew those hills well, he said, and had hunted there himself more than once. I welcomed his suggestion. We set out together an hour before dawn, and had a very long and tiring day. I was tremendously impressed by his skill and agility as a climber and by his stamina; he walked up-hill with beautiful ease of movement, tackled difficult places with a steady confidence which overcame them far more quickly than I could, and by the end of the day seemed to be as fresh as when we had started. I thought I had found the ideal man to come with us on Chakragil. He was intelligent, quiet and not excitable, and though, of course, he had never climbed on an ice-mountain, he was used to crossing high passes and living among valleys which were snow-covered in winter. I asked him if he would like to come with me for a couple of weeks to the Pamirs, explaining that the object of the trip was to climb one of the great snow-peaks, that he would have to carry a load, and would, of course, be well paid. He jumped at the idea, and the matter was settled without more ado.

Bill arrived back in Kashgar on 8th September. He was, for Bill, unusually excited. He had been into the South-western Cwm of Chakragil and was fairly confident that he had found a way of climbing on to the crest of the North Ridge. He could not be certain, for while in the cwm he had struck a patch of bad weather and the intermittent views that he had had of the surrounding mountains had left him so confused about the topography of the region that he was not even sure that he had identified Chakragil. Nor had he been able to see enough of the North Ridge to confirm my opinion of it.

As I was still expecting telegraphic instructions from the Governments of India and Pakistan about the future of the Consulate, which might require a fairly prompt reply, I did not feel justified in being away for very long. However, if necessary a messenger could be sent to fetch me back, and with that proviso I decided to allow myself a clear ten days, which, if the weather was kind, should give us time to attempt the peak. Taking with us Gyalgen, Mahmud and two Turkis, from whom we had hired pack-ponies, we started on 10th September and that evening reached Tashmalik, a large oasis at the southern edge of the plains.

From Tashmalik our way led for about ten miles up the valley of the Gez

River. The hills on either side of this, like all the foot-hills surrounding the Tarim Basin, were utterly barren, their weird conglomerate cliffs and arid nullahs in stark contrast to the miles of green oasis we had just left; that contrast which is the most characteristic scenic feature of Southern Sinkiang. The morning was clear, and the great snowy mass of Kungur now towered above us. The fluted ice-ridges of Chakragil looked glorious against the blue sky. The river was still in its summer spate, but here it flowed over a mile-wide bed, and was split into several channels. Even so, the current was so strong that it took us an hour to find places where the ponies could ford them. Before the Gez Valley was swallowed up in its great gorge, we turned to the westward, up the first large tributary, which was called Oui Tagh Jilga. This, too, was arid, except for stretches of tamarisk and briar jungle along the banks of the river. Some six miles up-stream the river had cut its way through a high barrier of conglomerate rock, which had been eroded into an extraordinary convolution of clean-cut ridges and canyons, very like those of the Tushuk Tagh Range, only on a smaller scale. Past this barrier we came to a wide stretch of cultivation surrounding the scattered village of Oui Tagh Aghiz. The land here had clearly been formed by the sedimentary deposits from a large lake, which had been dammed back by the conglomerate barrier before the river cut its way through to its present level. Stepping round the last corner of the defile, as through a doorway, the green fields and orchards presented a lovely and unexpected sight. When I had come here before, the fruit blossom had been out and the fields of young corn had been fringed with wide borders of wild iris.

On the third day we marched on up the Oui Tagh Jilga, past the entrance of the valley leading up to the North Face of Chakragil, and that afternoon we reached a group of *akois* set among the first of the fir trees near the snout of a glacier. We were warmly greeted by the inhabitants, with whom Bill had already made friends and whose manifold ills, real and imaginary, had been treated, apparently successfully, by the Doctor. After the usual feast of curds and cream, we went on, accompanied by a number of the local Kirghiz. We followed a steep path through the forest and eventually reached a wide grassy shelf, a couple of miles long, formed by an ancient lateral moraine and its attendant ablation valley. The shelf was used by the Kirghiz as a summer grazing-ground, and some *akois* were still there. It overlooked a great "concordia" of glaciers, which flowed down from a vast cirque of lofty mountains. Chakragil itself, tucked away in the left-hand corner of the cirque, was hidden behind a great rock peak, which Bill had named "Geometry Peak" from the extraordinary sharpness of the angles formed by its ridges. Several peaks of the cirque I recognized as forming part of the great panorama visible from Kashgar. From there, their forms had become so familiar to me, like part of the background pattern of a well-known picture, that it seemed strange to see them so close, the intricate detail of their structure, hitherto invisible, now dominating the scene.

The two aneroid barometers which Bill had brought from England had both been broken. But among the miscellaneous survey instruments left behind at the Consulate, I imagine by Sir Aurel Stein or perhaps by one of my predecessors with geographical tastes, were two hypsometers, or boiling-point thermometers. We had brought one of these with us. The solemnity of its use, setting it up, lighting the little spirit-lamp and waiting until it puffed like a toy steam-engine, lent a pleasant air of old-fashioned dignity to our expedition, and of course greatly entertained our hosts in the *akoi* that evening. It informed us that we were just over ten thousand feet above sea-level.

Bill, Gyalgen, Mahmud and I started early next morning, taking with us two tents and provisions for about four days. The two pack-ponies, in charge of one of the Turkis, carried the loads to the farther end of the two-mile terrace and a little beyond, until the ground became too broken for them to come any farther. Thereafter we shouldered the loads ourselves, and plodded on at a leisurely pace.

I always dislike intensely the idea of carrying a load, particularly when I am out of practice, as one always is on a short mountaineering expedition, and I

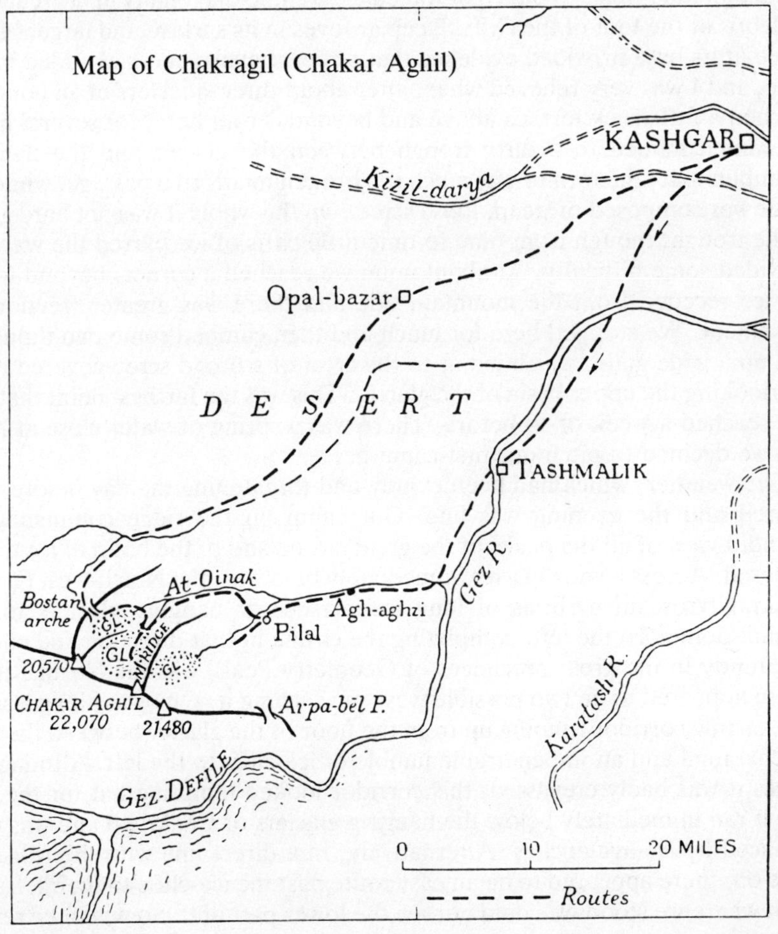

always try as far as I decently can to avoid it. But when circumstances make it unavoidable, I am always mildly surprised that the misery involved is so much less than I expected. In some situations it is always unpleasant; one is over flat country, but then I dislike walking over flat country even without a load, and fortunately I have rarely had to do so with one; another is in difficult jungle when you have to twist your body about and you cannot develop a rhythmic action. But under favourable conditions I even derive a certain sombre satisfaction from this form of toil; it is impossible to hurry, and impatience has to be subdued; one is forced to pay strict attention to that really very fascinating art of walking uphill, the main features of which are controlled and balanced movement and careful choosing of foot-hold; and, perhaps best of all, one has an excuse for frequent halts to admire the view. So it was today, and though the going was not easy, we managed, unless our hypsometer lied, to climb four thousand feet with remarkably little discomfort.

When we left the ponies, we were close to the huge rock precipices of Geometry Peak, which towered some six thousand feet above us. A broken ice-fall on the glacier to our right forced us to climb diagonally up a great cone of debris at the foot of the cliffs. Deep grooves in its surface and larger blocks of ice at its base provided evidence that a recent avalanche had added to the cone, and I was very relieved when, after about three-quarters of an hour, we reached a little rock terrace above and beyond. From here, for several hours we were confined to a dirty trough between the glacier and the flanking mountain-side; the former was much too broken to afford a passage, while the latter was composed of steep, loose scree. On the whole it was not hard going in the trough, though from time to time little cliffs of ice barred the way and provided some difficulty. At about noon we reached a corner, beyond which the ice receded from the mountain-side and there was greater freedom of movement. We stopped here for lunch and then climbed some two thousand feet up a wide gully, which led us to the crest of a broad scree-covered ridge overlooking the upper basin of the glacier. This was the farthest point that Bill had reached a week or so before. There was a spring of water close at hand and we decided to pitch our first camp here.

The weather, which had been cloudy and threatening the day before, had cleared and the evening was fine. Our camp on the ridge commanded a splendid view of all the peaks of the great cirque and of the basin of ice that it enclosed. Across a wide glacier immediately below us, the North-west Face of Chakragil rose in a series of long ice-terraces or hanging glaciers to the summit dome. To the left, completing the cirque in that direction and ending apparently in the great precipices of Geometry Peak, was the North Ridge. There appeared to be two possible ways of reaching it. One was along a steep and narrow corridor running up from the floor of the glacier between the face of Chakragil and an impenetrable jumble of ice-cliffs to the left. Although in places it was badly crevassed, this corridor looked tempting but for the fact that it ran immediately below the hanging glaciers of Chakragil and was thus menaced by ice-avalanches. Alternatively, in a direct line with the ridge we were on, there appeared to be an easy route past the ice-cliffs to their left; but from where we stood we could not see the lower part of it. So while the rest of us were pitching camp, Bill went on up the ridge to reconnoitre. He returned an hour later and reported that a narrow neck of ice connected the top of our ridge with the snow-slopes which we could see beyond. This was a great relief, for I had been contemplating the route up the corridor and had come to the conclusion that it would involve our spending too long a time under fire from the hanging glaciers for the risk to be justifiable.

While supper was cooking, we boiled our hypsometer. We discovered that, not unnaturally, the thermometer gave the same reading when immersed in boiling tea-water as in the ingenious little steam-engine provided by the makers, so we decided to lighten our loads by the weight of the latter. We would take for granted the height of the summit, where we would not be brewing tea. Our altitude worked out at 14,000 feet. We estimated that the crest of the North Ridge at the point where we would reach it was about three thousand feet above us. Providing the going was good, we could reasonably expect to carry a camp to there the next day. A final camp on the face of the mountain at about nineteen thousand five hundred feet should put us within easy reach of the summit, even if the snow conditions were much worse than we had reason to expect. Mahmud had gone quite well that day, and had made no complaint about his load, though I suspect that Gyalgen had seen to it that he carried the heaviest. He did not seem to be in the least daunted by the prospect of climbing this great ice-mountain, or of camping on its lofty ridges. To test him, I suggested that he should change places with Gyalgen and remain below; but he would not hear of it, and was evidently determined to win the rich reward I had offered him if we succeeded in reaching the top. The cloudless sky and the pink glow which filled the cirque at sunset gave promise of fine weather. We settled down for the night with high hopes.

We started at six o'clock the next morning, leaving behind one of the tents, Gyalgen's bedding and some food. Gyalgen came with us carrying a load as far as he could safely return alone; after which, he would go right down to the *akois*, taking with him the things we had left behind.

I always find that the events of a day spent in carrying a high camp up a mountain tend in retrospect to become telescoped in such a manner that it becomes difficult to distinguish them in their true perspective, and still harder to understand how the whole business took so long. In normal life, nine hours spent upon a single job seems to me a very long time (this may be because with me it so rarely occurs). But in this matter of carrying high camps, although individual hours may drag, at some point in the day, time seems to run together so that three o'clock, the hour at which one generally starts looking around for a suitable place to put the camp, suddenly appears out of a confused series of contrasting emotions. For the first hour I plod along in a mood of deep gloom, of self-pity and of dislike both for my companions and for the whole silly business of mountain climbing. I am stiff and tired, my legs and shoulders ache, in my hands and feet I detect undeniable symptoms of frostbite, the slopes above look impossibly long and steep, and my only desire is to lie down and sleep. The first halt works a subtle but profound change, and during the next spell, though it would be overstating the case to say that I am happy, I am not wholly insensitive to the grandeur of my surroundings, I am tolerant at least towards the minor shortcomings of my friends and willing to admit that mountaineering is not entirely unrewarding. Thereafter I swing between these emotional extremes. The quality of the snow, the moisture of my throat and the apparent progress of the party are among the factors motivating this change of mood; but there are evidently many others which escape the keenest introspection.

To begin with, on this day, all went very well. It was freezing hard and it would be several hours before the sun climbed above the North Ridge and started to soften the snow. The neck of ice at the top of our rock ridge carried us comfortably over a nasty ice-fall. The slopes beyond were in excellent condition. Mahmud seemed to be going rather slowly, but we evidently did not take this seriously enough to change our plans. It must have been about eleven o'clock and we had just hauled our baggage up the steep upper lip of a crevasse, when we decided that it was time for Gyalgen to leave us. We watched him down to easy ground, distributed his load amongst us and started on. Less than an hour later Mahmud began to show signs of distress. As the snow was beginning to get soft and Bill and I took it in turns to kick the steps, and as, too, we were having a little trouble in finding a way through the crevasses and small ice-cliffs which barred the way, the pace was in any case very slow, and he had plenty of time to rest. Even so, at about half-past one it became evident that he could not carry his load any farther. We relieved him of it, and while one of us was kicking the steps the other carried it up in relays. In spite of the delay, we had made such good progress that by three o'clock we reached a little hollow only fifty feet below the crest of the North Ridge. It was a snug little place, the bottom of a shallow crevasse, sheltered from the wind on three sides by ice-cliffs. We set to work to make camp, light the Primus and melt ice for tea.

Mahmud's collapse was a bitter blow. We had found a beautiful solution to the cardinal problem of reaching the North Ridge. The altitude of our camp turned out to be 17,500 feet, which was even higher than we had hoped to reach that day. A very moderate carry the next day would have placed us within easy reach of the summit, now only some four thousand five hundred feet above us. We still hoped that Mahmud might recover with a night's rest. But from the first the prospect was not very encouraging. He refused to eat anything, vomited frequently and in the intervals lay groaning on the floor of the tent. I was terribly sorry for him, but I could not help bemoaning the fact that if he had told us only an hour sooner that he was feeling ill, we could have sent him down with Gyalgen and gone on by ourselves.

We ate our evening meal, and then, oppressed by that strange, ethereal loneliness which settles upon a high camp at evening, we arranged ourselves as best we could for a long, uncomfortable night. At sunset a westerly wind started to blow with considerable force. In spite of our sheltered position, the noise of flapping canvas and of drift snow beating against the tent made sleep difficult. With three in a tent designed for two our space was cramped. For a long time I lay brooding upon our situation, in that futile, restless way that one does at night. Unless Mahmud made an unexpected recovery, it seemed that we had two courses open to us. We could attempt to reach the summit from this camp;

but we were not acclimatized to this altitude, and unless the snow were in excellent condition all the way we were hardly likely to succeed. The alternative was to take Mahmud down and return later; but we would probably have to take him down the whole 7,500 feet to the *akois*, and in that case we could not get back here for another three days, even if the weather held. It was already very late in the year and a heavy fall of snow would make even the North Ridge inaccessible. This, of course, was a potent reason for not staying on the mountain with a sick man. Of course, if Mahmud showed any sign of improvement by the morning, assuming that he was suffering from altitude, we might stay where we were for a day in the hope that on the following day he might be well enough to come up another couple of thousand feet with us, even without a load; for, clearly, we could neither leave him here without a tent nor go up ourselves without one.

These depressing speculations continued to revolve monotonously in my mind, while, in the brief lulls in the windstorm, I could hear poor Mahmud groaning and sometimes vomiting. He spent most of the night crouched on his hands and knees, whether in prayer or to relieve his sickness I could not tell. Though I slept a little, the night seemed interminable, and I have rarely been more glad to see the dawn. The wind dropped and the sun rose into a cloudless sky. While we were brewing tea, Bill and I discussed the situation. We agreed that before deciding anything we would go out for a breath of fresh air. A small mountain tent is a bad place for making decisions, for in it one's mind seems to become as cramped as one's body.

We roped up and climbed on to the crest of the North Ridge. We had grown accustomed to the panorama of the great glacier cirque to the west; fine though it was, it was nothing to the scene that now opened before us on the eastern side of the ridge. It was not a view of distance, for the plains to the north were misty and featureless and the mountains of the Kungur massif were hidden behind the eastern peak of Chakragil. It was the nearer objects and their peculiar arrangement that held us entranced. We looked straight down nine thousand feet, with nothing visible of the intervening precipice, to the grassy alps and the dark fir forest surrounding them, where my wife and I had camped some eighteen months before. They were still in shadow, but the air was very clear and as our eyes became accustomed to the gloom we could see tiny wreaths of smoke rising from the Kirghiz encampments. The *akois* themselves were invisible. To the right, suspended above this great abyss, close at hand and dazzling in the early morning sun, were the hanging glacier terraces, tier upon tier of them, supported by scores of slender buttresses of fluted ice, which formed the North Face of Chakragil. Two-thirds of this mighty precipice was now below us. The effect of depth, enhanced as it was by the delicately balanced poise of the vast and complex structure, was overwhelming. Beyond the topmost terrace we could see into a deep recess, a peaceful glen, which nestled beneath the mile-long ridge between the twin summits, its walls and floor forming a perfect curve of unbroken snow.

The crest of the North Ridge, though heavily corniced upon its eastern side, was broad enough to allow us to walk comfortably along it. It mounted at a gentle gradient and, some two thousand feet above us, merged into the great ice-dome of Chakragil. The climb would have presented not the slightest technical difficulty. We made our way along the ridge, partly to test the snow and partly to see the fantastic view to the east from a new angle. Our feet sank about nine inches into the snow. Even if this became no worse higher up, it would probably have made our progress too slow to reach the summit in a single day. But with another camp even fifteen hundred feet higher, we could hardly have failed to do so, providing the weather held for another thirty hours. But before we had left the camp we had little doubt that Mahmud would be able to go no farther, and we had almost resigned ourselves to the bitter disappointment of having to abandon our project when the summit was almost within our grasp. We stayed a while to gaze at what was in many ways the finest piece of mountain scenery I have ever seen. Then we returned to camp.

When we got back we found poor Mahmud still lying in the tent. We got him out and found that his condition was even worse than we had thought. He seemed scarcely able to stand; he was still vomiting frequently, and we now noticed that when he coughed, blood appeared on his lips. There was now no question but that we must get him down as soon as possible. Indeed, I felt profound relief that only one course was open to us; for I know of few more difficult decisions than those involving a choice between pressing and abandoning an attempt upon a mountain when the latter course is not absolutely necessary. We packed up our things and, leaving behind most of the food and the tin of kerosene, made them into two loads. Then we roped up and started down. Mahmud staggered to the edge of the hollow and collapsed. There was nothing we could do but to tow him along, which was not difficult for us, but must have been extremely unpleasant for him, for he often gathered momentum and slid or rolled past us and had to be pulled up at the end of the rope. Over the steep places we lowered him as gently as we could. He thought he was dying and asked us to leave him where he was. Once, when we halted for a long rest, he asked me for a pencil and paper and proceeded to write a brief letter which he asked me to deliver to his family when I got back.

Eventually we got him down to the head of the ridge on which we had camped two days before, by which time he had so far recovered as to be able to walk for short spells by supporting himself on our shoulders. I was convinced that he was suffering from nothing more serious than altitude sickness. This was confirmed, both by his quick recovery when we got down to lower levels and, when we got back to Kashgar, by a thorough examination by the Doctor, who could find nothing wrong with him. It was certainly the most severe attack of altitude sickness that I have ever witnessed. That the victim should have been a youngish man, so particularly tough and strong, who had spent all his life among mountains was certainly remarkable. But I have long ceased to wonder at manifestations of this capricious complaint.

On the evening of the following day, the weather showed unmistakable signs of a change for the worse. Our Kirghiz hosts told us that this was the beginning of the first autumn snowfalls, and announced their intention of moving down to lower pastures. They showed us an interesting pass to the north of the glacier cirque, and two of them were kind enough to accompany us to its summit. It led us into a long valley running northward to Yolchi

Moinak, which we had passed on our way back from Mustagh Ata the previous year. From there, we travelled again across the thirty-mile stretch of desert to Opal, and thence back to Kashgar.

We had reason, I think, to attribute our failure to reach the summit of Chakragil to ill luck. But for all that, we had shown a singular lack of imagination in devising our plan. It would have been far better if Bill had taken Gyalgen with him on his first trip, with the understanding that if he failed to find a route he would meet me ten days later – say, at the mouth of the Oui Tagh River – while if I did not find him there, I would come on up to the glacier cirque. Of course, we did not know of the existence of this at the time, but we could hardly have failed to meet. This would have given them more than a week's training at climbing to high altitudes, which would probably have been sufficient to enable Gyalgen to recover enough of his form to come with us on the mountain. They could have employed at least some of their time carrying loads up the lower part of the mountain. Perhaps this is being wise after the event, but I have a feeling that in the 'thirties we would have exercised more forethought.

We got back to Kashgar on 21st September. Bill had decided, instead of travelling via Hunza and Gilgit, to go westward from Misgar across the Chillinji Pass to Ishkumen and thence to Chitral. I would have liked very much to go with him on this journey, but two considerations prevented this. First, I could not get away until 10th October, and every week that he delayed lessened his chances of getting across the high passes on his route; secondly, I was anxious to visit the Mir of Hunza, with whom I had various matters to discuss. So we decided to go our separate ways and, if possible, to meet in Chitral before the end of November. He left Kashgar on 29th September.

As the day of my departure approached, I spent much time in sentimental reflection. During my years in Kashgar I had been accustomed each morning to ride ten or twelve miles before breakfast. Now I went over each of my half-dozen rides in turn, giving full rein to the exquisite nostalgia that each intimate landmark induced: the mill in the willow grove across the valley, where the boy used to blow his horn to announce that the miller was ready for fresh supplies of grain; the wide, green river-flats of Sogaluk, where in winter wild duck used to congregate in their thousands and where, on a frosty morning, the steam would rise from a hundred ice-girt pools into the early sunlight; the little grassy glade, down which I used to gallop at full speed, usually with thoughts of breakfast uppermost in my mind; the high loess bluff, where, on clear mornings, I would rein my pony and watch the sunrise on the Pamirs. It was all so familiar that it seemed incredible that I would never see any of it again; or, indeed, anything remotely like it, for I believe the countryside of South Sinkiang is unique. Three or four times during those last few days the mountains were clear and, looking at them, I was oppressed by regret for the number of things I had hoped to do and had not done. This was unreasonable, of course, for, although no doubt I had missed opportunities, even if I had had no duties to perform in Kashgar and had been able to give all my time to travel, I could not have covered the whole of that vast field.

I am still amazed at the great good fortune that gave me the chance to know something of Sinkiang and, having watched the recent turn of events, I shudder to think of the narrow margin by which I got that chance. For the Iron Curtain has already clanged down behind me, and it may be many decades before a Western traveller is free to travel there again.

My sorrow at leaving Kashgar was softened by the prospect of another six weeks' trek through the Pamirs, the Karakoram and the Hindu Kush. Apart from the break that it meant, I looked forward to this with the keenest pleasure. There are some aspects of a straightforward journey, providing it is done under the right conditions, that are more enjoyable than travelling through unknown country; just as there is delight to be found in climbing a well-known peak behind a guide, pleasure of a kind often lacking in the ascent of an unclimbed mountain. One is pleasantly free from the responsibility of finding the way, and of such tiresome decisions as to whether and when to turn back, how far to press forward each day and whether food and fuel supplies will last. Time and distance, because they are pre-ordained, cease to be matters of importance. One can relax into an untroubled absorption with the changing scenery, with the sheer delight of movement, with the satisfaction of food and rest.

As travelling companions I had Fateh Ali Khan, a Hunza who was in charge of our diplomatic courier service across the passes, and his three sons, while Lhakpa came with me as far as Misgar. Early in October we received word that the water in the Gez River was already low enough to allow the passage of caravans through the great defile between Kungur and Chakragil. So on the 10th, after a farewell party arranged by my staff in camp on the south bank of the Yamen Yar, we set out again for Tashmalik, where for the last time I saw the oases of the Tarim Basin. I had never travelled by the Gez route, and after we had passed the junction of the Oui Tagh Jilga, the way for the next two and a half days, along the bottom of that fantastic gorge, was new to me. The weather was rather bad and we saw little of the great ice-peaks that soared into the clouds above our heads. It was slow-going over the rocky floor of the gorge, and we had to ford the river dozens of times as it swung from side to side. In bays, long abandoned by the river, there were extensive jungles of willow and tamarisk; these provided delightful camp-sites, with abundant fuel for large camp-fires.

Beyond the gorge, we joined the route by which we had returned from Mustagh Ata the previous year, and for the next week or so we travelled through the typical Pamir country of wide, rounded river valleys, great stretches of grassland, lakes and ice-mountains. It was perfect country to ride through on a good pony, for over most of the way the surface was good enough to permit cantering. The pack-animals could not do more than twenty-five or thirty miles a day. I could cover this distance easily in three hours' riding, and the rest of the time I was free to spend as I chose; to idle in some pleasant spot on the way, to climb to a neighbouring hill-top and sit there for an hour or two, or to stop at a Kirghiz encampment for a bowl of milk. In the mornings, when we started, it was freezing hard, but when the sun had reached us it became pleasantly warm, though never too hot.

From the memory of days so crowded with movement and delight it is difficult to choose the highlights; for each enchanting moment was really inseparable from the whole, as is the breeze or the smell of heather from a Highland scene. At first, the mighty glaciers of the Kungur Range dominated the landscape. At Kara Kul I lay for four hours on a green meadow by the shore, the white shape of Muztagh Ata mirrored on the calm surface of the lake. At Subashi we stayed the night with our friends from Yam-bulak, and that evening while supper was being cooked I came out of their *akoi* for a stroll. The milking was nearly finished, and the sheep and goats clustered round the tents in their hundreds. In the valley it was already dusk, but across the river the huge snow-dome of the mountain, aflame in the light of the setting sun, was like molten metal against a dark-blue sky. Beyond the Ulugh Robat Pass, near one of the villages in the green Taghama Valley, we met a Kirghiz wedding procession and were invited to the wedding feast.

For five days the weather was fine, but as we reached the southern end of the Taghdumbash Pamir it broke, and beyond Dafdar we marched through a heavy and prolonged snowstorm. The little valley above Lupgaz, when we reached it, was deep in snow, so my last night in Sinkiang was spent in a bleak, cold camp. The next morning was clear again and the great peaks beyond the Mintaka Pass looked magnificent. The ponies had a struggle to get across the Pass in the new snow, but we had started early and by evening we reached a delightful grove of trees several miles below the glacier.

Then followed the part of the journey to which I had been looking forward most. I had never travelled through the Hunza Valley when the autumn colouring was at its best. I was afraid that I might now be too late; but, in fact, I had timed it to perfection. At first, where the tiny hamlets boasted only a few dozen apricots and poplars, the vivid patches of gold and red were small and comparatively rare; though, coming upon them suddenly round the corner of a gorge or high up on a vertical precipice, they were striking enough. But after two or three days, when we had travelled down to the more extensive villages, they gradually became a major part of the scene.

Ever since I first saw it in 1937, I have thought of the Hunza Valley as the ultimate manifestation of mountain grandeur. It was now eight years since I had been there and I found to my surprise that my memory had belittled rather than exaggerated its magnificence. I realized, I think, for the first time, how impossible it was to achieve anything like a full imaginative grasp of that country in a few days or weeks; but the realization was exhilarating, not overpowering. My heightened appreciation was due in part to the sudden change from the relatively gentle Pamir scenery we had just left, but in a large measure, too, to the exquisite loveliness of those autumn villages. For never do mountain forms show to such advantage as when they are set in contrast to beauty of another kind.

At five o'clock one evening I emerged from that long canyon where the Hunza River makes a right-angled sweep below Atabad. Baltit came suddenly into view: forty square miles of flaming red and gold, rising in terraces from the river to the base of the rock walls of the twenty-four thousand-foot Kanjut Peaks. In the distance down the valley Rakaposhi stood serene and clear.

THE MOUNT EVEREST RECONNAISSANCE EXPEDITION 1951

Everest 1951

THE MOUNT EVEREST
RECONNAISSANCE EXPEDITION 1951

First published by Hodder and Stoughton Limited, 1951

Contents

1 The Project *page* 595
2 The March 600
3 The Ice-fall 608
4 Exploratory Journeys 617

Maps
The route of the approach march 594
Explorations in the Everest district 609
The routes of the Gauri Sankar exploration 622

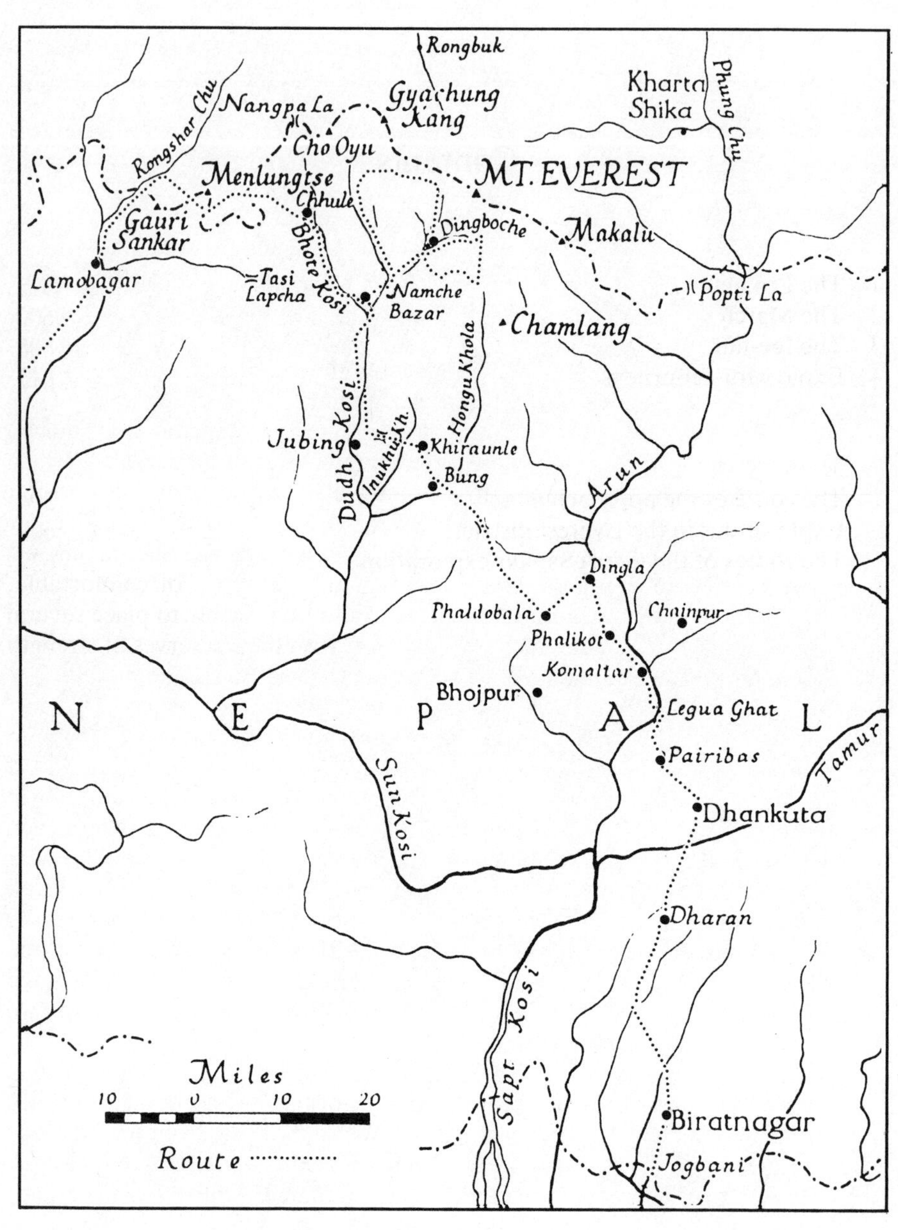

Rongbuk
Nangpa La
Gyachung Kang
Kharta Shika
Phung Chu
Rongshar Chu
Cho Oyu
Menlungtse
MT. EVEREST
Chhule
Gauri Sankar
Dingboche
Makalu
Bhote Kosi
Lamobagar
Tasi Lapcha
Namche Bazar
Popti La
Chamlang
Hongu Khola
Dudh Kosi
Jubing
Inukhu Kh.
Khiraunle
Bung
Arun
Dingla
Phaldobala
Chainpur
Phalikot
Komaltar
Bhojpur
N E P A L
Legua Ghat
Pairibas
Tamur
Sun Kosi
Dhankuta
Dharan
Sapt Kosi
Miles
10 0 10 20
Biratnagar
Route
Jogbani

CHAPTER ONE

The Project

WHEN, in 1924, Norton and Somervell so nearly reached the summit of Mount Everest, it was generally believed that the next expedition, taking advantage of the lessons they had learned, would most probably succeed. For, just as the 1922 parties, by attempting to climb the last 4,000 feet to the top in a single day, had completely under-estimated the physiological difficulties of climbing at great altitudes, so it seemed that the failure of the 1924 expedition was due to a simple, avoidable cause. That year the climbers had gone high too soon and had become involved in a series of struggles with the early spring blizzards, which had so far drained their strength that, when the time came to launch their attempts upon the summit, the climbers were already exhausted. In 1933 we were confident that, by carefully nursing the climbers and the Sherpas chosen to go high through the preliminary stages and by the use of comfortable, double-skinned tents at Camps 3 and 4, it would be possible to place several successive parties at a camp above 27,000 feet, with their reserves of strength largely unimpaired, and well able to overcome the last two thousand feet.

Once again we found that we had under-rated the resources of our opponent. We had been led by the experiences of the previous expedition to assume that at the end of May and beginning of June there would be a period of some two weeks of calm weather before the monsoon wrapped the mountain in a blanket of snow. Moreover, we had not fully realized the extent to which even a small deposit of new snow upon the rocks of the final pyramid would render them unclimbable. Our experiences in the nineteen thirties showed all too clearly that such a spell of favourable conditions immediately before the monsoon could not be relied upon. Indeed, it did not occur in any of the three years when attempts were made during that decade. In 1933 we had perhaps a fleeting chance, but both in 1936 and 1938 the monsoon was upon us before we had even established a camp on the North Col.

Even now we cannot assess the chances in any given year of meeting with a sufficiently late – or, as we used to think "normal" – monsoon to ensure favourable conditions for reaching the top. We cannot say, from the evidence we have, whether 1924 was an exceptional year, recurring perhaps only once or twice in a generation, or whether in the nineteen thirties we perhaps encountered a limited cycle of unfavourable seasons. Whatever the answer, it seemed that the problem of reaching the summit of Mount Everest from the north had been reduced to this one vital question. Three times men had climbed to more than 28,000 feet, unaided by oxygen apparatus; we believed that the climbing on the last thousand feet was no more difficult than that which had already been accomplished, but it was sufficiently difficult to demand good conditions of weather and snow; given these, there seemed to be no reason for failure, without them success would not be attained. Had it been possible, the obvious solution would have been to send out a small party each successive year until the right conditions occurred. There would have been no lack of personnel, and the modest expense would have been amply justified by physiological and other scientific research. Unfortunately, permission to do this could not be obtained from the Tibetan Government.

The attempt to climb Mount Everest, once an inspiring adventure, had become little more than a gambler's throw. To overcome this unhappy situation we had begun, as long ago as 1935, to consider the possibility of finding an alternative approach which would present a different kind of problem, one not so completely dependent for success upon the date of the monsoon.

From the mountains above the Kangshung Glacier, to the south-east, we had seen the ridge running up to the summit from the gap (the "South Col") between Everest and Lhotse. This clearly offered a much easier route up the final pyramid than that across the treacherous slabs of the North Face. It was broad and not so steep, while the dip of the strata would favour the climber. But was there any way of reaching the South Col? We had seen that the eastern side was impossible. The western side of the Col was unknown ground.

The Reconnaissance Expedition of 1921 had discovered in broad outline the geography of the south-western side of Mount Everest. The three great peaks of the massif, Everest, Lhotse (South Peak) and Nuptse (West Peak), together with their high connecting ridges, enclosed a basin which Mallory named the West Cwm. (Mallory had climbed a great deal in North Wales and for that reason he used the Welsh spelling of the word "combe".) Any approach to the South Col must lie up this hidden valley, which enclosed the whole of the southern aspect of Mount Everest.

On the 1935 Reconnaissance Expedition, when, with no intention of attempting to climb Everest, we had before us a wide field of mountain travel, our programme included an attempt to find a way to the West Cwm from the north. From the Lho La at the head of the Rongbuk Glacier, and also from a high col on the main watershed farther to the west, where we camped for two nights, we had close views of the entrance to the Cwm, a narrow defile flanked on the south by the great face of Nuptse and on the north by the western shoulder of Everest. Between these lofty portals the glacier of the Cwm poured in a huge ice-fall, a wild cascade of ice blocks, two thousand feet high. The upper part of the Cwm was screened from view by a northerly bend in the valley, so that we could not see either the South Col or the south face of Everest; nor could we find a practicable route down the precipices on the southern side of the watershed which would have enabled us to reach the foot of the ice-fall.

Thus the possibility of finding an alternative route up Mount Everest from the south-west could not be put to the test, for the only way of approaching the mountain from that side was through the valley of Sola Khumbu in Nepal.

That country had long been forbidden to Western travellers and there was, in those days, no chance of obtaining permission from the Government of Nepal to send an expedition to that area. Since the war, however, the Nepalese Government began to relax their policy of rigid exclusion, and from 1947 onwards several mountaineering and scientific expeditions – American, French and British – were permitted to visit various parts of the Nepal Himalaya. In the autumn of 1950, Dr. Charles Houston and his father, together with H. W. Tilman, paid a brief visit to the upper valleys of the Khumbu district. Houston and Tilman spent a day exploring the glacier flowing southward from the Lho La, but did not have time to reach the ice-fall.

In May, 1951, Michael Ward proposed to the Himalayan Committee (a joint committee of the Royal Geographical Society and the Alpine Club, which has handled all previous Everest Expeditions) that permission should be sought for a British expedition to go to Everest that autumn. His suggestion was energetically supported by Campbell Secord and W. H. Murray; formal permission was applied for and, on the assumption that it would be forthcoming, Murray began the preliminary work of organizing the expedition. I was in China at the time, and when I arrived home in the middle of June I had no idea of what was afoot; indeed, nothing was farther from my thoughts than taking part in a Himalayan expedition. After I had been in England for about ten days, I went to London and happened to call on Secord. He said, "Oh, you're back, are you? What are you going to do now?" I told him that I had no plans, to which he replied, "Well, you'd better lead this expedition." I said, "What expedition?" and he explained the position.

At first, I did not take the suggestion very seriously, for it seemed that, owing to the recent political disturbances in Nepal, it was unlikely that permission for an expedition would be forthcoming. But within a few days the Committee heard that, through the courtesy of the Nepalese Government and the good offices of Mr. Christopher Summerhayes, the British Ambassador at Katmandu, permission for the expedition had been granted. I found the decision to join the expedition a very difficult one to make. Having so lately emerged from Communist China, the freedom of England and the absence of suspicion, hatred and fear, were sheer delight, and the English summer a rare and treasured experience. I found it hard to leave all this and my family again almost immediately. Moreover, I had been away so long from the world of mountaineering that I doubted my value to the expedition.

On the other hand, for twenty years, ever since I had first known the Sherpas, I had longed, above all else, to visit their land of Sola Khumbu, through which the expedition would travel. I had heard so much about it from the Sherpas; indeed during our journeys together in other parts of the Himalaya and Central Asia, whenever we came upon a particularly attractive spot, they invariably said, "This is just like Sola Khumbu," and the comparison always led to a long, nostalgic discourse about their homeland. It required only an intelligent glance at the map and a little imagination to realize that their praise was not exaggerated; moreover, we had looked down into the upper valleys of Khumbu from the peaks west of Everest. Almost unknown to Western travellers, it had become, to me at least, a kind of Mecca, an ultimate goal in Himalayan exploration. So it was that I finally decided to accept the invitation to lead the expedition.

The possibility of finding a new approach to the summit of Mount Everest from the south-west had assumed a new significance to mountaineers all over the world from the time when the impending "liberation" of Tibet by the Chinese Communist armies had made the old line of approach inaccessible to citizens of Western countries. It was, however, highly improbable that such an alternative existed. No experienced mountaineer can be optimistic about the chances of finding a way up any great Himalayan peak. The vast scale of which these giants are built greatly increases the likelihood of the climber being faced by sheer impossibility – an unclimbable wall, slopes dominated by hanging glaciers, or avalanche-swept couloirs. In addition, his standard of performance is greatly reduced; the fact that heavy loads have to be carried a long way up the mountain to establish camps, the physical disabilities resulting from altitude, the disastrous consequences which threaten from bad weather – these are some of the factors which usually make it impossible for him to accept the challenge of a difficult ridge or face, or to commit himself to a spell of many hours of really hard climbing. When, as in this case, the search for a route is confined to one particular segment of the mountain, the chances of finding a practicable route are obviously still further reduced.

All that we knew of the South Face of Mount Everest and of the western side of the South Col was that they must be approached up a formidable ice-fall and through a narrow defile which was probably menaced by ice avalanches from the hanging glaciers on the immense precipices above. Beyond the defile was the unknown Cwm, whose southern containing wall, the 25,000-foot ridge connecting Lhotse with Nuptse, obscured all but the very summit of Everest from the south. We estimated that the floor of the Cwm was about 21,000 feet high, nearly 5,000 feet below the crest of the South Col. From the fact that, along the whole range, the mountains were far steeper on the southern side of the watershed than on the northern side, we inferred that the slopes below the col would not be easy. That was all we could guess. It did not present a picture upon which we could build great hopes. But the West Cwm was a freak of mountain architecture and there was no knowing what we might find there. I put the chances against our finding a practicable route at about thirty to one.

Clearly the expedition could only be a reconnaissance; moreover, the time and money at our disposal were not sufficient to organize an attempt to climb the mountain. If, despite the long odds, we found a possible route, we naturally hoped to send a further expedition the following spring to attempt it; for we still believed that, despite its many disadvantages, the spring was the only time of year to tackle the mountain. A case had been argued for making the attempt in the late autumn; that is, after the monsoon instead of before it. So far as I know, this idea had not gained the support of anyone who had been high on the mountain, but it had never been put to a practical test. There were many conflicting theories about the weather and snow conditions likely to be encountered in the autumn; there was little evidence on which to base these theories, and what evidence there was seemed equally conflicting. By visiting the mountain after the monsoon we hoped to furnish answers to some of these questions.

Preparations for the expedition had to be made in a great hurry. It was already July before I had made up my mind to go, and stores and equipment had to be ready for shipment to India by the end of that month. Before the war I used to boast that I could organize a Himalayan expedition in a fortnight. Things had changed since then. Essential materials for equipment, such as eiderdown for sleeping bags, windproof cloth and rope, were in short supply, and manufacturing firms were busy with priority orders. Whereas before the war it was possible at a moment's notice to obtain passages and cargo space on any of several ships sailing for India each week, especially in the off-season when we usually travelled, now sailings were infrequent and the ships always full. It seemed as though everyone we tried to contact was away on holiday. The problem of raising money to finance the expedition had to be solved quickly. It was a busy and confusing month, and there was little time to enjoy the summer woods at home. Fortunately, Bill Murray had done a great deal of the ground work already, and Campbell Secord allowed his house in Carlton Mews to be used as a dumping ground for stores and equipment as they accumulated. This was very hard on his wife, for the place became a sort of general office and Mrs. Secord had to bear the brunt of endless telephone calls from the press, equipment firms, applicants for a place in the party, inventors of helicopters and portable radio sets, food cranks, money lenders and members of the expedition. I remember especially the day before our stuff was due to go to the docks; nothing had been packed and we were still hopelessly involved in outside business such as arranging for equipment ordered from abroad to pass from the airport to the docks. I sent an S.O.S. to the W.V.S. to ask if they could send someone to come and pack for us. They responded promptly and worked with such efficiency that everything was packed and listed before evening.

The party had originally consisted of Bill Murray, Michael Ward, Tom Bourdillon and Alfred Tissières, one of the best-known Swiss climbers, who happened to be doing research work in Cambridge at the time. It was also hoped that Campbell Secord would be able to join the party. In its conception it was a purely private party, and, as I have said, the initiative lay with Ward, Murray and Secord. Unfortunately, in the end, neither Tissières nor Secord were able to accompany the expedition. When I was invited to take over the leadership, I stipulated that the Himalayan Committee should assume complete responsibility for financing the expedition and for all matters connected with press coverage. My reason for this was that, although private expeditions have a very great deal to recommend them, Everest expeditions attract a quite disproportionate amount of public interest, so that publicity requires a firm controlling hand. The Himalayan Committee entered into a contract with *The Times* for the publication and the syndication abroad of the official articles and dispatches dealing with the expedition. By this generous contract, *The Times* provided the bulk of the expedition's funds.

Murray and Ward sailed from Tilbury on 2nd August, 1951, taking with them all the stores and equipment. They reached Bombay on the 18th. Bourdillon and I flew to Delhi, arriving there on 19th August. Two days before

I left London a cable was received from the President of the New Zealand Alpine Club asking whether two members of the New Zealand Expedition, which was climbing in the Garhwal Himalaya that summer, might accompany our party. I also received a request from the Geological Survey of India to attach one of their officers, Dr. Dutt, to the expedition. I welcomed these suggestions.

CHAPTER TWO

The March

FROM India there are four ways of reaching Namche Bazar, the principal village in the district of Khumbu, where we proposed to make our base. The route from Darjeeling, generally used by the Sherpas, is long and very difficult during the monsoon. The route from Katmandu, though easier, is also rather long, while the cost in time and money of transporting a large quantity of baggage from India to the Nepalese capital would be considerable. By far the quickest way would be from Jainagar, the railhead north of Darbhanga in Bihar. But we were advised that it would be impossible to get from there to the foothills by lorry during the rains, while to march through the hot, swampy country would be most unpleasant. So we decided to travel from Jogbani, another railhead in North Bihar further to the east. Houston's party had gone by this route the previous year after the monsoon was over, and they had succeeded in reaching Namche in a fortnight from Jogbani.

Bourdillon and I reached Jogbani shortly before midnight on 24th August. We were met at the station by a jeep belonging to the Biratnagar Jute Mills. It was raining hard and, judging by the sodden state of the ground all round the little station, it seemed that it had been doing so for weeks. The road was so deep in mud that it took an hour to go from the station to the house of Mr. Law, the Chief Engineer of the Jute Mills, less than a mile away. This journey took us across the frontier into Nepalese territory. Mr. and Mrs. Law with Murray and Ward, who had arrived two days before, were waiting up for us. We were given a wonderful welcome in this Scottish home. The following day Colonel Proud, First Secretary of the British Embassy at Katmandu, arrived. He had been sent by the Ambassador to assist us and to accompany us as far as Dhankuta. His help was invaluable. He had brought with him Lieutenant Chandra Bahadur, an officer of the Nepalese Army, whose services had kindly been lent to the expedition.

On the 25th, too, Angtharkay arrived from Darjeeling. He is a very old friend of mine. We had been together on eight Himalayan expeditions before the war, and I had always regarded him as a man of quite outstanding character and ability. During the past few years he had set up a business in Darjeeling organizing treks in Sikkim for visitors. But he still went with major expeditions, though now as a Sirdar, or foreman. He was on the French expedition to Annapurna, and climbed to their highest camp. I had asked him to meet us in Jogbani so as to help with the transport to Namche, and later, of course, for work on the mountain. I had not seen him since 1939, when he was just a simple Sherpa porter, though a famous one, drawing the same pay as the others and carrying the same load. Now he had graduated to a different sphere. I was somewhat apprehensive of what I would find; for success tends to spoil these simple people at least as readily as it does the sophisticated. He had cut off the handsome pigtail that he used to wear and his clothes were distressingly smart, but I was relieved to find the same shy reticence and the same quiet humour that I remembered so well. There was no sign of dissipation and he looked no older; indeed, he had changed remarkably little in the last twelve years. It was curious that, in spite of his constant contact with Europeans, he had learnt practically no English.

Angtharkay had brought with him from Darjeeling twelve Sherpas, including a woman. They were all on their way to Sola Khumbu and were hoping to "work their passage" with us. We signed on four of them for the duration of the expedition and agreed to employ the others for the march at the same rates of pay as we gave to the local porters.

The next stage of our journey was a lorry drive of 30 miles to Dharan at the foot of the hills. We were told that with all the rain then falling the road would be impassable and that we would have to wait until the weather cleared. This was depressing news, for there seemed to be no reason why it should ever stop raining, though Mr. Law assured us that it would. In the meantime we were busy sorting out stores and equipment and packing them into 60-lb. loads for the march. Mr. and Mrs. Law were very kind and helped us in a great many ways, from arranging supplies of kerosene to sewing on buttons and mending socks. Another very pleasant contact we made was with Mr. B. P. Koirala, Home Minister of the Government of Nepal, and Mr. J. M. Shrinagesh, the Indian Political Adviser, who were setting out on a tour of Eastern Nepal.

On the evening of the 26th August it stopped raining and on the following morning a watery sun shone through the clouds. We set out in our hired lorry at 2.30 that afternoon. At Biratnagar, two miles away, there was an hour's delay while the driver collected supplies of petrol and tinkered with the engine. The lorry was besieged by people wanting a lift to Dharan, and by the time we left it was grossly overloaded. The road was in a deplorable state. Every few hundred yards the vehicle was brought to a standstill in deep mud, and each time we had first to dig trenches to free the wheels and then to spread bundles of grass and jute husks over the mud. It took us more than two hours to cover the first six miles. However, though it started to rain heavily again, conditions improved as we approached the hills. We reached Dharan long after dark, found a billet in an empty house and, after a long search, procured a meal in the bazaar.

The next morning we recruited coolies for the first part of the march. We found that the local practice was to pay coolies so much per seer (2 lb.) per stage. The men, therefore, preferred to carry 80-lb. loads instead of 60-lb., and we had to set about rearranging all our carefully packed baggage. While we were doing this a small boy came and asked if he could be signed on as "half a coolie." This tickled the Sherpas, and we gave him a box weighing 40 lb. He carried it so well that later I came to regret that all our porters were not boys.

These matters occupied the whole of the morning, and it was two o'clock in the afternoon before we began the first march. In a couple of miles we reached the foot of the hills. Here, as elsewhere throughout the length of the Himalayas, they rose abruptly from the plains for about 5,000 feet to the crest of the first range of foothills. We walked with our umbrellas up, for the sun was shining at last and it was very hot; but after a couple of hours we had climbed into low-hanging clouds where the air was deliciously cool and fresh. We spent the night in a small village just below the crest of the first range and started on at dawn on the 29th August. It had rained heavily all night, but now it had cleared somewhat, and as we crossed the ridge we had a glimpse of the Everest and Makalu massifs, 75 miles to the north, shining through a rift in the rain clouds. From the pass we descended 3,500 feet to the Tamur River and then climbed a similar height up the other side of the valley to Dhankuta, where we were provided with a tiny rest-house in a pleasant wood of tall pine trees. The following morning Colonel Proud started back on his journey to Jogbani.

Though we had covered a considerable distance, those first two marches had been very easy. The path was wide and well constructed, the porters had gone well and it had not rained at all during the day. So far, we had experienced nothing of the exasperation, the dismal toil of travel through the Himalayan foothills at the height of the monsoon. We soon began to suspect that it was not all going to be so easy. We had hoped that we would be able to persuade the Dharan coolies to remain with us, so that we could continue the march the very next day; but they refused and insisted on being paid off. What was worse, we had the very greatest difficulty in finding any fresh recruits. We sent the Sherpas into the bazaar and the Bara Hakim (local governor) sent *peons* into the outlying villages to engage the men. A few men arrived and agreed to go with us; but, finding that we were not ready to start, they drifted off again and disappeared. When this had happened several times, the situation began to seem desperate. By the time we had been in Dhankuta for forty-eight hours we felt as though we would never be on our way again. Various plausible but unhelpful explanations were advanced by the local authorities for the lack of coolies: a large military camp had been established nearby, and all the coolies were required to work there; owing to the recent disturbances in the country, the peasants were frightened to go far from their villages; because of the lateness of the rains, work on the land had fallen into arrears, with the result that the demand for labour was unusually heavy; no one ever travelled far during the monsoon if he could help it. Looking back, I would say that the last was the most likely explanation.

We could get curiously little information about the route ahead, and none that was reliable. We decided that a place called Dingla was to be our next objective. The country beyond that was, locally, a mere legend. Each person we asked held a different opinion as to how we should get to Dingla, while estimates of the time it would take varied between one day and a week.

It is remarkable at such times how, when the situation seems hopeless, all at once a solution presents itself. At about noon on the 1st September we suddenly found that there were no fewer than 17 coolies who were willing, though somewhat half-heartedly, to talk business. We required 25; but Angtharkay urged that we should start at once with the 17 before they had time to change their minds, and that he should follow with the remaining eight when he could get them. I was reluctant to split the party at such an early age, but it was obviously the wisest course to follow. Furthermore, the news that the expedition had moved on would certainly have a quick psychological effect upon the local carriers, who would immediately begin to think that they were missing a good thing.

Before starting, we went to say goodbye to the Bara Hakim and to thank him for his help and hospitality. He had just received a message from Jogbani to say that the two New Zealanders, E. P. Hillary and H. E. Riddiford, had arrived there. This was good news, for until then we had had no word of their whereabouts. We sent messages back to them and started on our way. In the evening we reached a ridge, some 6,000 feet high, overlooking the vast basin of the Arun River, where we spent the night in the little village of Paribas. Angtharkay arrived early the following morning. As we had expected, he had found no difficulty, once we had gone, in recruiting the remaining eight porters. Our march that day took us 5,000 feet down to the banks of the Arun.

At dawn on 3rd September we walked along a wide shore to a place called Legua Ghat, where there is a primitive ferry. A light mist hung low over the great river: this began to disperse as soon as the sun was up and we saw, far away up the valley, the gleam of snow peaks. The ferry consisted of a tree trunk hollowed out to make a clumsy canoe. It had a crew of three, two paddlers forward and a steersman aft, and could take seven passengers at one time, or an equivalent weight of baggage. As soon as the boat was cast off from the bank it was swept down by the current at an alarming speed. The paddlers worked furiously to get their frail craft across the river with a minimum loss of distance, for after each crossing it had to be towed laboriously back along the shore. The river was about 300 yards wide, and though there were no rapids for a mile or so downstream which allowed a substantial margin of error, the operation required considerable skill. It took from 7 a.m. until 2 p.m. to complete the ten double crossings necessary to transport ourselves, our coolies and our baggage across the river.

We were now less than 1,000 feet above sea level, and when we resumed the march that afternoon the heat was intense. There was no clearly defined route across the vast forested slopes of the valley. We made our way through steep rocky nullahs along a series of tiny tracks, which, branching and intersecting, connect the scattered hamlets. Often the tracks were so obscure that we lost them. The porters, carrying 80-lb. loads, went very slowly; even so, their speeds varied a great deal and it was impossible to keep everyone together. Thus, with such a diversity of tracks we soon lost contact with some sections of the party. At nightfall on 3rd September we reached a hamlet called Komaltar. Though it was only 4½ miles in a direct line from the ferry, it had taken nearly five hours to cover the distance. Nine of the local porters bivouacked in a stream-bed half a mile short of the hamlet and came in early next morning. The rest failed to turn up and, after sending back in search of them without success, we concluded that they had taken a different route. They reached Dingla more than a day after us.

For seven or eight miles we kept fairly close to the banks of the Arun, sometimes following a stretch of shore. The tropical forest and the dense undergrowth, the birds, the brilliantly coloured locusts, butterflies and other insects were typical of the deep river valleys of the Eastern Himalaya. We wore only shorts and sandshoes, with umbrellas to protect our heads from the heat. Whenever we came to a safe backwater, we used to plunge straight in and sit down for a few moments. The water was deliciously cool, though the refreshing effect did not last long. Even the Sherpas, who are afraid of water and who normally never immerse their bodies, began, at first timidly, then with great zest, to follow suit; all except poor Lhakpa, the woman, who looked on with obvious envy.

On the afternoon of 4th September we climbed 3,000 feet up through lovely country to a cluster of villages called Phalikot, and on the 5th, a relatively short march took us to Dingla, a large, scattered village perched among woods and terraced fields on a high ridge which commanded sweeping views across the Arun basin and, when the weather was clear, of the great snow ranges to the north.

At Dingla we again had great difficulty in recruiting porters. The Dhankuta men had been engaged as far as Dingla and refused to go any farther. We were delayed for four days. On 8th September, Hillary and Riddiford arrived. We now required 40 local coolies, for, besides the baggage brought by the New Zealanders, we had bought a quantity of rice and flour in case of a possible shortage in the country beyond. At last, on the evening of the 9th, after long and exasperating negotiations, enough men had been engaged. We gave them an advance of pay, and they promised to be ready to start soon after dawn the next day. But the next morning it was raining very heavily and they did not come until noon. However, after a couple of hours of tumult and confusion, we managed to allot them their loads and get them off.

Our next objective was the Salpa Bhanjyang, a 12,000-foot pass to the north-west leading over from the Arun basin to that of the Hongu Khola. The direct route was impassable owing to some steep mountain streams which were in spate and had swept away the bridges crossing them. This meant that we had to make a long detour to the south-west so as to reach the crest of the high watershed ridge, which we then followed to the pass. The detour cost us several extra days' marching. It was particularly annoying to discover that, if we had known this before, we could have reached the ridge much more quickly by travelling direct to it from Dhankuta via Bojhpur.

On 10th September we made our way along the path leading towards Bojhpur. This was easy and fairly level, but we had started so late and the porters went so slowly that by nightfall we had only reached the village of Phaldobala, four miles away. The next morning the porters refused to go on, saying that their loads were too heavy. According to the local custom, we had contracted to pay them by weight, and for this reason they had in the first place chosen to carry 80 lb. each rather than 60 lb. This meant that we had once again to rearrange all the loads and also to recruit more porters to carry the surplus. These operations, made no easier by the rain, occupied the whole of that day.

On the march to Dingla it had rained mostly at night and the days had been fine. This happy arrangement could not be expected to last, and by now it was raining for most of each day. We set off again on the morning of the 12th and climbed to the crest of the high, narrow watershed ridge. For three days we made our way slowly along it in a northerly direction, unable to see anything of our surroundings because of alternating spells of heavy rain and equally drenching Scotch mist. After a while we lost all sense of direction and distance; it was a curious sensation, blindly following this narrow crest, the ground on either hand falling steeply into the silent, forested depths below, while rocky peaks loomed, one after another, ahead. The undergrowth was infested with leeches; on a single twig a score of the creatures could be seen, stiff and erect, like a cluster of little black sticks, ready to attach themselves to our legs and arms and clothing as we brushed past.

The way consisted of a continuous series of long, steep climbs and descents. It was very hard work for the porters, for the track was slimy with mud and they slipped constantly, losing their balance under the shifting weight of their sodden loads. We spent the nights in little cowherds' shelters, mostly deserted, which were interspersed along the ridge. They kept out most of the rain, and fires lit inside discouraged the leeches from entering. Without them our lot would have been a great deal worse. One evening at sunset the mists slid down below the ridge, and for a while we saw, across a wide gulf of cloud, the great range of ice peaks.

At the Salpa Bhanjyang, which we reached on the morning of the 15th, we joined the route used by the Sherpas travelling between Khumbu and Darjeeling. Angtharkay told me that when he was last there, in December, 1947, it was so deep in snow that he had taken three days to cross it and that several Sherpas had died attempting to do so. It was a great help at last to have someone in the party who knew the way. From the pass we descended steeply for 7,000 feet to the Hongu Khola. At the village of Bung, on the farther side of the valley, we heard that the bridge across the next big river, the Inukhu Khola, had been washed away, and we had to choose between making a detour of three days to the south or attempting to build another bridge ourselves. We decided on the latter alternative.

From Bung we crossed another pass, about 10,600 feet high, to Khiraunle, which stands about 1,000 feet above the Inukhu Khola. Here we were told that several villages in the neighbourhood had been smitten by an epidemic of some virulent disease which killed its victims in four days. From a description of the symptoms, it seemed probable that it was bubonic plague. There was a village straight across the valley where 50 people had died during the past fortnight. The intervening gorge was so narrow that, though the place was the best part of a day's march away, we could with the naked eye see people moving about in it. We studied their movements with field glasses and saw that they were engaged in some activity which the Sherpas declared was a burial ceremony.

But the village of Khiraunle also provided some less depressing news. The local people were engaged in building a temporary bridge across the Inukhu Khola to take the place of the one that had been washed away, and this would be ready early the following morning. That day was the worst of the march. Heavy rain fell almost continuously. A way had to be cut through the dense undergrowth to enable the porters to climb down the precipitous slopes of the gorge to the point where the new bridge was built. This was only a few hundred yards downstream from the old bridge, but the intervening distance was impassable along the river bed. The new structure was a very flimsy affair, built in two sections, each spanning a formidable cataract and connecting one bank of the river with a central island. Each section was composed of two slender tree trunks, lashed together with green bark, and a bamboo handrail that would not have withstood a pressure of 10 lb. The river was rising rapidly, and before everyone was across, waves were splashing over the logs. Not long afterwards both sections of the bridge had been swept away, leaving the bamboo handrails flapping crazily in the spray.

We then had to climb a steep cliff to regain the track. In doing this we disturbed a hornets' nest. Not having been attacked myself, I was mystified by the ensuing confusion and panic until the party had reassembled on the track, 300 feet above the river. Two of the coolies had been stung so severely (one claimed seven stings) that they were already suffering from acute fever. Several others had swollen faces and eyes, while one man had disappeared. His load was located near the hornets' nest, and we thought that he had fallen down the cliff in his attempt to escape. I sent Angtharkay on to a village 2,000 feet above to get help, while Bourdillon, Ward and I climbed down the cliffs again and searched along the shore for the missing man, expecting to find his broken corpse. He had not fallen, however, and eventually he was found in a high fever sheltering in a cave. All the victims of this curious encounter recovered overnight.

The next day, the 19th, we crossed another 10,000-foot pass which took us into the valley of the Dudh Kosi. On the evening of 20th September the weather suddenly cleared and the monsoon seemed to have ended. After ten days of perpetual rain and mist, the clear air and warm sunlight were delicious. The forest was no longer oppressive, but light and green; the waterfalls sparkled as they cascaded down the precipices flanking the wide valley, threads of silver hanging from the ice spires 12,000 feet above our heads.

We were now in the country of the Sherpas, and a form of "Channel fever" animated Angtharkay and his companions. At each village through which we passed they were greeted by a crowd of their friends who took them off to some house to be fed and wined, to the accompaniment of eager chatter and full-blooded laughter. Of course, we came in for our share of this hospitality, which doubtless contributed to the magic of the scene. I began to wonder if, when eventually we reached our objective, any of us would be in a fit state to climb.

The valley split into two narrow gorges. The path, by a remarkable series of log platforms and ladders built in the cliff, followed the right-hand branch for half a mile, the lovely snow peak of Taweche framed between the vertical sides of the canyon, then climbed, zigzag, for 2,000 feet to the intervening ridge. Here, in a little fold in the mountainside, was Namche Bazar, 12,200 feet above sea level. We arrived there in the afternoon of 22nd September. The journey from Jogbani, which we had expected to cover in a fortnight, had taken us nearly four weeks.

Namche Bazar, which consists of about sixty houses, is the most important village in the district of Khumbu, for it is the last place of any size on the principal route from Eastern Nepal to Tibet, and is therefore a centre of trade between the two countries. It is the small metropolis of the Sherpas, who have close connections, both commercial and religious, with Tibet. They are themselves of Tibetan origin and are indistinguishable from the people of the great plateau to the north of the main range. They wear the same kind of clothes and have the same religious beliefs and customs, and, though they have a language of their own, they can all speak Tibetan. They lead a semi-nomadic life; each family owns a house and land in several villages at different altitudes and they move *en masse* from one village to another according to the seasons, to sow or harvest their fields of potatoes and barley. For this reason, it is common to find a village temporarily deserted while the inhabitants are working at another at a different level. They graze their sheep and goats and yaks in the high valleys, often several days' march from their villages.

We were given a great welcome in Namche, where we spent two days sorting out our stores and equipment and arranging for supplies of local food. I met many old friends from former expeditions, most of whom brought flagons of *chang* and stood by urging us to drink. We were provided with a house. Nearly all Sherpa houses are built on the same pattern. They are oblong, two-storied stone buildings, with carved wooden window frames and lattice windows. The front door leads into a dark stable, through which one has to grope, pushing past the oxen or yaks, to a steep wooden ladder leading to a short, narrow passageway on the upper floor. A right-hand turn at the top of the ladder leads to a latrine, a small dark room, with a hole in the middle of the floor which is otherwise deeply covered with grass or pine needles. The other end of the passage leads to the living-room, which occupies three-quarters of the upper floor. The alcove between the walled-in ladderway and the front wall is used as a kitchen. The fireplace is set on the floor, and an iron frame is used for holding the cooking pots above the fire. Beyond this is a couch reserved for the women. In the front wall to the right of the fireplace there is a line of windows. Beneath this a platform raised about a foot above the floor is covered with carpets and rugs. Here the men sit, crosslegged, behind a low wooden table. The seat of honour is at the end of the platform nearest the fire. The opposite wall, devoid of windows, is lined with shelves, full of great copper basins, wooden bowls, china cups, bamboo churns, and other cooking and eating utensils. The far end of the room is cluttered with bags of grain, ropes, wooden ploughs, mattocks and other farm implements. Beds are made up on the floor as they are required. Some houses belonging to well-to-do people have additional rooms furnished as small Buddhist shrines.

CHAPTER THREE

The Ice-fall

WE left Namche on 25th September, taking with us supplies for 17 days. In that time we hoped to make a thorough reconnaissance of the great ice-fall; if possible, to climb it into the West Cwm and to see whether or not there was a practicable route from there to the South Col. If we found a route we would then send down for more supplies, carry a camp into the Cwm and climb as far as possible towards the Col. If, as we expected, there proved to be no practicable route, we would then undertake an extensive exploration of the main range, the southern side of which was almost entirely unknown. We had engaged another five Sherpas, whom we equipped for work on the mountain, bringing the number up to ten. One of them was Angtharkay's young brother, Angphuter, whom I had last met in 1938, when as a lad of fourteen he had come across to Rongbuk from Namche and had carried a load to Camp 3 (21,000 feet) on Everest. Another fifteen men had been engaged to carry our baggage and supplies to our Base Camp at the head of the Khumbu Glacier.

We followed a path across the steep mountainside, 2,000 feet above the gorge of the Dudh Kosi, from which we had climbed three days before. On the way we met a very old friend of mine, Sen Tensing, whom I first met in 1935, when he had come across to Tibet to join the reconnaissance expedition. His peculiar appearance in the clothes we gave him had earned him the name of the "Foreign Sportsman". In the years that followed he had been my constant companion in various parts of the Himalaya and Karakoram. In 1936 I had taken him to Bombay, an adventure which he evidently still regarded as one of the highlights of his career. He had heard news of our approach while herding his yaks in a valley, three days' march away, and had hurried down to meet us, bringing gifts of *chang*, butter and curds. He came along with us, and for the rest of the day he regaled me with memories of the past.

After some miles the path descended into the gorge. We crossed the river by a wooden bridge and climbed steeply through the forest for 2,000 feet to the monastery of Thyangboche, built on the crest of an isolated ridge dominating the junction of the Dudh Kosi and the large tributary valley, the Imja Khola. The ridge was shrouded in mist that evening, and as it was growing dark when we reached the monastery we saw nothing of our surroundings. The monks welcomed us, and we found that a large Tibetan tent had been pitched for us on a meadow nearby.

During the past few days we had become familiar with the extraordinary beauty of the country, but this did not lessen the dramatic effect of the scene which confronted us when we awoke next morning. The sky was clear; the grass of the meadow, starred with gentians, had been touched with frost which sparkled in the early sunlight; the meadow was surrounded by quiet woods of fir, tree-juniper, birch and rhododendron silvered with moss. Though the deciduous trees were still green, there were already brilliant splashes of autumn colour in the undergrowth. To the south the forested slopes fell steeply to the Dudh Kosi, the boom of the river now silenced by the profound depth of the gorge. To the north-east, 12 miles away across the valley of the Imja Khola, stood the Nuptse-Lhotse ridge, with the peak of Everest appearing behind. But even this stupendous wall, nowhere less than 25,000 feet throughout its five-mile length, seemed dwarfed by the slender spires of fluted ice that towered all about us, near and utterly inaccessible.

We stayed in this enchanting spot till noon and visited the monastery during the morning. With its cloistered courtyard, its dark rooms smelling of joss sticks

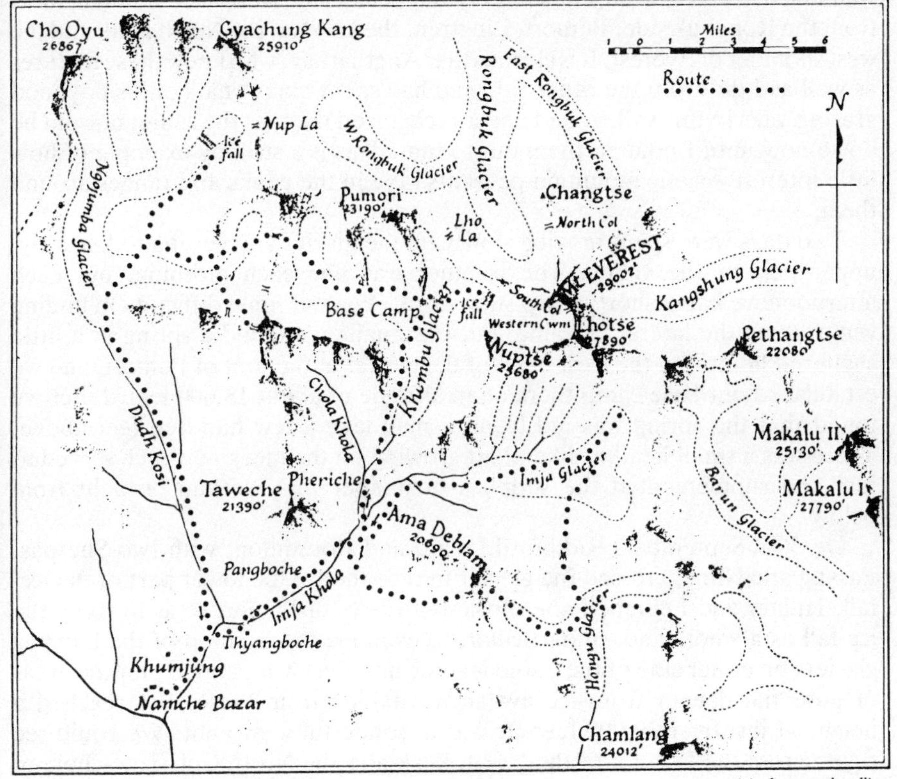

original map and spelling

and the rancid butter used for prayer lights, its terrifying effigies, its tapestries and its holy books bound between boards, it resembled most Tibetan monasteries in all save its setting. In the centre of the main room or shrine there were two thrones, one for the Abbot of Thyangboche, the other for the Abbot of Rongbuk. At that time the former was away on a visit to his colleague on the northern side of the great mountain, Chomolungma (Everest). Hanging in one of the windows of the courtyard, we were amused to find an oxygen cylinder. This had evidently been retrieved from the East Rongbuk Glacier by the Sherpas of one of the early Everest expeditions. It is now used as a gong which is sounded each evening at five o'clock as a signal for all the women who happen to be there to leave the monastery.

From Thyangboche the way led gently downwards through the woods and across the Imja Khola at a point where the river plunges as a waterfall into a deep abyss, overhung by gnarled and twisted trees with long beards of moss waving in the spray. Beyond the village of Pangboche we left the forest behind and entered highland country of heath and coarse grass. We spent the night of the 26th at Pheriche, a grazing village then deserted, and on the morning of the 27th we turned into the Lobujya Khola, the valley which contains the Khumbu Glacier. As we climbed into the valley we saw at its head the line of the main watershed. I recognized immediately the peaks and saddles so familiar to us from the Rongbuk side: Pumori, Lingtren, the Lho La, the North Peak and the west shoulder of Everest. It is curious that Angtharkay, who knew these features as well as I did from the other side and had spent many years of his boyhood grazing yaks in this valley, had never recognized them as the same; nor did he do so now until I pointed them out to him. This is a striking example of how little interest Asiatic mountain peasants take in the peaks and ranges around them.

Two days were spent moving slowly up the glacier and getting to know the upper part of the valley. The weather was fine each morning, but each afternoon we had a short, sharp snowstorm. We had some difficulty in finding water along the lateral moraine, but eventually we found a spring in a little sheltered hollow on the west bank of the glacier at the foot of Pumori, and we established our base camp there at an altitude of about 18,000 feet. Later we found that the spring was fed from a small lake a few hundred feet above. There was a small heather-like plant growing on the moraine which served as fuel and supplemented the supplies of juniper that we had brought from below.

On 30th September, Riddiford, Ward and Bourdillon, with two Sherpas, Pasang and Nima, crossed the glacier to reconnoitre the lower part of the ice-fall. Hillary and I climbed one of the buttresses of Pumori so as to study the ice-fall as a whole and, in particular, to examine the position of the hanging glaciers on either side of the gorge leading into the Cwm, and to plot the areas of potential danger from ice avalanches falling from these. We reached a height of just over 20,000 feet. It was a wonderful viewpoint. We could see right across the Lho La to the North Peak and the North Col. The whole of the north-west face of Everest was visible, and with our powerful binoculars we could follow every step of the route by which all attempts to climb the mountain had been made. How strange it seemed to be looking at all those well-remembered features from this new angle, and after so long an interval of time and varied experience; the little platform at 25,700 feet where we had spent so many uncomfortable nights, Norton's Camp 6 at the head of the north-east spur, the Yellow Band and the grim overhanging cliffs of the Black Band, the Second Step and the Great Couloir. They were all deep in powder snow as when I had last seen them in 1938. Straight across from where we stood, Nuptse looked superb, a gigantic pyramid of terraced ice.

But the most remarkable and unexpected aspect of the view was that we could see right up to the head of the West Cwm, the whole of the west face of Lhotse, the South Col and the slopes leading up to it. Indeed, a view from the interior of the Cwm itself could hardly have shown us more. We estimated that the floor of the Cwm at its head was nearly 23,000 feet, about 2,000 feet higher than we had expected. From there we could see that there was a perfectly straightforward route up the face of Lhotse to about 25,000 feet, whence, it seemed, a traverse could be made to the South Col. This long traverse would only be feasible in good snow conditions, and at present conditions were obviously anything but good.

The sudden discovery of a practicable route from the West Cwm to the South Col was most exciting. But we had come here to study the ice-fall, and this occupation soon sobered our spirits. The total height of this frozen cataract was about 2,000 feet. A rough transverse corridor divided it into two equal sections. The glacier descended from the Cwm in a left-hand spiral, so that the lower section of the ice-fall was facing our viewpoint while the upper half was largely in profile. With the field glasses we picked up two figures on the lower part. From their movements we recognized them, even at that distance, as Riddiford and Pasang. Of the others there was no sign. We heard later that they had taken a different route across the lower glacier and had been forced to turn back by a mass of ice pinnacles before reaching the foot of the ice-fall. Riddiford and Pasang had made splendid progress, though they were obviously having to work very hard in the soft snow. By two o'clock they had reached a point about four-fifths of the way up the lower section. Here they stayed for an hour and then returned.

Such excellent progress by a party of only two at the very first essay was in itself most encouraging. But from where we were standing, it looked as though the corridor above them was in danger of being swept throughout its length by ice avalanches falling from a great line of hanging glaciers on the left-hand wall of the gorge; it looked, indeed, as though the surface of the corridor was composed entirely of avalanche debris. The right-hand side of the lower ice-fall and of the corridor were clearly menaced from a mass of hanging glaciers in that direction, while our profile view of the upper ice-fall made it look very ugly. There was an easy way round the upper ice-fall to the left, but this was obviously a death-trap.

One of the many reasons why an attempt upon a great Himalayan peak offers so very much less chance of success than climbing a mountain of Alpine size is that a great part of the route has to be traversed again and again by parties of laden men carrying supplies to the higher camps. All objective dangers must be judged from this standpoint. The risk, say, of walking for ten minutes under an unstable ice-tower, which might be accepted by a party of two or three unladen mountaineers, is obviously increased a hundred-fold in the case of large parties of heavily laden men passing over the same ground dozens of times. The rules of mountaineering must be rigidly observed.

It now seemed that we would be faced with a most difficult decision: to abandon this wonderful new route to the summit of Everest that had appeared like a vision, this chance that we had scarcely dared to hope for, not because the way to it was beyond our powers, but because on a small section of the approach the party, and particularly the Sherpas, must repeatedly be exposed to the risk, however slight at each individual exposure, of extermination.

When we met Riddiford in camp that evening he was much more optimistic about the difficulties on the upper part of the ice-fall, but he had not been in a position to judge the avalanche danger. On the following day (1st October), while Bourdillon and Angtharkay repeated our visit to the Pumori ridge and climbed to a point some 300 feet higher, Hillary and I made a reconnaissance from another angle. This time we went up to the head of the glacier and climbed again to about 20,000 feet on a ridge of the peak bounding the Lho La on the west. From here, although we could not see into the Cwm, we had a much better view of the upper part of the ice-fall and of the corridor. We saw that, at this time of year at any rate, the avalanches from the left swept rather less than half the length of the corridor and that a crossing made at about its centre would be reasonably safe. We could also trace a good route through the upper part of the ice-fall.

On 2nd October, Riddiford, Hillary, Bourdillon and I, with three Sherpas (Pasang, Dannu and Utsering), took a light camp up to the foot of the ice-fall with the intention of making a concentrated attempt to climb from there into the West Cwm. At this time Murray and Ward were both still suffering from the effects of altitude and remained at the base camp for further acclimatization. The next day the weather was bad. It snowed gently most of the day and we stayed in our tents. The air about us was absolutely calm. At about ten o'clock we heard a dull roar which sounded like an Underground railway train. At first we thought it was a distant avalanche somewhere high up in the Cwm. We were quite accustomed to the thunder of these, falling intermittently all around us, from Nuptse, from the great ice-cliffs of the Lho La and from the ridges of Pumori. As a rule, the noise did not last more than a minute or two at a time. When, after a quarter of an hour, this distant roar was still maintained, we began to think that somewhere far away an entire mountainside must be collapsing. However, after an hour, even this theory seemed hardly tenable, and eventually we came to the conclusion that it must be caused by a mighty wind blowing across the Lho La and over the ridges of Everest and Nuptse. It went on throughout the day. No breeze ruffled the canvas of our tents.

The morning of the 4th was fine and very cold. We started soon after it was light. As we had anticipated, one of the difficulties of working on the ice-fall, particularly at this time of year, was the fact that the sun reached it so late in the day. At first, we were moving over hard ice, but as soon as we reached the ice-fall we were up to our knees in soft snow. Our feet became very cold, and once during the morning Hillary and Riddiford had to remove their boots, which were designed for their summer expedition and were only large enough for two pairs of socks, to have their feet massaged back to life. With Riddiford's tracks to follow, we had no difficulty in finding our way through the maze of crevasses and ice-walls. After 3½ hours' steady going, we reached his farthest point. Here Bourdillon, who was also still suffering a good deal from the effects of altitude, decided to stop and await our return. The place was just beside a prominent ice-tower which was thereafter known as "Tom's Serac". As the sun was now up, he would be able to keep warm enough.

Indeed, our trouble was now exactly the reverse. With the scorching glare of the sun on the fresh snow and the stagnant air among the ice-cliffs, it was rather like working in front of a furnace. This, combined with the altitude, very soon drained our energy and robbed all movement of pleasure. We shed all our upper garments except our shirts, but even so we poured with sweat, and before long our panting produced a tormenting thirst. The going now became far more complicated and laborious. Threading our way through a wild labyrinth of ice walls, chasms and towers, we could rarely see more than 200 feet ahead. The snow was often hip-deep, so that even with so many to share the labour of making the trail, progress from point to point was very slow. The choice of one false line alone cost us an hour of fruitless toil.

But technically the climbing was not difficult, and even if it had been we had plenty of time for the job. By the middle of the afternoon we seemed to be approaching the top of the ice-fall. We had decided to turn back not later than four o'clock in order to reach camp by six, when it would be getting too dark to see. Even that was running it rather fine, since it did not allow for accidents, such as the breaking of a snow bridge, and to become involved in such a complication after dark would be to run considerable risk of frostbite.

From the last line of seracs we looked across a deep trough to a level crest of ice marking the point where the glacier of the Cwm took its first plunge into the ice-fall, like the smooth wave above a waterfall. The trough was really a wide crevasse, partly choked by huge ice blocks, some of which appeared none too stable. Crossing it was the most delicate operation we had encountered.

By 3.50 we reached the final slope beyond the trough, less than 100 feet below the crest, from which we expected to have a clear view along the gently sloping glacier of the Cwm. We had to climb this diagonally to the right, so as to avoid a vertical brow of ice directly above. Pasang, whose turn it was, took over the lead; Riddiford followed and I came next. When we were on the slope it became obvious that the snow was most unstable and must be treated with great caution. By this time Pasang had advanced about 60 feet. Suddenly the surface began to slide downwards, breaking into blocks as it went. Pasang, who was at the upper edge of the break, managed with great skill to dive over it and ram his ice axe into the snow above. I was only a few yards from Hillary, who had a firm anchorage on an ice block at the beginning of the slope, and I was able without much difficulty to scramble off the moving slope back to him. Riddiford went down with the slope, and was left suspended between Pasang and me, while the avalanche slid silently into the trough. It was a nasty little incident, which might with less luck have had rather unpleasant consequences.

It was now high time to retreat. Going down was, of course, almost effortless compared with the labour of coming up. We had the deep trail to follow and we could jump or glissade down the innumerable little cliffs, each of which had cost a great deal of time and hard work to climb. It was after 5.30 when we reached Bourdillon, who had had a longer wait than he had bargained for, and was by now getting both cold and anxious. Soon after we had started down, the ice-fall became enveloped in mist. Later, this broke behind us and we saw, high above the darkening Cwm, the north face of Nuptse, a golden tracery of ice lit by the setting sun. We reached camp as it was getting dark, very tired after a strenuous day.

We were well satisfied with this reconnaissance. It was rather disappointing at the last moment to be denied a view into the Cwm from the top of the ice-fall, though in fact it would not have shown us much more than we had seen already. But we had climbed practically the whole of the ice-fall in a single day, despite abominable snow conditions and the fact that for the largest and most difficult part we had been working our way over entirely new ground. In time the route could certainly be greatly improved, and the climb would then be done in half the time and with less than half the effort. We thought that the snow conditions would probably improve, but even if they did not, the final slope could certainly be climbed and safeguarded by suspending lifelines from above. Finally, at this time of year at least, the route seemed to be reasonably free from the menace of ice avalanches. We had little doubt that, with a few days' work, we could construct a safe packing route up the ice-fall into the West Cwm.

We decided, however, to wait for a fortnight before attempting to do this. There were three reasons for this decision. The first was to allow time for snow conditions on the ice-fall to improve. Secondly, we had seen that there was still an enormous amount of monsoon snow lying on the upper slopes of Lhotse and Everest which would make it impossible to climb far towards the South Col, to say nothing of the possible risk of large snow avalanches falling into the Cwm from above. While we knew that at altitudes of 23,000 feet and above this snow would not consolidate, we had reason to believe that by the beginning of November a great deal of it would have been removed by the north-westerly winds which were already becoming established. Finally, half the party were badly in need of acclimatization before they could undertake any serious work even in the ice-fall. We spent the fortnight making journeys into the unexplored country to the west and south.

On 19th October, Hillary and I, who had been working together during this fortnight, returned to the Base Camp on the Khumbu Glacier. We had expected the others to get back on the same date, but they did not arrive until nearly a week later. On the 20th and 21st we took a camp to the old site at the foot of the ice-fall. This time we brought with us a large 12-man double-skinned dome tent designed for the Arctic. It was well worth the labour required to level a sufficiently large area of the ice surface on which to pitch it, for, after the tiny mountain tents we had been using hitherto, it was positively luxurious, and, having more room, we found it a great deal easier to get off to a really early start in the morning. On the 22nd we started work on the ice-fall. Snow conditions had improved slightly, but a number of new crevasses had opened up across our former route, and these caused us a little trouble to negotiate. However, by the end of the first day's work we had made a solid and completely safe route up as far as "Tom's Serac". Near this we marked out a site for a light camp from which to work on the upper part of the ice-fall, but we decided that for the present we would continue to work from our comfortable camp below.

On the 23rd we started early, taking with us Angtharkay and Utsering. It was a glorious morning. With every step of the way prepared, we climbed without effort, breathing no faster than on a country walk at home, and reached "Tom's Serac" in one hour and twenty minutes. We paused there for a brief rest that we hardly needed, while the sun climbed above the great Nuptse-Lhotse ridge to quicken the frozen world about us. We were in a mood of exultant confidence, for we expected that very day to enter the great Cwm.

But immediately above the Serac we ran into difficulties. A broad crevasse had opened across our former route, and it took us an hour and a half and a lot of very hard work to find a way across it. This check, though a salutary warning against over-confidence, was not serious, and it was not until we were over the crevasse that the real trouble began. Here, about one hundred yards from the Serac, we found that a tremendous change had taken place. Over a wide area the cliffs and towers that had been there before had been shattered as though by an earthquake, and now lay in a tumbled ruin. This had evidently been caused by a sudden movement of the main mass of the glacier which had occurred some time during the last fortnight. It was impossible to avoid the sober reflection that if we had persisted with the establishment of a line of communication through the ice-fall and if a party had happened to be in the area at the time, it was doubtful whether any of them would have survived. Moreover, the same thing might happen on other parts of the ice-fall.

With regard to our immediate problem, however, we hoped that the collapse of the ice had left the new surface with a solid foundation, though it was so broken and alarming in appearance. Very gingerly, prodding with our ice-axes at every step, with 100 feet of rope between each man, we ventured across the shattered area. The whole thing felt very unsound, but it was difficult to tell whether the instability was localized around the place one was treading or whether it applied to the area as a whole. Hillary was ahead, chopping his way through the ice blocks, when one of these, a small one, fell into a void below. There was a prolonged roar and the surface on which we stood began to shudder violently. I thought it was about to collapse, and the Sherpas, somewhat irrationally perhaps, flung themselves to the ground. In spite of this alarming experience, it was not so much the shattered area that worried us as the part beyond, where the cliffs and seracs were riven by innumerable new cracks which seemed to threaten a further collapse. We retreated to the sound ice below and attempted to find a less dangerous route. Any extensive movement to the left would have brought us under fire from the hanging glaciers in that direction. We explored the ground to the right, but here we found that the area of devastation was far more extensive. It was overhung, moreover, by a line of extremely unstable seracs.

We returned to camp in a very different frame of mind from the joyous mood in which we had climbed the lower part of the ice-fall only a few hours before. It seemed obvious that, though it might be a permissible risk for a party of unladen mountaineers, working on long ropes and taking every available precaution, to attempt the ice-fall, and even this was doubtful, we would not be justified in trying to climb it with a party of laden porters whose movements are always difficult to control. It looked as though, after all, we were to be faced with the decision which we had dreaded three or four weeks before: to abandon the attempt to reach the Cwm, not because the way was difficult, but because of a danger, which by the very nature of its underlying causes was impossible to assess with any certainty. In this case, however, it did not mean the total abandonment of the route; for the condition of ice-falls is subject to considerable seasonal variation, and it was not unreasonable to expect much better conditions in the spring than in the autumn. Nevertheless, it was a bitter disappointment not to be able to proceed with our plan of carrying a camp through into the Cwm and making a close examination of the route to the South Col. We agreed, however, to defer the final decision until we had made another reconnaissance of the ice-fall with the whole party.

The following day we again climbed the ridge near the Lho La. The view was not very encouraging, for we could see no way of avoiding the shattered area, which was in fact a belt stretching right across the glacier; though the upper part of the ice-fall above the corridor, so far as we could see, was undisturbed. On the 26th the rest of the party arrived back at the Base Camp, and on the 27th we all climbed the ridge of Pumori from which Hillary and I had first looked into the West Cwm on 30th September. We saw that a certain amount of monsoon snow had been removed by the north-west wind from the peak of Everest, though the north face of the mountain was still in an unclimbable condition. There was no apparent change in the snow conditions inside the Cwm, on Lhotse or on the South Col.

That evening we reoccupied the camp below the ice-fall, and on October 28th all six of us, together with Angtharkay, Pasang and Nima, set out for the ice-fall once more. Our chief object was that the others should examine the situation for themselves so that we could come to a united decision; though Hillary and I, too, were anxious to have another look at it. We arrived at the shattered area by the time the sun reached us. Only minor changes had taken place in the past five days, and this encouraged us, with great care, to cross it and make our way over the delicately poised seracs beyond. Pasang and Angtharkay made no secret of their apprehension and constantly pointed out to me that it was no place to take laden men. Beyond the corridor we found that the upper ice-fall was in a fairly stable condition, only one serac having collapsed across our former route. By ten o'clock we reached the final wall dominating the ice-fall. The steep slopes below this were in the same dangerous condition as they had been at the beginning of the month; but a fin of ice had become detached from the wall, and while other routes were being explored, Bourdillon succeeded in cutting steps up this, thus enabling us to reach the top of the wall. This was a fine effort, for it involved cutting his way through a deep layer of unstable snow into the ice beneath. By keeping to the edge of the fin, he was able to avoid any risk of a snow avalanche, but, as the whole thing overhung a profound chasm into which it might collapse, it was as well to avoid having more than one man on it at a time.

We now stood above the ice-fall, on the lip of the West Cwm, and we could look up the gently sloping glacier between the vast walls of Everest and Nuptse to its head. But we soon found that we had by no means overcome all the difficulties of entry into this curious sanctuary. A little way farther on a vast crevasse split the glacier from side to side, and there were indications of others equally formidable beyond. To cross these in their present state would have taken many days of hard work and a good deal of ingenuity, and unless we could carry a camp up to this point we were not in a position to tackle them. I have little doubt that in the spring they would be a great deal easier. We sat for nearly an hour contemplating the white, silent amphitheatre and the magnificent view across the Khumbu Glacier to Pumori, Lingtren and the peaks beyond the Lho La. Then we returned down the ice-fall.

The fact that we had now climbed the ice-fall without mishap made the decision to abandon the attempt to carry supplies through into the Cwm all the more difficult. We discussed it at great length. The next day Ward and Bourdillon climbed the ridge near the Lho La to satisfy themselves that there was no alternative route, while Hillary and I paid one more visit to the ice-fall. Angtharkay and Pasang were still convinced that it would be madness in the present conditions to try to carry loads through it, and unfair to ask the Sherpas to do so. There was nothing for it but to submit, hoping that we would get another chance in the spring.

CHAPTER FOUR

Exploratory Journeys

OUR failure to make a safe route up the ice-fall, and so to bring camps and supplies through into the West Cwm, disappointing though it was, had one great consolation, for it allowed us more time than we might otherwise have had to explore some of the great areas of unknown country along the southern side of the main range. During the period between our two visits to the ice-fall we divided into two parties. Murray, Riddiford, Bourdillon and Ward made their way westward from the Base Camp, up a long tributary glacier which took them past Pumori and along the southern side of the watershed. Apart from the exploration of the area, their chief object was to find a pass across the range to the north, which the Sherpas had told us about. We assumed that it must lead over to the West Rongbuk glacier, and it was hoped that the party might be able to climb Pumori from there. I was particularly interested in this alleged pass in view of our failure in 1935 to find any route across this part of the range. They found, however, that no such pass existed.

From the head of the tributary glacier they crossed a col which led them into the upper basin of the Dudh Kosi, at the head of which they found themselves in a mighty cirque formed by the two great mountains of Cho Oyu (26,750 feet) and Gyachung Kang (25,910 feet). On the eastern flank of this cirque was the Nup La, which had been reached by Hazard from the Tibetan side in 1924. For two days they climbed towards this col up an ice-fall, a good deal more difficult than the West Cwm ice-fall, though much less dangerous, before they finally gave up their attempt to reach the watershed. Then they descended the Ngojumbo Glacier and the valley of the Dudh Kosi to Namche.

Meanwhile, Hillary and I explored the country to the south of Mount Everest. Our chief objective was to find a way through the tangle of ranges to the Kangshung glacier which flows from the eastern flanks of Everest, and so to link up with the explorations of the 1921 Reconnaissance Expedition. In this project we were stimulated by the Sherpas' statement that at the head of the Imja Khola there was a pass leading over to Kharta in Tibet. We took with us a young man called Ang Dorje, who knew that valley well and who was most insistent that the pass existed. The upper basin of the Imja is contained on the north by the Nuptse-Lhotse wall and on the east and south by dozens of unnamed peaks between 20,000 feet and 24,000 feet high. When we reached its head we saw at once that there was no practicable way across the mountains to the east. Ang Dorje was not in the least abashed, and merely said that he had supposed that we, as mountaineers, would find a way. Turning southwards, however, we succeeded with some difficulty in crossing a col about 19,000 feet high over into the basin of the Hongu Khola, where we camped on the shores of a big lake. We looked across a wide basin to the Chamlang peaks. We were now well beyond the country known to the Sherpas, but we found evidence that the Hindu Nepalis from the south penetrated with their flocks to these valleys.

We crossed the Hongu basin to the eastward and found a pass, about 20,300 feet high, leading over to the great Barun Glacier flowing south-eastwards at the foot of Makalu (27,790 feet). From here, if we had had another three days' food with us, we could undoubtedly have reached the Kangshung. Another tempting project that presented itself, if only we had had the time and resources to undertake it, was to descend the Barun and to plunge into the great unexplored gorges leading down to the Arun River. But, once embarked upon this game of mountain exploration in these remote ranges, there is no end to its fascinating possibilities.

All this time the weather was fine and the period spanned the full moon. The nights were very cold. The mornings were sparkling clear; each afternoon cloud welled up out of the valleys and wrapped the peaks; each evening at sunset it dissolved. It was then, in camp, that we saw this stupendous country at its best, for each peak in turn was framed in shifting mists, its golden tracery of ice glowing in deep relief; no longer a mere part of a mountain massif, but floating in sublime isolation. Before the cloud had quite vanished, the moon would climb above some lofty crest, and presently all the peaks were there again, frozen against the night sky.

Returning across the Hongu basin, we crossed a third pass, also about 20,000 feet, on its western rim just to the south of the beautiful peak of Ama Dablam, which, as we had hoped, took us back into the valley of the Imja Khola. Finally, we crossed a high ridge running southward from Nuptse and so back to our Base Camp on the Khumbu Glacier.

Our third field of activity was the Gauri Sankar range, which we set out to explore at the beginning of November after work on the ice-fall had been abandoned. We went north-west from Namche along the valley of the Bhote Kosi. At Thame, Hillary, Riddiford and Dutt, who during October had been carrying out extensive geological investigations over a wide area, turned up a valley to the west and crossed the Tesi Lapcha. This pass, though involving some difficult ice-climbing, was known to and occasionally used by the Sherpas. It led through a mass of spectacular granite peaks over a northerly offshoot of the main range into a most remarkable gorge, known as the Rolwaling, running westward under the southern precipices of Gauri Sankar. The rest of us continued along the Bhote Kosi to the little grazing village of Chhule. From here Murray and Bourdillon, taking four days' food with them, went on to visit the Nangpa La, the pass by which the trade route crosses from Sola Khumbu to Tibet. It is approached on either side of the watershed up a long glacier and is situated in an extensive icefield at an altitude of more than 19,000 feet. It is, so far as I know, the highest pass on any trade route in the world. It carries a considerable volume of traffic throughout most of the year, and deep grooves worn in the glacier ice bear witness to the passage of countless yaks. No ponies are taken across, not because it is too high, for ponies are used extensively in the Karakoram Pass, which is not much lower, but because of a curious superstition that if anyone attempts to take a pony across, not only will the pony die, but the owner also will perish. It is by way of the Nangpa La that the Sherpas have their intimate contact with Tibet; large numbers of them cross it every year, not only to trade, but to make a pilgrimage to the Rongbuk Monastery. From near the pass, Murray and Bourdillon saw a possible way of climbing Cho Oyu.

From Chhule, Ward and I made our way westward into a group of high mountains whose position in relation to the main range was difficult to determine. After some time spent in reconnaissance, we found what seemed to be the only way through them, over a col which we subsequently named the Menlung La. Travelling very light and taking enough food for a week, we crossed this col together with Sen Tensing. It led over to a large glacier system, the main ice-stream of which was flowing southward, which suggested that we were still on the southern side of the main range. However, when we came to explore our new surroundings, we found that we were in a vast amphitheatre, in many respects very like the Nanda Devi basin, in the centre of which, completely isolated from the main massif, stood a most lovely peak of pale granite. It was the highest peak of the range, being somewhat higher than Gauri Sankar. We named it "Menlungtse". We found that the waters of the basin drained to the north-west and plunged directly into a system of tremendous canyons, the main artery of which we identified as the Rongshar. It is one of those remarkable rivers which, like the Arun, rise far to the north

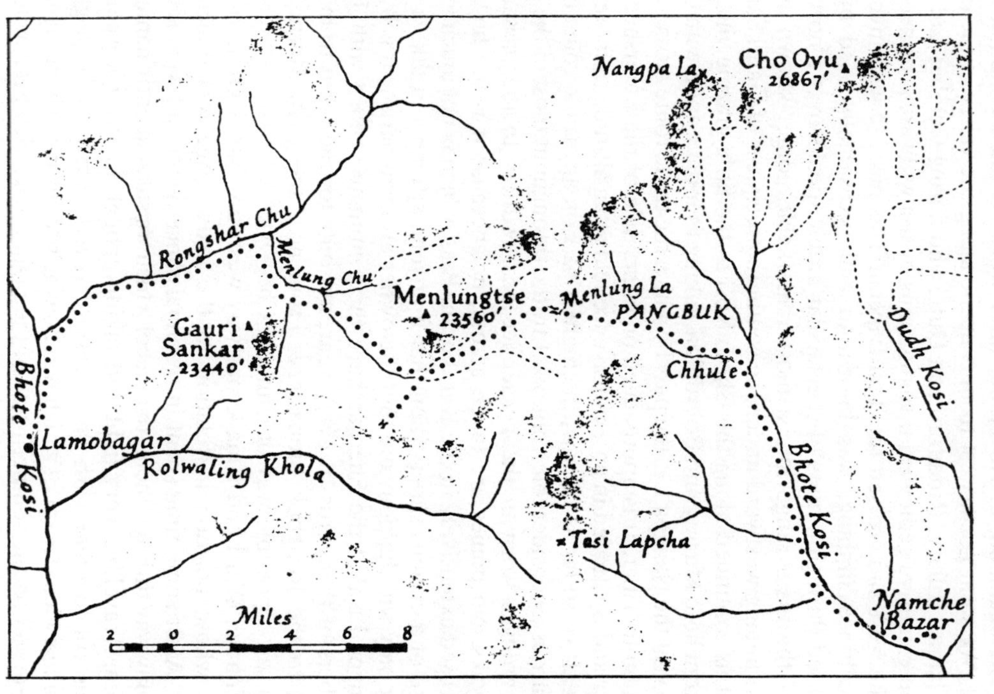

The routes of the Gauri Sankar exploration.

on the Tibetan plateau and have cut their way clean through the great Himalayan range. It is certainly one of the most spectacular gorges I have seen. We also succeeded in reaching the crest of the main range south of "Menlungtse" at a point about 19,500 feet high. From here we looked straight down 7,000 feet into the Rolwaling. Sen Tensing told me that this name was a Sherpa word meaning the furrow made by a plough. We were surprised to find that there was a way down the huge precipices into the gorge.

It was on one of the glaciers of the Menlung basin, at a height of about 19,000 feet, that, late one afternoon, we came across those curious footprints in the snow, the report of which has caused a certain amount of public interest in Britain. We did not follow them further than was convenient, a mile or so, for we were carrying heavy loads at the time, and besides we had reached a particularly interesting stage in the exploration of the basin. I have in the past found many sets of these curious footprints and have tried to follow them, but have always lost them on the moraine or rocks at the side of the glacier. These particular ones seemed to be very fresh, probably not more than 24 hours old. When Murray and Bourdillon followed us a few days later the tracks had been almost obliterated by melting. Sen Tensing, who had no doubt whatever that the creatures (for there had been at least two) that had made the tracks were "Yetis" or wild men, told me that two years before, he and a number of other Sherpas had seen one of them at a distance of about 25 yards at Thyangboche. He described it as half man and half beast, standing about five feet six inches, with a tall pointed head, its body covered with reddish brown hair, but with a hairless face. When we reached Katmandu at the end of November, I had him cross-examined in Nepali (I conversed with him in Hindustani). He left no doubt as to his sincerity. Whatever it was that he had seen, he was convinced that it was neither a bear nor a monkey, with both of which animals he was, of course, very familiar. Of the various theories that have been advanced to account for these tracks, the only one which is in any way plausible is that they were made by a langur monkey, and even this is very far from convincing, as I believe those who have suggested it would be the first to admit.

These various exploratory journeys gave us an intimate knowledge of a stretch of 60 miles of the Great Himalaya Range, in a country hitherto practically unknown to Western travellers. This form of mountaineering, the exploration of unknown peaks, glaciers and valleys, the finding and crossing of new passes to connect one area with another, is the most fascinating occupation I know. The variety of experience, the constantly changing scene, the gradual unfolding of the geography of the range are deeply satisfying, for they yield a very real understanding, almost a sense of personal possession, of the country explored.

LAND OF TEMPEST

Land of Tempest

First published by Hodder and Stoughton, 1963

Contents

1	A Strange Land	*page* 629
2	Some Pioneers	634
3	Lago Onelli	641
4	"Vulcan Viedma"	648
5	Seno Mayo	654
6	The Elusive Volcano	661
7	The Nunatak	667
8	Preparing for a Journey	672
9	Crisis in Punta Arenas	680
10	Voyage Through the Channels	687
11	The Landing	696
12	The Approach	703
13	The Reluctant Sledge	711
14	A Cheerless Christmas	717
15	On the Plateau	724
16	Familiar Landmarks	730
17	Cordon Darwin	738
18	The Journey's End	745
19	Land of Fire	749
20	"The Uttermost Part of the Earth"	756
	Addenda	
I	Further Travels in Patagonia and Tierra del Fuego	762
II	Crossing the North Patagonian Ice-cap	768
	Maps	
	The Great Lakes of Patagonia	636
	Tierra del Fuego: Cordillera Darwin	750

CHAPTER ONE

A Strange Land

HAVING a taste for strange country, I had long nursed a strong desire to visit Southern Patagonia; but the habit of travelling among the mountain ranges of Central Asia, like all agreeable habits, had been hard to break. Those ranges had provided an unlimited field, fresh opportunities kept occurring and each new venture suggested another batch of enticing projects; so Patagonia had receded ever further and more dimly into the future.

I once thought of applying for the job of British Consul in Punta Arenas, on the Straits of Magellan. I was Consul-General in Kunming at the time, and after a year of non-recognition by the Chinese Communist Government, it had become clear that I would have to move elsewhere. Having previously spent four years as a similar official in Kashgar, which had enabled me to travel in the Pamir, Kuen Lun and Tien Shan, it seemed an excellent way to achieve my purpose. However, I discovered that the post of Consul in Punta Arenas was an honorary one held by a local British resident. In any case, when I returned to England in the summer of 1951, I immediately became embroiled in the revival of the attempts to climb Everest, and soon found myself back in the Himalaya.

I celebrated my fiftieth birthday in the Karakoram. It was doubtless this melancholy event that impressed me with the urgency of making definite plans for an expedition to Patagonia before I became too senile for such an undertaking. Even so I might have done nothing about it, had it not been for Geoff Bratt.

Geoff was a young Australian student, working (in his spare time between more attractive activities) for his Ph.D at the Imperial College of Science. In 1957 the College had launched an expedition to the Karakoram and had invited me to lead it. Geoff was a member of the party and he had done much of the preliminary organization. We often shared a tent, and a great deal of varied discussion. Occasionally, of course, we talked of travel and exploration; and I found that he, too, was less interested in mountaineering for its own sake than as a means of getting to strange and little known parts of the world. On the subject of Patagonia it was not difficult to arouse his enthusiasm; his warmth brought mine to the boil and we agreed to go there together the following year.

Patagonia is not a country. The name refers to the whole of the mainland of South America south of the Rio Negro in Latitude 40° S. The bulk of this vast territory, lying in Argentina to the east of the Andes, consists of prairie, some of it flat, much of it hilly, nearly all of it dry, treeless and covered with coarse grass and open scrub. It is a stark, inhospitable land which, until late in the nineteenth century, was inhabited only by a few scattered Indian tribes. It was only then, towards the end of the century, that white men came, mostly direct from Europe or from the Falkland Islands, to settle there as sheep farmers, first along the Atlantic coast, then gradually further inland. Indeed the settlement of Patagonia is so recent that even today many of the *estancieros* are the sons and daughters of those original pioneers.

The Chilean part of Patagonia, except for a small area in the extreme south, is utterly different. Most of it is wild, rugged and uninhabited, a region of tempest and torrential rain, of fantastic geographical form and strange natural phenomena. The Pacific coast immediately west of the Andes, is split by a complex network of fjords which bite deep into the mainland and form an archipelago, a giant jigsaw of islands, 1,000 miles long. The climate is sub-antarctic, and the glaciation so extensive that, although the mountains are not particularly high, they are as spectacular as any in the entire range. There are two great Ice-caps, which are the only examples of their kind outside Polar regions. Many of the innumerable glaciers which radiate from these, flow down through dense "tropical forest" (as Darwin described it) and thrust their massive fronts into the intricate system of waterways surrounding them. Parrots and humming-birds inhabit these forests.

There was no lack of interesting objectives. Apart from scores of unclimbed peaks, much of the region had never been visited. For example, the whole of the northern half of the main Ice-cap was untrodden ground, and with two exceptions none of the glaciers on the western side of the range had been explored. Although most of the channels had been charted since the voyage of the *Beagle* in 1831, for hundreds of miles along this tortuous, uninhabited coast, no one had penetrated inland, while the interior of many of the islands was unknown. The eastern side of the range was comparatively well explored, but even there, there was much interesting work to be done.

That so much of the region still remains unexplored is due almost entirely to the physical difficulties of travel there, for during the last fifty years many attempts have been made to penetrate it. The chief problem is presented by the weather, which is said to be some of the worst in the world. Heavy rain falls for prolonged periods; fine spells are rare and usually brief, and above all there is the notorious Patagonian wind, the savage storms which often continue for weeks at a stretch, with gusts up to 130 m.p.h. The terrain too, is unusually difficult. Most parts of the main range, even many on the eastern side, can only be approached by water and, because of the weather, the use of small craft on the lakes and fjords is liable to be a hazardous business. The glaciers in their lower reaches are often so broken and crevassed that it is virtually impossible to travel on them, and lateral moraines rarely provide an easy line of approach, as they usually do in the Himalaya. In the foothills the forest often presents an impassable barrier, particularly on the western side of the range, where the wind has twisted the stunted trees into a low-lying mass of tangled trunks and branches. It is these obstacles which have prevented most expeditions to the area from achieving more than a limited objective or covering more than a very small proportion of the region.

The lakes of Southern Patagonia were explored towards the end of the last century by several expeditions, notably by that of Francisco Moreno, a distinguished Argentine geographer, who discovered Lago Argentino and Lago San Martin. The first expedition into the main range was made in 1914 by Dr. Frederick Reichert, who succeeded in reaching the head of the Moreno Glacier from Lago Argentino. Later, in 1916 and in 1933, he made two attempts to cross the main Ice-cap, the first from the head of Lago Viedma and the second from Lago San Martin. Though on both occasions he was frustrated by appalling weather conditions, he was able to bring back the first detailed accounts of the remarkable Plateau. Several more explorers have since tried to cross it. Another dominant figure in the exploration of the region was the redoubtable Salesian priest, Father Alberto de Agostini, who made no fewer than twelve expeditions to various parts of it, including the mountains of Tierra del Fuego, which have contributed the major part of our knowledge of the main range. The only complete crossing of the range had been made south of the Ice-cap by H. W. Tilman in 1956. During the course of his long voyage in *Mischief* he landed with two companions at the head of the Calvo Fjord on the Pacific side, and crossed the range to the front of the Moreno Glacier and back, a journey as the crow flies of twenty-five miles each way, which took them six weeks of arduous travel.

Geoff and I had first to decide upon the kind of expedition we were to take, and to begin with we were confronted by something of a vicious circle. Until we had formulated some clear objective we could hardly expect to receive financial support, and until we could discover the kind of work most likely to evoke support it was hard to choose an objective; particularly in view of our ignorance of local conditions. Neither of us cared very much what we did, so long as it gave us the chance to make the acquaintance of this fascinating region, and acquaintance that I hoped might ripen into terms of intimacy. In fact, I regarded this first trip as a reconnaissance, to learn something of problems and possibilities of exploratory travel with the view, later, to tackling a more ambitious venture. Eventually, after a good deal of research, we found the Trustees of the British Museum willing to send a botanist with us and to furnish a grant to cover his share of the cost. The man chosen for the job was Peter James and his assignment was to make a comprehensive collection of plants, lichens and mosses. This was a most valuable advance, for it gave us a nucleus upon which to build our plans.

Before the war, Tilman and I used to boast that we could work out our plans for an expedition to the Himalaya in half an hour on the back of an envelope. Basic simplicity was the keynote of all our ventures together; we knew exactly the weight of the food and equipment we would need, what we would have to take from England and what we could obtain locally and, above all, its cost. We were never more than a few pounds out in estimating our expenses. Planning an expedition to a new continent where inflation was rife was quite another matter, and Geoff and I soon found ourselves floundering in such a morass of uncertainties and conflicting advice that I began to wonder if we would ever get it organized. Moreover, Geoff was faced with the stern necessity of passing his final examinations in the summer of 1958, while I was engaged in forestry work in Shropshire; with the result that things moved slowly.

Fortunately, in July, John Mercer appeared on the scene. He had recently returned from his second visit to the Andes of Southern Patagonia and was anxious to go there again. Having heard of our plans he immediately offered to come with us; an offer we gladly accepted. With his first-hand knowledge to guide us, most of our troubles dissolved. A man of thirty-five, he had had a varied career as a geographer; his activities having ranged from a study of the glaciers of Baffin Land to an investigation of the population problems of Samoa. In 1949 he had made an attempt to cross the Ice-cap from the vicinity of Lago Viedma. His main reason for wishing to return to Patagonia was to continue a line of study which he had begun, the object of which was to determine the dates of successive periods of glacial advance. As Geoff himself was keen to do some glaciological work, this fitted in very nicely.

Peter Miles, the last member of the party to be recruited, was an Anglo-Argentine from Venado Tuerto in the Province of Santa Fé. A farmer by profession, he was a keen amateur naturalist, and he undertook to make collections of birds and insects both for the British Museum and for the Darwin Institute in Buenos Aires.

With this battery of scientific objectives we were able largely to finance the expedition with grants from the British Museum, and Percy Sladen Trust and the Mount Everest Foundation.

For our field of operations we chose the section of the range embraced by the western arms of Lago Argentino, largely because it was the most easily accessible. To begin with, Lago Argentino had a small town, El Calafate, on its shore, while none of the other lakes of Southern Patagonia had a town within hundreds of miles. Secondly it could be reached by air and by reasonably good roads. But by far the most important consideration was the fact that there was a Government launch operating on the lake, by means of which we would be able to reach our various bases. Our plan, which was indefinite and elastic, was to establish a series of these bases at the heads of the western fjords of the lake, spending three or four weeks at each, over a total period of three months.

Peter James, Geoff and I sailed for Buenos Aires from Tilbury on November 1. John travelled by way of the United States, where he had some private affairs to settle. In securing the cheapest available third class passages, we had been required by the shipping company to sign a document stating, in effect, that we realized what we were in for and that we would not complain. The reason became apparent when we reached Lisbon, where our meagre accommodation in the stern of the ship became congested with a multitude of Portuguese *émigrés* bound for Rio and Santos. The small saloon, particularly in bad weather, was rather like an underground train in the rush hour, and the noise was shattering. It was an interesting experience but scarcely enjoyable, and we were not sorry when, on the 23rd, we reached Buenos Aires, where we were met by Peter Miles.

We found ourselves staying at the City Hotel, one of the best in the capital, which provided a remarkable change from the slum conditions of the voyage. Normally we would have chosen a more modest establishment, but we were guests of the British Council, for whom I had undertaken to give some

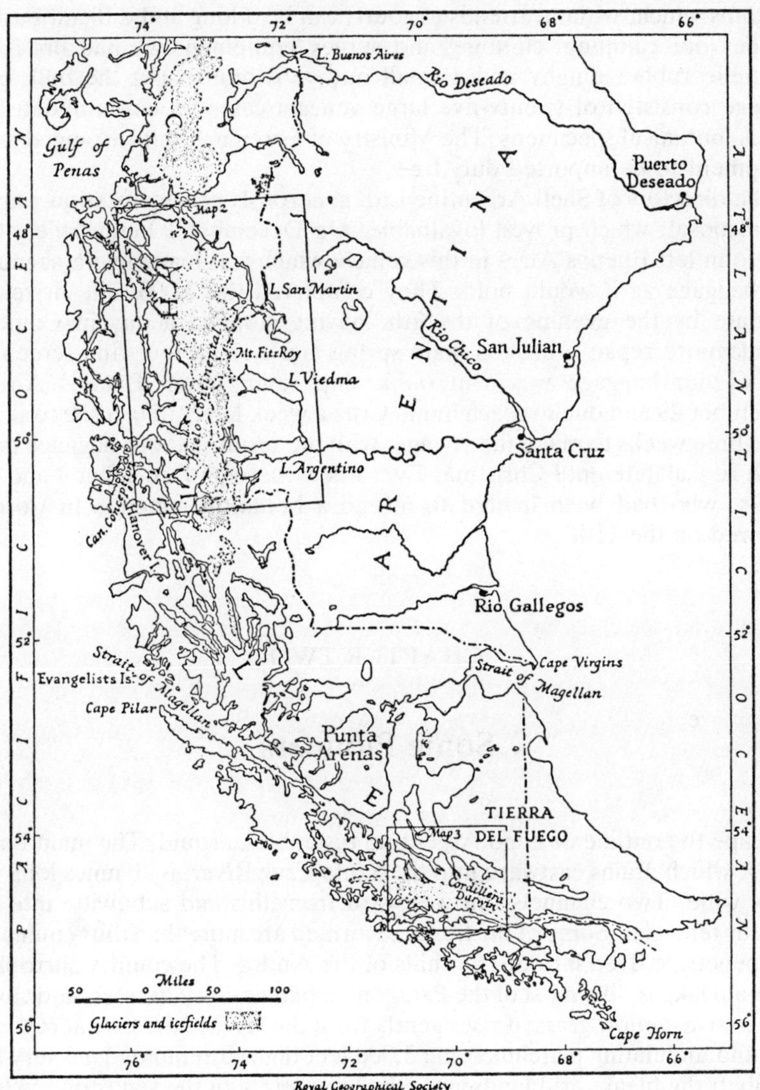

Royal Geographical Society

SOUTHERN PATAGONIA

lectures. Dr. MacKay, the representative of the Council, and his assistant Mr. Whistler, had made admirable arrangements for our stay, and we spent a busy week meeting a large number of people who could help and advise us. They also helped us to steer our baggage through the intricacies of the Argentine Customs which, without friends at court, can be a long and difficult business. Besides our camping, climbing and survey equipment we had brought an inflatable rubber dinghy and a small outboard motor; but the bulk of our luggage consisted of twenty-five large venesta cases to accommodate Peter James' botanical specimens. The Ministry of Foreign Affairs arranged for this equipment to be imported duty free.

The directors of Shell Argentine Ltd. generously placed a station-wagon at our disposal, which proved invaluable. On December 1 Peter Miles, Geoff and John left Buenos Aires in this vehicle which was loaded with as much of our baggage as it would hold. They completed the 2,000 mile drive to El Calafate by the evening of the 7th, having stopped a day in Comodoro Rivadavia to repair a broken main spring and a shattered wind-screen. The rest of our baggage was sent on a ship sailing from Buenos Aires on November 29 and due to reach Santa Cruz a week later. In fact she took more than three weeks to make the voyage, with the result that our baggage did not reach El Calafate until Christmas Eve. I flew there on December 4 and Peter James, who had been invited to attend a botanical congress in Cordoba, followed on the 11th.

CHAPTER TWO

Some Pioneers

In shape the outline of Lago Argentino resembles a squid. The main body of water, which drains eastward into the Santa Cruz River, is 40 miles long by 15 miles wide. Two channels run westward from this and subdivide into eight sinuous tentacles. Some of the fjords so formed are more than thirty miles long, and penetrate deep into the foothills of the Andes. The country surrounding the main lake is, like most of the Patagonian pampas, dry, treeless and covered with coarse, yellow grass; it rises gently from the level of the lake at 600 feet to hills and undulating plateaux some 3,000 feet high. It reminded me very much of Tibet: the bleak, arid landscape, the level strata of the sandstone hills, the clear, exhilarating air, the pale blue sky and the keen wind blowing from the glaciers.

El Calafate, which lies half-way along the southern shore of the main lake, consists of a few houses, mostly built of wood, with corrugated iron roofs. It seemed to me such a perfect replica of a Wild West film set, that I would hardly have been surprised to see a troop of cowboys galloping down the broad, dusty street, firing their six-shooters into the air. It has three small and, by modern standards, primitive hotels, and several stores which sell anything from onions to tweed suits, from gramophone records to farm implements. It is the only town within hundreds of miles, and it serves all the sheep *estancias* in the vicinity of the lake. It derives its curious name from a thorny bush, common on the Patagonian pampas, which has an edible berry like a blackcurrant. There is a local saying that any visitor who eats calafate berries is sure to return to Patagonia.

Though in that area there is little land left to be exploited for sheep raising, the country is sparsely populated. This is because the land is so poor, owing largely to the lack of rain, that on the average it requires four acres to keep one sheep; and as each *estancia* carries from 3,000 to 20,000 head, and some even more, the farmsteads themselves are few and far between. Some of the *estancias* are run by large companies, but for the most part they are owned by private individuals who comprise the cosmopolitan community. Among those we met were Britons, Spaniards, Germans, Danes, Norwegians, Hungarians, Turks and Yugoslavs.

The first *estanciero* I met was Carlos Santiago Dickie, generally known as "Charlie". He was wearing one of those old-fashioned caps with ear-flaps turned back over the crown. In his early sixties, his handsome, rather aristocratic face was framed by bushy grey side-whiskers which gave him something of the appearance of a Victorian country squire. His father had come to "the Lago" from the Falkland Islands in the early years of the century. He had a prodigious zest for life, and a fund of thrilling stories that would have kept the editor of a popular magazine in copy for a year or more. He told them with great fluency and with such enjoyment that they were frequently interrupted by gusts of Rabelasian laughter, which were usually accompanied by an eruption of sparks from his pipe, with the result that his clothes and (as I saw later) the cover of his favourite arm-chair were pitted with burns. Though I saw a great deal of him then and later, he never exhausted his repertoire, nor did I ever hear one of his stories repeated. His wife came from Shropshire and they had met in England during the First World War, when she was a nurse and he a wounded soldier. They had a widespread reputation for generosity and kindness, and I often heard it said that Charlie would give the shirt off his back to anyone who needed it. This was indeed high praise among people to whom generous hospitality is second nature.

Another couple that we were most fortunate to meet was Mr. and Mrs. Atkinson, whose Estancia Lago Roca lay near one of the southern arms of the lake. They immediately invited us to make it our base whenever and for as long as we liked. They were both keen naturalists and their knowledge of the flora and the birds of the region was of great value to Peter James and Peter Miles who, later, accepted their offer so literally that the living-room of the farm became littered with a wild confusion of drying plants and skins.

The most remote *estancia* in the district, and perhaps in Patagonia, is La Cristina, which lies at the head of one of the north-western arms of Lago Argentino. Almost surrounded by rugged mountains, the only practicable approach to it is by launch, and then only when the weather is calm enough to permit the voyage. When we reached El Calafate it had already been isolated

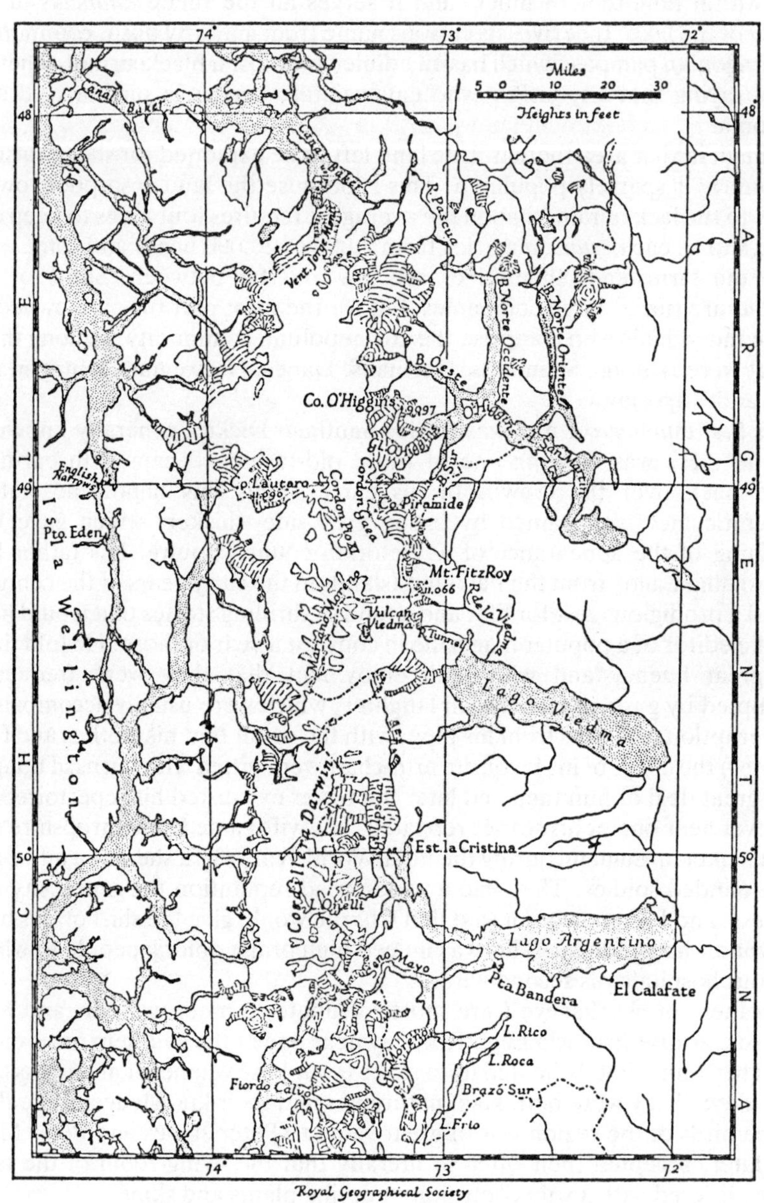

THE GREAT LAKES OF PATAGONIA

by constant storms for three months, but the owners, Mr. and Mrs. Masters and their son Herbert, were in daily communication by radio with the Dickies. When they heard of our arrival they invited us to come and stay with them as soon as possible. As we had been hoping to make our first base somewhere in that vicinity, this suited us admirably. They had a small steam launch which they offered to lend us, but it was old and not very seaworthy, and they advised us to come by Government launch as soon as the weather moderated.

This vessel was operated by the National Parks Administration, the director of which, Señor Tortorelli, we had met in Buenos Aires. He had very kindly issued instructions to the local authorities to place the launch at our disposal when we required it. It was kept at Punta Bandera, a small settlement on the lake shore, forty miles by road west of El Calafate, and at the entrance of the southern fjord system. This was a splendid place for Peter Miles to begin his work, for there were enormous numbers of waterfowl in the shallow, reedy lagoons surrounding it; among them black-headed swans, widgeon, teal, steamer ducks, flamingoes and several varieties of geese. None of the local inhabitants seemed in the least interested in shooting these birds, which would have been very easy prey.

The morning of December 13 was fine and calm. We set out in the launch from Punta Bandera at 8 o'clock, and half an hour later passed through a narrow passage, known as Hell's Gate, into the northern channel. Here the scene changed abruptly. The low-lying yellow pampas gave place to tall rock precipices and steep, forested slopes on either side of the fjord while, ahead, a mighty rampart of ice-peaks burst into view. These were the mountains of the Cordon Darwin, as that part of the main range is called. Even remembering that I was viewing them from only 600 feet above sea-level, I found it hard to believe that none of them was more than 10,000 feet high. We passed a score of icebergs, some smooth and rounded like giant mushrooms, some like craggy islands with cliffs of royal blue, one like a medieval castle with turrets and battlements standing more than 100 feet above the water. They were drifting eastward to the main lake; some of them would reach its farthest shore, to be stranded there, incongruous objects among the desert sand and scrub.

After a voyage of two and a half hours, the launch dropped anchor in a little landlocked bay at the southern end of the La Cristina valley. Herbert Masters was there to meet us when we came ashore and, having disembarked our baggage, we accompanied him to his house, a large bungalow with a corrugated iron roof, set in a garden gay with flowers and half surrounded by a grove of tall poplars. There we met his parents.

Mr. and Mrs. Masters were both eighty-two years old. They came from Southampton where he had been a seaman on a nobleman's yacht; but they had decided that this was no life for a married man, so in 1900, at the age of twenty-four, they had emigrated to Patagonia, where he had worked on various *estancias* to gain some knowledge of sheep farming. In those days it was a wild and desolate land; there were virtually no roads, the only means of transport were by horseback and bullock cart, and the journey from the coast to Lago Argentino took several weeks. It is difficult to imagine the impact of such conditions upon a young woman, brought up in an ordinary Victorian home, who had never left England before.

The valley was first visited in 1902 by H. Prichard, while on an expedition to discover the Giant Sloth, which was then believed to exist in Patagonia. The Masters came there not long afterwards, looking for a place to settle. They were captivated by its beauty, and immediately decided that it was to be their home. They acquired a lifeboat that had been salvaged from a wreck in the Straits of Magellan, and brought it to the lake by bullock cart, a journey of several hundred miles. Then, with none of the amenities which most of us take for granted as basic necessities, beyond the reach of medical help and with little resource save their courage, their staunch reliance upon themselves and each other, they calmly faced the years of toil and privation which they knew must intervene before they could win even a small measure of comfort and security. They named their *estancia* after their daughter, Cristina, who died there when still a young girl.

They started with a small flock of sheep. Living in tents before they had built themselves a house, they cleared and ploughed a small plot of land and planted the grove of poplars which now shields them from the wind-storms blowing down from the glaciers. Today they own 12,000 sheep which range over twenty square miles of country. They employ a *capitas* (headman) and a number of *peones*, mostly half-breed Chilean Indians, who do the shepherding and other work of the *estancia*. Their produce is taken to Punta Bandera in a barge towed by the steam launch (successor to the lifeboat). Their comfortable house, their well-appointed shearing sheds and farm buildings, are equipped with electricity generated by wind- and water-power. They have two cars which they keep in Punta Bandera and use once a year "to go to town", by which they mean Rio Gallegos, on the coast.

Their story, of course, is not unique, for such was the pattern of the lives of most people who came to settle in Patagonia, little more than half a century ago. But what a lesson it should be to us in our pampered modern society.

Mr. Masters was small and spare, and as active as most men in their prime. He held himself so erect that he always gave me the impression that he was leaning over backwards. He had lively, humorous eyes but a diffident, almost apologetic manner. But despite his apparent shyness, he made no attempt to hide his enormous pride in his wife, his "Señora" as he called her. He once came to me with a photograph of an attractive girl in Victorian dress and, with a conspiratorial wink said, "This is the one I left my home for." I replied, "Who wouldn't?" and meant it. Mrs. Masters looked very frail, as though it would hardly require a Patagonian wind to blow her away; and her hands were knotted with arthritis. But she ran her house with quiet efficiency and very little outside help; she cooked delicious meals and worked in her garden, which obviously gave her tremendous pleasure. In her face there was a look of profound serenity.

Herbert, their only son, was fifty-seven. He was well over six feet tall and so towered over both his parents. He had been educated at a British school in Buenos Aires, but otherwise had spent his whole life on the *estancia*. He was very clever with his hands, a gift for which he had plenty of scope. Perhaps his most remarkable achievement was the building of a launch, about forty tons displacement, from timber cut and seasoned on the *estancia*. It was beautifully made from plans taken from a magazine, and it had taken him several years to complete. It was not yet in use, as he was waiting the arrival of a motor which had been ordered from abroad, but he hoped that it would soon replace the old steam launch.

Chief among his varied interests, however, was his radio, which amounted almost to a passion. He had built a powerful transmitter with which he spent a great deal of his time talking to other "Hams" in every part of the globe. This was probably the origin of his extraordinary knowledge about distant lands, from Tibet to New Zealand, from the Congo to Alaska. Oddly enough he seemed to have no desire to travel. This hobby, of course, had practical value for he was in constant touch with El Calafate and Rio Gallegos and with various *estancieros* in the district, several of whom he had inspired with his enthusiasm. It was also a great joy to his mother to be able to have a cosy chat with Mrs. Dickie every morning at 10 o'clock.

It was easy to understand why the Masters had fallen in love with the valley as soon as they saw it, for it is an enchanting place. It lies in a climatic zone between the heavy precipitation of the main range and the dry conditions of the pampas to the east, so that while there is a great deal of forest, there is also plenty of open country. It is several miles wide and runs northward from the fjord to the foot of Cerro Norte, a beautiful peak standing at its head, twelve miles away. Its upper five miles contains Lago Pearson (named after the patron of Prichard's expedition), the source of a wide river that flows through flat grass-land to the fjord, and is joined by a tributary coming down over a series of fine waterfalls from another large lake, high up in the mountains. The valley is bounded on the east by forested slopes rising in a series of terraces to a range of barren mountains, which again reminded me of Tibet, particularly in the evening light when they glowed with soft and varied colour. To the west, the valley is contained throughout its whole length by a narrow ridge separating it from the Upsala Glacier. Its crest, which can be reached in an hour from the *estancia*, commands a superb view of that vast ice-stream: westward eight miles across it to the great peaks of the Cordon Darwin; southward to where it plunges on a three mile front into the waters of Lago Argentino; northward in an ever widening sweep to the Ice-cap itself. I little thought that, two years later, I would arrive at La Cristina after a journey from the Pacific coast across the whole length of that fascinating region.

The series of terraces on both sides of the valley, which cradle a score of small lakes among the forest, are formed by old lateral moraines, which mark the successive stages in the retreat of a glacier, which not so long ago filled the valley and was once united with the Upsala Glacier. The latter has itself retreated considerably in recent years, and when the Masters first came there it used to overflow the ridge at several points with long tongues of ice.

Though the bulk of our baggage had not yet arrived at El Calafate, we had the survey instruments and much of the camping equipment with us, so that a start could be made with the field work. On December 16, Geoff and John went to the farther shore of the north-western fjord, where they were to spend a fortnight working on the Upsala Glacier and its lower tributaries. They were taken there in the steam launch which was operated by the *capitas* and one of the farm hands. It was a remarkable contraption, like a sort of marine version of Stevenson's Rocket; the engine made a prodigious noise and steam issued from a dozen unlikely parts of the vessel's anatomy. Geoff enlivened their departure by falling into the water with a box of provisions which he was carrying aboard. He spent most of the three-hour voyage huddled in the minute boiler-room drying his clothes.

The rest of us spent ten delightful days in the La Cristina valley, which provided Peter James with an excellent opportunity to make a botanical survey of this intermediate zone. It contained a great variety of climatic conditions and he had to work extremely hard to cover the ground. He was out every day collecting from early morning until evening, while he spent most of each night sorting and pressing his specimens. Fortunately the Masters had an inexhaustible supply of old newspapers, for most of his drying equipment was contained in the baggage we had sent by sea. Peter Miles also had plenty to occupy him. Like Punta Bandera, the valley was teeming with waterfowl, and there were large numbers of plover and ibis, and a variety of birds of prey, such as condors, eagles, owls and hawks; but he was mainly interested in the smaller forest birds. Apart from foxes, wild animals seemed to be comparatively scarce, and we saw none of the small deer (huemul) which inhabit the forest, and are exceedingly shy. Herbert told us that there were still a great many pumas in the mountains, which killed a lot of sheep during the winter; but though he had shot plenty of them in his time, they were very hard to find.

On December 23, the Government launch came to fetch us and, bidding a most reluctant farewell to the Masters, we returned to Punta Bandera. From there we drove out to the Atkinsons' *estancia*, for Peter James had decided to spend the next fortnight collecting in the country surrounding Lago Roca and in the mountains to the south before tackling the flora of the rain forests in the main range.

The following day our baggage arrived in El Calafate, and Peter Miles and I spent Christmas Day unpacking it and transporting the collecting equipment to Lago Roca. Apart from some dehydrated meat and tea which we had brought from England, we obtained all the provisions that we required for our excursions into the mountains in El Calafate. We dealt mostly with a Yugoslav storekeeper named Tonko Simunovic, a huge man with courtly manners, who also acted as our banker and our post office. Letters we received were addressed to "c/o Tonko, Lago Argentino".

On December 26, Peter and I were taken in the Government launch to Onelli Bay on the coast of the north-westen fjord, ten miles south of Upsala Glacier front, where we had arranged to meet Geoff and John a couple of days later.

CHAPTER THREE

Lago Onelli

WE disembarked on a spit of land half a mile wide, separating Lago Onelli from Onelli Bay. It was covered with dense forest, which also clothed the steep mountainsides surrounding the bay and extended 2,500 feet above it. Like all the forest in Patagonia it was composed of *nothofagus*, which is said to be a first cousin to our beech, though personally I could see no resemblance. Though there are a great many varieties of this tree, only four extend to these southern latitudes; of these *Nothofagus Antarctica*, is the most common. Though we had seen plenty of woods at La Cristina, this was the first time we had been in the rain belt covering the main range, and the forest here was altogether different. There was a strange feel about it, eerie but not unfriendly, as though it belonged to another geological age, or perhaps to a Hans Andersen story.

As soon as the launch had departed, we went about making ourselves at home in a small clearing ten yards from the shore. Peter was a fastidious camper, and an excellent cook. Our stores were unpacked and neatly stored, while bunches of onions, garlic, and salami sausages, and backs of bacon were slung from poles. He was fond of his food, but for a man of his size (he weighed over seventeen stone) he did not eat a great deal, and could go for a long time with nothing at all. When I first met him in Buenos Aires dressed in his city suit, which looked as if it were about to burst, his sallow face under an Al Capone hat, he appeared corpulent, and I had grave doubts about his ability to survive an expedition of this sort. Now, in his rough expedition clothes, his appearance was completely transformed and he resembled the toughest of lumberjacks. I already knew that this was the real Peter Miles; physically immensely strong and very tough, well used to rough living and able to endure a great deal of hardship. He was a splendid companion, humorous and versatile in his talk (some, perhaps, might have thought he talked too much), an excellent raconteur and remarkably even-tempered.

It was a lovely evening and we cooked and ate our supper by a large fire, Peter was as thrilled as I was with our situation on the shore of this huge, uninhabited fjord, at the gateway to an unexplored part of the range. We slept on the beach, but in the night there was a sharp shower which sent us scrambling to our tent. But the rain did not last long, and by morning it was fine again. Indeed during the whole of our stay in the Onelli region we were blessed with a spell of weather very rare in Patagonia, and except for a few rain storms it was fine and almost windless the whole time.

We set off early to reconnoitre our surroundings, first making our way westward through the forest. Many years ago Mrs. Masters' brother had made a bold attempt to establish an *estancia* here to breed cattle; but he had abandoned the project together with much of his stock. As a result, the surrounding forest was inhabited by wild cattle and horses, which were confined to comparatively narrow bounds by the precipices and glaciers. Within these bounds, however, they had trampled a network of tracks, which was a great help to us in moving about.

When we reached the eastern shore of Lago Onelli we found that end of the lake so filled with icebergs that there was little water to be seen. We then went round to the northern shore and climbed up through the forest above it, making for a prominent hill standing 1,000 feet over the lake. On the way we had an alarming encounter with a wild bull. He was only a few yards away when we saw him, and he looked as if he was about to charge; however, he thought better of it and trotted off, bellowing, into the undergrowth.

As we had expected, the hill commanded a splendid view of the surrounding country. We could see the whole of the lake, which measured three miles by two miles. The entire western and north-western shores were occupied by the fronts of two great glacier systems, which joined each other a mile beyond. The western ice-stream, which we called the Onelli Glacier, entered the lake as a low, comparatively smooth tongue, but the northern front presented a continuous cliff of ice-standing 200 feet above the water. Every now and then as we watched, huge blocks of ice calved from this cliff and fell into the water with an impressive roar. The waves started by these avalanches spread right across the lake; though, from where we stood, they looked like ripples on a pond, we discovered later that this was not quite the case. The blocks of ice breaking from the glacier fronts drifted down the lake and pressed themselves into a confused mass at its eastern end, which we had seen that morning. Our first objective was to establish a base at the western end of Lago Onelli, and for this our rubber dinghy would be needed; for there was obviously no way round the northern side of the lake, and on its southern side there was a river to cross and also one place where a precipice fell sheer into the water. Returning to camp, we spent the afternoon unpacking the dinghy and motor, assembling them and going for a cruise in the bay to try them out.

The following morning we carried the dinghy and motor and 80 lb. of food through the forest and along the northern shore of Lago Onelli, until we found a narrow channel running through the mass of icebergs. Here we launched the boat, stowed the food and rowed cautiously through the channel until we reached the open water beyond. There we started the motor, set a course for the south-west corner of the lake and sat back to enjoy ourselves.

It was a perfect day, cloudless and still; the sun was so warm that we might have been on one of the Italian lakes. The blue water and the dark green forest, fringed with emerald at its upper limit, contrasted beautifully with the immense cirque of glaciers and ice mountains which opened to our view. We watched several avalanches falling into the lake from the glacier front, and we could now appreciate the size of the wave caused by the ice-blocks, some as large as houses, hitting the water; but by the time they reached us they had so broadened that we scarcely felt them. When we reached the south-west corner of the lake we found a little cove partly enclosed by the lateral moraine of the Onelli Glacier which projected far into the water. Bordering the cove there was a grassy glade covered with flowers, and sheltered on two sides by the forest and on the third by a high ridge of the moraine. We landed the stores at this delightful spot, which later became known as "Pedro's Camp".

It was only 1 o'clock when we started back, so we spent some time cruising along the northern and southern shores. When eventually we reached the packed icebergs towards the eastern end of the lake we found that the channel which we had come through that morning had widened, so instead of stopping the motor and getting out the oars, I merely throttled down to a slow speed. As we drew near to the point where we had embarked, we reached a narrow passage between two bergs. I was just about to stop the engine when the propeller guard struck a submerged ledge of ice; the motor was wrenched from its fastening and I turned in time to see it sinking beneath the surface. I made a grab at it, but it was just out of reach, and a moment later it disappeared.

At first I was not particularly worried, for by then we were only ten yards from the shore and I thought that we were in shallow water, though it was too heavily charged with glacier mud to see more than a foot below the surface. I scrambled on to the berg, of which the submerged ledge was part, and stayed there to mark the spot while Peter went ashore and returned with a twelve-foot pole. To our dismay we found that even with this we could not reach the bottom. We then discovered that the berg, which we had thought was grounded, was in fact afloat and had already drifted over the spot where the accident had happened, so that this was now impossible to locate. Neither of us was prepared to dive to the bottom of more than twelve feet of icy water and grope about beneath the ice, so there was nothing for it but to abandon our precious motor.

Very crestfallen we returned to camp, where we found that John and Geoff had arrived overland from their Upsala Camp, where they had spent a profitable time on their respective glaciological tasks. To save carrying it through the forest they had left most of their equipment behind; so the next day, while Geoff did a survey station on top of the hill we had climbed, and Peter began collecting, John and I took the dinghy round the coast to fetch it. The prospect of a twelve-mile row gave us cause to regret the loss of the motor; but again the day was fine and calm, and pulling gently over the smooth, sunlit water, which reflected the forest and the ice peaks around us, was a most pleasant occupation. After rounding the point of Onelli Bay we passed a number of very large icebergs drifting down from the Upsala Glacier front, with cliffs and caverns of vivid blue, some of them worn into fantastic shapes. We gave these monsters a wide berth, for sometimes weird noises would emanate from one or other of them; it would begin to pitch like a ship in a rough sea, and occasionally the whole mass would turn turtle causing a tremendous commotion in the surrounding water. As we approached it the glacier front itself was a spectacular sight, consisting of an ice cliff nearly three miles wide and 200 feet high, which was constantly calving fresh bergs into the fjord. We returned to camp by 6 o'clock.

Lago Onelli drained into the bay by a short but wide and rapidly flowing river. After supper that evening we struck camp and I ferried the party in three relays across the mouth of the river to the far side, and from there we carried the dinghy and our equipment through the forest to the south-east corner of Lago Onelli, which we reached at 11 o'clock as night was falling. It was mid-summer and we were in Lattitude 50° S, so that the night was very short, and it never became really dark, particularly when the sky was clear.

The next day I took the equipment in the dinghy, keeping close in to the southern shore of the lake, while the others walked along it as far as they could. I rowed to a point beyond the line of precipices which rose sheer from the water, unloaded my cargo on to some rocks a few feet above the water, and returned to ferry the others, one at a time, round the cliffs. While I was bringing John across we heard an avalanche fall from the glacier, two miles away across the lake. Five minutes later we reached the place where I had dumped the loads to find that a heavy swell was beating against the rocks where they lay and all but washing them away. We had to stand well off the shore, or the dinghy would have been ripped on submerged rocks now revealed by the back lash of the waves. At length the swell subsided and we were able to land and carry the equipment to a safe place in the forest above.

We were lucky to escape serious consequences resulting from my inexperience; for when the last man had been brought across and we were reloading the equipment into the boat, we heard a prolonged roar from across the lake and watched a series of ice towers collapse and crash into the water. It looked as though the glacier front were under an artillery bombardment. We hastily unloaded the boat and carried it and the equipment well clear of the lake. Five minutes later the waves came; this time they were many times larger than before and completely submerged the rocks where I had originally dumped the loads. The lesson was well and cheaply learnt.

We reached "Pedro's Camp" in the middle of the afternoon and pitched our tents on the soft grass of the meadow. There was ample firewood and a stream of clear water near by. After a brew of tea, Peter went off with his gun and butterfly net and Geoff set up his theodolite on the crest of the moraine.

The work on which John was engaged was unusual and fascinating. The history of most glaciers is marked by alternate periods of advance and retreat, and it is of great value to know when these periods occurred, not only to the glaciologist but also as evidence of past weather cycles. It is rarely possible to discover this information with any precision, but in wooded country when the advance of a glacier has penetrated the forest on either side, one often finds living trees that have been pushed over by the moraine marking the limit of the advance. By cutting an appropriate section from such a tree and studying the rings, one can determine the year when it was disturbed and thus date the climax of that particular advance. The technique has been employed with considerable success in North America, but it had never been tried in the Southern Hemisphere.

During the next two days, while Geoff was busy surveying the main glacier fronts, I went with John across the Onelli Glacier in search of suitable trees for his investigation. We camped in the forest beside a vast ice-fall forming part of the northern glacier system, where John obtained some excellent specimens from an old lateral moraine. The *nothofagus* there were unusually large, many of them fully eighty feet high. It seemed odd to be sitting in the dark shade of these ancient trees, looking out across a huge expanse of ice, riven and twisted and dazzling white. Another thing that never quite lost its strangeness for me was the sight of flocks of green parrots flying over these glaciers, uttering the same raucous cries that hitherto I had associated only with Indian jungles and such tropical places. Wrens were by far the most common birds in the forest; they used to perch a few feet away to scold us wherever we went. A species also much in evidence was a woodpecker, the male of which was crested with a beautiful red cockade. Occasionally we saw humming-birds hovering like large bees about the red flowers of the weigelia bushes, but they were comparatively rare.

The amazing spell of fine weather continued into the New Year. On January 1, Geoff, John, and I carrying three or four days' food, set out to explore the Onelli Glacier. We found the going so easy that in a few hours we had almost reached its upper basin, which consisted of a wide amphitheatre where a number of steep ice-falls coming down from the surrounding mountains converged onto the centre. The largest of these originated in a broad saddle, which we assumed must lie on the main continental watershed. Geoff and I were anxious to reach a point from which we could look into the unexplored country on the Pacific side of the range. For this purpose we had chosen a peak standing above the north-west corner of the amphitheatre, which seemed to be high enough to command a view over the saddle. Leaving the northern side of the glacier we plunged immediately into dense forest. It was slow, strenuous work forcing our way through this, for the ground was steep and broken by lines of cliffs which had been invisible from below, hidden by the trees. But it was considerably worse when we reached the "emerald band" at the upper limit of the forest. This was composed of a tangled mass of dwarf *nothofagus*, their twisted trunks trained by the prevailing wind to grow almost horizontally, their branches intertwined like ivy to form a kind of lattice about six feet deep. It was appalling stuff to struggle through, even with comparatively light loads; most of the time we were stepping from branch to branch; often our footholds would break and we became firmly entrapped in the mass beneath.

It was 8 o'clock by the time we had cleared this zone, and found a suitable ledge on which to pass the night. According to our aneroid the altitude was 2,800 feet, which seemed a paltry height to have reached after a long day's toil. All the same, our bivouac was a splendid view point, and as we ate our supper we watched the sunset colours spreading over a wide expanse of forest, glacier and lake to the rose-red mountains beyond the fjord. I was asleep long before dark, but I awoke at 1 o'clock. There was no moon; the Southern Cross and "Magellan's Cloud" were near the zenith, and the peaks around the amphitheatre were etched against a sky so brilliant with stars that here and there the ice shone with a phosphorescent glow.

We slept longer than we had intended and it was nearly 7 o'clock before we started. An hour's easy climbing took us up 1,400 feet, to the first buttress on the northern ridge of our mountain. John had injured his arm in the forest the day before and it was giving him some trouble; so, as it looked as though we were in for some hard rock-climbing, he decided to turn back. Geoff and I put on the rope, and after three or four difficult pitches, we reached the top of the buttress. From there the ridge swept upwards for 2,000 feet, steep, narrow and serrated. Though the rock was loose and we had to treat it with care, it was not particularly difficult, and we could move together most of the time. The sun was warm and the air was still. To our left we looked straight down into the great amphitheatre; to our right there was a vertical drop to a tributary of the Onelli Glacier, which was fed entirely by ice avalanches falling from the southern face of the mountain.

Climbing such a ridge in such conditions was sheer joy, and we were in high spirits when, at a height of 6,500 feet, we reached the point where it ran out into what appeared to be an easy snow slope leading to the summit. We found, however, that our troubles had not begun. The surface of the slope was unlike any I had ever seen; it was composed of balls of ice like large glass marbles, which slipped like quicksilver beneath our feet and threatened to carry us down on a rolling mass over the brink of the precipice below. At first we could find no way of dealing with this phenomenon; but after some experimenting, we discovered that, by flogging the surface with our ice-axes, we could cause it to avalanche in sections, and scoop steps in a comparatively compact layer beneath. It was a delicate operation and very hard work, and it took us nearly an hour to climb the first 100 feet; but beyond that the slope became less steep, and the ice marbles gradually gave place to soft snow.

At the top of the slope we were confronted by a more formidable obstacle, which had hitherto been hidden from us by the convexity of the slope. This was an ice-cliff running right across the face of the mountain, overhung by a cornice decorated with icicles, and separated from the snow below by a bergschrund, like a moat beneath a castle wall. At first it looked a hopeless proposition, and I felt a pang of disappointment that, after such an exhilarating climb, we were to be denied access to the summit, which a moment before had seemed within easy reach.

It was 12.30. A bank of cloud had begun to billow across the saddle from the west, but as this was a daily occurrence at this hour, it did not worry us. We still had ten hours daylight in hand. On close examination of the wall, we found that, towards the left, just at its lowest part, there was a break in the cornice and the bergschrund was spanned by a snow bridge. This happy combination of circumstances provided the one chance of climbing the wall, which at this point was only about twenty feet high.

I anchored myself securely below the lip of the bergschrund while Geoff made his way slowly across the bridge. The surface of the wall was composed of a deep layer of rotten snow which had to be hacked away before he could cut hand and foot holds in the ice beneath. We had no ice pitons and it was very difficult work, as he was constantly thrown off balance by the overhanging snow above. When he was half-way up, the step on which he was standing broke away and he fell. He landed on a snow bridge, which, to my amazement and relief, held him. But in falling he had driven his right crampon deeply into the flesh of his left leg between the calf and the shin.

It was a nasty wound and must have been painful, but now Geoff's blood was up and he firmly vetoed my suggestion that we should abandon the climb. So, having bound up his leg with a silk scarf, he took over my position, and I crossed the bridge to tackle the wall. I was more fortunate, and after a long struggle I was able to reach the top of the cliff, where I found myself on a slope of hard ice, 100 feet below the main west ridge of the mountain. I brought Geoff up, and at 2.15 we reached the crest, where we paused for a snack.

There was a cold breeze blowing from the north and, as our clothes were thoroughly soaked by contact with the wet snow on the wall, we were not inclined to linger. Also our goal was still a long way off. The ridge, however, was broad and easy, and, two hours later, at 4.15, we reached the summit, 8,100 feet high. To our surprise and delight we found we were standing on the continental divide. The weather to the west was not as clear as we might have wished, but looking down across the saddle we could see the dark tracts of forest on the Pacific side, broken in the far distance by a narrow arm of water which must have been the upper reaches of the Penguin Sound. The country to the north-west fell away gently in a wide glacier valley, very bleak and inhospitable. By contrast, the sunlit valleys of the Onelli basin looked warm and green and lovely.

We allowed ourselves only half an hour on the summit before starting to descend, for our time was running rather short. Climbing down the ice-cliff was more difficult than I had expected and I spent far too long over it. Geoff, however, decided to save time by jumping down from a point where the wall overhung the bergschrund. He cut steps down to the brink and stood contemplating the drop of nearly thirty feet with evident distrust. I suggested that he should cut an ice bollard, hitch the rope round it, and slide down. He was turning round to carry out this manoeuvre when his foot slipped. He just managed to swing himself round and leap forward so that he fell with his feet under him, and landed, shaken and winded but otherwise unhurt, on the soft snow slope, well clear of the bergschrund. After this spectacular performance we had no further excitement and, climbing down the ridge as fast as the unstable rock would allow, we reached our bivouac just before 10 o'clock, with plenty of daylight to spare. We were too tired to have much interest in food, but we consumed several pints of tea.

The sun was already high when we awoke the next morning, and for a long time we basked luxuriously in its warmth before rousing ourselves to prepare a leisurely breakfast. Starting at noon, we climbed down precipitous slopes to the "Avalanche Glacier", and that evening we joined John at a rendezvous on the southern side of the Onelli Glacier. From there we went up into the great amphitheatre where, in its farthest recesses we found little isolated pockets of forest, like dark green gems set in a wilderness of ice.

Our time in this fascinating valley was all too short, but we had arranged for the launch to pick us up on January 8, and we had to make our way back to Onelli Bay in time to meet it.

CHAPTER FOUR

"Vulcan Viedma"

RETURNING to El Calafate on January 8, we met Barny Dickinson and John Cotton, two Argentine mountaineers who, at my invitation, had come to join us for their summer holidays. We had intended to collect fresh supplies and go almost immediately to the head of Seno Mayo, the westernmost arm of Lago Argentino, for our second sortie into the main range. But one engine of the launch had broken down, and the captain was unwilling to venture out again until it had been repaired; as a result we had to defer this project for three weeks. We decided that Geoff, John and I would travel north to Lago Viedma in the station-wagon, which unfortunately was not large enough to take us all, while the other four went south-westward to the head of the Brazo Sur, and beyond to Lago Frio.

I was particularly anxious to visit the region around Lago Viedma to investigate the belief that there was an active volcano among the glaciers to the west. Since the discovery of the great lakes of Southern Patagonia there had been persistent reports of volcanic activity somewhere in the vicinity of the Ice-cap. For example, nearly fifty years ago some travellers had described showers of volcanic ash falling near the western end of Lago Viedma; deposits of volcanic ejecta had been found on several of the glaciers farther north; and, according to de Agostini and others, settlers near the shores of Lago San Martin had seen, on several occasions, columns of smoke rising from the Ice-cap to the west.

Dr. Reichert's expedition of 1933 had reached the Ice-cap by ascending the O'Higgins Glacier from the southernmost branch of Lago San Martin. For sixteen days they were confined to their tents on the edge of the Plateau by violent storms, and by the time these had abated their supplies were nearly exhausted. However, they pressed on westwards and reached a point close to the main divide. Visibility was still bad, but when they were at their farthest point, it cleared for a few minutes and they saw, looming out of the mist, "a volcanic cone, 3,000 metres high", from which clouds of steam were issuing. For some reason Reichert's discovery did not receive the recognition it deserved, and in the subsequent speculation about the existence and whereabouts of the volcano it seems to have been largely ignored. His route to the Ice-cap was followed twice, in 1957 and 1958, by parties led by Hugo Corbela, but no fresh evidence had emerged.

In 1954–5 the American Air Force made a series of survey flights over the range. Examining the photographs taken on these, Professor Keller of the University of Chile and Dr. Lliboutry, a distinguished French glaciologist, found what they thought to be an active vent on a large rock outcrop in the upper basin of the Viedma Glacier. Lliboutry himself flew over the place in 1952, and the observations he made seemed to confirm this belief. Describing them he wrote, "I distinctly saw a crater of ashes on a level with the glacier. At the firn line there is an irregular brown marking which could not be explained by any moraine deposit, and is perhaps the evidence of a relatively recent eruption of ashes." No one had ever visited this peculiar outcrop, which had come to be known as "Vulcan Viedma", and we were anxious to find out whether or not it really was a volcano erupting through an ice-sheet some thousands of feet thick.

We left El Calafate in the station-wagon on January 10. There was a fair earth road running northward along the valley of Rio Leon, the river by which Lago Viedma drains to Lago Argentino. But it involved the crossing of three ferries, one over Rio Santa Cruz and two over Rio Leon, and as the middle one was out of action we were forced to make a long detour to the east by a very rough pony track over the hills. There we saw large numbers of guanacos, long-necked animals resembling the llamas of Bolivia and Peru. Though in the more remote parts of Patagonia these creatures are still fairly plentiful, their numbers are now only a small fraction of what they were fifty years ago. They are large animals which can find little cover among the small scrub of pampas and are therefore easy to shoot; with the result that they have been mercilessly killed for their skins which, particularly those of the young beasts, make excellent rugs. They are supposed to be protected, but they are still being slaughtered, and there is grave danger that before long they will become extinct.

Another creature, extremely common both in the hills and the flat country bordering the lakes, was the rhea, the South American equivalent of the ostrich. When I first saw them, these huge birds looked singularly out of place against a background of glaciers. They have most peculiar breeding habits: a dozen or more females lay a single clutch of as many as sixty or seventy eggs; after which they take no further part in the matter, and leave the business of incubating the eggs and rearing the chicks entirely to the males. Unlike the guanaco, though they have been and are still hunted, their numbers do not seem to be diminishing.

Descending from the hills in the late afternoon we rejoined the road at a place called Punta del Lago, consisting of a store and an inn, at the eastern end of Lago Viedma. Continuing round the northern side of the lake, the road gradually deteriorated into a very rough track, which sometimes vanished for long stretches among the sand-dunes, rocks and scrub which composed the desolate landscape. The station-wagon suffered heavy punishment, and most of the time we were grinding along in bottom gear. Soon after leaving Punta del Lago we called at an *estancia* belonging to some friends of John, where we had dinner: then we drove on until dark and slept under the lee of a clump of calafate bushes.

At 8 o'clock the next morning we reached the Rio de Vuelta, which flows from the eastern valleys of the Fitzroy range. This was the end of the "motor road", for the swift river was spanned by a suspension bridge only wide enough to allow the passage of horses. At the bridge we found some twenty men, gathered round fires on which they were preparing their barbecue breakfasts. They were ranchers and *peones*, tough looking characters, from the scattered *estancias* across the river. They had come there that morning to meet the mail bus which was due to arrive from the Atlantic port of Santa Cruz, 250 miles away. We tried to enlist their help to transport our baggage to the foot of the range, now some fifteen miles away; but they were too absorbed in the enjoyment of their breakfast to take any interest in our problem, so we returned to a *puesta* that we had passed a couple of miles back.

Unlike most parts of Central Asia, where pack transport is usually available even in the most remote places, it is extraordinarily difficult to obtain in Patagonia. It took us the whole day to negotiate the hire of a horse and a man to come with it. By nightfall, however, we had overcome the stubborn opposition of the man in charge of the *puesta*, and the next day we reached Estancia Rio Tunnel, at the north-west corner of Lago Viedma.

The farm was owned by an old Norwegian lady and her three sons, all in their late thirties. Mrs. Halversen greeted us in a gruff, unsmiling manner, like a matriach who has a poor opinion of men in general; but we soon discovered that this air masked a most kindly disposition. “The Boys”, she told us, were away at one of the *puestas*; they were often absent for days at a time, and one never knew when they would be back; but meanwhile her *capitas* would have orders to do what he could for us. She was far from reticent, and as she bustled about her kitchen-cum-sitting-room, cooking and serving our meals, she spoke with much emphasis on such a bewildering variety of subjects and in such a strange mixture of Spanish, Norwegian and English, that it was very hard to follow the gist of the discourse.

We slept in one of the farm buildings, and after an early breakfast the *capitas* produced a pony to carry our baggage up the valley of the Rio Tunnel. As all the men on the farm were busy bringing in sheep for shearing, no one could be spared to accompany us, which meant that one of us would have to bring the pony back. As there was no pack-saddle available our baggage was put into an enormous canvas bag which was then slung across the pony’s back. It made an extremely awkward load which was constantly slipping to one side or the other, or becoming snagged on rocks or tree stumps. Fortunately for us the pony was a philosophical creature, and placidly submitted to our clumsy handling of him and his load.

The first section of the valley was a difficult gorge, and to avoid this we had to climb 2,000 feet up very steep grass slopes and over a col. Beyond this the path led across a precipitous scarp formed by a landslide. Here there were several passages where it was difficult enough for a man to find adequate foothold, let alone a badly loaded pony, and where a slip would have sent the animal plunging down to the river, 1,000 feet below. However, he displayed an astonishing aptitude for mountaineering, and we reached the other side of the scarp with no more serious mishap than the loss of part of our supply of sugar which, during one critical passage, had poured out of a hole in the canvas bag.

We now entered a beautiful open valley of gentle pastureland interspersed with patches of forest, dominated by the graceful spires of Fitzroy and Cerro Torre. After five hours' marching we reached a glacier lake enclosed by vertical rock walls. It was obvious we could take the pony no farther, so after a late lunch, while John and Geoff pitched camp in a pleasant glade, I rode back down the valley, using the folded canvas bag as a saddle.

The pony was as willing as he was even-tempered and I had no difficulty in urging him to a steady canter over the smoother parts of the way. At one point, as we were descending a steep slope, the improvised girth slipped and I fell head over heels down the slope. The friendly animal stopped and eyed me pityingly as I scrambled back and recovered the "saddle" from under his belly. After that I bore in mind the Tibetan dictum, "If your horse can't carry you up hill he is no horse; if you don't lead him down hill you are no man", and we reached the *estancia* with no further mishap, just in time for supper.

As soon as the meal was over I set out once more, despite the protests of Mrs. Halversen and the *capitas* who obviously thought I was mad. It was 8.45 and I still had two hours daylight before me. This time I made my way through the gorge, and climbing as fast as I could, reached the middle section of the valley as the last remnant of the light was fading from the surrounding snows. I slept on a soft bed of leaves in the forest, and was woken at dawn by gentle rain falling on my face. When I reached their camp two hours later, Geoff and John were still asleep.

After I had left them the previous afternoon, they had reconnoitred a complicated route through the glaciers blocking the head of the valley. This enabled us that day to reach a pass, 4,300 feet high, leading directly on to the Viedma Glacier. It was the pass that Reichert had discovered in 1916, on his first attempt to cross the Ice-cap. From there the Viedma Glacier appears as a vast triangular sheet of ice descending gently from the Plateau of which it forms a kind of lobe. It penetrates the eastern rim of the Plateau as an ice-stream nearly ten miles wide but contracts rapidly, and after flowing for twelve miles it reaches Lago Viedma on a front of two miles.

The general altitude of the Plateau itself is about 5,000 feet, but it is intersected by a number of separate ranges of much greater elevation. One of these, the Cordon Mariano Moreno, stretches for fifteen miles across the head of the Viedma Glacier, and contains peaks up to 11,600 feet. We had no difficulty in identifying the "Vulcan Viedma" lying close under the eastern flanks of this range; it looked like a long, black island in a sea of ice, and it was the only feature of its kind in the whole basin.

Early on the morning of January 15, carrying enough food for eight days, we climbed down 800 feet from the pass to the glacier, and set off towards the "Vulcan". Although the slope of the glacier was almost imperceptible, and its surface had appeared from the pass to be perfectly smooth, we found that much of it was so broken that it might have formed part of an ice-fall. A series of deep longitudinal valleys interesected by transverse crevasses, forced us to make long detours. Later we were confronted by a wide river flowing swiftly over the surface of the ice, and we had to explore far along its tortuous course to find a place where it was shallow enough to ford. We passed a number of spectacular "Moulins", huge circular shafts plunging vertically into the glacier, their smooth walls echoing the sinister roar of subterranean rivers. Geoff had brought a 600-foot line with a lead weight attached for measuring the depth of these monsters; but each time we tried the line became entangled, presumably by unseen cascades below, and we achieved little.

About three or four miles from the side of the glacier we came to a place where pumice was scattered on the surface of the ice over a very wide area. It was rapidly decomposing; most of it had already disintegrated into a fine silt, and even the largest lumps were so sodden that it was difficult to pick them up without crushing them. This suggested that the pumice was of fairly recent origin, for it would not be long before the whole lot was washed away. It was an exciting find, and even Geoff, who had been very sceptical about Lliboutry's discovery, was forced to admit that the outcrop we were approaching might after all turn out to be a volcano.

In the middle of the afternoon we reached a medial moraine which, running as straight as a Roman road down the centre of the glacier from the southern end of the "Vulcan", provided us with easy going. We were surprised to find that the heaps of debris, some of them thirty or forty feet high, contained no pumice, nor indeed any kind of volcanic rocks. As we went, we watched a dense bank of cloud pouring over the Mariano Moreno range from the west. So closely did it cling to the contour of the mountains, so sharply was its edge defined against the blue sky, that it might easily have been mistaken for part of the Ice-cap, but for its rapid movement as it cascaded across the main divide, plunged down the eastern side and vanished.

We reached the southern end of the "Vulcan" at 7.30, and pitched our tent under a massive, overhanging boulder. That night a storm broke with considerable violence, and continued, with occasional lulls, for more than a week. Had it come twelve hours earlier we would have had a very rough time reaching our objective against the wind and driving rain. As it was, under the lee of the outcrop and with the protection of our boulder, we lay in comparative comfort while it spent its first fury.

On the morning of the third day there was a lull in the storm and we ventured out to investigate the "Vulcan". It was three and a half miles long and perhaps a mile wide, with its highest point at the northern end standing some 1,500 feet above the surface of the glacier. A few hours sufficed to explore every part of it. It was composed almost entirely of sedimentary and metamorphic rocks, and there was no sign whatever of any volcanic or thermal activity, either contemporary or ancient. Wherever the mysterious deposits of pumice we had found on the glacier had come from, it was certainly not from here. I was already prepared for this disappointment by the absence of volcanic material on the medial moraine and by the nature of the rocks around our camp; but I had still been hoping for some freak phenomenon to be revealed on the northern part of the outcrop. Geoff on the other hand was delighted that his scepticism had been vindicted. Nevertheless the pumice had furnished one more piece of evidence of the existence of the elusive volcano somewhere in this great wilderness of ice.

Near its centre, the outcrop was almost bisected by a deep, circular valley, or amphitheatre, and it was obviously this that Lliboutry had mistaken for a crater. It contained a large lake-basin which was then almost empty; but a series of concentric shorelines and many stranded icebergs showed that from time to time the water was dammed back by the glacier on the eastern side of the outcrop to form a lake, 400 feet deep. On the southern part of the outcrop there were several smaller lakes with grassy shores, where we collected a dozen species of flowering plants and a variety of water insects. We were surprised to find, also, some animal droppings, probably those of deer or hares. We took some for identification, but unfortunately they had disintegrated by the time we got home.

In several places round the perimeter of the outcrop there were wide ravines, up to 100 feet deep, separating the rock from the glacier. At first we took them for "melt pits" (troughs formed by the rock becoming heated by the sun and melting the adjacent ice), and we were puzzled by their extraordinary size; for they were much larger than any I had found even in the Himalaya where the sun is far stronger. Later, however, we realized that they were not "melt pits" at all, but that these huge trenches had been scoured out of the solid glacier ice by the force of the wind.

That afternoon Geoff and I experienced an impressive sample of that wind. It had been comparatively calm for the previous hour or so, and we were just completing our investigation of the northern end of the "Vulcan" when, without any warning, the tornado struck with incredible violence. I did not see what happened to Geoff, but I was blown off my feet by the first blast. The wind whipped the snow from the surface of the glacier and hurled it along as a dense cloud of spray. As the temperature was well above freezing, the snow had melted by the time it reached us and in a few moments we were completely drenched, as though we had been subjected to the concerted aim of a fireman's hose. We were roped together, and fortunately only a few hundred yards directly to windward of a gap leading to the amphitheatre; so, although we could see nothing, we had only to allow ourselves to be hurled up the slope towards it. There, funnelled by the gap, the wind was stronger than ever and we had to crawl through on hands and knees until we reached a steep gully beyond. As we made our way back to camp, keeping well under the lee of the main ridge of the "Vulcan", over which the wind and spray still thundered, we speculated upon our chances of survival had we encountered such a storm on the peak above Lago Onelli.

Having investigated the "Vulcan", we had intended to attempt to climb one of the peaks of the Mariano Moreno range; but as the weather showed no sign of improving, we decided to travel right down the Viedma Glacier to some forest bordering its southern flank, where John could pursue his quest for trees that had been disturbed by the ice. The wind had abated by the next morning and, though it was still fairly strong, it was at our backs, helping rather than impeding us. We followed the medial moraine for ten miles, and it was only when we left it to cross to the side of the glacier that we ran into difficult ice. That evening we camped by a stream in a sheltered hollow, deep in the forest. Soon after we had got there the storm revived some of its former violence, which it maintained for the next thirty-six hours.

We built an enormous fire, feeding it with the largest of the dead tree-trunks that we could shift. A peculiarity of *nothofagus* wood is that it burns much more completely than most woods of the northern hemisphere, and it leaves so little ash, that however large a fire we made at night, it was always completely dead by the morning. During the day, from its warm environment, we watched with snug satisfaction the solid curtains of rain driving horizontally across the steep valleys above, and the tall trees bending with the wave-like rhythm of rippling corn.

On the second morning we awoke to a strange stillness. Though it was less than 2,000 feet above sea-level, the summer forest lay under a deep blanket of snow. Our stock of food was almost finished so, as John was satisfied with his collection of tree-sections, we set out across the glacier at 6.30 after a very meagre breakfast. There was a dense mist, and though we had reconnoitred a route the previous day we had some difficulty in finding our way through the shattered ice. By mid-morning the weather had changed back to its former régime of wind and rain, which lashed our faces and soaked our clothes; but at least we could see where we were going. At 3 o'clock we celebrated our arrival at the foot of the pass by consuming the last of our food, a tin of condensed milk. From there it was a long, weary plod over the pass to our former camp site by the Rio Tunnel, where we had left a cache of supplies. We reached it late in the evening, wet and tired and hungry.

The drenching rain did not encourage us to make a second sortie towards the Ice-cap, so we returned down the valley; and after two days at the north-west corner of the lake surveying the front of the Viedma Glacier, we started back to El Calafate.

CHAPTER FIVE

Seno Mayo

WHEN we returned to Lago Argentino on January 27, the hills at the far end of the lake were covered with snow to within a few hundred feet of the water's edge. The others were back at Lago Roca from their expedition to the south-west. They had had a rough time with the weather, but the two Peters had added valuable material to their collections, and they were busy drying and sorting their specimens, ably assisted by their long-suffering hostess. The launch had both engines working again, so on January 31, we all set out for the head of the Seno Mayo, taking with us provisions for a month. Cotton was nearly at the end of his holiday, and it was arranged that the launch should return to collect him after a few days.

The Seno Mayo is one of the most spectacular fjords of Lago Argentino. The narrow channel lies between precipitous forest, intersected by glaciers so steep that it looks as though the slightest disturbance would be enough to send them plunging bodily into the lake. At the head of the fjord, overshadowed by a magnificent rock spire known as Cerro Mayo standing 7,000 feet high above the water, the valley is blocked by a great ice-stream (the Mayo Glacier) which crosses it at right-angles and butts against the northern wall. Beyond this, the valley continues westward and penetrates so deeply into the main range that its actual head can only be half a dozen miles from the waters of one of the Pacific fjords. Apart from the botanical, zoological and glaciological work, our chief objective was to find a way into the basin of the upper valley, to explore it and, if time and weather allowed, to cross the range to the Pacific side.

We landed at noon on a wide, thickly wooded promontory jutting out from the southern shore of the fjord, a mile short of the glacier barrier. It was the first time that Peter James had been in the rain forest, and he was very excited by the abundance of flora, mosses and lichens. He could not wait to begin his collecting; and as soon as he set foot ashore he started running around like a terrier just released from its kennel, utterly oblivious of anything but his quarry. This intense absorption in his work was characteristic, and it never flagged throughout the whole expedition.

It was a fine afternoon and, after lunch, the rest of us set out to explore our lovely surroundings. Making our way through the forest to the far side of the promontory, we found that it was separated by a wide stretch of open water from the Mayo Glacier. Our passage along the southern shore was blocked by a vertical rock wall rising straight out of the lake for 3,000 feet and crowned with ice. This gigantic precipice was festooned with waterfalls which, in windy weather, never reached the base of the cliff, for they were caught at various levels by the stronger gusts and sent swirling upwards, so that the whole vast wall looked as though it were smouldering.

That evening Peter Miles and I went fishing in a creek beside the camp. In little more than an hour, using a spinner, we succeeded in landing eight rainbow trout, each weighing 2 or 3 lb. We cooked them by wrapping them in newspaper and baking them in the hot ashes of the camp fire.

The promontory provided the naturalists with an excellent base, from which they had easy access to the upper limits of the forest; so they decided to stay there. Its isolation from the Mayo Glacier, however, made it inconvenient for the rest of us; so, using the rubber dinghy, we ferried ourselves and our kit and fifteen days' food across to the northern shore of the fjord. There was a powerful westerly wind blowing, and it proved a difficult operation, which took us most of the day to complete. The wind was extraordinarily warm; this was a sure portent of storm, and during the next two days the weather was very rough. Indeed during the next three or four weeks there were only five days when it did not rain heavily, and calm spells were rare.

On February 2 we tried to find a way across the barrier formed by the Mayo Glacier. It was much more formidable than we had expected; everywhere the ice was broken and twisted into a chaotic mass of ridges and spires, intersected by a labyrinth of deep crevasses. It was impossible to choose a route for more than a few yards ahead; often we cut steps laboriously to the crest of a ridge only to find that we could not descend on the far side. Cotton was wearing a pair of clumsy, ill-fitting crampons, and three times he slipped and was only saved by the rope from falling into the chasms beneath. Matters were not improved by the wind and driving rain. By the middle of the afternoon we were barely half-way across, and our rate of progress was becoming slower and slower; so we abandoned the attempt and returned to camp, thoroughly soaked and cold.

For the next two days, when it rained incessantly, Cotton and I were both laid up with influenza and felt very sorry for ourselves. The launch was due to come on the 5th to fetch Cotton; and John, who had been suffering from toothache, decided to return to El Calafate with him. So, that morning, we ferried them across the fjord to the promontory.

Our camp on the northern shore had been badly chosen; it was exposed to the wind and was now very wet; so when we returned, Geoff, Barny and I cast around for a better home. Deep in the forest, not 200 yards from the shore, we found the ideal place. An overhanging cliff, 100 feet high, formed a roof over a wide area of dry, mossy ground, completely screened from the weather by thick undergrowth and tall trees. Several dead branches had fallen inside the cave, which provided us with enough dry firewood to last us for weeks; while twenty yards away there was a small lake of clear water. We lost no time in moving into this delightful abode where, free from the cramping confinement of tents, we could spread ourselves with complete abandon, and lie in luxurious comfort by a blazing fire.

In Barny we found an excellent companion. He was thoughtful and considerate, and had a most equitable temperament; he always seemed to be enjoying himself whatever the conditions and appeared quite imperious to discomfort, to minor personal misfortunes such as the loss of his pipe, and even to painful physical injury. He was slow in thought and in action, but his judgement was sound, and for us his more placid nature was most salutary. Geoff and I were prone to argue, often with considerable vehemence, over a wide range of subjects, from the behaviour of glaciers to abstract scientific or philosophical matters about which we knew nothing. Barny took no parts in these debates, but listened with an amused or, when we became particularly acrimonious, a puzzled expression on his face. But he was far from dull. Though it was not easy to draw him out, he had a wonderful fund of personal anecdotes; and, as a regular contributor to *Blackwood's Magazine*, he was a practised raconteur. As a bomber pilot during the war, he had been shot down over Germany, and some of his best yarns were of his attempt to evade capture by posing as a German officer, of his efforts to get out of various prison camps and of his eventual escape, some time after the war had ended, from his much harsher though less efficient confinement by the Russians. He told his tales with a kind of reluctant diffidence, and with a spontaneous humour, as if he had only just realized the comic side of his various predicaments.

On the 6th, Geoff and I tried to get round the barrier by climbing across the rock face against which the ice was pressing. To reach it we had to cross a small section of the glacier which demanded the use of crampons. Before tackling the rock, I left mine by a small tree in a place that I thought I could not mistake. A series of terraces enabled us to traverse nearly half a mile across the face and to reach a corner, from which we could see into the upper valley. But beyond this point the rock face was smooth and vertical, and we could go no farther; nor could we see any way through the tangled ice beneath us.

On the way back, I went to the place where I had thought I had left my crampons and found that they were not there. I was so certain that I had identified the right place, that I almost convinced myself that they had been removed by one of the condors that were circling overhead. This ludicrous theory delighted Geoff, and for a long time afterwards I had to suffer his taunts about my "cramponivorous condors". Two days later I found the wretched things neatly folded under another tree.

That evening I fished in a small lagoon which, though only a couple of hundred yards from the glacier, was fed by a stream from the forest. With my second cast, a particularly clumsy one, I caught a 4 lb. trout, which provided us with a substantial supper.

Our failure to cross the ice-barrier now faced us with the unpleasant alternative of climbing more than 2,000 feet up through dense, precipitous forest to look for a high-level route into the upper valley. Fortunately the next day was comparatively fine and we succeeded in reaching a prominent spur running down from the Cerro Mayo, where we did a theodolite station. From the spur we looked down a vertical cliff of some 2,000 feet to a lake, which formed a continuation of the fjord beyond the ice-barrier. We also had a clear view of the southern section of the basin and of a fairly low gap leading to the Pacific.

When we returned to the cave, we found that our camp had been visited by foxes. They had evidently had a wonderful time, for we found several bags of sugar and oats ripped open and the contents strewn all over the ground; while much of our cheese and nearly all our bacon had vanished.

The view from the spur had not been encouraging. The ground beyond looked so precipitous that Geoff and I had decided, before committing ourselves to the high-level route, to make one more attempt, the next day, to break through the ice-barrier. This time we kept close to the rock wall against which the glacier was pressing. By using some convenient rock ledges we made fair progress. Then, just as we seemed to have reached a complete impasse, with overhanging ice-cliffs hemming us in on all sides, we discovered a tunnel which ran for 200 yards under the ice and emerged beyond the cliffs. After some more strenuous climbing we struck better going and eventually reached a narrow inlet from the lake beyond. It lay between a mass of impassable ice-cliffs and a sheer rock wall, which was in fact the bottom of the precipice we had looked down the previous day. The only chance of making any further progress was by using the dinghy, but the inlet was so closely packed with small icebergs that we were very doubtful whether we could force a way through.

However, we decided to try, and the following day we returned with Barny, carrying our food and equipment together with the boat. We reached the inlet at 3.30. Inflating the dinghy, we found three punctures which had to be repaired. Then we started upon the most unusual combination of mountaineering and boating. The dinghy was not really big enough to take all three of us and the baggage as well. So first of all Geoff and I embarked with the baggage and by heaving at the icebergs and cutting away their edges with our ice-axes, we succeeded, with a good deal of labour, in clearing a channel to a rock ledge, twenty yards away. It had been intended that Geoff should land there with some of the baggage, and that I should take the boat back for Barny. But meanwhile the ice had closed the channel behind us, and it was obvious that I would not be able to clear it and propel the boat by myself. Fortunately, there was a wide crack running obliquely up the wall from the ledge, and by climbing this I was able to reach a point thirty feet immediately above the place where Barny was standing. From there I lowered a double rope, and by pulling on one while Barny heaved himself up with the other, he managed to reach me, and we climbed down the crack to join Geoff in the ledge.

After that we continued the voyage all together in the grossly over-loaded dinghy. Our main worry was that the boat would be punctured on some jagged edge as we shoved and hacked at the floating ice. One particularly large and stubborn monster forced us to disembark and carry the dinghy and the kit across it. We were reluctant to do so for the bergs were apt to capsize; indeed we had seen several of them do so on their own account. During the operation Barny's ice-axe fell into the water and was lost. He was unusually upset by this mishap, which surprised me, for he had already borne the loss of his whole supply of tobacco with complete equanimity, until I discovered that the axe was one he had borrowed from Cotton.

The total distance that we had to cover to the opposite shore of the inlet was not more than 300 yards; but it took us four hours of very hard work to get there. It was late in the evening when we landed, and blowing a full gale. We had just time before dark to fill the boat with rocks to prevent it from being blown away, and to scramble up into the shelter of the steep forest, where we spent a wet and uncomfortable night.

Having passed the barrier we had hoped to complete the journey to the head of the main valley mostly by water so as to avoid crossing the numerous steep ridges and cliffs along the shore. But the force of the wind and the roughness of the lake made this quite impossible in our tiny boat; so we were forced to continue by land. It was slow and very laborious work, for there were hardly any beaches along the lakeside, and we spent most of the time scrambling up steep slopes of tangled undergrowth and down into the ravines beyond; often covering the same ground several times, to find a way and then to relay our loads.

For some reason, Barny suffered the most; before long his coat was badly torn and what was left of his trousers hung in shreds about his bleeding legs. Geoff, however, was in his element. He had spent much of his early youth "bushwhacking" in the forests of his native Tasmania, and was justly proud of his ability, not only to get through any kind of scrub, but to find his way back with unerring precision. He had scored his greatest triumph some days before when, climbing through the forest to the spur, Barny had lost the rubber heel to his boot, and he had found it in the dense undergrowth on the way back.

While in the forest, of course, we did not feel the wind, but the noise that it made was most impressive; the individual gusts swept down the valley with a mighty roar like that of a major avalanche. On the night of the 10th, however, there was a lull, and the next morning dawned calm. It was already apparent that we could not attempt to cross the gap to the Pacific, and we now decided to seize the opportunity of the calm spell to make a long march to the head of the valley and back without our loads. The main reason for this decision was that there was one section of the route where the use of the boat was unavoidable. This was the neck of a big lagoon into which several glaciers flowed from the northern side of the basin. Even had it been possible to cross these glaciers, which we could see it was not, the detour involved would have taken many days.

We launched the dinghy and, rowing quickly along the shore, reached the mouth of the lagoon at 9 o'clock. By that time, however, it had started to blow again, and I was having such difficulty rowing against the wind that I decided to drop Barny on the eastern shore and return for him when I had taken Geoff across the channel, which was nearly half a mile wide. But the force of the wind and the size of the waves continued to increase, and I had a hard struggle to reach the western shore. By the time we had landed, it was obvious that if I returned to fetch Barny I might well be unable to get back again; and that if I failed to do so, Geoff would be stranded on the wrong side of the channel. Clearly we must both return forthwith, or go on and leave Barny behind for the rest of the day. With a guilty feeling that we were taking advantage of his good nature, we decided on the latter course. Of course he well understood the situation, and we learned later that he was trying to signal to us to go on without him.

We carried the boat well beyond the reach of the waves, filled it with boulders, and then pressed on as fast as we could, through intermittent squalls of heavy rain, to the head of the valley. There, in the shelter of a cirque of huge rock walls, we found that the vegetation was much more luxuriant and the trees far larger than any we had seen hitherto. Having reconnoitred a route up the glacier to the pass, in case one day we might have a chance of returning there, we started back at 2 o'clock.

When we returned to the lagoon in the late afternoon, the wind was blowing with great force and we had some difficulty in launching the boat. As soon as we removed the boulders holding it down, it was swept up like a kite, dragging us along with it. Once on the water we were sent skimming over the waves like a leaf, with little control over our direction.

Violent gusts came alternately down from the lagoon and down the main valley. Swirling spirals of spindrift warned us of their approach and as a rule we managed to turn the boat so that they hit us astern. One blast, however, caught us broadside and we nearly capsized. But our main efforts were directed at preventing ourselves from being driven into a bay packed with floating ice, from which it would have been difficult to extricate ourselves. There was a heavy swell beating against the eastern shore of the channel, and when we reached it we were hurled unceremoniously on to the rocks where we were welcomed by Barny. He was remarkably cheerful considering that he must have spent a miserable day. However, he had not wasted his time, for he had found an alternative route back to camp which, though it involved some difficult rock climbing, saved us many hours of toil and further aquatic adventures.

For the return journey, reluctant to repeat the passage through the ice-filled bay, we decided to attempt a high-level route which, in any case looked much less formidable from this side. Luckily, during the critical phases, the weather was calm; but on the last day the wind was as violent as ever, and we had to move roped together even on easy slopes. At one point Barny was blown off his feet and, in falling, injured his back. Though, as a result of this, he was largely crippled for the next few weeks he continued to maintain that the trip had been one of the most enjoyable he had ever experienced.

After a day's rest at the base camp, where the the naturalists were still hard at work with their collections, and Peter James was now approaching his total of 4,000 specimens of lichen and flowering plants, Geoff and I set out to reach the head of the Mayo Glacier. Once again we plunged into the maze of seracs and ice-ravines. It was exasperating work; hours of strenuous acrobatics resulted in little apparent progress, it was impossible to choose a route for more than a few yards ahead and we often had to return to try another line. Fortunately the day was fairly calm, though this gave us cause to wonder what the return journey might be like in really rough conditions. It was late in the evening when at last we broke through to relatively smooth ice, and at 9.30 we reached the side of the glacier below an isolated patch of forest.

Being tired and hungry we did not bother to look for a good camp site, but pitched our tent on the first piece of flat moraine we could find. Our carelessness was soon punished; for during the night there was a storm of wind and very heavy rain, and by morning the ground we were on had become the bed of a stream. The deluge continued for thirty-six hours without a pause; and when at last, on the second morning, it slackened to a drizzle, I climbed up into the forest to find a more congenial site. There I lit a fire, stripped off my anorak, sweater and shirt, and went back to fetch Geoff, whom I had left peacefully sleeping in his sodden sleeping-bag.

When, carrying the tent and the rest of the gear, we returned to the fire, it was still burning brightly, and my shirt and sweater were nearly dry; but my anorak was nowhere to be seen. Presently, however, I discovered a piece of charred material, two inches square, which was all that remained of the precious garment. Later Geoff used it to patch his trousers. The prospect of returning down the glacier in the sort of conditions we had lately experienced had already caused us some concern; now, bereft of my anorak, I found it distinctly bleak. Although I had already become accustomed to the peculiarities of the region, it did seem a little odd to be sitting comfortably in the forest and worrying about our ability to get down a short stretch of glacier below.

But the fates were kind; that very evening the weather suddenly cleared, and for the next three days there was not a breath of wind and scarcely a cloud in the sky. First we went up to the head of the Mayo Glacier to examine a peculiar moraine that we had seen there, which we found to have been formed by a colossal landslide from one of the neighbouring peaks. Then we discovered an easy pass to the head of the Ameghino Glacier, and climbed to the summit of a rock peak above it, where for three hours we sat in the warm sun gazing at a magnificent panorama of nameless mountains.

Mingled with our contentment there was some feeling of sadness, for our time together in that enchanting land was drawing to its close. For my part I was determined to return. The potion of the calafate berry had already cast its spell.

CHAPTER SIX

The Elusive Volcano

THE main purpose of my second visit to Patagonia in the southern summer of 1959–60 was to locate and investigate the mysterious volcano. There was little doubt that it must exist, and there was something most intriguing in the idea of this lonely vent hidden somewhere in the great expanse of the Ice-cap. For an active volcano is not normally an unobtrusive phenomenon, easily concealed. The problem of finding it had a strong appeal.

We had already followed one clue and found it to be false. But the "Vulcan Viedma" could not, in any case, have accounted for the volcanic deposits found on the O'Higgins Glacier some thirty miles farther north; nor for the eruptions reported to de Agostini by the settlers on the shores of Lago San Martin, for these were supposed to have been seen in the direction of the Ice-cap west of the lake.

Dr. Lliboutry, who devoted a section of his book *Nieves Y Glaciares de Chile* to a review of the question, was inclined to the opinion that the active vent or vents causing these phenomena were not located on any of the mountains rising above the Ice-cap, but rather that they were fissure volcanos erupting periodically though the ice-sheet itself, and covered by snow during their intervening periods of quiescence. He had noticed on the American Air Force photographs, a number of peculiar markings similar to those he had seen on the Viedma Glacier, on the various glaciers radiating from the northern part of the Ice-cap, which he identified as bands of volcanic ash. From a study of these and other evidence he concluded that the main focus of the eruptions was situated about Lat. 48° 50′ S, Long. 73° 40′ W; that is to say almost in the centre of the northern half of the Ice-cap, no part of which had ever been visited. Soon after my return I went to see Dr. Lliboutry in Grenoble, and he kindly discussed his views in detail. He was not, however, sanguine about the possibility of making a detailed exploration of the area overland, owing to the difficulty of the approach and the appalling weather conditions prevailing on the Ice-cap. He considered that the only practicable method would be by using helicopters, based at a point within striking distance of the area, and making sorties there during spells of fine weather. The cost of such an undertaking, however, would be enormous.

It is most strange, particularly in view of what transpired later, that the report of Dr. Reichert seems to have received so little consideration. Presumably this was because it was thought that his glimpse of the phenomenon was so brief that he and his companions might easily have mistaken snow blowing from a mountain-top for vapour issuing from a volcanic vent; and also because none of the other travellers, such as de Agostini and Corbela, who had been near the place he reached had seen a sign of anything that could be described as a "volcanic cone", let alone an erupting volcano. Nevertheless, a man of Reichert's standing as an explorer and scientist should have been given more credence.

My original intention was to investigate the area indicated by Lliboutry, and I proposed to attempt to reach it from the head of the Brazo Oeste (western arm) of Lago San Martin. Several valleys drained into this fjord from the west, and although, so far as I could discover, none of them had been explored, I hoped that one at least would afford access to the Ice-cap. A good deal of time and effort would no doubt be needed to find a way but, as the main obstacle to the exploration of any part of the Ice-cap was the violent wind, this route would have the advantage of involving the shortest distance to be travelled on the Plateau. Also the exploration of the valleys themselves would provide a most interesting secondary objective.

My plan was to establish an advanced base near the edge of the Plateau, and from there, lightly laden with a tent and a few days' food, to make a series of swift excursions on skis during spells of fine or moderate weather, so as to cover as much of the area as possible. In the light of my subsequent experience, this plan seems somewhat naïve; but my brief acquaintance with Patagonian winds, and still more the horrific stories that I had heard about conditions on the Ice-cap had so impressed me, that I did not contemplate a long sojourn on the Plateau itself.

It was not possible to reach the Brazo Oeste overland, and from the scanty information that I could get, it appeared that the only boat available on Lago San Martin was extremely unreliable. However, I was fortunate enough to obtain the loan of an inflatable boat known as a "Zodiac" manufactured by Messrs. R. F. D. Ltd., of Godalming. It was the ideal craft for the job. A replica of that used by Dr. Bombard for his crossing of the Atlantic, it was capable of withstanding almost any weather conditions, and a surprising amount of battering against rocks and ice. When assembled it was fifteen feet long, and though it could carry well over a ton, it could be packed up into a handy load. Also, the British Seagull Company lent me two 4-h.p. outboard motors.

Partly to circumvent the problem of finance, I decided to recruit my party from South America. First I invited Peter Miles. Though not a mountaineer, I had found him a most useful man to have on an expedition of this kind; and I hoped that, besides helping with the exploration of the valleys and carrying loads to our advanced base, he would be able to continue the zoological work he had done during the previous season. He was very keen to come again, but he had recently got married, and he asked if he could bring his wife, Martha, with him. He told me that she was strong and thoroughly used to rough conditions, having done a lot of deep-sea sailing. As a further recommendation he said that she was a very bad cook, and therefore would not mind our spartan diet. As I thought that Peter Miles would probably have to spend most of his time at the lower camps in the forest, I readily agreed to his proposal.

For the work on the Ice-cap I invited Jack Ewer, an Englishman teaching at the University of Chile in Santiago, and Peter Bruchhausen of the Antarctic Institute in Buenos Aires. Jack, who was forty, had had a lot of mountaineering experience and an expedition to Antarctica to his credit. Finally, while I was preparing things in London, Bill Anderson asked if he could join the party and offered to pay his expenses. Though he had not done much mountaineering, his experience for two years as leader of a party at Hope Bay in the Antarctic was sufficient qualification, and he was a great help to me in the preliminary organization.

At Rio, on my way out to Buenos Aires, I received a letter from Jack which contained some startling news. He told me that, with the co-operation of the Instituto Geographico Militar in Santiago, he had made an exhaustive study of the photographs taken by the American Air Force. He had found two pictures which had evidently escaped the notice of Professor Keller and Dr. Lliboutry, for they showed definite evidence of volcanic activity near the summit of the highest peak of a range named by de Agostini "Cordon Pio XI". The peak, which was called "Lautaro" by Lliboutry, stood high above the Plateau, well to the south of the area suggested by him, and in a position corresponding very closely to the "volcanic cone" seen by Reichert.

I had with me a photograph of Lautaro taken by Corbela; it bore no resemblance to a cone, and certainly did not look like a volcano. Moreover, remembering the "Vulcan Viedma" I was somewhat sceptical of Jack's discovery. However, when I met him in Buenos Aires and he showed me the pictures I had to admit that the evidence was too convincing to be ignored, and that we must divert our attention from the unexplored northern half of the Ice-cap to Lautaro, which could best be reached from the Brazo Sur (south arm) of the lake and up the O'Higgins Glacier. This change of plan altered the whole character of our task, for instead of finding a new route to the Plateau and there searching over a wide area of untrodden ground, we would be approaching by ways already traversed and aiming at a definite objective.

In the middle of December the party assembled in Buenos Aires where we bought most of our provisions. On the 22nd we embarked on a tanker bound for Comodoro Rivadavia, an oil town on the Atlantic coast of Patagonia, where we arrived on the 26th. Once again the Shell Company gave us generous and invaluable help, which solved our difficult problem of reaching Lago San Martin. Mr. de Wit, the Company's Manager, entertained us and provided us with three vehicles for the outward journey of 600 miles.

Leaving Comodoro at 7 o'clock on the 27th, we drove all day through undulating, semi-desert country along the coast, where the monotony of the landscape was relieved only by the sight of seals, guanacos, rheas and an occasional armadillo. San Julian, which we reached that evening, is a place of grim associations; for there Magellan's mutineers were left, presumably to die of slow starvation, and fifty years later Drake hanged Doughty, his second-in-command. To the modern traveller the country has a certain melancholy charm; but to those first voyagers, with the prospect only of appalling hardship and danger ahead of them, it must have seemed utterly dismal, and one cannot but feel some sympathy with the mutineers. Today San Julian is a port of some 3,200 inhabitants, and a centre of the local sheep industry. Like the other towns along the coast it is not a beautiful place.

From there we travelled westward for some 250 miles, through Tres Lagos, which consisted of a post office, a *gendarmerie* and a hotel-cum-store, and, late the next evening, we reached a place called Lago Tarr, near the south-east corner of Lago San Martin, where we found an inn.

Unlike Lago Argentino, Lago San Martin is almost completely surrounded by mountains, and its shores are very sparsely inhabited. Also it has no large, compact body of water, and consists rather of eight interconnecting fjords. Oddly enough, though it lies to the east of the Andes, it drains from its long north-western arm through the range to the Pacific.

Hitherto we had been travelling on a metalled road, but beyond Lago Tarr we followed a very rough track for another forty miles. Three times one of the vehicles got stuck in stream beds, and the last three miles of the track was a terrifying traverse across a steep unstable mountain slope. At 3 o'clock we reached a small *estancia*, El Condor, on the shores of the Maipu Fjord. The owner, Señor Fernandez, and his family received us with the usual open-handed hospitality that one finds everywhere in Patagonia.

Unlike the Brazo Oeste, the fjord from which I had originally intended to approach the Ice-cap, the Brazo Sur was accessible overland by a three-day journey across the mountains. However, as pack-horses were scarce, it was decided that Bill, Peter Bruchhausen and I should take the bulk of the baggage in the Zodiac, while the other three followed by land with the three animals our host could provide. Señor Fernandez expressed grave concern about our venturing on the lake in such a tiny craft, and I doubt if we succeeded in convincing him that it was seaworthy.

Fortunately, the storms, which had apparently been raging for the past few weeks, had now died down, and at 9 a.m. on New Year's Eve we started on our fifty mile voyage. The day was clear and still, and instead of the long cold struggle against powerful headwinds and drenching spray that we had anticipated, we found ourselves gliding over smooth water under a warm sun. By noon we had cleared the network of narrow channels at the exit of the Maipu Fjord and entered the main lake. I noticed that there was much less forest than I had seen among the inner fjords of Lago Argentino; at first the scenery reminded me of Lake Como, though on a very much larger scale. Gradually, however, the panorama of ice mountains opened to westward, clear except for some small white clouds that hung motionless over the higher peaks. At 4 o'clock we rounded a headland and were confronted to the south-west by a splendid view of the O'Higgins Glacier sweeping up from its broad front of ice-cliffs on a lake, to its source on the Ice-cap. Suddenly I noticed that one of the white clouds, far away in the background, seemed, unlike its neighbours, to be in a state of considerable agitation. We were able to observe it for an hour before it was lost to view; and three times we saw it shoot swiftly upwards to form a great mushroom-topped column. There appeared to be only one explanation for this peculiar phenomenon: that our volcano had chosen this very season to resume its activity!

At 6.15 we reached the mouth of a wide river connecting the Brazo Sur with the main lake, where there were two small farms, one on either side. Landing on the northern bank, we received a tempestuous welcome from a middle-aged woman who had run down from the farm at our approach. She embraced us as if we were dear relations whom she had not seen for years, and conducted us to her house, where we met her husband and daughter and two grandchildren.

Luis Mansilla was an elderly man with a sad, care-worn face; he rarely spoke and sat in meditative silence by the stove. It was clear that his household revolved about the dynamic personality of his wife, Doña Carmen, a woman of enormous vitality and, as we had already discovered, powerful emotions. She talked incessantly and displayed the volatile temperament of a *prima donna*; tears, laughter and passionate rage followed each other with such bewildering speed that Peter, our only linguistic contact, could find no explanation for her sudden changes of mood. She was for ever baking bread and a large tubful of dough was kept constantly in a corner of the kitchen: every now and then she would launch a vigorous attack, pummelling it like a boxer with a punch-ball, without the slightest interruption of her verbal flow. The finished article was always excellent.

The original settlers in this remote corner of Patagonia came there from Puerto Natales on the coast of southern Chile, nearly fifty years ago, making the long trek to their unknown destination by way of El Calafate and Tres Lagos. Doña Carmen had been there with her husband since 1925. One would imagine that, for a woman of her temperament, the loneliness must have been well-nigh intolerable; she told us that for the first seven years she had not seen another woman. Their present house, which had only been standing a few years, was built of rough timber and contained three very sparsely furnished rooms and a small kitchen. The walls of all these rooms were completely covered with newspapers, among which I was surprised to find several pages from English journals, twenty-five years old.

We hoped that we would be able to hire some pack-horses to help us on the next stage of our journey, and that evening, Peter broached the matter. However, the mere suggestion evoked such a storm of abuse from Doña Carmen that it was clear that a great deal of patient diplomacy would be needed to secure her co-operation. Our unexpected arrival had provided her with a heaven-sent opportunity to talk, and she was not prepared to let us go without a struggle. She painted a horrific picture of the hardship and dangers of the glacial regions above, which no one but a fool would wish to visit. In any case it was New Year's Eve and she flatly refused to discuss our plans until after the *fiesta* the following day.

Early next day the neighbours arrived from across the river, dressed in their Sunday best, and the assembled company settled down to a prolonged orgy of eating and drinking. At 11 o'clock Peter and I set out for a long walk to reconnoitre our surroundings. This was certainly a tactical mistake and we would have been better advised to curb our impatience and sacrifice our stomachs in the interest of goodwill. However, we partly atoned for our lapse when we returned in the evening to find the party still in progress, and our hosts and their guests in a distinctly mellow condition.

The next day Doña Carmen, suffering the normal reaction to the gaiety of the previous day, was in a difficult temper; but, by dint of much wood-chopping and hard work in her vegetable plot, we succeeded in so far mollifying her that she ordered her daughter, Maria, to go and catch three ponies. On January 3, with two of the ponies heavily laden with our baggage and Maria mounted on the third, we set out, accompanied by two foals. Following a steep, ill-defined track through the forest for three hours, we reached the crest of the ridge separating the valley of the Brazo Sur from that of the O'Higgins Glacier. On the way we experienced a great deal of trouble with the pack-ponies, whose awkward loads kept slipping under their bellies. Fortunately, Maria had inherited the philosophical temperament of her father; her mother would certainly not have tolerated our incompetence for a moment, and had she been our guide, we would soon have been left to our own devices.

From the crest of a ridge we descended to a shelf formed by an old lateral moraine of the O'Higgins Glacier, and made our way westward along it for several miles through pleasant, wooded country interspersed with grassy glades, until we reached the upper limit of the forest. There we chose a site for our first camp and dumped the loads. On the way back, Maria was shaken out of her habitual calm by the discovery that the two foals were missing. Mounted on one of the pack-ponies I accompanied her on a fruitless search, conducted at a breakneck speed through a trackless forest and over steep mountainsides, which only the onset of darkness forced her to abandon. We got back to the farm at 11.30 that night, by which time I was too tired to feel upset by the scolding of our irate hostess. The foals turned up on their own the following day.

On January 4, Jack and Peter and Martha Miles arrived from El Condor with five pack-ponies, accompanied by their owner, Aloyso Altamirando. A wizened brown nut of a man, with an expression of infinite resignation on his face, he had come to the lake with the original settlers nearly fifty years ago, and now farmed a small piece of land between El Condor and the Brazo Sur. With the help of his ponies we were able to carry up the rest of our baggage, and the next day, we set off after a touching farewell from Doña Carmen, who burst into tears at our departure.

So far things had gone remarkably well. In little more than a fortnight since leaving Buenos Aires, we were established at our first camp with provisions enough to last us for eight weeks. At this point, however, our satisfaction was marred by the departure of Bill Anderson. In an undertaking of this kind, when conditions must inevitably subject people's tempers to a good deal of strain, the mutual compatability of the members of the party is a matter of vital importance. It was already clear that Bill and I did not see eye to eye and as it was better that we should part company while it was still possible to do so, he went back with Altamirando and the ponies.

CHAPTER SEVEN

The Nunatak

OPPOSITE the site of our first camp, the O'Higgins Glacier, one of the largest flowing from the Ice-cap, was about two and a half miles wide. But it was in a state of rapid decline, and now flowed through a moraine trench (the top of which formed the shelf on which we had our first camp) between 800 and 1,000 feet deep. The sides of the trench were completely devoid of vegetation, which showed that they had not long been exposed. Altamirando told us that when he had first seen it in 1914, the surface of the glacier was almost level with the shelf. This would mean that the depth of the ice had decreased by some 800 feet in forty-seven years. Mrs. von Rensell Atkinson, who accompanied Dr. Reichert in 1933, has told me that the descent from the shelf to the glacier was then not more than 200 feet, which shows that the shrinkage had been far more rapid in the last twenty-seven years than during the previous twenty. Since 1933 the front of the glacier had retreated five miles. No other glacier that I have seen in Patagonia (or anywhere else for that matter) shows anything like this rate of decline. The extraordinary shrinkage of the O'Higgins Glacier is as difficult to explain as the fact that the Moreno Glacier, 120 miles farther south, has evidently not diminished appreciably during the last 200 years, while its neighbours have suffered a considerable net recession over the same period. Lliboutry suggests that the latter phenomenon might be explained by the shape of the Moreno's basin, which allows the unrestricted flow of the ice from the upper to the lower parts of the glacier. He admits that this explanation should also apply to the conditions of the Viedma Glacier, whose basin is quite as open, but which has retreated considerably; but he suggests that this apparent anomaly might be accounted for by thermal activity centred round the "Vulcan Viedma". As we have seen, the evidence for the existence of such activity has now been refuted, but the suggestion might be worth considering as an explanation of the phenomenal recession of the O'Higgins Glacier; though this would presumably imply that the present phase of volcanic activity on the Ice-cap began not much more than fifty years ago.

From our first camp onwards we had to carry everything ourselves, and the next two weeks was a period of hard work. We aimed at getting enough supplies to the Ice-cap to last us for a month; and this, together with our equipment (which included skis), necessitated three relays between each succeeding camp. In my original plan for the expedition I had not visualized Martha accompanying us far above the forest, though Peter, besides his zoological collecting, was to have helped with the exploration of the valleys leading to the Plateau from the Brazo Oeste. Now, however, with our change of plan, the situation was radically altered. They had both set their hearts on reaching the Ice-cap, and I could hardly expect them to be content to stay behind at the first camp for the six or seven weeks that we expected to be away. So I accepted their proposal to come with us and take their share in the work that lay ahead. Thereafter Martha, who had never done any back-packing before, carried a load of 30 or 40 lb. and bore the unpleasant conditions we met with as much stoicism as any of us.

First we had to descend 800 feet from the shelf into a curious bay of "dead" ice (i.e. ice which has been left stranded by the recession of the parent glacier) formed by a gap in the mountains, through which, a few decades ago, a portion of the O'Higgins Glacier had flowed to join a tributary of another glacier running down to the Brazo Sur. This minor ice-stream was now making a vigorous thrust over the "dead" ice, to form instead a tributary of the O'Higgins Glacier.

Our second camp, on the far side of the bay, was placed in a desolate waste of mud and boulders. We left there a cache of food together with one of our three tents. On our return in February we found that they had been buried by a mud avalanche. A mile or so beyond this place, following the edge of the glacier, we reached the entrance of a side valley. Formerly this had been occupied by a tributary glacier, but we found that its place had been taken by a large lake. With a good deal of difficulty we found our way round this obstacle, through a labyrinth of ice ridges, pinnacles and chasms not unlike the Mayo Glacier. This section of the route was a terrifying experience for poor Martha who was new to glacier travel and had not, of course, worn crampons until a few days before.

It was in this part that the rapid degeneration of the glacier was most apparent. There were day-to-day changes along our route, with new crevasses opening and ridges and pinnacles disintegrating; and when, a fortnight later, three of us had occasion to return there, it was obvious that a large part of the ice over which our route lay was about to collapse into the lake.

During all this time the weather was continuously bad, and strong wind and soaking rain were our daily portion. However, we were still sheltered from the full force of the westerly gales, which we could often see raging over the Ice-cap and, though conditions were most unpleasant, they were never bad enough to stop us.

On January 14 we reached the upper basin of the O'Higgins Glacier, where we established our fourth camp, and from there, on the 15th, Jack, Peter Bruchhausen and I reconnoitred forward to the edge of the Plateau. Returning to camp that evening, I fell into a hidden crevasse and dislocated my shoulder. Hanging on the rope with my right arm paralysed, I was quite unable to do anything to help matters. Fortunately, while Peter held the rope, Jack managed to reach down, grasp my arm and pull the joint back into place. The excitement of my situation must have acted as an anaesthetic, for I remember nothing but the relief of regaining the use of my arm and of being able to help my companions to extricate me. After that I rested for three days to give my shoulder a chance to recover, in which it was greatly helped by Martha's skilful massage, while Jack and the two Peters continued the work of relaying the loads.

On January 19 we carried the last relay to the edge of the Plateau, where we pitched our fifth camp on a comfortable ledge on a large rock outcrop. It commanded a superb view, and as by a lucky chance the weather had cleared we enjoyed that evening the first fruits of our toil. Northwards across the wide basin of the O'Higgins Glacier, the massive range of Cerro O'Higgins was delicately coloured in the golden twilight, looking with its remote summits, its armoury of hanging glaciers, as impressive as any Himalayan giant. To the north-west a vast sweep of almost level snow stretched away to some unexplored ranges on the northern part of the Plateau, and to the gently curved saddle, rimmed by a line of dark blue which gave us the impression that we were looking over to the Pacific. But for us, by far the most exciting part of the view was to the west, where the Cordon Pio XI rose steeply above the Plateau to a long line of peaks, silhouetted against the gaudy sunset sky. About 300 feet below the summit of the highest of these (Lautaro), the ice slope on the northern side was gashed by a black fissure, from which there flowed a steady stream of vapour, mounting virtually to a great height, then to be carried away by a southward air-current. It was a wonderful sight. Undoubtedly this was the volcano that Reichert had seen twenty-seven years before and about which there had been so much speculation.

It was still fine the next morning, and we set off on skis westward across the Plateau to lay a dump of three weeks' supplies. Soon after we started we saw an eruption of ash from the volcano, which blackened the snow over a large area of mountainside. As there was no wind it was very hot; the snow soon became soft and sticky and our loads seemed inordinately heavy. Peter Bruchhausen was suffering from acute pain in his foot, and in the afternoon Jack and I carried his load forward in relays. Nevertheless, we succeeded in covering two-thirds of the distance to the foot of the volcano before laying our dump; but we were all very tired when we returned to camp at 9.30 that evening.

The following morning was again clear, though there were unmistakable signs that the fine spell was about to end. I was most anxious that we should carry our camp forward to the dump without delay because I was afraid that a heavy fall of snow or drift might bury it, and although we had done our best to fix its position by compass bearings, it would, in any case, be difficult to find in thick weather. Also we had left ourselves rather short of food at our present camp. However, though we prepared for an early start, it was obvious that the party was in need of a rest, particularly Peter Bruchhausen who had had a hard struggle to get back the previous evening. So I decided to take a chance on the weather and give the party an off day, the first that Jack and Peter Bruchhausen had had since leaving the farm more than a fortnight before.

That night the weather broke and for the next four days the violence of the wind and driving sleet made it impossible to venture out on to the Plateau. On the fifth day, however, the storm abated, and we struck camp and set off in the afternoon hoping to reach the dump by nightfall. But Peter Bruchhausen found that, despite the enforced rest, his foot was worse; ski-ing caused him such agony that it was useless for him to attempt to come any farther. Reluctantly it was decided to send him back. He pleaded to be allowed to go alone, but that was obviously out of the question so, that very evening, Jack and I started to escort him down the glacier. We accompanied him as far as our first camp in the forest, where there was plenty of food, and from there he made his way slowly back to the settlement on the Brazo Sur. Later it was found that the cause of the trouble was a kind of cyst which had formed in the upper part of his foot; it continued to lame him until he was able to have it removed by a doctor.

His departure was very sad both for us and for him, for he was extremely keen, and was bitterly disappointed not to be able to take part in the work on the Ice-cap, particularly after he had borne his full share of the toil of the last few weeks. It was also a bad blow to our prospects of achieving much on the Ice-cap, for the mountaineering strength of the party, already depleted, was now severely weakened. Peter and Martha Miles were not mountaineers, and though this fact made their performance all the more remarkable, it would have been foolish, for example, to take them on an attempt to climb Lautaro in the conditions we were likely to meet. Nor, because of the complexity of the crevassed areas we had seen, was it a job for Jack and me to tackle on our own.

After some forced marches, Jack and I rejoined the others at the fifth camp, which we reached just in time to take advantage of another brief spell of clear weather. In it we made our way across the Plateau to a nunatak near the foot of the volcano, where, with supplies relayed forward from the dump, we established a well-stocked base, about half-way between Lago San Martin and the Eyre Fjord on the Pacific coast.

For the next fortnight the weather was very bad indeed, with heavy rain, some snowstorms and incessant wind, with occasional gusts of extreme violence. In one of these, two pairs of skis were blown away and never seen again. I do not believe that our small mountain tents would have survived for long in such conditions, had they not been protected from the full force of the wind by a rock cliff; though this had the minor disadvantage that when it snowed the tents were buried in drift.

One night, after a spell of particularly heavy rain, a pond two feet deep, formed on the concave platform occupied by the Miles' tent. Nothing could be done to drain it, so they brought their sodden sleeping-bags and squeezed themselves into our tent (designed for two), where we remained tightly packed until, thirty-six hours later, a lull in the weather enabled us to extricate their flooded tent and construct another platform for it. But three nights later they were in trouble again. A violent gust from an unexpected quarter tore their tent from its moorings, snapped most of its guy ropes and broke one of its poles. Once again they were forced to accept our meagre hospitality for two nights until the damage could be repaired. Both Peter and Jack were very large men, and we were so closely constricted that movement was almost impossible. This had some slight advantage in keeping us warm, because by then everything was wet; but sleep was difficult to achieve, and we spent most of these nights singing and talking. Peter had a good voice and a fine repertoire of songs, and as the party was composed of a Roman Catholic, a Protestant, a materialist and an agnostic we had plenty of scope for religious discussion.

When we had been at the nunatak for about ten days, a final disaster befell us. Instead of the usual Primus stoves, I had supplied the party with petrol stoves of a cunning and compact design. We had two of these with us, and for some time they had been causing trouble. Each had a right-angled section in the feed pipe, which became blocked, either by volcanic dust or lead in the petrol, or both, and as the pipe was welded on to the tank, it was impossible to clear the blockage. Finally, at about the same time, both stoves ceased to function altogether, and there was nothing we could contrive to remedy the situation. So thereafter, we had to subsist on uncooked food and cold drinks. Fortunately we did not have to melt snow for water, of which there was an ample supply on the nunatak.

We had planned to make a journey from our nunatak base into the unexplored northern part of the Plateau, where we expected that we might find more evidence of volcanic activity among the ranges there. Though Jack, a mighty optimist, would still have been more than willing to undertake it, I must confess that the battering that we had received from the weather had already robbed me of much of my zest for such an expedition. As for Peter and Martha, whose stoic endurances had been unfairly tested, and who in any case would have been left behind at the nunatak, there was little doubt as to where their inclinations lay. Now, however, with the failure of our stoves, even Jack was induced to admit that life on the open Plateau, with our obviously inadequate tentage and no means of cooking or melting snow, might well prove intolerable. So we decided to limit our objective to making a collection of rocks from such outcrops on the mountain that we could reach. In this task we were helped by the advent of one fine day.

Apart from a few minor mishaps, such as Peter and Martha falling into crevasses and Jack cracking a rib, our journey back was uneventful and increasingly pleasant as the rigours relaxed and one by one we savoured the delights of getting back to normal conditions.

Our return to the farm swept Doña Carmen into an ecstasy of emotional outpouring. It happened that I arrived an hour ahead of the others, so that I bore the full brunt of her rapture. She kept moving me about from one place to another, as though she were trying to find just the right position for a new piece of furniture, plying me with food and talking all the time. I was slightly mortified by her constant repetition of the phrase "Pobre viejo" ("Poor old man"), until I remembered how ancient my grey beard made me appear. It was quite a relief when the others arrived to divert her attention; though she continued to scold and cherish us like truant children whom she had despaired of ever seeing again.

A few days later we set sail in the Zodiac. One of the motors had been ruined by our clumsy handling and, despite a following wind, our speed was slower than on the outward journey. When we had been going an hour or so we were surprised to see a vessel approaching us. She turned out to be a boat, belonging to a strange character known as "El Catalan", which we had seen lying at the other end of the lake at the end of December; she had then been out of commission. When we came alongside we found that she was carrying an expedition from the University of Chile, led by Eduardo García. They were bound for Cerro O'Higgins. I was glad that Doña Carmen, whom we had left utterly dejected that morning, would so soon have company again.

That aftenoon the wind, which had been moderate before, freshened considerably. Low clouds raced overhead, and the grey water became uncomfortably rough. Peter succumbed to sea-sickness, and lay miserably in the bows; and we all became very cold. I was glad when we reached the calm of the narrow channels at the entrance of the Maipu Fjord, where we were overtaken by nightfall and ran the Zodiac ashore in a sheltered cove on a small wooded island. It was raining gently, but we soon had a large fire blazing, and were content to lie most of the night before its grateful warmth.

The achievements of the expedition had been disappointing. True, we had established beyond all doubt the existence and position of the mysterious volcano, thanks to the timely circumstance of its renewed activity; and we had collected enough material to learn something of its structure. That, certainly, had been our main objective; but with less miscalculation and a little more luck, we should have made much better use of a month's supplies carried to the Plateau with so much toil. We had covered little fresh ground, and we knew no more than before about the northern part of the Ice-cap, which was by far the largest part of this strange region. But we had learnt some valuable lessons; and when failure acts as a spur to fresh enterprise, it cannot be counted a total loss.

CHAPTER EIGHT

Preparing for a Journey

My first two expeditions to Patagonia had provided me with the experience I needed to attempt a more ambitious venture. There was no doubt as to my choice of an objective. The idea of landing somewhere on the uninhabited Pacific coast and making a journey across the unexplored northern half of the Ice-cap, stood out with challenging simplicity. I was anxious, too, to discover whether the volcanic activity which we had located that year extended to the northward, or whether it was an isolated phenomenon.

All the previous attempts to cross the Ice-cap farther south had been made from the Argentine side; and all of them, of course, had had to provide for the necessity of returning by the same route. To cross from the Pacific side, on the other hand, would involve no such necessity, as we would be travelling towards inhabited country. There was also the advantage that we would be going more or less with the prevailing wind, an extremely important factor.

The vital problem, however, was how to reach a suitable starting point on the Pacific coast. So far as I knew, this coast was uninhabited for several hundred miles in either direction. The nearest ports were Puerto Natales to the south and Puerto Montt to the north, both more than 500 miles away; and it would be extremely expensive to charter a suitable vessel from either to carry an expedition to its base. There is a fairly regular coastal traffic between Puerto Montt and Punta Arenas, and all the ships of less than 10,000 tons follow a route through the channels of the archipelago. It might be possible to arrange to be dropped by one of these ships at the entrance of one of the many fjords leading to the foot of the main range, and to complete the journey in a Zodiac boat. There were, however, several serious objections to this plan: in the first place it would be a hazardous operation unless we were lucky enough to strike a spell of fine weather at exactly the right moment, which was most unlikely; secondly, we would be severely limited in the amount of stores and equipment that we could take, and thirdly, it would mean that we would have to abandon the Zodiac and the outboard motors which could not possibly be carried across the Ice-cap. There was also the difficult problem of arranging for our evacuation from our base should we fail to get across.

On my way home in April 1960 I went to Santiago to discuss things with Jack. He was as enthusiastic as ever, but inclined to think that we should have a rest from Patagonia for a season, and spend his next long vacation exploring the volcanoes west of the Atacama desert instead. However, we discussed the question of landing an expedition at the head of one of the Pacific fjords with the President's Naval A.D.C., who seemed confident that the Chilean Navy would co-operate in such a project. I had plenty of time to consider the plan on the voyage home, and the more I thought about it the more exciting it seemed; so that by the time I reached England I was determined to attempt it the following season.

The choice of a starting point on the Pacific coast was one of fundamental importance. The Admiralty Chart showed no fewer than six fjords leading from the main north-south channel to the glaciers flowing down from the northern part of the Ice-cap, each offering a possible line of approach. Though they had all been charted at some time during the last 100 years, there appeared to be no recent data to show how far they were navigable. The Ice-cap could also be approached southward from the Canal Baker. This channel, which is more than 100 miles long, is the deepest inlet in the whole of that tortuous coastline. It has several branches; the most southerly of these, the Calun Fjord, contains the mouth of the Rio Pascua, which drains Lago O'Higgins. A few miles west of this afluent, the Jorge Monte Glacier, one of the largest in Patagonia, thrusts its massive front far out into the waters of the fjord.

After a careful study of the available data, I decided to approach the Ice-cap from this direction, a choice which offered several apparent advantages. In the first place the branches of the Canal Baker were far better charted than were the fjords to the south, and there was no doubt that a ship could safely reach a point within a few miles of the Jorge Montt Glacier. Secondly, the enormous size of this glacier suggested that it had an uninterrupted flow from the Ice-cap, which probably meant that the slopes leading up to the Plateau were comparatively gentle on the northern side. Thirdly, there was evidence that the glacier had shrunk considerably in recent decades, and in doing so it had probably left a strip of country free from forest, which might be a great help on the first stage of the journey. This argument would not apply to a glacier flowing through a less open valley.

The choice of the approach suggested an exciting extension to my original plan. Instead of merely crossing the northern section of the Plateau, I now envisaged a journey over the entire length of the Ice-cap to its southern extremity in the Cordon Darwin (a chain of mountains in the Cordillera Darwin) above Lago Argentino. The distance to be covered would be about 150 miles, twice that of the original plan and many times as long as any journey hitherto attempted in that part of the world. Certainly, the second half of it would be over ground previously covered and it was arguable that the extra time would be better spent in the unexplored northern sector; but as a large part of my object was to overcome the tyranny of wind and weather and the old bugbear of restricted travel, the idea of covering the whole region in one magnificent sweep had an irresistible appeal.

Jack agreed that the party should be composed of four members. It was important that we should all be competent mountaineers, and that at least one of the party should be a geologist. It was also most desirable that we should all have had some experience of the unpleasant conditions that we were likely to encounter, so that everyone would be well aware of what they were in for. After much deliberation we decided to invite two Chilean mountaineers, Eduardo García and Cedomir Marangunic, to join us. García (30) was the leader of the expedition that we had met on Lago O'Higgins. He had also been a member of the Japanese expedition to the mountains north of the Rio Baker in 1958, and of a Chilean expedition to Cerro Paine in 1959. With this experience he certainly knew what to expect. Marangunic (23) was a geologist, and he had been with García on Cerro O'Higgins. A Yugoslav by birth, his family had emigrated to Punta Arenas where they had adopted Chilean nationality; so he, too, was well acquainted with local conditions.

The key to the success of the venture lay in the choice of equipment. My previous experience had shown that the type of equipment used on mountaineering expeditions in the Himalayas was entirely inadequate against the rigours of the Patagonian climate. For example lightweight tents of the kind used for the high camps on Everest were quite incapable of withstanding torrential rain driven against them for hours on end by gale-force winds; and I was far from sure that they would not be destroyed by some of the more powerful gusts I had experienced in Patagonia. It was essential that we should have a tent with very high water-repellent qualities, that was capable of being pitched in the most violent wind, and strong enough and stable enough to withstand a prolonged battering from the most savage storms; otherwise, not only would life become quite intolerable, but we might find ourselves in a very precarious situation.

Jack urged that we should resort to the old-fashioned Pyramid tent used on the classic Antarctic sledge journeys, and still by no means obsolete. It is a double-skinned tent and its chief virtue is stability, for which, unlike most mountain tents, it does not rely upon its guys. Because of its shape the pressure of the wind tends to hold it down instead of lifting it up, and at the same time its poles are subjected to the minimum strain. With plenty of snow or other weights piled upon its skirts, or snowflaps, it can withstand an enormous force of wind. For its normal use on sledge journeys the ten-foot poles are made in single lengths, and are kept in place inside the canvas; it is then the easiest of all tents to pitch. But for mountaineers the Pyramid has several disadvantages, which account for the fact that they hardly ever use it. In the first place, it is very heavy; secondly, even when the poles are made in three sections, it packs into a very awkward load, and it is difficult to reassemble; finally, it requires a very wide platform on which to stand.

However, after listening to a great deal of conflicting advice on the subject from Polar explorers (much of it discouraging) I came round to Jack's view that the Pyramid was the only satisfactory solution to our tent problem. I ordered the standard model made by Camtors for the Falkland Islands Dependencies Survey. It was designed to accommodate three men, and was only just large enough to take the four of us. To increase the ground space appreciably would have meant adding considerably to the height of the tent, which would have made it harder to pitch and easier to blow down. The outer "skin" was made of Ventile 19, and the inner of a lighter fabric. Instead of a detachable groundsheet normally used, I had the tent made with a sewn-in groundsheet. The chief advantage of the former is that when the loads and the groundsheet have been packed up before striking camp, the tent can then be used as a latrine. I considered that we should forgo this luxury to secure greater protection from the wet; though, later, there were many moments when I questioned the wisdom of this choice. The tent weighed 60 lb; about twice as much as two 2-man mountain tents.

The question of clothing presented a difficult problem. At high altitudes, or indeed in any conditions of dry cold, however severe, it is a simple matter to provide complete protection: sufficient woollen, or better still, down undergarments, covered with a light windproof material are all that is required. But ordinary windproof cloth such as we had used on Everest is useless against hard-driven rain. I spent a great deal of time searching for a waterproof fabric that could be worn while doing hard physical work without becoming saturated with inside condensation. At length I came to the conclusion that no such material had yet been invented. "Gannex" cloth, which we had used the previous season, is devised to retard condensation so that if the garments can be ventilated at frequent intervals, they can be kept reasonably dry inside. Unfortunately, it is not possible to do this completely while carrying loads with the result that condensation is bound to occur locally (around the shoulders for example). However, the cloth had provided at least a partial solution to the problem, and I decided to use it again.

As the major part of the journey would be over the relatively flat surface of the Ice-cap, a sledge was one of the most important items of our equipment.

Sledge-hauling was a subject about which I knew almost nothing, and again I consulted the experts. The trouble was that none of the standard designs used in Polar regions was suitable for our purpose. Before we could use it, we expected to have to carry our sledge a very long way, through bogs and dense forest, over rough ground and shattered ice-falls, probably involving difficult mountaineering, and often exposed to a high wind. It was essential therefore that it should be collapsible, light, compact, easily portable and fairly tough. The advice of experts is usually conflicting, and I found that of Polar explorers to be no exception. Some told me, for example, that the Swedish "Pulka" sledge would be ideal for our purpose, others that it would be useless. Then there was the vexing problem of finding someone to make the sledge. I was still in the throes of indecision about six weeks before our baggage was due to be shipped to Punta Arenas, when I received a letter from John Bull, a young man who had been to the Antarctic with F.I.D.S. He told me that on hearing of my problem from Sir Vivien Fuchs, he had designed a collapsible sledge which could be made of fibreglass. He had consulted the Fibreglass Company of St. Helens who had agreed to make the sledge for nothing if he would provide them with a mould. I sent him a telegram and he spent the following week-end making the mould out of three-ply. The sledge arrived in London a few days before our baggage had to be sent to the docks. It was a strange-looking object, orange coloured and shaped like a shallow punt; it weighed 35 lb. and could be taken apart into four sections which fitted into each other like eggshells. On the bottom it had two narrow wooden slats to prevent it from slipping sideways.

Another question which I found hard to decide was whether or not to take skis. There could be no doubt about their value on the Ice-cap, where they would certainly save us a lot of hard work. But they are very awkward things to carry, particularly in thick forest and in a high wind. Jack, who has no half-hearted opinions, was strongly in favour of taking snowshoes instead. He had had some experience of using them in the Antarctic and considered that they were almost as good as skis for sledge-hauling. Though I discovered that very few of the experts shared this view, I decided to accept his judgement. It transpired, however, that there were no snowshoes available in Britain. Hillary told me that he had intended to get some for his expedition to the Himalaya and had scoured the country for them without success. In the end I approached Slazengers and asked if they would construct four pairs to my (or rather Jack's) specification. Their response was splendid; it seemed as though the entire staff took a personal interest in the matter; frequent discussions took place on the telephone between the works in Leeds and the London office and specimen snowshoes were sent to me by special messengers for my comment on various points.

Expedition food is always a fruitful topic for acrimonious discussion. There is a curious difference between Himalayan mountaineers and Polar explorers in their approach to this subject. While the latter have always been ready to accept a spartan ration for even their longest sledge journeys, a simple unvaried diet based entirely upon the nutritional value of the food, mountaineers usually insist that expedition food should be varied and palatable, and that their daily provisions should include a number of luxuries. This, I believe, is due to the tradition started by the early Everest expeditions and followed by most of the other classic expeditions to the great peaks of the Himalaya. It was thought that the climbers' appetites would be impaired by altitude and that everything possible must be done to tempt them to eat enough. The argument had some basis in fact; but the custom of lavish provisioning also arose from the fact that on these expeditions, transport was no real problem. We used to go to Everest, for example, with a cavalcade of 350 pack-animals, most of them carrying supplies that were far from essential. On the mountain itself there were innumerable porters available to carry our baggage; our advance was necessarily slow because of the need for acclimatization, so that a few days spent in carrying up extra food was a matter of little importance.

Like most traditions this one has been hard to break, and even today the idea of a basic food ration has not been widely accepted by mountaineers in the Himalaya. When, in the thirties, Tilman and I started our campaign to promote lightweight expeditions in that field, we were regarded as cranks in the matter of food. But our meagre diet was in the first place dictated by sheer necessity; then we discovered that, once we had got used to it, we were much better off with our simple fare. In fact we were only following the long established practice of Polar explorers.

Besides its primary value in saving weight, the basic ration makes it far easier to control the caloric intake of the party, and to ensure the maintenance of a balanced diet. Oddly enough it also seems to make people much more contented with their food, providing of course that the ration is sufficient for their needs. In my experience, which covers a very wide range of catering arrangements, I have always found that the more lavishly an expedition is victualled, the greater the variety of choice supplied, the more people complain about the food. I will not attempt to account for this curious psychological paradox.

I adopted the following ration scale (per man per day):

Sugar	8 ounces
Quaker oats	5 ounces
Wholemeal biscuit	4 ounces
Dehydrated meat	4 ounces
Butter	2 ounces
Cheese	2 ounces
Milk powder	4 ounces
Rum fudge	2 ounces
Soup powder	1 ounce
Potato powder	½ ounce
Total	32½ ounces

This provided about 4,500 calories. A supplementary supply of vitamins was taken in tablets. The exceptionally large amount of sugar allowed was, in a sense, a luxury; for sugar has a relatively low calorie/weight ratio; but I have found that it is always in very great demand on an expedition, even among people who do not normally consume much of it; presumaby because it is so rapidly converted into energy.

While I was engaged in procuring our food supplies, I had a great piece of luck. A firm of packers, Felber, Jucker and Co., was concerned with a process of vacuum packing food in a new plastic material called "Ralsin", which is extremely strong and almost as light as tissue paper. The head of the firm, Adrian Jucker, who happened by chance of hear of my plans, very kindly volunteered to pack our food in this way. When he explained the process to me I realized that it would provide the ideal solution to an old problem. Hitherto when calculating the logistics of a mountain journey at least 20 per cent had to be added to the weight of food carried to allow for packing; and on a long journey this amounted to a very considerable extra burden. But Ralsin was so light that its weight could be virtually ignored; moreover it was so strong that it could stand any amount of rough handling, and so impervious that it could be soaked in water indefinitely and still afford complete protection to the food inside.

A four-man/day ration of each food item was weighed into a Ralsin bag, which was then treated by the vacuum sealing machine. The effect of this on the food inside was to compress it into a hard, flat slab; though as soon as the bag was opened and the vacuum released, the food would expand again into its normal consistency. One of each item was put into a larger bag, which was also sealed and formed a day-pack for the party. The only items that were not dealt with in this way were the butter and the cheese which were shipped out in cold storage.

It was obviously impossible to make a precise estimate of how long the journey over the Ice-cap would take. The most important unknown factors were the difficulties we would encounter in reaching the Plateau and the extent to which our progess there would be impeded by the weather. The previous season it had taken us more than two weeks to carry all our baggage to the head of the O'Higgins Glacier, despite the fact that we had followed a known route and had been able to use pack transport through the forest. With neither of these two great advantages, it might easily take us twice as long to make our way up the Jorge Montt Glacier. I was well aware that we would be lucky if we got more than 10 per cent of reasonably fine weather during the journey; it was quite likely that we would get none at all. Before reaching the Ice-cap I reckoned that we would be able to press on regardless of the weather; but on the Plateau it would be a different matter, and there we might be held up for long periods, unable to move. However, the fact that the prevailing wind is from the north-west while we would be travelling on a southerly course, was very much in our favour.

In view of these unknown factors, it seemed best to base our estimates largely upon our carrying powers and to make our timetable fit in with this. Carrying 60-lb. loads we would be able to shift 720 lb. in three relays. The estimated weight of our equipment (tent, sledge, etc.), was 208 lb.; the balance of 512 lb. would provide enough food and fuel for fifty-five days. Assuming that it would take us three weeks to reach the head of the Jorge Montt Glacier, we would arrive on the Ice-cap with enough provisions for another thirty-four days, and a total weight of baggage of 525 lb., which was probably the maximum load that we could drag on the sledge. Thus a supply of food and fuel for fifty-five days was a convenient amount to start with. Unless the difficulties were very much greater than expected, eight weeks seemed a reasonable allowance of time in which to complete the crossing, and even this could be safely protracted for a week or so by cutting down our rations towards the end of the journey. I had sixty day-loads prepared, and took some additional food in bulk for dumping at our starting point in case we should fail to make the crossing and be forced to retreat.

The Chilean Navy offered to take the expedition from Punta Arenas to our chosen base on the southern shore of the Canal Baker, in a small vessel, *Micalvi*, used for servicing the navigation lights and maintaining contact with the few scattered settlements along the coasts. As my companions all worked at the University of Chile, their available time was restricted to the period of the long vacation, which in Chile is between mid-December and the beginning of March; so we had originally planned to start shortly before Christmas. Later it appeared that *Micalvi* would not be available then, and the time of our departure from Punta Arenas was put forward to about December 10; but they managed to get special permission to leave before the end of term.

I arranged for our stores and equipment to be shipped out on the Pacific Steam Navigation Company's M.V. *Salaverry*, which was due to sail from London at the end of October and to reach Punta Arenas on November 18. Everything was packed in two large crates which were ready to be taken to the docks on September 26, when I was notified that owing to a strike of tally clerks there was such congestion on the wharves, that no more cargo could be received. At first I was not greatly concerned, as there seemed to be plenty of time in hand. But as the strike dragged on, and there seemed little hope of a settlement, I became seriously alarmed that our baggage would arrive too late for our rendezvous in Punta Arenas. I heard that there was another ship sailing from Antwerp about October 20 for the same destination, and had almost decided to send the crates, which together weighed more than half a ton, over to catch it, when, on the 12th, I was told that *Salaverry* had gone to Glasgow to load, and that the baggage must be there to be put aboard not later than 14th. The crates were dispatched north by Express Delivery, though how the bulk of the ship's cargo could be sent all the way from London to Glasgow at such short notice I could not imagine. Then on 14th I heard that the Glasgow dockers were refusing to handle *Salaverry*'s cargo and the ship was being sent to Liverpool. However, at the last moment the strike ended, and a few days later I learnt, with enormous relief, that *Salaverry* had sailed with my precious crates on board. She was now expected to arrive at Punta Arenas on December 4, which still allowed a few days to spare for further delays.

CHAPTER NINE

Crisis in Punta Arenas

It was a dismal winter evening, with a raw wind and light rain, when I left London for Buenos Aires. Three days later, on November 30, having flown nearly half-way round the world, I arrived at Punta Arenas to find myself in similar conditions, except that the wind was more biting and the rain heavier. I was met at the airfield by William Booth, of the British Consulate and Cyril Jervis, who drove me to the town. A hotel room had been booked for me: but it seemed almost as cheerless as the weather outside and did nothing to dispel the impression that I was in a very remote corner of the world.

After lunch, clad in climbing boots, two heavy sweaters and an anorak, I summoned up the necessary resolution to go for a walk. Picking my way through a morass of mud and puddles which threatened to engulf my ankles, buffeted at each street corner by a piercing blast, I was not inclined, on that summer afternoon, to form a very favourable first impression of Punta Arenas ("Sandy Point"). Like all Patagonian towns that I had seen, it had an air of impermanence, as though it had been thrown together in a haphazard fashion for the temporary accommodation of a nomadic population. Certainly, unlike Rio Gallegos or Santa Cruz, it had some large and solid buildings that looked as though they had been built to stay, but for the rest one was reminded of a film version of a Klondyke gold-rush town, emerging from the grip of the long Arctic winter. It is only fair to add that when I saw it in the sunshine, and with my spirits warmed by the delightful hospitality of the inhabitants, this first jaundiced view was considerably modified.

I climbed up into the hills to the west and was soon out of sight of the town. Summer arrives late in these southern latitudes; the season was equivalent to the end of May in the northern hemisphere, and yet here, in Latitude 53°S., corresponding to that of Northern England, it seemed as though spring had scarcely begun. The country had the wild, bleak look of the Yorkshire moors on a stormy day in midwinter, snow lay still on the higher ground, and no flowers had yet ventured to bloom among the coarse grass tussocks. Some dead trees were scattered here and there, their skeleton branches bearded with lichen, and the harsh cries of the plovers overhead enhanced the melancholy of the scene. Out over the Straits of Magellan a few shafts of sunlight pierced the racing clouds and lit the grey sea with a lurid glow.

The next morning I called on Admiral Balaresque, Commander of the 3rd Naval Zone based on Punta Arenas. He had some very bad news to tell me. Apparently *Micalvi*, the ship that was to have taken us to the Canal Baker, had recently been driven ashore in a storm and so severely damaged that even if she were not a total loss, it would certainly be a very long time before she was in commission again. Moreover all the available ships in the area were heavily engaged in salvage operations, and the Admiral could see no prospect of being able to provide us with an alternative means of transport for at least a month or six weeks when, even if it were then forthcoming, it would probably be too late for my companions to embark on the expedition. He told me, however, that the main fleet was due to arrive at Punta Arenas that day from Valparaiso and was returning north about December 10; he thought it possible that the Commander-in-Chief might allow us to be taken to the Canal Baker in one of the smaller ships which could rejoin the fleet farther north. Naturally he could not promise anything but he generously offered to do anything he could for us.

I had lunch with Mr. and Mrs. Sven Robson at their house at Rio Seco, 12 kilometres along the coast from Punta Arenas. Their garden was a riot of colour such as I have rarely seen even in the best tended gardens in England. Robson was the Manager of the South American Export Company which operated a large meat-freezing plant at Rio Seco, and he also held the honorary post of British Consul. He very kindly invited me to stay at the staff guest house of the "Freezer". I moved to these comfortable quarters that afternoon, and spent most of the next few days walking in the hills and having long discussions with Cyril Jervis, the Chief Engineer of the "Freezer", who lived at the guest house.

Jervis was a man of decided views and a wide variety of interests. He spent much of his spare time operating his amateur radio, with which he communicated with other Hams in all parts of he world. One of his most regular contacts was Herbert Masters at Estancia La Cristina, at the head of the north-western branch of Lago Argentina, with whom he was on familiar terms despite the fact that they had never met. At that time Herbert was away in Rio Gallegos, and so "off the air"; but Jervis promised that when they next spoke to each other, he would tell him that we hoped to reach La Cristina from the Ice-cap during the first half of February. Less than a week later Jervis' radio was to play a decisive part in the shaping of our fortunes.

The latest news of *Salaverry* was that she was expected in Punta Arenas on December 6, and she was now so near the end of her voyage that there seemed to be no reason to fear a further delay. If we were to be taken north in a ship of the main fleet, it seemed that we would not be leaving before the 10th, which would allow plenty of time for unloading our baggage from *Salaverry* and checking over the stores and equipment. Meanwhile a letter from Jack informed me that he and the other two were extremely busy winding up their professional affairs in Santiago and had arranged to fly to Punta Arenas in a military plane on the 8th. It seemed to be cutting things a bit fine, but I assumed that they knew what they were about. With nothing to do but await events and keep my fingers crossed, I decided to go over to Tierra del Fuego to spend the week-end with my friends the Bridges; so I took a plane to Rio Grande on Saturday morning, the 3rd, having booked a passage on the next return flight on Tuesday the 6th, so as to be back in Punta Arenas in time for *Salaverry*'s arrival.

I was met at Rio Grande by Oliver and Betsy Bridges, who drove me to their *estancia*, Viamonte, on the Atlantic coast, forty miles farther south. On Sunday we went to lunch with their friend George, the Manager of the Tennessee Valley Oil Company's concession near Rio Grande. It was a most convivial party and I was feeling distinctly mellow when we started back at 3.30. On our way through the town, Oliver stopped at his agent's office to pick up his mail. Among this was an urgent telegram for me from Robson, sent an hour or so after I had left Punta Arenas the day before. It told me that arrangements had been made for the expedition to be taken to the Canal Baker on a frigate, which was under orders to sail at noon on Wednesday, the 7th; and that this was the last opportunity we would get. Robson also told me that he had informed Jack by telegram, and he advised me to return immediately.

That I must do so was obvious; but the next plane back (on which I was booked) was on Tuesday the 6th, and was not due to reach Punta Arenas until the late afternoon. This would allow me very little time to get the baggage off *Salaverry* (if she had arrived), deal with the customs formalities, which are apparently necessary even in a "free port", sort out the equipment, and have our fuel containers filled with paraffin. Moreover, in that part of the world, flight schedules are even less reliable than in Europe, and planes are often delayed by as much as twenty-four hours. Actually I was quite unaware of the real nature of the crisis until much later; which was a good thing for it saved me a very unpleasant thirty-six hours.

After discussing the matter at some length, Betsy suggested that we should go back to George and ask him to help me out. I was reluctant to ask such a favour from a comparative stranger, but there seemed to be no alternative. When we returned to the oil camp, George was sleeping off the effects of his own lavish hospitality; he was, however, generous enough not only to excuse our rude interruption of his siesta, but to offer very practical help. He said that if I returned at 9 o'clock the following morning he would arrange to have me flown in the Company's plane to a place called Sombrero, an oil town about 300 kilometres away. From there I would almost certainly be able to get a lift to Puerto Porvenir on the Magellan Straits, whence a ship sailed over to Punta Arenas every afternoon starting at about 4 o'clock. This appeared to solve my problem and I went back to enjoy another night at Viamonte with an easy mind.

The main island of Tierra del Fuego is divided between Chile and Argentina; the frontier runs from north to south roughly through the middle, with Rio Grande in Argentina and Sombrero in Chile. When I arrived at the oil camp on Monday morning, I found that a complication had arisen. Apparently international regulations stipulated that no plane was allowed to cross the frontier without at least twenty-four hours' notice; which meant that I could not be taken to Sombrero by air. However George very kindly supplied me with a car and a driver instead. This alternative arrangement took some time to make, and it was 11 o'clock before we set out, which meant that we would have to average at least 40 m.p.h. if I were to catch the ship. Much, of course, depended upon the condition of the road, which turned out to be far from good. Moreover the driver, who was obviously not at all pleased to have been given the job, was quite out of sympathy with my sense of urgency; and gradually my hopes sank as we bumped over the endless flat expanse of country.

At 1 o'clock we reached the Argentine frontier post, where I hoped that the formalities would not be unduly protracted. After examining our papers, the gendarme in charge informed us that no vehicle was allowed to leave the country without a special permit, which apparently we did not possess. He was quite unmoved by my entreaties, which were probably unintelligible anyway, and there was nothing for it but to turn back; a decision which the driver accepted with irritating complacency. We had covered about fifteen kilometres on the way back, travelling a great deal faster than before, when we met a large lorry bound for Sombrero. I decided to cadge a lift on it, for although I realized that there was no chance of catching the ship from Puerto Porvenir, I still hoped that there might be some alternative means of reaching Punta Arenas that day. I was squeezed in between the lorry driver and his mate, who were most friendly; and when I had made them understand that I was in a hurry, the huge vehicle began to travel at an incredible speed. At 4.30 we thundered into Sombrero. The whole town looked almost as if it had sprung up overnight.

Oliver had given me a letter of introduction to an Anglo-Chilean friend, Mr. Sutherland, an executive of the oil company in Sombrero. The driver knew where he lived and presently we stopped in front of a pleasant modern bungalow, which might have been one of a garden suburb in England. It stood near a church made of gaily painted wood and of a most unconventional design, which rather reminded me of a Walt Disney cartoon. Mr. Sutherland was away on the mainland, but his wife invited me in and sat me at a table spread for a very English tea. She spoke even less English than I Spanish; but Oliver's letter explained my problem, and having read it she started to make a series of telephone calls while I was charmingly entertained by her nine-year-old daughter. After tea Mrs. Sutherland appeared to have matters under control; indeed she seemed so confident that all would be well that I was quite content to leave myself in her capable hands without even bothering to find out what was happening.

At 6 o'clock a small bus, or *collectivo* arrived, and in this, the only passenger, I departed for my still unknown destination. An hour or so later, having covered some sixty kilometres, we reached a cluster of corrugated iron sheds near the shore of a wide lagoon; there was also a jetty with a tiny freighter alongside. The water of the lagoon and the gentle, arid hills surrounding it, reflected the golden light of the evening sun. This, I discovered, was Puerto Percy, used by the oil company for bringing equipment and supplies over from the mainland. I also learnt that the freighter was due to sail for Punta Arenas at 10 o'clock that night.

The little ship arrived at Punta Arenas at 2 o'clock in the morning and one of the crew escorted me to the Hotel de France where I was given a bed in a double room. At 3.30, just as I was dropping off to sleep, my room mate came in, still obviously enjoying the effects of his evening's entertainment, and in no way abashed to find that he had company. I rose at 6.30, dressed, shaved and swallowed some coffee; then I waited impatiently until 8 o'clock, which I felt was the earliest that I could decently telephone to Robson. It was then that I heard the shattering news.

Salaverry had been further delayed and was now expected to arrive on the 8th, twenty-four hours after the time fixed for the departure of the frigate *Covadonga* which was to take the expedition to the Canal Baker. Robson had been in consultation with the Admiral who had regretfully told him that *Covadonga*'s sailing could not possibly be delayed as this would affect the scheduled movements of the whole fleet. It seemed, in that sickening moment, as though our whole enterprise was on the verge of collapse.

There was, however, one chance that all was not yet lost. The Admiral had suggested that if we could get into contact with the Commander of *Salaverry*, Captain Thomas, and persuade him to co-operate, it might be possible either to transfer our baggage from *Salaverry* to *Covadonga*, when the two ships passed each other somewhere in the Channels, or for our baggage to be put ashore on one of the islands, where it could be picked up by the frigate on her way north. It appeared that the Commander-in-Chief had agreed to this proposal; but would Captain Thomas? It seemed a great deal to ask of any commander, particularly one whose ship was already several weeks late, to undertake, without the authority of his company, an operation which would certainly delay him still further and might involve some risk in those difficult and usually stormy waters; to say nothing of the extra work imposed upon himself and his crew. I imagine that there are very few who would not refuse such a request. Then there was the purely practical matter of whether such a manoeuvre were possible. But the most intractable question of all was this: would Captain Thomas be able to locate our two crates and get them out? They had been loaded in Glasgow as ordinary freight, he still had about 2,000 tons of cargo in his holds, most of which had been taken on during the voyage, so that it seemed more than probable that our baggage was somewhere near the bottom of its particular hold; and it would obviously be impossible to shift even 100 tons of cargo while still at sea. The more I pondered the situation, the more hopeless it seemed.

Meanwhile, however, one important obstacle had been removed. South American customs officials are not as a rule the easiest of people to persuade to deviate from their regulations (at least not by words alone); their bureaucratic instincts are usually well developed. To discharge cargo before it reached the port to which it was consigned, at some unspecified point on the coast, is a highly irregular procedure; and yet Robson had managed to obtain permission from the customs authorities in Punta Arenas for it to be done. This certainly was encouraging. Also, at Robson's request, Jervis had succeeded the previous evening in making contact with *Salaverry*, and had arranged for us to speak to Captain Thomas at 1.30 that afternoon.

I spent most of the morning at Naval Headquarters. The Admiral and his staff were extremely kind and went to a great deal of trouble considering the various aspects of the problem and working out alternative plans to submit to Captain Thomas should he be willing and able to co-operate. *Salaverry*'s position when Jervis had contacted her at 6 p.m. on Monday was in the northern part of the Gulf of Penas. Assuming a speed of fifteen knots she should have passed through the English Narrows by noon that day. Situated at the southern end of this channel there is a small meteorological station called Puerto Eden, the only inhabited locality for several hundred miles in either direction. It was also calculated that *Salaverry* and *Covadonga* would in all probability pass each other in the dark during the night of the 7th, when it would be extremely difficult to transfer the baggage, even in the unlikely event of fine weather. It was therefore thought that we would probably have to resort to the alternative plan whereby Captain Thomas would put our baggage ashore at an agreed point on the coast for us to pick up. After a careful study of the charts it was decided that the best place for this would be Fortescue Bay, an uninhabited inlet on the south-west coast of the Brunswick Peninsula which offered a protected anchorage and a sandy beach. I became so absorbed in these fascinating plans, that I almost forgot how very unlikely it was that they would be put into operation.

There was another important matter that I discussed with the Admiral. When it was arranged for the expedition to be taken to the Canal Baker in *Micalvi*, it had been agreed that the ship should pay a second visit to our landing-place about five weeks later, so that in the event of our failing to reach the Ice-cap, we could return there to be evacuated. Now, with the new arrangement, this plan had to be reconsidered, and it was evidently a problem that was causing the Admiral some concern. In view of the great courtesy shown us by the Navy, and the lengths to which they had gone to help us, I was most reluctant to press for a relief to be sent. On the other hand I was not quite happy at the prospect of starting the journey with no line of retreat. However, an unexpected solution presented itself.

For some years the Chilean Government had been working on a project to establish settlements at suitable points along the vast stretch of the country's southern coastline. I now discovered that comparatively recently one such settlement, composed of two families, had been established quite close to the point that we had chosen to land. This fact, of course, altered the whole position, for it meant that if we should fail to cross the Ice-cap, instead of being stranded in uninhabited country we would be able to fall back upon the settlement where at least we would find the means of survival for an indefinite period. So I told the Admiral not to bother to send a relief at least until the end of February, when it would be clear that we had failed to make the crossing, and that even then there would be no particular hurry.

Robson drove me out to Rio Seco for lunch. With the fate of the expedition about to be settled I felt slightly sick and had little appetite. After lunch we assembled in Jervis' room, and at 1.30 precisely he switched on his transmitter and began the rigmarole of repeating call signs. Presently, with some relief, I heard the voice of *Salaverry*'s radio operator, and Jervis and he began what seemed an interminable exchange of technical information about reception conditions. Then Jervis asked if Robson might speak to the Captain, and there was a long pause while the latter was brought from the bridge. After a further interchange of call signs, Captain Thomas came on the air addressing Robson. He had no idea, of course, what was afoot, and began by asking a number of questions about arrangements for the discharge of his cargo, which had then to be answered. I tried hard to judge the character of the man from his voice, and derived a good deal of comfort from its calm, good-humoured tone.

Then at last Robson broached the crucial issue. Briefly and clearly he explained the situation, outlining our project and emphasizing the vital part the Chilean Navy were playing in our plans. I could not have had a better advocate. I added my personal plea, and then waited, holding my breath, while the transmission was switched over. Captain Thomas began by saying that he was delighted to make my acquaintaince even if it were only on the air, and that he had always been keenly interested in the expeditions to Everest. He did not seem in the least put out by our extraordinary request, and without any hesitation went on to say that he would "do his damndest" to help us out. But he warned me that he could promise nothing; he had no idea where our crates were, and it was quite probable that they were in a part of the hold which could not be reached. He told us to contact him again at 4.30, by which time he would be able give us the answer. I did my best to thank him, and then told him of the Navy's proposal that he should put the baggage ashore at Fortescue Bay. He replied that he had never heard of the place, but that he would look into the matter and discuss it later if he had succeeded in extracing the crates; and with that the conversation closed. For the first time that day, despite the Captain's warning, I felt that there was a reasonable chance of the expedition starting. In my excitement I had quite forgotten to inquire about *Salaverry*'s position.

Meanwhile there was another question to worry about. Would the others arrive in time? On Saturday, Robson had sent a message to Jack through the British Embassy in Santiago telling him that they must reach Punta Arenas before noon on Wednesday; on Monday he received word from the Embassy, that the party had left that afternoon for Buenos Aires, presumably because there was no plane direct to Punta Arenas. There was an Argentine Airlines plane due to leave Buenos Aires at midnight on Tuesday and to reach Punta Arenas at 11 on Wednesday morning. It was the one I had come by the week before, and then it had arrived at noon. I could only hope that they would manage to get seats on this flight (not always an easy matter at short notice), and that the plane would be on time.

However, a pleasant surprise was in store for me: at 4 o'clock came the news that the others had arrived on the plane from Rio Grande. Speaking to Jack on the telephone I heard enough about their adventures to realize that it had been a very close call. He had not received Robson's message until late on Monday morning. There was a plane from Santiago to Punta Arenas on Tuesday, but on this there were no seats available. The Argentine Airlines Comet was due to leave for Buenos Aires in two hours' time and he decided to try to catch it in the hope of being able to take Tuesday night's plane to Punta Arenas. But there was a great deal to be done in that time: García and Marangunic had to be located and alerted; money for the long journey to be obtained from the bank; an Argentine visa to be secured; and a number of other matters to be seen to including his packing. They caught the Comet with no time to spare. When they reached Buenos Aires they found that there were no seats available on Tuesday's plane to Punta Arenas. However, they discovered that there was a plane belonging to a privately owned company, "Austral", leaving for Rio Grande in two hours' time from another airfield, twenty miles away. If this plane was on time it should arrive just in time for them to catch the one on to Punta Arenas. It did.

The unexpected arrival of the rest of the party seemed to be a good omen, Surely, I thought, our luck would not desert us now. All the same I was in a state of considerable nervous tension when we assembled in Jervis' room again at 4.30. Contact with *Salaverry* was established, and again there was a long exchange of technical talk between Jervis and the ship's operator, which I found hard to bear with patience, before Captain Thomas was allowed to speak. But at last he came through with the wonderful news that the crates had been found and brought out of the hold. He said that as they were far too big to be put into his ship's boats, they would have to be opened and the stores and equipment repacked into manageable parcels; to which I readily agreed.

The Captain told us that his ship was then approaching the northern entrance to the English Narrows, in thick weather. I immediately saw that yet another piece of good fortune had come our way; for this meant that *Salaverry* had not yet passed Puerto Eden, which seemed to be the perfect place to put our baggage ashore. The Captain agreed to my suggestion and while we discussed further details, Robson telephoned to the Admiral and secured his consent to the new arrangement. My somewhat inarticulate expression of thanks to Captain Thomas was cut short by his obvious desire to return to his bridge to supervise the difficult piece of navigation ahead of him.

A sense of enormous relief flooded over me, and with it a feeling of profound gratitude to all the kind people whose generous co-operation had overcome what had seemed, a few hours before, an impossible situation.

CHAPTER TEN

Voyage Through the Channels

THERE were several matters still to be dealt with on Wednesday morning. We had visited *Covadonga* the evening before to pay our respects to her Commander, Captain Roebke, who had asked us to come aboard at 12.30. We divided the chores between us, and having arranged to meet at 12.15 at Cedomir Marangunic's parents' home, a few minutes' walk from the quay, we spent a busy morning obtaining a supply of paraffin and hunting for temporary containers to put it in, making a number of small purchases and getting Argentine money from the bank against our eventual arrival in that country. Having also said my goodbyes, I arrived at the Marangunics' house at 12.18 to collect the others.

To my dismay I found that a luncheon party had been arranged in honour of the departing son of the house, to which we were invited together with several other friends and relations. I said that we could not possibly stop for lunch, as we were due on board the frigate in ten minutes. But my protests were cheerfully brushed aside, not only by our hosts but also by my companions. They mockingly suggested that I must have forgotten that I was now in Chile, where punctuality was not regarded with the same reverence as in England. Also, I was told that our host was acquainted with Captain Roebke, and that he was a very good chap, though this argument seemed a bit irrelevant. Chile or no Chile, it seemed to be a gross breach of manners to fail to comply with the Captain's request, to say nothing of the possibility of jeopardizing the whole expedition. On the other hand it seemed rather churlish to insist upon wrecking the family's farewell party, and not a very good beginning to my relationship with my Chilean companions. So, having been assured that it would not take more than a few minutes to consume the meal, I quickly capitulated.

As I feared, the luncheon proved to be an elaborate affair of many courses, slowly and formally served. Once having allowed it to begin, it was impossible for me to cut it short without being downright rude; and I had to curb my impatience as well as I could. It was 1.30 before we departed. When we reached the quay I saw to my horror that the frigate had gone, and was already some miles out to sea. For a ghastly moment I thought that she had sailed without us. However, there was a launch manned by naval ratings alongside the quay, and we were informed by a petty officer in charge, that *Covadonga* had merely gone out to box the compass.

It was a protracted operation, and when it was completed she returned to within a quarter of a mile of the quay, and we were taken out to her in the launch. We went forward to report to the Captain, who spoke perfect English and greeted me with these words:

"It's a pity, Mr. Shipton, that you couldn't keep the timetable we'd arranged. We may have a small navy but we take it seriously."

I would have been very glad if a trap-door had opened and swallowed me up. There was no possible reply to that withering reprimand. In the first place it was thoroughly deserved, and to have attempted an explanation would have made matters far worse. However, having delivered his broadside, Captain Roebke waved aside my muttered apologies and went on to make a charming little speech of welcome. He told us that he was honoured to have us in his ship, that he and his ship's company were entirely at our service and that he hoped we would make ourselves at home and consider ourselves free to visit his bridge whenever we wished to do so. Certainly these were no idle words, for throughout the voyage we were treated with delightful courtesy and everything possible was done to make us comfortable.

Covadonga headed due south into a stiff breeze and a choppy sea. To the west, the coast of the Brunswick Peninsula, the southernmost promontory of the American Continent, looked wild and bleak with the ragged clouds racing over its low hills. As I looked out over this stormy scene, I felt a great sense of joyous excitement. I could wish for nothing better than to be here on this warship at the start of a 600-mile voyage through the narrow channels of one of the most fantastic archipelagos on earth, bound for the best of all mountaineering adventures, a journey through an unexplored range. Life occasionally provides moments of complete happiness; this, for me, was one.

We had come aboard with a minimum of clothing, as we intended to abandon most of it as soon as we got the expedition equipment. As the others had brought practically no warm garments, they were provided with padded anoraks from the ship's stores. Jack and I were given berths in the ship's dispensary and the others occupied a cabin near by. We had our meals with the officers, most of whom spoke good English. After dinner that evening, I was handed a signal from Captain Thomas which said that our baggage had been repacked into twenty-seven parcels which had been put ashore at Puerto Eden. I drafted a message of thanks which Captain Roebke kindly undertook to signal to *Salaverry* as we passed her at about 2 o'clock in the morning. We went to bed early, and rocked by the gentle heaving of the ship, I went to sleep with a feeling of profound contentment.

When we came out on deck the next morning we were greeted by a biting wind. The scene had changed. Although we were still in the Straits of Magellan, we had rounded the southernmost cape and were heading north-west through a narrow channel between the mainland and the island of Santa Ines. On both sides the land rose precipitously from a belt of forest along the shore, and disappeared into the clouds some 2,000 feet above. Freshly fallen snow lay nearly down to the water's edge, which made it difficult to believe that we were within a fortnight of Midsummer Day.

For many hundreds of miles, the shores along this labyrinth of channels are uninhabited, and the interior of most of the islands is either completely unexplored, or very imperfectly known. Santa Ines is no exception. One of the largest islands of the archipelago, it is some 80 miles long and 50 miles wide and, though none of its mountains are more than 4,000 feet high, the central part of it appears to be covered by an extensive ice-sheet. Two expeditions have attempted to explore the interior of the island; they both failed to penetrate more than a few miles inland, partly because of the appalling weather conditions that they encountered, and partly because of the difficulty of the terrain.

During the morning we had a long discussion about our plans for the journey. We found that we were in agreement about most matters: but there was one most important exception. Eduardo and Cedomir approved of my choice of a landing-place, but Jack was most strongly of the opinion that we should land some fifteen miles farther east, near the mouth of the Rio Pascua. He reckoned that we were likely to run into considerable difficulties in the upper part of the Jorge Montt Glacier, which we could avoid by taking a more easterly route. We on the other hand considered that by following his route we were likely to be faced with weeks of hard work forcing our way through forest and over a subsidiary range of mountains. We debated the matter for a long time but in the end Jack, though he held to his basic contentions, agreed that the proximity of the settlement might perhaps be a decisive factor.

Meanwhile I was trying to get the measure of my two Chilean companions, and they, presumably, of me. To embark upon an undertaking of this sort with complete strangers may seem rash. But the choice of companions for an exploration is in any case something of a lottery, and my experience has taught me to mistrust my judgement in the matter. Normal acquaintance with a man, however close, is a very poor guide to whether or not he will be a suitable or even a tolerable companion on an expedition. Faults that may normally seem utterly trivial, often become nagging irritations in the enforced intimacy of an expedition; characteristics that may never appear in ordinary life can be distressingly or splendidly revealed in conditions of hardship, danger and physical or nervous strain. Some men who will rise magnificently to a crisis, may yet wilt under the stress of enforced inactivity. Then there is the diverse interplay of characters upon one another. A man may find himself with two companions, both of whom he likes very much, but who cannot tolerate each other. One of my most successful and delightful expedition partnerships was with a man who, I had been warned, was generally regarded as quite impossible to travel with. The argument of those who believe that an "arranged" marriage has at least as much chance of success as one based upon a love affair, seems to be applicable here.

I had taken an immediate liking to García and Marangunic when I met them in Punta Arenas, and for once my first impressions were confirmed and, on the whole, remained unaltered. García was thick-set, dark and fairly short. Though he seemed reserved at first, I soon discovered that he was a voluble talker, that he had a lively wit and was always ready with an amusing crack about the current situation. He had plenty of self-confidence, and although this was never unpleasantly obtrusive, he was not inclined to take advice. By profession he was an instructor in physical education, though his training had included the study of psychology. Marangunic was tall and spare. In build and to some extent in appearance he resembled Ed Hillary. His chief facial characteristic was his massive underhung jaw giving him the appearance of great determination, which indeed he had. He was quiet, slow of speech, but though he lacked the sparkling humour of Garćia, he was by no means dour, and his face was always ready to light up with a broad grin which caused his huge jaw to stick out even more. Like many determined people he was apt to be stubborn, though his obstinacy was tempered by a logical judgement; he never took up a position without careful thought, and he was generally right.

Jack had told me that neither of them could speak English, which had made me a bit apprehensive. However, I found that he was wrong. García spoke it fairly fluently, though quite ungrammatically; but he had a good deal of difficulty in understanding. Marangunic on the other hand could speak very little, but seemed to understand everything that was said. Thus with one speaking and the other understanding we got along splendidly. Following the modern English custom, Jack and I called them by their Christian names from the start; but though invited to follow suit they persisted throughout the expedition in calling us Mr. Ewer and Mr. Shipton.

We spent most of the day on the bridge, watching the frigate being steered along her tortuous course, past innumerable islets and an endless succession of passages, some in the form of narrow canyons, some wider than the main channel. Many of the features bore English names, such as Duke of York's Bay, Carrington Island, Smyth Channel and Cochrane Bight, evidence of the part played by British navigators in the monumental work of charting the vast maze of waterways. About noon we reached the western end of the Straits of Magellan, crossed a wide bay opening out to the Pacific Ocean, and then plunged into the still more intricate channels to the north. For most of the day it was stormy, and often we were hit by squalls of rain or sleet, which reduced visibility almost to zero. But towards evening the weather improved; the clouds lifted and the sun broke through, creating the complete arch of a brilliant rainbow against a distant squall, while far away to the east we caught glimpses of some ice-crested peaks framed by the dark green walls of a wide channel. This was the entrance to the Calvo Fjord, up which Tilman's *Mischief* had sailed to the foot of the main range.

I awoke early the next morning to find that the engines had stopped, and going out on deck I saw that the frigate was riding at anchor. We appeared to be in a lake, and not a very large lake either, for there was land close on every side. Though it was still only 6.30, the sun was already high and warm. It was a brilliantly fine morning; the air had a limpid clarity that is found only in those parts of the world subject to long spells of rain; the light and dark greens of the *nothofagus* forest, splashed here and there with clumps of white magnolias, the glacier-capped peaks of Wellington Island and the cloudless sky were mirrored in the still water about the ship. The contrast to the cold, tempestuous scene of the previous day was astonishing; it was as though we had sailed during the night into a new world of light and colour and peace.

On the westward shore, about half a mile away, there was a single concrete building with a wireless mast; this was the meterorological station of Puerto Eden. Three or four small boats had put out from the shore and were approaching the frigate. When they came alongside I saw that they were very flimsy craft, very roughly constructed. The occupants, two or three in each boat, were savage-looking people, men, women and children, clad in skin or ragged cloth garments, some with long, matted hair falling over their faces and shoulders. These were the Alacaluf Indians, of which there was a small number at Puerto Eden. They squatted motionless in their boats, gazing up at the frigate with expressionless mongoloid faces. Some of the boats contained piles of enormous mussels.

Our twenty-seven bundles of equipment and stores were brought on board, and we made a rough check of the contents before breakfast. The Captain had told us that we would stay at Puerto Eden for most of that day, to avoid reaching the upper part of Canal Baker in the dark; so, after breakfast the four of us were taken ashore in one of the ship's lifeboats, driven by an outboard motor. The meteorological station had a staff of three men who showed us over their sparsely furnished quarters. They were obviously delighted to have visitors, which in the circumstances was hardly surprising. They told us that their term of duty in this lonely post was two years. Though on that particular morning it was difficult to imagine a more lovely spot, their usual environment was very different. For months on end in the summer, rain and mist were their daily portion and this was the first time they had seen the sun for more than three weeks. In winter it was bitterly cold, and the nights were long. Apart from their routine duties, there was little for them to do; a certain amount of fishing in the channels, and occasionally a short hunting expedition, though the difficulty of the terrain prevented them going far from the station. However, they did not seem to be unduly depressed by their lot.

Accompanied by one of them, we went for a walk inland. There was no path, and we had not gone more than twenty yards from the station when we found ourselves floundering in a bog, sinking half-way to our knees in mud at every step. Beyond this we started climbing the steep, forested mountainside, and here we had to force our way through dense, tough undergrowth, clutched by thorny brambles and tripped by moss-hidden roots. This and the bog below provided us with a salutary reminder of the kind of country that we might have to penetrate in the early stages of our journey. Even without loads it was exhausting work, and the thought of doing it with 60 lb. on our backs was not a happy one. I began to wonder whether my estimate of three weeks to reach the Ice-cap would not prove to be wildly optimistic.

Sweating profusely we scrambled up 600 feet or so, and sat basking in the hot sun. Although from there the channels were now open to our view they still looked like a number of narrow, interconnected lakes, divided by scores of wooded islands and promontories, and it was hard to believe that they were a part of the Pacific Ocean, and that they would allow the passage of 10,000 ton vessels on a much frequented shipping route.

Returning to the station we visited some huts belonging to the Alacaluf, scattered along the shore. These people have from time immemorial inhabited the shores of the archipelago from the Gulf of Penas in the north to the western entrance to the Straits of Magellan, a distance of more than 500 miles. Though there is no evidence to show that they ever numbered more than a few thousand, since they were first encountered by western travellers their tribe has dwindled to pathetic proportions. It is estimated that there are now less than 200 scattered over the whole vast area. Some observers, however, say that these numbers are being held, and that there is no likelihood of the tribe becoming extinct in the foreseeable future.

Like other Patagonian Indians, such as the Ona and Yagan, they are exceedingly primitive and, as they have had little contact with civilized people, their way of life still remains almost unaltered. In 1888 the Salesians started a mission for the Alacaluf on Dawson Island at the southern extremity of the area; but it was not successful, mainly because any form of community life conflicted with their nomadic habits. Also it was found that when they congregated together for any length of time they were rapidly decimated by contagious diseases. Indeed, it is said that one of the main causes of the terrible decline of their population was measles, for them apparently a lethal disease. The people of the northern channels, around Wellington Island, had no regular contact with white men until the establishment of a lighthouse on San Pedro Island in 1932, and the meteorological station at Puerto Eden in 1936.

There can be few tribes in the world so completely lacking in organized community life. They have no clan system or chieftainship and they never attempt any form of agriculture or animal husbandry. They wander about the channels in small family units searching for food, and never stop long enough in one place to exhaust the supply. Sometimes, however, they will come together when a whale is found, either dead or trapped in land-locked waters. Then smoke signals are sent up to attract the attention of everyone who happens to be in the locality and the company thus assembled will remain together only so long as the meat lasts. Sometimes too, they will join in a combined raid on a sea-lion rookery when the creatures are whelping. It is only on these haphazard occasions that they unite to practise such tribal customs as initiation ceremonies.

Though nowadays they occasionally beg food from passing steamers, the Alacaluf still subsist almost entirely upon the natural products of their wild habitat. Their staple diet consists of shellfish, the meat of sea-lions and marine birds and a small quantity of berries and wild vegetables, such as fuchsia seed pods; but they also catch other sea creatures such as fish, porpoise and otter, and occasionally deer from the forest. Their food supply is inexhaustible and the most primitive methods of obtaining it are sufficient to meet their needs. This may partly account for the backward state of their development. Nor do they ever bother to store food for any length of time. They do not partake of regular meals, but eat whenever it is convenient and they feel so inclined. They cook all their food (except for sea-urchins which they eat raw) by roasting it on an open fire, and no utensils are used either for cooking or eating.

The smaller varieties of shellfish can be collected along the shore, but the large mussels, which seem to be their favourite form of food, are only found on the sea bottom. To procure these and giant barnacles from a depth of some fourteen feet or less they use spears, but in deeper water, up to about thirty feet, they dive to the bottom and collect the shellfish with their hands. This occupation is generally reserved for the women, who are considered to be better able to withstand the cold. After three or four dives these heroines hurry back to the shore and virtually sit on the fire.

Sea-lions are either harpooned or clubbed as they come ashore, but they are also caught in raw-hide nets placed aross the entrance of half-submerged caves where they are sheltering. Sea-birds, particularly cormorants, are mostly caught at night on rocky islets where they congregate to roost. The Indians blacken their faces and hands with charcoal, and hide close by until the birds have assembled and settled themselves for the night. Then they creep out and catch one bird after another, killing them by crushing their skulls with their teeth. Otters and deer are hunted with dogs, their only domestic animals.

The Alacaluf live in oval huts, about 12 feet by 8 feet in plan and some 6 feet high. To make them, a number of saplings are stuck into the ground around the perimeter, bent over and intertwined so as to form a dome-shaped framework; this is usually covered over with sea-lion skins, though if the supply is inadequate, bark, grass or ferns are used instead. The hut is like a primitive version of the *yort*, a dome-shaped tent used by Central Asian nomads. As in the *yort*, a fire is made in the middle of the floor and the smoke is supposed to escape through an aperture in the roof, though usually much of it remains inside; often the whole hut appears to be smouldering. The interior of the huts are kept warm and dry, and the people sleep on a soft litter of twigs. They have no idea of sanitation, and excretement may be found anywhere in the vicinity and even inside the huts.

They used to ignite fires with pyrite and flint, and although now most of them seem to have acquired matches, these are in such short supply that they still try to keep a fire burning continuously and even carry it with them on their journeys. All their travelling is done by water and land journeys are limited to short hunting trips; they never venture into the interior of the larger islands or the mainland. Formerly, despite the cold and damp, they used to go about naked except for a small skin mantle; now, though many of the children are still naked, most of the adults have cloth garments of some sort. As may be expected of people leading such unorganized lives, they have little awareness of time. Apart from day and night, summer and winter, units of time such as hours, weeks and months have no meaning for them. This is perhaps partly due to their inability to count beyond five; their word for "five" being synonymous with "many".

Despite the low level of their intellectual development and their lack of community life, the Alacaluf, in common with all primitive people, have a number of established customs, tribal rites and religious or superstitious practices. There appear to be no sexual taboos prior to marriage, and there is no form of marriage ceremony; when a man and a woman decide to live together the man simply joins the girl's family. Polygamy is not forbidden, but is not generally practised, except in cases of a man marrying two sisters or a widow and her daughter. During childbirth all the men leave the hut, and the husband, having put red paint on his face and right shoulder, a string of white feathers around his head and a white kelp goose skin across his breast, stands guard outside. Infants receive a good deal of affection but little sympathy when they hurt themselves. As soon as they are able to walk children are left largely to fend for themselves, and at the age of four they are expected to handle a shellfish spear and to cook for themselves.

When a death occurs, everyone at the encampment blackens his face with charcoal. The body is either buried or, more commonly, placed in a small cave under a cliff or sometimes just hidden in the undergrowth. Meat and shellfish are placed beside the body, and live coals are put in a miniature hut built near by. This practice seems to indicate a belief in some form of life after death. There is evidence, too, of a belief in a creator-god who causes a soul to enter the body of a newborn baby and to whom the soul returns after death; but it is doubtful whether this concept was derived from their original culture of whether it was acquired by contact with white men.

With their livelihood so dependent upon the elements, their search for food constantly impeded by storms and gales, it is not surprising that the Alacaluf have a great many superstitions concerning the weather. They believe, for example, that bad weather is caused by throwing sand or small pebbles at a hut or into the water; by killing a parrot or even looking at a flock flying overhead and when shellfish are eaten during a voyage, the shells must be kept until they can be deposited on land, well above high-water mark. Fine weather, on the other hand, is likely to be produced by throwing ashes on the water, and when a storm overtakes a canoe party they try to subdue it by throwing eggs into the sea; or if there are no eggs available an old basket is burned instead. To ensure a good season they will bury a large sea-lion tooth with a small white stone, and dig them up the following year.

It seemed odd to think of these people with their utterly primitive mode of life, their strange beliefs and customs, so little changed by the twentieth-century world outside, yet living in a comparatively accessible region and accustomed to the frequent passage of ships from Europe through the very heart of their homeland. I wondered if they would benefit, in terms of happiness, by civilization; but our contact with them was too brief to suggest an answer.

We returned to the frigate for lunch, at which we were served with a dish of the huge mussels we had seen in the Alacaluf boats. They were quite succulent and not as tough as they looked, though I found their taste rather nondescript. We spent the hot afternoon checking our stores and equipment, which we found complete, filling our plastic fuel containers with ten gallons of paraffin and fixing webbing bindings on to the snowshoes, while the crew took a keen interest in our activities. At the last job we showed ourselves most inept, and the Bo'sun came to our rescue with a variety of drilling and riveting tools.

Covadonga weighed anchor at 6 o'clock and, after a great shudder as her screws churned the water, she began to glide across the lagoon, through a narrow passage between two wooded islands and out into the channels beyond. The sky was still almost cloudless and the air so calm that no ripple disturbed the perfect reflections of mountain and forest whose colours were now beginning to deepen in the soft evening light.

After supper, at about 8 o'clock, we returned to the bridge to watch the vessel being steered through the English Narrows. By now the sun had sunk below the lofty crests of Wellington Island and all the land to the west was in deep shadow; but eastward, parts of the mainland shore and all the peaks beyond were still alight with its warm glow. At times it looked as though the ship were heading into a completely land-locked fjord; then suddenly she would swing through an angle of ninety degrees and glide into another passage that had opened unexpectedly on one side or the other. A cunning system of beacons had been arranged at various points, some on the shores, some high up on the mountain-sides; the moment and direction of any turn was indicated by a pair of beacons coming into line. Even for a landsman watching the operation in such rare fine weather, it was easy to imagine what a difficult piece of navigation it must be in the usual stormy conditions, with the wind deflected by the mountains into sudden hurricane gusts from any direction, with blinding squalls and with currents sent racing through the channels by the Pacific tides.

Having written half a dozen letters which were to be posted when the frigate reached Valparaiso, I went to bed at about midnight, tingling with excitement at the thought of what the next day would bring.

CHAPTER ELEVEN

The Landing

December 10. I awoke at 6.15 and, with no inclination to linger in bed, I dressed and went up to the bridge. Captain Roebke was there, muffled in a greatcoat and a thick woollen scarf and wearing a long-peaked, light blue baseball cap which seemed to be his regular head-gear when at sea. The frigate, now steering due east, was already far up Canal Baker, and I could distinguish the point of land which marked the place where the wide channel divided into its two upper fjord systems, one leading north-east to the mouth of the Rio Baker the other south-east to the Rio Pascua. We were less than three hours from our destination.

The weather had changed. There was a fresh northerly breeze, and though the sun was shining, a large part of the sky was covered by sultry-looking clouds. The Captain told me that he was expecting a storm within the next twenty-four hours, and that he was anxious to get through the Gulf of Penas, which was notorious for its rough seas, before it began to blow really hard. But it looked as though our luck, which had miraculously steered us through the various crises of the last week, was still holding. My enjoyment of the voyage had been slightly marred by a nagging worry that when we reached our destination, stormy weather might prevent our landing; for in this event we obviously could not expect the frigate to wait for better conditions. Now it was virtually certain that we had escaped this final hazard, though once again, it seemed, by a narrow margin.

After breakfast we carried our baggage to the port side of the ship and stacked it there, ready for disembarking; then we returned to the bridge to wait for the exciting moment when we would catch our first glimpse of the country which we would have to penetrate on the first stage of our journey. We had now entered the Calvo Fjord, which was similar to most of the channels through which we had been sailing for the last few days. Isla Francisca was close on the starboard side, ten miles long and densely forested, screening our view to the south. Then, as we rounded the eastern end of the island, the Jorge Montt Glacier suddenly appeared, curving upward in a mighty sweep from the gleaming peninsular of its shattered front, past a line of ice-peaks and vanishing over the far southern horizon. Twenty minutes later *Covadonga* dropped anchor off the northern shore of Isla Faro, which lay across the entrance of a deep bay.

While one of the boats was lowered and loaded with our baggage, we said good-bye to our hosts. I had been deeply touched by their friendliness and by their keen interest in every detail of our plans; now they seemed genuinely sorry to see us go, and they gave us an impressive send-off. We climbed down into the boat which was manned by a lieutenant and three sailors, the outboard motor was started and we were soon running at five knots before a gentle swell. We rounded the western corner of Isla Faro and the frigate disappeared from view. At that moment we heard three farewell blasts from her siren.

Only about forty years ago, the bay we were now in was almost entirely occupied by the Jorge Montt Glacier. Since then the ice had retreated about six miles, and although still extended far out into the water in the south-eastern corner, it had left a long strip of sandy shore at the southern extremity of the bay, which we could now see. This shore seemed to be the ideal place for our landing, and I was tempted to ask the Lieutenant to take us there. But it was important that we should establish contact with the settlers on whose goodwill we might be forced to rely in case of an emergency; and it would obviously be a good thing to do so while we were still guests of the Chilean Navy. We did not know exactly where the settlement was, but we thought it was located somewhere on the north-west shore of the bay. While we were discussing the matter, we caught sight of a rowing-boat nearly a mile astern in the direction of Isla Faro; so we turned about and made for it.

Its sole occupant was a middle-aged man, with an expression of infinite serenity on his handsome weatherbeaten face. He reminded me very much of a Scottish crofter. Without evincing any surprise or curiosity, he calmly and efficiently lashed his boat to ours as we came alongside, still travelling so fast that the resulting jerk on his rope very nearly pulled him overboard. He guided us past a promontory to an inlet on the western side of the bay, and thence about half a mile up a creek. There, in a sheltered forest clearing, we came upon the settlement. It appeared to consist of two solidly built log houses; but our visit was so brief that we never discovered whether there were more buildings behind.

The launch was run ashore on a small shingle beach, where we were greeted by two younger men, obviously very excited by our arrival which was also watched from the houses by two women and several small children. We off-loaded our baggage and stacked it on the beach, while the Lieutenant walked up to the houses accompanied by two of the *pobladores* (settlers). We inquired of the third whether he could lend us some horses to transport our baggage to the southern shore of the bay, for this was six miles away and it would take us several days of hard work to carry the loads there ourselves. The answer was that there were no horses available, that in any case it was very difficult to reach the end of the bay overland, but that we could be taken by boat the following day if the weather remained fine.

When the Lieutenant returned, however, he offered to take us in the launch before returning to the frigate. I was surprised by this generous offer, for it was already 11 o'clock, and I remembered that the Captain had told me he was anxious to get out of the Canal Baker and across the Gulf of Penas without delay. But I accepted without hesitation and our baggage was reloaded on to the launch. Meanwhile we distributed three jackets, three pairs of trousers and my old overcoat among the *pobladores*. They were delighted and evidently found it hard to believe that these valuable articles, most of them brand new, were really gifts. We also offered to supply them with sugar and coffee and a number of other luxuries if they would visit our base, which they said they would do in the course of the next day or two. With that we parted on excellent terms.

By then the tide had ebbed so far that we had considerable difficulty in heaving the launch off the beach. This done by the aid of levers, we set off down the creek. We had not gone more than 300 yards, when the motor stopped. It was soon discovered that the engine had seized, presumably from lack of oil, and that it was no further use. The launch was rowed to the shore, where our baggage was again off-loaded while a sailor ran back to the settlement. After a while he reappeared, coming down the creek with our friends, the *pobladores*, in two rowing-boats. Then the Lieutenant, who must have been feeling somewhat harassed but was too polite to show it, and the three sailors bid us a warm farwell and addressed their task of rowing the heavy launch five miles back to the frigate, where no doubt they would meet with a less friendly reception from their captain.

We distributed ouselves and our baggage, which with packing-cases and surplus stores must have weighed nearly half a ton, between the two rowing-boats, and started down the creek once more. When we rounded the headland into the bay, we were met by a stiff head-wind and a choppy sea. It was disappointing to find that the breeze had gone round to the south, but I was consoled by the thought that it would help the unfortunate crew of the launch. Jack and I were together with one of the *pobladores*. Our boat was a cumbersome affair and none too seaworthy. Little fountains of water gushed up between her timbers, and the rising tide in her bottom could only be kept at bay by fairly continuous baling. There was one pair of oars, and only room for one man to pull on them. The other boat, carrying our companions and the other two *pobladores*, had two pairs of oars, but it was evidently more cumbersome to row for we managed to haul ahead.

As we butted into the waves, an occasional shower of icy spray sweeping over us, it seemed to me that the wind was increasing; our progress appeared to be so slow that I began to wonder if we could cover the six miles to the southern shore of the bay. But our *pobladore* was quite unmoved and said cheerfully that it was fortunate that we had such a fine afternoon for the trip. All the same I was not sorry that we kept fairly close along the shore. He rowed solidly for the first hour, and then Jack and I took it in turns to relieve him. At first I was glad of the exercise for I felt very cold; but I was a great deal more glad when my spells came to an end and I had a chance to rest my aching forearms.

Gradually, as we came under the lee of some high cliffs at the south-western corner of the bay, the wind dropped and the water became calmer. Jack, who had a good command of Spanish, questioned the *pobladore* about his life in this remote place. He was formerly a merchant seaman, and he and his wife had come there from Puerto Natales with two other families three years before. With the assistance of the Chilean Government they had brought with them a couple of dozen sheep and the necessary tools for building their houses and for clearing and tilling the land. Their small flock had already increased to about sixty animals, and with their houses built and a small area of land under cultivation, they considered themselves fairly well established; but they had had a hard and sometimes anxious time. Two or three times a year they were visited by small Government vessels which brought them supplies of such things as flour and sugar in exchange for their wool. Of course this was not an economic proposition for the Government, whose object was to foster the settlement and development of this vast uninhabited coast. They had no other contact with the outside world.

They certainly did not seem discontented with their lot. Their conditions of life and their problems were probably not so very different from those of the Masters when, at the beginning of the century, they came to settle at La Cristina; but while the latter were strangers in a foreign land and for a time even more dependent upon their own resources, their climate was more agreeable and they could at least get out when they wanted to. As in the case of the Masters, I was deeply impressed by the determination and cheerful courage that had prompted these people to leave their homes to embark upon their lonely and hazardous quest of an independent life. I was sorry that we could not stay with them for a little while to see something of their strange Swiss Family Robinson existence; though I reminded myself that the opportunity to do so might still be forced upon us.

After three hours' rowing we reached the southern end of the bay and we ran the boats ashore near the point where a stream intersected the long sandy beach. The *pobladores* helped us to unload our baggage, and saying they would visit again either the next day or the day after, they departed on their return voyage. In fact, though they kept their promise, this was the last we saw of them.

It was now about 3.30. There was no wind; most of the cloud had vanished and the sun was deliciously warm. We could not have wished for a better afternoon for this long-anticipated moment of arrival at the starting point of our journey, nor for a more beautiful landing-place. The beach ran westward for half a mile to the line of tall cliffs which curved round the south-west corner of the bay, and eastward for nearly a mile to a massive wall of blue ice which, extending far out to sea, formed the end of the Jorge Montt Glacier. From the beach a wide plain extended inland for several miles. As this had only recently been abandoned by the ice (probably within the last hundred years) it was almost devoid of vegetation except for coarse grass and small scrub. From the cliffs at the western end of the beach a ridge ran up to a long mountain spar; the upper part of its steep forested slopes still held masses of winter snow, while lower down they were intersected by gleaming white ribbons of torrents and waterfalls. To the east the plain was bounded by the trunk of the glacier, which from the beach looked like an enormous white whale basking in the sun. Beyond the far end of the plain the glacier disappeared behind a range which, curving away to the right, climbed in a series of rounded steps to some high and distant peaks. It appeared to be separated from the western ridge by a wide valley. We called it "The Barrier Range".

Some three hundred yards from the beach we found an ideal camp site; a piece of flat ground of ample dimensions, close to the stream, but ten feet above it, which afforded reasonable protection from flooding, and surrounded on three sides by cliffs and hillocks of gravel and clay. Carrying our baggage over from the shore we became so hot that we took off our shirts, and by the time we had pitched the tents we were more than ready for a brew of tea.

We spent the rest of the afternoon and most of the evening unpacking our stores and equipment, checking them, separating the necessities from the surplus stuff which could be left behind and, as far as possible, making up individual loads to be carried forward. We were well aware of how lucky we were to be doing this in such perfect weather, for had it been pouring with rain or blowing half a gale or both, it would have been a difficult and unpleasant job. As it was, everything was tossed around with happy abandon, to be counted and sorted at leisure. To my relief nothing was found to be missing from my lists, for I had intended to make a final checking of the equipment at Punta Arenas, and having been denied that opportunity, I was slightly apprehensive that some small but vital item, such as prickers for the Primus stoves, or wax for the sledges, had been omitted. The only thing I had forgotten was a maximum-minimum thermometer, and for this oversight I received a stern reprimand from Jack.

The question of whether items of equipment were or were not necessary, or if not strictly necessary whether they might or might not be so useful as to be worth their extra weight, involved us in long and sometimes heated debate. Indeed, throughout most of the journey it continued to be something of a bone of contention. Remaining true to my deep-rooted prejudice in favour of travelling light, I usually found myself in a minority of one, and I had to fight so hard to uphold my principles that the others came to regard "Chuck it away" as my guiding precept or as a psychological oddity which must be humoured but at the same time kept under watchful restraint. In the weeks that followed, whenever anything was mislaid, one or other of the Chileans would invariably remark, "Ah! Mr. Sheepton chuck it away my spoon" or "my glove".

Jack, for example, had brought a plant press, and while I applauded his zeal for scientific investigation, I thought (or hoped) that there would not be sufficient opportunity for botanical collecting before we got on to the glacier to make it worth while carrying it all the way across the Ice-cap. After a stubborn struggle he agreed to abandon it on condition that he might retain some small bottles of alcohol which he had brought for collecting insects. Eduardo had brought a considerable weight of what is known to mountaineers as "ironmongery", including pitons and the like, used in extremely difficult climbing operations, beyond the scope of old-fashioned implements such as ice-axes and crampons. I could not imagine that we would attempt anything that would involve the use of these advanced technical appliances, and I pressed him to leave them behind. But Eduardo pointed out that they were the property of his club, and that they were practically irreplaceable in Chile. With this argument he won the day and the useless pieces of iron were carried all the way.

A more unusual gadget bought by the Chileans was a huge saw with villainous teeth. Its purpose was to enable us to cut large blocks of ice or snow from the surface of the glacier, with which to build igloos in case our tent was destroyed by a storm or blown away. Although neither the possibility of this contingency nor its ugly consequences had escaped me, I was very doubtful whether a saw would be of much help to us in building an igloo on the type of surface we were likely to meet. Much has been said and written about the construction of ice caves and houses, but, having never employed the technique myself, I have always supposed that it required special conditions, such as deep, hard snow for building, or a steel slope for tunnelling. However, the others were so sanguine about their ability with the aid of a saw in any conditions to whip up a comfortable residence in a couple of hours or so that, in view of my ignorance, I could hardly insist upon dispensing with this means of our salvation. So the monster remained with us, its jagged teeth a constant embarrassment while carrying loads and packing the sledges and a perpetual menace to the tent, the fuel containers and the ration bags; until one day, five weeks later, after a particularly severe blizzard, I noticed that it was no longer with us. Whether it was because by then my companions had acquired more confidence in the tent or less in their ability to build an igloo, its loss was not mourned; nor was I accused of having "chucked it away".

The presence of a considerable supply of surplus food, of course provoked further discussion. Our daily ration had been calculated with great care and it was generally admitted that its calorie and protein content was sufficient for our needs. The surplus food had originally been brought to stock a depot against the possibility of an enforced retreat; but I had now decided to hand it over to the *pobladores*, since if we were forced to return, we would in any case have to rely upon them for our sustenance. Besides such basic commodities as biscuits, sugar and oats, it also included a number of luxury items not in the ration, sweets, hot drink powder, lemonade powder, "energy tablets" and the like. Also Jack had found time during his brief stay in Punta Arenas to acquire a supply of bully beef and various packets of jelly and "pudding mix". He and Cedomir were both of the long, lean type of man that seems to be perpetually hungry, and the idea of leaving all these goodies behind caused them such anguish that in the end I agreed to allow some of them to be taken at least as far as the next camp where we might have a better idea both of our carrying capacity and of the difficulties ahead of us.

Remembering the disastrous failure of our stoves the previous year, I had decided this time to use the ordinary paraffin-burning Primus which, in my opinion, is still by far the best and most reliable kind of stove for light travel. I had brought a large one for regular use and a small one to be kept in reserve. We had been provided with an enormous supply of spare parts from which we made a careful selection, and jettisoned the rest. I have always found it difficult to estimate the consumption of paraffin over a given period; for so much depends upon such factors as how often water will be available and for how much of the time it will be necessary to melt snow, how much draught there will be inside the tent and how much the stove will be used for purposes other than cooking, such as drying clothes and warming the tent. We could safely predict that all these factors would be adversely disposed, and we decided to provide ourselves with a liberal allowance of a gallon per week, or eight gallons in all. This turned out to be almost exactly the right quantity. The fuel was carried in large plastic containers, one of which had been designed for use by the British Army in making parachute landings. We had a number of smaller plastic bottles to hold our current requirements.

Our personal belongings varied with the individual, the only stipulation being that each man should not have more than 20 lb. excluding his boots and Gannex suits. Mine consisted of 2 sweaters, 2 shirts, 2 pairs of pyjamas trousers, a string vest, 8 pairs of socks and 1 of gloves, balaclava helmet, sleeping-bag and air mattress, camera and 12 rolls of film, 1lb. tobacco, 2 pipes and 2 paper-backed books (*Madame de Pompadour* and *Cakes and Ale*). Our crampons were carried separately.

Long before we had finished sorting out the stores and equipment to be taken with us, it was clear that four relays would be needed to shift it. However, I was not particularly worried about this; for we were well ahead of our original timetable, and by carrying some extra food with us we could afford to take our time over the initial stages of the journey. If we ran into difficulties during the next ten days, it would be time enough to cut down our loads more ruthlessly. Our main concern was to reach the head of the Jorge Montt Glacier while there was still plenty of snow covering the ice-falls and crevassed areas. We had heard that the spring was late in arriving in Southern Patagonia, and that although parts of the country had suffered a drought, this did not apply to the mountainous areas to the west which on the contrary had experienced exceptionally heavy snowfall. These reports were confirmed by the deep deposits of winter snow that still lay in the forest a couple of thousand feet above us. It was most probable, therefore, that we would find good conditions on the upper part of the glacier at least until the end of December.

When everything had been sorted out and the tents pitched, we built an enormous fire of driftwood. It was the only camp fire we were to enjoy during the expedition. Besides the Pyramid, I had also sent an old Meade tent with the baggage from London. I had intended to leave this in Punta Arenas for use in my subsequent wanderings. Now, unfortunately, it would have to be abandoned, but at least it provided me with the luxury of a tent to myself during the few days spent at the first camp, and afforded the others a postponement of the cramped conditions to which we would have to accustom ourselves.

After supper I strolled down to the shore to enjoy the evening light and to ponder over our peculiar situation. There was no breeze, and the bay was too enclosed and too remote from the Pacific to allow the ocean swell to disturb its calm. For the most part the only sound was the gentle hiss of tiny waves breaking along the beach; but every now and then the peace was shattered by the thunderous roar of ice calving from the glacier front which, in the gathering dusk had assumed a sinister glow. Though the sky was streaked with cloud it appeared to hold no menace. It seemed that the Captain's gloomy prediction of twelve hours before had been wrong, and that we could look forward at least to another day of this holiday weather.

That moment can, I think, be counted among the highlights of my life; for then I was captured by the same surging excitement that I remember when I started for my first Alpine peak, for my first Everest Expedition and for the long trek across the Karakoram to Kashgar; or again when Tilman and I reached the upper gorge of the Rishi Ganga, and at our base camp in the Shaksgam Valley. All these were moments of anticipation, and although I have not always found that anticipation is better than fulfilment, it has a special quality (fear, perhaps, is part of it) that seems to make a more lasting impression on the mind.

The prospect of the journey across this strange Ice-cap was as exciting as any I have known; and to have been landed on this lonely shore and left to our own resources with no immediate means of retreat added a delicious tang to its savour. The fact that the task would be largely a contest, not against mountaineering difficulties, but against the notorious Patagonian weather, and that for most of the time we would be physically miserable, mattered not at all.

It was good to find that advancing years had not blunted my sensitivity to such feelings.

CHAPTER TWELVE

The Approach

I awoke at 1 o'clock to find heavy rain beating against the tent, and the canvas flapping angrily in the wind. It seemed incredible that less than four hours before I had been sitting on the shore enjoying the stillness of a perfect evening. But such unpredictable changes in the weather are only to be expected in Patagonia, so with a curse of resignation I buried my head in my sleeping-bag to protect it from the fine spray coming through the roof of the tent. I drifted back to sleep wondering vaguely how far *Covadonga* had progressed across the Gulf of Penas before the storm began. At 4 o'clock I woke again, to find it raining and blowing still harder. Above the noise of the storm, I could now hear the roar of the stream, which sounded so close and so loud that I wondered if after all the ten foot banks would be sufficient to contain the swollen torrent. I opened the door of the tent and looked out. It was already light, and as there appeared to be no immediate danger of a flood, I went back to bed.

We had intended to be off to an early start that morning, 5 o'clock I think was the time agreed upon, but now, in these conditions, it seemed a bit pointless, so I dozed on until 6.30 before rousing the others. We lingered over breakfast, vaguely hoping that the weather might moderate, but by 8 o'clock we could delude ourselves no longer; the holiday was over and we must turn out to face the harsh reality of our self-inflicted torment. As we splashed about in the mud, our hands numbed by the wind and rain, we realized again how lucky we had been to have had the opportunity of sorting things out in fine weather. Four sacks, each containing four 2-day food packs, had been strapped to our Yukon carrying-frames, and all we had to do was to shoulder our 60-lb. loads and start marching.

The cloud ceiling was down to about 1,000 feet, but through the driving rain we could still see the base of the mountains at the far end of the plain. Beyond the sand-dunes and moraine hillocks grouped around the shore, we reached a stretch of flat country, covered with tussocks of coarse grass. To our great relief the ground was firm, for we had been quite prepared to find here a wide expanse of bog, like the one that we had encountered at Puerto Eden, which would have taken us a very long time to cross. After three-quarters of an hour we found ourselves confronted by some low hills, formed by a series of *roches moutonnés*, or outcrops of rock worn smooth by glacier action, over which we had to climb.

When we reached the highest ridge of the hills, we looked down upon a lake about 4 miles long and nearly 2 miles wide, which was damned back from the sea by the trunk of the glacier. Its surface was half-covered with innumerable icebergs, of all shapes and sizes. Two of them were several hundred yards across, and as their surface still showed the original crevasse formation, they must have drifted away from the glacier without much fuss, which indicated that the eastern part of the lake was very deep.

We climbed diagonally across a series of ridges, some of them with deep clefts between, and made our way down to the western shore of the lake, which we followed for a quarter of a mile. Here we found thousands of waterfowl either feeding along the shore or sitting on the water a few yards from it. As we approached they kept rising into the air with a mighty beating of wings, circling overhead and settling again a few hundred yards away. Many of the birds, however, had young families, and remained behind to protect their chicks as they scurried into the water at our approach. The great majority were upland and ashy-headed geese, though there was also a number of steamer duck and several species of smaller birds including teal.

Despite the rain I was beginning to enjoy myself. My load was sitting comfortably on my hips, there was not too much drag on my untrained shoulders, and since the first hour or so I had got my second wind. It was exciting to see each new aspect of the way ahead and the ground was varied and interesting. Moreover this first stage was proving delightfully easy, and with no bog and no forest to impede us, we were making rapid progress inland.

The plain had merged into craggy moorland, intersected by deep gullies containing torrents, one of which was so swollen that we had some difficulty in crossing it. It stopped raining and the cloud ceiling broke and lifted, leaving small wreaths of mist clinging to the steep, forested slopes to our right, where the white ribbons had expanded into impressive cascades. Crossing the moorland, we reached a point where the ground fell away in front of us and we found ourselves looking up a long valley to the south-west. At its exit there was a wide, circular basin which lay between the high ground on which we stood and the base of the mountains to the south. This had once contained a lake which had formed behind a bank of old moraine, some 400 feet high; but the barrier had been breeched and now the river from the valley ambled sluggishly across the floor of the basin and drained through a narrow defile.

When we reached the river we found it to be some twenty yards wide and very deep, and it seemed as though we would have to make a detour into the valley, and possibly a long way up it, before finding a way across. This was not an agreeable prospect for, with all our baggage, the extra distance would have to be covered four times both ways. However, though it was still only 12.30, we decided to leave this problem until another day. We had reached a point from which it would be necessary, in any case, to make a thorough reconnaisance of the mountains ahead of us, before deciding upon our next line of advance. From a camp hereabouts, two of us could swim across the river and tackle this task, while the other two were exploring up-stream for a suitable place for a crossing with the baggage. So we dumped our loads on a high platform overlooking the river, and made our way back to camp, with the intention of bringing up another relay that afternoon.

It was very nearly 3 o'clock by the time we reached camp. I was feeling distinctly tired and regarded the prospect of carrying another load with abhorrence. Although they did not care to show it, I do not think that the others liked the idea any more than I did. But it was not raining and we had no real excuse for wasting the rest of the day, so after consuming one of Jack's tins of bully beef, we had a short rest and set out again carrying three sacks containing the remaining twelve 2-day ration packs and a load of fuel. However, I decided that on this second carry we should go only as far as the torrent that had held us up that morning, a little more than half-way up the river; a decision which my companions were very ready to accept. Even this was more than enough, for when at 8 o'clock we got back to camp, I felt very weary indeed, and after a half-hearted attempt to eat some supper I slunk away to my tent. I tried to console myself with the thought that we had made very satisfactory progress that day, but I was not really in a mood to take pleasure in anything, even in lying down.

The second day was a great deal less agreeable than the first. I awoke feeling very old and decrepit; my body ached all over as though it had been beaten with clubs and it required a great deal of resolution to get out of my sleeping-bag and into my damp clothes. I elected to carry the two sledges and the infernal saw, a gesture of ostentatious unselfishness which I soon regretted, for although together they weighed rather less than 60 lb. they made an awkward load which constantly threw me off balance, while the various sections drummed together with a maddening monotony. My pack-frame, which yesterday had felt reasonably comfortable, now seemed like an instrument of torture. A painful bruise had developed below the small of my back, upon which the frame bumped with merciless persistence, while the straps dragged at my aching shoulders. It was raining hard, mist obscured the view and there was no longer the excitement of treading new ground to counteract my misery.

The only consolation was that there was a calculable time-limit set upon this penance, for we knew exactly how many marching hours we had to do. I disciplined myself to refrain from looking at my watch for at least ten minutes at a time, and amused myself by trying to estimate how long it would take to reach various points in view. Each half-hour we stopped for an exquisite five minutes of rest which, I was gratified to notice, the others seemed to enjoy as much as I.

The torrent was still more swollen than it had been the day before, and the problem of crossing it with the two relays of loads caused a pleasant diversion. In any case I was beginning to feel better by then; my limbs had lost much of their stiffness, some semblance of vitality had returned to my wretched body, and by the time we reached the river with the second relay, I was even willing to admit to myself that the expedition might after all have some worthwhile purpose. The worst was over, and although I knew that it would be several days yet before I was fit enough to carry a load with any semblance of nonchalance, I could now look forward to a steady improvement in my condition.

However, the day had not yet finished with its quota of woe. On our way back across the *roches moutonnés* that evening, I carelessly stepped in a hole and sprained my right ankle. When we reached our camp we found that the *pobladores* had been there and had very kindly left a leg of mutton hanging from a stake. At first the Chileans were delighted by the prospect of a barbecue, but it was still raining heavily and none of us felt inclinded to build a fire with sodden pieces of driftwood, and still less willing to add it to his next day's load, so, alas, the generous gift was left untouched.

The following morning, December 13, my ankle was still so swollen and painful that Eduardo, who had assumed the role of the expedition's doctor, insisted that I must rest it for a day, and I was forced, with a fair show of reluctance, to agree. By then only four loads remained to be shifted, and it was decided that the other three, taking the Pyramid tent with them, should establish Camp 2 by the river, and that Jack and Cedomir should remain there to investigate the problem of the crossing, while Eduardo returned to spend the night with me. It was fortunate that we had the Meade tent to make this manoeuvre possible.

It was extremely irritating to be incapacitated as a result of my carelessness, and it was obvious that it would be some days before my ankle recovered completely. However, for the present I could at least assuage my conscience with the reflection that my companions would have a comparatively easy day; so, settling myself luxuriously against Eduardo's sleeping-bag, I became completely absorbed in Nancy Mitford's fascinating portrayal of court life in eighteenth-century France. At 2 o'clock Eduardo arrived back, soaking wet but as cheerful as ever. He massaged my foot and then entertained me for the rest of the evening with lively accounts of his various expeditions in the Andes.

My ankle was slightly less swollen the next morning, so after a leisurely breakfast, we strapped it tightly with an elastic bandage and prepared to start. Eduardo left a letter for the *pobladores* telling them to take over everything that we had left behind in the camp. This included some clothing, a pair of boots, the tent and a considerable quantity of sugar, tea, coffee, sweets, biscuits and various tinned foods. They must have been delighted.

Carrying only my personal belongings, I managed to hobble along at a reasonable pace. Though the weather was raw and bleak it was not raining, and with the whole day before us we could make long and frequent halts. Early in the afternoon, as we approached the end of the lake, we were delighted to see the Pyramid tent perched on top of the high moraine bank. This meant that the others had found a way of crossing the river, and when we reached the place where the loads had been dumped we found that they had all gone.

After a brief search we caught sight of some of them piled on the far bank near the point where the river entered the defile. On a strip of mud shore below, the fibreglass sledge lay assembled, with a climbing rope tied to either end, one of which, stretching across the river, was attached to an ice-axe driven into the mud on the near bank. This then, was the means by which Jack and Cedomir had made the crossing. I was surprised, because I would not have expected the joints of the sledge to be anything like watertight enough for it to be used as a boat. However, when we had hauled it across, we discovered that the joints had been cunningly sealed with wads of toilet paper.

Even so it was a delicate operation, particularly for the first man, to make the voyage. The sledge, which was shaped like a punt, was 8 feet long and only 6 inches deep. Eduardo sat in it and when I had heaved it gently off the shore we found that it floated with about an inch of freeboard. Fortunately, the river at this point was protected from the wind and very sluggish, so that there was scarcely a ripple on the water. Very gingerly Eduardo started to haul himself across by means of the rope attached to the far bank. He had progressed about four yards, when suddenly the sledge capsized hurling him into the water which was out of his depth. He scrambled out, while I hauled the upturned sledge back to the shore.

When he had recovered his breath and relieved his feelings with some violence, he stripped off his sodden clothes and boots and tried again. This time he lay prone in the sledge with his head forward, using one hand and his teeth to pull in the rope. About half-way across the sledge gave a lurch and shipped some water. For a moment I thought he was over again, but he managed to recover his balance and reached the far shore without further mishap. I then hauled the sledge back across the river, and loaded it with our belongings. I also took the precaution of stripping off all my clothes and my boots, which I sent across with the rest. Meanwhile Eduardo was sprinting up and down a stretch of beach, trying to restore some warmth to his naked body. When my turn came to make the crossing, all I had to do was to lie perfectly still in the sledge, doing my best to control my shivering, which might have been quite enough to upset the frail craft, while Eduardo pulled it across. All the same I was very relieved to reach the other side without a ducking in the icy water.

Having taken the sledge to a safe place well above the reach of the river, we climbed to the crest of the moraine bank. The tent had been pitched at a point a quarter of a mile farther on, near two little ponds which furnished our water supply. It commanded a splendid view north-west across the lake to the coast, and to the south across the basin to the steep, forested slopes of the Barrier Range. The cloud ceiling was down to about 1,000 feet and, although we could see several miles up the valley, its upper part was obscured. The moraine bank ran eastward for a mile or so, rising gently, and joined a prominent northerly spur of the Barrier Range, though it looked as if there might be a deep gap between it and the main massif.

Jack and Cedomir were away, presumably making a reconnaissance, so we settled ourselves into the tent, lit the Primus and brewed tea, which was just about ready when they returned. They had climbed most of the way up the spur but, finding themselves in thick mist, had returned without solving the problem of our next move. However we certainly could not complain, for their ingenious method of crossing the river had probably saved us several days' delay and a lot of hard work.

This was the first time that all four of us had occupied the Pyramid tent together, and as it was to be our home for nearly two months we were interested to see just how cramped our quarters were to be. It was originally designed as a three man tent for use in the Antarctic. The interior floor space was 8 feet square, and as our air mattresses were 2 feet wide there was just enough room for them to fit side by side. To begin with we lay with our heads along the back wall and about 6 inches from it. The mattresses were 6 feet long so that there was a corridor some 18 inches wide along the entrance wall, which was occupied by such things as the Primus, the current ration packs, boots and various other bits of personal gear. The space between the outer and inner entrance walls was used for stowing the cooking pots and flasks of fuel, and also, later, as a reservoir from which to refill the pots with snow.

There were three tapes stretched across the tent seven feet above the floor, which served as clothes lines on which to hang our wet garments. Theoretically the hot air rising from the stove and collecting in the apex of the tent (where there was a small ventilator) should have dried the clothes. I am told that in the Antarctic it does so most efficiently, but with us it never seemed to have the slightest effect, mainly, I suppose, because of the high humidity of the atmosphere even in the coldest weather. Nevertheless we all continued to hang up our clothes and often our boots, in the fond hope that they would dry. At least it provided us with a means of getting them out of the way.

Cedomir and I occupied the places along the side walls of the tent, while the others had the places between. The advantage of the outer berths was that we commanded the corners of the tent and could also dispose of small personal belongings such as pipes, diaries or books along the side walls. But this was outweighed by several serious disadvantages, and often in the weeks that followed I regretted my lack of foresight at the outset in not commandeering one of the inner berths. In very heavy rain the water came through the inner walls and trickled down them on to our sleeping-bags; in strong winds the flapping walls beat a constant tattoo upon our recumbent bodies; when drift-snow piled against the side of the tent its icy mass often pressed in upon us, further constricting our meagre living space; finally, we could not sit up without our heads and shoulders pressing hard against the damp and usually heaving walls. But on the whole we were well satisfied with our quarters.

To travel successfully in the mountains of Patagonia one must make up one's mind as far as possible to ignore the weather, and we were resolved to make this our basic principle. But we were now in a situation where it would be useless to advance without a thorough reconnaissance of the way ahead, and to make this we needed reasonable visibility. With the weight of baggage that we were carrying, a bad choice of route might involve us in endless delay and unnecessary toil. Our previous experience of Patagonian glaciers had shown that the ice on their lower reaches was usually extremely broken, and from what we had seen of the Jorge Montt it appeared to be no exception. Our aim therefore was to get on to it as far up as possible, preferably well above the present snow line. To do this it seemed that we would either have to cross the Barrier Range or find a way around its eastern end. If neither way proved feasible it was just possible that from the head of the valley we might find a pass across the western end of the range, which would lead us into the upper basin of the Jorge Montt.

Throughout the 15th it rained steadily, and for most of the day the cloud hung so low that we could barely see the lake, 400 feet below. Obviously nothing could be discovered in such weather, so we remained in our sleeping-bags with clear consciences, and as we still had a good deal of surplus food with us, we spent much of the time eating a variety of snacks. It was then that Eduardo began to develop a keen interest in English limericks and bawdy songs, which he sustained throughout the trip. He wrote them down in his diary and committed them to memory, reciting or singing them each evening, in what he called his English lesson. Misquoted in his Spanish accent, even the old schoolboy chestnuts sounded very funny. He was constantly demanding new material, and in time had compiled such a copious anthology that Jack and I were astonished at our own resourcefulness.

Late in the evening the rain stopped and we emerged from the tent for a breath of fresh air. The clouds had lifted and there was a brightness in the west as though somewhere the sun had succeeded in breaking through. The light was reflected on the floor of the basin in a vivid emerald, while in the opposite direction the livid forms of the icebergs seemed to be floating in a nebulous bowl of navy blue.

The improvement in the weather was maintained and by the morning it was comparatively fine. Though the sky was still overcast the peaks of the Barrier Range were clear and for the first time we could see the whole length of the south-western valley. There seemed to be little chance of finding a southward pass from its head, for it appeared to be flanked on that side by an unbroken wall. Fresh snow lay on the mountains and in the forests well below the 2,000 feet level.

At 7 o'clock Jack and Cedomir set off on a reconnaissance. There was no doubt that if the weather held until noon they would be able to reach a point on the Barrier Range high enough to see all that was needed; so Eduardo and I stayed behind and spent the morning bringing the rest of the loads up from the river, and airing the sleeping-bags and mattresses. We also weeded out the surplus food, and a few more pieces of unnecessary equipment, so that our baggage could now be shifted in three relays.

The others returned at 1 o'clock. They had made a thoroughly successful reconnaisance, and the news they brought was excellent. First they had climbed to the crest of the spur, beyond which, as we had already seen, there was a deep canyon, partly occupied by a tongue of ice from the glacier. Following it along they found that the spur led directly on to the eastern ridge of the Barrier Range. All this ground had been under ice so recently, that it was entirely free from the dense forest which covered the northern slopes, only a short distance away. Climbing diagonally up the ridge, they had reached a high point on its crest which commanded a view of the whole of the middle basin of the glacier including its western flank beyond the Barrier Range. Here there was a safe and easy corridor between the ice and the rock which would enable us to travel several miles along the side of the glacier without being forced on to it. But their most encouraging discovery was that only a short way beyond the corner of the range, along a line barely 2,000 feet above sea-level, the broken ice of the lower glacier disappeared beneath a smooth mantle of snow on which we would be able to use the sledges. Moreover their view had extended to the southern horizon where the head of the glacier, sweeping up in a broad ice-fall, disappeared over the rim of the Ice-cap. Though they thought that we might have some difficulty in climbing this ice-fall, there appeared to be no other serious obstacle in view.

After lunch we carried a relay of loads to the top of the spur, about 1,000 feet above. My ankle was still painful and I had to be careful where I trod. Reaching the crest we made our way along a series of terraces between long, whale-backed rocks until we reached a little tarn capped in a grassy hollow. It was a delightful spot, and as it was probably the last we would find before entering the icy world beyond, we decided to place our third camp there.

While the others started back, I went on 100 yards or so to the top of a knoll to get a view of the glacier. A few minutes later I returned to the tarn, and was removing my pack-frame from the load I had been carrying, when I heard a slight noise behind me. Looking round, I was astonished to see two huemul (a kind of deer about the size of chamois) gazing at me less than four yards away.

These creatures live in most parts of Patagonia where there is forest, but as a rule they are so shy that they are very rarely seen. In all the time that I had spent in the forests around Lago Argentino, Viedma and San Martin, though I had often come across their tracks, I had never set eyes on one of them. Yet these two had not been encountered by accident; they must have heard us arrive at the tarn ten minutes before and had come to see what was going on.

I rose slowly to my feet, expecting to see them turn and bolt; but not only did they hold their ground, they showed not the slightest sign of alarm. I advanced until I was about two yards from them; still there was no reaction. I had intended to see if I could actually touch one of them. I believe I could have done so, but I thought better of it, for I was so enchanted by their complete confidence that I was relucant to do anything that might destroy it. I tossed them a piece of biscuit that I had in my pocket, and they ignored the friendly gesture. After a few minutes they seemed to grow bored with me, and to my amazement they started to nibble at the grass. Presently one of them came across my piece of biscuit; he sniffed at it and left it alone.

I have often been in places where the wild life had never before been disturbed by human intrusion, but to find wild animals so completely without fear was a new and delightful experience. I left the huemul to their grazing and made my way back along the spur.

The following day, December 17, we brought up the rest of the loads in two relays and established Camp 3 by the tarn. That evening we received another visit from the huemul.

CHAPTER THIRTEEN

The Reluctant Sledge

EXACTLY a week had elapsed since our landing. So far things had gone so much more easily than we had expected that, although a certain amount of time had been wasted, we had reason to be satisfied with our progress. We had been most fortunate in our choice of an approach route, which had proved to be completely lacking in the two obstacles that we had most feared, bog and forest. Moreover, it looked as though the heavy deposits of winter snow still lying at a low altitude would afford us easy access to the upper part of the glacier. All the same it was a somewhat depressing thought that, in spite of our good fortune, we were still only five miles in a direct line from the coast, and little more than 1,000 feet above the sea.

There was a difference of opinion about the route we should follow beyond Camp 3. Jack was in favour of climbing round the end of the Barrier Range at a fairly high level to reach the trough beside the glacier. Cedomir on the other hand thought that we should cross the ravine on the eastern side of the spur, and climb the tongue of ice beyond, which he said, would lead us on to an easy section of the glacier. Eduardo and I, not having seen the ground, could not take part in this dispute; but after listening to both arguments, I exercised my casting vote in favour of the latter route, mainly because the fresh snow, which still lay on the lower slopes of the range, might cause us some trouble.

Intending to make a long carry on the 18th, we got away to an early start. We climbed diagonally down into the ravine so as to lose as little height as possible, and reached the ugly, sweating mass of the glacier tongue. For the most part the ice was deeply undercut, but there was one place where a semicircular ledge protruded like a giant tree fungus towards a convenient boulder, enabling us, with a long stride, to effect a lodgement on to it. The side of the tongue was steep for a couple of hundred feet, but the ice was rough and so encrusted with gravel that we could climb it without crampons. Gradually the slope eased off and before long we reached the crest of the tongue close to its junction with the main glacier.

I suddenly realized that despite my two days of enforced rest, I had already come to terms with my load. No doubt this was partly due to the interest of climbing on ice which held my attention, but it was no longer the loathsome taskmaster it had been, chaining me to a galley plank of unremitting toil. My movements had acquired some degree of balance and rhythm, some semblance of pleasurable control. Load-carrying was never among my favourite pastimes, but like other forms of hard labour, there is some satisfaction to be derived from its mastery.

Cedomir had been right. Though the glacier over to our left was badly shattered, the whale-back ridge of the tongue merged into a long corridor of unbroken ice along which we could now advance rapidly. Only an occasional crevasse crossed our path, and none of them was wide enough to present much difficulty. Moreover, we were climbing steadily and, only two hours after leaving camp, we reached the first patches of snow. Here we put on the rope and proceeded more cautiously, for although the snow was sufficient to conceal most of the crevasses it was thoroughly rotten. However, it deepened as we climbed and when we reached the head of the corridor we saw in front of us an unbroken sweep of solid spring snow disappearing into the mist.

Obviously this was the place to start using the sledges. We had brought neither of them with us, so we dumped our loads and, leaving a red flag fluttering from a tall bamboo staff to mark their position, we raced back down the glacier, reaching camp in time for an early lunch. That afternoon we carried up a second relay, which included the sledges, and returned in the evening in a mood of buoyant optimism, to spend our last night on dry land (relatively speaking).

I always find it something of a wrench to leave a land of growing things for a lengthy sojourn among the harsh monotones of glacier regions, the dead, scentless world of ice and snow. Though next morning it was raining as usual as we packed up the tent, and the grassy hollow where it had stood looked bleak and sad, at least it was green, and the forest in the mist below looked warm and friendly. I felt a sharp pang of nostalgia at the prospect of a long absence from the soft colours and sweet smells of vegetation. But in the early part of an expedition of this kind the outraged senses must make a long series of adjustments to changed conditions of living, and luckily the regret for each lost comfort is quickly forgotten.

The weather began to clear as we climbed on the glacier and, by 11 o'clock when we reached the dump, it was no longer raining. We set about assembling the fibreglass sledge which took us nearly an hour. Having never hauled a sledge before I had been looking forward keenly to this new form of exercise, and I was impatient at the delay. I do not know quite what I had been expecting; I think I had visualized pushing against a gentle restraint of the harness; a little monotonous perhaps and even tiring over a long period, but involving no really strenuous effort. Anyway it would be a delightful change from being weighed down by a load.

We still had some 700 lb. of baggage. It was obvious that we could not move it all at once, but we expected to be able to drag at least half of it quite easily on the fibreglass sledge, keeping Jack's sledge in reserve until the time came when we would be hauling a full 500-pound load. We were in for a rude shock.

At last the sledge was ready and loaded with half the baggage. We strapped on our snowshoes and walked up and down to try them out; they felt fine. Then we climbed into our harnesses, which consisted of 9-inch webbing belly-bands and shoulder straps, and took up our positions; the taller pair, Jack and Cedomir, on the longer traces in front, Eduardo and I behind. The great moment had arrived. The word was given, "Ready! go!" We took the strain; nothing happened. We heaved; still nothing happened. We might have been chained to a rock wall. Then at last with a mighty effort, our bodies lying on our harnesses at an angle of forty-five degrees, we managed to stagger forward for about five yards, when we came to a dead stop, the front of the sledge having ploughed deep into the soft, sticky snow.

Clearly we could not go on like this; so with one accord we sank down in the snow, panting hard, to consider the matter. The implications of our pathetic failure to haul even 350 lb. over this type of snow were all too obvious; and as they flashed across my mind I felt a sense of desperate frustration, verging on panic. As the snow conditions were not likely to improve and might well become worse, it looked as if we would have to continue this dreary business of relaying for most of the journey. But it was not the dreariness of the prospect that was worrying me. To be forced to continue relaying for the next five or six weeks would completely upset our timetable, and with it our provisioning. Secondly, it was very doubtful if relaying would be possible in the kind of weather that we must expect to meet on the Ice-cap.

However, it was no use dwelling on these gloomy thoughts, so we removed about 100 lb. from the sledge and tried again. This time, though with a great deal of effort, we managed to drag it along in fits and starts. We kept falling over our snowshoes which made it impossible to maintain the even pull necessary to keep the sledge moving smoothly. The action of walking in snowshoes is a kind of shuffle; lifting the toe and dragging the heel, and to perform this movement satisfactorily, it is necessary to keep the body upright. But to pull hard enough to move even our lightened sledge we still had to lean far forward, and this meant that at each step the toes of the shoes buried themselves in the soft snow. There was nothing for it but to give up using them until we could evolve a better technique. Without them, of course, we sank deeper into the snow, but at least we found that we could maintain a steady movement.

We struggled on for half an hour, in which time we covered about half a mile. Then we stopped, pitched the tent, and returned with the sledge for a second load. All this time we had been in mist, and it was only when we started back along our tracks that we realized that the slope up which we had hauled the sledge was a good deal steeper than we had thought. This at least was some comfort, for it partly accounted for the very great effort that the job had demanded.

The second and third relays were lighter than the first, and with a well-beaten trail to help us we had brought all the loads up to the tent by 4 o'clock. After that we bedded down and brewed some tea, which helped momentarily to revive our chastened spirits. But an atmosphere of depression hung over us that evening, and even Eduardo found little to laugh at. It was one of the few occasions that he neglected his "English lesson"; instead, he collaborated with Cedomir in calculating the probable rate of our future progress, the results of which were anything but encouraging. However, Jack's unshakeable confidence did much to dispel the gloom.

In the hope that snow conditions would be better early in the day, we decided to start getting up at 4.30 the next morning. I have acquired the ability to wake whenever I wish, so I had already assumed the unpopular role of morning rouser. It was usually a difficult task, and I am inclined to think that my nagging persistence in its execution was my principal contribution to the success of the expedition.

We found when we emerged from the tent that there had been a very slight frost during the night, and that though the snow was by no means firm, it was much less soggy than it had been the previous day. We had decided to assemble Jack's sledge, and by distributing the load between it and the "punt", we hoped to be able to drag more than we had managed the day before. It consisted of two runners, each 4 feet long and 6 inches wide, with a framework, 2 feet high and 3 feet wide, of wooden uprights and cross-slats. It took about two hours to put it together. We also removed the two wooden slats from the bottom of the fibrelgass sledge to reduce surface friction. The purpose of these slats was to prevent the sledge from slipping sideways while traversing a slope or in a cross wind. Though, later, we suffered a good deal from this, the slats were never replaced, partly because by then they were in regular use as extra tent pegs.

After applying a lavish coating of ski-wax to the sledges we loaded them with 300 lb., and attached Jack's to the back of the "punt". Then we took up our previous positions in the traces, and pulled. To our great relief the sledges moved forward smoothly, and with rather less effort than it had cost us to drag 250 lb. the previous day.

We marched on a bearing 4° West of South which, though we could not see it, we reckoned to be the direction of the middle of the upper ice-fall. A moderate north-westerly wind was blowing some sleet across our faces, but the clouds were several hundred feet above us, and visibility extended to about two miles; so we had no difficulty in maintaining our course with only occasional reference to the compass. The glacier at this point must have been at least eight miles wide, and though we could see the base of the mountains flanking it on the west, those on the eastern side were invisible.

It was very hard work, and before we had been going ten minutes my thighs had begun to ache. Also I was panting hard because of my inability to maintain any kind of rhythm, which is so essential to minimize fatigue in any form of physical activity. A practised climber, for example, should be able to walk up a steep slope, even in soft snow and carrying a heavy load, even when he is not particularly fit, without becoming out of breath, simply by moving with a precise and balanced rhythm. In a combined effort such as sledge-hauling, it is of course much more difficult to establish a good rhythm, particularly in soft snow or on a breakable crust; for the tall members of the team must adjust their natural strides to those of the shorter men, and there must be a quick and sympathetic response by the others when one man is checked by, say, a collapsing foothold. Later we began to improve in this respect, but on that first day we remained hopelessly uncoordinated, floundering along, sometimes pulling far more than our share of the load, sometimes with slack traces behind us. This of course resulted in an enormous waste of effort.

I decided to break the march up into half-hour spells, with five-minute halts between. The hand of my watch moved with maddening slowness, and I tried to keep my eyes off it as much as possible and think of other things. With the improved visibility I could now see that we were climbing steadily. It was difficult to estimate how much of the effort we were expending was due to the gentle upward slope, but it seemed reasonable to hope that when we reached the plateau, unless snow conditions there were very much worse, we might be able to drag 400 lb. This would include about three weeks' food and fuel which, even if further relaying proved impracticable, should be enough to enable us to reach the Viedma Glacier and to make our way down the Rio Tunnel. This at any rate was a comforting thought.

At the third halt someone suggested that we should reduce the length of the spells to twenty minutes; this met with general approval. The change had an excellent effect on morale, and for the next two hours life seemed relatively pleasant. We than had a half-hour halt for lunch, which consisted of biscuits, butter, cheese and fudge. At every second halting place we left a marker flag or a snowshoe stuck upright in the snow to guide us in thick weather, in case our tracks should become obliterated.

We came to a small ice-fall where we had to alter course and zig-zag through lines of crevasses, and up the steep slopes between. Here we had to exert all our energy to haul the sledges up, and in two places we had to detach them and pull them up separately. Every now and then one of us would fall into a crevasse up to his waist; then of course the sledges would stop and the victim, unable to move forward, would have to struggle out backwards. On one occasion, Jack's sledge ploughed its nose into a crevasse and stuck in a precarious position across a black abyss. A few weeks later in the season this little ice-fall would have caused us a lot of trouble. As it was, though it gave us a good deal of hard work, it presented no serious problem, and above it we emerged once more on to a smooth, gently inclined surface.

We stopped for one of our five-minute halts at about 2 o'clock. I had decided to do two more spells before dumping the load and returning. I was just about to announce this when Jack said that his legs felt like rubber, and suggested that we should "call it a day". I was a little surprised, because I had hardly ever heard Jack admit to being tired. In sledge-hauling it is very difficult to tell how much effort each member of the party is exerting. So long as you are careful to keep your trace taut, you might be pulling hardly at all, and yet escape notice. I expect all of us at one time or another suspected that one of our companions was not pulling his weight, particulary when the sledge seemed to be unusually heavy. But no one would ever suspect Jack of malingering; for he always threw every ounce of his very considerable energy into whatever he was doing. I had thought that he had probably been pulling harder than any of us for most of the time; now I was convinced of it; so I had no hesitation in accepting his suggestion, which had the hearty support of the other two.

As we were stacking the loads we noticed that the four-gallon Army fuel container was missing. It had been riding on Jack's sledge, and must, we thought have fallen off during one of the contretemps we had had on the ice-fall. We were somewhat alarmed, for as it contained half our fuel supply, its loss would have been serious. On the way back we found it resting on the lip of a crevasse.

We were all very tired, and although the way back was all downhill, and the empty sledges needed virtually no pulling, we sat down to rest several times. It seemed a very long way back to camp, which should, of course, have given me a good deal of satisfaction, but I could think of nothing but the cup of hot, sweet tea that I would be holding to my thirsty lips in the not too distant future.

When we reached the tent, we anchored the sledges against the possibility of a gale, and crawled in through the tunnel entrance. Most of our clothing was fairly wet, but our trouser legs, socks and boots were saturated from contact with the sodden snow; so we stripped off our lower garments before setting about the urgent business of lighting the Primus and brewing the nectar we craved. Snow had first to be melted and then more added until there was sufficient water to fill our three-pint pot, for nothing less would satisfy our needs. The process was exasperatingly slow.

I am something of a purist in the matter of tea-making and always insist that the water be brought fully to the boil before infusion; I believe that I would have to be dying of thirst before I would countenance any slackness in this respect. I do not, however, go to the length of taking a tea-pot on an expedition; for I find that, by throwing the tea-leaves into a pan of boiling water and then removing it from the fire, the result is quite as satisfactory as that produced by the standard method.

At last the water was bubbling to my satisfaction. The moment of bliss was almost at hand. Cups were held ready to receive the precious liquid, each with its quota of sugar and milk powder. I was about to throw in the tea-leaves, when the stove tilted, the pot slid off and emptied its entire contents over my naked feet.

I had been looking forward so passionately to that drink, that despite the pain, my first reaction was one of bitter disappointment, and it was a little while before the gravity of the disaster began to dawn on me. However, it was not lost on the others; after a moment's horrified silence, they began to express such concern that, though touched by their sympathy, I thought it slightly exaggerated.

Our small supply of medicines contained no specific remedy for burns, but feeling that something should be done, and with Eduardo's approval, I smeared by feet and ankles with Vaseline. Gradually the scalded flesh began to swell, a ring of huge blisters developed round my ankles, and the skin on top of my left foot withered and flaked away, leaving a raw surface like freshly cut meat. It was generally agreed that the wounds must be kept exposed to the air as much as possible.

Meanwhile a fresh supply of snow was melted, but when eventually the tea was ready, I found that my appetite for it had lost its edge. The tea disposed of, the preparation of the stew was put in hand. This constituted our main meal and was generally anticipated with lively enthusiasm. It took about an hour to prepare, which included melting the snow. First a four-ounce packet of soup powder was emptied into the water and boiled for ten minutes. We had three varieties, tomato, ox-tail and mushroom. Then three dehyrdated meat bars (16 oz. in all) were crumbled into the soup and allowed to boil for a further ten minutes. Finally, potato powder and Quaker Oats were added for thickening. I had brought several packets of various dried herbs, such as thyme, sage and bay leaves, which not only provided some variety of flavour, but completely extinguished that curiously uniform taste that grows more and more monotonous, and even repulsive, when a diet is confined to processed foods. We never grew in the least bit tired of that stew, and had no desire to exchange it for anything else.

We each had two eating utensils: a plastic mug with a capacity of about three-quarters of a pint, and a spoon. Hitherto I had been opposed to the use of plastic mugs on the grounds that they made the tea taste queer; but these, which had been brought from Santiago, were free from this defect. When all the cups had been completely filled with stew, there was always a small amount, half a dozen spoonfuls, left in the pot which was carefully divided between us at the end of the meal. Then one man was allowed to scrape the pot, a privilege always awarded to Jack or Cedomir.

After supper Eduardo bandaged my feet to protect them from contact with the inside of my sleeping-bag, and we settled down for the night, postponing any discussion of plans until we saw what the morning would bring. I tried with little success to keep my mind off my stupid accident and its possible consequences, and eventually, with the aid of a large dose of aspirin, fell asleep.

CHAPTER FOURTEEN

A Cheerless Christmas

SOON after it was light I removed the bandages to examine my feet. The right foot was comparatively unscathed, apart from a slight swelling of the flesh and the blisters round the ankle which looked like a kind of elephantiasis; the skin was not broken. The condition of the left foot, however, was not so good. It was very swollen and most of the upper surface of the foot was an open sore.

I could no longer delude myself that perhaps after all I had escaped injury bad enough to hold us up. It was quite obvious that I would be immobilized for several days at least. It was not that my foot would have been too painful to walk. With burns, as with frost-bite, there is serious danger of septicaemia, an affliction which would have placed, not only me, but all of us in a most unpleasant situation. It was imperative both to keep the wound dry and to avoid friction. Though we were supplied with canvas over-boots, or mutluks, it was impossible to walk even for half a mile through the sodden snow without our feet becoming saturated; and no system of bandaging, however ingenious, could avoid continuous rubbing against the upper surface of the foot. Galling though it was, there was nothing for it but to possess my soul in patience and to hope that the wound would soon heal.

It was pouring with rain and blowing quite hard, so I refrained from disturbing my companions, who woke at about 8 o'clock after eleven hours sleep. While tea was being brewed, we discussed plans to meet the new situation. First it was decided that they should have a day's rest. Then Jack suggested that they should spend the following day in an attempt to reach the upper ice-fall to find a route through it; but on further consideration he agreed that it was probably too far away for such a reconnaissance to be effective, particularly in bad weather.

Allowing for the food and fuel that would be consumed in the next two days, we estimated that 360 lb. of these still remained to be carried forward from Camp 4. We decided to reduce this by a further 25 lb. by abandoning most of our supply of cheese, which was contained in small tins and therefore had little food value relative to its weight. Cedomir lodged a strong protest against this decision, but he was overruled. The point was that if my companions could drag 250 lb. to the dump (Camp 5) the following day, they would then be able to take me along the day after, together with the remaining 85 lb., composed of the tent and our immediate necessities. The process would then be repeated as far as Camp 6, which we hoped would be close enough for work to begin on the ice-fall.

It was a dismal prospect having to lie like a useless log while the others did all the work, but they were so cheerful about it that the whole thing seemed to become a huge joke. Cedomir remarked that, what with a sprained right ankle and a scalded left foot, I was very lucky not to possess a third leg to invite a final calamity. Eduardo composed a song in Spanish about a man from the Himalaya who had a strange grudge against his feet which he was continually trying to mortify; this was clearly the explanation of the mystery of the prints of naked feet found on Himalayan snows. I was not able to judge the quality of the song, but it sounded fluent enough, and it certainly delighted its author.

The others left at 7.30 the next morning. I watched them from the entrance of the tent until they had gone about half a mile, when they disappeared over an undulation in the glacier. I was relieved to see that they were making fair progress. I settled down to kill time until they returned, regretting that I had not allowed myself a few more books. However I am a very slow reader, and with a system of rationing I managed to spin out my enjoyment of *Cakes and Ale* for several days. Also, Jack had lent me *Bleak House*, so on the whole I was reasonably well supplied. Fortunately I had an ample stock of tobacco, and as normally I would be unable to smoke much during the day, there was little danger of my running short.

At 11 o'clock I set forth on a necessary pilgrimage outside. As it was then not raining I put a mutluk on my right foot and left the other naked. Then, treading down the snow with the former I proceeded with a crab-like movement until I had reached a suitable distance from the tent. Later in the journey we suffered a good deal from constipation, this was due partly to the lack of roughage in our diet, but mainly to our reluctance to expose our persons to the wind and driving snow which caused us to discourage our natural inclinations for long periods. Our lesser needs were easily satisfied inside the tent by the use of plastic bottles.

So far we had experienced none of the gales that had been expected. In this we were very lucky indeed, for really rough weather now would have been much more difficult to deal with than it was later, when relaying was no longer necessary.

It rained hard throughout the afternoon, and the thought of the others struggling along in such dreary conditions, made me feel all the worse not to be with them. They arrived back at about 5.30, soaked through and tired, obviously having had a tougher time than before. Our tracks had disappeared and they had had to plough a fresh trail; also they had been pulling 8 lb. more per man. However, despite poor visibility, they had located the dump without trouble.

I felt somewhat cheered the next morning at the prospect of a move. There was little change in the condition of my foot, which was depressing, but although the wound was still raw and very sensitive, at least it looked clean and there was no sign of its becoming septic. Also the swelling was slightly reduced, and with my foot covered with a bandage and one sock (I normally wore three pairs of socks), I managed to get my boot on without causing undue pressure on the wound.

By the time we had packed up our bedding and the tent it was 9 o'clock. I sat in a comfortable nest of rucksacks prepared for me on the "punt", while the tent was tied on to Jack's sledge, the apex pointing forward. With the poles left in place it was ten feet long, so that it resembled a large calibre siege gun on a disproportionately small gun carriage. The weight on the sledges was slightly heavier than it had been the day before, and my companions probably did not derive much benefit from their tracks which, though visible, were largely covered by snow that had fallen during the night. However, as they would not have to return, they could afford to take longer rests between spells of pulling. I timed the spells, calling out the passage of five minute periods for the benefit of Jack and Eduardo who did not possess watches. It made me feel like an Eastern potentate driving a team of slaves.

I tried to help by using my ice-axe as a punt pole; I doubt if I did much good but I derived some satisfaction from the gesture, and at least it helped to keep me warm. Even so, after a couple of hours I was thoroughly chilled by the raw wind and driving sleet. When we reached the steep passages on the small ice-fall, despite Jack's protests, I got off the sledge and, treading very carefully in the tracks, hobbled along behind. The exercise provided a temporary relief to my stiff body; nevertheless I doubt if the others were more glad than I when eventually we reached the dump and established Camp 5.

During the next two days, Christmas Eve and Christmas Day, my morale sank to a low ebb. My foot, if it were healing at all, was doing so with maddening slowness. I am not well endowed with patience in such circumstances and I had become thoroughly exasperated by my role of a useless piece of baggage, by this infernal inactivity to which I could set no term. I was tempted to throw caution to the winds, and take a chance with my wretched foot. I doubt if my mood was improved by the fact that the others were in excellent spirits, and seemed to be thoroughly enjoying themselves. This of course was completely illogical, for obviously my own situation no less than theirs would have been far worse had they been reluctant and pessimistic. All the same I am ashamed to remember that I found it difficult to respond cheerfully to Eduardo's witticisms and good-natured sallies.

On the 24th they succeeded in reaching the foot of the ice-fall with the first relay, and on the 25th they carried up the second, again leaving only the tent and our immediate necessities and me to be shifted. Both days were long and hard, but they were evidently becoming accustomed to the exercise of sledge-hauling, and no doubt their technique was improving, for on both evenings they returned noticeably less tired than before. On both occasions the bad weather had prevented them from seeing much of the ice-fall, but at least they had seen no serious obstacle to begin with.

On the 26th I had another ride on the sledge. Though I became as cold and cramped as before, it was a very pleasant change from lying alone in the tent. I was eager to catch a glimpse of the ice-fall, but the visibility remained so restricted that I could see nothing of it. By then, however, having travelled diagonally across the glacier, we were quite close to its eastern side where a series of rock buttresses loomed through the mist. At the end of each spell of pulling, I retrieved the snowshoe or marker flag that had been left there on the first relay. When eventually we reached the last spell, I got off the sledge and walked behind, taking great care always to keep my left foot rigid and to place it on firmly beaten snow.

The possibility that they might climb the ice-fall the very next day, and so reach the edge of the Plateau, put the others in a particularly exuberant frame of mind that evening. They engaged in a lively discussion of plans, and in making various estimates of times, distances and weights. Jack produced a set of logistics based on the airy assumption that I would remain a passenger for the next three weeks. I thought this hardly tactful, but I was prepared to believe that it was not unkindly meant and refrained from violent comment. In any case the worst of my depression was over, and I was in a more benevolent mood than I had been for several days. This was partly because I was caught up in the general excitement at reaching the last obstacle before the Ice-cap, but mainly because my foot, far from having suffered by my walk that afternoon, was at last beginning to show signs of healing. I was secretly determined to get up the ice-fall under my own steam.

Someone suggested that the following day should be devoted to a thorough reconnaissance of the ice-fall to find the best way through it. After some discussion, however, the majority were in favour of taking some loads at least up the first part, so as to obtain some idea of the effort involved in hauling the sledge up the slopes. Accordingly the others set off at 7.30 with the fibreglass sledge laden with 200 lb. while I lay at the entrance of the tent to watch their progress. The weather was much improved. The sky was completely overcast, but it was not raining and the clouds had lifted to a couple of thousand feet above the glacier. However, I was too close under the ice-fall to see more than the first 300 or 400 feet of its central section, where a corridor of unbroken snow, running up between lines of crevasses, offered an obvious line of approach. To the east, the buttresses whose dim forms I had seen the previous day, had taken shape as a line of rock peaks flanking that side of the glacier. Beyond the right-hand end of this line I could see a formidable cascade of ice-cliffs, which merged with the main ice-fall and which I estimated to be about 2,000 feet high.

I watched the others making their way up the corridor. They were obviously finding it very hard work, but they were moving steadily, and after about an hour they reached the top, and disappeared over a ridge beyond. According to our aneroid, Camp 6 was 3,500 feet above sea-level. Assuming that the northern part of the Ice-cap was the same altitude as the southern (5,000 feet), the height of the ice-fall would be about 1,500 feet. I had little doubt that there was a way through, but to pass the time I worked out an alternative route up the right-hand buttress over the rock peak and descending to the top of the "cascade". It would take the best part of a week to perform the manoeuvre, as of course we would have to carry the sledges, but it seemed to be quite feasible. Then I lit the Primus and started to melt a supply of water for our evening meal.

At 10.30 I heard shouts, and looking out of the tent, I was surprised to see the others sitting on the sledge tobogganing down the corridor. Presently they arrived with the explanation of their early return. Above the place where I had seen them disappearing they had found a broad ramp running diagonally up to the left which, though it had been hard work hauling the sledge up through deep snow, had presented no technical difficulties. Beyond the top of the ramp, which they had reached in little more than two hours from the camp, there was a network of very large crevasses stretching as far as they could see. Though the ground was by no means steep, and though the crevasses seemed to be very well bridged, the snow was so soft that they came to the conclusion that it might be better to place Camp 7 at the top of the ramp, so as to tackle the next section of the ice-fall in the early morning. So they had decided to return, and after a cup of tea and an early lunch they carried up a second relay.

The next morning I announced my intention of walking up to the next camp. My foot was very much better; a reasonably solid scab had formed over the wound, which no longer hurt, and in fact was now itching exquisitely. With reasonable care I should be able to keep it dry and avoid rubbing off the scab. As I expected, my decision produced a strong protest from Jack who considered that my foot was still far from healed, and that my usual impatience was prompting me to take an unnecessary risk. However, the others were less averse to the idea which of course meant that the rest of the loads could be taken up in a single relay.

While the sledges were being loaded, I started slowly. It was a great joy to be moving again. The clouds had come down once more, but it was not raining or snowing and, though we were shrouded in dense mist, there was a feel of better weather in the air.

When we reached the dump at the top of the ramp, I suggested that, instead of pitching the camp there, we should go on through the ice-fall, with the tent and personal gear and whatever else could be taken on the fibreglass sledge. For it seemed to me that in view of the great depth of the snow, its condition was not likely to alter except for the worse. It was certainly arguable that a way through should first be found before attempting to take the sledge; but after some discussion my suggestion was adopted.

Cedomir went ahead on a twenty-foot climbing-rope, which was attached to the sledge and also lightly held by Jack. This enabled him to do his share of the hauling, and at the same time gave him sufficient freedom of movement to test the snow for hidden crevasses. It also minimized the chances of our standing on the same crevasse; though it could not ensure against it for, as we soon discovered, the crevasses were running in every direction. Jack was harnessed on a long trace, Eduardo on a short one, while I followed behind the sledge on a rope attached to Eduardo. It was not perhaps very sound mountaineering practice, but in the circumstances it was the best arrangement we could devise, and certainly it was less dangerous than carrying heavy loads.

Considering that we were barely 4,000 feet above the sea, and that it was already past midsummer, the amount of snow covering the ice was remarkable. It was obviously the remains of winter and spring falls which should have disappeared long before. We were most fortunate that it had not done so, for the ice-fall was very broken, and in normal summer conditions it would have been impossible to drag the sledges through it, and even walking might have been difficult. As it was, except for the major ice-cliffs and crevasses, the riven surface was smoothed to gentle undulations. Also, though the snow was soft and each of my companions was continually falling into hidden crevasses, it was sufficiently deep and packed to prevent a massive collapse of the bridges.

All the same it was extremely hard work for the others and often it was as much as they could do to keep the sledge moving. It was very galling not to be able to help them, but at least I was not riding on the sledge, which was something to be thankful for. They had to follow a tortuous course to avoid obstacles and, as visibility was still restricted to a few hundred yards, I kept an eye on the compass to maintain a general southerly direction.

Then suddenly, at 2 o'clock, the slope eased, no more crevasses were visible, the snow became less deep and presently we found ourselves walking over an almost level surface. It was difficult to believe that we had passed right through the ice-fall and were actually on the Plateau. For one thing, the aneroid registered our height as 4,500 feet, and we had been expecting to have to climb at least another 500 feet, which in those conditions would have taken a long time. We went on for a quarter of an hour, but met with no further obstacles and the flat, smooth surface continued to stretch away into the mist; so we decided to pitch camp.

At 6 o'clock, while supper was being prepared, we noticed that it was exceptionally cold, and that the light inside the tent, usually dim, had become uncommonly bright. Eduardo poked his head outside to investigate these phenomena and immediately gave a delighted yell. He then scrambled back. seized his boots and his camera and shot out of the tent, nearly upsetting the stove in his hurry. Peering after him through the tunnel entrance, I saw the cause of his excitement.

The mist had cleared. To the eastward, rising from a level horizon of snow, there was a line of fantastic peaks sparkling in sunlight against a background of pale-blue sky. Though their sides appeared to be completely vertical, they were almost entirely sheathed in ice, while their tops were crowned with immense mushroom-shaped cornices.

There was no longer any doubt that we had reached the Ice-cap, for it was also clear to the southward, and in that direction we could see nothing but gently undulating snow stretching away into the distance. This alone would have been sufficient cause for jubilation. It was December 28; only eighteen days had elapsed since our landing. Though the rim of the Plateau had been farther away than we had expected, the route to it had proved a great deal easier than we had dared to hope, and despite the time wasted as a result of my stupid accident, which had been minimized by the stalwart work of my companions, we were two days ahead of our schedule. Now, at the best possible moment, after weeks of rain and mist, it seemed that we were to be blessed with a spell of fine weather.

For the first time I felt absolutely confident in our ability to complete the journey across the whole length of the Ice-cap to Lago Argentino. We had food and fuel enough to last us for another thirty-seven days, and it seemed that nothing but a serious accident or the most diabolical weather could stop us now. We had reckoned on spending up to a week in an attempt to climb Lauturo, but that was a secondary project which could be embraced or rejected according to our situation when we arrived at the foot of the volcano.

So far of course we had been incredibly lucky in the matter of wind and we could hardly expect this state of affairs to continue indefinitely. We had yet to discover to what extent we would be immobilized by rough weather. I had always expected that we might be held up for a week at a time, but much would depend upon our ability, not only to travel, but to strike and pitch camp in the kind of wind we were likely to meet. Then there was the question of how long we would have to continue relaying. Obviously this would be impossible in really bad weather; but I was hopeful that we would soon be able to haul all our baggage together, and that in any case, even if we were forced to abandon some of our food, we would still be able to carry enough to see us through.

CHAPTER FIFTEEN

On the Plateau

THE clear sky brought a sharp frost for the night, and in the morning the first beams of the rising sun touched the tent at half-past four. Encouraged by this delightful novelty, and spurred by the prospect of a few hours of hard-frozen snow, my companions made an exceptionally rapid departure. Their task was to bring the rest of the loads through the ice-fall from the top of the ramp. I expected them to take the whole day to complete it.

I took the bedding outside to give it a much needed airing, and then sat down to study the view and to give my foot a dose of sunlight which I supposed might do it good. The air was still and the sky completely free from cloud. The deep trough of the Canal Baker was still visible over the northern rim of the Plateau, and beyond it I could now see the great peaks flanking the *Hielo Patagonico del Norte* ("North Patagonian Ice"). To the west, there was a range of rounded mountains which formed a low rim to the brimful basin of the Plateau ice. There were several gaps in it where the ice spilt over giving rise to the various glaciers flowing down to the fjords of the Pacific coast.

To the south, my view was limited by the slightly concave surface of the Plateau, but above it I could just see the ice crest of a far distant peak. It almost certainly belonged to the group of mountains we had seen from Nuntak the previous year, and a compass-bearing to it gave me the general direction we would be following.

The peaks to the east, now part of a vast sunlit landscape, looked less unearthly than they had appeared before. Then, as brilliant objects floating in the evening sky, they might have been twenty, thirty or forty miles away. I could see now that they were not more than eight miles distant and that they stood only about 2,000 feet above the Plateau; but they were still magnificent. The limpid air and the steep rays of the sun revealed more clearly the floral patterns of the ice draping their sheer sides.

This most lovely feature of the mountains of Southern Patagonia is caused by the winds, heavily charged with moisture, striking against exposed surfaces to form a coating of rime. It clings to vertical and even overhanging precipices as readily as it forms on gentler slopes, and its tensile strength is such that there seems to be no limit to its development. The steeper the slope the more it is exposed to the force of the wind, which results in the creation of wildly improbable shapes on the faces of the peaks and of immense cornices along the *windward* side of their summit ridges.

At 11 o'clock, while I was in the tent melting snow on the Primus, the others arrived. I was astonished when they told me that they had brought everything with them. The frozen snow had made their task a great deal easier than we had expected. The sun had been late in reaching the icefall, and they had managed to relay the loads through it before the surface had begun to melt. At the top, they had piled them all onto the two sledges and, Jack pulling his own and the other two the "punt", they had arrived triumphantly with some 400 lb. of baggage.

I made tea and handed it out to the others, and we all had lunch sitting on the sledges in our shirt-sleeves. The peace of the meal was disturbed by a final passage of arms with Jack about my foot. It had suffered little from my activity of the day before, and now looked and felt so much better that I had decided the next day to resume hauling, or at least to give it a trial. The announcement of my intention produced a strong reaction, including a discourse, couched I thought in somewhat patronizing terms, about my habitual impatience. I retorted with some heat, that I was the best judge of the situation, and that in any case it was my foot. On the latter point Jack rightly observed that we all had an equal stake in its welfare. He appealed to Eduardo as our medical adviser to use his restraining influence, but Eduardo tactfully changed the subject.

After lunch the others decided to take advantage of the fine weather and transport half the baggage forward for a couple of hours that afternoon. By then, of course, the snow had melted and the surface had reverted to its usual soft condition; but it was a great deal pleasanter to work in good visibility, and it seemed a pity to waste the opportunity. They set off at 1 o'clock. Two hours later the camp was enveloped in cloud, and by 5 o'clock when they returned, it was snowing. Our precious spell of fine weather had lasted less than twenty-four hours.

The next morning it was as thick as ever. Some sleet was falling, but there was still not much wind. We packed up the camp and started at about 8 o'clock. Jack hauled his own sledge, and the rest of us pulled the "punt". Formerly we had marched in pairs abreast, now we did so in line, with Cedomir out in front on a climbing-rope and Eduardo and I behind on a long and short trace respectively. It was a much better arrangement, for only one set of tracks was needed, and we could pull more evenly. My foot gave me no trouble, a relief equalled only by the satisfaction I felt at being able at last to do my share of the work. Despite my enforced rest I found the hauling a great deal less laborious than it had been ten days before.

The tracks of the previous day were barely visible, but the others had taken the precaution of marking the route with snowshoes, and in well under two hours we reached their dump. We added a couple of sacks of food, about 120 lb., to our load and went on, I held the compass and shouted directions to Cedomir, "left a bit" – "right a bit", to keep him on our chosen course of 4° West of South. We rested for five minutes after every half-hour of pulling.

At the third halt after the dump, Cedomir complained that he could not see properly. He was evidently suffering from a mild attack of migraine; so I took over the lead and Eduardo the compass. After a bit, Jack, who was following behind, pointed out that we were steering a very erratic course. We stopped to investigate the matter and discovered that the cause was Eduardo's ice-axe which was deflecting the compass needle; so he gave me the offending weapon to carry.

After two or three spells, I came to the conclusion that the climbing-rope made a very unsatisfactory towing line; partly because the elasticity of the nylon made it impossible to maintain an even strain, and partly because the waist loop was unsuited to the purpose. Now that we were on the Plateau the risk of falling into a crevasse was negligible, and it was therefore quite unnecessary for the leader to be on a climbing-rope; so I exchanged it for the harness and a long trace.

We decided to pitch camp at 2 o'clock to allow time to bring up the rest of the loads from the dump. This proved a wise precaution. Cedomir said that he was quite recovered and insisted upon going back with the others while I remained behind to perform the various camp chores, such as inflating the air-mattresses and melting snow. At about 4 o'clock the wind began to rise. Snow was falling and the mist was still dense; I became slightly apprehensive that, despite the markers, the others might have difficulty in finding the tent. They arrived before six, but even so the tracks had been almost obliterated.

Throughout the evening the force of the wind increased, and that night we were treated to a full-blooded Patagonian storm. For the first time I began fully to appreciate the qualities of the Pyramid tent, and I was devoutly thankful that I had followed Jack's suggestion to bring it. It gave a wonderful sense of security compared with the various types of mountain tent I had used hitherto. Its rigidity depended hardly at all upon its guy ropes; its shape ensured that the force of the wind, from whatever direction, was converted into a downward rather than a lateral pressure; the drift-snow piling up against its sides tended to perfect its streamlining, and the four poles, by meeting at the apex, had the maximum strength to support its weight.

Though by the morning the storm had abated, it was still fairly violent, and we were faced with a problem that had long been pending. It was obvious that we could not afford to be prevented from travelling by any but the most savage weather. But even in a comparatively mild blizzard relaying would be a hazardous procedure. In the first place our tracks would be erased almost immediately; with visibility restricted to, say, fifty yards, it would be very difficult to steer a return compass course with sufficient precision to ensure picking up our markers, unless they were placed at impossibly short intervals; and to lose our way would almost certainly be disastrous. Then there was the possibility of the dumps becoming drifted over and lost; and although perhaps this was not likely to happen within twenty-four hours, there was no guarantee that worsening weather would not prevent the second relay from being made for several days. But the most important factor was the direction of the prevailing wind which, particularly in bad weather, was from the north-west. One can often march, even in reasonable comfort, so long as the wind is coming more or less from behind when it is impossible to move in the opposite direction, facing the blinding drift. Thus it might happen that we would carry a relay forward, and find ourselves unable to return. In fact, as it turned out, in the weeks that followed there were few days when we could have travelled in a northerly direction.

Theoretically we now had about 550 lb. of baggage, not counting the weight of the sledges. In practice we had to drag more than this, for it was impossible to remove all the snow from the tent and the various sacks, which in any case were soaking wet; so that the total weight to be dragged must have been well over 600 lb. The question was whether we could manage such a load; this could only be answered by trial, and we decided to conduct some experiments before packing up the camp.

We emerged from the tent at 9 o'clock, to face the harsh world outside. Everything except the upper part of the tent was buried in snow, and our first task was to dig out the sledges with ice-axes and aluminium shovels. The snow was so wet that in ten minutes, our gloves were soaked. The most difficult job was extricating the traces. To prevent these from becoming entangled we had made a practice of leaving them stretched out in front of the sledges. They were now buried under two feet of snow which was so compact and heavy that they could not be freed by pulling, and we had to dig trenches along their whole length.

When, after nearly one hour and a half, in a strong wind and driving sleet, we had succeeded in extricating the sledges and the various loads, we scraped the bottom of the "punt", and applied a coat of ski-wax. Then we loaded it with the sacks of food, and Jack lay on top to act as a 200 lb. weight. After several trials, we found that three of us could just pull it with a load of 400 lb. In the existing conditions, however, Jack's sledge, in relation to its size, was more efficient; partly because the deep snow offered less frontal resistance to its runners. Laden with 150 lb. he was able to pull it without too much effort.

By the time we had concluded these experiments, it was nearly midday, and we were wet and cold. With the tent still to dig out and pack, it was obvious that there would not be time for more than a few hours sledging that day. We decided, therefore, to take a half holiday, and crawled back into the tent where, with the Primus giving full blast, we soon succeeded in creating an agreeable fug. It was comforting to know that we could now shift all our baggage together, and that we had finished with the monotonous back and forth business of relaying. Undoubtedly for the next week or so it would be extremely hard work, but our load would become lighter by about 10 lb. each day, and however slowly we went at first, our progress would surely be faster than it had been hitherto.

The next morning I roused the party at 3.30, when the first light of dawn was seeping faintly through the walls of the tent. The stove was lit in morose silence (verbal silence, that is, for the word was certainly not otherwise applicable in the roar of the wind and hammering of the tent canvas); after which most of the party dozed off again, until clouds of steam issuing from the pot gave the signal for further reluctant action.

Our breakfast invariably consisted of "brose" followed by tea. For the preparation of "brose" each man put 6 heaped tablespoons of oats, 2 of milk powder and two of sugar into his mug, mixed them together and added boiling water. For tea each man was allowed 2 heaped tablespoons of sugar. If anyone took more than his share, which occasionally happened in the early stages of the journey, his crime was discovered at the end of the day; and although the culprit could not then be detected, one hoped that his conscience was troubled enough to prevent a recurrence.

A few days later we had one of those contretemps, which in retrospect appear so incredibly petty that one is ashamed to recall them, but which seem to be inevitable when people are confined together at close quarters and in circumstances of some discomfort. A surprising amount of emotion is usually involved, and the difficulty at the time is to make an objective assessment of the importance of the issue, and to see clearly the extent to which one is actuated by sheer cussedness.

On this occasion the dispute arose over the position to be occupied by the stove during the preparation of breakfast. Hitherto a space was created for it between Jack and Eduardo in the middle of the tent. The point of this arrangement was that the heat from the stove would more effectively reach the clothes which were supposed to be drying aloft. I objected to it on three grounds: in the first place the creation of a space in the middle meant that Cedomir and I were squeezed even harder against our respective walls, which were usually wet and often pressed inwards by a cold mass of drift-snow, secondly the tendency of people to fall asleep again after the stove had been lit obviously increased the danger of fire and flood; thirdly, I could not get at the stove in that position, and as the party rouser it was a great deal easier for me to light the stove myself than to induce a reluctant response from my companions by shouting. My remedy was to place the stove in the corridor by the entrance, and for Cedomir and me to reverse our lying positions, so that we could easily reach it. This plan had the additional advantage that we could also reach the space between two walls of the tent for fresh supplies of snow which were constantly required for replenishing the pots.

For some reason Jack was bitterly opposed to this innovation, and for a while I refrained from pressing the matter; but with the worsening of the weather and the institution of earlier breakfasts, my sense of frustration got the better of me, and I decided to act. At the outset of the new régime Jack signified his disapproval by making full use of his considerable length to occupy as much of the corridor as possible with his feet, so that I had to lie across them to get at the stove (which I did as heavily as I could!). Primus stoves, like horses, are peculiarly sensitive to emotional atmosphere, and to succeed with them one must be thoroughly relaxed. I made three unsuccessful attempts to light the stove, each resulting in a conflagration. Jack's caustic comments suggested that he nursed a secret hope that I would set the tent on fire; but this was not gratified until some weeks later, when I burnt a hole in the inner entrance flap, and by then my system had won general approval.

On the whole, however, considering our constricted living-quarters, there were remarkably few of these quarrels, and I have rarely travelled with a set of more congenial companions. Eduardo's good humour was indefatigable; he was a tireless raconteur, and if occasionally I found his stories a bit tedious, it was only because the language difficulty made it hard to detect their point. Cedomir maintained an unruffled calm. He spoke little, but his obvious delight in Eduardo's jokes (and even Jack's and mine) was very touching.

When we emerged from the tent that morning the weather was still pretty rough, although the force of the wind showed signs of slackening. Visibility was very bad: ten yards away in any direction the white mist was indistinguishable from the snow. After thirty-six hours there was a great accumulation of drift-snow to dig away, so that it took us a long time to get the tent down and the sledges packed. Jack, with his usual insistence on doing more than his fair share of the work, loaded 170 lb. of baggage on to his sledge, leaving 380 lb. for the rest of us to drag on the "punt". I harnessed myself to the leading trace, with Cedomir behind me and then Eduardo; Jack followed behind the "punt". From now on the man on the leading trace acted as "helmsman". With a mighty heave we started.

I had been expecting to have to work hard; but the effort involved in keeping the sledge moving was a great deal more than I had bargained for, and I soon began to wonder how long I would be able to maintain it. I sank into the snow almost up to my knees, and the necessity of lifting my feet so high at each step while leaning forward at a steep angle was exhausting enough in itself without having to do my share of the pulling. I had to watch the compass constantly, for I found that if I took my eyes off it even for a few seconds, I was liable to swing as much as ten degrees off course. This meant that I could never look at the snow in front of me, with the result that I frequently stumbled. Before long the sweat was pouring down my face and (despite my shaggy eyebrows) into my eyes. With the combination of sweat and sleet my goggles became fogged, which made it difficult to see the compass. Every ten minutes I stopped for a rest, gasping for breath, with my head on my knees.

After an hour and ten minutes I handed over the lead to Cedomir. I was very relieved to find how much easier it was to follow behind him; to have the solid foundation of his tracks to step on, to see where I was putting my feet and to be able to concentrate my whole attention upon maintaining a steady pull on my trace. It seemed like a sinecure by comparison. For the rest of the day's march we worked in regular ten-minute spells of hauling, followed by a brief rest. The work of leading was divided between the three of us, each doing three consecutive spells in front.

At 11 o'clock we ate our day's ration of rum fudge, two ounces each, and at 1 o'clock we stopped for half an hour for lunch, which consisted of a four-ounce packet of biscuits each with butter. We sat under the lee of the sledges, but our underclothes were soaked with sweat, and although by then the wind had dropped to a stiff breeze, we soon became so chilled that there was no temptation to prolong the halt. We also had a small supply of glucose sweets (six a day each) which we sucked as we went along; they helped to keep thirst at bay. I used to try to preserve most of mine until after lunch to boost my flagging morale. Soon after 3 o'clock we all agreed that we had had enough for the day, so we off-loaded the sledges and set about the chilly task of making camp.

When the wind was very strong there was a considerable risk of the tent being blown away while we were pitching it. If this had happened it would probably have travelled a great deal faster than we could have followed, and there would have been nothing to stop its flight until it reached the eastern side of the Ice-cap. To prevent this disagreeable occurrence we followed a carefully prepared drill. First the tent was laid on the ground with the apex pointing into the wind, and the entrance uppermost. Then the near guy was securely fastened to an ice-axe which had been driven deep into the snow. While I sat on the apex to hold it down, the others spread the front "skirts", or snow-flaps, which were two feet wide, pegged them down with long aluminium spikes and weighted them with ration sacks. The next stage of the operation was the most critical. I held the rear guy and payed it out round the ice-axe as required, while Jack took charge of the apex and allowed it to rise until the others could crawl beneath the madly flapping canvas, grasp the rear corners of the "skirt", haul them back and peg them down. Then each took hold of one of the front poles and, as Jack allowed the apex to rise to the extent of his reach and let go, they planted them firmly in position.

When the tent had been trimmed, we shovelled snow on to the skirts and secured the five guys, which usually meant digging deep holes to reach snow compact enough to hold the pegs. To minimize the accumulation of drift-snow we built a barricade of snowshoes and Jack's sledge a few feet from the back, or windward side of the tent. Most of the baggage not required for the night was distributed along the skirts to supply added weight; the rest was stowed under the upturned "punt", which was secured to two ice-axes. In moderate weather the whole operation took about an hour to complete, but in really bad conditions it took considerably longer.

Chaos reigned inside the tent as we struggled to remove our sodden mutluks and boots, stripped off our clothes, inflated our mattresses and unpacked our bedding; but it was such a relief to be in out of the wind that no one minded. Then at last came the blissful moment when we were in our sleeping-bags clasping our mugs of tea. As soon as this had been disposed of we set about the preparation of the stew; and that in turn was followed by a final brew of "brose". Thus it was nearly 8 o'clock before we were ready to settle down for the night. Though it was still fully light, we had no difficulty in falling asleep; for we were all very tired but by no means dissatisfied with the day's work.

CHAPTER SIXTEEN

Familiar Landmarks

FROM now on, the pattern of our daily routine remained unaltered. Though gradually the dawn came later, I continued to rouse my companions at 3.30 each morning. The reason for this spartan procedure was that we always took such an infernal time to get started, and a late start was demoralizing. Jack always held firmly to the belief that the snow was in better condition before noon than after. Though I never disputed this theory, I was inclined to think that it was largely an illusion induced by fatigue towards the end of a day's march.

Each morning we aimed at being ready to start by 7 o'clock, but we rarely achieved this. Our reluctance to exchange the cosy warmth of our sleeping-bags for the chilly hospitality of our wet clothes was, of course, part of the reason. We tended to linger over breakfast and to grasp at any excuse to postpone the evil moment, such as polishing goggles or mending a mutluk. When our personal gear had been packed, three of us would crawl out of the tent, leaving Eduardo to deflate the mattresses, pack them and the pots, stoves and ration bags, and to clean the inside of the tent.

What really took the time was digging away the snow that had half buried the tent during the night and extricating the sledges and gear, a job which sometimes cost us more than three hours. Except on rare occasions drift-snow was always sweeping across the Plateau, stinging our faces and clogging our goggles so that it was difficult to see what we were doing; though we tried to work with our backs to the wind as much as possible. With temperatures hovering around freezing-point, the drift often melted and froze again, with the result that the skirts of the tent became encased in solid blocks of ice which had to be chipped away with ice-axes. We had to be very careful not to damage the tent. At some time during the first few days, someone put a shovel through the outer wall, but fortunately this accident was not repeated. The snowflap, however, came in for a severe battering, and before long it was torn across in several places.

The most unpleasant conditions for working were when the temperature was above freezing-point, for then the drift was wet, and our gloves, boots and trouser legs were soon saturated, and our hands and feet became unpleasantly cold. Dry drift was a comparative luxury. It was, of course, almost impossible to distinguish between real drift on the one hand and sleet or falling snow on the other; they all came at us more or less horizontally.

Once the digging operations had been completed, the task of packing up the tent and loading the sledges were comparatively simple; and the first few spells of hauling provided a welcome change, particularly as we then got warm. Our performance soon improved; on the very next march we lengthened our spells of hauling to fifteen minutes, and after a few days we were able to resume our old practice of twenty-minute spells.

We looked forward keenly to "elevenses", which I always announced with the cry of "fudge up", and usually to the lunch halt; but when the wind was particularly severe we postponed our lunch until after we had camped. By then, of course, we were ravenous and the task of pitching the tent became specially tedious. We never went on much later than 3 o'clock, and we sometimes stopped even earlier.

It might be supposed that this rigidly circumscribed routine was monotonous, but I do not think that any of us found it so. This was partly because of our constant preoccupation with chores that were both varied and of some immediate urgency, partly because we were so often in a state of looking forward with an almost passionate zest to the satisfaction of some bodily need such as food or rest or tea or warmth, and partly because of our absorption in the job in hand and our desire to improve our performance. Despite the loathsome prospect of getting up in the early morning, I remember looking forward keenly to the next day's march, hoping that snow conditions would be better, wondering how far we would get and what we might see. I certainly experienced none of the boredom and frustration I remember during the attempts to climb Everest, the endless coming and going over the same piece of ground, the long period of lying in a tent, too weak from oxygen-lack to enjoy physical activity or even food. Here we had no altitude to weaken us, and we became steadily fitter and more able to contend with our environment.

An important factor was our mental attitude to the weather. We had embarked upon the journey with the full realization that it would be the main hazard, the chief obstacle to be overcome. The numerous stories we had heard of travellers being storm-bound, unable to move for weeks at a time, had prepared us for the worst. For my part, I had been definitely scared of the wind, and had often tried to visualize what it would be like trying to pitch a tent in the kind of storm Geoff and I had experienced in the "Vulcan Viedma" two years before. But now that we were here, actually coping with the problems of the weather, we soon gained confidence in our ability not only to survive the worst it could do, but to travel in almost any conditions. This confidence enabled us to derive a positive pleasure, by no means masochistic, from the violence of the elements.

In some respects the weather was different from what we had expected. Unlike my previous experience of the Ice-cap, snowstorms were heavy and continuous, and rain was correspondingly rare. Though this resulted in a far greater density of drift which was tiresome on the march and caused us such a lot of hard work in the mornings, it had the advantage that the crevassed areas remained well covered. It was also a great deal colder; as a rule this did nothing to improve snow conditions, but at least we did not get so completely soaked as we had before. The previous year we used to regard a snowstorm followed by a frost as a sure herald of fine weather; this time, however, it was never the case.

A less welcome novelty was the dense mist which often persisted for days at a time and rendered navigation difficult. Most of the time on the northern part of the Ice-cap we had only a vague idea of our position, and were never quite sure of the course we should steer. But the most irritating thing about it was that we saw so little of our surroundings. Even this had its compensations, for when the mist did clear the scenic effect was dramatic and very moving.

On the afternoon of January 2 we made a landfall. The mist was less dense than usual; suddenly a dark mass loomed ahead of us and gradually assumed the form of a long line of cliffs. We altered course a few degrees to the westward, which appeared to take us nearly parallel to it, for when we camped an hour later it was still about the same distance away.

During the night the wind dropped, and with it the temperature. When I awoke in the morning it was so calm that there was not even a breeze to rustle the frost-encrusted tent canvas. After breakfast Jack and Cedomir set off to collect samples from the rock wall, the base of which was only just visible through the mist, leaving Eduardo and me to pack up the camp and load the sledges. It was an easy job that morning as very little drift had accumulated. As we worked the mist about us began to vanish, and the long, serrated crest of the wall slowly emerged, first as a shifting phantom, then in form so sharp that it still seemed to have no substance. The sun did not appear, but to the north-west there was a great expanse of pale-blue sky set in a golden frame, and a million crystals of frosted snow sparkled in the reflected light. There was nothing else in the scene, just the sky and the mist and that lonely rock standing in the midst of a vast expanse of snow, but its very simplicity gave me a sense of profound peace which alone would have made the whole journey worth while.

Jack and Cedomir were away for an hour and a half. They brought back specimens of granitic rock known as "Tonalite", of which the wall was composed. It was mainly white, but mottled with large black crystals of hornblende.

Our camp had been almost at the western end of the wall, from which extended a long snow hump. To get around the corner without making a long detour we had to haul the sledges over this, which involved us in a mile of uphill work. But the snow was good, and we had been so stimulated by the enjoyment of the morning and our hope of a spell of fine weather, that we were bursting with energy and high spirits. The hope, however, was short-lived; and before we had been going a couple of hours it had started to blow again, the temperature rose with lamentable effect on the snow, and heavy clouds raced low overhead.

For two days we passed through an archipelago of scattered rock peaks, rising like lofty islands out of the Plateau. We rarely saw their summits, but when they did appear, sheathed in glistening rime, looming out of the mist and swirling drift, they had the ethereal quality of a Chinese painting. This resemblance reminded me of the Chinese practice of displaying their pictures individually and not together in galleries, which they consider a barbarous custom calculated to spoil the effect of any masterpiece. Certainly with mountains their splendour and their beauty are enormously enhanced by visual isolation from their neighbours, and for this reason I have little liking for panoramas.

Cedomir came to the conclusion that all these peaks were composed of the same granite rock as the wall, which he had also found occurring in the vicinity of Cerro O'Higgins, and that it formed a massive intrusion extending right across this part of the range. The peaks undoubtedly formed part of the group where we had expected that we might find further evidence of volcanic activity, either recent or extinct. Though, of course, our observations were far too cursory to come to any definite conclusion, the presence of all this granite seemed to make it very improbable that any part of these mountains was of volcanic origin, and to suggest that Lautaro was after all an isolated phenomenon.

The patchy visibility, though greatly preferable to the perpetual blanket of dense fog we had had before, was sometimes confusing. On one occasion when I was in front with my eyes on the compass, I looked up and I had the distinct impression that the mist had cleared and that I saw a range of mountains very far ahead. I was quite convinced, not only of the reality of what I saw, but that I recognized the shape of the distant peaks. I let out an exultant shout, “Look! Lautaro”. I was very puzzled by the lack of response from my companions to this exciting announcement. Then, a few minutes later, my eyes suddenly snapped into true focus, and I realized that my distant range of mountains was in fact a line of crevasses about 100 yards away.

According to our aneroid we were now 5,600 feet high. One morning we suddenly found that the sledges had become very light, and we realized that we were going downhill. The incline was not perceptible to the eye, but it made a remarkable difference to the running of the sledges, and for two hours we scampered along at a fine speed. We reckoned that we must have reached the wide trough in the Ice-cap which we had seen the previous year running from east to west to the north of the Nunatak. It was an encouraging thought, for it meant that we were approaching the end of the first half of the journey.

The weather had become steadily worse. On the 7th, after a particularly heavy storm, we ran into bad *sastrugi*, a snow formation caused by the wind, rather like giant sand ripples, though instead of being smooth and firm, the ridges were usually crested with small ice cornices with soft snow beneath. It was exhausting work hauling the sledges over this rough terrain, for every few yards they buried their noses in soft banks of snow, and we had to go back to dig them out. For hours on end we seemed to make hardly any progress. Visibility was almost nil, and the leader, intent upon holding the course, kept stumbling over unseen obstacles. Jack’s sledge suffered severely; it was not really built for such rough treatment, and by 10 o’clock, it was on the verge of collapse. It was one of the days when we did not indulge in a lunch halt, and we were certainly not inclined to stop to effect the necessary repairs; so we piled Jack’s load on to the “punt”, tied his sledge on behind and all pulled together for the rest of the march. Jack was somewhat crestfallen. He was very proud of his sledge and though its performance both before and later provided ample justification for his pride, this setback was a sad blow.

This was the third consecutive day on which we had seen nothing but the snow immediately around us. We had supposed that the almost constant mist in which we had been travelling might be a phenomenon peculiar to the northern part of the Ice-cap, and that once we had crossed it, even if the weather was no more agreeable we might at least have better visibility. We could no longer cling to this comforting theory.

According to our reckoning we should now be very close to the northern buttresses and glaciers of the Cordon Pio XI, and we were most anxious to avoid blundering into them; for had we done so we might find ourselves amongst a complicated system of ridges and passages from which, in thick weather, we might have some difficulty in extricating ourselves. None of us had ever marched on a compass course for so long, through such featureless country and in such persistently bad visibility, and we had to admit the unpleasant possibility that we might have gone wildly astray. We were aiming for our old friend the Nunatak, with the intention of passing between it and the volcano, though it would be almost as convenient to pass to the east of it. In any case it would be far better to err to the left than to the right. Since passing the “Wall” we had been marching on a course 8° East of South, but two days before, with this in mind, we had altered it to 14°. There was an atmosphere of expectancy in camp that evening which did much to compensate for the toil and disappointment of a frustrating day.

The morning of the 8th was comparatively calm and Jack decided to repair his sledge, while the rest of us were packing up the camp. It was Cedomir who drew our attention to a dark form which could just be discerned through the blank whiteness of the mist. He and I both took a compass-bearing to it and we agreed that it lay 13° East of South, almost exactly on our line of march. Could it be the Nunatak? It was low on the horizon, which was encouraging, for I remembered that all the rock buttresses which we had seen on the northern side of Lautaro stood high above the Plateau. Yet it seemed almost incredible that, after weeks of almost blind travel, we had hit our target with such precision.

We loaded the sledges with unusual alacrity and started hauling, our suppressed excitement translated into redoubled effort. The mist was clearing and before long the rock began to take shape: two spurs rising steeply out of the snow plain to converge on the crest of a level skyline ridge. Suddenly I was convinced, beyond all shadow of doubt, that it was the Nunatak.

The party was in high spirits. We had reason to be well satisfied both with our performance and with our situtation. It was four weeks and a day since we had landed. We had completed the crossing of the whole of the northern half of the Ice-cap, no part of which had been visited before; and we had done so in better time than our most optimistic estimate. Except for one brief spell, the weather had been continuously bad and, although we had been very lucky to escape the wind on the Jorge Montt Glacier when we were most vulnerable to it, we had been able to travel in the worst of the storms so far. And now, despite the difficulties of navigation and our persistent uncertainty as to our whereabouts, we had hit off the Nunatak as accurately as though we had been following a well-marked path. There was, of course, a considerable measure of luck about this achievement; all the same, it was gratifying. Our only regret, a big one at that, was that we had seen so little on the way. From now on it was "money for old rope" as Jack put it. We would be travelling through known country, so that whatever the weather we should have no trouble in finding the way, and with lightening loads we would be able to travel increasingly fast.

The thoughts of my companions turned to the dump of food at our old camp on the Nunatak, and at each brief halt it was discussed, until somehow it was built up to a vision of gastronomic plenty. Jack and I had no clear recollection of what we had left there. I thought there were some meat bars, biscuits, sugar, oats and possibly some chocolate. Personally I had no interest in any of it except the sugar, and was secretly opposed to adding to our loads, but I was reluctant to damp the general enthusiasm and so held my peace.

We headed for the eastern side of the corridor. The Nunatak was a good deal farther away than it had appeared, and we were now pulling uphill, so it was noon before we reached a point abreast of its northern end. There we left the sledges and walked over to the familiar gully leading to our old camp. Remembering the network of crevasses guarding the base of the rock, we roped together, but this time there were none visible. Despite the unhappy memories that it evoked, Jack and I both confessed to feelings of nostalgia when we reached the old site.

It was buried under several feet of snow, and almost unrecognizable; so much so that we had great difficulty in locating the spot where we had left the dump. We dug in several places without success. As wc had neglected to bring shovels with us, the digging had to be done with ice-axes, and it was laborious work. The mood of *bonhomie* which had prevailed in the morning gradually evaporated. Eduardo, with unwonted asperity, remarked that in Chile when people left dumps of food they alway built cairns over them to mark the spot. A bitter wind was blowing over the ridge; I had left my sweaters on the sledge, and despite the digging I became miserably cold. Not having had my heart in the enterprise from the first, I was now thoroughly sick of the futile quest for food we did not need. But the look of angry disappointment on Cedomir's face, the strongest emotion I had ever seen it display, caused me to hold my tongue and redouble my efforts. At last, when even Cedomir's energy was beginning to flag, somebody's ice-axe struck a metallic reponse. It was a four-gallon paraffin tin lying in a rock crevice encased in ice. We wrenched it out and found another below. One of them contained 20 meat bars and a 2-lb. tin of butter, very rusty but apparently intact; the other was half full of an evil-smelling, glutinous substance which might once have been sugar, or oats or milk powder or a mixture of all three. The only other thing we found was a two-gallon fuel container from which the petrol had drained away. It seemed rather a meagre haul after all the build-up, but Jack and Cedomir were evidently delighted with the prospect of extra rations of butter and meat, Eduardo forgave our technical oversight and I was thankful to get away with the addition of only a few pounds of extra weight. So as we returned to the sledges to pitch our camp, our holiday mood was revived.

It was further enhanced by the prospect of fine weather, perfectly timed, we thought, for an attempt to climb Lautaro. The clouds lifted and shafts of sunlight broke through; to the north-east the peaks of Cerro O'Higgins appeared and the whole familiar scene was bathed in the soft colours of evening. Except for the lower buttresses, the volcano remained obscured, but it was evident that no major eruption had taken place during the past twelve months, and that this lonely vent had had no part in the cataclysm which had occurred in Central Chile, 500 miles farther north.

The following day we made our way through the corridor and camped near the spur coming down from the south ridge of Lautaro. We had intended to go far up into the great south-east coombe enclosed by the south and east ridges; but the promise of fine weather proved illusory once more, and before we had travelled the length of the Nunatak, the clouds were right down again and a powerful wind was driving the snow at us from behind. We knew that parts of the coombe were menaced by ice-avalanches from hanging glaciers on the surrounding ridges, and to have camped inside it without being able to see where we were would have been unwise.

We had twenty-seven days' food left, so that we could afford to spend at least a week waiting for a chance to climb Lautaro, and still allow ourselves nearly three weeks to complete the journey, which should be ample. We were now 6,500 feet above sea-level, and the summit of the mountain was about 5,500 feet above us. As the corridor was on the leeward side, an enormous quantity of drift-snow was constantly pouring into it from across the south ridge, so that we could hardly expect to find good conditions. Our snowshoes would help us in the lower part of the coombe, but the major part of the climb would be up the steep flank of the east ridge where there might be considerable risk of snow avalanches. Once on the crest of the south ridge, which was joined by the east ridge half a mile from the summit, we would be exposed to the full force of the wind. It would certainly be a long climb, probably very laborious, and possibly difficult; to attempt it we would need at least a day of settled weather, reasonable visibility and little wind.

We settled down to wait. As usual Jack was full of optimism, though I must confess that I saw little ground for it in view of our experience during the past month. The wind continued with unabated fury. Though it was probably no stronger than before, it was deflected by the mountain ridges into intermittent gusts, which came at us from all directions and seemed to lash the tent with increased venom. For the first two days we remained in our sleeping-bags, content to have an excuse to rest. With the stove going continuously we managed to get our clothes and boots reasonably dry. After that we took to making sorties in search of accessible rock outcrops from which to collect geological specimens. There was no risk of losing ourselves so long as we kept on a compass course from the foot of the spur. Sometimes we could see the steep snow slopes and hanging glaciers flanking the east ridge; with clouds of wind-driven snow racing across them in a series of sweeping spirals, they were an impressive sight. We never saw the upper part of the mountain, but a strong smell of sulphur which reached us from time to time suggested that the volcano was still mildly active.

On the evening of the fourth day, I suggested that we should abandon the attempt on the mountain and continue on our way.[1] There was no sign of an improvement in the weather, and it seemed most unlikely that the next three or four days would bring one. It would be better, I thought, to travel during the bad weather, and if during the next three weeks we were lucky enough to have a fine spell we would have time to use it; for anywhere along the route there would be plenty of opportunities for climbing and minor exploratory journeys. Eduardo and Cedomir agreed; but Jack had set his heart on Lautaro and was most reluctant to turn his back on it once more. For a man of his boundless energy, normally so impatient of delay, he had an admirable capacity for "sitting it out"; like Frank Smythe, he could retire within a cocoon of stoicism which rendered him impervious to the static endurance of unpleasant conditions.

After some discussion we agreed to a compromise: we would wait for another two days, and if by then there was still no improvement in the weather, we would resume our march.

[1]The peak was eventually climbed in 1964 by an Argentinian expedition. An Anglo-Argentinian group (Eric Jones, Mick Coffrey, Ernesto O'Reilly and Leo Dickinson) made the second ascent in 1973. This party also discovered and climbed another volcano. 10 miles north of the Lautaro, which they named Cerro Mimosa.

CHAPTER SEVENTEEN

Cordon Darwin

I was very glad when the morning of January 16 arrived. The weather was still atrocious, and I think that even Jack was resigned to the decision to abandon our hopes of climbing Lautaro. We steered a south-westerly course, heading for the upper basin of the Viedma Glacier. For the first couple of miles we were going down a gentle slope and, despite the soft snow, we raced along at a fine speed. By now the weight of our baggage was reduced to about 400 pounds, so that even on the level the exertion of hauling was very much less than it had been.

Before we had been going more than an hour, to our surprise we suddenly ran out of the mist into perfect visibility. To the north and east, Cerro Pyramid, the Cordon Gaea and even Cerro Gorra-Blanca, twenty-five miles away, were clearly in view. For a while we thought that the weather was changing, and we considered turning back. But although the clouds were high, the sky was heavily overcast, and the dark bank of fog from which we had emerged remained solid and immovable behind us. It was obvious that the storm was still raging on Lautaro, for although the main part of the mountain was completely hidden, we could see, towering above us, the end of the south ridge from which long streamers of snow were blowing.

The good visibility remained throughout the morning and early afternoon. It was a delightful change to have something to look at as we marched. To the east we could see through the gap leading into the valley of the Rio Electrico to gentle, russet hills far away beyond our world of ice and snow. But it was a fleeting respite; by the end of the march, we were beset once more by mist and driving sleet, and during the next two or three days, the weather became steadily worse, culminating in the most violent storm we experienced in the whole journey.

On the morning of the 18th, after a rough night, I was dressed before the others and emerged from a tent to start the usual digging operations. I could scarcely stand and had to crawl round to the back of the tent where, kneeling with my back to the wind, I began to work with the shovel. The snow was dry and powdery, and it whipped up into my face with such force and in such volume that I could not see what I was doing. After digging blindly for a quarter of an hour, I realized that I was achieving nothing, so I crawled back inside the tent. We waited until 9.30 and then decided to lie up for the day.

In the early afternoon the wind moderated, but it was then too late to start. In any case it was only a temporary lull, and towards evening the storm was renewed with even greater ferocity. The noise was shattering, and we had to yell at each other to make ourselves heard above the roar of the wind. Accustomed though I was by then to rough weather, I began to be uneasy, wondering if even the half-buried Pyramid could stand up to such a battering; I was quite sure that any other tent would have been destroyed.

While supper was being prepared, two of the walls of the tent suddenly sagged, and then started to flap madly. Jack and Cedomir dressed hastily, and crawled outside. It took them more than half an hour to re-fix the guys which had been wrenched from their moorings. When darkness had fallen, the same thing happened again, and this time Jack and I went out to deal with the situation. It was much warmer than it had been in the morning and the drift-snow had changed to drenching sleet. This was the main reason for the guys working loose, for the snow had thawed several feet below the surface. Soon afterwards, however, it began to freeze again and we had no further trouble.

I was awakened once in the night by a particularly violent gust, and lay for a while listening to the crazy racket with a certain amount of enjoyment. However, when I awoke again at the accustomed hour of 3.30, the wind appeared to have moderated, and we prepared to start. Conditions outside were little, if any, better than they had been the previous morning, but this time we persisted. The lower part of the tent was completely encased in ice, and it took so long to cut it away that it was 9 o'clock before we had finished loading the sledges.

We had gone about 100 yards when the surface suddenly changed to ice, as hard and smooth as a skating-rink, from which all vestige of snow had been swept away. I was in the lead with my eyes fixed on the compass so that I had no warning, with the result that my feet shot from under me and I fell heavily, dropping the compass which went sliding away like a curling stone. I got up, and forgetting I was in harness, tried to chase it, with the result that I crashed again. After that I crawled on all fours until I had recovered the compass which fortunately had come to rest against a patch of snow. I learnt later that my antics looked extremely funny and, by his repeated reference to the incident, Eduardo evidently came to regard it as one of the highlights of the trip.

The wind was swirling across our line of advance, and as soon as the "punt" was on the ice it was blown sideways and dragged all three of us over. After that Eduardo hitched his trace to the back of the sledge and pulled to windward. Even so it was very difficult to keep a straight course, and we went along in a crab-like fashion, with repeated falls, for a couple of hours, after which we found ourselves on snow again.

The wind was too strong for us to stop for lunch, and in the early afternoon it increased to such violence that, at 2.15, I decided that we had better pitch the tent while it was still possible. As it was, our drill came in for a severe testing. Fortunately, before we reached the most delicate part of the operation, it began to moderate. We thought that this was just a lull in the storm and worked as fast as possible to get the job done before it started up again. But the wind continued to diminish and by the time we had settled into the tent, it was no more than a gentle breeze. By 5 o'clock there was absolute calm.

As with the sudden cessation of an artillery barrage, the silence was uncanny, almost oppressive. It took some time to become accustomed to the strange tranquillity, and even when I awoke the next morning I had a sense of unreality, as if a fundamental part of life were missing.

The mist around us was clearing rapidly as we left the tent, and by the time we started we were in a sunlit corridor between two huge banks of cloud. Two miles away there was a rock buttress, the end of the north-easterly spurs of the Cordon Mariano Moreno. When we reached it we stopped for an hour while Cedomir collected samples. Across the corridor the cathedral spire of Fitzroy appeared through a gap in the eastern cloud-bank, surrounded by its glittering retinue of minarets.

At noon we reached the western end of the "Vulcan Viedma" where we were faced with a long slope up to a saddle between it and the Mariano Moreno. By then it was so hot that we decided to leave the toil up the slope until the cool of the morning. So we pitched the tent, leaving all our gear out to dry, and spent the afternoon basking in the sun; a delicious contrast to our situation twenty-four hours before. The great ice ramparts of the Mariano Moreno were clear; these and the vast coombes between reminded me of the south side of Mont Blanc. Over the long summit ridge there was the same closely fitting blanket of cloud that I had seen almost exactly two years before. Again it was flowing swiftly towards us like the crest of an enormous Niagara, plunging down the eastern precipices and vanishing in the clear air below; and yet the gale that was driving it did not disturb the stillness around us. When the sun sank behind it, the cloud-blanket was fringed with a flaming corona.

Cedomir said that he would like to spend a day examining the rocks of the "Vulcan", and as the rest of us were not averse to a spell of pottering about on dry land, I decided to grant his request, but with the proviso that we should first cross the saddle.

The morning of the 21st was very cold, but even on the hard-frozen snow it took an hour of very hard work to drag the sledges up the slope. At the crest of the saddle there was another of those remarkable chasms, 100 feet deep, scoured out of the solid glacier ice by wind action, which I had seen before at various points around the perimeter of the "Vulcan". Nowhere else have I encountered such spectacular examples of this phenomenon, and it seems that the wind in this particular locality must often attain exceptional force.

We could now look across the southern half of the Viedma glacier basin to the wide pass leading over to the Upsala. In the far distance beyond we saw the summit of one of the peaks of the Cordon Darwin standing above a dark mass of cloud. To the west of this range there is a high plateau which had been discovered by de Agostini, who named it "Altiplano Italia". We had already decided that, instead of going straight down the Upsala Glacier as we had originally intended, we would make our way on to this plateau, and from it attempt to climb one of the peaks of the range. With this in view we made a note of the bearing to the peak.

From the saddle we ran down the gentle slope beyond, and in half an hour reached a patch of moraine near a gap in the main ridge of the "Vulcan", where we pitched the tent. Then we glissaded 1,000 feet down into the circular hollow that Dr. Lliboutry had mistaken for the crater of a volcano. It was almost empty of water as it had been two years before, but the icebergs stranded at various levels around the basin showed that this was a seasonal state. Similar glacier-dammed lakes that I have met with in the Karakoram are full in the spring and drained in the summer, and it appeared that this one followed the same routine.

Cedomir spent the rest of the day examining the geology of the area, and Jack made a collection of plants and insects, while Eduardo and I wandered lazily about the basin, enjoying the hot sun and the perfect stillness about us. It was like being in a vast Greek amphitheatre with its concentric terraces, formed by a series of shore-lines, facing a high platform of glacier ice. Beyond the topmost shore-line, 400 feet above the bottom of the basin, there were flowers growing in protected crevices among the rocks.

It was still clear when we left the "Vulcan" the next morning and headed southward for the pass; but the weather was deteriorating rapidly, and before the morning was far advanced we were enveloped once more in mist and driving sleet. A great deal of the surface snow had melted during the past two days, and before long we began to have trouble with thinly covered crevasses. To prevent ourselves from falling into them, we put on our snowshoes for the first time since our abortive attempt to use them on the Jorge Montt Glacier. Although the sledges were still more heavily laden than they had been on that occasion, we had become so accustomed to hauling, that we now found no difficulty in manipulating the snowshoes.

On the 23rd we travelled through a severe storm, with almost no visibility all day, but were feeling full of energy after our sunny respite, and appeared to make excellent progress. That evening we discussed the question of how far we could go on in those conditions without the risk of blundering into the ridges and hanging glaciers of the Cordon Darwin. We decided to do so for another day, and then to wait for better visibility.

To our delighted surprise the very next day dawned brilliantly fine. For once we did not dally over breakfast, and we came out of the tent into the early sunlight to find ourselves surrounded by a stupendous view. There was not a cloud to be seen anywhere, and the storm-washed air was so clear that even the most distant mountains were sharply defined. To the east there was a slender spire rising from a beautifully symmetrical base; being so much closer, it looked almost as impressive as Fitzroy itself. To the west another range, immaculately white, rose out of the Plateau like a gigantic wave.

I was strongly tempted to head towards those nameless mountains and I still harbour some regret that I did not obey the impulse; for even one of their minor summits would command a fascinating view into the unseen country beyond. But they were a long way off in the wrong direction, and my companions had set their hearts on the Altiplano and the peaks of the Cordon Darwin, which stood in compelling grandeur to the south.

There had been a heavy frost and for once the surface of the snow was both hard and smooth. There was no need to wear snowshoes, and the sledges ran so easily that no effort was required to drag them. We made for a col between two nunataks, and strode along exulting in the cold air and the gentle, caressing warmth of the early sun, in the vast mountain world about us and in the sensuous awareness of our own physical well-being.

The slope on the far side of the col was comparatively steep and quite unbroken by crevasses, so we sat on the sledges and sped along at a fine speed for about half a mile to the bottom. By this time the sun had melted the surface of the snow, the dragging weight of the sledges increased, and the rest of the march to the northern end of the Cordon Darwin was hot and thirsty.

We camped in a glacier coombe enclosed by two ridges coming down from Cerro Don Bosco, the northernmost peak of the range. Immediately to the west there was a steep snow ramp running up between two ice-falls to the northern end of the Altiplano. We decided that if the weather held we would climb Cerro Don Bosco early the next morning before dragging the sledges up the ramp. The peak had been climbed from the Upsala Glacier three years before by a Polish expedition; indeed it was the only summit in the Cordon Darwin to have been reached; but as we were so well aware that the fine spell might end at any moment, we were determined to seize any opportunity for climbing that offered. For the same reason we were careful to site the camp exactly between two rock buttresses at the entrance to the coombe, so that by keeping a constant check on compass-bearings during the climb we would be able to find our way back even in a blizzard.

I woke the party at 2.30 the next morning and we were ready to start by 4 o'clock. Dawn was breaking, but many of the larger stars were still shining in a cloudless sky. There had been another sharp frost, and we walked rapidly over hard snow to the head of the coombe, keeping well out of the range of possible avalanches from a hanging glacier suspended high up on the western wall. Crossing a well-bridged bergschrund, we climbed an easy gully and over a rock spur, where we paused to put on our crampons. The rising sun found us threading our way through the séracs and cliffs of a small ice-fall. Beyond this, once more in frozen shadow, we made our way up a steep couloir between two overhanging ice buttresses, to the crest of the western ridge of the mountain.

After weeks of sledge-hauling, the varied rhythm, and balanced movements of mountaineering were sheer delight, and we climbed very fast, with complete disregard for economy of effort. The broad ridge was composed of a series of turrets of crystalline ice, which looked like giant fungi. They were steep but easy to climb and, at 7 o'clock, three hours after leaving camp we were on the summit of the mountain.

There was a strong westerly wind, but otherwise the weather was still fine and perfectly clear in every direction. To the southeast, across the wide valley of the Upsala Glacier, we saw the twisting channels of Lago Argentino and the golden pampas hills beyond. We greeted this first view of our objective with an excited cheer. In the opposite direction the view extended across the whole of the southern part of the Ice-cap, over which we had been travelling during the past week, to the distant ranges beyond. Westward was the Altiplano Italia and a score of peaks standing above it, brilliant against a dark background where the forested valleys of the Pacific lay in a vast well of shadow.

It was, however, our immediate surroundings that lent magic to the scene; for all about us there was an exotic statuary of ice, huge mushrooms and jutting gargoyles, sculptured in rime by the wind, each object composed of a delicate pattern of crystal flowers. Across a deep gap to the south was Cerro Murallon, a great square block of granite, 500 feet higher than the Don Bosco; its smooth, vertical sides festooned with a fantastic ice drapery like massive lace curtains; its flat summit ridge, perhaps 600 yards long, crowned by a line of ice minarets, sparkling in the sun.

Despite the wind, which was unusually cold, we stayed on the summit for nearly an hour before we began to descend the west ridge which offered an easy way down to the Altiplano. We had intended to go straight back to the camp, and to spend the afternoon hauling the sledges up the ramp. But it seemed a pity to waste such wonderful weather over such a dull task. A day like this was extremely rare; there was no knowing what the next day would bring, and it was more than probable that we would not have another opportunity to explore the Altiplano in good visibility. We still had more than twelve hours of daylight before us.

I suggested that we should cross the Altiplano while the snow was still hard, and climb a beautiful snow peak on the other side, which would give us a splendid view of the country to the west, but Cedomir was fired with an ambition to climb Cerro Murallon, and as the others seemed to favour this alternative, I decided to adopt it. The mountain appeared to be almost inaccessible from the north, but traversing round the western side we found a snow corridor running up under the vertical curtains of ice to the southwest face which was considerably less steep.

It was nearly midday when we reached the foot of the corridor, and we stopped there for lunch. Across the Altiplano we could now see through a wide gap to the left of the snow peak, to the vast tract of festooned country beyond. In the midst of this there was a wide channel westward into the far distance, sprinkled with icebergs which looked like tiny white dots on the surface of the water. It was the upper reaches of the Falcon Fjord. The weather was still fine, but clouds had begun to form over the forest far below.

As we climbed, the view to the south gradually expanded, until at last we could see the whole of the Altiplano and a magnificent semicircle of ice peaks enclosing it in that direction. The climbing was laborious because by then the snow was soft, but it was not difficult, and late in the afternoon we reached the summit ridge and looked down the sheer north face of the mountain. Immediately to our right was one of the ice towers, about 50 feet high which we had seen that morning from the Don Bosco. We reached the top of it without much difficulty and saw several more along the ridge to the east, one of which was higher than ours. But so far as we could judge, the true summit of the Murallon stood at the western end of the ridge about 300 yards away.

We had just decided to make our way back towards it, when suddenly we found ourselves enveloped in thick mist which had blown up from below. It was totally unexpected, for a moment before we had been under a clear sky and we had not seen any cloud in our vicinity. At first we thought that it was a small patch which had formed round the peak, and that it would soon clear again; so we climbed westward along the ridge as fast as we could against the stiff wind.

We gained height rapidly and when after a quarter of an hour the ridge levelled off and then began to fall away. I thought we had reached the summit. But suddenly a shape loomed a few yards ahead of us. It was an ice buttress about twenty-five feet high and almost vertical. Hoping to find an easy way from the back, we tried to pass it on the right, but were stopped by a bulge jutting out over a sheer drop into a cauldron of swirling mist. A similar obstacle stopped us on the left.

It would have been possible to climb the buttress direct in reasonable conditions, though even so it would have taken a long time. By then it had started to snow; it was obvious that the weather had turned bad, and we realized that we might well find ourselves in an ugly situation. It was nearly 5 o'clock. With visibility limited to a few yards it would be by no means easy to find the route down the mountain. The way back to camp was long and complicated, and if a severe storm developed it might be impossible to find it. Galvanized by these unpleasant thoughts we turned and ran back down the ridge.

We had some difficulty in finding the point at which we had reached it, for our tracks had already been obliterated. Then we plunged diagonally down the steep snow slopes on a south-westerly bearing. Below us to the left we knew that there was a sheer precipice falling to one of the tributaries of the Upsala Glacier and it was necessary to keep more and more to the right to reach the top of the corridor. But with the snow whipping up into our faces it was very hard to keep a sense either of direction or of distance. I was in front and was far from confident that I was going the right way. Fortunately at the critical moment we ran out beneath the cloud and saw the corridor below us. We raced down it and reached our lunch place where we paused for a brief rest.

We had a fleeting glimpse of the Altiplano and of the clouds pouring over the range before they enveloped us once more. From the lunch place we had previously taken a compass-bearing to the saddle between Don Bosco and Murallon so we had no difficulty in reaching it; but the way beyond was more complicated. In such weather it was impossible to retrace the route we had followed in the morning for it would have meant climbing most of the way up the west ridge of Don Bosco. The alternative was to make our way down to the Altiplano and circle round a series of buttresses which we could not see. It was a long, weary plod through soft snow, with sleet driving across our faces; but once again we were lucky, for another clearing of the mist enabled us to find the ramp leading down to the entrance of the coombe. There was still plenty of daylight when we reached camp, very tired and thoroughly wet.

Despite our failure, by a narrow margin of some twenty-five feet, to reach the summit of Cerro Murallon, it had been a wonderful day. Nevertheless I felt somewhat ashamed to have taken such a chance with the weather, for had it turned really bad our plight would have been serious. We had gone too far from our camp and the route back was much too complicated for us to be sure of being able to return to it in bad conditions.

CHAPTER EIGHTEEN

The Journey's End

THE fine spell, which had lasted more than thirty-six hours, was over and the noraml régime of wind and mist and driving sleet was re-established. The wind was uncommonly warm, always a bad weather portent, and the snow around us melted so rapidly that the following morning we found that the tent was perched on a pedestal almost two feet high.

We spent the 26th resting after our strenuous exertions of the previous day, and discussing our next move. Our plan to travel over the length of the Altiplano and to descend to the Upsala by way of the Bertachi Glacier, which had been explored by de Agostini, had lost much of its appeal. For we had already seen the whole of the Altiplano and all the mountains surrounding it, and there seemed little point in struggling over it in a blizzard. Jack was in favour of doing so on the slender chance that in the next two or three days the weather might improve enough to allow us to climb another of the peaks of the range; but the rest of us did not share his optimism. Perhaps the smell of the flesh-pots was already in our nostrils, sapping our resolution and blunting our appetite for further punishment. At any rate we decided, on a three to one vote, to descend direct to the Upsala Glacier and head for home. We agreed, however, that if the weather should improve, we would use our remaining five days' surplus food by making an excursion into the Darwin Range from the east.

There was a small glacier flowing eastward from the coombe and we made our way down it on the 27th. It was fairly steep and we hoped to be able to toboggan down on the sledges; but the surface was composed of a soggy morass of melting snow into which we sank almost to our hips, and we had to pull hard the whole way. On the 28th we made our way diagonally across the Upsala Glacier. The snow became thinner as we went, and we had to follow a tortuous course to avoid crevassed areas. About mid-morning we ran out on to bare ice which was so smooth that the sledges slid over it as if they were on ball-bearings, and we often had to run to prevent them from overtaking us.

On leaving the Cordon Darwin, we had crossed a sharply-defined weather frontier. Although the wind was strong and there were some sleet squalls, we had left the mist behind, an occasional gleam of sun broke through the clouds and conditions were altogether much more agreeable. The change of climate showed clearly on the eastern side of the Upsala Glacier, where all the rock walls and ridges were bare, and even the peaks of the Cerro Norte group, which were higher than many of those in the main range, held scarcely any snow or ice.

Gradually the surface of the glacier became more and more broken, and we knew that the time was fast approaching when we would have to abandon the sledges and continue with the loads on our backs; but we were determined to postpone that evil moment as long as possible. Throughout the afternoon the "punt" came in for a merciless bashing, for we leapt over wide crevasses at a run so that the sledge had sufficient momentum to carry it across and land on the other side with a crash. To prevent it from slipping into a chasm Eduardo hitched his trace to the back so that he could haul it sideways in either direction. Jack had to be more circumspect with his sledge, for although it was a great deal easier to control, it was nothing like so robust; and it was remarkable that he managed to keep up with us. Twice we had to off-load both sledges and carry them and the baggage in relays through a particularly bad area.

We were now heading straight down the glacier, close to its left-hand side and immediately above a deep ravine which separated the ice from its containing wall of red rock. At 6.30 we halted and, leaving the sledges, carried the loads down to the bottom of the ravine, where we pitched the tent on a little ice platform between two crevasses.

Early the next morning Cedomir and I set off on a geological excursion into the mountains to the east. After climbing 2,000 feet, we reached the crest of a ridge from which we looked down a sheer precipice into the valley of La Cristina. There was Lago Pearson, its near end surrounded by dark-green forest, and beyond we saw the river ambling through the wide, sunlit valley to the shore of Lago Argentino. To the east the walls of Cerro Norte, black and sinister, towered above us into the mist. Westward across the Upsala the Cordon Darwin was hidden by a monstrous wall of cloud. We got back to camp at 11 o'clock.

The flesh-pots were now so near that their call was irresistible; and as the weather on the main range showed no sign of improving, we all agreed to jettison our surplus provisions and take with us only sufficient for three more days. It was also decided to abandon the small sledge, which caused Jack obvious pain. We started at 1 o'clock, all four of us harnessed to the "punt". But the surface of the glacier was so broken that we made slow progress, and we would probably have done better carrying the loads.

We had worked over towards the middle of the glacier to avoid a mass of ice pinnacles on the left, and were making our way along a shallow trough between two pressure ridges. At 3.30 we reached a crevasse far too wide to jump, which extended right across the trough. It was obvious that we could take the sledge no farther, for the ice on either side was far too broken. By then snow was falling heavily, and as it would have taken us a long time to dismantle the tent and repack the baggage into portable loads, we decided to stop there for the night. Pitching the tent on the bare ice was a long job, for we had first to cut a large quantity of ice chips with which to weight it down.

We awoke on the morning of the 30th, to find the glacier covered with nine inches of fresh snow. It was still snowing and the bleak landscape was shrouded in mist. When we came to divide up the loads we found that we still had a distressing amount to carry; this was partly accounted for by Cedomir's geological collection, but it was also due to the Chileans' refusal to discard surplus items of equipment such as the spare rope and Primus and the empty fuel containers. We shouldered our heavy packs and bid a reluctant farewell to the "punt", which had played such a vital part in the success of the journey.

To the left of the trough there was a series of sharp ridges like waves about to break, running in a south-eastern direction. We climbed along one of these, which I had previously reconnoitred, and reached another trough close to the side of the glacier. In less than a quarter of a mile, however, we were confronted by a chaotic mass of séracs and ice-cliffs which we could not penetrate. The only way of passing it was to climb along another of the ice ridges which led us back up the glacier, with the result that after two hours of hard going we found ourselves close to the place from which we had started.

The rest of the morning followed a similar exasperating pattern. Each advance down the glacier was followed by long detours, often in the opposite direction, cutting steps down into a ravine and up the other side, or balancing along a slender crest of ice, unable to see where we were going. The fresh snow did not improve matters, for in the hollows deep drifts had collected, which hid the crevasses and blurred the outline of the ice bridges. At one point things looked so unpromising that, having dumped our loads, Cedomir and I went off in one direction and Eduardo and Jack in another to find a way through the maze. Our line proved hopeless and before long we found ourselves on an isolated spur from which we could not proceed in any direction. However, the others were more successful, and an hour later we were reunited at the dump with the prospect of better going ahead.

By the middle of the afternoon we had reached a stretch of comparatively smooth ice, and when, at 4 o'clock, we stopped to pitch the tent, we had reason to hope that we were through the worst, and that it would be our last camp on the glacier. In the evening the wind rose and by nightfall it was blowing very hard indeed. I was thankful that we were not in the Altiplano, where conditions must have been considerably worse. However, the tempest was short-lived and in the early morning the wind died away.

The mist, too, had gone and we could see far down the glacier to the col leading over to La Cristina. We were in a broad trough which ran gently down, smooth and straight, between pressure ridges of shattered ice, a mile or so from the left side of the glacier. No obstacle impeded us as we strode rapidly down the trough until, in a couple of hours, we had reached a point nearly opposite the col. Then we turned left on to the pressure ridges; but as we were following along the line of the crevasses we had little trouble in making our way through the forest of séracs, and by 11 o'clock we were glissading down the flank of the glacier into an ablation valley at the foot of the col.

The journey was virtually over. We were in no hurry to get anywhere. It was warm and a heavy lethargy crept into our bodies. Cedomir found that the rocks were full of fossils, and we spent a long time collecting them before we could summon the resolution to shoulder our loads again and start scrambling up the steep rocks to the pass. Two condors sailed overhead, the first creatures that we had seen since leaving the Jorge Montt, seven weeks before.

An hour later we were on a broad path, walking through enchanting woodland, our world alive again with the song of birds and the smell of growing things. We stopped frequently to lie on soft beds of moss and leaves, gazing up into the trees and taking deep gulps of sweet-scented air. The change of our environment was so sudden, the contrast so complete, that I sank into a kind of opiate trance, from which happy state I did not emerge for several days.

After stopping for an hour by a forest tarn to make tea, we left the path and scrambled down a steep grass slope to the shore of the bay where the old steam launch was riding at anchor. The sun was shining, and the warm, still air was heavy with the fragrance of herbs. Rounding a small headland we disturbed a flock of wild geese; and once across the river on the flat ground beyond, our ears were filled with the sound which, more than anything else, I shall always associate with Patagonia: the shrill, protesting cry of the plovers.

It was 6 o'clock when we reached the *estancia*. Mr. and Mrs. Masters were in the sitting-room and we tapped on the window to attract their attention. It must have given them something of a shock to see four bearded faces looking in at them, for I very much doubt if they recognized me at first; however they hurried out to greet us with apparent pleasure. It was wonderful to see the old couple again, looking as active as ever despite their eighty-four years. Mr. Masters ran off to fetch Herbert, while the old lady began immediately to prepare our supper. I suggested that we should feed ourselves and pitch our tent in the garden, but she vetoed the idea in a tone that permitted no argument. With no help in the house and no labour-saving devices, she accepted the extra task of providing for four hungry men with complete serenity, as no doubt, sixty years before, she had faced the job of building a home in this remote valley.

When Herbert arrived we gave him an account of the trip, while his parents were busy cooking and preparing our rooms. He had always taken a great interest in expeditions to the area, and he knew a great deal about the previous attempts that had been made to cross the Ice-cap. Cyril Jervis had told him over the radio that we had been landed on the shores of the Canal Baker and hoped to reach La Cristina, but he said that he had not thought for a moment that we would succeed; particularly as the weather had been exceptionally bad since the spring. Indeed, according to Mr. and Mrs. Masters, it had been by far the worst summer they remembered in the sixty years that they had been there; a piece of news that we found highly gratifying.

At 7.30 we sat down to dinner, served by the old couple who refused to allow us to do anything to help. It consisted of soup and a deliciously roasted joint of lamb, with potatoes and vegetables; and then, of all things, strawberries and cream. A couple of hours later came the final touch of perfection when we slid between clean sheets and turned out the electric light. Twenty-four hours before we had been in a blizzard in a wilderness of ice and snow.

The journey over the Ice-cap had taken fifty-two days. It had been an experience as completely satisfying as any I have known. Even the vileness of the weather was a source of some satisfaction, for it had been part of our purpose to accept its challenge and to prove our ability to travel securely even in its most savage moods. Above all, I now felt myself to be on terms of intimacy with this wild region which, to my mind, is the highest reward of any mountaineering venture.

CHAPTER NINETEEN

Land of Fire

PATAGONIA had proved a field of mountain adventure, far more fruitful than I had originally expected. As in the ranges of Central Asia, the horizon of "the untravelled world" was constantly expanding; the more, it seemed, one did the more there was left to do. Fresh projects kept occurring to my mind, each more compelling than the last. The potion of the calafate berry had certainly proved effective.

There was, however, a still more powerful lodestone farther south. For as long as I can remember I have been fascinated by Tierra del Fuego. Perhaps the intriguing name had something to do with it; or the remoteness of the place; or Darwin's description of the "savage magnificence" of the scene, the "mysterious grandeur" in the mountains. Whatever the main influence, I had long cherished an entrancing vision of lonely, storm-swept peaks, swathed in bands of cloud, protected from all intruders by massive, primeval forest, where exotic plants flourished as though in a tropical rather than a sub-Antarctic environment. When I came to examine the situation more closely, I was astonished to find how much of the mountain country was in fact still virgin ground, and the vision was quickly translated into a consuming desire to get there. Thus, emboldened by my experiences, in Patagonia where, I thought, conditions could not be so very different, I decided to take an expedition there in 1962 to explore and climb the highest ranges.

When Ferdinand Magellan was passing through the Straits which bear his name, he saw a large number of fires burning along the southern shore. They had probably been lit as rallying signals by the natives, who were no doubt astonished and terrified by the sudden appearance of his ships. This apparently was the origin of the name "Land of Fire". Magellan thought that it was part of a great southern continent stretching away into the Antarctic, and it was not until half a century later, when Drake, having passed through the Straits, was blown by north-westerly gales round Cape Horn back into the Atlantic, that it was realized that it was in fact an island.

A large part of Tierra del Fuego is flat or gently undulating, with open pampas in the north and well-forested land farther south. As in Patagonia it supports a flourishing sheep industry. The long southern coastline, however, is dominated by rugged mountainous country, which is really the final spur of the great chain of the Andes. Almost all the high mountains are situated on a large, uninhabited peninsula running westward from the main island for more than 100 miles between the Beagle Channel and Admiralty Sound.

At its western end stands Mount Sarmiento, which was climbed, after several abortive attempts, by an expedition led by de Agostini; but most of the Peninsula is occupied by the Cordillera Darwin which contains the highest peaks of Tierra del Fuego. This range covers an area that would easily accommodate the whole of the Mont Blanc and Pennine ranges of the Alps and most of the Bernese Oberland as well, while the extent of its glaciers must be far greater than those of the entire Alpine chain. Moreover, though the highest peaks are only some 8,500 feet they rise straight from sea-level, so that from the climber's point of view the mountains are equivalent in size to most of their Alpine rivals.

Yet, until 1962 almost the whole of this great range, with its scores of unnamed peaks, was untrodden ground. De Agostini had landed at several points along the northern coast and had climbed two peaks, "Italia" and "Frances" above the Beagle Channel on its southern side; but no one had penetrated to the interior. It was an alluring prospect for any mountaineer prepared to accept rough conditions.

For the Peninsula has a most evil reputation for weather. It is lashed by the same westerly gales that rage around Cape Horn, savage storms that bring

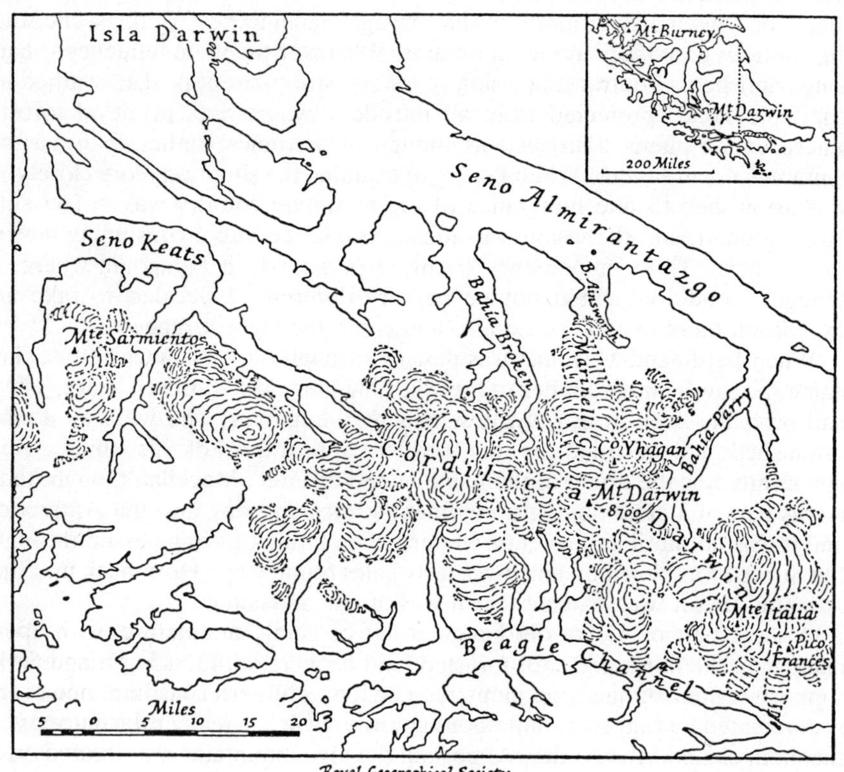

Royal Geographical Society

long spells of fog and rain and snow. But, as with the sea, part of the fascination of mountains lies in combating the elements that surround them. We accepted the challenge of the Himalayan giants partly because of the problems presented by the rarified atmosphere at great altitudes. Nor is the mountaineer a stranger to disappointment and frustration. How often, for example, did we set out to climb Mount Everest, repeated all the tedious preparations, made the long approach, only to find that a few feet of powder snow on the summit rocks had made our goal inaccessible? Yet we never thought the effort unrewarded. Certainly when I decided to go to the Darwin Range, I was well aware that we might spend nearly all our allotted time immobilized by foul weather, achieving nothing.

My companions on the Ice-cap had proved so good a team that I hoped that they would all join me in the new venture. Unfortunately Jack was unable to do so. To take his place Eduardo and Cedomir brought another Chilean mountaineer, Francisco Vivanco, known to his friends as "Pancho".

I equipped and provisioned the party in much the same way as before. Short skis, however, replaced the snowshoes and we took no sledge. Messrs. Burberry kindly provided our outer garments, and we had some light Terylene smocks, or "ponchos" as well. We also took a lightweight tent for high camps.

It was believed that the chief obstacle to gaining access to the interior of the Darwin Range would be the almost impenetrable barrier of bog and forest. We had found in Patagonia, however, that this kind of obstacle could often be overcome by careful choice of route, and by taking advantage of clear, firm ground left by retreating glaciers. The entire Peninsula is uninhabited. Though it is possible to approach it by land from the eastern end, it would take many weeks of difficult mountaineering to reach the highest peaks from that direction, so that the only practicable approach to these is by sea. Again the Chilean Navy kindly undertook to provide us with the necessary transport.

Like the whole coastline of Southern Chile the Peninsula is penetrated by a remarkable network of fjords. Many of them have been charted, and the outlines of the remainder have been plotted by aerial photographs. Cedomir and Eduardo made a careful study of these photographs, which proved invaluable in selecting a landing-place and a route to the interior. We chose a spot near the head of a fjord running twenty miles southward from an inlet known as Broken Bay in Admiralty Sound, the wide channel separating the north coast of the Peninsula from the mainland of Tierra del Fuego. The fjord had not been charted and, so far as I know, no one had been up it except perhaps the Yagan canoe Indians who used to inhabit these waters. In case it should prove impossible for a ship to reach the head of the fjord, and also to provide us with some degree of independent mobility at sea, I decided to take another Zodiac, similar to the one we had used on Lago San Martin two years before, and a 10 h.p. Evinrude motor. Both the boat and the motor were very kindly lent to me by the makers.

I reached Punta Arenas on January 13, 1962. My three companions were there to meet me, and we spent the next few days sorting out our stores and equipment which had just arrived from England, and which included a small wireless set. It is not my usual practice to take a radio on these expeditions. I grudge the weight and have always thought that in most emergencies a few pounds of extra food would be a greater asset. Also, in the event of the instrument failing to work, unnecessary alarm would be caused. On this occasion, however, I had been persuaded to take, at least as far as our landing-place, a small transmitter designed for sea rescue. With the help of the Naval signals officers in Punta Arenas we tested the machine and it was arranged that we should communicate with the Naval station on Dawson Island, half-way between Punta Arenas and Broken Bay, at 5.30 each evening while we were at our base. After that they would continue to listen for us at the same time each evening until we returned.

Admiral Balaresque had arranged for us to be taken to Broken Bay in the Naval Patrol Ship *Lientur*, and we set sail in the evening of January 18. The Admiral and his wife, whose son, Paul, was coming with us for the voyage, were at the quay to see us off.

By dawn the following day we were steaming up Admiralty Sound. A dismal scene greeted me as I came out on deck; mist hung low over the water, and the southern shore of the channel, though only half a mile away, was only just visible through the cold rain that was falling. Never at my best at 4 a.m., I felt profoundly depressed at the prospect of being left in this inhospitable land where, for all I knew, it might continue raining for the next six weeks. I returned below to cherish my last precious hours of warmth and comfort.

At 7 o'clock *Lientur* entered Broken Bay. Her speed was reduced and soundings taken. The water became steadily shallower, and five miles from the entrance of the bay it was found to be only two fathoms deep. The Captain could not risk going any further up the uncharted fjord, particularly in such poor visibility; so it was decided to put us ashore on the western side of the bay. We discovered later that the shallow water was caused by a reef of glacial moraine, and that the fjord beyond was very deep.

While our 800 pounds of baggage was being taken ashore in a lifeboat, we inflated and launched the Zodiac. Watched by most of the ship's company, I struggled for ten minutes to start the motor, until Paul Balaresque quietly drew my attention to the fact that I had connected the petrol feed pipe the wrong way round. After this convincing display of my inefficiency, we set off at high speed and overtook the ship's boat as it was entering the mouth of a small river which emerged from the dense forest along the shore. I had requested the Admiral to have us picked up on March 5 and it was now arranged that his place (which we called Ship Creek) should be our rendezvous.

We were still fifteen miles from our destination at the head of the fjord. Though it was still raining, there was no wind, and we decided to take advantage of the calm water and start immediately. As we were loading our stores and equipment into the Zodiac we heard three farewell hoots from *Lientur*, and watched her disappear into the mist, leaving us alone in the silent world.

At 10 o'clock we pushed the heavily laden Zodiac out of the creek and headed on up the fjord. As we started the motor, a sea-lion popped his whiskered head out of the water a few yards from the shore, looking like an old man of the sea, and gave a hoarse, irritable grunt. Negotiating the reef, we had to be careful to avoid dense masses of seaweed marking the submerged rocks which seemed to extend right across the fjord; but in the clear water beyond we cruised at a steady four knots.

Presently it stopped raining and the mist cleared, forming horizontal strands of cloud which lent an enchanting aura of mystery to the scene. To starboard, at the far end of a wide gulf, a vast glacier, also swathed in cloud-banks, swept down to the water on a wide front. Above it there was a silvery glint which came from the unseen snow peaks. It was thrilling to find my lifelong imaginings of this fabulous land so closely reproduced in reality.

Hundreds of black-and-white ducks rose from the water at our approach; apart from some steamer ducks and an occasional cormorant they were the only kind of waterfowl we saw. We encountered several pairs of dolphins, which played about us with the enormous zest of their kind. Though they came within inches of the boat, they never touched it.

The weather continued to clear; soon the sun came out, and one by one the great peaks appeared, floating incredibly high above the mist which still clung to the sombre forest on either shore. By 2.30, as we were approaching the head of the fjord, the last vestige of cloud had vanished. We landed at a point where the channel made a sharp turn to the west into an almost land-locked lagoon surrounded by a cirque of glaciers and mountains rising abruptly to 7,500 feet. The glass-smooth water of the lagoon was sprinkled with blocks of floating ice, calved from three great glacier fronts along its shore.

What an incredible contrast it was from the dreary scene of a few hours before! Standing on the shore gazing across at that glorious cirque, the warm sun caressing my naked shoulders, I felt that whatever the Darwin Range had in store for us this introduction was enough to make the whole venture worth while.

We spent the hot afternoon lazily sorting out the food and equipment to be taken with us, and stowing the boat and surplus gear in the forest. We had brought supplies to last for forty-five days; three days' food was left in the dump, and the rest was to be taken with us. Camp 1 was pitched in a meadow beside a river.

When we went to bed the sky was still perfectly clear. However, experience had taught us to expect nothing of the weather, and we were not surprised the next morning to find that it had broken. In mist and rain we began the task of carrying our loads, in three relays, up into the mountains. Our choice of a landing-place had been perfect; indeed any other would have cost us weeks of extra toil. As it was we found our way over a 3,000-foot pass on to the upper basin of the Marinelli Glacier which flows fifteen miles northward into Ainsworth Bay, and is probably the longest in the whole range. In six days we had established an advanced base (Camp 3) with all the loads, at the head of this great glacier.

We avoided the worst of the forest by climbing 800 feet up a rock ramp left by the shrinkage of a small glacier which came steeply down almost to the sea-shore at Camp 1. From Camp 2, in a wide grassy coombe at the upper edge of the forest, we looked down over the tree-tops and a tumbling ice-fall to the lagoon 1,500 feet below, and across to the tremendous cirque of mountains surrounding it. In fair weather or in foul it was one of the loveliest places I have ever seen.

During most of this time the weather was bad; but the morning of January 25, when we reached the pass with the first relay, was brilliantly fine and we were greeted by a splendid view of the whole length and breadth of the Marinelli Glacier and the scores of peaks surrounding it, including a lovely mountain standing above Parry Fjord which de Agostini had named "Luis de Savoya".

One of our chief purposes was to examine the geological structure of the range, and to make a collection of rock samples from appropriate places. This would best be served by crossing the range to the Beagle Channel. We had also set ourselves two other objectives: to climb the highest peak in the range and Luis de Savoya. In view of the predominance of foul weather we knew we must expect, this seemed a fairly ambitious programme. We would probably have been satisfied with the accomplishment of any one of our three objectives, and we scarcely hoped to achieve all three.

Our radio proved a complete failure. In normal conditions the station on Dawson Island should have been well within its range; but, presumably because of the high mountains surrounding us, we had failed to make ourselves heard from Camp 1. So we had reluctantly decided to hump the wretched machine, which weighed 20 lb., to Camp 2, hoping that we would have more success from a greater altitude. Again we failed, so we carried it on over the pass to Camp 3. But even there, at 3,000 feet, we could not establish contact. We had with us a small transistor set with which we could hear both Dawson Island and Punta Arenas calling us. Our silence seemed to be causing them increasing concern. Night after night while we were on the glacier, we heard them telling us to light fires, one if we were all right and two if we were in trouble. Presumably the idea was to send a plane to spot for the fires; but by then, of course, we had no means of complying with their request. Later, on two or three occasions, we were told that planes were being sent out the next day to look for us, and that we were to place ourselves in a conspicuous position; no easy thing to do among the towering mountains surrounding us. Anyway we did not see or hear anything of the planes.

On some Chilean maps of the area the name "Cerro Darwin" is applied to a peak standing above the Beagle Channel, presumably because it is the most prominent seen from that direction. So far we had not identified the highest mountain in the range, but we knew that it was one of a group of peaks at the head of the Marinelli Glacier. As it was obviously more appropriate that this should bear the name, we had decided to call it Mount Darwin.

Camp 3 was close to the northern side of the group, and we decided first of all to concentrate upon an attempt to climb this peak. The only direct approach to the group lay up a 2,000 foot ice-fall, not unlike the Khombu ice-fall on Everest. It looked so broken and complicated, however, that we did not fancy tackling it, heavily laden and in foul weather. The alternative was to make a long detour to the west in the hope of finding an easier line of approach. As we also hoped to find a route across the range in that direction, we decided to take three weeks' food with us.

On January 26 we started carrying our loads up another ice-fall. Using skis partly as a protection against falling into crevasses, we reached a broad snow ridge above the junction of two glaciers. There on the 29th we established Camp 4 (5,000 feet). The weather was continuously bad, our tracks were covered by wind and drifting snow almost as soon as we had made them, and our chief concern was to avoid losing our way among the crevasses. Nor, when they were hidden, was it very easy to determine in which direction they were running, and we had to be very careful to ensure that we were not all standing over the same crevasse at the same time. However, we only had one minor mishap, when Eduardo, who was in the lead, suddenly disappeared. Fortunately Cedomir was holding him on a tight rope and he did not drop far; for, as we found, it is much more difficult to extract a man from a crevasse when he is wearing skis.

From Camp 4, where we were held up for a day by a particularly severe tempest, we had to turn southwards to reach our objective. In a brief clearing, we saw in that direction a small saddle, 3,000 feet above us, accessible by way of a steep slope of what appeared to be wind-polished ice. Leaving a dump of twelve days' food, with the skis stuck upright in the snow to mark the spot, we set towards it. We had brought the light tent with us with the intention of using it for an attempt on Mount Darwin. But now that we were actually confronted with the prospect of facing the weather with such meagre protection, the prospect was so repulsive that we had no hesitation in leaving it behind, and accepting the burden of the Pyramid, even though this meant that we still had to carry in two relays. The ice slope was less steep than it appeared from below, but even so the Pyramid proved an awkward load; soaking wet and encrusted with frozen snow it must have weighed 80 lb.

The saddle was more than 8,000 feet high, only a few hundred feet below the highest summits of the range. We reached it with the second relay at 5.30 p.m. on February 1. A short while before the clouds had vanished, and we found ourselves looking eastward across a deep glacier coombe, on the opposite side of which was the highest peak of the group, our Mount Darwin. We were delighted to see that there was a feasible route down to the floor of the coombe, and from there up to the western face of the mountain.

The two other high peaks of the group flanked the head of the coombe; we called them Darwin II and III. The latter stood directly above the saddle, and Cedomir suggested that we should climb it there and then. As we had already done a hard day's work and had eaten nothing since breakfast, I reacted strongly against the idea. But the clear weather was such a rare occurrence, and it would probably not last for more than a few hours, that it seemed a pity to miss the chance of climbing our first peak. So we hurriedly pitched the tent on a ledge beneath a huge, overhanging ice-cliff, and set off.

No sooner had we started climbing up the ice ridge towards the peak than my fatigue and hunger vanished in the joy of unfettered movement, of the clear, cold air about me and of the rapidly expanding scene. We reached the summit as the sun was setting in a blaze of colour. East and west our view extended over the whole extent of the range, and southward far across the snow-capped islands beyond the Beagle Channel. In the long summer twilight we had plenty of time to return to our camp. The fine spell was indeed short-lived. That night there was a very heavy storm, from which the ice-cliff gave us very little protection. In the general confusion a bag containing two days' rations was blown away.

Descending 2,200 feet to the valley below we pitched camp at the western foot of Mount Darwin. Well protected by the high mountains surrounding it, the place seemed at first so peaceful after the storms to which we had been exposed that I called it the "Silent Coombe". Though it did not always live up to this name, it was on the whole a pleasant spot. We reduced our food ration by one-third and settled down to a ten-day siege. But the weather was liable to change at any moment, and we had to be ready to take advantage of any clearing.

The morning of February 4, though by no means fine, was at least comparatively calm; so we started up towards the summit, now some 3,000 feet above us, intending to reconnoitre the route, and to flag crucial sections. We encountered no great difficulty and succeeded in reaching the summit ridge, from which we looked down the sheer eastern face of the mountain into a boiling cauldron of cloud.

Our chance came the next morning, for the peak was clear and although it was blowing fairly hard the wind was not excessive. Helped by our step-cutting and route-finding of the day before, we climbed very fast and reached the top with five minutes to spare before it was once more enveloped in dense cloud. The deep contentment which came with the accomplishment of our first objective was enhanced that evening by the resumption of full rations.

CHAPTER TWENTY

"The Uttermost Part of the Earth"

ON February 6 we climbed Darwin II. Though the day was cloudless, a tremendous wind was now sweeping across the range from the south-west. As we were climbing the northern side of the mountain, however, we were largely protected from it until we were within 300 feet of the summit. Fortunately we were then on easy ground, for when we met the full force of the gale we were unable to stand and had to crawl forward on hands and knees, digging the picks of our ice-axes into the wind-packed snow. At one point, a large chunk of granite hurtled past Cedomir's head and buried itself in the snow a few feet ahead. It was hard to imagine where it came from, for we were near the top of the peak and there were no rocks in the vicinity. Cedomir added it to his collection, more for its sentimental than its scientific interest.

The actual summit was a pillar of ice, twelve feet high, and we each climbed it in turn while the others huddled on the lee side. We then descended to an ice plateau to the west from where we saw a large section of the southern side of the range, which was a great help in planning our crossing to the Beagle Channel. When we got back to the Silent Coombe we were wet through from head to foot as though we had been standing under a hose for some hours.

On the 7th we recrossed the saddle in mild weather, and on the following day pitched camp on a high pass on the main divide. From there we had to return to the dump at Camp 4 for more supplies. The pass was so wide and flat that there was some danger, if the weather was bad, of our missing the tent on the way back, for our tracks were obliterated almost as soon as they had been made. So we laid out a line of ski-sticks, placed fifty yards apart, on a compass-bearing at right-angles to our line of march.

The weather was constantly changing, and although fine spells were usually brief, they were much more frequent than they had been on the Ice-cap the year before. When they occurred, particularly in the early morning and evening, they brought to our surroundings that delicate colouring, that ethereal texture captured by Edward Wilson's paintings of the Antarctic.

We now had to cross a wide plateau to the west; so we had brought two pairs of skis from the dump, with which we constructed a sledge, as we preferred to drag our loads than to carry them. Most of the way we were in thick mist and had to find our way by compass, but on the 11th we descended below the cloud level and reached a high ridge running southward between two inlets from the Beagle Channel, nearly 4,000 feet below.

There was such a feeling of pleasurable excitement in the camp the next morning, that even breakfast seemed quite festive. At 7 o'clock, leaving the tent standing, we set off with cries of "*A la plage*" from my companions.

A swift glissade down a wide snow gully and a scramble down a series of cliffs brought us into a wide amphitheatre of gently sloping meadows sprinkled with white and yellow flowers. The surrounding precipices disappearing into the cloud, isolated us from the frozen world above. The sun broke through and the warm air was heavy with delicious scents. Even the struggle through the dense forest did not spoil the magic of the transformation. At 10.30 we reached the shore at a point where a large glacier flowed into the bay.

We allowed ourselves four hours on the shore before starting back a different way. By following the bed of a stream we penetrated the forest belt easily, but above this we were faced by a line of crags where we became involved in three hours of difficult rock climbing. As a result it was almost dark before we reached the camp.

On the return journey to our base on the Marinelli Glacier, though we had one fine day, the weather was extremely bad, with powerful winds and exceptionally heavy snowfalls, which made the going very laborious. For two days we were unable to move, and again we reduced our ration to conserve our food supplies. When, on the 19th, we reached Camp 4, we found that the dump was buried by six feet of fresh snow. As a precaution against this eventuality we had fixed its position by compass-bearings to surrounding objects, but even so we had to dig and probe for two hours before finding the tip of one of the upright skis.

We were afraid that our main depot at Camp 3 might have been similarly buried, for if so it would have been almost impossible to find, situated as it was on a flat, featureless expanse of snow at the head of the Marinelli Glacier.

Fortunately we had planted the twelve-foot aluminium wireless mast to mark the spot, and when we reached it the next day, we found that, although the mast had been snapped by the wind, it was still protruding above the surface. So perhaps the radio had been worth bringing after all!

We reckoned that we would have to start back on February 28 at the latest, so as to reach Ship Creek by March 5. This meant that we had seven days left to achieve our final objective, the ascent of Luis de Savoya.

On the 21st, after a long haul across the huge upper basin of the Marinelli Glacier, and a climb up a small ice-fall, we reached, late in the evening, what seemed to be a sheltered hollow at the foot of one of the granite buttresses of the mountain. Above us was a second ice-fall, and we had intended to carry our camp up this the next day, so as to get close enough to the top to reach it in a short spell of fine weather. However, that very evening the weather cleared and we decided to attempt the summit the next day if it was still fine.

Hitherto, fine evenings had always been followed by bad days, but when I awoke just before 3 o'clock the next morning and looked outside the tent, I saw the moon shining in a clear sky. I roused the others and we made a hasty breakfast. Though it was freezing hard, the snow had a breakable crust which made the going heavy. In spite of this we climbed rapidly, and achieved 1,000 feet in the first hour. Already the view had expanded over the mountains behind us. Sixty miles away stood the lovely spire of Sarmiento, ghostly white against the dark-blue shadows of the western sky; nearer at hand, the icy ramparts of Mount Darwin were already lit by the first rays of the rising sun.

We were now faced by a series of enormous crevasses which stretched right across the steep glacier, backed by vertical or overhanging walls. Each in turn seemed to present an impassable barrier; but each time the lucky chance of a slender snow bridge and a crack in the wall beyond enabled us to overcome the obstacle. The most difficult of the walls (led by Eduardo) took an hour and a half to surmount. Though it was inevitable, I found myself becoming increasingly impatient of the delay, for I could hardly believe that the fine weather would last much longer. Moreover, it was now obvious that we would not be able to carry our camp up this difficult ice-fall, and this might well be our last chance to climb the peak. However, when at last we reached the top of the ice-fall the sky was still cloudless and there was no wind.

After climbing a long slope of soft snow, we reached the crest of a steep ridge of hard ice. From there we looked straight down 7,000 feet to the blue waters of Parry Fjord and the dark-green forest surrounding it. At the top of the ridge there was a bulging wall of ice, which seemed to extend right across the upper face of the mountain. Traversing downwards to the left, however, we found a gangway leading to a col on the summit ridge, between two bosses which looked like giant cauliflowers. We chose the right-hand one, as it seemed to be the easier to climb, but when we reached the top we found that the other was a few feet higher. From where we stood the latter appeared to be overhanging on all sides; but having returned to the col and made our way round behind, we found a way of climbing it. We reached the summit at 12.30.

It had been an exciting climb, not because it was particularly difficult, but because the issue had been in doubt until the very last moment; and once again we were just in time, for the cloud had started to form about the highest peaks of the range, though this did nothing to detract from the splendour of the view. But we did not have long to admire it, for ten minutes later we ourselves were swathed in mist.

My companions were keen to change the name of the peak to one of local application. I suggested Cerro Yagan and we decided to adopt the name.

The descent was uneventful. There was still no wind and we could afford to take our time, and savour to the full the blissful sense of relaxation following the urgency of the past few hours. We were tired when we got back to camp and were looking forward to a long lie-in the next morning. But this was not to be. Around midnight I awoke to find a storm of unusual violence raging. The wind was coming at us in intermittent gusts, funnelled through the trough we were in, which continued to increase in force. At 3 o'clock I crawled outside to check the guys. Soon after 4.30, when it was quite light, the tent collapsed over our heads. We thought that two of the poles had snapped, but we discovered later that one side of the tent had been driven four feet into the hard-packed snow beneath. In the pandemonium of madly flapping canvas we managed to put on our boots and wind-proof suits and to collect our belongings. Then I crawled outside, stood up, and was immediately blown flat, while my balaclava was whipped off my head and disappeared, flying high over the rim of the ice-fall.

Our activities during the next two hours must have resembled one of those slapstick comedies of the old silent films. As we struggled to dismantle the tent and pack the loads, we were constantly being hurled to the ground. Cedomir's pack, weighing nearly 50 lb. was swept away and fell into a crevasse 200 yards off. Fortunately it lodged on a ledge twenty feet down and, by lowering Cedomir on the climbing-rope, we were able to recover it. Pancho's pack started on a similar escapade but he intercepted it with a neat rugger tackle. When at last we were ready, we started off, reeling and falling like drunks. Matters improved on the ice-fall which was comparatively sheltered, and although crossing the Marinelli Glacier we were again exposed to the wind, it blew steadily and not in those devastating gusts. Looking back at Cerro Yagan, seeing huge clouds of snow blowing off its flanks and hearing the roar of the wind among its ridges and corries, we were devoutly thankful not to be on the mountain in such conditions.

We had decided the night before to start back at once. We still had four days in hand; but Cedomir thought that he could most profitably spend the time examining the geology along the fjord. Also I had been asked by the British Museum to make a collection of *Collembola* from forest litter, and this would give me the opportunity of doing so. Moreover, we were all more than satisfied with the accomplishment of our three main objectives, and the prospect of some days of comparative idleness along those wooded shores made a powerful appeal.

That very evening we crossed the pass and reached the head of the valley leading down to the fjord, where we camped for the last time on the glacier, completely sheltered from that infernal wind. As we were cooking supper, a tiny owl flew in through the open door, flapped once around the tent and went out again to perch on the snow four feet away. There he sat for a quarter of an hour, gazing at us with his round, unblinking eyes. He was hardly bigger than a sparrow. It is hard to imagine what brought him up on the glacier, except, perhaps, sheer curiosity.

At 10.30 the next morning we reached Camp 2 in warm, sunny weather; and there we spent the rest of the day in idleness. If we had thought it a lovely place before, it seemed exquisitely beautiful now, with the meadows around the camp full of wild flowers, the peaks and glaciers of the cirque framed by a tracery of fresh green leaves and mirrored in the placid lagoon below. Once again our starved senses were ecstatically aware of the colour and the scents and the life around us.

On February 25 we reached the shore at Camp 1, and in the halcyon days that followed we cruised slowly down the fjord, stopping at one or other of the scores of charming little bays we passed, basking in the sun, diving into the icy water to fish for edible crabs among the forests of seaweed in the clear, deep pools at low tide, eating enormous quantities of mussels and sea-urchins and lying beside camp fires under the starlit sky. All this time the incredible spell of fine weather lasted, and every day the ice peaks of the Darwin Range were clear, reminding us of our newly-won possessions.

On the 27th we made our first and only radio contact with Dawson Island. The Naval Headquarters in Punta Arenas were immediately informed and they came back with the message that a ship would soon be sent to pick us up. This news was not altogether welcome, for it looked as though our lotus-eating was to be curtailed by several days. As it turned out, however, it was perhaps fortunate that we made that one contact; for about this time it was reported in several newspapers throughout the world that we were missing. How this story originated we never discovered; the Chilean Naval Authorities were certainly not responsible.

At 5.30 on March 2, as we were settling down in our camp at Ship Creek after another glorious day, we picked up a message from Dawson Island on the transistor radio to the effect that the patrol ship *Cabrales* had set out from Punta Arenas two days before to look for us, and asking us to light a fire beacon to guide her. We were extremely puzzled by this, and a bit disturbed; for the whereabouts of Ship Creek was known to the authorities and we could hardly have failed to notice a ship entering Broken Bay, even if she had not hooted or fired a gun to announce her arrival.

We hastily packed the camp, loaded the Zodiac and raced to the prominent headland farther along the shore. There, on a hill-top, we built a huge fire of driftwood, well soused with paraffin. We had just got it well alight, the flames leaping fifteen feet high, when Cedomir spotted a tiny object, apparently going past the entrance of the bay. Sure enough it was the ship: while we watched, we saw her alter course towards us and presently we heard the faint sound of her siren. We scrambled down the hill to the Zodiac and set off at full speed in the gathering dusk.

When we reached *Cabrales* and had been hauled aboard, we went forward to meet her commander. We were delighted to find that he was an old friend, Commander Rebolledo, who had been second-in-command of *Covadonga* when she had taken us to the Baker Channel the year before. Apparently he had not realized that we had a boat with us, and was very surprised when he caught sight of us, speeding towards him through the gloom. He told us that he had in fact left Punta Arenas two days before, but that he had had another assignment to discharge before coming to Broken Bay. Either we had misunderstood the message that we had picked up a few hours earlier, or it had been wrongly transmitted from Dawson Island.

The ship had turned and was now gliding through the dark silence towards the entrance of the bay. Astern we saw our fire still blazing on the now invisible headland. Beyond, between the black forested shores of the fjord, the mountains showed as a faint glow in the southern sky.

ADDENDA

I

Further Travels in Patagonia and Tierra del Fuego

first published in *The Alpine Journal*
Vol. LXVIII November 1963 No. 307

1. MOUNT BURNEY*

MOUNT Burney has often been referred to in scientific journals as the most southerly active volcano in South America. This belief was based on a somewhat vague report that in 1910 it was seen erupting. Some specimens of andesite lava had been collected from its western foot, near the shores of Mayne Channel; but apart from this little was known about the mountain, though it is often seen from ships passing through the channels.

In March, 1962, Marangunic and I attempted to reach it from the south-west. Lack of time and the difficulty of the terrain prevented our doing so; but the country we passed through was so attractive and our one glimpse of the mountain from ten miles away so intriguing, that I decided to devote the first part of my expedition this year to a further investigation of the area. This time John Earle came with me from England, and we were joined by Jack Ewer in Punta Arenas, where we arrived on January 5.

The easiest approaches to Mount Burney would be from the shores of Mayne Channel or Union Sound which bound the Muños Gamero Peninsula on the north-west and north respectively. But either of these would require sea transport, and although the Chilean Navy would have been willing to take us there as well as to the Beagle Channel later, there was no ship immediately available, and in any case I did not want to make too many demands on their hospitality. Besides this, I was anxious to explore the lakes we had discovered the previous year. So we decided again to approach the mountain from the south-west through the heart of the Muños Gamero peninsula. Once again I had brought a Zodiac inflatable craft and a 10 h.p. Evinrude outboard motor.

We set out from Estancia Skyring on January 9, the Zodiac laden with a month's provisions and forty gallons of petrol, and sailed along the coast to the neck of a mountainous peninsula which stretches twelve miles out into Skyring Sound. At this point we were met by a *peon*, whom Mr. Friedli had very kindly

*The mountain was climbed in 1973 by Shipton, Roger Perry, and Pete Radcliffe

sent from the estancia with four pack-horses; with the help of these we carried the boat and our baggage across the isthmus the following day in two relays. By this manoeuvre we avoided making the westward passage of Punta Laura at the end of the peninsula which, in a small boat in rough weather, is a difficult and somewhat hazardous operation.

Late in the evening of the 11th, after a stormy voyage, we reached the Passo del Indio, a narrow isthmus separating the north-western corner of Skyring Sound from the system of freshwater lakes occupying a large part of the Muños Gamero peninsula. It used to be crossed by the Alacaluf Indians to get their boats from Obstruction Sound to the southern channels. So far as I know, no one but the Alacaluf had crossed the isthmus until we did so last year. Indeed I am far from sure that we found the real 'Passo'; for the terrain is exceedingly complicated, and although it has been plotted from aerial pictures, the map is inaccurate. The following morning it took us six hours to carry our baggage across the isthmus. The boat, of course, gave us the most trouble; for, even with the wooden floor boards removed, it weighed nearly 150 lb., and was so bulky that it made an awkward load on a pack-frame.

In the afternoon when the voyage was resumed, the weather was calm, and we enjoyed a delightful cruise through the network of channels forming the eastern part of the lake system; past innumerable islets, like green, floating pin-cushions, and along forested shores, backed by sweeping mountain landscapes. From the water, the country looked gentle and friendly; but, then as before, it gave me a strange sense of loneliness, due no doubt to the knowledge that it was completely devoid of human habitation, and that for all its beauty, it was in fact far from kind. It would be horribly difficult to travel there without a boat.

By seven o'clock we had entered a narrow passage leading into the main lake. We had just selected a cove in which to spend the night, when the motor stopped and refused to start again; so we had to row ashore. This was the only time we experienced trouble with the motor, and it could not have happened at a more fortunate moment; on a calm evening, close to a good landing place. Had it occurred in the normal rough weather we might have found ourselves in an awkward situation. The next morning a strong southerly wind was blowing straight into our cove. We made repeated efforts to launch the Zodiac, but each time it was beaten back to the shore and swamped. So we spent the day in idleness, cursing our foolish choice of a camp site. However, at 8 p.m., while we were eating our supper, the wind dropped slightly; so we hurriedly packed up, and this time we succeeded in getting the boat through the breakers and the motor started. It was dark when, after another rough passage, we reached the western side of the main lake. The next morning we had an easy run along the lee shore to its northern extremity.

Our next task was to carry the boat and our gear to the new lakes we had found last year. I knew that the distance to the nearest point was not great, but I had no idea what the going would be like. If it had been dense forest all the way, it would have been a very long and laborious job. But we were delighted to find a long rocky spur, with open ground along its crest, which offered such easy going that in a day and a half we had completed the carry. On the next bit of the voyage we were forced to go so far westward that, with the mountains closing in on either side, I began to fear that I had been mistaken in thinking that the new lakes were interconnected, and that yet another and far more difficult portage would be necessary. However, at the last moment, a channel opened to starboard and we sailed through to the biggest of the lakes. The northern shore of this marked the end of our voyage; there we made our base in surroundings which, apart from the glaciers, might well have been in the Scottish Highlands.

On the 16th we set out across a great plain which we had seen last year stretching northward to the coast. It was largely devoid of forest and, as we had rightly inferred from this, it was very swampy. Marangunic had thought that it might have been formed by huge deposits of volcanic ash filling a wide channel which had once connected the lakes with the sea; but the swamp and the deep beds of peat made it difficult to obtain much evidence to support this theory.

We started with eighteen days' food, and our normal equipment was augmented by two ciné cameras and some 3,000 feet of film, as part of John's object in joining the expedition was to make a film record of it. Thus we had too much to carry at once and we had to relay. Because of the swampy nature of the ground, the going on the plain was laborious and unpleasant; but on the second day we reached the south-easterly spurs of Mount Burney which were heavily forested. That evening we camped amid the most glorious surroundings, in a wide basin formed by the East face of the mountain and a range of wooded foothills, and filled with a lovely mixture of glacier, forest, lakes and meadows, some of which were richly strewn with wild flowers.

We were now faced with the problem familiar to most of us in a bad Alpine season; whether to wait for a chance to climb our peak, or to keep moving and to risk missing such a chance. The upper part of Mount Burney was hidden in cloud; but there seemed to be a way of reaching it up the South-east ridge. If our sole object had been to climb the mountain, we would no doubt have taken a camp up this ridge and waited for a clearing. Our main purpose, however, was to explore as much of the mountain and surrounding country as possible; so we decided to concentrate on making a journey right round the mountain, hoping that any spell of fine weather that might occur would find us in a position to make the ascent. As it turned out, this was the right decision, for not once during the sixteen days that it took us to make the tour did the weather clear.

At first the way led us over a wide ice-sheet, and thereafter across a long series of ridges and combes, many of which contained glaciers. The cloud ceiling usually remained around 2,500 or 3,000 feet and, as for the most part we were travelling slightly below this level, we had a series of fine views over the channels flanking the peninsula on the north and north-west. Our camps were usually pleasantly sited near the upper edge of the forest. The weather was generally what one might expect in a bad summer in the Lake District, though colder, and occasionally we experienced severe gales.

We kept close under the faces of the mountain; those not covered with ice seemed to be composed entirely of *tuff*; some of them were most spectacular. We found very few outcrops of andesite lava, though the moraines were largely composed of this material. So far as we could judge, the area covered by the volcano and its subsidiary cones, is about twenty-four miles in circumference. We found no evidence of recent activity.

Eventually we reached the south-eastern combe of the mountain. This was the side of Burney that I had seen last year and, although this time we could not see the peaks of the summit ridge, I was no less impressed by the splendid ice-face, which seemed to belong to a mountain of quite a different order of magnitude. The valley below was very beautiful; it was drained by a wide river which we followed through the forest to the plain, whence we reached the place where we had left the boat. We were then blessed by a spell of milder weather, and the voyage back through the lakes to Skyring was wholly delightful.

2. MOUNT BOVÉ

From the summits of the peaks we climbed in the Darwin Range of Tierra del Fuego last year, we saw the mountains lying at the eastern end of the peninsula. They looked very fine, and we thought that two of them, Bové and Roncagli, might be as high as Mount Darwin itself, if not higher. Like the central part of the range, this group was largely unexplored, and I had decided to spend the second half of my expedition this year in the region, approaching it from the Beagle Channel.

When we returned to Punta Arenas from Mount Burney, John and I were joined by Peter Bruchhausen, who had been with me in Patagonia three years before, and Claudio Cortez, a medical student from Santiago. Once again the Chilean Navy had generously agreed to transport us to our chosen base, and on February 12 the four of us embarked on their ship *Cabrales*.

The voyage took us through a labyrinth of channels characteristic of the whole coastline of southern Chile. The following morning we passed close to Mount Sarmiento, a land-mark well known to the early navigators of the Magellan Straits, and we saw its lovely ice-spring piercing the banks of cloud which hung low over the coast. For much of the day the scenery resembled the Western Isles of Scotland as, in the eastern part of the archipelago, the forest is sparse and confined to a few sheltered valleys. Early in the morning of the 14th, we were put ashore with a month's provisions in a little bay known as Olla.

Since dawn it had been raining heavily; the precipices flanking the Beagle Channel and the massive glaciers cascading down to the water's edge had presented a sombre spectacle. As soon as we landed, however, the weather cleared and the scene was transformed. Under a warm sun and a cloudless sky, Olla Bay was idyllic. A wide, sandy beach, backed by forest, stretched in a half-mile crescent around the turquoise water of the lagoon. The peace was only disturbed by the boisterous behaviour of a party of sea-lions further along the shore. The tide was low and we collected large quantities of mussels which we ate for breakfast. Then, resisting the temptation to linger in this lovely place, we started inland, carrying supplies for seven days.

Our chief objective was to climb Bové which, seen both from Mount Darwin and from the eastern end of the Beagle Channel, appeared to be the highest peak of the group. A few years ago an attempt had been made to reach it from the east by a party of Argentine mountaineers; they had failed largely because of the weather. De Agostini's party had landed at Olla Bay when they climbed Pico Italia.[1] A map of the area reproduced in his book, *Sfingi di Ghiaccio*, had led us to suppose that we could reach the western face of Bové from the head of the Italia glacier, and so, lacking any other information about the mountain, we decided to approach it from that direction.

Our way through the forest was made easy by well-worn guanaco tracks (later, on several occasions we encountered herds of these creatures on the high glacier moraines; they are, I believe, distant relatives of the camel); and at 7.30 that evening we camped on a ridge far above the tree-line. Meanwhile, Peter, who had been lagging behind, and whom I had last seen only a couple of hundred feet below the camp, had disappeared. Getting no reply from our shouts, and thinking that he must have by-passed the camp, John and I set off up the ridge. It was almost dark and raining gently when we returned after a fruitless search. But a little later, shortly before 10.30, Claudio found Peter lying on a ledge quite close to the camp, recovering from a long attack of vomiting, during which he must have lost consciousness. Evidently he was allergic to mussels.

Two days later we reached the head of the Italia glacier. The weather was bad, but we saw enough to realise that there was no way of reaching Bové from that direction; so we returned to Olla Bay, loaded the Zodiac with our baggage, and moved our base eastward along the coast. We had been fortunate only to waste four days in this abortive reconnaissance; for in the mountains of Tierra del Fuego, where for weeks on end the surrounding country may be shrouded in mist, or movement prevented by gales, route-finding is apt to be a long and frustrating business.

Our second sortie was more successful; we found an excellent route into the range, and on February 21 we established a camp near the head of the Francés glacier at the southern foot of Bové. As we approached it, moreover, the weather cleared and we saw that there was a way of reaching the summit from that direction. This was a great relief, for it meant that we would thus be saved many days of further reconnaissance and load-carrying. Later we discovered that any alternative approach would have been either impossible or a great deal more difficult. As it was, we had now only to sit tight and await a chance to climb the mountain, using any brief clearing of the weather to familiarise ourselves with the route so as to save time when such a chance occurred.

We found that there was a remarkable absence of névé even in the highest glacier basins and that the surfaces were nearly all composed of hard ice. Though, as a rule, this made it a lot easier to move around locally, it presented us with a considerable problem in pitching the tent securely on open glacier; indeed it would have been impossible to do so in a high wind. This factor would have prevented us from travelling as freely as we did last year. I suspect that such conditions are quite exceptional even so late in the season. We experienced some severe storms, and our pyramid tent suffered a tremendous battering. I know of no other type of tent that could have withstood such

[1]In *A.J.* 67. 259, I stated that this party had climbed Pico Francés as well as Pico Italia; this, however, is not the case.

weather, and there were times when I doubted even its ability to do so.

At dawn on the 25th it was calm, but rain was falling heavily. However, this stopped by 9 a.m. and we set out, not expecting to get far, as the mountain was still wrapped in cloud. The lower part of the route led up a wide gully, a thousand feet high. We had already reconnoitred this and found it to be full of the debris of avalanches falling from a line of hanging glaciers. However, by climbing very steep ice on the left flank of the gully, we were able to avoid the danger, and eventually reached the crest of the West ridge of the mountain. Though there was little visibility, it was still calm and we sensed an improvement in the weather; so we went on.

The ridge was composed of a mounting series of huge ice bosses, like gigantic cauliflowers, poised on a narrow crest, overhanging on either side. One after another they loomed above us until, shortly before 3 p.m., we reached the top of the highest. To make sure that this was the summit of the peak, we continued along the ridge; but before we had gone far the curtain of mist in front of us parted, and we looked down a sheer drop of several thousand feet to a large glacier flowing eastward. A number of such clearings occurred while we were on the summit, which revealed the view in sections. The most exciting of these was to the north where we saw Roncagli standing above a group of fine granite spires. It seemed to be somewhat lower than Bové (whose height we estimated at 8,100 feet), but from this direction it looked a difficult mountain to climb.

We were fortunate to reach the summit when we did, for during the descent we were once again in thick cloud. Moreover, soon after we reached the camp the calm spell ended, and that night the roar of the wind and the racket of frozen drift lashing the walls of the tent emphasised our luck. But we were to have another break. On March 1 we climbed Pico Francés (7,900 feet) and, arriving at the summit at five o'clock on a perfect evening, we had a superb view of the whole range as far west as Mount Darwin, and eastward for seventy miles along the Beagle Channel. Though it was late and very cold, we stayed there for an hour and a half. Beyond the sparkling clusters of ice crystals, like veined leaves, characteristic of these summit ridges, we saw, far below, the coves of Devil's Island, green and blue in the warm sunlight.

Our return to the coast was hampered by foul weather. On one occasion during a storm shortly before leaving the glacier, I fell into a crevasse, where I remained for three-quarters of an hour until I and my load could be extricated. By then the wind was very violent and, blinded by drift and often knocked over by the more powerful gusts, we had a good deal of difficulty in moving on down.

Reaching our base with several days to spare before our rendezvous with the Chilean Navy on March 15, we spent a pleasant time cruising about the channel visiting various sea-lion rookeries along the forested shores. One morning we met two ships of the Chilean Antarctic Flotilla. They stopped to investigate our strange craft, and Claudio, anxious to get home in time for his final examinations, took this unexpected opportunity of a lift back to Punta Arenas. The rest of us awaited the arrival of a small vessel, *Beagle*, which took us to Puerto Williams, a small naval base in the eastern part of the Beagle Channel.

II

Crossing the North Patagonian Ice-cap

first published in *The Alpine Journal*
Vol. LXIX November 1964 No. 309

THE crossing of the Hielo Patagonico del Norte was a natural sequel to our journey over the southern Ice-cap in 1960/61. I knew that it would have to be done some time, but for two summers it was shelved in favour of the Fuegan mountains. We sometimes used to discuss it on that first journey and, on the few days that we were confined to our tent in the Darwin Range, Garcia used to pass the time by drawing us maps of the general layout of the region and discussing the problems of access and egress. For he had some personal knowledge of the area, having taken part in the sixteen-man Japanese-Chilean Expedition that, in 1958, had climbed Arenales, a mountain standing near its south-eastern edge. Though he had played a major part in pioneering the way and in the work of establishing the lower camps, he had been left out of the parties that reached the summit, which had naturally caused him keen disappointment. When I met him with Marangunic in Santiago in April 1963, they suggested that we should tackle the new crossing the following season.

The project involved much the same problems as we had met before; there was no reason to expect better weather conditions and, though the distance to be covered was not so long, the way would be more complicated because of several high passes that we would have to cross in the latter part of the journey. Also, after leaving the glaciers we would still have a long way to go before reaching habitation, and this meant that we would have to carry a rubber dinghy with us for crossing rivers and lakes. On the other hand an approach to the ice-cap from the north-west was known: several parties had made their way up from Laguna San Rafael on the Pacific coast in their attempts on Mount San Valentin before that mountain was finally climbed in 1952.[1] In addition, Garcia's knowledge of a route into the range from the south-east provided us with a line of escape. Our reasons for making the journey in that direction were the same as before: we would be travelling from an uninhabited region towards habitation, and with the prevailing wind.

We decided to start in November in the hope that we would find an abundance of winter snow which would both provide good conditions for

[1]See *A.J.* 59. 432.

sledging and cover the crevassed areas. An additional advantage was that my companions would return in time to spend part of their summer vacation with their families. I wrote to the Minister of Education and the Director of the Geological Institute in Santiago, to request their release a month before the end of the summer term, and received favourable replies from both. The fourth member of the party was recruited by Garcia and Marangunic; he was a young Spaniard, Miguel Gomez, who had come three years before with a Spanish expedition to the Peruvian Andes, and had been in South America ever since. He proved an excellent choice; a first rate mountaineer, always cheerful and always ready to do the most unpleasant jobs and to carry the heaviest loads.

This time we took skis with us but, apart from these and the boat, I equipped the party in the same way as before. We had another collapsible fibre-glass sledge, and a light wooden one. Our food, too, was much the same, though I increased the daily sugar ration from 8 oz. to 9 oz. per man. Our equipment and food were packed in a single wooden case, and shipped to Valparaiso. I joined my companions on November 15 in Santiago, where I found that the Air Force had made arrangements for our departure on the 21st.

Although we had obtained official permission to import our baggage free of duty, it was November 19 before Marangunic and I could go down to Valparaiso to claim it from the customs. Even then we had to negotiate a mass of formalities, and the issue remained in doubt until late that evening. The next morning in Santiago we opened the case and found that it had previously been broken open and a number of things stolen, including two pairs of climbing boots, two pairs of crampons, all our windproof trousers, most of our supply of tea and eight days' rations. As a result, we spent a busy day repairing our losses.

Once again we received invaluable assistance from the Chilean government. On the 21st we were flown in an Air Force 'Otter' to Puerto Montt, and the following morning we were provided with two 'Beachcraft' planes to take us from there to Puerto Aisen. As soon as we arrived, we called on Señor Atilio Cosmelli, the Governor of Aisen Province, who received us with charming courtesy and was kind enough to take a keen interest in our project. He had already arranged for our departure that very afternoon in a small motor vessel, *Devine*.

The voyage through the channels from Puerto Aisen to Laguna San Rafael should have taken a day and a half. Unfortunately, at about noon on the 23rd, when we were still some seven hours' sailing from our destination, *Devine's* transmission shaft snapped. Luckily, the wind, which had been strong throughout most of the morning, had subsided, and the crew of three, with the aid of the dinghy and a small outboard motor, were able to tow the helpless vessel to a nearby island, where she was made fast to some overhanging trees.

Luckily, too, *Devine* carried a radio, and the captain was able to send a message to Aisen informing the Governor of our plight. He immediately despatched a privately owned vessel, *Alicia*, to our rescue, which reached us late in the evening of the 24th. We spent much of the intervening time catching fish, which was useful as we were already living on expedition rations.

The crew of *Alicia* were under the impression that they had been sent to fetch us back to Aisen. However, after a strenuous discussion, in which our cause was championed by the captain of *Devine*, and a further exchange of radio messages with Aisen, they agreed to take us on. These negotiations resulted in a late start in the morning of the 25th, and as *Alicia* could only make five knots it was nearly 5 p.m. before we reached the mouth of the Rio Tempanos, the narrow five-mile channel leading to Languna San Rafael. The crew of *Alicia* said that they had been told in no circumstances to attempt the passage of this channel, and they proposed to land us near its mouth.

Although this was only some ten miles from the San Rafael glacier, the country between was composed of swamp and dense forest, and it would have taken us at least a week to reach it with all our gear, and probably a great deal longer. This would have seriously upset our timetable and left us short of food for the journey. Fortunately, largely due to the good offices of *Devine's* captain, the crew once again yielded to our entreaties. On the ebb tide there was a strong current running against us through the channel, carrying with it a number of large ice-bergs. However, we made the passage without mishap and at eight o'clock we were put ashore at the south-east corner of the lagoon.

In the 1920's an attempt had been made to dig a canal from the southern end of Laguna San Rafael to the channels leading to the Gulf of Penas with the purpose of providing shipping with a protected passage along that part of the coast. The project was abandoned because of the swampy nature of the ground. At the same time the government had built a large, three-storied hotel on the shore of the lagoon, at the point where we landed. The cost must have been enormous. Presumably the idea was to attract visitors to that remote and lonely spot; but apart from the spectacle of the San Rafael glacier, thrusting its ice-cliffs into the lagoon on a two-mile front, it would have offered few of the amenities required by the average tourist. The building was completed but never used, and there it stands, a bizarre object in that wild, uninhabited land. However, it provided us with welcome shelter from the heavy rain that persisted throughout the night.

Our satisfaction at having, after all, reached this place received a rude shock when we discovered that a kit-bag, containing the sledge-harness, ski skins, priming fuel and several other important items, had been left on board. Though not disastrous, this loss darkened our horizon considerably. However, when we awoke at 5.30 the next morning, we were astonished to see *Alicia* approaching the shore. She had anchored near the upper entrance of the Rio Tempanos, the passage of the channel being too dangerous to attempt in the dark; our kit-bag had been found and was now being returned. This action of the crew was most generous, considering that we had already put them to a great deal of extra trouble, and persuaded them to disobey the instructions of their owners. By it they had nothing to gain and a great deal to lose. They even refused any remuneration. Such kindness is typical of these people.

The glacier was still four km. away, across an alluvial plain. Previous parties had apparently had no difficulty in reaching it, but lately a river issuing from the near flank of the glacier had spread its delta over the plain, and we had to cross a series of meandering streams. This was not difficult with our rubber dinghy, but it took us two days to transport our baggage to the corner where the glacier emerged from the mountains. There, on the 27th we established our first camp on a raised beach, sheltered by cliffs and luxuriant forest, with provisions enough for forty-three days.

Unlike most Patagonian glaciers, the San Rafael has shrunk very little, and the ice presses close against the forest on the precipitous slopes flanking it. Though by no means steep, its whole surface is a chaotic mass of séracs and crevasses; so the only way up it was along the narrow trough between the forest and the glacier, though we were frequently forced on to the ice for long stretches, and the going was sometimes hard. For the first stage we carried the loads in four relays. Our second camp (1,200 ft.) was pitched on an ice-platform among the séracs, as we could find no suitable ledge in the forest.

The second stage took us through to the upper basin of the glacier, and beyond our third camp (2,300 ft.), which we established on December 6, the going was easier. For the next five days we made our way eastward through a series of crevassed areas. We had hoped that so early in the summer these would be well covered; but the winter snowfall had evidently been exceptionally light and the crevasses were much more open than we had expected. Sometimes we used the small sledge, but mostly the going was too rough and we had to carry. Route-finding was complicated, though luckily at this stage we were not much bothered by mist. Indeed during the first fortnight of the journey the weather, judged by Patagonian standards, was not at all bad; there was no severe wind and we had five fine days.

On December 11 we reached the plateau, and were then able to bring both sledges into operation. For two days, however, our progress was very slow, as we encountered several more badly crevassed areas. On the morning of the 13th, for example, after an uninterrupted run of an hour and a half, we suddenly found ourselves in the midst of a perfect maze of fissures, mostly concealed by a shallow covering of rotten snow. Though, of course, our skis were a great help in bridging the crevasses, it was difficult to determine their direction, and we had to exercise great care to avoid the risk of all of us falling into the same one. Moreover we were then in dense mist with visibility restricted to a few yards. However, this proved to be the last of these obstacles, and for the next five days we were able to steer a straight course, 10° east of south.

For two days the weather was bad and we marched mostly on a compass bearing; but though we experienced some discomfort from driving sleet and melting drift, which made us very wet, the wind was not severe, and by dawn on the 16th it was fine once more. For the next three days we travelled along a flat corridor ten miles wide, between two ranges of granite peaks, their exciting shapes, which reminded me very much of the Karakoram, constantly appearing and disappearing among banks of shifting cloud. These peaks offer a wonderful new field of mountaineering, for there are scores of them, and most will demand a very high standard of climbing. Moreover one of the ranges should not be too difficult of access from the east. With the sledges running easily over good snow, with plenty of time in between spells of pulling to sit in the warm sun, and enjoying these glorious surroundings, this part of the journey was sheer delight.

On the 18th we reached the foot of a col leading south-west across a northerly spur of the Arenales group. We had been lucky that the fine spell had enabled us to find it without difficulty, for that night the weather broke. On the 19th we were confined to our tent by a storm and, although the 20th was not much better, a temporary lull in the morning encouraged us to set out for the pass; and a few brief clearings later in the day enabled us to find a route and to carry half our loads to its crest. The rest were brought up the following day. We now entered a vast basin of glaciers which combine in a large ice-stream flowing southwards to the Baker Channel. Our objective was a depression in the range south of Arenales, which Garcia had seen from the east and which would lead us on to the route followed by his 1958 expedition; we called it the Arenales col. Crossing a second pass and keeping close under the main range, we reached the foot of it on the 24th.

It had been our intention to leave a dump at this point, and to go on with the small sledge carrying a week's provisions with the object of climbing two mountains, Pared Norte and Pared Sur, near the southern end of the range. But we were behind our schedule and, estimating the time that it would take to cross the col and reach habitation, with a reasonable allowance for delay by bad weather, we reckoned that we had only four days' food to spare and that this would hardly give us time to attempt either of the peaks. So we decided to go straight to the col, and use the time climbing from there. In fact events showed us to have been over-cautious, particularly as during the next ten days we had some of the best weather of the whole trip.

Christmas morning was still and cloudless. We packed up the camp and started at 6.45 a.m., following a route that Garcia and Gomez had reconnoitred the previous evening. There had been a sharp frost during the night (−11°C) and the snow was in perfect condition. Carrying 50 lb. each, we climbed 3,000 feet to the col (about 7,850 feet) in 2 hr. 20 min. Then, having deposited our loads on the broad snow-saddle, we set off at ten o'clock to climb Cerro Arco (9,950 feet), a mountain two miles away to the south. A powerful wind embarrassed us on the steep ice-slopes below the summit, but the weather remained clear and from the top we had a wonderful view of Arenales to the north, across the basin of the Rio Baker to Mount San Lorenzo, fifty miles away to the south-west, and over the great glaciers to the west. Pared Norte and Pared Sur, to the south, looked splendid, and we regretted that we were not to make their closer acquaintance. When we got back to the col we dug a pit in which we pitched the tent, and built a high snow wall round it for protection from the wind.

It was still clear early the next morning, but in the gaudy sunrise there were ominous signs that a storm was about to break. So, as we only had one more day's food with us, we raced down to the dump at the foot of the col, where we collected the remainder of our baggage, except for the small sledge which we decided to abandon. We were only just in time, for half an hour later the storm broke with considerable violence and everything was blotted out in mist and blinding drift. It would have been almost impossible to locate the dump in such conditions.

The snow was soft that day, which was lucky as it meant that our deep downward tracks survived the gale just long enough to guide us over the lower and most complicated section of the route. The upper section was more or less straight and we could follow a compass bearing. Even so I was very doubtful if we would manage to hit off the right part of the col and find the tent, largely hidden within its snow wall. The climb back to the col was most unpleasant, for we were soon soaked to the skin by melting drift driven against us with tremendous force, and we were often blown over by the more violent gusts. When, however, we reached the col, whether by luck or by accurate navigation we found the tent and wasted no time in scrambling through the entrance. The inside immediately became a shambles of sodden garments, slushy snow and pools of water, and we spent until ten o'clock that night drying out. The storm continued to rage until about that time, when it ceased as suddenly as it had begun.

When we awoke at five o'clock the next morning, it was very cold. Though the sun was shining, the weather again looked threatening, and we thought we were in for another storm: many of the peaks were capped by mushroom-shaped clouds and the distant views were suffused with an inky blue. We decided to move down to a wide combe, 400 feet below the col, at the southern foot of Arenales. The wet snow which had half buried the tent the day before had frozen into a solid block of ice; it was a long job digging this away, and we were not ready to start until 10.30. By then all the clouds had vanished and the day was gloriously fine.

Garcia was keen to seize the opportunity of climbing Arenales (11,277 feet) which had been denied him on the Japanese expedition. So, though there were two other fine peaks within our reach, we decided to forgo the chance of another first ascent. We dragged the sledge down into the combe, and set off for the mountain shortly before eleven o'clock. It was a climb of 4,800 feet, but conditions were excellent and it was not difficult. A bitter south-westerly wind kept us moving fast and we reached the summit at 2.40. From there we had a superb view over the ice-cap and the ranges to the north as far as San Valentin.

When we got back to the sledge, we went on down the combe so as to take advantage of the clear weather, as there seemed to be only one line through the crevasses, which would have been very difficult to find in bad visibility. The following day we made our way along a terrace between two formidable ice-falls. Garcia had warned us that the Japanese expedition had encountered great difficulty here, negotiating a series of immense crevasses. But that had been in March and we hoped that at the end of December we would have less trouble. Even so, the two-mile passage took us all day. The crevasses were among the largest I had ever seen; once again I was thankful we were equipped with skis, for some of the chasms were spanned only by the slenderest of bridges and the snow was soft. Beyond the terrace we had a short section of ice-fall to negotiate, followed by the descent of a 2,000 foot rock-wall; but with Garcia to guide us these obstacles presented no great difficulty, even in bad weather. After that we had some ten miles to go to the snout of the Colonia glacier, which we reached on January 2.

Our final obstacle was Lago Colonia, some six miles long and flanked on both sides by steep precipices. The rubber dinghy, which had survived the journey without a single puncture, was too small to take us all with our luggage;

in fact we would have had to make three relays. Except on rare occasions it would have been impossible to row the boat back against the prevailing westerly wind; moreover even in calm weather a strong wind was liable to spring up without warning. We therefore constructed a raft with our air mattresses and skis. This carried one man and the baggage, and was towed behind the dinghy which accommodated the rest of us. For oars we used snow-shovels fixed to the end of poles and, until it became too rough, an anorak was hoisted over each craft to serve as a sail.

At first it was relatively calm, but the wind and the waves increased as we went. We kept close to the precipitous southern shore, though there were few places where we could have landed. About half way, however, there was a small beach where we put in for some refreshment. The second part of the voyage was most exciting, for it was very rough. However we managed to maintain our direction and eventually we reached the far end of the lake, where we were hurled unceremoniously ashore by the breakers. There we lit a mighty fire, to dry ourselves and to celebrate the end of our journey.

Two or three miles beyond the end of the lake we found some untenanted houses, and we had to go another ten miles down the Rio Colonia before we reached a small farm where we could hire some pack ponies. For the next few days we marched in comfort and deep contentment along broad valleys flanked by snow peaks, through mile upon mile of green meadows and woods where wild strawberries abounded. The sun shone and the air was clear and still. Always we met with the same generous hospitality and kindness, which is everywhere to be found in Patagonia; always we were fed, housed, provided with transport and accompanied on the next stage; payment for these services, if it was accepted at all, was a secondary consideration and not even the poorest people seemed to expect it.

We crossed the Rio Baker, a noble river as wide as the Danube at Budapest, below its junction with the Rio Colonia. From there we marched to the Rio Cochrane, another tributary of the Baker, where there was a gendarmerie post with a radio station. A message was transmitted to the Air Force post at Balmacera, and a few hours later a Beachcraft arrived to collect us.

The journey had gone remarkably smoothly. This was very largely due to the skill and efficiency of my companions, for much of the detailed planning, particularly in the field, was theirs. Normally, I believe, this part of Patagonia is not more favoured by fine weather than the parts further south. If this is the case, we were extremely lucky; in the six weeks occupied by the crossing we had fifteen fine days; the good spells occurred when we most needed them and the bad spells were comparatively short and rarely severe. Altogether it had been a glorious trip, full of variety, through some of the loveliest mountain country I have seen in Patagonia or anywhere else. The region still offers wide scope for those who enjoy untravelled ground; for mountaineers it is an almost untouched field.[2]

[2]The general location of the area described is latitude 47°S., longitude 73°W.

APPENDICES

APPENDIX I

The 1935 Everest Reconnaissance

A section of the paper *'The Mount Everest Reconnaissance'* by Eric Shipton which he read to the Royal Geographical Society in December 1935 and later published in the Geographical Journal Vol LXXXVII, No. 2, February 1936.

The expedition arrived in the Everest region after an initial period of climbing and surveying in the Nyonno Ri range . . .

The whole party [Shipton, Bill Tilman, Edwin Kempson, Charles Warren, Edmund Wigram, Dan Bryant (NZ) and Karma Paul (Liaison Officer)], with the exception of Karma Paul, left the Rongbuk Monastery on July 6 in gloriously fine weather, taking with us sufficient food for five weeks, and forty Tibetans to carry our gear as far as Camp II. We left Spender and his cameras, together with a few of the older and more experienced Sherpas, at the old base camp and went on ourselves to Camp I the same day. While we made our way up the glacier to Camp III the weather continued fine and the north face of Everest became quite black and soon began to resemble the mountain in its pre-monsoon aspect. The days were hot and windless, the nights clear and cold, and it was difficult to imagine how the slopes of the North Col could be in anything but perfect condition by the time we reached them. Bryant unfortunately now became ill and had to be left behind at Camp I, to follow up when he had recovered.

We reached Camp III on July 8 without much incident or effort and had enough food there to last us for three weeks, having dumped the rest at Camp II. The next day the weather became unpleasant, though very little snow fell. We spent the day moving camp farther up towards the North Col. A few hundred yards above Camp III, in fact within sight and hail of it, we came upon the body of Maurice Wilson. It was evident that he had died in his sleep from exhaustion and not from starvation, as he had found a dump of food which had been left in 1933 and which was still well stocked.

A great deal has been said about the danger of snow avalanches on the North Col. Exactly why these slopes should differ from any others at a similar altitude it is difficult to say, but the memory of the disastrous avalanche of 1922 is partly responsible for the extreme caution with which subsequent parties have tackled them. *We* regarded the North Col with the same respect and were determined not to run any risk with snow which we considered to be in the least bit doubtful. Kempson had had very considerable experience of winter snow conditions in the Alps, while I imagined I was familiar with a fairly wide range of Himalayan snows. The weather conditions for the past week had been ideal for packing the snow, and although we examined carefully each section of our route we could not detect anywhere the slightest tendency to avalanche. In detail the aspect of the North Col had changed considerably since 1933. The middle section of our old route, known to us as the Punch Bowl, and the 30-foot wall above it were contorted beyond recognition into a mass of tottering séracs, which would have rendered the 1933 route exceedingly difficult, if not impracticable. A tongue of ice a few hundred feet to the right had protruded somewhat and now provided us with comparatively easy access to the old site of Camp IV. The ledge on which this camp had been had now completely disappeared, and the ice was far too steep for us to think of pitching a tent. In the upper section great bulges of ice forced us to traverse right across the face before we could climb to the crest of the col which we reached at a point very close to the site of our old Camp IVa. The big Arctic tent and the food dump which we had left in 1933 were buried under some 8 feet of (presumably) monsoon snow. For three days we worked on the ice slopes of the North Col and by July 12 we had established a camp at the foot of the north-east ridge and stocked it with sufficient food and fuel to last us for fifteen days. It was occupied by Kempson, Warren, and myself, and nine Sherpas. Our plan was to take a light camp up to 26,000 feet and from there to investigate the snow conditions on the slabs of the upper part of the mountain and to reconnoitre some of the ground about which there has been so much debate.

We had established ourselves on the North Col in less than a week after leaving Rongbuk, and it seemed advisable to spend the next two or three days in rest and acclimatization. The weather was bad and we were worried by a nasty wind which was particularly fierce at night. We spent four uncomfortable days waiting for better weather, during which time we went some way up the ridge. As time was of no particular object and our job was to keep a watch on the mountain during the whole of the monsoon, we had made up our minds that we should not force our way up in bad weather. It seemed a waste of time to hang about doing nothing, so we decided to leave on the North Col all the food and fuel we had with us and what tents and equipment we could spare and descend to Camp III to spend our time climbing other peaks in the vicinity until the weather improved. We could then return to the North Col without being obliged to carry anything further up there. With this plan in view we started to descend on the morning of July 16. Although the weather had been bad, only a few inches of new snow had been deposited on the mountain during our stay on the North Col and although we tackled the slopes below with extreme caution they did not seem to have altered materially since we had last seen them. We descended in two parties: Kempson and I were in front with five Sherpas, while Warren was some way behind with the other four. We had not gone far before we were brought up short at the brink of a sudden cut-off which stretched for several hundred yards in either direction. This indicated that an enormous avalanche had recently broken away largely along the line of our ascending tracks. In fact the whole face of the slope had peeled off to a depth of 6 feet. This was an alarming discovery and there followed a somewhat heated debate as to whether we should retreat to the North Col or carry on down. The others advocated the former course; but it seemed to me that if, as we had reason to suppose, the avalanche had occurred on the previous night its track must indicate a temporary line of strength, and it was not likely that another avalanche would fall immediately, while if we returned to the North Col we would later have to face a risk which we had no means of gauging. Anyway my argument was the simpler to put into effect and so we crept down with our hearts in our mouths and reached the glacier unharmed.

To my mind the incident had considerable significance. As I have said, very little new snow indeed had been deposited on the slopes and this cannot have had any appreciable effect on the stability of the old snow which we had unanimously agreed seemed perfectly sound. And yet the avalanche had occurred along our ascending route. That merely indicated that we were not competent to judge the stability of monsoon snow at these altitudes. Anyway I decided there and then to abandon our stores and have nothing further to do with the North Col during the monsoon. Later we were to have substantial evidence that the monsoon snow does not either disappear or consolidate at an altitude higher than 23,000 feet in the region of Mount Everest. We were thus able to provide a definite answer to one of the chief problems which we had come out to solve. In my opinion the only time of year that one can reasonably hope to reach the summit of Mount Everest is during the exceedingly short interval between the end of the winter gales and the arrival of the monsoon. In 1933 there was no such interval.

When we reached Camp III we found a note from Tilman saying that he and Wigram had gone down to Camp II to bring up more food. They had climbed two peaks of over 22,000 feet in the neighbourhood. On the next day, the 17th, we moved a camp up to the head of a big unnamed glacier which flows into the East Rongbuk from the east. From here we climbed the peak known as Khartaphu – 23,600 feet high. We carried the light theodolite with us, but before we could reach the summit clouds had rendered it impossible to do any useful work. However we managed to get some fine views into the country to the east which later proved to be very useful to us. We also took some telephotos of the summits of Everest and Makalu. We descended to Camp II the next day where we met Spender. He had completed several stations on both sides of the Main Rongbuk Glacier and had obtained sufficient data to enable him to draw a large-scale plan of the north face of Everest and to calculate with sufficient precision the altitude of any point on that face, both of which achievements will be extremely useful in planning a fresh assault on the mountain.

The party was now divided into two. Spender, Kempson, and Warren were to attempt to explore the country lying between the East Rongbuk Glacier and the Doyal La while the rest of us remained in the vicinity of Camp II. We moved across to the east and climbed the much-photographed Kellas Rock Peak,

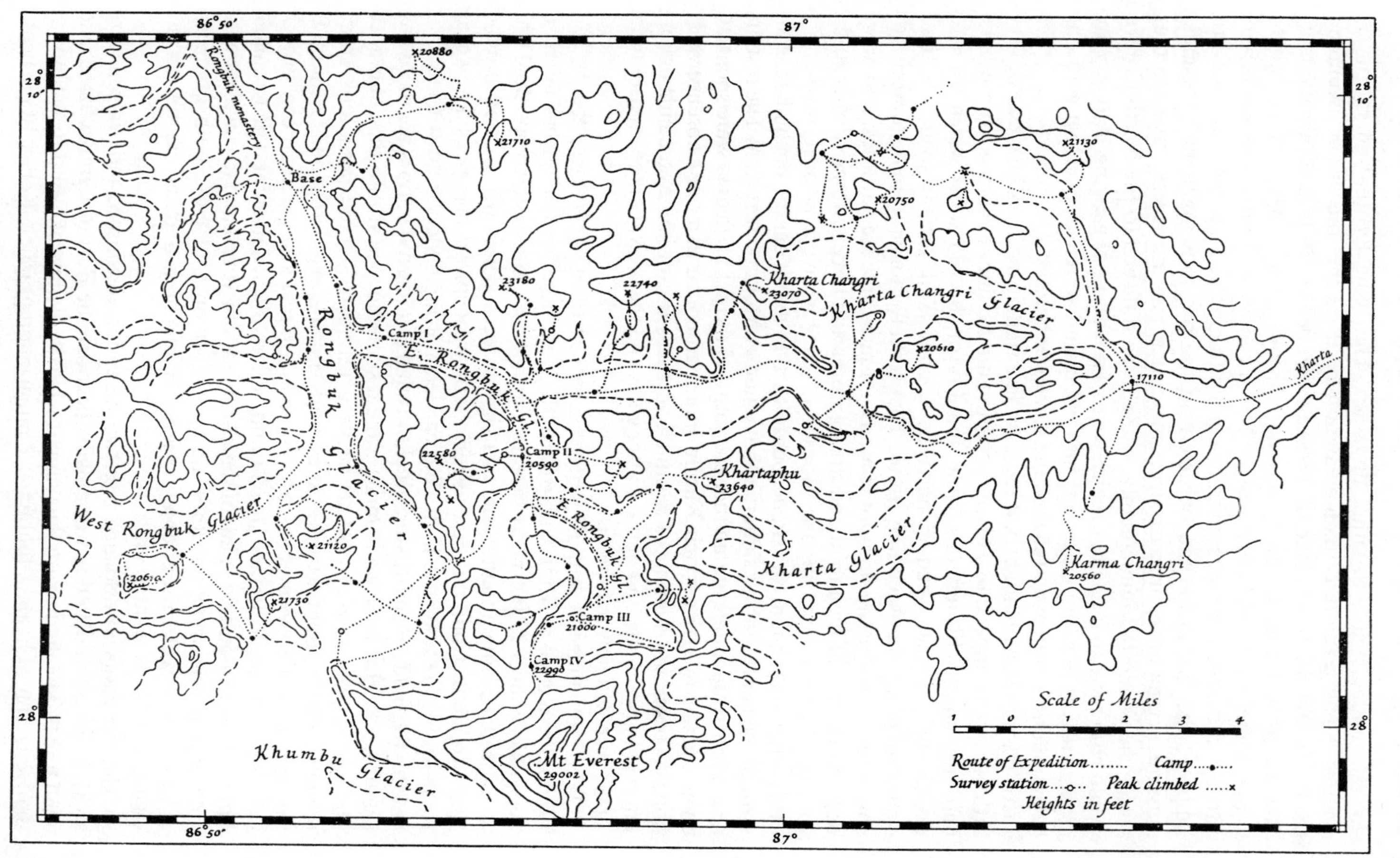
86°50'
87°
28° 10'
Rongbuk monastery
Base
×20880
×21710
×23180
×22740
Kharta Changri
×23070
Kharta Changri Glacier
×20750
×21130
×20610
17110
Kharta
Camp I
E. Rongbuk Gl.
Rongbuk Glacier
West Rongbuk Glacier
22580
Camp II
20590
Khartaphu
×23640
E. Rongbuk Gl.
Kharta Glacier
Karma Changri
20560
×21120
20610
×21730
Camp III
21000
Camp IV
22990
Mt Everest
29002
Khumbu Glacier
28°
Scale of Miles
1 0 1 2 3 4
Route of Expedition
Camp
Survey station
Peak climbed
Heights in feet

23,000 odd feet. This mountain has so often appeared in newspapers under the name of "Mount Everest" that we experienced quite a thrill in reaching its summit. There, as on Khartaphu, we found that there was a very marked and sudden change in the quality of the snow as we reached 23,000 feet. The snow on the ridges below was good and safe, but that lying above 23,000 feet had always to be treated with the utmost caution. After returning to Camp II we climbed the beautiful ice peak which rises above it – it is 22,580 feet high. After this we explored the little valley which joins the main Rongbuk Valley on the east, and climbed two more peaks of 21,000 feet in the neighbourhood. This was done in order to be able to supplement with photographs the work which Spender had done in this valley a fortnight before. We returned to Rongbuk on the 31st and were surprised to find that Kempson was already there. A series of misfortunes had prevented them from completing the task they had set out to do. Their food supply had run short; they had encountered vile weather which seems to pour up through the Arun Gorge during the whole of the monsoon; two of their Sherpas had developed dysentry, and Spender himself had developed a complaint with disturbingly similar symptoms. However they had done some very good work. Spender had completed several good stations in the vicinity of what had come to be known as the Kharta Changri Pass, while Kempson and Warren had climbed two peaks of over 22,000 feet, up one of which they had taken the light photo-theodolite. They also climbed the beautiful peak of Kharta Changri which is just over 23,000 feet high. The rest of the party arrived in heavy rain that evening and the next two days were spent in devouring the luxuries which Karma Paul had collected in our absence and which consisted of two sheep, twenty-one dozen eggs, and a little rancid butter. Tewang and Namgir, the two sick Sherpas, were discharged. The party was greatly weakened by the departure of Kempson, who had to return to England.

Our next intention was to examine the western side of the mountain. Although Mallory in 1921 had visited the watershed in two places he had experienced bad weather while doing so and had not seriously commented on the mountaineering aspect of the southern side. Another task we had was to report on the feasibility of the suggested route up the north-west ridge of the mountain. Tilman, Wigram, Bryant and I left Rongbuk on August 3 making towards the head of the main Rongbuk Glacier. Warren stayed behind with Spender who was still sick. Some days later these two followed us up and completed Spender's work on the north-western aspect of the mountain. After two days' march up the west side of the main valley we divided our forces into two. Tilman and Wigram were to attempt to cross the Lho La to the foot of the Western Cwm while Bryant and I went up the West Rongbuk Glacier. We climbed two peaks, one a fine fluted-ice peak which commanded one of the most magnificent mountain views I have seen, the other Lingtren Nup up which we managed to take the theodolite for a round of angles and photographs. After this we took a camp on to the crest of the watershed and stayed there for two stormy nights. On August 10 from this camp we climbed the triangulated peak, 21,730 feet. The day was an adventurous one. Conditions rendered the climb a very delicate job; on the descent while we were making our way along a narrow ice ridge I heard a roar like a heavy gun going off, felt a jerk of the rope round my waist which nearly cut me in two, and found myself standing alone on the ridge. Bryant had broken away a bit of cornice, had gone down with it, and was now almost hanging on the other end of the rope some way below the crest of the ridge; but he had retained possession of his axe and was thus able cut his way back to me. Later in the descent we got involved in a small snow avalanche which, fortuantely, we were expecting. Early on the following morning, having spent an entertaining night trying to drown the noise of the wind with some of Bryant's extraordinary repertoire of comic songs, we erected the theodolite with considerable difficulty on the crest of the pass and took a round of angles and photographs. Unfortunately the photographs were spoilt by the film jamming in the camera. However we secured several somewhat cloudy views over that interesting section of Nepal which the Sherpas refer to rather vaguely as Solu Khumbu. We also saw up into the myserious Western Cwm. No descent is possible on the southern side of this col, and we were sorely tempted to try to find an exit from the basin of the West Rongbuk Glacier to the west but we had agreed to reassemble at Rongbuk on August 14. On our return there we learnt that Tilman and Wigram had found that there is no route southward from the Lho La, and having climbed a peak in its vicinity, had crossed a difficult pass lying immediately north of the North Peak and descended direct to Camp II. They had then climbed two more 22,000-foot peaks before returning to Rongbuk. While at the head of the main glacier they had found time to examine thoroughly the lower section of the north-west ridge which had been strongly recommended as an alternative route up Mount Everest. They were both convinced that an attack from this quarter would not offer the slightest chance of success. From the mountaineering standpoint these two had put up a fine performance.

After two days' rest we set off once more up the East Rongbuk Glacier, having instructed Karma Paul to meet us in three weeks at Kharta with such surplus gear as remained. Our first objective was the North Peak, though Tilman's report of increasingly bad snow conditions above 22,000 gave us some misgivings as to the advisability of attempting a peak of nearly 25,000 feet at this time of year, and we bitterly regretted having left this until so late. We had two main objects in climbing the peak: one was to be able to secure some telephotographs of the upper part of Everest from its summit, the other was to collect further evidence of the behaviour of monsoon snow at these extreme altitudes. From Camp II we made our way up to and along the great horseshoe ridge of the mountain. We found that the snow was in a frightful condition and the higher we got the worse it became. We had three camps on the mountain, the highest of which we placed at about 23,200 feet, almost directly above the North Col. In order to reach it we had to flog our way through snow up to our waist. The weather was bad and at this camp we spent one exceedingly unpleasant night. Our primus stove ceased to function as the jets were too large for that altitude and we could not melt enough snow for drinking. The next morning we started at dawn but found that the snow was worse than it had been below and soon we were floundering in a seemingly bottomless morass. From where we were we could look down on to the North Col and could see that the large Whymper tents which we had left there in July were now buried under fresh snow. The final ridge of the North Peak we found to be very sharp and under the existing snow conditions it was impossible to reach the summit, and we were regretfully compelled to abandon the struggle. When we regained the East Rongbuk glacier the next day we found Spender waiting for us in the central trough, having completed with much difficulty two stations in the Eastern Cwm.

The next fortnight was spent in making a high level route between the East Rongbuk Glacier and the Doya La above Kharta. It was certainly the most delightful two weeks of the expedition and yielded the most interesting geographical results. We crossed the Kharta Changri pass to what Spender with his arctic terminology had called the Ice Cap Station. Indeed the upper glaciers of this district appear to resemble closely those of the Greenland ice cap. But in their lower reaches they are very Himalayan in character and take a great deal of negotiating. From here we had a delicious time crossing new passses, climbing peaks and unravelling the most interesting mountain topography. The mornings were generally fine, which allowed us to work in camera stations at suitable points all along our route. When we reached the Doya La we experienced again that indescribable pleasure of coming down to living things after a long sojourn in high glacier regions. The smell of grass and flowers was almost intoxicating. On September 6 we reached Kharta, where we hired ponies and hurried as fast as these would carry us to the Choten Nyima La. We spent the remainder of our time climbing in the little-visited Dodang Nyima Range of North Sikkim. As is generally the case, the results of the expedition fell short of our hopes, but our inability to wander far afield enabled us to do more mountaineering than we had intended. Twenty-six peaks, all over 20,000 feet high, had been climbed, the summits of only two of these had previously been reached.

APPENDIX II

Explorations in the Karakoram, 1939

A section of Eric Shipton's paper 'Karakoram 1939' which Dr R. Scott Russell read to the Royal Geographical Society on 4 March, 1940. The full text appears in *The Geographical Journal*, Vol XCV, No 6, June 1940.

The party had approached up the Hispar Glacier with the plan of setting up a central camp on Snow Lake near the Hispar Pass . . .

. . . On August 12 a relay of loads was taken to the top of the Hispar pass, and on the 13th we all occupied a camp there. Two days were spent on top of the pass, during which [Peter] Mott, [Edrik] Fountaine, and I occupied several high triangulation stations. Fazal Ellahi made use of some of the stations for his plane-table survey, and [Scott] Russell and [Campbell] Secord ascended the peak on the Biafo-Hispar watershed north of the Hispar pass that had been climbed by the Workmans in 1908. There is no doubt whatever that it was the same peak. We had with us several photographs of it taken by the Workmans from near the Hispar pass. But whereas they estimated the height at 21,300 feet, both our triangulated height for it and Fazal Ellahi's height worked out at 19,400 feet. The weather was perfect and we all got very extensive views from our various stations, reaching as far as Haramosh and K2. Russell and Secord spent four hours on top of the watershed peak taking photographs, rays, and vertical angles to all the points of interest with the Wild plane-table outfit. The height for the Hispar pass worked out at 16,910 feet, and our fixing placed it 7 miles to the west of its position on the old map. This shortens the length of the Hispar glacier to 30 miles.

On August 15 we descended to the Snow Lake. The failure of the Nagir coolies had forced us to abandon much of our fuel supply on the Hispar glacier. This necessitated a radical alteration of the original plan and the postponement of several projects in the vicinity of the Snow Lake. We spent four days working there, during which time Fazal Ellahi got well started with the survey of the Biafo. At this time of year the upper glacier consisted mostly of dry ice and was perfectly safe to move about on, so on August 19 we left Fazal Ellahi with all the available food and fuel, four porters and his personal servant, to continue his work. Fountaine, Secord, and I descended the Biafo glacier in three days to Askole, while Mott and Russell crossed the pass discovered by Tilman in 1937 to the Cornice glacier. Travel on the Biafo glacier is remarkably easy, as the smooth white ice extends from its upper reaches almost to the snout. Except for camping, we made no use of the extensive ablation valleys which stretch for 20 miles up the glacier and are well filled with grass and fuel. In these ablation valleys were many bear tracks, though we never saw any of the creatures themselves. At Askole, Secord left us to return to Srinagar, and Fountaine and I started with three weeks' food for the Panmah glacier. I was pleased to find that our dealings with the men of Askole in 1937 had left them with confidence and an apparent affection for us, and there was considerable competition among them to accompany us, which was a welcome change after our recent experience with the Nagiris.

The lower Panmah is typical of most of the valleys of the district. It is desolate and barren, and its bed is filled with gravel and mud deposits, with large alluvial fans split up by the present streams into high cliffs and deep gorges. Typical also are the frequent oases: grassy glades, willow and rose thickets irrigated by spring water. The largest of these is the grazing ground of Panmah, which is about 12 miles up the valley, at the snout of the glacier.

We had with us the Zeiss photo-theodolite, and began the survey of the Panmah glacier system with a high station west of Panmah on August 25. Meanwhile the porters moved our camp a few miles up the glacier to the foot of our second station, which we occupied the next day. The weather then broke. We moved our camp across the main glacier to a point opposite the junction of the Choktoi glacier. We were confined to this camp for three days. Angtharkay shot several ibex, which kept us well supplied with meat for the next fortnight or three weeks. On the 30th the weather cleared, and on that day we did a station about 2500 feet above the camp and moved up towards Skinmang at the junction of the Chiring with the main glacier. On August 31 Fountaine, with two Sherpas, went up the Chiring glacier and camped at about 17,000 feet. The next morning he continued up the glacier and soon saw a low col beneath a spur of the mountain that we had identified as Spender's Changtok Peak, which would obviously have led to the north branch of the Sarpo Laggo glacier. Since the view from the col was likely to be limited, he decided to continue up the glacier to a high col two miles to the south, the summit of which he reached without difficulty. The descent down the other side to the Sarpo Laggo glacier was no more difficult. The view to the east included Skyang Kangri (Staircase), K2, Broad Peak, and the Gasherbrum Peaks; to the west the 'Ogre' group, Kanjut, and many other giants. The pass he was on (the long-sought 'New Muztagh Pass') affords a very easy means of communication across the main Asiatic watershed; certainly the quickest and easiest known route between Askole and the Shaksgam river. On the following day Fountaine climbed to the head of another branch of the upper Chiring glacier and reached a col leading to a tributary of the Panmah glacier. From the head of this however there seemed to be a practicable route to the Trango glacier. Compass bearings and photographs from both these cols will be a great help in drawing the map.

Meanwhile on August 31 I climbed a peak some miles up the Chiring glacier on its northern side. The peak was about 19,600 feet high and commanded a magnificent view of the whole district while providing me with an admirable survey station. On September 1 I climbed another small peak above the Drenmang glacier for the same purpose, and saw far up the Nobande Sobande glacier. It is difficult to know why this glacier is so named, for it is really a continuation of the Panmah. Nor did the name convey anything to the local men. I found many bear tracks along the side of the glacier up as far as the Drenmang. Skinmang, where I had my camp, is a delightful spot flanked by gentle grass-covered slopes which stretch for many miles, and watered by clear streams. On September 2 I crossed the Panmah glacier again and fixed another station 2000 feet above its western bank. Fountaine joined me that evening after three days of strenuous mountaineering.

We then moved down the main glacier, surveying on the way, and camped on the 3rd on the right bank of the Choktoi glacier. On the 4th we carried heavy loads 8 miles up the Choktoi, taking with us a large supply of juniper fuel. Travelling was easy, over smooth white ice. We now discharged the Balti coolies. When we entered the upper basin we were met by a stupendous view of the granite peaks of the Ogre group standing a sheer 7000 feet above the glacier. As we rounded the corner, one after another the ice spires crowning the knife-sharp ridges of the peaks flicked into view, brilliantly translucent in the afternoon sun. The walls flanking the right bank of the glacier were so steep and unbroken that we had great difficulty that evening in climbing to a point sufficiently high for a suitable station. The next day we climbed high above the opposite bank, and on the 6th we reached a small peak, about 18,500 feet, on the Nobande-Choktoi watershed. The weather was fine and our view extended far over the ranges to the north, while to the south the Ogre group showed its full magnificence. We moved to the head of the Choktoi, completed our survey of it, and moved camp to the crest of the col between the Choktoi and the

Shimshal
LUPGHAR SAR
MALANGUTTI SAR
DISTEGHIL SAR
YAZGHIL DOMS
YAZGHIL GLACIER
BALTIT
MOMUHIL SAR
NAGAR
Buri Harar
TRIVOR
Gharesa Glacier
YUKSIN GARDEN PEAK
YUTMARU SAR
KUNYANG GLACIER
PUMARI CHHISH
KUNYANG CHHISH
Buattar Glacier
Barpu Glacier
Hispar
Khani Basa Glacier
DIRAN
HISPAR GLACIER
Miar Glacier
MAKRONG CHHISH
SPANTIK
Uyum
(Nushik La)
Bolcho La
Kero Lungma Glacier
MALUBITING
CHOGO LUNGMA GLACIER
Haramosh Glacier
LAILA
Haramosh La
Arandu
KAPULTUNG KUNG
PEAK 1/43M
HARAMOSH

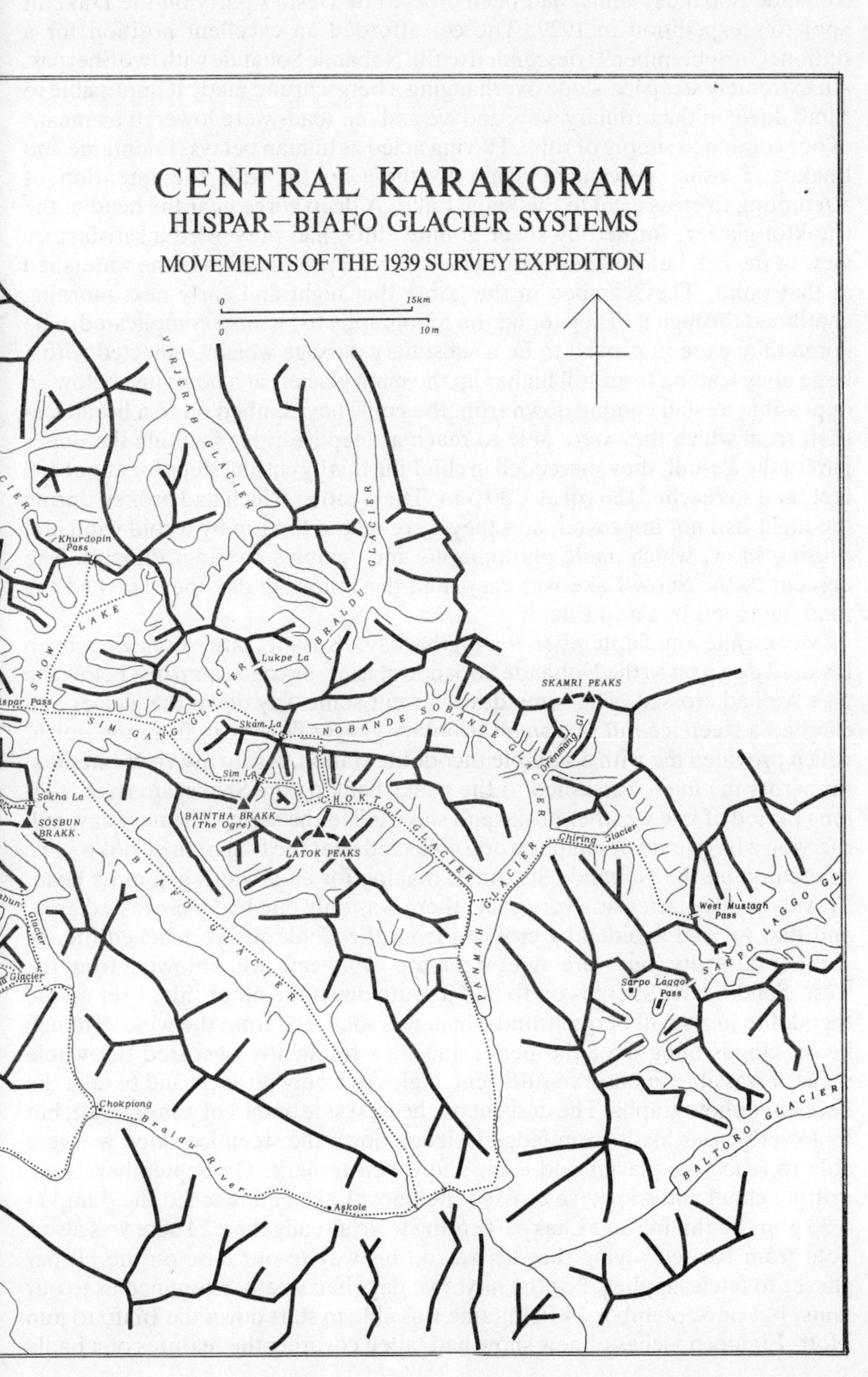
CENTRAL KARAKORAM
HISPAR–BIAFO GLACIER SYSTEMS
MOVEMENTS OF THE 1939 SURVEY EXPEDITION
0
15km
0
10m
VIRJERAB GLACIER
BRALDU GLACIER
Khurdopin Pass
SNOW LAKE
Lukpe La
SKAMRI PEAKS
Hispar Pass
SIM GANG GLACIER
Skam La
NOBANDE SOBANDE GLACIER
Drenmang Gl
Sim La
CHOKTOI GLACIER
Sokha La
SOSBUN BRAKK.
BAINTHA BRAKK (The Ogre)
LATOK PEAKS
Chiring Glacier
BIAFO GLACIER
PANMAH GLACIER
West Mustagh Pass
SARPO LAGGO GL
Sarpo Laggo Pass
Chokpiong
Braldu River
Askole
BALTORO GLACIER

Nobande Sobande, which had been crossed by Desio's party on the Duke of Spoleto's expedition in 1929. The col afforded an excellent position for a station. On September 9 I descended to the Nobande Sobande with two Sherpas. An extremely steep ice-slope overhanging a bergschrund made it impossible to climb down in the ordinary way, and we and our loads were lowered by means of our combined supply of rope. Having acted as human belays, Fountaine and Lhakpa Tensing descended again to the Choktoi with the intention of attempting to cross a col to the Snow Lake. A deep gorge near the head of the Choktoi glacier, formed by sheer granite cliffs, had prevented a satisfactory view of the col, but we knew that there was a deep depression in the watershed at that point. They camped in the gorge that night and early next morning continued through it. They found the topography to be most complicated. The gorge they were in proved to be a subsidiary passage which connected with a large alley leading from still higher up the main glacier, at a point just below an impossible ice-fall coming down from the col. They climbed on to a broad ice-shelf from which they were able to reach a steep ice-ridge flanking the upper part of the ice-fall. they succeeded in climbing this by cutting steps for about 500 feet, and so reached the col at 1.30 p.m. The weather which had broken during the night had not improved, and they were met at the top by a cold wind and drifting snow, which made photographs and compass bearings difficult. The descent to the Snow Lake was easy, and the following day they reached the food dump left by Fazal Ellahi.

Meanwhile on September 9 Angtharkay, Kusang, and I, having been lowered down on to the Nobande Sobande glacier, pitched camp just below the pass we had crossed. The same day we went some way down the glacier and climbed a steep ice-fall of a small tributary glacier flowing in from the north, which provided me with a suitable theodolite station. Again my view extended far across the main watershed to the peaks flanking the Shaksgam river. Our long period of fine weather broke and snow fell in the night. The next day, still carrying a large load of juniper wood collected near the foot of the Choktoi, we pushed on up the Nobande Sobande, making for an obvious gap at its head. Travel on this glacier was very easy; there was only one badly crevassed area, and that we had avoided by crossing from the Choktoi. We reached the col without difficulty, but were met on the top by a heavy wind blowing from the west. Sending the Sherpas on to find a route down the other side, I set up the theodolite in a small bergschrund which was sheltered from the wind. Though heavy clouds hung over the peaks and mist frequently obscured the whole scene, I was able to observe sufficient angles to fix my position and to take the necessary photographs. The descent on the west side of the col was difficult, but by lowering our loads from ledge to ledge down the steep ice-slope we were able to reach the glacier and camp there before dark. On September 11, in drifting cloud and snow, we crossed the Snow Lake and reached the dump at 4.30 p.m. Fountaine and Lhakpa Tensing were already there. There was also a note from Russell saying that he was on his way to our base on the Hispar glacier to fetch supplies. For the next two days bad weather confined us to our tents, but on September 14 Fountaine was able to start down the Biafo to join Mott. Eighteen inches of new snow had fallen covering the features of a badly crevassed area below us, and he had considerable difficulty in the first part of his journey. Late in the evening of the 15th Russell and two Sherpas arrived from across the Hispar pass, which was heavily covered by new snow. He brought news of the out-break of war, which he had heard by wireless. The news, though not altogether unexpected, was a considerable shock. We had been in the field only a few months, but European politics already seemed very remote, and it was hard to realise the meaning of the disaster. It seemed obvious that we must abandon the expedition, but the party was too widely separated for immediate recall, and as less than a month was necessary for the completion of our summer programme, I decided to carry on until we were reassembled in Gilgit. First we had to wait for Fazal Ellahi's party, so that we could make a combined crossing of the Hispar pass, which was likely to become difficult with further snowfalls. He was due back at the dump on September 22.

Russell and I with our three Sherpas went up to the northern glacier of the Snow Lake to explore a way across the main watershed. I had hoped that one of us would be able to make a route to Shimshal, for such a passage would have been extremely interesting, but in the present circumstances a further division of the party seemed hardly justified. After two days we camped at the foot of a steep ridge which led up to the watershed. We were held up there by another heavy fall of snow, but on September 20 we made an ascent of the ridge, which presented us with a fine day's mountaineering and a task that took us all our time to accomplish. Angtharkay and Lobsang came with us to help with the work, but even so we were obliged to leave the theodolite half-way up and did not reach the top until 4.30 p.m. We found ourselves on the crest of the main watershed at a point about 19,500 feet high overlooking a wide snow basin on the northern side. This basin was obviously one of the upper feeders of the Khurdopin. Our regret at having decided not to attempt the complete crossing was intensified by the fact that a gentle snow slope was all that separated us from the Khurdopin glacier, which would have led us to Shimshal. The view from the pass was magnificent and extremely interesting. We took rounds of photographs and compass bearings, but a bitter wind and the lateness of the hour prevented us spending long on top. The descent was much easier than the ascent, and by going hard we succeeded in reaching camp before it was too dark to see.

Before going down the next day we climbed to a point which gave us a view of some of the peaks across the eastern wall of the Snow Lake, to which we took angles. We reached the dump on the 22nd, and our arrival there coincided almost exactly with the arrival of Fazal Ellahi's party. He had completed the survey of the entire Biafo glacier and its tributaries from source to snout. His map is a beautiful piece of work. On September 23 we all crossed the Hispar pass to our dump at Kanibasar. From here, on the 24th, Russell set out for Gilgit with telegrams to inform those interested in us of our movements, and to place our services at the disposal of the Government. He had certain physiological experiments to complete at Makorum, but he reached Gilgit on October 3. Meanwhile I stayed with Fazal Ellahi to supervise the completion of his survey of the Hispar basin. First we went up the Kanibasar glacier, where we camped for three nights. Fortunately the weather had improved and held for the next fortnight. I was very glad to have the opportunity of being with Fazal Ellahi for a long time while he was at work. I was impressed by the skill with which he chose his stations, the speed and neatness with which he worked, the accuracy of his fixings, and the extraordinary energy which he displayed. Next we went up the Jutmaru glacier, and here, as on the Kanibasar, we found that the topography bore little resemblance to that portrayed on the existing maps. The watershed at the heads of both these glaciers was very high indeed, and at only one place did I see a chance of reaching it; though there was not time to attempt to do so. At the head of the Jutmaru we followed for miles the tracks of some creature in the fresh snow. The tracks were a good deal bigger than those made by our boots, and though I suppose they must have been made by bear they did not in the least resemble the bear tracks we had seen in the mud at the sides of the Biafo and Panmah glaciers. The difference was possibly due to the melting of the snow. Fazal Ellahi having completed his work, we returned to Nagir on October 12. At Minapin, one march below Nagir, we met Inayat Khan who, having finished the survey of the areas allotted to him (the whole of the Hispar valley from and including the Kunyang glacier to the Hunza river), had come down to survey the Minapin glacier which he had just completed. We reached Gilgit on the 15th, where we found the rest of the party waiting for us.

I had not seen Mott for two months. On August 19 he and Russell had left the camp on the Snow Lake and set off southwards towards the gap in the West Biafo Wall, which constitutes the only practicable pass from the Biafo to the much-discussed Cornice and Garden glaciers (the local names for which are Sokha and Solu respectively). Tilman had first crossed the pass in the 1937 Shaksgam Expedition and exploded the myth, originated by the Workmans, of an enclosed Cornice glacier. It was not at first clear which route Tilman had followed, so the day before they began the journey Russell and I had reconnoitred the most likely col. They camped the first night at the foot of the short glacier leading up to the col, and on the following morning started early. The first part of the ascent was easy, but for the last 300 feet there was a steep ice-slope and some hard step-cutting was necessary. Tilman chose a more gradual route that brought him some way above and south of the lowest part of the col, but he had difficulty in getting down the far side. It was necessary to relay their loads up the final slope and, while the Sherpas were bringing up the remaining loads, Mott attempted to obtain a plane-table fix on the col. Falling snow and the lack of any fixed points for resection made this impossible. The descent from the col presented no difficulties, and they threaded their way easily down the icefall to the dry glacier below. They were now at the head of a narrow valley shut in by giant precipices of rock and snow. A mile from the pass the glacier turned to the left and a steep bluff prevented any futher view. When the Workmans, and later Tilman, looked down from a high col at the eastern head of the Sosbun it would have in fact appeared enclosed owing to the curtaining effect of this bluff, but it is hard to understand how the Workmans explained the source of the Kuschuchun Lungma river which they crossed at Bisil.

Mott and Russell's first camp over the pass was on the north side of the glacier, and 2 miles from its head. They found some fuel and a welcome bed of grass after weeks spent above the snow-line. The following day Mott began the survey. There were no fixed points visible, so that he was obliged to lay out a base of assumed length and carry out the whole of this part of the survey to an unknown scale and a relative system of heights. Later, on the Solu, he fixed the scales by tying on to two fixed points which were triangulated on the South Hispar Wall, and while at Askole redrew the map to its correct scale with true contours instead of form-lines. Azimuth he obtained by simple observations on Polaris. The whole of this survey would have been rendered far more difficult, if not impossible, without the assistance of the Wild telescopic alidade which enabled him to carry out a graphical triangulation, and fix the relative system of heights with considerable accuracy.

One of the most pleasant aspects of the Sokha and Solu glaciers is the amount of vegetation on the lower slopes. Flowers of every colour and form were a constant delight to the eye during the climbs to the survey stations, and provided Russell with a magnificent field for his botanical work, while a mass of willow and juniper served as an endless source of fuel.

Six miles down the Sokha glacier from the pass a steep and very crevassed tributary glacier descended from a cirque surrounded by gothic pinnacles of rock which Mott was to see again from the west arm of Sosbun. There are two further tributary glaciers joining the Sokha on the south side. Russell ascended the most westerly of these in the hope of finding a pass over the watershed, but the col he reached (16,500 feet), contrary to expectations, proved to be on a subsidiary ridge south of which a stream led down to the Basha valley.

On the sixth day the party descended the ablation valley on the right bank of the Sokha glacier, reaching the Solu which they crossed, and made camp in the ablation valley on its west bank. The following morning, while Russell continued his botanical collecting, Mott proceeded up the Solu far enough to see round the bend, a mile from its head, where the glacier takes a sharp turn to the east. From his plane-table station, on a hillside surrounded by willows, grass and flowers, he could see the whole of the basin hemmed in by the Biafo rock wall, and the col Tilman reached from the Snow Lake. It is doubtful whether a descent west from the col is possible owing to the very formidable ice fall at the head of the Solu. Tilman did not attempt it. They came across many fresh bear tracks, which are common in this area, though the animals themselves were not seen.

On August 27 they moved down to the snout of the Solu glacier where there is quite a large grazing village named Dabados, where they were able to buy fresh food. They spent two days there rounding off the survey of the two glaciers, and then descended to the Basha valley, whence they travelled to Askole by the normal route. At Askole Russell left Mott and proceeded up the Biafo to meet me on the Snow Lake. Mott returned down the Askole valley as far as Chokpiong to survey the Hoh Lungma and Sosbun glaciers. From his first station on a ridge west of the Hoh Lungma nullah he was fortunately able to pick up Kanjut Sar and Conway's Ogre which, with Ganchen, gave him a perfect fix. The view from this station was magnificent, the whole area to be surveyed being visible. Four main glaciers drain into the Hoh Lumba river. The largest of these, the Sosbun, flows southwards and, at its head, splits into two arms which are divided by a narrow rock ridge. The western arm flows beneath the pinnacles the party had previously seen from the Sokha glacier. It was from a col above its western arm that the Workmans and Tilman looked down on to the head of the Sokha. Tilman took the western arm of the Sosbun for the Hoh Lungma, but according to local tradition the name refers to the glacier flowing north-east from Ganchen. The Hoh Lungma is joined by another glacier, flowing from the west, named the Tsilbu. Two weeks later Fountaine ascended this glacier and crossed a col (17,000 feet) at its head to the Basha valley. South of the Hoh Lungma a smaller glacier, the Chongahanmung, drains into a wide sandy flat. In Spender's compilation the name Zarn glacier appears to refer to this glacier. Owing to bad weather it was two days before Mott was able to get a second fixing. There were several heavy snowfalls and the temperature dropped. At the end of a week he completed the survey of the Hoh Lungma and its adjacent glaciers and moved camp to the divide of the Sosbun. From the top of the ridge he was again able to check his position in relation to Kanjut Sar. Fountaine meanwhile had descended the Biafo glacier after leaving me on the Snow Lake, and on September 18 met Mott in the Hoh Lungma valley just below the glacier.

It had been intended that Mott and Fountaine should work together from now on. But unfortunately Mott had developed a form of septic rash which forced him to lie up for several days, and as the time for the return of the expedition to Gilgit was drawing close, it was decided to abandon the proposed survey of the Kero Lungma glacier. When he was somewhat better, Mott completed his work in the Hoh Lungma area and made his way back to Gilgit *via* Rondu and Astor, crossing the Ganto La (above the Basha valley) and Harpo La on the way. Lhakpa, who was suffering from severe toothache, remained with Mott while the other two Sherpas went with Fountaine.

The latter party made their way up the Hoh Lungma glacier and camped about a mile from a steep col at the head of the Tsilbu, which is flanked by Hikmul on the south and a low rock ridge on the north. The next day they set out to cross the col (later named the Hikmul pass). The first one and a half hours were through deep snow, but after that the ground steepened and they had to cut their way up an ice-slope covered by a thin layer of loose snow. After negotiating two difficult bergschrunds, some rocks and a steep gully, they reached the top of the col, from which Fountaine took a round of photographs and bearings. To the east the Ogre Peaks could be seen, while westwards they had a fine view up the Chogo Lungma glacier to Haramosh. It was surprising to see that a few miles from its snout there was a right-angled bend in the glacier. After descending the col on the other side they reached the snout of the glacier by evening. The valley they were in was exceedingly steep and dropped 8000 feet from the col they had crossed to the Basha valley, in a distance of less than 4 miles. This made the descent to the village of Bisil difficult. From Bisil to Arandu the party had further trouble owing to the fact that a rope bridge between the two places was down.

From Arandu Fountaine the two Sherpas started up the Chogo Lungma on September 26 to attempt to cross the Haramosh pass at its head. They took with them enough food for ten days and carried heavy loads. They followed an ablation valley which ran along the northern bank of the glacier and provided them with an easy route. On the first day they camped early, about 3 miles up the glacier, so that they might prepare a large supply of *tsampa* in order to conserve their paraffin when they got beyond the wood fuel in the higher reaches of the glacier. The next day they continued up the ablation valley, which was wide and well wooded. About 5 miles above its snout the main valley took a decided turn to the north, confirming what they had seen from the Hikmul pass. They passed several deserted shepherd villages during the day and camped that night by the last willow tree on the north side of the glacier, about 10 miles from the snout. They had left the last of the juniper 2 miles lower down. Here again they found a great number of bear tracks. A little farther on they left the ablation valley and proceeded up a band of white ice on the glacier. At about this point a large glacier joins from the south, at the head of which they saw a col which on their side appeared to be practicable. On the night of September 28 they camped on the south bank, at a point about 2 miles below the junction of Haramosh. On this side of the glacier at about 13,500 feet there was still plenty of willow. The following day they went up the Haramosh glacier and camped on its north bank about 5 miles below their pass, which they reached on September 30 after a laborious trudge through deep snow. The view down the other side of the Haramosh pass presented a dramatic contrast from the great glacier they had just come up. Directly below them at the foot of a steep rock face was a thick jungle. The willow and birch trees in their autumn foliage filled the bottom of the valley with gold and red for 4 miles, where the colour changed to the dark green of pine forest. Beyond this deep well of colour Dobani stood in splendid isolation. To the south stood the mighty cliffs of Haramosh draped in hanging glaciers. Later from one of these they saw an avalanche fall which travelled 4 miles down the valley. They climbed down the rock face, which was quite difficult, and in places dangerous owing to falling stones and ice, and reached the valley 4500 feet below by nightfall. Three days later they reached Gilgit, when for the first time they heard news of the war . . .

APPENDIX III

Eric Earle Shipton (1907–77)

by Charles Warren

The Alpine Club obituary notice first published in *The Alpine Journal* Vol. 83 No. 327 1978

The appearance of an obituary notice on Eric Shipton in *The Times* at the end of March 1977 must have come as a shock to many of his friends. One had got into the habit of thinking of Eric as the grand old man of mountain exploration who went on for ever whilst, as the years passed by, he became ever more distinguished-looking in personal appearance and bearing.

I remember attending a committee meeting of the Club at which, in the absence of the President, Shipton was in the chair. An item under discussion was nominations for the next Presidency. Suggestions were being made, but then, suddenly, we all saw the light and realized that the obvious heir to the throne was in our midst. His protestations that he might be in Patagonia were brushed aside and we convinced him that we wanted a President who was still active in the field and that any defection from club functions while he was *on active service*, so to speak, could be looked after by the V.P.'s.

I suppose that with Howard Somervell, that great man, Eric Shipton must have been one of our most distinguished Presidents of recent years. Certainly he was deeply respected by young and old alike, both for his great achievements, continued activities and, above all, for the integrity of his outlook on mountaineering matters. A speech that he made at an annual dinner during his Presidency was one of the finest Elder Statesman pronouncements on a mountaineering philosophy that the Club has ever been given and the Editor of the *AJ*, realising its significance, captured it for the pages of the Journal.

One of the splendid things about Eric Shipton was that, although he ended up by being a highly professional explorer, he always managed to retain the emotional integrity of the old master amateurs towards mountaineering as a sport. Never, at any time, was he willing to sell his soul for a mess of mass-media pottage. Talking of a small expedition he took to Patagonia he says: 'My own motive for launching it was to satisfy a desire, of many years standing, to make the acquaintance of this strange region: for, like Tilman, I had long been intrigued by its remarkable geography.' This kind of statement explains a great deal about Eric. It tells us why he became our greatest mountaineer explorer instead of just the 'conqueror' of Everest; a title that would have made him feel acutely embarrassed. And although many of us would have liked him to have been the leader of the expedition that made the first ascent of Mount Everest, I for one, can understand why he was not, eventually, chosen to do so – the truth of the matter is that, by that time, his heart was not truly in it. Having discovered the route to the top by way of the South Col he had really played his part, as the great explorer he was. For him it was the discovery that counted, not the conquest.

Shipton was undoubtedly one of the greatest mountaineer explorers there has ever been. One could enumerate his exploits indefinitely, but fortunately for us he has placed them on record, for our delectation, in the admirable books he wrote; and in his numerous articles in journals. Two of his books have become mountaineering classics. His first, *Nanda Devi*, was pronounced by Winthrop Young – 'among the best books of adventure known to me'. But the one that has always appealed to me most of all is *Upon That Mountain*. On a front end-paper of my copy I find that I have pencilled: 'Possibly Eric's best book; and certainly the one that states his mountaineering philosophy in his most forthright manner. This is what we heard so often from his lips during the Tibetan Everest expeditions.'

But now, to become more personal, what kind of person was Eric? The first time I heard of him was when I was an undergraduate at Cambridge in the great days of the CUMC. He was then active in the Alps and stories of his extrication from a 'moulin' on the Mer de Glace and of an entangled adventure on the Aiguille Ravanel were then legendary. But it was not until 1935 that I first became personally acquainted with him, when he invited me to join his now famous and at the time little publicized, but most successful, Reconnaissance expedition to Mount Everest.

This must surely have been one of the most enjoyable, as well as the most scientifically productive, of all Everest expeditions. We were instructed to examine post-monsoon snow conditions on the mountain, which we did up to a height of 7000m. And then, having established that they became impossible above that altitude, and highly dangerous on the slopes below the North Col, we retreated and proceeded to explore and map the environs of Everest in a systematic manner.

Not the least enjoyable aspect of this expedition was the part played by its members in helping Michael Spender, our professional surveyor, with his photogrammetric survey. We all took part in this; which inevitably involved exploration of new country and ended up with first ascents of 24 mountains of over 6000m in height. Shipton was in his element in all of this, and it was in the course of these explorations that he and Dan Bryant, the New Zealander, climbed a peak on the watershed to the west of Mount Everest which gave them the glimpse of the Western Cwm which led to Eric's epoch-making suggestion that an approach to the mountain up the Khumbu glacier might turn out to be the best way to the summit.

In the course of three expeditions through Tibet to the mountain I spent much time talking to, and arguing with, Eric and this was most stimulating. He always delighted in taking up the opposite point of view in any discussion, arguing that black was white just for the Devil of it. His reasoning was often wrong; but in the course of these arguments something stimulating always came out of them so that the journeys across Tibet and the long hours sitting about in tents on the mountain were never dull when one was with him. In the course of such conversation I learnt that his great regret was that he had never had the opportunity of a formal training in anything once he had left school. He would have liked to have been trained as a surveyor, a geologist, a zoologist, or what-you-will in the line of his general interests of exploration, and at the time I knew him closely I gathered that this worred him and made him feel insecure. But the marvel is that through sheer integrity of outlook he trained himself to become the World's greatest mountain-explorer. Perhaps it was just because of his lack of formal training in one narrow field that Eric, who was a dreamer of dreams, became the great man he was. At heart he was a poet and, although he did not actually write poetry, his books were full of the stuff that poets' dreams are made of. Despite his lament over his lack of a specific professional training he managed to establish a reputation as a natural philosopher on mountain exploration. His many published statements on the subject have left us in no doubt about his thinking on the matter. And it is interesting that some recent exploits on very big mountains have tended to endorse his constantly expressed contention that small expeditions, even to the World's greatest mountains, are potentially capable of being as successful as large and expensive ones.

For those of us who have had the pleasure of travelling and arguing with Eric Shipton in some remote mountain ranges, the news of his unexpected death brought sorrow, and feelings of sadness at our loss. One is consoled however by the certain knowledge that he has joined the ranks of the immortals amongst our brethren of the Mountain World.

APPENDIX IV

Selected Bibliography

All publications originate from London unless otherwise noted.

Other books by Shipton

The True Book About Everest (Muller, 1955) also published as *Men Against Everest* (Prentice-Hall, New Jersey, 1956) A children's book.

That Untravelled World (Hodder and Stoughton, 1969) An autobiography.

Tierra del Fuego – The Fatal Lodestone (Charles Knight, 1973)

Books with mountaineering information or comment

H. W. Tilman – The Seven Mountain-Travel Books (Diadem, 1983)
An omnibus edition incorporating four books in which Tilman describes climbs with Shipton.

Kamet Conquered by F. S. Smythe (Gollancz, 1932)

Everest 1933 by Hugh Ruttledge (Hodder and Stoughton, 1934)

Camp 6 by F. S. Smythe (Hodder and Stoughton, 1937)

Everest: The Unfinished Adventure by Hugh Ruttledge (Hodder and Stoughton, 1937) The official account of the 1936 expedition.

Mountain Prospect by Scott Russell (Chatto and Windus, 1946)
Contains a long account of the 1939 Karakoram Expedition.

The Antique Land by Diana Shipton (Hodder and Stoughton, 1950).

The Story of Everest by W. H. Murray (Dent, 1953)

To the Third Pole by G. O. Dyhrenfurth (Werner Laurie, 1955)
Provides a contemporary analysis of the early Everest expeditions.

Abode of Snow by Kenneth Mason (Rupert Hart Davis, 1955)
Similarly informed analysis of Shipton's expeditions by another expert commentator.

High Adventure by Edmund Hillary (Hodder and Stoughton, 1955)
Contains some penetrating observations about the 1951 Everest Reconnaissance Expedition.

The Book of Modern Mountaineering by Malcolm Milne (Arthur Barker, 1968)
Includes an illustrated chapter by Shipton 'The Patagonian Andes and the Cordillera Darwin'.

Another Ascent of the World's Highest Peak (Foreign Languages Press, Peking, 1975) The first undisputed ascent of the North Ridge with many interesting photographs.

In the Throne Room of the Mountain Gods by Galen Rowell
(Sierra Club Books, San Francisco/Allen and Unwin, 1977)

Everest by Walt Unsworth (Allen Lane/Houghton Mifflin, Boston 1981)
A comprehensive history – essential background reading.

Springs of Enchantment by John Earle (Hodder and Stoughton, 1981)

Alpine Journal articles in addition to those in this book.

Mount Kenya by P. Wyn Harris (*AJ*, November 1929). An account of his climbs with Shipton.

The Kamet Expedition by F. S. Smythe (*AJ*, November 1931). Includes several interesting photos that do not appear in 'Kamet Conquered'.

Mountains of the Moon by E. E. Shipton (*AJ*, May 1932)

Lasher Plain by E. E. Shipton (*AJ*, May 1934). An illustrated account of the crossing from Tibet to Sikkim with Lawrence Wager in 1934.

The Nanda Devi Basin by E. E. Shipton (*AJ*, May 1935)

Survey of the Nanda Devi District by E. E. Shipton (*AJ*, May 1937). Not to be overlooked as other references to this trip are so skimpy. Good photos of Dunagiri. See also *HJ* Vol. IX 1937.

The Shaksgam Expedition by E. E. Shipton (*AJ*, May 1938). Includes photos of the Aghil Range that do not appear in 'Blank on the Map'.

The Karakoram Expedition, 1939 by R. Scott Russell (*AJ*, November 1940)

High Pasture by G. F. Peaker (*AJ*, May 1944). Alpine anecdotes involving Shipton.'. . . it is generally held that no amateur, however able, is as good as the best guides at feats of sheer endurance. I am inclined to think that Shipton comes near to being the exception to this Rule ... he was a very remarkable goer . . .'

The Arch by E. E. Shipton (*AJ*, May 1948)

Mustagh Ata by E. E. Shipton (*AJ*, May 1948)

Bogda Ola by E. E. Shipton (*AJ*, November 1950)

The Reconnaissance of Mount Everest, 1951 by W. H. Murray (*AJ*, November 1952)

The Cho Oyu Expedition, 1952 by R. C. Evans (*AJ*, May 1953)

Crossing the Patagonian Ice-cap by H. W. Tilman (*AJ*, November 1956).

The Imperial College Karakoram Expedition, 1957 by E. E. Shipton (*AJ*, November 1958)

Two Visits to the Andes of Southern Patagonia by Eric Shipton (*AJ*, November 1960). Activities around Lago Argentino with photos that are not in 'Land of Tempest'.

Some reflections on Modern Climbing by Eric Shipton (*AJ*, May 1967). Shipton was President of the Alpine Club at this time – this is the substance of his speech at the 1966 Annual Dinner.

A Visit to Alaska by Eric Shipton (*AJ*, May 1967)

Mount Burney by Eric Shipton (*AJ*, 1975)

Review of Walt Unsworth's Everest book by Peter Lloyd (*AJ*, 1982). Contains another long analysis of the 1953 leadership crisis.

Sir Percy Wyn Harris an obituary notice by Sir Jack Longland (*AJ*, 1982). There are several relevant comments including the assertion that Wyn Harris's and Shipton's final bid to reach the North Col in 1936 was as a result of goading by Frank Smythe . . . '[he] taunted them with cowardice'.

Geographical Journal articles in addition to those in this book.

Photographic Surveys in the Mount Everest Region by Michael Spender (*GJ*, October 1936).

The Mount Everest Expedition of 1938 by H. W. Tilman with Appendix – The Gyangkar (Nyonno Ri) Range by E. E. Shipton (*GJ*, December 1938).

The Shaksgam Expedition of 1937 (*GJ*, April 1938)

The Karakoram Survey 1939: A New Map by P. G. Mott (*GJ*, September 1950)

Everest: The Reconnaissance of the Southern Route by E. E. Shipton (*GJ*, June 1952)

The Expedition to Cho Oyu by Eric Shipton (*GJ*, June 1953)

Norton of Everest: An Appreciation by Eric Shipton (*GJ*, March 1955)

Explorations in Patagonia by Eric Shipton (*GJ*, September – December 1959)

Volcanic Activity on the Patagonian Ice-cap by Eric Shipton (*GJ*, December 1960)

Eric Shipton – an obituary notice (*GJ*, July 1977). Other lengthy obituaries appeared in *The Times*, 30 March 1977, *The American Alpine Journal*, 1978 and *Mountain* 55, 1977.

The Himalayan Journal Vols VII, VIII, IX, X, XI, and XX also contain references to various expeditions which are often more thoroughly illustrated than the *AJ* and *GJ* versions.

APPENDIX V

Shipton's Mountaineering Record 1922–1973

Relevant pages in the text and books noted at the end of each item

c.1922/23
Later school years – passion for Geography (particularly volcanoes) inspired by writings of Whymper and Tyndall. Visited Pyrenees with family – fascinated by the Cirque de Gavarnie. pages 315–320

1924
Norway and Alps: Mountain-walking in the Jotunheimen with Gustav Sommerfelt. December First climbs: a guided ascent of the Gross Lohner and the Tschingelochtighorn above Adelboden. pages 320–322

1925
Alps Easter A solo climb up a gully on cliffs above Lake Como and a guided attempt on Monte Disgrazia. First alpine season in the Dauphiné guided by Elie Richard. pages 321–329

1926
Alps Another intensive season with Elie Richard page 329

1927
Lake District and Alps Easter spent rock-climbing with Gilbert Peaker and then the first part of the alpine season climbing in the major French ranges with Peaker. Later in the season they moved to Zermatt where they hired the noted guide Theophile Theytaz and completed several major climbs including the Zmutt Ridge. pages 330–331

1928
Alps Very active fourth alpine season with Peaker and H. M. Kelly: Matterhorn by the Zmutt Ridge descending the Italian Ridge; Haute Route; traverse of Drus and Grepon; Requin. Rochefort Ridge with Jack Longland and George Trevelyan; Aig Verte with Graham MacPhee. pages 333–334

1929
East Africa: Mt Kenya January, with Percy Wyn Harris and Gustav Sommerfelt. Attempts on the North East Face of Batian and South Ridge of Nelion. Shipton and Wyn Harris then made the first ascent of Nelion by South East Face followed by traverse to Batian. All three climbers repeated this climb shortly afterwards. pages 336–350

East Africa: Mt Kenya November, with Pat Russell. Repeated the Nelion-Batian route and made first ascent of the South East Gully of Point John. page 352

1930
East Africa: Kilimanjaro Near success on Kibo and ascent of Mawenzi with Bill Tilman. page 352

East Africa: Mt Kenya First ascent of West Ridge of Batian with Bill Tilman. The pair also climbed two pinnacles above the Mackinder Valley, the North West Face of Point Piggott and the South Gully of Midget Peak. On the latter climb they were lucky to escape disaster during the descent when Tilman fell, became unconscious, and had to be lowered to a ledge by Shipton who was unbelayed. pages 325–363

1931
India (Garhwal): The Kamet Expedition June-August, with Frank Smythe (leader), Bentley Beauman, E. St.J Birnie, Raymond Greene and R. Holdsworth, Lewa, Achung, Nima Tendrup, Nima, Pasang Bhotia, Nima Dorje, Ondi, Nerbu, Kesar Singh and others. The expedition made the first ascent. The summit (25,447 ft.) was reached by Smythe and Holdsworth, and Shipton and Lewa on June 21 and by Birnie, Greene and Kesar Singh two days later. On July 8 Shipton and Nima climbed a 19,500 ft. peak.

The expedition moved to the Arwa Valley where Shipton took part in eight more first ascents. see *Kamet Conquered* by F. S. Smythe and *That Untravelled World.*

1932
East Africa: Ruwenzori January. Ascents of the main summits of Mts Speke, Baker and Stanley (mostly 3rd ascents) with Bill Tilman. pages 364–369

1933
Tibet: Mount Everest Expedition March-June with Hugh Ruttledge (leader), Frank Smythe, Percy Wyn Harris, Lawrence Wager, Jack Longland, Tom Brocklebank, Colin 'Ferdie' Crawford, E. St.J. Birnie, Raymond Greene, George Wood-Johnson, W. McLean, E. C. Thompson, Hugh Bousted, E. O. Shebbeare, W. Smijth-Windham, Karma Paul, Lhakpa Chedi, Lewa, Nursang, Sonam Topgye, Nima Tendrup, Pasang Bhotia, Pasang Kikuli, Pasang Dorje, Kusang, Da Tsering, Angtharkay and others. The expedition established Camp 6 at 27,400 ft. in late May and two summit attempts followed (by Wyn Harris and Wager, and Smythe and Shipton). Both were stopped by poor snow conditions in the Great Couloir at about 28,100 ft. (on the second attempt only Smythe reached this point, Shipton having returned to Camp 6 earlier). Various peaks were climbed at the end of the expedition: Ruttledge, Crawford, Shipton and Brocklebank climbed one of 22,340 ft. above the Rapiu La, and Shipton and Brocklebank climbed a 22,000 ft. peak above Camp 1. pages 369–394

Tibet/Sikkim: Lasher Plain July, with Lawrence Wager, Pasang Bhotia, Sonam, Aila and others. They broke away from the returning Everest expedition to attempt a crossing from the Lasher Plain to Sikkim. Climbed a 20,000 ft. peak in the Nyonno Ri range, then made the second ascent of Lhonak Peak (21,260 ft.). see Bibliography

1934
India (Garhwal): Nanda Devi and Badrinath ranges with H. W. Tilman, Angtharkay, Pasang Bhotia and Kusang. May/June. First passage of the upper Rishi Gorge to gain access to the Nanda Devi Sanctuary. Explored the northern section making the ascent of a 21,000 ft. peak (possibly Sakram) and two attempts on a 23,000 ft. peak. They also reached three cols on the eastern rim. pages 47–97 and 401–412.

July. The party then moved to the Badrinath range where they crossed the watershed by a pass at the head of the Arwa Valley to reach Chatarangi Bamak Glacier, and then the Gangotri Glacier and Gaumukh. pages 99–112 and 413

August. The party crossed the Badrinath/Kedarnath watershed by a difficult pass at the head of the Satopanth Glacier. pages 113–136 and 413–415

September. They returned to the Nanda Devi Sanctuary where they climbed a short distance up the South Ridge of Nanda Devi. Shipton, Angtharkay and Kusang then made the first ascent of Maiktoli (22,320 ft.) and finally all five climbers left the Sanctuary via the dangerous Sunderdhunga Col. pages 137–152 and 415–419

1935

Tibet: Mt Everest Reconnaissance Expedition May/August, with Shipton as leader and Dan Bryant, Michael Spender, Charles Warren, Edwin Kempson, Edmond Wigram, Bill Tilman, Karma Paul, Angtharkay, Rinsing, Tensing, Pasang Bhotia, Kusang, Sen Tensing and eleven other sherpa porters. After a brief exploration of the Nyonno Ri range, the expedition arrived at the East Rongbuk Glacier where the body of Maurice Wilson was found. A 'reconnaissance in force' was mounted on the North Ridge but soon abandoned in the face of poor snow conditions. Members of the expedition then climbed over twenty peaks around the northern flanks of Everest. Shipton's ascents included Kellas's Rock Peak 23,000 ft. (with Tilman and Wigram), Khartaphu 23,640 ft. (with Warren and Kempson) and peaks of the Lingtren group (with Bryant).
pages 421–429 and 777–783

1936

Tibet: Mt Everest Expedition March/June with Hugh Ruttledge (leader), Eric Shipton, Frank Smythe, Percy Wyn Harris, Edwin Kempson, Edmond Wigram, Charles Warren, Peter Oliver, Noel Humphreys, John Morris, Jim Gavin, W. Smijth-Windham, Karma Paul, Jemadar Lachiman Singh, Pasang Bhotia, Tsering Tarkay, Rinsing, Ondi, Tewang, Ang Tsering, Nursang, Angtharkay, Da Tsering and others. The attempt failed at the North Col in the face of repeated heavy snowfalls. Shipton and Wyn Harris had a lucky escape from a slab avalanche below North Col. pages 429–430

India: Nanda Devi Sanctuary August/October. An Indian survey expedition led by Major Osmaston, with Fasil Eligh (probably the Fasal Ellahi of the 1939 Karakoram expedition) and others. Shipton joined as route advisor. Sherpas included Angtharkay, Sen Tensing, Gyalgen, Ang Dawa, Rinsing and Tensing Norgay (who was ill for part of the trip). Shipton accompanied Osmaston into the Sanctuary and while the former surveyed the latter explored. A 21,770 ft. peak on the eastern rim was climbed, the col below the South Ridge of Changabang (Shipton's Col) was reached from the Changabang Glacier (with Angtharkay and Ang Dawa). Shipton, Angtharkay and Sen Tensing then left the Inner Sanctuary and moved to the Rhamani Glacier where they attempted the South West Ridge of Dunagiri (reaching 23,184 ft.), crossed the Bagini Pass, reconnoitred the northern approaches to Dunagiri and finally surveyed the glacier and valley below Nanda Ghunti. see *Bibliography*

1937

India (now Pakistan) and China: The Shaksgam Expedition May/September with Bill Tilman, John Auden, Michael Spender, Angtharkay, Lhakpa Tensing, Sen Tensing, Lobsang, Ila, Nukku, Angtensing and others. A major survey expedition to the northern extremities of the range. This was reached by a long approach march crossing the Sarpo Laggo Pass. From a base camp in the Shaksgam Valley the party explored and mapped the Aghil Range and the northern approaches to K2. They proceeded up the Skamri (Crevasse) Glacier, exploring and mapping as they advanced. The climbers then split into groups. Tilman led a small team west across Snow Lake to investigate the enigma of the Cornice Glacier, Auden return to Askole via the Nobande Sobande Glacier and Shipton and Spender with Angtharkay and others mapped and explored the Braldu Glacier system before returning via Shimshal and Hunza. A number of minor peaks were climbed. pages 141–304 and 436–451

1938:

Tibet: Mount Everest Expedition April/June with Tilman as leader and Noel Odell, Charles Warren, Peter Lloyd, Peter Oliver, Frank Smythe, Karma Paul, Angtharkay, Kusang, Pasang Bhotia, Tensing Norgay, and others. Another abortive attempt.
see *Everest, 1938* and pages 430–451

1939
India (now Pakistan): The Karakoram Survey Expedition July/October In collaboration with the Survey of India. Shipton was leader with surveyors Peter Mott, Fazal Ellahi and Inayat Khan and mountaineers Edrik Fountaine, Scott Russell, Campbell Secord and A. F. Betterton, with Angtharkay, Kusang and others. The expedition made a comprehensive survey of the Hispar, Biafo, Sosbun, Sokha/Solu, Kero Lungma, Chogo Lungma, Panmah, Choktoi, Nobande Sobande and Snow Lake glacier systems. Several minor peaks were climbed. pages 451–454 and 786–79

1941
China: Kashgar Range September, with Lhakpa Tensing and others. A visit to the Bostan Terek valley to view 18,000 ft. granite peaks. Shipton (accompanied for part of the way by Lhakpa) climbed the second highest peak in the group. pages 476–485

1942
China: Bogdo Ola group September. Brief visit with Michael Gillett and Lhakpa Tensing revealed possibilities for a later expedition. pages 543–562

1947
China: Tushuk Tagh Range near Kashgar January, with Diana Shipton, Lhakpa, Gyalgen and a local man, Uzman Akhun. A successful campaign to penetrate the range to reach a huge natural arch that could be seen from the distant plains. pages 508–515

China: Mustagh Ata August, with Bill Tilman and Gyalgen. The trio came close to success on this 24,758 ft. peak by an easy but long route. pages 516–558

1948
China: Bogdo Ola group July, with Bill Tilman, Lhakpa Tensing and Agasha. They circumnavigated the massif gaining various vantage points on its ridges – notably c.17,000 ft. on the East Ridge. pages 553–574

China: Chakragil (Chakar Aghil) September, with Bill Tilman, Gyalgen and a local man, Mahmud. They made an attempt on the North Ridge of this 22,071 ft. peak, reaching a height of 17,000 ft. pages 575–585

1951
Nepal: The Mount Everest Reconnaissance Expedition August/October with Shipton as leader and Mike Ward, Bill Murray, Tom Bourdillon, Ed Hillary, Earle Riddiford, Angtharkay, Pasang Bhotia, Nima, Sen Tensing and six other sherpas. They climbed the Khumbu Icefall and studied the Western Cwm from the slopes of Pumori establishing the feasibility of a route up the mountain from Nepal. The climbers also made a series of exploratory travels among the mountain groups to the south-east and south-west of Everest, crossing cols in the Baruntse area to the south-east and in the Cho Oyu and Gauri Sankar groups to the west. pages 595–622

1952
Nepal: The Cho Oyu Expedition March/June, with Shipton (as leader), Charles Evans, Campbell Secord, Alf Gregory, Tom Bourdillon, Ray Colledge, Griffith Pugh and the New Zealanders, Ed Hillary, George Lowe and Earle Riddiford. After an initial reconnaissance the party made an attempt on the West Face from the Nangpa La and reached ice-cliffs at 22,500 ft. before retreating. The expedition then concentrated its activities to the west of Nangpa La where they climbed eleven mountains between 21,000 and 23,000 ft. In June, Hillary, Lowe, Evans and Shipton with eight porters made a long journey to the Hongu Basin, where they climbed two 22,000 ft. peaks and thence

past Makalu to a col overlooking the Kangshung Glacier in Tibet. They returned by the Barun Valley. see *That Untravelled World* by Eric Shipton.

1957

Pakistan: The Imperial College Karakoram Expedition July/September, with Shipton as leader, Keith Miller, Geoff Bratt, Brian Amos, Graham Budd, Roger Cratchley, Peter Grimley, Chris Gravina and Mr Qureshi (Survey of Pakistan). Surveying on the Bilafond, Lolofond, Siachen, Teram Shehr and K12 glaciers. see *Bibliography*

1957/58

Argentina: Patagonia November/February, with Geoff Bratt, John Mercer, Peter Miles, Peter James, Barney Dickinson and John Cotton. Exploratory trips up several glaciers at the heads of Lagos Viedma and Argentino. A difficult 8,000 ft. peak above the Onelli Glacier was climbed by Shipton and Bratt. pages 641–660

1959/60

Argentina: Patagonia December/January, with Peter and Martha Miles, Jack Ewer and Peter Bruchausen. An expedition up the O'Higgins Glacier to the foot of Cerro Lautero. Bad weather prevented an attempt. pages 661–671

1961/62

Chile: South Patagonian Ice-cap November/January, with Jack Ewer, Eduardo García and Cedomir Marangunic, assisted by the Chilean Navy. The party made a fifty-two day trek along the Ice-cap from the Jorge Montt Glacier to the Upsala Glacier making ascents of Cerros Don Bosco and Murallon. pages 672–637

Chile: Tierra del Fuego January/February, with Eduardo García, Cedomir Marangunic and Francisco Vivanco, assisted by the Chilean Navy. From a base on the Marinelli Glacier, they crossed the Cord. Darwin making the first ascents of Cerro Yagen (7,500 ft.), Mount Darwin (8,700 ft.) and Darwin II and III. pages 738–756

Chile: Patagonia/Mount Burney March, with Cedomir Marangunic and 'Ricardo'. An unsuccessful attempt to approach the mountain from the south-west. page 738

1963

Chile: Patagonia/Mount Burney and Tierra del Fuego January. Jack Ewer and John Earle. They circled Mt. Burney but poor weather prevented an attempt. pages 762–763

February/March, with John Earle, Peter Bruchausen, Claudio Cortez, assisted by the Chilean Navy. From Olla Bay the party climbed Mount Bové (8,100 ft.) and Pico Francis (7,900 ft.). pages 764–767

1964/65

Chile: North Patagonian Ice-cap December/January, with Eduardo García, Cedomir Marangunic and Miguel Gomez. Starting from the San Raphael Glacier they made a six-week crossing of the Ice-cap to the Rio Cochrane, making the first ascent of Cerro Arco (9,950 ft.) and the second ascent of Cerro Arenales (11,227 ft.). pages 768–779

1966

USA (Alaska): Mount Russell June/July, with H. Adams-Carter, Bob Bates, Don Anderson, Larry McDade, Larry Carter and Russ MacAusland. An attempt on the unclimbed East Ridge which failed at c.11,000 ft. see *Bibliography*

1973

Chile: Patagonia/Mount Burney February/March, with Roger Perry and Pete Radcliffe, and British and Chilean Navy support. The first ascent of the mountain by a route up the West Spur. see *Bibliography*